Industrial Relations and Labour Laws

About the Authors

Piyali Ghosh is an Assistant Professor with School of Management Studies, Motilal Nehru National Institute of Technology (MNNIT) Allahabad. She has earned her PhD from MNNIT Allahabad, MBA from University of Allahabad and MA (Economics) from CSJM University, Kanpur. Dr. Ghosh has earlier been associated as member of faculty with Birla Institute of Technology and Science (BITS) Pilani and Institute of Management Technology (IMT) Ghaziabad, and has been teaching courses on Industrial Relations & Labour Legislations, Human Resource Management, Business Ethics & Corporate Governance and Managerial Economics. Her research interest lies in Industrial Relations, Training & Development and Employee Engagement. Dr. Ghosh has worked on an international project on women entrepreneurs spanning several countries and is presently working as a principal investigator in a project on housing for urban homeless poor funded by HSMI-HUDCO, New Delhi. She has co-authored a book on *Managerial Economics*, has more than 20 research papers published in national and international journals and has presented over 10 research papers in various conferences.

Shefali Nandan is an MBA with specialization in Human Resource Management (HRM) from Lucknow University, Lucknow and earned her PhD in the area of HRM from Dr. Hari Singh Gour Central University, Sagar, Madhya Pradesh. She also holds a Master's degree in Chemistry and has qualified UGC-NET. With a teaching experience spanning over thirteen years, Dr. Nandan is currently teaching Business Management at School of Management Studies, Motilal Nehru National Institute of Technology Allahabad. Her teaching areas include Industrial Relations & Labour Legislations, Human Resource Management, Organisational Behaviour, Change Management and Cross-Cultural Management. Earlier, she has taught postgraduate and undergraduate courses in Business Management at Dr. Hari Singh Gour University, Sagar, for more than four years. She has 45 national and international publications to her credit. She has worked on an international project on women entrepreneurs that covered 18 countries and is currently working as co-principal investigator in a project on *Investment Patterns of Urban Poor* funded by Indian Council for Social Science Research. Dr. Nandan has been a resource person for training at various organizations including Jawaharlal Nehru Police Academy, Sagar. Her research is primarily focused on labour issues, performance appraisal and human resource development. Other areas of her work include corporate change management, women entrepreneurship, gender issues and other issues of social interest.

Industrial Relations and Labour Laws

Piyali Ghosh
School of Management Studies
Motilal Nehru National Institute of Technology Allahabad

Shefali Nandan
School of Management Studies
Motilal Nehru National Institute of Technology Allahabad

McGraw Hill Education (India) Private Limited

Published by McGraw Hill Education (India) Private Limited,
Registered Office: Anjana Complex No: 5/90 A, Butt Road, St. Thomas Mount, Chennai – 600016,
Tamil Nadu, India.

Industrial Relations and Labour Laws

Twelfth reprint 2025

Print Edition
ISBN-13: 978-93-392-0304-7
ISBN-10: 93-392-0304-6

E-book Edition
ISBN-13: 978-93-392-0305-4
ISBN-10: 93-392-0305-4

13 14 15 16 17 IBH 29 28 27 26 25

Typeset at The Composers, 260, C.A. Apt., Paschim Vihar, New Delhi 110063 and
Printed and Bound in India at IBH Print & Bind Pvt. Ltd., Plot No. 81, Ecotech -12, Greater Noida, U.P.

Visit us at: www.mheducation.co.in
Toll free in India: 1800 103 5875
Write to us at: support.india@mheducation.com
CIN: U80302TN2010PTC111532

This book is

For my parents.
If it weren't you, I wouldn't have come so far.

Piyali Ghosh

Dedicated to my inspiring grandmother
for enhancing my understanding of life, and my parents
for their unconditional love and support.

Shefali Nandan

Foreword

Growth of industries is very essential for the economic development of a nation. Industries can flourish only when there is a healthy relationship between management and workers — the two most important components of any organization. Today, the relationship between management and workers has undergone a huge change due to factors like globalization, extensive use of technology, revolution in information and communication technology and changes in the nature of jobs. Outsourcing has become very popular and composition of workforce is changing. It is therefore essential to understand industrial relations from a new perspective in this changed scenario. It is essential for a practising manager and for a future manager to comprehend various dimensions of management-workers relations along with various labour legislations governing and regulating this relationship to find optimum and lawful solutions to problems related to workers.

Industrial Relations and Labour Laws by Dr. Piyali Ghosh and Dr. Shefali Nandan takes a comprehensive view of various aspects of industrial relations and discusses labour legislations in a lucid manner. The book covers issues that are relevant in current scenario. Each chapter is well planned that begins with its objectives and builds on the topic with the help of researches in the area. The layout of the chapters has been designed creatively, where 'Spotlight' in the chapters highlight important concepts and definitions, while 'Reflection' connects it with previous chapters.

The section on industrial relations has very deftly integrated current problems and issues related to management-workers relations in today's business environment with traditional concepts. It explains the changes that have taken place in various aspects of industrial relations over a period of time. Labour Legislations have been discussed with proper introduction to each legislation and using a simple language, including recent amendments. The real-life cases and caselets in each chapter help the readers understand the nuances of the topics.

The book will address the needs of not only students and professionals in the field but may also prove to be of interest to anyone who wishes to understand the subject. I congratulate the authors for making an excellent effort in bringing a clear understanding of the subject through this book and wish them all the best in their endeavours.

(S. K. Khare)
Former General Manager (Employee Relations)
Indian Oil Corporation Limited
Marketing Division, Head Office, Mumbai

Preface

The subject of industrial relations basically deals with the relationship between management and workers in an organizational set-up. With the current dynamic business environment and organizations witnessing fast changes since the past few decades, the concept of industrial relations could not remain insulated. Labour-management relations are gaining new hues; labour legislations are getting amended in tandem with the times, and new legislations are getting enacted. It is in this backdrop that the title *Industrial Relations and Labour Laws* has been designed and developed.

The blueprint of this title had been drawn in our minds a few years back and this book is an outcome of our thought process, analysis and interpretation of the subject. Through our experience of teaching industrial relations and labour legislations as a part of the curriculum of MBA programme, we have come across a general perception that the concept of industrial relations is changing shades and shapes with factors like growth of the service sector, emergence of new kinds of jobs, changes in the structure and functions of trade unions, and use of new technologies. Thus, today there is a need to look at the relationship between management and workers with a new perspective. It is this fresh standpoint that is the focal point of this title. It prepares the students of business management, practicing managers and professionals to understand the various dimensions of the issues that lead to friction between labour and management in the current scenario and help them find solutions to the problems governing labour-management relations.

While designing the structure of the book and critically analysing some of the existing titles on this subject, we realised that the book should be neither too bulky, nor too concise, without compromising on the quality of the content. At a time when the country has been witnessing violent strife between workers and management in big industrial houses like Maruti Suzuki, Jet Airways and Hyundai Motors, we have included real-life cases from such industries, to help readers connect with theory and also to keep them abreast with the recent changes in the industrial relations scenario of the nation. We have endevoured to maintain a balance between the usage of academic citations, latest available data and examples from real life.

The book is divided into two sections: Section I covers industrial relations and Section II covers labour legislations. The section on industrial relations, spanning from Chapter 1 to Chapter 13, covers aspects like trade unions, collective bargaining, industrial discipline, dispute settlement, industrial safety and health, and international perspective on industrial relations. An additional feature is that pertinent recommendations of the Second National Commission on Labour have been included at appropriate places in the chapters.

Section II covers labour legislations in India and runs from Chapter 14 to Chapter 26. All major labour legislations have been included in this section. It has been observed that students of business management, especially, may not find interest in the legal jargons that usually are indispensable part of Acts. Care has, therefore, been taken to explain all the Acts in simple and lucid language. Keeping pace with the recent developments in the legislative framework of the country, 'The Sexual Harassment of Women at Workplace (Prevention, Prohibition and Redressal) Act, 2013' has also been included as an Appendix.

A special feature of this book is "Case Corner" containing real-life legal cases and business situations that have been given at appropriate places in each chapter. Another aspect is 'Spotlight' in each chapter that highlights the important concepts in the chapter. 'Reflection' is a connecting link with concepts discussed in earlier chapters. Other learning aids include desired knowledge competencies at the beginning of each chapter, end-of-chapter summaries and case studies, discussion questions and exercises, glossary, and an extensive list of references for further study.

To sum up, the aim of this book is to provide a rich repository of both theoretical concepts and their practical application. Emphasis has been laid on critical thinking and creative analysis of situations related to labour-management dynamics. This book will benefit students of business management, human resource management, personnel management, industrial relations and law. The book will also act as a reference for practicing managers and consultants, and as an invaluable guide for UGC-NET aspirants. We sincerely hope that the book will be highly useful to all the readers and would contribute to increasing their understanding of the subject.

Piyali Ghosh
Shefali Nandan

Publisher's Note

We value your views, comments and suggestions and hence look forward to your communication at *info.india@mheducation.com.* Please feel free to report piracy issues, if any.

Acknowledgements

Writing a book of this magnitude is an enormous task which requires contribution of many helping hands. First of all, we are grateful to Almighty for giving us the inspiration to commence on this journey and the strength to complete it.

As a subject Industrial Relations and Labour Laws has earned many opinions. Some find it interesting, though a lot many see it as difficult more because it delves into the intricate realms of human behaviour at work. This book is designed to unlock the doors to the challenging yet fascinating world of industrial relations. It was close to two years in writing, but cumulatively around ten years in the making. We are thankful to students, practitioners and all others whose need for a comprehensive repository on Industrial Relations and Labour Laws provided us with the motivation to write this book.

We express our heartfelt gratitude to Dr. Geetika, Professor and Head, School of Management Studies, Motilal Nehru National Institute of Technology Allahabad, for her constant guidance and support in our endeavour. Her insights on the subject have gone a long way in adding value to every chapter. This book would not have taken its present form without the inputs from our other colleagues who helped in improving the contents of the book. We appreciate their valuable suggestions. Students are a teacher's best critics. We are thankful to all our students as queries of these young minds drove us to explore new dimensions of the topics covered in the book.

Our sincere thanks go to Shri S. K. Khare, former General Manager (Employee Relations), Indian Oil Corporation Limited, for agreeing to write the Foreword and for being so enthusiastic about our work. We are grateful to all the copyright holders, organizations and individuals for their permission to use their works in the book. Each source of our cases and examples has been acknowledged at the point of usage. We owe much to by Shri Abhijit Majumdar, Faculty, Indian Institute of Coal Management, Ranchi, who extended support in allowing access to the rich repository of labour-related journals in the library of the Institute. His profound practical knowledge of disciplinary proceedings in public sector enterprises has also assisted in shaping several issues in the book.

We cannot thank our families enough for supporting and encouraging us in every possible way and makings things convenient for us so that we could fully concentrate on our task of book writing.

We acknowledge the contribution of the reviewers in the form of invaluable comments and suggestions that proved to be instrumental in enhancing the value of the book. We are indebted to all others who have directly and indirectly helped us in bringing the book to its present form. Finally, we thank the publishing team whose support, efforts, diligence and pains taken round the clock helped the book see light of the day.

We hope our readers discover how interesting Industrial Relations and Labour Laws can be.

Piyali Ghosh
Shefali Nandan

Contents

PART B
LABOUR LAWS

PART

INDUSTRIAL RELATIONS

1

Industrial Relations: An Overview

Desired Knowledge Competencies

- To describe the concept and evolution of industrial relations.
- To discuss the theoretical perspectives in industrial relations.
- To identify the impact of globalisation and technology on industrial relations.

CONCEPT OF INDUSTRIAL RELATIONS

An industry has two main components: management (including the owner or the capitalist) and labour. The concept of industrial relations may be said to have come into being with the need to manage the relations between labour and management in industry. This need emerges because on one side there is management (on behalf of the capitalist) that invests money and procures various inputs with the objective of reaping profits, while on other side, there is labour that toils hard for the production of goods and services and gets compensation in return. Their objectives may sometimes clash with each other and such a situation may prove to be detrimental to the interests of not just the two parties involved but that of the community as a whole. However, if they work in harmony, the outcome of the efforts of labour and management may contribute to the development of the economy and would benefit the entire community.

The concept of industrial relations is characterised as collectivist and pluralist in nature. It has been traditionally viewed as the relationship between employers and their representatives and workers and their representatives, emerging out of work. However, the modern approach to industrial relations includes not only relationships between workers, between workers and employers, and between employers and employers, but also various processes involved in these relationships, such as organising of workers, workers' participation in decision making, dispute settlement, collective bargaining, etc. Yoder (cited in Singh and Kumar, 2011, p. 5) defined industrial relations as the "relationship between management and employees, or among employees and their organisations, that characterise or grow out of employment." Many scholars have viewed industrial relations in a narrow sense and have focused on specific aspects of this relationship. Flanders (1970, p. 86), a British industrial relations scholar, defined industrial relations as "a study of the institutions of job regulation." Hyman (1975, p. 12) considered "struggle for power" as an inherent feature of industrial relations and proposed industrial relations as "the study of processes of control over work relations", with focus on collective actions of workers' organisations. Johri (1969) (as cited in Monappa, 1999, p. 8) defines industrial relations as "the relation between an employer and employee in the course of running of an industry and may project itself to spheres which may transgress to the areas of quality control, marketing, price fixation, and disposition of profits among others." According to Singh (1968, p. 9), industrial relations "involve a study of the State, the legal system, the workers' and employers' organisations at the institutional level; and of the patterns of industrial organisation (including management), capital structure (including technology), compensation of the labour force, and the study of market forces—all at the economic level."

The economic, political, social and technological environment of a country affects its industrial relations framework. Work and workplaces are affected by norms, rules, and regulations created by various institutions and organisations (e.g., organisations of employers and government agencies). The institutions which devise and implement this network of rules are an important component in the study of industrial relations (Bray and Wailes, 1997). Thus industrial relations cannot be separated from the institutional framework, which is mainly made up of government agencies responsible for creating policies and rules governing industry and labour. The involvement of government agencies gives rise to tripartite nature of industrial relations, with labour, management and the State as the three actors.

In India, industrial disputes on wages, employment conditions, working conditions, retrenchment, lay-off, production, etc. may be resolved through bipartite processes with involvement of both workers and management. But when it is not possible to resolve disputes at this level, the State intervenes, and then it takes a tripartite form. The rationale for State intervention is to achieve cooperation and social justice (e.g., prevention of exploitation of sweated and child labour). The State also acts as a regulatory body for industrial relations in India.

Spotlight

Industrial relations serve the means by which various interests involved in the labour market are accommodated, primarily for the purpose of regulating employment relationships.

Taking the above definitions and concepts into consideration, we may define industrial relations as a means by which the various interests involved in the labour market are accommodated, primarily for the purpose of regulating employment relationships.

INDUSTRIAL RELATIONS AND THE CONSTITUTION OF INDIA

The Constitution of India provides the basic guidelines for creating the industrial relations system of the country. The Fundamental Rights and the Directive Principles of State Policy in the Constitution act as the basis for labour policy. Any policy, rule or law, under any circumstances, cannot violate the Fundamental Rights. In fact, these rights have been ensured through various labour legislations and include: the right to equality (Article 14), prohibition of discrimination (Article 15), the rights to freedom of speech and association (Article 19), the rights to life and personal liberty (Article 21), prohibition of traffic in human beings and forced labour (Article 23), and prohibition of employment of children in factories, etc. (Article 24).

Spotlight

The Fundamental Rights and the Directive Principles of State Policy enshrined in the Constitution of India act as the basis for labour policy in the country.

The Directive Principles of State Policy enshrined in the Constitution act as guidelines for the State in creating such industrial relations system in the country as provides equity, justice and welfare for workers. These guidelines require that the State should aim to: secure a social order for the promotion of welfare of people (Article 38); direct its policies towards securing adequate means of livelihood for all citizens through various means including equal pay for equal work, protection of health and strength of workers, and protection of childhood and youth from exploitation (Article 39); have a legal system to promote justice on the basis of equal opportunity and provide free legal aid through suitable legislation (Article 39A); secure right to work, to education, and to public assistance in cases of unemployment, old age, sickness, disablement, and undeserved want (Article 41); secure just and humane conditions of work and maternity relief (Article 42); secure work, living wage, decent standard of life, etc., to people (Article 43); and secure participation of workers in the management of undertakings engaged in any industry (Article 43A).

HISTORY OF INDUSTRIAL RELATIONS IN INDIA

We will study the evolution of industrial relations in India by dividing it into two phases: pre-Independence phase and post-Independence phase.

Pre-Independence Phase

The history of industrial relations in India can be traced back to the time of emergence of industries. Though the Industrial Revolution in Europe had begun during the eighteenth century and by the nineteenth century industries were well established, in India beginning of modern industries was during the mid-nineteenth century. Indigo plantations, established in 1831, may be said to be the first industry in India. Later, a cotton mill was established in 1851 in Bombay (now Mumbai) and jute manufacturing was started in 1855 in Calcutta (now Kolkata).

During the early phase of industrialisation there was a clear divide between capitalists and labour. Capitalists or employers were in a commanding position; their sole concern was to earn and maximise profits. Workers were treated merely as tools of production. They subsisted on meager wages, had long working hours, and lived in poor conditions; there were hardly any laws to protect them. To get rid of such poor working and living conditions, workers gradually begun to organise themselves and protest against the atrocities inflicted upon them by the employers. This laid the seeds of trade unionism. The year 1860 marked the beginning of labour unrest in India to protest against the oppression of indigo cultivators in Bengal, followed by instances of labour unrest observed in Nagpur (in 1877), Bombay and Surat. However, due to unequal distribution of power between labour and employers, the former had to suffer for protesting, by way of dismissals, victimisation, etc.

Enactment of the Factories Act, 1881 was an important milestone in the evolution of industrial relations, as it ushered in a force that awakened workers. Several workers' organisations had begun to take form by this time, and in 1890, the first workers' association, named Bombay Mill Hands Association, was established with the efforts of N.M. Lokhande. After this several other associations were formed, though it was not easy for these organisations to get legal recognition. The Trade Unions Act that came into existence in 1926 contained provisions for registration of trade unions.

Spotlight

The Bombay Mill Hands Association, formed in 1890, was the first workers' association in India.

Meanwhile, certain developments at international level too had an impact upon workers and employers. The World War I (1914-1918) resulted in price rise, which enabled employers to generate profits. However since wages remained the same, workers had to face a situation of economic distress. Labour unrest increased and a number of strikes took place, prominent amongst which were the strikes of workers of Textile Labour Association Ahmedabad in 1917, led by Mahatma Gandhi and the strikes at Madras (now Chennai) by workers of Buckingham and Carnatic Mills in 1910 and 1921. Formation of the International Labour Organisation (ILO) in 1919 gave a boost to the labour movement. Around this time another significant development took place in the form of establishment of the All India Trade Union Congress in 1920. A number of labour legislations were enacted, including the Workmen's (now Employees') Compensation Act, 1923 and the Trade Unions Act, 1926. The Economic Depression in 1929 worsened the condition of workers, as a result of which labour unrest grew and there were a number of strikes and lock-outs deteriorating labour-management relations. Government's intervention during this time to control labour unrest was the beginning of the tripartite nature of industrial relations.

The Second World War (1939–1945) again resulted in price rise, profits for capitalists, and poor living conditions for labour. Since the establishment of tripartite consultative machinery in 1942, the principle of tripartite structure of industrial relations was gradually evolved and refined, that shaped the industrial relations machinery in India. Many developments took place in the years that followed the World War II. The Indian National Trade Union Congress was formed in 1947. A number of legislations were enacted during this phase, including the Industrial Employment (Standing Orders) Act, 1946, and the Industrial Disputes Act, 1947.

Post-Independence Phase

Immediately after Independence the emphasis of the Government of India was to contain labour unrest and increase industrialisation for growth and generation of employment. A Tripartite Conference was convened in 1947 in which the Industrial Truce Resolution was adopted. It required management and labour to agree to maintain industrial peace and prevent any work stoppages during the next 3 years to promote industrial growth. The Labour Relations Bill of 1950 introduced the concept of collective bargaining. Though the Bill could not be passed, nonetheless, it initiated a thought process towards non-legal bipartite approach of solving industrial disputes.

Emphasis was laid on industrial peace in the First Five Year Plan (1951-1956), which had set targets for all round development of the nation. The Plan also mentioned about methods of settling disputes between labour and management through tripartite bodies, the need for a grievance procedure and the importance of works committees. The Second Five Year Plan (1956-1961) evolved norms, codes and methods for achieving harmony and discipline in industry. It spelt out the need for union recognition and to end unresolved disputes through voluntary arbitration, rather than compulsory adjudication. Schemes for workers' participation in management were evolved during this period, including Joint Management Councils in 1958. The Indian Labour Conference held in 1957 emphasised on maintaining discipline in industry and the Code of Discipline was evolved in 1958. The Workers' Education Scheme was also initiated in 1958 to support industrialisation.

Spotlight
The First Five Year Plan emphasised on achieving industrial peace.

Spotlight
The Code of Discipline was established during the Second Five Year Plan.

In the Third Five Year Plan (1961-1966), specifically during Chinese aggression on India, the Industrial Truce Resolution was adopted in 1962, in which labour and management resolved to settle disputes peacefully and pledged to increase production. Central Wage Boards, Safety Councils and the Model Grievance Procedure were initiated during this period. An important event during this Plan was the appointment of the First National Commission on Labour that took a comprehensive view of industrial relations in the country in its report. The first half of the decade of 1970s, during the Fourth Five Year Plan (1969-1974), saw a lot of industrial strife. Political interference in trade unions had increased by this time. Efforts for maintaining industrial peace initiated in the early years of Independence proved to be inadequate. The Government declared Emergency in 1975 to control the ongoing volatile economic conditions in the country and to maintain peace. Right to strike was suspended during the emergency period. The subsequent Five Year Plans made some brief mention of issues related to industrial relations. The Industrial Policy Resolution of 1980 reaffirmed the earlier resolution of 1956. We have touched on government policies on labour and the Five Year Plans in detail in Chapter 10.

Notable changes in the industrial relations scenario in the country took place with the adoption of the New Industrial Policy of 1991, that aimed at liberalisation of the economy. The policy put the responsibility on the Government to equip workers with adequate skills in order to deal with technological changes. It considered workers as equal partners in economic growth and emphasised upon training and workers' participation in management.

In the changed business scenario, trade unions have taken up varied functions and have adopted a participative approach, shifting from the traditional militant approach. We have analysed such traditional and new functions of trade unions in Chapter 3.

THEORETICAL PERSPECTIVES

Several theories and perspectives have been proposed to understand the concept of industrial relations and the rationale behind the beliefs and actions of labour and management. We will discuss some of the prominent ones in this section.

Systems Model

The Systems Model proposed by Dunlop in the 1950s views industrial relations system as consisting of three actors: management, workers and their formal and informal organisations, and government agencies. These actors function in an environment that is made up of technology, labour, markets, and various power equations in the society. Dunlop believed that all the three constituent actors, at least to some extent, are affected by environmental factors. Within this environment all these actors interact to work and to determine the rules that help in running the industrial relations system.

The three unique factors in Dunlop's model are: external environmental forces acting upon the labour-management relationship; specific characteristics in labour-management-government interactions; rules arising out of and at the same time governing existing employment relationships between the three actors; and a shared understanding of rules that gives stability to the entire system.

Dunlop viewed the above-mentioned arrangement of industrial relations as a system, wherein the components are interacting and interdependent, while freely giving and receiving information from the external environment for dealing with certain issues and are together responsible for certain outputs. Thus industrial relations may be viewed as a social sub-system operating within environmental constraints.

Spotlight

The Systems Model views industrial relations as a social sub-system comprising labour, management and the State, functioning within environmental factors.

Unitary Perspective

The essence of the Unitary Perspective is that the enterprise is a social system or a unitary organisation made up of management and workers, both having the common objectives of achieving high efficiency and high profits that would ultimately benefit all, and hence there exists no conflict. Management adopts a leadership role and holds the responsibility to design such policies as are beneficial to workers, management and all the other stakeholders. It must also work to promote loyalty amongst employees.

Spotlight

Unitary Perspective considers management and workers as having the same objectives and any conflict between them as an anomaly.

According to this theory, all the actions and ideas of management and the State are right and rational, while the actions and beliefs of workers that are conflicting with management and the State are irrational. In fact, even trade unions are an outcome of imperfections in common understanding of shared interests between workers and management. The main characteristics of the Unitary Perspective are:

- Management is the main authority in an organisation and there is no conflict of interest between management and trade unions.
- Both the parties must work together to achieve their common objectives.
- Trade unions are not essential for the well-being of workers or for managing conflicts.

The unitarist view sees employer-employee relations as essentially harmonious, punctuated only by occasions of temporary and illegitimate conflicts. Conflict is thus an anomaly and a dysfunctional aspect of working that disturbs harmony and hence could be eliminated.

However, this theory fails to recognise that power is unequally distributed between workers and management in an organisation and that this inequality in itself may generate conflict. It views conflict as a negative force rather than as an opportunity to achieve harmony. Further, it adopts a normative approach as it believes in the common interest of all stakeholders but does not propose ways to identify these common interests.

Pluralist Theory

Conceptually the Pluralist Theory of Flanders is the opposite of the Unitary Theory. According to this approach, an organisation is the sub-system of a social system, and is made up of two divergent groups, *viz.*, management and trade unions, each having its own interests and perception of the social structure. However, these two interconnected groups have a common objective of the maintenance and growth of the organisation by making use of the process of bargaining. Any conflict that arises between the groups is over distribution of profits, and is natural and inevitable. The Pluralist Theory views conflict between workers and management as difficult to reconcile and that conflict itself is not wrong. The focus should be on 'how to handle it' rather than 'how to avoid it'. State intervention may be required if the conflict cannot be handled by workers and management. Thus, the pluralistic perspective takes the view that the potential for conflict is inherent in the employment relationship, but is manageable and can be contained by an appropriate network of rules and regulations. Pluralist perspective emphasises the use of various conflict resolution techniques that involve the parties in conflict and other stakeholders.

> **Spotlight**
> The Pluralist Perspective views conflict as a natural outcome in an organisation due to the presence of groups with divergent interests.

One of the main drawbacks of the Pluralist Theory is its over-emphasis on rules and procedures. Though rules and laws can be made to resolve conflicts, they cannot adapt to changing conditions at workplace (Gennard and Judge, 2002). In fact, rules need to be reviewed and changed from time to time in order to be effective. Also, the focus of this theory is too much on workers' interests, and that can jeopardise the effectiveness of collective bargaining processes.

Radical Perspective

The Radical Perspective is inspired by the Marxist view on capitalism. It considers work and working conditions in an organisation as exploitative to workers. Class conflict exists in society and conflict between labour and management is simply a part of it. The followers of Radical Perspective consider organisations as representing the oppressive nature of the general societal structure. Conflict is unavoidable in organisations as management represents the interests of capitalists who want to maximise profit at the cost of workers. Even the modern practices of improving employee-management relations like employee empowerment or gain-sharing, are viewed as solely motivated by the objective of benefiting management.

Followers of Radical Perspective view industrial relations in terms of an enduring structural conflict between employers and those who sell their labour to the employers. Temporary accommodations to this conflict, according to radicals, do little more than controlling employees in their exploited position and secure the stability of a system that continues to favour employers.

TRADE UNIONISM

Trade unionism refers to the whole gamut of activities related to trade unions, including their structure and functions. Very often the terms 'labour movement' and 'trade union movement' are used synonymously, but it may be understood here that the former has a wider connotation. Trade union movement may be seen as a sub-set of labour movement, and is largely a by-product of industrialisation. According to Tannenbaum (1951), trade unionism is a natural outcome and an inherent feature of a capitalistic society, while labour movement refers to awakening of labour class for their rights as workers and as human beings. To secure their rights, workers found it convenient and useful to organise themselves and fight as a body rather than demanding their rights individually, which would have less impact on employers. Gradually these organisations got consolidated and started fighting for their legal status. This struggle of workers to associate and get recognition for their organisations is referred to as the trade union movement. Unions represent workers and adopt various means like strikes, *gheraos,* etc., to pressurise employers. Traditionally, the role of trade unions was considered to fight for workers' rights, but with changing times they have witnessed a number of changes in their roles. We will talk about various aspects of trade unions in India in Chapters 3 and 4.

ORGANISATION OF INDUSTRIAL RELATIONS IN INDIA

The framework for industrial relations in India is formed by a number of labour legislations in the country that contain obligations and duties for both employers and workers. Under the Constitution of India, labour is a subject in the Concurrent List, which empowers both the Central and State Governments to enact legislations subject to certain matters being reserved for the Centre.

EXHIBIT 1.1 LABOUR JURISDICTION: CONSTITUTIONAL STATUS

Union List	*Concurrent List*
Entry No. 55: Regulation of labour and safety in mines and oil fields	Entry No. 22: Trade Unions; industrial and labour disputes
Entry No. 61: Industrial disputes concerning Union employees	Entry No. 23: Social security and insurance employment and unemployment
Entry No. 65: Union agencies and institutions for professional, vocational or technical training.	Entry No. 24: Welfare of labour including conditions of work, provident funds, employers invalidity, and old age pension and maternity benefit
	Entry No. 25: Vocational and technical training of labour

(Adapted from: www.constitution.org/cons/india/shed07.htm accessed on 29/1/2014.)

Spotlight
Industrial relations system in India is tripartite in nature.

Industrial relations in India revolve around three actors: employers, workers and their trade unions, and the State. This three-pronged (or tripartite) structure tries to balance the power equation between management and workers. According to Brandes (1976, p. 6, as cited in Wad, 1996, p. 16), tripartite structure helps in managing "a continuing tug of war between big labour and big business with government seeking to prevent either side from gaining predominance". Many tripartite bodies have been set up in India for joint consultation between the representatives of government, employers and workers. These bodies, such as the Indian Labour Conference (ILC), the Standing Labour Committee (SLC), and Industrial Committees provide a forum to discuss and resolve the issues related to labour. We have covered tripartism as a statutory measure for resolving industrial disputes and various tripartite bodies in India in chapters 8 and 10.

The role of the State is protective for labour, the weaker partner in industrial relations. The Government is not only a policy maker; it is also an employer in public sector enterprises. It initiates and ensures proper implementation and administration of policies and legislations for workers' welfare, social security, health and safety. Chapter 10 also features an elaborate discussion on the role of State, Labour policies in the Five Year Plans, and provisions and welfare measures for women and child labour. In view of the large proportion of workforce employed in the unorganised sector, the Government of India has been making efforts to provide social security to workers in this sector too. Various aspects of labour welfare and social security have been dealt with in Chapter 10, while the concept of industrial health and safety has been explored in detail in Chapter 13.

There are certain bipartite arrangements like collective bargaining (covered in Chapter 5) for managing relations between workers and management. The emphasis of bipartite methods is on settling any dispute between management and workers through mutual dialogue and on failure at this level tripartite methods of resolving disputes may be resorted to. The Industrial Disputes Act, 1947 has provisions for such methods of settling disputes with the intervention of the Government. These include conciliation officer, board of conciliation, voluntary arbitration, and compulsory arbitration. There are Labour Courts, Industrial Tribunals, and National Tribunals in which compulsory arbitration proceedings take place. Various dimensions of disputes in industry and dispute settlement have been dealt with in chapters 7 and 8 respectively.

Industrial discipline is very essential for maintaining peace and harmony in industry. Various methods are available for disciplining employees. There is a procedure for initiating enquiry against employees. The principle of natural justice must be adhered to in the process of initiating and conducting enquiry. Grievance settlement mechanisms exist in organisations for settling grievances at individual level. In fact, the First National Commission on Labour had even proposed a Model Grievance Procedure. The concepts of discipline, grievance and grievance handling have been covered in Chapter 6.

The Government of India has sought to involve workers in decision making through various schemes for workers' participation. Works Committees, Joint Management Councils, Joint Consultative Committees, shop councils and joint councils are methods that have evolved from time to time for achieving effective workers' participation in management. We will elaborate on workers' participation in management and related aspects in Chapter 11.

Labour Administration Machinery

In India the Ministry of Labour & Employment controls labour-related issues. The Ministry has four attached offices, namely, Office of the Directorate General of Employment and Training, New Delhi; Office of the Chief Labour Commissioner (Central), New Delhi; Labour Bureau, Chandigarh and Shimla; and Directorate General of Factory Advice Service and Labour Institutes, Mumbai. Besides there are ten subordinate offices: Directorate General of Mines Safety, Dhanbad, and Offices of the Welfare Commissioners in nine cities in India; four autonomous organisations: Employees' State Insurance Corporation, Employees' Provident Fund Organisation, VV Giri National Labour Institute, and the Central Board for Workers' Education; and other adjudicating and arbitration bodies.

NATIONAL COMMISSIONS ON LABOUR

Two National Commissions on Labour have been established in the country so far to review various labour-related issues and give recommendations. The first Commission was set up to study the industrial relations scenario in the country when the industrialisation process had been initiated by the Government for economic development. The Second Commission on Labour was set when the process of economic liberalisation had been initiated. Let us give a brief overview of both the Commissions in this section.

Spotlight

Two National Commissions on Labour have been set up India to review the industrial relations scenario in the country.

First National Commission on Labour (1969)

The First National Commission on Labour was set up on 24 December, 1966 under the Chairmanship of Justice PB Gajendragadkar. The Commission studied and analysed the industrial relations in India and its various dimensions for the first time both in the organised and unorganised sectors. It submitted its report in August, 1969. The issues covered in the report included labour welfare, wages, wage policy, bonus, social security, workers' training and education, workers' and employers' organisations, and industrial relations machinery.

Recommendations of the First National Commission on Labour resulted in amendment of certain labour laws, including the Workmen's (now Employees') Compensation Act, 1923 (like removal of wage ceiling for coverage); the Industrial Disputes Act, 1947 (mainly in respect of unfair labour practices); the Employees' State Insurance Act, 1948 (in terms of enhancement in the wage limit for exemption from payment of employees' contribution); the Factories Act, 1948 (like making penalties more stringent for violation of safety requirements and provision of welfare facilities); and the Employees' Provident Funds and Miscellaneous Provisions Act, 1952 (namely enhancement in the rate of contribution and making default of dues a cognizable offence).

The Commission's recommendations have been instrumental in enactment of certain laws, like the Contract Labour (Regulation and Abolition) Act, 1970; the Limestone and Dolomite Mines Labour Welfare Fund Act, 1972; the Iron Ore, Manganese Ore and Chrome Ore Mines Labour Welfare Fund Act, 1976; the Equal Remuneration Act, 1976; and the Child Labour (Prohibition and Regulation) Act, 1986.

The recommendations of the Commission have also brought about certain changes in government policies and programmes in some areas like wage policy and minimum wages, vocational training, labour statistics and research, and workers' education.

Second National Commission on Labour (2002)

Spotlight

The Second National Commission on Labour recommended the creation of an umbrella legislation to provide social security to unorganised sector workers.

As specified earlier, vast changes took place in the economy due to the policy of liberalisation-privatisation-globalisation adopted by the Government of India in 1991. With the opening up of the economy, the business environment suddenly became very dynamic. In view of the changes taking place in the industrial relations scenario, the Government felt the need to set up another National Commission on Labour. Thus, the Second National Commission on Labour was established in 1999 under the chairmanship of Ravindra Varma. The Commission submitted its report to the Government in 2002, in which it made a comprehensive analysis of issues related to labour by taking into consideration the impact of globalisation, need for change in the existing labour laws, dynamics of the Indian labour system, progress of industrial development after Independence, etc. The Commission gave recommendations related to review of laws, social security measures, women workers and child labour, wages, skill development, labour administration, unorganised sector, etc. To ensure the welfare of workers in the unorganised sector, it proposed an umbrella legislation for social security of workers in this sector. The Ministry of Labour & Employment drafted the Unorganised Sector Workers Bill, 2004, which, *inter alia*, envisages provisions for safety, social security, and health and welfare matters. The recommendations of the Second National Commission on various labour-related issues feature in the respective chapters of the book.

INDUSTRIAL RELATIONS IN MODERN ERA

The industrial relations system in India has undergone a sea change in the post-liberalisation phase. The last two decades have witnessed notable transformation in the way business is done. Physical boundaries between nations are no longer an obstruction for business; multinational organisations are emerging in large numbers and are continuously expanding; concern of employers towards the rights and interests of workers is increasing; and workers are much more aware of their surrounding environment and are awakened towards their rights as compared to the pre-Independence period. New management systems are emerging that are designing novel ways of managing worker-management relations.

Initially the scope of industrial relations was limited, more or less, to procuring and securing workers' rights by trade unions. Now this scope has expanded to all those aspects of work-related activities that require interactions between workers and management. Workers, through their representatives, participate in decision making in the enterprise to find ways to enhance firm performance and to discuss discipline-related issues, training of workers, etc. Thus workers have come a long way from olden times when they were treated merely as a tool for production to a time when they have a voice in decision making on issues that affect them.

Changing nature of business has also given rise to new issues for collective bargaining. Business organisations are now hiring employees on contract basis as expenses incurred on such workers are lesser as compared to permanent employees. Due to this, job security has emerged as an important issue in collective bargaining besides wages, work conditions, etc. The various dimensions of labour and employment in the present scenario have been covered in Chapter 2.

Spotlight

The scope of industrial relations has expanded to aspects of work-related activities that require interaction between workers and management.

Impact of Globalisation

Globalisation is the process of interconnecting people across the world on various dimensions including cultural, economic, political, technological and environmental aspects (Greenberg and Baron, 2008). It has become a defining characteristic feature of the world as we see it in the twenty-first century. The process of globalisation influences not only macro-level economic policies, but also arrangements at enterprise-level. It has brought a remarkable shift in the traditional system of industrial relations and has changed the dimensions of the relationship between management and workers. The boundaries of doing business, initially limited within a country, have now expanded across nations, bringing about economic interdependence between countries. In addition, as pointed out by Michael Camdessus, ex-Managing Director of International Monetary Fund, increased competition in market has resulted in change in products traded, with a shift to more skill-intensive products in developing countries and less skill-intensive products in developed countries (Camdessus, 1996).

To support these changes there have been a number of modifications in work arrangements in organisations so that they can sustain themselves. This has had a considerable impact on the employer-employee relationship and has also altered the roles played by trade unions. Camdessus (1996) has summarised the situation as "......really traumatic when workers through lack of the ability or means to learn new skills, or because they are too old to change, lose their jobs. Trade unions have a role to play to help workers re-train, ensure that social entitlements are fulfilled and are maintained at an adequate level..."

Spotlight

Globalisation has resulted in increased migration of workers within the country and across nations.

Globalisation has resulted in multinational corporations (MNCs) establishing their operations in other countries where locals are hired. Cross-cultural issues are bound to emerge in such a scenario, adding a new dimension to existing worker-management relations. Labour migration is another related aspect, which needs to be dealt by employers today. With increasing job opportunities, workers' migration is taking place not just within a country from village to cities, but from one country to another, for improved living standards.

Enterprises have been seeking ways to optimise their operations in order to strengthen their competitiveness by reducing costs on labour and other resources. This has been done by identifying the core strengths and functions to maintain competitiveness and subcontracting peripheral functions to external organisations, downsizing, and adopting technology to substitute labour. Besides, companies are joining hands through mergers and joint ventures to get strategic advantages. Such situations have created a volatile environment for employment.

The economic liberalisation programme in India has encouraged MNCs from developed nations to enter India with sophisticated technology. There has been a steady growth of the tertiary sector in recent years, which has created new employment opportunities; at the same time shrinkage of the primary sector has also been witnessed. MNCs have been detrimental to the growth of indigenous products and have been responsible for displacement of people engaged in traditional sectors. The reports of a large number of suicides by weavers in Andhra Pradesh, Tamil Nadu, etc. are a testimony to this phenomenon (Report of the Second National Commission on Labour, 2002).

The relationship between labour and management has seen a lot of changes in such a scenario. MNCs based in economically developed industrialised countries are opening up operations in resource-rich developing countries, where they get cheap labour. This situation has created changes in various aspects of labour standards in different industries and regions as trade unions take a comparative view of existing wages, welfare and other related issues that affect industrial relations. Keeping in mind the need to understand industrial relations in other countries in a networked economy today, we have included certain dimensions of industrial relations in other countries in Chapter 12.

Industrial Relations and Technological Change

Besides the various outcomes of globalisation that have affected industrial relations as talked about in the previous section, technological change has been an important aspect that has had a significant impact on labour-management relations. New technology is adopted by organisations for various reasons like cost-cutting, achieving better product quality, time saving, efficiency and gaining competitive advantage. Whatever the objective may be, adoption of technology affects wide-ranging aspects in an organisation, including human resource, employment, job profiles, work arrangements, employee attitude, training and industrial relations (Kanawaty, Gladstone, Prokopenko and Rodgers, 1989).

With intensifying competition in markets, product/service quality has become a deciding factor in increasing customer base and ultimately decides profits generated by an organisation. Customers always demand quality at lesser price. 'Benchmarking' and quality standards (like ISO, BIS, 6 Sigma, etc.) are increasingly being adopted. Demand in the market fluctuates and enterprises need to be very responsive and flexible while catering to the needs of customers in terms of product quality and prices. Adoption of better technology can ensure quality and reduce costs. Production processes and schedules need to be adapted according to the demand. With the integration of modern production technology and information technology (IT), enterprises are trying to handle the vagaries of market with flexibility in their operation schedules. With integrated computerised systems, it has become possible to coordinate operations in different units located across countries to manage supply and demand in the market. Work methods like *kanban* (an approach for incremental process improvement) and 'just-in-time' are being adopted in companies to maintain efficiency and to respond to customer needs in time.

What needs to be noted is that whatever change is brought about in production technology, it ultimately goes down to workers, as they have to learn and adapt to new ways of working. It generates apprehensions in them regarding job security, economic benefits, change in habits, redundancy and skill obsolescence. These apprehensions are not unfounded. Workers have to learn new skills, build new capabilities, and need to be trained to operate new machines. Embracing new technologies has increased the demand for skilled employees. Thus employee training and retraining issues arise with technological advancements. Many private sector organisations in India are responding by taking initiatives to enhance the skill-level of their workforce. Fear about job security may affect management-worker relations and may also result in labour unrest. Management needs to handle such situations deftly; workers may be made partners through their representatives in bringing about such changes in an enterprise.

Spotlight

Technological changes have resulted in obsolescence of skills, thus stressing on need for training and retraining.

Exhibit 1.2 Skill Development Initiatives by Government and Private Sector in India

The outcome of globalisation of the Indian economy has been rapid economic growth, with changes in technology and work processes, leading to an increase in demand for skilled manpower. The Government of India has taken several steps to meet this demand. There were 1,896 Government Industrial Training Institutes (ITIs) in the country as on 1st January, 2007, out of which 500 are being upgraded into Centres of Excellence under a scheme launched in 2005-2006 and up- gradation of the remaining has been done through Public Private Partnership since 2007-2008. Tata Motors is an example of private companies involved in such partnership. This scheme was initiated with an objective of improving the quality of vocational training in the country to make it demand-driven so as to ensure better employability of graduates. The private sector has been taking various initiatives on its own and in collaboration with the Government and international entities, to upgrade in-house training facilities and also to provide training to potential employees to make them job-ready.

In early 2008, the Government formed the "Coordinated Action on Skill Development" with a 3-tier institutional structure consisting of: Prime Minister's National Council, the National Skill Development Coordination Board (NSDCB), and the National Skill Development Corporation (NSDC), with the objective of creating skilled workforce. The Prime Minister's National Council on Skill Development has a vision to create 500 million skilled people by 2022 through skill systems.

(Adapted from: FICCI (n.d). Skill Development: Sector Profile. Retrieved from www.ficci.com /sector/74/ Project_docs/ SectorProfile.pdf on 1/2/2014.)

Use of information technology has changed the way business is done, and the modes of interaction with employees, customers, suppliers and stakeholders. IT has also resulted in increased awareness of workers regarding labour laws, their rights, working conditions in other enterprises in the same industry and other industries, and so on. IT facilitates them to interact and discuss issues with worker leaders in other regions of the country and the world. In other words, information technology has helped in widening the vista for workers and in opening up their minds for their broader roles in an enterprise.

Concerns of cost cutting have forced enterprises to seek novel ways of operations, of which outsourcing has become very popular. Systems of contracting and sub-contracting have altered the traditional systems of production and the established pattern of employer-worker relationship, reducing the need for workers in enterprises. There has been an increasing trend in the number of informal workers. These changes have influenced trade union membership and have adversely affected their bargaining power.

INDUSTRIAL RELATIONS AND HRM/HRD

Human Resource Management (HRM) is a process that helps in proper utilisation of the existing workforce in an organisation and creation of such work conditions and systems as can result in better employee efficiency. According to Cascio and Aguinis (2005, p. 4), "HRM is concerned with managing of staff, retention, development, adjustment, and change in order to achieve both individual and organisational objectives." Limited to enterprise-level, the focus of HRM is to carry out organisational functions of recruitment, selection, maintenance and separation with effectiveness and efficiency so as to achieve organisational objectives and motivate employees. HRM may be considered to be individualistic in approach.

Human Resource Development (HRD), on the other hand, may be seen as a sub-set of HRM. Werner and Desimone (2006, p. 15) define HRD as "a set of systematic and planned activities designed by an organisation to provide its members with the opportunities to learn necessary skills to meet current and future job demand." Rao (1985) believes that the process of HRD helps employees in identifying and using their potentials for self and/or organisational development, and develops such organisational culture as supports team work and collaborations among sub-units which contributes to the professional wellbeing and motivation of employees. Thus, the process of HRD is developmental in orientation with the objective to improve and enhance employee capability and competence through their development, in order to gain competitive advantage. The focus of every aspect of HRD is on developing a skilled and superior workforce through continuous learning so that the organisation can satisfy its customers.

Industrial relations, though concerned with employer-worker relations, may be seen to be different from HRM/HRD in several ways. It has a wider scope than HRM as its objective is to achieve improved relations between workers and management at various levels, starting from unit-level, through enterprise-level, regional-level, and finally at the national-level. Industrial relations issues may have involvement of workers across the industry, for example strike by workers of a unit may be joined by workers of other units/enterprises too in the form of sympathetic strike. Further, industrial relations is inherently collectivist in nature as it considers management and workers as two bodies distinct in every aspect of their relation. Another difference is that while industrial relations is tripartite in character, though some of its processes are bipartite too (e.g., collective bargaining), HRM/HRD lacks any such feature and simply involves devising of policies to maintain an efficient workforce in an organisation so as to ultimately get competitive advantage. Moreover, HRM/HRD policies are designed by the management and changed from time to time; industrial relations issues, on the contrary, are mostly governed by labour laws that cannot be modified by management or workers while regulating their relations.

Despite these differences, industrial relations and HRM/HRD cannot be seen as totally different concepts. Both address employee-related concerns, though industrial relations as an area is construed to be dealing with labour/blue-collar employees and HRM/HRD is concerned with white-collar/managerial staff. Issues like employee welfare policies, grievance handling and training of workers are of common concern to HRM/HRD and industrial relations. In the modern industrial scenario, improving quality of work life of employees is also seen as a common concern. As mentioned above, HRM/HRD helps in maintaining, utilising and developing available skilled workforce that also involves motivating workers through rewards and other methods. This helps in maintaining harmonious work relations. It has been already explained that the scope of industrial relations today has expanded to all aspects of interactions between workers and employers that include HR functions like performance appraisal, recruitment and selection, compensation, training, etc. Thus industrial relations and HRM/HRD may be integrated for general development, motivation and welfare of workers and for achieving harmonious employee-management relations.

Spotlight

HRM/HRD and industrial relations may be integrated to improve employee efficiency and competence level and to maintain harmony in work environment.

PRINCIPLES OF LABOUR LEGISLATIONS

Out of the two main players in industry, i.e., labour and management, labour has always been the weaker one. The factory system had certain evils attached to it that affected the already weak labour. The need for labour laws emerged from the need to manage the "problems relating to human relations arising out of large scale development of factory system which has emerged in consequence of industrial revolution" (Mishra, 1999, p. 2). The sole concern of employers was to increase production and productivity without any focus on improving the condition of workers, who were largely illiterate and poor and unaware of their rights. To support their families they had to accept whatever meager wages were offered. The State had no interference in the relation of employer and labour. Gradually when conditions worsened too much, the government was forced to intervene to improve the condition of workers.

The labour laws of independent India derive their origin and guidelines from the Constitution of India and from the beliefs and ideologies of leaders of the struggle for Independence. The Indian Constitution guarantees social equality and social justice to all the citizens. These are the two basic principles on which labour laws are based. According to Mishra (1999), social justice implies two things: first, fair distribution of profits between owner and workers in an industrial enterprise and second, providing safe and healthy work conditions to workers. According to Article 38 of the Constitution, "the State shall strive to promote the welfare of the people by securing and protecting as effectively as it may, social order in which justice, social economic and political, shall inform all the institutions of the national life." Social equity refers to equality between different social groups such as rich and poor; male and female, and young, old and children, religious groups, people belonging to different castes, etc. There must be no discrimination in terms of opportunity, wage distribution, benefits, etc., between different social groups. Article 39 enshrines such principles of social equity.

Spotlight

Two important principles of labour legislations in India are social equity and social justice.

Labour legislations have also been significantly influenced by the Conventions and Recommendations of the ILO, recommendations of the National Commissions on Labour, and deliberations of various sessions of the Indian Labour Conference and the International Labour Conference. These legislations aim at maintaining harmony and discipline in industry so as to promote the growth of the national economy. Though they have been enacted to protect workers, workers have their share of obligations too in maintaining peaceful working conditions in industry. Labour legislations in India may be broadly classified into the following five categories:

- **Regulatory legislations** (e.g., the Trade Unions Act, 1926 and the Industrial Disputes Act, 1947)
- **Wage-related legislations** (e.g., the Payment of Wages Act, 1936 and the Minimum Wages Act, 1948)
- **Welfare legislations** (e.g., the Factories Act, 1948, the Plantation Labour Act, 1951 and the Mines Act, 1952)
- **Protective legislations** (e.g., the Bonded Labour System (Abolition) Act, 1976 and the Child Labour (Prohibition and Regulation) Act, 1986)
- **Social security legislations** (e.g., the Employees' Compensation Act, 1923, the Employees' State Insurance Act, 1948 and the Maternity Benefit Act, 1961)

Chapters 14 to 26 exhaustively cover some of the important labour legislations.

SUMMARY

- The concept of industrial relations may be said to have emerged with the need to manage the relations between labour and management in industry. It has traditionally been viewed as the relationship between employers or their representatives on one side and workers and their representatives on the other, emerging due to work.
- The Constitution of India provides the basic guidelines for creating the industrial relations system. The Fundamental Rights and the Directive Principles of State Policy in the Constitution act as the basis for labour policy.
- The history of industrial relations can be traced back to the time of emergence of industries in India. Enactment of the Factories Act, 1881 was an important milestone in the evolution of industrial relations, as it worked as a catalyst that awakened workers. Several workers' organisations had begun to take form by this time.
- World War I and World War II resulted in price rises due to which employers generated profits, and workers faced situations of economic distress. This led to increase in labour unrest and strikes. Formation of ILO in 1919 gave a boost to labour movement.
- A lot of emphasis was laid on industrial peace during the First Five Year Plan (1951-1956). The first half of the decade of 1970s, during the Fourth Five Year Plan (1969-1974), saw a lot of industrial strife.

- Dunlop viewed industrial relations as a system consisting of three actors: management, workers and the government, that functions in an environment made up of technology, labour, markets, and various power equations in the society.
- The Unitary Theory views work enterprise as a social system made up of management and workers with common objectives and no conflict. The Pluralist Perspective views an organisation as made up of groups of people with divergent objectives and hence considers that conflict is natural. Radical Perspective is inspired by the Marxist view about capitalism that considers conditions and work in organisations as exploitative to workers.
- Industrial relations system in India is tripartite in nature. The First National Commission on Labour was set up in 1966 which, for the first time, studied and analysed the industrial relations in the country. The Second National Commission on Labour was set up in 1999, which analysed the industrial relations in India in the era of globalisation.
- The concepts of HRM/HRD and Industrial Relations may be integrated to create an efficient and motivated workforce working in a harmonious environment.
- The era of globalisation and liberalisation has had a deep impact on labour in India as it has resulted in increased competition, quality consciousness, cost awareness, downsizing and technological changes. It has also generated the need for skill-development in workers.
- Two important principles of labour legislations in India are social equity and social justice. Labour legislations may be broadly divided into five categories: regulatory legislations, wage related legislations, welfare legislations, protective legislations, and social security legislations.

Key Concepts

Systems model	Pluralistic perspective	HRM
Unitary perspective	Directive principles	Labour legislations
Tripartism	National commission on labour	Globalisation

Bibliography

Bray, M. and Wailes, N. "Institutionalism and Industrial Relations Theory". In Bramble, T. et.al (Eds.), *Current Research in Industrial Relations*, Brisbane: AIRAANZ; (1997) pp 55-66. Retrieved from http://mngt.waikato.ac.nz/departments/Strategy%20and%20Human%20Resource%20Management/Airaanz/old/conferce/pdf/bray%26wai.pdf on 1/2/2014.

Camdessus, M. The Impact of Globalization on Workers and their Trade Unions. Address at the Six-teenth World Congress of the International Confederation of Free Trade Unions (ICFTU) Brussels, 26th June,1996. Retrieved from http://www.imf.org/external/np/sec/ mds/ 1996 /mds 9613.htm on 1/2/2014.

Cascio, W. F. and Aguinis, H. *Applied Psychology in Human Resource Management,* New Delhi: Prentice Hall of India; 2005.

Flanders, A. *Unions and Management*. London: Faber and Faber; 1970.

Gennard, J. and Judge, G. *Employee Relations*. London: CIPD Publishing; 2002.

Greenberg, J. and Baron, R. A. *Behavior in Organisations,* 9th edition, New Delhi: Pearson Education Limited; 2008.

Hyman, R. *Industrial Relations: A Marxist Introduction*. London: Macmillan; 1975.

Kanawaty, G., Gladstone, A., Prokopenko, J. and Rodgers, G. Adjustment at the Micro Level, *International Labour Review*, Vol. 128, No. 3, pp. 269-296, 1989.

Mishra, S. N. *Labour and Industrial Legislations*. Allahabad: Central Law Publications;1999.

Monappa, A. *Industrial Relations*. New Delhi: Tata McGraw Hill;1999.

Rao, T.V. Integrated Human Resource Development System. In Goodstein, L. D. and Pfeiffer, J.W. (Eds.), *The 1985 Annual Developing Human Resources*, p. 227. San Diego, CA: University Associates; 1985.

Singh, P. N. and Kumar, N. *Employee Relations Management*, New Delhi: Pearson Education; 2011.

Singh, V. B. *Climate for Industrial Relations*. Bombay: Allied Publisher; 1968.

Tannenbaum, F. *A Philosophy of Labour*. New York: Alfred A. Knopf; 1951.

Wad, P. *Enterprise unions: From Backward to Vanguard Unionism? Theory and Evidence from Industrialized and Industrializing Countries: USA, Japan, South Korea, Mexico, India, and Malaysia*, Copenhagen Business School, Department of Intercultural Communication and Management. 1996.

Werner, J. M and Desimone, R. L. *Human Resource Development,* New Delhi: Cengage Learning; 2006.

Review Questions

Objective Type Questions

I. State True or False

(i) Bombay Mill Hands Association was founded by Mahatma Gandhi.
(ii) HRD is a sub-set of HRM.
(iii) The Code of Discipline was evolved during the Third Five Year Plan.
(iv) The Second National Commission on Labour recommended an umbrella legislation for unorganised sector workers.
(v) The Mines Act, 1952 is a protective legislation.

Answers: (i) False, (ii) True, (iii) False, (iv) True, (v) False

II. Fill in the Blanks

(i) The concept of industrial relations is collectivist and ____ in nature.
(ii) The First National Commission on Labour submitted its report in _________.
(iii) Two important principles of labour legislations in India are social equity and social ______.
(iv) Radical perspective is inspired by the ______ views about capitalism.
(v) Collective bargaining is a _____ arrangement.

Answers: (i) pluralist, (ii) 1969, (iii) justice, (iv) Marxist, (v) bipartite

Discussion Questions

1. What do you understand by the concept of industrial relations?
2. Explain the following:
   (a) Impact of globalisation on industrial relations
   (b) Dunlop's model of industrial relations
   (c) Principles of labour legislations in India
3. Compare the pluralist and the unitary approaches to industrial relations. Which one seems to be more realistic to you?

4. Trace the history of industrial relations in India.
5. Discuss the role of the State in industrial relations in India.
6. Highlight the impact of technology on labour-management relations.
7. Elucidate the underlying principles of labour legislations in India.
8. There is a need to integrate HRM, industrial relations and HRD in modern business scenario. Do you agree with the statement? Justify your answer.
9. Explain how does the system of industrial relations in India draw its elements from the Constitution?
10. Needs of workers in post-liberalisation era are different from those in pre-liberalisation period in India. Discuss.

CASE STUDY

Labour Problems at Toyota-Kirloskar

Background In 1997, the Toyota Motor Corporation of Japan had entered into collaboration with the Kirloskar Group in India and established its motorcar manufacturing unit, Toyota Kirloskar Motors Limited (TKML) at Bangalore, Karnataka with a capital investment of Rs. 7 billion. Initially both Toyota and Kirloskar held equal shares, but the share of Toyota increased in steps to 99:1 in 2003, resulting in a complete takeover by Toyota Motors. The total strength of the workforce in the production line in TKML was 1,819, encompassing both regular and contract workers. TKML is the main assembling unit while Toyota Kirloskar Auto Parts Ltd. (TKAPL) and Toyota Techno Park are the manufacturing units of auto parts. The employees' unions in TKML and TKAPL have played an important role in the labour affairs. Union interventions were successful in improving the work conditions, introduction of good attendance allowance and policy issues relating of labour welfare. Bargaining through the union has been instrumental in wage revision and introduction of mediclaim and shift allowance.

There were a large number of contract workers at TKML and TKAPL and hence job security had emerged as an important issue. These contract workers, due to reasons like uncertainty of employment, were not organised. This lack of organisation had significant repercussions on wages, working conditions and labour relations in terms of differentials between regular and contract workers. Workload, harassments and stressful conditions were also found to be higher for contract workers. The TKML followed 'kanban' or 'just-in-time' and other methods in production that are known to create higher levels of workload and stress. Performance appraisal system at TKML was very subjective and resulted in discriminatory management practices. All these factors were generating dissatisfaction amongst the workers.

The Struggle

The unrest in Toyota Kirloskar started with the discriminatory and unfair labour practices of the management in terms of salary revision, irrational disciplinary actions and non-confirmation of trainee team members. In 2001, TKML announced a hike of Rs. 300 for team members in response to a long-standing demand of the workers for salary revision. This nominal increase was unacceptable to the employees and they protested. The management finally agreed to discuss the issue with some representatives of the employees and solved the problem temporarily, but a majority of the employees were not satisfied with the decision of the management, and they decided collectively to continue with their protest.

The management applied pressure tactics by starting disciplinary action against the leaders and suspended three workers, accusing them of non-performance and instigating violence. Workers continued their protest. In order to destabilise the collective action of the workers and to prevent the formation of an employees' union, the management suggested constituting an association by the name Team Member Association (TMA) in the unit. Despite differences of opinion amongst workers, the TMA was formed with 15 elected members. In the meantime, a team member, who was very active in the struggle, was terminated for non-performance. Disciplinary action against the workers continued. The workers sought explanations through the TMA from the management for the suspension of workers. But the management refused to entertain the TMA as a body for bargaining and negotiation; it considered the functions of the TMA to be restricted to issues of workers' safety and welfare. This led to another strike, which continued for 12 days.

Repeated disciplinary actions by the management and the incapability of the TMA to counter them prompted the workers to register the TMA as a trade union. The employees' union in TKML, affiliated to Centre of Indian Trade Unions (CITU), was formally registered in July, 2001. The workers organised themselves under the banner of Toyota Kirloskar Motors Employees' Trade Union and submitted a charter of demands to the management, that included revoking of the decision of suspensions and terminations. Some of the demands of the employees' union were settled in a tripartite meeting organised by the Assistant Commissioner of Labour, Bangalore. However, the demand of revoking the suspensions and dismissals was not settled in the meeting. The termination of workers continued. On termination of service of a trainee, the union began a fresh agitation and as a result jobs of two of the office bearers of the union were terminated. The workers immediately went on strike that lasted for 52 days with the demand to re-appoint the two union leaders. It was at this juncture that the Government of Karnataka categorically included Toyota Kirloskar in the Public Utility Services (PUS) and redefined the norms of PUS by amending the First Schedule of the Industrial Dispute Act, 1947, in 2001. The strike was therefore called off.

The management started suspending union leaders selectively on the charge of non-performance. This triggered off fresh agitation and several union members were suspended on different pretexts, beginning from January, 2004. Two charters of demand presented by the union in a gap of few months were turned down by the management, which accepted only the wage revision demand in the first charter. Strike notice was served by the union. Protests continued outside the premises of the company and grew in proportion. At this stage, the Minister for Labour, Government of Karnataka held a discussion with the union members and management for resolving the issue. The management did not revoke the suspension of the workers. Discussions with the Deputy Labour Commissioner also did not bring any result. The strike, which had started on 6th January 2006, subsequent to the suspension of three employees for 'severe misconduct', was a part of the long struggle of the workers against the practices of victimisation in the unit.

(Adapted from: George, S. (n.d.) Workers' Struggle in Toyota Kirloskar Motors, India: Changing Capital Labour Relations in Transnational Corporations, Labour File, Vol. 4 No. 1, pp. 34-37. Retrieved from www. labourfile. org/ArticleMore.aspx?id=268 on 1/2/2014.)

Review Questions

1. Discuss the key issues in the case that gave rise to labour problems at TKML.
2. Analyse the role of the concerned trade union in the case.
3. What steps should the management at TKML have taken to improve industrial relations in the organisation?

2

Indian Labour Force

Desired Knowledge Competencies

- To explain the concept of labour force and review its growth in India.
- To analyse sectoral distribution of employment and major occupations in India.
- To describe various characteristics of the Indian labour force.
- To discuss the labour administration machinery in India.

INTRODUCTION

Labour is the physical or mental effort of human beings that undertakes any production process; it is known as the primary factor of production. As a corollary, labour force is an inseparable aspect of the economy of a nation. Ever since industries came up, there have been efforts to understand work and workers in order to improve efficiency and increase productivity. Changes in social, economic, political and technological environments of a nation bring about changes in the nature of its workforce. This chapter provides a basis for understanding the structure, composition and trends of the labour force of India.

According to the definition adopted by the 66th Round of National Sample Survey (2009-2010), labour force comprises persons who are either 'working' (or employed) or are 'seeking or available for work' (or unemployed). As defined by the Manual on Labour Statistics (I) 2012, brought out by the Central Statistics Office, Ministry of Statistics and Programme Implementation, Government of India, labour force covers the current economically active population consisting of the employed and the unemployed. The Manual further explains the economically active population as including all persons of both the sexes who provide labour for the production of economic goods and services during a specified time-reference period as defined by the United Nations system of national accounts and balances. These persons must also fulfill the requirements for inclusion among those who are either employed or unemployed. The Manual also discusses the term 'employed' as defined by the International Labour Organisation (ILO),

Spotlight

Labour force includes the current economically active population comprising the employed and the unemployed.

as encompassing all persons above a specific age, who during a specified brief period, either 1 week or 1 day, were in the following categories:

a. Paid Employment

(i) at work: persons who, during the reference period, have performed some work for wage or salary, in cash or in kind;
(ii) with a job but not at work: persons who, having already worked in their present job, were temporarily not at work during the reference period and had a formal attachment to their job.

b. Self-Employed

(i) at work: persons who, during the reference period, have performed some work for profit or family gain, in cash or in kind;
(ii) with an enterprise but not at work: persons with an enterprise, which may be a business enterprise, a farm or a service undertaking, who were temporarily not at work during the reference period for any specific reason.

The term "some work" used here may be interpreted as work for at least an hour.

Workers in India can be broadly divided into 3 categories: self-employed, casual wage labour, and regular salaried/wage employees (Ministry of Labour & Employment, 2010). These categories may be explained as follows:

> **Spotlight**
> Workers in India are broadly categorised as self-employed, casual wage labour and regular salaried/wage employees.

a. Regular Salaried/Wage Employees

These are individuals who work in farm or non-farm enterprises of others (both household and non-household) on full time or part time basis and receive salary/wage on a regular basis, which could be either time wage or piece wage or even salary. This category also includes paid apprentices.

b. Casual Wage Labour

A person who is casually engaged in others' farm or non-farm enterprises (both household and non-household) is casual wage labour. Wages are received according to the terms of the daily or periodic work contract.

c. Self-Employed

Persons who run their own farm or non-farm enterprises or are engaged in any profession or trade independently on their own account or with 1 or a few partners are said to be self-employed. There are 3 categories of self-employed persons, as follows:

(i) ***Own-account Workers:*** These are self-employed persons who run their enterprises on their own account or with 1 or a few partners and, who by and large, do not hire any labour.
(ii) ***Employers:*** Employers are self-employed persons who operate on their own account or with 1 or a few partners and who, by and large, run their enterprise by hiring labour.
(iii) ***Helpers in Household Enterprises:*** These are self-employed persons (mostly family members) who are engaged in their household enterprises, working full time or part time, assisting a related person living in the same household in running the enterprise. They do not receive any regular salary or wage in return for the work performed.

Let us take a quick look at some more terms to understand the dynamics of labour force in India. These are measures used by the National Sample Survey Office (NSSO), Ministry of Statistics and Programme Implementation to collect data on employment, and include: Usual Status, Current Weekly Status and Current Daily Status, which may be understood as follows:

a. Usual Status (US)

Usual Status reflects the status of a person as belonging to the labour force, if he/she had been either working or looking for work during the major part of the 365 days preceding a survey by the NSSO. Usual Status is divided into 2 categories: Principal Status and Subsidiary Status. Principal Status (PS), also called Usual Principal Status (UPS), is the activity accounting for majority of a person's time over the year, and such workers are called principal status workers. Subsidiary Status (SS) refers to any activity other than the principal activity undertaken on a short-term basis, and such workers are called subsidiary status workers. These categories taken together constitute total employment on the basis of Usual Principal and Subsidiary Status (UPSS), or Usual Status.

Spotlight

Usual Status is divided into 2 categories: Principal Status and Subsidiary Status.

b. Current Weekly Status (CWS)

Current Weekly Status is the activity status of a person during a period of 7 days preceding the date of a survey conducted by NSSO. A person is considered as a worker if he has been involved in an economic activity at least for 1 hour on any day of the reference week.

c. Current Daily Status (CDS)

Current Daily Status is determined on the basis of a person's activity status on each day of the reference week. A person is taken to be employed for the full day if he/she has worked for 4 hours or more during the day.

GROWTH AND SIZE OF INDIAN LABOUR FORCE

Demographic profile of a country has an important bearing on the structure of its labour force. According to the 1991 Census of India, the economically active population stood at 285.9 million and the estimated labour force had grown by more than 65 million since 1981. The findings of the 'Key Indicators of Employment and Unemployment in India 2011-12' released by the NSSO, based on the data collected in its 68th Round (2011-2012), reveal that according to the Status (PS+SS), the workforce at national level has increased from 459.0 million as on 1st January 2010 (NSS 66th Round), to 472.9 million as on 1st January, 2012 (NSS 68th Round), indicating a growth of about 13.9 million. Further, the Report to People on Employment, 2010 has made a projection of growth of the labour force to 574 million in 2014-2015. As per the projections of the 2011 Census report, the ongoing demographic changes in the country are likely to contribute to increasing size of the labour force. There is a projected increase in the proportion of population in the working age group (15-59 years) from approximately 58 per cent in 2001 to more than 64 per cent by 2021 (Ministry of Labour & Employment, 2010). The period from the first half of the last decade, i.e., 1999-2000 to 2004-2005, has witnessed an employment growth of 2.9 per cent per annum, with a significant growth in employment for women both in rural and urban areas.

According to NSSO 68th Round (2011-2012), currently about 40 per cent of the population belongs to the labour force, with 41 per cent in rural areas and 37 per cent in urban areas. The distribution of workforce in rural and urban areas is presented in Table 2.1, which indicates that a higher percentage of workforce is available in rural areas.

Table 2.1 Distribution of Workforce at All-India Level

	Rural (in millions)		*Urban (in millions)*	
	Male	*Female*	*Male*	*Female*
NSS 66th Round	231.9	104.5	99.8	22.8
NSS 68th Round	234.6	101.8	109.2	27.3

(Adapted from: Key Indicators of Employment and Unemployment in India, 2011-2012)

If we see the distribution of workforce in self employed, casual wage labour and regular salaried/wage employees, in 2009-2010 the total self-employed were estimated to be 51 per cent; casual workers stood at 33.5 per cent, and regular wage/salaried employees were 15.6 per cent at the national level (Table 2.2). During 2011-2012, there was an increase in self-employed workers, and regular wage/salaried employees, while casual labour saw a decline.

Table 2.2 Distribution of Usual Status (PS + SS) Workers (per cent) according to Employment Status at National Level

	Self-employed	*Casual labour*	*Regular wage/salaried employees*
2009-2010	51.0	33.5	15.6
2011-2012	52	30	18

(Adapted from: Key Indicators of Employment and Unemployment in India, 2009-2010 and Key Indicators of Employment and Unemployment in India, 2011-2012)

Distribution of workers by status of employment (Table 2.3) shows that in rural areas, the proportion of self-employed had declined from more than 60 per cent in 2004-2005 to 54.2 per cent in 2009-2010. About 11 per cent of the rural self-employed have been found to work as casual labour also, to supplement their household income. Similarly, the proportion of self-employed had declined in urban areas by more than 4 per cent from 45.4 per cent in 2004-2005 to 41.1 per cent in 2009-2010. As an outcome, the proportion of all wage workers in rural areas increased from approximately 40 per cent in 2004-2005 to 46 per cent in 2009-2010. A similar increase in wage workers is evident in urban areas.

The Second Annual Report to People on Employment (Ministry of Labour & Employment, 2011) estimates the all-India unemployment rate to be 3.8 per cent, according to the UPS approach. The global economic slowdown that begun in 2007 had a profound impact on employment conditions in many countries of the world. Even in India, employment growth had slowed down considerably between 2004-2005 to 2009-2010, but there was no net employment loss. In fact, as per the findings of NSSO 66th Round (2009-2010), 6.4 million persons were added to the total employment during this period. The total employment (UPSS) stood at 465.5 million in 2009-2010 (Ministry of Labour & Employment, 2011). It is significant to note that unemployment rate in India has declined during the period 2004-2005 to 2011-2012. It stood at 2 per cent at all-India level in 2011-2012, with 3 per cent in urban areas and 2 per cent in rural areas (Key Indicators of Employment and Unemployment in India, 2011-12).

TABLE 2.3 Percentage Distribution of All Workers by Status of Employment (Self-employed, Regular Employees and Casual Workers) in Rural and Urban Areas in Different Years

	Years			
	1993-1994	*1999-2000*	*2004-05*	*2009-2010*
Rural				
Self-employed	58.0	55.8	60.2	54.2
All wage workers *	42.0	44.2	39.9	45.9
Regular	6.5	6.8	7.1	7.3
Casual	35.6	37.4	32.8	38.6
Urban				
Self-employed	42.3	42.2	45.4	41.1
All wage workers*	57.7	57.8	54.5	58.9
Regular	39.4	40.0	39.5	41.4
Casual	18.3	17.7	15.0	17.5

*Note: *All wage paid is the sum of regular and casual workers.*
(Adapted from: NSSO, 1996, NSSO, 2001, NSSO, 2006, NSSO, 2011)

SECTORAL DISTRIBUTION AND MAJOR OCCUPATIONS IN INDIA

Indian economy can be divided into 3 major sectors: primary (including agriculture), secondary (including manufacturing), and tertiary (including services). As an impact of globalisation, and with growing industrialisation in the country, the share of tertiary sector in the economy has been continuously increasing over the years from about 49 per cent in 1991 to about 62 per in 2006-2007 (Paul et al., 2009) and has remained at the highest among all the 3 sectors. Growth in agricultural and industrial sectors had registered a sharp decline in 2008-09 over the previous year. Though the growth of these sectors has improved by 2010-2011, still it has been less than that of the tertiary sector (Ministry of Labour & Employment, 2011).

From 2009-2010 to 2011-2012 employment in the tertiary sector, in general, has increased, while it showed a decrease in agriculture. According to the 'Key Indicators of Employment, 2011-12', among the workers in Usual Status, about 49 per cent is enagaged in the agricultural sector, 24 per cent in the secondary sector and the rest 27 per cent in the tertiary sector. Table 2.4 shows the data on sectoral distribution of workers in India across different years. In 2009-2010, the contribution of agriculture to total employment had declined by approximately 5 per cent as compared to that in 2004-2005. Although the share of agriculture in India's GDP has come down, 49 per cent of the workforce, majority of which are wage labourers, still continues to depend on this sector (NSSO Survey 2011-2012).

Spotlight
Employment in the tertiary sector has increased from 2009-2010 to 2011-2012.

There was a marginal decline in the share of the manufacturing sector in 2009-2010 as compared to that in 2004-2005. The service sector (including hotels, restaurants and trade, and public administration and community services) registered a marginal increase in share in 2009-2010, though the share of the service sector in total employment has increased from less than 20 per cent in 1993-1994 to more than 25 per cent in 2009-2010. Sectors that have experienced a major increase in share of employment in 2009-2010 were construction and financing & real estate, with the former registering a phenomenal increase. Between 1993-1994 and 2009-2010, the share of construction in the country's total employment has increased by more than 3 times.

TABLE 2.4 Percentage Distribution of Workers (UPSS) by Industrial Classification of Sectors of Employment during Different Years

Sectors	*Distribution of workers (%)*			
	1993-94	*1999-2000*	*2004-05*	*2009-10*
Agriculture	64.75	59.84	58.44	53.20
Sub-Total	**64.75**	**59.84**	**58.44**	**53.20**
Mining & quarrying	0.72	0.57	0.60	0.60
Manufacturing	11.35	12.09	11.69	11.00
Utilities	0.36	0.32	0.30	0.30
Construction	3.12	4.44	5.59	9.60
Sub-Total	**15.55**	**17.42**	**18.18**	**21.50**
Hotels, restaurants and trade	7.42	9.40	10.29	10.80
Transport, storage and communication	2.76	3.70	3.80	4.30
Financing and real estate	0.94	1.27	1.50	2.10
Public administration and community services	8.58	8.36	7.79	8.10
Sub-Total	**19.70**	**22.73**	**23.38**	**25.30**
Total	**100.0**	**100.0**	**100.0**	**100.0**

(Adapted from: Second Annual Report to the People on Employment, 2011)

Workforce in India is characterised by a clear rural-urban divide. Majority of the population is found in rural areas, and hence also the labour force, though, for obvious reasons, majority of people in rural areas are engaged in agricultural activities, while those in urban areas are engaged in the tertiary sector (Table 2.5).

TABLE 2.5 Employment in Different Sectors from 2009–2010 to 2011–2012

Sector	*Rural*				*Urban*			
	Male		*Female*		*Male*		*Female*	
	2009-10	*2011-12*	*2009-10*	*2011-12*	*2009-10*	*2011-12*	*2009-10*	*2011-12*
Agriculture	63	59	79	75	6	6	14	11
Secondary	19	22	13	17	35	35	33	34
Tertiary	18	19	08	8	59	59	53	55

(Adapted from: Key Indicators of Employment and Unemployment in India, 2011-2012)

Organised Sector/Regular Employment

The organised or formal sector in India basically consists of public sector enterprises and private sector organisations. This sector employs less than 10 per cent of India's workforce. According to the estimates of the Ministry of Labour & Employment (2010), around two-thirds of the total organised sector employment was in the public sector and the rest in private sector, largely corporate manufacturing and a variety of services. Regular employment (or organised sector employment) in India has grown at a slower rate in comparison to total employment, implying faster growth of employment in the unorganised sector. This is evident from the findings of various surveys.

Spotlight

Organised sector employment in India has grown at a slower rate in comparison to total employment.

The 2001 Census showed that the organised sector comprised just 7 per cent of the workforce. There has been no significant change in the proportion of regular employed, for both males and females, over the years. However, a change in this trend was observed and there was a marginal increase in the proportion of regular employment from 14 per cent in 1999-2000 to 15.6 per cent in 2009-2010. One of the possible reasons for this increase, as put by Kundu and Mohanan (2009), may be the need of the emerging sectors to meet global competition.

Unorganised Sector Employment

The term 'informal sector' was first used by the International Labour Organisation in 1972, to denote a wide range of small and unregistered economic activities. At the 15th International Conference of Labour Statisticians (January 1993), the informal sector was considered to be the one that "may be broadly characterised as consisting of units engaged in the production of goods or services with the primary objective of generating employment and incomes to the persons concerned. These units typically operate at a low level of organisation, with little or no division between labour and capital as factors of production and on a small scale. Labour relations, where they exist, are based mostly on casual employment, kinship or personal and social relations rather than contractual arrangements with formal guarantees" (Kolli, n.d., p. 4).

In India, the Report on Conditions of Work and Promotion of Livelihoods in the Unorganised Sector, 2007, published by the National Commission for Enterprises in the Unorganised Sector (NCEUS), has defined unorganised workers as those who work in the households or unorganised enterprises without any security of employment or social security provided by employers. The NCEUS (2007) has also provided a structure to the informal sector in India, by classifying the workforce into the following segments:

(a) Unorganised non-agricultural workers
   (i) Wage workers in non-agricultural sector
   (ii) Self-employed workers in non-agricultural sector
   (iii) Women workers in non-agricultural sector
(b) Other disadvantaged workers (migrant, child, and bonded labour)
(c) Agricultural workers
   (i) Agricultural labourers
   (ii) Farmers

The unorganised sector (often referred to as the informal sector) plays a pivotal role in the economy of India, by providing employment to a high proportion of socially and economically underprivileged sections of the

Spotlight

Unorganised workers work in households or unorganised enterprises; they do not have any security of employment or social security.

society. The NSS 62nd Round indicated that workers in unorganised informal enterprises constituted 92.4 per cent of all workers. According to another estimate, informal employment accounted for 95.5 per cent of total employment in 2004-2005, with 1.5 per cent each in public and private corporate sectors (National Statistical Commission, 2012). The growth in employment in the Indian economy is largely due to increase in the informal sector, irrespective of whether the employment is in the organised or unorganised sector. For example, the growth in employment of 61 million (from 362 million to 423 million) has been of informal employment in the organised sector (NCEUS, 2007).

Another prominent trend has been that of increased casualisation in work. Casual wage labour forms a part of the unorganised sector. These workers lack social security benefits, and do not even have a regular job contract. Studies indicate that sub-contracting arrangement of work in the unorganised sector is increasingly becoming popular as it ensures longer hours of work without higher pay. This is an outcome of globalisation and capital-centric growth policies (Bhaduri and Patkar, 2009). Agriculture is the main sector where the majority of casual labour is absorbed, followed by the manufacturing and service sectors respectively. At the national-level, the largest proportion of casual labour is involved in growing of food grain crops, followed by general constructions activities.

The informal workforce in India faces a host of problems. It has low rate of education, and low awareness, and a majority of it works under poor working conditions. There is no job security or social security. The most vulnerable sections of the society belong to this sector. 'Inclusive growth' has remained an agenda of the Government of India since quite some time. To attain the objective of inclusive growth there has been a perceived need for improving the quality of work life and raising the level of living standard of workers, particularly those who occupy a pivotal position in the overall growth process of the country. In this regard the Unorganised Sector Workers' Social Security Bill, 2007 aims at providing social security to unorganised sector workers. The *Rashtriya Swasthya Bima Yojna* is another social security measure introduced by the Government for these workers in the recent years, which provides health insurance cover to workers below the poverty line in any empanelled hospital in the country.

Spotlight

The *Rashtriya Swasthya Bima Yojna* provides health insurance cover to the unorganised sector workers below the poverty line in any empanelled hospital in the country.

CHARACTERISTICS OF INDIAN LABOUR

India's vast labour force has its own unique features. It is diverse in terms of religion, caste, gender, culture, education level, skill level, area of working (rural and urban), and so on. These features have not only affected its growth and development, but have also affected the overall industrial relations scenario in the country. Certain important characteristics of Indian labour force are discussed in this section.

Caste System

Caste has been the one of the most significant discriminating factors in the Indian labour market. The country has a deep rooted caste system that influences not only the day-to-day activities of people, but also affects the occupations they choose. Medhora (1965) pointed out that the Indian caste system has been so pervasive in every aspect of life of people that it determines not just access to opportunities and choice of economic activities of a person, but also his social status. In olden times, the Indian society was

Spotlight

In ancient times the Indian society was divided into 4 ***varnas*** or castes on the basis of economic activities: ***brahmins***, ***kshatriyas***, ***vaishyas*** and ***shudras***.

divided into 4 *varnas* or castes on the basis of economic activities: *brahmins*, who took up religious and educational activities; *kshatriyas*, who were experts in warfare; *vaishyas*, the trading community; and *shudras*, who were supposed to take up the so called lowly jobs like scavenging. *Shudras* were forced to live in segregation and were often an exploited category. Occupations were hereditary and there was very little or no occupational mobility. Some impact of this pattern of division of society, as in ancient times, exists even today, though these socio-cultural rigidities are decreasing in impact with changing times. Government resorted to the policy of reservation for the 'not so privileged' categories of people in the social system with a view to provide them with equal opportunities in terms of education and employment. Thus, today labour force in India consists of people who belong to Scheduled Castes (SCs), Scheduled Tribes (STs), Other Backward Classes (OBCs), and so on. Table 2.6 shows that there has been an increase in the percentage of people involved in regular employment in various social groups over the years. At all-India level, the UPS rates of participation in the labour force for the SC, ST and OBC groups are 55.9 per cent, 59.7 per cent, and 53.3 per cent respectively, as against 48.5 per cent for the general category (Ministry of Labour & Employment, 2011).

TABLE 2.6 Percentage of Workers in Regular Employment in Different Social Groups (1999–2000, 2004–2005 and 2009–2010)

Social Group	*1999-2000*	*2004-2005*	*2009-2010*
SC	10.42	12.37	12.94
ST	6.79	6.73	7.73
OBC	11.59	12.05	13.28
Others	21.65	21.46	23.89
All	14.01	14.25	15.59

(Adapted from: Second Annual Report to the People on Employment, 2011)

EXHIBIT 2.1 DISCRIMINATION IN THE INDIAN PRIVATE SECTOR

A field experiment was carried out to seek evidence on discrimination in Indian job market. The study analysed responses to job applications sent to private sector firms to ascertain the effect of caste and religious backgrounds in the process of job market selection. 3 responses were sent to each call–as an upper caste Hindu, as a Dalit, and as a Muslim. The identities were differentiated only by the names on the applications, which otherwise were similar in all other respects. The companies chosen were securities and investment companies; pharmaceutical and medical sales; computer sales, support and IT services; manufacturing; accounting firms, automobiles sales and financing; marketing and mass media; agriculture sales; construction and banking. The study found that job applicants with a Dalit or Muslim name were less likely to have a positive application outcome than equally qualified persons with a high caste Hindu name.

(Adapted from: Thorat S. and Attewell P. "The Legacy of Social Exclusion", Economic and Political Weekly, 2007, Vol. 48 No. 41, pp. 4141-4145.)

Education Level

There is a low literacy rate in the labour force in India and spreading even basic education is still a challenging task. NSSO (2007) reveals a direct link between level of education and regular employment, indicating that as the level of education rises, the percentage of regular employment increases. The all-India school drop-out rates have been reported as 27 per cent, 40.6 per cent, and 49.3 per cent in the year 2010-2011 for classes I-V, I-VIII, and I-X respectively (Amirtham and Kundupuzhakkal, 2013). The school drop-outs usually join the pool of unorganised labour, and this in turn explains the large size of unorganised sector in India.

Gender

Let us now take a look at the gender dimension of labour force in India. In general, women's participation in the labour market has been typically low in India. According to the Annual Report to the People on Employment (2010), bulk of employment in India is concentrated in the agricultural sector. In rural areas, agriculture constitutes up to 68 per cent of the total employment, engaging approximately 81 per cent female workers and 66 per cent male workers. Employment growth rate and labour force growth rate of females are lower than that of males. According to the Second Annual Employment and Unemployment Survey 2011-2012, conducted by the Labour Bureau, Ministry of Labour & Employment, the Female Work Participation Rate (FWPR) is estimated to be 23.6 per cent at all-India level under the UPS approach, as compared to the Male WPR of 75.1 per cent. There has also been a long term downward trend in the FWPR for rural areas, with the downslide more pronounced in the case of UPS workers. The proportion of UPS workers among rural females consistently fell between 1983 and 2009-2010, except in 2004-2005. Another interesting observation is that out of the 3 employment categories of workers recorded by the NSS, a higher proportion of female workforce is always in the self-employed group. Also, rural female workforce comprises a large proportion of unpaid workers, consistently above 40 per cent since the period 1993-1994 to 2007-2008, with an all time high of 48 per cent in 2004-2005. The share of paid or income-earning self-employed has been around 15 per cent. Another striking feature is that casual labour accounts for the majority of the paid female workforce in rural areas (Mazumdar and Neetha, 2011).

Spotlight

Employment growth rate and labour force growth rate of females are lower than that of males.

If we look at the compound annual growth rate (CAGR) of labour force during the period 2004-2005 to 2009-2010, it is higher for urban persons than for rural persons for all workers, but there has been a decrease in CAGR of female workers, both in rural and urban areas, the decrease being higher in rural areas (Table 2.7). Total female employment had declined by about 1 million in urban areas and by nearly 19 million in rural areas. Subsidiary status workers, that comprise usually the most vulnerable section of workforce, showed a prominent decline in employment. It may be concluded from the available data that a large proportion of the decline in total employment during 2004-2005 to 2009-2010 is accounted for by the decline in the subsidiary status employment of women workers.

TABLE 2.7 Number of Workers (in millions) and their CAGR in 2004–2005 and 2009–2010

	Principal status workers (measured as UPS)			*Subsidiary status workers (measured as subsidiary workers)*			*All workers (measured as UPSS)*		
Rural	***2004-2005***	***2009-2010***	***CAGR***	***2004-2005***	***2009-2010***	***CAGR***	***2004-2005***	***2009-2010***	***CAGR***
Male	213.5	228.0	1.31	4.5	4.1	–1.98	218.5	232.1	1.21
Female	91.4	81.2	–2.34	33.0	24.0	–6.19	123.8	105.2	–3.20
Total	304.9	309.2	0.28	37.5	28.7	–5.61	342.3	337.9	–0.26
Urban									
Male	90.1	102.8		2.68	1.4 0.7	–11.73	91.6	103.4	2.45
Female	20.4	20.9	0.47	4.8	3.2	–7.80	25.2	24.1	–0.89
Total	110.5	123.7	2.28	6.2	4.0	–8.61	116.8	127.7	1.80
Rural + Urban									
Male	303.6	330.7	1.73	5.9	4.8	–3.92	310.1	335.5	1.59
Female	111.8	102.1	–1.80	37.8	27.9	–5.89	149.0	130.0	–2.69
Total	415.4	432.8	0.82	43.7	32.7	–5.63	459.1	465.5	0.28

(Adapted from: NSSO, 2006, NSSO, 2011)

The main reasons that have been pointed out for the low participation of women in the labour force are that wage rates of women are lower than that of men in many occupations and that women are denied of many occupations though they are capable of working with same competence as men (Planning Commission, 2008). Other reasons include failure to recognise many of the women-centric work (such as cooking, collection of fuel and fodder, house and utensils cleaning, etc.) as economic activities, social and family compulsions, and patriarchal nature of the society. Despite this, it must be noted that women's participation in labour market has significantly increased in recent years, particularly in urban areas (Ministry of Labour & Employment, 2011).

Liberalisation has brought a lot of changes in the Indian economy, that have had a significant impact upon the state of women's employment. These changes include increasing informalisation of the economy; sub-contracting and outsourcing to developing countries; and growth of export-oriented manufacturing (Nihila, 1999; Neetha, 2002). As observed by Ghosh (2004), a term that is now being used to characterise the labour force that is required for these jobs is 'feminisation'. The principal characteristics of feminisation are: a move towards casualisation of labour, shift to part-time or piece-rate contracts, and higher freedom of hire and fire. Under these situations women seem to be the preferred choice for employers since they are available at lower wages and are easier to 'manage'.

It is interesting to note that though the percentage of regular female employees is relatively low as compared to males in both rural and urban India, it has been increasing over the years. As per the Annual Employment Review (2010), published by Director General of Employment and Training, Ministry of Labour & Employment, there has been an increase in women's employment in the organised sector from 4.93 million in March 2004 to 5.53 million in March 2009. This could partly be due to increase in demand for domestic workers, who are categorised as regularly employed (Paul et al., 2009). However, the percentage of regular male workers showed no significant change from 1999-2000 (17.2 per cent) to 2009-2010 (17.7 per cent), as shown by NSSO survey (Ministry of Labour & Employment, 2011).

Migratory Character

In recent years, with increased mobility of population, the study of migration characteristics has assumed significant importance. Any movement which involves change of residence from one village or town to another village or town is known as migration. Historically speaking, migration as a new source of employment appeared after the Organisation of Petroleum Exporting Countries (OPEC) had sharply increased crude oil prices in 1974. The Middle East oil-exporting countries begun huge development programmes based on their large oil revenues and hence required skilled and unskilled labour. Many workers from India migrated to these Gulf countries during that period in search of lucrative jobs. In recent times, there has been a widespread migration of labour from villages to towns as well. Globalisation may be seen as the prime reason for this trend. New job opportunities lure the youth to move to towns. Farmers, especially from the upper caste, who constitute the bulk of the agricultural community, are the worst hit. While the family members from the lower communities, including women and children, engage themselves in agricultural activities, the upper caste women keep away from such activities as these are considered below their dignity. Therefore such farmers are forced to migrate to cities to earn their living. Migration is not just taking place from rural to urban areas, or of skilled workers to Gulf countries; there has been migration of professionals to emerging sectors like Information Technology (IT), and of doctors, engineers and scientists to other developed countries for better career opportunities and higher earnings.

Spotlight

Migration refers to any movement which involves change of residence from one village or town to another village or town.

EXHIBIT 2.2 PROBLEMS OF LABOUR MIGRATION

Migration of labour to towns in the State of Bihar has created problems for farmers who were on the threshold of a bumper paddy crop after a spell of drought for 2 years. Lack of labour made harvesting a daunting task. The ever-increasing trend of labour migration is mainly an offshoot of rich cash offered to the migrants and also the lucrative commission and perks earned by the brokers, who act as a conduit between the labour and the employers from other States. These touts, a good number of them who are mostly unemployed youths from the villages, earn nothing less than ₹50,000 to ₹0.2 million every year.

Bihar Institute of Economic Studies reveals that migration among the Musahar community was alarming. It attributes the reason to the poor performance of the Mahatma Gandhi National Rural Employment Guarantee Act that had promised employment to workers. Roughly 4 lakh labour, comprising nearly 5 per cent of the district's total population, have migrated to States like Uttar Pradesh, Punjab, Haryana and West Bengal. While majority of them prefers to work in brick kilns, only a small minority is into harvesting work in these States.

(Adapted from: Sinha, S. B. (2011). Labour migration leaves farmers high and dry. Retrieved from www.articles.timesofindia.indiatimes.com/2011-11-23/patna/30432685_1_labour-migration-contractors on 18/7/2014.)

Absenteeism and Labour Turnover

Absenteeism and labour turnover are common problems in Indian industries. Absenteeism rate amongst workers in an industry is an indicator of the level of their job satisfaction, morale and commitment to job. It directly affects the productivity of the individual worker as well as the entire industry. There are multiple implications of high levels of absenteeism on an organisation, besides decrease in productivity. These include reduction in quantity of output and decrease in quality of product or service that may result in loss of customer base and ultimately affect profits adversely. Reasons for high level of labour turnover could be poor human resource policies of the organisation, dissatisfaction with salary/wage, long working hours, low career growth opportunities, better opportunities offered by competitors, and personal variables like family responsibilities, particularly in case of women.

Spotlight

Absenteeism rate amongst workers in an industry is an indicator of the level of their job satisfaction, morale and commitment to job.

There has been a consistent increase in the rate of absenteeism of workers. The Annual Survey of Industries (2009-2010) reports that the rate of absenteeism at all-India level has increased to 8.75 per cent during 2009 from 8.65 per cent during 2008 (Ministry of Labour & Employment, 2013). In 2007 it was 8.34 per cent and was still lower at 7.99 per cent in 2006 (Ministry of Labour & Employment, 2012). The highest absenteeism rate amongst the directly employed regular workers during 2009 was reported in the industry group 'Manufacture of Tobacco Products' (15.64 per cent) and the lowest in 'Water Collection, Treatment and Supply' (1.59 per cent). At all-India level, 66.85 per cent factories had reported labour turnover in their units during 2009, the highest being 96.43 per cent in the industry group 'Manufacture of Man-made Fibres', followed by 94.74 percent in 'Mining and Quarrying' (Ministry of Labour & Employment, 2013).

Move towards Informalisation

From the discussion in the previous sections it is clear that there is a shift towards forced informalisation of labour in the Indian economy. This move has been necessitated by the changing economic and global business scenario. It is becoming tough for the workers, new and old, to get secure employment. Informal jobs are increasing even in the organised sector. Those with full time regular jobs are forced to move to part-time or casual, low-paid jobs in the unorganised sector. This can be seen from the growing trend in outsourcing of manufacturing from the large scale sector to the small and medium sector. This is also one of the reasons for the de-industrialisation of most of the industrial centers. Big companies hire casual labour or outsource their requirements of materials, etc. Operating at the level of small scale industries is advantageous to big companies as most of the laws for protecting employment are not enforced in these industries. Another advantage is that these industries are exempted from paying taxes for the first 5 years. This trend may be seen as an outcome of liberalisation, which has resulted in increased competition at all levels and organisations are forced to make such strategies as would help them reduce costs and increase profits. The overall effect is the growth of the informal sector.

Child Labour

Considered as a vulnerable group in the Indian labour market, child labour, according to the Child Labour (Prohibition and Regulation) Act, 1986, constitutes the work done by children below 14 years of age. States like Andhra Pradesh, Uttar Pradesh, Karnataka, Orissa, West Bengal, Madhya Pradesh and Delhi and are having relatively higher concentration of child labour. Giri (2005) has identified the causes and impact of child labour. While the causes include poverty, illiteracy, lack of education, lack of unionism, migrated population and large family size, the impact of child labour on human resource development was found in the form of exploitation, low earnings of workers, and low career options.

Spotlight

Child labour constitutes the work done by children below 14 years of age.

Elimination of child labour has been a policy concern for the Government of India not only from the perspective of development of children, but also for maintaining labour standards. The Government has launched several direct and indirect measures to control this problem. The National Policy on Child Labour was formulated in 1987, aiming to eradicate child labour and protect all children from exploitation.

EXHIBIT 2.3 CHILD LABOUR IN GLASS INDUSTRY

The district of Firozabad is known for its glass industry. The products of the glass industry broadly include glass bangles, glass hardware, products for science laboratories, automobiles, domestic purposes, etc. Glass manufacturing takes place in hazardous conditions. Temperature as high as 1400°C to 1600°C is used during the manufacturing process which increases the ambient temperature up to 50ºC in manufacturing sheds.

A large number of children are engaged in various processes of glass works. These children are as young as 5-6 years. Maximum number belongs to the age group of 8-12 followed by 13-16. The operations which involve majority of child labour are carried out in the informal sector outside the factory at household levels and godowns. These processes include *Jhalai* (straightening of bangles), *Jurai* (joining), *Murai* (designing by use of forceps), *Katai* (designing by grinders), polishing, *Chaklai* (sorting), packaging in small cardboard boxes and transporting the bangles from the place of one process to another. Children are preferred as they have no bargaining power, and are more active, agile and disciplined. Poverty of the family pushes them into this work. The working conditions cause injury to health and often result in physical disabilities.

(Adapted from: Chandra, A. (2009). Child Labor– A Study from Anthropological Perspective with Special Reference to Glass Industry, Firozabad, Anthropologist, Vol. 11 No. 1, pp. 15-20.)

EMPLOYMENT IN EMERGING SECTORS

The Indian economy has witnessed phenomenal changes ever since liberalisation was introduced more than 2 decades ago. The developments that have taken place as a result have given a boost to the economy and have consequently affected the labour market in a significant manner. Increased exports from India have led to an increase in employment opportunities in the export-oriented sectors. Some of the high employment potential sectors include IT, IT Enabled Services, engineering goods, gems and jewellery, hospitality and health care, automobile, mining, readymade garments, textiles and handicrafts. Expansion and dealings across borders have provided an impetus for introduction of modern technologies that provides a reason for skill enhancement of the Indian workforce. Certain new sectors are also emerging that are providing good employment opportunities. As observed earlier in the chapter, the service sector is growing in size; many of the above mentioned emerging sectors belong to the service sector. According to the Ministry of Labour & Employment (2010), a large number of people are employed in the retail sector, which includes both the organised and unorganised labour market (7.1 per cent). The second largest labour market comprises the construction industry (5.9 per cent). This sector is male dominated (7.7 per cent) and pro-urban in terms of employment, employing nearly 8.7 per cent of the urban and 5 per cent of the rural workers.

LABOUR ADMINISTRATION MACHINERY

The ILO Convention No. 150 has defined labour administration as "public administration activities in the field of national labour policy" (Labour Administration, n.d.). The government of any nation applies international labour standards through its national laws and policies. It is therefore essential that a country maintains a robust and active labour administration system or machinery that holds the responsibility for formulating and implementing labour policies. Casale and Sivananthiran (2010) propose that labour administration system encompasses all public administration bodies responsible for and/or engaged in labour administration, which may include ministries, departments of ministries, public agencies (state level, regional, or local agencies), or any other form of decentralised administration, and any institutional framework for the coordination of the activities of such bodies, and for consultation with and participation by employers and workers and their organisations.

Looking at the history of labour administration in India we find that during the late nineteenth century, matters pertaining to labour administration were enforced through Magistrates. There were only a few laws in existence to regulate labour conditions (e.g., Fatal Accidents Act, 1855; Workmen's Breach of Contract Act, 1859; Employers and Workmen (Disputes) Act, 1860, etc.). Labour administration was done on a temporary and casual basis as there was no fixed policy on labour issues. The Government of India Act, 1919, for the first time, gave some shape to labour administration and defined in some detail the distribution of legislative and administrative powers between the central and provincial governments. Generally, the Central Government could enact labour laws relating to mines, railways, major ports, seamen, and international and inter-provincial emigration, and the provincial governments could deliberate on labour matters pertaining to factories, plantations, public works, inland vessels, labour disputes, labour welfare, and housing, but under the control of the Central Government.

Spotlight
Labour falls in the concurrent list of the Constitution of India.

Today, India has a fixed system of labour administration with a well-defined structure. Labour falls in the Concurrent List of the Constitution of India. This means that both the Central Government and the State governments have the power to make laws on this subject. Machinery for administering labour issues exists both at the central and State levels.

Labour Administration Machinery of the Central Government

The highest authority with respect to labour issues lies with the Ministry of Labour & Employment, while the Secretary, Ministry of Labour & Employment, holds the executive authority. The Ministry has 4 attached offices and 10 subordinate offices, in addition to 4 autonomous organisations, several adjudication bodies and 1 arbitration body. Apart from the Ministry of Labour & Employment, Ministries specialised for certain industrial sectors (for example the Ministry of Power and the Ministry of Mines) cover aspects of labour administration such as safety and specific aspects of social security and labour welfare, with respect to defined groups of workers.

Spotlight
The highest authority with respect to labour issues lies with the Ministry of Labour & Employment.

The Chief Labour Commissioner (CLC) at the Central level controls the implementation of provisions of labour legislations. The organisation of the Chief Labour Commissioner (Central), known as the Central Industrial Relations Machinery (CIRM), was set up in April 1945, as an outcome of the recommendation of the Royal Commission on Labour in India. It was entrusted with the responsibility of preventing and settling industrial disputes, enforcing labour laws and promoting the welfare of workers in the undertakings of the Central Government. The Chief Labour Commissioner's office has the responsibility to enforce the Industrial Disputes Act, 1948, the Payment of Wages Act, 1936, and rules made in respect of mines, railways, air transport services and docks, wharves and jetties in major ports, Industrial Employment (Standing Orders) Act, 1946, the Minimum Wages Act, 1948, the Maternity Benefit Act, 1961, the Payment of Bonus Act, 1965, the Contract Labour (Regulation and Abolition) Act, 1970, the Payment of Gratuity Act, 1972, the Equal Remuneration Act, 1976, the Inter-state Migrant Workmen (Regulation of Employment and Conditions of Service) (RE&CS) Act,1979, the Child Labour (Prohibition and Regulation) Act, 1986, the Labour Laws (Exemption from Furnishing Returns and Maintaining Registers by Certain Establishments) Act, 1988, the Indian Railway Act, 1989, the Building and Other Construction Workers (RE&CS) Act, 1996, Chapter VI-A of the Indian Railway Act, 1989, Hours of Employment Regulations for Railway Employees, 1961 (now known as Railway Servants (Hours of Work and Period of Rest) Rules, 2005 w.e.f. 28.02.2005), MES Contractors Workers Regulations, and the Maternity Benefit (Mines and Circus) Rules, 1963, for organisations where the Central Government is the appropriate government (*www.clc.gov.in*). The CLC is responsible for enforcing labour legislation with respect to wages, remuneration, child labour, contract labour, migrant labour, working time, industrial disputes, and maternity benefits in the industries and establishments for which the Central Government is the appropriate Government.

Each State in India has a Labour Minister who heads the Department of Labour of that State. The Secretary of the Department has the executive authority. Though many agencies and government departments such as Chambers of Commerce, Factory and Mines Inspectorate, Social Insurance Directorate, and the Department of Human Resource Development and Education are involved in labour administration, but it is primarily the responsibility of the Department of Labour to formulate, develop and execute labour policies.

Spotlight

Labour Commissioner at State-level has the responsibility of ensuring proper implementation of the provisions specified in labour legislations.

Labour Commissioner at State-level has the responsibility of ensuring the proper implementation of the provisions specified in labour legislations. The Labour Commissioner has multiple responsibilities that include inspection of factories, conciliation, and hearing of various review applications of aggrieved parties under various labour laws. The Commissioner may act as appropriate Government for granting sanction for prosecution, besides functioning as a competent authority for issuing orders under various provisions of the Industrial Disputes Act, 1947, and other labour legislations. At State-level below the Labour Commissioner are the Joint Labour Commissioner, the Assistant Labour Commissioner, and other officers.

Department(s) Responsible for Labour Inspection

The Directorate General, Factory Advice Service and Labour Institutes (DGFASLI) and the Chief Labour Commissioner are attached offices of the Ministry of Labour & Employment. The CLC is responsible for enforcing labour legislations related to working conditions, as discussed above, whereas the DGFASLI is responsible for carrying out inspections related to occupational safety and health issues.

Spotlight

The DGFASLI is responsible for carrying out inspections related to occupational safety and health.

At State-level, the Inspectorates of Factories, under the control of State Labour Departments, enforce the Factories Act, 1948 in their respective States. The Directorate General of Mines Safety conducts safety and health inspections with respect to safety and health regulations in mines and oilfields. There are Inspectors who carry out safety and health inspections and those related to other issues in respect of labour. There are also special inspectorates in some States covering particular industries, for example, the Plantation Inspectorate in Kerala. Labour Inspectors may conduct inspections on receiving a complaint or in cases where it is deemed necessary to ensure the safety of workers. Powers of Inspectors are limited to filing complaints in the courts of law but Inspectors can issue a prohibition order in such conditions at places like construction sites, mines etc., where there is a danger to life—safety and health of the workers or of the public— until measures have been taken to remove the cause of the danger to the Inspectors' satisfaction. Inspectors may consult the trade unions or workers' representatives during inspections.

The Director General of Inspection in the Central sphere is authorised to exercise the powers of an Inspector as well as a quasi-judicial authority, and holds the power to impose fines on offending employers.

Some Central laws are enforced by the Central Government and others by the State governments. Nature of the establishment or sector decides whether it will be governed by Central or State Government. For example, factories, boilers and electricity fall under concurrent legislative powers, whereas railways, highways, major ports, mines and oilfields come under the competency of the Union.

Local Divisions

For the purpose of effective labour administration, there are 18 regions across the country, each headed by a Regional Labour Commissioner. The DGFASLI has both its headquarters and the Central Labour Institute in Mumbai and 4 Regional Labour Institutes at Chennai, Kanpur, Kolkata and Faridabad. It works in coordination with its Central and Regional Labour Institutes. The activities of DGFASLI include mainly framing policies and plans, and executing the programmes pertaining to safety, health and welfare of workers in industries and docks; it also maintains liaison with national and international agencies for its activities.

Summary

- Labour force includes the current economically active population comprising the employed and unemployed.
- Workers can be broadly divided into 3 categories—self-employed, casual wage labour and regular salaried/wage employees. At the national-level majority of the workers belong to self-employed category.
- Certain measures used by the National Sample Survey Office to collect data on employment are: Usual Status, Current Weekly Status and Current Daily Status.
- Majority of workforce in rural areas is employed in the primary sector, while majority in urban areas is employed in the tertiary sector.
- The organised sector employs less than 10 per cent of India's workforce. Regular employment or organised sector employment in India has grown at a slower rate in comparison to total employment.
- Indian economy is showing a trend of movement towards informalisation as a result of changing economic and global business scenario. Informal employment accounts for major proportion of total employment. There has been faster growth of employment in the unorganised sector.
- Migration of labour from rural to urban areas is a common feature. Migration of professionals to countries abroad is also taking place in search of better career and earning opportunities.

- Workforce is India is highly variegated. Heterogeneity exists mainly with respect to gender, area of working (rural/urban), skill and caste. Indian labour force is characterised by low education level and shows a tendency towards absenteeism and turnover.
- Women have a low participation rate in the labour force. Many socio-cultural factors are responsible for this situation. There is also a prevalence of child labour in India.
- Labour falls in the Concurrent List of the Indian Constitution.
- The labour administrative machinery in India is well-structured, with the Ministry of Labour & Employment at the Centre as the apex body.
- The Chief Labour Commissioner (Central) controls the implementation of provisions of labour legislations. DGFASLI is responsible for carrying out inspections related to occupational safety and health issues.

Key Concepts

Self-employed	Regular salaried employees	Informalisation
Usual status	Child labour	Absenteeism
Casual wage labour	Labour administration	Migration

Bibliography

Amirtham, N. S. and Kundupuzhakkal, S. "Gender Issues and Dropout Rates in India: Major Barrier in Providing Education for All", *Educationia Confab*, 2013, Vol. 2, No. 4, pp. 226-233. Retrieved from http://www.confabjournals.com/confabjournals/images/6520138445228.pdf on 18/7/2014.

Bhaduri, A. and Patkar, M. "Alternative Industrialization", *Economic and Political Weekly, 2009, Vol.* 44, No.1, pp.10-15.

Casale, G. and Sivananthiran A. Fundamentals of Labour Administration, 2010. Retrieved from http://www.ilo.org/wcmsp5/groups/public/@dgreports/@dcomm/@publ/documents/article/wcms_120687.pdf on 18/7/2014.

Central Statistics Office. *Manual on Labour Statistics (I) 2012*. Ministry of Statistics and Programme Implementation, New Delhi: Government of India; 2012.

Ghosh, J. Informalisation and Women's Workforce Participation: A Consideration of Recent Trends in Asia, 2004. Retrieved from http://www.networkideas.org/ featart/apr2004/ Women_informal_work.pdf on 17/7/2014.

Giri, G. D. Impact of Child Labour and Human Resource Development with Special Reference to Automobile Workshops in Mumbai. *Ninth Digest of Indian Labour Research*, 2005, p. 10. Labour Bureau, Ministry of Labour & Employment, Chandigarh/Shimla: Government of India. Retrieved from http://labourbureau.nic.in/Ninth_Digest_Mar_2011.pdf on 18/7/2014.

http://clc.gov.in/estb/shtm/functions.php on 16/7/2014.

http://www.ilo.org/labadmin/info/WCMS_156047/lang--en/index.htm

Key Indicators of Employment and Unemployment in India, 2011-12: Retrieved from http:// pib.nic.in/newsite/erelease.aspx?relid=96641 on 8/7/2014.

Kolli, R. Concepts, Definitions and Sub-classifications of Informal Sector and Informal Employment, n.d.. Retrieved from http://www.uneca.org/sites/default/files/uploaded-documents/ACS/AGEIS2013/ageis2013-discussions-concepts-eca-chap2_en.pdf on 18/7/2014.

Kundu, A. and Mohanan, P. C. *Employment and Inequality Outcomes in India*, 2009. Retrieved from http://www.oecd.org/dataoecd/54/51/42546020.pdf on 17/7/2014.

Labour Administration. Retrieved from http://www.ilo.org/global/topics/labour-law/labour-administration/lang--en/index.htm on 18/7/2014.

Major Concepts and Definitions: NSS 61st Round. Retrieved from http:// mospi.nic.in/ mospi _new / upload/ nsso/concepts_61R.pdf on 18/7/2014.

Mazumdar, I. and Neetha, N. "Gender Dimensions: Employment Trends in India, 1993-94 to 2009-10", *Economic and Political Weekly*, 2011, Vol. 46, No. 43, pp. 118-126.

Medhora, P. B. "Entrepreneurship in India," *Political Science Quarterly*, 1965, Vol. 80, No. 4, 558-580

Ministry of Labour & Employment. *Annual Report to the People on Employment*, New Delhi: Government of India; 2010.

Ministry of Labour & Employment. *Second Annual Report to the People on Employment,* New Delhi: Government of India; 2011.

Ministry of Labour & Employment. *India Labour Year Book 2009 and 2010*, Labour Bureau, Chandigarh/ Shimla: Government of India; 2012.

Ministry of Labour & Employment. *Annual Survey of Industries, 2009-10, Vol. II: Report on Absenteeism, Labour Turnover, Employment & Labour Cost*, Chandigarh/Shimla: Labour Bureau, Government of India; 2013.

Ministry of Statistics and Programme Implementation. Key Indicators of Employment and Unemployment in India, 2009-10, National Statistical Organisation, National Sample Survey Office, Government of India; 2011.

National Commission for Enterprises in Unorganised Sector. *Conditions of Work and Promotion of Livelihoods in the Unorganized Sector,* New Delhi: Government of India; 2007.

National Sample Survey Office. *Employment and Unemployment in India, 1993-94.* 50th Round, July 1993-June1994, Report 409, New Delhi: Government of India; 1996.

National Sample Survey Office. *Employment and Unemployment Situation in India 1999–2000.* 55th Round, July 1999–June 2000, Report No. 458, Part I and II and Unit Level Data. New Delhi: Government of India; 2001.

National Sample Survey Office. *Employment and Unemployment Situation in India 2004-05,* 61st Round, July 2004–June 2005, Report No. 515, Part I and II and Unit Level Data. New Delhi: Government of India; 2006.

National Sample Survey Office. *Informal Sector and Conditions of Employment in India, July 2004-June 2005.* Report No. 519, 61st Round, Ministry of Statistics and Programme Implementation, New Delhi: Government of India; 2007.

National Sample Survey Office. *Employment and Unemployment Situation in India,* 62nd Round, July 2005– June 2006, Report No. 522, New Delhi: Government of India; 2007.

National Sample Survey Office. *Report on Key Indicators of Employment and Unemployment in India, 2009-10,* 66th Round, National Statistical Organisation, Ministry of Statistics and Programme Implementation, New Delhi: Government of India; 2011.

National Statistical Commission. *Report of the Committee on Unorganised Sector Statistics,* New Delhi: Government of India; 2012.

Neetha, N. "Flexible Production, Feminisation and Disorganisation: Evidence from Tiruppur Knitwear Industry", *Economic and Political Weekly,* 2002, Vol. 37, No. 21, pp. 25-31.

Nihila, M. "Marginalisation of Women Workers: Leather Tanning Industry in Tamil Nadu", *Economic and Political Weekly,* 1999, Vol. 34 Nos. 16 and 17, pp. 17-24.

Paul B., G. D., Bhirdikar, K, Shabnam, S., Mukherjee, P., Krishna, M., Bhardwaj, R, Purandaran, K. and Venkatesha, M. R. *India Labour Market Report, 2008,* Mumbai: Adecco-TISS Labour Market Research Initiatives, Tata Institute of Social Sciences; 2009.

Planning Commission. *Eleventh Five Year Plan 2007-12*, New Delhi: Government of India; 2008.

Survey on Employment and Unemployment. Retrieved from http://pib.nic.in/newsite/ erelease .aspx?relid=86062 on 18/7/2014.

Review Questions

Objective Type Questions

I. State True or False

(i) The CAGR of labour force during the period 2004-2005 to 2010-2011 was higher for rural persons, than for urban persons.
(ii) The office of the CLC(C) was established in 1947.
(iii) Secondary sector employs the highest percentage of workforce in rural areas.
(iv) Activities of the DGFASLI are mainly related to occupational safety and health issues of workers.
(v) Own account workers do not hire any labour.

Answers: (i) False, (ii) False, (iii) True, (iv) True, (v) True

II. Fill in the Blanks

(i) The National Policy on Child Labour was incepted in __________.
(ii) The Ministry of Labour & Employment has __________ attached offices.
(iii) The unorganised sector is referred to as the __________ sector.
(iv) A person must work at least for __________ hours a day to be considered employed for the day.
(v) Absenteeism reflects level of job satisfaction, morale and __________ to job.

Answers: (i) 1987 (ii) 4 (iii) informal, (iv) 4 (v) commitment

Discussion Questions

1. Define the following terms: (i) Labour force (ii) Usual status (iii) Casual labour
2. Analyse the growth of labour force in India, highlighting the changes in employment in the primary, secondary and tertiary sectors of the economy.
3. What are the important characteristics of Indian labour force? Discuss the reasons for the migratory character of Indian labour.
4. Discuss the structure of labour administration machinery in India.
5. Write a brief note on child labour in India.
6. What are the powers and responsibilities of the Centre and States in labour administration?
7. What have been the reasons for declining trend in employment in the organised sector in India? What, according to you, are its implications for the economy?
8. Analyse the employment status of women in India. Give reasons for their low participation in labour force.
9. How can you categorise workers on the basis of employment status?
10. There is a clear urban-rural divide in the labour force in India. Comment on the statement with relevant facts and figures.

CASE STUDY

Indian Migrants to the Gulf Countries

Indian migrants have been working in the Gulf countries, mostly at low positions in oil companies, since the time oil was discovered there in the 1930s, and the their number gradually increased till the 1970s. After a sudden rise in price of oil in 1973, there was a huge demand for workers in these countries due to infrastructural development activities being taken up there. A large numbers of migrant workers from Asia were found going to the 6 Gulf Cooperation Council (GCC) countries of Saudi Arabia, Bahrain, Kuwait, Oman, Qatar, and the UAE. India and Pakistan provided most of the unskilled labour. Gradually the migrants from India further increased and Indian migrants became the largest in number. Later, after the Kuwait war of 1990–1991, Indians even replaced non-national Arabs in the Gulf, like the Jordanians, Yemenis, Palestinians and Egyptians. By 2006, Indian migrant population to the Gulf had crossed 3.5 million.

After the mid 1970s, in order to control the rapid growth of migrants, the GCC countries imposed a number of restrictions such as: foreign nationals cannot own any business or land and they can have business only in partnership with the locals. It gradually became difficult for the workers even to take families with them. Though the demand for professionals has gradually increased in these countries, yet a large chunk of migrants comprises semi-skilled or unskilled workers. These workers, who are employed as housemaids, cooks, gardeners, cleaners etc., have been reported to be working and living in wretched conditions. They live in cramped rooms with no facilities for kitchen or toilet. They have to bear unfriendly weather conditions and hardly get any opportunity for socialisation. Female workers working as housemaids even face sexual abuse. There is no protection of any local labour law for them. Long separation from their families and adverse living conditions break them emotionally and physically.

Back home, these workers face exploitation on another front. These unskilled and semi-skilled workers work under short contracts (rarely exceeding 2 years). They come back home after their contract ends and search for a new job contract begins. Many recruitment and placement agencies, in collusion with potential employers, take advantage of illiterate workers who are hardly aware of laws and their rights and so have to suffer in many ways. These agents and employers deduct money from the wages of the workers in the name of various types of fees and withhold their passport. They provide them with inadequate medical and other facilities at work, and even use them for carrying smuggled goods.

A large proportion of the migrant workers come from the south Indian States of Kerala, Tamil Nadu, Andhra Pradesh and Karnataka, other States being Maharashtra, Punjab and Rajasthan. It was estimated that by 2005 1 out of every 3 or 4 Indians living in Gulf was from Kerala. Towards the end of 1990s, it was believed that migration had improved the condition of poor families in Kerala and appeared to be one factor that seemed to have done better than agricultural reforms, trade union activities, and welfare legislations. This was one aspect of the situation. Very soon the side effects of migration in the State of Kerala had begun to be felt. One was increase in unemployment rate due to rise in education and the other was migration of workers from other States to Kerala to replace the workers who had emigrated. Education rate increased seemingly because the youth of Kerala watched other emigrated workers. They too, like other emigrants, wanted to get jobs in Gulf countries and earn a lot of money to lead a happy life. To realise this dream they were motivated to get educated, more so, when secondary education was made compulsory for migrants in many Gulf countries.

The emigrated Indian workers to the Gulf countries have had an impact upon the economy of the country. They have been sending huge remittances to their homes in India. This has been one of the significant aspects of their migration. In the mid 1970s, remittances from the migrated Indians to the developed countries had increased, but later on, its share gradually decreased as they were joined by their families. Remittances from Gulf continued to increase and reached to US $21,700 million in 2004. In 1999-2000, it contributed 3 per cent to the GDP. In the middle of 1991, when India faced a serious balance of payment crisis, remittances from migrants to the Gulf countries played an important role in bringing the country out of the crisis.

The phenomenon of worker migration has been perceived to have resulted in both gains and losses. Married men who left their families and went away, leaving the household responsibility to their wives, made many women expert in 'home management'. The children of these workers can get better education and facilities. But the flip side is that it also resulted into social and psychological problems, for example, a feeling of loneliness experienced by the family members of these workers who moved to unknown destinations in foreign countries for the sake of giving good social status and a better life to their family back home.

(Adapted from: Khadria, B. India: Skilled Migration to Developed Countries, Labour Migration to the Gulf. In S. Castles and R. D. Wise (eds.) Migration and Development: Perspectives from the South, Geneva: IOM; 2008, pp. 79-112.)

Review Questions

1. What are the problems faced by the migrant workers in Gulf countries?
2. Discuss the socio-economic dimensions of the phenomenon of migration of workers to the Gulf countries.
3. What according to you can be the impact of workers' migration upon the labour market of India?

3

Trade Unions: Concept, Evolution and Functions

Desired Knowledge Competencies

- To explain the concept of trade unions, their objectives and types.
- To discuss the notable theories of trade unions and the methods unions adopt.
- To review the evolution of unions in India and study their structure.
- To outline the range of functions performed by unions.

INTRODUCTION

Trade unions are an inseparable part of the industrial relations system of any nation, having their own sets of objectives or goals to achieve, and each having its own strategy, based on its ideology, to reach those goals. Unions are an instrument for promoting the cause of the working class; they allow workers to demand their rights and voice their grievances in a legitimate manner.

There is an interesting treatise on the causes that had fuelled the labour movement and hence contributed to the birth of trade unions. Hoxie (1921) proposes that unions are an outcome of common interpretation by workers of social situations in which they lived, and the aims, policies and methods of unions acted as a remedy to these conditions. Perlman (1928) attributes the birth of trade unionism to job consciousness and scarcity of employment. Tannenbaum (1951) suggests that while machine was the cause, labour movement was the result.

Evidences suggest that seeds of trade unionism were sown with the beginning of industrialisation, to be more specific, the Industrial Revolution. Industrialisation brings with itself 2 diametrically opposite phenomena: on one hand, workers pick up the necessary skills that lead to enhanced productivity, and on the other hand, automation reduces the labour needed for a given level of output, thus throwing workers out of employment. Thus industrialisation casts insecurity in the minds of workers due to fear of obsolescence and loss of employment. Following the age-old adage that unity is strength, workers as a consequence of such insecurity demand more wages and better working conditions through their collective actions. Thus a trade union is born. To sum up, the growth of unions across the world can be traced back to the growth of industrial organisations. Though the concept of unions had originated in the context of blue-collar manual workers, it has eventually extended to cover white-collar employees also, including supervisors and managers.

Spotlight
Trade union movement is a by-product of Industrial Revolution.

According to the International Labour Organisation (ILO), trade unionism is a means for workers to liberate themselves from poverty and social exclusion; they provide a forum to workers to express their views. Trade unions are supposed to play an important role in maintaining harmonious relations between management and labour. Their purpose is to make an attempt to provide a dignified life to workers, while fulfilling their obligations towards management. In situations in which interests of workers and management clash, trade unions play a crucial role in negotiating with the management to maintain industrial peace and harmony.

The following sections cover the concept of trade unionism, objectives, types and functions of unions, and the various methods they adopt to achieve their objectives. We have also deliberated upon eminent theories of trade unionism. Separate sections have been devoted to the history and evolution of trade unionism and structure of unions in India.

DEFINITIONS OF TRADE UNIONS

Trade unions have been defined by several authors and institutions at different points of time. Sidney and Beatrice Webb (1920, p. 1) define trade union as "a continuous association of wage earners for the purpose of maintaining or improving the conditions of their working lives". Dankert (1948, p. 1) proposed that "a trade union is a continuing organisation of employees established for the purpose of protecting or improving, through collective action, the economic and social status of its members". Cole (1955, p. 13) defines a trade union as "an association of workers in one or more professions carried on mainly for the purpose of protecting and advancing the members' economic interest in connection with their daily work". According to Yoder (1974, p. 159), a trade union is "a continuing, long-term association of employees formed and maintained for the specific purpose of advancing and protecting the interests of members in their working relationships". The International Labour Organisation defines a trade union as an organisation of employees, usually associated beyond the confines of 1 enterprise, established for protecting or improving, through collective action, the economic and social status of its members.

Spotlight
According to ILO, a trade union is an organisation of employees, usually associated beyond the confines of 1 enterprise, established for protecting or improving through collective action, the economic and social status of its members.

According to Section 2(h) of the Trade Unions Act, 1926, a trade union can be defined as "any combination, whether temporary or permanent, formed primarily for the purpose of regulating the relations between workmen and employers, or between workmen and workmen, or between employers and employers, or for imposing restrictive conditions on the conduct of any trade or business, and includes any federation of two or more trade unions".

Stated in simple terms, trade unions are voluntary associations formed by employees to safeguard their interests through collective actions. Combining the various definitions, we get the following characteristics of a trade union:

- It is an association of workers or employers.
- It is voluntary in nature; hence an employee has a choice to join or not to join a union.

- Such an association is continuous in nature.
- It is formed for improving the conditions of workers, and to protect and promote all kinds of interests, namely, economic, political and social, of its members through collective actions; the dominant interest is, however, economic.
- It also aims at establishing harmonious relationship between management and workers.

Spotlight

Trade unions are voluntary associations formed by employees, to safeguard their interests through collective actions.

OBJECTIVES OF TRADE UNIONS

Trade unions were primarily formed for protecting the interests of workers.

The aims and objectives of major trade unions in India are seen to vary according to their political ideologies (Ratnam, 2006). Nevertheless, the broad objectives of unions are:

- **Ensuring Rights to Workers:** An important objective of unions is to ensure rights to workers. Trade unions had actually emerged for this purpose, since a single worker may not be effective to demand for better terms and conditions of work from management; bargaining power is greater as a group or association. Towards this end, unions also offer legal representation to their members. They oppose any such policy or action of management, or even the government, that is perceived as a potential threat to workers' interests and rights.

EXHIBIT 3.1 FURORE OVER NEW MANUFACTURING POLICY

The Center of Indian Trade Unions (CITU) has strongly opposed the new National Manufacturing Policy approved by the Union Cabinet, and has termed it as an attempt by the Government to give backdoor entry to the so-called labour reform of 'hire and fire' that is being pressed by business houses through the creation of new manufacturing zones. The Center believes that "the National Manufacturing Policy will create new islands of lawlessness with bountiful concessions to business houses and absolute jungle raj in implementation of labour laws of the land". It said that the Government cannot unilaterally change the labour laws legislated by the Parliament through executive policy or order, and announced that it would oppose any such action.

CITU pointed out that the new policy would also be discriminatory against those industries which do not operate from these special zones, whereas those manufacturing in these zones would take undue advantage of the concessions offered by the Government. It has also laid down that this is a kind of disregard shown by the Government to the basic norm of industrial democracy, and that the Government must consult with central trade unions before taking any decision on such labour-related issues.

(Adapted from: www.thehindu.com/business/Industry/article2577119.ece accessed on 23/10/2014.)

- **Securing Economic Interests of Workers:** Trade unions were formed to save workers from oppression. Getting fair wages/remuneration is a right of workers. Unions continuously strive to ensure that workers are getting wages according to the going-rate. Besides wages, they safeguard other economic interests of workers, like bonus and compensation for accidents.

- **Participating in Management:** Participation implies a process of sharing power and authority between labour and management (Verma, 1987). Workers, through their elected representatives, participate in the decision-making process of an organisation. Unions negotiate with the employer to find out solutions to any difference of opinion between the union and management over issues like pay, working hours, etc. This process supports creation of a democratic environment in an organisation, and ensures that the interests of workers are not overlooked and that workers have a voice in decisions impacting them.

Spotlight

Objectives of trade unions include ensuring rights to workers, securing economic interests of workers, participating in management, providing welfare of workers and their families, and contributing to national development

- **Ensuring Welfare of Workers and their Families:** Besides ensuring rights to workers, welfare activities are also taken up by trade unions for workers and their families, so as to provide them with a decent living. Unions make it certain that employers fulfill their obligations regarding statutory welfare activities and amenities for workers.

EXHIBIT 3.2 OPPOSITION OF PRIVATISATION AT AMTS

Gujarat Mazdoor Sabha, the trade union of the Ahmedabad Municipal Transport Service (AMTS), has sought High Court intervention, challenging further privatisation and restraining AMTS from going ahead with its Request for Proposal (RFP) that had invited private operators to operate 550 buses with private staff. The Public Interest Litigation (PIL) has claimed that under the Bombay Provincial Municipal Corporations Act, 1949, AMTS is duty-bound to provide services to people, and setting up and maintaining infrastructure and human resource are its statutory duties; privatisation of its services is against the law, the PIL contended. Also, awarding contract to private players for managing buses would render its daily wagers, contract drivers and conductors jobless. It was also submitted that the Industrial Tribunal, by an award, has granted payment of wages to temporary and daily wagers of AMTS at par with permanent workmen, and the privatisation bid is just to frustrate the award of the Industrial Court, the petitioner argued.

(Adapted from: www.articles.timesofindia.indiatimes.com/2011-12-27/ahmedabad/30561252_1_amtsahmedabad-municipal-transport-service-temporary-conductors accessed on 27/10/2014.)

- **Contributing to National Development:** According to the recommendations of the First National Commission on Labour (1969), trade unions must aim not only at championing the cause of workers, but also at rendering constructive cooperation in the formulation and implementation of plans and policies relating to national development.

REASONS FOR JOINING UNION

We have mentioned earlier that trade unions are voluntary associations and therefore it is not mandatory for a worker to join a union. This brings us to a pertinent question: why would a worker join a trade union? Right from the beginning of the trade union movement, it has been very evident that workers tend to collude when they have a demand from, or a grievance against their employer. Trade union has always been a platform to workers to promote their interests; workers could not have attained much success if they dealt with such issues individually.

Waddington and Whitson (1997) classify the reasons for joining trade unions as individual benefits and collective reasons. Individual benefits include training and education, industrial benefits and professional services like free legal advice and financial services. Collective reasons comprise mutual support, improved wages and working conditions, peer-group pressure and belief in union organisation.

> **Spotlight**
>
> *Costs of Joining Union:* Membership fee (monetary) and time devoted to union activities (non-monetary).
>
> *Benefits of Joining Union:* Safeguard against victimisation by management, facilitation of redressal of grievances, sense of security, greater bargaining power and power of representation.

A worker's decision to join a union can be ascertained purely on the basis of cost-benefit analysis of such a decision. While costs may include membership fee (monetary) and time devoted to union activities (non-monetary), benefits of unionisation may include safeguard against victimisation by management (Mills, 1994; Modi, Singhal and Singh, 1995); facilitation of redress of grievances (Modi, Singhal and Singh, 1995); sense of security; greater bargaining power; and power of representation. As pointed out by Schnabel (2003), it is the balance of costs and benefits combined with the expectations about the degree to which the union would be able to realise the collective, social and ideological motives that would determine the actual membership decision.

The various reasons that may be instrumental behind a worker joining a trade union may be as follows:

- **Greater Bargaining Power:** A worker possesses very little bargaining power as an individual. Pursuing an issue as a cohesive group instead of an individual would have greater prospects of being heard and addressed to. Workers can, as members of a union, participate in matters that affect their lives through collective bargaining agreements between union and management.
- **Sense of Security:** Workers as individuals may feel exposed to the whims and fancies of top management decisions. However, union membership instills a sense of security among them to safeguard from uncertainties in income and other hazards.
- **Other Reasons:** Other reasons behind joining a union may be negotiation for wages and working conditions, protection from unforeseen exigencies like accidents and illness, etc. Gratification of social and psychological needs and "social pressure" (Mills, 1994; Modi, Singhal and Singh, 1995) may also be other rationale for joining union.

> **Spotlight**
>
> *Reasons behind Joining Unions:*
> - Greater bargaining power
> - Sense of security
> - Other reasons

Following the model proposed by Schuler and Youngblood (1986), there are 3 separate conditions that influence an employee's decision to join a union, namely: dissatisfaction, lack of power and union instrumentality. These are explained here briefly.

- **Satisfaction of Employee:** Satisfaction of an employee at work is contingent upon 2 types of contracts: employment contract (pertaining to conditions of employment like wages, hours of work, etc.) and psychological contract (consisting of unspecified expectations of the employee about reasonable working conditions, nature of supervision, empowerment, etc.). An employee's level of satisfaction would be determined by the degree to which the organisation fulfils these contracts.
- **Powerlessness:** Contrary to what seems to be obvious from the above discussion, an employee would not join union when he perceives dissatisfaction. In fact, when he is dissatisfied, an

employee would first try to resolve the reason by himself. Now, the degree of success of such an individual attempt would depend on 2 features of the job: *essentiality* and *exclusivity*.

Essentiality refers to how important or critical the job is to the overall success of the organisation, while exclusivity refers to how difficult it is to replace an employee (Schuler and Youngblood, 1986). If an employee has greater degree of essentiality and exclusivity, he would be in a commanding position and would be likely able to force his employer to improve the situation. Low essentiality and exclusivity would render an individual's attempt as unsuccessful. In other words, an employee would not be able to remove his cause(s) of dissatisfaction if he is not exclusive and can be substituted easily, and in such a case he is in a state of powerlessness. It is under such circumstances that the employee would wish to overcome his dissatisfaction through other means, including joining a union, which may address the reason(s) behind dissatisfaction through a common forum.

> **Spotlight**
> *Essentiality* refers to how important or critical the job is to the overall success of the organisation. *Exclusivity* refers to how difficult it is to replace an employee.

- **Instrumentality:** Instrumentality refers to the degree to which an effort would lead to desired outcomes. In this context, we may explain instrumentality to be a calculative or utilitarian relationship with unions based on a cognitive assessment of the costs and benefits pertaining to union representation (Newton and Shore, 1992). According to Brett (1980), workers feel bound to their unions simply because of the rewards that these unions secure for them. A worker may thus determine if a union is instrumental in removing his dissatisfaction. For this, he may compare the costs and benefits of union membership; if the benefits outweigh costs, the employee would join the union. However, in many cases an employee may not be able to ascertain such benefits and costs, and opt for joining union without any such evaluation and comparison.

TYPES OF TRADE UNIONS

Trade unions differ in their purposes, membership pattern of workers and level of operation. Let us talk about the different types of unions on these bases in this section.

Classification on the Basis of Purpose

Following the philosophy of Hoxie, unions may be classified on the basis of their purposes and functions, as follows:

> **Spotlight**
> *Classification of Unions on the Basis of Purpose:*
> - Reformist Unions
> - Revolutionary Unions
> - Predatory Unions

- ***Reformist Unions:*** These are the unions that seek to improve the existing economic and social conditions of workers, without attempting to uproot or drastically change the existing system. Examples are unions associated with the American Federation of Labour (AFL) and the Congress for Industrial Organisation (CIO) in USA. Hoxie's business unionism and friendly or uplift unionism belong to this category.
- ***Revolutionary Unions:*** These are the unions that seek to destroy and abolish the existing economic and social order by means of some kind of force, with an objective of improving the status of workers. The means adopted by these unions may be revolution or exercise of political strength.

  Thus a revolutionary union may be either *anarchist union* or *political union*.

- ***Predatory Unions:*** These stick to no particular means and adopt any method to fulfill their purpose. They may be of 2 types: *hold up-union*, formed by combination of employee and employer, both not abiding by any principles, concerned with their own benefit, without any concern for outsiders; and *guerilla unions*, that work against employers, and are controlled by a 'boss'. They use violence and other secret methods to achieve their objectives.

Classification on the Basis of Membership Pattern

Trade union members may all belong to the same trade/craft or different crafts; they may also be blue-collar or white-collar employees. Thus on the basis the types of membership, trade unions may be classified as: occupational or craft unions, industrial unions, general unions, and blue-collar and white-collar unions.

- ***Occupational/Craft Unions:*** The earliest form of trade unions found were *craft unions*, which comprised members from the same craft or trade. It is obvious that such unions operated purely for the interests of the members of the specific craft. Further, since the membership of such unions is open only to those belonging to a particular craft, craft unions may be quite small in size. These unions are found in modern times also, such as pilots' associations, etc. In India, the Singareni Collieries Engineering Workers Union, affiliated to the Hind Mazdoor Sabha, and the Navigators Union of Air India are examples of craft unions.
- ***Industrial Unions:*** Size of craft unions was small, since they were restricted to a single craft or trade. Eventually with increase in work complexities, such unions begun to collude amongst themselves, and thus emerged *industrial unions*. The focus area of such unions is broader, as they are no longer limited to the interests of a particular craft; they aim to represent all employees in a specific industry, regardless of their type of work. An industrial union would comprise all workers in an industry with different skill sets, namely, skilled, semi-skilled, and unskilled, engaged in a particular industry or enterprise. The United Automobile Workers (UAW) is an industrial union in USA, representing skilled craft workers, assembly line workers and unskilled workers in all of the major American automobile companies. The Textile Labour Association Ahmedabad is one of the most famous industrial unions in India. The Steel Employees Trade Union (SETU) (affiliated to CITU) is another example.
- ***General Unions:*** With their origin in the early nineteenth century in Great Britain, *general unions* are for skilled and unskilled workers performing different jobs in different industries, employments or crafts, while industrial unions are for different workers in the *same* industry. GMB and the Transport and General Workers' Union (TGWU) are examples of general unions in Great Britain. Jamshedpur Labour Union and the National Union of Municipal and General Workers are examples of general unions in India.
- ***Blue-Collar and White-Collar (Managerial) Unions:*** A further classification of unions can be made within this category, on the basis of the level of employees as members of a union. For this we would first need to explain the concept of blue and white-collar workers

  Blue-collar workers are those who are at the operative level, employed at the production floor, or in maintenance shops; they are paid on piece-rate or time-rate basis. Unions representing such workers are regarded as *blue-collar unions*. White-collar employees,

Spotlight

Blue-collar Workers
- operative level
- employed at the production floor
- unions representing such workers regarded as *blue-collar unions*

White-collar Employees
- non-manual workers
- paid on a monthly basis
- unions representing such workers regarded as *white-collar unions*

on the contrary, do not work on the shop floor; they are non-manual workers who are paid on a monthly basis. Unions representing such workers are regarded as *white-collar unions*. White-collar employees are distinct from their blue-collar counterparts in aspects like educational background, higher social status and occupational position. As such their unions are usually regarded as "guilds" or "associations" or "officers' associations", possibly to distinguish them from workers' unions. The primary objective of formation of such associations is similar to that of trade unions, i.e., to protect the interests of officers. We find ample evidence in the history of Indian trade unionism that white-collar employees were initially shy of unionising at the beginning; they have eventually formed strong unions. Examples of such unions are the All India Bank Officers' Association and the Airports Authority Officers' Association (India), a recognised multi-cadre association of the Airports Authority of India (AAI).

Classification on the Basis of Level of Operation

The organisational pattern of a trade union federation is usually a 3-tier structure, comprising enterprise-level unions, industry-level unions and national-level federations.

> **Spotlight**
> *Classification of Unions on the Basis of Level of Operation:*
> - Plant-level unions
> - Industry-level unions
> - National federations

- ***Plant-level Unions***: A *plant-level union* is, as is suggestive from the name, is a union that operates at the factory or plant level.
- ***Industry-level Unions:*** An *industry-level union* operates at the industry-level, comprising several factories or enterprises.
- ***Regional-level Federations:*** These are organisations of all the constituent unions in a particular State or region.
- ***National Federations:*** These are national-level bodies to which plant-level unions, local-level unions and regional-level unions may get affiliated.

Apart from these, there may be another type of unions, namely, *agricultural unions*, comprising agricultural workers. The Khet Mazdoor Union of AITUC, Bharatiya Khet Mazdoor Union (BKMU), and All India Agricultural Workers Union (AIAWU) are examples of agricultural unions operating in India.

STRUCTURE OF TRADE UNIONS IN INDIA

Structure of a trade union refers to the organisation of the union and the pattern of linkages of various units within that union. The level of operation of unions, as discussed in the previous section, also forms the basis for understanding the structure of trade unions. The organisational pattern of a trade union federation in India is usually a 4 tier structure, comprising plant (or enterprise)-level unions, local-level federations, regional-level federations and national-level federations, as depicted in Figure 3.1.

> **Spotlight**
> *Structure of Unions in India:*
> - Plant (Enterprise)-level unions
> - Local-level federations
> - Regional-level federations
> - National federations

- ***Plant-level Unions:*** Operating at the factory or plant level, *plant (or enterprise)-level unions* comprise the first tier in the structure. A single plant may have several such unions, as the Trade Unions Act, 1926 allows any 7 workers to come together to form a union. Enterprise-level unions can be of 2 kinds: those having affiliation with national-level federations, and those that are independent (i.e., without any affiliation). The Rourkela Shramik Sangh, the recognised trade union body of the Rourkela Steel Plant, is an example of plant-level unions.

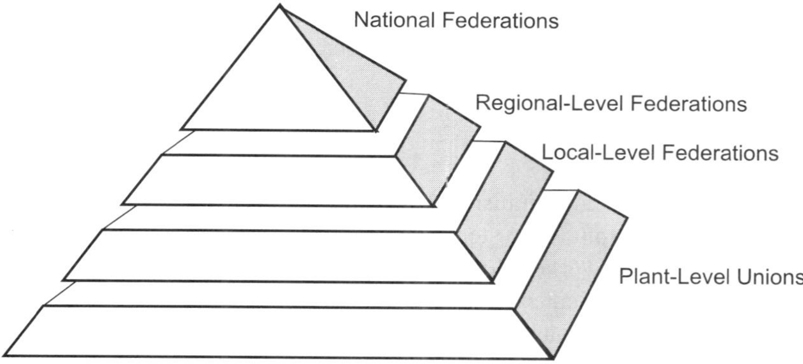

Figure 3.1 *Structure of Trade Unions in India*

- ***Local-level Federations:*** Plant-level unions in a particular craft or industry at the local-level may constitute a *local-level federation*. This is the second tier from below, and is above the plant-level unions. The local federation holds together the local, plant-level unions in a particular craft or industry. Such a federation may be independent, or affiliated to either some regional-level or national-level federation.
- ***Regional-level Federations:*** Federations of all the constituent unions in a particular State or region forms *regional-level federations*. Such federations are a vital component in the structure of unionism in a vast country like India where language, customs, religion, geography and impact of political factors vary from region to region. These federations may have 2 types of members: affiliating plant-level unions and affiliating local federations. Many regional political parties may have their own trade union wings. Telugu Desam in Andhra Pradesh and Trinamul Congress in West Bengal are 2 such examples of regional political parties.
- ***National Federations:*** Constituting the highest level in the 4 tier structure of trade unions in India, *national federations* are the *central* or *apex* organisations that act as coordinating bodies, to which plant-level unions, local unions or regional-level unions may get affiliated. These federations may have their own regional or State-level coordinating bodies to which plant-level unions may get affiliated. Examples of such organisations in India are the Indian National Trade Union Congress (INTUC) and All India Trade Union Congress (AITUC). Detailed structure and working of certain national-level federations have been taken up in the next chapter.

THEORIES OF TRADE UNIONS

As mentioned earlier, trade unions have many objectives to fulfill. Extensive researches have been conducted, and several theories have been proposed to explain the approaches adopted by different unions and the motives behind their objectives and functioning. Some of the eminent theories are:

- Marxian Class Conflict Theory
- Webb's Theory of Industrial Democracy
- Cole's Theory of Union Control of Industry
- Hoxie's Theory of Functional Classification of Unionism
- Tannenbaum's Sociological Theory
- Common's Environmental Theory
- Perlman's Theory of Scarcity Consciousness

- Kerr and Associates' Protest Theory
- Simon's Theory of Monopolistic, Anti-Democratic Trade Unionism
- Mahatma Gandhi's Trusteeship Theory

Marxian Class Conflict Theory

Karl Marx was the founder of communism. According to him, trade unions are an outcome of the capitalist system, and are an important instrument in the struggle between workers (proletariat) and capitalist class (bourgeoisie). He believed that capitalism results in 3 outcomes which aid in the growth of labour movement, namely tendency of accumulation of wealth with capitalists; tendency for depression of wages and resultant problems of workers; and inevitability of economic crises. Therefore the labour class must continue its struggle to abolish capitalism.

> **Spotlight**
> Marxian Class Conflict Theory
> - Unions are an important instrument in the struggle between workers and capitalist class
> - Labour class must continue its struggle to abolish capitalism

In his *Communist Manifesto,* Marx stated that competition divides the interests of workers, but the cause of maintaining wages gives them a common reason to unite and present resistance against capitalists. Unions must organise workers to eliminate competition among themselves for employment. They should generate awakening amongst workers to abolish the wage system as a whole, and contribute to the decay of capitalism.

Marx was of the opinion that unions facilitate workers to get gainful employment, and hence perform the function of protecting their wages; however, they must not restrict themselves to fulfillment of these narrow objectives. He proposed that trade unions must provide orientation towards changing the social structure and propounded revolutionary and radical means to bring about this change.

Perceiving that outside guidance and support is necessary for the working class, Marx defined a role for intellectuals to imbue social and political awakening in the working class. He suggested that trade unions by themselves cannot do anything beyond economic struggle; therefore they must be ready to accept guidance from outside, in order to get permanent gains and establish a socialist state.

Webb's Theory of Industrial Democracy

Sidney and Beatrice Webb, authors of the title *Industrial Democracy* published in 1897, were leaders in the Labour Party in Great Britain. They witnessed trade unions emerging not from any particular institution, but from every opportunity for the meeting together of wage earners of the same occupation. According to the Webbs, the chain of supply involves the worker, employer, wholesaler, retailer and customer. The pressure created by the customer due to comparative prices in the market increases at every link in the chain, which finally accumulates at the employer's level, who is eventually forced to lower the costs of production by reducing wages and other inputs. Thus, the ultimate sufferers are the workers, and to protect their interests, they unionise. Therefore market pressures and competition lead to the formation of trade unions.

> **Spotlight**
> *Webbs' Theory of Industrial Democracy*
> - Market pressures and competition lead to the formation of trade unions
> - Unions are the prime agents of industrial democracy

Unions sought to establish 'Common Rules' which refer to efforts in making firms pay workers at least a minimum wage and provide certain minimum working conditions in terms of working hours, safety measures, leaves, etc.

The Webbs rejected the Marxist concept of a 'classless society': Though both opposed the capitalist system, but unlike Marx, the Webbs advocated peaceful means to establish a socialist society. They believed that trade unionism was neither a temporary function which arose as an outcome of industrial development, nor a means to overthrow capitalism. They proposed that unions were the prime agents of industrial democracy in bringing equality between employers and workers in terms of bargaining power, by giving voice to workers.

Unions do not just exist to give economic benefits to their members; a larger purpose of their existence is to reconstruct the society by replacing capitalism with a form of socialism and have a permanent function to fulfill in the democratic State.

Cole's Theory of Union Control of Industry

G. D. H. Cole is celebrated in the history of industrial relations for his work *The World of Labour*, published in 1913. His approach to trade unionism is somewhere between those of the Webbs and Marx. Cole believed that unionism exists to carry on class struggle. He has suggested that the control of industry should be in the hands of the true producers, namely, workers, in partnership with the State. This is in sharp contrast to revolutionary methods proposed by Marx.

Hoxie's Theory of Functional Classification of Unionism

Robert F. Hoxie is amongst the earliest to have argued that trade unionism has evolved differently across socio-psychological factors. Economic factors, according to him, are not the only reason for the growth of trade unionism. He proposed that workers with similar thinking and economic conditions tend to develop similar interpretations of problems and solutions, and this is the outcome of group psychology. Further, Hoxie provided a different approach of understanding the concept of trade unions by classifying unionism on the basis of functions, as follows:

> **Spotlight**
>
> *Hoxie's Classification of Unionism:*
> - Business Unionism
> - Friendly/Uplift Unionism
> - Revolutionary Unionism
> - Predatory Unionism
> - Dependent Unionism

- ***Business Union:*** Also regarded as *bread-and-butter unionism*, business unions working on this ideology are concerned with improving wages and working conditions, rather than changing political and social situations in which workers live. Thus these unions are trade-conscious rather than class-conscious. They stress on immediate goals and display an instrumental orientation. Such unions accept the capitalistic system and wage structures, rather than questioning them, and in that they are conservative in nature. The means they adopt to seek their goals are collective bargaining and industrial action (like strikes).
- ***Friendly or Uplift Union:*** The primary aim of unions following this principle is to contribute towards better life of workers by elevating their moral, intellectual and social life. Thus these unions are trade-conscious, and they advocate methods like cooperative enterprises, profit-sharing, etc. They use collective bargaining and political actions as means to achieve their objectives.
- ***Revolutionary Union:*** These unions adopting revolutionary methods belong to this category of unionism. They are class-conscious. They follow the dictums of Marx and reject private ownership of productive resources and wage system. They are radical in approach, and use a combination of industrial and political actions to achieve their objectives. The ultimate aim of such unions is to replace the capitalistic system with a socialistic system. Hoxie has divided revolutionary unionism into 2 categories on the basis of objectives and methods of unions: one adopting *socialistic approach (unionism),* with focus on socialist ideologies, and the other adopting *quasi-anarchy approach (unionism)* that practices means like strikes, sabotage and violence.

- ***Predatory Unionism:*** The unions belonging to this category are leader-based, instead of member-based; they do not follow any ideology, and adopt any method to secure better wages and benefits for members. These unions may even join hands with employers for mutual benefit. They may be either trade-conscious or class-conscious.
- ***Dependent Unionism:*** In this type of unionism the unions are dependent on the support of workers and other labour groups. They are usually of 2 types: *company unions* (that depend entirely on employer), and *label unions* (that depend upon the label imprinted on the products made by the union members and such products find a ready market among unionists and union sympathisers).

Hoxie believed that trade unions may not exactly be like any 1 of the 4 he has proposed. The methods and objectives of a trade union are dependent upon the beliefs of the competing groups within the union. He was also of the opinion that though the effect of trade unionism is ultimately bringing democracy in industry, but systems within trade unions hardly depict any democracy.

Tannenbaum's Sociological Theory

Frank Tannenbaum, a professor with the Columbia University, USA, proposed the Sociological Theory of trade unionism. The Industrial Revolution had disrupted the older way of life and also put the life of workers into threat. Workers became totally dependent on machines and employers made them feel insecure. They responded by self-defence through trade unions. According to Tannenbaum, "the initial organiser of the trade union movement is the shop, the factory, the mine, and the industry. The agitator or the labour leader merely announces the already existing fact." Thus the emergence of trade unions was spontaneous, and in fact, inherent in the growth of capitalism; he proposed that machine is the cause, and labour movement is the result. The employer acted as a catalyst in the process of organising workers into a self-conscious group, and trade unionism emerged as a means to restore the organic life and dignity that workers enjoyed before the advent of capitalism.

Spotlight

Tannenbaum's Sociological Theory

- Machine is the cause, and labour movement is the result
- Unions try to gain monopoly over labour supply to industry

According to Tannenbaum, unions have become very powerful bodies that try to gain monopoly over labour supply to industry. They tend to bargain with employers over wages and those firms that cannot pay wages are driven out. He also believed that unions cannot remain isolated and they gradually begin to perform the functions of the management, because every activity of management affects workers in some way or the other.

Tannenbaum was of the opinion that trade unionism did not challenge capitalism; rather it civilised capitalism and integrated workers through collective bargaining. The real essence of the trade union movement could be appreciated only by seeing the role it has played in the lives of workers in the transition from a simple society to a complex industrial and urban economy.

Commons' Environmental Theory

John R. Commons was a professor of Economics at the University of Wisconsin, USA. His approach to trade unionism was based on environmental factors, and hence his theory is regarded as the "Environmental Theory of Labour Movement". Factors like free land, market expansion and resultant competition, and immigration with influx of races, nationalities and languages, according to Commons, had delayed the American labour movement, and were responsible for the rise and fall of trade unions. Commons believed that unionism is a protective device for workers who had to be shielded from the harshness of the market. Collective bargaining was an instrument of class struggle, and Commons proposed that ultimately there would be partnership between employers and employees.

Perlman's Theory of Scarcity Consciousness

Perlman, an economist at the University of Wisconsin, USA, was an associate of Commons. He had extensively studied trade unionism in USA and authored the title *A History of Trade Unionism in United States* in 1922, in which he argued that *scarcity consciousness*, expressed by sharing job opportunities, had motivated American unionism. Perlman's theory attributes the emergence of trade unionism to the "scarcity consciousness" of workers, which implies "economic pessimism of the manual group". He was of the opinion that scarcity of opportunities was a universal psychology, typical among manual workers. Scarcity consciousness emerged because of the fact that the economic position of workers could not be improved beyond an ordinary standard of living, and this gave rise to job-conscious unionism, wherein unions controlled job opportunities. Based on studies conducted in 4 countries, namely, USA, UK, Germany and France, Perlman proposed 3 factors that controlled union activities: *first*, the resistance power of capitalism; *second,* the role of intellectuals; and *third,* the degree of maturity of trade unions. Unions established certain job rights, which they would then ration amongst the members through various regulations related to employment conditions, like working hours, seniority, etc.

> **Spotlight**
>
> *Perlman's Theory of Scarcity Consciousness*
>
> - Trade unionism emerged out of the "scarcity consciousness" of workers
> - Unions and collective bargaining are the essential components of the democratic society.

In his path-breaking monograph, *Theory of the Labour Movement* (1928), Perlman proposed that unions and collective bargaining are the essential components of a democratic society. Workers must organise unions and engage in class struggle against their employers. According to Perlman, workers lacked cohesiveness and class-consciousness. Neither did they join unions to further the cause of the labour class, nor were they willing to make sacrifices to make the unions a strong organisation. Unions therefore capitalised on the self interests of certain workers and attempted to maintain an intact organisation of workers by focusing on their economic needs.

Unions accept the legitimacy of capitalism, though they aim to limit its excesses, and they must strive to establish job rights for workers. Perlman proposed a pragmatic approach to be adopted by unions in improving the economic condition of workers through social and economic reforms. He believed that intellectuals and non-manualists (outsiders) undermined the approach of trade unions. They attempted to impose their beliefs on labour movement and believed that the condition of the labour class could only be remedied if it adopted their ideologies.

Kerr and Associates' Protest Theory

Kerr, Dunlop, Harbison and Myers used the term 'labour organisation' for trade unions. They observed that labour studies have been conducted mostly in Western capitalist countries, and hence were of the opinion that to understand the actual nature of labour organisations, one must not be restricted to the views proposed on the basis of such studies. These thinkers believed that the protest of the labour class against industrialisation is a universal phenomenon, as industrialisation puts a universal demand and a change is required in the relationship of worker and his work and that with the cultural environment. Kerr and associates proposed that a new recruit dislikes discipline and perceives that the compensation received is commensurate with his efforts or his needs. The dynamic industrial system is unable to provide him with security. He then protests against this system in the form of turnover, sabotage, absenteeism, etc. Unionism is an organised form of such protests against the ills of the system, as a natural aspect of industrialisation.

Spotlight

Kerr and Associates' Protest Theory

- Unionism is an organised form of protest against the ills of the system
- 5 ideal types of leadership of industrialisation process are dynastic elite, middle class, revolutionary intellectuals, colonial administrators and nationalist elites

Kerr and associates suggested that leadership of the industrialisation process is taken by one of the following 5 ideal types:

- ***Dynastic Elite:*** Under this leadership, unions undertake social functions at plant-level and indulge in political activities challenging the workers. Usually such unions are class-conscious and adopt revolutionary means to achieve their objectives.
- ***Middle Class:*** Unions undertake regulation of management at the local-level under this leadership, along with independent political activities that do not challenge employers. Such unions embrace reformist approach.
- ***Revolutionary Intellectuals:*** The main function of unions in this type of leadership is to act as an instrument to educate and lead workers with an objective of improving production and political activities. Such unions are affiliated to centralised federations.
- ***Colonial Administrators:*** Such unions are anti-colonial and are led by nationalists and independent leaders. They fight for independence and thus are a part of independence movement.
- ***Nationalist Elite:*** Nationalist in nature, these unions are led by nationalist leaders. They try to achieve a balance between economic development and protection of workers' interests.

Simons' Theory of Monopolistic, Anti-Democratic Trade Unionism

The contribution of Simons in theories of trade unionism can be linked to his seminal work on the theory of order. As a pronounced adherent of democracy as the ideal form of government, (1945/48) Simons describes democracy as "government by discussion" and depicts consensus as the key prerequisite for the orderly functioning of the democratic process. According to his theory, the general framework within which private individuals are free to transact is to be designed in a manner which maximally destroys the power concentration in the economy (in all fields of economic policy) and in government itself (by federalism, decentralisation and the rule of law). Simons (1944/48) denounced trade unionism on the ground that it is monopoly founded on violence, and also claimed that "monopoly power has no use, save abuse".

Mahatma Gandhi's Trusteeship Theory

Mahatma Gandhi believed in the philosophy of *Sarvodoaya*, which attempts to establish class harmony. He proposed that trade unions are not just meant for carrying on the struggle for wages and working conditions, but they must act like reformist organisations built with the belief that labour and capital must exist in harmony, instead of opposing each other. Unions must uplift workers and help in their all-round development, including teaching supplementary occupations, in order to reduce uncertainties during periods of hardship.

According to Gandhian thought, social order is based on social necessity and not on personal greed. Resources are to be shared by everybody and wealth is for those who generate it. Thus one who controls resources is not the owner, but the trustee. The concept of trusteeship implies stewardship without ownership, and therefore it presumes that a capitalist is a trustee for those on whom he depends for the making, retention and enhancement of his capital. Gandhi proposed that a capitalist should keep minimum wealth for himself and give the rest to the trust for the greatest good of all.

Spotlight

Gandhi's Trusteeship Theory:

- *Sarvodoaya* establishes class harmony
- Trusteeship implies stewardship without ownership

Gandhi did not advocate workers' participation in politics because they are not awakened enough for the purpose and also because political leaders may exploit and use them for their own interests.

Gandhi differs from Marx in the sense that the latter believed in destruction of the exploitative social order, but Gandhi talks of a constructive order based on reformation of such exploiters. While Marx advocated a violent method, Gandhi adopted non-violent means, though he did not oppose peaceful strikes. According to Gandhi, strikes should be used as the last resort, when all peaceful negotiations, conciliation and arbitration are exhausted. He believed that respect for mutual rights and responsibilities can settle all disputes. Gandhi added the concept of social trusteeship to socialism and State-regulated trusteeship, and proposed that *ahimsa* or non-violence, peaceful conduct of relations and positive cooperation can lead us to the correct path of industrial relations.

HISTORY AND EVOLUTION OF TRADE UNIONS IN INDIA

The trade union movement in India can be traced back to the period when industrialisation begun in the country in the 1850s, with the establishment of cotton mills in Bombay (now Mumbai) (1851) and jute mills in Calcutta (now Kolkata) (1855) (Singh, 1965). Consequently, this may be considered as the period for emergence of the working class in India. However, the factory system created a lot of problems for workers. Emphasis was on increasing production, with little or no concern for workers; they lived and worked in poor conditions at meager wages, which lead to widespread discontentment. This situation itself provided an impetus to the development of a system that would mitigate the problems of workers.

The early years of the labour movement were fraught with difficulties. Strike committees, naming themselves as trade unions, would demand the privileges of unions, without any means of discharging responsibilities thereof. With such turbulent years in the beginning, unions have traversed a long journey so far, and the country has seen a steady rise in the number of unions, with increase in their membership base, as also their funds.

We have divided the span of more than 16 decades of trade union movement in India into 3 phases: pre-World War I, post-World War I, and post-Independence. The objective of this section is to trace the origin and development of trade union movement in India. We have also portrayed the characteristics of the labour movement and the factors which were instrumental behind the growth of this movement in each of these phases.

Spotlight

Phases of Trade Union Movement in India:

- Pre-World War I
- Post-World War I
- Post-Independence
  - Phase I (1947 to mid-1960s)
  - Phase II (mid-1960s to 1979)
  - Phase III (1980 to 1991)
  - Phase IV (1991 to 2000)
  - Phase V (2000 and beyond)

Pre-World War I

Industrialisation in India in the 1850s during British rule had ushered in benefits for capitalists, but resulted in acute misery of workers, who were made to work hard for long hours under poor conditions. 1860 marked the beginning of labour unrest in India, to protest against the oppression of indigo cultivators in Bengal. In 1875 Sarobji Shapurji made a protest in Bombay against poor working conditions of workers (Giri, 1959). The first Factory Commission was appointed in 1875, and to improve the situation of workers in India, the British government passed the Factories Act in 1881. However, this Act was inadequate to address the issues of women and child labour; this eventually led to the next Factory Commission in 1884. In 1885, the Indian National Congress was born with A. O. Hume as its president. Its leaders took up the cause of the working class. This gave a strong impetus to labour movement in India. In the year 1890, N. M. Lokhande sponsored the first labour organisation in India, the Bombay Mill Hands Association, as its president. However, the Association was not a trade union in its true sense, as it had no existence as an organised body, and no formal roll of members or funds or rules to support its structure and functioning.

A number of workers' associations were formed during this period. Some of the important ones are: the Amalgamated Society of Railway Servants in India and Burma (1897), the Printers Union, Calcutta (1905), the Bombay Postal Union (1907) and the Kamgar Hityardhak Sabha and Service League (1910). These organisations or associations were not trade unions in the real sense, as they did not have any specific aims and objectives, and they worked primarily for the welfare of workers. The post-1890 period was also marked by several strikes. The most notable ones are the 2 strikes in Bombay in 1894, the first big strike of mill workers of Ahmedabad in 1895, and the strike in jute industries at Calcutta in 1896. It may be mentioned here that in 1911 the Factories Act was passed to regulate the working conditions in industrial set-ups at that time.

The most notable features of the trade union movement in this phase are that the movement was essentially led by social reformers and not by workers, and that the unions which were operational in this phase were not unions in the true sense.

Post-World War I

Several authors have classified this period as the era of formation of modern trade unionism. Social, economic and political changes were taking place around the world during World War I (1914–1918). These developments gave further impetus to the growth of the trade union movement in India. Movement for independence from British rule and labour movement were going on side by side, both getting support and boost from each other. Masses were awakening and becoming aware of the political conditions in the country. With a sharp rise in the prices of essential commodities and a "wage lag" (Sinha, Sinha and Shekhar, 2006), condition of workers was going worse. The Russian Revolution of 1917 also greatly influenced the labour movement in India. The stage was all set for the emergence of trade unions that could voice their demands through militant activities. The first organised trade union in India, the Madras Labour Union, primarily an association of textile workers, was formed in 1918 by B. P. Wadia. Meanwhile, the International Labour Organisation was formed in 1919 with India as the founder member, and the Textile Labour Association Ahmedabad was formed in 1920 under the leadership of Anusuya Ben Sarabhai and Shanker Lal Banker. Other notable unions that came up in this period were the Indian Seamen's Union, Calcutta Clerks' Union and All India Postal and RMS Association.

Rising prices, without a commensurate increase in wages, despite the huge profits made by employers, fuelled a new awakening in this phase. Growth of trade unions was accompanied by a large number of strikes, beginning in 1918 and continuing up to 1920, mainly as a protest to the largely deteriorating condition of workers. Several unions were formed after this, including the All India Trade Union Congress (1920) and the Railway Men's Federation, recognised by the Railway Board, (1922). Similarly, the All India Union of Postal and Telegraph Employees was also formed, and it got recognition from the Director General of Posts and Telegraphs.

Labour uprisings were taking place in many parts of the world. Due to the resultant pressure created, coupled with interventions by the ILO, several industrial legislations were passed during this period. The agitation for legislation for trade unions had begun under N. M Joshi, also called the "Father of Trade Union Movement" in India. The Trade Unions Act was finally passed in the year 1926. This was an important milestone in the evolution of trade unions, as the Act gave legitimate status to unions, and association of workers was made a lawful activity. This was followed by the Trade Disputes Act, 1929, which provided for *ad hoc* Conciliation Board and Court of Enquiry for the settlement of trade disputes. Meanwhile, a split took place in AITUC, namely, leftist and rightist. The All India Trade Union Federation, a wing of the AITUC, was formed in 1929. Efforts were made to unify the split sections of AITUC in the interest of the labour movement. Another split in 1931 led to the formation of All India Red Trade Union Congress.

The Great Depression during this period greatly affected the already suffering workers. There were mass retrenchments, lay-offs and wage-cuts. A large number of strikes took place to resist this. The maximum unrest was witnessed in Bombay (Verma, 1987). In 1935, the All India Red Trade Union Congress merged itself with AITUC; further in 1938, an agreement was made between the National Trade Union Federation (NTUF) and AITUC, and consequently NTUF affiliated itself with AITUC. The year 1938 saw the most important State enactment, namely, the Bombay Industrial Disputes Act, 1938, providing for setting up of an Industrial Court, and prohibiting strikes and lock-outs under certain conditions. The Act laid down compulsory recognition of unions by an employer, and gave the right to workers to get their cases represented either through a representative union, or where no representative union existed in the industry or center or unit, through elected representatives of workers, or through the Government Labour Officer. However, the scope of the Act was limited only to certain industries in the province.

The Second World War broke out in 1939, bringing with itself the same kind of chaos as the First World War. India, like many other parts of the world, was going through economic and political turmoil. In November, 1941, the second split took place in AITUC when the radicals left the party and the Indian Federation of Labour (IFL) was formed with M. N. Roy as the General Secretary. The Federation aimed to mobilise the support of the working class for ensuring uninterrupted production services in industries. By the time the World War II came to an end, the Indian trade union arena had 2 major central federations: AITUC, under the control of the Indian Communist Party, and IFL, under the domination of the Radical Democratic Party.

The year 1946 saw another milestone in labour relations, with the enactment of the Industrial Employment (Standing Orders) Act, 1946. The objective of the Act was to bring uniformity in the condition of employment of workmen in industrial establishments, and thus minimise instances of industrial conflicts. The Act requires employers in industrial establishments wherein 100 or more workmen are employed, or were employed on any day of the preceding 12 months, to define with sufficient precision the conditions of employment under them, and to make the said conditions known to workmen employed by them. Another important State-level enactment that was passed was the Bombay Industrial Relations Act, 1946, aimed at regulating the relation of employers and employees, making provision for settlement of industrial disputes. Meanwhile, the end of the Second World War marked a new phase of misery to the working class, with unemployment, shortage of consumer goods and soaring prices.

The obvious consequence was large scale strikes. The most notable one was the strike of the All India Postmen and Lower Grade Staff Union in 1946, which went on for more than 3 weeks.

Post-Independence

India became independent on 15 August 1947. A significant development in this period was the First Pay Commission, appointed in May 1946, to mainly address the demand for revision of salaries of Government servants in the face of rising prices. Following Bhattacherjee (1999), we divide the post-Independence phase further into the following phases: Phase I (1947 to mid-1960s), Phase II (mid-1960s to 1979), Phase III (1980 to 1991) and Phase IV (1991 to 2000), and extend it to Phase V (2000 and beyond). Let us describe each of these phases briefly here.

- ***Phase I (1947 to mid-1960s):*** This phase corresponds to an era of State planning and setting of up of public sector enterprises to provide employment to people. The State played an important role and intervened in issues like determination of wages and working conditions. The period 1946-47 was marked by increase in the number of industrial disputes, which led to the enactment of the Industrial Disputes Act, 1947. This Act introduced compulsory adjudication on a permanent basis. Another important landmark in the trade union movement was the establishment of INTUC in May 1947, with Sardar Vallabhbhai Patel as its first president. Eventually INTUC became the most dominant of all central federations in terms of membership, and in 1948, the Government of India recognised it as the most representative among central federations. Thus INTUC got the right to nominate workers' delegations to the ILO.

  Meanwhile socialists belonging to the AITUC moved out and formed the Hind Mazdoor Panchayat (HMP) in 1948, which later became the Hind Mazdoor Sabha (HMS). In 1949, the United Trade Union Congress (UTUC) was formed under the leadership of Mrinal Kanti Bose, a Marxist, with the objective to create a classless society and non-political unionism. Hence by 1949, there were 4 central federations carrying the baton of the trade union movement in India: AITUC as the senior-most union, INTUC, HMS and UTUC. In 1954, Bharatiya Mazdoor Sangh (BMS) was formed under the aegis of the Jan Sangh Party, presently known as the Bharatiya Janata Party. The year 1960 saw several amendments in the Trade Unions Act, 1926, including minimum membership subscription; further amendments were incorporated in 1964. By 1965, a splinter group of socialists, headed by George Fernandes, formed the second Hind Mazdoor Panchayat.
- ***Phase II (mid-1960s to 1979):*** This period was marked by economic stagnation and political turmoil. Employment slowed down, inter-union rivalries increased and there was widespread industrial conflict. The split in the communist movement divided AITUC, leading to the formation of the Center of Indian Trade Unions (CITU) in 1970 by the Marxist Communist Party. UTUC was also split into 2 along ideological lines, the splinter group calling itself UTUC (Lenin Sarani). The Hind Mazdoor Sabha and the Center of Indian Trade Unions emerged as important trade unions during this phase, which also saw the emergence of women in trade unions when the Self Employed Women's Association (SEWA), the trade union of women in the unorganised sector, was formed in 1972, under the guidance of Ms Ela Bhatt. In the same year, 3 central trade union organisations, namely, HMS, INTUC and AITUC agreed to establish a National Council of Central Trade Union Organisations to enhance understanding and cooperation in the activities of the central unions, to promote the interests of the working class and to further the trade union movement.

During the late 1970s, there was a major change in the growth of independent employees' unions and economic unionism, mainly in the new capital intensive industries. Datta Samant rose as an influential trade union leader in this period. His approach was revolutionary. He resorted to long strikes, sometimes overreaching economic demands, bypassing legalistic struggle and by significantly using violence against opponent workers and trade union centers.

- ***Phase III (1980 to 1991):*** This corresponds to a period of segmented and uneven economic development, witnessing the phenomenon of decentralised bargaining and independent trade unionism. Inter-State and inter-regional variations in the nature of labour-management became very obvious. The Trade Unions (Amendment) Bill was introduced in the Lok Sabha in 1982. It proposed to make several amendments in the Act, like a minimum qualifying membership of 10 per cent of workmen (subject to a minimum of 10) employed in an establishment where a trade union is proposed to function, with a view to reduce multiplicity of unions.
- ***Phase IV (1991 to 2000):*** This was the transition phase between traditional and modern methods of trade unionism. Economic reforms in India were introduced in 1991, which had a great impact on the way businesses are run, and ultimately affected workers and unions. The advent of globalisation in India required the replacement of rigid and stabilised systems with more flexible ones, open to changes. The roles and functions of trade unions had to be adapted with the new requirements, like workers' training for adoption of new technology and issues related to the Voluntary Retirement Schemes. Regional trade union organisations affiliated to regional political parties such as DMK, AIADMK and MDMK in Tamil Nadu and the Shiv Sena in Maharashtra also emerged during this phase. The year 1999 saw a consensus among leading trade union federations like BMS, AITUC, CITU and INTUC to provide protection to the domestic industries, strengthening of public sector units by revival and amendment of labour legislations. *(Adapted from: Economic Times, New Delhi, 14/2/1999.)*
- ***Phase V (2000 and beyond):*** The recent phase is characterised by political instability, with no single party being able to emerge as the majority. The coalition government, with a number of political parties, is forced to follow a combination of ideologies that appeases every party in the coalition. The Trade Unions Act, 1926 underwent several amendments in 2001, which became effective on and from 9th January 2002. As per such amendments, no trade union of workmen shall be registered unless at least 10 per cent or 100, whichever is less, subject to a minimum of 7 workmen engaged or employed in the establishment or industry with which it is connected, are the members of such trade union on the date of making of application for registration. Further, a registered trade union of workmen shall at all times continue to have not less than 10 per cent or 100 of the workmen, whichever is less, subject to a minimum of 7 persons engaged or employed in the establishment or industry with which it is connected, as its members.

It is in this phase that the Government opened up the economy for Foreign Direct Investments. Further, the World Trade Organisation (WTO) rules and policies on trade liberalisation (for instance, implementation of product patents regime from 1st January 2005) had their own impact on business. Besides increasing the percentage of their shareholding, several foreign companies acquired Indian companies by buying controlling interests. Thus Coca Cola bought Parle Drinks, while Hindustan Lever took over Tata Oil Co. Ltd. At the same time, a number of Indian-owned companies went into the hands of foreign investors.

It would be rather iterative to say that workers are naturally the ones who are directly affected by such changes. The employment scenario has changed dramatically in this phase, with a shift from formal to informal sector, which has had an impact on the membership status of trade unions. This phase has also seen the onset of the economic recession beginning in the year 2007. Large scale lay-offs and retrenchments have taken place, and unions are being vigilant for any injustice being caused to employees, and are found to oppose it vehemently. A good example of this is the mass retrenchment of Jet Airways staff that had to be repealed due to strike by the union of its employees. Trade unions are also adopting pragmatic practices to keep pace with changes in technology, and are hence getting involved into supportive and developmental roles, thus moving ahead of their traditional militant role. This phase is also witnessing increased participation of women in trade unions.

FUNCTIONS OF TRADE UNIONS

Trade unions were seen as a 'military school' for class war by Engels (Hyman, 1971). Traditionally the role of unions has been to safeguard economic interests, secure better conditions of work and life, fight against exploitation and arbitrariness by management, and to ensure fairness and equity in employment contexts. During the long history of the trade union movement many positive changes have taken place in workers' conditions. Several legislations have been passed in order to ensure a better life to workers. Working class itself has become better educated. Today due to developments in the Information and Communication Technology, workers have become better informed and are aware of the forces that impact their industry. They are directly involved with the economic system of production, and over the years they have come to a position where they can influence not only the employment conditions and policies of an organisation, but also labour policies at national-level. Unions have seen a quantum change in their roles and functions; they have been performing a plethora of functions, some of which have been more prominent than others at different phases of their evolution. Ewing (2005) has identified that over the course of time trade unions have developed 5 principal functions: service, representation, regulatory, governmental and public administration, with more emphasis being placed recently on service, governmental and public administration functions.

Since many important central trade unions are wings of political parties, they are bound to be affected by the ideology of their respective parties. For instance, some unions that are influenced by Leftist principles aim at changing the capitalist system as a whole. However, irrespective of their political affiliation, the generic functions of unions in the current scenario may be categorised as primary and new functions.

Primary Functions

Scholars and practitioners have been debating since long over what are the primary functions of a trade union. While it is commonly comprehended that the primary function of a union is to protect the economic interest of workers (Hoxie, 1921; Perlman, 1928), many are of the opinion that the most basic function of a union is to build up its own organisation, and to give weight to its collective actions; once this function is accomplished, other functions follow.

> **Spotlight**
> The primary function of a union is to promote and protect the interests of its members in all aspects of their working life, including improvement in their civic environment (*First National Commission on Labour, 1969*)

Considering the fundamentals of unionism, there is an unequal distribution of wealth and power in all organisations. The basic function of unions is thus to reduce this inequality. According to the First National Commission on Labour (1969), the principal function of a union is to promote and protect the interests of its members in all aspects of their working life, including improvement in their civic environment. Extant research reveals the following as the primary functions of trade unions:

- To secure fair wages for workers; unions ensure that they are not exploited in any way, particularly in economic terms.

- To offer responsive cooperation in improving levels of production, productivity, discipline and high standards of quality.
- To improve working and living conditions, and to represent workers' interests in various fora (Freeman and Medoff, 1984).
- To enlarge opportunities for promotion and training.
- To promote integration of workers' interests with their industries.
- To cooperate in and facilitate technological advancement by broadening workers' understanding of underlying issues.

EXHIBIT 3.3 DEMAND FOR WELFARE BOARD FOR IT SECTOR EMPLOYEES

Majority of the employees in the Information Technology (IT) sector in Kerala are unorganised and therefore subjected to exploitation. Many of them are forced to work for over 12 hours a day for low wages. Government agencies such as the Kerala State IT Mission, Keltron, Information Kerala Mission, Akshaya and IT@School are alleged to be functioning as commission agents to enter into contracts for getting the work done by low-paid workers in the small-scale IT units. The Association of IT Employees (AITE) believes that exploitation in the private sector is now being extended to the Government IT sector. It has hence urged the Kerela Government to set up a welfare board for those working in this sector. It has also asked the Government to announce minimum wages for employees in the IT and allied sectors. The Association is trying to pressurise the Government to provide job security for IT workers under the Government agencies such as the IT Mission and Information Kerala Mission; strengthening of e-governance; and expansion of e-district programmes to the entire State.

(Adapted from: www.thehindu.com/todays-paper/tp-national/tp-kerala/article2590509.ece accessed on 2/10/2014.)

New Functions

Spotlight

New Functions of Unions:

- Communication
- Welfare activities
- Education
- Training
- Research
- Social work

The last few decades have witnessed a lot of turbulence in the global business environment in the form of redefined national boundaries, influence of WTO in national business laws, policy matters, economic recession and so on. This has resulted in changes in employment patterns and emergence of new sectors in the economy. Such changes have had a direct impact on the way trade unions are functioning. Rapid advancements in technology and successive revisions in pay have undoubtedly improved workers' conditions within the organised sector, but mostly at the cost of loss of control over jobs (Ratnam, 2006). Except for SEWA, little success has been noted in organising workers in the small-scale enterprises, as well as in other segments of the informal sector. All such factors have necessitated a paradigm shift in the roles of trade unions; from predominantly bargaining institutions, they have become specialised agencies, representing the voice and interests of labour. They have redefined their roles and functions to match with new issues facing the workers, management and organisations.

In addition to their traditional bargaining activities, unions now have a newly acquired voice and representative function. Many of them are trying to increase their value by providing a variety of services to their members, as well as to the community to which they belong. Such services range from providing legal and financial advice to improving skills of workers (Ghosh, Nandan and Gupta, 2009). These new functions of unions, also called ancillary functions (Monappa, 2000), can be categorised into the following groups:

- ***Communication***: Many large unions publish newsletters and/or magazines, with the main aim of clarifying their policy or stance on certain principal issues, as well as to pass on information about their activities. For example, *The Indian Worker* is a fortnightly bilingual publication of INTUC.
- ***Welfare Activities***: A number of trade unions are engaged in various welfare activities, such as providing housing and schooling facilities for the wards of workers establishing cooperative societies for promoting thrift among workers and providing consumer items at discounted prices. Unions are also playing an instrumental role in advocating against social evils like child labour, and in counseling employees on various matters. This apart, unions are being catalytic in promotion of cultural and recreational activities. The Textile Labour Association Ahmedabad has ventured to organise self-employed women in SEWA and has even started banking activities for this purpose.
- ***Education:*** Education makes workers aware of their surrounding environment. Unions strive to launch educational programmes for workers to enhance their knowledge of the work environment and to inform them about issues regarding their rights and responsibilities, about procedures and systems that exist in the workplace for redressing grievances, and similar issues.
- ***Training of Workers:*** Trade unions also provide training to workers in order to enhance their efficiency and effectiveness. This function has gained greater relevance in the current scenario when changes in technology are taking place very fast and obsolescence of skills is a routine phenomenon. For example, unions in India and Bahrain have joined hands to tackle exploitation of workers from Kerala and to make them aware of their rights when they land in Bahrain and other Gulf countries in search of employment opportunities. The General Federation of Bahrain Trade Unions Bahrain's main trade union body, and INTUC have come together to push for a pre-departure training programme for workers before they leave Kerala.

(Adapted from: www.financialexpress.com/news/india-bahrain-trade-unions-join-hands-to-protect-workers/891310/ accessed on 23/10/2014.)

Exhibit 3.4 Rourkela Shramik Sangh: Towards Skill Enhancement

The Rourkela Shramik Sangh (RSS), the recognised trade union body of Rourkela Steel Plant (RSP), has put forth its demand to the management of the Steel Authority of India Ltd. to send workers abroad for enhancement of their technical skills. This would equip them to better understand the need for maintaining the quality of work in the ongoing expansion and modernisation process of RSP.

(Adapted from: Economic Times, 24 August, 2010.)

- ***Research:*** Union negotiators require updated information to be collected systematically and analysed meticulously at the bargaining table. They also need to backup their wage demands with knowledge of the industry, of productivity, and of comparative industry practices. Many unions conduct their own research to this effect, laying emphasis on practical problems, especially day-to-day affairs at work. The Indian Labour Research Center is the research wing of the Bharatiya Mazdoor Sangh, and is actively engaged in such research.

- ***Social Work:*** Besides undertaking activities for worker welfare, many of the trade unions are even engaged in social work. For example, the Bharatiya Mazdoor Sangh encourages its workers to undertake social and constructive work, along with day-to-day union activities.

Exhibit 3.5 Union Participation in Managing Change

A number of labour leaders had established the Center for Workers Management (CWM) with the understanding that a change of culture in the labour movement as well as at management level is required in order to ease the strain in management-labour relations. A visionary plan was developed by CWM to bring about a change in the role of trade unions in a scenario in which privatisation is taking place. This was implemented in a limited number of large private enterprises, and about 30 firms responded to this initiative. Kamani Tubes Ltd. at Mumbai and Kamani Metals Ltd. (with plants in Mumbai and Bangalore) were the first to get involved in this plan.

The Supreme Court had ruled in favour of the labour movement initiative of transforming Kamani Tubes that had gone bankrupt due to mismanagement, into a workers' cooperative. Workers then raised a considerable sum of money to build a new financial asset structure. Leadership, rather than management, was provided by CWM in defending the enterprise's interests with respect to commercial banks, supervisory boards imposed by the Government of India, and courts of law.

Though, due to the economic situation 1990 onwards and various other problems like weak management, this attempt could not be successful, nonetheless, it provided an example of shift in the role of trade unions from militant orientation to development orientation.

(Adapted from: www.ilo-mirror.library.cornell.edu/public/english/bureau/inst/papers/1999/dp100/ accessed on 25/10/2014.)

METHODS OF ACHIEVING OBJECTIVES

The history of trade union movement bears evidence to myriads of methods adopted by unions to achieve their objectives. Such means may be peaceful or equipped with agitation and revolution, depending upon the ideologies followed by the trade unions. The Webbs propose the following methods adopted by unions: *collective bargaining, mutual insurance* and *legal enactments*. Pressure tactics including strikes, picketing, *gherao* and boycott are also often used to achieve the objectives.

- **Mutual Insurance:** Unions have since long tried to provide insurance and other benefits to their members, which act as a security against casualties and also contribute to improvement in the conditions of workers. This method implies that in exchange of fees that members pay, unions render certain services to them. It involves creation of a common fund to which every member is required to contribute, and the fund thus created is to be used for schemes for mutual benefit. Such benefits would enable unions to prevent workers from accepting employment on terms and conditions injurious to the trade (Ironside and Seifert, 1995).

Spotlight

Under mutual insurance, unions provide insurance and other benefits to their members, which act as a security against casualties and contribute to improvement in the conditions of workers.

The Webbs referred to the method of mutual insurance adopted by trade unions as acting as a "friendly society", that would provide insurance and other forms of assistance to members. Trade unions in Great Britain and USA are known to have provided mutual insurance to their members. British unions in the nineteenth century provided their members with insurance against unemployment, sickness, accidents, pensions for retired members and funeral expenses. The method of mutual insurance in Great Britain predominantly involved craft unions. Unions in USA have also provided benefits to their members from out of their funds, to meet economic uncertainties.

Mutual insurance is not a primary purpose of trade unions, neither does it have any actuarial basis or legal standing; in fact, this function can be performed better by other social and private bodies. But for union purposes, reserve funds are valuable because such funds enable the union of workmen to acquire wealth that binds them into a cohesive body.

Webb and Webb (1920) were of the opinion that unions adopted insurance policies primarily to strengthen the working-class organisation. They proposed the following advantages of mutual insurance (Boyer, 1988):

- Insurance benefits motivated hesitant recruits to join unions.
- These benefits were a powerful instrument for maintaining discipline among the members, and for enforcing on all the decisions of the majority.
- It results into commitment and loyalty towards the union, as members who had contributed to the benefit fund for several years would not want to be separated from the union as that would imply the forfeiture of old age and funeral benefits.
- Unemployment benefits adopted by unions helped in preventing unemployed members from accepting employment with wages below standard rate.
- These funds were a moral influence in negotiating with employers, thus enhancing bargaining power of the union.

The amount and number of benefits that can be provided by any trade union as a part of mutual insurance would essentially depend upon the funds of the union created through contribution by its members. This method is not very popular in India because of weak financial condition of unions and lack of sufficient advancement of trade unions as compared to countries like UK and USA. However, certain big unions like the Textile Labour Association Ahmedabad and Rashtriya Mill Mazdoor Sangh, Bombay have undertaken welfare measures for members.

Mutual insurance policies have undoubtedly attracted young workers to unions, observed Boyer (1988); despite their large scale acceptance, these policies gradually waned out, and unions in capitalist countries have shifted their focus to collective bargaining.

- **Collective Bargaining:** Collective bargaining came to be adopted as a method for achieving trade union objectives after unions received legal recognition and came to be recognised as legitimate representatives of workers. It is a method by which unions protect, safeguard and improve the conditions of the lives of their members. Under this method, trade union representatives bargain with the employer over terms and conditions of employment like wages, hours of work, incentives, working conditions, etc. An individual worker is not as influential and effective as a group in negotiating the terms and conditions of work. Due to this reason, collective bargaining came to be recognised as a useful method adopted by unions to achieve their objectives. Union representatives bargain with the employer and enter into an agreement, which is known as a collective agreement; such an agreement may deal with a single issue, or may include multiple issues. Negotiations may be conducted at different levels: they could be at local or plant level, where union representa-

Spotlight

Collective bargaining is a method by which unions protect, safeguard and improve the conditions of the lives of their members, by bargaining with employers over terms and conditions of employment.

tives negotiate with the management at factory or unit level, or at regional or national level. Though bargaining with a single employer is commonly found, employers may also unite for the purpose of bargaining.

Collective bargaining as a method has succeeded in introducing an element of industrial democracy; it enables workers to participate in the decision making process on the issues influencing them in industry, which was earlier the sole prerogative of the employers.

Collective bargaining has succeeded in the field of industries and labour management, particularly in countries like USA and UK, where trade unionism is very well developed. In Indian scenario, trade unions are mostly affiliated to political parties, and hence are controlled by such parties, regarded as "outsiders". It is the presence of such outsiders that influences the process of bargaining, and often contributes to the failure of the collective bargaining process.

Failure to reach an agreement through collective bargaining may result in the adoption of other means like strike or lock-out. We shall be dealing with collective bargaining as a process in further detail in Chapter 5.

- **Legal Enactments/Political Actions:** Legal enactments and political actions also help trade unions achieve their objectives. Unions send their representatives to legislatures to present the views and concerns of workers and convince the political leaders to enact laws for securing better working and living conditions. Once enacted, these laws define the legal rights of workers, and the industry has to abide by such laws.

Spotlight
Legal enactments affect the working class in general, while mutual insurance and collective bargaining impact the members or employees of a particular plant, industry or craft.

How is legal enactment or political action different from mutual insurance and collective bargaining? As the Webbs opined, mutual insurance allows unions to aid needy members directly, and collective bargaining focusses on negotiating with employers on issues pertaining to workers, while legal enactments emphasise on securing laws that would mandate general and specific work regulations at all levels of the government. Thus the impact of legal enactments is on the working class in general, while that of both mutual insurance and collective bargaining is restricted to the members or employees of a particular plant, industry or craft.

Labour laws on dispute settlement, labour welfare, social security, wages, working conditions, employment of women and children, etc. have contributed immensely to ensuring rights to workers and improving their conditions. The International Labour Organisation has played an important role in influencing enactment of labour laws; workers' representatives are sent to ILO to participate in various meetings of the body along with government representatives.

Affiliation to political parties dates back to the early history of trade unionism; political connections help unions gain power and influence. Since the time of their inception, trade unions in India have sought to affiliate themselves to one political party or the other. AITUC, the first trade union of India, is affiliated to the Communist Party of India; INTUC is associated with the Indian National Congress.

- **Direct Action:** When unions fail to achieve their objectives through any of the means discussed above, they resort to direct action, which refers to exerting pressure on employers by resorting to tactics like strikes, boycott, blockade, etc. Before we take up some of these tactics in brief, let us specify here that direct action leads to loss of productivity, and involves not only the employer and workers, but also suppliers, consumers and other stakeholders; hence this method must be avoided and used only as the last resort.

Spotlight
Direct action exerts pressure on employers through tactics like strikes, boycott, blockade, *gherao*, etc.

Strike refers to collective withdrawal from work by the members of a union. It is a powerful weapon in the hands of a union to get its demands accepted. Picketing is an action taken by union members to prevent employees from attending work after a strike has been called. Boycott refers to the rejection by workers of specific products or services provided by the employer. *Gherao* (literal meaning: confinement) is the confinement of managerial personnel within a small space, till the management is compelled to give a more favourable decision. Blockade refers to obstruction of products, etc. at a certain point by workers, though it does not involve any stoppage or reduction in production. We shall be telling more about all these tactics in the chapter on industrial disputes.

Other means of direct action may include mass subordination, demonstration, postering, etc.

RECOMMENDATIONS OF THE NATIONAL COMMISSIONS ON LABOUR

The First National Commission on Labour (1969) had encouraged the formation of national federations, as these would be more effective at collective bargaining forums and also as agencies to which educational and research activities for the benefit of workers in the concerned industries could be entrusted.

According to the recommendations of the Second National Commission on Labour (2002), federations of trade unions, as also central organisations of trade unions and federations in India should be covered within the definition of trade unions, and be subject to the same discipline as a primary trade union. The same dispensation shall apply to employer's organisations, as also employees' organisations. Further, the Commission was not in favour of craft-based or caste-based organisations of workers or employees or employers.

SUMMARY

- Trade unions are association of workers (or employers) formed on a continuous basis; they are a means to provide workers a medium to express their demands and views.
- The main objective of unions is to ensure workers' rights, safeguard economic interests, participate in management, make provision for welfare of workers and their families and contribute to national development.
- The various reasons that may influence a worker in joining union are: greater bargaining power, sense of security, gratification of social and psychological needs, negotiation for wages and working conditions, protection from unforeseen exigencies like accidents and illness, etc.
- Trade unions can be classified on the basis of their purposes, membership pattern of workers and level of operation.
- Notable theories proposed to explain the approaches and functioning of trade unions are: Marxian Class Conflict Theory, Webb's Theory of Industrial Democracy, Cole's Theory of Union Control of Industry, Hoxie's Theory of Functional Classification of Unionism, Tannenbaum's Sociological Theory, Common's Environmental Theory, Perlman's Theory of Scarcity Consciousness, Kerr and Associates' Protest Theory, Simon's Theory of Monopolistic, Anti-Democratic Trade Unionism and Mahatma Gandhi's Trusteeship Theory.
- Evolution of trade unionism in India can broadly be divided into 3 phases: pre-World War I, post-World War I and post-Independence. The post-Independence phase may be further studied under 5 distinct periods.

- Traditionally trade unions were supposed to have militant functions; over the years, such functions have undergone many changes, with focus shifting towards ensuring welfare and developmental aspects of workers.
- Primary functions of trade unions are: securing fair wages for workers; offering responsive co-operation in improving levels of production and productivity, discipline, and high standards of quality; improving working and living conditions and representing workers' interests in various fora; exploring opportunities for promotion and training, etc.
- New functions of unions include: communication, welfare activities, education and training of workers, research and social work, etc.

Key Concepts

Trade union	Class conflict theory	AITUC
Trusteeship theory	Direct action	Plant-level union
Managerial unions	Mutual insurance	Instrumentality
Craft union	Industry-level union	INTUC

Bibliography

Bhattacherjee, D. *Organized Labour and Economic Liberalization India: Past, Present and Future*. Geneva: International Institute for Labour Studies (ILO); 1999.

Boyer, G. R. "What Did Unions Do in Nineteenth-Century Britain?" [Electronic version]. *Journal of Economic History*, 1988, Vol. 48, No. 2, pp. 319-332.

Brett, J. M. "Why Employees Want Unions?", *Organizational Dynamics*, 1980, Vol. 8, pp. 47-59.

Cole, G. D. H. *An Introduction to Trade Unionism*, London: George Allen & Unwin Ltd., 1955 p. 13.

Dankert, C. E. *Contemporary Unionism*, New York: Prentice Hall Inc., 1948 p. 1.

Ewing, K. D. "The Function of Trade Unions", *Industrial Law Journal,* 2005, Vol. 34, Issue 1, pp. 1-22.

Freeman, Richard B., and James L. Medoff. *What Do Unions Do?* New York: Basic Books, 1984.

Ghosh, P., Nandan, S. and Gupta, A. "Changing Role of Trade Unions in India: A Case Study of NTPC, Unchahar", *Asian Academy of Management Journal*, 2009. Vol. 14 No. 1, pp. 37-57

Giri, V. V. *Labour Problems in Indian Industry*, Asian Publishing House, Bombay, 1959.

Government of India, *Report of the National Commission on Labour (1969).*

Government of India, *Report of the National Commission on Labour (2002).*

Hoxie, R. F. *Trade Unionism in the United States*, New York: Russel & Russel, 1921.

Hyman, R. *Marxism and the Sociology of Trade Unionism*, Pluto Press, London, 1971.

ILO. International Workers' Symposium on "The Role of Trade Unions in the Global Economy and the Fight against Poverty', Geneva, 17th–21st October 2005.

Ironside, M. and Seifert, R. V. *Industrial Relations in Schools*, Routledge, London, 1995.

Kerr, C., Dunlop, J. T., Harbison, F. and Myers, C. A. *Industrialism and Industrial Man: The Problems of Labour and the Management of Economic Growth*, Harvard University Press, Cambridge, MA, 1960.

Mills, D. Q. *Labor Management Relations,* McGraw Hill Book Company, New York, 1994.

Modi, S., Singhal, K. C. and Singh, U. C. "Workers' Participation in Trade Unions", *Indian Journal of Industrial Relations*, 1995. Vol. 31 No. 1, July, pp. 40-58.

Monappa, A. *Industrial Relations,* Tata McGraw Hill, New Delhi, 2000.

Newton, L. A. and Shore, L. M. "A Model of Union Membership: Instrumentality, Commitment and Opposition", *Academy of Management Review*, 1992, Vol. 17 No. 2, pp. 275-298.
Perlman, S. *A Theory of Labour Movement*, New York: Macmillan, 1928.
Ramaswamy, E. A. *Worker Consciousness and Trade Union Response,* Oxford University Press, New Delhi, 1988.
Ratnam, C. S. V. *Industrial Relations,* Oxford University Press, New Delhi, 2006.
Schnabel, C. Determinants of Trade Union Membership, in Addison, John T./Schnabel, Claus (eds.): *International Handbook of Trade Unions*, Cheltenham, 2003.
Schuler, R.S. and Youngblood, B.S.A. *Effective Personnel Management*, 2nd ed., West Publishing Company, New York, 1986.
Simons, H. C. (1944/48). "Some Reflections on Syndicalism", reprinted in: *Economic Policy for a Free Society*, Chicago, pp. 121-159.
Simons, H. C. (1945/48). "Introduction: A Political Credo", reprinted in: *Economic Policy for a Free Society*, Chicago, pp. 1-39.
Singh, V. B. "Trade Union Movement", in Singh, V. B. (Ed.) *Economic History of India 1857–1956,* Allied Publishers, Mumbai, 1965.
Sinha, P. R. N., Sinha, I. B. and Shekhar, S. P. *Industrial Relations, Trade Unions, and Labour Legislation*, Pearson Education, New Delhi, 2006.
Tannenbaum, F. *A Philosophy of Labour*, New York: Alfred A. Knopf, 1951.
Verma, P. *Labour Economics and Industrial Relations*, New Delhi: Tata McGraw Hill, 1987.
Waddington, J. and Whitson, C. "Why Do People Join Unions in a Period of Membership Decline?" *British Journal of Industrial Relations, 1997,* Vol. 35 No. 4, pp. 515-546.
Webb, S. and Webb, B. *Industrial Democracy,* London: Longmans, 1920.
Webb, S. and Webb, B. op. cit., p. 1.
Yoder, D. *Personnel Management and Industrial Relations*, New Delhi: Prentice Hall of India, 1974, p. 159.

Review Questions

Objective Type Questions

I. State True or False

(i) The Textile Labour Association Ahmedabad is a craft union.
(ii) Tannenbaum has classified trade unions on the basis of their functions.
(iii) N. M. Lokhande had sponsored the first labour organisation in India.
(iv) INTUC is affiliated to the Communist Party of India.
(v) Blockade means rejection of specific products/services provided by the employer by workers.

Answers: (i) False, (ii) False, (iii) True, (iv) False, (v) False

II. Fill in the Blanks

(i) In mutual __________ a common fund is created in which every member contributes.
(ii) Under dynastic __________ leadership, unions undertake social functions at the plant-level.
(iii) ____________ unions may join hands with employers for mutual benefit.
(iv) Mahatma Gandhi's theory of trade union was based on the philosophy of ____________.
(v) The First Factory Commission was appointed in ____________.

Answers: (i) insurance, (ii) elite, (iii) predatory, (iv) Sarvodaya, (v) 1881

Discussion Questions

1. Trade unions are an important component of the modern industrial relations system of a nation. Do you agree with the statement? Justify your view.
2. Define a trade union. List the various objectives of trade unions.
3. Write a critical note on the role of trade unions in uplifting the condition of workers.
4. Analyse the driving forces behind the development of trade unions in India.
5. Discuss the important events in the evolution of trade unions in India in the pre-World War I and post-World War I periods.
6. Examine the impact of the process of economic liberalisation on trade unionism in India.
7. Compare Marxist Theory of Class Conflict and Webbs' Theory of Industrial Democracy. Which one do you think is more relevant in today's context? Why?
8. Classify the functions of trade unions. How have these functions changed over time?
9. Explain the elements of powerlessness and instrumentality that may drive an employee towards joining a trade union.
10. Write short notes on:
    (i) Tannenbaum's Sociological Theory
    (ii) Hoxie's Theory of Functional Classification of Unionism
    (iii) Gandhi's Trusteeship Theory

Role of Unions: Traditional and Beyond

National Thermal Power Corporation (NTPC) Limited, a 'Navratna' public sector unit and the largest power generating company of India, was incorporated in the year 1975. NTPC's core business is engineering and operation of power generating plants. With a strong employee base, NTPC has won several distinctions of being one of the best employers in India.

Trade Unions at NTPC, Unchahar

There are around 1,200 employees at the Unchahar Power Station (hereon also referred to as Plant or Power Station), in the State of Uttar Pradesh, of which 693 are in workmen grade. The role of trade unions assumes critical significance in the success of the Power Station. At the apex level, union-management relations at NTPC are governed through the National Bipartite Committee (NBC) consisting of 4 Central Trade Union Organisation (CTUO) nominees, viz., AITUC, BMS, CITU and INTUC, with representatives of unions from various projects/stations on one side, and management representatives on the other. Following are the major unions at the Plant.

(i) NTPC Power Karamchari Sangh: Affiliated to CITU and inspired by CPI (Marxist), the Sangh follows Communist philosophy. It negotiates with the management on the workers' interests and problems. With its inception at the Unchahar Station in the year 1992, the Sangh now boasts of 310 members as per the last elections held. It is animated by the goal of organising workers to further their interests in economic, social and political matters. The methods adopted by this union are legislation, demonstrations, agitations and intensification of the class struggle.

(ii) NTPC Employees' Union: Affiliated to INTUC, the Employees' Union has adopted the ideologies of the Congress Party, and negotiates with the management at the plant-level. There are 140 members in the Union as per the last elections held. The main objectives of the Employees' Union are: to secure greater participation of workers in the management of the enterprise; to improve the conditions at work; and to provide various social security measures. The means adopted for the furtherance of these objectives are peaceful, through the process of law and negotiations.

(iii) NTPC Mazdoor Sangh: The NTPC Mazdoor Sangh is affiliated to the Bharatiya Mazdoor Sangh, and has adopted the principles of the Bharatiya Janta Party. It also negotiates with the management at plant-level. The methods employed by the Mazdoor Sangh are legitimate, peaceful and democratic.

(iv) NTPC Electric Employees' Union (EEU): Affiliated to INTUC, EEU has adopted its constitution from the philosophies of Congress. It is in the minority since it got less than 10 per cent votes in the last elections held, and hence it does not negotiate with the management at a large level. Purpose of formation of this union was to organise those workmen/employees of electricity organisations of Uttar Pradesh, namely, the UP Power Corporation, NTPC Unchahar Electricity Production Departments, and The Cooperative Electric Society Ltd., who do not fall under executive and supervisory categories.

Other recognised unions of the Plant are Feroze Gandhi Urja Thermal Power Plant (FGUTPP) Pariyojna Karamchari Sangh (Independent), FGUTPP Pravidhik Karamchari Sangh (Independent), UP Vidyut Mazdoor Sangh (affiliated to Bharatiya Mazdoor Sangh) and NTPC Shramik Sangh (affiliated to UTUC). Unions that are not recognised include the UP Vidyut Panchayat and NTPC Workers' Association.

Role of Trade Unions at NTPC, Unchahar

Trade unions at NTPC not only act as machinery to voice employee grievances and problems before the management, but they also have a fair involvement in welfare measures for workers. They actively participate in discussions with the management at different levels regarding safety, work conditions and various other worker-related issues. Meetings are held from time to time, in which management and union representatives discuss and try to resolve several issues, the primary among which are issues pertaining to labour welfare. Welfare activities of the workers at Unchahar Power Station are divided into 2 broad categories: plant welfare and township welfare.

Plant Welfare Under this category, there is a provision for facilities of canteen, drinking water and restrooms for employees.

Township Welfare The Plant has welfare bodies like Union Working Committees, Employee Welfare Association and Township Advisory Development Committee, which look into the affairs of township welfare. Aspects related to entertainment like cable TV facilities, reading rooms, music halls, sports and theatres are being taken care of by the representative trade union. Besides, there are facilities like activity center for children, and Sports Council which organises various sports events like cricket, football, table tennis, etc. for the employees. There are 3 schools in the township, the infrastructure of which is provided by NTPC. All other expenses of the schools are met by their tuition fee. There are different clubs and associations that organise various events and celebrations. Different types of programmes on aspects like technical skills, safety and information management systems are organised by the Employee Development Center for the employees (including workers).

Thus there is involvement of management and union representatives towards the welfare of workers and their families. They are trying to promote workers' interests and thus bring about their overall development.

(Adapted from: Ghosh, P., Nandan, S. and Gupta, A. "Changing Role of Trade Unions in India: A Case Study of NTPC, Unchahar" Asian Academy of Management Journal. 2009, Vol. 14 No. 1, pp. 37-57.)

Questions

1. What are the functions performed by trade unions at NTPC, Unchahar?
2. Are the roles of trade unions at NTPC, Unchahar different from the traditional roles of unions as discussed in the chapter? Justify your stand with suitable examples.
3. What other developmental functions do you suggest to be performed by modern unions?

4

Trade Unions in India: Various Issues

Desired Knowledge Competencies

- To develop an understanding of the objectives, ideologies and other aspects of Central Trade Union Organisations in India.
- To review trade union membership in India and its recent trends.
- To identify the problems encountered by unions and the contemporary issues of trade unionism in India.
- To comprehend the concept of employers' organisations in Indian context.

INTRODUCTION

In the years following India's Independence there has been an increase in the total number of trade unions and their federations. Membership of unions has also increased over time. However, union activities have been more or less confined to the organised sector, more so in public sector enterprises, from which over 70 per cent of union membership is drawn.

The process of liberalisation and globalisation has ushered in a series of structural changes in the Indian economy. Perhaps the most notable of such changes are disinvestment of the public sector and introduction of new work practices like outsourcing and contractual employment. The past decade has also witnessed the emergence and expansion of new sectors including retail, Information Technology (IT) and business process management (BPM). These are human capital-intensive sectors comprising knowledge workers, who have a unique style of working and are generally averse to joining unions. All these factors have resulted in marginalisation of the labour movement as a whole and have eventually contributed to the weakening of trade unions.

In this chapter we will talk about the objectives and ideologies of notable Central Trade Union Organisations (CTUOs) in India, besides touching upon the issue of trade union membership. Many social, political, legal and economic factors are found to affect the functioning of unions leading to a number of problems related to multiplicity of unions, leadership, finances, etc. This chapter makes a critical analysis of such problems faced by unions. Certain other contemporary issues like membership of women in trade unions and the impact of globalisation on unions have also been covered in a separate section.

CENTRAL TRADE UNION ORGANISATIONS IN INDIA

Before we talk about the Central Trade Union Organisations in details, let us briefly explain the concept of recognition of a union as a CTUO. The criteria laid down by the Ministry of Labour & Employment, Government of India for trade unions to be recognised as CTUOs are as follows:

- Their affiliates must be spread over at least 4 States and in 4 industries, and
- They must have a minimum of 5 lakh (i.e., 0.5 million) members.

The strength of a CTUO is taken to be the combined membership of all registered unions affiliated to that CTUO. Once recognised, the Government gives a CTUO representation in various fora like the International Labour Organisation (ILO), international and national conferences, development councils, tripartite bodies, committees, etc. on the basis of the results of General Verification. We shall be explaining the concept of General Verification subsequently in the chapter in context of union membership.

In this section we shall be discussing some of the important CTUOs in terms of their objectives, membership patterns and other details. The Self Employed Women's Association has also been included mainly because it has established itself as a successful association of women workers, in spite of being relatively younger than the other CTUOs.

All India Trade Union Congress

The All India Trade Union Congress (AITUC), the first trade union in India, was founded in the year 1920 at Bombay (now Mumbai), with Lala Lajpat Rai as its first president. Up to 1945, Congressmen, socialists and communists worked under the flag of AITUC; subsequently the union split up on account of difference in political ideologies. Since then, it has been associated with the Communist Party of India. AITUC has been a key player in the labour movement and has also played a crucial role in India's struggle for freedom.

Objectives AITUC aims to achieve the following objectives by peaceful and legitimate means:

- To establish a socialist state in India.
- To socialise and nationalise the means of production, distribution and exchange as far as possible.
- To improve the economic and social conditions of workers.
- To protect and further the interests, rights and privileges of workers in matters related to employment.
- To safeguard and promote workers' right to freedom of speech, freedom of press, freedom of association, freedom of assembly, right to strike and right to work.
- To abolish political/economic practices based on caste, creed, community, race or religion, and to fight against all forms of social oppression and injustice.
- To oppose all forms of atrocities and harassment against women at workplace.

Membership Any union seeking affiliation to AITUC must, on application, pay an annual contribution and special levies, as per rules. The membership of AITUC is about 3.6 million. The unions affiliated to it are from the organised sector like textile, engineering, coal, steel, road transport and electricity board, as well as from the unorganised sector, such as *beedi*, construction and head-load workers, *anganwadi*, local bodies and handloom. Recently a number of agricultural workers' unions have affiliated themselves to AITUC.

Spotlight
AITUC was formed in 1920.

Structure The structure of AITUC comprises affiliated unions, a general council including office bearers, working committee of the general council and State bodies.

Hind Mazdoor Sabha

The Hind Mazdoor Sabha (HMS) was founded in Calcutta (now Kolkata) during a trade union conference from 24th to 26th December 1948, with R.S. Ruikar as the first president. The key factor behind the emergence of this union was the realisation that the trade union movement must be freed from misuse of unions by political parties in meeting their own interests. Affiliated to the International Trade Union Confederation (ITUC)—which represents 175 million workers in 153 countries and territories and has 308 national affiliates—the HMS has been functioning as an independent and democratic trade union centre, free from the pulls and pressures of political parties, employers and the government. However, HMS may not be construed to be apolitical; it denounces the concept of a market-driven economy and privatisation as a one-stop solution to the problems in the economy.

Spotlight
Socialists of AITUC moved out and formed the Hind Mazdoor Panchayat in 1948, which later became the Hind Mazdoor Sabha.

Objectives As per the philosophy of this union, free market is solely profit-oriented and has no social concerns. For a country's balanced development with equity, the state should play a regulatory role. In this pursuit, following are the broad objectives of HMS:

- To ensure all-round development of workers and their families. For this HMS encourages and assists unions affiliated to it to take up non-traditional activities which address social evils like child labour and generates awareness on issues like gender equality, environment protection, adult literacy, etc.
- To make endeavours towards having a single unified trade union movement.
- To promote industrial democracy, workers' education and cooperative movement.
- To build the trade union movement as an effective instrument of the country's socio-economic transformation with social justice.

Membership As per the findings of the General Verification conducted by the Ministry of Labour & Employment, with year 2000 as the year of reckoning, HMS had a membership of 3,342,213 in 2002 (13 per cent of the total trade union membership in the country). It has members from a cross section of industries like textiles, iron and steel and coal mining, spread over 23 States.

Structure HMS has affiliates at State-level from various industries, which in turn have affiliations from regional and plant-level unions. The office has an elected president at the top, followed by vice presidents, general secretaries and chief advisors.

Indian National Trade Union Congress

The Indian National Trade Union Congress (INTUC) is the trade union wing of the Indian National Congress. It came into existence on 3rd May 1948, after a resolution to this effect was passed by the central board of the Hindustan Mazdoor Sevak Sangh on 17th November 1947. Many attribute the birth of INTUC as a historic necessity to voice the genuine demands of the working class, keeping in view national interest as well.

INTUC is guided by Gandhian Sarvodaya philosophy, and is associated with ILO since 1949. It is inspired by the idea of transforming its beliefs with changing times, which can enable it to tackle the problems and contemporary issues related to workers. These include: promoting egalitarianism in the society; community welfare; maintaining and strengthening links with the unions of other countries having the same employer, as in the case of multinational firms; focus on improving the working conditions and the general quality of life for workers; and training and research for workers.

> **Reflection**
> INTUC was established on 3rd May 1947. It was recognised by the Government of India in 1948 as the most representative among the central federations.

Objectives The objectives of INTUC are:

- To establish an order of the society that promotes all-round growth and development of its individual members and eliminates exploitation and inequality.
- To organise the society in such manner as to ensure full employment and the best utilisation of its manpower and other resources.
- To secure increasing association of workers in the administration of industry and their full participation in its control.
- To promote the social, civic and political interests of the working class.
- To place industry under national ownership and control in suitable form in order to realise the aforesaid objectives in the quickest time.

Membership Any registered trade union may seek affiliation to INTUC. Each affiliated union has to pay to the union the prescribed annual affiliation fee per member on the basis of membership on its rolls on the close of the preceding year, subject to a minimum of ₹100. The Working Committee may grant concession in the rate of affiliation fee in respect of unions functioning in *beedi,* fisheries, agriculture and such other industries in the unorganised sector. As per the provisional statistics of the Ministry of Labour & Employment, the membership figure of INTUC stood at 3.9 million in 2002.

Structure The union has a president at the top, followed by the general secretary and treasurer. There are affiliated State branches, each having its own president.

Bharatiya Mazdoor Sangh

The Bharatiya Mazdoor Sangh (BMS) was founded on 23rd July 1955 under the leadership of Dattopantji Thengdi. BMS was not the result of any split in the existing trade union organisations, unlike in the cases of almost all other unions. Hence it had the formidable responsibility of building its organisational structure from the grassroot level.

BMS does not believe in class concept and is non-political in nature. The grounded philosophy of this union is that a trade union can exert

> **Reflection**
> BMS was formed under the aegis of the Jan Sangh Party, presently known as the Bharatiya Janata Party.

influence on management and policies of government only when it adopts the principle of non-political trade unionism. With its productivity-orientation, BMS rejects the idea of State control and proposes the restriction of State control to inevitable sectors like defence. However, the union strongly supports public accountability of each individual. It denounces coercive methods and adheres to constructive approach in all its struggles; in this context the philosophy of BMS is strikingly different from that of class struggle proposed by Marx.

Objectives The aims and objectives of the Bharatiya Mazdoor Sangh are:

- To establish such order of the society in which there shall be security of, among other things, full employment and maximum production; economic democracy, development of autonomous industrial communities, and provision of work with living wage to every individual.
- To enable workers in realising the above objectives by assisting them in organising themselves in trade unions; directing and coordinating the activities of affiliated unions and bringing unity in the trade union movement.
- To secure and preserve for the workers their legitimate rights, including the right to strike as the last resort for redressing grievances; good conditions of living, a living wage and due share in the profits in their respective industries as partners; and enforcement, amendment and enactment of new labour legislations.
- To inculcate in workers a sense of responsibility towards their industry and nation.
- To educate workers through seminars, lectures, training programmes, etc.
- To bring out publications in the interest of workers and to encourage labour research. BMS has established the *Bharatiya Shram-Shodh Mandal*, a research-based institution in 1980 to promote objective studies based on impartial examination of facts and developments in the industrial field.
- To contribute to ameliorate the social, economic, cultural, civic and general conditions of the workers and bring about welfare of their families.

BMS has set up the '*Paryavaran Manch*' in 1995 to pragmatise the activities of trade unions, earlier limited to issues related to wages, bonus etc. It is also engaged in multiple activities directed towards the upliftment of the working class. The non-political ideology of BMS has now gained currency and is finding acceptance even at international levels.

Membership As of the year 2002, the total membership of BMS stood at 2,15,797, and the union claims to have presence in all the States of India, with more than 5,000 affiliate unions in all the 44 industries classified by the Ministry of Labour & Employment.

Structure BMS has a president, vice presidents, general secretary, a few other secretaries, department in-charges (each looking after various departments of the union office like media, external affairs, etc.), zonal organising secretaries (where each zone comprises several States) and in-charges of federation groups formed by grouping together federations from different industries (for example, railway, defence and postal federations form 1 group).

Self-Employed Women's Association

The Self Employed Women's Association (SEWA) is a registered trade union of about a million women workers in the informal sector. It was founded in 1972 by Ela Bhatt, a lawyer and union organiser. SEWA grew out of the Textile Labour Association Ahmedabad, India's oldest and

Spotlight
SEWA is a trade union of women in the unorganised sector, formed in 1972.

largest union of textile workers. It is an organisation of poor, self-employed women workers, who earn a living through their own labour or small businesses. Established with the purpose of assisting women belonging to households of mill workers and with its focus on training and welfare activities, SEWA has now stretched its wings, and today it is a national union with members from nine States—Gujarat, Madhya Pradesh, Bihar, Kerala, Uttar Pradesh, Rajasthan, Delhi, West Bengal and Uttarakhand. It is guided by the Gandhian principles of *satya* (truth), *ahimsa* (non-violence), *sarvadharma* (integrating all faiths) and *khadi* (propagation of local employment and self-reliance). SEWA is both an organisation and a movement in itself. The SEWA movement is an amalgamation of 3 movements: the labour movement, the co-operative movement and the women's movement. It has adopted the strategy of struggle and development by the joint action of unions and cooperatives.

Objectives The objectives of SEWA are:

- To organise women workers for full employment.
- To promote self-reliance among women.

Membership Several States, namely, Gujarat, Madhya Pradesh, Bihar, Kerala and Uttar Pradesh have registered State-level unions under SEWA. Members of all these unions are women workers from the informal sector. The union is open for membership to self-employed women workers from all over India. In 2008, SEWA organised workers from 124 trades and occupations, and reported an all-India membership of 9.6 million. The membership fee is ₹5 per year.

Structure Each of the State-level unions of SEWA is its affiliate. The union is governed by a 2 tier level of elected representation. The members of each trade elect their representatives in the ratio of 1 representative per 100 members. These representatives then form the trade council *(Pratinidhi Mandal)*. In addition, and parallel to the trade council, are the trade committees *(Dhandha Samiti)* in each trade. A trade committee has no fixed number of members; the number usually varies from 15 to 50. Members of trade councils are members of their respective trade committees as well. The organiser of a trade group is the Member Secretary of the trade committee of that group. Besides, each State-level union has representation in SEWA through the national council.

UNIONISATION OF WORKERS AND UNION MEMBERSHIP

Trade unionism in India has experienced a steady growth with support from both society and government. The number of registered trade unions and membership of unions both have increased steadily after Independence, except for a few periods. The most authentic source of the number of unionised workers in India is the General Verification of membership of trade unions affiliated to CTUOs, and is an exercise undertaken by the Chief Labour Commissioner (CLC) (Central), on the directions of the Ministry of Labour & Employment. The purpose of such verification is to determine the representation of CTUOs in various national and international councils, committees, conferences etc. General Verification of CTUOs was earlier conducted in 1980, followed by another in 1989,

Spotlight

General Verification is an exercise undertaken by the CLC (Central) to determine membership of trade unions affiliated to CTUOs.

and the latest in 2002. Results of the same were published by the Ministry of Labour & Employment in 1985, December 1996 and January 2008 respectively. The total number of unionised workers has shown an average annual growth rate of 5.35 per cent between 1989 and 2002 (Table 4.1). The process of the next verification has already been initiated by the Ministry. So far, 2 meetings of the Standing Committee on General Verification comprising representatives from various CTUOs have been held under the chairmanship of the CLC (Central) and the date of reckoning for fresh General Verification was decided as 31st December 2011.

TABLE 4.1 Unionised Workers in India

Year	*1989 (in millions)*	*2002 (in millions)*	*Increase (in millions)*	*Average Annual Growth Rate*
Unionised workers *(including Agricultural and Rural Workers)*	12.27	24.60	12.33	5.35
Unionised workers *(excluding Agricultural and Rural Workers)*	10.54	17.13	6.39	3.74

(Adapted from: John, J. Overall Increase and Sectoral Setbacks: Lessons from Central Trade Union Verification 2002 Data, Labour File, Vol. 5 Nos. 1 and 2, pp. 13-25, 1992.)

Though the number of registered trade unions has increased from 1989 to 2002, the percentage of unions submitting returns has decreased, and in 2002 it was merely 11.4 per cent of the total number of trade unions. The total membership, excluding Agricultural and Rural Workers (A&RW), of all CTUOs has increased in absolute terms from 10,541,932 in 1989 to 17,131,529 in 2002, registering an increase of 62.51 per cent at an average annual growth rate of 3.74 per cent. It may be noted here that agricultural unions may or may not be included during the General Verification. In 2002, the data on A&RW has been presented as an industrial-sector category and has been considered while calculating the membership of CTUOs. Consequently the total number of members of a CTUO now includes the members that a union might have among A&RW.

Overall, trade union membership does not show any fixed pattern in terms of increase or decrease. For example, the pattern of growth of trade unions from the year 1991 to 2008 shows that there has been a continuous rise in the number of unions from 1991 to 2007, except in 2004, when there was a slight decrease, and then a decrease in 2008. The percentage of unions submitting returns decreased to 9.7 in 2003, from 11.4 in 2002 and then to 7.0 per cent in 2004 (Table 4.2). This could also be due to the fact that membership is calculated only for those trade unions that are submitting returns and total membership calculated is dependent upon membership of these unions only. The membership of trade unions increased from 5.42 million in 2000 to 9.57 million in 2008, though there was a notable fall in 2003, 2004 and 2007 over the previous years. Average membership per union has also shown a remarkable decrease in 2002, 2003, 2004 and 2008. This decrease may be attributed factors like changing employment patterns, growth of service sector and rise in informalisation of labour in the country. Other reasons could be fragmentation of major unions and rise of independent unions at unit-level.

Table 4.2 Growth of Registered Trade Unions and their Membership Status (1991 to 2010)

Year	Number of Registered Trade Unions	Number of Unions Submitting Returns	Membership of Unions Submitting Returns					Average membership per union
			Men		Women		Total Membership ('000)	
			Number ('000)	% to total	Number ('000)	% to total		
1991	53535	8418 (15.7)	5507	90.3	594	9.7	6100	725
1992	55680	9165 (16.5)	5148	89.6	598	10.4	5746	627
1993	55784	6806 (12.2)	2636	84.1	498	15.9	3134	460
1994	56872	6277 (11.0)	3239	79.1	856	20.9	4095	652
1995	57952	8162 (14.1)	5675	86.8	863	13.2	6538	801
1996	58988	7242 (12.3)	4250	75.9	1351	24.1	5601	773
1997	60660	8872 (14.6)	6504	87.8	905	12.2	7409	835
1998	61992	7403 (11.9)	6104	84.2	1145	15.8	7249	979
1999	64817	8152 (12.6)	5190	81.0	1218	19.0	6408	786
2000	66056	7253 (11.0)	4510	83.2	910	16.8	5420	747
2001	66624	6531 (9.8)	4392	74.8	1481	25.2	5873	899
2002	68544	7812 (11.4)	5102	73.2	1871	26.8	6973	893
2003	74649	7258 (9.7)	4854	77.3	1423	22.7	6277	865
2004	74403	5252 (7.1)	2954	87.0	443	13.0	3397	647
2005	78465	8317 (10.6)	6334	72.6	2385	27.4	8719	1048

(Contd.)

2006	88440	8471	7754	86.5	1206	13.5	8960	1058
		(9.6)						
2007	95783	7408	5751	73.0	2126	27.0	7877	1063
		(7.7)						
2008	84642	9709	7420	77.5	2154	22.5	9574	986
		(11.5)						
2009	22284*	3861	4388	67.7	2092	32.3	6480	1678
		(17.3)						
2010	18602*	2937	3185	62.5	1912	37.5	5097	1735
		(15.8)						

Note:

i. Figures in Column 2 are estimated by incorporating the latest available information of the non-responding States.

ii. Figures in brackets in Column 3 denote percentage of unions submitting returns to total number of registered unions.

iii. The figures are exclusive of federations in all the statements.

iv. The data is based on the returns received.

(Adapted from: www.labourbureau.nic.in accessed on 26/2/2014.)

Let us now briefly analyse the membership status of CTUOs as per the results of the General Verification. Looking back in time we can see that in 1924 there were just 167 trade unions in India with a quarter million members. According to the figures available with the Government, there are presently 12 CTUOs with total membership of 0.248 million. The central trade unions have shown a massive increase in their membership as per the latest verification report prepared by the Chief Labour Commissioner (Central). 3 new bodies have been graded with the status of central unions, as their membership has crossed the mandatory 0.5 million. All other CTUOs existing earlier have shown an increase in membership from the previous date of reckoning, that is, 1989, with Bharatiya Mazdoor Sangh leading the list. A comparison of the membership of CTUOs between the years 1980, 1989 and 2002 has been shown in Table 4.3.

TABLE 4.3 Membership of Central Trade Union Organisations

S. No.	*Name of Trade Union*	*Membership with Date of Reckoning as on 31.12.1980*	*Membership with Date of Reckoning as on 31.12.1989*	*Membership with Date of Reckoning as on 31.12.2002*
1.	INTUC	22,36,128	26,92,388	39,54,012
2.	BMS	12,11,345	31,16,564	62,15,797
3.	HMS*	7,62,882	14,80,963	33,38,491
4.	United Trade Union Congress - Lenin Sarani (UTUC-LS)	6,21,359	8,43,256	13,73,268
5.	National Labour Organisation (NLO)	2,46,540	1,38,877	—
6.	United Trade Union Congress (UTUC)	1,65,614	5,84,523	6,06,935
7.	Trade Unions Co-ordination Centre (TUCC)	1,23,048	2,30,139	7,32,760

(Contd.)

8.	National Front of Indian Trade Unions (NFITU)	84,123	5,29,762	6,03,219
9.	AITUC	3,44,746	9,38,486	34,42,239
10.	CITU	3,31,031	17,75,220	26,78,473
11.	Hind Mazdoor Kisan Panchayat (HMKP)*	—	3,516	—
12.	Indian Federation of Free Trade Unions (IFFTU)	—	428	—
13.	SEWA	—	—	6,88,140
14.	Labour Progressive Front (LPF)	—	—	6,11,506
15.	All India Central Council of Trade Unions (AICCTU)	—	—	6,39,962
	TOTAL	61,26,816	1,23,34,142	2,48,84,802

*Hind Mazdoor Kisan Panchayat (HMKP) merged with HMS on 23rd October 2010
(Adapted from: www.labour.nic.in/ir/Implementation-I.htm accessed on 2/3/2014.)

PROBLEMS OF TRADE UNIONS IN INDIA

Unions in India are too fragmented; they split up due to various reasons. Earlier unions were affiliated to different political parties each having its own ideology. Consequently the splits in unions tended to be on ideological grounds. However, more recently, leadership issues have become the main reasons for their fragmentation, thus weakening unions. Adoption of downsizing strategies by decentralising production and by sub-contracting various operations to small businesses have led to reduction in the growth of jobs in the organised sector and a consequent increase in the share of the informal sector in industrial employment. Regular workers are being replaced by contract workers to reduce wage costs so that business firms could compete in the market. This has accentuated the process of weakening of trade unions (Datt, 2008), as majority of union membership comes from the organised sector. Other issues that weaken the structure and functioning of trade unions include declining membership, poor finances, influence of politics, dominance of outside leadership, multiple subscriptions of union membership and inter and intra union rivalries arising out of multiplicity of unions (Das, 1999), both at macro and firm levels. Moreover, intense competition within the product market and instability of the labour market have made the job of unions very difficult. In this section we will analyse some of the glaring problems of trade unions in India.

Recognition of Trade Unions

Existence of a strong and recognised trade union is an essential ingredient for industrial peace. A serious flaw in the legislations related to trade unions in India is the absence of any recognition process for unions. The Industrial Disputes Act, 1947 does mention the term "recognised unions", but it does not prescribe any procedure for recognition. The Trade Unions Act, 1926 also does not address this issue. Except for Andhra Pradesh, Gujarat, Madhya Pradesh, Maharashtra, Rajasthan and West Bengal, there are no State enactments regarding the recognition of trade unions. Lack of any central enactment may result in employers ignoring or even by-passing representative unions while entering into various agreements or settlements, to the disadvantage of majority of workers. This undermines the collective bargaining rights of workers and eventually threatens industrial peace (Menon, 2010).

There have been many instances of strikes by workers on the issue of recognition. In the year 2010, more than 7,000 workers of Foxconn, a Taiwan-based manufacturer of electronics components, went on a strike in the city of Sriperambudur. These workers were demanding the recognition of their union, Thozilalar Sangam (FITS), affiliated with the Stalinist Communist Party of India (Marxist) by the management, for all labour-related discussions. Foxconn management, with the full support of the Tamil Nadu Government responded with police attacks against the striking workers, including repeated mass detentions, which led to the arrest of more than 300 workers (Kumar and Kumar, 2010).

Exhibit 4.1 Strike at Maruti Suzuki's Manesar Plant

Around 2,000 young workers at Maruti Suzuki's Manesar facility in Haryana went on a wildcat sit-down strike from 4th to 17th June 2010. The motive was to put pressure on the management, demanding recognition for a new union, the Maruti Suzuki Employees Union (MSEU), mainly consisting workers at the Manesar plant. According to the striking workers, the existing Maruti Udyog Kamgar Union (MUKU) which is mainly dominated by those working at Maruti's Gurgaon plant was not able to represent the workers at Manesar. There was no notice of the strike to the management; workers stopped production completely and stayed inside the factory for nearly a fortnight.

The Manesar plant produces cars like the A-Star, Dzire and SX4. The strike postponed the production of 13,200 cars and caused a loss of about ₹6 billion (US$133 million/100 million Euros). Maruti Suzuki's sales figures for June dropped by 23 per cent; this incidentally was the sharpest fall in the past 2 and a half years. In July, the management announced to shift a production-line back from Manesar to Gurgaon plant. Workers continued the strike despite the police stationed within the factory premises and ignoring the official declaration by the Haryana Government on 10th June that the strike was illegal.

(Adapted from: www.gurgaonworkersnews.wordpress.com/gurgaonworkersnews-no-941/ accessed on 30/3/2014.)

Leadership

Trade union leadership is an important issue that seeks serious attention. Most of the unions have affiliation with political parties and union leaders are often used as means by these parties to their political ends. These leaders may be internal or even external and they usually work on honorary basis. An external leader is one who is not a full time employee of the organisation, and hence does not emerge from amongst the workers. Such a leader may be working for than 1 union and may find little time for each.

There are advantages and disadvantages with both the types of leadership. An external leader has better knowledge of the trends and practices in other organisations in the industry, and therefore may prove to be more effective on the bargaining table. If he is a politician or a person with strong political links, especially with the ruling party, then he may be able to provide some advantages either in terms of policy or of implementation of administrative actions. On the other hand, his involvement with

Spotlight

An external leader is not a full time employee of the organisation, and hence does not emerge from amongst the workers.

plant-level problems would be much less, as he is not on the shop floor to understand the intricate issues applicable to a particular plant. Since an external leader does not belong to the organisation, he lacks the required depth of understanding of working of the unit. In contrast, internal leaders have first-hand experience of day-to-day problems faced by workers, and are available and more easily accessible to workers.

Multiplicity of Unions and Inter-Union Rivalry

The provision in the Trade Unions Act, 1926 that 7 or more workers can form a trade union has resulted in multiplicity of trade unions at every level. Another reason behind union multiplicity is affiliation with rival political parties. As put up by Mathur and Mathur (1957, p. 201), "The clay of unionism is possibly effervescent industrial labourers, but the sculptors chiseling it into shape have certainly been members of political parties." Every union tries to impress upon the workers that it is their true representative, and in an attempt to increase membership and gain power, each tries to lure the members of other unions. In such a scenario, instead of working in the interest of workers, union leaders tend to indulge in a different power play. Thus there may be inter-union rivalry which ultimately weakens the trade union movement as a whole, reducing the bargaining power of workers in securing their rights. Another problem that arises out of multiplicity of unions at plant-level is that the management may face problems in identifying which one would be the representative union of workers for the purpose of collective bargaining. Rift amongst unions themselves may put workers at disadvantage when it comes to pressuring the management to meet their demands.

Declining Membership

Growth in membership of trade unions in India has not been in the same proportion as the growth of employment. With shift of employment to the unorganised sector and employment in the organised sector being almost stagnant, union membership has been severely affected. Sub-contracting has emerged as a typical employment practice, whereby workers are no longer in any employment relationship, rather they are involved in a contractual relationship. This is also contributing to declining membership in trade unions.

Exhibit 4.2 Increasing Informalisation of Labour

With the recent move towards forced informalisation of labour, new entrants to the labour market cannot hope to get secured employment. Those with permanent jobs are being pushed into insecure, low-paid jobs in the unorganised sector. This can be seen from the growing trend in outsourcing of manufacturing from the large-scale sector to the small and medium sector. For example, there has been a gradual shrinking of employment and production in the Hindustan Unilever Limited (HUL) factory at Sewri in Mumbai, leading ultimately to the total closure of the factory. Despite this, HUL products are increasing manifold. This is so because the conglomerate has shifted its production from large factories to small-scale industries located in industrial estates in different parts of the country.

(Adapted from: Bhowmik, S.K. (n.d.). Labour Rights Deficits in the Service Sector, (Commentary - The State of Labour) Labour File, Vol. 6, No. 1, pp. 24-26.)

The new pattern of unionisation points towards a shift from organisation of workers in a region or industry to the emergence of independent unions at the enterprise-level. These unions are mainly concerned with enterprise-level issues, with no forum to link them with national federations that could secure for them a voice at national policy-making levels. Also, with increasing demand for skilled workers, especially in the IT sector, a new class of managers and skilled workers is being recruited in business firms with lucrative compensation packages and offers for frequent promotions on performance or merit basis. These workers place individual interest at a higher level than group interest; they do not prefer to be members of trade unions; rather they form their own associations to seek larger benefits.

Low Finances

Trade unions need to perform a variety of functions in the process of rendering services and fulfilling their goals. As such, a sound financial position is an essential ingredient for their effective functioning. However trade unions in India are plagued with the problem of a weak financial base. According to the statistics of the Ministry of Labour & Employment, the total income including previous year's closing balance of trade unions had decreased from ₹1,387 million in 2000 to ₹1,105 million in 2007; total expenditure had decreased from ₹594 million to ₹430 million during the same period.

There are several factors contributing to the financial problems faced by unions. The primary source of finance for unions is member subscription fee. Since members are mostly poor workers who live on meager wages/salary, this fee is deliberately kept low, though the amount of fee varies across unions. There is another very interesting aspect that is responsible for low finances of Indian trade unions. Multiplicity of unions is resulting in a competitive situation, where each union tries to keep its membership fee low in order to increase its membership. The situation becomes more precarious when many a times there are defaulters who would not pay their fees timely. Due to low finances, trade unions not only find it difficult to meet their expenses, but also have to face other kinds of problems. For example, the Trade Unions Act, 1926 allows for half of the office bearers of any union as outsiders. However, a feeble financial structure incapacitates a union from supporting its staff. This leads to increased dependence of these unions on national-level trade unions to which they are affiliated, which are in turn affiliated to political parties; thus indirectly they get controlled by political parties. Unions may even get dependent on management for finances; this may result in co-optation. Under this situation unions cannot raise their voice and fight against management for issues related to workers. Thus the entire purpose of their existence may get defeated.

Keeping in perspective the costs imperative in collection of membership fees, including the time spent thereby and the reluctance on the part of workers to pay the fee, no matter how small the amount may be, many organisations have adopted the *check-off system*. Under this system, subscription dues of a worker are directly deducted from his/her pay by the employer, before disbursement. Thus the amount of union subscription deducted is given directly to that union in favour of which the member worker has given written consent for deduction of subscription. The check-off method finds application in General Verification by which the management verifies the membership of a union on the basis of subscriptions given by the workers to the different unions operating in the organisation.

Spotlight

Check-off is a system in which management extends the facility of deducting the union subscription fee from the salary of the member worker, and paying the amount to the concerned union.

CONTEMPORARY ISSUES

Changes taking place in the internal and external business environment have a direct or indirect impact on trade unions. Increased literacy level, dual career families, greater participation of women in workforce, shifting demographics, escalating aspirations of the working class and many other factors are contributing to transformations in the composition, beliefs and functioning of unions. Economic slowdown also has had a great influence on the role of unions, as it usually results in decreased production levels, retrenchment and mass lay-offs. In addition, removal of trade barriers and opening up of the Indian economy for foreign companies has also directly affected unions. Another issue that asks for attention is the role of women in unions today. The increasing participation of women in trade unions and the impact of globalisation on unions have been discussed in the following sub-sections.

Women in Trade Unions

Characterised by low level of unionisation, India has one of the lowest trade union densities in the entire Asia-Pacific region, and more alarmingly, this density is on the decline. In this context, participation of women in unions is an issue that cannot be overlooked. While women are known to have actively participated in many union activities and struggles, their growth within unions, however, does not have many instances to cite. Sectors like textiles and engineering that were spearheads in the trade union movement in India were essentially male-dominated. As a corollary, women's role in the movement was also not much significant, and hence does not fetch many illustrations. In the 1960s, Anusuiya Ben was the union leader of Calico Mills. Later, Ela Ben organised women in the unorganised sector to form SEWA. In a similar manner, Jaya Arunachalam organised women working in the unorganised sector in 4 Indian southern States under the Working Women's Forum.

A striking characteristic of the current phase of the labour movement in India is the increasing participation of women in trade unions. As evident from Table 4.2, female membership of trade unions submitting returns saw nearly 4 times increase from just 0.5 million in 1991 to 2.1 million in 2008, though this growth rate has not been uniform. Later, both 2009 and 2010 have witnessed fall in women's membership, though not significant. The trends are encouraging as far as participation of women in the workforce and their involvement in unions is concerned. Yet the bitter reality is that women's membership is still low. When compared, it can be seen that male membership in 1991 stood at around 5.5 million and at 3.1 million in 2010 with no fixed pattern of increase or decrease.

Let us explore some of the reasons behind such low female participation in union activities. Studies are suggestive that women are predominantly (as high as 96 per cent) engaged in the informal sector, where wages and working conditions are lower than the formal sector and there is no clear employer-employee relationship. Thus many of the segments like agriculture and domestic work in cities, where women usually outnumber men, are not covered by most of the legislations in the country. Unionisation of men in its own is low in the informal sector; hence the status of unionisation of women is still lower. There are very little or no women workers in some geographical regions and certain industries. Among all industries, agriculture, hunting and forest industry had the highest proportion (57.07 per cent) of women workers, whereas the lowest proportion (1.99 per cent) of women was found in wholesale and retail, repair of motor vehicles, motorcycles and personal and household goods in the year 2003. In 2004 the least (2.14 per cent) representation of women was in the electricity, gas and water supply industry, while fishing industry registered the highest proportion (56.36 per cent) of women members *(Statistical Profile of Women Labour, 2009-2011).*

Sometimes restrictions on work timings and nature of work (for example, night shifts or work involving hazardous conditions) do not allow for employment of women workers in many jobs. Perhaps the best example would be underground mines, wherein women workers are banned from working. Such restrictions and bans have further affected the employment rate of women.

Martens and Mitter (1994) point out that the lack of interest in unionism among women workers is not as a result of any inherent characteristics of women, but because of the culture of mainstream trade unions that does not sufficiently address the needs and problems of working women, like child care, sexual harassment, etc. As a consequence, women either remain unorganised or mobilise themselves in informal associations. Of the very few who join unions, even a fewer participate actively in union activities. Some other reasons behind the under-representation of women in unions are as follows:

- **Family responsibilities:** The Indian society expects a woman to fulfill family responsibilities even if she is employed. Childcare is considered to be the sole responsibility of the mother. Such commitments pose hindrances to any woman who has to thus balance her work and family and it becomes difficult for her to find time for union activities. "The fact that some jobs can only be done outside employees' normal working hours (settling individual problems, inter-professional meetings, etc.) means that trade union activity encroaches on the time generally set aside for personal life" (Mario, 2002, p. 231), and round-the-clock availability may not be feasible for women.
- **Socio-cultural inhibitions:** Social taboos and cultural inhibitions in the Indian sub-continent inhibit a woman from assuming a public profile as a representative of any union. There is patriarchal control within unions that restricts women from moving into roles of authority (Ramaswamy, 1998). Similarly engagement in union activities in a male-dominated ambience is also looked down upon.
- **Male dominated culture of unions:** ILO (2000) has identified male-dominated culture of unions as a barrier to increase in women's membership. The functioning of unions is in tune with masculine ways. The timings at which union meetings are arranged are usually beyond normal working hours, and such meetings may even continue till late hours, which makes it all the more difficult for women union members to attend. Further, male member workers often use union jargons, and discussions are loaded with sexist language (Ratnam and Jain, 2002), where women member may feel 'out of the place'.
- **Emergence of new jobs**: Women are particularly affected by the growth in new types of jobs. Many multinational corporations have evolved a vendor system of sub-contracting for their production. Depending on the nature of work, some of these vendors either employ women workers in large numbers or give out work to home-based workers mostly through contractors (Jhabwala and Sinha, 2002). This is likely to reduce the access of women to trade union activities.
- **Lack of physical infrastructure**: Union offices often lack proper physical infrastructure (including childcare facility and rest rooms), which may be inconvenient for women members to attend meetings and other activities at the office premises. Further, women may be constrained by lack of safe and affordable transportation facilities from union office to home.
- **Other reasons**: As compared with men, women have lesser access to formal education and training, which hinders their gaining confidence to shoulder responsibilities and assume leadership roles in unions.

Studies indicate that India has taken a lead in organising women in the unorganised sector through various modes that include trade unions, cooperatives and self-help groups (ILO, 1994; Datt, 1997). Almost all major central trade unions have established internal cells or subcommittees for working women, directed at taking up the specific problems of women members; but there is still a long way to go.

Globalisation and Trade Unionism

The era of economic liberalisation in India was initiated in the year 1991 during the Prime Ministership of P.V. Narasimha Rao. One of the obvious outcomes of this policy was increase in market competition for the domestic firms, which were now required to compete not only with other domestic players, but also with international firms in terms of quality, price and technology. Firms thus adopted cost-cutting in order to compete in the market by resorting to practices like downsizing, outsourcing and replacing regular employees with contract employees to save expenses on workforce. Large scale retrenchments were taking place. Since public sector organisations could not retrench employees, some of them reduced fresh recruitments and introduced the scheme of voluntary retirement, also known as the Golden Handshake Scheme; examples of such organisations include State Bank of India and the Indian Telephone Industries. As a result of such initiatives, there has been a huge decline in public sector employment, which led to reduction in employment in the organised sector. Privatisation of State enterprises by the process of disinvestment has further contributed to decline in employment. The consequences on workers were many, and perhaps the most serious one was decline in job security.

The phased economic liberalisation process has touched every aspect of the economy. With increasing demands for more skilled workers, especially in the IT sector, a new class of managers and skilled workers called knowledge workers are now in demand. For these highly paid workers, being members of trade unions is not important. They have needs different from traditional factory workers and to promote their interests they form their own associations. In recent years, workers of various industries have chosen to form their own independent unions which are not affiliated to any political party and these function as independent bodies. Examples include the National Co-ordination Committee of Electricity Employees and Engineers, and unions formed in banks, insurance companies and financial institutions.

This new environment has had a far reaching impact on trade unions and has weakened their power. It has also added new responsibilities and crafted out new roles for unions, which must now review their old objectives and policies, redefine their functions to embrace the changes, and prepare workers to meet the challenges of the changed business environment. The new functions of trade unions have already been reviewed in detail in Chapter 3.

EMPLOYERS' ORGANISATIONS

Employers and their organisations are an important component of the industrial relations system of any modern society, though these organisations have not been very successful in seeking as wide attention as have workers and their organisations have (Alexander, 1972). Employers' organisations are a formal body of employers, from the same or from different sectors, set up with the objective to champion and further the interest of employers, represent them at various fora, and advise them to improve the conditions of conducting trade and maintaining harmonious industrial relations.

The earliest employers' organisation in India was set up during British rule; it was the first chamber of commerce, known as the Calcutta Chamber of Commerce, started by an English businessman in 1833 at Kolkata. About half a century later, Indians organised a chamber of their own and the first Indian Chamber of Commerce, named the Native Merchants' Chamber of Coconada, was set up at Coconada, Andhra Pradesh, in 1885. After 2 years the Bengal National Chamber of Commerce and Industry was established at Kolkata

Spotlight

Some notable employers' organisations in India are: ASSOCHAM, FICCI, EFI, CII, AIOE, AIMO and NASSCOM.

(Alexander, 1972). Post-Independence, India saw the emergence of employers' associations primarily in industries like jute, textile and engineering in response to labour enactments (Ratnam and Verma, 2011). In fact, there has been a significant growth in these organisations after Independence.

Employers' organisations are different from trade unions, as the latter are made up of workers. On the contrary, employers' organisations comprise individual companies though they fall within the purview of the definition of trade unions as given in the Trade Unions Act, 1926. They may be registered under any of these 3 legislations: Indian Societies Registration Act, 1860; Trade Unions Act, 1926; and Indian Companies Act, 1956.

The Council of Indian Employers (CIE) is the umbrella organisation for Indian employers. It was formed when the Employers' Federation of India (EFI) (established in 1933) was amalgamated with the All India Organisation of Employers (AIOE) in 1956. CIE was joined by the Standing Conference of Public Enterprises (SCOPE) in 1973. The Council of Indian Employers is not registered under any Act of the country, but all its 3 constituents are registered individually under some Act or the other. CIE is fully recognised by the Government of India and other national and international bodies and apex employers' associations dealing with labour and social policy issues. EFI represents Indian employers at ILO in Geneva and at the International Organisation of Employers (IOE)— a world body of employers in Geneva— the largest representative organisation of the private sector all over the world with 157 national employers' organisations across 44 countries.

Some of the most notable employers' organisations in India are the Associated Chambers of Commerce (ASSOCHAM), the Federation of Indian Chambers of Commerce and Industry (FICCI), the Employers' Federation of India (EFI), the Confederation of Indian Industries (CII), the All India Organisation of Employers (AIOE), the All India Manufacturers' Organisation (AIMO) and the National Association of Software and Services Companies (NASSCOM). We would be talking about only 4 of these organisations here in detail, namely, ASSOCHAM, FICCI, EFI and NASSCOM.

Associated Chambers of Commerce and Industry of India

The Associated Chambers of Commerce and Industry of India, India's apex industry body, was established in 1920 by promoter chambers, representing all regions of India. It has membership of over 0.2 million companies and professionals across the country. ASSOCHAM represents the interests of industry and trade. It establishes an interface with the Government on policy issues and interacts with other international organisations. ASSOCHAM is represented in all national and local bodies. It acts as a voice of the industry and conveys its stance and opinions relating to various issues including public-private partnerships for economic development.

> **Spotlight**
> Established in 1920, ASSOCHAM represents the interests of industry and trade.

ASSOCHAM members represent trade (national and international), industry (domestic and international), professionals (e.g., chartered accountants, lawyers and consultants), trade and industry associations and other chambers of commerce. The services it provides to its members include offering expert advice, analysis of legislations, organising workshops, seminars for generating awareness and facilitating interaction, etc.

The objectives of ASSOCHAM are to promote trade by representing industry at various national and international fora; enhancing competitiveness; and disseminating information about national and international policies.

Federation of Indian Chambers of Commerce and Industry

> **Spotlight**
> FICCI, established in 1927, aims at enhancing overall efficiency of Indian industry.

The Federation of Indian Chambers of Commerce and Industry is the largest and oldest apex business organisation in India. It was founded by G.D. Birla and Purushottam Das Thakurdas in 1927. It is a non-government, not-for-profit organisation. FICCI has membership from various sectors including manufacturing, gems and jewellery, chemical, mining, power and retail. These members are from the corporate sector, both private and public, including small and medium enterprises and MNCs. FICCI enjoys an indirect membership of over 2,50,000 companies from various regional chambers of commerce and has tie-ups with over 200 industry associations and chambers across the globe.

FICCI has the vision of being the thought leader for industry; to be an advocate for policy change; and to take steps for ensuring effective implementation. Its main objectives are: to enhance efficiency of Indian industry; to promote global competitiveness of its members; and to expand business opportunities both in domestic and foreign markets. It strives to achieve these objectives through a range of activities that include: providing help in arbitration, advising on economic affairs, conducting research on economic issues, carrying out consumer research, assisting in technology commercialisation, offering B2B solutions, maintaining relations with customers and generating awareness for maintaining quality of products and services.

Employers' Federation of India

> **Spotlight**
> EFI is an apex body of employers' organisations and industries.

The Employers' Federation of India was established in 1933, as an association of autonomous organisations of industries in India, with the purpose of defending, promoting and championing the interests of employers. EFI is an apex body of employers' organisations and industries that plays an important role in matters concerning labour, human resource management, industrial relations and other related issues. It was initially registered under the Indian Companies Act, 1956. Later it was unregistered and registered again in 1963 under the Trade Unions Act, 1926.

The Federation represents employers' concerns and views at various tripartite fora of the Ministry of Labour & Employment, such as the Standing Labour Committee, Indian Labour Conference and other industry committees and sub-committees at State and national levels. It is a key constituent of CIE, along with AIOE and SCOPE. EFI represents Indian employers at the international level as a member of the Confederation of Asia-Pacific Employers and IOE.

The principal goals and objectives of the Employers' Federation of India include regulating and maintaining harmonious relations between employers and workers; promoting and protecting the legitimate interests of employers; collecting and disseminating information affecting employers; supporting employment generation; helping accelerate labour reforms; and improving policies to enhance competitiveness.

National Association of Software and Services Companies

> **Spotlight**
> NASSCOM is an association of companies belonging to the IT and BPM industries. Its main objective is to facilitate and promote trade in software and services.

The National Association of Software and Services Companies is an association of companies belonging to the IT and BPM industries in India. It was set up in 1988 with the objective of facilitating and promoting trade in software and services. It is a not-for-profit organisation registered under the Indian Societies Act, 1860. NASSCOM is a global trade body with 1,350 members as in the year 2012, of which over 250 are global companies from US, UK, European Union, Japan and China. The member companies are in the business of software development, software services, software products, IT-enabled/BPM services and e-commerce. Membership with NASSCOM enables an organisation to engage and drive 'thought leadership' in their various activities. It gives a member the boost to address challenges and build strategies as a part of a growth-led, competitive and sustainable industry.

NASSCOM is engaged in several initiatives like policy advocacy in collaboration with the Government of India, membership engagement including mentoring small and new members, development initiatives like research and organising forums, global trade development, entrepreneurship, etc. Its mission is to establish India as a centre for innovation and professional services; to increase India's skill pool; and to use Information and Communication Technology for a balanced and inclusive growth.

RECOMMENDATIONS OF THE SECOND NATIONAL COMMISSION ON LABOUR

The following are some of the important recommendations of the Second National Commission on Labour (2002) regarding trade unions:

- Only that union which has at least 10 per cent members amongst the workers of a unit should have the right to represent individual workers. To meet this requirement, Section 36 of the Industrial Disputes Act, 1947 must be amended accordingly.
- A worker who is not a member of any trade union will have to pay an amount equal to the union subscription rate, which may be credited to a statutory welfare fund.
- Central organisation of trade unions and federations should be covered within the definition of trade union.
- Craft-based or caste-based unions shall not be allowed to be registered.
- Check-off system must be made compulsory for an establishment employing 300 or more workers.
- Recognition of any union should be on the basis of check-off system. A trade union with 66 per cent support must be accepted as the single negotiating agent, and if none of the unions has 66 per cent support, then unions that have the support of more than 25 per cent should be given proportionate representation.
- Recognition once granted should be valid for a period of 4 years.
- Organisation of the Chief Labour Commissioner (Central) should be responsible for verifying the membership of unions affiliated to Central Trade Union Organisations for the purpose of giving representation in national and international conferences and committees, as also of unions for the purpose of recognition under the Code of Discipline.

SUMMARY

- A CTUO is a union that has affiliates spread over at least 4 States and a minimum of 0.5 million members. At present there are 12 Central Trade Union Organisations in India.
- The All India Trade Union Congress, founded in 1920, was the first trade union in India. Its main objective is to establish a socialist state in India.
- The Hind Mazdoor Sabha was founded in 1948. It denounces the concept of market-driven economy.

- The Bharatiya Mazdoor Sangh was founded in 1955. It believes in a classless society and is non-political in nature. BMS has the highest membership as per General Verification of 2002.
- SEWA, founded in 1972, is a trade union of women in the informal sector of the Indian economy. Its primary objective is to promote self-reliance among women.
- Trade unionism in India has experienced a steady growth, with increase in the number of registered unions and their membership, but for a few periods of exception.
- Unions in India are facing a number of problems like recognition, low finances, multiplicity, inter-union rivalry, leadership issues and declining membership. Though recognition of unions is essential for industrial peace, there is no legislation in India prescribing the process of recognition. Union leadership may be internal or external, both having their advantages and disadvantages. Multiplicity of unions in India results in inter-union rivalry that adversely affects the interests of workers.
- The problem of low finances increases the dependence of unions on national-level unions, which are affiliated to political parties. This increases political control over unions.
- Membership of women in unions in India is still low. This is due to various reasons like family responsibilities, socio-cultural inhibitions, male-dominated culture of unions, emergence of new jobs and lack of physical infrastructure at union offices.
- Globalisation has had a great impact upon trade unions as it has resulted in the emergence of new sectors and new type of workforce with different aspirations. This has forced unions to review their objectives and roles.
- Employers' organisations are a formal body of employers from the same or different sectors, set up with the objective to further their interest, and maintaining harmonious industrial relations. Some of the prominent employers' organisations in India are ASSOCHAM, FICCI, EFI and NASSCOM.
- ASSOCHAM was established in 1920; it represents the interest of industry and trade. FICCI was established in 1927 with the objective of enhancing overall efficiency of Indian industry. EFI was established in 1933 and strives to regulate harmonious relations between employers and employees. NASSCOM was set up in 1988. It is an association of IT and BPM companies in India.

Key Concepts

Central Trade Union Organisation
Union membership
Union recognition
AITUC
Union multiplicity
INTUC
BMS
HMS
Employers' organisations
Check-off
ASSOCHAM
NASSCOM

Bibliography

Alexander, K.C. "Employers' Organisations in India", *Economic and Political Weekly,* Vol. 7, No. 9 (26th February), pp. M37–M41, 1972.

Das, H. "Trade Union Activism—Avoidable or Inevitable?" *Indian Journal of Industrial Relations*, Vol. 35 No. 2, pp. 224-236, 1999.

Datt, R. *Organizing the Unorganized Workers*, New Delhi: Vikas Publishing House, 1997.

Datt, R. "Emerging Trends in Trade Union Movement", *Mainstream*, 2008 (3rd May), Vol. 46, No. 20. Retrieved from http://www.mainstreamweekly.net/article678.html on 30/3/2014.

ILO. *The Role of Trade Unions in Promoting Gender Equality and Protecting Vulnerable Women Workers*. November 2000. First Report, ILO-ICFTU Survey; International Labour Organisation. Retrieved from http://www.ilo.org, on 14/3/2014.

Jhabwala, R. and Sinha, S. "Liberalization and the Woman Worker", *Economic and Political Weekly*, 2002 (25th May), pp. 2037–2044, 2002.

Kumar, A. and Kumar, N. K. *Government Seeks to Crush Strike of Foxconn Workers in India*, 2010. Retrieved from https://www.wsws.org/en/articles/2010/10/foxc-o25.html on 14/3/2014.

Mario, C. as cited in "Women in Trade Unions: Making the Difference", p. 21. Retrieved from www.etuc.org/sites/www.etuc.org/genre_an_080403.pdf on 14/3/2014.

Martens, M.H. and Mitter, S. (Eds.) "Women in Trade Unions: Organizing the Unorganized", Geneva: International Labour Office, 1994.

Mathur, A. S. and Mathur, J. S. *Trade Union Movement in India,* Allahabad: Chaitanya Publishing House, 1957.

Menon, S. "Labouring for Rightful Bargain", *Business Standard,* 2010 (Oct 30). Retrieved from *http://www.business-standard.com/india/news/labouring-for-rightful-bargain/413162* on 15/3/2014.

Ramaswamy, U. "Organising with Gender Perspective". in Datt, R. (Ed.) *Organising the Unorganised Workers*. New Delhi: Vikas Publishing House, 1998.

Ratnam, C.S.V. and Verma, A. "Employment Relations in India" in Bamber, G.J., Lansbury, R.D. and Wailes, N. (Eds.). *International and Comparative Employment Relations: Globalisation and Change*, 5th ed., London: Sage.

Ratnam, C.S.V. and Jain, H.C. "Women in Trade Unions in India", *International Journal of Manpower*, Vol. 23, No. 2, pp. 277–292, 2002.

www.aituc.org
www.assocham.org
www.bms.org.in
www.efionline.in
www.ficci.com
www.hms.org.in
www.nasscom.org
www.sewa.org
www.labour.nic.in

Review Questions

Objective Type Questions

I. State True or False

(i) As per the 2002 General Verification, the Bharatiya Mazdoor Sangh has the largest membership.
(ii) Punjab has a State-level enactment for the recognition of unions.
(iii) SEWA is governed by a 3 tier structure of elected representation.
(iv) The Second National Commission on Labour recommends check-off system to be compulsory for an establishment employing 300 or more workers.
(v) Hind Mazdoor Sabha was founded by Dattopantji Thengdi.

Answers: (i) True, (ii) False, (iii) False, (iv) True, (v) False

II. Fill in the Blanks

(i) The ___________ Chamber of Commerce was the first chamber of commerce in India.
(ii) SEWA was founded by Ela Bhatt in ___________.
(iii) INTUC is guided by Gandhian ___________ philosophy.
(iv) External leaders of unions work on ___________ basis.
(v) ___________ unions may or may not be included during the General Verification.

Answers: (i) Kolkata, (ii) 1972, (iii) Sarvodaya, (iv) honourary, (v) agricultural

Discussion Questions

1. Discuss the objectives and ideologies of INTUC, AITUC and BMS. Highlight the similarities and differences between the functioning styles of these unions.
2. Why is the issue of recognition of trade unions important for Indian industrial relations scenario?
3. Write short notes on:
   (a) Multiplicity of trade unions in India
   (b) Check-off system
   (c) Self Employed Women's Association
4. Write a critical note on 'women in trade unions in India'.
5. Internal and external leadership for trade unions have their own advantages and drawbacks. Comment on the statement.
6. Globalisation has had a profound impact upon unions. Do you agree with the statement? Give reasons in support of your opinion.
7. What are employers' organisations? Elaborate on any 2 employers' organisations in terms of their objectives and functioning.
8. Analyse the problems facing trade unions in India. Which problem, according to you, poses the most serious threat to unions today? Why?
9. Study the pattern of union membership in India in terms of gender. What reasons can you assign to this pattern?
10. Do you think the recommendations of the Second National Commission on Labour would be able to improve the condition of trade unions in the country? How?

Women Workers in the Indian Garment Industry: A Long Road Ahead

Working Conditions The garment industry in India, particularly in the export sector, has very poor conditions of work, typical of the informal and unorganised sector. Manufacturing of garments for export is spread all over the country, though it is mostly concentrated in urban areas. The industry mainly consists of 2 types of units: independent, small proprietary units at one end, and sub-contracting units at the other. A large proportion of end jobs are also given out to home-based workers. The methods of production and work organisation are heterogeneous. The production process is broken down into separate functions that are performed in different locations and managed by different parties such as export agents, contractors and sub-contractors. In general, core processes such as design, cutting and sampling are centralised, while other jobs like sewing, button stitching, thread cutting, embroidery and washing are sub-contracted. Extensive sub-contracting has deeply fragmented the industry, leaving the workers with no permanent linkages. Most of the fabricators (i.e., workshops) are unregistered small units without any legal backing. Since work is seasonal, production units are usually dismantled when there is no work. These units are located in crowded areas and working conditions are poor with little lighting and insufficient ventilation.

There is a large number of women workers in these garment manufacturing units. They have quite a heterogeneous profile; very few of the women who work in large fabricators are technically trained and literate and are employed in specialised jobs. Most of the women are unskilled—working as checkers and helpers—and not listed in the records. Division of labour continues to be affected by customs and traditions and seems to be benefitted little by technology. Women's work contains a large component of piece-rated work and some of skilled work 'here and there' within a framework of employment which itself is casual and informal. A large number of women in the industry are invisible as home-based workers, getting work from the contractors and sub-contractors, often having little interaction with the principal employer. With the exception of large units, wages are piece-rated. Studies reveal that women get lower wages than men even when they do similar work. Although policy prescribes that all garment units must be registered and conform to legislative prescriptions, reality reveals large-scale evasion. There is a huge feeling of job insecurity due to the constant fear of closure of units. Any attempt to organise the workers results in units being closed down and relocated elsewhere. Frequent closures also result in worker mobility that is horizontal and not vertical.

Trade Unions and Women While women suffer as casual and marginal workers with low skills and poor wages in production processes of the garment manufacturing units, the perception that management and even unions have about women's work is not very encouraging. The general discernment is that apart from their nimble fingers, women's expertise does not lie in the skilled operations in spinning, carding, weaving, designing and cutting in this industry. Trade unions do not seem to have made appreciable efforts and have not been forthcoming in taking up the issue of women's employment or their rights. Their major focus has instead been on problems relating to wages, fringe benefits and production.

Women themselves have come forward with their issues at individual, departmental and even plant-levels to protect their employment. While these women leaders have been active in their respective departments, few have even been a part of the wider trade union movement and decision-making processes. Yet, the performance of women workers in trade unions of the garment industry has been far from satisfactory. The burden of household responsibilities and the culture of the wider society do not encourage women to be active in unions. Their small number is another reason for this condition. More importantly, women in this industry are mainly engaged as reelers and cone winders, and hence they do not have the clout that spinners or weavers have either with the management or with trade unions.

Most union leaders admit that the task of organising women workers in garments, handlooms and power looms is in itself arduous. Statistics about women's employment levels are sometimes mentioned in the charter of demands that trade unions put up to employers, but are rarely discussed in the bargaining forums. The small number of women workers seems to be of little concern for the unions, but a few organisations such as SEWA in Ahmedabad and Annapurna Mahila Mandal in Mumbai have organised women who have been displaced, and have turned them into home-based and self-employed workers. Especially SEWA has organised women in several trades and has been making relentless efforts for appropriate legislation for self-employed and home-based women workers. It has given considerable thrust to worker education programmes to educate their members on their rights. Such efforts, however, have continued to remain mere innovative experiments, and are too few in number to meet the challenges of the numerous workers. The need of the hour is to combine the organising principles and beliefs of trade unionism and a spirit of cooperative ideology to bring substantial changes in the existing conditions.

(Adapted from: Ramaswamy, U. and Darala, S. (1992). "Women in the Indian Textile and Garment Industry", in Klemp, L. and Friedrich, B. R. (Eds.), Women Textile Workers Demand Justice: On the Situation of the Textile and Garment Industry in the Countries of the South, Germany: Ebert Foundation.)

Review Questions

1. Enumerate the problems faced by the women working in the garment industry. Which of these do you think require immediate attention?
2. What role can trade unions play to mitigate the problems of these workers?
3. What are the hindrances in women joining and working as effective union members? What role can trade union leaders play to remove these hindrances?

Annexure I: Criteria of Recognition of Trade Unions under Code of Discipline

The Code of Discipline (or 'Code') comprises guidelines aimed at maintaining harmony in industry in India; it came into effect in 1958 and is voluntary in nature. The process of recognition of trade unions has been prescribed in the Code, though it is not binding upon the companies to adopt it.

Where there is more than 1 union, the union claiming recognition in an establishment should have been functioning for at least a year after registration, but where there is only 1 union, this condition would not apply. The membership of the union should cover at least 15 per cent of the workers in the establishment concerned. Only those workers who have paid their subscriptions for at least 3 months during the period of 6 months immediately preceding the reckoning would be counted as members. A union may claim to be recognised as a representative union for an industry in a local area if it has membership of at least 25 per cent of the workers of that industry in that area. When a union has been recognised, there should be no change in its position for a period of 2 years. Where there are several unions in an industry or establishment, the one with the largest membership should be recognised.

A representative union for an industry in an area should have the right to represent the workers in all the establishments of the industry. If a union of workers in a particular establishment has a membership of 50 per cent or more workers of that establishment, it should have the right to deal with matters of purely local interest, for instance, handling of grievances pertaining to its own members. All other workers who are not members of that union might either operate through the representative union for the industry or seek redress directly. In the case of trade union federations which are not affiliated to any of the central organisations of labour (i.e, CTUOs), the question of recognition would have to be best dealt with separately. Only that union which observes the Code of Discipline would be entitled to recognition.

5

Collective Bargaining

Desired Knowledge Competencies

- To discuss the concept and significance of collective bargaining.
- To explain the process of bargaining and the levels at which collective bargaining takes place.
- To analyse the hindrances in collective bargaining in India.
- To identify the essentials of a successful process of collective bargaining in India.

INTRODUCTION

Workers and employers in any industrial relations system have devised several tools to manage conflicts between them and thus maintain harmonious relations with each other. The process of collective bargaining is one such tool that strives at arriving at peaceful settlement of any dispute existing between the two parties. There can be numerous issues of dispute between workers and management, including conditions of work, wages, hours of work, and so on. We have covered disputes and their underlying causes in Chapter 7. Workers, either at individual level, or as a group, may have demands from the management, which, if not fulfilled, may brew disputes. Instead of each individual worker negotiating with the management to get his/her demands fulfilled, it was found that if negotiation is done in a collective manner, it can be beneficial for both workers and management, and the impact would be much deeper and wider. Trade unions take up such issues on behalf of their members and negotiate with management. Thus there is collective interest involved in negotiations.

The concept of collective bargaining had originated with the emergence of trade unions. When there were no trade unions, workers were at disadvantage as an individual worker had no power to influence the employer to listen to the problems and accede to the demands. Nonetheless, the rise of trade unionism changed the scenario, as workers were now able to put forth their problems in a collective manner. This was the genesis of collective bargaining. The term 'collective bargaining' was first used by the economic theorist Beatrice Webb in Britain in 1891 to describe the process in which representatives of a group of workers conduct the bargaining of the sale of their labour on behalf of the whole group of workers (*www.eurofound.europa.eu*). This concept was first used in USA by Gompers.

The beginning of collective negotiations in India may be traced back to the period of 1920s, when, with the interventions of Mahatma Gandhi, efforts were being made to reach an agreement between the textile workers of Textile Labour Association Ahmedabad and management to settle disputes in textile mills in Ahmedabad. With the growth of trade unionism and passing of the Trade Unions Act, 1926, workers' associations got a legal status in the form of registered trade unions, which could now formally bargain with employers. Later, when the Constitution of India was formed, it granted freedom of association as a fundamental right through Article 19(c). Freedom of association ensures that workers and employers can form associations that can represent workers to negotiate labour-management relations. Before the Industrial Disputes Act, 1947 came into existence, collective bargaining was practiced only in rare cases, but with the passing of the Act, the practice of collective bargaining got a fillip. Initially statutory status was given only to settlements that were arrived in conciliation proceedings and were binding in nature. However, by an amendment to the Industrial Disputes Act, 1947 in the year 1956, bilateral agreements between workmen or their trade unions and employers also got statutory recognition and enforceability. Some of the pioneering collective agreements that took place at that time were the agreements related to bonus between TISCO and Tata Workers' Union in 1956, between Indian Tea Association and Indian Tea Planters' Association representing the management and Hind Mazdoor Sabha and Indian National Trade Union Congress representing the workers in 1956 and between Bata Shoe Company Ltd., Calcutta and Bata Mazdoor Union (beginning in 1948 and contracted from time to time).

CONCEPT AND DEFINITION OF COLLECTIVE BARGAINING

The term collective bargaining is made up of two terms: 'collective', indicating an activity by a group of people and 'bargaining', indicating negotiation. Putting them together, we may simply say that collective bargaining involves a negotiation between groups to arrive at a common agreement. It denotes participation of workers and management in the process of reconciliation of their conflicting interests through peaceful negotiations. The process denotes industrial democracy, in which workers voice their interests, demand their rights and participate at an equal platform with the management in arriving at an agreement. Collective bargaining is the first step in finding a peaceful solution to the problems existing between labour and management. So, it may be seen as a technique to maintain industrial harmony.

Ever since the concept came into existence, collective bargaining has been defined by many researchers. We shall be referring to some of these definitions in order to analyse the nature of the process.

The International Labour Organisation (ILO) Right to Organise and Collective Bargaining Convention (No. 98), 1949 describes collective bargaining as "voluntary negotiation between employers or employers' organisations and workers' organisations, with a view to the regulation of terms and conditions of employment by collective agreements" (Silva, 1996). According to another definition (International Labour Office, 1960, p. 3), collective bargaining stands for "the negotiations about working conditions and terms of employment between an employer, or a group of employers, or one or more employers' organisations, on the one hand, and one or more representative workers' organisation on the other with a view to reaching agreement."

Spotlight

Collective bargaining is voluntary and formal by nature, and involves of 2 parties negotiating for work, working conditions or terms and conditions of employment.

Some authors describe collective bargaining in terms of the steps involved in it. For example, according to Beach (1979, p. 96), collective bargaining "involves the process of union organisation of employees; negotiation administration, and interpretation of collective agreements, covering wages, hours of work, and other conditions of employment; engaging in concerted economic action and dispute settlement procedures." Dunlop (1958) focused on the issues involved in the process while defining collective bargaining as a system which sets, modifies and administers workplace rules; a procedure to determine the amount of compensation and distribution of economic benefits for employees; a method of resolving disputes during the pendency of an agreement, and also determining if strike or lock-out should be resorted to after the expiry of an agreement. Perlman (1936) believes that collective bargaining is not just meant to demand wage raise, improvement in working conditions and terms of employment, or to establish democracy at workplace. It serves a bigger purpose. It is a technique through which the weaker and lower class of the society exerts pressure and demands for itself more of 'social sovereignty', welfare, security and liberty.

We may thus define collective bargaining as a voluntary and formal process of negotiation between one or more organisation(s) of workers and the organisation of the employer regarding work, working conditions or terms and conditions of employment, and thereby also serves as a means of establishing industrial democracy.

Exhibit 5.1 Collective Bargaining and Industrial Jurisprudence

Collective bargaining in India has been a subject matter of industrial adjudication since long, and has been defined by law courts at different points of time.

In *Karnal Leather Karamchari Sangathan vs. Liberty Footwear Co.* [(1989) 4 SCC 448] the Supreme Court had observed that, "Collective bargaining is a technique by which dispute as to conditions of employment is resolved amicably by agreement rather than coercion." According to the Apex Court, collective bargaining forms the basis to bring about social justice in the Industrial Disputes Act, 1947.

In *Bharat Iron Works vs. Bhagubhai Balubhai Patel and Others* (1976 SCR (2) 280) it was held that "Collective bargaining, being the order of the day in the democratic, social welfare State, legitimate trade union activities, which must shun all kinds of physical threats, coercion or violence, must march with a spirit of tolerance, understanding, and grace in dealings on the part of the employer. Such activities can flow in healthy channel only on mutual cooperation between the employer and the employees and cannot be considered as irksome by the management in the best interests of its business. Dialogues with representatives of a union help strike a delicate balance in adjustments and settlement of various contentious claims and issues."

(Adapted from: www.indiankanoon.org/doc/77506/ accessed on 10/1/2014; Collective Bargaining Process in India: A Critique. Retrieved from www.articles base.com/organisational-articles/collective-bargaining-process-in-india-a-critique-539870.html on 10/1/2014.)

From the above discussion we can conclude that collective bargaining has the following characteristics:

- It is a *process*. There are several sequential steps or phases in collective bargaining, beginning with presentation of a list of demands, followed by negotiations and signing of a collective agreement, which leads to administration of the contract.
- It is a *bipartite* process involving 2 parties. Negotiations take place between workers and their employers.
- It is a *collective* activity. Groups of workers and employer(s) are involved in this process, and both parties act collectively.

- *Negotiations* form the basis of collective bargaining. The process involves mutual 'give and take' between labour and management through discussions that may result in compromising and accommodating situations for the other party.
- Collective bargaining is a *formal* process by which employers and unions of workers decide to resolve their conflicts and disputes.
- The process aims at establishing *industrial democracy* as it provides workers a forum to demand their rights.
- The underlying objective of collective bargaining is always to resolve the issues between labour and management through a dialogue, and to come to an agreement rather than strike, lock-out or other methods of coercion that disrupt industrial harmony. Thus it helps in promoting *industrial peace*.
- *Cooperation* and understanding between management and labour are the basic requirements for the success of collective bargaining.

SIGNIFICANCE OF COLLECTIVE BARGAINING

Collective bargaining enables management and workers to negotiate on the terms and conditions of employment for establishing amicable relationship and helps prevent industrial disputes, which are harmful for both the parties. The significance of collective bargaining may be understood from the observation of the Report of the Second National Commission on Labour (2002, p. 329) that "employment relations are best regulated, not by provisions of law, but on the basis of agreed procedures and systems that the managements and unions are able to arrive at, on the basis of what is commonly described as 'collective bargaining' or negotiations." In fact, researches have indicated that countries where collective bargaining is highly prevalent tend to have lesser inequality in wages and lesser problems of unemployment. Such countries have fewer instances of strikes, which are shorter in comparison with countries that make lesser use of collective bargaining (ILO, n.d.). Republic of Korea was able to successfully face the Asian financial crisis and South Africa made a peaceful transition from the phase of apartheid into post-apartheid era due to well-established collective bargaining (Aidt and Tzannatos, 2002). Thus collective bargaining is important not only for workers and management, but also for a nation.

> **Spotlight**
> Wages in the organised sector in India are decided mostly by collective bargaining.

Wages in the organised sector in India are decided mostly by collective bargaining, and much depends on the bargaining strength of the management and trade unions. Unions symbolise workers' right to organise. Collective bargaining is a technique through which unions put forth their demands collectively and make their collective voice heard when decisions affecting their work-life are made, and thus promote industrial democracy.

Significance of the process of collective bargaining has been succinctly portrayed by the Supreme Court in *Ram Prasad Vishwakarma vs. Industrial Tribunal* (1961 SCR (3) 196) as: "It is well known how before the days of collective bargaining labour was at a great disadvantage in obtaining reasonable terms for contracts of service from his employer. As trade unions developed in the country and collective bargaining became the rule the employers found it necessary and convenient to deal with the representatives of workmen, instead of individual workmen, not only for the making or modification of contracts but in the matter of taking disciplinary action against one or more workmen and as regards all other disputes."

(Adapted from: www.indiankanoon.org/doc/1616269/ accessed on 15/1/2014.)

We will now explain the significance of collective bargaining for employers, workers, industry and the nation as a whole.

For Employers

- ***A means to resolve issues peacefully*:** Collective bargaining helps to resolve issues existing between workers and employers peacefully. This saves time that can otherwise be used gainfully in the production process and eliminates a lot of hassles.
- ***A chance to understand workers' perspective*:** Sitting with workers' representatives across the table and having a dialogue with them provides the management with an opportunity to get an insight into workers' perspectives and problems. This also minimises the pitfalls of a unilateral decision.
- ***Belief in participative management*:** In the process of collective bargaining workers participate in finding solutions to problems and disputes. The very fact that management is negotiating with workers proves the belief of management in participative management and respect for workers and their rights.
- ***A means to increase productivity*:** Conflict resolution through law courts results in long drawn battles in which a lot of time and money are expended. If an agreement could be reached through a bipartite meeting between workers and management, the resources saved as a result can be utilised for increasing productivity. In fact, measures for increasing productivity often form the terms of agreement between workers and management. The type of bargaining in which the workers' demands are agreed upon in return for increase in efficiency on their part is called *productivity bargaining*.

Spotlight

In a productivity bargaining agreement workers' demands are agreed upon in return for increase in their efficiency.

- ***A mechanism to improve public image*:** If an organisation is able to resolve its conflicts with workers through dialogue, it creates a positive public image for itself at national and international levels.

For Workers

- ***A legitimate platform*:** Collective bargaining provides a platform to workers to present their demands and concerns in a legitimate manner to employers.
- ***Equal status*:** The process of collective bargaining offers an equal status for workers vis-à-vis their employers. It ensures that labour is not merely a tool in the hands of employers for increasing production. Collective bargaining empowers workers to object to the conditions existing in the organisation and demand improvement through negotiations.
- ***Exercising rights*:** Collective bargaining allows workers to exercise their rights to organise themselves, choose their representatives and demand their legitimate benefits and rights assured to them through various legislations.
- ***Solidarity among workers*:** Collective bargaining can be successful only if there is unity amongst workers. Thus it requires workers to act as a united body that can pressurise the employer to concede to their demands.
- ***Improved facilities*:** Employers want to increase their profits through cost cutting, which may even amount to reduction in facilities for workers or denial of new benefits for them. Workers can demand for improvement of working conditions and oppose cutting down of their existing benefits and facilities through the mechanism of collective bargaining.

- ***Strengthening the position of trade unions as bargaining agents*:** In *Tamilnad Electricity Workers' Federation vs. Madras State Electricity Board* (AIR 1965 Mad 111) the Madras High Court had observed that the whole theory of organised labour and its statutory recognition in industrial legislation is based upon the unequal bargaining power that prevails between the employer and an individual (or disunited) workman. Collective bargaining is the foundation of the trade union movement, and it is in the interest of labour that statutory recognition has been accorded to trade unions and their capacity to represent workmen who are members of these unions.

  (Adapted from: www.indiankanoon.org/doc/1190603 accessed on 16/1/2014).

  Thus whenever union leaders represent workers and negotiate with employers for their demands to be met or concessions to be granted, it reaffirms the position of a union in its role as a protector of the interests of workmen and their legitimate representatives.
- ***Improved quality of work-life*:** Since the process of collective bargaining aims at bringing about equality, improving overall work conditions, increasing facilities and bringing democracy in work sphere, its ultimate outcome is enhancing quality of work-life of workers.

For Industry

- ***Means to industrial peace*:** As mentioned earlier, the process of collective bargaining helps in promoting peace and harmony by acting as a tool to resolve conflicts at a basic level between workers and employers, without the intervention of any third party. Employers and representatives of workers negotiate to resolve their differences together by sitting across the bargaining table, rather than by indulging in exercising undue pressure tactics like *gherao*, pelting, etc.
- ***Facilitation of modernisation and restructuring*:** Liberalisation of the Indian economy has resulted in changes in organisations in terms of technology, professionalisation of systems and processes and restructuring. Trade unions today are adopting new roles that include involvement in educating and training workers. Multi-employer bargaining may facilitate modernisation and restructuring (OECD, 1994). Occupational training for workers in a particular industry may be regulated by a bargaining process involving multiple employers at industry level. Such training may be funded by collective financing, as in countries like Australia (Mitchell and Scherer, 1993) and France (Goetschy and Rozenhlatt, 1992).
- ***Continuous production and profits:*** Industrial unrest is detrimental to the growth of any industry. Strikes, lock-outs, *gheraos,* etc. result in huge losses in production and ultimately affect profits. Such undesirable situations may be eliminated through peaceful negotiations.

For Nation

- ***Increase of productivity*:** Collective bargaining helps in avoidance of instances of strikes and lock-outs and resultant work stoppages. It assists in improving relations between employers and workers and helps in maintaining industrial peace and harmony. These conditions help in improving productivity at national level.
- ***Strengthening of the economy:*** Successful collective bargaining results in increased production, enhanced employment, better work conditions, improved wages and growth in industries. All these contribute to strengthening the economy of a country. Thus constructive agreements result in fairer economic development (ILO, 2004).

- ***Establishment of democracy in industrial relations system***: As observed by several researchers (Windmuller, Albeda, Albage and Blanpain, 1987; Traxler, 1991), collective bargaining replaces unilateral decision-making by the employer and hence introduces an element of industrial democracy by giving workers an opportunity to state their terms of working.

Spotlight
Collective bargaining introduces an element of industrial democracy.

Exhibit 5.2 Collective Bargaining between General Motors Corporation and the United Auto Workers

A historic collective bargaining agreement took place between one of the world's leading automobile manufacturers, General Motors Corporation (GMC), USA and the United Auto Workers (UAW) in late 2007. GMC was under huge pressure due to its declining market share with the entry of Japanese auto companies in USA. In addition to other financial issues, the company was facing under-funded pension liabilities and rising employee and retiree healthcare costs. A nation-wide strike involving 74,000 UAW employees was called over job security concerns and retiree healthcare costs. The work stoppage affected 82 domestic General Motors assembly plants for 2 full days. An agreement was reached on a 4-year contract, and workers returned to work the same day. The Union ratified the contract with 65 per cent approval. Under the new contract, the company was required to establish a new healthcare trust to pay for retiree healthcare that would be funded by General Motors and managed by UAW. Employees were required to make quarterly fund contributions. GMC also agreed to stop outsourcing of positions for the duration of the contract. The agreement was seen by the management to be innovative, as it would provide a basis for improved competitiveness.

(*Adapted from:* Schildkraut, J. L. (2008). Profiles of Significant Collective Bargaining Disputes in 2007, Bureau of Labor Statistics. *(Adapted from: Schildkraut, J. L. (2008). Profiles of Significant Collective Bargaining Disputes in 2007, Bureau of Labor Statistics. Retrieved from: GM UAW Workers Ratify Historic Contract www.bls.gov/opub/cwc/cb 20080520ar01p1.html on 12/1/2014; www.wardsauto.com/news-amp-analysis/gm-uaw-workers-ratify-historic-contract on 18/1/2014.)*

LEVELS OF COLLECTIVE BARGAINING

Bargaining in different sectors may take place at different levels. In no country does it take place only at one level. Depending upon the coverage of the terms of agreement and involvement of unit-level, enterprise-level, regional-level or national-level trade unions, collective bargaining may take place at unit/plant level, enterprise-level, industry or national level.

Unit/Plant-level Negotiations that take place at unit/plant-level result in decentralised agreements. Sometimes such negotiations take place with trade union federations at company-level, involving representatives of unions of different plants of an establishment. As we have mentioned earlier, the agreement between TISCO and Tata Workers' Union in 1956 was the first unit-level agreement in India.

Enterprise-level Such negotiations take place between management and enterprise-level union representatives, and affect all workers across all the units of the enterprise.

Industry-level Industry or sector-level negotiations cover various companies in an industry. There may be involvement of one or more employers' organisations and trade union federations in such bargaining. Industry-level bargaining includes a range of bargaining patterns and results in standardisation of the terms of employment and working conditions in 1 industry or sector. Depending upon the issues covered, bargaining may take place at sub-regional, regional or sometimes even at national-level. An advantage associated with such multi-employer bargaining is that the collective agreements at industry-level tend to standardise wages and working conditions and hence produce a 'latent cartelisation' among employers as they eliminate wages from competition (OECD, 1994).

Cotton, jute, textiles and transport are some industries in India in which such agreements commonly take place. Though the oil sector was nationalised way back in the 1970s, industry-level bargaining does not take place in this sector. Even if collective bargaining occurs at plant or enterprise-level, the oil coordination committees are able to achieve a great deal of standardisation in pay and service conditions (Government of India, 2002).

National-level National-level negotiations usually take place in the industries or sectors which are controlled by the Government. Collective negotiations at this level generally involve more than 1 national-level trade union federations and employers' organisations. Examples of sectors in the Indian economy where national-level bargaining is common are iron and steel, postal department, banks, ports and docks, etc. Most of the mining industries such as coal, iron ore, copper, bauxite and zinc, the oil sector and the cement industry have evolved a system of national-level negotiations and settlements (Government of India, 2002).

Economy-level bargaining is an extension of national-level bargaining. "Economy-wide bargaining may be a bipartite or tripartite form of negotiation or "concertation" between union confederations, central employer associations and government agencies" that provides a basis for

Spotlight
Economy-level bargaining is an extension of national-level bargaining.

Exhibit 5.3 Levels of Collective Bargaining in other Countries

Levels at which collective bargaining takes place may differ across countries. The existence of strong employers' organisations and powerful trade unions in many industrialised nations, particularly in Europe, has resulted in many important negotiations and agreements being concluded at the national or industry-level, and some at enterprise-level. Collective bargaining at enterprise-level has been more common in USA, barring certain sectors like coal, steel, trucking and construction. In Japan enterprise-level bargaining has been more common, while national-level bargaining appears to be an exception. This trend is due to the structure of unions which are enterprise-based. In many Asian countries enterprise-level bargaining has been more common as compared to national and industry-level bargaining. This is because of relatively low rate of unionisation, which does not support national-level agreements, and due to this reason employers' organisations in such countries rarely get involved in collective bargaining. In Japan such collective negotiations taking place at unit-level and other participative methods at shop-floor level (such as joint consultation), have resulted in increased productivity by considering specific conditions existing in an enterprise.

(Adapted from: Silva, S. (1996). Collective bargaining negotiations, International Labour Organisation, ACT/EMP Publishers, p. 3. Retrieved from www.ilo.org/public/english/dialogue/actemp/downloads/publications/srscbarg.pdf on 2/1/2014.)

lower-level bargaining on the terms of employment, with the objective of fulfilling macroeconomic goals (OECD, 1994, p. 170).

In India there has been a trend towards decentralisation of collective bargaining in the key sectors, so that it takes place usually at enterprise or unit-level, rather than at industry-level. Factors that have contributed to this trend include privatisation of the public sector and increasing infomalisation in the organised sector (Pratap, n.d).

PROCESS OF COLLECTIVE BARGAINING

The actual process of bargaining involves 3 steps: pre-bargaining preparations by management and unions, bargaining and contract administration. These steps have been described in this section.

I. Pre-bargaining Preparations by Management and Unions

Both management and unions have to make in-depth preparation for the actual negotiations. Let us elaborate on the preparation of each.

Preparations by management After a charter of demands has been presented to the management by workers, the former must begin the following preparations:

(i) The management must make a careful study of the charter and decide the objectives for collective bargaining and the gains expected from this process. The objectives may be to enhance productivity, to increase production level, to improve relations with workers, to gauge workers' attitude towards management actions, and so on.

(ii) A team for negotiation comprising members with expertise in different areas must be finalised. It may include people like the human resource manager, an expert in industrial relations and labour legislations, a financial expert, production in-charge and others as necessary. The team leader must be given the authority to take decisions during the negotiation meeting within given limits, so that decisions may be taken instantly rather than waiting for approval from higher authorities, thus delaying the process.

(iii) Management must also try to identify if there is any 'hidden agenda' of workers that they may bring up at the negotiation table. This can be done by collecting information related to absenteeism, grievance issues, suggestions, turnover and disciplinary actions from different departments of the organisation. Other than this, management must collect figures on production, sales, loss by wastage, costs incurred, relevant expenditures, company performance in past years, etc. Hard facts in support of arguments are important in convincing the other party. For example, if sales are going down and workers are demanding increase in wages and salary, record of declining sales may help in convincing workers to review their demand.

(iv) Management must gather data on practices prevalent in industry on the issues present in the charter of demand and other factors that may impact the bargaining process. For example, if it is a demand related to increasing facilities for worker welfare, management must find out the facilities provided by other organisations in the same industry. Proper 'homework' by management is essential for putting forth its arguments emphatically.

(v) Since it is a bargaining process whereby both the parties are expected to 'give up' something to 'take' something, management must also try to gauge the extent to which workers are willing to accommodate and 'give up' on each of the demands. Though considered to be 'not very ethical', many companies resort to cooptation to get the inside story of the other party. Cooptation refers to the situation when management tries to influence one or more of the union member(s) by offering them promotion or other benefits, in exchange for information about union strategies or for influencing workers, so as to get advantage during the negotiation process.

Preparations by workers Just like management, workers and their trade unions also need to make elaborate and in-depth preparations for their success in collective bargaining. Union leadership plays an important role in this process. While preparing the charter of demands, trade union leaders must ensure that it includes the interests of all categories of workers, including women workers, skilled workers, unskilled workers, etc. A term called *intra-organisational bargaining* is used for a situation when there is a need for bargaining within a worker body due to differences between various worker-groups (or even within the existing groups in management).

> **Spotlight**
> Intra-organisational bargaining is used to resolve conflicts between various groups within a worker body or within management.

The demands must be related to real issues, rather than those 'created' by union leaders in order to simply prove that they are the 'real' leaders of workers. If this is not ensured, a trade union cannot be considered a true representative of workers.

While preparing the charter of their demands, unions must carefully make an in-depth study of the practices existing in the industry. They must collect information from internal as well as external sources in order to justify their demands and pressurise the management for accepting such demands. Workers and their unions must also try to find out the level to which the management would be ready to bend and make concessions.

II. Bargaining

When management analyses union demands, these could come out to be of 3 types: those that can be accepted unconditionally, those that can be partly accepted, and those that must be rejected. For demands that can be accepted unconditionally, the outcomes would be positive, while rest of the situations need to be handled deftly by management representatives at the bargaining table. Management may accept some demands partly and in return may put forth its demands on workers. Another possibility may be that it accepts some demands and buys time to consider others without direct refusal. Outright refusal may result in problems as workers may resort to pressure tactics like strike.

If negotiations are not successful, the next round of discussions would need to be planned. Deadlock must be avoided as it ultimately results in loss for both the parties.

> **Spotlight**
> Distributive bargaining is a zero-sum game.

Before we move on to the third and final step in the bargaining process, we will take a look at some of the processes related with collective bargaining.

Distributive bargaining Distributive bargaining involves bargaining over economic issues like wages, salaries and bonus. Here one party gains at the cost of the other party, so it results in a *win-lose* situation and hence is a zero-sum game. Such a situation generates negative feelings in the losing side and may even breed mistrust and unhealthy labour-management relations. This type of bargaining is also known as *conjunctive bargaining*.

Integrative bargaining This type of bargaining involves a situation in which either both the parties have something to gain, or at least none of the parties loses anything. Thus it is a *win-win* situation for both. For example, during economic slowdown management may demand increase in working hours in return for job security. This is the most ideal situation. This type of bargaining is sometimes known as *cooperative* or *interest-based bargaining*.

Attitudinal structuring Attitudinal structuring means changing the attitudes and beliefs of workers and management regarding each other, so as to create an environment of mutual trust. This is required in the following situations:

- When it is a *lose-lose* situation, i.e., when none of the parties is ready to accommodate the interests of the other party. In such a situation, negotiations come to a dead end and resultantly both the sides have to lose.
- When there is a *win-lose* situation that generates bitterness in the losing party.

Under both the situations the involved parties need to change their attitude in order to avoid generation of any hostility.

Good faith bargaining The principle of good faith bargaining is that both the parties meet each other with the intent to constructively communicate with each other over the issues of dispute and make honest attempts to arrive at a collective agreement. There is a readiness to make concessions, though it neither requires any party to shelve its own interests, nor does it compel any party to necessarily agree to a proposal, nor does it require any of the parties to make any undue concession. The principle of good faith is violated when:

- any of the sides indulges in *surface bargaining*, in which the meeting is simply an eye-wash without any intention of reaching an agreement, or
- the parties involved indulge in any unfair labour practice during negotiation and while administering the contract, or
- the employer refuses to meet with union representatives, or
- the employer refuses to provide any information to union, that can be used for holding discussions and negotiations.

Spotlight

In good faith bargaining employers and workers' representatives negotiate with each other with the honest intent to reach a mutually beneficial agreement.

III. Contract Administration

Once an agreement is signed between the trade union and management, the final phase in the process of collective bargaining is marked by contract administration. The parties must understand that they have come together to reach an agreement for improving the existing conditions. Thus, to achieve this objective they must administer the contract properly. The process of administering is included in the contract itself.

The management team and union representatives must make all the employees aware of the terms and conditions in the contract, so that everybody may understand what is expected of them. Collective bargaining agreements must contain formal procedures for resolving grievances that may arise over the interpretation and application of the terms of contract. Efforts must be made by workers and management to resolve these grievances at lower levels. Otherwise methods like conciliation, arbitration or ultimately adjudication may be resorted to. All these methods of settlement of disputes have been covered in Chapter 8.

PREREQUISITES OF SUCCESSFUL BARGAINING

For collective bargaining to be successful, there are certain conditions that must exist to provide a strong base and to support the process. First, there must be support from the legal and political system of the country. Second, the attitude of the negotiating parties must be such that there is a willingness to reach an agreement and to accept and implement it. Also, for workers to get their demands accepted, their unions must be strong and powerful so as to exert pressure on the employer to listen to and accept their demands. These prerequisites for successful bargaining are reviewed as follows:

Legal and Political Framework

Workers must enjoy the right to organise and bargain. There must be a supportive legislation system to promote the use of bilateral negotiations as a means to resolve conflicts. The legal and political framework of the country must recognise the method of collective bargaining at par with other methods of settling disputes like conciliation, arbitration, etc. The Supreme Court of India has time and again encouraged the use of this process and has recognised the sanctity of bilateral agreements.

Prakash (1991) has cited 2 examples in this context. In the case of *State of Bihar vs. D.N. Ganguli* (1959 SCR 1191), the Apex Court held that it would be wholly unreasonable for an Industrial Tribunal to which the matter may be referred for adjudication, to insist upon adjudication of a dispute on merits even after it has been informed that such dispute has been amicably settled between the parties. In such cases it should immediately make an award in terms of the settlement.

In the second case, namely that of *Sirsilk Ltd. vs. Government of Andhra Pradesh* (AIR 1964 SC 160), though an award had already been sent for publication to the Government by the Industrial Tribunal for its enforcement under the Act, the Court gave preference to a settlement arrived between the parties to the dispute. It was noted that there is no dispute left between the parties once they arrive at such a settlement, and therefore the Tribunal's award itself should not be enforced by the Government by publishing it, as required under Section 17 of the Industrial Disputes Act, 1947.

The Trade Unions Act, 1926 provides workers the right to organise and form a union, though India has not yet ratified ILO Conventions No. 87 and No. 98. The former is regarding Freedom of Association and Protection of the Right to Organise, and the latter is regarding Right to Organise and Collective Bargaining. Certain other measures like schemes for workers' education, tripartite conferences, Code of Discipline, formation of joint management councils, works committees and shop councils, and the existence of grievances redressal machinery act as measures to promote collective bargaining. The Industrial Truce Resolution of 1962 has also influenced the growth of collective bargaining as it required management and workers to cooperate with each other in every possible way and resolve their disputes in a peaceful manner through mutual discussions, conciliation and voluntary arbitration (Singh and Bhatia, 2000).

Attitudinal Framework

Employers and trade union representatives must form a supportive attitude for negotiating with each other. Nature of the relationship between employer and workers affects the collective bargaining process. Management will indulge in bargaining at an equal level if it has respect for workers' rights. Existence of mutual trust is thus an essential ingredient in the bargaining process. Style of management is another factor affecting the willingness to use collective negotiations; negotiations have better chances to be successful if management believes in participative style. It is very essential that both the sides keep a flexible attitude and consider the concerns of the other side with an open mind. There is a need for proper coordination within and between different levels of employers' organisations and union federations for successful implementation of agreements.

Existence of Strong Trade Unions

For collective bargaining to be successful there must be a strong trade union that can put up the demands of workers emphatically and exert pressure on the employer to accept their demands. In fact, a strong union is a *sine qua non* for collective bargaining.

HINDRANCES TO COLLECTIVE BARGAINING

We have specified earlier that existence of a strong trade union is one of the prerequisites for successful collective bargaining. A proper legal framework is essential for the formation of strong unions and for their recognition. Pratap (2011) has observed that most of the famous workers' struggles in 2009-2010 were either on the issue of formation or of recognition of trade unions for collective bargaining. Workers of Hyundai Motors India Ltd. and MRF Tyres had struggled for recognition of their unions. Further, problems faced by trade unions directly affect their bargaining power. Such problems include falling union memberships, low finances, multiplicity, etc. Changing factors in the business environment due to economic liberalisation also have direct and indirect impact on trade unions. Let us quickly have a look at all such inhibitors to successful collective bargaining.

Multiplicity of Unions

The problem of multiplicity of unions weakens their bargaining power. There can be numerous small unions existing in an establishment, but none of them may actually be strong enough to pressurise the employer to accept workers' demands. Moreover, multiplicity gives rise to rivalry between unions, which divides their power, and management stands at an advantage in such a situation. The already weak workers' group loses its strength further. Multiplicity poses another challenge for collective bargaining. Workmen in a unit or plant may be members of different unions. When a collective agreement is signed, it is assumed that all the interested parties are participating in it and that they have consent in the agreement. Every union, irrespective of whether or not it represents the majority, is supposed to be an interested party. Now, workmen may not choose to be the members of any union, and one or more unions may, for reasons of their own, may also not like to be a part of the settlement.

According to Section 2(p) of the Industrial Disputes Act, 1947, settlement refers to a settlement arrived at in the course of conciliation proceeding that may be held by a conciliation officer or Board of Conciliation under the Act. It also includes a written agreement between the employer and workmen arrived at otherwise than in the course of conciliation proceeding where such agreement has been signed by the parties thereto in such manner as may be prescribed. A copy thereof must be sent to an officer authorised in this behalf by the appropriate Government and the conciliation officer. Section 18(3) mentions that a settlement arrived at by agreement between the employer and workman otherwise than in the course of conciliation proceeding shall be binding on the parties to the agreement. Thus it may be implied that collective agreements are binding on all workmen, as conciliation officer's presence is supposed to ensure that the agreement is *bona fide*.

The Amendment to the Trade Unions Act, 1926 in 2001, enforced with effect from 9th January 2002 provides for reducing multiplicity of unions. It requires at least 10 per cent or 100 workmen, whichever is less, subject to a minimum of 7 workmen engaged or employed in an establishment, to be the members of a union before its registration.

Lack of Legislation on Recognition of Trade Unions

The Trade Unions Act, 1926 provides only for the procedure for registration of unions. There are no provisions in either the Trade Unions Act, 1926 or the Industrial Disputes Act, 1947 regarding recognition of trade unions as bargaining agents. Although the provision relating to recognition of trade unions was sought to be incorporated in the Act by introducing Chapter IIIA through the Trade Unions (Amendment) Act 1947, but it has not yet been put into operation. Only certain States like Maharashtra, Gujarat, Madhya Pradesh and Rajasthan have made provisions for recognition of unions in their laws. In the absence of any proper statute for recognition of a bargaining agent, employers may refuse to bargain with a particular trade union and select the one of its 'choice' for negotiations.

Unless the process of collective bargaining is given a strong support in the form of statutory provisions, it will be difficult to popularise the use of this process in resolving disputes.

External Leadership

According to the Trade Unions Act, 1926 half of the total number of office bearers of any union can be outsiders. An outsider cannot understand the problem as a factory worker would, and so such a person may not be as effective while negotiating with employers. Even employers may not be very forthcoming in negotiating with a person who is hardly aware of the day-to-day happenings in the plant or workplace.

Most of the trade unions are affiliated to political parties and many a times leaders of these parties assume leadership positions in the unions. Employers may be averse to the idea of any person from a political party becoming a union leader as this would amount to political interference in the activities of the establishment. Thus involvement of outsiders may indirectly result in weakening of the roots of collective bargaining in industry.

Informalisation of Economy

The process of globalisation and liberalisation has resulted in increased competition for business firms at domestic as well as international levels. Firms are finding the employment of casual labour or temporary workers more beneficial mainly for 2 reasons. First, it is difficult for these workers to form their registered unions. Second, most of the labour laws do not apply to casual labour, hence such workers fall outside the ambit of many statutory benefits that are required to be provided to permanent workers. The phenomenal increase in the number of casual labour has resulted in reduced membership of trade unions and has affected their strength.

> **Spotlight**
> The proportion of informal jobs has been increasing in both public and private sector enterprises in India.

Another issue that is worth mentioning here is that since workers in the unorganised (or informal) sector do not have a registered trade union, they cannot reap the benefits of collective bargaining. This is a grave situation, since majority of workers in India belong to the informal sector. The Report of the Second National Commission on Labour (2002, p. 602) notes that "collective bargaining has not been able to get any visible space in the unorganised sector.... this is a sector in which workers do not have protection or adequate bargaining power". In the Third India-EU Seminar on Employment Relations and Resolution of Conflicts (2008), the key elements of an effective collective bargaining system for the informal sector have been identified, some of which are highlighted here:

- There must a procedure to recognise representative workers' organisations of informal workers.

- Such representative organisations must work with full autonomy for collective bargaining, without dependence on any other agency.
- Keeping in mind the *ad hoc* nature of the job of informal workers and hence that of their organisations, such mechanisms must be evolved as they can deal with change of legal persona of either the workers or management to ensure continuity.
- There is a need for development of innovative pressure tactics like legal action or public demonstrations in place of strikes, which may act as the last resort for informal workers.

RECOMMENDATIONS OF THE SECOND NATIONAL COMMISSION ON LABOUR

The Second National Commission on Labour (2002) has given certain recommendations on the issue of collective bargaining. Some of the important ones are mentioned here briefly.

- Every worker must be ensured the right to organise and form trade unions and the right to collective bargaining.
- Trade unions must be strengthened and collective bargaining must be encouraged in the country.
- A settlement entered into with a recognised negotiating agent must be binding on all workers. Provisions must be made in the law for determining negotiating agents, particularly on behalf of workers.
- It is essential to recognise that collective bargaining or negotiations could be at different levels, namely at establishment-level, at corporate-level, at industry-level, at regional-level, at national-level and so on.
- Since benefits of collective settlements are received by all workers in an establishment, whether or not they are members of any trade union, therefore it is desirable that a provision may be introduced in the law according to which, a worker who is not a member of any union will have to pay an amount equal to the subscription rate of the negotiating agent or the highest rate of subscription of a trade union not involved in the negotiation process.
- An integrated labour judiciary system must be set up, with Labour Relations Commissions as a constituent body. These Commissions, amongst their other duties, should be responsible for the task of identifying collective bargaining or negotiating agents.
- Workers' education programmes must be so designed that they help workers understand their rights and their environment, so that their bargaining power may be improved.
- Demand for bonus in excess of prescribed annual bonus, either on the basis of profits earned in the accounting year or on the basis of production or productivity will be determined by collective bargaining.
- Competent bodies in the national system of labour administration should make their services available to employers' and workers' organisations, as may be appropriate under national laws or regulations or national practice, with a view to promoting the regulation of terms and conditions of employment by means of collective bargaining.
- The vital role of trade unions in collective bargaining must be duly recognised in any institutional arrangement.
- A comprehensive Industrial Relations Law is proposed, that will contain provisions for collective bargaining on issues relating to finances, wage structure, fringe and other benefits, bonus, housing, medical facilities, overall recruitment and personnel policies and norms and resolution of disputes pertaining to the areas of collective bargaining.

Summary

- The term 'collective bargaining' was first used by the economic theorist Beatrice Webb in 1891 in Britain. The process of collective bargaining strives at arriving at peaceful settlement of any dispute between labour and management.
- The Trade Unions Act, 1926, the Industrial Disputes Act, 1947 and certain provisions of the Constitution of India give a boost to the process of collective bargaining in India.
- Collective bargaining is a voluntary and formal process of negotiation, and it also serves as a means of establishing industrial democracy. The process is important for management as it provides a means to resolve issues peacefully, a chance to understand workers' perspective, to prove their belief in participative management, increase productivity and improve public image.
- Collective bargaining provides a legitimate platform to workers to present their demands to employers at an equal status and exercise their rights. It promotes solidarity amongst workers and renders them an opportunity to get improved facilities and better quality of work life. Moreover, it strengthens the position of trade unions as bargaining agents.
- The actual process of bargaining involves 3 steps: pre-bargaining preparations by management and unions, bargaining and contract administration.
- Both management and unions must carefully prepare their own demands and study the demand(s) of the other party through extensive research of practices existing in industry in order to decide their stance during negotiation.
- From the perspective of an employer, union demands can be of 3 types: those that can be accepted unconditionally, those that can be partly accepted and those that must be rejected.
- For effective bargaining, attitudinal structuring may be required and bargaining must be done in good faith. Integrative bargaining results in a *win-win* situation, while distributive bargaining results in a *win-lose* situation.
- The process of administering an agreement must be included in the contract itself. For proper contract administration the management team and trade union representatives must make aware all the employees about the terms and conditions in the contract, so that all may understand what is expected of them.
- Prerequisites for successful bargaining include existence of a supportive legal and political framework, supportive attitudinal framework of both employer and trade unions and existence of a strong trade union.
- Depending upon the coverage of the terms of agreement and involvement of unit-level, regional-level or national-level trade unions, collective bargaining may take place at the enterprise, industry or national level. In India unit-level bargaining is the most common.
- Factors that pose as hindrance for success of collective bargaining include multiplicity of trade unions, lack of uniform legislation for recognition of unions, external leadership and increase in number of informal workers as compared to regular workers.

Key Concepts

Bargaining	Intra-organisational bargaining	Industrial democracy
Charter of demands	Negotiation	Plant-level bargaining
Trade union recognition	Integrative bargaining	Contract administration

BIBLIOGRAPHY

Aidt, T. and Tzannatos, Z. *Unions and Collective Bargaining: Economic Effects in a Global Environment*, Washington, DC: World Bank; 2002.

Beach, D. S. *Management of People at Work*, New York: Macmillan; 1979.

Dunlop, J.T. *Industrial Relations System*, New York: Henry Holt and Company; 1958.

Goetschy, J. and Rozenblatt, P. "France: The Industrial Relations System at a Turning Point?" In Ferner, A. and Hyrnan, R. (Eds.), *Changing Industrial Relations in Europe,* Oxford: Blackwell; pp. 357-394; 1992.

Government of India, Report of National Commission of Labour, Vol. 1, Part I; 2002.

Government of India, op. cit., p. 329; 2002.

Government of India, op. cit., p. 602; 2002.

http://www.eurofound.europa.eu/emire/IRELAND/COLLECTIVEBARGAINING-IR.htm on 10/1/2014.

ILO. *A Fair Globalization: Creating Opportunities For All*, Geneva: World Commission on the Social Dimension of Globalization; 2004.

ILO. *Collective Bargaining*. Retrieved from http://www.ilo.org/global/ standards/ subjects-covered-byinternational-labour-standards/collective-bargaining/lang--en/index.Htm on 10/1/2014.

ILO. *Collective Bargaining. A Worker's Education Manual*, p. 3; 1960.

Mitchell, R. and Scherer, P. "Australia: The Search for Fair Employment Contracts through Tribunals" In Hartog, J. and Theeuwes, J. (Eds.), *Labour Market Contracts and Distributions: A Cross National Comparison*, North Holland: Elsevier; 1993.

OECD. "Collective Bargaining: Levels and Coverage", *Employment Outlook,* Paris: OECD; pp. 167-194; 1994.

OECD. "Collective bargaining: Levels and Coverage". *Employment Outlook,* p. 170. Paris: OECD; 1994.

Perlman, S. "The Principles of Collective Bargaining", *Annals of the American Academy of Political and Social Sciences,* 1936, Vol. 84, pp. 154-159.

Prakash, A. Trade Unions and Collective Bargaining In India. *Central India Law Quarterly*, Vol. 4 No. 1, 1991. Retrieved from *http://indiankanoon.org/doc/633664/* on 10/1/2014.

Pratap, S. *Trade Union Repression in India*, Asia Monitor Resource Centre. Retrieved from *http://www.amrc.org.hk/node/1201.2011* on 11/1/2014.

Pratap, S. Shrinking spaces for collective bargaining in India. Retrieved from *http:// workerscentre.files. wordpress.com/2011/07/shrinking-spaces-for-collective-bargaining-in-india.pdf. (n.d.)* on 10/1/2014.

Silva, S. *Collective Bargaining Negotiations*. International Labour Organisation, ACT/EMP Publishers, p.3. Retrieved from *http://www.ilo.org/public/english/dialogue/ actemp/downloads/publications/srscbarg.pdf.1996* on 14/1/2014.

Singh, N. and Bhatia, S.K. *Industrial Relations and Collective Bargaining: Theory and Practice*, New Delhi: Deep and Deep Publication; 2000.

Third India-EU Seminar on Employment Relations and Resolution of Conflicts, (New Delhi – September 22-23, 2008. Retrieved from *http://labour.nic.in/upload/uploadfiles/files/ Divisions/LC&ILAS/50604135551f2dseminarSep222308.pdf* on 8/1/2014.

Traxler, F. The Logic of Employers' Collective Action. In Sadowski, D. and Jacobi. D. (Eds.), *Employers Associations in Europe: Policy and Organisation*, pp. 29-50, Nomos Vaerlagsgesellschaft, Baden-Baden; 1991.

Windmuller, J. P. Albeda, W., Albage L. G., and Blanpain, R. *Collective Bargaining in Industrialized Market Economies: A Reappraisal*. Geneva: ILO; 1987.

Review Questions

Objective Type Questions

I. State True or False

(i) Collective bargaining in India usually takes place at national-level.
(ii) The Second National Commission on Labour has recommended provision in legislations for determining negotiating agents.
(iii) Intra-organisational bargaining is bargaining within management or workers' groups.
(iv) Distributive bargaining is a zero-sum game.
(v) Cooptation is a method of achieving better understanding between management and workers.

Answers: (i) False, (ii) True, (iii) True, (iv) True, (v) False

II. Fill in the Blanks

(i) In ________ bargaining both the parties involved may have something to gain.
(ii) ________ -level bargaining is an extension of national-level bargaining.
(iii) Attitudinal _________ refers to changing the attitudes and beliefs of workers and management regarding each other.
(iv) Steps involved in bargaining process are ______, bargaining and contract administration.
(v) _____ in the organised sector in India are decided mostly by collective bargaining.

Answers: (i) integrative, (ii) economy, (iii) structuring, (iv) preparation, (v) wages

Discussion Questions

1. Define collective bargaining. State the salient features of the process of collective bargaining.
2. Explain the significance of collective bargaining for both management and labour.
3. The process of collective bargaining is important for establishing industrial democracy. Comment on the statement.
4. Analyse the steps involved in collective bargaining.
5. Explain the following terms:
   (a) Distributive bargaining
   (b) Integrative bargaining
   (c) Attitudinal structuring
6. Discuss the shortcomings in the Trade Unions Act, 1926 that pose as hindrance for collective bargaining in India.
7. Analyse the prerequisites for the success of collective bargaining.
8. Write short notes on the following:
   (a) Good faith bargaining
   (b) Statutory framework for collective bargaining in India
   (c) Levels of collective bargaining
9. What can be the outcomes of a bargaining process? What, according to you, is the most desirable outcome and why?
10. How do you think the recommendations of the Second National Commission on Labour can help improve the scenario of collective bargaining in India?

Labour Unrest at Manesar

Maruti Suzuki India Ltd. (MSIL), earlier known as Maruti Udyog Ltd. (MUL), came into existence in 1981 as a public sector enterprise. It became a joint venture between MUL and Suzuki Motor Company, Japan in 1983. In 2002 the Government of India sold its share and the company was privatised, after which MUL changed its name to Maruti Suzuki India Ltd. The first plant was started in Gurgaon, Haryana in 1984 and the second was set up in Manesar in the year 2006. There were about 950 regular workers, 400 trainees, 700 contract workers and 400 apprentices at the Manesar plant.

Poor working conditions and the structure of wage payment led the Manesar workers to demand a union with the name Maruti Suzuki Employees Union (MSEU) towards end-2010 or early-2011 to negotiate with the management. MSEU had filed an application with the Labour Department of Haryana Government to get registered. The company wanted the workers to be part of the existing union, i.e., Maruti Udyog Kamgar Union (MUKU), supposedly formed by cooperation between labour and management and active at the Gurgaon plant. When the company officials forced them to join MUKU, all the workers, including apprentices and contract workers (who were not members of either of the 2 unions), struck work by going for a sit-in strike on 4th June 2011. On 6th June 2011, the company dismissed 11 workers, including the 4 office bearers of the proposed union on grounds of indiscipline and striking work. The strike, supported by the All India Trade Union Congress, was joined by the workers of the neighbouring factories in sympathy. The strike ended after 13 days with joint negotiations. MSEU signed its first agreement with the management and the terminated workers were reinstated. According to the agreement, both workers and management decided to cooperate with each other.

After this strike the management changed the department of many workers; workers perceived this action as one of victimisation. Meanwhile, their application for a separate union registration was rejected by the Labour Commissioner. Through August 2011 workers adopted a go-slow policy. The impact was 50 per cent production cut in the plant. The management took a strict stance and on 29th August 2011 the company locked the factory. Workers were denied entry into factory premises unless they signed a good conduct bond, to which they refused. The company terminated the services of 18 trainees; 44 regular workers were either suspended or fired. During this period, the company hired contract workers, got its supervisors to work on the shop floor, allowed 170 workers who signed the bond to get in, and started production.

Negotiations at this stage were made complex by the varied political influences on workers. Deep resentment amongst workers had set in and they favoured leaders with a more radical approach. An agreement was signed on 1st October 2011, under the terms of which, the workers agreed to sign the good conduct bond, and management committed not to work with malice against workers. But this agreement was allegedly breached by the management. As a part of the agreement, MSIL had agreed to take back all the workers. However the 44 regular workers who were dismissed earlier would now only be suspended and internal investigations would be conducted against them. Later the management refused to re-engage about 1,000 casual/contract workers who had also participated in the strike. When workers came back to work on 3rd October 2011, they demanded taking back of all contract workers and the 44 suspended workers.

Another sit-in strike began on 7th October 2011 with the demand to reinstate the contract workers. Workers of 3 more Suzuki companies in the Gurgaon–Manesar belt joined the agitating workers in a sympathetic strike. The strike was declared as illegal and was called off following a tripartite agreement between the management, workers and the Haryana Government on 19th October 2011. Terms of settlement included setting up of a Grievance Redressal Committee and a committee for labour welfare, taking back of 64 permanent workers though another 30 would remain suspended, reinstatement of around 1,200 casual workers, and that a Labour Officer from the State Government will be a permanent invitee to the Grievance Redressal Committee to review its proceedings.

Workers again applied for union registration and this time the government labour authorities granted the registration and as a pro-active HR initiative, management of MSIL also recognised the union. Later, in March 2012, the union of workers was registered as Maruti Suzuki Workers Union (MSWU), which presented its charter of demands to the management in April 2012, that included an item of 'regularisation of contract workers'. Several futile meetings took place between the union and management in the next 2 months, as management was resistant to the demand on contract workers. In a tense environment, a disturbance was triggered off by a conflict between a worker and a manager around mid-July 2012, and a worker was suspended. The union protested and demanded reinstatement of the worker. Negotiations begun between the management and the union leaders, but violence broke out. The incident resulted in the death of a senior HR executive and left around 100 officials injured on 18th July 2012. MSIL dismissed 546 employees in connection with the violent labour unrest at its Manesar facility.

The Special Investigation Team formed by the Haryana Government came to the conclusion that the violent incident at the Manesar plant was solely due to internal issues between the management and workers.

(Adapted from: Sruthijith, K. K. and Chauhan, C. P. (2011, Oct 17). Workers strike thrice in five months, How Maruti Suzuki lost connect with them.

Retrieved from www.articles.economictimes.indiatimes.com/2011-10-17/news/30290122_1_manesar-plantmaruti-suzuki-s-manesar-maruti-s-manesar;

The Times of India (Oct 21, 2011). Strike at Maruti Suzuki's Manesar plant ends; 64 workers to be taken back.

Retrieved from www.timesofindia. indiatimes.com/business/india-business/Strike -at- Maruti-Suzukis-Manesar-plant-ends-64-workers-to-be-taken-back/articleshow/ 10438357.cms;

Mukherjee, S. (2012, November 7). Maruti works to stall labour trouble at Manesar. Retrieved from www.businessstandard.com/article/companies/maruti-works-to-stall-labour-trouble-at-manesar-112110700027_1.htm;

Kaushik, A. (n.d.). Case Study–Maruti Disaster: The HRs Blister.

Retrieved from: www. businessmanager.in/most_read.php?most_read_id=27;

www.indiatoday.intoday.in/story/aituc-backs-strike-at-maruti-plant-in-manesar/1/141347.html accessed on 26/1/2014.)

Review Questions

1. Enumerate the reasons for problems between labour and management at Maruti's Manesar plant.
2. Why do you think the collective bargaining process has repeatedly failed in the given case?
3. What steps could have been taken by management and union leaders to ensure the success of the collective bargaining process.

6

Industrial Discipline and Grievance Handling

Desired Knowledge Competencies

- To understand the concept of industrial discipline, grievance and grievance handling.
- To comprehend ways of handling indiscipline at work.
- To identify methods of discovering grievance at work and the legal framework of grievance handling in India.
- To describe the Code of Conduct and the Model Grievance Procedure.

INTRODUCTION

Any organisation aspiring to have a stable workforce needs to be aware of the actions it can take to deal with indiscipline of its employees, and equally, of the actions which employees can take to voice grievances they may have. Issues related to discipline and grievance redressal are time consuming and potentially costly and can damage employee relations and the image of the organisation as a good employer, if not handled properly. Nevertheless, many employers have to deal with these issues at some point of time or the other. The human resource approach tends towards a dislike of rules and procedures, in favour of a more individualised approach (Foot and Hook, 1999). However, organisations need to comply with legislations in managing their workforce, and hence discipline and grievance, though being individual issues in the area of industrial relations, must not be treated individually. This chapter deals with industrial discipline and grievance handling with the underlying philosophy that disciplinary and grievance procedures promote good management practices and are invaluable tools to address performance issues in any organisation.

INDUSTRIAL DISCIPLINE

Employees are vital resource for any organisation and often a crucial differentiating factor from its competitors. Employees must not only work together as a team to achieve organisational success, but also adhere to the rules and regulations of the organisation and conduct themselves in accordance with the standards of acceptable behaviour. Discipline refers to the process of systematically conducting of business by the organisational members who regulate their behaviour in accordance to the established rules and norms of the organisation.

No organisation can function properly and prosper without an effective disciplinary system; in fact, industrial discipline is essential for the smooth running of an organisation and also for the maintenance of industrial peace and harmony. Employee behaviour forms the basis of discipline in an organisation; discipline is a useful tool with the management for developing, improving and stabilising the behaviour of its workforce. Discipline with reference to employees implies complying with the predefined rules and regulations of the organisation, i.e., to conform to the code of conduct established by the organisation. Some commonly found disciplinary issues include absenteeism, tardiness, malingering, pilferage, damaging property, tampering with safety devices, misuse of equipment and other company resources, bribery, alcoholism, insubordination and negligence. Let us now understand the concept of discipline.

Concept and Meaning of Discipline

The term "discipline" can have various connotations. According to Calhoon (1963), discipline is the force that prompts individuals or groups to observe rules, regulations, standards and procedures deemed necessary for an organisation. Tead (1933) defines discipline as the orderly conduct of affairs by the members of an organisation who adhere to its necessary regulations because they desire to cooperate harmoniously in forwarding the end which the group has in view, and willingly recognise that to do this their wishes must be brought into a reasonable unison with the requirements of the group in action.

Spotlight
In an organisational set up discipline is a process of modulation of human behaviour for desired performance.

Summing up, discipline may be defined as an attitude which aims at inculcating restraint and orderly behaviour. In an organisational set-up, discipline connotes a state of order that must be adhered to by the members and a process of modulation of human behaviour for desired performance. It may also be looked upon as an employee's self-control process, which prompts him/her to cooperate willingly with organisational rules and standards.

Nature of Discipline

Spotlight
Under negative discipline employees adhere to rules and regulations in fear of punishment.

Maintaining discipline at work ensures the successful attainment of organisational objectives. There are 2 broad aspects of discipline: positive discipline and negative discipline. *Negative discipline* is somewhat traditional in approach, under which employees adhere to rules and regulations in fear of punishment. Such punitive action may be in form of penalties, fines, demotions or transfers. Thus fear of punishment dissuades employees from disregarding the norms and rules at work. Employees do not perceive organisational goals as their own goals and there is a lack of a feeling of oneness with the organisation.

Positive discipline, on the other hand, implies discipline without punitive actions. It involves creation of an atmosphere in the organisation whereby employees willingly conform to the established rules and regulations. A shift in approach from negative discipline, paving the way for the concept of positive discipline, can be attributed to changes at workplace like increase in the level of education and awareness of the working class and growth of trade unionism. The main aim of positive discipline is to inculcate self-discipline among employees, so that they adhere to the organisational rules and regulations not due to any fear of punishment but due to the inherent desire to ensure congruence of individual objectives with group objectives and harmony in achieving organisational goals. Such discipline can be achieved through appropriate rewards and effective leadership.

Indiscipline

Employees may indulge in defiant behaviour when they violate organisational rules and norms, and such violation may prove to be detrimental to the functioning of the organisation. The term 'indiscipline' generally refers to such violation of or non-conformity to formal or informal rules and regulations in an organisation. Some of the causes for indiscipline are: unfair practices by management (like irregularities in payment of wages, discrimination in wages, ineffective handling of grievances, etc.); policies and procedures of the organisation (like non-compliance with wage legislations and promotional and transfer policies); absence of code of conduct; lack of effective leadership; communication barriers; and politicised trade unionism. Other reasons may include deliberate delay in disciplinary proceedings, imposition of punitive measures like transfer to an inconvenient place at a short notice, aggressive attitude of trade unions, etc. Whatever be the cause(s), indiscipline brings with itself adverse effects on the morale of the workforce, thus affecting individual and organisational performance in a negative way. Hence organisations ensure preventive and curative measures on the earliest symptoms of indiscipline.

Spotlight

Indiscipline refers to violation of or non-conformity to formal or informal rules and regulations in an organisation.

Misconduct

Before we move on to the ways of handling indiscipline, let us quickly touch upon a related concept, namely, misconduct. In a generic sense, misconduct refers to any unacceptable or improper behaviour by an individual. In an organisational context, misconduct is disobedience of some established and defined rules and breach of discipline on the part of an employee; it is violation of rules. Bhatia (2003) defines misconduct as a behaviour which is in breach of the accepted and expected norms of conduct; it presupposes wrongful intention and is not merely an error in judgment. Typical examples of misconduct by an employee would include habitual absenteeism and taking or giving bribes.

In *Shardaprasad Onkarprasad Tiwari vs. Divisional Superintendent, Central Railway Nagpur Division, Nagpur* and *Satubhe K. Vaghele vs. Moosa Raza* [(1969) 10 Guj LR 23], the High Court has noted the definition of misconduct in Stround's Judicial Dictionary, as: "Misconduct means, misconduct arising from ill motive; acts of negligence, errors of judgment, or innocent mistake, do not constitute such misconduct."

(Adapted from: www.indiankanoon.org/doc/1454648 accessed on 25/12/2013.)

Spotlight

Acts of misconduct can be performed even outside the premises of an establishment and beyond duty hours, subject to the provisions in the standing orders of the concerned establishment.

An act of misconduct by an employee is prejudicial to the interest of the employer and is likely to damage its reputation. What is notable here is that such acts can be performed even outside the premises of an establishment and beyond duty hours, subject to the provisions in the standing orders of the concerned establishment. The onus lies with the management to determine in its standing orders as to what all shall constitute acts of misconduct and to define the quantum of punishment for each of them.

It has been held in *A. L. Kalara vs. The Project and Equipment Corporation of India Ltd.* (1984 AIR 1361) that standing orders or rules require an employer to define with sufficient precision the terms of employment, particularly those pertaining to the definition of misconduct. Further, it would not be open to the employer to treat any act as misconduct, unless it was precisely so defined previously. No doubt, this is a salutary principle of law enunciated by the Supreme Court for guidance of all Courts and parties.

(Adapted from: www.indiankanoon.org/doc/1606318/ accessed on 25/12/2013.)

As per Schedule I of the Industrial Employment (Standing Orders) Act, 1946, relating to Model Standing Orders, the following acts and omissions on the part of workers shall be treated as misconduct:

(a) willful insubordination or disobedience, whether alone or in conjunction with others, to any lawful and reasonable order of a superior;
(b) theft, fraud or dishonesty in connection with the employers' business or property;
(c) willful damage to or loss of employers' goods or property;
(d) taking or giving bribes or any illegal gratification;
(e) habitual absence without leave or absence without leave for more than 10 days;
(f) habitual late attendance;
(g) habitual breach of any law applicable to the establishment;
(h) riotous or disorderly behaviour during working hours at the establishment or any act subversive of discipline;
(i) habitual negligence or neglect of work;
(j) frequent repetition of any act or omission for which a fine may be imposed to a maximum of 2 per cent of the wages in a month;
(k) striking work or inciting others to strike work in contravention of the provisions of any law or rule having the force of law.

We would be talking more about the Industrial Employment (Standing Orders) Act, 1946 and its various provisions in Chapter 16.

EXHIBIT 6.1 MISCONDUCT OUTSIDE THE PREMISES OF AN ESTABLISHMENT

In *M/s Glaxo Laboratories Ltd. vs. Workmen* (AIR 1984 SC 505) a worker had been chargesheeted for assaulting a coworker while the latter was coming to his office. The incident had occurred in a bus outside the premises of the establishment, but it had nexus to the disputes in the office. It had the effect of subversive of discipline and hence the management chargesheeted the worker for violating of a particular standing order which read as follows: "…assault or any act subversive of discipline….committed within the premises of the establishment". The worker was ultimately dismissed from service, but the High Court ordered reinstatement on the ground that the act committed by him was not a misconduct because it was committed not within the premises of the establishment. The management thereafter filed a Special Leave Petition (SLP) in the Supreme Court.

The Supreme Court held that any act committed outside the premises of the establishment, even if it is subversive of discipline, does not amount to misconduct, unless it has been specifically incorporated as misconduct in the standing orders of the establishment. The Court disfavoured liberal interpretation of standing orders and held that wherever there are penal consequences, standing orders would be strictly construed.

(Adapted from: www.indiankanoon.org/doc/1513240/ accessed on 24/12/2013.)

Handling Indiscipline

Discipline implies obedience, orderliness and maintenance of proper subordination on the part of employees. Employees who cannot be self-motivated to maintain such discipline may require some degree of extrinsic disciplinary action in the form of penalty or punishment. Stated in simple terms, employees who indulge in defiant behaviour are dealt with disciplinary proceedings, which refer to the steps taken by an employer to decide as to what and whether any penalty is warranted against an employee. Whenever an employee is sought to be awarded any penalty or dismissed, the employer, either himself or through a representative, holds disciplinary enquiry to ascertain as to whether the proposed penalty or dismissal is warranted. Article 311 of the Constitution of India puts limitation in the matter of award of major penalty or dismissal, by which no person who is a member of a civil service of the Union or on all-India service or a civil service of a State can be dismissed except after an enquiry that informs him of the charges against him and given a reasonable opportunity of being heard in respect of such charges. Therefore holding of disciplinary proceeding is a necessary pre-condition to impose any penalty.

> **Spotlight**
> Holding of disciplinary proceeding is a necessary pre-condition to impose any penalty.

In case of employees working in Public Sector Undertakings (PSUs), holding of disciplinary enquiry (also termed as departmental enquiry) is mentioned in the Conduct Discipline and Appeal (CDA) Rules and under the Certified Standing Orders. Even in case of employees of private sector establishments, holding of departmental enquiry is laid down in the standing orders framed under the Industrial Employment (Standing Orders) Act, 1946. Such standing orders have the force of law and constitute statutory terms of employment in an establishment. In this connection let us touch upon the concept of vigilance here. The term "vigilance" means watchfulness and covers all kinds of deviations from standards of integrity as well as improper exercise of administrative discretion, nepotism, favouritism and conduct unbecoming of a public servant. Vigilance is an important tool with the management of any PSU to increase its productivity and profitability by plugging any seepage in its resources. It thus acts as a profit-generating centre for an enterprise.

Disciplinary actions, whether in PSUs or private sector, must conform to the following principles:

- **Principle of natural justice:** Natural justice in common sense means "that which is founded in equity, in honesty and right." The main ingredients of natural justice are:
    - *Nemo judex in causa sua*: This means that no one should be made a judge in his own cause or the rule against bias.
    - *Audi alteram partem*: This means "Hear the other side". In other words, this pertains to the rule of fair hearing or the rule that no one should be condemned unheard.

  The principle of natural justice is firmly grounded in Articles 14 and 21 of the Constitution of India. Article 311 of the Constitution also follows this principle. The principle of natural justice must guide all enquiries and actions; this means that no person should be appointed to conduct an enquiry who himself is interested in the outcome, either as an aggrieved party or because he is hostile to the person proceeded against, or for any other reason. Overall, justice must not only be done, but should also seem to be done.
- **Principle of impartiality or consistency**: This principle implies that under identical situations where even the extenuating circumstances are alike, there should be no marked difference in the action taken.
- **Principle of impersonality or consistency:** The disciplinary authority should not have a sense of elation or triumph or sadistic pleasure when a recalcitrant or delinquent employee is brought to book.

Steps in Disciplinary Procedure

The essential steps in a disciplinary procedure are as follows:

(i) ***Complaint and Preliminary Enquiry:*** The disciplinary procedure must be initiated by a complaint against indiscipline of the employee concerned (also regarded as the "charged officer" adverse to the interest of the company. Let us mention here that before starting the process of discipline it is essential to hold a preliminary enquiry to know if a *prima facie* case of indiscipline and misconduct exists or not. Thus the preliminary enquiry report of the complaint must indicate ground(s) as to whether there is substance in the complaint, calling for disciplinary action. When an employee is alleged to have committed any of the offences mentioned in the standing orders or service rules or under common law, the departmental manager must make a report, indicating action recommended. The management must thereafter depute a responsible officer of the company to enquire into the misconduct. On examining both sides of the case, the enquiry officer must ascertain if there is a *prima facie* case for chargesheet, in which case, the accused must be chargesheeted. If the offence committed is only of minor magnitude, the employee may be excused or given warning orally or in writing.

Spotlight

The preliminary enquiry report of a complaint must indicate ground(s) as to whether there is substance in the complaint, calling for disciplinary action.

(ii) ***Issue of Chargesheet:*** Once the *prima facie* case of misconduct on the part of the concerned employee is established, the management should proceed to issue a chargesheet to him/her. A chargesheet can be issued by the Appointing Authority or authority higher than the Appointing Authority or Disciplinary Authority (DA) or by an authority senior in rank to the concerned employee, with the specific approval of the Appointing Authority or Disciplinary Authority. A chargesheet is merely a notice of the charge on the employee and provides the employee with an opportunity to explain his/her conduct; therefore chargesheet is generally known as a 'show cause notice'. It needs to be drafted in a plain and simple language which can be understandable easily by the employee; charges also need to be specific, with a separate charge for each allegation and without any vagueness.

(iii) ***Consideration of Explanation:*** In the next stage, on receipt of the written statement of defence of the charged officer against the chargesheet served, the explanation furnished should be considered by the Disciplinary Authority as to whether the reply of the charged employee is satisfactory or not. In case the reply is found to be satisfactory, there is no need to proceed with the disciplinary case and the chargesheet can be withdrawn on the basis of facts showing innocence of the employee. On the contrary, if the DA is not satisfied with the employee's explanation, it can proceed with disciplinary enquiry. As another consequence, if the charged officer admits the charge, the employer can warn him/her or award punishment without further enquiry.

(iv) ***Suspension Pending Enquiry:*** In case the charge against the delinquent employee is grave and of serious nature, a suspension order may be served on the employee along with the chargesheet. As per the provisions of the Industrial Employment (Standing Orders) Act, 1946, the suspended employee must to be paid a subsistence allowance equal to one-half of wages for the first 90 days of suspension and three-fourths of wages for the remaining period of suspension if the delay in the completion of disciplinary proceedings is not due to the employee's conduct. It must be noted here that what is grave as a charge would be the sole discretion of the management, and must be decided in accordance with the Code of Discipline.

Spotlight

The Industrial Employment (Standing Order) Act, 1946 has provision for subsistence allowance to a suspended employee.

(v) ***Holding of Enquiry:*** The Appointing Authority or an authority not subordinate to the charged officer and delegated with the powers as the Disciplinary Authority can appoint the Inquiring Authority (IA) and Presenting Officer (PO) and a notice to this effect should be given to the concerned employee. The Inquiring Authority must preferably be of a rank higher than that of the charged employee or at least of equal rank. It should be of good knowledge and ability to assess the evidence to marshal the enquiry proceedings with due regards to the principle of natural justice. A copy of the chargesheet along with copy of article of charge, imputation of charge, list of documents and a list of witnesses must be given to the IA. The Presenting Officer must present the case before the IA through oral and documentary evidences. Further, the charged officer must be given sufficient notice to represent his/her case and make submission in own defence. Fair opportunity should be given to the employee to cross-examine the witnesses.

(vi) ***Order of Punishment:*** The Standing Orders or service rules of the organisation must provide that any employee who is adjudged to be guilty of misconduct is liable to be dismissed without notice, or discharged, or suspended from work with loss of pay for a specified period, or fined or warned, depending on the seriousness of the offence. Before making a final order in the case, the DA shall forward a copy of the IA's report to the charged officer, to enable the latter to make a representation against the report, if he/she so desires. On receipt of the representation, if any, the DA shall record its findings against each article of charge as to whether in his opinion the charge stands proved or not. In case the Disciplinary Authority does not agree with findings of the IA on any article of charge, it shall also record the reasons for it while recording findings. The DA may remit the enquiry report to the IA in case a clear finding is not possible or there is any defect in the report of the IA against any article of charge. The DA, having regard to the aforesaid, shall record reasons that in its opinion which penalty(s) commensurate to the article of charge proved against the employee, would meet the ends of justice and accordingly issue the penalty order in a speaking manner. While deciding the nature of disciplinary action, the charged employee's previous records, precedents, effects of the action on other employees, etc. have to be considered.

(vii) ***Appeal:*** Appeal may be preferred by the officer against the penalty awarded on him/her in case the punishment is not convincing and acceptable to him/her to the Labour Court or Industrial Tribunal. The criteria that a Labour Court or Industrial Tribunal would seek to establish when a case is being adjudicated by it is whether a proper domestic enquiry had been conducted or not, whether the principle of natural justice was observed or not, whether the enquiry proceedings were unbiased or not, and whether the affected party was heard in good faith or not.

Remedies lie in the appropriate court of law for the charged employee if he/she is aggrieved with the decision of the Appellate Authority and when he/she has exhausted all the channels of appeal in his/her disciplinary case.

It has been held in *Adinath s/o Narayanrao Jadhav vs. Chief General Manager* (WP 2511.95.J. dated 14/1/2012) that in the case of departmental inquiries it is a settled law that even if one of the acts of misconduct is established and is of serious nature, courts cannot interfere in the quantum of punishment.

(Adapted from: www.indiankanoon.org/doc/192670095/ accessed on 25/12/2013.)

Exhibit 6.2 Acceptance of Resignation Prior to Disciplinary Proceedings

A preliminary enquiry was being conducted against an employee working in a government company for some misconduct, who, on coming to know of the same submitted resignation enclosing a draft of an amount equivalent to 3 months' pay. The rules of the organisation provide its management a right not to accept resignation if any disciplinary proceedings are commenced against an employee. There is a further rule that any employee should give 3 months' notice or 3 months' pay in lieu of such notice, if he submits resignation. After receiving the resignation letter, the personnel department submitted this matter to the vigilance department, which advised the former not to accept the resignation, but to suspend him immediately in view of the investigation being conducted by the vigilance department on the complaints received against the employee. The personnel department accordingly suspended him and subsequently a chargesheet was issued to the delinquent employee.

The employee challenged the commencement of disciplinary proceedings. The High Court dismissed his writ petition, subsequent to which, he filed an SLP in the Supreme Court. The contention of the employee is that he had resigned from his job by paying an amount equivalent to 3 months' pay in accordance to the rules. By that time no disciplinary proceedings were pending against him. The management cannot hence refuse the acceptance of resignation; therefore the actual acceptance is a mere formality. The management contended that as the employer is a government company and the vigilance department is expected to follow the Central Vigilance Manual, which directs non-acceptance of resignation if any case was being investigated by the vigilance department. It was also contended that the Government of India has issued executive instructions to follow the said manual and the management is bound by such executive instructions, even though these do not form a part of the rules framed by the company. The Supreme Court held that when once an employee submits his resignation by paying 3 months' pay, there cannot be any departmental proceedings, even if the employee submitted resignation knowing fully well that showcause notice was being issued.

(Adapted from: V. P. Gindroniva vs. State of Madhya Pradesh (AIR 1970 SC 1494) www.indiankanoon.org/doc/108995/ accessed on 23/12/2013.)

Forms of Punishment

In establishments covered by the Industrial Employment (Standing Orders) Act, 1946 the model standing orders or certified standing orders may specify the various forms of punishment for different acts of misconduct. As is obvious, misconduct of lesser gravity would fetch lesser form of punishment. Let us specify here that standing orders limit the management in awarding punishment from only those specified in the standing orders. Let us talk about the alternate forms of punishment here.

> **Spotlight**
> The model standing orders or certified standing orders may specify the various forms of punishment for different acts of misconduct.

- **Warning:** Warning may be oral or written. An oral warning is a verbal interaction between the delinquent employee and his/her supervisor, wherein they discuss the problem behaviour and the expectations on the part of the management to change such defiant behaviour. Such a warning is issued as an informal reprimand; it may not have serious implications. When in writing, a warning forms a part of an employee's service record and is reflective of the conduct and efficiency of the employee during his/her tenure with the organisation. Hence a written warning is more official and may even summarise the previous oral attempts, if any. It can be referred to by the management in case of a promotion due for the employee concerned. A warning, as is suggestive of the term, serves to be a reminder to an employee to be vigilant in future. A written warning can also be used in awarding severe punishment in future in case of habitual repetition of the same offence.

- **Penalties:** On the basis of the conclusions arrived at in the disciplinary proceedings, if any or all of the charges leveled against the charged officer are proved, then the management may impose appropriate penalty on him/her as per rules. The penalty levied should normally be imposed for good and sufficient reasons, commensurate with the gravity of the misconduct of the employee concerned. Management has the sole discretion to decide the appropriate penalty for a particular misconduct, subject to the obvious qualification that the penalty should not be unduly excessive. Minor penalties may include censure; withholding of promotion; withholding of increments of pay with or without cumulative effect; and recovery from pay or such other amount as may be due to him, of the whole or part of any pecuniary loss, caused to the company by negligence or breach of orders. Reduction to a lower grade or post or to a lower stage in a time scale and dismissal from service are examples of major penalties.

EXHIBIT 6.3 QUANTUM OF PUNISHMENT

A police constable was chargesheeted on the ground of using abusive language against his superior officer. The disciplinary authority (DA) appointed an enquiry officer, who eventually submitted a "not guilty" report. DA disagreed with the same and issued a notice to the chargesheeted employee, stating such disagreement. No reasons thereof were given. Ultimately the said employee was dismissed from service. The High Court did not interfere, and the employee filed an SLP in the Supreme Court, contending that if DA disagrees with the "not guilty" report, it should give reasons thereof; opportunity should be given to represent against the tentative reasons. He further contended that the punishment was excessive.

The Supreme Court held that the disciplinary authority was required to give tentative reasons for the said disagreement. Also that no straight formula could be evolved in adjudging whether abusive language in the given circumstances would warrant dismissal from service. The Supreme Court finally set the dismissal order aside, but suggested reduction of 2 increments.

(Adapted from: Ram Kishan vs. Union of India and Others (1996 AIR 255) www.indiankanoon.org/doc/1307831/ accessed on 23/12/2013.)

- **Suspension:** Suspension from duty means keeping an employee away from workplace temporarily for reasons of discipline, though it does not mean removal from service. The suspended employee shall not enter the work premises during the period of suspension without the permission of the Disciplinary Authority or any other competent authority; he/she shall not leave the station without the written permission of the competent authority. Such an employee is not granted any leave during the period of suspension. However, an employee suspended pending enquiry shall be paid subsistence allowance admissible to him/her, as per provisions of the Industrial Employment (Standing Orders) Act, 1946, already referred to in an earlier section.

Suspension of an employee from duty often arises under the following situations:

- **Suspension Pending Domestic Enquiry:** We have already explained this under steps in disciplinary proceedings. Such suspension is till investigations are pending, though at this stage it cannot be called a punishment. Under normal circumstances the order of suspension is issued along with chargesheet, but if it is not possible, the charge-sheet must follow within 7 days of issue of suspension order. The Disciplinary Authority also has the right to keep a charged employee under suspension if he/she is accused in a court of law for any criminal offence, until the disposal of the trial.
- **Punitive Suspension:** The Disciplinary Authority may decide to punish a charged officer by way of suspension for the acts of misconduct committed by him/her after the conclusion of domestic enquiry. In case of punitive suspension, the suspended employee is prohibited from performing duties and wages of such employee are withheld for the period of suspension, since it is a punishment imposed on him/her.

- **Dismissal and Discharge:** Both the terms 'discharge' and 'dismissal' refer to termination of service of an employee and are used only when other measures have failed to change unacceptable behaviour. The literal meaning of the term dismissal is 'to let go' or 'to relieve from duty'; it is a punishment for some misconduct, though discharge is not always a punishment. Agarwal (1978) defines discharge to be termination of service by giving agreed notice or payment and acceptance of money in lieu of such notice. Removal from service in the form of discharge does not disqualify an employee from re-employment in the organisation, whereas dismissal from service does disqualify him/her from such re-employment. In fact, the stigma that is attached to the expression 'dismissal' may make it practically impossible for the person concerned to obtain another employment, unlike the case of discharge. Thus dismissal is considered to be the severest of all the penalties. Removal or dismissal is due to gross misconduct on the part of an employee. In case of dismissal, the employer can withhold the contribution of the employee to provident fund, bonus and gratuity payable and other dues, in order to make good of the loss caused to the organisation by his/her misconduct. In other words, a dismissed employee loses all termination benefits. *Discharge simplicitor* refers to termination of services of an employee for loss of confidence and trust. Since it is a termination, it does not carry any stigma of misconduct, but chances of victimisation of the employee cannot totally be eliminated here.

> **Spotlight**
> Dismissal is due to gross misconduct on the part of an employee.

As Chhabra and Suri (2007) have pointed out, disciplinary proceedings are essential to dismiss an employee, though the employer may or may not do so for discharging an employee. An employee can be discharged by giving a reasonable notice, as provided in the standing orders or contract of service, without being served with a charge sheet, receiving explanation thereof and holding an enquiry, as is usually done for dismissing an employee. No order of removal or dismissal from service shall be made by an authority lower than the appointing authority of the employee concerned, notwithstanding the fact that such appointing authority might have subsequently delegated the power of appointment of employees of the category or rank to which the employee belongs to such lower authority.

Code of Discipline in Industry

In the 15th Indian Labour Conference held in July 1957 the question of discipline in industry was discussed at length and certain general principles to be followed by both labour and management for their mutual interest as also for the common interest of the society and the nation were laid down through tripartite consultation. Applicable to both public and private sector enterprises, the Code of Discipline is a set of self-imposed and mutually agreed upon voluntary principles of discipline and relations between the management and workers in the industry. It is a code of conduct both for workers and management, and it provides for the voluntary and mutual settlement of disputes through mutual negotiation, voluntary arbitration and conciliation without the interference of an outside agency. While it dissuades both parties from unilateral action, the Code induces them to make the best use of the existing machinery for the settlement of disputes. Thus the Code of Discipline compels both the parties in dispute not to indulge in any strike or lock-out without exploring the avenues for the voluntary and mutual settlement of any possible misunderstanding or dispute. In this manner, it lays emphasis on an atmosphere of mutual regard and respect, in order to maintain harmonious relations and promote industrial peace.

Spotlight

The Code of Discipline lays emphasis on an atmosphere of mutual regard and respect for maintaining harmonious relations and promoting industrial peace.

The basic objectives of the Code of Discipline are to:

- emphasise upon the employers and employees to recognise each other's rights and obligations;
- promote constructive criticism between the parties concerned at all levels;
- maintain discipline in the industry;
- avoid work stoppages and litigation;
- eliminate all forms of coercion, intimidation and violence in industrial relations;
- facilitate the free growth of trade unions; and
- secure settlement of disputes and grievances by mutual negotiation, conciliation and voluntary arbitration

To maintain discipline in industry there has to be a just recognition by employers and workers of the rights and responsibilities of either party, as defined by the laws and agreements (inducting bipartite and tripartite agreements arrived at all levels from time to time) and a proper and willing discharge by either party of its obligations consequent on such recognition. Towards this end, management and unions agree on not indulging into various actions, summarised as follows (Dhingra and Verma, 1995):

Management and Union(s) Agree that

- no unilateral action should be taken in connection with any industrial matter and such matter should be settled at appropriate level;
- the existing machinery for settlement of disputes should be utilised with the utmost efficiency;
- affirming their faith in democratic principles, they bind themselves to settle all future differences, disputes and grievances by mutual negotiation, conciliation and voluntary arbitration;
- there should be no strike or lock-out without prior notice;
- neither party will have recourse to coercion, intimidation, victimisation or go-slow tactics;
- they will avoid litigation, sit-down and stay-in strikes and lock-outs;
- they will promote constructive cooperation between their representatives at all levels and as between workers themselves and abide by the spirit of agreements mutually entered into;
- they will establish upon a mutually agreed grievance procedure which will ensure speedy and full investigation leading to settlement;
- they will abide by various stages in the grievance procedure and take no arbitrary action which would by-pass this procedure; and
- they will educate the management personnel and workers regarding their obligation to each other.

Management Agrees

- not to increase work-load unless agreed upon or settled otherwise;
- not to support or encourage any unfair labour practice such as interference with the right of employees to enroll or continue as union members; discrimination, restraint or coercion against any employee because of recognised activity of trade unions; victimisation of any employee and abuse of authority in any form;
- to take prompt action for settlement of grievances and implementation of settlements, awards, decision and orders;
- to display in conspicuous places in the undertaking the provisions of the Code in local language;
- to distinguish between actions justifying immediate discharge and those where discharge must be preceded by a warning, reprimand, suspension or some other form of disciplinary action and to arrange that all such disciplinary action should be subject to an appeal through normal grievance procedure;
- to take appropriate disciplinary action against its officers and members in cases where enquiries reveal that they were responsible for precipitate action by workers leading to indiscipline; and
- to recognise the union in accordance with the criteria evolved at the 16th Session of the Indian Labour Conference held in May 1958.

Union Agrees

- not to engage in any form of physical duress; not to permit demonstrations which are not peaceful and not to permit rowdyism in demonstration; that their members will not engage or cause other employees to engage in any union activity during working hours, unless as provided for by law, agreement or practice;
- to discourage unfair labour practices such as negligence of duty, damage to property, interference with or disturbance to normal work and insubordination;
- to take prompt action to implement awards, agreements, settlements and decisions;
- to display in conspicuous places in the union offices, the provisions of this Code in the local language(s); and
- to express disapproval and to take appropriate action against office bearers and members for indulging in action against the spirit of the Code.

GRIEVANCE HANDLING

Employees have their own sets of aspirations and expectations from their employers. Whenever there is any incongruence between such expectations and what an employee actually gets from the organisation, he/she experiences a feeling of dissatisfaction or discontentment. A grievance is formed due to difference between employees' expectations and management policies or practices. Grievance is not a rare feeling when it comes to someone's job. Perhaps it is inherent in human nature to be dissatisfied about something or the other. The most commonly found reason of grievance is pay; if it is not pay structure, then some other aspect of work, say work environment, relation with superior or peer group, etc., with which an employee may have dissatisfaction and hence have grievance.

In the area of employment relations, employee dissatisfaction is commonly divided into 2 broad categories: *organised* and *unorganised dissatisfaction* (Green, 1987; Rose, 2004). Organised dissatisfaction leads to collective form of conflicts like strikes, go-slows and work-to-rule as attempts made by workers to change whatever condition is deemed to be unsatisfactory (Salamon, 2000; Rose, 2004). On the other hand, unorganised form of conflicts refers to individual-based forms of behaviour which are less-strategically oriented to the achievement of change (Mills, 1994; Fossum, 2000; Rose 2004).

Definition of Grievance

The International Labour Organisation (ILO) defines grievance in an exhaustive way to include any complaint either by a worker, or a group of workers, or a trade union, or by an employer, or a group of employers, or an employer's organisation, regarding some specific aspect of the employment relationship, or in case of workers, regarding employment conditions, or employer's policy and practices. Britton (1982) proposes that a grievance is any dispute that arises between an employer and employee, which relates to the implied or explicit terms of an employment agreement. The First National Commission on Labour (1969) in India has visualised grievances as being those "arising out of complaints affecting one or more individual workers in respect of their conditions of work and not disputes over matters of general applicability to all" (Paragraph 24.23). D'Cruz (1999) defines grievance as a matter raised by an employee to express dissatisfaction with management behaviour, and as an attempt to bring out changes. Grievance is any dissatisfaction regarding work and workplace filed by employee formally to his immediate supervisor (Rose, 2004). On the other hand, Michael Jucius defines grievance as any discontent or dissatisfaction, whether expressed or not, whether valid or not, and arising out of anything connected with the company that an employee thinks, believes, or even feels as unfair, unjust, or inequitable. What is noteworthy is that, according to Jucius, grievance may or may not be expressed, though Rose (2004) proposes that grievance is a written allegation.

Spotlight

The First National Commission on Labour (1969) visualises grievances as "arising out of complaints affecting one or more individual workers in respect of their conditions of work and not disputes over matters of general applicability to all".

Fairness at work is one of the pivotal aims of employment relations. Fairness, however, is a relative term, and is expected by every employee from his/her employer. When an employee feels something is unfair in the organisation, he/she is said to have a grievance. Whatever be the cause of such grievance, it is surprising that any such feeling of dissatisfaction or grievance may be real or imaginary. In fact, it may so happen that an employee may not be able to ascertain on his/her own as to what is/are the reason(s) behind such dissatisfaction. And this may be due to ignorance, lack of knowledge of duties and rights, or even mental blocks. Thus grievance may be any real or imaginary feeling of injustice that an employee may perceive concerning his/her employment relations. This may become a tricky situation for any organisation, as it may not always be feasible for the management to understand the real reason behind dissatisfaction and grievance.

Spotlight

Grievance may be overtly expressed, verbally or in writing, or may be kept within.

A grievance may take various forms; it may be overtly expressed, verbally or in writing, or it may be covert or kept within. The latter may have serious implications in itself because unexpressed grievance may result in frustration and detachment, ultimately affecting employee performance. In such cases the onus is on the management to perceive that employees have some grievance, and then ascertain the reason(s) behind such grievance. Mere discontent or dissatisfaction is not grievance; it may initially find expression in the form of a complaint. But if such a complaint remains unattended by the management, an employee would eventually feel a lack of justice or fairness on the part of management. This would increase his/her dissatisfaction, and eventually such dissatisfaction would assume the status of a grievance. According to Ratnam (2006), a complaint becomes a grievance under the following 3 conditions:

(i) When an employee feels that some injustice has been done to him/her.
(ii) When the complaint is formally expressed, either in verbal or written form.
(iii) When it is related to the policies, procedures and practices of the organisation.

There are several ways in which employees may express their dissatisfaction; such expressions may even go to the extent of aggression and hostility. Other manifestations may include absenteeism, indiscipline, etc. If there is a manifestation of dissatisfaction, then it would be relatively easier for the management to address such issues; the situation may become difficult if the management is not able to perceive the real reason behind grievance. Why is it important for management to identify the factors that fuel employee grievance? Any unheard grievance would lead to symptoms like absenteeism, low morale and less enthusiasm towards work, and all of these would lead to serious problems like low productivity and poor work quality. As such it becomes imperative on the part of management to identify such symptoms and take corrective actions, such that whatever behaviour is manifested is not repeated again. Perhaps, the adage "a stitch in time saves nine" says it all: if the management is able to identify the symptoms and ameliorate any grievance at individual-level, this would prevent the issue getting extended any further and affecting a larger group of workers.

Nature and Causes of Grievance

A grievance may be expressed by a single worker, or by several workers, or even by a union of workers, if the subject matter of grievance is of such nature that it may affect several workers of the organisation, in which case it no longer remains restricted to a grievance. Ratnam (2006) proposes that when individual grievances are not redressed and other workers are also affected by the same situation, then it becomes a collective grievance, which normally comes under the purview of collective bargaining. As laid down in the Model Grievance Procedure by the First National Commission on Labour, "complaints affecting one or more individual workers in respect of their wage payments, overtime, leave, transfer, promotion, seniority, work assignment, and discharge would constitute grievance where points of dispute are of general applicability or of considerable magnitude, they will fall outside the scope of this procedure".

Although their nature is found to vary across organisations, in general grievances fall under the following categories in most Indian organisations (Ratnam, 2006): promotions (matters related to supersession, promotion, seniority and fixation of pay); compensation (issues on increments, payment and recovery of dues); amenities (like inequitable distribution, entitlement and medical benefits); service matters (like transfers, continuity of service and superannuation); disciplinary action (including punishment, fines and victimisation); nature of job (like allocation of job); condition of work (like safety and hazards); and leave.

Handling of Grievances

By now it must be clear that any grievance in an organisation, whether explicitly expressed or not, must be addressed by the management with immediate effect. In fact, management is required to take appropriate steps to eliminate the cause(s) of such grievance, so as to ensure employees are committed to their work and to the organisation. Now there is a difference between how small and large organisations deal with issues of dissatisfaction leading to grievance. In small organisations handling of grievances is often devoid of any formal mechanism. In such an informal system grievance may be dealt with by the intervention of managers, who discuss such issues with their subordinates and sort these problems out. Large organisations, on the contrary, have a formal mechanism for grievance redressal. Grievances may be handled by a single official or may even include an entire department that would deal exclusively with employee grievances. A

Spotlight

A formal grievance handling system provides an avenue to employees to vent their grievances; it assigns certain individuals to hear and refer or resolve employee grievances, usually at fixed times.

formal system provides an avenue to employees to vent their grievances; it assigns certain individuals to hear and refer or resolve employee grievances, usually at fixed times. Such a procedure indirectly helps to improve relations between the parties to the collective agreement (Thomson, 1974), renders justice (Balfour, 1984) and improves perceptions of fairness and equity (Lewin and Peterson, 1988). The grievance procedure also serves as the mechanism by which management and union representatives can 'bargain' over the applicability of the terms in question (Thomson and Murray, 1976; Lewin, 1983). Both union officials and managers invest their time and energy in grievance procedures to ensure that employees' complaints are dealt with in an effective manner (Bemmels and Lau, 2001). Such a formal system tends to be procedural and ritualised In fact, employees may become disillusioned with the effectiveness of the mechanism if the system takes long time to find a workable solution to the grievance expressed. We would be talking more about a formal system of grievance handling in a subsequent section.

According to the First National Commission on Labour (1969), a grievance procedure should be simple and have the provision for at least 1 appeal. The Commission recommends a formal grievance procedure to be introduced in units employing 100 or more workers. Paragraphs 24.29 and 24.30 of the recommendations suggest that a grievance procedure should normally provide 3 steps: submission of a grievance by the aggrieved worker to the immediate superior, appeal to the departmental head/manager, and appeal to a bipartite grievance committee representing the management and the recognised union. In rare cases where unanimity eludes the committee in the third step, the matter may be referred to an arbitrator. The Commission prescribes 3 conditions necessary for any formal or informal system of grievance handling, namely: satisfaction of the individual worker, reasonable exercise of authority by the manager and participation by unions (Paragraph 24.29).

Discovering Grievances

Understanding grievances is always a difficult task for managers when there is no explicit manifestation. Managers need to be sensitive in understanding what may be bothering employees. In the absence of a formal mechanism, a useful source of information on grievances and the causes therein would be the grapevine. In fact, in organisations in which there is no formal grievance handling mechanism, employees may approach the trade union for removal of their grievances. As such, union may be another source of information on issues of grievance. Let us focus on some of the most common ways of discovering grievances.

- **Direct Observation:** In this method a manager generally observes any change in the behaviour of subordinates affecting their performance. Examples of changes in behaviour may include absenteeism, indiscipline, lack of enthusiasm at work, etc. Needless to say, this method would necessitate a manager to be sensitive to the difficulties subordinates may face at work and empathise with them. A manager must also be efficient enough to observe changes in behaviours and other traits that may actually hint at a hidden issue of dissatisfaction.
- **Gripe Box:** The gripe box serves as an innovative way to discover grievances; it is a facility to employees to file complaints about anything that is causing dissatisfaction, maintaining their anonymity. These boxes are kept at prominent locations in the organisation or factory premises for the convenience of employees to express their feelings or opinion about any aspect of the organisation. In many organisations employees are apprehensive of expressing their grievances in fear of facing the wrath of the management. Under such circumstances the gripe

> **Spotlight**
> The gripe box is a facility to employees to file complaints about anything that is causing dissatisfaction, maintaining their anonymity.

box method is particularly useful, as it encourages an employee to provide information without the fear of being reprimanded or victimised.

- **Open Door Policy:** In this technique employees are encouraged to enter a manager's chamber and express their grievance. This is a democratic way of securing information about grievances at work.
- **Exit Interview:** When an employee leaves an organisation for greener pastures, it often intrigues the management as to what instigated the employee to leave the present job. An exit interview is a useful source of information on such reasons. These interviews are nothing but interactions between the departing employee and management. The outcome of such interviews can provide valuable insights into what are the problem areas which compel an employee to leave, and in what all areas the organisation needs improvement. Exit interviews can thus go a very long way in improving work conditions if the management addresses the problem areas, thereby ensuring employee retention.
- **Opinion Surveys:** Management can also conduct surveys at intervals to gauge the areas in which employees may be having grievances. This can be a proactive method to take corrective actions before dissatisfaction takes the shape of grievance.

Exhibit 6.4 ILO Standards on Grievance Handling

Recommendation No. 130 (1967) on the Examination of Grievances deals with a special category of labour disputes: grievances of one or several workers against specific aspects of their employment conditions or labour relations. The grounds for a grievance may be any measure or situation that concerns employer-worker relationship or that is likely to affect the conditions of employment of one or more workers in the enterprise, if the situation appears to be contrary to the provisions of collective agreement, individual employment contract, national laws or other rules. In case grievance procedures are established through collective agreements, the parties involved should be encouraged to promote the settlement of grievances using those procedures, abstaining from any action which would impede the effective functioning of such procedures.

Recommendation No. 130 explicitly calls for workers' organisations and workers' representatives to be associated on an equal basis with employers and their organisations in the establishment and implementation of grievance procedures. The Recommendation also highlights the various elements that form the basis of grievance procedure in any enterprise. An attempt should be made initially to settle the grievance directly between the workers or group of workers and the immediate supervisor. In the event of failure to settle the grievance at the initial level, the worker should have the right to have the case considered at a higher level, depending on the nature of the grievance as well as structure of the enterprise. Grievance procedures should be so formulated and applied that there is a possibility for settlement of dispute at every level. They should also be expeditious and simple. Workers concerned in any grievance should have the right to take part directly in the grievance procedure. During the procedure, workers may be assisted or represented by a trade union representative or any other person of his/her choice, in conformity with national law and practice.

(Adapted from: Lee, Chang-Hee (2006). "Industrial Relations and Dispute Settlement in Vietnam", ILO Discussion Paper. Retrieved from: www.apirnet.ilo.org/resources/industrial-relation-dispute-sttlement-in-vietnam on 24/12/2013.)

- **Grievance Procedure:** A formal and systematic grievance procedure is perhaps the best way to understand what all aspects of the organisation are causing dissatisfaction to employees. It gives employees an avenue to vent their grievances. Presence of a robust grievance mechanism instills confidence in employees about their grievances being heard and corrective actions to be taken. In absence of such a procedure, employees may not be able to express their grievances, and this may eventually lead to union intervention, which may disrupt the harmony between employer and employees.

It may be noted here that there is no perfect method among those specified above. An organisation may actually use more than one of these ways to discover causes of grievances among employees.

Legal Framework of Grievance Handling in India

If we look back in time at the historical evolution of grievance handling in Indian organisations, we would find the first official reference to grievance in legislation given in the Model Standing Orders of the Industrial Employment (Standing Orders) Act, 1946. As per Clause 29 of the First Schedule of the Act, all complaints arising out of employment, including those related to unfair treatment or wrongful exaction on the part of an employer or his agent, shall be submitted to the manager or any other person specified in this behalf, with the right to appeal to the employer. Standing orders regulate the conditions of employment, discharge, grievances, misconduct, disciplinary actions, etc. of workmen, and faulty or inadequate application and administration of the standing orders by an employer may lead to grievances and misconduct, which may have adverse effect on industrial relations.

Section 49 of the Factories Act, 1948 provides for the appointment of such number of welfare officers as may be prescribed by State Governments in every factory employing 500 or more workers. One of the duties of such welfare officers is to bring to the notice of the factory management the grievances of workers, individuals as well as collective, with a view to securing their expeditious redressal and to act as a liaison officer between the management and workers. The Industrial Disputes Act, 1947 has included Section 9C in Chapter IIB, that prescribes setting up of a Grievance Settlement Authority for the settlement of industrial disputes connected with an individual workman employed in every industrial establishment in which 50 or more workmen are employed or have been employed on any day in the preceding 12 months. The Industrial Disputes (Amendment) Bill, 2010 passed by the Rajya Sabha on 3rd August 2010 seeks to establish 1 or more Grievance Redressal Committee within an industrial establishment having with 20 or more workmen, with 1 stage appeal at the head of the establishment for resolution of disputes arising out of individual grievances. With this amendment, a workman will get one more alternative grievance redressal mechanism for the resolution of his/her disputes within the organisation itself, with minimum necessity for adjudication. Setting up of a Grievance Redressal Committee would in no way affect the right of a workman to raise a dispute on the same issue under the provisions of the Industrial Disputes Act, 1947.

> **Spotlight**
> Setting up of a Grievance Redressal Committee would not affect the right of a workman to raise a dispute on the same issue under the provisions of the Industrial Disputes Act, 1947.

Model Grievance Procedure

The 15th Session of the Indian Labour Conference held in 1957 had emphasised on the need for an established grievance procedure for the country as a whole, that would be acceptable to unions as well as to management. In response to this, the Model Grievance Procedure was drawn up in the 16th Session of the Indian Labour Conference in 1958 in pursuance of the Code of Discipline. We have already explained the Code of Discipline under industrial discipline in this chapter. The procedure drawn up has successive time-bound steps with access to the next stage if satisfaction is not obtained in the previous stage. Let us describe the Model Grievance Procedure here in detail.

The process of grievance redressal, as per the "Model", starts with a grievant worker who can make a verbal complaint to the supervisor or any other manager designated for the purpose. The supervisor must give a reply to the grievant within 48 hours of lodging of the grievance. If the reply or solution offered is satisfactory, the process of redressal ends there. However, if the employee is not satisfied, he/she can move the grievance to the departmental head or any other designated officer within 72 hours (or 3 days) after the receipt of the reply. If the employee is satisfied, the matter would end there; otherwise the grievance is referred again within 72 hours to the Grievance Committee, which must be a joint committee of at least 2 or 3 workers and 2 or 3 managers. The Committee would get a time limit of 7 days to consider the matter and suggest a suitable solution. If the decision given is unanimous, then it has to be implemented with immediate effect. If the grievant continues to remain dissatisfied, he/she can proceed further within another 72 hours to appeal to the Chief Executive of the enterprise or the head of the establishment, who gets 3 days to consider the problem. If the suggestion given by such authority satisfies the employee concerned, the problem is solved. If not, the grievant has 3 options: he/she may file a revision petition to the management for a complete review of the entire matter, or proceed for conciliation by moving the government labour procedure for redressal, or ask for voluntary arbitration. Whichever of these options is chosen by the grievant marks the final step in the process, since it is not possible to carry the redressal any further. Figure 6.1 gives a succinct explanation of the entire process.

Spotlight

The Model Grievance Procedure has successive time-bound steps with access to the next stage if satisfaction is not obtained in the previous stage.

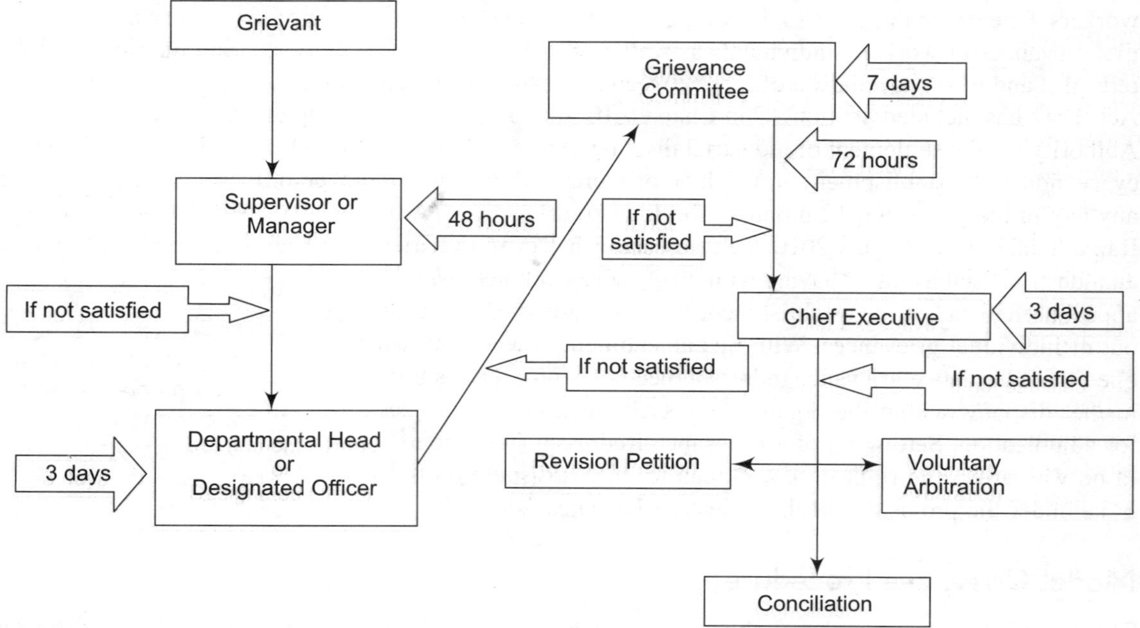

Figure 6.1 *Model Grievance Procedure*

Recommendations of the Second National Commission on Labour

The Second National Commission on Labour (2002) recognises right to redressal of grievance as among those rights that are inalienable and hence must accrue to every worker under any system of labour laws and labour policy. Every establishment to which the general law of employment relations applies, i.e., those with 20 or more workers, shall establish a Grievance Redressal Committee consisting of equal number of representatives of workers and employers. Such committee shall not be larger than 10 members or smaller than 2 members, depending on the employment size of the establishment, as may be prescribed. 1 member of the committee may be designated as the Chairman and another as the Vice Chairman. A system may be established to ensure that 1 of them is from the management, and the other from among employees' representatives. The Grievance Redressal Committee shall be the body to which all grievances of a worker in respect of his employment, including his non-employment, will be referred for decision within a given time frame. Where the worker is not satisfied with the decision of the committee, he shall be free to seek arbitration of the dispute by an arbitrator, to be selected from a panel of arbitrators to be maintained in the manner prescribed, or seek adjudication of the dispute by the Labour Court. The decision of the Labour Court or the arbitrator shall be final.

As regards resolution of disputes between employers and workers, the Commission has recommended that all matters pertaining to individual workers, be it termination of employment or transfer or any other mater, be determined by recourse to the Grievance Redressal Committee, conciliation and arbitration or adjudication by the Labour Court. These disputes need not be elevated to the rank of 'industrial disputes' which would then take the form of collective disputes. Individual disputes may be taken up by the affected workers themselves or by any registered trade union of which the worker is a member, provided the union has at least 10 per cent membership amongst the workers in that establishment, by referring the dispute to the Grievance Redressal Committee for a decision. Where the Committee is not able to settle the dispute within 30 days, or if no such committee is in existence, the dispute may be referred for arbitration to a mutually agreed Arbitrator or Conciliation Officer or to a Lok Adalat or Labour Court in the prescribed manner.

Spotlight

The Second National Commission on Labour (2002) has recommended that disputes pertaining to individual workers need not be elevated to the rank of 'industrial disputes', which would then take the form of collective disputes.

Summary

- Industrial discipline is essential for the smooth running of an organisation and also for the maintenance of industrial peace and harmony.
- Discipline on account of employees implies complying with the predefined rules and regulations of the organisation, i.e., to conform to the code of conduct established by the organisation. Maintaining discipline at work ensures the successful attainment of organisational objectives.
- There are 2 broad aspects of discipline: positive discipline and negative discipline. Negative discipline is traditional in approach, under which employees adhere to rules and regulations in fear of punishment. Positive discipline implies discipline without punitive action.
- In organisational context misconduct is disobedience of some established and defined rules and breach of discipline on the part of an employee. Disciplinary actions against misconduct must conform to principle of natural justice, principle of impartiality or consistency, and principle of impersonality or consistency.

- The essential steps in a disciplinary procedure are: complaint and preliminary enquiry, issue of charge sheet, consideration of explanation, suspension pending enquiry, holding of enquiry, order of punishment and appeal.
- Various forms of punishment are warning, penalties, suspension and discharge. In establishments covered by the Industrial Employment (Standing Orders) Act, 1946, model standing orders or certified standing orders may specify the various forms of punishment for different acts of misconduct. Misconduct of lesser gravity would fetch lesser form of punishment.
- To maintain harmonious relations and promote industrial peace, the Code of Discipline has been laid down which applies to both public and private sector enterprises. It specifies various obligations for both management and workers with the objective of promoting cooperation between their representatives.
- Grievance is any discontent or dissatisfaction, whether expressed or not, whether valid or not, and arising out of anything connected with the company that an employee thinks, believes or even feels as unfair, unjust or inequitable.
- As per the First National Commission on Labour (1969), a grievance procedure should be simple and have the provision for at least 1 appeal. It should ensure that it gives a sense of satisfaction to the individual worker, reasonable exercise of authority to the manager, and participation to unions.
- The Model Grievance Procedure was drawn up in the 16th session of Indian Labour Conference in 1958. The procedure has successive time-bound steps, with access to the next stage, if satisfaction is not obtained in the previous stage.

Key Concepts

Discipline	Charge sheet	Disciplinary proceeding suspension
Misconduct	Model grievance procedure	Code of discipline
Discharge/Dismissal	Natural justice	

Bibliography

Agarwal, S. L. *Labour Relations Law in India*, Meerut: MacMillan; 1978.

Balfour, A. "Five Types of Non-Union Grievance Systems", *Personnel*, March-April 1984, Vol. 61, No. 2, pp. 67-76.

Bemmels, Brian and Lau, Dora C. "Local Union Leaders' Satisfaction with Grievance Procedures", *Journal of Labor Research*, 2001,Vol. 22 No. 3, pp. 653-667.

Bhatia, S. K. *Constructive Industrial Relations and Labour Laws*, New Delhi: Deep and Deep Publications; 2003.

Britton, R.L. *The Arbitration Guide*, NJ: Englewood Cliffs, Prentice-Hall; 1982.

Calhoon, R.D. *Managing Personnel*, California: Harper and Row, 1963.

Chhabra, T. N. and Suri, R. K. *Dynamics of Industrial Relations*, New Delhi: Pentagon Press; 2007.

D'Cruz, M.N. *A Practical Guide to Grievance Procedure, Misconduct and Domestic Inquiry*, Kuala Lumpur: Leeds Publication; 1999.

Dhingra, L.C. and Verma, A.S. "The Code of Discipline in Industry, 1958," *Central India Law Quarterly*, Retrieved from http://indiankanoon.org/doc/1747153/; 1995 on 25/12/2013.

Foot, M. and Hook, C. *Introducing Human Resource Management*, United Kingdom: Longman Group; 1999. Paperback.

Fossum, J.A. *Labor Relations: Development, Structure, Process*, 7th edition, USA: McGraw-Hill; 2000.
Green, G.D. *Industrial Relations,* 2nd edn., London: Pitman Publishing; 1987.
Lewin, D. "Theoretical Perspectives on the Modern Grievance Procedure, New Approaches to Labor Unions", *Research in Labor Economics*, 1983, Greenwich, CT: JAI Press, Supplement 2, pp. 127-147.
Lewin, D. and Peterson, R. B. *The Modern Grievance Procedure in the United States*, New York: Quorum Books; 1988.
Mills, D.Q. *Labor-Management Relations*, 5th edition, Singapore: McGraw Hill Book Co.; 1994.
Ratnam, C. S. V. *Industrial Relations*, New Delhi: Oxford University Press India; 2006.
Report of the National Commission on Labour, Ministry of Labour & Employment.
Rose, E. *Employment Relations*, 2nd edition, England: Prentice Hall, 2004.
Salamon, M. *Industrial Relations: Theory and Practice*, 4th edition, Great Britain: Prentice Hall; 2000.
Tead, O. (1933). *Human Nature and Management*, 2nd edn., McGraw Hill Book Co. Inc., New York.
Thomson, A.W.J. *The Grievance Procedure in the Private Sector*, Ithaca, NY: Cornell University; 1974.
Thomson, A.W.J. and Murray V. F. *Grievance Procedure*, Westmead, England: Saxon House; 1976.

Review Questions

Objective Type Questions

I. State True or False

(i) The minimum number of members of a Grievance Redressal Committee must be 10.
(ii) If the order of suspension has not been issued along with chargesheet, the latter must follow within 7 days of issue of suspension order.
(iii) Dismissal and discharge are not any type of punishment.
(iv) *Nemo judex in causa sua* pertains to the rule of fair hearing.
(v) The exit interview is a democratic way of securing information about grievances at work.

Answers: (i) False, (ii) True, (iii) False, (iv) False, (v) False

II. Fill in the Blanks

(i) The Grievance Committee has a time limit of ____________ days to consider a grievance.
(ii) As per Model Standing Orders absence without leave for more than ____________ days is an act of misconduct.
(iii) Subsistence allowance for a suspended employee is equal to one-half of his wages for the first ____________ days of suspension.
(iv) The Code of Discipline dissuades both the parties from ____________ action.
(v) ____________ is considered the severest penalty.

Answers: (i) 7, (ii) 10, (iii) 90, (iv) unilateral, (v) dismissal

Discussion Questions

1. What are the principles that disciplinary proceedings must adhere to?
2. Clearly describe the process of grievance redressal as per the Model Grievance Procedure.
3. Discuss how the Code of Conduct promotes industrial peace and harmony.
4. Define indiscipline. What are the reasons contributing to indiscipline at work?

5. What are the most common ways of discovering grievances? Which of them, according to you, would be the most effective in a software company?
6. Define misconduct. Which acts as per the Industrial Employment (Standing Orders) Act, 1946 are considered to be those of misconduct?
7. Give a step-wise description of a disciplinary procedure.
8. What are the different types of suspension? What are the restrictions on a suspended employee?
9. What are the recommendations of the Second National Commission on Labour on grievances and their redressal?
10. Distinguish between:
    (a) Positive punishment and Negative punishment
    (b) Discharge and Dismissal

Taking Bribe at Workplace

The appellant is aggrieved against the order of the learned Single Judge dated 21st April 2008, passed in WP(S) No. 5477 of 2007, whereby the appellant's writ petition challenging the award dated 5th June 2007 passed by the Labour Court, Jamshedpur has been dismissed.

The facts reveal that the petitioner in this case was caught red-handed on 24th January 1995 taking bribe of ₹150 when he was on duty in shift 'E'. The Labour Court, after considering the evidence of the parties, held that the petitioner was in fact caught red-handed taking bribe and the amount of ₹150 was also recovered immediately thereafter. The punishment inflicted upon the workman was upheld by the award. The learned Single Judge also, after considering the facts of the case, dismissed the writ petition.

The counsel for the appellant submitted that the appellant was assigned the duty of receiving goods only and therefore there was no occasion and there could not have been any reason for taking as well as giving bribe in the present case. It was also submitted that another person was earlier caught red-handed taking bribe, but he had been reinstated in service. The counsel for the appellant further submitted that there is no sufficient evidence on record on the basis of which it can be inferred that money was taken as bribe in view of the defence of the appellant taken in the departmental proceeding and before the Labour Court. The defence of the appellant was that at about 11.00 am on 24th January 1995, the concerned supplier came to the workman and asked for an amount of ₹150 to attend some urgent work. The said person normally and in past also had taken some money from the appellant. In the instant case, the supplier returned the said money of ₹150. The workman also admitted that at that time he was surrounded by other workmen and other persons of the respondent company and ₹150 was recovered from him. According to the counsel for the appellant, so far as demanding and taking of bribe is concerned, there is no evidence in view of the stand taken by the appellant.

It will be relevant to mention here that the writ petition was admitted on 2 counts. Firstly, whether the order of termination can sustain in law on the ground of non-examination of the person from whom the appellant is alleged to have received the illegal gratification. Secondly, whether the punishment was proportionate to the guilt, as the allegation is of taking bribe of ₹150 only.

The counsel for the respondent had submitted that the person from whom the amount was taken was examined in departmental proceedings and therefore the first ground does not survive. It was also submitted that the defence taken by the appellant also is unbelievable due to the fact that the appellant himself had lodged complaint against the person from whom, as he was saying, was receiving the money back.

It is undisputed that on 24th January 1995, while on duty, the appellant had taken ₹150 from a person and admittedly, that person was a supplier of goods to the company. If the Labour Court, after appreciation of the evidence, has rejected the defence stand of the appellant that it was a case of return of money by the supplier to the appellant, then it is a pure question of fact.

Review Questions

1. Do you think that the decision of the Labour Court, after appreciation of the evidence, is tenable?
2. Looking at the post which the petitioner was holding of receiving goods of the other parties for the respondent-company, do you think that the misconduct of accepting the amount of ₹150 as bribe is grave enough to be awarded a punishment of dismissal?
3. Do you think that the petitioner ought to be discharged or dismissed?

(Adapted from: Dudhnath Ram vs. Management of M/s Tata Iron and Steel Co. Ltd. [(2012) LLR 814] www.indiankanoon.org/doc/142687700/ accessed on 26/12/2013.)

Industrial Conflict and Disputes

Desired Knowledge Competencies

- To comprehend the concepts of industrial conflict and dispute.
- To discuss the various views of conflicts and the underlying reasons of industrial disputes.
- To outline the typology of strikes and the concepts of lock-out, *bandhs* and *gheraos*.
- To develop an understanding of the trend of industrial disputes in India.

INTRODUCTION

The entire gamut of industrial relations revolves around a cycle of expectations and aspirations, which depends on cooperation and teamwork. This cycle often creates a series of conflicting situations due to the divergent interests of employers and employees. When any such conflict is allowed to exist for long, it has negative implications for an organisation. Under the unitary approach to industrial relations, workplace conflict is seen as a temporary aberration resulting from poor management, and is considered not only as unnecessary, but also as destructive. The pluralistic approach however views conflicts between the management and workers as inevitable and, in fact, conducive for growth. The Marxist approach considers conflicts to be the outcome of the capitalist society.

Industrial dispute, on the other hand, refers to any disagreement between workers and employers on a wide range of issues like wages, working conditions and other employment matters. Disputes may also arise due to disagreement between rival unions regarding issues like jurisdiction, or even between employers and employers. Conflict and dispute are intertwined in industrial relations. In this chapter we would discuss both these concepts within the ambit of labour legislations in India.

INDUSTRIAL CONFLICT

Referred to as a "dramatic expression of the relationship between capital and labour (Korpi and Shalev, 1979, p. 164), conflict is inherent in the interests of capital and labour as parties to the employment relationship. There are different views on what conflict is all about. Coser (1967, p. 8) has defined conflict as "A struggle over values and claims to scarce status, power and resources, in which the aims of the opponent are to neutralize, injure or eliminate the rivals". Willmot and Hocker (2001, p. 41) look at conflict as "an expressed struggle". It is apparent that the phenomenon of conflict in both these definitions has negative and destructive hues. On the contrary, Deutsch (1973) and Rahim (1983) consider conflict as "confronting interests" or "incompatible activities" existing between the parties involved in social situations. Thomas (1992, p. 265) considers conflict as "the process which begins when one party perceives that another has frustrated, or is about to frustrate, some concern of his". This definition is broad enough to include a wide variety of conflict phenomena.

When people work together, conflict becomes an integral and in fact a normal part of doing business. Organisational conflict refers to an interactive process manifested in incompatibility, disagreement or dissonance within or between social entities (i.e., individual, group, organisation, etc.) (Rahim, 2002). It includes interpersonal, inter-group and inter-organisational conflicts. Numerous factors may be responsible for conflicts at workplace. In fact, there can be more than one reason that may come into play to give rise to a single instance of conflict. Hence it is not always easy to ascertain or single out the particular cause(s) involved. What may be more intriguing is that the apparent reason(s) behind any unrest may conceal the deep-seated and more fundamental causes. Nevertheless, the factors responsible for organisational conflicts can be clubbed under the following heads:

- **Industry-related factors:** These factors include industry-related policies or practices pertaining to employment, wage, hours of work, terms and conditions of employment, rights and obligations of employers and workers, etc.
- **Organisation-related factors:** Such factors .may include wages (e.g., wage structure; deductions from wages; incentives; allowances); work-related issues (e.g., authoritarian administration; methods of job evaluation; physical working conditions; usage of technology and machinery; plant layout); terms of employment (e.g., hours of work; shift working; promotion; leave rules; layoff; retrenchment; dismissal; job security); union issues (e.g., recognition of union; membership of union; subjects of collective bargaining); unfair practices (e.g., non-implementation of labour laws and regulations; ambiguity in standing orders; violation of collective agreements), etc.

Spotlight

Factors behind organisational conflicts can be clubbed under:

- *Industry-related factors*
- *Organisation-related factors*
- *Individual-related factors*
- *Government-related factors and*
- *Miscellaneous factors*

- **Individual-related factors:** These factors are related to the personality and behaviour of an individual worker, like habits; behavioural maladjustments; lack of scope for self-expression and participation, etc.
- **Government-related factors:** These include changes in economic policies and regulations; improper implementation of labour legislations; changes in administrative machinery, etc.
- **Miscellaneous factors:** Other factors that may be instrumental in industrial conflicts are the growing intervention of political parties in union activities; unstable political situation; inter-union rivalry; clashes within union; change in ownership of establishment, etc.

However, this list is not exhaustive. With increase in complexities of jobs, emergence of new industries and growing awareness level of workers, the goals, expectations and aspirations of both workers and employers are expanding their domains. Such new expectations and aspirations would invoke new kinds of clashes between the two groups and the causes of conflicts would continue to increase in number and complexities.

All the reasons behind organisational conflicts can be summed up in accordance to the perspective of Rahim (2002), who proposes that organisational conflicts are likely to happen when the parties involved:

- are required to engage in an activity that is incongruent with their needs or interests.
- hold behavioural preferences that are incompatible with the implementation of each other's preferences.
- want some mutually desirable resource that is short in supply.
- possess attitudes, values, skills and goals that are appropriate for directing their behaviour but contradict the attitudes, values, skills and goals held by others within an organisation.
- have contradictory preferences regarding their joint actions.

Views on Conflict

Traditional View The traditional view, dated in the 1930s and 1940s, was primarily based on attitudes that prevailed about group behaviour. It had a negative, rigid and formalistic approach to conflict. Conflict was considered dysfunctional and had to be avoided at all costs by role players (Slabbert, 2004), primarily because of the adverse effects it could have on organisational productivity. The classical writers believed that conflict is indicative of malfunctioning within the organisation and that it represents management's failure to bind the workers and organisation together in a cohesive unit. Conflict was denounced because conflicting groups would not cooperate in getting tasks completed. Managers would also have to devote extra efforts and time in resolving conflicts. All of these would lead to losses in productivity and hence the traditional view recommended suppression of conflicts.

> **Spotlight**
> The traditional view had a negative, rigid and formalistic approach to conflict.

Modern View The modern approach to conflict originated in the discourses of the human relations theorists, who proposed that conflict is a natural phenomenon that is inevitable and should be managed as such (Reynecke, 1997). Conflict is natural and inevitable because organisations are composed of individuals with different and divergent values, goals and perceptions. Faulty policies and structure of the organisation leading to blockage in communication also contribute to conflicts at work. Because of its inevitability in any organisational set up, conflict must be resolved amicably to achieve good human relations. Overall, the human relations school perceived conflict as harmful and advised resolution of conflicts in the interest of the organisation and its members.

The modern view proposes that conflict is not only a positive force in a group, but is also necessary for a group to perform effectively. Conflict should be measured in terms of functionality, i.e., whether it is functional or dysfunctional. A functional conflict encourages the group to work for the attainment of its goals, improves its performance and contributes to personal growth of the members and to overall organisational growth. A dysfunctional conflict is destructive in nature as it hinders group or individual performance. Thus it is inappropriate to say that conflict is all good or bad. In fact, the modern approach encourages conflict on the ground that a minimum level of conflict is necessary to keep the organisational members alert and creative. It provides stability to a group and helps in the identification of power centers in and between groups (Chhabra and Suri, 2007). Conflict is also viewed to be integral to the process of change; a harmonious group that exhibits cooperation is prone to become static and non-responsive to change and innovation. The onus would lie on the group leader to allow any conflict to happen in order to make the group members innovative and imaginative. Further, conflicts must be kept under control to avoid their dysfunctional consequences.

> **Spotlight**
> As per the modern view, conflict should be measured in terms of functionality.

> **Reflection**
> Pluralistic perspective views conflict as a natural outcome of interactions between divergent groups in an organisation.

INDUSTRIAL DISPUTES

An industrial dispute may be defined as a disagreement or difference of opinion between management and workers over issues like pay, working conditions and other terms of employment. However, it would be wrong to suppose that industrial disputes are limited to employees and employers. Disputes also include any disagreement between worker and worker and between employer and employer. All these aspects are neatly summarised in the definition of industrial disputes as per Section 2(k) of the Industrial Disputes Act, 1947 as "any dispute or difference between employers and employers, or between employers and workmen, or between workmen and workmen which is connected with the employment or non-employment or the terms of employment or with the conditions of labour, of any person." We would be talking about the Act and its various provisions in detail in Chapter 15.

Spotlight
Section 2(k) of the Industrial Disputes Act, 1947 defines an industrial dispute as any dispute or difference between employers and employers, or between employers and workmen, or between workmen and workmen, which is connected with the employment or non-employment or the terms of employment or with the conditions of labour, of any person.

Disagreement or difference fuelling an industrial dispute could be on any matter concerning workers, either individually or collectively, connected with employment, like inequitable wage structure, or non-employment, or with the conditions of labour, like poor working conditions. When an industrial dispute occurs, both the parties try to pressurise each other and often adopt coercive methods to have their demands fulfilled. Management may resort to lock-outs, while workers may call on strikes, picketing or *gheraos*. Whatever be the method adopted, disputes lead to negative repercussions. Such implications of industrial disputes have been explained in a subsequent section. Let us first understand the differences between seemingly similar terms, namely conflict and dispute, and individual dispute and industrial dispute.

Difference between Conflict and Dispute

Is there any difference between conflict and dispute? Many a times these two terms have been found to be used interchangeably. Conflict is considered to be an unavoidable fact of organisational life; it is somewhat general as a concept. However, when conflict acquires concrete and specific manifestations, it becomes an industrial dispute, i.e., industrial conflict is general, whereas industrial dispute is specific. More specifically, the term 'industrial dispute' is used in the literature including government publications to denote work-stoppage as well as those differences between labour and management that are settled through the industrial relations machinery (Chhabra and Suri, 2007). Be it dispute or conflict, either must be resolved for harmonious labour-management relations. When workers and their unions take an issue of conflict to the management for the purpose of negotiation, such a conflict becomes a matter of industrial dispute.

Spotlight
Industrial conflict is general, whereas industrial dispute is specific.

Difference between Individual Dispute and Industrial Dispute

There is a large divergence of opinions as to whether a dispute between an individual worker and employer (i.e., an individual dispute) can be considered as an industrial dispute under Section 2(k) of the Industrial Disputes Act, 1947. Let us analyse some relevant judgments to clarify the difference.

It would be worthwhile to note the provisions of Section 2A, added as per an amendment in the Industrial Dispute Act, 1947 in the year 1965. According to this section, where any employer discharges, dismisses, retrenches or otherwise terminates the services of an individual workman, any dispute or difference between that workman and his employer connected with, or arising out of, such discharge, dismissal, retrenchment or termination shall be deemed to be an industrial dispute, notwithstanding that no other workman or any union of workmen is a party to the dispute.

In *The Newspapers Ltd vs. The State Industrial Tribunal, U.P.* [(1957) SCR 754] the Court held that any dispute between an employer and a single workman does not fall within the definition of "industrial dispute" under the U.P. Industrial Disputes Act, 1947. Though the applicability of the said Act to an individual dispute, as opposed to a dispute involving a group of workmen, is excluded and if workmen as a body or a considerable section of them make a common cause with the individual workman, then such a dispute would be an industrial dispute.

The Court has held in *D. N. Banerji vs. P. R. Mukherjee and Others* [(1953) SCR 302] that the words "industrial dispute" seemingly imply that the dispute must be such as would affect large groups of workmen and employers on issues such as wages, bonuses, allowances, pensions, provident fund, number of working hours per week, holidays and so on. Even with reference to a business, we would hardly opine that there is an industrial dispute where an employee is dismissed by his employer and the dismissal is questioned as wrongful. But at the same time, having regard to the modern conditions of society where capital and labour have organised themselves into groups for the purpose of fighting their disputes and settling such disputes on the philosophy that in union is strength, and with collective bargaining becoming a powerful tool in the hands of unions, a single employee's case might develop into an industrial dispute when it is taken up by the trade union of which he is a member and there is a concerted demand by the employees for redress. Such an issue may not be limited to a single establishment or a factory, but may cover the industry as a whole in a case where the grievance, if any, passes from the domain of an individual complaint into a general complaint on behalf of all the workers in the industry. In such widespread extension of labour unrest even an industrial dispute in a particular business becomes a large scale industrial dispute, which the Government cannot afford to ignore as a minor trouble to be settled between the particular employer and workman concerned.
(Adapted from: www.indiankanoon.org/doc/162306/ accessed on 15/2/2014.)

MANIFESTATION OF CONFLICT

Workers resort to various methods like strikes, go-slow and work-to-rule as a manifestation of their discontentment and conflict with the employer, while lock-out is the weapon in the hands of the employer to manifest an industrial dispute. Let us elaborate on each of these weapons now.

> **Reflection**
> Through direct action unions exert pressure on employers through tactics like strikes, boycott, blockade, ***gherao***, etc.

Strike

A strike is a powerful weapon in the hands of workers and their trade unions to get their demands accepted. A strike generally involves quitting of work by a group of workers for the purpose of pressurising their management. Section 2(q) of the Industrial Disputes Act, 1947 defines a strike as "a cessation of work by a body of persons employed in any industry acting in combination or a concerted refusal, or a refusal under a common understanding, of any number of persons who are or have been so employed to continue to work or to accept employment".

We have already referred to strikes under the method of direct action adopted by unions in Chapter 3. Let us talk about the types of strikes here.

Types of Strikes

There can be several bases of classifying strikes. Let us explain types of strikes in terms of such bases.

I. On the Basis of Consent of Union

(a) *Authorised strikes:* Strikes which are called with the consent of the union are authorised strikes.

(b) *Unauthorised strikes:* An unauthorised strike, popularly known as a lightning strike or a "wildcat strike" is one which is called without prior consent of the union concerned and without giving proper notice to the employer. Hence a wildcat strike is an unofficial strike. Such a strike is normally the outcome of an emotional upsurge due to provocative circumstances between employer and workers. Many authors are of the opinion that such strikes occur in violation of the no-strike pledge in collective bargaining agreements. The characteristic feature of this type of withdrawal of labour, as Srivastava (1990) points out, is that workmen suddenly withdraw their labour and bargain afterwards. The union concerned is under obligation to use its best efforts to end a wildcat strike.

Spotlight

A wildcat strike is an unofficial strike.

Such strikes are prohibited in public utility services under the Industrial Disputes Act, 1947 and in all industrial establishments in public utility services in Uttar Pradesh, Maharashtra, Madhya Pradesh and Gujarat, where notice of strike is required to be given. We shall be deliberating about regulation of strikes and notice of strike in Chapter 15. Further, the standing orders of an industrial establishment generally require notice of strike. Since no notice is required in industrial establishments other than public utility concerns, a question therefore arises whether a wildcat strike would be misconduct or unjustified in such establishments; this is a subject-matter of judicial controversy (Srivastava, 1990).

Exhibit 7.1 Wildcat Strike at Maruti Suzuki

A wildcat strike had exploded on 4th June 2011 and continued till 17th June 2011 at the Manesar plant of Maruti Suzuki, with around 2,000 workers demanding the recognition of a new union, namely, Maruti Suzuki Employees Union (MSEU), formed by those working at the Manesar plant, and for improving working conditions and wages of the workers.

Without previous notice to strike, the workers brought production to a complete halt. They spent almost two weeks in the factory. The strike delayed the production of 13,200 cars and the company was hit in a phase of full production capacity. Damages caused were worth 100 million Euros to the company. The workers continued with the strike, even though it was officially declared illegal on 10th June and police were stationed within the factory.

The outcome was however a defeat for the majority of the workers, with their most important goal, i.e., improvement in wages not being attained. Instead, the agreement with the management contained a penalty wage cut of two days per strike day. The agreement also included re-employment of the eleven union members who had been fired during the protests, though subject to investigation.

(Adapted from: www.de.labournet.tv/node/6048, www.libcom.org/news/india-wildcat-strike-maruti-suzuki-continues-may-spread-09062011 accessed on 28/2/2014.)

II. On the Basis of Tactics Used to Halt Work

(a) *Ordinary strike:* This type of strike is characterised by employees quitting their workplace during prescribed working hours; the striking workers also prevent others from coming to work. Rallies, picketing and demonstrations are also made by the workers to draw the attention of the management to their grievances and demands.

(b) *Slow-down strike:* In this type of strike, the striking workers remain on their jobs. They do not stop work as such, but restrict the volume of output produced in an organised manner. If we go by the definition of strike as provided by the Industrial Disputes Act, 1947, in slow-down there is no "cessation of work" or "refusal to continue to work" or "refusal to accept employment". Nevertheless the economic implications of slow-down are very serious as adoption of such techniques raises the costs of production. These strikes are resented by employers on grounds of immorality.

Exhibit 7.2 Slow-down at IISCO, Burnpur

The workers of Indian Iron and Steel Co. (IISCO) Ltd. had started a slow-down on 19th January 1953 at the Burnpur unit without any declared reason or demand from the management. The company had no knowledge of the intrigues and the animosities which had engendered the trouble until 10th February 1953. It was also unable to recognise the Action Committee which was set up as a representative body, as the Committee was not constituted by any lawful election and especially as it had been actively engaging in subversive activities, including the slow-down of production.

On account of the continued illegal stoppage of work, 'slow down' tactics and strikes indulged in by the workmen despite the advice of their union, IISCO issued a notice dated 23rd August 1953 that in consequence of the illegal strike the management had no option other than declaring a lock-out of the entire works except the special shifts with effect from 24th August 1953.

(Adapted from: Labour Trouble at Burnpur, The Economic Weekly, 15th August, 1953. Retrieved from www.epw.in/system/files/pdf/1953.../labour_trouble_at_burnpur.pdfý, www.indiankanoon.org/doc/1919374/ on 28/2/2014.)

Let us throw light on "go-slow" here as a variant of slow-down, in which workers deliberately slow-down the pace of production by pretending to be engaged in the factory. As Mamoria et al. (2008, p. 231) point out, "The go-slow is a technical word which is used to describe the tactics of workers when they intentionally reduce the speed of work to adopt dilatory tactics to reduce production or efficiency while pretending to be engaged in the factory." There is no "cessation of work" or "refusal to continue to work" or "refusal to accept employment" in such type of strikes as well. Workers adopt the practice of "go-slow" to circumvent the statutory restrictions on strike; however, when they are disciplined for misconduct, these workers assert that the practice amounts to strike (Srivastava, 1990).

In *M/s Bharat Sugar Mills Ltd vs. Shri Jai Singh and Others*, the Supreme Court had observed that: "Go slow which a picturesque description of deliberate delaying of production by workmen pretending to be engaged in the factory is one of the most pernicious practices that discontented or disgruntled workmen sometime resort to. It would not be far wrong to call this dishonest. For, while thus delaying production and thereby reducing the output the workmen claim to have remained employed and thus to be entitled to full wages." Besides, go-slow is likely to be much more harmful than total cessation of work by strike. This is because while during a strike much of the machinery can be fully turned off; however during go-slow the machinery is kept going on at a reduced speed, which is often extremely damaging to machinery parts.

(Adapted from: www.indiankanoon.org/doc/774563/ accessed on 28/2/2014.)

(c) *Quickie:* In a quickie workers remain at their work stations, but halt their work for a brief while, say a few minutes to a few hours (Sinha, Sinha and Shekhar, 2006). The implications of such work-stoppage, even though for a few minutes, can be very serious, especially in assembly-line production.

(d) *Sit-down strike:* In a sit-down strike a group of workers keeps control over the production facilities; these workers stop production and refuse access to the owners or to any one else desiring to work. Thus workers do not absent themselves from their place of work when they are on strike, though they do not work. It is a strike in the traditional sense, to which is added the element of trespass by strikers upon the property of the employer. A sit-down strike is also known as a 'pen down' or 'tool down' strike.

Another variant of a sit-down strike is a "sit-in" strike. In this type of strike an organised group of protesting workers sits and occupies an area where it is not wanted and refuses to move out until its demands are met. In *The Punjab National Bank Ltd. vs. its Workmen* (1960 SCR (1) 806) the employees of the appellant Bank had commenced a pen-down strike followed by a general strike, pending arbitration of an industrial dispute between them. In considering whether this pen-down strike is actually a strike within the scope of Section 2(q) of the Industrial Disputes Act, 1947 or not, the Court held that on a plain and grammatical construction of the definition of a strike it would be difficult to exclude a strike where workmen enter the premises of their employment and refuse to take their tools in hand and start their usual work. Refusal under common understanding to continue to work is undoubtedly a strike and if in pursuance of such common understanding the employees had entered the premises of the Bank and refused to take their pens in their hands that would surely be a strike under Section 2(q). The main grievance of the Bank is that these employees not only sat in their places and refused to work, but they would also not vacate their seats when asked to do so by their superior officers. Such conduct may introduce an element of insubordination. The Court was finally of the opinion that the pen-down strike in which the employees had participated cannot be said to be outside Section 2(q) of the Act.

> **Spotlight**
> In a sit-in strike an organised group of protesting workers sits and occupies an area where it is not wanted and refuses to move until its demands are met.

(Adapted from: www.indiankanoon.org/doc/1395554/ accessed on 26/2/2014.)

Let us sort out the difference between quickie and sit-downs. The basic distinction between these two variants of strikes is the duration involved. Obviously a quickie is for shorter duration than a sit-down. The similarity between the two is in the stoppage of work.

(e) *Stay-in strike:* A stay-in strike is one in which the striking workers report to their duties, but refuse to work and they do not leave the plant premises. The owner of the plant (or factory) is deprived of the use of the plant and the machinery and further operations are at a halt. Besides, the owner has to incur additional expenditure on the safety and security of the plant and machinery when the striking workers remain inside the factory or establishment.

(f) *Work-to-rule strike:* Work-to-rule is a kind of concerted activity in which employees remain on job, but perform their work literally in accordance with the rules prescribed for the purpose. These work-

> **Spotlight**
> In work-to-rule employees remain on job, but perform the work literally in accordance with the rules prescribed for the purpose.

ers decline to do anything not mentioned therein, take permissible time off the job, and perform their work to the letter in such a manner that it results in slowing the work down.

> **Spotlight**
> The terms "stay-in strike", "sit-down strike", "pen-down strike", and "tool-down strike" are often used synonymously.

As Srivastava (1990) observes, usually under work-to-rule, rules of work are stretched and followed in such a manner that under the shelter of complying with rules the very purpose of these rules, namely, harmonious working for maximizing production, is frustrated. As such, workers literally work according to rules but in spirit they work against; in substance they amount to "work against rule". Work-to-rule is generally employed as an alternative to a traditional strike, particularly in situations when the latter cannot be called. It amounts to bringing about a lot of pressure on the management by the employees.

EXHIBIT 7.3 WORK-TO-RULE AT NEYVELI LIGNITE CORPORATION

The employees of Neyveli Lignite Corporation (NLC) gave up their 13-days-old strike and returned to work soon after the Tamil Nadu Government clinched the deal with the Securities and Exchange Board of India to buy 5 per cent NLC shares at ₹500 crore. However, in response to this deal, the employees have decided to adhere to the work-to-rule procedures. The rules stipulate eight-hour shift for employees, with rightful breaks in between for refreshment. Prior to the strike the employees and workers never went by the clock but would always put in extra work of about two to two-and-half hours daily beyond their shift obligations. The foremen, numbering about 2,000, used to work extra hours to facilitate smooth change over from one shift to the other as it would normally take some time before the fresh batch of employees would replace the previous batch by a practice that is termed as "man-to-man relieving".

According to S. Rajavanniyan, General Secretary of the Labour Progressive Front (Neyveli Unit), the proposed action of the employees should not be construed as either a threat to the management or an anti-management move. He specified that "Taking time-off is indeed the legal right of the employees which they will duly exercise hereafter." The employees and the workforce in the mines and thermal power stations would unfailingly take the tea/tiffin break in such manner that during such intervals the officials could not take over, as the entire functionality would be with the employees. Rajavanniyan reiterated the point that "it would not be a vengeful act but a rightful act on the part of the employees as provided under the law."

(Adapted from: Strike given up, but NLC staff to go by work-to-rule, Neyveli, 17th July, 2013, Retrieved from www.thehindu.com/news/national/tamil-nadu/strike-given-up-but-nlc-staff-to-go-by-worktorule/ article4923643 on 28/2/2014.)

(g) *Sick-in strike:* The sick-in (also known as sick-out) is an interesting variant of a strike; instead of calling a conventional strike, a majority or all the workers call in sick simultaneously. The employer cannot initiate any action against such workers because these workers do not break any rules; they just avail of their sick leave that they are entitled to, on the same day. Sick-in is thus a good way to strike without striking; it provides a signal to the employer of the repercussions if the workers really went on strike.

However we should specify here that the expressions "stay-in strike", "sit-down strike", "pen-down strike", and "tool-down strike" are often used as synonymous to each other.

III. On the Basis of Miscellaneous Purposes

(a) *Sympathetic strike:* As the name itself suggests, a sympathetic strike is borne out of sympathy; the striking workers do not have any grievance against their employer. However they join the other group of workers, whether the latter are on strike or not, to express their solidarity and commonness to the cause of these workers.

Exhibit 7.4 Expressing Solidarity to the Maruti Cause

The strike by workers of Maruti Suzuki at its Manesar factory was under threat to spread to other auto and component makers in the Manesar-Gurgaon belt, which makes about half of all the cars and bikes in the country. The demand placed by Maruti workers for an independent workers' union had struck a sympathetic chord among workers in neighbouring units including Hero Honda, Honda Motorcycle and Scooter India (HMSI), Rico Auto, Omaxe Auto and Lumax Industries. Unions of these companies are now threatening to strike work against their respective companies.

The secretary of HMSI Employees' Union said that "We have decided to call a one day strike to protest against the indecisive Maruti management. We will give them some time before taking a final call on the issue." The president of Rico Auto's workers' union at the Daruhera plant near Manesar said that "If Maruti Suzuki fails to act on workers' demands, we will resort to a strike at our plants in coming days." The president of Employees' Union at Hero Honda's Daruhera plant said that "We will extend all support to Maruti employees and may go on strike to express our solidarity. If required, we will come to a common location and protest for joint demands."

(Adapted from: www.libcom.org/news/india-wildcat-strike-maruti-suzuki-continues-may-spread-09062011 accessed on 28/2/2014.)

(b) *Hunger strike:* Hunger strike features fasting by some or all the striking workers for a limited period. However, the ulterior motive of workers involved in the strike is to exert moral pressure on the management for acceptance of their demands and to attract the attention of the public. Srivastava (1990) holds the view that the usage of hunger strike as a weapon is complicated because, like the term 'strike', it is used to describe all protest fasts, whether or not the particular protest activity is in furtherance of an industrial dispute. Typical examples are of students on hunger strike to press their demands against educational authorities, political leaders on hunger strike to compel the government to redress their grievances, and sections of the community on hunger strike in support of their stand against various authorities or bodies.

> **Spotlight**
> Workers on hunger strike intend to exert moral pressure on the management for acceptance of their demands and to attract the attention of the public.

(c) *Jurisdictional strike:* Typically American in concept, jurisdictional strike is an outcome of a dispute between the members of different unions over work assignments or disagreement between two or more unions as to which of them should have the exclusive right to bargain collectively with the employer. Needless to mention, such strikes can occur only in such establishments that have multiple trade unions which are rivals.

(d) *Economic strike:* As is evident from the name itself, this type of strike is initiated to enforce the economic demands of workers, such as wages, bonus and various types of allowances.

(e) *Token strike:* A token strike is generally of a very short duration intended to convey the strength of feeling of workers on a disputed issue. It serves more as a kind of signal for the real threat

EXHIBIT 7.5 HUNGER STRIKE: SATYAGRAHA

In *Pipraich Sugar Mills Ltd vs. Pipraich Sugar Mills Mazdoor Union [(1956-57) X FJR 4113 LAT]* certain workmen who held key posts in the factory went on hunger strike on a holiday at the residence of the Managing Director of the factory and continued to do so on other working days. The Labour Appellate Tribunal observed that the mere fact that the hunger strike was staged on a holiday does not reduce the essential characteristics of a strike from this hunger '*satyagraha*'. This is because the intention of the strikers was to continue the strike till their demands were met or till they died of starvation. It was not claimed on behalf of the *satyagrahi* workers that they did present themselves for their duty on 2nd April 1953. So it must be held that the '*satyagraha*' was continued on 2nd April 1953 and amounted to 'strike'.

(Adapted from: www.indiankanoon.org/doc/1252531/ accessed on 26/2/2014.)

of a strike ahead in case the demands of the workers are unheeded by the employer. The motive behind such a strike is moral persuasion.

(f) *Political strike:* Political strikes are called with the objective of challenging the government or influencing its policy decisions in favour of the working class. Such strikes are not the outcome of any industrial dispute.

(g) *General strike:* General strikes are wide-spread in terms of coverage and scope, with participation of members of all or most of the unions in a region or an industry. These strikes are usually directed to create political pressure on the government, and in this sense general strikes are similar to political strikes.

(h) *Picketing and Boycott:* Picketing is an action taken by union members to prevent employees from attending work after a strike has been called. It is accompanied by patrolling of striking workers in front of the premises of the employer and displaying banners and placards to show their protest verbally. Picketing is a tool in the hands of workers to generate public awareness of their dispute with their employer. Peaceful picketing is not illegal; however adoption of coercive methods and persuasion by threat or violence may fail to restrict picketing within peaceful limits.

Boycott refers to the rejection by workers of specific products or services provided by the employer. As per Mamoria et al. (2008), a boycott is an appeal for voluntary withdrawal of cooperation, and so it is persuasive in nature, but negative in approach; however, picketing is positive in approach as it involves adopting necessary and adequate measures to prevent cooperation by others in the normal functioning of a business.

(i) *Gherao:* The term *gherao* literally means encirclement. In *Jay Engineering Works Ltd. and Others vs. State of West Bengal and Others* (AIR 1968 Cal 407), the Court has defined *gherao* as a physical blockade of a target, either by encirclement or forcible occupation. It has described two kinds of *gherao*. The ordinary kind is encirclement and blockade of an industrial establishment, where the person *gheraoed* is generally in managerial or supervisory position present at the premises. Blockade can also be outside the premises on a public thoroughfare; the persons blockading may trespass into the land belonging to an industrial establishment. The second kind of *gherao* is encirclement in depth, i.e., forcible possession of the industrial establishment and ouster of the real owner and the managerial and other staff. A *gherao* can last for several hours or even days, and the staff are prevented from going out pending fulfillment of the demands of workers.

(Adapted from: www.indiankanoon.org/doc/140181/ accessed on 28/2/2014.)

Spotlight

A *gherao* is a physical blockade of a target, either by encirclement or forcible occupation.

According to the First National Commission on Labour (1969), *gheraos* strike at the very root of trade unionism apart from their adverse effects on industry and the economy of the country. The Commission hence deprecated resort to *gheraos* which invariably tend to inflict physical duress on the person(s) affected and not only endanger industrial harmony but also create problems of law and order. If such means are to be adopted by workers for realisation of their claims, trade unions may come into disrepute; it is hence the duty of all union leaders to condemn this form of labour protest as harmful to the interests of the working class itself. As per the Commission, *gheraos* cannot be treated as a form of industrial protest since they involve physical coercion rather than economic pressure, thus affecting national interest in the long run. The incidence of *gherao* was initiated amidst violent trade unionism in West Bengal, followed by Kerala, though it is not much in practice nowadays.

Blockade under *gherao* is occasionally supplemented by assault, criminal trespass, mischief to person and property, unlawful assembly and various other criminal offences. Many a times the offences reported are cruel and inhuman, e.g., confinement in a small space without lights or fans and for long periods without food or communication with the outside world. The persons confined are beaten, humiliated by abuse and not allowed even to answer calls of nature and subjected to various other forms of torture. In short the officials "*gheraoed*" are completely at the mercy of the besiegers. The Court has held that workers have no right to resort to coercive methods like wrongful restraint, wrongful confinement and criminal trespass, which are all cognizable offences as per the Indian Penal Code. Often such strikes are referred to as "secondary action'. The legality of such strikes is found to vary across countries.

(Adapted from: www.indiankanoon.org/doc/140181/ accessed on 28/2/2014.)

(j) *Secondary strike:* Secondary strikes are those in which pressure is not applied against the primary employer, but against some third person who has good trade relations with the employer and thus the latter incurs losses.

(k) *Bandh:* The literal meaning of the term *bandh* is "closed", implying that everything is to be closed during a *bandh*.

In *Communist Party of India (M) vs. Bharat Kumar and Others* [(1998)1 SCC 201] the Kerala High Court has laid down that: "… which the organiser of a bandh, call for a bandh, they clearly express their intention that they expect all activities to come to a standstill on the day of the bandh." A call for a *bandh* is different from that for a general strike or a *hartal*. The Court further held that: "The intention of the callers of the *bandh* is to ensure that no activity either public or private if carried on that date… It is no doubt true that while calling for a *bandh* it is not also announced that any citizen not participating in the *bandh* will be physically prevented or attacked." However experience has shown that when any attempt is made to move out, such a person has been threatened with harmful consequences.

In *Railway Board, New Delhi vs. Niranjan Singh* (AIR 1969 SC 966), the Supreme Court has observed that: "The fact that the citizens of this country have freedom of speech, freedom to assemble peaceably and freedom to form associations or unions does not mean that they can exercise those freedoms in whatever place they please. The exercise of those freedoms will come to an end as soon as the right of someone else to hold his property intervenes. Such limitation is inherent in the exercise of those rights." Keeping this verdict in perspective and if the call for *bandh* and holding of it entails restriction on the fundamental freedoms of the citizen, the court, in *Rama Prasad Sarkar vs. The State of West Bengal* (WP 23617 (W) of 2013), has held that no political party has the right to call for *bandh* on the plea that it is part of its fundamental right of freedom of speech and expression. Moreover, nothing stands in the way of political parties calling for a general strike or *hartal* that is not accompanied by express or implied threat of violence to enforce it. It is not possible to accept that the calling of a *bandh* is the only measure to demonstrate the protest of a political party to a given decision or in a given situation.

(Adapted from: www.indiankanoon.org/doc/87610222/ accessed on 28/2/2014.)

Lock-out

The use of the term "lock-out" to describe the instruments of economic coercion in the hands of employers dates back to 1860s; as a practice lock-out is younger than its counterparts in the hands of workers, i.e., strike, by about a hundred years (Srivastava, 1990). Formerly lock-out as an instrument of coercion was resorted to by an employer or group of employers to ban union membership; later lock-out was declared generally by a body of employers against a strike at a particular establishment by closing all factories until strikers would return to work. Section 2(l) of the Industrial Disputes Act, 1947 defines lock-out as "the temporary closing of a place of employment or the suspension of work, or the refusal by an employer to continue to employ any number of persons employed by him". As mentioned earlier in the chapter, lock-out is a weapon in the hands of the employer to coerce labour to come down in their demands, thus restraining their militant spirit.

Spotlight

Section 2(l) of the Industrial Disputes Act, 1947 defines a lock-out as "the temporary closing of a place of employment or the suspension of work, or the refusal by an employer to continue to employ any number of persons employed by him".

In *Presidency Jute Mills Co. Ltd. vs. Presidency Jute Mills Co. Employees' Union* [(1952) LAT 62] the Court has held that the Industrial Disputes Act, 1947 treats strikes and lock-outs on the same basis as counterparts of each other. If we look at these instruments of industrial disputes, we can find plentitude of negative impacts of each. It is just that in lock-out it is the employer who first draws the sword. Neither a strike, nor a lock-out would severe the relation of employer and workers. The Supreme Court describes a lock-out as the antithesis of strike.

(Adapted from: www.indiankanoon.org/doc/301159 accessed on 25/2/2014.)

We shall be discussing the other aspects of lock-out, including notice of lock-out by an employer on any public utility service and illegality of a lock-out in the chapter on Industrial Disputes Act, 1947.

ANALYSIS OF TRENDS IN CONFLICT IN INDIAN INDUSTRY

The Industrial Relations machineries at both Centre and State levels under the aegis of the Ministry of Labour & Employment strive on a continuous basis towards maintenance of harmonious industrial relations in the country. The Departments of Labour in the States and Union Territories and Regional Labour Commissioners (Central) are responsible for collecting basic information in respect of work-stoppages from the affected primary units in the State and Central Spheres respectively, whenever such occurrence of a work-stoppage becomes known either directly or from supplementary sources like police records. Such information is furnished in standard format to the Labour Bureau, Ministry of Labour & Employment, on or before the 25th of each succeeding month. The statistics on industrial disputes brought out by the Labour Bureau include information in respect of those temporary work-stoppages only which include strikes, lock-outs and *gheraos* followed by lock-outs, and involving 10 or more workers, whether directly and/or indirectly. Work-stoppages which involve less than 10 workers are not included in such records. Similarly, political strikes, sympathetic demonstrations, etc. are also not included, as they are not connected with any specific dispute, grievance or demand of workers of an industrial establishment and are beyond the competence of their employer to redress. The figures thus collated form the basis for the Ministry to monitor the extent of industrial harmony on a regular basis.

Figures for 2010 provided by the Labour Bureau reflect that there were 371 industrial disputes (strikes and lock-outs), in which 10,74,473 workers were involved and 2,31,30,527 man-days were lost. Of the total disputes, 334 (90.03 per cent) involving 4,47,640 (41.66 per cent) workers and 2,16,18,156 (93.46 per cent) man-days lost were in State Sphere. Statistics on industrial disputes during the year 2010 in Central Sphere by States reveal that the highest number of disputes (7 each), was recorded in Tamil Nadu and West Bengal. Workers involved and man-days lost were the highest in West Bengal and Tamil Nadu as 185,747 workers and 657,636 man-days respectively. Incidentally there was no case of lock-out reported in Central Sphere during the year.

With the exception of some notable disputes in reputed establishments like Maruti Suzuki and Air India, the overall industrial relations climate has generally remained peaceful and cordial. The number of incidences of strikes and lock-outs which stood at 389 in 2007 has exhibited a declining trend and was at 182 *(provisional)* in 2012. The man-days lost on account of these disturbances had registered a notable dip from 27.17 million in 2007 to 1.79 million in 2012 *(provisional)*; the figures have however shown variations over this period. Spatial or industry-wise dispersion of the incidences of strikes and lock-outs has shown widespread variation among different States and Union Territories. The major reasons for these industrial disputes have been wage and allowance, bonus, personnel, indiscipline and violence and financial intermediaries (excluding insurance and pension funds). Table 7.1 provides figures of industrial disputes (all strikes and lock-outs) for the years 2005 to 2013.

TABLE 7.1 Industrial Disputes (All Strikes and Lock-outs) from 2005 to 2013

Year	*Disputes*	*Workers Involved*	*Man-days Lost ('000)*
2005	456	2,913,601	29,665
2006	430	1,810,348	20,324
2007	389	724,574	27,167
2008	421	1,579,298	17,433
2009	345	1,867,204	17,622
2010	371	1,074,473	23,131
2011 (P)*	389	734,723	14,332
2012 (P)*	276	1,225,042	3,390
2013 (P)* (Jan. to June)	79	221,258	1,360

Adapted from: Indian Labour Journal, Vol. 54 No. 3, May 2013 and Indian Labour Journal, Vol. 54 No. 9, September 2013

**(P): Provisional and based on the returns/clarifications received in the Bureau till 31st July 2013.*

The figures are clearly reflective of a decline in the number of disputes over the years. The number of workers involved in such disputes is seen to have a fluctuating trend.

EFFECTS OF INDUSTRIAL DISPUTES

Whatever by the type adopted, strikes have far-reaching impacts on not only the employers, but also the striking workers themselves, the consumers of the products of the affected industry, the suppliers to the establishment(s) and the economy as a whole. Though a lock-out is in the hands of the employer, but otherwise its consequences are similar. Let us enumerate the effects of industrial disputes as a whole in this section.

Effects on Workers

The most immediate impact of industrial disputes on the workers is through their wages. The question that would come in sequence is that whether striking workers should be entitled to wages from their employer or not. The Supreme Court has held in *Syndicate Bank and Another vs. K. Umesh Nayak* (AIR 1995 SC 319) that the right of workmen to receive strike wages is when the strike is not only legal, but is also justified. What needs to be understood here is that every strike is not illegal, and that workers enjoy the right to resort to strike in order to express their grievances or demands. The Court has opined in *All India Central Government Health Scheme Employees' Association (Delhi Branch) vs. Union of India and Others* (WP(C) No. 5471 of 2008) that if the strike is illegal, there is no question of payment of any wages. Even if a strike is legal, but unjustified, there have been instances in which courts have refused wages for the period of such illegal strike. It hence follows as a corollary that where the strike is illegal or unjustified, the concerned workmen would not be entitled to strike wages. In addition, as held in *Crompton Greaves Ltd. vs. Workmen* (AIR 1978 SC 1489), whenever workers would resort to the use of coercion, violence or acts of sabotage during the strike period, they would render themselves disentitled to claim wages for the strike period.

Spotlight

When the strike is illegal or unjustified, the concerned workmen would not be entitled to strike wages.

(Adapted from: www.indiankanoon.org/doc/1650811/ accessed on 28/2/2014.)

The entire discussion hence boils down to the simple fact that workers would normally not earn wages for the period for which the dispute would continue, and this loss of earnings exerts tremendous pressure on their own selves and their dependents. With an already low level of earning, workers would seldom have any savings to fall back on. They may even get into debt traps to sustain their livelihood. Workers also suffer from physical injuries in case there are incidents of violence during the industrial dispute. Facing the wrath of the employer in the form of victimisation is another risk that workers may be exposed to. There have been instances when union leaders who are actively involved in protests and strikes have been suspended on various charges (Das and Gupta, 2013).

Such losses can of course be made good of if the dispute ends at a favourable note for the agitating workers. They can get rid of their hardships following increase in wages and other allowances, subject to the demands put forth by the workers and their fulfillment by the management.

Effects on Employers

The very first impact of an industrial dispute on the employer is stoppage of work, which, in turn, affects production adversely. As per the provisional figures obtained by the Labour Bureau (*Source: Indian Labour Journal, Vol. 5 No. 9, September 2013, p. 898)*, there were 276 instances of industrial disputes (strikes and lock-outs taken together) during 2012 in both State and Central spheres. Work-stoppages as a consequence involved 1,225,042 workers with a time-loss of 3.39 million man-days. Though large in themselves, these figures are still redeeming, as against 389 disputes involving 734,723 workers with a time-loss of 14.33 million man-days during 2011 (*provisional*). In 2012 the public sector had accounted for 1.71 million man-days or 50.43 per cent of the total time-loss. Among the States, Tamil Nadu alone was responsible for a time loss of 0.82 million man-days (i.e., 24.25 per cent), followed by Haryana, West Bengal, Kerala, Andhra Pradesh and Karnataka with 0.38, 0.37, 0.33, 0.28 and 0.26 million man-days respectively of the total time loss. Amongst the various industry divisions, 'manufacturing' had registered a time-loss of 1.55 million man-days (i.e., 45.65 per cent of the total time-loss).

As a simple rule of economics, the average cost of production goes on increasing during any industrial dispute leading to work-stoppage due to fixed expenses that continue to be incurred though the variable costs (e.g., wages and cost of raw materials) are nil during the stoppage. It also results in a fall in sales, leading to a fall in profits. Stoppage of production not only reduces the profit-making capacity of the employer, but also affects delivery commitments. Idle machinery may get dysfunctional during the phase of work stoppage. The employer may also have to incur additional expenses on the safety and security of the factory premises during the period of unrest. Losses may be incurred due to destruction of property and physical intimidation if the dispute takes a violent turn. Economic costs of a dispute are escalated in case the dispute ends with a decision favouring the economic demands of the workers.

Apart from the immediate economic effects, industrial disputes may have non-economic implications like loss of goodwill of the employer and bitter labour relations. Psychological distress out of the dispute can also have a bearing on the employer's peace of mind. Incidences of disputes may mar the image of the establishment as a good employer to prospective job applicants.

The employer can resort to various methods in order to make good of the economic loss as a result of a dispute. The unsold stock of goods in the inventory can be sold during the dispute to meet prior business commitments. The employer can speed up production with additional facilities and overtime. Following the principles of economics, whereby excess demand for a commodity fetches a higher price, the commodity produced by the employer can be sold at a higher price once the dispute is resolved. In case the employer has multiple plants, production facilities can be shifted to the other plant(s) which are out of the ambit of the dispute. The employer can simply conduct a cost-benefit analysis in such a case. As Sinha, Sinha and Shekhar (2006) point out, if the employer ascertains that the costs of agreeing to the terms of the agitated union are less than the anticipated costs of the dispute, the employer would avert the strike or alternately face the strike. However, the analysis may come out to be incorrect and the dispute may turn to be in favour of the workers, thus imposing additional expenses on the employer.

Effects on Other Stakeholders and Economy

The effects of industrial disputes are not restricted only to the two parties involved in such dispute, i.e., workers and employers; disputes have their impact on others as well, like the consumers of the commodity, suppliers to the establishment which is facing the dispute, and the economy as a whole. The direct effects of a strike on the affected firm may be only one component of the total impact resulting from the action; the existence of indirect or "spillover" effects can have important implications for the economic performance of competing firms as well (McDonald and Bloch, 1999). Customers of the affected commodity also face inconveniences due to limited supply of the commodity in the market. The more essential the commodity the greater would be the inconvenience. Strikes and lock-outs in public utility services create greater inconvenience to the public at large. As long as the dispute continues and production is halted, the business of the suppliers to the affected firm would also suffer. Prolonged industrial disputes also lead to wastage of national resources and thus have an adverse effect on national productivity and national income. Overall there is an air of negativity and bitterness in the industrial relations of the country.

Exhibit 7.6 Nationwide Bank Strike: Crippling Trade and Industry

Public sector bank employees had embarked on a two days' countrywide strike on August 22 and 23 2012, in opposition to the proposed reforms in the Banking Regulation Act, that would ease mergers and allow more private capital, including foreign investment in the banking sector. The strike was called by all major unions, including the All India Bank Employees' Association and the All India Bank Officers' Association under the banner of the United Forum of Bank Unions (UFBU). Traders and industrialists raised their protests against the strike that was scheduled on a Wednesday and Thursday, Monday already being a gazetted holiday.

The UFBU declared the strike to be successful on the very first day, with all public and private sector banks and even rural banks closing their shutters in opposition of the reforms. Though ATMs remained operational, they were apprehended to run out of cash by the end of the second day of the strike.

(Adapted from: Banks down shutters, trade and industry suffer, The Telegraph, Ranchi, 23/8/2012.)

Summing up the discussion we may say that the issue of industrial peace has assumed vital importance to the Government. The effects of industrial disputes are a reminder that unless there is a proper equilibrium between the capabilities and demands of the employers and the legitimate expectations of the working class, not only these two parties to dispute but also the industry, the general public and the economy as a whole would have to bear all the consequences.

Summary

- Conflict is inherent in the interests of capital and labour as parties to the employment relationship. Industrial dispute refers to any disagreement between workers and employers on issues like wages, working conditions and other employment matters, between rival unions, or even between employers and employers.
- Factors behind organisational conflicts can be clubbed as: industry-related factors, organisation-related factors, individual-related factors, government-related factors, and miscellaneous factors.
- The traditional view on conflict has a negative, rigid and formalistic approach to conflict and as per the modern view, conflict is considered to be an unavoidable fact of organisational life and should be measured in terms of functionality.
- Conflict is somewhat general as a concept; when conflict acquires concrete and specific manifestations, it becomes an industrial dispute.
- Workers resort to various methods like strikes, *gherao,* go-slow and work-to-rule as a manifestation of their discontentment and conflict with the employer. A strike is a powerful weapon in the hands of workers to get their demands accepted by the management. Strikes can be classified on the basis of consent of union, techniques adopted, generic purpose, etc.
- A lock-out is the weapon in the hands of the employer to manifest an industrial dispute. It is the employer who initiates a lock-out. Neither strike nor lock-out can severe the employer-employee relation in an organisation.
- Whatever is the form of manifestation of disputes, both strikes and lock-outs have far-reaching impacts not only on the workers but also on the employers, the consumers of the products of the affected industry, the suppliers to the establishment(s), and the economy as a whole.

- Unless there is a proper equilibrium between the capabilities and demands of the employers and the legitimate expectations of the working class, not only these two parties to dispute but also the industry, the general public and the economy as a whole would have to bear all the resultant adversities.

Key Concepts

Industrial conflict	Go-slow	Boycott
Work-to-rule	Picketing	Lock-out
Gherao	Strike	*Bandh*
Industrial dispute	Sympathetic strike	Sick-in strike

Biliography

Chhabra, T. N. and Suri, R. K. *Dynamics of Industrial Relations*, New Delhi: Pentagon Press; 2007.

Coser, L.A. *Continuities in the Study of Social Conflict*, New York: Free Press; 1967.

Das, K.S.L.and Gupta, D. *Industrial Conflict and Collective Labour Relations: A Case of Toyota Kirloskar India* (2001-2006). *International Journal of Engineering, Business and Enterprise Applications*, 2013, Vol. 3 No. 2, pp. 121-125.

Deutsch, M. *The Resolution of Conflict*, New Haven: Yale University Press; 1973.

Korpi, Walter, and Shalev, Michael. "Strikes, Industrial Relations and Class Conflict in Capitalist Societies", *The British Journal of Sociology*, June 1979,Vol. 30, No. 2, pp. 164-187.

Mamoria, C. B., Mamoria, S., and Gankar, S. V. *Dynamics of Industrial Relations,* New Delhi: Himalaya Publishing House; 2008.

McDonald, J. T. and Bloch, H. "The Spillover Effects of Industrial Action on Firm Profitability", *Review of Industrial Organization*, Sep. 1999, Vol. 15, Issue 2, pp. 183-200.

Rahim, M.A. "A Measure of Styles of Handling Interpersonal Conflict", *Academy of Management Journal*, 1983,Vol. 2, pp. 368–376.

Rahim, M.A. "Toward a Theory of Managing Organizational Conflict", *The International Journal of Conflict Management*, 2002, Vol. 13, No. 3, pp. 206-235.

Ratnam, C. S. V. *Industrial Relations*, New Delhi: Oxford University Press India; 2006.

Reports of the National Commission on Labour, Ministry of Labour & Employment and Rehabilitation, Government of India, 1969.

Report of the National Commission on Labour (2002, 1991-1967), New Delhi, Academic Foundation, 2003.

Reynecke, L. *The Relation between Personality Dimensions and Styles to Handle Interpersonal Conflict*, Unpublished Masters Dissertation, 1997.

Sinha, P. R. N., Sinha, I. B. and Shekhar, S. P. *Industrial Relations, Trade Unions, and Labour Legislation*, New Delhi; Pearson Education; 2006.

Slabbert, A. D. "Conflict Management Styles in Traditional Organisations", *The Social Science Journal*, 2004,Vol. 41 No. 1, pp. 83-92.

Srivastava, Suresh C. Strikes and Lock-outs in India: Law and Policy, *Central India Law Quarterly*, 1990; *http://indiankanoon.org/doc/608849/.*

Statistics on Industrial Disputes, Closures, Retrenchments and Lay-offs in India during the Year 2010, Labour Bureau, Ministry of Labour and Employment, Government of India.

Thomas, K.W., Conflict and Conflict Management: Reflections and Update, *Journal of Organisational Behaviour*, 1992, Vol. 13, pp. 265-275.

Willmot, W.W. and Hocker, J. L. *Interpersonal Conflict*, New York; McGraw- Hill; 2001.

Review Questions

Objective Type Questions

I. State True or False

(i) General strikes are similar to political strikes.
(ii) The traditional view of conflicts is proposed by human relations theorists.
(iii) Workers involved in a legal strike can get strike wage even if the strike is unjustified.
(iv) Terms of employment can be categorised as an individual-related reason of conflicts.
(v) A quickie is for shorter duration than a sit-down.

Answers: (i) True, (ii) False, (iii) False, (iv) False, (v) True

II. Fill in the Blanks

(i) Work-stoppages which involve less than ____ workers are not included in records compiled by the Labour Bureau.
(ii) A ______ is persuasive in nature, but negative in approach.
(iii) Encirclement in ____ involves forcible possession of the industrial establishment and ouster of the real owner.
(iv) Modern view proposes conflicts to be measured in terms of ____.
(v) In ___ strikes no pressure is applied against the primary employer.

Answers: (i) ten, (ii) boycott, (iii) depth, (iv) functionality, (v) secondary

Discussion Questions

1. How is *gherao* different from *bandh*? Discuss the consequences and legality of both as per legislation.
2. Explain picketing and boycott as methods of direct action adopted by workers. How are these methods dissimilar to each other?
3. Discuss the different approaches to viewing organisational conflict.
4. What are the various techniques of strike that workers can adopt in case they cannot functionally call a strike? Why such methods are considered immoral by employers?
5. What are the most common reasons of conflicts at work? Read the exhibit on strike in Maruti Suzuki and attribute appropriate reasons to the strike.
6. Industrial disputes do not occur in vacuum. Elaborate on the statement in light of the various effects of disputes.
7. Discuss the various types of strikes on the basis of generic purposes.
8. What are the circumstances under which a dispute between an individual worker and an employer can be considered as an industrial dispute?

9. "A lock-out is the antithesis of strike." Discuss.
10. Distinguish between:
    (a) Sit-in and Sick-in strikes
    (b) Sympathetic and Jurisdictional strikes
    (c) Work-to-rule and Go-slow

Air India: Grounded by Strikes

The national carrier of India, Air India (AI) is reeling under one problem or the other. Steeped in losses and thriving on taxpayers' heard-earned money, AI pilots struck work yet again on 7th May 2012, over demands for better career progression. The airlines management took a tough stand by sacking 101 pilots, including 10 office bearers of the Indian Pilots' Guild (IPG), the 450-member association of erstwhile AI pilots which was also derecognised. This marked the sixth strike in the company since 2009 and the fourth by its pilots in less than a year. The IPG reacted with the allegation that the management had created a 'hostile environment' by sacking the striking pilots and also derecognizing the Guild. The management took a hard stand with the opinion that the pilots have been in complete disobedience of the court's orders for the last two months and they need to call off the strike first before talking to the management regarding their demands. The 58 days' protracted strike by Air India pilots was finally called off in early July 2012 after the Delhi High Court asked them to join duty within 48 hours and advised the airline management to sympathetically consider their grievances, including the aspect of reinstatement of those pilots whose services were terminated as a consequence of their strike.

Last May when pilots had struck work by calling in sick, the national carrier had lost around ₹200 crores. The airline management had initially given pilots time till 6.00 pm to return to work; it eventually decided to act sooner and sent a team of doctors to check on the claims of the 'sick' pilots. It soon became apparent that no one needed a medical report on the pilots to know that 'sick leave' was just an excuse to be on strike. With around 300 pilots having reported sick, the Government reacted by sacking 10 of the striking pilots. It also derecognised the IPG, and sealed its offices. It was decided not to talk to the sacked pilots. On 9th May the Delhi High Court declared the strike illegal. The initial repercussions of the pilots calling in sick affected three international flights; however the airline was reported to have managed the situation by operating all the international flights in the afternoon of the particular day the pilots had reported sick. Flights on long-haul routes are operated by the agitating pilots who were demanding first class travel in routes that cost the airline the heaviest.

Pilots of AI, the highest paid employees of the organisation, are reportedly the biggest trouble-mongers for the management. An AI captain earns somewhere around ₹6-12 lakhs a month. Pilots get to stay in five-star hotels on outstation duty and spend up to 3 nights for every flight they operate. Travel allowances of pilots are provided by the company.

The national carrier is plagued by several problems including poor management, excess manpower, apathetic attitude of its employees, few routes to fly, governmental red-tapism and bureaucracy, and last, but not the least, the 'infamous' and ill-conceived merger of AI and Indian Airlines. The Government is perturbed by the inconvenience faced by the passengers. The latest strike leading to cancellation of AI Express flights has jeopardised the career of several hundred poor workers migrating to the Gulf for job opportunities. The agitation of the pilots has affected operations of seven prime international destinations in North America and Europe. It has led to a daily loss to the tune of ₹10-15 crores in addition to the existing operating losses of ₹21 crores. Overall the AI has incurred a record loss of ₹7,853 crores in 2011-2012. Its outstanding loans and dues amount to more than ₹70,000 crores, with no option left with the Government than clearing a ₹30,000 crores helpline from taxpayers' money in order to keep the airline alive.

(Adapted from: Srivastava T., Flight disruptions on global routes a blessing in disguise for AI? Hindustan Times, Lucknow, 14/5/2012; Air India pilots end strike after 58 days, The Times of India, New Delhi 4/7/2012; Baweja, H., Sacked AI pilots may not be taken back as govt. talks tough, Hindustan Times, Lucknow, 13/5/2012; Srivastava T., Time for Govt. to Let the Maharaja Go? Hindustan Times, Lucknow, 12/5/2012.)

Review Questions

1. Do you think that it was rational on the part of the pilots to have reported sick? Was the airline justified in taking action against the striking pilots? On what grounds would you defend your answer?
2. What are the effects of the strikes called by the pilots of AI?
3. Looking at the condition of the airline, what suggestion would you give to drag AI out of troubled waters?

Settlement of Industrial Disputes

Desired Knowledge Competencies

- To discuss various ways of settlement of industrial disputes.
- To describe different statutory and non-statutory measures of dispute settlement.
- To develop an understanding of the processes involved in conciliation machinery, reference of disputes to adjudication machinery, etc.

INTRODUCTION

We have already discussed industrial disputes, the underlying causes of disputes and their all-pervasive impact on workers, employers, consumers, suppliers and the economy in Chapter 7. A dispute is not an end in itself; every conflict or dispute must be followed by its settlement, leading to cooperation, thus completing a full cycle. The effects of industrial disputes necessitate striking a proper balance between the capabilities and demands of employers on the one hand and the legitimate expectations of workers on the other, to ensure cordial industrial relations and lasting industrial peace. Settlement of disputes thus assumes paramount importance in the domain of industrial relations. Both employers and workers should strive to settle any discontentment or rift in their mutual relation with the help of the preventive machinery. Whenever the preventive machinery fails, the dispute settlement machinery should be brought into operation by the government to settle disputes. Overall, such machinery should be fair and independent for the peaceful settlement of industrial disputes to ensure the establishment and maintenance of good industrial relations. In this chapter we would elaborate on prevention and settlement of disputes and the machinery involved therein, within the realm of labour legislations in India.

PREVENTION AND SETTLEMENT OF DISPUTES

The simplest way to settle any dispute between an employer and workers is by mutual discussions; this process is termed as "bargaining". If such a bargaining process faces obstacles then the parties involved may ask for the intervention of a third party; the settlement process in such a case is known as bargaining with conciliation. However, it is not necessary that the dispute gets settled at this stage.

In case it is continued, the parties would have two possible options. They may either resort to coercive methods to arrive at a settlement, or may refer the dispute to a third party for a process known as 'arbitration'. We have exhaustively covered strikes and lock-outs as coercive methods of settling industrial disputes in Chapter 7. The focus of this chapter is on the ways to prevent and settle disputes beyond such coercive methods.

There are several perspectives of looking at prevention and settlement of industrial disputes. We have mentioned about preventive and settlement machineries in the previous section. Understanding the implications of industrial disputes and to protect the interests of the working class, the management of industrial establishments and the society, the Government has designed certain mechanisms (statutory and non-statutory) to prevent the occurrence of disputes and ensure their settlement. The statutory machinery comprises the following: Works Committee, conciliation, Court of Inquiry at the central and State-levels, and adjudication authorities consisting of Labour Courts, Industrial Tribunals and National Tribunals. With the sharp growth in the number of laws and litigations, the legal system is under great pressure. In order to reduce this already heavy pressure on courts efforts need to be made to resolve disputes by resorting to Alternative Dispute Resolution (ADR) methods, before they reach the court (Medha, n.d.).

Spotlight

Arbitration, conciliation and mediation are the most popular tools of Alternative Dispute Resolution.

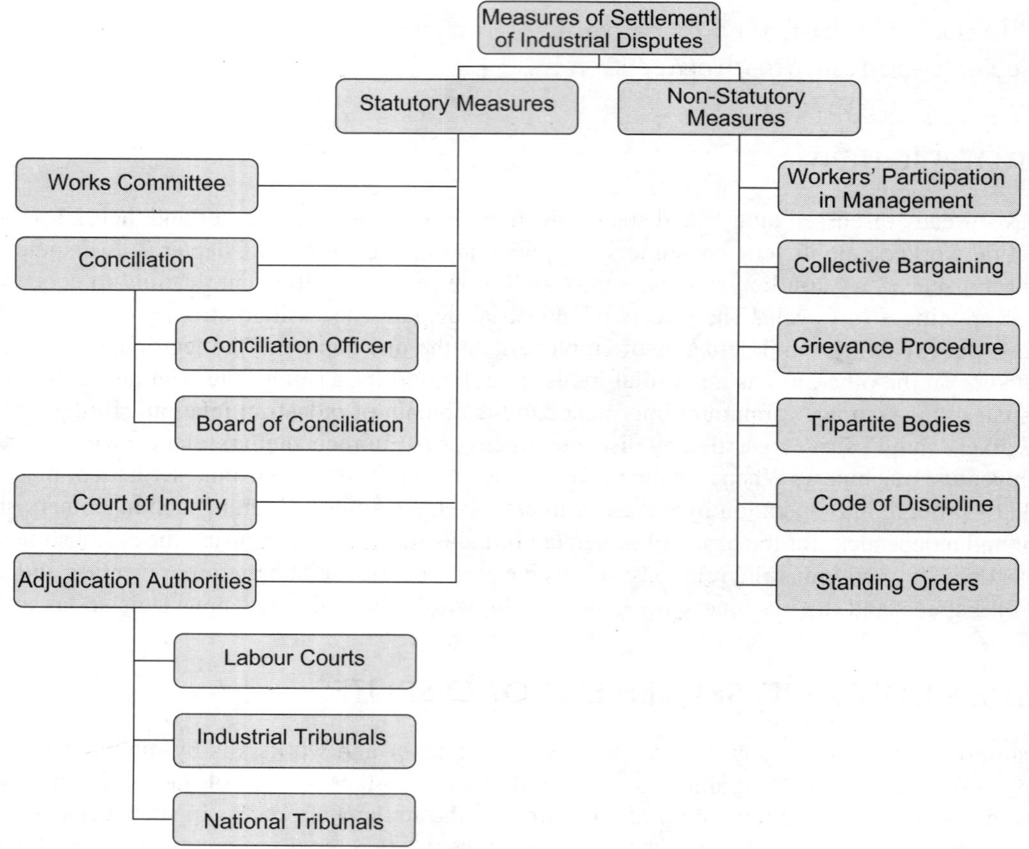

Figure 8.1 *Measures of Settlement of Industrial Disputes*

Arbitration, conciliation and mediation are the most popular tools of Alternative Dispute Resolution. However, the ADR is considered to be in an experimental phase in India. Hence is the necessity of non-statutory measures for the prevention of industrial disputes internally. These measures consist of: Workers' Participation in Management (WPM), collective bargaining, grievance procedure, tripartite bodies, Code of Discipline and Standing Orders. Tripartite bodies include the Indian Labour Conference (ILC) and Standing Labour Committee (SLC) operating at national-level; Wage Boards and Industrial Committees functioning at industry-level; and State Labour Advisory Boards at State-level.

We can also develop an insight into dispute settlement from the point of view of the stages involved in the process of settlement, i.e., settlement with State-intervention and without State-intervention. We have explored this perspective in a subsequent section. Figure 8.1 depicts the various statutory and non-statutory measures of settling industrial disputes, to be explained in the very next section.

I. Statutory Measures of Settlement of Industrial Disputes (or Settlement Machinery)

Various statutory measures to settle industrial disputes given in the Industrial Disputes Act, 1947 have been explained here. The sections mentioned at appropriate places imply those given in the Act.

(i) Works Committee [Section 3] A Works Committee is bipartite in composition. The Statement of Objects and Reasons appended with the Industrial Disputes Bill, 1946 refers to Works Committee as an institution for the prevention and settlement of industrial disputes. The duties of such committees were specified to include removal of causes of friction between the employer and workmen in the day-to-day working of an establishment and to promote measures for securing amity and good relations between them. It was also mentioned in the Statement that industrial peace will be the most enduring where it is founded on voluntary settlement, and that Works Committees would render recourse to the remaining machinery provided for in the Bill for the settlement of disputes as infrequent.

Section 3 of the Industrial Disputes Act, 1947 mandates any industrial establishment employing 100 or more workmen to constitute a Works Committee consisting of representatives of employers and workmen engaged in the establishment. Further, the number of representatives of workmen in the Committee shall not be less than the number of representatives of the employer. The workers' representatives shall be chosen in the prescribed manner from among the workmen engaged in the establishment and in consultation with their trade union, if any. It shall be the duty of the Works Committee to promote measures for securing and preserving amity and good relations between the employer and workmen and, to that end, to comment upon matters of their common interest or concern and endeavour to compose any material difference of opinion in respect of such matters. These bipartite committees are empowered to settle differences between workers and their employers and thus they act as a safety valve in settling disputes. We shall be talking briefly about bipartite committees in the section on dispute settlement with the intervention of the State. Both Central and State Governments have framed relevant rules under the Industrial Disputes Act, 1947 concerning the size of Works Committee, selection of representatives of workers, terms of office, etc.

Spotlight

Section 3 of the Industrial Disputes Act, 1947 mandates any industrial establishment employing 100 or more workmen to constitute a Works Committee.

However, let us specify here that we have included Works Committees under statutory measures of dispute settlement, as the establishment of such committees is a legal binding on organisations. At the same time, Works Committees are also considered as an integral component of Workers' Participation in Management. Hence we have mentioned these committees under non-statutory measures of dispute settlement as well.

(ii) Conciliation The dictionary meaning of the term 'conciliation' is "bringing of opposing parties or individuals into harmony". As one of the most important methods of dispute settlement, conciliation refers to the process of reconciling the views of parties to a dispute and bringing them to an agreement. The first step in conciliation is the selection of a qualified conciliator, who is a neutral third party. In the next step, a decision is taken as to who will attend the conciliation and the cost to be incurred in the process. The parties are thereafter encouraged to explain their case and share their feelings. The process involves discussions among the parties in the presence of the conciliator, with the objective of exploring equitable resolutions, thus paving the way for a mutually acceptable settlement. The role of the conciliator is to simply listen to the parties and identify the issues without being judgmental. Thus the conciliator does not decide anything on behalf of either of the parties, but essentially provides a supportive role in finding a viable solution. The conciliator facilitates negotiations between the disputing parties and helps them in understanding both their conflicts and interests. A brainstorming session follows and possible solutions are explored. At the final stage when the parties reach a consensus, a written agreement is drawn up. The process of conciliation is not binding on the parties till they sign this agreement, which has the effect of an arbitration award.

> **Spotlight**
> A conciliator facilitates negotiations between disputing parties and helps them understand their conflicts and interests to arrive at a mutually acceptable agreement.

Conciliation Machinery The conciliation machinery, as provided under the Industrial Disputes Act, 1947, is analysed here briefly. Section 4 provides for the appointment of Conciliation Officers, to whom the industrial disputes shall be referred for conciliation. As per provisions of Section 11, a Conciliation Officer enjoys the powers of a Civil Court; he examines all facts relevant to the disputed matter and then gives his judgment. He is charged with the duty of holding conciliatory proceedings for the purpose of bringing about a fair and amicable settlement of any industrial dispute without delay, as given in Section 12. On the failure to arrive at a settlement, the Conciliation Officer shall send a full report to the appropriate Government.

> **Spotlight**
> Conciliation Officer enjoys the powers of a Civil Court.

The Act also empowers the Government to appoint a Board of Conciliation for promoting the settlement of disputes [Section 5(1)] where the Conciliation Officer fails to do so within 14 days. The Board of Conciliation is a tripartite ad hoc body consisting of a Chairman and two to four other members. The mode and procedure of the functioning of the Board are similar to those of the Conciliation Officer. As per Section 10(3), where the dispute is referred to the Board, the appropriate Government may prohibit the continuance of any strike or lock-out in connection with such dispute which may be in existence on the date of reference.

> **Spotlight**
> The Board of Conciliation is a tripartite ad hoc body consisting of a Chairman and 2-4 other members nominated by the parties to the dispute.

Section 13 of the Act provides that when a dispute has been referred to the Board of Conciliation, the Board may take suitable steps to induce the parties to come to a fair and amicable settlement. If a settlement is arrived at, the Board is required to send a report and a memorandum of the settlement signed by the parties to the appropriate Government. If no such settlement is arrived at, the Board is required to send a full report to the appropriate Government, along with its recommendations for the determination of the dispute. It is required to submit its report within two months of the date of the reference of the dispute, or within a shorter period, as determined by the appropriate Government.

Section 19 of the Industrial Disputes Act, 1947 lays that settlement comes into operation on the date agreed upon by the parties to the dispute and in case no date is agreed upon, the date on which the memorandum of settlement is signed by the parties to the dispute. A settlement is binding for such period as is agreed upon for a period of six months from the date which the memorandum of settlement is signed by the parties to the dispute. According to Section 18(2), a settlement arrived at in the course of conciliation proceedings shall be binding on the following:

(a) all parties to the industrial dispute,
(b) all other parties summoned to appear in the proceedings as parties to the dispute,
(c) the employer, his heirs and successors of the establishment to which the dispute relates, and
(d) all workmen who were employed in the establishment or part of the establishment, to which the dispute relates, on the date of the dispute and all persons who subsequently become employed in that establishment or part thereof.

As per Section 20(2), a conciliation proceeding shall be deemed to have concluded in the following circumstances:

(a) in case a settlement is arrived at, when a memorandum of settlement is signed by the parties to the dispute,
(b) in case no settlement is arrived at, when the report of the Conciliation Officer is received by the appropriate Government or when the report of the Board is published under Section 17, or
(c) when a reference is made to a Court, Labour Court, Tribunal or National Tribunal under Section 10 during the pendency of conciliation proceedings.

(iii) Court of Inquiry [Section 6] In case the conciliation proceedings fail to settle an industrial dispute, a Court of Inquiry is appointed by the appropriate Government, as provided in Section 6 of the Industrial Disputes Act, 1947.

According to Section 6(2), a Court of Inquiry may consist of one or more independent persons as the appropriate Government may appoint; where it consists of two or more members, one of them shall be appointed as the Chairman. Sub-section 3 empowers the Court having the prescribed quorum to act even if the Chairman or a member is absent; however, the Court shall not act if the services of the Chairman have ceased to be available and till a new Chairman has been appointed. Section 11(5) empowers a Court of Inquiry, if it so thinks fit, to appoint one or more persons having special knowledge of the matter under consideration as assessor(s) to advise it in the proceeding before it. Under Section 14 the Court shall inquire into the matters referred to it and report thereon to the appropriate Government within six months from the date of commencement of inquiry.

(iv) Adjudication The ultimate legal remedy for the settlement of an unresolved dispute is marked with the reference of such a dispute to adjudication by the appropriate Government. Adjudication may be described as the process which involves intervention by a third party appointed by the appropriate Government, with or without the consent of the parties to the dispute, for the purpose of settling such a dispute. If both parties to the dispute agree to refer the dispute for adjudication at their own accord, then such reference of dispute to adjudication is considered voluntary; however it is compulsory when reference is made to adjudication without the consent of either or both the parties.

Spotlight

Adjudication involves intervention by a third party appointed by the appropriate Government, with or without the consent of the parties to the dispute, for settling the dispute.

Adjudication Machinery The Industrial Disputes Act, 1947 empowers the appropriate Government to provide a three-tier adjudication machinery with the following constituents: Labour Courts, Industrial Tribunals and National Tribunals. Let us talk about each of these constituent members of the machinery in details now.

(a) Labour Courts Labour Courts as a component of the adjudication machinery apart from Industrial Tribunals came into existence under the Industrial Disputes (Amendment and Miscellaneous Provisions) Act, 1956, by which the original Section 7 was substituted by a new one. The present Section 7 empowers the appropriate Government to constitute one or more Labour Courts for the adjudication of industrial disputes relating to any of the following matters (as enlisted in the Second Schedule of the Act) and for performing such other function as may be assigned to them under the Act:

1. The propriety or legality of an order passed by an employer under standing orders;
2. The application and interpretation of standing orders;
3. Discharge or dismissal of workmen including re-instatement of, or grant of relief to, workmen wrongfully dismissed;
4. Withdrawal of any customary concession or privilege;
5. Illegality or otherwise of a strike or lock-out; and
6. All matters other than those specified in the Third Schedule.

According to Section 7(2), a Labour Court shall consist of only one person who shall be appointed by the appropriate Government. Sub-section 3 of Section 7 provides that no person shall be appointed as the presiding officer of a Labour Court, unless:

1. he is, or has been, a judge of a High Court; or
2. he has, for a period not less than three years, been a District Judge or an Additional District Judge; or
3. he has held any judicial office in India for not less than seven years; or
4. he has been the presiding officer of a Labour Court constituted under any Provincial Act for not less than five years.

As the Court mentions in *Ramkrishan Ramnath Bidi Factory vs. Labour Court, Nagpur* [(1963) ILLJ 417 Bom], the Labour Court is essentially an authority for the avowed purpose of adjudication of industrial disputes, and would be governed by all the principles of industrial adjudication. *(Adapted from: www.indiankanoon.org/doc/751360/ accessed on 2/1/2014.)*

We shall be reviewing the powers and duties of Labour Court in Chapter 15, under the Industrial Disputes Act, 1947.

(b) Industrial Tribunals Industrial Tribunals were created for the first time by the Industrial Disputes Act, 1947. Section 7A of the Act empowers the appropriate Government to constitute one or more Industrial Tribunals for the adjudication of industrial disputes relating to any matter, whether specified in the Second Schedule or the Third Schedule and for performing such other functions as may be assigned to them under the Act. Similar to a Labour Court, a Tribunal shall consist of only one person to be appointed by the appropriate Government. Further, a person shall not be qualified for appointment as the presiding officer of a Tribunal unless he is, or has been, a Judge of a High Court, or he has, for a period of not less than three years, been a District Judge or an Additional District Judge. It is provided by Section 7A(4) that the appropriate Government may appoint two persons as assessors to advise the Tribunal in the proceedings before it.

In *The Bharat Bank Ltd., Delhi vs. The Employees of the Bharat Bank Ltd., Delhi and the Bharat Bank Employees' Union Delhi* (AIR 1950 SC 188), the Supreme Court had considered the question as to whether an Industrial Tribunal constituted under the Industrial Disputes Act, 1947 was a Court for the purpose of Article 136 of the Constitution. It was held that though the Tribunal has all the trappings of a Court, but its award was not appealable to the Apex Court. *(Adapted from: www.indiankanoon.org/doc/653417/ accessed on 3/1/2014.)*

The Industrial Tribunal is a judicial body that is responsible for the adjudication of industrial disputes relating to any matter whether specified in the Second Schedule or the Third Schedule of the Industrial Disputes Act, 1947. Matters related to the Second Schedule have already been covered under Labour Courts. Those related to the Third Schedule are as follows:

1. Wages, including the period and mode of payment;
2. Compensatory and other allowances;
3. Hours of work and rest intervals;
4. Leave with wages and holidays;
5. Bonus, profit sharing, provident fund and gratuity;
6. Shift working otherwise than in accordance with standing orders;
7. Classification by grades;
8. Rules of discipline;
9. Rationalisation;
10. Retrenchment of workmen and closure of establishment; and
11. Any other matter that may be prescribed.

Spotlight

Industrial Tribunal is responsible for the adjudication of industrial disputes relating to any matter specified in the Second or Third Schedule of the Industrial Disputes Act, 1947.

Industrial Tribunals, as given in Section 11, shall have the same powers vested in a Civil Court when trying a suit, in matters like: enforcing the attendance of any person and examining him on oath; compelling the production of documents and material objects; issuing commissions for the examination of witnesses, etc. A Tribunal shall hold its proceedings expeditiously and shall submit its award to the appropriate Government within the specified period (Section 15).

(c) National Tribunals As per Section 7B of the Industrial Disputes Act, 1947, the Central Government may constitute one or more National Tribunals for the adjudication of industrial disputes which involve questions of national importance or are of such a nature that industrial establishments situated in more than one State are likely to be interested in, or are affected by them. In other words, these tribunals are meant for those disputes which, as is suggestive of the name, involve issues of national importance or issues which are likely to affect the industrial establishments of more than one State. It is thus evident that the span of jurisdiction of National Tribunals is wider than those of the other two components of the adjudication machinery discussed earlier.

Sub-section 2 of Section 7B provides that a National Tribunal shall consist of only one person to be appointed by the Central Government; sub-section 3 lays that a person shall not be qualified for appointment as the presiding officer of a National Tribunal unless he is, or has been, a Judge of a High Court. Similar to Industrial Tribunals, the Central Government may, if it so thinks fit, appoint two persons as assessors to advise the National Tribunal in the proceeding before it. According to the provisions of Section 7C, presiding officers of National Tribunals should be independent persons, below the age of 65 years. We shall be taking into account the powers and duties of National Tribunals in Chapter 15.

Spotlight

The procedures and powers of different authorities under Section 11 of the Industrial Disputes Act, 1947 are equally applicable to Conciliation Officers, Board of Conciliation, Court of Inquiry, Labour Court and Tribunals.

It may be noted here that the procedures and powers of different authorities laid down under Section 11 of the Act are equally applicable in the case of Conciliation Officers, Board of Conciliation, Court of Inquiry, Labour Court and Tribunals.

Exhibit 8.1 Central Government Industrial Tribunal-cum-Labour Courts

The Central Government Industrial Tribunal-cum-Labour Courts (CGIT-cum-LCs) are set up as per the provisions of the Industrial Disputes Act, 1947 for adjudication of industrial disputes arising in the Central Sphere. The objective of setting up CGIT-cum-LCs is maintaining peace and harmony in the industrial sector. Due to increasing awareness about their rights and about labour laws among the workers, there is a gradual increase in the number of cases being filed under the Industrial Disputes Act, 1947 before these courts. Restructuring of workforce with the application of latest technology in the industries has also resulted in retrenchment, declaration of surplus, etc., which has further led to an increase in workers' grievances. The CGIT-cum-LCs aim at quick and timely disposal of industrial disputes through adjudication, such that industrial growth does not suffer on account of any widespread industrial unrest.

There are 22 CGIT-cum-LCs set up in various States, out of which 10 are under Non-Plan and 12 under Plan Scheme. The CGIT-cum-LC No.1, Mumbai and CGIT-cum-LC, Kolkata also function as National Tribunals. These courts are headed by presiding officers who are selected from amongst serving or retired High Court Judges or District or (serving or retired) Additional District Judges.

(Adapted from: www.labour.gov.in/content/division/central-govt-industrial-tribunal.php accessed on 2/1/2014.)

Reference of Disputes to the Adjudication Machinery [Section 10] Now that we have explained the three-tier structure of the adjudication machinery, let us quickly describe the process of reference of disputes to the adjudication machinery. The appropriate Government may refer an unresolved dispute to a Labour Court or Industrial Tribunal or National Tribunal for adjudication. We have already specified that any matter which is important for the industry as a whole and is listed in the Second or Third Schedule may be referred for adjudication to a Labour Court or Industrial Tribunal. However, as per Section 10(1)(d), where a dispute is pertaining to a matter specified in the Third Schedule, and is not likely to affect more than one hundred workmen, the appropriate Government may refer it to a Labour Court. In case a dispute involves any question of national importance or is of such nature that industrial establishments situated in more than one State are likely to be interested in or be affected by the dispute, then as per Section 10(1A), the Central Government may refer such dispute or any relevant matter that is related to the dispute to the National Tribunal. Further, sub-section (2) of this section provides that where the parties to an industrial dispute apply in the prescribed manner, whether jointly or separately, for a reference of the dispute to a Board, Labour Court, Tribunal or National Tribunal, the appropriate Government, if satisfied that the persons applying represent the majority of each party, shall make the reference accordingly.

II. Non-Statutory Measures of Settlement of Disputes (or Preventive Machinery)

(i) Workers' Participation in Management Workers' Participation in Management is a mechanism by which the workers of an establishment are allowed to participate actively in the decision-making process of the establishment and to have a say in its management. Hailed as a powerful behavioural tool, WPM promotes a sense of belongingness in workers and checks any kind of exploitation of workers by the owners or top management. Workers involve themselves in the management of an organisation by way of information sharing, joint consultation and suggestion schemes. Thus WPM is essentially democracy at work, and is instrumental in reducing industrial unrest and in ensuring higher productivity, increased commitment and overall increased growth of the economy.

The various forms of WPM prevalent in India are: *Works Committee, Joint Management Council, Shop Council, Joint Council* and *Unit Council*. Works Committees are intended to promote measures for securing and preserving cordial relations between employer and workmen and to opine on matters of common interest or concern. These committees comprise equal number of representatives of employers and employees in the industry concerned. *Joint Management Councils* are established in any establishment employing 500 or more workers and have equal representation of workers and management. These councils are charged with the general duty of promoting and assisting in the management of the undertaking in a more efficient, orderly and economical manner, ensuring amiable relations between the employer and workers and building understanding and trust between them. These councils were established for the first time in 1950; further, since 1975 the two-tier participation called *Shop Councils* at shop-level and *Joint Councils* were introduced. *Shop Councils* have been incorporated in big industrial establishments employing more than 500 workers, with each council having equal representation of workers and management. The functions of these councils are to achieve increased production, productivity and overall efficiency of the shop or department, eliminate wastage, utilise capacity and manpower of the establishment to the optimum level, and to support the management in achieving the monthly or yearly production targets. *Joint Councils* are prescribed for every industrial unit employing 500 or more workers. These councils are responsible for the settlement of matters unresolved by *Unit Councils*. Each organisation shall decide on the number of councils to be set up for the services it has, in consultation with the recognised union(s). A *Unit Council* is required to be set up in each unit of an organisation or service employing 100 or more persons. Such a council would have equal number of representatives of workers and management as its members. The number of *Unit Councils* and the departments to be attached to each council of the establishment is to be decided by the employer in consultation with the recognised union(s). The decisions of *Unit Councils* are to be taken on the basis of consensus and not by a process of voting.

Spotlight
The various forms of WPM in India are: *Works Committee, Joint Management Council, Shop Council, Joint Council* and *Unit Council*.

For detailed explanation of Workers' Participation in Management and its various aspects, refer to Chapter 11.

(ii) Collective Bargaining Collective bargaining is the term used to describe a situation in which "the essential conditions of employment are determined by a bargaining process undertaken by representatives of a group of workers on the one hand and of one or more employers on the other" (Yoder, 1959). It includes negotiation, administration and enforcement of written contracts between workers and their employers and the process of resolving labour-management conflicts.

Reflection
Collective bargaining is a voluntary and formal bipartite process.

We have explained collective bargaining and its various facets in Chapter 5.

(iii) Grievance Procedure The First National Commission on Labour (1969) in India visualised grievances as being those "arising out of complaints affecting one or more individual workers in respect of their conditions of work and not disputes over matters of general applicability to all". An organisation establishes a grievance procedure to give avenue to an employee to file his/her dissatisfaction (Mante-Meija and Enid, 1991). The Model Grievance Procedure was drawn up in the

16th Session of the Indian Labour Conference in 1958, in pursuance of the Code of Discipline. This procedure has successive time-bound steps, with access to the next stage, if satisfaction is not obtained in the previous stage. The Commission has also prescribed the following three conditions for any formal or informal system of grievance handling: satisfaction of the individual worker, reasonable exercise of authority by the manager and participation by unions.

Reflection
Code of Discipline laid down that management and unions will establish, upon a mutually agreed upon basis, a grievance procedure that would ensure speedy and full investigation of a grievance, leading to settlement.

Successful handling of grievances helps an organisation to contain matters of discontentment and thus prevent industrial disputes as a cumulative effect. We have elaborated on grievance and grievance handling in Chapter 6.

(iv) Tripartite Bodies The term "tripartite" refers to representatives of three bodies. Industrial peace being an area of concern, the Government of India, after Independence, had laid stress on the need for consultation between the representatives of labour, management and the Government in tripartite and bipartite forums. With its tripartite structure, the International Labour Organisation (ILO) has been a proponent of strong tripartite cooperation, in which the "social partners" play an important role in shaping government policy on a wide range of issues (Trebilcock, n.d.). In response to the constant pressure of the ILO to implement tripartite structures in the area of industrial relations, the Government of India constituted various tripartite bodies like the Indian Labour Conference, the Standing Labour Committee and Industrial Committees to deliberate on various issues relating to labour and management that would have formidable impact on the country's labour policies and legislations. Tripartism and its evolution in India have been covered extensively in Chapter 10.

The principal aim of the tripartite consultative machinery is "to bring the parties together for mutual settlement of differences in a spirit of cooperation and goodwill" (Chhabra and Suri, 2007, p. 178). The tripartite Indian Labour Conference and its tripartite Standing Labour Committee are the premier policy advisory bodies in the field of industrial relations at the national-level, constituted to suggest ways to prevent industrial disputes. The Government had adopted the annual tripartite conference, initially known as the Tripartite National Labour Conference, held for the first time in the year 1942, on the model of the International Labour Conference. It was subsequently renamed as Indian Labour Conference since 1944. The underlying philosophy was to attain active and willing cooperation of capital and labour post-World War II through State-consultation with these two partners of industrial production during such annual conferences. As an apex national-level tripartite body, the ILC is the testing ground of tripartite consultations. The primary functions of the ILC are: to promote consistency in labour legislations; to streamline the procedure for settlement of industrial disputes; and to discuss matters of national importance between employers and workers. The ILC advises the Government on any matter referred to it for advice, considering suggestions made by the States and representatives of the organisations of workers and employers (Chhabra and Suri, 2007). The 45th Session of the Indian Labour Conference was held on 17th and 18th May 2013.

Spotlight
The Indian Labour Conference and Standing Labour Committee are premier tripartite bodies at the national-level.

Reflection
Presently there are 44 national-level tripartite committees in India.

EXHIBIT 8.2 45TH SESSION OF THE INDIAN LABOUR CONFERENCE

The Indian Labour Conference occupies a predominant place in the functioning of the Ministry of Labour & Employment, as a part of its commitment to tripartism. It is a unique forum which brings together the voice of the social partners in designing government policies and programmes.

The 45th Session of the Indian Labour Conference was held at New Delhi on 17th and 18th May 2013, at a crucial time when the world economy was still struggling to sail through the ripple effects of the global economic slowdown. The purpose of this conference was to take certain decisive and crucial steps for the upliftment of the working class. In the meeting of Standing Labour Committee held in January 2013 before the Conference, the following four agenda items for the 45th Session were finalised: service conditions, wages and social security for various categories of workers employed in different Central and State Government schemes; social security with special reference to assured pension with indexation for all workers including self-employed workers; labour law for micro and small enterprises; and measures to improve employment and employability. The selection of the agenda items is a fair indicator of the main concerns of the various stakeholders associated with the subject of labour. Increasing 'Quality Employment' and 'Extending Outreach of Social Security Net' are the two broad areas receiving continuous attention of the tripartite constituents.

(Adapted from: www.pib.nic.in/newsite/erelease.aspx?relid=96048 accessed on 2/1/2014.)

Spotlight
A meeting of the SLC takes place as a prelude to the ILC.

The main function of the Standing Labour Committee is to consider such issues as may be referred to it by the Plenary Conference or the Central Government and to advise on such matters, taking into account the suggestions made by the Government, workers and employers. A meeting of SLC takes place as a prelude to the Indian Labour Conference to review the Action Taken Report of the conclusions of the preceding Labour Conference and also to decide upon the agenda items of the forthcoming Labour Conference.

Both ILC and SLC consist of representatives of the Central Government, governments of States and Union Territories and representatives of employers and workers' organisations nominated by the Central Government in consultation with all-India organisations of workers and employers. These two bodies work with minimum procedural rules in order to facilitate free and fuller discussions among the members (Report of the National Commission on Labour, 1969).

Spotlight
Awards given by Wage Boards are non-statutory in nature.

Reflection
The first Wage Board in India was set up for the cotton textile industry.

In the 1950s and 1960s the Government had constituted various Wage Boards in appreciation of the problems which arise in the arena of wage fixation. Operating at industry-level, these Wage Boards are tripartite in character, in which representatives of workers, employers and independent members participate and finalise the recommendations. Eventually it was felt that the Government need not set the wage rates in respect of employees in different sectors, and that wage-fixation can be left to the concerned industry; however wages are still decided by the Wage Boards for journalists and non-journalist newspaper and news-agency employees. Since the awards given by Wage Boards are non-statutory in nature, recommendations made by these Boards are not enforceable under the law. The importance of the non-statutory Wage Boards has hence declined over a period of time and no non-statutory Wage Board was set up after 1966, with the exception of sugar industry, in which the last such Board was constituted in 1985 (*www.labour.nic.in*).

Exhibit 8.3 Wage Boards in the Newspaper Industry

The Working Journalists and other Newspaper Employees (Conditions of Service) and Miscellaneous Provisions Act, 1955 (hereinafter referred to as 'the Act') provides for regulation of conditions of service of working journalists and non-journalist newspaper employees. Sections 9 and 13C of the Act provide for constitution of two Wage Boards for fixing or revising the rates of wages in respect of working journalists and non-journalist newspaper employees respectively. The Central Government shall, as and when necessary, constitute Wage Boards, which shall consist of the following members:

- Three persons representing employers in relation to newspaper establishments;
- Three persons representing working journalists for Wage Board under Section 9 and three persons representing non-journalist newspaper employees for Wage Board under Section 13C.
- Four independent persons, one of whom shall be a person who is, or has been a judge of High Court or the Supreme Court, and who shall be appointed by the Government as the Chairman thereof.

Since 1955, the Government of India has constituted six Wage Boards for newspaper employees. In 2007 the Government constituted two Wage Boards (referred to as Majithia Wage Boards), one for working journalists and other for non-journalist newspaper employees, as the sixth Wage Board as per the provisions of the Act. The Majithia Wage Boards submitted their final report on 31st December 2010.

(Adapted from: www.labour.nic.in/content/division/wage-board.php accessed on 3/1/2014.)

The concept of Industrial Committees as tripartite bodies with equal representation from employers and workers sides had emerged in the Indian Labour Conference of 1944. The very first Industrial Committee was formed in the year 1948 in the plantation industry, which is considered to be one of the industries having the highest labour absorption in the country. This was followed by other industries like coal mining, jute, minerals other than coal, leather, cotton textiles, etc. The basic objective behind setting up of these committees was to deal with problems specific to the industries in which they were set up.

State Labour Advisory Boards, as is indicated by the name itself, are tripartite bodies set up in nearly all States, with equal representation of workers and employers to advise the State Governments on all matters pertaining to labour. A typical example is the State Level Child Labour Advisory Board established in various States to look into issues related to child labour.

(v) Code of Discipline The Code of Discipline is a set of self-imposed and mutually agreed upon voluntary principles of discipline and cordial relations between management and workers of both public and private sector enterprises. In the 15th Indian Labour Conference held in July 1957, certain general principles to be followed by both labour and management for their mutual interest as also for the common interest of the society and the nation were laid down through tripartite consultation. The Code of Discipline was finally approved by the 16th Indian Labour Conference held in the next year. It is a code of conduct both for workers and management, and it provides for the voluntary and mutual settlement of disputes through mutual negotiations, voluntary arbitrations and conciliations, without the interference of an outside agency. The First National Commission on Labour (1969) had observed that the Code had worked in its initial stages with a certain degree of success and then fell into disuse. The Commission was also of the opinion that with the removal of the important provisions relating to recognition of unions, setting up of grievance machinery and unfair labour practices from the Code and incorporating them in the proposed legislation, the Code would have no useful function to perform.

Reflection
There are 3 sets of principles in the Code of Discipline: the first set of principles is for both management and unions; the second set is for management; and the third one is for union.

(vi) Standing Orders The Standing Orders of any establishment regulate the conditions of employment of a worker from the stage of his entry to the establishment to that of exit from the establishment. The Industrial Employment (Standing Orders) Act, 1946 was passed so that employers of industrial establishments define with sufficient precision the conditions of employment under them and to also make the said conditions known to workmen employed in such establishments. Standing Orders define the conditions of employment in an organisation and matters related to discharge, misconduct, etc. and act as a code of conduct for workers during their tenure with their employer. Thus Standing Orders form a regulatory pattern for industrial relations.

Spotlight
Standing Orders form a regulatory pattern for industrial relations.

STAGES IN THE SETTLEMENT OF INDUSTRIAL DISPUTES

As mentioned earlier, we can also view the process of settlement of disputes in terms of the stages involved in lines with Sinha, Sinha and Shekhar (2006). For this purpose, we may split the process into two parts: settlement with State-intervention and without State-intervention. However, most of the stages as per this classification have previously been reviewed under statutory and non-statutory measures of settling disputes. Settlement without State-intervention includes collective bargaining and voluntary arbitration. Settlement with State-intervention includes: compulsory setting up of bipartite committees; compulsory collective bargaining; initiation of compulsory investigation; compulsory conciliation and mediation; and compulsory arbitration and adjudication. This section features explanation of all these measures.

I. Settlement without State Intervention

(i) Collective Bargaining We have already touched upon collective bargaining as a non-statutory measure in a previous section.

(ii) Voluntary Arbitration Let us first understand the concept of arbitration here. Generally speaking, arbitration refers to the process by which the parties to any dispute submit their differences to the judgment of an impartial person (or group) appointed by mutual consent or by any statutory provision. An arbitration system authorises a third party to decide how a dispute should be resolved (Padhi, 2012). Arbitration process may be either binding or non-binding. Binding arbitration produces a third party decision that the parties to the dispute must follow, even though they may disagree with the decision. Non-binding arbitration, on the other hand, produces a third party decision that the parties concerned may not accept.

Spotlight
In arbitration the parties to a dispute submit their differences to the judgment of an impartial person (or group) appointed by mutual consent or by any statutory provision.

Arbitration finds application in the settlement of conflicts since quite a long time in India. Mahatma Gandhi had propagated the practice of voluntary arbitration in the textile industry in Ahmedabad. In fact, the Textile Labour Association Ahmedabad provides for voluntary arbitration. In 1957 provisions for voluntary arbitration were inserted in Section 10A of the Industrial Disputes Act, 1947. Arbitration was incorporated in the Code of Discipline in 1958. In the Indian Labour Conference in 1962 it was decided that arbitration would be preferred after conciliation method fails, except in cases where the employer prefers adjudication.

Spotlight

In voluntary arbitration the parties willingly and by mutual consent refer their dispute to a third party.

In voluntary arbitration the parties willingly and by mutual consent refer their dispute to a third party, known as the arbitrator, under such circumstances in which both parties disagree on their own argument and they feel that any bargaining process is ineffectual and coercive methods would not yield positive outcomes. An arbitrator may be a single person or a panel. As per Section 10A of the Industrial Disputes Act, 1947, there must be an arbitration agreement signed by the parties thereto. Employers and workmen who are not parties to the arbitration agreement but are concerned in the dispute, shall be given an opportunity of presenting their case before the arbitrator(s). The arbitrator(s) shall investigate the dispute and submit to the appropriate Government the arbitration award signed by the arbitrator(s). However, the award given by the third party is not binding on the parties to dispute, whereby the significance of voluntary arbitration is diluted. Nevertheless, it is usually a less expensive and speedier method of settling a dispute than resolving it in court.

The First National Commission on Labour (1969) had foreseen that with the growth of collective bargaining and the general acceptance of recognition of representative unions and the improved attitude of management, there would be wider acceptance of voluntary arbitration. It had even advised employers to encourage voluntary arbitration and wean away reluctant employers from recourse to third party intervention.

II. Settlement with State Intervention

Role of State Before we get into the details of the process of settlement of industrial disputes, let us understand the role of State in dispute settlement. Industrial peace being a serious issue, the Government makes continuous efforts to ensure peaceful and harmonious industrial relations. The Industrial Disputes Act, 1947 is reflective of this very concern of the State. In *Narendra Kumar Sen vs. All India Industrial Disputes (Labour Appellate) Tribunal* [(1953) 55 Bom. LR 125], the Court has observed that the Act was passed with the following objectives: to bring about industrial peace in the country; to avoid conflicts between employers and labour; to prevent strikes and lock-outs; and to ensure that production does not suffer by reason of constant and continuous labour troubles.

Reflection

Existence of the State in industrial relations has been proposed by Dunlop.

Industrial relations are not restricted to the concern of labour and management alone; the State is an equally important stakeholder. Justification of the need for intervention of the State in industrial disputes is guided by the question as to whether the dispute is of such magnitude as to disturb industrial peace and hamper production. Thus the concern of the State in matters relating to labour, especially settlement of industrial disputes, is a product of its obligations to protect the interests of working class, while at the same time boosting the manufacturers, thus fostering economic growth.

In *Workmen of Dimakuchi Tea Estate vs. The Management of Dimakuchi Tea Estate* [(1958) AIR 353], the Court is of the opinion that if the Government considers that the workmen have no such interest as would lead them to disturb industrial peace by strike, or otherwise if the dispute was not ended, it might not, in its discretion, refer the dispute for adjudication by a tribunal. It must be left free to decide as it thinks best in the interest of the country. *(Adapted from: www.indiankanoon.org/doc/1198151/ accessed on 1/1/2014.)*

The following are the ways in which State intervention is possible in settlement of industrial disputes:

(i) Compulsory setting up of bipartite committees
(ii) Compulsory collective bargaining
(iii) Initiation of compulsory investigation
(iv) Provision for conciliation and mediation
(v) Compulsory arbitration and adjudication

Let us describe each of these measures now.

(i) Compulsory Setting up of Bipartite Committees As is evident from the name itself, a bipartite committee is made up of two parties: representatives of workers and their employer at the plant-level or at industry-level. The bipartite machinery to settle industrial disputes in India was established as early as in 1920; a few joint committees were set up by the Government of India in Indian Railways and Government Printing Presses. TISCO in Jamshedpur was the pioneer in private sector to set up joint committees. Chapter 10 provides a comprehensive coverage of bipartism in Indian context.

(ii) Compulsory Collective Bargaining To refuse to bargain collectively in good faith by a recognised trade union and an employer has been included in the list of unfair labour practices in the Fifth Schedule of the Industrial Disputes Act, 1947. Collective bargaining has been explained earlier in this chapter. However, in certain cases, the State may intervene and mandate workers and employers to enter into a formal collective bargaining process through their representatives; the underlying objective is to ensure that the parties settle their disputes through mutual discussions and negotiations before they resort to coercive methods.

> **Spotlight**
> The State may encourage and even force workers and employers to enter into a formal collective bargaining process.

Exhibit 8.4 Bipartite Committees in Coal India Ltd.

In Coal India Ltd. (CIL) and its subsidiaries there is a well established forum of representation of the management and trade unions for interaction and redressal of issues related to employment, safety, grievances and welfare-related matters. The following joint bipartite committees are operating at different levels in the Maharatna: Joint Consultative Committee, Welfare Committee, Safety Committee, Industrial Relation Meetings (structural meetings with unions) and Joint Bipartite Committee for the Coal Industry (JBCCI) Apex Level. Of these, JBCCI, constituted by the Government of India, consists of 5 Central Trade Unions and the management of Coal Companies i.e., CIL and its subsidiary companies, Singareni Collieries Co. Ltd., Tata Iron and Steel Company and Indian Iron and Steel Company. The wage structure and other conditions of service, including fringe benefits, welfare measures, etc. of the non-executive cadre employees in the coal industry are settled by bipartite wage negotiations by JBCCI.

(Adapted from: www. coal.gov.in/0203CHAPTER%20X.pdf accessed on 3/1/2014.)

(iii) Initiation of Compulsory Investigation Court of Inquiry is a statutory machinery responsible for investigation into matters of industrial dispute. We have detailed about Courts of Inquiry, their structure and functioning under statutory measures of dispute settlement.

(iv) Provision for Conciliation and Mediation 'Conciliation' and 'mediation' are two terms that are often used interchangeably. ILO (1983) has defined conciliation as "the practice by which the services of a neutral third party are used in a dispute as a means of helping the disputing parties to reduce the extent of their differences and to arrive at an amicable settlement or agreed solution. It is a process of orderly or rational discussion under the guidance of the conciliator." Brown and Marriott (2011) view mediation as a facilitative process in which the disputing parties engage the assistance of an impartial third party, the mediator, who helps them to try to arrive at an agreed resolution of their dispute. According to these authors, the mediator has no authority to make any decisions that are binding on them, but uses certain procedures, techniques and skills to help them to negotiate an agreed resolution of their dispute without adjudication. The authority of the mediator vests on the approval of the parties that he should facilitate their negotiations.

> **Spotlight**
> Conciliation is a process of orderly or rational discussion under the guidance of the conciliator.

The Parliament of India has made a clear distinction between conciliation and mediation by way of two distinct statutes. Section 30(1) of the Arbitration and Conciliation Act, 1996 permits the arbitral tribunal to "use mediation, conciliation or other procedures" for the purpose of reaching settlement; this makes it evident that the two terms are used with different connotations. As per the various provisions in the Act, the 'conciliator', apart from assisting the parties to reach a settlement, is also permitted to make "proposals for a settlement" and "formulate the terms of a possible settlement" or "reformulate the terms" (Rao, n.d.). The Civil Procedure Code (Amendment) Act, 1999 also speaks of 'conciliation' and 'mediation' as different concepts. Several authors opine that the role of the 'conciliator' in India is pro-active and interventionist, while the role of the 'mediator' is restricted to that of a 'facilitator'. Nevertheless, both these terms refer to some kind of third-party intervention in voluntary settlement of disputes.

(v) Compulsory Arbitration and Adjudication We have talked about voluntary arbitration under settlement of disputes without intervention of State, whereby the parties willingly and by mutual consent refer their dispute to a third party, known as the arbitrator. Compulsory arbitration, on the other hand, is a non-binding, adversarial process in which parties to the dispute have to accept the arbitration without any willingness on their part. In case one of the parties feels aggrieved by any act of the other, it may apply to the appropriate Government to refer the dispute to adjudication machinery. The State may decide to adopt compulsory arbitration to resolve a dispute under circumstances in which it thinks that industrial production should not be compromised due to work-stoppage as a consequence of a strike or lock-out. Thus, under compulsory arbitration, the parties are forced to arbitration by the State when they fail to arrive at a settlement by a voluntary method. In this process one or more arbitrators hear the arguments of the parties to the dispute and issue a non-binding judgment on the merits after an expedited hearing. Compulsory arbitration leaves no scope for strikes and lock-outs; it takes away a party's right to have any dispute with the other party.

> **Spotlight**
> In compulsory arbitration the parties to the dispute have to accept the arbitration without any willingness on their part.

RECOMMENDATIONS OF THE SECOND NATIONAL COMMISSION ON LABOUR

Following are the recommendations of the Second National Commission on Labour (2002) on matters pertaining to settlement of industrial disputes:

- It is necessary to provide a minimum level of protection to managerial and other employer against unfair dismissals or removals through adjudication by Labour Court or Labour Relations Commission or arbitration.
- Presently Central legislations relating to labour relations are the Industrial Disputes Act, 1947, the Trade Unions Act, 1926 and the Industrial Employment (Standing Orders) Act, 1946. In addition, there is the Sales Promotion Employees Act, 1976 and some other Acts for particular trades or employments, besides State-level enactments The Commission recommends that provisions of all these laws may be judicially constituted into a single law called the Labour Management Relations or the Law on Labour Management Relations.
- In case of socially essential services like water supply, medical service, sanitation, electricity and transport, when a dispute is not settled through mutual negotiations, there may be a strike ballot. If the ballot shows that 51 per cent of workers are in favour of a strike, it should be taken that a strike has taken place, and the dispute must forthwith be referred to compulsory arbitration.
- A system of Labour Courts, Lok Adalats and Labour Relations Commissions has been envisaged as the integrated adjudicatory system in labour matters.
- Labour Courts and Industrial Tribunals should be merged, and this system will deal not only with matters arising out of employment relations but also trade disputes in matters such as wages, social security, safety and health, welfare and working conditions and so on.
- Industrial disputes that are not settled in conciliation should go for either voluntary arbitration or by arbitrators maintained by the Labour Relations Commission or adjudication. In the case of essential services the dispute should go for compulsory arbitration; in other cases, it should go for adjudication. Arbitrators should be chosen from eminent persons in industry, conciliators, trade unionists and labour judiciary.
- Labour Courts must be given powers to issue decrees or initiate contempt proceedings for non-implementation or non-compliance of awards.
- A Central Labour Relations Commission (LRC) should be set up for establishments in Central-Sphere, and a State Labour Relations Commission should be set up for those in the State-Sphere. Above both the Central and State Labour Relations Commissions, there will be the National Labour Relations Commission to hear appeals against the decisions of the two other Commissions. The National LRC, Central LRC and the State LRCs will be autonomous and independent.
- To make conciliation effective, it is necessary to improve the status, competence and calibre of conciliation officers through proper recruitment, training and placement. A Labour and Judicial Service can be formed.
- Voluntary resolution of disputes should be encouraged over legalistic approach of settlement of disputes through adjudication. Labour administration should encourage better human resource management practices.
- There should be a legislative framework for voluntary dispute settlement. A basic prerequisite is to place a system of recognition of negotiating agency on the statute. The responsibility of conducting verification of trade union membership for recognition of trade unions should be vested in the Central and State LRCs.

- The Works Committee required to be constituted under Section 3 of the Industrial Disputes Act, 1947 should be substituted by an Industrial Relations Committee to promote in-house dispute settlement.
- The Indian Labour Conference should be an effective forum for review, consultation and formulation or evolution of perspective and policies; it has to be as representative as possible. Some means must be found to include representatives from the unorganised sector and from central organisations that are not affiliated to central trade union federations.
- In lines with the proposals in the Draft Indian Labour Code for the strengthening of the Indian Labour Conference, the ILC can be used as a sounding board for proposals of legislations. Suggested functions of the ILC would include: review of labour situation; consideration of Conventions and Recommendations of the ILO for adoption; sounding board for legislative proposals, etc.
- The ILC should set up Tripartite Standing Committees to consider and review problems, legislations and implementation into main areas.
- Labour disputes between a foreign invested enterprise and its employees may be settled through consultations between the concerned parties, failing which, the parties may apply to the labour dispute mediation committee of the enterprise. Further, if mediation fails, the parties may apply to the labour dispute arbitration committee. Either party that is not satisfied with the adjudication of arbitration may bring the case to the people's court of the district or country where the enterprise is located within 15 days upon the reception of the adjudication.

Summary

- Settlement of disputes is of paramount importance in the domain of industrial relations. Both employers and workers should strive to settle any discontentment or rift in their mutual relation with the help of the preventive machinery, failing which the Government should intervene with the dispute settlement machinery.
- There are several perspectives of looking at prevention and settlement of industrial disputes: statutory and non-statutory measures of settlement; preventive and settlement machinery; and settlement with or without State intervention.
- The statutory machinery comprises the following: Works Committee, Conciliation, Court of Inquiry at the central and State levels, and adjudication authorities consisting of Labour Courts, Industrial Tribunals and National Tribunals.
- The non-statutory machinery is used for the prevention of industrial disputes, and consists of: workers' participation in management, collective bargaining, grievance procedure, tripartite bodies, Code of Discipline and Standing Orders.
- Tripartite bodies include the Indian Labour Conference and Standing Labour Committee operating at national-level; Wage Boards and Industrial Committees functioning at industry-level; and State Labour Advisory Boards at State-level.
- The process of settlement of disputes can be split into two parts: settlement with State-intervention and without State-intervention. Settlement without State-intervention includes collective bargaining and voluntary arbitration.
- Settlement with State-intervention includes: compulsory setting up of bipartite committees; compulsory collective bargaining; initiation of compulsory investigation; provision for conciliation and mediation; and compulsory arbitration and adjudication.
- Recommendations of the Second National Commission on Labour (2002) include: amalgamation of all Central legislations related to labour relations into a single law; establishment of legislative framework for voluntary settlement of disputes, etc.

Key Concepts

Settlement
Arbitration
Adjudication
Conciliation
Indian Labour Conference
Tripartite bodies
Bipartite bodies
Labour Court
Conciliation officer
Tribunal
Court of Inquiry
Mediation

Bibliography

Brown, H. and Marriott, A. *ADR Principles and Practice*, London; Sweet and Maxwell; 2011.

Chhabra, T. N. and Suri, R. K. . *Dynamics of Industrial Relations*, New Delhi: Pentagon Press; 2007.

Government of India, Consultative Machinery in the Labour Field (Bulletin), p. 7.

Mante-Meija, Enid, A. "Designing an Instrument for Resolving Individual Conflict in 'Total' Institution", *Knowledge and Policy*, 1991,Vol. 4, No. 3, pp. 58-73.

Medha N. (n.d.) Alternative Dispute Resolution in India: A Study on Concepts, Techniques, Provisions Problems in Implementation and Solutions. Retrieved from: www.fdrindia.org/publications/AlternativeDisputeResolution PR Pdf accessed on 1/1/2014.

Padhi, P. K. *Labour and Industrial Laws*, New Delhi; PHI Learning Pvt. Ltd.; 2012.

Report of the National Commission on Labour, 1969, Ministry of Labour & Employment and Rehabilitation Government of India.

Reports of National Commission on Labour (2002, 1991-1967), New Delhi: Academic Foundation; 2003.

Sinha, P. R. N., Sinha, I. B. and Shekhar, S. P. *Industrial Relations, Trade Unions, and Labour Legislation*, New Delhi; Pearson Education; 2006.

Trebilcock, A. (n.d.) Labour Relations and Human Resources Management: An Overview. Retrieved from:www.ilocis.org/documents/chpt21e.htm on 3/1/2014.

www.labour.nic.in/content/division/majithia-wage-board.php on 3/1/2014.

ILO: Conciliation Services: Structures, Functions and Techniques Labour-Management Relations Series, No. 62, Geneva: ILO; 1983.

Yoder, D. *The Outlook in Industrial Relations*, University of Minnesota Minneapolis: Industrial Relations Center; 1959.

Rao (n.d.) Retrieved from http://lawcommissionofindia.nic.in/adr_conf/concepts%20med%20Rao%201.pdf on 3/1/2014.

http://labour.nic.in/content/division/wage-board.php on 2/1/2014.

Review Questions

Objective Type Questions

I. State True or False

(i) Awards given by Wage Boards are non-statutory in nature.
(ii) A unit council is set up in each unit of an organisation employing 500 or more persons.
(iii) The role of the conciliator is restricted to that of a facilitator.
(iv) The Tripartite National Labour Conference was renamed as Indian Labour Conference since 1944.

(v) A dispute may be referred to the Board of Conciliation if the Conciliation Officer fails to settle it within 14 days.

Answers: (i) True, (ii) False, (iii) False, (iv) True, (v) True

II. Fill in the Blanks

(i) The authority of the _____ is conferred on the approval of the parties to the dispute.
(ii) A _______ arbitration produces a third party decision that the parties to the dispute must follow.
(iii) The first Industrial Committee was formed in the ______ industry.
(iv) The Central Government may appoint ______ assessors to advise the National Tribunal in the proceeding before it.
(v) Labour Court may adjudicate on matters in the _______ Schedule of the Industrial Disputes Act, 1947.

Answers: (i) mediator, (ii) compulsory, (iii) plantation, (iv) two, (v) Second

Discussion Questions

1. Explain the mechanism of conciliation machinery and its role in settlement of industrial disputes.
2. Critically analyse the role of State in dispute settlement.
3. Explain the concepts of arbitration and voluntary arbitration. What are the strengths and weaknesses of voluntary arbitration?
4. Discuss the structure and span of operation of Industrial Tribunals. How are Industrial Tribunals different from National Tribunals?
5. What are the different tripartite bodies that are involved in settlement of industrial disputes? Explain the functions of each.
6. Elaborate on the recommendations on settlement industrial disputes made by the Second National Commission on Labour.
7. Differentiate between arbitration and adjudication. Which one, according to you, is a better measure to ensure lasting industrial peace?
8. Discuss the three-tier structure of the adjudication machinery for settlement of disputes.
9. Explain the measures of State-intervention in dispute settlement.
10. Distinguish between:
    (a) Conciliation and Mediation
    (b) Compulsory arbitration and Voluntary arbitration
    (c) Joint Management Council and Joint Council

Settlement of Industrial Disputes: the Situation in West Bengal

West Bengal has been one of the five States in India which have accounted for over 50 per cent of the total Indian workforce in the industrial and service sectors in 2006. The major industries in the State are leather, tea, jute, engineering and paper. There is substantial public sector presence in West Bengal and in more recent years an emerging joint sector as well.

Significantly, there is no law on collective bargaining or on union recognition at the all-India level and different States have framed their own laws. But enforcement is not easy, since employers are not homogeneous. The State Government also does not have a large enough body of inspectors to enforce legislative provisions. In the organised sector trade unions apply pressure on management to enforce legislative provisions. Bargaining takes place at various levels, that too only once in 3 to 4 years, although there is no national-level agreement on any issue. Since there is a significant number of industry-wide agreements in the State, there have to be mechanisms at the plant or establishment level through which industrial relations problems can be tackled. Wages, major allowances and productivity levels are determined at the industry-level, but smaller agreements on detailed issues may be signed from time to time at the plant-level. There would not be contradictions between these agreements, because the issues dealt with would be different. This is clearly demonstrated in the case of jute and steel industries. The industry-level agreement in the jute industry includes vague clauses on productivity and mentions merely that cooperation is required from unions. The company-level or unit-level agreements, on the other hand, have ample details on specific outputs, machines, operations and processes.

Wages are fixed in different ways in the organised and unorganised sectors. For the organised sector there are two methods. If we include all units registered under the Factories, Mines or Plantations Acts, then the organised sector is large. But in reality large establishments in the organised sector are those which implement the major legal requirements for employment and labour and employ 100 or more workers. Those employing below this number can be clubbed as smaller units in the organised sector but have characteristics very similar to that of the unorganised sector. The method of collective bargaining is used to fix wages in large-sized organisations and a mixture of unilateral (by the employer), collective negotiations and statutory methods is used for the smaller units, depending on the size of the workforce and the degree of unionisation.

Joint labour management bodies at the enterprise-level are as follows:

Works Committees: A Works Committee is a statutory body for all manufacturing units employing 100 or more workers with worker representatives elected on the basis of departmental constituencies and not nominated by unions. The main industries where this body still exists are jute and engineering, that too without holding regular elections. Very few other industries even constitute such bodies. In others, they may have existed at one time, but have fallen into disuse. Up to December 2006, the West Bengal Government had ordered 1,005 establishments to constitute Works Committees through elections; only 119 units were compliant. Even though this is a tool of industrial relations, there appears little urgency in this matter.

Industrial Relations Committees: These committees are formed voluntarily by enterprises, especially in large central public sector undertakings, to resolve day-to-day problems at the local level. They are not required by any statute and have been set up by management of various enterprises with trade union concurrence.

Joint decision-making bodies: These bodies exist in those enterprises, again mainly the public sector steel plants, where participative management has been formally introduced. This is also not required by any statute and can be looked upon as a strategy in industrial relations.

The total number of disputes raised in West Bengal for conciliation fell steadily from 3,103 in 1994 to 2,053 in 2002, and 1,852 in 2003. Lock-outs have however increased. Statistical data also indicate that even the percentage of disputes disposed off by the Labour Directorate is declining from a substantial 45 to 50 per cent between 1994 and 2001, to just 37 to 38 per cent in the post-2002 period. This declining tread does not mean that relations between management and unions have become very harmonious; instead it implies that both parties have perceived that it is better to resolve disputes amicably and jointly, so that employees do not lose wages and employers production. Such a trend of industrial disputes could also indicate reduced dependence on the State labour machinery. Unions too are in no position to agitate for workers' benefits since workers themselves prefer to get smaller benefits rather than face industrial closure. This has happened in the case of some strikes, for example in the jute industry, where workers have pressurised unions to call off strikes after a very short period.

The State Government refers to all government intervention in dispute settlement as tripartism. Industry-wide settlements in jute, tea and engineering are all tripartite. The main tripartite body operating in West Bengal is the State Labour Advisory Board which discusses issues that have defied solution in other forums and suggests possible methods for solution.

(Adapted from Sen, R. (2009). The Evolution of Industrial Relations in West Bengal, ILO Subregional Office for South Asia, New Delhi. Retrieved from www.ilo.org/wcmsp5/groups/public/@asia/@ro-bangkok/@sronew_delhi/documents/publication/wcms_123342.pdf on 1/1/2014.)

Review Questions

1. Sketch the statutory dispute settlement machinery in West Bengal on the basis of the case.
2. What do the figures on industrial disputes suggest about the effectiveness of the non-statutory measures of dispute settlement over the statutory ones?
3. Comment on collective bargaining prevalent in the State of West Bengal.

9

Labour Welfare

Desired Knowledge Competencies

- To describe the concept of labour welfare and trace its evolution in India.
- To discuss the theories of labour welfare.
- To outline the types of labour welfare measures.
- To explain the concept of workers' education and training.

INTRODUCTION

Labour welfare is an important aspect of industrial relations. Welfare activities in an industry encompass not only workers, but their families also, as well-being of a worker cannot be seen in isolation (Report of the Committee on Labour Welfare, 1969). The Royal Commission on Labour (1931) was of the view that, "the term welfare as applied to industrial workers is one which must be necessarily elastic, bearing a somewhat different interpretation in one country from another, according to the different social customs, the degree of industrialisation and the educational development of workers"(cited in Sharma, 2004, p. 298). Labour welfare is a broad term encompassing various benefits, amenities and facilities provided by employers to workers and their families, over and above wages/salaries. It helps in improving safety, general well-being and efficiency of workers.

The concept of labour welfare finds its origin in the Directive Principles of State Policy enshrined in the Constitution of India. Article 38 directs the State to secure a social order for the promotion of the welfare of people. Article 41 requires that within the limits of its economic capacity and development, the State shall make effective provisions for securing the right to work, to education, and to public assistance in case of unemployment, old age, sickness and disablement, and in other cases of undeserved want. Article 42 mandates that the State should make provision for securing just and humane conditions of work and for maternity relief. According to Article 43, the State shall endeavour to secure, by suitable legislation or economic organisation or in any other way, to all workers, agricultural, industrial or otherwise, work, a living wage, conditions of work ensuring a decent standard of life and full enjoyment of leisure and social and cultural opportunities. According to Article 47, the

State should regard the raising of the level of nutrition and the standard of living of its people, and improvement of public health, as among its primary duties.

Labour welfare refers to "Such facilities and amenities as adequate canteens, rest and recreation facilities, sanitary and medical facilities, arrangements for travel to and from and for accommodation of workers employed at a distance from their homes, and such other services, amenities and facilities including social security measures as contribute to conditions under which workers are employed" (Report of the Committee on Labour Welfare, 1969, p. 24). We may thus define labour welfare as the whole range of benefits, amenities and facilities, including social security, provided by employers to workers besides their wages/salaries, that helps in maintaining and improving their health, safety and quality of life.

Spotlight

Labour welfare refers to the whole range of benefits, amenities and facilities, including social security, provided by employers to workers besides their wages/salaries, that helps in maintaining and improving their health, safety and quality of life.

EVOLUTION OF THE CONCEPT OF LABOUR WELFARE

The concept of labour welfare, as we understand today, has developed over a period of time. The evolution of labour welfare in India may be broadly divided into 3 phases. This section provides a depiction of all these phases.

Phase I: 1850–1900

This was the phase when industrialisation was growing and labour was exploited by employers for increased profits by way of long working hours, poor working conditions, no job security and low wages. Some enactments were passed by the government during this phase, with the objective of improving the working and living conditions of workers. Though these had limited scope, but a beginning was nevertheless made. The Apprentices Act, 1850 aimed at helping poor children to learn trades and crafts; the Fatal Accidents Act, 1853 had the provision for giving compensation to families of workers who lost their lives; and the Merchant Shipping Act, 1859 had provisions for the health of seamen. Enactment of the Indian Factories Act, 1881 was a significant step towards labour welfare, though it was limited in scope and was applicable only to factories employing not less than 100 persons.

Phase II: 1900–1947

During this phase the efforts of expanding the scope of labour welfare gained some momentum. The Indian Factories Act passed in 1911 had a wider scope in terms of applicability, working hours for children and provisions for health and safety. The discontentment caused among workers due to conditions arising out of World War I (1914-1918), the Russian Revolution of 1917, and setting up of the International Labour Organisation (ILO) in 1919 gave impetus to welfare activities taken up by employers and the State. The Government of India passed the Indian Factories (Amendment) Act, 1922 with wider applicability; the amended Act contained provisions for limiting the working hours for both men and women, and other welfare provisions for women and children. The Workmen's (now Employees') Compensation Act, 1923 introduced provisions for compensation in case of injury at work, resulting in disablement or death. The Royal Commission on Labour (1931) had a considerable influence on welfare activities in the

Spotlight

The Royal Commission on Labour (1931) had a considerable influence on welfare activities in India.

country. With its recommendations, the Factories Act, 1934 came into force; this Act reduced the working hours for children and women and provided for crèches at workplace. It also recommended health insurance and maternity benefits. The Indian Dock Labourers Act was passed in 1934, providing for safety at working places on shore and of any regular approaches over a dock, wharf, quay or similar premises. The Labour Investigation Committee (also known as the Rege Committee) was appointed by the government in 1944 to investigate into labour welfare measures. In its report submitted in 1946, the Committee recommended extension of the scope of labour welfare to include measures like education, healthcare, relief in case of old age and death, etc.

After World War II, many welfare measures were introduced in enterprises. In 1942, welfare officers were appointed in the Labour Department by the government. Welfare activities were initiated for mica and coal mine workers and their families (Sharma, 1998) and a welfare fund was created for coal mine workers in 1944.

EXHIBIT 9.1 EARLY INITIATIVES IN LABOUR WELFARE IN INDIA

Tata Steel was the first to establish labour welfare practices in India, even before these were made statutory laws across the world. Tata Steel, even in its nascent years, brought in social scientists like Sidney and Beatrice Webb to work on welfare schemes. In fact, some of the initiatives introduced by the company were not only the first of their kind in India, but also in many Western countries at that time. Apart from building housing blocks for its employees, and offering civic amenities and infrastructure, the company introduced 8-hour working days as early as 1912; free medical aid was started in 1915; initiatives like leave with pay, Workers' Provident Fund Scheme and Workmen's Accident Compensation Scheme were introduced in 1920; maternity benefits were offered as early as in 1928. Profit sharing bonus was granted for the first time in the country by the company in 1934, and a scheme of retiring gratuity was introduced for the Tata employees in 1937.

(Adapted from: Chattopadhyay, S.S. (2008, Jun. 21-Jul. 04). Steel with soft core, Frontline, 25(13). Retrieved from www.frontline.in/static/html/fl2513/stories/20080704251310600.htm on 17/4/2014.)

Phase III: 1947 Onwards

After India attained Independence, industrialisation begun and employment level started increasing. The Government was concerned for improving the condition of workers. Many welfare legislations were enacted towards this end, including the Factories Act, 1948, the Plantations Labour Act, 1951, the Mines Act, 1952, the Contract Labour (Regulation and Abolition) Act, 1970, etc. Labour Welfare Funds were created for workers under legislations like the Coal Mines Labour Welfare Fund Act, 1947, the Iron Ore Mines Labour Welfare Cess Act, 1961 and the *Beedi* Workers Welfare Fund Act, 1976. Welfare provisions for workers in almost every industry were made in industry-specific legislations like the Merchant Shipping Act, 1958, the Motor Transport Workers Act, 1961 and the *Beedi* and Cigar Workers (Conditions of Employment) Act, 1966, etc. In addition to these legislations, many other welfare and social security legislations were enacted by the Central Government and various State Governments.

OBJECTIVES OF LABOUR WELFARE

Labour welfare activities are a reflection of the nature of industrial relations of a nation. The main objective of such activities is to improve the condition of workers, and thereby enhance productivity of an enterprise. Other objectives are to improve employee morale and preserve efficiency level of workers by providing a richer quality of life and improved standard of living to workers and their families. Welfare activities directly or indirectly aim at reducing absenteeism and labour turnover in industries. Welfare measures contribute to the maintenance of industrial peace (Mamoria and Mamoria, 1980) and enhance the image of an employer (Thomas, 1990); this induces many employers to embark on labour welfare activities.

Spotlight

Labour welfare activities may be guided by humanitarian, utilitarian or paternalistic approach.

There may be three approaches that underlie the welfare activities taken up by employers. These are discussed as follows:

- **Humanitarian approach:** This may viewed as a sense of social responsibility of employers towards workers and concern for providing such amenities as would help workers live a life with frugal level of comfort.
- **Utilitarian approach:** Under utilitarian approach expenditure on welfare amenities are seen as investment that would preserve employee efficiency for the benefit of an organisation.
- **Paternalistic approach:** The paternalistic approach propagates an employer as the guardian of workers, who undertakes welfare activities due to a sense of responsibility towards them and to protect them.

THEORIES OF LABOUR WELFARE

Several theories have been proposed to explain how and why labour welfare measures are undertaken. Some of the important theories are briefed here.

- **Police Theory:** This theory assumes that owners and managers of industrial undertakings have a lot of wealth and power, which they use for their own benefits. They overlook and neglect the welfare of workers, and even exploit workers for their own advantage. The State must enact legislations that would coerce employers to provide for workers' welfare in the form of minimum wages, healthcare, good working conditions, etc. The basis for taking up welfare activities is fear and compliance.
- **Philanthropic Theory:** Humanitarian by approach, this theory is based on the assumption that welfare measures are undertaken with the objective of providing benefits to workers for improving their condition. Many philanthropists believed that investment in labour welfare will be ultimately beneficial for industry.
- **Paternalistic or Trusteeship Theory:** This theory is paternalistic in approach and proposes that the owner of an industrial undertaking is the guardian or 'father' of all the workers. The employer owns the property and profits which he uses for the benefit of workers and the society as a whole. Due to lack of awareness, workers know little about their rights. Though not bound, the employer must take care of the interests of workers. Mahatma Gandhi strongly believed in the trusteeship theory.

Spotlight

The philanthropic theory assumes that welfare measures are undertaken with the objective of providing benefits to workers for improving their condition.

- **Placating Theory:** The placating theory believes that as workers are becoming more aware of their rights, they are adopting a militant attitude to pressurise employers for higher wages and improved working conditions. Given such situations, undertaking welfare measures can appease workers and peaceful industrial relations can be attained.

- **Public Relations Theory:** This theory proposes that welfare activities of an industrial undertaking not only help in improving relations between workers and employer, but also in enhancing public relations. When labour welfare measures of an undertaking are publicised, they create goodwill in the society. Sales and profits of such an establishment may go up. Thus it gives two-way benefits to employers: increased profits and better industrial relations. This theory may be said to be based on the utilitarian approach.
- **Functional Theory:** Utilitarian by approach, this theory rests on the assumption that welfare measures help to preserve the efficiency and productivity of workers. Also known as the efficiency theory, the functional theory propagates the essentiality of collaboration between union and management with the common objective of increasing production, as such a collaboration would benefit employers in getting higher profits and workers in earning higher wages.
- **Religious Theory:** This theory is based on the belief that doing good deeds is an investment. In this context, investing in labour welfare is a good deed that would reap fruits in future. Pain and problems are a result of sins done in the past. Providing benefits to workers in the form of canteens, health benefits, crèches, etc. can also help in atonement of sins.

TYPES OF LABOUR WELFARE

Welfare amenities provided to workers may be of several types, namely, voluntary, statutory and mutual. Certain facilities are taken up voluntarily by employers for the benefit of workers because of the feeling of humanitarianism, irrespective of statutory requirements. There are other facilities that are to be provided by employers because of statutory requirements. Some welfare measures are mutual in nature, in which both workers and employers contribute.

Statutory measures may be of two types (Sills, 1968):

- Measures which have to be provided irrespective of the size of the organisation or the number of people employed therein. These include washing, storing and drying of clothes, first-aid, drinking water, and latrines and urinals.
- Measures which are to be provided subject to employment of specified number of people, such as canteens, rest shelters, crèches and ambulance rooms.

> **Spotlight**
> Intra-mural facilities are provided within the premises of an establishment; extra-mural facilities are provided outside such premises.

Statutory measures may also be categorised as: *welfare legislations* that provide for general well-being and some degree of comfort, and *social security legislations* that are protective in nature.

Depending upon whether welfare amenities are provided within the premises of an establishment or outside, welfare measures may be of two types: *intra-mural* and *extra-mural*. Intra-mural facilities are those that are provided by the employer to the workers within the premises of an establishment, e.g., drinking water, canteen, rest room, crèche, etc. Extra-mural facilities are provided outside the premises of an establishment, e.g., housing, transport, etc.

Statutory Welfare Measures

The Government of India has laid down various labour enactments from time to time, many of which contain provisions for worker welfare. These measures have to be taken up by an employer as a legal obligation and any negligence in implementing these provisions results in penalty. Some of the important legislations include the Factories Act, 1948, the Industrial Disputes Act, 1947, the Payment of Bonus Act, 1965, the Plantations Labour Act, 1951, the Mines Act, 1952, the *Beedi* and Cigar Workers Act, 1966, the Contract Labour (Regulation and Abolition) Act, 1970, the Motor Transport Workers Act, 1961, the Merchant Shipping Act, 1958, the Dock Workers (Safety, Health and Welfare) Scheme, 1961 and the Inter-State Migrant Workmen (Regulation of Employment and Conditions of Service) Act, 1979. It may be mentioned here that ILO Recommendations have had a deep impact upon labour welfare enactments in India. Welfare provisions contained in some of the Acts are specified here.

Exhibit 9.2 Recommendation Concerning Welfare Facilities for Workers

The R102-Welfare Facilities Recommendation, 1956 (No. 102) adopted on 26th June 1956 by the General Conference of ILO, convened at Geneva by the Governing Body of the International Labour Office is as following:

Whereas it is desirable to define certain principles and establish certain standards concerning the following welfare facilities for workers:

(a) feeding facilities in or near the undertaking (canteen, buffet and trolley, mess room and other suitable rooms, mobile canteens, other facilities, use of facilities);
(b) rest facilities in or near the undertaking and recreation facilities excluding holiday facilities;
(c) transportation facilities to and from work where ordinary public transport is inadequate or impracticable.

The Conference also recommended that the provisions should be applied as fully and as rapidly as national conditions allow, by voluntary, governmental, or other appropriate action, and that each Member should report to the International Labour Office as requested by the Governing Body concerning the measures taken to give effect thereto.

(Adapted from: (www.ilo.org/dyn/normlex/en/f?p=NORMLEXPUB:12100:0::NO::P12100_ INSTRUMENT_ID: 312440 accessed on 17/4/2014.)

The Factories Act, 1948

This is a legislation dedicated to labour welfare and it contains extensive provisions for workers' health, safety and welfare. Chapter 14 discusses all such provisions in detail. Annexure I gives the number of canteens, shelters, rest rooms and welfare officers (which are statutory requirements under the Act) in factories in the year 2010.

The Mines Act, 1952

The issue of health and safety of mine workers is governed by the Mines Rules, 1955 (hereinafter referred to as 'Rules'), created under the jurisdiction of the Mines Act, 1952. Under the Act and the Rules, an employer has to provide the following facilities for the health and welfare of mine workers: adequate and suitable shelters for taking food and rest at every mine where 50 or more persons are employed (Section 62 of the Rules); canteens in mines employing 250 or more workers (Section 64 of the Rules); appointment of a welfare officer in mines employing 500 or more workers and where the number of workers in a mine exceeds 2,500, such welfare officer to be assisted by a suitably qualified additional welfare officer for every additional 2,000 persons or part thereof employed (Section 72 of the Rules); sufficient supply of cool and wholesome drinking water (Section 19 of the Act); sufficient number of latrines and urinals separately for males and females in every mine (Section 20 of the Act); and maintenance of first-aid boxes or cupboards in every mine and first-aid rooms in mines employing more than 150 workers (Section 21 of the Act).

The Plantations Labour Act, 1951

The welfare measures that are to be provided to plantation workers by employers are: clean and wholesome drinking water (Section 8); separate latrines and urinals for male and female workers (Section 9); medical facilities for workers as prescribed by the State Government (Section 10); one or more canteens in every plantation ordinarily employing 150 workers (Section 11); crèches in plantations employing 50 or more women workers (Section 12); recreational facilities for workers and their children (Section 13); educational facilities for children of workers employed in any plantation between the age of 6 and 12 exceeding 25 in number (Section 14); housing facilities for every worker and his/her family residing in the plantation (Section 15); workers to be provided with prescribed number and type of umbrellas, blankets, raincoats or other like amenities for protection from rain or cold (Section 17); and appointment of a welfare officer in plantations employing 300 or more workers (Section 18).

The Contract Labour (Regulation and Abolition) Act, 1970

A contractor is liable to provide the following amenities to contract labour: canteen, wherein contract labour numbering 100 or more is ordinarily employed (Section 16); rest room wherein contract labour is required to halt at night in connection with the working of the establishment (Section 17); arrangements for sufficient supply of wholesome drinking water, latrines and urinals, washing facilities (Section 18); and first-aid facilities (Section 19). In case of failure on the part of the contractor to provide these facilities, the principal employer is liable to provide the same.

The Merchant Shipping Act, 1958

Welfare provisions in the Act include: supply of sufficient provisions and drinking water of good quality (Section 168); maintenance of proper weights and measures on board (Section 171); supply of beddings, towels, medicines, medical stores, and provision of surgical and medical advice (Section 172); crew accommodation (Section 175); appointment of Seamen's Welfare Officer at such ports in or outside India as the Government may consider necessary (Section 13); setting up of an advisory board to be called the National Welfare Board for Seafarers for advising the Central Government on the measures to be taken for promoting the welfare of seamen (whether ashore or on board ship) generally, and in particular the establishment of hostels or boarding and lodging houses for seamen, the establishment of clubs, canteens, libraries and other like amenities for the benefit of seamen, the establishment of hospitals or the provision of medical treatment and of educational and other facilities for seamen (Section 218).

SOCIAL SECURITY

The concept of social security is based on the principles of human dignity and social justice (ILO, 1969). According to ILO (2005, p. XXI), "Social security is the protection that a society provides to individuals and households to ensure access to health care and to guarantee income security, particularly in cases of old age, unemployment, sickness, invalidity, work injury, maternity or loss of a breadwinner." Thus we may define social security as assurance provided by the State against various types of adverse situations to which individuals may be exposed in events like old age, sickness, financial distress, disablement, unemployment, maternity or death. Social security may be of two types: social insurance and social assistance. A social assistance scheme provides financial benefits to persons of small earnings as a right, which can sufficiently fulfill the minimum standard of need; its source of finance is taxation. ILO defines a social insurance scheme as one that provides benefit for persons of small earnings granted as a legal right in amounts which is the combined contributory effort of the insured person, the employer and the State (as cited in Mishra, 1999, p. 10). Social security measures are significant for a nation to achieve the goal of a welfare state and to maintain the efficiency of workers. ILO has been instrumental in setting standards of social security. The Social Security (Minimum Standards) Convention adopted in 1952 embodies universally accepted basic principles and common standards of social security.

Spotlight

Social insurance schemes provide benefits to persons of small earnings in the form of amounts contributed by the insured, his employer and the State.

Some of the important social security legislations in India are the Employees' Compensation Act, 1923, the Minimum Wages Act, 1948, the Employees' State Insurance Act, 1948, the Employees' Provident Fund and Miscellaneous Provisions Act, 1952, the Maternity Benefit Act, 1961 and the Payment of Gratuity Act, 1972. These Acts have been covered as separate chapters in this book.

Social Security for Unorganised Workers

As discussed in Chapter 2, the majority of the workforce in India consists of workers in the unorganised sector. They are involved in activities like agriculture, construction, mining, manufacturing and services. On account of lack of organisation and unionisation due to low literacy and awareness levels, these workers do not get adequate social security and welfare.

Reflection

Unorganised workers are engaged in the informal sector and do not have any social security.

Many of the unorganised workers, particularly agricultural labour, work under highly insecure conditions. There are no social security measures for these workers for maintaining basic living standards and risk coverage, especially in crisis situations such as unemployment, sickness or disablement. Neither there is any law to ensure suitable and safe working conditions. Even the working hours are not fixed and wages are governed by local factors. The situation is the same in the case of migrant labour and forced labour. The only exceptions are the Governments of Gujarat, Kerala, Karnataka and Madhya Pradesh, which have insurance schemes for the landless agricultural labour.

The unorganised sector does not get much benefit out of the existing framework of labour laws. However, the Minimum Wages Act, 1948 stands out as a legislation that is widely applicable to unorganised workers, including agricultural labour. The Act empowers both Central and State Governments to fix or revise the minimum rates of wages in respect of scheduled employments under their respective jurisdiction. The basic objective of minimum wage fixation is to improve the standard of living of these workers. We have talked about the Act exhaustively in Chapter 18.

Some welfare schemes are being implemented by the Central Government for specific occupational groups of the unorganised sector, such as *beedi* workers, non-coal mine workers, cine workers, handloom weavers, fishermen, etc. Certain initiatives of the Government like the National Rural Employment Guarantee Act, 2005, the National Rural Health Mission and the *Sarva Shiksha Abhiyaan* address the problems of employment, health and education, respectively. Some of the State Governments and non-governmental organisations have also been implementing welfare programmes for certain categories of unorganised workers. Despite various efforts, there is still a wide gap in coverage of such workers under social security measures.

WELFARE FUNDS

Labour welfare funds have been set up by the Government to provide welfare and social security to workers in certain industries. There are 5 welfare funds governed by different legislations, which are administered by the Ministry of Labour & Employment; their corresponding legislations are:

- The Mica Mines Labour Welfare Fund Act, 1946
- The Limestone and Dolomite Mines Labour Welfare Fund Act, 1972
- The Iron Ore, Manganese Ore and Chrome Ore Mines Labour Welfare Fund Act, 1976
- The *Beedi* Workers Welfare Cess Act, 1976
- The Cine Workers' Welfare Fund Act, 1981

The purpose of these welfare funds is to provide housing, medical care (prevention of diseases), transportation, water supply, educational and recreational facilities, social insurance and security to workers employed in non-coal mines and *beedi* industry and to cine workers. For building and construction workers, the welfare boards and welfare funds are required to be set up by the concerned State Governments.

Spotlight

Labour welfare funds have been set up by the Government to provide welfare and social security to workers in certain industries.

Welfare funds fall broadly in two groups: tax (cess)-based and contributory. The Central Government funds are tax-based, while welfare boards for mine workers, *beedi* and cigar workers, etc. are financed by the cess levied on these commodities. Under the *Beedi* Workers Welfare Cess Act, 1976, a fixed cess is levied per thousand *beedis* manufactured. Similarly there is a cess for building and construction workers. Cess is levied on the mica mines and under other welfare laws on mine products on the basis of quantum of production. Under the Cine Workers Welfare Cess Act, 1981, cess is levied on the basis of production of films and not on the basis of collection.

Among the different States, Kerala has set up more than 20 welfare funds for workers in the unorganised sector, including toddy workers, agricultural workers, handloom workers, auto-rickshaw workers, cashew workers, construction workers, motor transport workers, some artisans and others. These funds provide a wide range of benefits including old age benefit, medical care, education, assistance for marriage, housing, etc. to the beneficiaries. The funds set up by the Kerala Government are mostly contributory, and hence are similar to social insurance. The schemes are administered by autonomous boards and are financed by contributions from employers, workers and others. In Maharashtra, the Mathadi Boards exist for various groups of headload workers. The Tamil Nadu Welfare Fund established under the State law for manual workers has established labour welfare centres that provide childcare facilities and tailoring classes for the wives and wards of workers.

LABOUR WELFARE PRACTICES IN INDIA

Labour welfare in India is carried out by the efforts of Government, employers, trade unions and voluntary organisations. We have already mentioned the legislations enacted and enforced by the Central Government that have provisions for labour welfare earlier in this chapter. These apart, there are labour laws enacted and enforced by various State Governments, which apply to respective States. A typical example is of the Shops and Establishments Act, enacted by every State to regulate conditions of work and provide for statutory obligations of employers and rights of employees in the unorganised sector and other employments in their jurisdiction. The Government may introduce new welfare provisions or amend the existing ones while implementing the recommendations made by bodies like National Commission on Labour and Pay Commission. Child Care Leave for employees of Central Government was introduced as a result of recommendations of the Sixth Central Pay Commission, with effect from 1st September 2008. Women employees having minor children may be granted Child Care Leave by a competent authority for a maximum period of 2 years (i.e., 730 days) during their entire service for taking care of up to 2 children, less than 18 years of age, whether for rearing or taking care or any other needs like examination, sickness, etc. During the period of such leave, women employees shall be paid leave salary equal to pay drawn immediately before proceeding for leave. It may be availed of in more than 1 spell. Child Care Leave shall not be debited against leave account; such leave may also be allowed in the third year as leave not due (without production of medical certificate).

Employers, depending upon their capacity, make different welfare facilities available to workers. Large establishments provide facilities even beyond the level required by laws, while small ones may just provide statutory benefits. Non-statutory or voluntary benefits provided by employers to workers include loans for purposes like house building; recreational facilities; education of children; purchasing of personal vehicle; conveyance; leave travel concession; fair price shops; and many other such facilities.

Amongst voluntary organisations, there are some social organisations like the Bombay Social Service League, the Seva Sadan Society, the Maternity and Infant Welfare Association and the Young Men's Christian Association, that undertake voluntary welfare activities like night schools, promotion of public health, organising recreational activities and lectures, etc. (Agalgatti, 2008).

Spotlight

Labour welfare is considered to be a new function of trade unions.

Though trade unions have limited financial resources, they are actively undertaking labour welfare activities within their means. A notable example is of the Textile Labour Association Ahmedabad, which provides maternity care, education and development of children, workers' education and training programmes, medical and healthcare, recreation, etc. The Rashtriya Mill Mazdoor Sangh, Mumbai provides similar amenities to workers and their families. The Mazdoor Sabha, Kanpur, the Railwaymen's Union and Indian Federation of Labour in Uttar Pradesh are some other trade unions that are engaged in labour welfare by providing facilities like legal defence and running of cooperative societies. The Steel Employees' Welfare Association at Bhilai provides social security to workers of the Bhilai Steel Plant in the form of financial assistance to the families of deceased member-workers and assistance to member-workers for medical care, retirement, etc. (Agalgatti, 2008). Trade unions at the Unchahar plant of National Thermal Power Corporation were found to have a fair involvement in labour welfare activities (Ghosh, Nandan and Gupta, 2009).

WORKERS' EDUCATION AND TRAINING

Education is important for workers as it helps them improve their understanding in a holistic manner regarding their status problems and rights and responsibilities in various roles as workers, as union members, as consumers and as citizens (Peterson, 1952). The Indian workforce is characterised by low level of education. The Government of India had realised the need for educating workers to ensure large scale industrialisation in the country after Independence, and towards this end, it initiated the Workers' Education Scheme in 1958. This scheme was administered by the Central Board of Workers' Education (CBWE), which is an autonomous body under the Ministry of Labour & Employment, registered under the Societies Registration Act, 1860. The CBWE gets grants-in-aid from the Ministry of Labour & Employment to operate its activities.

Spotlight

The scheme for workers' education is administered by the Central Board of Workers' Education, an autonomous body under the Ministry of Labour & Employment.

The objective of the Workers' Education Scheme is to create a well-aware and disciplined workforce in the organised, unorganised and rural sectors (*www.labour.nic.in*). The First National Commission on Labour (1969) had observed that the beneficiaries of the Workers' Education Scheme were found to show more interest in union activities than others who did not receive education under the Scheme (National Commission on Labour Recommendations, n.d.). Educated workers were also found to have high interest in participation in management activities (Sethi, 1973, as cited in Sen, 2012). The Indian Institute of Workers' Education (IIWE) was established by the CBWE in March 1970 at Mumbai as the apex training institute. To achieve its objectives, various training programmes are conducted by the CBWE for the workers of formal and informal sectors at national, regional and unit levels through a network of 50 regional and 9 sub-regional Directorates spread in various parts of the country (*www.cbwe.gov.in*).

Under the Constitution of India, vocational training is a concurrent subject. The term 'vocational training' refers to lower level education and training for the population of skilled or semi-skilled workers in various trades; however, it does not enhance their level with respect to general education (Goel, n.d.). The national vocational training system provides training for development of skills. The Central Government is responsible for developing policies and training schemes at the national level, setting of training standards, procedures, certification, etc. The National Council for Vocational Training (NCVT), a tripartite body under the Ministry of Labour & Employment, supervises training activities. It has representation from employers, workers and Central/State Governments. State Councils for Vocational Training are constituted at State-level monitoring training programmes by the respective State Governments. Training is provided through Industrial Training Institutes (ITIs), run by State Governments, and through various industrial establishments that provide apprentice training.

The main vocational training schemes consist of Craftsmen Training Scheme, Apprenticeship Training Scheme, Training of Skilled Workers and Supervisors, Training of Craft Instructors, Training of Women, Staff Training and Research, Development of Instructional Materials and Hi-Tech Training Scheme. Since women constitute a significant part of the workforce, women's vocational training has also been given special attention. The Directorate General of Employment and Training has launched the Women's Vocational Training Programme in 1977.

Some of the challenges faced by the Government in training workers include uneven distribution of ITIs in different parts of the country; small coverage of persons including both school pass-outs and drop-outs, trade obsolescence, lack of training infrastructure and inadequate number of experienced staff (Chandra, 2004). In view of the tremendous growth of the service sector in India, skills need be imparted to workers by introducing appropriate training schemes for enhancing their employability in this sector.

LABOUR RESEARCH

Labour research is an activity aimed at collecting, analysing and disseminating knowledge about various dimensions of labour by using scientific methods. Globalisation, changing work technology, information technology, socio-economic factors, etc. are affecting the nature of workforce and adding new dimensions to it. This calls for labour research.

Spotlight

Labour research is an activity aimed at collecting, analysing and disseminating knowledge about various dimensions of labour by using scientific methods.

Nanda (2011) has classified labour research into three categories: *basic* (concerned with theoretical and conceptual studies related to labour economics), *applied* (the objective of which is to give such findings as can help solve existing labour problems), and *administrative* (that aims at providing data for the work of the Government and that is related to other agencies associated with labour management and welfare).

The Government of India relies on scientifically conducted researches in formulating its policies (Ministry of Labour & Employment, 2011). The main purposes of most of the labour research undertaken by the Government are: to identify measures to solve problems, to assist in devising policies, and to comprehend and understand the depth of the socio-economic conditions of workers for comparison at national and international levels. Research on labour-related issues is conducted by several bodies in the country. The Ministry of Labour & Employment has a separate research division. The National Labour Institute also conducts labour research. This apart, State Governments have their research studies. The Second National Commission on Labour (2002) has expressed the need for coordination between all these bodies to enhance the effectiveness of labour research.

LABOUR STATISTICS

Labour statistics provide an insight into the socio-economic development of a country; such statistics are necessary for planning developmental activities and improving the industrial relations scenario of a nation.

The Report of the Second National Commission on Labour (2002) lists the following government agencies engaged in collection, compilation and dissemination of labour statistics in the country:

- Ministry of Labour & Employment and its affiliates Directorate General of Factory Advice Service and Labour Institutes, Employees' State Insurance Corporation and Employees' Provident Fund Organisation).
- Other agencies (Office of the Registrar General of India, National Sample Survey Office, Planning Commission and State Governments).

> **Spotlight**
> The Labour Bureau is the main agency in India engaged in collecting statistics on different aspects of labour.

Of these, the Labour Bureau is the main agency engaged in collecting statistics on different aspects of labour since its inception in 1946. It also conducts labour research by way of studies and surveys covering the unorganised sector, SC/ST labour in urban areas, women workers and contract labour; occupational wage surveys in the organised sector; family budget enquiries; rural labour enquiry; Annual Survey of Industries; and the Digest of Indian Labour Research. The Labour Bureau is also responsible for the collation, collection and publication of statistics and related information on wages, earnings, productivity, absenteeism, labour turnover, industrial relations, working and living conditions, evaluation of working of various labour enactments, etc. Since the informal sector employs a major proportion of the workforce in many countries (including India), a resolution concerning statistics of employment in the informal sector was adopted by the 15th International Conference of Labour Statisticians in 1993. The Resolution requires that countries in which the informal sector has a significant role in the national economy should develop a comprehensive system for collecting statistics on employment in this sector, so as to create a statistical database for various uses. This system should contribute in the improvement of labour statistics, macroeconomic analyses, planning, policy formulation for the informal sector in specific and economy in general, and in integration of the informal sector with the development process. Such a system would also help in developing assistance programmes for workers in this sector. The Resolution emphasises the need for monitoring of such data every year and an in-depth examination every 5 years.

Exhibit 9.3 ILO Convention and Recommendation on Labour Statistics

The ILO Convention No. 160 and Recommendation No. 170 concerning Labour Statistics adopted in 1985 contain the general provisions regarding collection, compiling and publication of basic labour statistics. Such statistics should include the following subjects:

(a) Economically active population, employment, where relevant unemployment, and where possible visible under-employment;
(b) Structure and distribution of the economically active population, for detailed analysis and to serve as benchmark data;
(c) Average earnings and hours of work (hours actually worked or hours paid for) and, where appropriate, time rates of wages and normal hours of work;
(d) Wage structure and distribution;
(e) Labour cost;
(f) Consumer price indices;
(g) Household expenditure or, where appropriate, family expenditure and, where possible, household income or, where appropriate, family income;
(h) Occupational injuries and, as far as possible, occupational diseases; and
(i) Industrial disputes.

(Adapted from: R170-Labour Statistics Recommendation, 1985 (No. 170). Retrieved from www.ilo.org/dyn/normlex/en/f?p=NORMLEXPUB:12100:0::NO::P12100_INSTRUMENT_ID:312508 on 17/4/2014.)

EMPLOYMENT SECURITY AND MANAGEMENT OF REDUNDANCIES

Employment security implies that a worker enjoys permanent employment without any fear of losing job. The policy of economic liberalisation in India had resulted in intense competition and to meet this challenge organisations adopted several strategies, including technological upgradation and restructuring, which often gives rise to redundancy. The Oxford Dictionary defines redundancy as 'the state of being no longer in employment because there is no more work available' (*www.oxforddictionaries.com*). Budget constraints and/or change in work technology may be the major drivers of redundancy.

An employer may terminate a worker's employment for reason of redundancy in accordance with the Industrial Disputes Act, 1947, which refers to such termination as 'retrenchment'. Section 2(oo) of the Act defines retrenchment as the termination of workmen's services by the employer for any reason other than termination by way of disciplinary action; retirement (whether voluntary or superannuation); non-renewal of the term of contract; and continued ill-health. The prime reasons for retrenchment have been found to be financial stringency, shortage of raw material, shortage of power and lack of demand for the product (Ministry of Labour & Employment, 2013).

Spotlight

Employers may terminate a worker's employment for reason of redundancy, in accordance with the Industrial Disputes Act, 1947, which defines such termination as 'retrenchment'.

It may be noted that employers are prohibited from terminating the employment of a female employee at any time during maternity leave or pregnancy, where the employee would have otherwise been entitled to maternity benefit or medical bonus under the Maternity Benefit Act, 1961.

Employees may also be separated from work by way of lay-off or closure. Lay-offs, retrenchment and closure are three separate concepts and reflect increasing degrees of severity (Debroy, 2012). Section 2(kkk) of the Industrial Disputes Act, 1947 defines lay-off as the failure, refusal or inability of an employer on account of shortage of coal, power, or raw materials, or accumulation of stock, breakdown of machinery, natural calamity, or for any other connected reason, to give employment to a workman whose name is borne on the muster rolls of his industrial establishment and who has not been retrenched. Closure is defined in Section 2(ff) of the Act as the permanent closing down of a place of employment or a part thereof, and is taken as one which may have occurred due to industrial disputes or also because of reasons other than industrial disputes, such as financial stringency, shortage of power or raw material or coal, inter or intra union rivalries, accumulation of stock, lack of demand, breakdown of machinery, indiscipline, violence, etc.

In general, there has been a decrease in the number of units retrenching workers and the number of workers affected thereby (Table 9.1). In the year 2010, there were 13 cases of retrenchment in the Central and State spheres, in which 559 workers were affected. This reflects a decrease of 55.17 per cent in respect of retrenchments, as well as 79.24 per cent in respect of the number of workers retrenched over the previous year. Similarly, during the year 2010, 23 cases of lay-off, showing a decline of 53.06 per cent from the previous year, were reported, which affected 1,494 workers and resulted in a time-loss of 1,46,978 man-days. During this period, number of workers laid-off and man-days lost had also decreased by 89.64 per cent and 47.69 per cent respectively as compared to the previous year (Ministry of Labour & Employment, 2013). During 2010, 42 industrial units were closed, thus affecting 2,401 workers, as compared to 68 units closed in 2009, affecting 3,571 workers. This decrease in the number of units and persons affected may be taken as an indication towards increasing informalisation of labour, as employing informal workers saves an employer from the burden of paying compensation for retrenchment or lay-off.

TABLE 9.1 Number of Units Effecting Retrenchment and Workers Retrenched therein between 2001 and 2010

Year	*Number of Units*	*Number of Workers Affected*
2001	133	3668
2002	98	3975
2003	74	2911
2004	38	2944
2005	35	2184
2006	24	884
2007	23	264
2008	19	1748
2009	29	2693
2010	13	559

Adapted from: Ministry of Labour & Employment (2013)

Managing Redundancy

- **Need Assessment:** An employer must ensure that there is a genuine need for redundancy. For this, a works committee may be consulted on issues related to retrenchment. However, the employer has no obligation to follow any such recommendation.
- **Employee Entitlements:** An employer is required to provide 1 month's notice to any retrenched workman indicating the reasons for retrenchment. The State-specific Shops and Establishments Act specifies notice requirements for all non-workmen employees. Most States usually require employers to provide at least one month's notice or the period specified in the employment contract. Employers are required to pay retrenchment compensation equivalent to 15 days' average pay for every year of continuous service to all workmen who are made redundant. For non-workmen, the amount payable is specified in the contract of employment or the relevant Shops and Establishments Act. Gratuity is also payable under the Payment of Gratuity Act, 1972 to all employees (whether "workmen" or not) with more than 5 years of continuous service.

RECOMMENDATIONS OF THE SECOND NATIONAL COMMISSION ON LABOUR

The Second National Commission on Labour (2002) has given several recommendations for labour welfare and social security, some of which are mentioned in this section.

- The need for crèches not to depend on the number of women workers or the number of children (up to 6 years of age). Every establishment employing 20 or more workers must run a crèche properly manned and equipped either singly or in association with other employers and/or local bodies.
- Enactment of a general law relating to hours of work, leaves and working conditions at workplace.
- Integration of the present laws on welfare outside the workplace, as far as possible, with the laws on social security.
- Ratification of Article 4 of the ILO Convention No. 177 of 1996 on promotion of equality of treatment and other rights of for home-workers, including right to organise, occupational safety and health, remuneration, social security, etc. would offer substantial safeguards to millions of workers.
- Simplification of judicial procedures related to statutory provisions that would enable unorganised workers to obtain legal redress.
- Introduction of a system of registration for domestic workers; these workers should be entitled to benefits of all the schemes that the Commission has recommended for self-employed workers.
- Transformation of welfare funds into instruments of social security by way of: expanding their coverage; broadening the range of benefits; modifying the financial arrangements for providing benefits and decentralising the administration of the funds; and setting up of a Central Fund from which welfare and social security measures for women workers should be financed.
- Establishing a separate wing for unorganised workers in Labour Departments, with adequate number of women employees.
- Formulation of an umbrella-legislation for workers in the unorganised sector that should be capable of being implemented and monitored easily.
- Conversion of the Employees' Compensation Act, 1923 from an employers' liability scheme to a social insurance scheme. Its coverage should be progressively extended to cover more

employments and classes of employees. Further, the restrictive clauses in Schedule II of the Act should be removed.

- Extension of the existing provisions for maternity benefit in the organised sector so as to be applicable to all women workers; establishments to which this Act is not applicable may be brought within its scope on priority basis by following the National Industrial Classification. The Commission also perceived the need for a separate legislation on maternity benefits for women in the organised sector. Such legislation may be implemented through welfare funds or area-based schemes.
- Professionalisation of the management of the Employees' State Insurance (ESI) Scheme. The provision of funeral expenses in the Scheme may be substituted by the term 'emergency expenses' so as to include care of the sick and elderly members. The Employees' State Insurance Corporation has, therefore, to take a decision to de-link employment injury and maternity benefits from medical benefits, and to extend the application of the ESI Scheme for the purposes of these benefits throughout the country. Alternatively, separate social insurance schemes confined to these benefits will have to be evolved.
- Need for a law to place all the provident funds under a common regime; the Employees' Provident Funds and Miscellaneous Provisions Act, 1952 may be made applicable to all classes of establishments, subject to such exceptions as may be considered necessary for specified reasons.
- Integration of the Payment of Gratuity Act, 1972 with the Employees' Provident Funds and Miscellaneous Provisions Act, 1952 and its conversion into a social insurance scheme. An Unemployment Insurance Scheme may be introduced as a part of the Employees' Deposit Linked Insurance Scheme.
- Setting up of a Department of Social Security within the Ministry of Labour & Employment, which would provide policy inputs and secretarial services to the National Authority and the same be set up for States.

Summary

- Labour welfare may be viewed as the whole range of benefits, amenities and facilities including social security provided by employers to workers. Such benefits are provided besides wages/salaries of workers and help in maintaining and improving their health, safety and quality of life.
- The concept of labour welfare finds its origin from Articles 28, 41, 42, 43 and 47 of the Directive Principles of State Policy.
- Labour welfare activities may be guided by humanitarian, utilitarian or paternalistic approach.
- Various theories explaining the reasons for existence of labour welfare are: police theory, paternalistic theory, religious theory, philanthropic theory, placating theory, public relations theory and functional theory.
- Welfare measures may be categorised as statutory, voluntary and mutual, or as intra-mural and extra-mural; provisions in enactments constitute the statutory measures.
- Social security is an assurance provided by the State against various types of adverse situations to which individuals may be exposed in events like old age, sickness, financial distress, disablement, unemployment, maternity or death. Social security may be of two types: social insurance and social assistance.
- Unorganised sector workers in India do not enjoy any social security by way of labour enactments, with the exception of the Minimum Wages Act, 1948.

- Besides employers, trade unions and certain voluntary organisations are also involved to some extent in labour welfare in India.
- The scheme for workers' education initiated in 1958 is administered by the Central Board of Workers' Education (CBWE); the national vocational training system provides training for developing skills.
- The Labour Bureau is the main agency in India engaged in collecting statistics on different aspects of labour.
- Labour welfare funds have been set up by the Government to provide welfare and social security to workers in certain industries; 5 legislations govern such welfare funds.
- Redundancy of workforce may arise due to cost constraints and change in technology. An employer may terminate a worker's employment by reason of redundancy in accordance with the Industrial Disputes Act, 1947, which defines such termination as 'retrenchment'.

Key Concepts

Intra-mural	Social insurance	Welfare fund
Extra-mural	Retrenchment	Labour statistics
Social security	Workers' education	Labour research
Labour welfare	Social insurance	Redundancy

Bibliography

Agalgatti, B. B. *Labour Welfare and Industrial Hygiene*. Pune: Nirali Prakashan; 2008.

Chandra, R. *Social Development in India*. New Delhi: Isha Books; 2004.

Debroy, B. "India's Segmented Labour Markets, Inter-State Differences, and the Scope for Labour Reforms" in Debroy, B., Bhandari, L., Aiyer, S.S.A. and Gulati, A. (Eds.) *Economic Freedom of the States of India,* New Delhi : Academic Foundation; 2012, pp. 75-82.

Ghosh, P., Nandan, S. and Gupta, A. "The Changing Roles of Trade Unions in India: A Case Study of National Thermal Power Corporation (NTPC)", Unchahar, *Asian Academy of Management Journal,* 2009,Vol. 14, No. 1, pp. 37–57.

Goel, V.P. (nd). *Technical and Vocational Education and Training (TVET) System in India for Sustainable Development*. Retrieved from http://www.unevoc.unesco.org/up/India _Country_Paper.pdf

ILO, *Safety and Health in the Iron and Steel Industry*, Geneva: International Labour Office; 2005, p. XXI.

ILO, Approaches to Social Security, 1942, p 80, quoted in *Report of the National Commission on Labour*; 1969, p. 162.

Mamoria, C. B. and Mamoria, S. *Labour Wefare, Social Security and Industrial Peace in India*, New Delhi: Kitab Mahal Distributors; 1980.

Ministry of Labour & Employment. *Report of the Committee on Labour Welfare*. Government of India; 1969, p. 24.

Ministry of Labour & Employment. *Ninth Digest of Indian Labour Research, 2010,* Chandigarh/Shimla: Labour Bureau, Government of India; 2011.

Ministry of Labour & Employment. *Statistics on Industrial Disputes, Closures, Retrenchments and Lay-Offs in India during the Year, 2010*, Chandigarh/Shimla: Labour Bureau, Government of India; 2013.

Mishra, R. S. *Labour Legislations*. Allahabad: Central Law Publication; 1999.

Nanda, B.N. Ninth Digest of Labour Research, Labour Bureau, Chandigarh/Shimla Ministry of Labour & Employment, Government of India, 2011.

National Commission on Labour-Recommendations, http://cbwe.gov.in/recommendations/national-commission-on-labour--recommendations.aspx accessed on 17/4/2014.

Peterson, F. *American Labor Unions: What they are and how they work*, New York: Harper and Brothers; 1952.

Report of the Committee on Labour Welfare, Vol. I, Ministry of Labour, Employment and Rehabilitation, Department of Labour & Employment, p. 24, Government of India; 1969.

Report of the Royal Commission on Labour, Calcutta: Central Publications; 1931.

Sen, R. (2012). Employee Participation in Management, Working Paper 40, ILO, Geneva. Retrieved from http://www.ilo.org/wcmsp5/groups/public/---ed_dialogue/---dialogue/documents/publication/wcms_187873.pdf on 18/4/2014.

Sharma, R. K. *Social Problems and Welfare*, New Delhi:Atlantic Publishers and Distributors; 1998.

Sharma, R. K.. *Indian Society, Institutions and Change*, New Delhi: Atlantic Publishers and Distributors; 2004.

Sills, D. L. *International Encyclopedia of Social Sciences,* USA: The MacMillan Company and the Free Press; 1968,Vol. 15, pp.228-245.

Thomas, H.S. *Understanding Personnel Management*, New York: CBS College Publishing; 1990.

CBWE, http://labour.nic.in/content/orgnisation/cbwe.php accessed on 17/4/2014.

CBWE, http://www.cbwe.gov.in/about-us.aspx accessed on 17/4/2014.

http://www.ilo.org/wcmsp5/groups/public/dgreports/dcomm/documents/publication/wcms_067588.pdf accessed on 17/4/2014.

Review Questions

Objective Type Questions

I. State True or False

(i) The Industrial Dispute Act, 1947 includes termination by means of disciplinary action in the definition of the term retrenchment.
(ii) The philathrophic theory of labour welfare is based on humanitarian approach.
(iii) The Mines Act, 1952 has the provision for appointment of a welfare officer in mines employing 200 or more workers.
(iv) Provisions of the Factories Act, 1948 apply to workers of the unorganised sector.
(v) Under the Cine Workers Welfare Cess Act, 1981 cess is levied on the basis of collection.

Answers: (i) False, (ii) True, (iii) False, (iv) False, (v) False

II. Fill in the Blanks

(i) A social ________ scheme provides financial benefit to persons of small earnings as a right.
(ii) The Labour Investigation Committee, also known as the ______ Committee, was appointed by the Government to investigate into labour welfare measures.
(iii) Welfare funds fall broadly in two groups: tax-based and ______.
(iv) ___________ facilities are provided outside the premises of an establishment.
(v) Crèches must be provided in plantations employing ______ or more women workers.

Answers: (i) assistance, (ii) Rege, (iii) contributory, (iv) extra-mural, (v) 50

Discussion Questions

1. Define 'labour welfare'. How can you categorise the various types of welfare measures?
2. Sketch the evolution of labour welfare in India.
3. Describe the theories of labour welfare that are based on utilitarian approach and humanitarian approach.
4. Write short notes on the following:
   (i) Provisions in the Constitution providing a basis for labour welfare
   (ii) Collection of labour statistics in India
   (iii) Recommendations of the Second National Commission on Labour on social security legislations in India
5. What is the significance of labour research for the economy of a nation?
6. What is redundancy and why does it occur? What aspects must be kept in mind while managing redundancy in an establishment?
7. What is the significance of social security? Discuss the current scenario of social security for unorganised labour in India.
8. Discuss how workers' education and training is administered in India.
9. What are the provisions for labour welfare in the Plantations Labour Act, 1951 and in the Mines Act, 1952?
10. What are the various welfare funds in India? Discuss the benefits that such funds offer to workers.

Protection of the Rights of Jethwai's Mine Workers

The State of Rajasthan has numerous kinds of metallic and non-metallic minerals. The workforce employed in the State's mining industry is second only to agriculture. The workers in mining predominantly constitute *adivasis* (tribals) and *dalits* (low castes). These seasonal mine workers engage in hard labour for 12 to 13 hours a day. They work in hazardous conditions, with temperature as high as 50°C in summers and freezing cold in winters. They are prone to a number of occupational diseases and physical injuries due to the poor safety conditions; the mines lack basic facilities and do not provide even statutory benefits to the workers. The employers, i.e., the mine owners, are least concerned about the plight of the workers, as their main motive is earning profit.

There is a blatant violation of laws and safety measures in most of the mining activities of the State. For example, certain mining companies operate on illegal or expired leases; they practice improper dumping of mine debris; and pay less than the minimum wage to mine workers. Mine owners try to increase profitability by paying miners less for long hours of work and frequently fail to pay cess or royalties. Small huts are provided to miners as shelters that can barely accommodate them or protect them from weather. It appears to be a tough task for the State Mining Department to control the situation probably due to lack of political will and the actual resources to fully monitor and control the operations of thousands of leases spread across Rajasthan. This neglect has further aggravated the already oppressive working conditions of a large number of people. Majority of mine workers are males. Women are engaged mainly in activities like clearing debris and pebbles from the mines. They are usually paid far less than male workers. Contravening all the norms of the Child Labour

(Prohibition and Regulation) Act, 1986, children are engaged in work under hazardous conditions and are exploited in every manner.

Jethwai, a small village in the Jaisalmer district of western Rajasthan, is predominantly a Bhil tribal village. Apart from Bhils, there are many migrant workers from the neighbouring districts of Jodhpur, Barmer and Ajmer. A large majority of Jethwai's population is engaged in one sort of mining-related activity or the other. Migrant population is preferred by mine owners as they are often more compliant, and rarely complain about unfair treatment or violation of their rights as they fear losing job. Since they are worried about earning their living, such migrant workers agree to work for much lower wages and rarely participate in village-based activities.

In general the mining industry only reserves some 4 to 5 per cent of total production costs for labour. The mine owners pay wages in two different ways: daily-wages and piece-rate wages. Although the mine operators guarantee wages to their workers at the end of every month, usually such wages are not paid regularly, and workers may have to wait for several months to get their wages. To support their families and in circumstances like marriages, illness or funerals, these mine workers have to borrow large amounts of money from mine owners. Unable to pay off the loan, they very often are pushed into debt bondage, when they are forced to work off their debts. They are given lower wages on this account. This situation arises as these workers do not have any other source of financial support. If they change jobs they are required to repay the whole debt or, often, the new employer repays the debt and the loan is transferred.

Safety conditions in the minefields are far from satisfactory. Accidents frequently take place in mines due to the primitive manual tools like heavy hammers, chisels, etc. used by the workers. Frequent accidents result in high rate of injuries and number of deaths every year. Even in this situation the mine workers have no assistance and are forced to borrow from mine owners, and thus falling into debt trap. Family members of deceased workers get very little compensation, largely being left to fend for themselves.

Disillusioned with the Government's apathy and the attitude of mine owners, a group of environmentalists, lawyers and activists came together to form the Mine Labour Protection Campaign (MLPC) in 1994 with the objective of improving the lives and working conditions of Rajasthan's mine workers. The MLPC began its work with the determination to protect the rights of mine workers, promote environmental justice, provide adequate healthcare, ensure occupational safety and guarantee fair wages. After remaining dormant for some time, the Campaign became active again in 1999 with the formation of a series of mine workers' unions in Rajasthan. In 2001, the Stone Mineworkers' Union (Pathar Khan Mazdoor Union) was formed with a total of 95 members. It had the objective to protect the miners' rights and ensure them safe working conditions. The union worked to ensure that mine workers received payments on time, and were provided with safe working conditions, adequate housing, regular employment, and a legally binding assurance for full compensation in the case of fatal and non-fatal accidents.

The Mine Labour Protection Campaign encouraged Jethwai's mine workers to take ownership of mining resources by forming a cooperative. This was seen as an effort to give mine workers a sense of dignity and a stake in their own land. Their cooperative, the Pathar Khan Shramik Theka Sahkari Samiti Ltd. (PKSTSSL) was formed in 2002. It aimed to help the mine workers take up mining leases, and is one of India's first mining co-operatives for the indigenous people. The PKSTSSL engages in profit-earning activities from mining activities. One of the basic principles of the cooperative is that any profit earned must be distributed equally among all the cooperative members. The wages of workers have increased significantly as compared to that paid by private mine owners. The cooperative has been earning considerable profits ever since successful acquiring of leases to extract minerals, though private mine owners create problems for them. The PKSTSSL educates workers on their legal rights related to fair wages, working hours and other benefits. Mine workers of cooperative-owned mines have facilities like clean drinking water and proper shelter rooms.

Inspired by this cooperative, the women of the village have formed their own Self Help Group (SHG) that helps its members in developing skills for making products like candles, detergents, etc., and then selling them through SHG shops, thus becoming independent and supporting their households.

(Adapted from: Sengupta, R. (2007). Protection the Rights of Jethwai's Mineworkers – An MLPC Intervention, Rajasthan, India: Artisanal and Small-Scale Mining in Asia-Pacific Case Study Series. Retrieved from www.asmasiapacific.org/download_file.php?uid=92 on 18/4/2014.)

Review Questions

1. Discuss the problems faced by the mine workers of Rajasthan, as reflected in the case.
2. Which labour laws do you think are contravened in this case?
3. According to you how effective has the MLPC been in mitigating the problems of the mine workers?
4. Discuss the role played by the PKSTSSL in improving welfare of the mine workers. What lessons can mine owners of Rajasthan learn from this cooperative?

ANNEXURE I Number of Canteens, Shelters, etc., Crèches and Welfare Officers in Factories during 2010

Canteen			*Shelters, Rest Rooms, and Lunch Rooms*	
Number of factories required to provide canteens as per notification under Section 46	Number of factories which have provided canteens as under Section 46	Number of factories in which canteens are run by contractors	Number of factories wherein more than 150 workers are ordinarily employed	Number of factories which have provided shelter or rest room and lunch
4950	2727	3320	5860	10846

Crèches		*Welfare Officers (WOs)*			
Number of factories where more than 30 women workers are ordinarily employed	Number of factories which have provided crèches as required under Section 48	Number of factories wherein more than 500 or more workers are ordinarily employed	Number of factories where WOs are required to be appointed	Number of factories which have provided WOs as required under Section 49	Number of WOs appointed
4128	3316	1448	1905	1385	1725

Adapted from: Ministry of Labour & Employment (2013). Statistics of Factories 2010, Labour Bureau, Chandigarh/Shimla: Government of India.

10

Wages, Government Policies on Labour and Five Year Plans

Desired Knowledge Competencies

- To explain the role of State in the realm of industrial relations and of concepts related to wage and theories of wage.
- To discuss the mechanism of tripartism, especially in Indian context.
- To analyse labour policies in Five Year Plans and labour reforms in India.
- To outline provisions and welfare measures for women and child labour in India.

INTRODUCTION

Harmonious relations between workers and employers and lasting industrial peace are the desired goals in all industrialised economies. However, the responsibility of ensuring such harmony is not restricted to employers and workers and their trade unions. The State, as the third stakeholder in industrial relations, takes steps through appropriate legislations and other machinery to ensure industrial peace. The role of State in settlement of industrial disputes in India has been broadly covered in Chapter 8. However, settlement of disputes is actually a fraction of the overall role the State plays in shaping the industrial relations framework, which we shall be elaborating in this chapter. The concept of tripartism involving three parties (i.e., trade unions of workers, employer and the government) as a participative mechanism for settlement industrial disputes has also been discussed in Indian context.

Wages paid to labour are a source of their livelihood and a cost to the employer at the same time. This chapter presents the different theories of wages and elaborates on Wage Boards, their evolution in India and their functions. The Planning Commission was set up by a resolution of the Government of India in March, 1950. It was charged with the responsibilities of assessing all resources of the country, augmenting deficient resources, formulating plans for the most effective and balanced utilisation of resources and determining priorities *(www.planningcommission.nic.in)*. The Five Year Plans, formulated, executed and monitored by the Planning Commission,

Spotlight

The Planning Commission was set up by a resolution of the Government of India in March, 1950.

form an integral component of the planning process in India. Issues pertaining to employment and employability considered critical for a labour-abundant country like India, and labour policy (including industrial relations, employment, wages, welfare, working conditions and productivity) have always occupied pivotal position in the Five Year Plans. Initiating with the First Five Year Plan (1951-1956), the Planning Commission has travelled a long way, with the on-going Twelfth Five Year Plan (2012-2017). We have captured various policies and recommendations related to labour across all the twelve Five Year Plans in this chapter. Separate sections have been devoted to deliberations on labour law reforms, and provisions and measures meant for women workers and child labour.

ROLE OF STATE IN INDUSTRIAL RELATIONS

The State is an endogenous player of the industrial relations system (Aoki et al., 1997 as cited by Jeong. 2010) of any nation. The existence of State is projected in the one of the most widely accepted approaches to the analysis of industrial relations proposed by Dunlop (1958). Yesufu (1985) describes State intervention as entailing all actions, whether direct or indirect, by which a government promotes, sustains or participates to influence or determine the conditions of employment and the relations between those directly involved in the employment contract (i.e., employers or managers on one hand, and employees or trade unions on the other).

Four distinct roles of the State that affect industrial relations are identified by Jeong (2010) as: a third party regulator of labour relations; a regulator of markets; an establisher of the welfare system; and its own employer and policymaker. Ratnam (2006) observes that the role ascribed to the State in industrial relations depends on the ideological, political and socio-economic bent of the State, and that it varies depending on the level of development or industrialisation and the level of interactions.

Reflection

As per Dunlop, an industrial relations system consists of three sets of actors: managers and their organisations, workers and their organisations, and governmental agencies.

According to Silva (n.d.), following are the commonly found means of State intervention:

- *Statute law* represents the most direct means of State intervention and is one of the specific means used by the State to condition industrial relations outcomes. Statutory regulation of minimum terms and conditions such as minimum wages, working conditions, safety and health, social security and protection are integrated with the terms and conditions in contracts of employment, which employers must conform to.
- The system of *labour courts, tribunals or arbitration* is a more indirect method through which the State influences industrial relations.
- *Administrative role* is another method of State intervention, e.g., as conciliator or mediator.

Ratnam (2006) suggests the following as the major means of State intervention in industrial relations: policy framework in the sphere of labour and labour management relations; legislation (including both hard laws and soft laws); and institution (classified as facilitative, executive, and judicial). Otobo (2000) has noted five areas that are the most frequently subjected to State regulations, namely: employment and manpower development; wages and salaries; union government and administration; collective bargaining; and industrial conflict.

In Indian context, the First National Commission on Labour (1969 p. 307) has observed that "The concern of the State in labour matters emanates as much from its obligations to safeguard the interests of workers and employers as to ensure to the community the availability of their joint product/service at a reasonable price. The extent of its involvement in the process is determined by the level of social and economic advancement, while the mode of interventions gets patterned in conformity with the political system prevailing in the country and the social and cultural traditions of its people".

TRIPARTITE MODEL OF INDUSTRIAL RELATIONS

Concept of Tripartism

As the term suggests, tripartism involves three parties that participate in settlement of matters of industrial dispute. The three participants are the trade unions of workers, employer and the government, with the pivotal role played by the government. Tripartism promotes the idea of partnership between labour and management and rests on the following principles (*www.indialabourarchives.org*):

> **Spotlight**
> Tripartism plays a vital role in settlement of disputes when bipartism fails in reaching a consensus.

- Management and workers should share a relation of partnership and synergy.
- The community as a whole must be responsible for protecting the interests of workers, so that they enjoy their due share in the fruits of development of the nation.

Tripartism operates at industry and national levels. As a mechanism it plays a vital role in settlement of disputes especially when bipartism does not help in reaching a consensus. Meetings of the participants are conducted to review all aspects of a dispute, advise each other and try reaching a consensus by peaceful means.

Evolution of Tripartite Bodies in India

The need for consultation on labour matters in lines with the International Labour Organisation (ILO) was recommended by the Royal Commission on Labour in India (also known as the Whitley Commission) in 1931. The Commission envisaged a statutory organisation that should be large enough to ensure adequate representation of the divergent interests of the parties involved; however, such an organisation was also projected as not to be too large to stifle individual contributions by the members to the discussion. The Commission had recommended that the representative of employers, workers and government should meet regularly. Further, worker members should be elected by their registered trade unions and employers' representatives should be elected by their associations. However, the then British government did not immediately accept these recommendations. The Government of India Act, 1935, which was an important milestone in itself, placed the subject of labour in the Concurrent List. The Centre and the Provinces having concurrent jurisdiction with respect to matters in the Concurrent List were thus empowered to enact their own legislation with respect to labour among other matters. It was in the wake of such events that the need for tripartite consultation was perceived by both employers and workers' representatives. During the Second World War separate consultations with the representatives of labour and employers were held successively in 1941 and 1942 by the Government. The experience of these consultations highlighted the necessity of holding joint meetings of the representatives of these three entities on a common platform. The objective of such meetings was seen to be the resolution of disputes and clearing of differences between workers and employers by means of constructive discussions and mutual understanding.

In the year 1942, India set up two tripartite bodies on the model of the International Labour Conference, the Tripartite National Labour Conference, which was eventually named as the Indian Labour Conference (ILC) and the Standing Labour Advisory Committee, re-named later as

> **Spotlight**
> ILC and SLC are the first two tripartite bodies set up in 1942 in India.

the Standing Labour Committee (SLC). After Independence, the Government of India put emphasis on the need for consultation between the representatives of labour, management and the government in tripartite and bipartite forums. India ratified the Tripartite Consultation (International Labour Standards) Convention, 1976 (No. 144) concerning tripartite consultations to promote the implementation of International Labour Standards in 1978, the same year it was adopted by the ILO. At present there are 44 national-level tripartite committees in the country.

Tripartite Bodies in India

The *Indian Labour Conference* and the *Standing Labour Committee* are two important national-level tripartite bodies that play a significant role in shaping the industrial relations framework of the country. The objectives set before these two tripartite bodies at the time of their inception in 1942 were:

(i) promotion of uniformity in labour legislation;
(ii) laying down of a procedure for the settlement of industrial disputes; and
(iii) discussion on all matters of all-India importance between employers and employees. (Report of the First National Commission on Labour, p. 311)

Reflection

In response to the pressure of the ILO the Government of India had constituted various tripartite bodies (other than ILC and SLC), and a number of industry-specific tripartite committees.

The ILC was instituted to advise the Government on matters brought to its notice by the Government itself. The First National Commission on Labour (1969) had noted that earlier the SLC used to deliberate on its own or over such matters that were sent to it by the ILC and the latter would make the final recommendations. However, eventually both the ILC and the SLC have become deliberative bodies, ILC being more representative. Both these tripartite bodies consist of representatives of the Central Government, Governments of States and Union Territories and representatives of Employers and workers' organisations nominated by the Central Government in consultation with all-India organisations of workers and employers. The meetings of the ILC are held annually, whereas the SLC meets as and when necessary.

The decision to constitute *Industrial Tripartite Committees* or *Industrial Committees* with equal representation from employers and workers sides was mainly the outcome of tripartite deliberations at the ILC in 1944. The functions of these committees are to study and debate on problems related to labour and specific to an industry, with a view to ensure better understanding between labour and management, and to advise the Government in solving problems related to such industry. Industrial Committees are found in industries like plantation, coal mining, jute, minerals other than coal, leather, cotton textiles, etc.

Reflection

The first Industrial Committee was formed in 1948 in the plantation industry.

Wage Boards were constituted by the Government at the industry-level in the 1950s and 1960s to solve the problems related to wage fixation. These boards have representatives of workers, employers and independent members who participate and finalise the recommendations. We shall be explaining the functions, composition and other aspects of Wage Boards in a subsequent section.

State Labour Advisory Boards are tripartite advisory bodies set up in nearly all States to provide a forum of the representatives of the Government, employers and employees for discussing problems in order to maintain and promote harmonious industrial relations and to increase production.

Other notable tripartite committees are: the Central and State Advisory Committees to advice the Government on the administration of welfare funds; the Steering Committee on Wages to study trends in wages, production and prices and assist in laying down principles to guide wage-fixing authorities; the Central Implementation and Evaluation Machinery to assess the extent of non-implementation of labour legislations, awards, etc.; the Central Board of Workers' Education, an autonomous body under the Ministry of Labour & Employment that administers the Workers' Education Scheme; and the Special Tripartite Committee constituted in 1992 to study the impact of the New Industrial Policy on labour-related problems and for making useful recommendations.

Reflection

State Labour Advisory Boards have equal representation of workers and employers.

LABOUR AND FIVE YEAR PLANS

This section presents the thrust areas and various policies and recommendations related to labour from the First Five Year Plan (1951-1956) to the on-going Twelfth Five Year Plan (2012-2017) *(www.planningcommission.nic.in)*.

First Five Year Plan (1951–1956)

In the context of labour, the primary objective of the First Five Year Plan was to increase employment opportunities and to raise the standard of living of the masses. Towards this end, primary attention was given to the rural sector of the Indian economy on account of the magnitude and seriousness of the problem in the sector. Measures were directed towards ensuring a better distribution of the educated labour force among different occupations, thus diverting workers from 'crowded' occupations to those where there is a shortage.

The First Five Year Plan emphasised the need for overall industrial peace in industry and the ultimate oneness of interest; it propagated the virtue of harmonious relations between capital and labour. The Plan encouraged mutual settlements, collective bargaining and voluntary arbitration. It was observed that it is incumbent on the State to arm itself with legal powers to refer disputes for settlement by arbitration or adjudication, on failure of efforts to reach an agreement by other means. The Plan concentrated on five aspects of labour policy: industrial relations, wages, working conditions, employment & training and productivity.

Second Five Year Plan (1956–1961)

Driven by the objective of developing a socialist pattern of the society, the Second Five Year Plan was framed with suitable alterations in the existing labour policy. The underlying principle of the Plan was that a socialist society is built up not solely on monetary incentives, but also on the ideas of service to society and the willingness on the part of the latter to recognise such service. Therefore the creation of industrial democracy was considered a pre-requisite for the establishment of a socialist society.

Provision was made for the certification of employers' associations as representatives of industry in an area. Any agreement entered into by such associations would then be binding on all members as well as on non-members of the associations. The Plan emphasised the need for industrial discipline. The necessity of a suitable framework for labour legislations and enforcement machinery was considered in the Second Five Year Plan for ensuring industrial peace. For this, the importance of preventive measures, including the last stage of mutual negotiations, namely conciliation, for achieving industrial peace was stressed upon. Emphasis was also placed on facilitating the stages of mutual negotiations and voluntary arbitration.

The Plan recommended appointment of a wage commission and an authority like a tripartite wage board, consisting of equal representatives of employers and workers, to be instituted for individual industries in different areas. The Employees' Provident Fund (EPF) Scheme, which was instituted on a statutory basis during the First Five Year Plan, was extended in the Second Plan phase to cover industries and commercial establishments having 10,000 or more workers in the country as a whole. The main development programmes proposed under the Plan were: expansion of training of craftsmen and instructors, the Employment Service Organization and the Central Labour Institute; financing of housing schemes; and setting up of a Film Unit.

Third Five Year Plan (1961–1966)

The development of industrial relations in the Third Five Year Plan was contingent on the foundations created by the working of the Code of Discipline. Full awareness of the obligations under the Code to all the constituents of the central organisations of employers and workers was emphasised in the Plan.

Reflection

The Workers' Education Scheme, initiated in 1958, is administered by the Central Board of Workers' Education.

The Third Plan stressed on increasing the application of the principle of voluntary arbitration for resolving differences between workers and employers. It spelt out the need to strengthen workers' participation in management through Works Committees and Joint Management Councils. A large scale expansion of the Workers' Education Scheme was also visualised for the period of the Third Plan. Apart from minimum wage, the Plan suggested to fix fair wages for different classes of workers. An urgent consideration was given to the conversion of the various Provident Fund schemes into a statutory scheme for old age, invalidity and survivorship pension-cum-gratuity. Emphasis was given on the problem of safety at workplace. The Plan proposed to set up a Standing Advisory Committee to promote measures for bringing down the incidence of accidents in factories and a National Mine Safety Council for safety education and propaganda in the mining industry.

Fourth Five Year Plan (1969–1974)

The Fourth Five Year Plan did not have any fresh direction or any shift in the Government's industrial relations policy; it further extended the training and employment schemes implemented in the previous Plan. The activities of the Employees' State Insurance (ESI) Corporation were proposed to be expanded. Greater emphasis was placed on promoting safety practices and on the development of indigenous mine safety equipment. Stress was laid on strengthening labour administration for better enforcement of labour laws. The Fourth Plan recommended that studies should be undertaken to get estimates on unemployment and information on different segments of the labour force. It laid considerable emphasis on labour-intensive schemes such as roads, minor irrigation, soil conservation, rural electrification, village and small scale industries, housing and urban development.

Fifth Five Year Plan (1974–1979)

The Fifth Five Year Plan laid emphasis on generation of employment, labour welfare and greater mobility of labour especially from labour surplus to labour starved areas. The Plan stressed on strengthening industrial relations and conciliation machinery, better enforcement of labour legislations, research in labour and labour statistics, and undertaking studies in the field of wages and productivity.

Sixth Five Year Plan (1980–1985)

One of the principal objectives of the Sixth Five Year Plan was the progressive reduction of unemployment in the country. Labour force estimates were obtained through surveys by the National Sample Survey Office (NSSO) on the basis of usual status participation rates. Special attention was paid to women and educated manpower both for the purpose of analysis of the existing employment market and for the formulation of suitable policies for these categories.

Seventh Five Year Plan (1985–1990)

The emphasis of the Seventh Plan was on employment and manpower policy. Technological upgradation, modernisation and scientific advances in production process in organised industry, agriculture and small industry were envisaged as the essence of growth of productivity. The Plan also ensured suitable arrangements and adjustment policies in terms of education, training, retraining and re-orientation of workers to avoid dislocation effects and to ensure smoothening of the process of technology adoption.

Eighth Five Year Plan (1992–1997)

The Eighth Plan aimed mainly at reducing unemployment. The Plan echoed concerns of the earlier Plan with particular reference to workers' participation in management, skill, training, productivity, equitable wage policy and the informal sector. It also expressed concerns about rationalisation of the regulatory framework with a view to provide reasonable flexibility for workforce adjustment for effecting upgradation of technology and improvement in efficiency.

Ninth Five Year Plan (1997–2002)

The Ninth Five Year Plan attempted to create conditions for improvement in labour productivity in general and for provision of social security. It aimed at reducing the number of laws which determine the relations between workers and employers so that a much smaller number of laws can reach out to the entire workforce.

Attempts at providing social security were targeted specifically at the poor through special employment generation programmes and provision of free or heavily subsidised basic needs like health, nutrition, housing and education. Efforts were made to extend the coverage of the National Social Assistance Programme to the casual and self-employed workers in the informal sector both in rural and urban areas with the objective to cover the economically active population outside the organised sector. The Ninth Plan directed efforts to modify the existing National Child Labour Project (NCLP) by establishing special schools to provide non-formal education, vocational training, supplementary nutrition, stipend, healthcare, etc. to children withdrawn from employment.

Tenth Five Year Plan (2002–2007)

Unemployment was a major concern in the Tenth Plan; hence provision of gainful employment opportunities was a thrust area. During the Plan period efforts were made to ensure universal access at least to primary health care facility and to promote vocational training as a measure to generate employment opportunities.

Spotlight

Provision of gainful employment opportunities was a thrust area of the Tenth Plan.

The Tenth Plan envisaged reorganisation and strengthening of the Labour Department. It also undertook affirmative measures to eradicate child labour by way of the Child Rehabilitation Scheme that included identifying child labour, providing vocational education to children and paying them stipend, and their placement in appropriate jobs or helping them in self-employment.

Eleventh Five Year Plan (2007–2012)

The employment strategy for the Eleventh Plan was to ensure rapid growth of employment while ensuring an improvement in the quality of employment, especially in the unorganised sector. The aim was to achieve substantial increase in the share of regular employment, with a reduction in that of casual employment. Employment of women was encouraged in this Plan period. The Eleventh Plan highlighted the significance of programmes for skill development to aid the desired growth in employment. Services like Information Technology (IT) enabled services, telecom and tourism were identified to have prospects for high growth in output and for creation of new employment opportunities. Need for ensuring a under provision of social security and welfare of unorganised workers was also perceived in the Plan period.

Twelfth Five Year Plan (2012–2017)

The focus of the Twelfth Five Year Plan is to improve the outreach of skill development, both quantitatively and qualitatively; to bridge the spatial, sectoral regional and gender divides; and to have an institutional mechanism focused solely on skill development. The Plan has stressed on provision for necessary support mechanisms to enable the financial requirements/skill loans for poor students (i.e., the Credit Guarantee Fund). As regards issues of employment, the Plan has suggested an outcome-based approach to ensure that employability created is manifested in immediate, measurable and tangible employment or self-employment of trainees.

The Twelfth Five Year Plan has recommended activating the State Skill Missions and making them nodal points for receiving most of the skill-related funding from Centre. Greater interaction is encouraged among industry academia and skill providers to narrow the demand-supply gap of skilled manpower. The intervention of IT is clearly evident from the following thrust areas of the Twelfth Five Year Plan: development of Information and Communication Technology (ICT)-based real time labour market information system; development of an online national register of skilled persons; all employment exchanges to come online and act as pro-active counseling and placement centres; and setting up of a National Skill Registry having the facility to link various databases across Ministries and States. Other focus areas of the Plan include: focus on training of trainers; promotion of Public Private Partnership; and development of a model on the informal sector that reaches out to people.

LABOUR POLICY AND LABOUR LAW REFORMS

> **Spotlight**
> Currently there are 45 labour legislations in India.

Labour policy in India is mainly based on labour laws. The dignity of human labour and the need for protecting and safeguarding the interest of labour has been enshrined in various articles of the Constitution of India. As we have mentioned earlier, labour is a subject in the Concurrent List in the Constitution, which empowers both the Central and State Governments to enact legislations. As a result, a large number of labour legislations have been enacted at Central and State levels that cater to different aspects of labour, including employment, occupational health and safety, fixing of minimum wages, payment of wages, compensation against injury at work leading to disablement or death, bonded labour, various categories of labour (namely, contract labour, women labour, child labour, migrant labour, etc.), settlement and adjudication of industrial disputes, social security (including provident fund, gratuity, bonus, etc.), industry-specific categories of workmen (like mines, plantations, *beedi,* and cigar, etc.). India has 45 labour legislations as on date, including the latest Sexual Harassment of Women at Workplace (Prevention, Prohibition and Redressal) Act, 2013. A complete list of all these laws has been provided in the appendix of the chapter. Apart from these laws, both Central and State Governments have formulated Rules to facilitate implementation of these laws. We have mentioned some of these Rules in relevant parts of this chapter. The Planning Commission observes that laws need to be reviewed from time to time, especially in a dynamic context, and hence stresses on the review or updating of labour laws on a continuous basis in order to bring them in tune with the emerging needs of the economy, including attaining higher levels of productivity and competitiveness, increasing employment opportunities and attracting more investment for growth.

It is obvious from this deliberation that the entire gamut of labour legislations, both at Central and State levels, the Rules appended with many of these laws, the enormous number of sections and clauses within each Act and their implementation invite an element of complexity in the industrial relations framework.

Flexibility in labour laws is an important matter to ensure all pervasive structural reforms. Further, the growing dynamism in the Indian labour market has also brought with itself notable instances of labour disputes in big industrial houses like Maruti Suzuki and Honda Motorcycle. In the face of such circumstances, more flexibility in labour laws has been widely perceived as an urgent need.

Datta and Sil (2007) observe that the main accusation against the labour laws in India, especially by employers, is that they are excessively pro-worker in the organised sector; this has led to serious rigidities with adverse consequences in terms of performance of this sector and the operation of the labour market. Thus growth of output in the organised sector is not leading to a proportionate growth in employment, which is compelling employers to resort to more capital intensive production processes. This brings us to an interesting dichotomy: labour laws that are meant to protect the jobs of the workers are themselves impeding the scope for creation of more job opportunities in future.

The Planning Commission and different committees have been recommending reform of labour laws by highlighting the need for flexibility in the existing laws that would give impetus to the industry to compete in international markets. Let us now understand the perspective of employers and workers on this issue. Employers view flexibility as a pre-requisite for promoting economic growth and generating jobs, whereas trade unionists consider this as a strategy of employers for profit maximisation and reduction in the bargaining power of unions, without commensurate employment opportunities (Datta and Sil, 2007). Unless we have labour reforms, as Debroy (2001) portrays, India's comparative advantage of enormous labour abundance will not be adequately utilised because of the high wage lands created by the labour legislation in the organised sector.

Spotlight

The Planning Commission and different committees have been recommending reform of labour laws by highlighting the need for flexibility.

AMENDMENT PROPOSALS AT VARIOUS STAGES OF CONSIDERATION

Updating labour laws is a continuous process and changes are implemented in these laws from time to time by the Government to bring the various provisions in tandem with the emerging needs of the economy. The Working Group on Labour Laws and Other Regulations for the Twelfth Five Year Plan (2012-017) set up by the Planning Commission has given recommendations on amending certain legislations, some of which have been discussed in this section. (*www.planningcommission.nic.in)*

Following are some of the amendments proposed for various labour legislations in india:

- The Minimum Wages Act, 1948 may be amended, to, inter-alia, make the National Floor Level Minimum Wage statutory and applicable to all "other" employments.

- The Contract Labour (Regulation and Abolition) Act, 1970 is proposed to be amended to ensure that in case contract labour performs the same or similar kind of work as those directly appointed by the principal employer, such a worker shall be entitled to the same wage rates, holidays, hours of work and social security provisions. Further, whenever a contract worker is engaged through a contractor, the contract agreement between the principal employer and the contractor must clearly indicate the wages and contribution towards social security schemes and other benefits to be paid by the contractor to the contract labour concerned.
- The Factories Act, 1948 must be amended to introduce new terms like 'hazardous substance', 'disability', etc.; to redefine certain other terms; and to add new provisions on health, safety, hazardous process, welfare, working hours for adults, employment of young persons, annual leave with wages; and penalties & procedures, including provision of flexibility in the matter of employment of women during night in factories.
- The Employees' Provident Fund and Miscellaneous Provisions Act, 1952 may be amended to bring down the threshold limit of workers from the existing '20 and above' to '10 and above' as regards coverage of establishments.

RECOMMENDATIONS OF THE WORKING GROUP

On the basis of views of various stakeholders (i.e., employers, workers and State Governments) the Working Group has given broad recommendations on labour legislations, some of which have been mentioned under specific heads in this section.

I. Consolidation, Simplification and Rationalisation of Labour Laws

The Working Group has agreed with the suggestion of the Second National Commission on Labour (2002) and National Commission for Enterprises in the Unorganised Sector (NCEUS) (2007) that labour laws should be consolidated in the following cognate groups to reduce their multiplicity that would ensure better enforcement and more effective compliance:

- **Laws Governing Industrial Relations:** The Working Group has recommended consolidation of the laws pertaining to industrial relations (i.e., the Industrial Disputes Act, 1947, The Industrial Employment (Standing Orders) Act, 1946 and the Trade Unions Act, 1926) into one law, i.e., the Industrial Relations Act.
- **Laws Governing Wages:** The legislations governing wages (i.e., the Equal Remuneration Act, 1976, the Minimum Wages Act, 1948, the Payment of Bonus Act, 1965 and the Payment of Wages Act, 1936) may be consolidated into one Act, named the Payment of Wages Act.
- **Laws Governing Social Security:** There are more than one definition of a single concept available across legislations. The Working Group has hence recommended that the definitions of establishments, eligibility criteria, etc. in the various social security legislations (i.e., the Employees' State Insurance Act, 1948, the EPF and Miscellaneous Provisions Act, 1952 and the Payment of Gratuity Act, 1972) may be harmonised for purposes of consolidation.
- **Laws Governing Working Conditions and Welfare:** The Working Group has recommended clubbing of the Acts on working conditions and labour welfare (i.e., the Factories Act, 1948, the Maternity Benefit Act, 1961, the Workmen's (now Employees') Compensation Act, 1923, the Contract Labour (Regulation and Abolition) Act, 1970 and the Inter-State Migrant Workmen (Regulation of Employment and Conditions of Service) (RECS) Act, 1979).
- **Welfare Cess Laws:** The Working Group opines that all Cess Acts and Welfare Fund Acts may be clubbed into one Act.

II. Common Definitions

At present different terminologies and definitions used in various labour laws lead to confusion and complications in the effective compliance and enforcement of these laws. One of the pre-requisites for codification or consolidation of labour laws is thus to have common definitions.

III. Protecting Interest of Workers in the Unorganised Sector

The Working Group has recommended provisions of minimum living wage, improved regulatory activities, basic social security and labour welfare schemes, and improved health and safety facilities to workers in the unorganised sector.

IV. Amendments in Certain Acts

Certain Acts like the Minimum Wages Act, 1948, the Contract Labour (Regulation and Abolition) Act, 1970 and the Factories Act, 1948 have far reaching impact on the living standards of workers and have certain proposed amendments at various stages of consultation. Such considerations have been recommended to be put on fast track during the Twelfth Five Year Plan.

V. Enhancing Eligibility Criteria and Indexing of Benefits

The eligibility criteria in terms of wage ceiling in Acts like the Payment of Wages Act, 1936, the ESI Act, 1948, the EPF and Miscellaneous Provisions Act, 1952 and the Employees' Compensation Act, 1923, etc. should be reviewed at a given periodicity, say 3 to 5 years, considering the erosion in the wage ceiling limits through amending the rules rather than the Acts.

VI. Improving Enforcement of Labour Laws

The Working Group has suggested a complete review of the strength of the enforcement machinery of labour legislations; creation of an All India Service for labour administration; induction of greater professionalism, etc. Holding *Lok Adalats* has also been encouraged to enable faster disposal of cases. A database should be built on all aspects relating to industrial relations and the officers of the Labour Departments should have access to such database through computer connectivity. In addition to codification and simplification of labour laws, the Working Group also suggested for creating an online 'single window system' for making compliance simple and user friendly and for bringing transparency.

VII. Easing Compliance Burden of Labour Laws

For minor offences for which punishment by way of fine is provided, a senior officer of the Labour Department should be empowered to adjudicate these cases. This would reduce the time taken in disposing complaints and also lessen the burden on courts. The Working Group has recommended identification of the reasons for non-implementation of certain Acts.

PROVISIONS FOR WOMEN WORKERS IN VARIOUS LEGISLATIONS

Chapter 2 portrays the increase in participation of women at workplace. With Government sources like Census (2011) and National Sample Survey (68th Round) confirming a rise in the work participation rate for women, the Government has been playing a crucial role in protecting the class of women workers through policy measures and legislations. Some of the important provisions for safeguarding the interests of working women as available in various legislations have been compiled in this section.

Employment

- Section 27 of the Factories Act, 1948 prohibits employment of women in any part of a factory for pressing cotton in which a cotton-opener is at work.
- Section 46(1)(a) of the Mines Act, 1952 prohibits employment of women in any part of a mine which is below ground.

Remuneration

- Article 39 of the Constitution of India envisages that the State shall direct its policy, among other things, towards securing equal pay for equal work for both men and women. The Equal Remuneration Act, 1976 gives effect to this constitutional provision. It provides for the payment of equal remuneration to men and women workers and for the prevention of discrimination on the ground of sex against women in the matter of employment and for matters connected therewith or incidental thereto.
- A Central Advisory Committee has been set up at the Centre under the Equal Remuneration Act, 1976 to advise the Government on providing increasing employment opportunities for women and generally reviewing the steps taken for effective implementation of the Act.

Health and Safety Measures

Sections 22(2) and 34(2) of the Factories Act, 1948 provide for health and safety of women workers. These sections have been dealt with in details in Chapter 14.

Prohibition of Night Work

Section 66(1)(b) of the Factories Act, 1948, Section 25 of the Beedi and Cigar Workers (Conditions of Employment) Act, 1966 and Section 46(1)(b) of the Mines Act, 1952 stipulate working hours for women between 6 AM and 7 PM.

Provisions for Separate Latrines and Urinals

Provisions for separate latrines and urinals for female workers exist in: Section 19 of the Factories Act, 1948; Section 20 of the Mines Act, 1952; Section 9(1) of the Plantations Labour Act, 1951; Rule 51 of the Contract Labour (Regulation and Abolition) Act, 1970; and Rule 42(1) of the Inter-State Migrant Workmen (RECS) Central Rules, 1980.

Provisions for Separate Washing Facilities

Provisions for separate washing facilities for female workers are given in: Section 42(1)(b) of the Factories Act, 1948; sub-section (1) of Rule 57 of the Contract Labour (Regulation and Abolition) Act, 1970; and Rule 43(1) of the Inter-State Migrant Workmen (RECS) Act, 1979.

Provisions for Crèches

Provision for crèches exists under the following legislations:

- Section 48(1) of the Factories Act, 1948 mandates every factory employing more than 30 women workers to provide and maintain suitable room(s) for the use of children under the age of 6 years of such women. As per sub-section (2) of the Section, these rooms must have adequate accommodation, adequate lighting and ventilation and maintained in a clean and sanitary condition, under the charge of women trained in the care of children and infants.
- As per Section 12(1) of the Plantations Labour Act, 1951, in every plantation wherein 50 or more women workers (including those employed by any contractor) are employed, or where the number of children of women workers (including women workers employed by any contractor) is 20 or more, there shall be provided and maintained by the employer suitable rooms for the use of children of such women workers.
- Section 14(1) of the Beedi and Cigar Workers (Conditions of Employment) Act, 1966 mandates the provision and maintenance of suitable room(s) for the use of children under the age of 6 years of female employees in industrial premises where more than 50 female employees are ordinarily employed.
- Section 35(1) of the Building and Other Construction Workers (RECS) Act, 1996 provides for suitable room(s) for the use of children under the age of 6 years of female building workers in every place wherein more than 50 such female workers are ordinarily employed.
- As per Rule 44(1) of the Inter-State Migrant Workmen (RECS) Act, 1979, in every establishment where 20 or more workmen are ordinarily employed as migrant workmen and in which their employment is likely to continue for 3 months or more, the contractor shall provide and maintain two rooms of reasonable dimensions for the use of the children of these workers under the age of 6 years.

Maternity Benefit

- The Maternity Benefit Act, 1961 regulates the employment of women in certain establishments for periods specified before and after childbirth and provides maternity benefit and certain other benefits. We have covered the various provisions of this Act in Chapter 17.
- The Building and Other Construction Workers (Regulation of Employment and Conditions of Service) Act, 1996 provides for maternity benefit to female beneficiaries of the Welfare Fund.

Other Measures

Training and Education With participation of women increasing steadily in the workforce, it has been realised by policy makers and social thinkers alike that the process of social development cannot afford to ignore the needs, interests and aspirations of women. Another major concern in the 1970s has been gender inequalities and inequities. Women's vocational training thus assumed special attention to the Government of India, and the Women's Vocational Training Programme (WVTP) was designed and launched under the Directorate General of Employment and Training (DGET) in 1977 to mainstream women into economic activities of the nation. The Programme aims to promote both self-employment and wage-employment of women in industry as semi-skilled or skilled and highly skilled workers by way of increasing their participation in skill-training facilities.

Reflection

The DGET is the apex organization for development and coordination of vocational training programmes at national level.

Training institutes exclusively for women have been set up under Central and State sector schemes. Under the Central sector, the DGET has set up 11 institutes, comprising one National Vocational Training Institute (NVTI) for Women at Noida and 10 Regional Vocational Training Institutes (RVTIs) for Women at Mumbai, Bangalore, Thiruvananthapuram, Hisar, Indore, Kolkata, Tura, Allahabad, Vadodara and Jaipur.

EXHIBIT 9.1 ACTIVITIES OF THE WOMEN'S VOCATIONAL TRAINING PROGRAMME

Institutionalized skill training is offered to women under the Women's Vocational Training Programme at basic (under Craftsmen Training Scheme [CTS]), advanced and post-advanced levels (both under Craft Instructors Training Scheme [CITS]). The Women Target Groups (Regular Training) for different categories are:

- For CTS: Training facilities offered in engineering and non-engineering skill courses; minimum age is 14 years; no bar on upper age; minimum qualification is pass in 10th or 12th class under the 10+2 system, depending on the training area opted.
- For CITS: Women having National Trade Certificate in relevant trade; no upper age limit.

The programmes under CTS are implemented by the Central Government, State Governments and Union Territories. In the Central Sphere the Women's Vocational Training Programme is implemented through a network of 11 institutes (1 National Vocational Training Institute for Women and 10 RVTIs). Under the State sector, vocational training is organised through a network of Women Industrial Training Institutes (ITIs)/private Women ITIs/Women Wings in General ITIs, which are directly under the administrative control of the respective State Governments. The curriculum for the training courses is designed in consultation with the industry and is modified as and when required.

(Adapted from: www.womentraining.gov.in/general/act.HTM accessed on 4/6/2014.)

Sexual Harassment of Women Workers

EXHIBIT 9.2 SEXUAL HARASSMENT OF WOMEN WORKERS: THE LEGAL PERSPECTIVE

In its landmark judgment in *Vishakha and Others vs. State of Rajasthan and Others* (AIR 1997 SC 3011) the Supreme Court of India has categorically held that any incident of sexual harassment results in violation of fundamental rights of gender equality and the right to life and liberty. Thus any such incident is a clear violation of the rights guaranteed under Articles 14, 15, 19(1)(g) and 21 of the Constitution of India, which are enforceable under Article 32 of the Constitution. The Apex Court has further observed that sexual harassment includes such unwelcome sexually determined behaviour as physical contacts and advances, sexually coloured remarks, showing pornography and sexual demands, whether by words or actions. Such conduct can be humiliating and may constitute a health and safety problem. Equality in employment can be seriously impaired when women are subjected to gender-specific violence such as sexual harassment at workplace, and safeguards against sexual harassment are implicit therein.

(Adapted from: www.indiankanoon.org/doc/635207/ accessed on 6/6/2014.)

The Sexual Harassment of Women at Workplace (Prevention, Prohibition and Redressal) Act, 2013 provides for protection against sexual harassment of women at workplace and for the prevention and redressal of complaints of sexual harassment and for matters connected therewith or incidental thereto. The Act received the assent of the President of India on 22nd April, 2013 and has come into force on and from 9th December, 2013. We have included this Act as an appendix to the book.

POLICIES AND PROVISIONS FOR CHILD LABOUR

The affirmative attitude of the State towards prevention of child labour is evident from various Articles in the Constitution of India. Article 21A, under the title Right to Education, says that the State shall provide free and compulsory education to all children of the age of 6 to 14 years in such manner as the State may determine by law. Article 24 prohibits employment of children below the age of 14 years in any factory or mine or in any other hazardous occupation. Article 39(e) states that the health and strength of workers, men and women, and the tender age of children are not abused and that citizens are not forced by economic necessity to enter avocations unsuited to their age or strength.

State intervention in various dimensions to eradicate employment of children has resulted in instances of child labour witnessing record decline in the last few decades, both in terms of magnitude and workforce participation rate. Table 9.1 presents the details of inspections carried out, prosecutions launched and convictions made under the Child Labour (Prohibition and Regulation) Act, 1986 between 2007 and 2012 on the basis of data received from various States.

Table 9.1 Enforcement Figures on Child Labour

Year	*Number of Inspections*	*Number of Prosecutions*	*Number of Convictions*
2007	363927	12705	617
2008	355629	11318	763
2009	317083	11418	1312
2010	239612	8998	1308
2011	84935	4590	774
2012**	25040	589	167

**Information yet to be received from many States.

(Adapted from: www.labour.nic.in, accessed on 4/6/2014.)

On the basis of data generated by the National Sample Survey Office (2009-2010), working children in India are estimated at 49.84 lakhs. Further, as per the Report of the Working Group on Employment, Planning and Policy for the Twelfth Five Year Plan, the percentage of child labour has been found to have declined steadily from 6.2 per cent in 1993-1994 to 3.3 per cent by 2004-2005 to 2.4 per cent in 2007-2008 and finally to 2 per cent in 2009-2010. An inspection of the figures published by the Global Report on Child Labour published by ILO in 2006 revealed that the activity rate of children in the age group of 5-14 years stood at 19.4 per cent in the Asia Pacific Region in 2000, though in India the activity rate of children is 5 per cent as per 2001 Census (Ministry of Labour & Employment, 2012-2013, p. 91). However, child labour still exists in different industries and the Government has to play a proactive role in the eradication of this menace.

Spotlight
The National Policy on Child Labour was declared in August, 1987.

The National Policy on Child Labour, declared in August, 1987, contains a three-pronged action plan for tackling the problem of child labour. As a part of the *legislative action plan*, the Government of India has enacted the Child Labour (Prohibition and Regulation) Act, 1986 to prohibit the engagement of children below the age of 14 years in 18 occupations and 65 processes and to regulate the conditions of work of children in certain other employments. The onus of enforcement of the various provisions of the Act lies with the State Governments, as provided in Section 2 of the Act. The Government monitors the enforcement of the legislation from time to time. Special drives on enforcement and awareness generation are also launched regularly.

Rescue and repatriation is another crucial component of the legislative policy. During inspections and raids conducted under the Act, child labour is identified and rescued; rehabilitative measures are set forth thereafter by way of repatriation in case of migrant child labour; and bridge education is provided with the ultimate objective of mainstreaming such children into the formal system of education. The Government also provides pre-vocational training to the rescued children.

As a part of the *convergence action plan*, a Core Group on convergence of various welfare schemes and general development programmes of the Government for benefiting children has been constituted under the aegis of the Ministry of Labour & Employment. The primary aim of the Core Group is to ensure that the families of child labour are given priority for their upliftment. The Government is aware of the fact that poverty and illiteracy are the root cause of child labour; hence it is necessary that educational rehabilitation of children is supplemented with economic rehabilitation of their families, so that they are not compelled by economic circumstances to send their children to work.

Under *project-based action plans*, the National Policy on Child Labour also envisages launching of projects for the welfare of working children in areas of high concentration of child labour. With regard to educational rehabilitation, the Government has implemented the National Child Labour Project (NCLP) Scheme in 1988. The Scheme seeks to adopt a sequential approach towards rehabilitation of children working in hazardous occupations and processes in the first instance. A survey of child labour engaged in such occupations is conducted, following which, children are to be withdrawn and then put into special schools, to be eventually mainstreamed into formal schooling system. Project Societies at the district level are fully funded for opening of such special schools or Rehabilitation Centres. As per figures revealed by the Ministry of Labour & Employment, presently about 7,311 special schools are in operation, with enrolment of 3.2 lakh children. About 8.95 lakh children have already been mainstreamed into the formal system since inception of the NCLP.

EXHIBIT 9.3 ERADICATING CHILD LABOUR THROUGH CONVERGENCE OF SCHEMES

The Ministry of Labour & Employment is taking various proactive measures by converging schemes of different Ministries. Some of such schemes are highlighted here.

The Ministry of Women and Child Development is working in supplementing the efforts of this Ministry in providing food and shelter to the children withdrawn from work through their schemes of shelter homes, etc. The Ministry of Human Resource Development (MHRD) is working in collaboration with the Ministry of Labour & Employment for providing mid-day meal to the National Child Labour Project Scheme school children, teachers' training, supply of books, etc. under the *Sarva Shiksha Abhiyan* and mainstreaming of NCLP children into the formal education system. Convergence has also been made with Ministries of Rural Development, Urban Housing and Poverty Alleviation and Panchayati Raj for covering these children under the various income and employment generation schemes for their economic rehabilitation. In each State one officer from the State Department of Labour has been nominated as Anti Human Trafficking Unit (AHTU) to act as link officer for coordinating with the MHRD in that State for the prevention of trafficking of children. The Ministry of Railways is also contributing in similar convergence by generating awareness and restricting child trafficking.

Further, the Ministry of Labour & Employment is implementing a pilot project named "Converging against Child Labour: Support for India's Model" in collaboration with ILO and SRO Delhi, funded by the US Department of Labour. The project aims at contributing to the prevention and elimination of hazardous child labour, including trafficking and migration of children for labour. It is covering two districts each in Bihar, Jharkhand, Gujarat, Madhya Pradesh and Orissa for 42 months.

(Adapted from: www.labour.gov.in/upload/uploadfiles/files/Divisions/childlabour/PolicyofGovernmenon-theissueofChildLabour.pdf accessed on 5/6/2014.)

WAGES

The term 'wage' refers to a payment made under contract by an employer to a worker in lieu of the services rendered by the latter. The most commonly accepted unit to measure such service is time. Wages may thus be paid on basis of hours, days, month or even year.

Over time thoughts on wages have developed from mere *subsistence theory* and *standard of living theory* to broader aspects of human resource management, and wages and salary are now clubbed as compensation (Geetika, Ghosh and Choudhury, 2011). Let us quickly touch upon the concepts of money wage and real wage here, before we move on to the theories of wages. *Money wage* is evaluated with reference to the money that is paid, instead of the equivalent purchasing power; it is also known as nominal wage. However, money wage may not depict what a worker really earns; it is real wage that determines the standard of living of a worker. *Real wage* is income of a worker after taking into consideration the effects of inflation on his/her purchasing power.

Spotlight

Money wage is evaluated with reference to the money that is paid; real wage considers the effects of inflation on purchasing power.

THEORIES OF WAGES

Subsistence Theory

Proposed by David Ricardo, the subsistence theory states that the price of labour depends on the subsistence of labour. Wages tend to settle at a level that is just sufficient to maintain the bare minimum subsistence level of a worker and his/her dependents. Such price, according to Ricardo, is equal to the amount of commodities necessary for the existence of a worker and his/her family. If wages rise above the subsistence level, workers are encouraged to marry and have large families, which would eventually add to the labour force, bringing wages down to the subsistence level. If however wages fall below this level, marriages and births are discouraged and impoverishment would increase death rate. This would again lower labour supply, until wages rise to the subsistence level.

The subsistence theory is completely outdated and has no practical application, especially in developed countries. It also ignores the importance of demand for labour and the role of trade unions in determining wages.

Wages Fund Theory

According to the Wages Fund Theory proposed by J. S. Mill, wages depend upon two quantities, namely, the fixed wage fund (or circulating capital) set aside for the purchase of labour and the number of workers seeking employment. Since the wage fund is fixed, only a reduction in the number of workers could raise wages. There is another dimension to the fixed wage fund: if trade unions of workers succeeded in raising wages in one trade that could only be possible at the expense of another. Therefore unions cannot raise wages for the labour class as a whole.

This theory has been widely criticised on several grounds, the strongest of them being that wages are not necessarily paid out of circulating capital alone. The Wages Fund Theory is applicable at best in an under-developed country that has capital deficiency, and stands rejected now.

> **Spotlight**
> The wage fund (or circulating capital) is fixed.

Purchasing Power Parity Theory

The classical economists, most notably Pigou, had argued that a cut in wages during unemployment and depression in the economy would help in restoring full employment. This viewpoint was criticised by Keynes, who propounded a new theory applicable to the economy as a whole and not particularly wages. Keynes considered determination of wage rate from a macro viewpoint, as an income for the wage earners. If the wage rate is high, workers would have more purchasing power, which, in turn, would increase the aggregate demand for goods and the level of output. Conversely, if the wage rate is low, purchasing power of labour would be less, which would lower the aggregate demand. Low aggregate demand would have an adverse impact on the level of employment and output. Therefore a cut in the wage rate instead of removing unemployment and depression would further accentuate the problem.

Residual Claimant Theory

The Residual Claimant Theory has been proposed by Walker, according to whom, wages are the residue after the other factors of production have been paid. In other words, after rent, interest and profit have been paid, the remainder of the total output would go to workers as wages. Several authors consider this theory to be optimistic, as it suggests the possibility of increase in wages through increased efficiency of workers, whereas the Subsistence Theory and Wages Fund Theory were pessimistic in approach. However this theory has been rejected by economists on several grounds.

Marginal Productivity Theory

One of the most prominent of neoclassical theories of wages, the marginal productivity theory, is associated initially with John Bates Clark and was developed later by Marshall, Jevons and Walras. It is basically a theory of distribution, and can be applied to any factor of production, although it has been most prominently used for determination of wages.

The marginal productivity theory rests on the assumptions of a perfectly competitive market and profit maximisation motive of employers. It postulates that demand for labour is determined by the value of output of an additional worker. The marginal product of labour is the amount by which the output would be increased if a unit of labour was increased, with the quantities of other factors of production remaining constant.

> **Spotlight**
> As per the marginal productivity theory, demand for labour is determined by the value of output of an additional worker.

Since the employer works for profit, therefore he would like to pay as low as possible, and definitely not more than the marginal productivity of the factor (here labour). Due to perfect competition, no factor input would be willing to accept a return lower than its marginal productivity. Thus in an open market marginal productivity determines the equilibrium factor price (here wage).

The marginal productivity theory invites criticism on account of the assumption of perfect competition. Further, labour is assumed to be perfectly mobile, which does not hold in the real world. Because of such reasons this theory becomes just a theoretical explanation of wage determination, whereas in real life wages are determined by other considerations like efficiency of labour, bargaining and negotiation.

Bargaining Theory of Wages

Proposed by John Davidson, this theory of wage determination is based on negotiations between employers and unions, with the assumption that the two parties, labour and employer, have conflicting objectives. Each wants the maximum share of the firm's profits and is aware of the costs of a strike and the risks of participating in one.

Efficiency Wage Theory/Hypothesis

The term 'efficiency-wages' was coined by the noted economist, Alfred Marshall. The efficiency wage hypothesis is a complete digression from the marginal productivity theory explained earlier. It postulates that in certain situations employers may find it more beneficial to pay wages to their workers higher than their marginal revenue product. The underlying idea is that the value of a worker may depend on how much he/she is paid, because richer workers are more productive or better motivated to avoid unemployment. This theory is more modern and practical in approach as it takes a holistic view of wages.

Demand and Supply Theory

According to this theory, wages are determined by the interaction of demand and supply, just like any commodity. Demand for labour partly reflects productivity of labour and partly the market value of the product at different levels of production. Factors that determine the demand for labour include derived demand, elasticity of demand for labour and technical progress. Supply of labour, on the other hand, depends on the number of workers and the number of hours per day they are prepared to work. It is governed by the prevailing wage rate in the market and preference of labour for leisure. Workers earn to meet their needs, which may include basic necessities of food, clothing and shelter, education and health and entertainment of self and dependents.

> **Spotlight**
> The labour supply curve is backward bending beyond a particular wage.

Due to the trade-off between hours of work and hours of leisure, the supply curve of labour is not normally upward sloping, but is backward bending beyond a particular wage.

WAGE BOARDS

The concept of industry-level Wage Boards has been introduced in Chapter 8 as a non-statutory measure of settlement of industrial disputes. We have also touched on this topic in this chapter under tripartite bodies in India. This section presents a brief description of evolution of Wage Boards in India, their structure and functions and a critical evaluation of their role in Indian industrial relations.

Evolution of Wage Boards in India

Tracing the evolution of Wage Boards in India we can see that as early as 1931 the Whitley Commission on Labour had recommended the setting up of a Wage Board for the determination of wages in lines with concern of the ILO to evolve an international instrument for minimum wage fixation. Subsequently the First Five Year Plan also drew a scheme for permanent wage boards to be set up in each State with a tripartite composition and dealt with at the level of the Central Government. This was envisaged in the Second Plan as well. Finally the Wage Board system was introduced in March, 1957; the very first of its kind was set up for the cotton textile industry in the name of Central Wage Board. This was followed by establishment of such boards in other industries like sugar, cement, and jute. Though Wage Boards were initially meant to deal with the problems which arise in wage fixation, eventually it was felt that wage fixation can be left to the concerned industry without State intervention. As on date, wages are decided by Wage Boards for journalists and non-journalists newspaper and news-agency employees. Since 1955, the Government has constituted six wage boards for these employees, presented in Table 9.2.

Spotlight

The first Wage Board in India was set up for the cotton textile industry in 1957.

TABLE 9.2 Wage Boards for Working Journalists and Non-Journalist Newspaper Employees

S. No.	*Industry*	*Date of Appointment*	*Date of Submission of Final Report to Govt.*	*Date of Acceptance of Recommendation by Govt.*
1.	Wage Board for Working Journalists	2.5.1956	NA	11.5.1957
2.	(a) Wage Board for Working Journalists	12.11.1963	17.7.1967	27.10.1967
	(b) Wage Board for Non-Journalists Newspaper Employees	25.2.1964	17.7.1967	18.11.1967
3.	(a) Wage Board for Working Journalists	11.6.1975	13.8.1980	26.12.1980 &
	(b) Wage Board for Non-Journalists Newspaper Employees	6.2.1976		20.7.1981
4.	Wage Board for Working Journalists and Non-Journalists Newspaper Employees	17.7.1985	30.5.1989	31.8.1989
5.	Wage Board for Working Journalists and Non-Journalists Newspaper Employees	2.9.1994	25.7.2000	5.12.2000 and 15.12.2000
6.	Wage Board for Working Journalists & Non-Journalists Newspaper Employees	24.5.2007	31.12.2010	11.11.2011

(Adapted from: www.labour.nic.in, accessed on 4/6/2014.)

Constitution of Wage Board

A Wage Board is tripartite by structure, consisting of a chairperson, an equal number of representatives of employers and employees (two members each) and two other independent members (an economist and a consumers' representative) nominated to the Board. The Chairman is appointed by the appropriate Government in consultation with the Chief Justice of the High Court concerned or the Supreme Court of India. Any person who is or has been eligible to be appointed as a Judge of a High Court shall be qualified for appointment as the Chairman. Usually a Member of Parliament is nominated to represent consumers. The appropriate Government appoints workers' and employers' representatives on the recommendations of the most representative workers' and employers' organisations respectively in the sector concerned.

Functions of Wage Board

A Wage Board adjudicates industrial disputes referred to it with the assistance of independent members. As per the First National Commission on Labour (1969), a Wage Board serves as an effective machinery for determination of wages, and for this purpose it attempts to fix wages within the broad framework of the Government's economic and social policy. It is required to work out a wage structure based on the principles of fair wages formulated by the Committee on Fair Wages. In addition to the considerations relating to fair wages, a Wage Board must take into account the following aspects:

(i) the needs of the industry in a developing economy,
(ii) the system of payment by results,
(iii) the special characteristics of the industry in various regions and areas,
(iv) the categories of workers to be covered (this may be according to the definition in the Industrial Disputes Act, 1947), and
(v) the working hours in the industry.

Besides, a Board may be assigned additional tasks like working out the principles that should govern payment of bonus and framing of gratuity schemes to workers in the concerned industry.

Exhibit 9.4 Role of Wage Boards

In *Sindhudurg District Central Cooperative Bank Ltd., Kudal vs. Sindhu Sahakari Bank Karamchari Sanstha* ((1997) IILLJ 1217 Bom) the Court has observed that Wage Board is a platform where the conflicting and contradictory views of employers and workmen are sought to be harmonized within the narrowest possible limit in the presence of the Chairman, with an impartial attitude to reach harmonious decisions. The very object of constituting a tripartite Wage Board can bring to bear on the discussions and examinations of the questions by persons having a close and intimate knowledge of the working of the industries. The presence of such persons in the Board leads to competent handling of industrial disputes. Thus the Board ensures more acceptable decisions. The decisions of the Board are also based on the spirit of compromise.

It has been pointed out that from the time these Boards have been incepted, the efforts of the Chairman and members have gone a long way in maintaining harmonious industrial relations in the undertakings appearing before them. Such decisions, when taken unanimously, are naturally and legally free from appeal to the higher Courts. In this spirit, they have greater value in terms of collective bargaining and industrial peace than decisions imposed on the parties by a single statutory authority like the Industrial Court. The scheme of Wage Boards thus introduces a dual adjudication process, which is a unique feature of this tripartite machinery: one is to plead their case and the other is to decide their case.

(Adapted from: www.indiankanoon.org/doc/885322/ accessed on 1/6/2014.)

Evaluation of Wage Boards

The Committee on the functioning of the system of Wage Boards set up by the First National Commission on Labour (1969) had identified major problems from which Wage Boards suffer, some of which are discussed here:

- A section of employers' organisations opposed this single machinery for wage fixation in all types of industrial undertakings and preferred collective bargaining or adjudication for wage determination. The composition and functioning of the Boards was also criticised.
- Wage Boards take an unduly long time. Their working can be improved only if procedural delays are removed.
- Majority of the recommendations of these boards are not unanimous; such recommendations should be implemented only if they are unanimous.
- Workers' organisations were generally dissatisfied about the manner of working of the Boards on grounds of time taken, ad hoc increase in emoluments, that too on the lower side recommended by these boards, the non-statutory nature of recommendations and adjudication in the event of non-implementation.

The Committee made some important recommendations, including selection of the Chairman of a Wage Board by common consent of the organisations of workers and employers in the industry concerned; functioning of the Boards essentially as a machinery for collective bargaining; assistance by technical assessors and experts; setting up of a Central Wage Board in the Union Ministry of Labour on a permanent basis to serve all Wage Boards through the supply of statistical and other material and lending of necessary staff, etc. (Report of the First Commission on Labour, 1969).

The importance of non-statutory Wage Boards has declined over time since recommendations made by these boards are not enforceable under the law. Simultaneously trade unions have grown in strength and are themselves able to negotiate their wages with the management. No non-statutory Wage Board has been set up after 1966, with the exception of the sugar industry, in which the last such Board was constituted in 1985 *(www.labour.nic.in)*. Nevertheless, Wage Boards have succeeded in promoting industry-wise negotiations and have thus ensured industrial peace.

RECOMMENDATIONS OF THE SECOND NATIONAL COMMISSION ON LABOUR

The Second National Commission on Labour (2002) has made certain significant recommendations in the areas of labour legislations, women and child labour and wages. We have included some of these recommendations in this section.

Labour Laws

- The organised sector should be defined as consisting of establishments which have a minimum employment limit. Whatever be such limit, certain provisions like maternity benefit, child care, employees' compensation, medical benefits and other elements of social security and safety must be applicable to all workers, irrespective of the employment size of that establishment or the nature of its activity.

- The Government may lay down a list of highly paid jobs like airline pilots who are presently deemed as workmen category as being outside the purview of the laws relating to workmen and included in the proposed law for the protection of non-workmen.
- The existing set of labour laws should be broadly grouped into four or five groups of laws pertaining to industrial relations, wages, social security, safety and welfare and working conditions.
- Coverage as well as definition of the term 'worker' should be the same in all groups of laws, subject to the stipulation that social security benefits must be available to all employees including administrative, managerial, supervisory and others excluded from the category of workmen and others not treated as workmen or excluded from the category of workmen. The Commission preferred the gender-neutral expression 'worker' instead of the currently used word 'workman' that we find in the Industrial Disputes Act, 1947 and some other Acts.
- To rationalise and simplify the existing labour laws it was proposed that persons engaged in domestic service are better covered under the proposed umbrella legislation, particularly in regard to wages, hours of work, working conditions, safety and social security.

Women Workers

- The laws and systems of social security should prevent and eliminate discriminatory attitudes and practices towards women workers. All recommendations for policies meant for this segment of the workforce must be combined with an enhancement of their own strength, i.e., women's empowerment.
- A separate wing should be set up in the Labour Departments for unorganised workers with adequate number of women employees.
- A Central Fund must be set up from which welfare and social security measures for women workers should be financed. A Welfare Fund should be set up with employers' contribution in the form of a cess with provisions for maternity leave for women agricultural labour.
- The existing provisions for maternity benefit in the organised sector should be extended to be applicable to all women workers. There is a need for separate legislation for providing maternity benefits to women in the unorganised sector. Its implementation is possible through Welfare Funds or area-based schemes. A statutory scheme for the implementation of maternity entitlements should cover all women under income criteria. The scheme should provide financial support for childbirth, childcare and breast-feeding in the first few months of the child's life. Funds to support such a scheme should be raised from a basket of sources.
- Both underground work in mines and work between certain hours for women workers must be prohibited. There need not be any restriction on night work for women if their number in any shift in an establishment is not less than five and if the management is able to provide satisfactory arrangements for their transport, safety and rest after or before shift hours.
- Labour legislation should include provisions for crèches where there are 20 or more workers, irrespective of the gender of the worker.

Child Labour

- Public action is recommended to be mobilised along all fronts to change the attitude towards child labour and to build public pressure against hiring children. The entire strategy would have to be based on promoting the norm that no child should work and that all children should be in schools.

- An indicative law on child labour was proposed to replace the existing Child Labour (Regulation and Prohibition) Act, 1986.
- The age group of over 3 years must be included to ensure that children of disadvantaged groups have equality of opportunity in the school system.
- Special efforts should be made to identify, develop and investigate low-cost, community-based approaches; to analyse their impact on the overall development of children and to validate and legitimise them on the basis of evaluation.

Wages

- State Governments should specify minimum wages for an unskilled category of worker and these wages should be the same for all industries. Whatever the employment, notification should prescribe the same minimum wage to all. The Minimum Wage Committee may fix the minimum wage for a region, to be made applicable to all employments in that region.

Summary

- The State is an endogenous player of the industrial relations system of any nation. Tripartism involves three parties (i.e., trade unions of workers, employer and government) that participate in settlement of matters of industrial dispute. In India the main tripartite bodies are: ILC, SLC, Industrial Committees, Wage Boards and State Labour Advisory Boards.
- The Planning Commission and different committees have been recommending reform of labour laws in India by highlighting the need for flexibility that would give impetus to the industry to compete in international markets.
- The main recommendations regarding amendment of labour laws are: consolidation, simplification and rationalisation, common definitions in laws, provisions of minimum living wage, improved regulatory activities, basic social security and labour welfare schemes, and improved health and safety facilities to unorganised workers.
- Amendment is recommended in certain key acts like the Minimum Wages Act, 1948, the Contract Labour (Regulation and Abolition) Act, 1970 and the Factories Act, 1948.
- Government has been playing a crucial role in protecting the class of women workers through policy measures and legislations. Some important provisions for safeguarding the interests of working women available in various legislations are in the categories of prohibition of employment, provision for equal remuneration, health and safety measures, prohibition of night work, provisions for conservancy, separate washing facilities, crèches and maternity benefit. Other important provisions are related with training and education and sexual harassment of women workers.
- The National Policy on Child Labour contains a three-pronged action plan for tackling the problem of child labour: legislative action plan, convergence action plan, and project-based action plan.
- As a part of the legislative action plan, the Government has enacted the Child Labour (Prohibition and Regulation) Act, 1986 to prohibit the engagement of children below the age of 14 years in 18 occupations and 65 processes and to regulate the conditions of work of children in certain other employments.
- The term 'wage' refers to a payment made under contract by an employer to a worker in lieu of the services rendered by the latter. Wages may be paid on basis of hours, days, months or even year.
- Various wage theories are subsistence theory, wages fund theory, purchasing power parity theory, residual claimant theory, marginal productivity theory, bargaining theory, efficiency wage theory/hypothesis and demand and supply theory.

- A Wage Board is tripartite by structure, consisting of a chairperson, an equal number of representatives of employers and employees (two members each) and two other independent members (an economist and a consumers' representative). A Wage Board is required to work out a wage structure based on the principles of fair wages formulated by the Committee on Fair Wages.
- The Five Year Plans, formulated, executed and monitored by the Planning Commission, form an integral component of the planning process in India. Issues pertaining to labour policy (including industrial relations, employment, wages, welfare, working conditions and productivity) occupy pivotal position in the Five Year Plans.

Key Concepts

Tripartism	State intervention	Labour policy
Child labour	Five Year Plan	Labour law reforms
Wage theory	Planning Commission	Minimum wage

Bibliography

Datta, R. C. and Sil, M. *Contemporary Issues on Labour Law*, Mumbai: Tata Institute of Social Studies; 2007.

Debroy, B. Why We Need Law Reform, 2001, http://www.indiasemimar.com/2001/497/497%20bibek%debroy.htm, accessed on 4/6/2014.

Dunlop, J.T. *Industrial Relation System*, New York: Holt and Company; 1958.

Geetika, Ghosh, P. and Roy Choudhury, P. *Managerial Economics*, 2nd edition, New Delhi: Tata McGraw Hill; 2011.

Jeong, D. Y. The Role of the State in Industrial Relations, *Seoul Journal of Business*, 2010, Vol. 16, No. 2, pp. 95-125.

NCEUS Conditions of Work and Promotion of Livelihood, in the Unorganised Sector, New Delhi: Government of India; 2007.

Otobo, D. *Industrial Relations: Theory and Controversies*, Lagos: Malthouse Press Ltd., 2000.

Ratnam, C. S. V. *Industrial Relations*, New Delhi: Oxford University Press India; 2006.

Reform in India: An Overview, Discussion Paper No. 5/2007, ATLMRI Discussion Paper, Tata Institute of Social Sciences, Retrieved from http://skillingindia.com/pdf/Contemporary%20Issue%20on%20Labour%20Law%20Reform%20in%20India%20An%20overview.pdf, accessed on 5/6/2014.

Report of the National Commission on Labour (2002, 1991–1967) New Delhi: Academic Foundation.

NSSO Employment and Unemployment Situation in India, (July 2011–June 2012), Vol. 554 of 68th Round NSSO, MOSPI, Government of India, January 2014.

Silva, De S. R. (n.d.) Elements of a Sound Industrial Relations System, *International Labour Organization, ACT/EMP Publishers, Retrieved from http://www.ilo.org/public/english/dialogue/actemp/downloads/publications/srseleme.pdf on 6/6/2014.*

Yesufu, T. M. *The Dynamics of Industrial Relations: The Nigerian Experience*, Ibadan, Nigeria: University Press Ltd.; 1982.

http://www.ilo.org/public/english/standards/relm/ilc/ilc95/pdf/rep-i-b.pdf, accessed on 5/6/2014 www.planningcommission.nic.in

Review Questions

Objective Type Questions

I. Write True or False

(i) No non-statutory Wage Board has been set up after 1966, excepting the jute industry.
(ii) Meetings of the ILC and SLC are held annually.
(iii) The Residual Claimant Theory is pessimistic in approach.
(iv) The Factories Act, 1948 mandates provision for crèches in every factory employing more than 30 women workers.
(v) Money wage is also known as nominal wage.

Answers: (i) False, (ii) False, (iii) False, (iv) True, (v) True

II. Fill in the Blanks

(i) So far the Government has constituted ____ wage boards for working journalists and non-journalist newspaper employees.
(ii) According to Ricardo, the price of labour depends on the ______of labour.
(iii) Rescue and ____ is a crucial part of the legislative policy adopted by the Government for eradication of child labour.
(iv) The development programmes proposed under the Second Five Year Plan included financing of _____ schemes.
(v) The proposed National Skill ______ would have the facility to link various databases across Ministries and States.

Answers: (i) six, (ii) subsistence, (iii) repatriation, (iv) housing, (v) Registry

Discussion Questions

1. Discuss the functioning of tripartism in industrial relations. State the objectives and role played by the main tripartite bodies in India.
2. What shift in focus of the Government is reflected in terms of labour policy and recommendations in the Five Year Plans? Discuss in the light of all the Five Year Plans formulated so far.
3. What do you understand by the role of State in industrial relations? What could be major means of State intervention?
4. What are the major issues in labour law reforms in India? Discuss specifically in context of social security legislations.
5. How can the recommendations of the Second National Commission on Labour help in ameliorating the condition of child labour in India? How pro-women are the various recommendations?
6. Critically compare the various theories of wage. Which one, according to you, is the most relevant in current business environment? Which theory would be the most inapplicable?
7. Elucidate the concept of a Wage Board, highlighting its composition and main functions.
8. Discuss the initiatives taken by the Government of India to eradicate child labour.
9. Compare the perspectives of different stakeholders in industrial relations on flexibility in labour legislations. Do you consider bringing about flexibility as necessary?
10. Discuss the various provisions for women workers under different legislations.

CASE STUDY

Child Labour in India: Justice Denied

Children are not any commodity; they are precious and one of the most important assets for any nation. The welfare and development of any community is largely contingent on the health and well-being of its children. However, it is a matter of disgrace that millions of children today are forced to work in various economic activities in return of very nominal wages. As domestic help they have to clean clothes and floors, cook food and take care of children in the house. Children also work as bonded labour out of perceived obligations to landlords or money lenders, to whom they are mortgaged for small loans taken for purposes like treatment of sickness and social ceremonies. Thus the provision of child labour becomes a part of a family rent or debt settlement.

Practically there in no industry in which children do not work. More specifically, as many as 90 per cent of children in the carpet industry in Mirzapur in the State of Uttar Pradesh have been bonded, i.e., sold into virtual slavery. They also have to work in exploitative and hazardous conditions. According to an estimate, approximately 50,000 children ranging from 3.6 to 15 years of age work in the match and fireworks industries in and around Sivakasi in the State of Tamil Nadu, perhaps the most publicised center of child labour in India. As many as 150 to 200 children are loaded in buses and vans which start off from 3 to 5 in the morning from neighbouring villages within a radius of about 20 miles, to get to the factories at 6 AM or 7 AM. These children return home between 6 and 9 in the evening. They work for about 12 hours daily in dark sheds, handling dangerous and toxic chemicals, but effectively are away from home for 15 hours. Three quarters of these child workers are girls. Each village in the neighbourhood of Sivakasi has an agent who enrolls the children and ensures that they are awake when the transport arrives. These agents receive a monthly salary of ₹150. They may give an advance of up to ₹200 per child labour enrolled to the parents; the advance is then deducted from the child's salary. In the glass industry of Firozabad in Uttar Pradesh almost 25 per cent of the total workers are not even of 15 years of age. They have to undertake almost all the processes involved in bangle making, including carrying molten glass from the furnace to adult workers and back to the furnace, in which temperature approaches 700 degree Centigrade. Children who are often hired along with their parents for construction work also have to engage in hard physical labour while digging earth, carrying head loads of mud and mortar, breaking stones and soldering heavy iron rods.

The ILO has also pointed in its studies that millions of children work under exploitative conditions. They are beaten up, treated cruelly, and provided little food and insufficient rest. No medical treatment is made available to these children by their employers. Some child workers have even been found to go to the extent of consuming liquor, opium, *ganja* and *charas*. Such a disturbed and undisciplined childhood makes criminals out of innocent children. They are denied education and their development is retarded, as they work long hours in the fields, glass factories, carpet weaving industry and in homes.

The causes behind this problem are many. Undoubtedly the existence of child labour in India, in most of the cases, is the gift of poverty; but there are certain other causative dimensions. The social structure is also one of reasons; child labour is mostly from the scheduled castes, scheduled tribes and other backward classes and religious minorities. Policy makers argue that the State ought not to intervene in the issue of child labour, since poor parents depend upon the income of their children, and hence it is a matter of social justice that the children of the poor are allowed to work.

(Adapted from: Gupta, S. (1999). Child Labour is Violative of Rights of the Child, www.indiankanoon.org/doc/1496959/ accessed on 4/6/2014.)

Review Questions

1. Comment on the condition of child labour as portrayed in the case.
2. What are the reasons for the rampant prevalence of child labour in the country?
3. The legislation on child labour seeks only to *regulate* child labour but does not consider it entirely unacceptable. Would you agree with this statement? Defend your argument.

APPENDIX

Labour legislations in India can be presented in the following four broad categories:

- **Labour laws enacted and enforced by the Central Government:** These include, in chronological order of their year of enactment: The Mica Mines Labour Welfare Fund Act, 1946; The Employees' State Insurance Act, 1948; The Mines Act, 1952; The Employees' Provident Fund and Miscellaneous Provisions Act, 1952; The Limestone and Dolomite Mines Labour Welfare Fund Act, 1972; The Iron Ore Mines, Manganese Ore Mines and Chrome Ore Mines Labour Welfare (Cess) Act, 1976; The Iron Ore Mines, Manganese Ore Mines and Chrome Ore Mines Labour Welfare Fund Act, 1976; The Beedi Workers Welfare Cess Act, 1976; The Beedi Workers Welfare Fund Act, 1976; The Cine Workers Welfare Fund Act, 1981; The Cine Workers Welfare (Cess) Act, 1981; The Dock Workers (Safety, Health and Welfare) Act, 1986; and The Sexual Harassment of Women at Workplace (Prevention, Prohibition and Redressal) Act, 2013.
- **Labour laws enacted by Central Government and enforced by both Central as well as State Governments:** Chronologically these include: The Payment of Wages Act, 1936; The Industrial Employment (Standing Orders) Act, 1946; The Industrial Disputes Act, 1947; The Minimum Wages Act, 1948; The Maternity Benefit Act, 1961; The Apprentices Act, 1961; The Payment of Bonus Act, 1965; The Contract Labour (Regulation and Abolition) Act, 1970; The Payment of Gratuity Act, 1972; The Equal Remuneration Act, 1976; The Inter-State Migrant Workmen (Regulation of Employment and Conditions of Service) Act, 1979; The Cine Workers and Cinema Theatre Workers (Regulation of Employment) Act, 1981; The Child Labour (Prohibition and Regulation) Act, 1986; The Labour Laws (Exemption from Furnishing Returns and Maintaining Registers by Certain Establishments) Act, 1988; The Building and Other Constructions Workers' (Regulation of Employment and Conditions of Service) Act, 1996; and The Building and Other Construction Workers Cess Act, 1996.
- **Labour laws enacted by the Central Government and enforced by State Governments:** Such laws, arranged in order of their respective years of enactment are: The Workmen's (now Employees') Compensation Act, 1923; The Trade Unions Act, 1926; The Children (Pledging of Labour) Act, 1938; The Employers' Liability Act, 1938; The Weekly Holidays Act, 1942; The Factories Act, 1948; The Plantations Labour Act, 1951; The Working Journalists and Other Newspapers Employees (Conditions of Service) and Miscellaneous Provisions Act, 1955; The Employment Exchange (Compulsory Notification of Vacancies) Act, 1959; The Motor Transport Workers Act, 1961; The Personal Injuries (Emergency Provisions) Act, 1962; The Personal Injuries (Compensation Insurance) Act, 1963; The Beedi and Cigar Workers (Conditions of Employment) Act, 1966; The Sales Promotion Employees (Conditions of Service) Act, 1976; The Bonded Labour System (Abolition) Act, 1976; The Unorganized Workers' Social Security Act, 2008.
- **Labour laws enacted and enforced by the State Governments which apply to respective States:** These include, among others, The Shops and Establishments Acts.

Workers' Participation in Management

Desired Knowledge Competencies

- To comprehend the concept of workers' participation in management and its levels.
- To understand the objectives and need for workers' participation in management.
- To outline the forms of workers' participation in management.
- To develop an insight into workers' participation in India.

INTRODUCTION

There has been an increasing concern in industrial establishments for involving workers in organisational matters, particularly in those aspects that have an impact upon them. Workers' participation generally encompasses different forms of workers' involvement in decision-making pertaining to various activities of an organisation. It may be understood as an advanced form of cooperation between labour and management. Participation may also exist at higher levels, i.e., industry or sector-level and even at national-level through tripartite bodies. The idea of workers' participation had originated in Europe (Ozaki and Trebilcock, 2011). A beginning in this direction was made when the concept of 'industrial democracy' was proposed by Sydney Webb and Beatrice Webb. Cole (1917) believed that political democracy could be achieved by extending democracy to industry. It is important to understand that 'industrial democracy' and 'workers' participation' are two distinct terms. The difference between the two has been clarified in a succinct way by Rasmussen (2009, p. 494), according to whom, participation, "whether it involves having a say in decisions or sharing in financial benefits, does not necessarily give employees (individually or collectively) any control over those decisions …Although participating employees have potential influence within an organisation, management is free to ignore their views and opinions if it so chooses. Underlying the idea of industrial democracy, in contrast, is the possibility of employee control of various aspects of the enterprise's operations."

Spotlight
The concept of industrial democracy was given by Sydney and Beatrice Webb.

Simultaneously, an interesting relationship is observed between workers' participation in management (WPM) and industrial democracy. WPM is a means for establishing industrial democracy, and the belief of management in industrial democracy may actually act as a precursor for bringing about workers' participation in management. If an employer wants workers' involvement and commitment, specific mechanisms, structures and institutions would be required through which they can participate and function in a democratic set up (Pateman, 1970; Rhodes and Steers, 1981). The nature of participation may differ across enterprises in terms of power given to workers, as it may range from just being consultative to co-determination of certain matters together with the management. Whatever the mode may be, it allows employees to control their work and working conditions to a certain extent (Strauss, 1998).

Thus, we may define workers' participation in management as the sharing of decision-making power by workers through their representatives in the entire range of activities of an organisation, by direct or indirect involvement. Participation usually takes place through joint committees of workers and management. Workers' participation may be known by different names in different countries, for example in Germany it is termed as co-determination, while in Yugoslavia it is known as self-management. In India, the beginning of joint committees of workers and employers begun in 1920, when the Government of India constituted joint committees in railways and Government printing presses. A similar joint committee was formed in the Tata Iron and Steel Works, Jamshedpur. A joint committee was also constituted in the Carnatik Mill in Madras (now Chennai) in 1922 (Ministry of Labour & Employment, 2002).

> **Spotlight**
> WPM is defined as sharing of decision-making power by workers through their representatives in the entire range of activities of an organisation, by direct or indirect involvement.

The Government of India considers workers' participation as an important means to achieve social justice and economic prosperity. The Industrial Policy Resolution adopted by the Government in 1956 declared that in a socialist democracy, labour is a partner in the common task of development, and should be asked to participate in it with enthusiasm (Ministry of Labour & Employment, 2002, p. 1282).

OBJECTIVES AND NEED OF WORKERS' PARTICIPATION IN MANAGEMENT

The objectives of workers' participation in management may differ from one country to another, depending upon the socio-economic context. In India, soon after Independence, the Government had initiated various schemes for workers' participation as a necessary ingredient for the growth of industrialisation and to create a socialist society through this process. In Germany one of the objectives of 'co-determination' was prevention of exploitation of workers by management (Virmani, 1978). In Japan the objective of 'joint consultation' is to share information between workers and management on various issues ranging from management to working conditions in the organisation (Shimada, 1994).

In general, some of the general objectives of workers' participation in management are:

- **Sharing of power:** Power in industrial establishments has, as a practice, remained in the hands of management. Participation is actually a distribution of social power in industry so that it tends to be shared among all those who are engaged at work, rather than getting concentrated in the hands of a few (Mamoria, Mamoria and Gankar, 2008). Including workers in decision-making gives them the opportunity to share power with management.
- **Stimulate cooperation:** Through the process of WPM both management and workers come together with the objective of identifying problems of the organisation and cooperate with each other in finding solutions to these problems.
- **Increase labour-management communication:** Regular meetings between labour and management help in maintaining interaction between them. It creates a system of communication and consultation by formal and informal means, by which workers are kept informed about the affairs

of the organisation. It provides a forum through which they express their opinion and contribute to management decisions (Eaton, 1995).

- **Empowerment of employees:** The process of WPM facilitates employee empowerment by giving them a voice in matters that affect them.
- **Promotion of industrial peace:** Association of management and workers ensures better understanding between them. It changes the feelings and attitude of workers such that suspicion gives way to mutual trust and a stable relationship, a sense of belongingness and participation are built up, that would result in industrial peace (Davis, 1997).

The Second Five Year Plan (1956-1961) had emphasised the importance of association of management with labour. Such association helps in increasing productivity for the general benefit of employees, enterprise and community. It gives employees clarity in understanding their role in the working of the industry and the process of production. Association satisfies the urge of workers for self-expression, as also observed by French (1987), thus leading to industrial harmony, better relations and increased cooperation. Studies have shown that participation in management increases job satisfaction and decreases work apathy (e.g., Saini, 1983 and De, 1984 as cited in Gani, 1991, p. 48); such participation also reduces industrial conflicts (Thakur and Sethi, 1972 and Chaudhari, 1981, as cited in Gani, 1991, p. 48).

Spotlight
The Second Five Year Plan (1956-1961) had emphasised the importance of association of management with labour.

Shimada (1994) considers WPM important as it fulfills the following needs:

- **Productivity and quality improvement:** The purpose of workers' participation in management is to increase their involvement in the production process, generate a sense of belongingness and help in improvement of quality. This improves their efficiency and strengthens their abilities, which results in productivity increase.
- **Labour adjustments:** Changing business conditions require modifications in work structure and work schedules, and introduction of new technology. Work adjustments may require transfer of workers to new jobs in the same or to a different plant and sometimes even their retrenchment and lay-off. Such readjustment plans are discussed in joint consultations in Japan before they are actually implemented. Thus workers are informed *a priori* about the situation, though the issues may be negotiated later through collective bargaining.
- **Adaptation to economic changes:** Participation and communication with workers at various levels aid organisations in moderating the effects of economic shocks and help both management and workers in better adjustments. With cooperation of workers, organisations have been found to be able to adjust wages and working hours more flexibly, thereby leading to more stability. Participation also gives a sense of employment security to workers.

TYPES AND FORMS OF WORKERS' PARTICIPATION IN MANAGEMENT

Types of Workers' Participation in Management

The International Labour Organisation (ILO) suggests the following types of participation (*www.ilo.org*):

- **Direct participation:** Direct participation may take place through teams and workers' assemblies consisting of all employees.
- **Indirect or representative participation:** Workers may participate indirectly through their trade unions, works councils, joint consulta-

Spotlight
According to ILO, types of workers' participation may be direct, indirect and financial.

tive committees and various other committees like occupational health and safety committees, employee representation on board, etc.

- **Financial participation:** Such participation takes place through profit-sharing or stock ownership, or various combinations of these forms.

Sen (2012) classifies the methods of participation adopted by various enterprises into the following three types:

- **Superficial participation:** Such participation comprises information-sharing and suggestion schemes.
- **Intermediate participation:** Intermediate participation involves collective bargaining in both traditional and non-traditional areas and consultation on restricted issues.
- **Real participation:** Such participation covers consultation on unrestricted issues and co-determination on both restricted and unrestricted issues. Real participation gives workers 'voice' in every aspect of running of an enterprise, and hence may be equated to democracy. Bhattacharya (1986, p. 173) defines "industrial democracy as the exclusive control of productive organisations by their total workforce on the basis of equality of vote." This means that workers do not merely have a superficial participation. They participate with the management at an equal level in deciding issues on the governance of core issues of the enterprise.

Monappa (1995) has identified four types of participation: consultative, associative, administrative and decisive. Other ways of distinguishing WPM may be on the basis of its advisory and mandatory nature, and as a voluntary or statutory measure.

Forms of Workers' Participation in Management

There are various forms of workers' participation, like information-sharing, consultation, association, joint decision-making and implementation (Klein, 1987). Some forms give employees influence (by way of giving a say), while others provide them power (by way of potential control) (Rasmussen, 2009). These forms are used in different types of WPM. The types of workers' participation deliberated about in this section may involve the following forms:

- **Works Committee:** The concept of Works Committee has already been introduced as a dispute settlement measure in Chapter 8. The term 'works committee' describes arrangements for the representation of workers, usually at the plant or unit-level, although they may exist at higher levels (company, group of companies, industry, nations or group of nations). Extensive use of such committees, also known as works councils, workers' committees and cooperation committees, is well established in a number of European countries such as Belgium, Denmark, France, Germany and the Netherlands.
- **Collective Bargaining:** In collective bargaining workers' representatives negotiate with the representatives of management on issues like wages, working conditions and other labour-related issues through exchange of dialogue. It involves active participation of workers. Collective bargaining results in collective agreements, which lay down certain rules and conditions of service in an establishment. Such agreements are normally binding on the parties.

  > **Spotlight**
  > Collective bargaining is the process in which representatives of workers and management negotiate on issues related to labour.

  Theoretically speaking, collective bargaining is based on the principle of equality of power, but in actual practice, each party tries to overpower the other and get the maximum advantage for itself by using means like threats, strikes, lock-outs and other direct actions, if necessary. Thus collective bargaining represents the confrontational aspect of labour-management relations, different from works committee that is based upon mutual cooperation. Collective bargaining and its various aspects have been dealt with exhaustively in Chapter 5.

- **Suggestion Schemes:** Many organisations have implemented suggestion schemes as a form of WPM, in which workers are encouraged to give their suggestions on various issues and problems related to production and administration. Accepted suggestions may even be rewarded. Here workers have no power and employers are under no pressure to accept the suggestions.

EXHIBIT 11.1 SUGGESTION SCHEME IN MARUTI SUZUKI INDIA LEADS TO SAVINGS

Maruti Suzuki India Ltd., India's largest car manufacturer, has implemented the Suggestion Scheme for its employees, which has benefited the company in various ways. This scheme rewards employees for their suggestions and was adopted from the parent company Suzuki Motor Corporation.

The Suggestion Scheme, which is based on a Japanese practice of engaging employees, has seen participation of employees across levels, plants, facilities and business functions, in improving work practices within the company. The number of suggestions has been increasing steadily over the years and so has been the saving resulting therefrom. In the year 2011-12, over 320,000 suggestions were offered by the employees, which lead to cost savings of over ₹294.2 crore. Savings of ₹354 crore were registered during the financial year 2012-13, with over 3.96 lakh suggestions from the employees received during this period.

Most suggestions relate to improving quality and reducing costs, ways to speed up operations, improving efficiencies and streamlining supplies. Some of them have even helped improve efficiencies of the robots that are used on the shop floor. The Scheme has also been beneficial in improving ergonomics in the shop floor and in reducing fatigue of the workers, along with various other benefits. The company has been making innovations in the Suggestion Scheme. An online version, *Sujhav Sangrehika*, has also been made available to employees; it gives real time updates on an employee's suggestions.

(Adapted from: Pathak, K. Suggestion Scheme from Employees Leads to Savings for MSIL, Business Standard. Retreived from www.business-standard.com/article/companies /suggestion -scheme -from-employeesleads-to-savings-for-msil-113053100634_1.html. on 24/10/2014.)

- **Quality Circle:** Quality Circles (QCs) are small groups of six to twelve volunteers from the same work area, who meet regularly to identify, analyse and solve quality and performance-related problems in their area of responsibility (Munchus, 1983). QCs may be viewed as a participative management technique that had originated in Japan. They are based on the principles of voluntary participation and collaborative decision-making (Gray, 1993).

  Successful implementation of a QC programme requires that workers must have interest in the programme; they must believe that their support and participation would benefit themselves as well as the organisation; participants in a QC must be well-trained in human and technical skills (Wood, Hull and Azumi, 1983).

  QCs have been criticised as a limited form of empowerment as employees can take decisions only in specific areas, due to which they cannot enjoy the real power (Turban, 1985; Gray, 1993; Tang and Butler, 1997; Abo-Alhol, Ismail, Sapuan and Hamdan, 2006).

Spotlight

Quality Circle is a participative management technique in which small teams of usually 6 to 12 employees are voluntarily formed to identify and solve quality and performance-related problems.

- **Stock Ownership:** Many employers and governments have been known to propose workers' stock ownership as a method of participation. This could increase workers' control over industry, since they become shareholders of the company. In USA there have been many experiments with what is referred to as Employee Stock Options Plan (ESOP). In India, ESOPs were pioneered by Infosys. National Aluminium Company Ltd. (NALCO) was the first company amongst public sector organisations to have started ESOPs (*www.deccanherald.com*).

LEVELS OF WORKERS' PARTICIPATION IN MANAGEMENT

Worker involvement in labour-related affairs may take place at different levels, namely, at the level of enterprise or industry or region or nation or even at international level. This section gives a brief overview of such levels of participation.

- **Unit or Enterprise-level:** Workers' participation in decisions through modes like collective bargaining and works committees takes place at unit or enterprise-level.
- **Industry-level:** Workers discuss and decide upon issues related to the entire industry through their representatives in industrial committees, wage boards, etc.
- **Regional-level:** Workers' participation may occur at the regional-level through bodies like State Labour Advisory Boards.
- **National-level:** At the national-level there is a tripartite labour machinery, which comprises representatives of employers, employees and government. Various problems of industrial relations and policy-related issues are analysed and decided at this level.
- **International-level:** Workers are represented at international-level in conferences, seminars and in bodies like ILO.

We have talked about all these measures in detail in Chapter 8.

WORKERS' PARTICIPATION IN MANAGEMENT IN INDIA

The need for some form of worker involvement in the management of an enterprise was felt in the mid-1950s and 1960s in India, well after Independence. This was realised more by the Government than by employers to ensure rapid industrialisation. However, there was no urge as such among unions for greater involvement in the management of industrial enterprises. It was observed by Punekar (1957) that workers' participation in those times would take the form of joint committees for such functions as safety measures, social and cultural activities, production and productivity, personnel counseling, control of working conditions, auditing, profit sharing, recruitment and dismissal and overall management of an enterprise. Since then several forms of participation have emerged, some of which are elaborated here.

Shop Councils and Joint Councils

In 1975 a scheme of shop councils and joint councils was formulated by the Government. This was applicable to all enterprises in manufacturing and mining employing 500 or more people in the public, private and cooperative sectors, irrespective of whether joint consultative machineries had been set up and were functioning in such enterprises.

In the same year, in accordance with this scheme, during the Emergency period in the country the Constitution was amended and Article 43A was introduced, that formed part of the Directive Principles of State Policy. The purpose of this amendment was to increase productivity, promote industrial peace, and inculcate a sense of involvement among the workers. It directed the State to take suitable measures to ensure participation of workers in the management of industrial establishments.

Shop Council The two-tier scheme of 1975 provided for the appointment of shop councils in each department or shop of an enterprise. The employer was expected to set up a shop council in consultation with the recognised union or other registered unions of workers, depending upon the local conditions.

Each council consists of an equal number of representatives of employers and workers. The employer determines the number of members in each council in consultation with union. Employers' representatives are nominated by the management from among the persons employed in the unit concerned, while all representatives of workers are required to be from amongst those engaged in the shop or department concerned. The manner of representation was not specified in the two-tier scheme.

Spotlight

Shop council exists at shop floor level, consisting of an equal number of representatives of employers and workers.

Each shop council is supposed to function for 2 years and meet at least once a month. The chairman of the council is nominated by the management and the vice-chairman by the workers. Decision-making is by consensus and decisions have to be implemented within a month.

The functions of shop councils are to assist the management in achieving production targets, improving production, productivity and efficiency, eliminating wastage and utilising capacity and manpower to the optimum level. They should specifically identify areas of low productivity, study absenteeism and recommend measures for their improvement. The councils should also concern themselves with safety, working conditions, discipline and two-way communication.

Joint Council The Scheme of 1975 envisaged that there should be one joint council for a single plant, its constitution being similar to that of shop councils. The chief executive of the unit would be the chairman; the vice-chairman was to be nominated by the worker members of the council. The joint council was required to meet at least once in 3 months. Any one of the council members could be the secretary of the council.

The functions of joint councils were to discuss production and productivity, achieve efficiency, eliminate wastage, arrest absenteeism, ensure safety measures, etc.; the physical conditions of working and welfare measures are the other areas of their concern. These councils were expected to ensure a two-way flow of communication between the management and workers. They must also give suggestions for improving the skills of workers and for providing adequate facilities for training.

Spotlight

Joint council exists at plant-level, and is required to hold meetings at least once in a quarter.

In 1977 the Government of India introduced another scheme for participation; this scheme was meant for commercial and service organisations having large scale public dealings, such as hospitals and post and telegraph, which employ 100 or more workmen. Under this scheme, unit councils and joint councils were to be set up. The functions of unit and joint councils under this scheme were almost similar to those laid down under the 1975 scheme, with the exception that emphasis was also laid in the new scheme on discipline, elimination of pilferage and all forms of corruption.

Since the scheme was flexible in nature, various forms of workers' participation had emerged with respect to levels of participation, size of councils, duration of schemes, frequency of meeting and mode of selection of representatives. This probably explains the initial increase in the number of enterprises controlled by the Central Government, which had adopted this scheme. By 1977-78, 545 Central Government undertakings, 167 State Government undertakings, 1,132 private enterprises and 99 cooperative sector units had introduced this scheme (Gupta, 1979). However there was a sharp decline in the number of units or enterprises having shop and joint councils after 1979.

Both the schemes (1975 and 1977) generated a lot of confusion and controversy due to various reasons including lack of criteria for determining representation, exclusion of grievance redressal, restrictions imposed on consideration of work-related issues, inadequate sharing of information, lack of a supportive and participative culture and indifference of management. Improper handling of schemes by union leaders also contributed to the ineffective functioning of many forums and their eventual decline.

Works Committees

Section 3(1) of the Industrial Disputes Act, 1947 provides for the setting up of a Works Committee consisting of representatives of management and employees in every industrial establishment employing 100 or more workmen. The objective of the committee, according to sub-section 2 of Section 3, is "to promote measures for securing and preserving amity and good relations between the employer and workmen and to that end, to comment upon matters of their common interest or concern and endeavour to compose any material difference of opinion in respect of such matters".

The Act provides that the total number of representatives in the Works Committee, including those of the employer, should not exceed 20, and that the number of representatives of workers should not be less than that of the employer. The workers' representatives are to be chosen from among the workmen engaged in the establishment, in consultation with their registered trade union, if any.

> **Spotlight**
> The total members in a Works Committee should not exceed 20, and the number of representatives of workers should not be less than that of the employer.

The main duties of Works Committee are: to promote measures for securing and preserving harmonious industrial relations; discuss matters of common interest or concern; and endeavour to compose any material difference of opinion between the employer and workmen in respect of such matters.

The 17th Session of the Indian Labour Conference held in 1959 reviewed the functions of Works Committees and approved a list of functions which could be assigned to such committees. Accordingly Works Committees were allotted discussions on lighting, ventilation, temperature, sanitation, drinking water, canteens, dining and rest rooms, medical and health services, safe working conditions, administration of welfare funds, educational and recreational activities and encouragement of thrift and savings among workers.

According to the statistics presented in the Report of the First National Commission on Labour (1969), the number of Works Committees set up in 1951 was 1,142, which rose to 2,574 in 1959-60, when 4,730 committees were required to be set up. Further there were 3,133 committees in 1965-66, as against 5,091 committees that were required to be set up.

Joint Management Council

Soon after the adoption of the Industrial Policy Resolution by the Government in 1956, which exhorted public sector enterprises to set an example in workers' participation, a tripartite committee was set up. It visited UK, Sweden, France, Belgium, West Germany and Yugoslavia, and recommended the setting up of Joint Management Councils (JMCs) in all undertakings. The scheme was to be voluntary and consultative in nature. These councils were to deal with all matters except those falling within the area of collective bargaining, such as wages, bonus, hours of work, etc.

> **Spotlight**
> A Joint Management Council could be set up in undertakings employing at least 500 workers.

The objectives of JMCs are to identify measures to build up trust and understanding and hence promote cordial relations between management and labour; increase productivity; secure effective welfare and other facilities; and train workers in understanding and sharing responsibilities. JMCs generally function as a consultative body.

A JMC has equal representation from workers and management. The size of the Council should be restricted to 12 persons, the majority of workers' representatives ideally with workers themselves. Outside members, if inducted by the local trade unions, should not exceed 25 per cent of the workers' representatives.

Following are the criteria to be followed in selecting undertakings in which JMCs should be established:

- The undertaking should have well-established and strong trade unions.
- There should be willingness among employers and workers or their unions for establishing JMCs.
- The size of the undertaking in terms of employment should be at least of 500 workers.
- The employer, if in the private sector, should be a member of one of the leading employers' organisations and the trade union should be affiliated to one of the central federations.

The scheme prescribed that JMCs are entitled to be consulted on certain specified matters that included administration of standing orders and their amendments as and when needed, retrenchment, rationalisation, closure and reduction in or cessation of operations. In some matters the management is expected to share information with the Council, like the general economic situation of the concern, the state of the market, production and sales programmes, methods of manufacture and work, annual balance sheet and profit and loss statements, as well as long-term plans for expansion. In other matters, administrative responsibilities have to be given to JMCs, like welfare and safety measures, vocational training and apprenticeship schemes, suggestion schemes, schedules for working hours, breaks and holidays, etc.

Spotlight

Joint Management Councils were meant to be voluntary and consultative in nature.

It was initially decided that JMCs would be set up in 50 selected enterprises, to be gradually expanded to others, using the experience of the first 50. But ultimately the total number never exceeded 140, and even that gradually decreased (Sen, 2010). The main problem was management's reluctance to share decision-making with workers, which lay at the root of the failure of JMCs and the schemes that followed (Sheth, 1972).

A tripartite seminar in 1958 had emphasised a basic requirement for establishing JMCs. "The Seminar was convinced that Joint Councils will thrive only in an atmosphere of mutual confidence and goodwill. It took note of the gradual improvement in the attitude of employers and trade unions towards each other and felt that there was a need for continuous educative work both on the side of labour and management" (Ministry of Labour & Employment, 1969, p. 344).

The First National Commission on Labour, which reviewed the working of JMCs, observed that there was not much support for these councils. The Commission held the view that "when the system of recognition of Trade Unions becomes an accepted practice both management and unions would themselves gravitate towards greater cooperation and set up JMCs" (Ministry of Labour & Employment, 1969, p. 345).

Exhibit 11.2 Workers' Participation in Management at Tata Steel

Tata Iron and Steel Company at Jamshedpur set up a three-tier machinery in 1956 after an agreement reached with the recognised unions. The components of the machinery were:

- *Joint Consultative Council of Management* is the highest level, which comprises 10 representatives of management and an equal number of workers. It meets once in every 3 months, and its main function is to advise management on issues pertaining to production, welfare, financial matters, etc.
- *Joint Works Council* has 12 members each from workers and management. It meets once every month and its functions include studying production problems, monitoring functioning of other committees, etc. It also coordinates the activities of the Departmental Councils.
- *Joint Departmental Council* exists at the lowest level and operates at the level of every department or a combination of two or more departments. It has representation from both management and workers. Size of the council may vary between 4 to 10 members. It meets once in 15 days. Suggestions received from employees are analysed in a meeting for further action.

Apart from these councils, there are various other forums like the General Safety Committee, the Safety Appliances Committee, the Suggestion Box Committee and the Canteen Management Committee.

(Adapted from: Venkataramana, P. Workers' Participation in Management, Chaman Enterprises, New Delhi, 2007.)

Worker Director

Another means of workers' participation in management is having a representative of workers, regarded as Worker Directors, in the Board of Directors of an enterprise. Involvement of workers at such a high level gives them equality with the management. They directly participate in making of a policy and monitoring its implementation at organisational level. Worker Directors thus act as lining pin between workers and top management. They look into issues put up at board level with workers' perspective, and at the same time, communicate management's perspective to the workers.

The Nationalised Banks (Management and Miscellaneous) Scheme, 1970, initiated by the Government in 1970, provided for the appointment of a Worker Director and a Director representing the officers' cadre on the Board of each nationalised bank. The Worker Director was to be a nominee of the recognised union.

Spotlight

Worker Director is the nominee of the recognised union representing workers at the board of directors of an organisation.

For introducing Worker Directors in banks statutory amendments were made in 1973 in the State Bank of India Act, 1959 and the Banking Regulation Act, 1969, that provided for the appointment of one Worker (non-executive) Director and one Non-Worker (officer/executive) Director in each bank. Implementation of the scheme was delayed both by managements of various banks and unions. Unions protested against Officer Directors, contending that officers were in any case represented. The performance of Worker Directors was also a concern, as they rarely spoke in the board meetings. Workers felt their number was too small to make an impact, and in many cases the Worker Directors felt intimidated by the presence of many Non-Worker Directors, who all came from social and educational strata superior to that of workers

(Ghosh and Gupta, 1992). At that time most of the recognised unions in Public Sector Undertakings (PSUs) controlled by the Centre were affiliated to Indian National Trade Union Congress (INTUC). Hence it became easy to nominate the national INTUC president or the general secretary on most boards. By the 1990s the scheme had almost come to an end, and if we consider steel industry, by that time, the lone employee director was in IISCO, West Bengal (Sen, 2010).

Joint Consultative Machinery

The Joint Consultative Machinery (JCM) was set up in 1966 by the Government on the basis of the recommendations of the Second Pay Commission constituted in 1959; the prime motive was to facilitate communication and cooperation between the Government and its employees. The Commission defined the objectives of the machinery as "promoting harmonious relations and securing the greatest measure of cooperation between the government in its capacity as employer and the general body of its employees in matters of common concern and with the object further of increasing the efficiency of public service" (Ministry of Labour & Employment, 2002, p. 1284).

The scheme of Joint Consultative Machinery, established mainly on the model of the Whitley Councils in the UK, provides a platform for constructive dialogues between representatives of workers and management for peaceful resolution of all disputes in organisations where the Government is the employer. The objective of the scheme was to promote harmonious relations and ensure cooperation in matters of common concern, which would further increase the efficiency of the public service and welfare of employees. The scheme is non-statutory and mutually agreed upon between the management and employees.

Spotlight

The Joint Consultative Machinery was set up to facilitate communication and cooperation between the Government and its employees.

The JCMs have three-tier structure, e.g., office-level, department-level and national-level councils. Meetings of JCM must be held at least once in 4 months. There is a provision for compulsory arbitration on certain matters such as pay and allowances, hours of work and leaves, in case there is a disagreement at the national-level JCM.

Another scheme was notified in December 1983 for Central PSUs excluding those which are run by Government Departments because they already had an existing stricture of JCMs. The functions of such councils to be set up under this scheme included consultation on production facilities, storage facilities, material, economy, operational problems, wastage control, safety issues, quality improvement, planning, implementation and fulfillment of monthly targets, development of new products, encouragement to and consideration of suggestions, work system, profit and loss statement, balance sheet, operational expenses, absenteeism, administration of social security schemes, workers' training programmes, issues pertaining to women, and welfare issues like housing, medical benefits, transport facility, canteens, etc.

Besides the methods of participation covered in this section, many Indian companies have also adopted methods like quality circles and suggestion schemes for workers' participation.

Challenges in Implementing Workers' Participation in Management in India

The various schemes for workers' participation in India have not been able to deliver the desired results, as they have faced a number of challenges. Bisht (1986) found several reasons for the failure of participative schemes, which include: non-commitment of the management to the schemes; alienation of workers arising from non-implementation of decisions; and a general apathy among workers.

One central element of all such participative institutions is sharing of information (Bernstein, 1982; Cornforth, Alan, Jenny and Spear, 1988; Lawler III, 1989); management is often reluctant to share information or even responsibility with workers. Sethi (1973 cited in Sen, 2012, p. 11) observed that "managers ... do not think that participation will unleash the creative talents of their subordinates. On the contrary, they seem to have a rather low opinion about their subordinates' ability to understand and participate in organisational decision-making."

Often there are perceived differences in social status, education and awareness between management and workers that create a barrier for bringing them at an equal level. This obstructs transparency and trust. Certain variables related to workers also affect their willingness to participate. Sethi (1973) found that interest to participate was the highest among educated workers. Bisht (1986) reported that workers in the age group of 30 to 40 years were the ones who are the most interested in participation.

A regular communication flow between unions and management is an essential ingredient for the success of WPM. A mere scheme of participation without an accompanying system of regular communication does not work. Moreover, participation of workers must not be just in occasional situations; it needs to be sustained as a regular practice. The concept of WPM can be successful only if management and workers adopt it in the spirit with which the measures thereof are formulated. There are certain pre-requisites for this participation to be successful; existence of a powerful trade union is the most important of them. Worker representatives must feel strong enough to put forth their points of view in front of the more powerful management. Employers must also support workers' participation by considering them as equal partners in the working of organisations. If management wants a serious and meaningful contribution of workers in decision-making, it must educate them by sharing the complete and right information.

RECOMMENDATIONS OF THE SECOND NATIONAL COMMISSION ON LABOUR

The Second National Commission on Labour (2002) has given certain observations regarding WPM in India. We will highlight some of the important ones here.

- Though employers' organisations in India have been against introducing schemes of WPM by law, such schemes as established by law have been successful in countries like Germany, Japan and many member nations of the European Union. A legal base should be provided for institutionalising WPM in India, particularly in the context of liberalisation and globalisation.
- There is a need for mutual dialogues between workers and management for improving industrial relations, worker welfare and efficiency of organisations in view of changing technology, organisation structures and global competition.
- In many countries a well-structured system of WPM exists where frequent interactions give rise to clearer understanding of common interests. Modern means of communication have made it easier to procure and exchange information related to processes of organisations.
- Changing nature of work and technology require greater understanding of the need for voluntary and imaginative cooperation, which can come with awareness of the common objectives and the identity of interests.
- In today's scenario there is a need to have an appropriate system that can ensure contact, cooperation and co-determination at as many levels as possible from the plant-level to the board-level.

Summary

- The term 'workers' participation' is generally used to encompass various forms of workers' involvement in decision-making, usually at plant-level or corporate-level. Workers' participation in management may be seen a means for establishing industrial democracy and a belief of management in industrial democracy.
- Objectives of WPM are sharing power, promoting cooperation, increasing communication between labour and management, ensuring employee empowerment and promoting industrial peace. Need for WPM arises as it helps to improve productivity and quality, to bring about labour adjustments and to support organisations in adapting with economic changes.
- Forms of WPM may be classified as direct, indirect and financial participation. Other classifications may be superficial, intermediate and real participation; advisory and mandatory participation; and voluntary or statutory participation.
- Various methods of workers' participation include Works Committee, collective bargaining, suggestion schemes, quality circles and stock ownership.
- Collective bargaining is the process by which workers' representatives negotiate with the representatives of management through dialogue on issues like wages, work, working conditions and other labour-related issues.
- Quality Circle is a participative management technique in which small teams of 6 to 12 workers in an enterprise are voluntarily formed to identify and solve quality or performance-related problems.
- Workers' involvement in labour-related affairs may take place at different levels, namely, enterprise-level, industry-level, regional-level, national-level and international-level.
- In 1975 a scheme of shop councils and joint councils was formulated by the Government. This was applicable to all enterprises in manufacturing and mining, employing 500 or more workers in the public, private and cooperative sectors.
- Shop council exists at shop floor or department-level, consisting of an equal number of representatives of employers and workers; joint council exists at plant-level, and is required to hold meetings at least once in a quarter.
- The Industrial Disputes Act, 1947 provides for the setting up of a Works Committee consisting of representatives of management and employees in every undertaking employing 100 or more workmen to promote healthy relations between employers and workmen.
- Recommended by a tripartite committee of the Government, joint management councils could be set up in undertakings employing at least 500 workers. The objectives of JMCs are to promote cordial relations between management and labour and to build up trust and understanding between them.
- A Worker Director is the nominee of a recognised union who would represent workers at the Board of Directors of the organisation.
- The Second Pay Commission had recommended the setting up of Joint Consultative Machinery to facilitate communication and cooperation between the Government and its employees.
- The challenges for success of WPM in India include reluctance of employers to share power and information, lack of interest among workers to participate, etc.

Key Concepts

Joint Consultative Machinery
Works Committee
Joint council
Joint Management Council
Suggestion scheme
Industrial democracy
Shop council
Worker Director
Quality Circle

Bibliography

Abo-Alhol, T. R., Ismail, M. Y., Sapuan, S. M. and Hamdan, M. M. "Effects of Quality Circle Participation on Employee Perception and Attitude in Five Malaysian Companies", *Journal of Scientific and Industrial Research,* 2006,Vol. 65, No.12, pp. 970-976.

Bernstein, P. Necessary Elements for Effective Worker Participation in Decision-making. In Lindenfeld, F. and Whitt, J.R. (Eds.), *Workplace Democracy and Social Change,* Boston, MA:Porter Sargent; 1982, pp. 51-81.

Bhattacharya, J.B. *Participative Management and Industrial Democracy – Concepts and Practices,* Calcutta: Omega; 1986.

Bisht, N.S. *Participative Management in India,* New Delhi: Shree Publishers; 1986.

Cornforth, C., Alan, T., Jenny, L. and Spear, R. *Developing Successful Worker Cooperatives*, London: Sage; 1998.

Cole, G. D. H.. *Self-Government in Industry*, London: G. Bell and Sons; 1917.

Davis, T. R. V. "Open Book Management–Its Promises and Pitfalls", *Organisational Dynamics*, Winter, 1997,Vol. 25, No. 3, pp. 7-19.

Eaton, J. "Employee Buyouts in Canada", *British Journal of Industrial Relations*, 1995,Vol. 33 No. 3, pp. 417-458.

French, J. L. "Employee Perspectives on Stock Ownership: Financial Investment or Mechanism of Control?" *Academy of Management Review*, 1987,Vol. 12, No. 3, pp. 427-435.

Gani, A. *Labour-Management Relations: A Study of Textile Industry in Jammu and Kashmir*: New Delhi; Concept Publishing Company; 1991.

Ghosh, P. K. and Gupta, P. K. "Efficacy of Employees' Directors in State Bank of Indore–A Case Study", *Indian Journal of Industrial Relations*, 1992,Vol. 27, No. 4, pp. 412–418.

Gray, G. R. "Quality Circles: An Update", *SAM Advanced Management Journal*, 1993, Vol. 58, pp. 41-47.

Gupta, K. L. *Industrial Democracy in Public Sector Enterprises in India*, Aligarh: Navman Prakashan; 1979.

http://www.deccanherald.com/content/143639/nalco-first-psu-introduce-esop.html accessed on 2/10/2014.

http://www.ilo.org/public/english/iira/study/workers accessed on 4/10/2014.

http://planningcommission.nic.in/plans/ planrel/fiveyr /2nd /2planch27.html accessed on 2/10/2014.

Klein, K. J. "Employee Stock Ownership and Employee Attitudes: A Test of Three Models", *Journal of Applied Psychology*, 1987,Vol. 72, No. 2, pp. 319-332.

Lawler III, Edward, E. Participative Management in the United States: Classics Revisited. In Corndis, J. Lammers and Gyorgy, Szell (Eds.), *International Handbook of Participation in Organisations, Vol. I, Organisational Democracy: Taking Stock*, New York: Oxford University Press; 1989.

Mamoria, C.B., Mamoria, S. and Gankar, S.V. *Dynamics of Industrial Relations*, 16th editon, New Delhi: Himalaya Publishing House; 2008.

Ministry of Labour and Employment. Report of the Second National Commission on Labour, 2002

Monappa, A. *Industrial Relations*, New Delhi: Tata McGraw Hill; 1995.

Munchus III, G. "Employer-Employee Based Quality Circles in Japan: Human Resource Policy Implications for American Firms", *Academy Management Review*, 1983,Vol. 8, pp. 255-261.

Ozaki, M. and Trebilcock, A. Forms of Worker Participation. Geneva: International Labor Organisation, 2011. Retrieved from http://www.ilo.org/oshenc/part-iii/labor-relations-and-humanresource-management/item/202-forms-of-workers-participation 2011 on 28/10/2014.

Pateman, C. *Participation and Democratic Theory*, London: Cambridge University Press; 1970.

Punekar, S. D. "Workers' Participation in Management", *Economic Weekly*, 1957, June, pp. 745-749. http://www.epw.in/system/files/pdf/1957_9/24/workers_participation_in_ management.pdf on 28/10/2014.

Rasmussen, E. *Employment Relations in New Zealand*, New Zealand: Prentice Hall; p. 494, 2009.

Report of National Commission on Labour/2002, 1991-1967, Academic Foundation, New Delhi.

Rhodes, S. and Richard, M. S. "Conventional vs. Worker Owned Organisations", *Human Relations*, 1981,Vol. 34, No. 12, pp. 1013–1035.

Sen, R. *Employee Participation in Management*. Working Paper 40, Geneva:ILO;2012. Retrieved from http://www.ilo.org/wcmsp5/groups/public/---ed_dialogue/---dialogue/documents /publication/wcms_187873.pdf on 21/10/2014.

Sen, R. *Industrial Relations–Text and Cases*, 2nd edition, New Delhi:Macmillan India; 2010.

Sethi, K. C. "Workers' Participation in Management", *The Economic Times*, 14 August 1973, p. 5.

Sheth, N.R. *Joint Management Councils: Problems and Prospects*, New Delhi: Shri Ram Centre for Industrial Relations; 1972.

Shimada, H. *Worker Participation in Management Decision-making*. A draft prepared for Conference on International Evidence Commission on the Future of Worker-Management Relation, 1994. Retrieved from http://digitalcommons.ilr.cornell.edu/cgi/ viewcontent.cgi?article=1432&context=key_workplace on 4/10/2014.

Strauss, G. "Workers' Participation and US Collective Bargaining". In Corndis, J. L. and Gyorgy, S. (eds.), *International Handbook of Participation in Organisation*, Vol. I, Organisational Democracy: Taking Stock, New York: Oxford University Press; pp. 227–247, 1998.

Tang, T. L. P. and Butler, E. "Attributions of Quality Circles' Problem-Solving Failure: Differences among Management, Supporting Staff, and Quality Circle Members", *Public Personnel Management*, 1997, Vol. 26, pp. 203-225.

Turban, E. "Do Quality Circles Pay?" *Training and Development Journal*, 1985,Vol. 39, pp. 10-12.

Virmani, B. R. *Workers' Participation in Management*, New Delhi:MacMillan; 1978.

Wood, R., Hull, F. and Azumi, K. "Evaluating Quality Circles: The American Application", *California Management Review*, 1983,Vol. 26, pp. 37-53.

Review Questions

Objective Type Questions

I. State True or False

(i) Joint council must meet once in 4 months.
(ii) State Labour Advisory Boards are a forum for workers' participation at national-level.
(iii) Formation of Quality Circles in industrial establishments is a statutory requirement in India.
(iv) WPM and industrial democracy are similar concepts.
(v) Intermediate participation comprises consultation on restricted issues.

Answers: (i) False, (ii) False, (iii) False, (iv) False, (v) True

II. Fill in the Blanks

(i) The concept of industrial democracy was given by __________ and Beatrice Webb.
(ii) The number of members of joint management council should not be more than __________.
(iii) The term for a shop council is __________ years.
(iv) __________ participation comprises information-sharing and suggestion schemes.
(v) Meetings of JCM must be held at least once in __________ months.

Answers: (i) Sydney, (ii) 12, (iii) 2, (iv) superficial, (v) 4

Discussion Questions

1. Explain the concept of WPM and its relation with industrial democracy.
2. Highlight the objectives and need of workers' participation in management.
3. Outline the various methods of participation in management.
4. Differentiate between shop council and joint council.
5. Discuss the structure and functions of Works Committee.
6. Write short notes on:
   (i) Joint Management Council
   (ii) Joint Consultative Machinery
   (iii) Worker Director
7. Discuss the relevance of suggestion schemes and collective bargaining as methods of workers' participation in management.
8. What are the challenges in successful achievement of workers' participation in management?
9. WPM helps in maintaining industrial peace. Do you agree? Why?
10. How can quality circle be considered as a method of workers' participation in management?

Workers' Participation in Management in a Cooperative

New Central Jute Mills (NCJM), an undertaking of an employees' cooperative credit society in West Bengal operating in the private sector. It has about 7,000 employees, out of which almost 60 per cent are migrants from rural areas of Bihar and Uttar Pradesh. Most of the employees have been living in the company premises for more than 10 years.

The cooperative was formed from the remnants of a deserted family-owned company. In April 1986, the former owners declared lock-out on the ground of 'labour unrest' that had lasted for about a year. The workers suffered a lot during this period. Socio-economic conditions were becoming poor as the main business of the locality, i.e., jute mills, was in poor condition. Following a discussion with the Managing Director (MD) of the company, the local government and local political leaders, a cooperative of the remaining employees, who were around 2,500, was formed primarily to save the workers' jobs. Thus in April 1987 the employees took over and the company resumed its operations. Some employees who had left, came back. The cooperative got its legal existence in 1989. The management consulted the All Union Advisory Committee (AUAC) of trade union representatives before holding discussions with external agencies like financiers, governmental agencies, local government, etc.

Though the cooperative became a legal body, workers could not accept the new system, as they viewed it as a 'game' of union leaders and the management to take away their money. This doubt was deepened when some workers could not sell off their shares, as the shares were made non-transferable. Neither the management nor the union leaders clarified the doubts of workers regarding financial matters. Workers of the plant complained that union representatives were not concerned with the problem at shop floor level. The MD felt the need to involve workers in decision-making at the plant-level, which would also increase their interest in work. Thus a Plant Level Consultative Committee (PLCC) was constituted in 1989 with the objective to provide a platform for democratic decision-making, to share problems and remove misunderstandings with management, and to enhance interest of workers in their work.

Along with PLCC, there were four more modes of workers' participation:

1. **Joint memorandum of all unions meeting:** All union representatives and committee members used to have a joint meeting to deliberate on issues of common interest, usually through consensus. The memorandum of the meeting was distributed to workers.
2. **Union group meeting:** This meeting between union leaders and union members was to make them aware of shop-level problems in the various sections.
3. **Works Committee meeting:** This was intended for exploring problems primarily related to workers' welfare and work conditions, which helped in creating awareness among the leaders regarding shop-floor conditions, so that they could be taken up with shop floor managers or supervisors.
4. **Gate meeting:** This meeting served as a platform for general information sharing and venting off grievances by workers.

These meetings served as information channels and helped in increasing workers' involvement in their work. Disciplining process improved considerably after evolution of these meetings. A process for settling disciplinary issues was developed, that involved settling issues at the plant-level between management and workers, without the need to refer it to Labour Office.

But despite all efforts, discontent grew amongst workers as the cooperative was not able to provide full wages/salary on a regular basis. They noticed that union representatives were spending most of their time in attending these meetings and they hardly worked. In addition, these representatives were given some extra allowances, whereas workers were not even given full wages. Moreover, workers came to know of the plans of the management to increase production using contract labour. This generated a feeling of job insecurity amongst casual workers, and with the objective to protect their interests they formed their own union called *Shramik Samiti*. The *Sharmik Samiti* accused both management and union leaders of not being concerned about welfare of workers, and demanded that members of the *Samiti*, who did not get jobs through the year, be given jobs rather than jobs going to outside workers. Many workers left their union and joined the *Samiti*. They also opposed union's role in disciplining. From that time, issues discussed in PLCC also changed and 'payment of wages' became a frequent matter of discussion. Unions were also accused of biased attitude in nominating workers for PLCC, who knew nothing about the real problems of workers. Therefore unions were forced to nominate shop-floor workers. These workers often took up the issue of wages at the meetings, to which the Committee Chairman showed displeasure. This resulted in disturbances in meetings, which gradually increased. Demonstrations, etc. by workers gained intensity and disrupted normal working. Ultimately the *Sharmik Samiti* was invited to attend the Board meeting. Gradually normalcy returned. There was a period of stability between 1991 and 1994. But outside, the entire jute industry was hit by labour unrest.

Committees like PLCC, Works Committee, etc. were all active. Financial issues were also taken up in PLCC meetings, though it was considered a higher-up matter by management. Discussions took place on rationalisation of employment and consequent increase in workload. Some joint memoranda were signed and distributed to workers for their information and the workers were asked to clarify their doubts with their respective sectional union leaders.

Reduction in number of employees and increased workload was taken into account at the PLCC meeting. Union representatives explained the rationale for job reduction to the worker mass in gate meetings and in union group meetings. Workers opposed any change in workload, but due to pressure from the operating agency and urgency of the situation, the management went ahead. Unions tried to convince workers of the situation and finally workers accepted workload change. Many permanent workers even volunteered to be transferred to new jobs with additional responsibilities. Some came up with suggestions on sharing of new responsibilities.

This was followed by a period of turbulence during 1994-1996. The cooperative was not making the expected progress and financiers became reluctant in continuing their support. It became difficult to pay timely wages or any other financial support to workers. There was a general lack of trust and management refused to talk about issues of wages in PLCC. Differences emerged between workers on one side and union representatives and management on the other. Due to disruptions the frequency of holding PLCC meetings decreased and ultimately the cooperative had to be cancelled as became more of a platform for fighting than amicable discussions.

(Adapted from: Kandathil, G. M. and Varman, R. (2002). Contradictions of Workers' Participation: Case Study of a Workers' Owned Jute Mill, 11th Conference of the International Association for the Economics of Participation (IAFEP), Catholic University of Brussels, Brussels, 4-6 July, 2002. www.ocean.st.usm.edu/~w300388/brussels/kand.pdf, accessed on 24/10/2014.)

Review Questions

1. Give an account of the various modes of workers' participation in management at NCJM.
2. Identify the reasons for labour problems at NCJM. Is trade union playing a positive or negative role in the entire situation? Explain citing suitable instances from the case.
3. Suggest ways of improving the scenario of workers' participation in the cooperative.

12

Industrial Relations: International Perspective

Desired Knowledge Competencies

- To discuss the nature of industrial relations in different countries.
- To comprehend the characteristics of trade unions and collective bargaining in other countries.
- To identify international practices in labour welfare and workers' participation in management.
- To outline the structure and functioning of the International Labour Organisation.

INTRODUCTION

The beginning of the process of industrialisation in Europe had initiated the labour movement that gradually grew and spread to different countries, having varying degrees of impact. Labour and management are the two most important aspects of an industry. The nature of relationship between them depends upon the legal, political, economic, social and cultural contexts of a country, and hence industrial relations system is found to vary from one country to another.

In Asia most of the countries have been under foreign dominance in the past, and when they became independent, the governments' approach towards economic development was the deciding factor in shaping the industrial relations systems in these countries. Governments commonly became the largest employer and hence influenced labour-management relations. The political developments in each of these nations were also different. With democratisation in many East Asian countries such as Korea, Indonesia and the Philippines in the late 1980s and 1990s, development of independent trade union movements and collective bargaining has picked up (Yoon, 2009).

Spotlight

Industrial relations system of a country is shaped by the unique legal, political, economic, social and cultural factors of the country.

If we take a look at industrial relations system in the European Union (EU) at the Union level, it has specific features which relate to various economic, political and social developments in the EU. These features include the European social dialogue, the European Employment Strategy, the Charter of Fundamental Rights of the European Union, cross-border coordination of collective bargaining, macroeconomic dialogue and the European Works Councils (*www.eurofound.europa.eu*).

Industrial relations systems and practices are shaped by three main actors: government, workers and their unions, and employers/employers' organisations. In many Asian countries, for instance, governments have had a significant impact on industrial relations. On the contrary, in Continental Europe, workers' unions in some countries (e.g., Germany and the Nordic countries) have been found to have a major influence on shaping industrial relations, while in USA it has been more employer-driven (De Silva, 1997).

The role and functions of trade unions also depend upon the country context. The extent to which trade unions take up the responsibility to promote the interests of their members and that of community, and the mode they adopt to pressurise employers depend not only on their strength, but also the socio-economic compulsions and industrial structure in the nation. Labour legislations existing in a country have an important role to play in this connection.

Various aspects of labour-management relations like labour welfare, workers' participation in management (WPM), labour laws, etc. are markedly distinct across countries and these give a unique shape to the industrial relations in these countries. The affluence of a country will determine if labour welfare has to be imposed upon employers or if they willingly undertake such activities. In general, the amount of benefits provided to workers will be contingent on the economic condition of the country. Different modes of workers' participation in management have been discussed in Chapter 11. The extent and nature of workers' involvement in decision-making in industrial undertakings depend on government policies and nature of trade unions and hence vary from country to country.

The International Labour Organisation (ILO) plays an important role in shaping labour-management relations at the international level. Many of ILO's Conventions and Recommendations have influenced labour legislations in member-countries. India is a founder-member of ILO and industrial relations in India, to a considerable extent, have been influenced by ILO.

In this chapter we will discuss aspects of industrial relations in some select countries and the impact of ILO on Indian industrial relations.

NEED FOR UNDERSTANDING INTERNATIONAL INDUSTRIAL RELATIONS

We have already mentioned that the industrial relations system in a country is influenced by the unique characteristics of its environmental factors. In light of this view, such a system which has been successfully implemented in one country may or may not be successful in another one. Despite this fact, it is essential to be aware about practices in other nations. It is important to learn from successful models in other countries and identify the aspects that may be replicated in order to improve labour-management relations in a country. Today in the era of globalisation, when business organisations are expanding across boundaries of their nations, they hire local people. In this context, understanding industrial relations scenario and practices in other countries would help in managing operations and workforce of the enterprise in these countries successfully.

Perhaps the best example of learning from the practices in other nations and implementing such learning in designing own industrial relations system in Indian context is when after Independence, the Government of India had formed a tripartite committee that visited UK, Sweden, France, Belgium, West Germany and Yugoslavia to learn the prevalent practices and on returning the committee made certain recommendations. It agreed upon the constitution, functions and administration of Joint Councils and also recommended the setting up of Joint Management Councils.

INTERNATIONAL INDUSTRIAL RELATIONS SYSTEMS: A COMPARATIVE FRAMEWORK

In this section we will study the industrial relations systems in other regions/countries including the European Union, the United States of America and several Asian countries with respect to characteristics like bipartism/tripartism, trade unionism, collective bargaining, workers' participation in management and labour welfare.

Bipartism/Tripartism

Industrial relations system in a country in general may have a bipartite or tripartite nature. In many of the Asian countries the State has adopted a paternalistic approach and considers itself as protector of workers and holds itself responsible for their welfare. This is because most of these countries are still developing economies and a practice of pluralism may not be very helpful in achieving economic development. In fact, industrial relations in these countries have been shaped by the active role of the State in their industrial development. Their governments intervene directly or indirectly (through formal mechanisms and institutions like adjudication, labour tribunals, etc.) in labour issues. The main objectives are to protect the weak labour and to maintain harmony in industry.

Spotlight

In many Asian countries the State has adopted a paternalistic approach and considers itself as the protector of workers and responsible for their welfare.

In the EU we may analyse industrial relations at two levels: at EU level and at the level of member-countries. At the EU level, there may take place a dialogue between European-level trade union federations and employers' organisations in the form of discussions, consultation etc., that may be either bipartite (involving only unions and employers' organisations), or tripartite (where there is intervention of the European Commission). Across EU member-countries, both bipartite and tripartite agreements take place. Tripartite agreements are common and may be practiced for deciding wage policy and similar issues in some countries like Ireland, Italy and Portugal, or aspects like employment and social security in countries like Portugal and Spain. Bipartite agreements between unions and employers at inter-sectoral level are commonly done for laying down guidelines for lower-level bargaining on pay and work conditions in Belgium, Finland and Greece. UK has a few such formal systems (Carley and SPIRE Associates, 2001).

In Japan tripartite discussions and consultations commonly take place at national-level. Issues like labour legislations or major labour policy changes are usually discussed in tripartite councils and consensus is arrived at before reaching a final decision. However changes initiated in 1995 in the process of revision of labour laws have diluted the powers of Rengo, a major trade union confederation (Nakamura, n.d.). We have talked about Rengo in further details in the very next sub-section on trade unions.

USA is characterised by the absence of bipartite or tripartite formal institutions or mechanisms for any dialogue at national-level. There is no representative employers' organisation. The government may bring together trade unions and employers'/business organisations for consultation or discussion on specific issues through means like seminars and conferences. The Department of Labour may also consult trade unions and employers'/business organisations separately.

Trade Unions

Reflection

Trade unions came into existence mainly to promote workers' interests at workplace.

Trade unions negotiate with employers over wages and working conditions primarily through collective bargaining. When this method fails, they resort to strikes and other pressure tactics to get their demands accepted. Trade unions in general are concerned with a wide range of economic and social issues—from wages to workers' rights.

An important feature of trade unionism in EU is a high degree of unity and coherence at continent level, but there is huge diversity and sometimes division at national-level. All the major trade union confederations in EU countries and outside EU are members of the European Trade Union Confederation (ETUC). Certain European industry federations that group most of the major EU trade unions in their respective sectors, are also affiliated to the ETUC. A number of trade union organisations are also affiliated to the European Confederation of Independent Trade Unions.

At country-level in EU the pattern of trade union organisation varies. For instance, in Austria and Germany there are a few industrial unions that comprise a single dominant confederation. There are a few other small workers' organisations in Germany but none in Austria. In UK and Ireland, on the other hand, there is a single major national centre but the number of member unions is larger and these unions are industrial, general and occupational unions. In Belgium, France, Italy, Luxembourg, the Netherlands, Portugal and Spain there are multiple confederations that differ on their views related to various issues, mainly political and religious.

Exhibit 12.1 Models of Industrial Relations System in European Union

Following are the four main models of industrial relations systems that exist in European Union nations:

i. **Nordic corporatism**: The Nordic corporatism model features high levels of trade union membership, negotiations at industry-level (sectoral) and relatively centralised bargaining arrangements. Generally social groups are more integrated into the system and union density is high. Hence collective agreements apply to majority of workers, without the need for government intervention. This model is followed in Scandinavian countries like Denmark, Finland and Sweden.

ii. **Social partnership**: This model is based on existence of employers' associations and trade union confederations as it depends on strong negotiating parties who can make agreements survive. The social partnership model exists in countries like Austria, Belgium, Germany, Luxembourg, the Netherlands and Slovenia.

iii. **Liberal pluralism**: Labour-management relations are largely based at company-level and can be confrontational (with the exception of Ireland's social pacts). In general, there are fewer laws concerning the labour market, social security, etc. Union density rates tend to be lower and therefore collective bargaining coverage is restricted, as negotiations are not centralised and there is no legal means of extending company-level deals industry-wide. This model is followed in Ireland, UK, Cyprus and Malta.

iv. **State-centred**: Governments in this model exercise more control; unions and employers are also accommodated to a certain extent to avoid social confrontation. Union density is often lower in these countries, but collective bargaining coverage may be wider because of the potential for extension of agreements to non-unionised workplace both by law and via employers' associations. It exists in France, Greece, Italy, Portugal and Spain.

(Adapted from: European Trade Union Confederation (2010). Trade unions and industrial relations in EU. Brussels. Retrieved from www.etuc.org/IMG/pdf/TURKISH_4.pdf on 27/92014.)

The number of major confederations in these countries varies from 2 in Portugal and Spain to 5 in France, many of them being made up of several sectoral trade union federations. In Italy and France, there are other major trade unions besides these large confederations. In Nordic countries there are separate confederations for workers in different occupations, made up of industrial and occupational unions, whereas in Greece, separate confederations exist for public and private sectors, each made up of different types of unions.

The structure of trade unions in USA is almost similar to that in Ireland and UK. The apex body is the American Federation of Labor and Congress of Industrial Organizations (AFL-CIO), which is made up of a large number of industrial and occupational unions. There are a few other unions that are not affiliated with the AFL-CIO umbrella.

Asian countries have both similarities and differences in their trade union structure and functioning. China and Vietnam have a communist regime. In China workers are represented by the All China Federation of Trade Unions and in Vietnam by the Vietnam General Confederation of Labour, both being the official national centres of trade unions and affiliated with the ruling parties. At a lower level there are sectoral unions and regional unions. Regional unions are formed on the basis of administrative hierarchy, at district, city and State levels, and are more important than sectoral unions. All these lower level unions work under the official national federation, while enterprise-level trade unions work under the management.

Japan and Korea have had strong enterprise-level unions. Japanese trade union organisations have a three-tier structure: enterprise-based unions, industrial federations and the national center at the top. In the past national trade union centres were divided but were later united in 1989 into a national centre called the Japanese Trade Union Confederation, or Rengo, which organises majority of the unionised workers. Various enterprise-level unions that are organised into sectoral unions are the members of Rengo and, in this respect, trade union structure in Japan resembles that in France. Rengo works with the national government and employers' organisations on issues including labour standards, tax systems and social security, that cannot be dealt with at the industry or enterprise-level. Table 12.1 gives the basic trade union organisation in the EU, Japan and USA.

TABLE 12.1 Basic Trade Union Organisation: EU, Japan and USA

	Mainly industry/sector organisational structure	***Mixed (industry/general/ occupational) organisational structure***
Single main confederation	Austria, Germany, EU level	Ireland, UK, USA
Multiple confederations (divided on religious/political/organisational lines)	Belgium, France, Italy, Japan, Luxembourg, the Netherlands, Portugal, Spain	Denmark, Finland, Greece, Norway, Sweden

Adapted from: Carley and SPIRE Associates, 2001

A common trend across the EU (at both European and national levels), Japan and USA has been towards consolidation and merger of trade union organisations; consequently the number of industry federations affiliated to ETUC (in EU) and to AFL-CIO (in USA) has declined. A similar trend is seen in union membership across the industrialised market economies in recent decades, which is largely due to a decline in employment in the traditionally high-unionisation manufacturing industry and the growth of lower-unionisation services sector, increasing levels of contract employment and even corporate restructuring. This decrease has been witnessed in countries like France, the Netherlands, UK, USA and Japan.

Collective Bargaining

The collective bargaining process and levels therein may differ across countries depending on the extent of involvement of the State in industrial relations, the issues 'open' for negotiation and the strength of trade unions.

Enterprise-level bargaining is a common approach in East Asian countries. In Malaysia and Singapore the governments have adopted a policy of enterprise or 'in house' unionism for securing cooperation, though sectoral bargaining is also picking up gradually. Both these governments have imposed restrictions on collective bargaining as in both the countries certain issues like transfer, promotion, retrenchment, lay-off, etc. are considered management prerogatives and collective agreements on these issues require certification by the Industrial Court, which can even refuse the certification if the provisions are harmful to the national interest. Government intervention is sanctioned in Korea, Japan, Thailand and the Philippines when industrial disputes pose a threat to the growth of the national economy. Due to legal restrictions on workers in most of the countries in East Asian region, collective bargaining in the public sector is not much developed. The fragmented nature of trade unions in countries like Cambodia, Indonesia and the Philippines weakens their strength and limits their power in collective bargaining. Even at the national-level, they have little impact in influencing the policies. In China, the process has developed in a real sense only after 2000.

The mechanism of coordination of collective bargaining at Union level in the EU has been devised to avoid downward pressure on wage costs. However, issues like pay and work conditions are not subject to collective bargaining at sectoral or inter-sectoral EU level. In many States centralised national bargaining has been replaced by more decentralised systems of bargaining, but there is still a role for national-level bargaining. The Member States have widely differing dominant systems of collective bargaining over pay and working conditions. It is at the company-level in Bulgaria, Czech Republic, UK and Poland; at industry-level in Austria, Germany and the Netherlands; at company and industry-level in Spain, Sweden, Norway, Italy and France; at national-level in Belgium, where it sets framework. Industry and national levels co-exist in countries like Norway and Slovenia and bargaining takes place at all the three levels in Finland (Coordination of Collective Bargaining, *www.eurofound.europa.eu*). However, despite these differences and a widely-observed trend towards the decentralisation of bargaining, it can be said that most countries have relatively centralised systems. There are countries like UK and most of the countries of Central and Eastern Europe where industry-level bargaining has largely disappeared, particularly in the private sector, and company-level negotiations predominate (*www.worker-participation.eu*).

Under the Federal National Labor Relations Act, 1935 (or Wagner Act), workers in USA have gained the right to bargain collectively over wages, hours of work and other terms and conditions with their employers. Historically collective bargaining in USA is rooted deeply in the values of industrial democracy (Summers, 1978). The predominant bargaining-level for pay and all other issues is the individual company. Inter-sectoral or sectoral bargaining is virtually unknown in USA (with some exceptions at industry-level). Many unions seek to conduct 'pattern bargaining', whereby an agreement is arrived at in a particular company or companies and then extended to other firms in the sector.

The predominant bargaining level in Japan for pay and all other issues is the individual company; inter-sectoral or sectoral bargaining just like in USA is virtually non-existent. Enterprise-level bargaining is characterised by almost complete autonomy of the employer and enterprise-based unions, with no external participation (Shirai, 1999 as cited in Oh, 2006, p.15). However, it may be noted that there is coordination from both trade union and employers' sides during the annual spring-time negotiations or *Shunto*. The pattern followed in these negotiations is that major manufacturers in leading industries are the first ones to participate in bargaining, followed by other large companies and later by small enterprises.

Collective bargaining may be said to be much more centralised in EU than Japan and USA, though there is no uniformity between the members of EU (UK, for example, has a highly decentralised bargaining structure).

Exhibit 12.2 Spring Labour Offensive: A Centralised Collective Bargaining System in Japan

With the objective of overcoming the limitations of enterprise-based unions in Japan, the Spring Labour Offensive (known as *Shunto*) began in 1956 as an annual unified struggle by labour unions in all industries, in which they come up with the central demand of simultaneous wage increases. This system has had a significant impact in shaping the Japan's economy and industrial relations system. However under a prolonged national depression since the 1990s the Spring Labour Offensive experienced significant changes over the last decades. Rengo changed its name from 'the Spring Labour Offensive' to 'The Spring Struggle for a Better Life', indicating its changed objectives and character. Now its objectives also include comprehensive improvement of workers' living standards. The Spring Labour Offensive has shown diversification of demands that include shorter working hours, lump sum payments, welfare benefits and change in management policies.

(Adapted from: Oh, H. (2006). Report on the Survey on Industrial Relations in East Asia: Collective Bargaining in Japan. ILO- Japan Multi-Lateral Project, 2006. Thailand: ILO.)

LABOUR WELFARE AND SOCIAL SECURITY

The Report of the First National Commission on Labour (1969) observed that there are several factors deciding the standards of welfare facilities in organisations located in different countries, viz., an understanding of human dignity; pressure from labour; level of industrial prosperity and support from public opinion. Many facilities that have to be enforced by law in developing countries may be a matter of daily life in developed countries and are provided by employers without waiting for a demand from workers. Thus welfare amenities provided to workers essentially depend on the level of economic development of a country.

The emphasis and scope of social security system also varies across countries, depending on government policies and the amount of benefits may be said to depend upon the economic status of the nation.

Social security schemes in Japan include the public pension system to provide income security for the elderly, survivors and persons with disability. Healthcare systems to protect public health include health insurance, public health and maternal and child health systems. There are provisions of care services and financial support for persons with disabilities, a system to protect workers through employment insurance, work-related accident insurance, etc. Universal health insurance was implemented in both South Korea and Taiwan during the 1990s. Both the countries provide pension benefits. In addition to the Basic Livelihood Allowance Programme, the Mother-Child Welfare Scheme and long-term elderly care, South Korea provides unemployment insurance that also covers part-time workers, most of whom are women (Lee and Park, 2003; Tchoe, 2003).

In the EU there are rules regarding social security at EU level, but these rules do not replace national systems with a single system. EU countries have their own social security legislations that decide their specific beneficiaries and benefits, though EU has framed certain common rules to protect social security rights of citizens when moving within Europe (EU 28 Member States, Iceland, Liechtenstein, Norway and Switzerland). Nevertheless, a lack of common norms has resulted in a large disparity in social protection between EU Member States (Dijkhof, 2011).

Reflection

Social security is assurance provided by the State against various types of adverse situations to which individuals may be exposed in events like old age, sickness, financial distress, disablement, unemployment, maternity or death.

National insurance in UK accounts for over half of the expenditure on social security in the country (Spicker, n.d.). Social security benefits in UK include income support for people with low income, job seeker's allowance, child benefit, housing benefit that supports in paying all or part of house rent, council tax benefit, disability living allowance, invalid care allowance, state pension etc. French social security benefits can be categorised into five branches: sickness, maternity, paternity and death; accidents-at-work and occupational-diseases; retirement; family benefits; and unemployment benefits (*www.cleiss.fr*). The Belgian social security system is based on the payment of social contributions that finance the social security system. Employer and employee both contribute to the social security fund. Social security is provided in events of sickness, unemployment, incapacity for work through sickness or invalidity, accidents at work and industrial disease, family allowances and pensions. The self employed can also claim social security for which they pay a social contribution (*www.belgium.be*).

In USA there are two principal federal programmes offering support for the elderly: Old Age, Survivor's and Disability Insurance (OASDI), commonly known as Social Security, and Medicare. Social Security provides retirement income to the elderly, while Medicare provides health insurance coverage for the aged and disabled and is funded partly by payroll taxes and premium payments by retirees, and rest by the federal government. In addition, the Supplemental Security Income (SSI) programme serves as a safety net to ensure that the elderly and disabled have a minimum level of income if their pension benefits are very low or if they do not qualify for Social Security. These apart, USA has a wide second-tier of private pension plans and plans sponsored by employers (Velloso, 2006).

WORKERS' PARTICIPATION IN MANAGEMENT

The idea of workers' participation had originated in Europe, though its systems and forms profoundly differ from one country to another. Chapter 11 discusses various forms of WPM. If we look at the institutional set up of workers' participation in various countries like Germany, Japan and many of the EU member nations, we can clearly deduce that they have been established by law. A number of developing countries have also adopted legislative initiatives with a view to having works councils or similar structures set up (e.g., Pakistan, Thailand and Zimbabwe) as a means of promoting labour-management cooperation. Extensive use of works councils, sometimes called workers' committees, cooperation committees, etc. is well established in several European countries such as Belgium, Denmark, France, Germany and the Netherlands.

Spotlight

Board representations are a common form of workers' participation in EU.

Board representations are also a common form of workers' representation in EU. The majority of EU Member States have provisions in their legislation for some kind of employee representation at board-level (Kluge and Stollt, 2007, as cited in Rehfeld et al., 2011, p. 14).

Workers' participation may have a direct form as in Japan and USA, or indirect form, prevalent in Germany and Australia. In Germany co-determination occurs at plant-level through workers' councils. In many Japanese companies a consensus is sought at all levels before taking a decision. It is called *ringi.* Through this process employees put considerable influence in decision-making. Though it slows down the decision-making process, but it ultimately results in quick implementation of decisions. Workers' participation in USA stands, in general, for negotiation, administration and collective bargaining, and is based on free choice. Unlike in Germany (where the German Work Councils Act, first passed in 1952 and subsequently amended, provides a legal basis for representation), the law does not impose a system of representation by requiring the creation of works council, but protects employees in choosing whether or not to have a system of representation and in choosing a union that represents them (Summers, 1978).

Reflection

Co-determination aims at preventing exploitation of workers by management.

EXHIBIT 12.3 WORKS COUNCIL IN GERMANY

The Works Council in Germany represents interests of employees within an establishment. Elected separately for manual and non-manual workers, it enjoys certain rights to information, consultation and co-determination. Co-determination covers participation in arrangements on health and safety at work, deciding 'social plan' in situations like plant closure, setting guidelines for staff selection and appraisal, in-service training, etc. In the areas of obligatory collective co-determination like accident prevention and health protection, works rules, working time, fixing of performance-related pay rates, and others, the employer cannot take action without the Works Council's agreement. The Council can refer a matter to the establishment-level arbitration committee for enforcement. Works Council is empowered to conclude works agreements at the enterprise-level and can initiate complaints where it believes the agreement is not being honoured.

(Adapted from: www.ilo.org/oshenc/part-iii/labor-relations-and-human-resource-management/ item/202 -forms-of-workers-participation Retrieved on 28/9/2014.)

Quality circles comprise a form of worker participation originated in Japan and adopted in many countries. They are generally expected to achieve two goals: enhancement of quality and productivity, and fostering of a sense of participation in decision-making among workers, resulting in better industrial relations. Emphasis has been placed more on the former in Japan and on the latter in Europe and North America. Another difference is that while circle leaders are normally appointed by management in Japan, they are often elected in Germany.

Reflection

Quality circles are based on the principles of voluntary participation.

INTERNATIONAL LABOUR ORGANISATION

The International Labour Organisation is a specialised agency of the United Nations Organisation (UNO) that aims at improving labour standards at global level. It has a tripartite structure having representatives of governments, employers and workers, and provides a forum for discussion of labour issues and policies. Currently the ILO has 185 Member States.

Origin

> **Spotlight**
> The main objectives of ILO are to establish social justice for maintaining peace and harmony in the world, and to promote human and labour rights.

The ILO was created in 1919, as part of the Treaty of Versailles that brought an end to World War I. ILO's main objectives are to establish social justice for maintaining peace and harmony in the world, and to promote human and labour rights. Its Preamble states that:

1. Whereas universal and lasting peace can be established only if it is based upon social justice;
2. And whereas conditions of labour exist involving such injustice hardship and privation to large numbers of people as to produce unrest so great that the peace and harmony of the world are imperiled; and an improvement of those conditions is urgently required;
3. Whereas also the failure of any nation to adopt humane conditions of labour is an obstacle in the way of other nations which desire to improve the conditions in their own countries.

> **Spotlight**
> The General Conference of ILO in its 26th Session in 1944 brought out the 'Declaration of Philadelphia', which was incorporated into ILO's Constitution.

In its 26th Session in 1944, the General Conference of ILO brought out the 'Declaration of Philadelphia', which was incorporated into ILO's Constitution. It reaffirmed the principles of ILO, which are as following:

- labour is not a commodity;
- freedom of expression and of association are essential to sustained progress;
- poverty anywhere constitutes a danger to prosperity everywhere;
- the war against want requires to be carried on with unrelenting vigour within each nation, and by continuous and concerted international effort in which the representatives of workers and employers, enjoying equal status with those of governments, join with them in free discussion and democratic decision with a view to the promotion of the common welfare.

The Declaration set forth the ten objectives of ILO, which are:

- Full employment and the revising of standards of living.
- The employment of workers in the occupation in which they can have the satisfaction of giving the fullest measure of their skill and make their contribution to the common well being.
- The provision, as means to the attainment of this end, and under adequate guarantees for all concerned, of facilities for training and the transfer of labour, including migration for employment and settlement.
- Policies in regard to wages and earning, hours and other conditions of work calculated to ensure a just share of the fruits of progress to all, and a minimum living wage to all employed and in need of protection.
- The effective recognition of the right of collective bargaining, the cooperation of management and labour in the continuous improvement of productive efficiency and the collaboration of workers and employers in social and economic measures.
- The extension of social security measures to provide a basic income to all in need of such protection and comprehensive medical care.
- Adequate protection for the life and health of workers in all occupations.
- Provision for child welfare and maternity protection.
- The provision of adequate nutrition, housing and facilities for recreation and culture.
- The assurance of equality of educational and vocational opportunity.

Membership

The States that were the members of ILO on 1st November 1945, any original member of UNO and any State that attained membership of the United Nations by a decision of the General Assembly may become a member of the ILO. The concerned State must give its formal acceptance of the obligations of the Constitution to the Director-General of the International Labour Office, also referred to hereafter as 'the Office'. The General Conference of the ILO may also admit a State as member by a vote of two-thirds of the delegates attending the session, including two-thirds of the Government delegates present and voting.

Reflection
India is a founder member of the ILO.

The Constitution of ILO provides that any member of ILO may withdraw its membership after giving notice to the Director-General of the Office. Such notice shall take effect 2 years after the date of receipt, subject to the condition that the member has fulfilled all financial obligations arising out of its membership at that time.

Structure

ILO carries out its functions through three main bodies: the International Labour Conference, the Governing Body and the International Labour Office.

The International Labour Conference The International Labour Conference is also called as the international parliament of labour. Its main function is to set labour standards and general policies of ILO. It provides a forum for discussion of social and labour-related issues. It also adopts the ILO's budget and elects the Governing Body. The Conference meets once a year in Geneva and has been continuing to meet every year since its first session in 1919, except for the interruption due to World War II. The annual meeting is attended by the delegates of governments, workers and employers of ILO Member States. The delegation of each Member State consists of two government delegates, one employer delegate, a worker delegate and their respective advisers. Generally the government representatives are ministers and officials responsible for labour affairs, while the employer and worker delegates are nominated by the respective government in agreement with organisations of employers and workers important at national-level. Every delegate has equal rights and has one vote.

Spotlight
The International Labour Conference sets labour standards and general policies of ILO.

The Governing Body The Governing Body is the executive body of the ILO. It meets thrice in a year. Its main functions are to: take decisions on ILO policy; decide agenda of the International Labour Conference; scrutinise the budget of the ILO for submission to the Conference; elect the Director-General of the Office; and look after the implementation of the Recommendations and Conventions of ILO.

Spotlight
The Governing Body elects the Director-General of the Office.

The work of the Governing Body and that of the Office are aided by tripartite committees covering major industries. The Governing Body is also supported by committees of experts on such matters as vocational training, management development, occupational safety and health, industrial relations, workers' education and special problems of women and young workers.

It has 56 titular members (28 governments, 14 employers, and 14 workers) and 66 deputy members (28 governments, 19 employers and 19 workers). Out of 28 titular government seats, 10 are permanently held by States of chief industrial importance. Since 1922 India has been holding one of these 10 seats. The other government members are elected by the Conference every 3 years. The employer and worker members are elected in their individual capacity.

Prior to the adoption of a Convention or Recommendation, the Governing Body ensures proper preparation on the subject and adequate consultation of the concerned members by means of a preparatory conference or other means.

International Labour Office The International Labour Office is the Secretariat of the ILO. The Office has a Director-General, who is elected every 5 years by the Governing Body. The Director-General is responsible for the efficient conduct of the Office and other duties as may be assigned. It is the centre of the activities of ILO. It has headquarters in Geneva and many field offices around the world. The Office has a research and documentation centre. Some of the important functions of the International Labour Office include the following:

(i) Collection and distribution of information on all matters related to labour conditions in the world, particularly those subjects which it proposes to bring before the Conference with the objective to conclude international Conventions and Recommendations.

(ii) Conduct of research on certain matters as may be ordered by the Conference or by the Governing Body.

(iii) As per the directions of the Governing Body the Office must:

   (a) prepare the documents on the various items of the agenda for the meetings of the Conference;

   (b) provide assistance to governments at their request in framing of laws and regulations on the basis of the decisions of the Conference, and in improvement of administrative practices and systems of inspection;

   (c) carry out the duties regarding the effective observance of Conventions;

   (d) prepare and bring out publications on problems labour and employment of international interest.

In general, the Conference or the Governing Body may assign other powers and duties to the Office from time to time.

Conventions and Recommendations

ILO draws international labour standards that are legal instruments and set out basic principles and rights at work. These standards may either take the form of *Conventions*, which are legally binding international treaties that may be ratified by Member States, or *Recommendations*, which act as non-binding guidelines. In many cases, a Convention lays down the basic principles to be implemented by ratifying countries, while a related Recommendation supplements the Convention by providing more detailed guidelines on how it could be applied. Recommendations can also be autonomous, i.e., not linked to any Convention.

Spotlight

ILO Conventions are international treaties and are instruments which create legally binding obligations on the countries that ratify them.

Conventions and Recommendations are drawn up by representatives of governments, employers and workers and are adopted at the International Labour Conference. Once a standard is adopted, Member States are required under the ILO Constitution to *submit* them to their competent authority (normally the parliament) for consideration. In the case of conventions, this means consideration for *ratification*. If it is ratified, a Convention generally comes into force for that country a year after the date of ratification. Ratifying countries have to apply the Convention in their laws and practice and must report on its application at regular intervals. If the countries violate the Convention they have ratified, there is a provision of moving representation and complaint against them.

Spotlight

ILO Recommendations are non-binding and set out guidelines that provide an orientation to national policies and actions.

If a member has ratified any International Labour Convention and later withdraws from the membership of ILO, such withdrawal shall not affect the continued validity for the period provided for in the Convention of all obligations arising thereunder or relating thereto.

India and the International Labour Organisation

The ILO Recommendations and Conventions have provided useful guidelines and framework for the evolution of legislative and administrative measures for the protection and advancement of the interest of workers in India. India has so far ratified 43 Conventions of ILO, including the 4 core Conventions (out of the total 8), which are Forced Labour Convention (No. 29), Abolition of Forced Labour Convention (No. 105), Equal Remuneration Convention (No. 100), Discrimination (Employment Occupation) Convention (No. 111). Annexure I presents the list of ILO Conventions ratified by India.

Regarding the ratification of any Convention, India has adopted a policy that first the national laws and policy will be brought into conformity with the provisions of the Convention, which is done through an amendment. The entire process of ratification begins when the Director-General of International Labour Office sends a certified copy of the Convention or Recommendation to the Central Government, which then circulates it to all the State Governments, concerned Ministries of the Government of India and the employers' and workers' organisations. These bodies give their observations and suggestions. The Central Government then prepares a statement on action proposal which is placed before the Parliament for discussion. Copies of the statements are thereafter forwarded to the ILO and to the State Governments, and employers' and workers' organisations.

Many provisions in various labour legislations in India have been incorporated as a result of ratification of ILO Conventions by the Government. Thus provisions regarding working hours and weekly rest were incorporated in protective legislations like the Factories Act, 1948, the Mines Act, 1952, the Plantations Labour Act, 1951 and the Beedi and Cigar Workers (Conditions of Employment) Act, 1966 as a result of ratification of Hours of Work (Industry) Convention, 1919 in 1921 and the Weekly Rest (Industry) Convention (No. 14), 1921 in 1923. Many Conventions and Recommendations related to health, safety and welfare have resulted in incorporation of provisions in the Factories Act, 1948 and other welfare Acts. Similarly, the Minimum Wage Fixing Machinery Convention (No. 26), 1928 and the Minimum Wage Fixing Machinery Convention (No 121), 1970 have influenced the Minimum Wages Act, 1948. Several Conventions on employment of children and young persons and that of women have been ratified by India, and appropriate provisions have been included in relevant Acts.

Spotlight

Many provisions in various labour legislations in India have been incorporated as result of ratification of the ILO Conventions by the Government.

Conventions and Recommendations of ILO on social security like Workmen's Compensation (Occupational Diseases) (No. 18), 1925 and Equality of Treatment (Accident Compensation) (No. 19), 1925 have been ratified by India and the provisions of these two conventions have been incorporated into the Workmen's (now Employees') Compensation Act, 1923 and the Employees' State Insurance Act, 1948. Many provisions in the Employees' Provident Fund and Miscellaneous Provisions Act, 1952 and the Payment of Gratuity Act, 1972 are a result of other Conventions related to old age benefits like Old Age Insurance (Industry) Convention (No. 35). Conventions aimed at promoting and regulating harmonious industrial relations namely, Rural Workers Organization Convention (No. 141), 1975, Tripartite Consultation (International Labour Standards) Convention (No. 144) have also been ratified, with the former being included in the Trade Unions Act, 1926 and the latter in the Minimum Wages Act, 1948 and the Employees' State Insurance Act, 1948.

Even the Conventions not ratified and many Recommendations related to such Conventions have influenced labour legislations. For example, certain provisions of Employment Injury Benefits Convention (No. 121), 1964 and Workmen's Compensation (Occupational Diseases) Recommendation (No. 24), 1925 have been incorporated in the Employees' Compensation Act, 1923. Thus the ILO Conventions and Recommendations play an important role in shaping Indian industrial relations by way of influencing labour legislations.

SUMMARY

- Legal, political, economic, social and cultural factors have an impact on all the actors in industrial relations scenario, i.e., employers, workers and the government of a country. Hence industrial relation systems differ across countries.
- It is important to learn from successful models in other countries in order to improve labour-management relations in a country.
- The governments in most Asian countries intervene directly or indirectly in labour issues. While USA is characterised by the absence of bipartite or tripartite formal institutions or mechanisms for any dialogue at national level, EU countries have both bipartite and tripartite systems.
- In EU the pattern of trade unionism varies in different member countries, from a few industrial unions comprising a single dominant confederation in Austria and Germany to multiple confederations in Belgium, France, Italy, etc.
- Japan and Korea have strong enterprise-level unions; USA has a strong confederation to which many of workers' unions are affiliated.
- Enterprise-level collective bargaining is a common approach in East Asian countries; in many EU States centralised national bargaining has been replaced by more decentralised systems of bargaining, but there is still a role for the national-level bargaining. The predominant bargaining level for pay and all other issues in USA is that of the individual company.
- The mechanism of coordination of collective bargaining at European level in EU has been devised to avoid downward pressure on wage costs.
- Social security schemes in Japan include the public pension system to provide income security for the elderly, survivors and disabled persons.
- In EU there are rules regarding social security at EU level, but these rules do not replace national systems with a single system. These countries have their own social security legislations.
- Workers' participation may have a direct form, as in Japan and USA or indirect form, as in Germany and Australia. In Germany co-determination occurs at plant level through workers' councils.
- ILO is a specialised agency of UNO that aims at improving labour standards at global level, having a tripartite structure. It carries out its functions through three main bodies: the International Labour Conference, the Governing Body and the International Labour Office.
- ILO's Recommendations and Conventions have had a strong impact on Indian labour legislations.

Key Concepts

European Union
Works council
International Labour Conference
Governing Body
International Labour Office
Convention
Recommendation
Rengo
Ratification

Bibliography

Carley, M. and SPIRE Associates. 2001. Industrial Relations in the EU, Japan and USA, 2000. Retrieved from http://www.eurofound.europa.eu/eiro/2001/11/feature/tn0111148f.htm on 14/9/2014.

Coordination of Collective Bargaining. Retrieved from http://www.eurofound.europa.eu/areas/ industrialrelations/dictionary/definitions/coordinationofcollectivebargaining.htm on 14/9/2014.

De Silva, S. "The Changing Focus of Industrial Relations and Human Resource Management". Paper presented at the *ILO Workshop on Employers' Organizations in Asia-Pacific in the Twenty-First Century*, Turin, Italy, 5-13 May 1997. Bureau For Employers' Activities, International Labour Office , Geneva. Retrieved from http://www.ilo.org/public/ english/dialogue/actemp/downloads/ publications/srsirhrm.pdf on 15/9/2014.

Dijkhof , T. 2011. *International Social Security Standards in the European Union: The Cases of the Czech Republic and Estonia*. Antwerp: Intersentia.

EU System of Industrial Relations. Eurofound. Retrieved from http://www.eurofound.europa.eu /areas/industrialrelations/dictionary/definitions/eusystemofindustrialrelations.htm, on 14/9/2014.

Government of India. *Report of the National Commission on Labour*. Ministry of Labour, Employment and Rehabilitation; 1969.

http://www.belgium.be/en/family/social_security_in_belgium/. Retrieved on 12/9/2014.

http://www.cleiss.fr/docs/regimes/regime_france/an_0.html. Retrieved on 12/9/2014.

Lee, H.K. and Park, Y.R. "Families in Transition and the Family Welfare Policies in Korea". Paper presented at the Canada-Korea Social Policy Research Symposium, Seoul, November 22-23, 2003.

Nakamura, K. (n.d.). "Decline or Revival?: Japanese Labor Unions". The Japan Institute for Labour Policy and Training. Retrieved from http://www.jil.go.jp/english/ JLR/documents/2007 /JLR13_ nakamura.pdf on 12/9/2014.

Oh, H. "Report on the Survey on Industrial Relations in East Asia: Collective Bargaining in Japan". ILO- Japan Multi-Lateral Project, 2006. Thailand: ILO; 2006, p. 15.

Rehfeld,U. et al. *Employee Involvement in Companies under the European Company Statute*, p. 14. Dublin: European Foundation for the Improvement of Living and Working Conditions. 2011. Retrieved from http://www.eurofound.europa.eu/pubdocs/2010/78/en/1/EF1078EN .pdf on 17/9/2014.

Spicker, P. (n.d.). *An Introduction to Social Policy*. Retrieved from: http://www2.rgu.ac.uk/publicpolicy/ introduction/socialsecurity.htm?CFID=74676815&CFTOKEN=90868932&jsessionid=5030 116d835bf605f340387c685433346651TR on 20/9/2014.

Summers, C. "Worker Participation in Corporate Management -The United States Version". *Journal of Comparative Corporate Law and Securities Regulation*, 1978, Vol. I, pp. 157-186.

Tchoe, B. "Long-term Care Policy for the Elderly in Korea". Paper presented at the Canada-Korea Social Policy Research Symposium, Seoul, 22-23 November, 2003.

Velloso, H. Social Security in the United States: Overview and Outlook. UNO. 2006. Retrieved from http://www.eclac.org/publicaciones/xml/0/27160/lcw89i.pdf on 14/9/2014.

Worker-participation.eu. "Collective Bargaining". Retrieved from http://www.worker-participation.eu/National-Industrial-Relations/Across-Europe/Collective-Bargaining2 on 14/9/2014.

Yoon, Y. "A Comparative Study on Industrial Relations and Collective Bargaining in East Asian Countries". *Industrial and Employment Relations Department*. Geneva: International Labour Office; 2009.

Review Questions

Objective Type Questions

I. State True or False

(i) Tripartite discussions and consultations commonly take place at national-level in Japan.
(ii) An important feature of trade unionism in the EU is high degree of unity and coherence at continent level, as well as at national level.
(iii) ILO Conventions create legally binding obligations on the members which ratify them.
(iv) Japanese trade union organisations have a two-tier structure.
(v) The International Labour Office is the Secretariat of ILO.

Answers: (i) True, (ii) False, (iii) True, (iv) False, (v) True

II. Fill in the Blanks

(i) The ILO was created in ______________.
(ii) Co-determination is a common form of worker participation found in ______________.
(iii) Many trade unions in USA seek to conduct ______________ bargaining, whereby an agreement achieved in a particular company or companies is extended to other firms in the sector.
(iv) The ______________ corporation model features industry-level negotiations.
(v) Korea has strong ______________ -level unions.

Answers: (i) 1919, (ii) Germany, (iii) pattern, (iv) Nordic, (v) enterprise

Discussion Questions

1. Why do industrial relations systems vary across countries? Highlight the need to understand industrial relations in an international perspective.
2. Discuss the bipartite and tripartite nature of industrial relations in international perspective
3. Compare trade unionism in Asian countries and in the European Union.
4. Discuss the characteristic features of Japanese industrial relations system.
5. Differentiate between:
   (i) Workers' participation in UK and in Japan
   (ii) ILO Conventions and Recommendations
   (iii) Functions of the Governing Body and the International Labour Office
6. How can the process of collective bargaining differ in different countries? Explain giving suitable examples.
7. Discuss the social security practices in the European Union and USA.

8. Formation of European Union has given more or less uniformity in various dimensions of labour-management relations in the member countries. Critically analyse the statement.
9. Outline the structure of ILO.
10. Discuss the impact of ILO on Indian labour legislations.

Challenges for Workers' Participation in the United Kingdom

Trade unions are a strong force in the British public sector and key private sector companies, but with changing times, trade union membership is declining at workplaces and so unions have not remained as the only means for workers 'voice'. Various alternative approaches have been evolved for this purpose that include direct involvement and communication methods, employee engagement, consultative committees and non-union and hybrid forms of consultation.

In the mid-twentieth century there existed big trade unions, with large membership base, that participated in collective bargaining and thus regulated work conditions and employment. Unions participate in decision-making through consultative committees or partnership agreements and recognised trade unions play a statutory role in finding solutions to issues related to collective redundancy and business transfers. Trade unions not only represent workers in collective bargaining but also give individual representation in grievance and disciplinary matters, and even in work organisation and training issues. Such a trend is declining now as the density of membership and the use of collective bargaining process both have fallen in public and private sector companies in recent years. Though unions are still a strong force in British industrial relations and are functioning actively in the public sector and within many large companies in the private sector in key industries (like vehicle manufacturing, aerospace and banks), but due to various changes in internal and external environment of organisations they no longer remain the only 'voice' of workers, as about three quarters of the employed people are not union members and have no access to union representation at work. In a large part of private sector and small part of the public sector recognised unions do not even exist. There is a representation gap for a large number of employees and they have expressed doubts about union effectiveness in giving voice to workers.

Significant changes in employment relations in the past two decades have given rise to new methods in UK by which employees receive regular information about their organisation and can have a voice. Besides formal meetings of employers and trade union representatives, direct communication and involvement have become common. Researches have shown that the more the voice workers have in organisations, the better it is for increasing productivity and decreasing absenteeism; and the voice systems that combine direct forms of involvement with indirect forms through representative bodies increase organisational commitment.

Indirect methods like Consultative Committees especially in the private sector, whether non-union or combining union and non-union representatives in a 'hybrid' body are becoming common and are operating alongside direct methods of involvement. There has been a remarkable growth in the use of direct communication in the last 25 years, having face to face meeting with employees. The preference for direct methods has been found to be strong.

A drawback of methods like Consultative Committees and joint negotiating committees is that that they are less frequent than the direct methods like team briefing sessions and workforce meetings. But direct methods too have limited scope in terms of time limitations, and for meaningful dialogue, which is important for real participation.

The advent of social media may change the way employers communicate with staff and open up new opportunities for employees to link with each other. Social media can help employees gain a stronger collective voice as employees can respond rapidly to issues discussed in Consultative Committees.

Consultative Committees have a long, if not very distinguished, history in British employment relations. Such a committee must have representatives of employees, drawn from recognised trade unions or directly elected by employees, or both. Trade unions have not been very positive towards these committees and prefer collective bargaining as a participation process as they fear that Consultative Committees might be used as their substitutes.

Though employers favour various forms of employee involvement but their object to legal enforcement of Consultative Committees especially where these appear to limit their prerogatives. In 2004, only around a quarter of workplaces with 200 or more employees did not have a Consultative Committee. It is interesting to note that two-thirds of these committees were non-union and only 11 per cent were organised exclusively by the recognised unions. Around 1 in 5 were 'hybrids', having a mixture of union and non-union representatives. The power of these committees depend upon the attitude of management towards them, that may be decided to discuss important organisational decisions with them or may simply take them as a means of communication with workers. Management is always the dominant partner in consultation since it is they who are setting the key parameters to the agenda. In 2008, the Information and Consultation of Employees Regulations came fully into force for undertakings with 50 or more employees. The way the regulations are drawn up in UK gives considerable freedom to choose the form and frequency of consultation.

Regarding the non-union Consultative Committees, there is evidence that managers often discuss a wider range of issues with these committees and take their views seriously. It is important to recognise that non-union representatives, for the most part, have a more restricted role than their union counterparts since their only function is to attend Consultative Committees. Consultation is a very different process from collective bargaining as it does not rely on arriving at agreement since the purpose is to discuss management plans and allow employees to raise matters concern. Where unions engage in both collective bargaining and consultation, the processes are often complementary. The resultant pattern of relationship is usually referred to as a 'partnership'. Scotland is an example where there is a country-wide 'Labour-Management Partnership' in the National Health Service.

In several hybrid councils trade unions have maintained their collective bargaining role but took part with non-union representatives in the Consultative Committee. A drawback with the hybrid form is the role of non-union members. If management wants a serious consultation with workers it must have an authoritative body to talk with, the one that represents workers in real sense. A confidential issue can be discussed with a representative, not the delegate, whose authority and powers are limited. Collective consultation in union and non-union organisations has the capacity to provide a meaningful forum where employees have access to senior managers and are able to express their opinion on major decisions which have implications for the workforce. The necessary requirements for active consultation to be developed include readiness and preparedness of management to share information on major changes in time with workers, and discussion of a wide range of issues. Employee representatives need to be able to develop a collective voice, and consultation has to be supported by a culture of mutual cooperation and trust.

(Adapted from: Purcell, J. and Hall, M. (2012). Voice and Participation in the Modern Workplace: Challenges and Prospects. Acas Future of Workplace Relations discussion paper series. Retrieved from www.acas.org.uk/media/pdf/g/7/Voice_and_Participation_in_the_Modern_ Workplace_challenges_and_prospects.pdf on 27/9/2014.)

Review Questions

1. What are the challenges in employee participation in management in UK?
2. Discuss the various direct methods that are being used for giving 'voice' to workers in UK. Evaluate their advantages and disadvantages.
3. Compare the suitability of direct methods vis-à-vis indirect methods of employees' participation in management in UK? Which method do you think has the potential of giving better 'voice' to workers?

Annexure I: ILO Conventions Ratified by India

Convention	*Year of ratification*
C001: Hours of Work (Industry) Convention, 1919 (No. 1)	1921
C002: Unemployment Convention, 1919 (No. 2) Not in force	1921
C004: Night Work (Women) Convention, 1919 (No. 4) (Not in force)	1921
C005: Minimum Age (Industry) Convention, 1919 (No. 5)	1955
C006: Night Work of Young Persons (Industry) Convention, 1919 (No. 6)	1921
C011: Right of Association (Agriculture) Convention, 1921 (No. 11)	1923
C014: Weekly Rest (Industry) Convention, 1921 (No. 14)	1923
C015: Minimum Age (Trimmers and Stokers) Convention, 1921 (No. 15) (Not in force)	1922
C016: Medical Examination of Young Persons (Sea) Convention, 1921 (No. 16)	1922
C018: Workmen's Compensation (Occupational Diseases) Convention, 1925 (No. 18)	1927
C019: Equality of Treatment (Accident Compensation) Convention, 1925 (No. 19)	1927
C021: Inspection of Emigrants Convention, 1926 (No. 21) (Not in force)	1928
C022: Seamen's Articles of Agreement Convention, 1926 (No. 22)	1932
C026: Minimum Wage-Fixing Machinery Convention, 1928 (No. 26)	1955
C027: Marking of Weight (Packages Transported by Vessels) Convention, 1929 (No. 27)	1931
C029: Forced Labour Convention, 1930 (No. 29)	1954
C032: Protection against Accidents (Dockers) Convention (Revised), 1932 (No. 32)	1947
C041: Night Work (Women) Convention (Revised), 1934 (No. 41) (Not in force)	1935
C042: Workmen's Compensation (Occupational Diseases) Convention (Revised), 1934 (No. 42)	1964
C045: Underground Work (Women) Convention, 1935 (No. 45)	1938
C080: Final Articles Revision Convention, 1946 (No. 80)	1947
C081: Labour Inspection Convention, 1947 (No. 81) Excluding Part II	1949
C088: Employment Service Convention, 1948 (No. 88)	1959
C089: Night Work (Women) Convention (Revised), 1948 (No. 89) Has ratified the Protocol of 1990	1950
C090: Night Work of Young Persons (Industry) Convention (Revised), 1948 (No. 90)	1950
C100: Equal Remuneration Convention, 1951	1958
C105: Abolition of Forced Labour Convention, 1957	2000
C107: Indigenous and Tribal Populations Convention, 1957 (No. 107)	1958
C108: Seafarers' Identity Documents Convention, 1958 (No. 108)	2005
C 111: Discrimination (Employment and Occupation) Convention, 1958	1960
C115: Radiation Protection Convention, 1960 (No. 115)	1975
C116: Final Articles Revision Convention, 1961 (No. 116)	1962

(*Contd.*)

Convention	*Year of ratification*
C118: Equality of Treatment (Social Security) Convention, 1962 (No. 118)Has accepted Branches (a) to (c)	1964
C122: Employment Policy Convention, 1964	1998
C123: Minimum Age (Underground Work) Convention, 1965 (No. 123) Minimum age specified: 18 years	1975
C127: Maximum Weight Convention, 1967 (No. 127)	2010
C136: Benzene Convention, 1971 (No. 136)	1991
C141: Rural Workers' Organizations Convention, 1975 (No. 141)	1977
C144: Tripartite Consultation (International Labour Standards) Convention, 1976	1978
C142: Human Resources Development Convention, 1975 (No. 142)	2009
C147: Merchant Shipping (Minimum Standards) Convention, 1976 (No. 147)	1996
C160: Labour Statistics Convention, 1985 (No. 160) Acceptance of Article 8 of Part II has been specified pursuant to Article 16, paragraph 2, of the Convention.	1992
C174: Prevention of Major Industrial Accidents Convention, 1993 (No. 174)	2008

13

Industrial Health and Safety

Desired Knowledge Competencies

- To discuss the concept of and need for industrial health and safety.
- To identify the causes of accidents and ways to avoid them.
- To develop an understanding of the statutory and non-statutory measures for maintaining workers' health and safety.

INTRODUCTION

Ever since the Industrial Revolution begun and expanded in Europe and later to different parts of the globe, there have been concerns regarding occupational health and safety. With increasing industrialisation and advancements in technology, dangers of manual jobs have undoubtedly been reduced, but risks of new kinds have developed. As machines and processes are becoming technologically advanced, they are also becoming more complicated, inviting potential hazards to the health of workers and safety at workplace. The new economic order has resulted in demands for higher productivity, leading to work stress, besides the pressure to deal with mechanisation. Health and safety are the responsibility of management as well as workers, and negligence on the part of either of the two may result in risk to human life.

Let us first understand the concept of industrial health and safety before we move on to the various related aspects at workplace. The term 'industrial health' encompasses all the measures undertaken to promote physical well-being, maintain sanitation at workplace and prevent occupational diseases amongst workers. Industrial safety includes all the activities undertaken to generate awareness amongst workers and implementation of safety measures so as to prevent accidents in industry. It may be noted here that the term 'occupational safety and health' (OSH) has the same connotation as 'industrial safety and health'. OSH has been defined by Alli (2008, p. vii) as "the science of anticipation, recognition, evaluation and control of hazards arising in or from the workplace that could impair the health and well-being of workers, taking into account the possible impact on the surrounding communities and the general environment". In this chapter we shall use both the terms interchangeably.

Spotlight

Industrial safety includes all the activities undertaken to generate awareness among workers and implementation of safety measures so as to prevent accidents in industry.

The Government of India recognises that health and safety of workers has a positive impact on their productivity and on the economic and social development of the nation. The National Policy on Occupational Safety and Health is drawn out of various parts of the Constitution of India. For example, the Directive Principles of State Policy provide safeguards to workers; Article 24 prohibits employment of children below 14 years for work in any factory or mine or in any other hazardous employment; Article 39 requires the State to direct its policy towards securing the health and strength of workers, men and women, and the tender age of children and that they are not abused at workplace; Article 42 directs the State to make provision for securing just and humane conditions of work and for maternity relief. Thus the Constitution assures occupational health and safety to all workers, irrespective of their age, gender or sector of employment. On the basis of these Directive Principles and various international instruments, the Government is committed to regulate all economic activities for the management of safety and health risks at workplace, and to provide measures to ensure healthy and safe working conditions for every working person in the nation.

Spotlight

The National Policy on Occupational Safety and Health is drawn out of various parts of the Constitution of India.

NEED FOR INDUSTRIAL HEALTH AND SAFETY

Maintaining healthy and safe work conditions is a need for every organisation, small or big. A negligent attitude towards these aspects may result in various types of problems for organisations and workers. According to the Health and Safety Authority (HSA), Ireland, accidents and ill-health can result in losses to an organisation in terms of money, time, skill and public image, besides the hassle of being involved in legal proceedings (*www.hsa.ie*). We will throw light on these issues here in turn.

- **Financial loss**: Whatever may be the nature of accident or ill-health resulting out of work, an organisation has to bear heavy cost for it. There could be a loss of physical assets like machine and material, besides harm to workers. Moreover, a large amount of compensation is required to be paid to the victims in compliance with legal enactments. Besides these direct costs, there may be indirect costs arising out of accidents. There is loss of productivity; manpower lost is required to be replaced through fresh recruitment and these workers must be trained before they start working on machines or equipment. Such recruitment and training process would again have cost implications.
- **Time loss**: When an accident takes place, work may be stalled for some period. Time and efforts are also required for fulfilling formalities laid down in the Employees' Compensation Act, 1923 (discussed in Chapter 26). A typical example is of notice as per Section 10(1) of the Act, by which no claim for compensation shall be entertained by a Commissioner unless notice of the accident has been given in prescribed manner as soon as practicable after the accident and unless the claim is preferred before him within 2 years of the occurrence of the accident. Production may get behind schedule as a result of such activities.
- **Skill loss**: Employee skill is an asset for any company and is, in fact, a differentiating factor with other companies in the same industry. Little negligence on the part of management or workers may result in accidents or ill-health, causing partial or permanent disablement in workers, and in many cases, even death. Thus an organisation loses its human asset and skills due to these conditions.
- **Hassles of legal proceedings:** Involvement in legal proceedings may consume a lot of time, energy and resources for an organisation. For example, in the case of Union Carbide disaster in Bhopal, it took 26 years for the verdict of the Supreme Court of India to see the light of the day (Business Standard, 2011).

- **Tarnished public image**: Accidents at workplace not only result in material losses, but also tarnish the public image of the organisation.

ACCIDENTS

Let us now try to understand the meaning of the term Heinrich, Peterson and Roos (1980) describe an accident as an event that is both unplanned and uncontrolled, in which the action or reaction of an object, substance, person or radiation results in personal injury or the probability thereof. Raouf (2011) defines an accident as any unplanned occurrence which results in injuries, fatalities, loss of production or damage to property and assets. Haddon (1964) views an accident as an unexpected occurrence of physical damage to any animate or inanimate structure. According to Ghiselli and Brown (1948), an accident is an event that takes place without foresight, and results in some type of personal injury and/or damage to equipment and property. Combining all these definitions, we propose an accident to be *any unexpected occurrence where there is causation or probability of damage to physical objects and injury to living beings.*

Spotlight

Accidents are unexpected occurrences with causation or probability of damage to physical objects and injury to living beings.

Causes of Accidents

Accidents do not occur without any reason; there are preceding circumstances involving humans, situations and machines that result in accidents. Sometimes there is an inherent risk involved in the nature of the job itself. The International Labour Organisation (ILO) defines risk as "a combination of the likelihood of an occurrence of a hazardous event and the severity of injury or damage to the health of people caused by this event".

Many theories for explaining the causation of accidents have been developed, that include domino theory, multiple causation theory, accident proneness theory, pure chance theory and energy transfer theory. According to the domino theory developed by Heinrich, Peterson and Roos (1980), all accidents could be modeled with a chain of five factors. This theory was so named as the series of factors giving rise to an accident was compared with a row of dominoes knocking each other down (Figure 13.1). The sequence is as follows:

1. Ancestry and social environment, causing
2. Fault of the person, resulting in

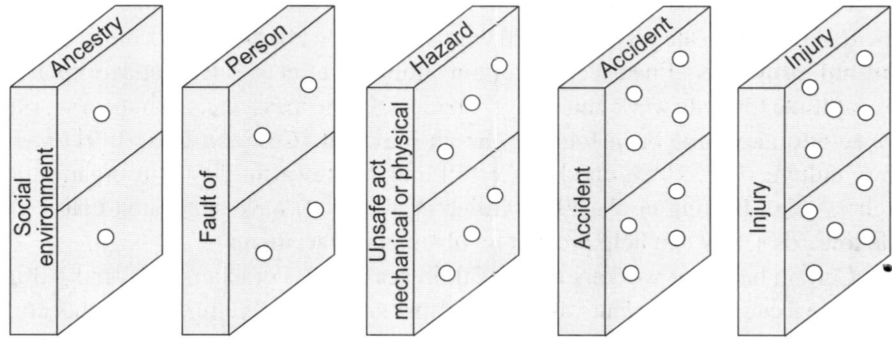

Figure 13.1 *Domino's Theory of Accident*
Source: Heinrich, Peterson and Roos, 1980

3. Unsafe act and/or mechanical or physical hazard, causing
4. Accident, resulting in
5. Injury

Petersen (1971), in his book 'Technique of Safety Management', took a wider view of causes of accidents and proposed the 'multiple causation model'. This model says that reasons of accidents are a number of contributing factors, causes and sub-causes, which combine together in a random fashion to cause an accident.

The factors giving rise to accidents may be divided into two categories: human factors and mechanical factors.

I. Human Factors

Human factors include those causes of accidents which are related in some way to individuals and account for one of the most important causes of accidents. For example, it was reported that 62 per cent of the accidents between 1994 and 2004 in Indian Railways were caused due to failure of railway staff (Amitabh, n.d). The reason for occurrence of human error may be attributed to both physical and psychological factors (Cooper and Volard, 1978). Human errors have been differentiated by Reason (1990) as: *active failures*, that immediately precede an accident usually caused by frontline workers and *latent failures*, that precede active failures and are usually management-related factors, e.g., poor supervision. According to Male (2003), human factors contribute to causation of accidents in various ways which include, among other aspects, designing the job and the way of managing various systems like training procedures, etc. Human factors are found at two levels: worker-related and management-related.

a. Worker-Related Factors Worker-related factors are causes of accidents that originate from physical, psychological and behavioural aspects of workers. Some of the important causes are elaborated here as follows:

> **Spotlight**
> Worker-related factors are those causes of accidents that originate from physical, psychological and behavioural aspects of workers.

(i) **Personality variables**: The accident proneness theory says that some people are more likely to have accidents due to the presence of certain permanent personality variables. This theory was supported by Klumb (1995), who had observed that the majority of people never have accidents, a lesser percentage has one accident and a still lesser percentage experiences large number of accidents. It is the third category of people who possess the characteristics of accident-proneness.

(ii) **Attitudinal problems**: Presence of certain attitudes affects safety at workplace. A general careless attitude towards work and things, laziness, clumsiness, etc. all impact workplace safety. Employee attitudes have been found to be an indicator (Cox and Cox, 1991) and component of safety culture (Lee, 1995, cited in Correll and Andrewarth, 2000) in organisations. Several researchers (e.g., Barling et al., 2002; Gillen et al., 2002) have suggested that a more positive attitude towards safety can help prevent involvement in accidents.

(iii) **Habits:** Certain habits of workers may result in accidents. For example, coming drunk to workplace may be a cause of accidents. Irritable temper and quickly getting into fights are other habits that may directly or indirectly lead to involvement in accidents. Life patterns may also affect safety at workplace. Sleeping late at night may result in sleepiness at workplace, thus threatening safety.

(iv) **Stress:** Stress is an emotional state that results from the self-perceived inability of a person to bridge the gap between a desired state and the present state, when the outcomes are important for him/her. There is a direct relationship between job stress and occupational accidents (Trimpop et. al., 2010). Organisations consider stress as related to workers' lifestyle, personality and psychological variables, while unions find its roots in excessive or conflicting work demands and poor supervision (Causes and cures for stress still misunderstood, 1990). Work overload is supposed to be the prime cause of industrial stress, which may generate a feeling of anger, fatigue, confusion and anxiety in workers (Goetsch, 1993). The indirect effect of stress may be on safety attitudes, as workers may deviate from safe work practices and are likely to commit more errors if they are under pressure to increase production (Clarke and Cooper, 2004).

Spotlight
A direct relationship exists between job stress and occupational accidents.

(v) **Unsafe Acts:** Unsafe acts may be understood as those human actions that arise out of errors that are potentially hazardous and can cause an accident. These human errors occur when workers deviate from the standard job procedures and hazard control processes, which may expose them to the risk of accidents (Joel, 1997).

b. Management-Related Factors Management-related factors include reasons of accidents that originate from the actions of management. In such causes management is responsible for decision making. As mentioned earlier, latent failures result from management actions, which may ultimately culminate into an accident. Some important management-related causes of accidents are explained here.

(i) **Laxity in implementation of safety norms:** A casual attitude of management towards safety may ultimately result in accidents. Most accidents take place because small issues are either neglected or overlooked. Overlooking smaller details in design of plant and equipment often leads to accidents. Physical layout of the workplace or work location, the condition of tools, equipment and materials that do not meet safety standards create unsafe conditions at work (Abdelhamid and Everett, 2000). Safe working is also an attitude, as already told above. Laxity or non-seriousness on the part of management may result in the development of undesirable attitude among workers regarding safety. Stringent implementation of safety norms must be exercised and strict actions must be taken against workers flouting safety norms, otherwise it may convey a negative message to workers. The Directorate General of Factory Advisory Services and Labour Institutes (DGFASLI), an attached office of the Ministry of Labour & Employment, advises factories on various problems related to safety, health, efficiency and well-being of workers. It receives information from time to time relating to factories covered under the provisions of the Factories Act, 1948 from States and Union Territories. This information can be used for knowing the State-wise status of health and safety, and compliance level with statutory standards in factories, and for estimation of various trends. Statistics on the status of compliance with statutory provisions based on such data is given in Annexure I.

(ii) **Inadequate training:** Employees working on machinery of any kind and those handling hazardous materials must be properly trained before they are put on job. Lack of proper training in terms of time or content regarding use of machines, safety equipment and gadgets is a potential threat and may be a precursor to accidents.

(iii) **Flaws in job design:** Work overload, which is a cause of workplace stress, may be a flaw of job design, resulting in accidents, ill health and injuries. Ergonomics need to be considered while designing jobs. According to the International Ergonomics Association (IEA), "Ergonomics (or human factors) is the scientific discipline concerned with the understanding of the interactions among humans and other elements of a system, and the profession that applies theoretical principles, data and methods to design in order to optimise human well-being and overall system performance". IEA further states that ergonomists contribute to the design and evaluation of tasks, jobs, environments and systems to make them compatible with the needs, abilities and limitations of people.

(iv) Unsound recruitment policies: Selecting the right person for a job is a factor that cannot be ignored in maintaining workplace safety (Male, 2003). When management fails to understand the importance of good recruitment and selection policies, the chances of selection of a wrong person are high. This may aggravate the chances of human errors at work. Some of the important aspects to be considered in a candidate for person-job fit are physical characteristics (body size and shape, strength and posture), senses (vision, hearing and touch), mental abilities and work experience (Health and Safety Executive, 2013).

(v) Poor supervision: Lack of proper and regular monitoring may result in problems escaping the attention of supervisors. Workers must be monitored if they are using safety gadgets or if they are complying with safety rules or not. All mechanical equipment must be checked periodically for their workability. Ignoring any of these aspects may be dangerous for safety.

Exhibit 13.1 Chernobyl Disaster

On 26th April 1986, a test was conducted at the Chernobyl Nuclear Power Station, Ukraine, in former Soviet Union. During the test a sudden surge of power caused an explosion, releasing a cloud of radiation into the environment. Emergency actions were taken and later the damaged unit was completely covered in a temporary concrete structure, called the "sarcophagus," to limit further release of the radioactive material. The precise causes of the accident are not clear, but the general belief is that the disaster was caused by both reactor design flaws and operator error.

In the aftermath, 28 out of 600 workers at the site were killed by severe radiation effects within the first 4 months, while 106 workers suffered from acute radiation sickness due to high radiation doses. About 2,00,000 workers involved in the cleanup operation in 1986 and 1987 also received high doses of radiation (between 1 and 100 units against the average annual radiation dose for a US citizen of about 0.6 unit).

As a result of the accident, inhabited areas of Belarus, the Russian Federation and Ukraine were contaminated with radiations. Many children and adolescents in the area drank milk contaminated with radioactive iodine. A number of thyroid cancer cases were detected among these children and a few of them even died.

(Adapted from: Nuclear Regulatory Commission (n.d.). Backgrounder on Chernobyl Nuclear Power Plant Accident United States. Retrieved from ww.nrc.gov/reading-rm/doc-collections/ fact-sheets/chernobyl-bg.html on 20/9/2014; Chernobyl Nuclear Accident. Retrieved from www.environment.about.com/od/ chernobyl/p/ chernobyl.html on 18/9/2014.)

II. Mechanical Factors

Mechanical factors may be understood as those causes of accidents that do not involve any human error. These include failure of machines and control systems and problems in safety gadgets.

(a) Failure of machines and control systems: Sometimes accidents occur even when no human fault is involved due to machine failure at some crucial juncture of work process.

(b) Problems in safety gadgets: Faulty design or poor quality of safety gadgets like helmets, gloves, respirators and the like are another reason of accidents.

Figure 13.2 summarises the various causes of accidents described so far.

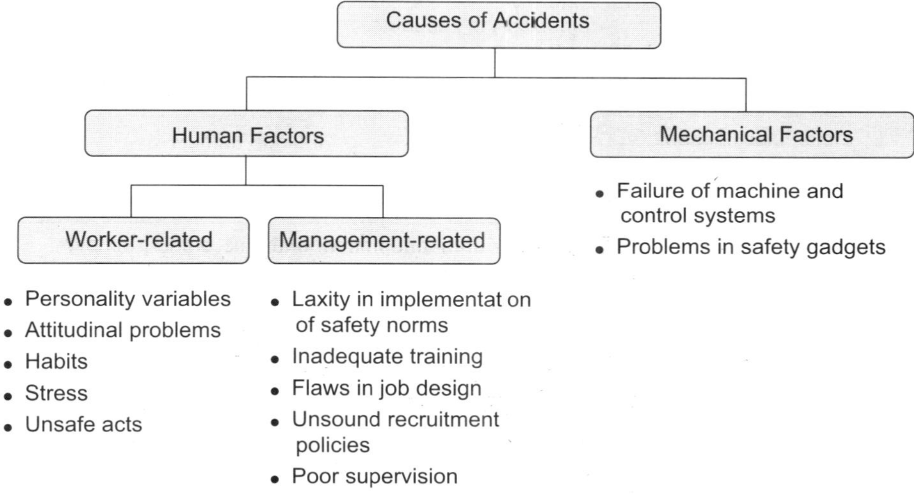

Figure 13.2 *Causes of Accidents*

OCCUPATIONAL HAZARDS AND DISEASES

Occupational hazard may be defined as a risk to the health or life of an employee associated, inherent in the nature of an occupation or work environment. Different types of works have different types of risks associated with them. For example, mining and excavation work has certain unique hazards associated with it that become the cause of majority of accidents in mines. Cause-wise analysis of fatal accidents in coal and non-coal mines in India for the period 1996-2000 has revealed that causes like roof-fall, dumpers and trucks, and rope haulage in coal mines and side-fall, fall of persons, dumpers/trucks and fall of objects in non-coal mines contribute a major share of the fatal accidents (*www.dgfasli.nic.in*). Besides this, the environment in the underground coal mines exposes workers to some specific health hazards.

Spotlight

Occupational diseases are the diseases occurring as a result of prolonged working in certain occupations.

An occupational disease is not characterised merely by the disease itself, but by a combination of a disease and exposure, as well as an association between the two (Karjalainen, 1999). Occupational diseases may be seen as another type of occupational hazard. It may be defined as a disease occurring as a result of prolonged working in an occupation. According to the ILO (2009), these are the disease known, under prescribed conditions, to arise out of exposure to substances or dangerous conditions in processes, trades or occupations. The ILO List of Occupational Diseases (Revised 2010), approved in the 307th Session of the ILO Governing Body, includes a wide range of internationally recognised occupational diseases that range from illnesses caused by physical, chemical and biological agents to occupational cancer. Mental and behavioural disorders have found a place in this list for the first time.

It has been established that certain diseases are prevalent in certain industries and processes (Krishnan, 1997). Some of these are mentioned in Table 13.1.

TABLE 13.1 Some Common Occupational Diseases and Industry/Process of their Prevalence

Disease	*Industry/Process of Prevalence*
Byssinosis	Textile industry
Pneumoconiosis	Coal workers
Silicosis	Coal workers, stone quarrying and slate pencil manufacturing units
Mercury poisoning	Charco-alkali plants
Dermatitis	Mineral oil handling
ECG abnormalities	Viscose rayon industry
Lead poisoning	Lead handlers, printing and battery manufacturing

Adapted from: Krishnan, 1997

In India about 10 million workers employed in mining, construction and various industries are exposed to silica dust. Some studies show that silicosis prevalence rates are 54.6 per cent among slate pencil workers and 35.2 per cent among stonecutters, while pneumoconiosis prevalence rate among coal-workers is 18.8 per cent (ILO, 2013). Similarly, workers employed in the textile industry are exposed to unhealthy levels of cotton dust, particles of pesticides and soil, resulting in respiratory disorders like asthma and a fatal disease called byssinosis (also known as brown lung). Nowadays computers are commonly used at workplace and it has been found that working on computers has occupational hazards associated with it. Prolonged use of computer can cause musculoskeletal problems, as corroborated by several studies (e.g., Karlqvist et al., 2002; Jensen et al., 2002). Duration of computer work was found to be positively associated with neck and shoulder problems, while intensive use of mouse pointer has been found to be associated with hand and wrist problems. The list of notifiable diseases provided in the Factories Act, 1948 is presented in Annexure II.

EXHIBIT 13.2 NOISE-INDUCED HEARING LOSS IN COAL MINING

Noise-Induced Hearing Loss (NIHL) is an occupational illness in coal mining owing to high level of noise exposure due to the usage of heavy equipment, drilling of rocks and confined work environment. Barriers to reducing NIHL include: gaps in knowledge of noise dose/source relationships, unavailability of effective noise controls and need for worker education and empowerment. A related issue is the difficulty of communication in noisy workplaces by both hearing impaired and normal hearing workers. The Hearing Conservation Programme aims at overcoming such barriers in an attempt to reduce NIHL in the mining industry.

(Adapted from: Imteyaz, A., Ansari, F. and Dey, U. K. (2011). Prevention of Noise-Induced Hearing Loss for Coal Mines, Electronic Diagnostic and its Management, Coal Mining Technology and Management, May-August, 2011,Vol. 15 No. 5, pp. 1-6.)

Occupational diseases may cause permanent disablement and their cure is usually not available. However most of these diseases can be prevented by adopting appropriate occupational health measures. The ILO has its own Code of Practice that serves as a guideline for safety and health for employers, workers and public authorities in various sectors like construction, iron and steel industries, agriculture and forestry.

Exhibit 13.3 ILO Code of Practice on Safety and Health in the Iron and Steel Industry: Some Recommendations

In consistence with national laws and regulations, there should be:

- existence of a joint commitment between the competent authority, employers, workers and their representatives,
- establishment of criteria for classifying substances that are used and produced in the production of iron and steel that may be hazardous to health,
- monitoring of the safety and health requirements of comparable national or international iron and steel-making facilities by Labour Inspectorates for further development and improvement of safety measures,
- responsibility of employers to maintain workplaces, plant, equipment, tools and machinery, and should organise work so as to eliminate or control workplace hazards and risks, and
- right to workers and their representatives to participate in the process of consultation and cooperate with employers concerning all aspects of safety in the production of iron and steel specified in this code.

(Adapted from: ILO (2005). Code of Practice on Safety and Health in the Iron and Steel Industry, Sectoral Service Programme, Geneva: International Labour Office.)

TRENDS IN OCCUPATIONAL DISEASES AND ACCIDENTS

Occupational health and safety is an important issue all over the world. According to estimates by the ILO, approximately 2.3 million deaths occur every year globally because of occupational accidents and work-related diseases, which means that over 6,000 workers die every day because of their work (*www.ilo.org*). About 0.4 million people die in India every year due to work-related problems (Al-Tuwaijri, 2008).

Certain occupational diseases occur more frequently than others. On the basis of parameters like: the frequency of occurrence of the illness or injury, its severity in individual cases and its potential for prevention, the National Institute of Occupational Safety and Health, United States of America, has identified certain leading occupational diseases. Of these, occupational lung disease has been found to be the most prevalent and includes diseases like silicosis, asbestosis, byssinosis and occupational asthma. Occupational cancer stands at the second number, followed by cardio-vascular diseases; disorder of reproduction, neurotoxicity, noise induced hearing loss, dermatological conditions and psychological disorders also feature in the list (*www.nihfw.org*).

Estimates by the World Health Organisation indicate that out of 11 million cases of occupational diseases in the world, a significant proportion of 1.9 million cases (17 per cent) comes from India and out of 0.7 million deaths in the world 0.12 million (17 per cent) is contributed by India (*www.nihfw.org*). The DGFASLI had reported 1,454 fatal and 30,035 non-fatal injuries in 2010, using records from registered factories which employed about 5 per cent of total workforce (*www.dgfasli.nic.in*). Table 13.2 presents statistics on industrial injuries for a decade (2001-2010); there is no clear trend and figures are fluctuating for different years.

TABLE 13.2 Industrial Injuries in Factories, their Incidence and Frequency Rates

Year	*Number of Injuries*		*Incidence Rate (Per Thousand Workers Employed)*		*Frequency Rate (per One Lakh Man Days Worked)*	
	Fatal	*Non-fatal*	*Fatal*	*Non-fatal*	*Fatal*	*Non-fatal*
2001	627	28,364	0.07	3.24	0.19	8.67
2002	540	20,453	0.13	4.88	0.16	6.14
2003	525	16,432	0.08	2.50	0.11	3.33
2004	562	15,020	0.05	1.33	0.08	2.21
2005	613	14,163	0.09	1.97	0.05	1.21
2006	1,068	18,844	0.13	2.28	0.08	1.3
2007	821	14,469	0.10	1.81	0.09	1.64
2008 (P)	1,369	32,570	—	—	—	—
2009 (P)	1,509	31,584	—	—	—	—
2010 (P)	1,454	30,035	—	—	—	—

P: provisional

(Adapted from: www.labour.nic.in/upload/uploadfiles/files/Divisions/LC%26ILAS/RajaRam.pdf. Retrieved on 2/9/2014; Ministry of Labour & Employment, Labour Pocketbook 2010 and 2011, Labour Bureau, Chandigarh/ Shimla: Government of India, DGFASLI www.dgfasli.nic.in/fact_stat09.htm, Retrieved on 2/9/2014.)

(Adapted from: www.labour.nic.in/upload/uploadfiles/files/Divisions/LC%26ILAS/RajaRam.pdf. Retrieved on 2/9/2014; Ministry of Labour & Employment, Labour Pocketbook 2010 and 2011, Labour Bureau, Chandigarh/ Shimla: Government of India, DGFASLI www.dgfasli.nic.in/fact_stat09.htm. Retrieved on 2/9/2014.)

STATUTORY SAFETY MEASURES

There is no single legislation in India that addresses every aspect of occupational health and safety; in fact several legislations cover this issue in a fragmented manner. For mining, construction, manufacturing and ports there are separate legislations that cover the health and safety issues of workers in these industries. The Factories Act, 1948 is a comprehensive Act that covers the health, safety and welfare of workers working in a factory as defined by the Act. We will talk about all such provisions in detail in Chapter 14. Provisions in some of the other Acts regarding health and safety of workers are covered here.

Plantations Labour Act, 1951

The Plantations Labour Act, 1951 applies to all tea, coffee, rubber and cinchona plantations. The objective of the Act is to regulate working conditions and provide for welfare of workers in plantations. Chapter III contains provisions for health of workers. It provides for arrangement of clean and wholesome drinking water (Section 8), separate latrines and urinals in sufficient number for males and females in every plantation (Section 9) and medical facilities for workers and their families (Section 10). If any accident occurs in the plantation that causes death or any bodily injury to a worker, by reason of which the worker is prevented from working for a period of

Spotlight

Chapter III of the Plantations Labour Act, 1951 contains provisions for health of workers.

48 hours or more immediately following the accident, the employer is required to inform the authorities in the prescribed form (Section 32A). The Act was amended with effect from 1st June 2010 to provide safety and occupational healthcare to plantations workers. The Plantations Labour (Amendment) Act, 2010 provides a new Chapter IVA to cover all aspects of safety and occupational health of workers in plantations. It includes provisions regarding safety measures to be adopted in the use, handling, storage and transport of insecticides, chemicals and toxic substances, as given in Section 18A(1). The amended Act also empowers State Governments to make rules for prohibiting or restricting employment of women or adolescents in using or handling hazardous chemicals, provided in Section 18A(2).

Every employer shall ensure that every worker in plantation employed for handling, mixing, blending and applying insecticides, chemicals and toxic substances, is trained about the hazards involved in different operations in which he is engaged, the various safety measures and safe work practices to be adopted in emergencies arising from spillage of such insecticides chemicals and toxic substances and such other matters as may be prescribed by the State Government [Section 18A(4)].

Section 18A(6) provides that every employer shall maintain health record of every worker who is exposed to insecticides, chemicals and toxic substances which are used, handled, stored or transported in a plantation, and every such worker shall have access to such record.

Mines Act, 1952

The objective of the Mines Act, 1952 is to regulate the working conditions and safety of miners. Chapter V of the Act (sections 19 to 27) contains provisions for health and safety of workers. It provides for arrangement of clean and wholesome drinking water for workers at suitable points (Section 19), properly maintained urinals and latrines separately for males and females in the mines (Section 20), and easily accessible first-aid boxes [Section 21(1)]. The Act grants certain powers to the Inspectors in Section 22 to maintain and monitor safety of mine workers, and suitability of conditions in mines for employment. Section 22A(1) empowers inspectors to prohibit employment under certain situations where the employer has failed to comply with the provisions relating to safety. Section 23 lays down the provision for notice to be given by the owner, agent or manager of a mine of the occurrence of an accident, in a prescribed manner and place. The Central Government is empowered to appoint a court of enquiry in case of accidents (Section 24). Section 25 mandates notification by the owner, agent or manager of a mine if any person employed in the mine contracts any notified disease. The Central Government, as per Section 26, has the power to direct investigation of causes of notified disease(s) that have been or suspected to have been contracted in a mine.

Spotlight

The objective of the Mines Act, 1952 is to regulate the working conditions and safety of miners.

The Shops and Establishments Acts

The Shops and Establishments Act is a State-enactment. Each State has framed its own rules for the Act. The main objective these State-level legislations is to provide statutory obligation and rights to employees and employers in the unorganised sector of employment, i.e., shops and establishments, and to maintain the working conditions of employees in 'shops' and 'establishments' as defined in the Act. There are provisions for maintaining health of workers in these Acts. For example, Chapter VIII of the Bombay Shops and Establishments Act, 1948 provides for health and safety of employees by way of cleanliness, ventilation, lighting, precautions against fire and first-aid in sections 39, 40, 41, 42 and 42A respectively.

Spotlight

The Shops and Establishments Act is a State-enactment.

Similarly Chapter V of the Tamil Nadu Shops and Establishments Act, 1947 has provisions for health and safety of workers, specifically cleanliness (Section 20), ventilation (Section 21), lighting (Section 22), and precautions against fire (Section 23).

NON-STATUTORY SAFETY MEASURES

Certain non-statutory safety measures may be voluntarily taken up by organisations to maintain safety, explored in this section.

- **Discipline**: Maintaining proper discipline at workplace ensures safety. Workers must adhere to discipline and follow the prescribed norms for maintaining workplace safety. However, over-adherence to discipline may have just the opposite outcomes; in fact workers may not report injury due to fear and disciplinary actions may evoke resentment. It was found that workers' reporting of work-related injuries was reduced by 50 per cent when management had disciplined them for reporting injury experiences (Lipscomb et al., 2013). Therefore management must be careful while maintaining discipline. In this regard, the 'hot stove rule' of McGregor (1967) may prove to be useful. Though widely practiced as a generic rule to ensure discipline, this rule may be extended to safety issues by drawing an analogy between touching a hot stove and disciplining employees on safety aspects. According to this rule, there are four characteristics which must be applied for maintaining discipline. These can be explained in context of safety as follows:

> **Spotlight**
> The 'Hot Stove Rule' may be extended to safety issues by drawing an analogy between touching a hot stove and disciplining employees on safety aspects.

  - **Immediate feedback:** When you touch a hot stove, you burn your hand. The burn was immediate and the pain was a result of your action. You cannot blame the hot stove for burning your hand; rather you would understand your fault and learn a lesson of not repeating the act. Similarly, management must take immediate action against indiscipline and ensure that it is not directed at any person, but his/her actions.
  - **Prior warning:** The red hot stove was a warning in itself that whosoever touches it would get burnt. You ignored the warning and touched it; hence you got punished. Similarly, if any employee, despite knowing safety rules and regulations of the organisation, chooses to ignore the warning, he/she will have to pay the penalty as the organisation had already made its employees aware of the consequences.
  - **Consistency:** Every time you touch a hot stove, you get burnt. Management must also be consistent in disciplining unsafe acts of works.
  - **Impersonal nature:** You touched the hot stove and got burnt. It was not directed against you, but your actions; anyone who touches a hot stove would feel the same pain. Whosoever touches the hot stove, will get burnt. Management must adopt the same approach. Discipline must be directed against the act, not the person.
  - **Training:** Knowledge of hazards provided by worker training programmes is presumed to result in fewer incidents and accidents (Montgomery, 2002). Safety training, coupled with other interventional activities such as inspections and safety meetings, is often implemented at work sites to prevent the occurrence of accidents, or to reduce their likelihood, or severity as part of a safety and health programme (Iyer et al., 2005).

  The Industrial Safety Division of the DGFASLI aims at achieving improvement in working conditions and safety standards of factories and docks through training, consultancies, field studies and surveys. Specialised training courses are conducted for senior managers, safety officers, supervisors, trade union officials and safety committee members from the industry. The Division has made significant contributions in generating national-level awareness on safety and development of infrastructure on safety at national-level through competency building. We would be talking more about DGFASLI and its various functions in details in the very next section.

- **Counseling:** Employee counseling may prove to be helpful in changing human variables like safety attitude and habits; it also assists employees in dealing with stress and improving their efficiency. Counseling can be a part of Employee Assistance Programmes which are widely used in organisations today. These programmes help employees in enhancing their performance.
- **Creating a safety climate and safety culture:** The term 'safety culture' can be understood as referring to the content and context of employee behaviour in organisations, while 'safety climate' is used to refer to values, attitudes and perception of employees regarding safety (HSE, 2005). The Health and Safety Executive further identifies the five indicators of safety climate in an organisation as: leadership, two-way communication, employee involvement, learning culture and attitude towards blame. Of these, employee involvement can be either formal or informal. Formal involvement can be through trade unions and various committees on safety, while informal participation can be through consulting workers in decision-making on safety issues (Krishnan, 1997). A good safety climate (and culture) plays a significant role in maintaining safety. Kirkcaldy et al. (1999) suggest that the general atmosphere or culture for safety in an organisation may play a role in mitigating the effects of stress. Moreover, training can result in the desired behavioural changes in employees only if they desire such change. This desire can be inculcated through if a supporting work climate exists in the organisation (Kirkpatrick and Kirkpatrick, 2006).

Spotlight

Safety climate of an organisation refers to values, attitudes and perception of employees regarding safety.

- **Generating awareness:** Organisations may conduct workshops and special awareness sessions at regular intervals on occupational safety and health issues. Safety posters and slogans are other means to generate awareness about significance of safety amongst workers.

ADMINISTRATION OF INDUSTRIAL SAFETY AND HEALTH

Occupational health and safety in India is managed at three levels: Central-level, State-level and plant-level. The Centre and States have jurisdiction over different subject matters present in different lists in the Seventh Schedule of the Constitution of India. Welfare of workers falls in the Concurrent List. At present there is no agency or Department of the Government of India that is exclusively responsible for matters of occupational health and safety. As discussed in Chapter 2, the DGFASLI provides assistance to the Ministry of Labour & Employment in formulating national policies on occupational health and safety in factories and docks. It also advises factories on various problems concerning safety, health, efficiency and well-being of employees at workplace. The Director General, DGFASLI is also the Chief Inspector of Dock Safety under the Dock Workers (Safety, Health and Welfare) Act, 1986 in respect of major ports. The Directorate General of Mines Safety deals with safety and health issues of mine workers. The inspectors of the respective States working under the Directorate of Industrial Safety and Health inspect occupational health services at State-level. At plant-level healthcare is provided either by the management or through the social security programme of the Employees' State Insurance (ESI)

Spotlight

The DGFASLI assists the Ministry of Labour & Employment on health and safety issues in factories and docks.

Scheme, under the Employees' State Insurance Act, 1948. The ESI Scheme is administered by an apex corporate body called the Employees' State Insurance Corporation (ESIC), headquartered at New Delhi.

RECOMMENDATIONS OF THE SECOND NATIONAL COMMISSION ON LABOUR

One of the objectives of the Second National Commission on Labour was to suggest rationalisation of the existing labour legislations in the organised sector. In its report submitted in 2002, the Commission has given several recommendations for improving health and safety at workplace. Some of the important recommendations are as follows:

- Grouping of existing set of labour laws into four or five groups of laws pertaining to industrial relations, social security, safety and welfare of the working class.
- The Commission has suggested the term 'omnibus law' to be enacted, providing for different rules and regulations on safety applicable to different activities.
- Setting up of a Commission on Occupational Safety and Health by the Central and State Governments and formulation of a Model Safety and Health Policy for organisations. The National Commission has also mentioned that organisations that adopt this model must constantly review and revise it on the basis of their experiences.
- Emphasis on the need to strengthen measures for occupational safety and health in industries. Towards achievement of this goal, the DGFASLI may focus special attention to the hazardous chemical industry.
- Formation of a National Board for attaining proper coordination amongst various bodies dealing with the issues of safety and occupational health, functioning under different Ministries.
- Occupational Safety and Health (OSH) have to be the responsibility and duty of the employer. The employer in consultation with workers should set out in writing an OSH policy specific to his organisation which must be communicated and be readily accessible to all workers.
- A competent institution, perhaps on the lines of the Occupational Safety and Health Commission of the USA, should be nominated to formulate, implement and periodically review a national policy for the establishment and promotion of OSH Management Systems in organisations.
- A disaster management plan must be formulated at every unit and industrial estate and at the city, district, state and national levels. A safety audit policy and programme should be developed.
- Workers engaged in the agricultural sector have to be educated about potential hazards by imparting knowledge about their work, means to identify work-related risk factors and information on first-aid.
- The amendments made in the Factories Act, 1948, after the Bhopal gas tragedy, should be extended to organisations other than factories. The amendments which have been made should be implemented properly.

SUMMARY

- Increase in industrialisation and advancements in technology have resulted in increase in occupational risks and hazards.
- The Indian Constitution ensures healthy and safe working conditions to all men and women in the country. The National Policy on Occupational Safety and Health is derived from various parts of the Constitution of India.

- Accidents are unexpected occurrences where there is causation or probability of damage to physical objects and injury to living beings. There is a need to prevent accidents and ill-health, as they may result in losses to an organisation in terms of money, time, skills and public image, besides involving it in legal proceedings.
- Causes of accidents may be put into two categories: human factors and mechanical factors. Human factors are related to workers, like personality variables, attitude, habits, stress and unsafe acts; those related to management include failure to implement safety norms, improper job design, inadequate training, flawed recruitment policies and poor supervision. Mechanical factors include failure of machines and control systems and problems in safety gadgets.
- Occupational hazards are the dangers inherently associated with a particular occupation. These include occupational diseases, which are diseases that arise due to exposure to certain work environment. Occupational diseases common in India are silicosis, pneumoconiosis, byssinosis, etc.
- There is no single legislation in India to cover the issue of occupational health and safety; several legislations have provisions for health and safety of workers in general and particular to industries.
- Occupational safety and health can be ensured through statutory and non-statutory measures. Statutory measures include certain labour enactments like the Plantations Labour Act, 1951, that covers health and safety of plantation workers and the Mines Act, 1952, that addresses health and safety issues of mine workers. States have framed their own rules and regulations in the State-level Shops and Establishments Acts.
- Non-statutory measures for maintaining workplace safety and health include maintaining proper discipline, training of workers, counseling and generating awareness amongst workers.
- The DGFASLI assists the Ministry of Labour & Employment on health and safety issues in factories and docks. The Directorate General of Mines Safety deals with safety and health issues of mine workers. The Inspectors of the respective States working under the Directorate of Industrial Safety and Health inspect occupational health services at the State-level.
- The Second National Commission on Labour has given several recommendations for improving health and safety of workers at workplace, including: grouping of existing set of labour laws into four or five groups of laws pertaining to industrial relations, social security, safety and welfare of working class; setting up of a Commission on Occupational Safety and Health by the Central and State Governments and formulation of a Model Safety and Health Policy for organisations, etc.

Key Concepts

Accident
Hot Stove Rule
Occupational disease
Unsafe act
DGFASLI
Industrial health
Occupational hazard
Safety climate
Domino theory

Bibliography

Abdelhamid, T. S. and Everett, J. G. "Identifying Root Causes of Construction Accidents", *Journal of Construction Engineering and Management*, 2000, January/February, pp. 52-60. *Retrieved from http://faculty.kfupm.edu.sa/CEM/jannadi/Identifying-Root-Causes-Of-Constuction-Accident.pdf on 12/9/2014.*

Alli, B.O. *Fundamental Principles of Occupational Health and Safety.* International Labour Office, Geneva: ILO; 2008.

Al-Tuwaijri, A., Fedotov, I., Feitshans, I., Gifford, M., Gold, D., Machida, S., Nahmias, M., Niu, S. and Sandi, G. "Beyond Deaths and Injuries: the ILO's Role in Promoting Safe and Healthy Jobs". Seoul, Korea: XVIII World Congress on Safety and Health at Work; June,2008. Retrieved from http://www.ilo.org/wcmsp5/groups/public/---dgreports/---dcomm/documents/ publication/wcms_094524.pdf on 14/9/2014.

Amitabh. Rail Accidents Due to Human Errors–Indian Railways Experience. (n.d.). Retrieved from www.intlrailsafety.com/capetown/3_024_amitabh.doc, on 15/9/2014.

Barling, J., Loughlin, C. and Kelloway, E. K. "Development and Test of a Model Linking Safety-Specific Transformational Leadership and Occupational Safety", *Journal of Applied Psychology*, 2002,Vol. 87, pp. 488-496.

Business Standard. Bhopal Gas Tragedy Survivors Unhappy with SC Decision. May 12, 2011. Retrieved from http://www.business-standard.com/article/economy-policy/bhopal-gas-tragedy-survivors-unhappy-with-sc-decision-111051200093_1.html on 20/9/2014.

Causes and Cures for Stress still Misunderstood. *Occupational Health and Safety Letter,* November 28, 1990,Vol. 20, No. 24.

Clarke, S. and Cooper, C. L. *Managing the Risk of Workplace Stress, Health and Safety Hazards*, London/New York : Routledge; 2004.

Cooper, K. and Volard, S. V. "The Influence of the Individual on Industrial Accidents, Accident Prevention", 1978,Vol. 5, No. 5, pp. 45-49.

Correll, M. and Andrewarth, G. Positive Safety Culture: Key to a Safer Meat Industry, 2000, p 7. Retrieved from http://www.safework.sa.gov.au/uploaded_files/meatCulture LiteratureReviewV81.pdf on 19/9/2014.

Cox, S. and Cox, T. The Structure of Employee Attitudes to Safety: A European Example, *Work & Stress*, 1991, Vol. 5, pp. 93-106.

Existing Setup of Occupational Safety and Health in the Work Place. Retrieved from http://www.dgfasli.nic.in/working_group/chap_1.htm on 14/9/2014.

Ghiselli, E.E. and Brown, Clarence, W.*Personnel and Industrial Psychology*, USA: McGraw Hill Book Company Ltd.; 1948.

Gillen, M., Baltz, D., Gassel, M., Kirsch, L. and Vaccaro, D. Perceived Safety Climate, Job Demands, and Coworker Support among Union and Non-Union Injured Construction Workers, *Journal of Safety Research*, 2002,Vol. 33, pp. 33-51.

Goetsch, D. L. *Industrial Safety and Health: In the Age of High Technology for Technologists, Engineers and Managers*, Macmillan Publishing Company, New York. 1993.

Haddon, W. *Accident Research: Methods and Approaches*, New York: Harper & Row; 1964.

Health and Safety Executive. *Ergonomics and Human Factors at Work*. 2013. Retrieved from http://www.hse.gov.uk/pubns/indg90.pdf on 14/9/2014.

Health and Safety Executive. *A Review of Safety Culture and Safety Climate Literature for the Development of the Safety Culture Inspection Toolkit*. Human Engineering: Research report 367. 2005. Retrieved from http://www.hse.gov.uk/research/rrpdf/rr367.pdf on 12/9/2014.

Heinrich, H. W., Peterson, D. and Roos, N. *Industrial Accident Prevention*, 5th edition, New York: McGraw-Hill; 1980.

http://www.hsa.ie/eng/Workplace_Health/Accidents_and_Behaviour/. Retrieved on 25/9/2014.

IEA. http://www.iea.cc/01_what/What%20is%20Ergonomics.html, retrieved on 25 September 2013.

ILO. *Prevention of Occupational Diseases*. 2013. Retrieved from http://www.ilo.org/wcmsp5/groups/public/---ed_protect/---protrav/-safework/documents/publication/wcms_208226.pdf on 21/9/2014.

ILO. List of Occupational Diseases Occupational Safety and Health Series, No. 74, Revised 2010. Retrieved from http://www.ilo.org/safework/info/publications/WCMS_150323/lang--en/index.htm on 8/9/2014.

ILO. *Identification and Recognition of Occupational Diseases: Criteria for Incorporating Diseases in the ILO List of Occupational Diseases*. Meeting of Experts on the Revision of the List of Occupational Diseases (Recommendation No. 194). Geneva. 27–30 October, 2009. Retrieved from http://www.ilo.org/wcmsp5/groups/public/@ed_protect/@protrav/@safework/documents/meetingdocument/wcms_116820.pdf on 9/9/2014.

ILO. *Code of Practice on Safety and Health in the Use of Machinery*. n.d. Retrieved from http://www.cen.eu/cen/Sectors/Sectors/Machinery/Documents/ILO%20code%20of%20practice.pdf on 9/9/2014.

Karjalalainen, A. International Statistical Classification of Diseases and Related Health Problems (ICD-10) in Occupational Health, *World Health Organization*, 1999. Retrieved from http://www.who.int/occupational_health/publications/en/oehicd10.pdf on 10/9/2014.

Iyer, P. S., Haight, J. M., Del Castillo, E., Tink, B. W. and Hawkins, P.W. "A Research Model Forecasting Incident Rates from Optimized Safety Program Intervention Strategies", *Journal of Safety Research,* 2005, Vol. 36, pp. 341-351.

Jensen, C., Finsen, L., Søgaard, K. and Christensen, H. Musculoskeletal Symptoms and Duration of Computer and Mouse Use, *International Journal of Industrial Ergonomics*, 2002, Vol. 30, No. 4, pp. 265-275.

Joel, L. *The Handbook of Maintenance Management*, New York: Industrial Press; 1997.

Karlqvist, L., Tornqvist, E.W., Hagberg, M., Hagman , M. and Toomingas, A."Self- reported Working Conditions of VDU Operators and Associations with Musculoskeletal Symptoms", *International Journal of Industrial Ergonomics*, 2002,Vol. 30, No. 4, pp. 277-294.

Kirkcaldy, B., van den Eden, P., Trimpop, R. and Martin, T. "Modeling Psychological and Work-Situation Processes that Lead to Traffic and On-Site Accidents", *Disaster Prevention and Management*, 1999,Vol. 8, No. 5, pp. 342-350.

Kirkpatrick, D. L. and Kirkpatrick, J. D. *Evaluating Training Programs: The Four Levels*, San Francisco: Berrett-Koehler Publishers, Inc.; 2006.

Klumb, P. L. "Cognitive Failures and Performance Differences: Validation Studies of a German Version of the Cognitive Failures Questionnaire", *Ergonomics*, 1995, Vol. 38, No. 7, pp. 1456-1467.

Krishnan, N. V. *Safety Management in Industry*, Mumbai: Jaico Publishing House; 1997.

Lipscomb, H. J., Nolan, J., Patterson, D., Sticca, V. and Myers, D. J. Safety, Incentives, and the Reporting of Work-Related Injuries among Union Carpenters: "You're Pretty Much Screwed if You Get Hurt at Work", *American Journal of Industrial Medicine,* 2013,Vol. 56, pp. 389-399.

Male, G.E. Safety of Industrial Lift Trucks: A Survey of Investigated Accidents and Incidents, *Health and Safety Executive*, Special Inspector Reports, April 1997-March 2001, 2003.

McGregor, D. *The Human Side of Enterprise*, New York: McGraw-Hill; 1967.

Montgomery, J. F. "Safety and Health Training". In Plog, B. A., Quinlan, P.J. (Eds.), *Fundamentals of Industrial Hygiene*, Itasca, Illinois: National Safety Council; 2002, pp. 680-681.

National Institute of Health and Family Welfare. Retrieved from http://www.nihfw.org/NDC/DocumentationServices/NationalHealthProgramme/NATIONALPROGRAMMEFORCONTROL.html on 18/9/2014.

Petersen, D. *Techniques of Safety Management*, New York: McGraw-Hill; 1971.

Raouf, A. "Theory of accident causes". In Jorma, S. (Ed.) *Accident Prevention, Encyclopedia of Occupational Health and Safety*, Jeanne Mager Stellman, Editor-in-Chief, International Labor

Organization, Geneva. 2011. Retrieved from http://www.ilo.org/oshenc/part-viii/accident-prevention/item/894-theory-of-accident-causes on 15/9/2014.
Reason, J. *Human Error,* Cambridge: Cambridge University Press; 1990.
Trimpop R., Kirkaldy B., Athansou J. and Cooper C. Individual Differences in Working Hours, Work Perceptions and Accident Rates in Veterinary Surgeries, *Work Stress,* 2010,Vol. 14, pp. 181-188.
http://www.dgfasli.nic.in/info1.htm
http://www.ilo.org/global/topics/safety-and-health-at-work/lang--en/index.htm. Retrieved on 15/9/2014.

Review Questions

Objective Type Questions

I. State True or False

(i) Safety climate refers to the content and context of employee behaviours in organisations.
(ii) Article 24 of the Indian Constitution prohibits employment of children below 14 years from working in any factory, mine or in any hazardous employment.
(iii) Active failures are usually management-related factors behind an accident.
(iv) As per the Employees' Compensation Act, 1923, no claim for compensation shall be entertained by a Commissioner unless it is preferred within 2 years of the accident.
(v) Occupational diseases may cause permanent disablement, but are usually curable.

Answers: (i) False, (ii) True, (iii) False, (iv) True, (v) False

II. Fill in the Blanks

(i) Worker-related causes of accidents originate from physical, psychological and _______ aspects of workers.
(ii) The __________theory of accidents proposes five incidents occurring in a series, leading to accidents.
(iii) ________ is a study of interaction between humans and work to optimise human well-being and enhance work performance.
(iv) The four characteristics to maintain discipline as per the hot stove rule are: immediate feedback, prior warning, ______ and impersonal nature.
(v) _________is an occupational disease prevalent in the textile industry.

Answers: (i) behavioural, (ii) domino, (iii) Ergonomics, (iv) consistency, (v) Byssinosis

Discussion Questions

1. Define the following terms: i. Accident, ii. Stress, Industrial health, iv. Safety climate, and v. Ergonomics.
2. Explain the various human factors that are responsible for occurrence of accidents at workplace.
3. Explain the domino's theory of cause of accidents.
4. Discuss the provisions of the Plantations Labour Act, 1951 pertaining to safety of plantation workers.
5. What is the role of job-design in causing or preventing accidents at workplace? Explain with the help of an example.

6. Write short notes on:
   (i) Occupational disease
   (ii) Mechanical factors causing accidents at workplace
   (iii) Need for industrial health and safety
7. Explain the administrative set-up in India for maintaining health and safety of workers.
8. Discuss various non-statutory measures for maintaining occupational health and safety.
9. What is the 'hot stove rule'? How can it be used in preventing accidents in industries?
10. What structural and functional changes in the administrative machinery for health and safety in India have been recommended by the Second National Commission on Labour?

The Union Carbide Disaster

The Background Union Carbide Corporation (UCC) was one of the largest industrial companies in the United States during 1984, having operations in three dozen countries, including India. A chemical plant in Bhopal was operated by Union Carbide India Limited (UCIL), where a little over 50 per cent was owned by Union Carbide Corporation. In the late 1960s, the Bhopal plant produced the pesticide Sevin. Later the plant started using an advanced technology that used methyl isocyanate (MIC) imported from the United States, for producing Sevin and another pesticide, Temik. Due to combined impact of factors like government's efforts to achieve industrial self-sufficiency and increasing competition in the chemical industry, a plant for manufacturing methyl isocyanate was constructed at Bhopal by UCIL in the late 1970s, at the outskirts of the city. The process to be used was sophisticated but also hazardous. Due to crop failures and famines in the 1980s, farmers' capacity to purchase pesticides had decreased. The UCIL plant was decided to be sold out due to decreased profitability, but in absence of ready buyers it was decided that the plant would be dismantled and established in another developing country. Till this plan was to be materialised, the facility continued manufacturing with poor standards of safety equipment and procedures as compared to those in its sister plant in West Virginia. The local government was aware of the potential risks and safety problems but avoided any action as the plant was already struggling for survival and was a big employer.

The Disaster In the night of 2nd December 1984, a series of small events led to a big disaster. At 11.00 pm an operator at the plant noticed some leakage of MIC gas and increasing pressure inside a storage tank. The tank was apparently filled beyond the recommended capacity; and the storage tank supposed to be held in reserve for excess MIC was already full. The vent-gas scrubber, which is a safety device designed to neutralise toxic discharge from the MIC system, had been turned off earlier due to problems in its parts. Many of the equipment apparently had faulty valves and due to fault in a valve, 1 ton of water, which was used for cleaning internal pipes, got mixed with 40 tons of MIC. The coolant from the refrigeration unit that was used to cool the MIC storage tank had been emptied and drained-off for use in another part of the plant. Pressure and heat from the vigorous chemical reactions in the tank continued to build up. The equipment and instruments in use in the plant, including temperature and pressure gauges were highly unreliable, so much so that workers even ignored if they showed any abnormal readings. Even the warning systems in the plant were not working properly. The same seemed to have happened that night. The gas flare safety system also had also been not working for some time. At around 1.00 am on 3rd December, a safety valve stopped working and that led to escape of a plume of MIC gas into the environment in the early morning, when the city was fast asleep. The poisonous gas caused coughing and painful irritation of eyes of the residents of areas around the plant. It resulted into a large numbers of injury and deaths of humans and animals. Approximately 3,800 people died immediately and local hospitals were full of affected people. Local residents were unaware of the gas that caused so many casualties, its effects and ways to escape. This fact further aggravated the crisis and gave way to a catastrophic situation. These events that led to accident were preceded largely by certain errors and acts of negligence which could have otherwise been prevented.

The Aftermath There were immediate as well as long term health effects of exposure to MIC. These included respiratory, ocular, gastrointestinal, genetic, psychological and neuro-behavioural effects. As per the reports of Government of India, more than half a million people were exposed to the gas and an estimated 10,000 persons died. About 15,000 to 20,000 died prematurely due to the effects of MIC in the next two decades. There was loss of not just human life, but many animals and birds had also died.

Immediately after the disaster, the UCC began attempts to shun the responsibility for the gas leak, putting the onus on to UCIL, stating that the plant was wholly built and operated by the Indian subsidiary. There were long drawn law suits and other legal entanglements besides disputes in the figures of dead and injured people. In a settlement mediated by the Indian Supreme Court, the UCC agreed to pay a compensation amount of $470 million to the Indian Government to be distributed to the victims. The Government later filed a petition in the court seeking a higher compensation to the victims on account of doubtful assessments made earlier. However, Dow Chemicals, which owns Union Carbide since 2001, has opposed the petition.

The Lessons Learnt There are certain lessons that may be learnt from this entire disaster. Governments of developing countries and international agencies must focus on the responsibility of companies for accident prevention, particularly with respect to plant location and design. Industries should not be allowed to be situated close to residential areas. Local bodies and agencies need to be provided with sufficient financial support so that they can arrange for necessary medical facilities and other essential help in times of industrial accidents. The medical services in any city where there are hazardous industries located, should have proper facilities to deal with such emergencies as occurred in Bhopal. Safety legislations must have proper provisions for maintaining safety of in every type of industrial facility.

Provisions regarding hazardous processes were incorporated in the Factories Act, 1948 only after Bhopal disaster. Medical facilities at the time of the accident were not sufficient in Bhopal to deal with the amount of casualty that took place. Development of industries have to be accompanied by proper disaster management plans by authorities and where there is no proper infrastructure or technical expertise to manage such disasters, industries should not be allowed to be established. Lessons learnt from the Bhopal tragedy must be used to prevent any such accident in future.

(Adapted from: Broughton, E. (2005). The Bhopal disaster and its aftermath: a review. Environmental Health, Vol. 4 No. 6. Retrieved from www.ncbi. nlm.nih.gov/pmc/ articles/ PMC1142333/ on 24/9/2014.)

Review Questions

1. Enumerate the causes for the accident at the UCIL Bhopal plant in December, 1984.
2. If you were the safety in-charge of UCIL, what actions would you have taken after the leakage of MIC was reported to you?
3. What lessons can be learnt from the Bhopal Disaster?

Annexure I: Statistics about Health and Safety Measures in Factories in India (2009)

Registered Factories	324,761
Working Factories	270,294
Employment	
Total	13,100,129
Men	11,340,366
Women	1,759,763
Safety Officers	2,642
Welfare Officers	3,096
Factory Medical Officers	6,809
Safety Policy	14,681
Safety Committees	12,995
On-site Emergency Plans	1,920
Total Injuries	33,093
Fatal Injuries	1,509

Adapted from: www.dgfasli.nic.in/fact_stat09.htm accessed on 15/9/2014.

Annexure II

Following are the notifiable diseases mentioned in Schedule II of the Factories Act, 1948, inserted by the Factories (Amendment) Act, 1987.

1. Lead poisoning or its sequelae
2. Lead tetra-ethyl poisoning or its sequelae
3. Phosphorus poisoning or its sequelae
4. Mercury poisoning or its sequelae
5. Manganese poisoning or its sequelae
6. Arsenic poisoning or its sequelae
7. Poisoning by nitrous fumes
8. Carbon bisulphite poisoning
9. Benzene and its derivatives poisoning or its sequelae
10. Chrome ulceration or its sequelae
11. Anthrax
12. Silicosis
13. Poisoning by halogens or its derivatives of hydrocarbons
14. Pathological manifestation due to radium, radioactive substances, or X-rays
15. Primary epitheliomatous cancer of the skin
16. Toxic anemia
17. Toxic jaundice due to poisonous substances
18. Oil acne or dermatitis due to mineral oil or its derivatives in any form
19. Byssinosis
20. Asbestosis

21. Occupational or contact dermatitis caused by direct contact with chemical or paints. It could be primary irritants or allergic sensitisers.
22. Noise induced hearing loss
23. Beryllium poisoning
24. Carbon monoxide
25. Coal miner's pneumoconiosis
26. Phosgene poisoning
27. Occupational cancers
28. Isocyanates poisoning
29. Toxic nephritis

PART B

LABOUR LEGISLATIONS

14

The Factories Act, 1948

An Act to consolidate and amend the law regulating labour in factories

Desired Knowledge Competencies

- To understand the forces contributing to the evolution of the Factories Act, 1948.
- To have knowledge of the extent, commencement anc application of the Factories Act, 1948, and of the various definitions given under the Act.
- To grasp relevant concepts like factory, hazardous process, health and safety and welfare.

INTRODUCTION

The Industrial Revolution had ushered in a sea of changes in the techniques of production. Though the waves of the Revolution hit Indian shores much later, its onset nevertheless saw a remarkable rise in employment in factories. Workers in those times largely lacked any formal education and training and hence fell easy prey to the capitalists by way of low wages and poor working conditions. There was a dire need for a social welfare legislation governing working conditions in factories. It is in such a backdrop that the Factories Act, 1948 was passed.

BACKDROP OF THE FACTORIES ACT, 1948

The Indian Factories Act, 1881, hailed as the first labour law in India, lacked suitable provisions for inspection and enforcement. With the growth of factories there was a rising demand for a stricter piece of legislation. On the basis of the recommendations of the Factories Commission appointed by the Government of India in 1890, the Factories Act, 1891 was passed; it was amended subsequently in the years 1911, 1923, 1926 and 1931 (*Adapted from: www.indiankanoon.org/doc/151775/ accessed on 20/12/2013*). In 1929, the Government appointed the Royal Commission on Labour. The primary objectives of the Commission were to enquire into and report the existing conditions of labour in industrial undertakings and plantations in British India, especially matters pertaining to their health, efficiency and standard of living. The Commission produced its report in 1931. One recommendation in this report was to appoint Labour Officers in order to establish liaison with employers. These officers were expected to ensure that industries followed sound recruitment practices and that employees were provided with good working conditions, canteen facilities, fair price shops, recreation, medical and housing facilities, etc.

The Factories Act, 1934 aimed at regulation of labour employed in the factories in India. It revealed a number of defects which hampered the effective administration of factories. However, the provisions relating to safety, health and welfare of workers were found to be inadequate and failed to reach out to the large masses of workers employed in workplaces beyond the scope of the Act. In view of the growing industrial activities in the country, a complete overhauling of the Act was essentially called for. The Indian Factories Act was amended by the Factories Amendment Acts 1935, 1937, 1940, 1941, 1944, 1945, 1946 and 1947 (*Adapted from: www.indiankanoon.org/doc/151775/ accessed on 15/12/2013*). The Factories Bill having been passed by the Legislature received the assent of the President of India on 23rd September 1948. It came into force on 1st April 1949 as The Factories Act, 1948. This legislation was enacted by the Parliament to consolidate and amend the law regulating labour in factories. The primary objective of the Act is to protect workers employed in factories against industrial and occupational hazards. The Act obliges the occupier of every factory to abide by and observe the several regulatory measures provided by the Act in the interest of health, safety and welfare of the workers working therein (*Adapted from: www.indiankanoon.org/doc/770619/ accessed on 15/12/2013*).

"The Factories Act, as the preamble recites, is an Act to consolidate and amend the law regulating labour in factories. The Act requires that the workers should work in healthy and sanitary conditions and for that purpose it provides that precautions should be taken for the safety of workers and prevention of accidents. Incidental provisions are made for securing information necessary to ensure that the objects are carried out and the State Governments are empowered to appoint inspectors, to call for reports, and to inspect the prescribed registers with a view to maintain effective supervision. The duty of the employer is to secure the health and safety of workers and extends to providing adequate plant, machinery and appliances, supervision over workers, healthy and safe premises, i.e., good working facilities and conditions and extends to giving reasonable instructions. Detailed provisions are therefore made in diverse chapters of the Act imposing obligations upon the owners of the factories to maintain inspecting staff and for maintenance of health, cleanliness, prevention of overcrowding and provision for amenities such as lighting, drinking water, etc. Provisions are also made for safety of workers and their welfare, such as restrictions on working hours and on the employment of young persons and females, and grant of annual leave with wages." *(Adapted from: www.indiankanoon.org/doc/154064/ accessed on 29/12/2013.)*

Since enactment, the Factories Act, 1948 has been amended several times, as follows:

1. The Repealing and Amending Act, 1949.
2. The Adaptation of Laws Order, 1950.
3. The Repealing and Amending Act, 1950.
4. The Part B States (Laws) Act, 1951.
5. The Factories (Amendment) Act, 1954.
6. The Central Labour Laws (Extension to Jammu and Kashmir) Act, 1970.
7. The Factories (Amendment) Act, 1976.
8. The Factories (Amendment) Act, 1987.

ABOUT THE ACT

CHAPTER I: PRELIMINARY

Short Title, Extent and Commencement (Section 1)

1. This Act may be called the Factories Act, 1948.
2. It extends to the whole of India.
3. It shall come into force on the 1st day of April, 1949.

Interpretation (Section 2)

In this Act, unless there is anything repugnant in the subject or context,-

Adult [Section 2(a)] Adult means a person who has completed his eighteenth year of age;

Adolescent [Section 2(b)] Adolescent means a person who has completed his fifteenth year of age but has not completed his eighteenth year;

Calendar Year [Section 2(bb)] Calendar year means the period of 12 months beginning with the 1st day of January in any year;

Child [Section 2(c)] Child means a person who has not completed his fifteenth year of age;

Competent Person [Section 2(ca)] Competent person in relation to any provision of this Act, means a person or an institution recognised as such by the Chief Inspector for the purposes of carrying out tests, examinations and inspections required to be done in a factory under the provisions of this Act having regard to:

(i) the qualifications and experience of the person and facilities available at his disposal; or
(ii) the qualifications and experience of the persons employed in such institution and facilities available therein, with regard to the conduct of such tests, examinations and inspections, and more than 1 person or institution can be recognised as a competent person in relation to a factory;

> **Spotlight**
> Section 2(b) defines an adolescent as a person who has completed 15 years, but not 18 years of age.

Hazardous process [Section 2(cb)] Hazardous process means any process or activity in relation to an industry specified in the First Schedule where, unless special care is taken, raw materials used therein or the intermediate or finished products, bye-products, wastes or effluents thereof would:

(i) cause material impairment to the health of the persons engaged in or connected therewith, or
(ii) result in the pollution of the general environment:

Provided that the State Government may, by notification in the Official Gazette, amend the First Schedule by way of addition, omission or variation of any industry specified in the said Schedule;

Young person [Section 2(d)] Young person means a person who is either a child or an adolescent;

Day [Section 2(e)] Day means a period of 24 hours beginning at midnight;

Week [Section 2(f)] Week means a period of 7 days beginning at midnight on Saturday night or such other night as may be approved in writing for a particular area by the Chief Inspector of Factories;

Power [Section 2(g)] Power means electrical energy or any other form of energy which is mechanically transmitted and is not generated by human or animal agency;

Prime mover [Section 2(h)] Prime mover means any engine, motor or other appliance which generates or otherwise provides power;

Transmission machinery [Section 2(i)] Transmission machinery means any shaft, wheel, drum, pulley, system of pulleys, coupling, clutch, driving belt or other appliance or device by which the motion of a prime mover is transmitted to or received by any machinery or appliance;

Machinery [Section 2(j)] Machinery includes prime movers, transmission machinery and all other appliances whereby power is generated, transformed, transmitted or applied;

Manufacturing process [Section 2(k)] Manufacturing process means any process for:

(i) making, altering, repairing, ornamenting, finishing, packing, oiling, washing, cleaning, breaking up, demolishing, or otherwise treating or adapting any article or substance with a view to its use sale, transport, delivery or disposal, or
(ii) pumping oil, water, sewage or any or other substance; or
(iii) generating, transforming or transmitting power; or
(iv) composing types for printing, printing by letter press, lithography, photogravure or other similar process or book binding; or
(v) constructing, reconstructing, repairing, refitting, finishing or breaking up ships or vessels; or
(vi) preserving or storing any article in cold storage;

In *Qazi Noorul Hasan Hamid Hussain Petrol Pump vs. Deputy Director, E.S.I. Corporation* [(2003) (96) FLR 1090], it is stated that the definition of "manufacturing process" in the Factories Act, 1948 does not depend upon and is not co-related with any end-product being manufactured out of a manufacturing process. It includes even repair, finishing, oiling, or cleaning process with a view to its use, sale, transport, deliver, or disposal. Pumping oil, water or sewage under Section 2(k)(ii) does not mean that it may result into outcome of any processed product for sale. The words "manufacturing process" cannot be restricted to an activity which may result into manufacturing something or production of a commercially different article, and cannot be interpreted in a narrow sense in respect of an Act which is meant for the purposes connected with social welfare.

(Adapted from: www.indiankanoon.org/doc/1830087/ accessed on 19/12/2013.)

In *State vs. Ardeshir Hormusji Bhiwandiwala* [(1956) 58 BOMLR 66], the respondent is the occupier of Wadia Mahal Salt Works at Wadala where salt is made, and an important question is that whether the sale is made as a result of any manufacturing process within the meaning of clause (k)(i) of Section 2. It has been argued by the respondent that no manufacturing process is done on these salt works as there is no intervention of human agency and no work is being done by a human hand or by power machinery.

The Court agrees that the workmen employed on these salt works are separating the sea-water from the sea, without which separation the salt as produced on these works would not be produced. Such separation is also a treatment of the sea-water, given to it with a view to make its product an article of use, sale, transport etc. within the meaning of clause (k)(i). The scraping out of the salt, its sacking for the purpose of grading the salt into crystals of various sizes, its packing into gunny bags for its transport and delivery or disposal are all done by the workmen. In these circumstances, the Court held that a manufacturing process is being carried on upon these salt works.

(Adapted from: www.indiankanoon.org/doc/769962/ accessed on 15/12/2013.)

Worker [Section 2(l)] Worker means a person employed, directly or by or through any agency (including a contractor) with or without the knowledge of the principal employer, whether for remuneration or not, in any manufacturing process, or in cleaning any part of the machinery or premises used for a manufacturing process, or in any other kind of work incidental to, or connected with, the manufacturing process, or the subject of the manufacturing process but does not include any member of the armed forces of the Union;

Spotlight
Worker, as per Section 2(l), is a person employed, directly or by or through any agency (including a contractor) with or without the knowledge of the principal employer, whether for remuneration or not.

In *Rohtas Industries Ltd vs. Ramlakhan Singh and Others* [(1978) AIR 849], the Court held that reading clause (1) of Section 2 of the Act, together with clause (k) and (m) thereof, it is clear that a person to be a worker within the meaning of the Act must be a person employed in the premises or the precincts of the factory. Raw materials used in the manufacturing process for producing paper and its various products will be a "subject of the manufacturing process" within the meaning of clause (1) of Section 2. In this case, the respondent was not working in a manager's capacity. Though he was not employed "in any manufacturing process or in cleaning any part of the machinery or premises used for a manufacturing process", he was engaged in a work which was connected with the "subject of the manufacturing process" and therefore, he was a factory worker within the meaning of clause (1) of Section 2 of the Act.

(Adapted from: www.indiankanoon.org/doc/813955 accessed on 25/12/2013.)

Factory [Section 2(m)] Factory means any premises including the precincts thereof:

(i) whereon 10 or more workers are working, or were working on any day of the preceding 12 months, and in any part of which a manufacturing process is being carried on with the aid of power, or is ordinarily so carried on, or
(ii) whereon 20 or more workers are working, or were working on any day of the preceding 12 months, and in any part of which a manufacturing process is being carried on without the aid of power, or is ordinarily so carried on,

Spotlight
Factory does not include a mine or a mobile unit belonging to the armed forces of the Union, railway running shed or a hotel, restaurant or eating place, as given in Section 2(m).

but it does not include a mine subject to the operation of the Mines Act, 1952, or a mobile unit belonging to the armed forces of the Union, railway running shed or a hotel, restaurant or eating place.

Explanation I For computing the number of workers for the purposes of this clause all the workers in different groups and relays in a day shall be taken into account;

Explanation II For the purposes of this clause, the mere fact that an Electronic Data Processing Unit or a Computer Unit is installed in any premises or part thereof, shall not be construed to make it a factory if no manufacturing process is being carried on in such premises or part thereof;

In *Bharat Electronics Ltd. vs. B.E.L. Head Office Staff Association* [(2000) (85) FLR 364] the Court holds that in order to fall within the meaning of the expression "factory", there should be a premises including precincts thereof and in that premises there must be a "manufacturing process" that is carried on with the help of workmen, with or without the aid of power. The word "premises" in a generic term means an open land or land with buildings. The term "precincts" means the space enclosed by the walls or other boundaries of a particular place or building and more vaguely, the region lying immediately around a place without distinct reference to any enclosure. The concept "manufacturing process" is also defined under the Act and the legislative definition of this expression is the subject matter of judicial interpretation in a number of cases. The Courts have given a wide meaning to this expression. Therefore for an "establishment" to fall within the meaning of the expression "factory", the same should satisfy all the requirements envisaged in Section 2(m) of the Factories Act, 1948.

(Adapted from: www.indiankanoon.org/doc/1120520/ accessed on 28/12/2013.)

The definition of the expression "factory" specifically provides that it shall not include a hotel, restaurant or eating place. In *Lal Bavta Hotel Aur Bakery Mazdoor Union vs. Ritz Private Ltd.* [(2007) IIILLJ 201 Bom], the counsel appearing for the appellant submitted that sub-clause (i) of clause (m) of the Factories Act, 1948 is attracted since more than 10 workers have been working in the precincts of the establishment wherein a manufacturing process within the meaning of Section 2(k) is carried out. However, the Court held that this submission would not advance the case of the appellant for the simple reason that the statutory definition of the expression "factory" provides firstly what the definition means and secondly what it does not include. Once a hotel, restaurant or eating place is deemed by the statute as not to be included within the definition of the expression "factory", such an establishment shall stand excluded from the definition. Under these circumstances, the establishment of Ritz Hotel being a hotel would not fall for classification as a factory under Section 2(m) of the Factories Act, 1948.

(Adapted from: www.indiankanoon.org/doc/1463479/ accessed on 15/12/2013.)

In *State vs. Ardeshir Hormusji Bhiwandiwala* [(1956) 58 BOMLR 66], the respondent is the occupier of Wadia Mahal Salt Works at Wadala where salt is made, and an important question raised is that whether the site where the salt works are situated is "premises" within the meaning of clause (m) of Section 2. The Court observes that just as under the Employees' Compensation Act, 1923, "premises" includes lands and the employer is liable to pay compensation to his employees' dependents, whether the accident to the employee in the course of his employment occurs in the employer's building or on his land, so also it is reasonable to assume that while putting the Factories Act, 1948 on the Statute Book, the Legislature had intended that the occupier of a factory, whether the factory is situated in a building or on an open land, would similarly be liable if the accident occurred to his workman in the course of his employment either in a building or on an open land.

(Adapted from: www.indiankanoon.org/doc/769962/ accessed on 15/12/2013.)

CASE CORNER

In *Gujarat Electricity Board vs. State of Gujarat and Another* [(1984) IILLJ 370 Guj], the Gujarat Electricity Board has challenged the directions contained in the order passed by the second respondent. State of Gujarat is the first respondent. According to the petitioner, it is engaged in the business of generation, supply and distribution of electrical energy. Apart from thermal power stations, the petitioner has also got several sub-stations where high voltage is converted into low voltage with the help of transformers and other devices installed therein. However no generation of electricity is done at the sub-stations. The petitioner contends that the sub-stations, whether big or small, are not factories and therefore the provisions of the Factories Act, 1948 (or the Act) cannot apply to them. Since the office of the Factories Inspector was raising an objection in this connection and was insisting that the said sub-stations should be registered as factories even though no manufacturing activity was done at such-substations, the petitioner had addressed a letter to the first respondent (State) and had requested the Government to instruct the Chief Inspector of Factories not to compel the petitioner to get the sub-stations registered as factories under the said Act. The second respondent opined that the workmen employed in the sub-stations are engaged in "manufacturing process" in a "factory" within the meaning of sections 2(k) and 2(m) of the Act and sub-stations employing 10 or more workers would be covered within the definition of a "factory" under Section 2(m)(i) of the Act and so would require registration under the said Act.

In the petition it was urged on behalf of the respondent that there was no transformation of electric energy received at the two sub-stations, that the sub-stations worked only to reduce energy from a high to a low potential, and that the process should not be regarded as transformation of energy within the meaning of Section 2(k)(iii) of the Act. It was further submitted that all the three processes, i.e., generation, transformation and transmission of electric energy took place only at the power station and not at the sub-station. The Court accepted the submission and hence the petitioner was not required to get all its sub-stations registered as factories.

(Adapted from: www.indiankanoon.org/doc/100506/, accessed on 21/12/2013.)

Occupier [Section 2(n)] Occupier of a factory means the person who has ultimate control over the affairs of the factory.

Provided that:

(i) in the case of a firm or other association of individuals, any 1 of the individual partners or members thereof shall be deemed to be the occupier;

(ii) in the case of a company, any 1 of the directors shall be deemed to be the occupier;

(iii) in the case of a factory owned or controlled by the Central Government or any State Government, or any local authority, the person or persons appointed to manage the affairs of the factory by the Central Government, the State Government or the local authority, as the case may be, shall be deemed to be the occupier:

Provided further that in the case of a ship which is being repaired, or on which maintenance work is being carried out, in a dry dock which is available for hire:

1. the owner of the dock shall be deemed to be the occupier for the purposes of any matter provided for by or under:
   (a) Section 6, Section 7, Section 7A, Section 7B, Section 11 or Section 12;
   (b) Section 17, in so far as it relates to the providing and maintenance of sufficient and suitable lighting in or around the dock;
   (c) Section 18, Section 19, Section 42, Section 46, Section 47 or Section 49, in relation to the workers employed on such repair or maintenance;
2. the owner of the ship or his agent or master or other officer-in-charge of the ship or any person who contracts with such owner, agent or master or other officer-in-charge to carry out the repair or maintenance work shall be deemed to be the occupier for the purposes of any matter provided

for by or under Section 13, Section 14, Section 16 or Section 17 (save as otherwise provided in this proviso) or Chapter IV (except Section 27) or Section 43, Section 44 or Section 45, Chapter VI, Chapter VII, Chapter VIII or Chapter IX or Section 108, Section 109 or Section 110, in relation to:

(a) the workers employed directly by him, or by or through any agency; and
(b) the machinery, plant or premises in use for the purpose of carrying out such repair or maintenance work by such owner, agent, master or other officer-in-charge or person;

In *West India Steel Company Ltd. vs. Azeez* [(1990) IILLJ 133 Ker], a workman who is the president of a trade union, caused obstruction to the work in the factory for about 5 hours, when a particular worker was deputed for work in the millets clearing section. The Court observed that inside the factory a worker is bound to obey the reasonable instructions given to him by the superiors and is bound to carry out the duties duly assigned to him. The mere fact that he is a trade union leader does not confer on him any impunity in that regard. Orders given or instructions issued by managerial superior can be disobeyed or disregarded by the workers only at their peril. A trade union can espouse the cause of the workmen for change in the existing pattern of discharge of duties; workers can even resort to lawful agitations for vindicating their rights. But its officials are not entitled to order a workman to stop his work or otherwise obstruct the work of the establishment.

(Adapted from: www.indiankanoon.org/doc/723265/ accessed on 24/12/2013.)

Prescribed [Section 2(p)] Prescribed means prescribed by rules made by the State Government under this Act;

Shift [Section 2(r)] Where work of the same kind is carried out by 2 or more sets of workers working during different periods of the day, each of such sets is called a "group" or "relay" and each of such periods is called a "shift".

References to Time of Day (Section 3)

In this Act references to time of day are references to Indian Standard Time, being 5 and a half hours ahead of Greenwich Mean Time:

Provided that for any area in which Indian Standard Time is not ordinarily observed the State Government may make rules:

(a) specifying the area,
(b) defining the local mean time ordinarily observed therein, and
(c) permitting such time to be observed in all or any of the factories situated in the area.

Power to Declare Different Departments to be Separate Factories or Two or More Factories to be a Single Factory (Section 4)

The State Government may, on its own or on an application made in this behalf by an occupier, direct, by an order in writing and subject to such conditions as it may deem fit that for all or any of the purposes of this Act different departments or branches of a factory of the occupier specified in the application shall be treated as separate factories or that 2 or more factories of the occupier specified in the application shall be treated as a single factory:

Provided that no order under this section shall be made by the State Government on its own motion unless on opportunity of being heard is given to the occupier.

Power to Exempt during Public Emergency (Section 5)

In any case of public emergency the State Government may, by notification in the Official Gazette, exempt any factory or class or description of factories from all or any of the provisions of this Act, except Section 67, for such period and subject to such conditions as it may think fit:

Provided that no such notification shall be made for a period exceeding 3 months at a time.

Explanation For the purposes of this section "public emergency" means a grave emergency whereby the security of India or of any part of the territory thereof is threatened, whether by war or external aggression or internal disturbance.

Approval, Licensing and Registration of Factories (Section 6)

1. The State Government may make rules:
   (a) requiring, for the purposes of this Act, the submission of plans of any class or description of factories to the Chief Inspector or the State Government;
   (aa) requiring the previous permission in writing of the State Government or the Chief Inspector to be obtained for the site on which the factory is to be situated and for the construction or extension of any factory or class or description of factories;
   (b) requiring for the purpose of considering application for such permission the submission of plans and specifications;
   (c) prescribing the nature of such plans and specifications and by whom they shall be certified;
   (d) requiring the registration and licensing of factories or any class or description of factories, and prescribing the fees payable for such registration and licensing and for the renewal of licences;
   (e) requiring that no licence shall be granted or renewed unless the notice specified in Section 7 has been given.
2. If on an application for permission referred to in clause (aa) of sub-section (1) accompanied by the plans and specifications required by the rules made under clause (b) of that sub-section, sent to the State Government or Chief Inspector by registered post, no order is communicated to the applicant within 3 months from the date on which it is so sent, the permission applied for in the said application shall be deemed to have been granted.
3. Where a State Government or a Chief Inspector refuses to grant permission to the site, construction or extension of a factory or to the registration and licensing of a factory, the applicant may within 30 days of the date of such refusal appeal to the Central Government if the decision appealed from was of the State Government and to the State Government in any other case.

Explanation A factory shall not be deemed to be extended within the meaning of this section by reason only of the replacement of any plant or machinery, or within such limits as may be prescribed, of the addition of any plant or machinery if such replacement or addition does not reduce the minimum clear space required for safe working around the plant or machinery or adversely affect the environmental conditions from the evolution or emission of steam, heat or dust or fumes injurious to health.

Spotlight
Occupier must send written notice to the Chief Inspector at least 15 days before he begins to occupy or use any premises as a factory, as per Section 7(1).

Notice by Occupier (Section 7)

1. The occupier shall, at least 15 days before he begins to occupy or use any premises as a factory, sent to the Chief Inspector a written notice containing:

(a) the name and situation of the factory;
(b) the name and address of the occupier;
(bb) the name and address of the owner of the premises or building (including the precincts thereof) referred to in Section 93;
(c) the address to which communications relating to the factory may be sent;
(d) the nature of the manufacturing process:
   (i) carried on in the factory during the last 12 months in the case of factories in existence on the date of the commencement of this Act, and
   (ii) to be carried on in the factory during the next 12 months in the case of all factories;
(e) the total rated horse power installed or to be installed in the factory, which shall not include the rated horse power of any separate stand-by plant;
(f) the name of the manager of the factory for the purposes of this Act;
(g) the number of workers likely to be employed in the factory;
(h) the average number of workers per day employed during the last 12 months in the case of factory in existence on the date of the commencement of this Act.
(i) such other particulars as may be prescribed.

2. In respect of all establishments which come within the scope of the Act for the first time, the occupier shall send a written notice to the Chief Inspector containing the particulars specified in sub-section (1) within 30 days from the date of the commencement of this Act.
3. Before a factory engaged in a manufacturing process which is ordinarily carried on for less than 180 working days in the year resumes working, the occupier shall send a written notice to the Chief Inspector containing the particulars specified in sub-section (1) at least 30 days before the date of the commencement of work.
4. Whenever a new manager is appointed, the occupier shall send to the Inspector a written notice and to the Chief Inspector a copy thereof within 7 days from the date on which such person takes over charges.
5. During any period for which no person has been designated as manager of a factory or during which the person designated does not manage the factory, any person found acting as manager, or if no such person is found, the occupier himself, shall be deemed to be the manager of the factory for the purposes of this Act.

General Duties of the Occupier (Section 7A)

1. Every occupier shall ensure, so far as is reasonably practicable, the health, safety and welfare of all workers while they are at work in the factory.
2. Without prejudice to the generality of the provisions of sub-section (1), the matters to which such duty extends, shall include:
   (a) the provision and maintenance of plant and systems of work in the factory that are safe and without risks to health;
   (b) the arrangements in the factory for ensuring safety and absence of risks to health in connection with the use, handling, storage and transport of articles and substances;
   (c) the provision of such information, instruction, training and supervision as are necessary to ensure the health and safety of all workers at work;
   (d) the maintenance of all places of work in the factory in a condition that is safe without risks to health and the provision and maintenance of such means of access to, and egress from, such places as are safe and without such risks;

Spotlight

Section 7A(1) mandates that every occupier shall ensure the health, safety and welfare of all workers while they are at work in the factory.

(e) the provision, maintenance or monitoring of such working environment in the factory for the workers that is safe, without risks to health and adequate as regards facilities and arrangements for their welfare at work.

3. Except in such cases as may be prescribed, every occupier shall prepare, and, as often as may be appropriate, revise, a written statement of his general policy with respect to the health and safety of the workers at work and the organisation and arrangements for the time being in force for carrying out that policy, and to bring the statement and any revision thereof to the notice of all the workers in such manner as may be prescribed.

General Duties of Manufacturers, etc., as Regards Articles and Substances for Use in Factories (Section 7B)

1. Every person who designs, manufactures, imports or supplies any article for use in any factory shall:
   (a) ensure, so far as is reasonably practicable, that the article is so designed and constructed as to be safe and without risks to the health of the workers when properly used;
   (b) carry out or arrange for the carrying out of such tests and examination as may be considered necessary for the effective implementation of the provisions of clause (a);
   (c) take such steps as may be necessary to ensure that adequate information will be available:
      (i) in connection with the use of the article in any factory;
      (ii) about the use for which it is designed and tested; and
      (iii) about any conditions necessary to ensure that the article, when put to such use, will be safe, and without risks to the health of the workers:

   Provided that where an article is designed or manufactured outside India, it shall be obligatory on the part of the importer to see:
   (a) that the article conforms to the same standards if such article is manufactured in India, or
   (b) if the standards adopted in the country outside for the manufacture of such article is above the standards adopted in India, that the article conforms to such standards.
2. Every person, who undertakes to design or manufacture any article for use in any factory, may carry out or arrange for the carrying out of necessary research with a view to the discovery and, so far as is reasonably practicable, the elimination or minimisation of any risks to the health or safety of the workers to which the design or article may give rise.
3. Nothing contained in sub-sections (1) and (2) shall be construed to require a person to repeat the testing, examination or research which has been carried out otherwise than by him or at his instance in so far as it is reasonable for him to rely on the results thereof for the purposes of the said sub-sections.
4. Any duty imposed on any person by sub-sections (1) and (2) shall extend only to things done in the course of business carried on by him and to matters within his control.
5. Where a person designs, manufactures, imports or supplies an article on the basis of a written undertaking by the user of such article to take the steps specified in such undertaking to ensure, so far as is reasonably practicable, that the article will be safe and without risks to the health of the workers when properly used, the undertaking shall have the effect of relieving the person designing, manufacturing, importing or supplying the article from the duty imposed by clause (a) of sub-section (1) to such extent as is reasonable having regard to the term of the undertaking.
6. For the purposes of this section, an article is not to be regarded as properly used if it is used without regard to any information or advice relating to its use which has been made available by the person who has designed, manufactured, imported or supplied the article.

Explanation For the purposes of this section, "article" shall include plant and machinery.

CHAPTER II: INSPECTING STAFF

Inspectors (Section 8)

1. The State Government may, by notification in the Official Gazette, appoint such persons as possess the prescribed qualification to be Inspectors for the purposes of this Act and may assign to them such local limits as it may think fit.
2. The State Government may, by notification in the Official Gazette, appoint any person to be a Chief Inspector who shall, in addition to the powers conferred on a Chief Inspector under this Act, exercise the powers of an Inspector throughout the State.

2A. The State Government may, by notification in the Official Gazette, appoint as many Additional Chief Inspectors, Joint Chief Inspectors and Deputy Chief Inspectors and as many other officers as it thinks fit to assist the Chief Inspector and to exercise such of the powers of the Chief Inspector as may be specified in such notification.

2B. Every additional Chief Inspector, Joint Chief Inspector, Deputy Chief Inspector and every other officer appointed under sub-section (2A) shall, in addition to the powers of a Chief Inspector specified in the notification by which he is appointed, exercise the powers of an Inspector throughout the State.

3. No person shall be appointed under sub-section (1), sub-section (2), sub-section (2A) or sub-section (5) or, having been so appointed, shall continue to hold office, who is or becomes directly or indirectly interested in a factory or in any process or business carried on therein or in any patent or machinery connected therewith.

Spotlight

As per Section 8(4), every District Magistrate shall be an Inspector for his district.

4. Every District Magistrate shall be an Inspector for his district.
5. The State Government may also, by notification as aforesaid, appoint such public officers as it thinks fit to be additional Inspectors for all or any of the purposes of this Act, within such local limits as it may assign to them respectively.
6. In any area where there are more Inspectors than 1 the State Government may, by notification as aforesaid, declare the powers which such Inspectors shall respectively exercise and the Inspector to whom the prescribed notices are to be sent.
7. Every Chief Inspector, Additional Chief Inspector, Joint Chief Inspector, Deputy Chief Inspector, Inspector and every other officer appointed under this section shall be deemed to be a public servant within the meaning of the Indian Penal Code, and shall be officially subordinate to such authority as the State Government may specify in this behalf.

Powers of Inspectors (Section 9)

Subject to any rules made in this behalf, an Inspector may, within the local limits for which he is appointed,

(a) enter, with such assistants, being persons in the service of the Government, or any local or other public authority, or with an expert as he thinks fit, any place which is used, or which he has reason to believe is used, as a factory;

(b) make examination of the premises, plant, machinery, article or substance;

(c) inquire into any accident or dangerous occurrence, whether resulting in bodily injury, disability or not, and take on the spot or otherwise statements of any person which he may consider necessary for such inquiry;
(d) require the production of any prescribed register or any other document relating to the factory;
(e) seize, or take copies of, any register, record or other document or any portion thereof, as he may consider necessary in respect of any offence under this Act, which he has reason to believe, has been committed;
(f) direct the occupier that any premises or any part thereof, or anything lying therein, shall be left disturbed (whether generally or in particular respects) for so long as is necessary for the purpose of any examination under clause (b);
(g) take measurements and photographs and make such recordings as he considers necessary for the purpose of any examination under clause (b), taking with him any necessary instrument or equipment;
(h) in case of any article or substance found in any premises, being an article or substance which appears to him as having caused, or is likely to cause danger to the health or safety of the workers, direct it to the dismantled or subject it to any process or test (but not so as to damage or destroy it unless the same is, in the circumstances necessary, for carrying out the purposes of this Act), and take possession of any such article or substance or a part thereof, and detain it for so long as is necessary for such examination;
(i) exercise such other powers as may be prescribed.

Provided that no person shall be compelled under this section to answer any question or give any evidence tending to incriminate himself.

Certifying Surgeons (Section 10)

Spotlight

Section 10 empowers the State Government to appoint qualified medical practitioners to be certifying surgeons.

1. The State Government may appoint qualified medical practitioners to be certifying surgeons for the purposes of this Act within such local limits or for such factory or class or description of factories as it may assign to them respectively.
2. A certifying surgeon may, with the approval of the State Government, authorise any qualified medical practitioner to exercise any of his powers under this Act for such period as the certifying surgeon may specify and subject to such conditions as the State Government may think fit to impose, and references in this Act to a certifying surgeon shall be deemed to include references to any qualified medical practitioner when so authorised.
3. No person shall be appointed to be, or authorised to exercise the powers of, a certifying surgeon, or having been so appointed or authorised, continue to exercise such powers, who is or becomes the occupier of a factory or is or becomes directly or indirectly interested therein or in any process or business carried on therein or in any process or machinery connected therewith or is otherwise in the employ of the factory:

   Provided that the State Government may, by order in writing and subject to such conditions as may be specified in the order, exempt any person or class of persons from the provisions of this sub-section in respect of any factory or class or description of factories.
4. The certifying surgeon shall carry out such duties as may be prescribed in connection with-
   (a) the examination and certification of young persons under this Act;
   (b) the examination of persons engaged in factories in such dangerous occupations or processes as may be prescribed;

(c) the exercising of such medical supervision as may be prescribed for any factory or class or description of factories where:
   (i) cases of illness have occurred which it is reasonable to believe are due to the nature of the manufacturing process carried on, or other conditions of work prevailing, therein;
   (ii) by reason of any change in the manufacturing process carried on or in the substances used therein or by reason of the adoption of any new manufacturing process or of any new substance for use in a manufacturing process, there is a likelihood of injury to the health of workers employed in that manufacturing process;
   (iii) young persons are, or are about to be, employed in any work which is likely to cause injury to their health.

Explanation In this section "qualified medical practitioner" means a person holding a qualification granted by an authority specified in the Schedule to the Indian Medical Degrees Act, 1916, or in the Schedules to the Indian Medical Council Act, 1933.

CHAPTER III: HEALTH

Cleanliness (Section 11)

1. Every factory shall be kept clean and free from effluvia arising from any drain, privy or other nuisance, and in particular:
   (a) accumulation of dirt and refuse shall be removed daily by sweeping or by any other effective method from the floors and benches of workrooms and from staircases and passages, and disposed of in a suitable manner;
   (b) the floor of every workroom shall be cleaned at least once in every week by washing, using disinfectant, where necessary, or by some other effective method;
   (c) where a floor is liable to become wet in the course of any manufacturing process to such extent as is capable of being drained, effective means of drainage shall be provided and maintained;
   (d) all inside walls and partitions, all ceilings or tops of rooms and all walls, sides and tops of passages and staircases shall:
      (i) where they are painted otherwise than with washable water-paint or varnished, be repainted or re-varnished at least once in every period of 5 years;
      (ia) where they are painted with washable water-paint, be repainted with at least 1 coat of such paint at least once in every period of 3 years and washed at least once in every period of 6 months;
      (ii) where they are painted or varnished or where they have smooth impervious surfaces, be cleaned at least once in every period of 14 months by such method as may be prescribed;
      (iii) in any other case, be kept whitewashed or colourwashed, and the whitewashing or colourwashing shall be carried out at least once in every period of 14 months;
   (dd) all doors and window frames and other wooden or metallic framework and shutters shall be kept painted or varnished and the painting or varnishing shall be carried out at least once in every period of 5 years;

> **Spotlight**
> The floor of every workroom shall be cleaned at least once in every week by washing, using disinfectant, where necessary, or by some other effective method, as given in Section 11(1)(b).

(e) the dates on which the processes required by clause (d) are carried out shall be entered in the prescribed register.

2. If, in view of the nature of the operations carried on in a factory or class or description of factories or any part of a factory or class or description of factories, it is not possible for the occupier to comply with all or any of the provisions of sub-section (1), the State Government may by order exempt such factory or class or description of factories or part from any of the provisions of that sub-section and specify alternative methods for keeping the factory in a clean state.

Disposal of Wastes and Effluents (Section 12)

1. Effective arrangements shall be made in every factory for the treatment of wastes and effluents due to the manufacturing process carried on therein, so as to render them innocuous, and for their disposal.
2. The State Government may make rules prescribing the arrangements to be made under sub-section (1) or requiring that the arrangements made in accordance with sub-section (1) shall be approved by such authority as may be prescribed.

Ventilation and Temperature (Section 13)

1. Effective and suitable provision shall be made in every factory for securing and maintaining in every workroom:
   (a) adequate ventilation by the circulation of fresh air, and
   (b) such a temperature as will secure to workers therein reasonable conditions of comfort and prevent injury to health;

   and in particular:
   (i) walls and roofs shall be of such material and so designed that such temperature shall not be exceeded but kept as low as practicable;
   (ii) where the nature of the work carried on in the factory involves, or is likely to involve, the production of excessively high temperatures, such adequate measures as are practicable shall be taken to protect the workers therefrom, by separating the process which produces such temperatures from the workroom, by insulating the hot parts or by other effective means.
2. The State Government may prescribe a standard of adequate ventilation and reasonable temperature for any factory or class or description of factories or parts thereof and direct that proper measuring instruments, at such places and in such position as may be specified, shall be provided and such records, as may be prescribed, shall be maintained.
3. If it appears to the Chief Inspector that excessively high temperatures in any factory can be reduced by the adoption of suitable measures, he may, without prejudice to the rules made under sub-section (2), serve on the occupier, an order in writing specifying the measures which, in his opinion, should be adopted, and requiring them to be carried out before a specified date.

> **Spotlight**
> Effective and suitable provision shall be made in every factory for securing and maintaining adequate ventilation in every workroom by the circulation of fresh air, as provided in Section 13(1)(a).

Dust and Fume (Section 14)

1. In every factory in which, by reason of the manufacturing process carried on, there is given off any dust or fume or other impurity of such a nature and to such an extent as is likely to be injurious

> **Spotlight**
> As per Section 14(1), an exhaust appliance shall be applied as near as possible to the point of origin of the dust, fume or other impurity, and such point shall be enclosed so far as possible.

or offensive to the workers employed therein, or any dust in substantial quantities, effective measures shall be taken to prevent its inhalation and accumulation in any workroom, and if any exhaust appliance is necessary for this purpose, it shall be applied as near as possible to the point of origin of the dust, fume or other impurity, and such point shall be enclosed so far as possible.

2. In any factory no stationary internal combustion engine shall be operated unless the exhaust is conducted into the open air, and no other internal combustion engine shall be operated in any room unless effective measures have been taken to prevent such accumulation of fumes therefrom as are likely to be injurious to workers employed in the room.

Artificial Humidification (Section 15)

1. In respect of all factories in which the humidity of the air is artificially increased, the State Government may make rules,
   (a) prescribing standards of humidification;
   (b) regulating the methods used for artificially increasing the humidity of the air;
   (c) directing prescribed tests for determining the humidity of the air to be correctly carried out and recorded;
   (d) prescribing methods to be adopted for securing adequate ventilation and cooling of the air in the workrooms.
2. In any factory in which the humidity of the air is artificially increased, the water used for the purpose shall be taken from a public supply, or other source of drinking water, or shall be effectively purified before it is so used.
3. If it appears to an Inspector that the water used in a factory for increasing humidity which is required to be effectively purified under sub-section (2) is not effectively purified he may serve on the manager of the factory an order in writing, specifying the measures which in his opinion should be adopted, and requiring them to be carried out before specified date.

Overcrowding (Section 16)

1. No room in any factory shall be overcrowded to an extent injurious to the health of the workers employed therein.
2. Without prejudice to the generality of sub-section (1), there shall be in every workroom of factory in existence on the date of the commencement of this Act at least 9.9 cubic metres and of a factory built after the commencement of this Act at least 14.2 cubic meters of space for every worker employed therein, and for the purposes of this sub-section no account shall be taken of any space which is more than 4.2 meters above the level of the floor of the room.
3. If the Chief Inspector by order in writing so requires, there shall be posted in each workroom of a factory a notice specifying the maximum number of workers who may, in compliance with the provisions of this section, be employed in the room.
4. The Chief Inspector may by order in writing exempt, subject to such conditions, if any, as he may think fit to impose, any workroom from the provisions of this section, if he is satisfied that compliance therewith in respect of the rooms is unnecessary in the interest of the health of the workers employed therein.

Spotlight

Section 16(1) provides that no room in any factory shall be over crowded to the extent of injurious to the health of the workers.

Lighting (Section 17)

1. In every part of a factory where workers are working or passing there shall be provided and maintained sufficient and suitable lighting, natural or artificial, or both.
2. In every factory all glazed windows and skylights used for the lighting of the workrooms shall be kept clean on both the inner and outer surfaces and, so far as compliance with the provisions of any rules made under sub-section (3) of Section 13 will allow, free from obstruction.
3. In every factory effective provision shall, so far as is practicable, be made for the prevention of:
   (a) glare, either directly from a source of light or by reflection from a smooth or polished surface;
   (b) the formation of shadows to such an extent as to cause eye-strain or the risk of accident to any worker.
4. The State Government may prescribe standards of sufficient and suitable lighting for factories or for any class of description of factories or for any manufacturing process.

Drinking Water (Section 18)

1. In every factory effective arrangements shall be made to provide and maintain at suitable points conveniently situated for all workers employed therein a sufficient supply of wholesome drinking water.
2. All such points shall be legibly marked "drinking water" in a language understood by a majority of the workers employed in the factory, and no such point shall be situated within 6 meters of any washing place, urinal, latrine, spittoon, open drain carrying sullage or effluent or any other source of contamination unless a shorter distance is approved in writing by the Chief Inspector.
3. In every factory wherein more than 250 workers are ordinarily employed, provision shall be made for cooling drinking water during hot weather by effective means and for distribution thereof.
4. In respect of all factories or any class or description of factories the State Government may make rules for securing compliance with the provisions of sub-sections (1), (2) and (3) and for the examination by prescribed authorities of the supply and distribution of drinking water in factories.

Spotlight

No point of drinking water shall be situated within 6 meters of any washing place, urinal, latrine, spittoon, open drain carrying sullage or effluent or any other source of contamination, as given in Section 18(2).

Latrines and Urinals (Section 19)

1. In every factory:
   (a) sufficient latrine and urinal accommodation of prescribed types shall be provided conveniently situated and accessible to workers at all times while they at the factory;
   (b) separate enclosed accommodation shall be provided for male and female workers;
   (c) such accommodation shall be adequately lighted and ventilated, and no latrine or urinal shall, unless specially exempted in writing by the Chief Inspector, communicate with any workroom except through an intervening open space or ventilated passage;
   (d) all such accommodation shall be maintained in a clean and sanitary condition at all times;
   (e) sweepers shall be employed whose primary duty it would be to keep clean latrines, urinals and washing places.

2. In every factory wherein more than 250 workers are ordinarily employed:
   (a) all latrine and urinal accommodation shall be of prescribed sanitary types;
   (b) the floors and internal walls, up to a height of 90 centimetres of the latrines and urinals and the sanitary blocks shall be laid in glazed tiles or otherwise finished to provided a smooth polished impervious surface;
   (c) without prejudice to the provisions of clauses (d) and (e) of sub-section (1), the floors, portions of the walls and blocks so laid or finished and the sanitary pans of latrines and urinals shall be thoroughly washed and cleaned at least once in every 7 days with suitable detergents or disinfectants or with both.

Spotlight

As per Section 19(2)(a), in every factory wherein more than 250 workers are ordinarily employed all latrine and urinal accommodation shall be of prescribed sanitary types.

3. The State Government may prescribe the number of latrines and urinals to be provided in any factory in proportion to the numbers of male and female workers ordinarily employed therein, and provide for such further matters in respect of sanitation in factories, including the obligation of workers in this regard, as it considers necessary in the interest of the health of the workers employed therein.

Spittoons (Section 20)

1. In every factory there shall be provided a sufficient number of spittoons in convenient places and they shall be maintained in a clean and hygienic condition.
2. The State Government may make rules prescribing the type and the number of spittoons to be provided and their location in any factory and provide for such further matters relating to their maintenance in a clean and hygienic condition.
3. No person shall spit within the premises of a factory except in the spittoons provided for the purpose and a notice containing this provision and the penalty for its violation shall be prominently displayed at suitable places in the premises.
4. Whoever spits in contravention of sub-section (3) shall be punishable with fine not exceeding ₹5.

CHAPTER IV: SAFETY

Fencing of Machinery (Section 21)

1. In every factory the following, namely:
   (i) every moving part of a prime mover and every flywheel connected to a prime mover, whether the prime mover or flywheel is in the engine house or not;
   (ii) the headrace and tailrace of every water-wheel and water turbine;
   (iii) any part of a stock-bar which projects beyond the head stock of a lathe; and
   (iv) unless they are in such position or of such construction as to be safe to every person employed in the factory as they would be if they were securely fenced, the following, namely,
      (a) every part of an electric generator, a motor or rotary convertor;
      (b) every part of transmission machinery; and
      (c) every dangerous part of any other machinery,

   shall be securely fenced by safeguards of substantial construction which shall be constantly maintained and kept in position while the parts of machinery they are fencing are in motion or in use:

Provided that for the purpose of determining whether any part of machinery is in such position or is of such construction as to be safe as aforesaid, account shall not be taken of any occasion when:

(i) it is necessary to make an examination of any part of the machinery aforesaid while it is in motion, or as a result of such examination, to carry out lubrication, or other adjusting operation while the machinery is in motion, being an examination or operation which it is necessary to be carried out while that part of the machinery is in motion, or

(ii) in the case of any part of a transmission machinery used in such process as may be prescribed (being a process of a continuous nature the carrying on of which shall be, or is likely to be, substantially interfered with by the stoppage of that part of the machinery), it is necessary to make an examination of such part of the machinery while it is in motion or, as a result of such examination, to carry out any mounting or shipping of belts or lubrication or other adjusting operation while the machinery is in motion,

and such examination or operation is made or carried out in accordance with the provisions of sub-section (1) of Section 22.

2. The State Government may by rules prescribe such further precautions as it may consider necessary in respect of any particular machinery or part thereof, or exempt, subject to such condition as may be prescribed, for securing the safety of the workers, any particular machinery or part thereof from the provisions of this section.

CASE CORNER

In *J.B. Mangharam and Co. and Another vs. E.S.I. Corporation* [(1970) ILLJ 460 MP], the first appellant is a well-known manufacturer of confectionary and the second appellant is the manager of the company. An employee of the said firm met with an accident while working on the power press machine used for cutting tin by pressing the die, and his four fingers were partly cut when the die fell on his hand. This employee was insured and since the injury was an employment injury having arisen in the course of his employment, the Employees' State Insurance Corporation (or, the Corporation) paid a sum as partial disablement benefit. The Corporation claimed reimbursement from the firm on the ground that at the time of the accident the machine was not provided with a guard at the die and as such the firm had contravened the provisions of Section 21 of the Factories Act, 1948.

The simple issue here is whether a guard was necessary or not. The Court observed that in the ordinary process of its working, the hand of a workman can very easily go under the die through negligence or otherwise in the absence of the guard. The object of the guard is to prevent the hand of the workman coming under the die in an unwary moment, thereby ensuring his safety. The tin has to be manipulated by hand close to the die while operating the machine and the hand is bound to be injured if it comes under the die in the course of its operation. The die is, therefore, clearly a dangerous part of the machinery requiring a guard. Since the firm had failed to provide a guard at the die, it had contravened Section 21 of the Factories Act, 1948.

(Adapted from: www.indiankanoon.org/doc/49245/ accessed on 24/12/2013.)

Work on or near Machinery in Motion (Section 22)

1. Where in any factory it becomes necessary to examine any part of machinery referred to in Section 21, while the machinery is in motion, or, as a result of such examination, to carry out:
   (a) in a case referred to in clause (i) of the proviso to sub-section (1) of Section 21, lubrication or other adjusting operation; or
   (b) in a case referred to in clause (ii) of the proviso aforesaid, any mounting or shipping of belts or lubrication or other adjusting operation,

   while the machinery is in motion, such examination or operation shall be made or carried out only by a specially trained adult male worker wearing tight fitting clothing (which shall be supplied by the occupier) whose name has been recorded in the register prescribed in this behalf and who has been furnished with a certificate of his appointment, and while he is so engaged:
   (a) such worker shall not handle a belt at a moving pulley unless:
      (i) the belt is not more than 15 centimeters in width;
      (ii) the pulley is normally for the purpose of drive and not merely a fly-wheel or balance wheel (in which case a belt is not permissible);
      (iii) the belt joint is either laced or flush with the belt;
      (iv) the belt, including the joint and the pulley rim, are in good repair;
      (v) there is reasonable clearance between the pulley and any fixed plant or structure;
      (vi) secure foothold and, where necessary, secure handhold, are provided for the operator; and
      (vii) any ladder in use for carrying out any examination or operation aforesaid is securely fixed or lashed or is firmly held by a second person.
   (b) without prejudice to any other provision of this Act relating to the fencing of machinery, every set screw, bolt and key on any revolving shaft, spindle, wheel or pinion, and all spur, worm and other toothed or friction gearing in motion with which such worker would otherwise be liable to come into contact, shall be securely fenced to prevent such contact.
2. No woman or young person shall be allowed to clean, lubricate or adjust any part of a prime mover or of any transmission machinery while the prime mover or transmission machinery is in motion, or to clean, lubricate or adjust any part of any machine if the cleaning, lubrication or adjustment thereof would expose the woman or young person to risk of injury from any moving part either of that machine or of any adjacent machinery.
3. The State Government may, by notification in the Official Gazette, prohibit, in any specified factory or class or description of factories, the cleaning, lubricating or adjusting by any person of specified parts of machinery when those parts are in motion.

Spotlight
No woman or young person shall be allowed to clean, lubricate or adjust any part of a prime mover or of any transmission machinery while it is in motion, as given in Section 22(2).

Employment of Young Persons on Dangerous Machines (Section 23)

1. No young person shall be required or allowed to work at any machine to which this section applies, unless he has been fully instructed as to the dangers arising in connection with the machine and the precautions to be observed and:
   (a) has received sufficient training in work at the machine, or
   (b) is under adequate supervision by a person who has a thorough knowledge and experience of the machine.

2. Sub-section (1) shall apply to such machines as may be prescribed by the State Government, being machines which in its opinion are of such a dangerous character that young persons ought not to work at them unless the foregoing requirements are complied with.

Striking Gear and Devices for Cutting off Power (Section 24)

1. In every factory:
   (a) suitable striking gear or other efficient mechanical appliance shall be provided and maintained and used to move driving belts to and from fast and loose pulleys which form part of the transmission machinery, and such gear or appliances shall be so constructed, placed and maintained as to prevent the belt from creeping back on to the fast pulley;
   (b) driving belts when not in use shall not be allowed to rest or ride upon shafting in motion.

Spotlight

Section 24(1) forbids driving belts not in use from resting or riding upon shafting in motion.

2. In every factory suitable devices for cutting off power in emergencies from running machinery shall be provided and maintained in every workroom:

   Provided that in respect of factories in operation before the commencement of this Act, the provisions of this sub-section shall apply only to workrooms in which electricity is used as power.
3. When a device, which can inadvertently shift from "off" to "on" position, is provided in a factory to cut off power, arrangements shall be provided for locking the device in safe position to prevent accidental starting of the transmission machinery or other machines to which the device is fitted.

CASE CO

In *Jayathilal Dhanji and Co. Oil Mills vs. Employees' State Insurance Corporation* [(1961) IILLJ 542 AP] the appellant, Jayathilal Dhanji and Company Oil Mills, runs an oil mill in Hyderabad. In their employment was an unskilled worker, whose duty was to feed the oil mill by pouring groundnut seeds into the crushing machine that worked apparently by a belt, moved by a power driven shaft. The belt was mounted on to a pulley fixed to it as usual. On the date of the accident the crushing machine was running without being fed by any seeds, the stock being exhausted. In absence of the mechanic and fitter, the employee concerned, on finding that the crushing machine was running unnecessarily with the possible consequence of serious damage to it, went down from the place where he was working, to shift the belt off the moving pulley connected to the crushing machine. In the absence of the necessary equipment to safely facilitate such disconnection, the said employee tried to kick the belt of the moving pulley so that it may slip and get loose and the crushing machine may thus be stopped. In doing so, by accident, his leg got caught between the pulley and the belt and he was pulled up to a height of about 6 feet from where he fell down and died instantaneously.

This is a case of a clear non-compliance with the statutory requirements contained in Section 24 of the Factories Act, 1948. Instead of complying with the section and providing the equipment indicated therein, this factory would effect the movement of the belt with some rod, or other crude contrivance which was obviously unsafe. Hence there is no doubt that the appellant is guilty of negligence in not complying with the safety rules laid down in Section 24 of the Act applicable to the factory in question.

(Adapted from: www.indiankanoon.org/doc/1929472/ accessed on 23/12/2013.)

Self-acting Machines (Section 25)

No traversing part of a self-acting machine in any factory and no material carried thereon shall, if the space over which it runs is a space over which any person is liable to pass, whether in the course of his employment or otherwise, be allowed to run on its outward or inward traverse within a distance of 45 centimeters from any fixed structure which is not part of the machine:

Provided that the Chief Inspector may permit the continued use of a machine installed before the commencement of this Act which does not comply with the requirements of this section on such conditions for ensuring safety as he may think fit to impose.

Casing of New Machinery (Section 26)

1. In all machinery driven by power and installed in any factory after the commencement of this Act:
   (a) every set screw, bolt or key on any revolving shaft, spindle, wheel or pinion shall be so sunk, encased or otherwise effectively guarded as to prevent danger;
   (b) all spur, worm and other toothed or friction gearing which does not require frequent adjustment while in motion shall be completely encased, unless it is so situated as to be as safe as it would be if it were completely encased.
2. Whoever sells or lets on hire or, as agent of a seller or hirer, causes or procures to be sold or let on hire, for use in a factory any machinery driven by power which does not comply with the provisions of sub-section (1) or any rules made under sub-section (3), shall be punishable with imprisonment for a term which may extend to 3 months or with fine which may extend to ₹500 or with both.
3. The State Government may make rules specifying further safeguards to be provided in respect of any other dangerous part of any particular machine or class or description of machines.

Prohibition of Employment of Women and Children near Cotton-openers (Section 27)

No woman or child shall be employed in any part of a factory for pressing cotton in which a cotton-opener is at work:

Provided that if the feed-end of a cotton-opener is in a room separated from the delivery end by a partition extending to the roof or to such height as the Inspector may in any particular case specify in writing, women and children may be employed on the side of the partition where the feed-end is situated.

> **Spotlight**
> No woman or young person shall be employed in any part of a factory for pressing cotton in which a cotton-opener is at work, as given in Section 27.

Hoists and Lifts (Section 28)

1. In every factory:
   (a) every hoist and lift shall be:
      (i) of good mechanical construction, sound material and adequate strength;
      (ii) properly maintained, and shall be thoroughly examined by a competent person at least once in every period of 6 months, and a register shall be kept containing the prescribed particulars of every such examination;
   (b) every hoist-way and lift-way shall be sufficiently protected by an enclosure fitted with gates, and the hoist or lift and every such enclosure shall be so constructed as to prevent any person

or thing from being trapped between any part of the hoist or lift and any fixed structure or moving part;

(c) the maximum safe working load shall be plainly marked on every hoist or lift, and no load greater than such load shall be carried thereon;

Spotlight

Section 28(1)(c) mandates that the maximum safe working load shall be plainly marked on every hoist or lift.

(d) the cage of every hoist or lift used for carrying persons shall be fitted with a gate on each side from which access is afforded to a landing;

(e) every gate referred to in clause (b) or clause (d) shall be fitted with interlocking or other efficient device to secure that the gate cannot be opened except when the cage is at the landing and that the cage cannot be moved unless the gate is closed.

2. The following additional requirements shall apply to hoists and lifts used for carrying persons and installed or reconstructed in a factory after the commencement of this Act, namely:
   (a) where the cage is supported by rope or chain, there shall be at least 2 ropes or chains separately connected with the cage and balance weight, and each rope or chain with its attachments shall be capable of carrying the whole weight of the cage together with its maximum load;
   (b) efficient devices shall be provided and maintained capable of supporting the cage together with its maximum load in the event of breakage of the ropes, chains or attachments;
   (c) an efficient automatic device shall be provided and maintained to prevent the cage from over-running.
3. The Chief Inspector may permit the continued use of a hoist or lift installed in a factory before the commencement of this Act which does not fully comply with the provisions of sub-section (1) upon such conditions for ensuring safety as he may think fit to impose.
4. The State Government may, if in respect of any class or description of hoist or lift, it is of opinion that it would be unreasonable to enforce any requirement of sub-sections (1) and (2), by order direct that such requirement shall not apply to such class or description of hoist or lift.

Explanation For the purposes of this section, no lifting machine or appliance shall be deemed to be a hoist or lift unless it has a platform or cage, the direction or movement of which is restricted by a guide or guides.

Lifting Machines, Chains, Ropes and Lifting Tackles (Section 29)

1. In any factory the following provisions shall be complied with in respect of every lifting machine (other than a hoist and lift) and every chain, rope and lifting tackle for the purpose of raising or lowering persons, goods or materials:
   (a) all parts, including the working gear, whether fixed or movable, of every lifting machine and every chain, rope or lifting tackle shall be:
      (i) of good construction, sound material and adequate strength and free from defects;
      (ii) properly maintained; and
      (iii) thoroughly examined by a competent person at least once in every period of 12 months, or at such intervals as the Chief Inspector may specify in writing; and a register shall be kept containing the prescribed particulars of every such examination;
   (b) no lifting machine and no chain, rope or lifting tackle shall, except for the purpose of test, be loaded beyond the safe working load which shall be plainly marked thereon together with an identification mark and duly entered in the prescribed register; and where this is not practicable, a table showing the safe working loads of every kind and size of lifting machine or chain, rope or lifting tackle in use shall be displayed in prominent positions on the premises;

(c) while any person is employed or working on or near the wheel track of a travelling crane in any place where he would be liable to be struck by the crane, effective measures shall be taken to ensure that the crane does not approach within 6 metres of that place.

2. The State Government may make rules in respect of any lifting machine or any chain, rope or lifting tackle used in factories:
   (a) prescribing further requirements to be complied with in addition to those set out in this section;
   (b) providing for exemption from compliance with all or any of the requirements of this section, where in its opinion, such compliance is unnecessary or impracticable.
3. For the purposes of this section a lifting machine or a chain, rope or lifting tackle shall be deemed to have been thoroughly examined if a visual examination supplemented, if necessary, by other means and by the dismantling of parts of the gear, has been carried out as carefully as the conditions permit in order to arrive at a reliable conclusion as to the safety of the parts examined.

Explanation In this section:

(a) "lifting machine" means a crane, crab, winch, teagle, pulley block, gin wheel, transporter or runway;

(b) "lifting tackle" means any chain sling, rope sling, hook, shackle, swivel, coupling, socket, clamp, tray or similar appliance, whether fixed or movable, used in connection with the raising or lowering of persons, or loads by use of lifting machines.

Revolving Machinery (Section 30)

1. In every factory in which the process of grinding is carried on there shall be permanently affixed to or placed near each machine in use a notice indicating the maximum safe working peripheral speed of every grindstone or abrasive wheel, the speed of the shaft or spindle upon which the wheel is mounted, and the diameter of the pulley upon such shaft or spindle necessary to secure such safe working peripheral speed.
2. The speeds indicated in notices under sub-section (1) shall not be exceeded.
3. Effective measures shall be taken in every factory to ensure that the safe working peripheral speed of every revolving vessel, cage, basket, flywheel, pulley, disc or similar appliance driven by power is not exceeded.

Pressure Plant (Section 31)

1. If in any factory, any plant or machinery, or any part thereof is operated at a pressure above atmospheric pressure, effective measures shall be taken to ensure that the safe working pressure of such plant or machinery or part is not exceeded.
2. The State Government may make rules providing for the examination and testing of any plant or machinery such as is referred to in sub-section (1) and prescribing such other safety measures in relation thereto as may in its opinion be necessary in any factory or class or description of factories.
3. The State Government may, by rules, exempt, subject to such conditions as may be specified therein, any part of any plant or machinery referred to in sub-section (1) from the provisions of this section.

Floors, Stairs and Means of Access (Section 32)

In every factory:

(a) all floors, steps, stairs, passages and gangways shall be of sound construction and properly maintained and shall be kept free from obstructions and substances likely to cause persons to slip, and where it is necessary to ensure safety, steps, stairs, passages and gangways shall be provided with substantial handrails;

(b) there shall, so far as is reasonably practicable, be provided and maintained safe means of access to every place at which any person is at any time required to work;

(c) when any person has to work at a height from where he is likely to fall, provision shall be made, so far as is reasonably practicable, by fencing or otherwise, to ensure the safety of the person so working.

Spotlight

When any person has to work at a height from where he is likely to fall, Section 32(c) says that provision shall be made by fencing or otherwise, to ensure the safety of the person so working.

Pits, Sumps, Openings in Floors, etc. (Section 33)

1. In every factory every fixed vessel, sump, tank, pit or opening in the ground or in a floor which, by reason of its depth, situation, construction or contents, is or may be a source of danger, shall be either securely covered or securely fenced.
2. The State Government may, by order in writing, exempt, subject to such conditions as may be prescribed, any factory or class or description of factories in respect of any vessel, sump, tank, pit or opening from compliance with the provisions of this section.

Excessive Weights (Section 34)

1. No person shall be employed in any factory to lift, carry or move any load so heavy as to be likely to cause him injury.
2. The State Government may make rules prescribing the maximum weights which may be lifted, carried or moved by adult men, adult women, adolescents and children employed in factories or in any class or description of factories or in carrying on any specified process.

Protection of Eyes (Section 35)

In respect of any such manufacturing process carried on in any factory as may be prescribed, being a process which involves:

(a) risk of injury to the eyes from particles or fragments thrown off in the course of the process, or

(b) risk to the eyes by reason of exposure to excessive light,

the State Government may by rules require that effective screens or suitable goggles shall be provided for the protection of persons employed on, or in the immediate vicinity of, the process.

Precautions against Dangerous Fumes, Gases, etc. (Section 36)

1. No person shall be required or allowed to enter any chamber, tank, vat, pit, pipe, flue or other confined space in any factory in which any gas, fume, vapour or dust is likely to be present to such an extent as to involve risk to persons being overcome thereby, unless it is provided with a manhole of adequate size or other effective means of egress.

2. No person shall be required or allowed to enter any confined space as is referred to in sub-section (1), until all practicable measures have been taken to remove any gas, fume, vapour or dust, which may be present so as to bring its level within the permissible limits and to prevent any ingress of such gas, fume, vapour or dust and unless–
   (a) a certificate in writing has been given by a competent person, based on a test carried out by himself that the space is reasonably free from dangerous gas, fume, vapour, or dust; or
   (b) such person is wearing suitable breathing apparatus and a belt securely attached to a rope the free end of which is held by a person outside the confined space.

Precautions Regarding the Use of Portable Electric Light (Section 36A)

In any factory:

(a) no portable electric light or any other electric appliance of voltage exceeding 24 volts shall be permitted for use inside any chamber, tank, vat, pit, pipe, flue or other confined space unless adequate safety devices are provided; and

(b) if any inflammable gas, fume or dust is likely to be present in such chamber, tank, vat, pit, pipe, flue or other confined space, no lamp or light other than that of flame-proof construction shall be permitted to be used therein.

Explosive or Inflammable Dust, Gas, etc. (Section 37)

1. Where in any factory any manufacturing process produces dust, gas, fume or vapour of such character and to such extent as to be likely to explode on ignition, all practicable measures shall be taken to prevent any such explosion by:
   (a) effective enclosure of the plant or machinery used in the process;
   (b) removal or prevention of the accumulation of such dust, gas, fume or vapour;
   (c) exclusion or effective enclosure of all possible sources of ignition.
2. Where in any factory the plant or machinery used in a process such as is referred to in sub-section (1) is not so constructed as to withstand the probable pressure which such an explosion as aforesaid would produce, all practicable measures shall be taken to restrict the spread and effects of the explosion by the provision in the plant or machinery of chokes, baffles, vents or other effective appliances.
3. Where any part of the plant or machinery in a factory contains any explosive or inflammable gas or vapour under pressure greater than atmospheric pressure, that part shall not be opened except in accordance with the following provisions, namely:
   (a) before the fastening of any joint of any pipe connected with the part or the fastening of the cover of any opening into the part is the cover of any opening into the part is loosened, any flow of the gas or vapour into the part of any such pipe shall be effectively stopped by a stop-valve or other means;
   (b) before any such fastening as aforesaid is removed, all practicable measures shall be taken to reduce the pressure of the gas or vapour in the part of pipe to atmospheric pressure;
   (c) where any such fastening as aforesaid has been loosened or removed effective measures shall be taken to prevent any explosive or inflammable gas or vapour from entering the part or pipe until the fastening has been secured, or, as the case may be, securely replaced:
   Provided that the provisions of this sub-section shall not apply in the case of plant or machinery installed in the open air.

4. No plant, tank or vessel which contains or has contained any explosive or inflammable substance shall be subjected in any factory to any welding, brazing, soldering or cutting operation which involves the application of heat unless adequate measures have first been taken to remove such substance and any fumes arising therefrom or to render such substance and fumes non-explosive or non-inflammable, and no such substance shall be allowed to enter such plant, tank or vessel after any such operation until the metal has cooled sufficiently to prevent any risk of igniting the substance.
5. The State Government may by rules exempt, subject to such conditions as may be prescribed, any factory or class or description of factories from compliance with all or any of the provisions of this section.

Precautions in Case of Fire (Section 38)

1. In every factory, all practicable measures shall be taken to prevent outbreak of fire and its spread, both internally and externally, and to provide and maintain:
   (a) safe means of escape for all persons in the event of a fire, and
   (b) the necessary equipment and facilities for extinguishing fire.
2. Effective measures shall be taken to ensure that in every factory all the workers are familiar with the means of escape in case of fire and have been adequately trained in the routine to be followed in such cases.

Spotlight

Section 38(2) mandates effective measures to ensure that in every factory all the workers are familiar with the means of escape in case of fire and have been adequately trained in the routine to be followed.

3. The State Government may make rules, in respect of any factory or class or description of factories, requiring the measures to be adopted to give effect to the provisions of sub-sections (1) and (2).
4. Notwithstanding anything contained in clause (a) of sub-section (1) or sub-section (2), if the Chief Inspector, having regard to the nature of the work carried on in any factory, the construction of such factory, special risk to life or safety, or any other circumstances, is of the opinion that the measures provided in the factory, whether as prescribed or not, for the purposes of clause (a) of sub-section (1) or sub-section (2), are inadequate, he may, by order in writing, require that such additional measures as he may consider reasonable and necessary, be provided in the factory before such date as it specified in the order.

Power to Require Specifications of Defective Parts or Tests of Stability (Section 39)

If it appears to the Inspector that any building or part of a building or any part of the ways, machinery or plant in a factory is in such a condition that it may be dangerous to human life or safety, he may serve on the occupier or manager or both of the factory an order in writing requiring him before a specified date:

(a) to furnish such drawings, specifications and other particulars as may be necessary to determine whether such building, ways, machinery or plant can be used with safety, or
(b) to carry out such tests in such manner as may be specified in the order and to inform the Inspector of the results thereof.

Safety of Buildings and Machinery (Section 40)

1. If it appears to the Inspector that any building or part of a building or any part of the ways, machinery or plant in a factory is in such a condition that it is dangerous to human life or safety, he may serve on the occupier or manager or both of the factory an order in writing specifying the measures which in his opinion should be adopted and requiring them to be carried out before a specified date.
2. If it appears to the Inspector that the use of any building or part of a building or any part of the ways, machinery or plant in a factory involves imminent danger to human life or safety, he may serve on the occupier or manager or both of the factory an order in writing prohibiting its use until it has been properly repaired or altered.

Maintenance of Buildings (Section 40A)

If it appears to the Inspector that any building or part of a building in a factory is in such a state of disrepair as is likely to lead to conditions detrimental to the health and welfare of the workers, he may serve on the occupier or manager or both of the factory an order in writing specifying the measures which in his opinion should be taken and requiring the same to be carried out before such date as is specified in the order.

Safety Officers (Section 40B)

1. In every factory:
   (i) wherein 1,000 or more workers are ordinarily employed, or
   (ii) wherein, in the opinion of the State Government, any manufacturing process or operation is carried on, which process or operation involves any risk of bodily injury, poisoning or disease, or any other hazard to health, to the persons employed in the factory,

   the occupier shall, if so required by the State Government by notification in the Official Gazette, employ such number of Safety Officers as may be specified in that notification.
2. The duties, qualifications and conditions of service of Safety Officers shall be such as may be prescribed by the State Government.

> **Spotlight**
> As per Section 40B, Safety Officers must be employed in every factory wherein 1000 or more workers are ordinarily employed.

Power to Make Rules to Supplement this Chapter (Section 41)

The State Government may make rules requiring the provision in any factory or in any class or description of factories of such further devices and measures for securing the safety of persons employed therein as it may deem necessary.

CHAPTER IVA: PROVISIONS RELATING TO HAZARDOUS PROCESSES

Constitution of Site Appraisal Committees (Section 41A)

1. The State Government may, for purposes of advising it to consider applications for grant of permission for the initial location of a factory involving a hazardous process or for the expansion of any such factory, appoint a Site Appraisal Committee consisting of:
   (a) the Chief Inspector of the State who shall be its Chairman;

(b) a representative of the Central Board for the Prevention and Control of Water Pollution appointed by the Central Government under Section 3 of the Water (Prevention and Control of Pollution) Act, 1974;

(c) a representative of the Central Board for the Prevention and Control of Air Pollution referred to in Section 3 of the Air (Prevention and Control of Pollution) Act, 1981;

(d) a representative of the State Board appointed under Section 4 of the Water (Prevention and Control of Pollution) Act, 1974;

Spotlight

The Site Appraisal Committee, as per Section 41A(2), shall make its recommendation to the State Government within a period of 90 days of the receipt of such application in prescribed form.

(e) a representative of the State Board for the Prevention and Control of Air Pollution referred to in Section 5 of the Air (Prevention and Control of Pollution) Act, 1981;

(f) a representative of the Department of Environment in the State;

(g) a representative of the Meteorological Department of the Government of India;

(h) an expert in the field of occupational health; and

(i) a representative of the Town Planning Department of the State Government,

and not more than 5 other members who may be co-opted by the State Government who shall be:

(i) a scientist having specialised knowledge of the hazardous process which will be involved in the factory,

(ii) a representative of the local authority within whose jurisdiction the factory is to be established, and

(iii) not more than 3 other persons as deemed fit by the State Government.

2. The Site Appraisal Committee shall examine an application for the establishment of a factory involving hazardous process and make its recommendation to the State Government within a period of 90 days of the receipt of such application in the prescribed form.
3. Where any process relates to a factory owned or controlled by the Central Government or to a corporation or a company owned or controlled by the Central Government, the State Government shall co-opt in the Site Appraisal Committee a representative nominated by the Central Government as a member of that Committee.
4. The Site Appraisal Committee shall have power to call for any information from the person making an application for the establishment or expansion of a factory involving a hazardous process.
5. Where the State Government has granted approval to an application for the establishment or expansion of a factory involving a hazardous process, it shall not be necessary for an applicant to obtain a further approval from the Central Board or the State Board established under the Water (Prevention and Control of Pollution) Act, 1974 and the Air (Prevention and Control of Pollution) Act 1981.

Compulsory Disclosure of Information by the Occupier (Section 41B)

1. The occupier of every factory involving a hazardous process shall disclose in the manner prescribed all information regarding dangers, including health hazards and the measures to overcome such hazards arising from the exposure to or handling of the materials or substances in the manufacture, transportation, storage and other processes, to the workers employed in the factory, the Chief Inspector, the local authority within whose jurisdiction the factory is situate and the general public in the vicinity.
2. The occupier shall, at the time of registering the factory involving a hazardous process lay down a detailed policy with respect to the health and safety of the workers employed therein and intimate such policy to the Chief Inspector and the local authority and, thereafter, at such intervals as may

be prescribed, inform the Chief Inspector and the local authority of any change made in the said policy.

3. The information furnished under sub-section (1) shall include accurate information as to the quantity, specifications and other characteristics of wastes and the manner of their disposal.
4. Every occupier shall, with the approval of the Chief Inspector, draw up an on-site emergency plan and detailed disaster control measures for his factory and make known to the workers employed therein and to the general public living in the vicinity of the factory the safety measures required to be taken in the event of an accident taking place.
5. Every occupier of a factory shall:
   (a) if such factory engaged in a hazardous process on the commencement of the Factories (Amendment) Act, 1987, within a period of 30 days of such commencement; and
   (b) if such factory proposes to engage in a hazardous process at any time after such commencement, within a period of 30 days before the commencement of such process,

   inform the Chief Inspector of the nature and details of the process in such form and in such manner as may be prescribed.
6. Where any occupier of a factory contravenes the provisions of sub-section (5), the licence issued under Section 6 to such factory shall, notwithstanding any penalty to which the occupier or factory shall be subjected to under the provisions of this Act, be liable for cancellation.
7. The occupier of a factory involving a hazardous process shall, with the previous approval of the Chief Inspector, lay down measures for the handling, usage, transportation and storage of hazardous substances inside the factory premises and publicise them in the manner prescribed among the workers and the general public living in the vicinity.

Specific Responsibility of the Occupier in Relation to Hazardous Processes (Section 41C)

Every occupier of a factory involving any hazardous process shall:

(a) maintain accurate and up-to-date health records or, as the case may be, medical records, of the workers in the factory who are exposed to any chemical, toxic or any other harmful substances which are manufactured, stored, handled or transported and such records shall be accessible to the workers subject to such conditions as may be prescribed;

(b) appoint persons who possess qualifications and experience in handling hazardous substances and are competent to supervise such handling within the factory and to provide at the working place all the necessary facilities for protecting the workers in the manner prescribed:

Provided that where any question arises as to the qualifications and experience of a person so appointed, the decision of the Chief Inspector shall be final;

(c) provide for medical examination of every worker:

   (a) before such worker is assigned to a job involving the handling of, or working with, a hazardous substance, and

   (b) while continuing in such job, and after he has ceased to work in such job, at intervals not exceeding 12 months, in such manner as may be prescribed.

Power of Central Government to Appoint Inquiry Committee (Section 41D)

1. The Central Government may, in the event of the occurrence of an extraordinary situation involving a factory engaged in a hazardous process, appoint an Inquiry Committee to inquire into the

standards of health and safety observed in the factory with a view to finding out the causes of any failure or neglect in the adoption of any measures or standards prescribed for the health and safety of the workers employed in the factory or the general public affected or likely to be affected, due to such failure or neglect and for the prevention and recurrence of such extraordinary situations in future in such factory or elsewhere.

2. The Committee appointed under sub-section (1) shall consist of a Chairman and 2 other members and the terms of reference of the Committee and the tenure of office of its members shall be such as may be determined by the Central Government according to the requirements of the situation.
3. The recommendations of the Committee shall be advisory in nature.

Emergency Standards (Section 41E)

1. Where the Central Government is satisfied that no standards of safety have been prescribed in respect of a hazardous process or class of hazardous processes, or where the standards so prescribed are inadequate, it may direct the Director-General of Factory Advice Service and Labour Institutes or any institution specialised in matters relating to standards of safety in hazardous processes, to lay down emergency standards for enforcement of suitable standards in respect of such hazardous processes.
2. The emergency standards laid down under sub-section shall, until they are incorporated in the rules made under this be enforceable and have the same effect as if they had been incorporated in the rules made under this Act.

Permissible Limits of Exposure of Chemical and Toxic Substances (Section 41F)

1. The maximum permissible threshold limits of exposure of chemical and toxic substances in manufacturing processes (whether hazardous or otherwise) in any factory shall be of the value indicated in the Second Schedule.
2. The Central Government may, at any time, for the purpose of giving effect to any scientific proof obtained from specialised institutions or experts in the field, by notification in the Official Gazette, make suitable changes in the said Schedule.

Workers' Participation in Safety Management (Section 41G)

1. The occupier shall, in every factory where a hazardous process takes place, or where hazardous substances are used or handled, set up a Safety Committee consisting of equal number of representatives of workers and management to promote cooperation between the workers and the management in maintaining proper safety and health at work and to review periodically the measures taken in that behalf:

   Provided that the State Government may, by order in writing and for reasons to be recorded, exempt the occupier of any factory or class of factories from setting up such Committee.
2. The composition of the Safety Committee, the tenure of office of its members and their rights and duties shall be such as may be prescribed.

Spotlight

As per Section 41C(1), a Safety Committee must consist of equal number of representatives of workers and management to promote cooperation in maintaining proper safety and health at work.

Right of Workers to Warn about Imminent Danger (Section 41H)

1. Where the workers employed in any factory engaged in a hazardous process have reasonable apprehension that there is a likelihood of imminent danger to their lives or health due to any accident, they may bring the same to the notice of the occupier, agent, manager or any other person who is in charge of the factory or the process concerned directly or through their representatives in the Safety Committee and simultaneously bring the same to the notice of the Inspector.
2. It shall be the duty of such occupier, agent, manager or the person in charge of the factory or process to take immediate remedial action if he is satisfied about the existence of such imminent danger and send a report forthwith of the action taken to the nearest Inspector.
3. If the occupier, agent, manager or the person in charge referred to in sub-section (2) is not satisfied about the existence of any imminent danger as apprehended by the workers, he shall, nevertheless, refer the matter forthwith to the nearest Inspector whose decision on the question of the existence of such imminent danger shall be final.

In *Mangesh G. Salodkar vs. Monsanto Chemicals of India Ltd.* the Court views that the Factories Act, 1948 contains detailed provisions for ensuring the welfare of workers and for guarding against unhygienic and dangerous conditions of work. Special provisions have been made for regulating hazardous processes and these are supplemented by other salutary provisions. The right of workers to be fully informed on issues concerning health and to participate in safety management are instances of rights which are constitutionally recognised and implemented by legislation. Ignorance is a powerful barrier to the fulfilment of socio-economic rights. In matters of workers' safety, such ignorance of rights is compounded by the economic necessity of sustaining livelihood. Economic necessity poses a serious constraint upon workers complaining about conditions of work. The choice is between economic death, as industrial law often describes the consequences of termination, or disease, debilitation and death caused by working in a hazardous environment. Prospective workers have no bargaining power to scrutinise working conditions; present workers are chilled into silence, and workers are lost in the oblivion of faded memories. The regulatory authority entrusted with the task of enforcing statutory standards designed to promote health, safety and welfare of workers therefore has a vital role to play in the achievement of statutory norms. Absence of information by way of updated medical records results in a virtual denial of access to justice.

(Adapted from: www.indiankanoon.org/doc/961204/ accessed on 23/12/2013.)

CHAPTER V: WELFARE

Washing Facilities (Section 42)

1. In every factory:
   (a) adequate and suitable facilities for washing shall be provided and maintained for the use of the workers therein;
   (b) separate and adequately screened facilities shall be provided for the use of male and female workers;
   (c) such facilities shall be conveniently accessible and shall be kept clean.
2. The State Government may, in respect of any factory or class or description of factories or of any manufacturing process, prescribe standards of adequate and suitable facilities for washing.

Facilities for Storing and Drying Clothing (Section 43)

The State Government may, in respect of any factory or class or description of factories, make rules requiring the provision therein of suitable places for keeping clothing not worn during working hours and for the drying of wet clothing.

Facilities for Sitting (Section 44)

1. In every factory suitable arrangements for sitting shall be provided and maintained for all workers obliged to work in a standing position, in order that they may take advantage of any opportunities for rest which may occur in the course of their work.
2. If, in, the opinion of the Chief Inspector, the workers in any factory engaged in a particular manufacturing process or working in a particular room are able to do their work efficiently in a sitting position, he may, by order in writing, require the occupier of the factory to provide before a specified date such seating arrangements as may be practicable for all workers so engaged or working.
3. The State Government may, by notification in the Official Gazette, declare that the provisions of sub-section (1) shall not apply to any specified factory or class or description of factories or to any specified manufacturing process.

First-aid Appliances (Section 45)

1. There shall in every factory be provided and maintained so as to be readily accessible during all working hours first-aid boxes or cupboards equipped with the prescribed contents, and the number of such boxes or cupboards to be provided and maintained shall not be less than 1 for every 150 workers ordinarily employed at any 1 time in the factory.
2. Nothing except the prescribed contents shall be kept in a first-aid box or cupboard.
3. Each first-aid box or cupboard shall be kept in the charge of a separate responsible person who holds a certificate in first-aid treatment recognised by the State Government and who shall always be readily available during the working hours of the factory.
4. In every factory wherein more than 500 workers are ordinarily employed there shall be provided and maintained an ambulance room of the prescribed size, containing the prescribed equipment and in the charge of such medical and nursing staff as may be prescribed and those facilities shall always be made readily available during the working hours of the factory.

Spotlight

As per Section 45(1), first-aid boxes or cupboards equipped with the prescribed contents must be provided and maintained in every factory so as to be readily accessible during all working hours.

Canteens (Section 46)

1. The State Government may make rules requiring that in any specified factory wherein more than 250 workers are ordinarily employed, a canteen or canteens shall be provided and maintained by the occupier for the use of the workers.

Spotlight

In every factory with more than 250 workers ordinarily employed, canteen(s) shall be provided and maintained by the occupier for the use of the workers, as prescribed in Section 46(1).

2. Without prejudice to the generality of the foregoing power, such rules may provide for:
   (a) the date by which such canteen shall be provided;
   (b) the standards in respect of construction, accommodation, furniture and other equipment of the canteen;
   (c) the foodstuffs to be served therein and the charges which may be made therefor;
   (d) the constitution of a managing committee for the canteen and representation of the workers in the management of the canteen;
   (dd) the items of expenditure in the running of the canteen which are not to be taken into account in fixing the cost of foodstuffs and which shall be borne by the employer;
   (e) the delegation to the Chief Inspector, subject to such conditions as may be prescribed, of the power to make rules under clause (c).

In *J.K. Cotton Spinning & Weaving Mills Co Ltd. vs. Badri Mali and Others* (1964 (3) SCR 724) it has been held that the responsibility of provision and maintenance of a canteen in or near the factory is not only a provision but also one of maintenance. The work of a canteen is therefore not only incidental to, but is also absolutely necessary and integral to the operation of a factory employing 250 or more workmen.

(Adapted from: www.indiankanoon.org/doc/999519/ accessed on 27/12/2013.)

CASE CORNER

In *Hari Shankar Sharma and Others vs. M/s Artificial Limbs Manufacturing Corporation and Others* [Appeal (civil) 7731 of 1997] the first respondent, a Government of India undertaking, had set up a canteen for the employees of its factory. From time to time agreements were entered into between the first respondent and different contractors to prepare and serve foodstuffs and other refreshments at the canteen, one of whom is the second respondent herein. During the pendency of the contract with the second respondent, the appellants raised an industrial dispute claiming to be regular workmen of the first respondent.

It was submitted that the first respondent was bound by Section 46 of the Factories Act, 1948 (referred to now onwards as the Act) to set up the canteen and that the State Government had by notification specified the factory of the first respondent under the provisions of Section 46(1) of the Act. It was contended that since the first respondent was statutorily obliged to provide and maintain a canteen for the use of its employees, the same was part of its establishment and therefore the appellants who were employed in such canteen were the employees of the first respondent. It is the appellant's case that the various terms in the contract between the contractor and the first respondent clearly showed that the appellants were under the direct supervision and control of the first respondent. This, along with the fact that the appellants had continued to be employed in the canteen despite several changes of contractors, showed that the appellants were the employees of the first respondent.

Before the Labour Court the contractor stated in cross-examination that he used to supervise and control his employees and pay their salaries. Even the witnesses for the appellants stated that their salaries were paid by the contractor. The appellants' witnesses also said that the second respondent brought the raw material, while the witnesses of the first respondent said that the latter had no hand in the selection of the employees of the canteen. The prescribed procedure for appointing employees of the first respondent was not applied to them. The first respondent neither recorded their attendance nor paid them their salaries. The Labour Court also noted that the appellants' witnesses were unable to identify or name any officer of the first respondent, who they claimed supervised their work. After a detailed analysis of the evidence, the Labour Court concluded that the appellants were not the employees of the first respondent.

(Adapted from: www.indiankanoon.org/doc/1324023/ accessed on 21/12/2013.)

Shelters, Rest Rooms and Lunch Rooms (Section 47)

1. In every factory wherein more than 150 workers are ordinarily employed, adequate and suitable shelters or rest rooms and a suitable lunch room, with provision for drinking water, where workers can eat meals brought by them, shall be provided and maintained for the use of the workers:

   Provided that any canteen maintained in accordance with the provisions of Section 46 shall be regarded as part of the requirements of this sub-section:

   Provided further that where a lunch room exists no worker shall eat any food in the work room.
2. The shelters or rest rooms or lunch rooms to be provided under sub-section (1) shall be sufficiently lighted and ventilated and shall be maintained in a cool and clean condition.
3. The State Government may:
   (a) prescribe the standards in respect of construction, accommodation, furniture and other equipment of shelters, rest rooms and lunch rooms to be provided under this section;
   (b) by notification in the Official Gazette, exempt any factory or class or description of factories from the requirements of this section.

Spotlight

Section 47(1) provides that where a lunch room exists no worker shall eat any food in the work room.

Creches (Section 48)

1. In every factory wherein more than 30 women workers are ordinarily employed there shall be provided and maintained a suitable room or rooms for the use of children under the age of 6 years of such women.
2. Such rooms shall provide adequate accommodation, shall be adequately lighted and ventilated, shall be maintained in a clean and sanitary condition and shall be under the charge of women trained in the care of children and infants.
3. The State Government may make rules:
   (a) prescribing the location and the standards in respect of construction, accommodation, furniture and other equipment of rooms to be provided under this section;
   (b) requiring the provision in factories to which this section applies of additional facilities for the care of children belonging to women workers, including suitable provision of facilities for washing and changing their clothing;
   (c) requiring the provision in any factory of free milk or refreshment or both for such children;
   (d) requiring that facilities shall be given in any factory for the mothers of such children to feed them at the necessary intervals.

Spotlight

As per Section 48(1), in every factory employing more than 30 women workers, suitable room(s), shall be provided and maintained for the use of children under the age of 6 years of such women.

Welfare Officers (Section 49)

1. In every factory wherein 500 or more workers are ordinarily employed the occupier shall employ in the factory such number of welfare officers as may be prescribed.
2. The State Government may prescribe the duties, qualifications and conditions of service of officers employed under sub-section (1).

Spotlight

As per Section 49(1), in every factory employing 500 or more workers, the occupier shall employ the prescribed number of welfare officers.

Power to Make Rules to Supplement this Chapter (Section 50)

The State Government may make rules-

(a) exempting, subject to compliance with such alternative arrangements for the welfare of workers as may be prescribed, any factory or class or description of factories from compliance with any of the provisions of this Chapter;

(b) requiring in any factory or class or description of factories that representatives of the workers employed in the factory shall be associated with the management of the welfare arrangements of the workers.

CHAPTER VI: WORKING HOURS OF ADULTS

Weekly Hours (Section 51)

No adult worker shall be required or allowed to work in a factory for more than 48 hours in any week.

In *M/s Richa and Company vs. Shri Suresh Chand* [W.P.(C) No.10744/2006], the working hours of the petitioner's firm were initially 9.30 AM to 6 PM, including a tea break from 4 PM to 4.15 PM. From 1st July 2002 the management changed the working hours from 9.30 AM to 6.15 PM, implying that the working hours per day of the workmen were increased from 7 hours 45 minutes to 8 hours. This increase of working hours is in compliance with Section 51 of the Factories Act, 1948, which contemplates and mandates that working hours in a factory shall not be more than 48 hours in a week.

(Adapted from: www.indiankanoon.org/doc/135068522/ accessed on 24/12/2013.)

Weekly Holidays (Section 52)

1. No adult worker shall be required or allowed to work in a factory on the first day of the week (hereinafter referred to as the said day), unless:
   (a) he has or will have a holiday for a whole day on 1 of the 3 days immediately before or after the said day, and
   (b) the manager of the factory has, before the said day or the substituted day under clause (a), whichever is earlier:
      (i) delivered a notice at the office of the Inspector of his intention to require the worker to work on the said day and of the day which is to be substituted, and
      (ii) displayed a notice to that effect in the factory:

   Provided that no substitution shall be made which will result in any worker working for more than 10 days consecutively without a holiday for a whole day.

2. Notices given under sub-section (1) may be cancelled by a notice delivered at the office of the Inspector and a notice displayed in the factory not later than the day before the said day or the holiday to be cancelled, whichever is earlier.
3. Where, in accordance with the provisions of sub-section (1), any worker works on the said day and has had a holiday on one of the 3 days immediately before it, that said day shall, for the purpose of calculating his weekly hours of work, be included in the preceding week.

CASE CORNER

In *Motor and Machinery Manufacturers Ltd. vs. State of West Bengal and Others* (AIR 1964 Cal 262), the appellant is a public limited company that employs about 600 workmen at its factory Kolkata (erstwhile Calcutta), which is a factory within the meaning of the Factories Act, 1948 and is governed by the provisions of the said Act. The workmen of the factory except a few monthly paid staff get their wages calculated on hourly basis for all working days excepting those days that are covered by sickness, annual leave and festival holidays under different provisions of the Act. They enjoy 12 paid festival holidays in a calendar year and also get the usual weekly holiday on Sunday, which is a holiday without pay. In the year 1959, 22nd March was a Sunday and 24th and 25th March were declared holidays on account of Holi festival. Considering that it would be convenient both to the workmen and the company if the intervening day, namely, 23rd March 1959 which was a working day could be declared a holiday, the appellant company declared it as a holiday and further declared with a view to compensate the loss of wages for 23rd March 1959, that Sunday, the 29th March 1959, would be a working day. Notice as required by the Act declaring that the factory would remain closed on 23rd March 1959, was given on 9th March 1959. The appellant company was informed by the Factory Inspector upon whom this notice was served that the notice was not strictly in conformity with the provisions of law, the appellant company, by a notice dated 20th March 1959, cancelled the previous notice and declared that the factory would remain closed as already declared on 23rd March 1959, but would remain open in lieu thereof on 12th April 1959, which was a Sunday. On 6th April 1959, the workmen of the factory and/or their union wrote a letter to the appellant company contending *inter alia* that no reasons had been ascribed for declaring 23rd March 1959, a full working day, as a holiday and so the workmen were entitled to a compensation holiday under Section 53 of the Factories Act, 1948. This contention was disputed by the appellant company in response to which, the Industrial Tribunal, West Bengal held that the workmen working on daily wages basis on the plea "no work no pay" would be entitled to get one day's wages by way of compensation for 23rd March 1959. The appellant company moved the Court, which pointed out that the appellant company had not followed the provisions of Section 52 of the Act and their action in declaring 23rd March 1959 as a substituted holiday for making Sunday 12th April a working day was not warranted by the provisions of Section 52 of the Act.

(Adapted from: www.indiankanoon.org/doc/1893085/ accessed on 26/12/2013.)

Compensatory Holidays (Section 53)

1. Where, as a result of the passing of an order or the making of a rule under the provisions of this Act exempting a factory or the workers therein from the provisions of Section 52, a worker is

deprived of any of the weekly holidays for which provision is made in sub-section (1) of that section, he shall be allowed, within the month in which the holidays were due to him or within 2 months immediately following that month, compensatory holidays of equal number of the holidays so lost.

2. The State Government may prescribe the manner in which the holidays for which provision is made in sub-section (1) shall be allowed.

Daily Hours (Section 54)

Subject to the provisions of Section 51, no adult worker shall be required or allowed to work in a factory for more than 9 hours in any day:

Provided that, subject to the previous approval of the Chief Inspector, the daily maximum specified in this section may be exceeded in order to facilitate the change of shifts.

Spotlight

No adult worker shall be required or allowed to work in a factory for more than 9 hours in any day, as given in Section 54.

Intervals for Rest (Section 55)

1. The periods of work of adult workers in a factory each day shall be so fixed that no period shall exceed 5 hours and that no worker shall work for more than 5 hours before he has had an interval for rest of at least half an hour.
2. The State Government or, subject to the control of the State Government, the Chief Inspector, may, by written order and for the reasons specified therein, exempt any factory from the provisions of sub-section (1) so however that the total number of hours worked by a worker without an interval does not exceed 6.

Spread Over (Section 56)

The periods of work of an adult worker in a factory shall be so arranged that inclusive of his intervals for rest under Section 55, they shall not spread over more than 10 and a half hours in any day:

Provided that the Chief Inspector may, for reasons to be specified in writing, increase the spread over up to 12 hours.

Night Shifts (Section 57)

Where a worker in a factory works on a shift which extends beyond midnight:

(a) for the purposes of sections 52 and 53, a holiday for a whole day shall mean in his case a period of 24 consecutive hours beginning when his shift ends;
(b) the following day for him shall be deemed to be the period of 24 hours beginning when such shift ends, and the hours he has worked after midnight shall be counted in the previous day.

Prohibition of Overlapping Shifts (Section 58)

1. Work shall not be carried on in any factory by means of a system of shifts so arranged that more than 1 relay of workers is engaged in work of the same kind at the same time.
2. The State Government or subject to the control of the State Government, the Chief Inspector, may, by written order and for the reasons specified therein, exempt on such conditions as

may be deemed expedient, any factory or class or description of factories or any department or section of a factory or any category or description of workers therein from the provisions of sub-section (1).

Extra Wages for Overtime (Section 59)

1. Where a worker works in a factory for more than 9 hours in any day or for more than 48 hours in any week, he shall, in respect of overtime work, be entitled to wages at the rate of twice his ordinary rate of wages.
2. For the purposes of sub-section (1), "ordinary rate of wages" means the basic wages plus such allowances, including the cash equivalent of the advantage accruing through the concessional sale to workers of foodgrains and other articles, as the worker is for the time being entitled to, but does not include a bonus and wages for overtime work.
3. Where any workers in a factory are paid on a piece-rate basis, the time rate shall be deemed to be equivalent to the daily average of their full-time earnings for the days on which they actually worked on the same or identical job during the month immediately preceding the calendar month during which the overtime work was done, and such time rates shall be deemed to be the ordinary rates of wages of those workers:

   Provided that in the case of a worker who has not worked in the immediately preceding calendar month on the same or identical job, the time rate shall be deemed to be equivalent to the daily average of the earning of the worker for the days on which he actually worked in the week in which the overtime work was done.

   Spotlight
   Ordinary rate of wages does not include a bonus and wages for overtime work.

   Explanation For the purposes of this sub-section in computing the earnings for the days on which the worker actually worked such allowances, including the cash equivalent of the advantage accruing through the concessional sale to workers of foodgrains and other articles, as the worker is for the time being entitled to, shall be included but any bonus or wages for overtime work payable in relation to the period with reference to which the earnings are being computed shall be excluded.
4. The cash equivalent of the advantage accruing through the concessional sale to a worker of foodgrains and other articles shall be computed as often as may be prescribed on the basis of the maximum quantity of foodgrains and other articles admissible to a standard family.

   Explanation 1 "Standard family" means a family consisting of the worker, his or her spouse and 2 children below the age of 14 years requiring in all 3 adult consumption units.

   Explanation 2 "Adult consumption unit" means the consumption unit of a male above the age of 14 years; and the consumption unit of a female above the age of 14 years; and that of a child below the age of 14 years shall be calculated at the rates of 0.8 and 0.6 respectively of one adult consumption unit.
5. The State Government may make rules prescribing:
   (a) the manner in which the cash equivalent of the advantage accruing through the concessional sale to a worker of foodgrains and other articles shall be computed; and
   (b) the registers that shall be maintained in a factory for the purpose of securing compliance with the provisions of this section.

CASE CORNER

In *Heavy Vehicles Factory Employees Union Represented by its General Secretary and Another vs. Union of India Represented by its Secretary to Government, Ministry of Defence and Others* (2012 LLR 358), the petitioner is a registered and recognised union representing various categories of employees. The employees who were working under the third respondent-establishment contended that they were all along in receipt of overtime allowances whenever they were detained for duty beyond the normal working hours of 48 hours in a week, and the said allowances were calculated and computed by including all allowances admissible to the employees (like House Rent Allowance, City Compensatory Allowance, Transport Allowance, etc.), as per the provisions of the Factories Act, 1948.

The first respondent issued a memorandum stating that House Rent Allowance, Travelling Allowance and Small Family Allowance would stand excluded for the purpose of computation of overtime allowance, without assigning any reason therein for exclusion of the same. Aggrieved by the order, the employees and the union filed original applications before the Central Administrative Tribunal, which dismissed their applications. On appeal, the Court observed that in the absence of any rule to exclude the allowances from the definition of the basic wages, as given in sub-section (2) of Section 59, when the section excludes only two items, viz. bonus and wages for overtime work, the action of the first respondent in excluding the said allowances is without any authority and such items should be included.

(Adapted from: Chadha and Co., Labour Law Update, April and May 2012.)

Restriction on Double Employment (Section 60)

No adult worker shall be required or allowed to work in any factory on any day on which he has already been working in any other factory, save in such circumstances as may be prescribed.

Notice of Periods of Work for Adults (Section 61)

1. There shall be displayed and correctly maintained in every factory in accordance with the provisions of sub-section (2) of Section 108, a notice of periods of work for adults, showing clearly for every day the periods during which adult workers may be required to work.
2. The periods shown in the notice required by sub-section (1) shall be fixed beforehand in accordance with the following provisions of this section, and shall be such that workers working for those periods would not be working in contravention of any of the provisions of sections 51, 52, 54, 55, 56 and 58.
3. Where all the adult workers in a factory are required to work during the same periods, the manager of the factory shall fix those periods for such workers generally.
4. Where all the adult workers in a factory are not required to work during the same periods, the manager of the factory shall classify them into groups according to the nature of their work indicating the number of workers in each group.
5. For each group which is not required to work on a system of shifts, the manager of the factory shall fix the periods during which the group may be required to work.
6. Where any group is required to work on a system of shifts and the relays are not to be subject to predetermined periodical changes of shifts, the manager of the factory shall fix the periods during which each relay of the group may be required to work.
7. Where any group is to work on a system of shifts and the relays are to be subject to predetermined periodical changes of shifts, the manager of the factory shall draw up a scheme of shifts where-

under the periods during which any relay of the group may be required to work and the relay which will be working at any time of the day shall be known for any day.

8. The State Government may prescribe forms of the notice required by sub-section (1) and the manner in which it shall be maintained.
9. In the case of a factory beginning work after the commencement of this Act, a copy of the notice referred to in sub-section (1) shall be sent in duplicate to the Inspector before the day on which work is begun in the factory.
10. Any proposed change in the system of work in any factory which will necessitate a change in the notice referred to in sub-section (1) shall be notified to the Inspector in duplicate before the change is made, and except with the previous sanction of the Inspector, no such change shall be made until 1 week has elapsed since the last change.

Register of Adult Workers (Section 62)

Spotlight

A register of adult workers shall be maintained by the manager of every factory, as laid down in Section 62(1).

1. The manager of every factory shall maintain a register of adult workers, to be available to the Inspector at all times during working hours, or when any work is being carried on in the factory, showing:
   (a) the name of each adult worker in the factory;
   (b) the nature of his work;
   (c) the group, if any, in which he is included;
   (d) where his group works on shifts, the relay to which he is allotted;
   (e) such other particulars as may be prescribed:

   Provided that, if the Inspector is of opinion that any muster roll or register maintained as part of the routine of a factory gives in respect of any or all the workers in the factory the particulars required under this section, he may, by order in writing, direct that such muster roll or register shall to the corresponding extent be maintained in place of, and be treated as, the register of adult workers in that factory.

1A. No adult worker shall be required or allowed to work in any factory unless his name and other particulars have been entered in the register of adult workers.

2. The State Government may prescribe the form of the register of adult workers, the manner in which it shall be maintained and the period for which it shall be preserved.

Hours of Work to Correspond with Notice under Section 61 and Register under Section 62 (Section 63)

No adult worker shall be required or allowed to work in any factory otherwise than in accordance with the notice of periods of work for adults displayed in the factory and the entries made beforehand against his name in the register of adult workers of the factory.

Power to Make Exempting Rules (Section 64)

1. The State Government may make rules defining the persons who hold positions of supervision, or management or are employed in a confidential position in a factory or empowering the Chief Inspector to declare any person, other than a person defined by such rules, as a person holding position of supervision or management or employed in a confidential position in a factory if, in the opinion of the Chief Inspector, such person holds such position or is so employed, and the

provisions of this Chapter, other than the provisions of clause (b) of sub-section (1) of Section 66 and of the proviso to that sub-section, shall not apply to any person so defined or declared.

Provided that any person so defined or declared shall, where the ordinary rate of wages of such person does not exceed the wage limit specified in sub-section (6) of Section 1 of the Payment of Wages Act, 1936, as amended from time to time, be entitled to extra wages in respect of overtime work under Section 59.

2. The State Government may make rules in respect of adult workers in factories providing for the exemption, to such extent and subject to such conditions as may be prescribed–
   (a) of workers engaged on urgent repairs, from the provisions of sections 51, 52, 54, 55 and 56;
   (b) of workers engaged in work in the nature of preparatory or complementary work which must necessarily be carried on outside the limits laid down for the general working of the factory, from the provisions of sections 51, 54, 55 and 56;
   (c) of workers engaged in work which is necessarily so intermittent that the intervals during which they do not work while on duty ordinarily amount to more than the intervals for rest required by or under Section 55, from the provisions of sections 51, 54, 55 and 56;
   (d) of workers engaged in any work which for technical reasons must be carried on continuously from the provisions of sections 51, 52, 54, 55 and 56;
   (e) of workers engaged in making or supplying articles of prime necessity which must be made or supplied every day, from the provisions of Section 51 and Section 52;
   (f) of workers engaged in a manufacturing process which cannot be carried on except during fixed seasons, from the provisions of Section 51, Section 52 and Section 54;
   (g) of workers engaged in a manufacturing process which cannot be carried on except at times dependent on the irregular action of natural forces, from the provisions of sections 52 and 55;
   (h) of workers engaged in engine-rooms or boiler-houses or in attending to power-plant or transmission machinery, from the provisions of Section 51 and Section 52;
   (i) of workers engaged in the printing of newspapers, who are held up on account of the breakdown of machinery, from the provisions of sections 51, 54 and 56.

Explanation In this clause the expression "newspapers" has the meaning assigned to it in the Press and Registration of Books Act, 1867;

   (j) of workers engaged in the loading or unloading of railway wagons or lorries or trucks from the provisions of sections 51, 52, 54, 55 and 56;
   (k) of workers engaged in any work, which is notified by the State Government in the Official Gazette as a work of national importance, from the provisions of Section 51, Section 52, Section 54, Section 55 and Section 56.

3. Rules made under sub-section (2) providing for any exemption may also provide for any consequential exemption from the provisions of Section 61 which the State Government may deem to be expedient, subject to such conditions as it may prescribe.
4. In making rules under this section, the State Government shall not exceed, except in respect of exemption under clause (a) of sub-section (2), the following limits of work inclusive of overtime:–
   (i) the total number of hours of work in any day shall not exceed 10;
   (ii) the spread over, inclusive of intervals for rest, shall not exceed 12 hours in any one day:

   Provided that the State Government may, in respect of any or all of the categories of workers referred to in clause (d) of sub-section (2), make rules prescribing the circumstances in which, and the conditions subject to which, the restrictions imposed by clause (i) and clause (ii) shall not apply in order to enable a shift worker to work the whole or part of a subsequent shift in the absence of a worker who has failed to report for duty;

(iii) the total number of hours of work in a week, including overtime, shall not exceed 60;

(iv) the total number of hours of overtime shall not exceed 50 for any one quarter.

Explanation "Quarter" means a period of three consecutive months beginning on the 1st of January, the 1st of April, the 1st of July or the 1st of October.

5. Rules made under this section shall remain in force for not more than 5 years.

In *State of Gujarat vs. Kansara Manilal Bhikhalal* [(1964) SCR (7) 656], the Court holds that Section 59 cannot be considered in isolation; it has to be read with Section 64, where the State Government has been given the power to make exempting rules. Under these rules a departure from the provisions of sections 51, 52, 55 and 56 can be made but only in accordance with the rules so framed. For example, overtime work may be taken from workers engaged on urgent repairs in spite of the provisions of sections 51, 54, 55 and 56, but must be in accordance with Rule 91 and the urgency which is referred to in this section and the rule is 'an urgency relating to the factory and not an urgency felt by the constituents of the factory'. A departure from the hours of work as laid down in Section 61(2) can only be made in cases in which the exempting provisions of the rules cover the case and not otherwise.

(Adapted from: www.indiankanoon.org/doc/1459249/ accessed on 24/12/2013.)

Power to Make Exempting Orders (Section 65)

1. Where the State Government is satisfied that, owing to the nature of the work carried on or to other circumstances, it is unreasonable to require that the periods of work of any adult workers in any factory or class or description of factories should be fixed beforehand, it may, by written order, relax or modify the provisions of Section 61 in respect of such workers therein, to such extent and in such manner as it may think fit, and subject to such conditions as it may deem expedient to ensure control over periods of work.
2. The State Government or, subject to the control of the State Government, the Chief Inspector, may by written order exempt, on such conditions as it or he may deem expedient, any or all of the adult workers in any factory or group or class or description of factories from any or all of the provisions of sections 51, 52, 54 and 56 on the ground that the exemption is required to enable the factory or factories to deal with an exceptional press of work.
3. Any exemption granted under sub-section (2) shall be subject to the following conditions, namely:
   (i) the total number of hours of work in any day shall not exceed 12;
   (ii) the spread over, inclusive of intervals for rest, shall not exceed 13 hours in any one day;
   (iii) the total number of hours of work in any week, including overtime, shall not exceed 60;
   (iv) no worker shall be allowed to work overtime, for more than 7 days at a stretch and the total number of hours of overtime work in any quarter shall not exceed 75.

Explanation In this sub-section "quarter" has the same meaning as in sub-section (4) of Section 64.

Further Restrictions on Employment of Women (Section 66)

1. The provisions of this chapter shall, in their application to women in factories, be supplemented by the following further restrictions, namely:

(a) no exemption from the provisions of Section 54 may be granted in respect of any woman;
(b) no woman shall be required or allowed to work in any factory except between the hours of 6 AM and 7 PM.

Provided that the State Government may, by notification in the Official Gazette, in respect of any factory or group or class or description of factories, vary the limits laid down in clause (b), but so that no such variation shall authorise the employment of any woman between the hours of 10 PM and 5 AM;

(c) there shall be no change of shifts except after a weekly holiday or any other holiday.

2. The State Government may make rules providing for the exemption from the restrictions set out in sub-section (1), to such extent and subject to such conditions as it may prescribe, of women working in fish-curing or fish-canning factories, where the employment of women beyond the hours specified in the said restrictions is necessary to prevent damage to, or deterioration in, any raw material.
3. The rules made under sub-section (2) shall remain in force for not more than 3 years at a time.

Spotlight

No woman shall be required or allowed to work in any factory except between 6 AM and 7 PM, as per Section 66(1)(b).

CHAPTER VII: EMPLOYMENT OF YOUNG PERSONS

Prohibition of Employment of Young Children (Section 67)

No child who has not completed his fourteenth year shall be required or allowed to work in any factory.

Spotlight

As per Section 67, no child who has not completed his fourteenth year shall be required or allowed to work in any factory.

Non-adult Workers to Carry Tokens (Section 68)

A child who has completed his fourteenth year or an adolescent shall not be required or allowed to work in any factory unless:

(a) a certificate of fitness granted with reference to him under Section 69 is in the custody of the manager of the factory, and
(b) such child or adolescent carries while he is at work a token giving a reference to such certificate.

Certificates of Fitness (Section 69)

1. A certifying surgeon shall, on the application of any young person or his parent or guardian accompanied by a document signed by the manager of a factory that such person will be employed therein if certified to be fit for work in a factory, or on the application of the manager of the factory in which any young person wishes to work, examine such person and ascertain his fitness for work in a factory.
2. The certifying surgeon, after examination, may grant to such young person, in the prescribed form, or may renew:
   (a) a certificate of fitness to work in a factory as a child, if he is satisfied that the young person has completed his fourteenth year, that he has attained the prescribed physical standards and that he is fit for such work;
   (b) a certificate of fitness to work in a factory as an adult, if he is satisfied that the young person has completed his fifteenth year, and is fit for a full day's work in a factory:

Provided that unless the certifying surgeon has personal knowledge of the place where the young person proposes to work and of the manufacturing process in which he will be employed, he shall not grant or renew a certificate under this sub-section until he has examined such place.

3. A certificate of fitness granted or renewed under sub-section (2):
   (a) shall be valid only for a period of 12 months from the date thereof;
   (b) may be made subject to conditions in regard to the nature of the work in which the young person may be employed, or requiring re-examination of the young person before the expiry of the period of 12 months.
4. A certifying surgeon shall revoke any certificate granted or renewed under sub-section (2) if in his opinion the holder of it is no longer fit to work in the capacity stated therein in a factory.
5. Where a certifying surgeon refuses to grant or renew a certificate or a certificate of the kind requested or revokes a certificate, he shall, if so requested by any person who could have applied for the certificate or the renewal thereof, state his reasons in writing for so doing.
6. Where a certificate under this section with reference to any young person is granted or renewed subject to such conditions as are referred to in clause (b) of sub-section (3), the young person shall not be required or allowed to work in any factory except in accordance with those conditions.
7. Any fee payable for a certificate under this section shall be paid by the occupier and shall not be recoverable from the young person, his parents or guardian.

Effect of Certificate of Fitness Granted to Adolescent (Section 70)

1. An adolescent who has been granted a certificate of fitness to work in a factory as an adult under clause (b) of sub-section (2) of Section 69, and who while at work in a factory carries a token giving reference to the certificate, shall be deemed to be an adult for all the purposes of chapters VI and VIII:

1A. No female adolescent or a male adolescent who has not attained the age of seventeenth year but who has been granted a certificate of fitness to work in a factory as an adult, shall be required or allowed to work in any factory except between 6 AM and 7 PM:

Provided that the State Government may, by notification in the Official Gazette, in respect of any factory or group or class or description of factories:

(i) vary the limits laid down in this sub-section so, however, that no such section shall authorise the employment of any female adolescent between 10 PM and 5 AM;
(ii) grant exemption from the provisions of this sub-section in case of serious emergency where national interest is involved.

2. An adolescent who has not been granted a certificate of fitness to work in a factory as an adult under the aforesaid clause (b) shall, notwithstanding his age, be deemed to be a child for all the purposes of this Act.

Working Hours for Children (Section 71)

1. No child shall be employed or permitted to work, in any factory:
   (a) for more than 4 and a half hours in any day;
   (b) during the night.

Explanation For the purpose of this sub-section "night" shall mean a period of at least 12 consecutive hours which shall include the interval between 10 PM and 6 AM.

Spotlight

Section 71 provides that no child shall be employed or permitted to work in any factory for more than 4.5 hours in any day and during night.

2. The period of work of all children employed in a factory shall be limited to 2 shifts which shall not overlap or spread over more than 5 hours each; and each child shall be employed in only 1 of the relays which shall not, except with the previous permission in writing of the Chief Inspector, be changed more frequently than once in a period of 30 days.
3. The provisions of Section 52 shall apply also to child workers and no exemption from the provisions of that section may be granted in respect of any child.
4. No child shall be required or allowed to work in any factory on any day on which he has already been working in another factory.
5. No female child shall be required or allowed to work in any factory except between 8 AM and 7 PM.

Notice of Periods of Work for Children (Section 72)

1. There shall be displayed and correctly maintained in every factory in which children are employed, in accordance with the provisions of sub-section (2) of Section 108 a notice of periods of work for children, showing clearly for every day the periods during which children may be required or allowed to work.
2. The periods shown in the notice required by sub-section (1) shall be fixed beforehand in accordance with the method laid down for adult workers in Section 61, and shall be such that children working for those periods would not be working in contravention of any of the provisions of Section 71.
3. The provisions of sub-sections (8), (9) and (10) of Section 61 shall apply also to the notice required by sub-section (1) of this section.

Register of Child Workers (Section 73)

1. The manager of every factory in which children are employed shall maintain a register of child workers, to be available to the Inspector at all times during working hours or when any work is being carried on in a factory, showing:
   (a) the name of each child worker in the factory;
   (b) the nature of his work;
   (c) the group, if any, in which he is included;
   (d) where his group works on shifts, the relay to which he is allotted; and
   (e) the number of his certificate of fitness granted under Section 69.

1A. No child worker shall be required or allowed to work in any factory unless his name and other particulars have been entered in the register of child workers.

2. The State Government may prescribe the form of the register of child workers, the manner in which it shall be maintained and the period for which it shall be preserved.

> **Spotlight**
> Section 73(1) lays down that the manager of every factory in which children are employed must maintain a register of child workers.

Hours of Work to Correspond with Notice under Section 72 and Register under Section 73 (Section 74)

No child shall be employed in any factory otherwise than in accordance with the notice of periods of work for children displayed in the factory and the entries made beforehand against his name in the register of child workers of the factory.

Power to Require Medical Examination (Section 75)

Where an Inspector is of opinion:

(a) that any person working in a factory without a certificate of fitness is a young person, or
(b) that a young person working in a factory with a certificate of fitness is no longer fit to work in the capacity stated therein,

he may serve on the manager of the factory a notice requiring that such person or young person, as the case may be, shall be examined by a certifying surgeon, and such person or young person shall not, if the Inspector so directs, be employed, or permitted to work, in any factory until he has been so examined and has been granted a certificate of fitness or a fresh certificate of fitness, as the case may be, under Section 69, or has been certified by the certifying surgeon examining him not to be a young person.

Power to Make Rules (Section 76)

The State Government may make rules:

(a) prescribing the forms of certificates of fitness to be granted under Section 69, providing for the grant of duplicates in the event of loss of the original certificates, and fixing the fees which may be charged for such certificates and renewals thereof and such duplicates;
(b) prescribing the physical standards to be attained by children and adolescents working in factories;
(c) regulating the procedure of certifying surgeons under this Chapter;
(d) specifying other duties which certifying surgeons may be required to perform in connection with the employment of young persons in factories, and fixing the fees which may be charged for such duties and the persons by whom they shall be payable.

Certain Other Provisions of Law not Barred (Section 77)

The provisions of this Chapter shall be in addition to, and not in derogation of, the provisions of the Employment of Children Act, 1938.

CHAPTER VIII: ANNUAL LEAVE WITH WAGES

Application of Chapter (Section 78)

1. The provisions of this Chapter shall not operate to the prejudice of any right to which a worker may be entitled under any other law or under the terms of any award, agreement (including settlement) or contract of service:

   Provided that if such award, agreement (including settlement) or contract of service provides for a longer annual leave with wages than provided in this Chapter, the quantum of leave, which the worker shall be entitled to, shall be in accordance with such award, agreement or contract of service, but in relation to matters not provided for in such award, agreement or contract of service or matters which are provided for less favourably therein, the provisions of Sections 79 to 82, so far as may be, shall apply.
2. The provisions of this Chapter shall not apply to workers in any factory of any railway administered by the Government, who are governed by leave rules approved by the Central Government.

Annual Leave with Wages (Section 79)

1. Every worker who has worked for a period of 240 days or more in a factory during a calendar year shall be allowed during the subsequent calendar year, leave with wages for a number of days calculated at the rate of:
   (i) if an adult, 1 day for every 20 days of work performed by him during the previous calendar year;
   (ii) if a child, 1 day for every 15 days of work performed by him during the previous calendar year.

Spotlight

Every adult worker who has worked for a period of 240 days or more in a factory during a calendar year shall be allowed during the subsequent calendar year, leave with wages for a number of days calculated at ₹1 per day for every 20 days of work performed by him during the previous calendar year, as provided in Section 79(1)(i).

Explanation 1 For the purpose of this sub-section:
   (a) any days of lay off, by agreement or contract or as permissible under the standing orders;
   (b) in the case of a female worker, maternity leave for any number of days not exceeding 12 weeks; and
   (c) the leave earned in the year prior to that in which the leave is enjoyed,

shall be deemed to be days on which the worker has worked in a factory for the purpose of computation of the period of 240 days or more, but he shall not earn leave for these days.

Explanation 2 The leave admissible under this sub-section shall be exclusive of all holidays whether occurring during or at either end of the period of leave.

2. A worker whose service commences otherwise than on the first day of January shall be entitled to leave with wages at the rate laid down in clause (i) or, as the case may be, clause (ii) of sub-section (1) if he has worked for two-thirds of the total number of days in the remainder of the calendar year.
3. If a worker is discharged or dismissed from service or quits his employment or is superannuated or dies while in service, during the course of the calendar year, he or his heir or nominee, as the case may be, shall be entitled to wages in lieu of the quantum of leave to which he was entitled immediately before his discharge, dismissal, quitting of employment, superannuation or death calculated at the rates specified in sub-section (1), even if he had not worked for the entire period specified in sub-section (1) or sub-section (2) making him eligible to avail of such leave, and such payment shall be made:
   (i) where the worker is discharged or dismissed or quits employment, before the expiry of the second working day from the date of such discharge, dismissal or quitting; and
   (ii) where the worker is superannuated or dies while in service, before the expiry of 2 months from the date of such superannuation or death.
4. In calculating leave under this section, fraction of leave of half a day or more shall be treated as 1 full day's leave, and fraction of less than half a day shall be omitted.
5. If a worker does not in any one calendar year take the whole of the leave allowed to him under sub-section (1) or sub-section (2), as the case may be, any leave not taken by him shall be added to the leave to be allowed to him in the succeeding calendar year:

   Provided that the total number of days of leave that may be carried forward to a succeeding year shall not exceed 30 in the case of an adult or 40 in the case of a child:

   Provided further that a worker, who has applied for leave with wages but has not been given such leave in accordance with any scheme laid down in sub-sections (8) and (9) or in contravention of sub-section (10) shall be entitled to carry forward the leave refused without any limit.

6. A worker may at any time apply in writing to the manager of a factory not less than 15 days before the date on which he wishes his leave to begin, to take all the leave or any portion thereof allowable to him during the calendar year:

   Provided that the application shall be made not less than 30 days before the date on which the worker wishes his leave to begin, if he is employed in a public utility service as defined in clause (n) of Section 2 of the Industrial Disputes Act, 1947:

   Provided further that the number of times in which leave may be taken during any year shall not exceed 3.
7. If a worker wants to avail himself of the leave with wages due to him to cover a period of illness, he shall be granted such leave even if the application for leave is not made within the time specified in sub-section (6); and in such a case wages as admissible under Section 81 shall be paid not later than 15 days, or in the case of a public utility service not later than 30 days from the date of the application for leave.
8. For the purpose of ensuring the continuity of work, the occupier or manager of the factory, in agreement with the Works Committee of the factory constituted under Section 3 of the Industrial Disputes Act, 1947, or a similar Committee constituted under any other Act or if there is no such Works Committee or a similar Committee in the factory, in agreement with the representatives of the workers therein chosen in the prescribed manner, may lodge with the Chief Inspector a scheme in writing whereby the grant of leave allowable under this section may be regulated.
9. A scheme lodged under sub-section (8) shall be displayed at some conspicuous and convenient places in the factory and shall be in force for a period of 12 months from the date on which it comes into force, and may thereafter be renewed with or without modification for a further period of 12 months at a time, by the manager in agreement with the Works Committee or a similar Committee, or as the case may be, in agreement with the representatives of the workers as specified in sub-section (8), and a notice of renewal shall be sent to the Chief Inspector before it is renewed.
10. An application for leave which does not contravene the provisions of sub-section (6) shall not be refused, unless refusal is in accordance with the scheme for the time being in operation under sub-sections (8) and (9).
11. If the employment of a worker who is entitled to leave under sub-section (1) or sub-section (2), as the case may be, is terminated by the occupier before he has taken the entire leave to which he is entitled, or if having applied for and having not been granted such leave, the worker quits his employment before he has taken the leave, the occupier of the factory shall pay him the amount payable under Section 80 in respect of the leave not taken, and such payment shall be made, where the employment of the worker is terminated by the occupier, before the expiry of the second working day after such termination, and where a worker who quits his employment, on or before the next pay day.

Spotlight

Section 79(12) provides that the unavailed leave of a worker shall not be considered in computing notice period before discharge or dismissal.

12. The unavailed leave of a worker shall not be taken into consideration in computing the period of any notice required to be given before discharge or dismissal.

Wages during Leave Period (Section 80)

1. For the leave allowed to him under Section 78 or Section 79, as the case may be, a worker shall be entitled to wages at a rate equal to the daily average of his total full time earnings for the days on which he actually worked during the month immediately preceding his leave, exclusive of any

overtime and bonus but inclusive of dearness allowance and the cash equivalent of the advantage accruing through the concessional sale to the worker of foodgrains and other articles.

Provided that in the case of a worker who has not worked on any day during the calendar month immediately preceding his leave, he shall be paid at a rate equal to the daily average of his total full time earnings for the days on which he actually worked during the last calendar month preceding his leave, in which he actually worked, exclusive of any overtime and bonus but inclusive of dearness allowance and the cash equivalent of the advantage accruing through the concessional sale to the workers of foodgrains and other articles.

2. The cash equivalent of the advantage accruing through the concessional sale to the worker of foodgrains and other articles shall be computed as often as may be prescribed, on the basis of the maximum quantity of foodgrains and other articles admissible to a standard family.

Explanation 1 "Standard family" means a family consisting of a worker, his or her spouse, and two children below the age of 14 years requiring in all three adult consumption units.

Reflection

Standard family means a family consisting of a worker, his/her spouse and 2 children below the age of 14 years requiring in all 3 adult consumption units.

Explanation 2 "Adult consumption unit" means the consumption unit of a male above the age of 14 years; and the consumption unit of a female above the age of 14 years and that of a child below the age of 14 years shall be calculated at the rates of 0.8 and 0.6 respectively of one adult consumption unit.

3. The State Government may make rules prescribing:
   (a) the manner in which the cash equivalent of the advantage accruing through the concessional sale to a worker of foodgrains and other articles shall be computed; and
   (b) the registers that shall be maintained in a factory for the purpose of securing compliance with the provisions of this section.

Payment in Advance in Certain Cases (Section 81)

A worker who has been allowed leave for not less than 4 days, in the case of an adult, and 5 days, in the case of a child shall, before his leave begins, be paid the wages due for the period of the leave allowed.

Mode of Recovery of Unpaid Wages (Section 82)

Any sum required to be paid by an employer, under this Chapter but not paid by him shall be recoverable as delayed wages under the provisions of the Payment of Wages Act, 1936.

Power to Make Rules (Section 83)

The State Government may make rules directing managers of factories to keep registers containing such particulars as may be prescribed and requiring the registers to be made available for examination by Inspectors.

Power to Exempt Factories (Section 84)

Where the State Government is satisfied that the leave rules applicable to workers in a factory provide benefits which in its opinion are not less favourable than those for which this Chapter makes provision it may, by written order, exempt the factory from all or any of the provisions of this Chapter subject to such conditions as may be specified in the order.

Explanation For the purposes of this section, in deciding whether the benefits which are provided for by any leave rules are less favourable than those for which this Chapter makes provision, or not, the totality of the benefits shall be taken into account.

CHAPTER IX: SPECIAL PROVISIONS

Power to Apply the Act to Certain Premises (Section 85)

1. The State Government may, by notification in the Official Gazette, declare that all or any of the provisions of this Act shall apply to any place wherein a manufacturing process is carried on with or without the aid of power or is so ordinarily carried on, notwithstanding that:
   (i) the number of persons employed therein is less than 10, if working with the aid of power and less than 20 if working without the aid of power, or
   (ii) the persons working therein are not employed by the owner thereof but are working with the permission of, or under agreement with, such owner:

   Provided that the manufacturing process is not being carried on by the owner only with the aid of his family.
2. After a place is so declared, it shall be deemed to be a factory for the purposes of this Act, and the owner shall be deemed to be the occupier, and any person working therein, a worker.

Explanation For the purposes of this section, "owner" shall include a lessee or mortgagee with possession of the premises.

Power to Exempt Public Institutions (Section 86)

The State Government may exempt, subject to such conditions as it may consider necessary, any workshop or workplace where a manufacturing process is carried on and which is attached to a public institution maintained for the purposes of education, training, research or reformation, from all or any of the provisions of this Act:

Provided that no exemption shall be granted from the provisions relating to hours of work and holidays, unless the persons having the control of the institution submit, for the approval of the State Government a scheme for the regulation of the hours of employment, intervals for meals, and holidays of the persons employed in or attending the institution or who are inmates of the institution, and the State Government is satisfied that the provisions of the scheme are not less favourable than the corresponding provisions of this Act.

Dangerous Operations (Section 87)

Where the State Government is of opinion that any manufacturing process or operation carried on in a factory exposes any persons employed in it to a serious risk of bodily injury, poisoning or disease, it may make rules applicable to any factory or class or description of factories in which the manufacturing process or operation is carried on:

(a) specifying the manufacturing process or operation and declaring it to be dangerous;

(b) prohibiting or restricting the employment of women, adolescents or children in the manufacturing process or operation;

Spotlight

Section 87(b) prohibits or restricts the employment of women, adolescents or children in the manufacturing process or operation of a factory that has a serious risk of bodily injury, poisoning or disease.

(c) providing for the periodical medical examination of persons employed, or seeking to be employed, in the manufacturing process or operation, and prohibiting the employment of persons not certified as fit for such employment and requiring the payment by the occupier of the factory of fees for such medical examination;
(d) providing for the protection of all persons employed in the manufacturing process or operation or in the vicinity of the places where it is carried on;
(e) prohibiting, restricting or controlling the use of any specified materials or processes in connection with the manufacturing process or operation;
(f) requiring the provision of additional welfare amenities and sanitary facilities and the supply of protective equipment and clothing, and laying down the standards thereof, having regard to the dangerous nature of the manufacturing process or operation.

CASE CORNER

The Tamil Nadu Fireworks and Amorces Manufacturers Association vs. The Principal Secretary to Government, Department of Labour & Employment, Chennai [Writ Petition (MD) No. 7156 of 2012], points out an interesting fact that the Factories Act, 1948, does not define the expression "dangerous operations", but that the very scheme of Section 87 of the Act gives a clear indication of what would constitute dangerous operations. Moreover, a careful analysis of Section 2(cb) and Section 87 would show that they are not mutually exclusive. The focus of Section 2(cb) is on materials, whether raw materials or finished or semi-finished products or wastes or effluents. But the emphasis of Section 87 is on process or operation. Interestingly, Section 2(cb) does not deal with hazardous products or materials, but with "hazardous process", though its focus is on materials. Section 87, on the other hand, is more homogenous, as it refers to process or operation. Therefore every hazardous process would certainly be a dangerous operation, if it exposes the employees to the serious risk of bodily injury. But every dangerous operation need not necessarily be a hazardous process unless the conditions prescribed in Section 2(cb) are satisfied.

Manufactories of fireworks use raw materials and get finished and semi-finished products and by-products that would certainly cause material impairment to the health of the employees. Similarly they also use a manufacturing process or operation which by itself exposes the employees to the serious risk of both bodily injury and poisoning. In such circumstances, the classification of manufactories of fireworks as those carrying on "hazardous process" within the definition of the expression under Section 2(cb) does not take the manufacturing process or operation carried on in those factories beyond the classification contained in Section 87 for a dangerous operation. In other words, manufactories of fireworks satisfy the prescriptions contained in both the sections, thereby becoming obliged to follow the statutory requirements prescribed for a hazardous process industry and for a dangerous process industry as well.

(Adapted from: www.indiankanoon.org/doc/64318123/ accessed on 25/12/2013.)

Power to Prohibit Employment on Account of Serious Hazard (Section 87A)

1. Where it appears to the Inspector that conditions in a factory or part thereof are such that they may cause serious hazard by way of injury or death to the persons employed therein or to the

general public in the vicinity, he may, by order in writing to the occupier of the factory, state the particulars in respect of which he considers the factory or part thereof to be the cause of such serious hazard and prohibit such occupier from employing any person in the factory or any part thereof other than the minimum number of persons necessary to attend to the minimum tasks till the hazard is removed.

2. Any order issued by the Inspector under sub-section (1) shall have effect for a period of 3 days until extended by the Chief Inspector by a subsequent order.
3. Any person aggrieved by an order of the Inspector under sub-section (1), and the Chief Inspector under sub-section (2), shall have the right to appeal to the High Court.
4. Any person whose employment has been affected by an order issued under sub-section (1), shall be entitled to wages and other benefits and it shall be the duty of the occupier to provide alternative employment to him wherever possible and in the manner prescribed.
5. The provisions of sub-section (4) shall be without prejudice to the rights of the parties under the Industrial Disputes Act, 1947.

Notice of Certain Accidents (Section 88)

1. Where in any factory an accident occurs which causes death, or which causes any bodily injury by reason of which the person injured is prevented from working for a period of 48 hours or more immediately following the accident, or which is of such nature as may be prescribed in this behalf, the manager of the factory shall send notice thereof to such authorities, and in such form and within such time, as may be prescribed.
2. Where a notice given under sub-section (1) relates to an accident causing death, the authority to whom the notice is sent shall make an inquiry into the occurrence within 1 month of the receipt of the notice or, if such authority is not the Inspector, cause the Inspector to make an inquiry within the said period.
3. The State Government may make rules for regulating the procedure at inquiries under this section.

Notice of Certain Dangerous Occurrences (Section 88A)

Where in a factory any dangerous occurrence of such nature as may be prescribed occurs, whether causing any bodily injury or disability or not, the manager of the factory shall send notice thereof to such authorities, and in such form and within such time, as may be prescribed.

Notice of Certain Diseases (Section 89)

1. Where any worker in a factory contracts any disease specified in the Third Schedule, the manager of the factory shall send notice thereof to such authorities, and in such form and within such time, as may be prescribed.
2. If any medical practitioner attends on a person who is or has been employed in a factory, and who is or is believed by the medical practitioner to be, suffering from any disease specified in the Third Schedule, the medical practitioner shall without delay send a report in writing to the office of the Chief Inspector stating:
   (a) the name and full postal address of the patient,
   (b) the disease from which he believes the patient to be suffering, and
   (c) the name and address of the factory in which the patient is, or was last, employed.

3. Where the report under sub-section (2) is confirmed to the satisfaction of the Chief Inspector, by the certificate of a certifying surgeon or otherwise, that the person is suffering from a disease specified in the Third Schedule, he shall pay to the medical practitioner such fee as may be prescribed, and the fee so paid shall be recoverable as an arrear of land-revenue from the occupier of the factory in which the person contracted the disease.

Spotlight

Failure by any medical practitioner to comply with Section 89(2) is punishable with fine up to ₹1,000, as provided in Section 89(4).

4. If any medical practitioner fails to comply with the provisions of sub-section (2), he shall be punishable with fine which may extend to ₹1,000.
5. The Central Government may, by notification in the Official Gazette, add to or alter the Third Schedule and any such addition or alteration shall have effect as if it had been made by this Act.

Power to Direct Enquiry into Cases of Accident or Disease (Section 90)

1. The State Government may, if it considers it expedient so to do, appoint a competent person to inquire into the causes of any accident occurring in a factory or into any case where a disease specified in the Third Schedule has been, or is suspected to have been, contracted in a factory, and may also appoint 1 or more persons possessing legal or special knowledge to act as assessors in such inquiry.
2. The person appointed to hold an inquiry under this section shall have all the powers of a Civil Court under the Code of Civil Procedure, 1908, for the purposes of enforcing the attendance of witnesses and compelling the production of documents and material objects, and may also, so far as may be necessary for the purposes of the inquiry, exercise any of the powers of an Inspector under this Act; and every person required by the person making the inquiry to furnish any information shall be deemed to be legally bound so to do within the meaning of Section 176 of the Indian Penal Code.
3. The person holding an inquiry under this section shall make a report to the State Government stating the causes of the accident, or as the case may be, disease, and any attendant circumstances, and adding any observations which he or any of the assessors may think fit to make.
4. The State Government may, if it thinks fit, cause to be published any report made under this section or any extracts therefrom.
5. The State Government may make rules for regulating the procedure at inquiries under this section.

Power to Take Samples (Section 91)

1. An Inspector may at any time during the normal working hours of a factory, after informing the occupier or manager of the factory or other person for the time being purporting to be in charge of the factory, take in the manner hereinafter provided a sufficient sample of any substance used or intended to be used in the factory, such use being:
   (a) in the belief of the Inspector in contravention of any of the provisions of this Act or the rules made thereunder, or
   (b) in the opinion of the Inspector likely to cause bodily injury to, or injury to the health or, workers in the factory.
2. Where the Inspector takes a sample under sub-section (1), he shall, in the presence of the person informed under that sub-section unless such person wilfully absents himself, divide the sample

into 3 portions and effectively seal and suitably mark them, and shall permit such person to add his own seal and mark thereto.

3. The person informed as aforesaid shall, if the Inspector so requires, provide the appliances for dividing, sealing and marking the sample taken under this section.
4. The Inspector shall:
   (a) forthwith give 1 portion of the sample to the person informed under sub-section (1);
   (b) forthwith send the second portion to a Government Analyst for analysis and report thereon;
   (c) retain the third portion for production to the Court before which proceedings, if any, are instituted in respect of the substance.
5. Any document purporting to be a report under the hand of any Government Analyst upon any substance submitted to him for analysis and report under this section, may be used as evidence in any proceedings instituted in respect of the substance.

Safety and Occupational Health Surveys (Section 91A)

1. The Chief Inspector, or the Director General of Factory Advice Service and Labour Institutes, or the Director General of Health Services, to the Government of India, or such other officer as may be authorised in this behalf by the State Government or the Chief Inspector or the Director General of Factory Advice Service and Labour Institutes or the Director General of Health Services may, at any time during the normal working hours of a factory, or at any other time as is found by him to be necessary, after giving notice in writing to the occupier or manager of the factory or any other person who for the time being purports to be in charge of the factory, undertake safety and occupational health surveys and such occupier or manager or other person shall afford all facilities for such survey, including facilities for the examination and testing of plant and machinery and collection of samples and other data relevant to the survey.
2. For the purpose of facilitating surveys under sub-section (1) every worker shall, if so required by the person conducting the survey, present himself to undergo such medical examination as may be considered necessary by such person and furnish all information in his possession and relevant to the survey.
3. Any time spent by a worker for undergoing medical examination or furnishing information under sub-section (2) shall, for the purpose of calculating wages and extra wages for overtime work, be deemed to be time during which such worker worked in the factory.

Explanation For the purposes of this section, the report, if any, submitted to the State Government by the person conducting the survey under sub-section (1) shall be deemed to be a report submitted by an Inspector under this Act.

CHAPTER X: PENALTIES AND PROCEDURE

General Penalty for Offences (Section 92)

Save as is otherwise expressly provided in this Act and subject to the provisions of Section 93, if in, or in respect of, any factory there is any contravention of any of the provisions of this Act or of any rules made thereunder or of any order in writing given thereunder, the occupier and manager of the factory shall each be guilty of an offence and punishable with imprisonment for a term which may extend to 2 years or with fine which may extend to ₹1 lakh or with both, and if the contravention is continued after conviction, with a further fine which may extend to ₹1,000 for each day on which the contravention is so continued:

Provided that where contravention of any of the provisions of Chapter IV or any rule made thereunder Section 87 has resulted in an accident causing death or serious bodily injury, the fine shall not be less than ₹25,000 in the case of an accident causing death, and ₹5000 in the case of an accident causing serious bodily injury.

Explanation In this section and in Section 94 "serious bodily injury" means an injury which involves, or in all probability will involve, the permanent loss of the use of, or permanent injury to, any limb or the permanent loss of, or injury to, sight or hearing, or the fracture of any bone, but shall not include, the fracture of bone or joint (not being fracture of more than 1 bone or joint) of any phalanges of the hand or foot.

Spotlight

Serious bodily injury does not include the fracture of bone or joint (not being fracture of more than 1 bone or joint) of any phalanges of the hand or foot.

Liability of Owner of Premises in Certain Circumstances (Section 93)

1. Where in any premises separate buildings are leased to different occupiers for use as separate factories, the owner of the premises shall be responsible for the provision and maintenance of common facilities and services, such as approach roads, drainage, water supply, lighting and sanitation.
2. The Chief Inspector shall have, subject to the control of the State Government, power to issue orders to the owner of the premises in respect of the carrying out of the provisions of sub-section (1).
3. Where in any premises, independent or self-contained, floors or flats are leased to different occupiers for use as separate factories, the owner of the premises shall be liable as if he were the occupier or manager of a factory, for any contravention of the provisions of this Act in respect of:
   (a) latrines, urinals and washing facilities in so far as the maintenance of the common supply of water for these purposes is concerned;
   (b) fencing of machinery and plant belonging to the owner and not specifically entrusted to the custody or use of an occupier;
   (c) safe means of access to the floors or flats and maintenance and cleanliness of staircases and common passages;
   (d) precautions in case of fire;
   (e) maintenance of hoists and lifts; and
   (f) maintenance of any other common facilities provided in the premises.
4. The Chief Inspector shall have, subject to the control of the State Government, power to issue orders to the owner of the premises in respect of the carrying out the provisions of sub-section (3).
5. The provisions of sub-section (3) relating to the liability of the owner shall apply where in any premises independent rooms with common latrines, urinals and washing facilities are leased to different occupiers for use as separate factories:

   Provided that the owner shall be responsible also for complying with the requirements relating to the provision and maintenance of latrines urinals and washing facilities.
6. The Chief Inspector shall have, subject to the control of the State Government, the power to issue orders to the owner of the premises referred to in sub-section (5) in respect of the carrying out of the provisions of Section 46 or Section 48.

7. Where in any premises portions of a room or a shed are leased to different occupiers for use as separate factories, the owner of the premises shall be liable for any contravention of the provisions of:
   (i) Chapter III, except sections 14 and 15;
   (ii) Chapter IV, except sections 22, 23, 27, 34, 35 and 36:
   Provided that in respect of the provisions of sections 21, 24 and 32 the owner's liability shall be only in so far as such provisions relate to things under his control:
   Provided further that the occupier shall be responsible for complying with the provisions of Chapter IV in respect of plant and machinery belonging to or supplied by him;
   (iii) Section 42.
8. The Chief Inspector shall have, subject to the control of the State Government, power to issue orders to the owner of the premises in respect of the carrying out the provisions of sub-section (7).
9. In respect of sub-sections (5) and (7), while computing for the purposes of any of the provisions of this Act the total number of workers employed, the whole of the premises shall be deemed to be a single factory.

Enhanced Penalty after Previous Conviction (Section 94)

1. If any person who has been convicted of any offence punishable under Section 92 is again guilty of an offence involving a contravention of the same provision, he shall be punishable on a subsequent conviction with imprisonment for a term which may extend to 3 years or with fine which shall not be less than ₹10,000 but which may extend to ₹2 lakh or with both:
   Provided that the court may, for any adequate and special reasons to be mentioned in the judgment, impose a fine of less than ₹10,000.
   Provided further that where contravention of any of the provisions of Chapter IV or any rule made thereunder or under Section 87 has resulted in an accident causing death or serious bodily injury, the fine shall not be less than ₹35,000 in the case of an accident causing death and ₹10,000 in the case of an accident causing serious bodily injury.
2. For the purposes of sub-section (1), no cognizance shall be taken of any conviction made more than 2 years before the commission of the offence for which the person is subsequently being convicted.

Penalty for Obstructing Inspector (Section 95)

Whoever wilfully obstructs an Inspector in the exercise of any power conferred on him by or under this Act, or fails to produce on demand by an Inspector any registers or other documents in his custody kept in pursuance of this Act or of any rules made thereunder, or conceals or prevents any worker in a factory from appearing before, or being examined by, an Inspector, shall be punishable with imprisonment for a term which may extend to 6 months or with fine which may extend to ₹10,000 or with both.

Penalty for Wrongfully Disclosing Results of Analysis under Section 91 (Section 96)

Whoever, except in so far as it may be necessary for the purposes of a prosecution for any offence punishable under this Act, publishes or discloses to any person the results of an analysis made under

Section 91, shall be punishable with imprisonment for a term which may extend to 6 months or with fine which may extend to ₹10,000 or with both.

Penalty for Contravention of the Provisions of Sections 41B, 41C and 41H (Section 96A)

1. Whoever fails to comply with or contravenes any of the provisions of sections 41B, 41C or 41H or the rules made thereunder, shall, in respect of such failure or contravention, be punishable with imprisonment for a term which may extend to 7 years and with fine which may extend to ₹2 lakh, and in case the failure or contravention continues, with additional fine which may extend to ₹5,000 for every day during which such failure or contravention continues after the conviction for the first such failure or contravention.
2. If the failure or contravention referred to in sub-section (1) continues beyond a period of 1 year after the date of conviction, the offender shall be punishable with imprisonment for a term which may extend to 10 years.

Offences by Workers (Section 97)

1. Subject to the provisions of Section 111, if any worker employed in a factory contravenes any provision of this Act or any rules or orders made thereunder, imposing any duty or liability on workers, he shall be punishable with fine which may extend to ₹500.
2. Where a worker is convicted of an offence punishable under sub-section (1), the occupier or manager of the factory shall not be deemed to be guilty of an offence in respect of that contravention, unless it is proved that he failed to take all reasonable measures for its prevention.

Penalty for Using False Certificate of Fitness (Section 98)

Whoever knowingly uses or attempts to use, as a certificate of fitness granted to himself under Section 70, a certificate granted to another person under that section, or who, having procured such a certificate, knowingly allows it to be used, or an attempt to use it to be made, by another person, shall be punishable with imprisonment for a term which may extend to 2 months or with fine which may extend to ₹1,000 or with both.

Spotlight

Fine for permitting double employment of child is up to ₹1,000, as per Section 99.

Penalty for Permitting Double Employment of Child (Section 99)

If a child works in a factory on any day on which he has already been working in another factory, the parent or guardian of the child or the person having custody of or control over him or obtaining any direct benefit from his wages, shall be punishable with fine which may extend to ₹1,000 unless it appears to the Court that the child so worked without the consent or connivance of such parent, guardian or person.

Detention of Occupier in Certain Cases (Section 100) Repealed by the Factories (Amendment) Act, 1987.

Exemption of Occupier or Manager from Liability in Certain Cases (Section 101)

Where the occupier or manager of a factory is charged with an offence punishable under this Act, he shall be entitled, upon complaint duly made by him and on giving to the prosecutor not less than 3 clear days' notice in writing of his intention so to do, to have any other person whom he charges as the actual offender brought before the Court at the time appointed for hearing the charge; and if, after the commission of the offence has been proved, the occupier or manager of the factory, as the case may be, proves to the satisfaction of the Court:

(a) that he has used due diligence to enforce the execution of this Act, and
(b) that the said other person committed the offence in question without his knowledge, consent or connivance,

that other person shall be convicted of the offence and shall be liable to the like punishment as if he were the occupier or manager of the factory, and the occupier or manager, as the case may be, shall be discharged from any liability under this Act in respect of such offence:

Provided that in seeking to prove as aforesaid, the occupier or manager of the factory, as the case may be, may be examined on oath, and his evidence and that of any witness whom he calls in his support shall be subject to cross-examination on behalf of the person he charges as the actual offender and by the prosecutor:

Provided further that, if the person charged as the actual offender by the occupier or manager cannot be brought before the Court at the time appointed for hearing the charge, the Court shall adjourn the hearing from time to time for a period not exceeding 3 months and if by the end of the said period the person charged as the actual offender cannot still be brought before the Court, the Court shall proceed to hear the charge against the occupier or manager and shall, if the offence be proved, convict the occupier or manager.

Power of Court to Make Orders (Section 102)

1. Where the occupier or manager of a factory is convicted of an offence punishable under this Act the Court may, in addition to awarding any punishment, by order in writing require him, within a period specified in the order (which the Court may, if it thinks fit and on application in such behalf, from time to time extend) to take such measures as may be so specified for remedying the matters in respect of which the offence was committed.
2. Where an order is made under sub-section (1), the occupier or manager of the factory, as the case may be, shall not be liable under this Act in respect of the continuation of the offence during the period or extended period, if any, allowed by the Court, but if, on the expiry of such period or extended period, as the case may be, the order of the Court has not been fully complied with, the occupier or manager, as the case may be, shall be deemed to have committed a further offence, and may be sentenced therefor by the Court to undergo imprisonment for a term which may extend to 6 months or to pay a fine which may extend to ₹1,000 for every day after such expiry on which the order has not been complied with, or both to undergo such imprisonment and to pay such fine, as aforesaid.

CASE CORNER

In *State of Gujarat vs. Sudhir Mehta* [(1998) 1 GLR 560], the Factory Inspector, Adipur-Kutch, visited the factory of Milton Pvt. Ltd. at Gandhidham and noticed that there were 1,083 women workers working therein, out of whom some had children below the age of 6 years. According to the Factory Inspector, Milton Pvt. Ltd. had contravened the provisions contained in sections 48(1) and 102(2) of the Factories Act, 1948 (for short "the Act") as the women workers were not provided with a suitable room, viz. creches (*Ghodiaghar*) for the use of their children under the age of 6 years. Further according to the Factory

Inspector, the room in the said factory which was shown as *Ghodiaghar* was stored with cupboard, cotton waste, etc. and it could not be used for the purpose it was meant for.

The Court observed that women workers are compelled to carry their young children along with them far away from their respective homes at the factory where they are working. In absence of *Ghodiaghar*, these children were either left in open or at some unsuitable places exposed to all sorts of noises, smokes, air pollution, heat, moving machineries, dust and sometimes even to the leakages of harmful gases. "It is good that the Parliament has made a provision for providing crèches; even otherwise, on humanitarian ground also even if there was no such Legislative provision, it is indeed the duty of the factory owners to take care of the minor children of their women workers." Thus, not to provide *Ghodiaghar* is an offence of very grave and serious nature. Further, breach of the relevant provisions of the Act cannot be considered to be trivial, more particularly when the offence alleged is a continuing one in view of the provisions contained in sub-sections (1) and (2) of Section 102 of the Act not complied with.

(Adapted from: www.indiankanoon.org/doc/1409680/ accessed on 27/12/2013.)

Presumption as to Employment (Section 103)

If a person is found in a factory at any time, except during intervals for meals or rest, when work is going on or the machinery is in motion, he shall until the contrary is proved, be deemed for the purposes of this Act and the rules made thereunder to have been at that time employed in the factory.

Onus as to Age (Section 104)

1. When any act or omission would, if a person were under a certain age, be an offence punishable under this Act, and such person is in the opinion of the Court *prima facie* under such age, the burden shall be on the accused to prove that such person is not under such age.
2. A declaration in writing by a certifying surgeon relating to a worker that he has personally examined him and believes him to be under the age stated in such declaration shall, for the purposes of this Act and the rules made thereunder, be admissible as evidence of the age of that worker.

Onus of Proving Limits of What is Practicable, etc. (Section 104A)

In any proceeding for an offence for the contravention of any provision of this Act of rules made thereunder consisting of a failure to comply with a duty or requirement to do something, it shall be for the person who is alleged to have failed to comply with such duty or requirement, to prove that it was not reasonably practicable or, as the case may be, all practicable measures were taken to satisfy the duty or requirement.

Cognizance of Offences (Section 105)

1. No Court shall take cognizance of any offence under this Act except on complaint by, or with the previous sanction in writing of, an Inspector.
2. No Court below that of a Presidency Magistrate or of a Magistrate of the first class shall try any offence punishable under this Act.

Limitation of Prosecutions (Section 106)

No Court shall take cognizance of any offence punishable under this Act unless complaint thereof made within 3 months of the date on which the alleged commission of the offence came to the knowledge of an Inspector:

Provided that where the offence consists of disobeying a written order made by an Inspector, complaint thereof may be made within 6 months of the date on which the offence is alleged to have been committed.

Spotlight

Where an offence consists of disobeying a written order made by an Inspector, Section 106 provides that complaint thereof may be made within 6 months of the date on which the offence is alleged to have been committed.

Explanation For the purposes of this section:

(a) in the case of continuing offence, the period of limitation shall be computed with reference to every point of time during which the offence continues;

(b) where for the performance of any act time is granted or extended on an application made by the occupier or manager of a factory, the period of limitation shall be computed from the date on which the time so granted or extended expired.

Jurisdiction of a Court for Entertaining Proceedings, etc., for Offence (Section 106A)

For the purposes of conferring jurisdiction on any court in relation to an offence under this Act or the rules made thereunder in connection with the operation of any plant, the place where the plant is for the time being situate shall be deemed to be the place where such offence has been committed.

CHAPTER XI: SUPPLEMENTAL

Appeals (Section 107)

1. The manager of a factory on whom an order in writing by an Inspector has been served under the provisions or this Act or the occupier of the factory may, within 30 days of the service of the order, appeal against it to the prescribed authority, and such authority may, subject to rules made in this behalf by the State Government, confirm, modify or reverse the order.
2. Subject to rules made in this behalf by the State Government (which may prescribe classes of appeals which shall not be heard with the aid of assessors), the appellate authority may, or if so required in the petition of appeal shall, hear the appeal with the aid of assessors, one of whom shall be appointed by the appellate authority and the other by such body representing the industry concerned as may be prescribed:

   Provided that if no assessor is appointed by such body before the time fixed for hearing the appeal, or if the assessor so appointed fails to attend the hearing at such time, the appellate authority may, unless satisfied that the failure to attend is due to sufficient cause, proceed to hear the appeal without the aid of such assessor or, if it thinks fit, without the aid of any assessor.
3. Subject to such rules as the State Government may make in this behalf and subject to such conditions as to partial compliance or the adoption of temporary measures as the appellate authority may in any case think fit to impose, the appellate authority may, if it thinks fit, suspend the order appealed against pending the decision of the appeal.

Display of Notices (Section 108)

1. In addition to the notices required to be displayed in any factory by or under this Act, there shall be displayed in every factory a notice containing such abstracts of this Act and of the rules made thereunder as may be prescribed and also the name and address of the Inspector and the certifying surgeon.
2. All notices required by or under this Act to be displayed in a factory shall be in English and in a language understood by the majority of the workers in the factory, and shall be displayed at some conspicuous and convenient place at or near the main entrance to the factory, and shall be maintained in a clean and legible condition.
3. The Chief Inspector may, by order in writing served on the manager of any factory, require that there shall be displayed in the factory any other notice or poster relating to the health, safety or welfare of the workers in the factory.

Service of Notices (Section 109)

The State Government may make rules prescribing the manner of the service of orders under this Act on owners, occupiers or managers of factories.

Returns (Section 110)

The State Government may make rules requiring owners, occupiers or mangers of factories to submit such returns, occasional or periodical, as may in its opinion be required for the purposes of this Act.

Obligations of Workers (Section 111)

1. No worker in a factory:
   (a) shall wilfully interfere with or misuse any appliance, convenience or other thing provided in a factory for the purposes of securing the health, safety or welfare of the workers therein;
   (b) shall wilfully and without reasonable cause do anything likely to endanger himself or others; and
   (c) shall wilfully neglect to make use of any appliance or other thing provided in the factory for the purposes of securing the health of safety of the workers therein.
2. If any worker employed in a factory contravenes any of the provisions of this section or of any rule or order made thereunder, he shall be punishable with imprisonment for a term which may extend to 3 months, or with fine which may extend to ₹100, or with both.

Right or Workers, etc. (Section 111A)

Every worker shall have the right to:

(i) obtain from the occupier, information relating to workers' health and safety at work,

(ii) get trained within the factory wherever possible, or, to get himself sponsored by the occupier for getting trained at a training centre or institute, duly approved by the Chief Inspector, where training is imparted for workers' health and safety at work.

(iii) represent to the Inspector directly or through his representative in the matter of inadequate provision for protection of his health or safety in the factory.

General Power to Make Rules (Section 112)

The State Government may make rules providing for any matter which, under any of the provisions of this Act, is to be or may be prescribed or which may be considered expedient in order to give effect to the purposes of this Act.

Powers of Centre to Give Directions (Section 113)

The Central Government may give directions to a State Government as to the carrying into execution of the provisions of this Act.

No Charge for Facilities and Conveniences (Section 114)

Subject to the provisions of Section 46 no fee or charge shall be realised from any worker in respect of any arrangements or facilities to be provided, or any equipments or appliances to be supplied by the occupier under the provisions of this Act.

Publication of Rules (Section 115)

1. All rules made under this Act shall be published in the Official Gazette, and shall be subject to the condition of previous publication; and the date to be specified under clause (3) of Section 23 of the General Clauses Act, 1897, shall be not less than 45 days from the date on which the draft of the proposed rules was published.
2. Every rule made by the State Government under this Act shall be laid, as soon as may be after it is made, before the State Legislature.

Application of Act to Government Factories (Section 116)

Unless otherwise provided this Act shall apply to factories belonging to the Central or any State Government.

Protection to Persons Acting under this Act (Section 117)

No suit, prosecution or other legal proceeding shall lie against any person for anything which is in good faith done or intended to be done under this Act.

Restrictions on Disclosure of Information (Section 118)

1. No Inspector shall, while in service or after leaving the service, disclose otherwise than in connection with the execution, or for the purposes, of this Act any information relating to any manufacturing or commercial business or any working process which may come to his knowledge in the course of his official duties.
2. Nothing in sub-section (1) shall apply to any disclosure of information made with the previous consent in writing of the owner of such business or process or for the purposes of any legal proceeding (including arbitration) pursuant to this Act or of any criminal proceeding which may be taken, whether pursuant to this Act or otherwise, or for the purposes of any report of such proceedings as aforesaid.

3. If any Inspector contravenes the provisions of sub-section (1) he shall be punishable with imprisonment for a term which may extend to 6 months, or with fine which may extend to ₹1,000, or with both.

Restriction on Disclosure of Information (Section 118A)

1. Every Inspector shall treat as confidential the source of any complaint brought to his notice on the breach of any provision of this Act.
2. No inspector shall, which making an inspection under this Act, disclose to the occupier, manager or his representative that the inspection is made in pursuance of the receipt of complaint:

   Provided that nothing in this sub-section shall apply to any case in which the person who has made the complaint has consented to disclose his name.

Act to Have Effect Notwithstanding Anything Contained in Act 37 of 1970 (Section 119)

The provisions of this Act shall have effect notwithstanding anything inconsistent therewith contained in the Contract Labour (Regulation and Abolition) Act, 1970, or any other law for the time being in force.

CASE CORNER

The Court has pointed out in *Government of Andhra Pradesh and Others vs. Bhadrachalam Paper Boards Ltd. and Andhra Steel Corporation* [(1991) ILLJ 115AP] that the words within brackets, namely, "including a contractor" in the definition of worker in Section 2(l) of the Factories Act, 1948 (or, "the Act") were added by the Factories (Amendment) Act, 1976. The effect of the said amendment is that even a worker engaged through a contractor and working in a factory would come under the definition of worker for the purpose of the Act. All the beneficial provisions in the Act shall apply to such workers as well. This was done evidently to ensure that the benefits of the several regulatory and welfare measures (e.g., canteen as per Section 46) provided by the Act shall extend even to contract labour.

The Factories Act, 1948 contains far more elaborate and extensive provisions made in the interest of health, safety and well-being of workers than the provisions contained in the Contract Labour (Regulation and Abolition) Act, 1970 and the Rules made thereunder. Contract labour working in most of the factories would be governed both by the Acts. Section 119 of the Factories Act, reintroduced by the aforesaid Factories (Amendment) Act, 1976, was enacted with a view not to deprive contract labour of the better facilities provided by the Factories Act.

Interestingly, there is no provision in the Factories Act for the abolition of contract labour in any factory or other establishment to which the Act applies. This aspect is dealt with only by Section 10 of the Contract Labour Act. In such a situation, it cannot be concluded that the Factories Act contains any provision inconsistent with Section 10 of the Contract Labour Act. If so, the power of the appropriate Government under Section 10 is not affected or curtailed in any manner by Section 119 or by any other provision in the Factories Act. In the absence of any inconsistency both the Acts will apply and continue to apply to a factory or establishment to which they apply. It would be evident that several factories governed by the Factories Act would also be "establishments" for the purpose of the Contract Labour

Act, the result being both the Acts will be attracted. Section 119 of the Factories Act gives an overriding effect to the provisions of the Factories Act, notwithstanding anything inconsistent therewith contained in the Contract Labour Act. However this section does not say that the Contract Labour Act shall not apply to the factories to which the Factories Act applies. Both the enactments contain provisions in the interests of health, safety and well-being of workers. Only to the extent of inconsistency between the provisions of both enactments it is provided that the Factories Act shall have primacy.

(Adapted from: www.indiankanoon.org/doc/770619/ accessed on 25/12/2013.)

Repeal and Savings (Section 120)

The enactments set out in the Table appended to this section are hereby repealed:

Provided that anything done under the said enactments which could have been done under this Act if it had then been in force shall be deemed to have been done under this Act.

ADMINISTRATION OF THE ACT

The Factories Act, 1948 is administered by the Ministry of Labour & Employment, Government of India through its Directorate General Factory Advice Service and Labour Institutes (DGFASLI) and by the State Governments through their factory inspectorates. DGFASLI was set up with the objective of advising the Central and State Governments on administration of the Factories Act and coordinating factory inspection services in States. It serves as a technical arm to assist the Ministry in formulating national policies on occupational safety and health in factories and docks. DGFASLI also advises factories on various problems concerning safety, health, efficiency and well-being of workers. We have talked about DGFASLI in Chapter 13.

SUMMARY

- The primary objective of the Factories Act, 1948 is to protect workers employed in factories against industrial and occupational hazards. For this purpose it imposes upon occupiers certain obligations to secure employment for workers in conditions conducive to their health and safety.
- Factory, as per Section 2(m), means any premises including the precincts thereof, whereon 10 or more workers are working, or were working on any day of the preceding 12 months, and in any part of which a manufacturing process is being carried on with the aid of power, or is ordinarily so carried on.
- As per Section 7A, every occupier shall ensure, so far as is reasonably practicable, the health, safety and welfare of all workers while they are at work in the factory.
- Chapter II lays down various provisions related to inspecting staff, namely, Inspectors (Section 8, powers of Inspectors (Section 9) and certifying surgeons (Section 10).
- Chapter III has provisions related to health, including cleanliness (Section 11), disposal of wastes and effluents (Section 12), ventilation and temperature (Section 13), dust and fume (Section 14), artificial humidification (Section 15), overcrowding (Section 16), lighting (Section 17), drinking water (Section 18), latrines and urinals (Section 19) and spittoons (Section 20).

- Safety provisions in Chapter IV include fencing of machinery (Section 21), work on or near machinery in motion (Section 22), employment of young persons on dangerous machines (Section 23), striking gear and devices for cutting off power (Section 24), self-acting machines (Section 25), casing of new machinery (Section 26), prohibition of employment of women and children near cotton-openers (Section 27), hoists and lifts (Section 28), lifting machines, chains, ropes and lifting tackles (Section 29), revolving machinery (Section 30), pressure plant (Section 31), floors, stairs and means of access (Section 32), pits, sumps, openings in floors, etc. (Section 33), excessive weights (Section 34), protection of eyes (Section 35), precautions against dangerous fumes, gases, etc. (Section 36), precautions regarding the use of portable electric light (Section 36A), explosive or inflammable dust, gas, etc. (Section 37), precautions in case of fire (Section 38), power to require specifications of defective parts or tests of stability (Section 39), safety of buildings and machinery (Section 40), maintenance of buildings (Section 40A), safety officers (Section 40B), and power to make rules to supplement this Chapter (Section 41).
- Hazardous processes are dealt with exclusively in Chapter IVA with provisions relating to constitution of Site Appraisal Committees (Section 41A), compulsory disclosure of information by the occupier (Section 41B), specific responsibility of the occupier in relation to hazardous processes (Section 41C), power of Central Government to appoint Inquiry Committee (Section 41D), emergency standards (Section 41E), permissible limits of exposure of chemical and toxic substances (Section 41F), workers' participation in safety management (Section 41G) and right of workers to warn about imminent danger (Section 41H).
- Welfare provisions in Chapter V include washing facilities (Section 42), facilities for storing and drying clothing (Section 43), facilities for sitting (Section 44), first-aid appliances (Section 45), canteens (Section 46), shelters, rest rooms and lunch rooms (Section 47), crèches (Section 48), welfare officers (Section 49) and power to make rules to supplement this Chapter (Section 50).
- Chapter VI has provisions for working hours of adults weekly hours (Section 51), weekly holidays (Section 52), compensatory holidays (Section 53), daily hours (Section 54), intervals for rest (Section 55), spread over (Section 56), night shifts (Section 57), prohibition of overlapping shifts (Section 58), extra wages for overtime (Section 59), restriction on double employment (Section 60), notice of periods of work for adults (Section 61), register of adult workers (Section 62), hours of work to correspond with notice under Section 61 and register under Section 62 (Section 63), power to make exempting rules (Section 64), power to make exempting orders (Section 65) and further restrictions on employment of women (Section 66).
- Employment of young persons in Chapter VII covers prohibition of employment of young children (Section 67), non-adult workers to carry tokens (Section 68), certificates of fitness (Section 69), effect of certificate of fitness granted to adolescent (Section 70), working hours for children (Section 71), notice of periods of work for children (Section 72), register of child workers (Section 73), hours of work to correspond with notice under Section 72 and register under Section 73 (Section 74), power to require medical examination (Section 75), power to make rules (Section 76) and certain other provisions of law not barred (Section 77).
- Chapter VIII has provisions for annual leave with wages, namely application of Chapter (Section 78), annual leave with wages (Section 79), wages during leave period (Section 80), payment in advance in certain cases (Section 81), mode of recovery of unpaid wages (Section 82), power to make rules (Section 83) and power to exempt factories (Section 84).
- Chapter IX includes special provisions like power to apply the Act to certain premises (Section 85), power to exempt public institutions (Section 86), dangerous operations (Section 87), power to prohibit employment on account of serious hazard (Section 87A), notice of certain accidents

(Section 88), notice of certain dangerous occurrences (Section 88A), notice of certain diseases (Section 89), power to direct enquiry into cases of accident or disease (Section 90), power to take samples (Section 91) and safety and occupational health surveys (Section 91A).

- Penalties and procedure are covered in Chapter X, including general penalty for offences (Section 92), liability of owner of premises in certain circumstances (Section 93), enhanced penalty after previous conviction (Section 94), penalty for obstructing Inspector (Section 95), penalty for wrongfully disclosing results of analysis under Section 91 (Section 96), penalty for contravention of the provisions of sections 41B, 41C and 41H (Section 96A), offences by workers (Section 97), penalty for using false certificate of fitness (Section 98), penalty for permitting double employment of child (Section 99), exemption of occupier or manager from liability in certain cases (Section 101), power of Court to make orders (Section 102), presumption as to employment (Section 103), onus as to age (Section 104), onus of proving limits of what is practicable, etc. (Section 104A), cognizance of offences (Section 105), limitation of prosecutions (Section 106), and jurisdiction of a court for entertaining proceedings, etc., for offence (Section 106A).
- Chapter XI deals with supplemental provisions, including appeals (Section 107), display of notices (Section 108), service of notices (Section 109), returns (Section 110), obligations of workers (Section 111), right of workers, etc. (Section 111A), general power to make rules (Section 112), powers of Centre to give directions (Section 113), no charge for facilities and conveniences (Section 114), publication of rules (Section 115), application of Act to Government factories (Section 116), protection to persons acting under this Act (Section 117), restrictions on disclosure of information (Section 118), restriction on disclosure of information (Section 118A), Act to have effect notwithstanding anything contained in Act 37 of 1970 (Section 119) and repeal and savings (Section 120).
- The Factories Act, 1948 is administered by the Ministry of Labour & Employment through DGFASLI and by the State Governments through their factory inspectorates.

Key Concepts

Occupier
Hazardous process
Artificial humidification
Health
Safety
Welfare
Working hours
Canteens
Chief Inspector
Site Appraisal Committee
Young persons
Annual leave

Bibliography

www.business.gov.in/legal_aspects/factories_act.php

Review Questions

Objective Type Questions

I. State True or False

(i) A factory must have at least 1,000 workers for welfare officers to be employed.
(ii) The periods of work for an adult worker shall not spread over more than 10.5 hours in any day.

(iii) An adult worker allowed leave for not less than 4 days shall be paid the wages due for the period of the leave allowed before his leave begins.
(iv) Every hoist and lift shall be thoroughly examined by a competent person at least once in every period of 12 months.
(v) Notification by the State Government to exempt any factory in any case of public emergency shall not be for a period exceeding 6 months at a time.

Answers: (i) False, (ii) True, (iii) True, (iv) False, (v) False

II. Fill in the Blanks

(i) No point of drinking water shall be situated within ___ meters of any washing place.
(ii) Periods of work for adult workers must not exceed _____ hours a day.
(iii) A certificate of fitness granted or renewed shall be valid only for a period of ______ months from the date thereof.
(iv) Contravention of any of the provisions of this Act shall make the occupier punishable with imprisonment up to ___ years.
(v) Adult consumption unit includes consumption unit of a male above ______ years of age.

Answers: (i) 6, (ii) 5, (iii) 12, (iv) 2, (v) 14

Discussion Questions

1. What are the rights conferred to workers on various issues as per the Factories Act, 1948?
2. What are the general duties of the occupier of a factory?
3. Discuss the provision for canteen facility according to this Act.
4. Describe the various provisions related to employment of women and children in factories.
5. Explain the concept of weekly and compensatory holidays.
6. How can you elucidate "dangerous operations" as defined by the Act?
7. Discuss the concept of annual leave with wages in details.
8. Explain the overriding role of the Factories Act, 1948 in context of contract labour.
9. What is a Site Appraisal Committee? What are the functions of such a committee? Discuss its structure.
10. What are certificates of fitness? Discuss provisions related to such certificates.

CASE STUDY-I

The respondent in this case is the manager of Jubilee Mills, a factory as defined by Section 2(m)(i) of the Factories Act, 1948 (hereinafter, "the Act"). He was accused that having failed to securely fence the shaft and pulleys which formed part of the transmission machinery of the carding department, he had contravened the provisions of the Act and hence committed an offence punishable under the Act.

In the last week of March 1957, some carding machines in the carding department of the said factory were being shifted to some other place when the machinery was not in motion. The belt of the carding machine No. 108 was lying idle on the hanger which was over 12′ above the ground level.

The pulley which was to be shifted was also 12′ above the ground level. Below the hanger there was a steam pipe which was about 7′3″ from the ground level. Instructions had been issued to do the work of shifting only during the recess when the shaft and pulleys were not in motion. About 2 or 3 minutes before the recess on the day of the accident, 1 workman placed a ladder against the steam pipe, climbed the ladder and sat on the steam pipe when the shaft and pulleys were in motion. In breach of the said instructions he stood up on the steam pipe and attempted to take the belt which was lying idle on the hanger on the other side of the shaft and the pulley, and in doing so he was entangled in the belt and the moving shaft. The workman was taken out from the shaft by cutting the belt and taken to the hospital, where he died within half an hour.

It was not disputed, nor can it be disputed, that the shaft and the pulleys formed part of "the transmission machinery". The charge against the accused was that he had failed to securely fence the shaft and the pulleys. The appellant contended that the safety aimed at, whether by fencing or by position or by construction, is absolute safety and that the shaft and the pulleys in this case where not, by their position, absolutely safe to every person employed in the factory. The respondent pleaded not guilty and his defence was that the said shaft and the pulleys did not require being fenced because they were in such a position as to be safe to every person employed in the factory as they would be if they were securely fenced. The respondent also stated that on several occasions when the belts would go out of position and they had to be re-adjusted or mounted, that at the time of mounting, the guards would have to be removed and re-fitted, involving great loss of time and that the said activities would naturally hamper production and keep the machinery idle. It is also not disputed on behalf of the respondent that the safety provided for in the Act is absolute safety. What is contended is that whether the shaft and pulleys were safe by construction, and if safety, though absolute, can be only against foreseeable risks and dangers and not otherwise.

(Adapted from: State vs. L.C. Patel [(1959) 61 BOMLR 1021] www.indiankanoon.org/doc/351357/ accessed on 28/12/2013.)

Review Questions

1. Do you think that the respondent is guilty of the offence with which he has been charged?
2. Were the shaft and pulleys safe by construction? Was there in any foreseeable risk in the present case?
3. Which all sections of the Factories Act, 1948 are relevant in this case?

CASE STUDY-II

This case is on the basis of a writ petition filed by the VST Industries Canteen Workers' Union, represented by its Secretary, seeking a mandamus directing the first respondent to treat the members of the petitioner-Union, who are the employees of the canteen established under Section 46 of the Factories Act, 1948 (or, the Act) by the first respondent (i.e., VST Company Ltd.) as the employees of the first respondent-company. The petition also seeks a consequential direction to tender all monetary and other benefits accrued and acquired by treating them as such.

It is stated that VST Company Ltd. employs nearly 2,050 persons excluding the canteen staff for manufacturing cigarettes. In fulfillment of the requirement under Act, the first respondent had also established a canteen and is maintaining it within the factory premises. The first respondent had been managing the canteen up to the year 1982, after which it introduced contract system for maintaining the canteen so established. It is stated that the workmen employed by the first respondent for maintaining the canteen from 1937 till 1982 are adjusted in various departments by the first respondent. The respondent has 5 other associate units which also have canteens established and maintained by regular staff and they are all given all benefits excepting the members of the petitioner-Union working in VST Company Ltd. at Hyderabad. Presently the canteen is run by Blue Star Enterprises. It is stated that the management of the canteen has been entrusted to contractors from time to time. The personnel working in the canteen are retained by all these contractors. They have been paid salaries through these contractors and the same is also counter-signed by the nominee of the principal employer as required under the Act. These workmen have been tendered Employees' State Insurance and Employees' Provident Fund benefits. It is further stated that contractors have not issued any appointment orders to the members of the petitioner-Union, who have also been issued identity cards by the Welfare Officer of VST. Such identity cards are renewable from year to year.

It is further stated that the first respondent has provided building along with furniture, utensils, gas, electricity, water supply and other cutlery for the canteen. The contractor is only instrumental in preparing the food and serving it to the employees. The rates of such items are also prescribed by the management. In this perspective it is stated that the contractor has no role to play and it is only the first respondent which runs the canteen in fulfillment of the requirement contemplated under Section 46 of the Act. It is therefore contended that the first respondent shall treat the members of the petitioner-Union as its employees and pay them regular salaries and other benefits as are given to the other regular employees.

(Adapted from: VST Industries Canteen Workers' Union vs. Vazir Sultan Tobacco Co. Ltd. and Another [(1998) IIILLJ 450 AP] www.indiankanoon.org/doc/56008/ accessed on 25/12/2013.)

Review Questions

1. The first respondent has stated that the canteen workers are not the employees of the management as they are only appointed by the contractor and that the salaries are also paid by Blue Star Enterprises. Do you think that the first respondent can be held to be the employer for the members of the petitioner-Union?
2. On what grounds can the contractor evade the responsibility of running the canteen?

15

The Industrial Disputes Act, 1947

An Act to make provision for the investigation and settlement of industrial disputes, and for certain other purposes.

Desired Knowledge Competencies

- To portray the evolution of the Industrial Disputes Act, 1947.
- To comprehend the various definitions given under the Act.
- To discuss relevant concepts like authorities under the Act and their procedures and powers, reference of disputes to such authorities, etc.

INTRODUCTION

Prior to the enactment of the Industrial Disputes Act as a Central legislation for settlement of industrial disputes in the year 1947, industrial disputes were settled as per the provisions of the Trade Disputes Act, 1929. However, several shortcomings were revealed in exercising the various provisions of the 1929 Act. A specific defect was in context of restraints imposed on the rights of strike and lock-out in public utility services, whereas there was no provision to render the proceedings institutable under the Act for the settlement of an industrial dispute, either by reference to a Board of Conciliation or to a Court of Inquiry, conclusive and binding on the parties to the dispute. This defect along with other flaws required a fresh legislation (*Source: The Industrial Disputes Act, 1947: Bare Act*). Accordingly the Industrial Disputes Bill, 1946 was introduced in the legislature and was referred to the Select Committee.

BACKDROP OF THE INDUSTRIAL DISPUTES ACT, 1947

The Statement of Objects and Reasons of the Act *(Source: The Gazette of India, 1946, Part V, pp. 239-240)* refers to Rule 81A of the Defence of India Rules, which empowers the Central Government to refer industrial disputes to adjudicators and to enforce their awards. The Industrial Disputes Bill embodies the essential principles of Rule 81A, which have proved to be generally acceptable to both employers and workmen, mostly retaining the provisions of the Trade Disputes Act, 1929 intact.

The two institutions for the prevention and settlement of industrial disputes provided for in the Bill are: *Works Committees* and *Industrial Tribunal*. Works Committees were required to be constituted in every industrial establishment employing 100 or more workmen to promote measures for securing amity and good relations between employers and workers. On the other hand, a reference to an Industrial Tribunal would be considered relevant where both the parties to an industrial dispute apply for such reference and also where the appropriate Government considers it expedient so to do. An award of a Tribunal may be enforced either partially or wholly for a period not exceeding a year.

Spotlight

The two institutions for the prevention and settlement of industrial disputes provided for in the Industrial Disputes Bill, 1946 are: *Works Committees and Industrial Tribunal*.

Reorientation of the administration of the conciliation machinery provided in the Trade Disputes Act, 1929 was also envisaged in the Industrial Disputes Bill. Conciliation was made compulsory in all disputes in public utility services and optional for other industrial establishments. Time limits were prescribed for conclusion of conciliation proceedings with the objective of expediting these proceedings. Another new feature of the Bill was prohibition of strikes and lock-outs during the pendency of conciliation and adjudication proceedings of settlements reached in the course of conciliation proceedings. Further, awards of Industrial Tribunals were declared binding by the appropriate Government. The Industrial Disputes Bill also empowered the appropriate Government to declare, if public interest or emergency so requires, by notification in the Official Gazette, any industry to be a public utility service, for such period, if any, as may be specified in the notification.

On the basis of the recommendations of the Select Committee (*Report of the Select Committee, Gazette of India, Part V, pp. 33-35*) amendments were made in the original Bill and the legislature passed the Industrial Disputes Bill, 1947. Though the Bill received the assent of the President and came on the Statute Book on 11th March 1947, the Industrial Disputes Act, 1947 came into force on and from 1st April 1947.

Since enactment, the Industrial Disputes Act, 1947 has been amended several times, as follows:

1. The Indian Independence (Adaptation of Central Acts and Ordinances) Order, 1948
2. The Industrial Disputes (Banking and Insurance Companies) Act, 1949
3. The Adaptation of Laws Order, 1950
4. The Repealing and Amending Act, 1950
5. The Industrial Disputes (Appellate Tribunal) Act, 1950
6. The Industrial Disputes (Amendment and Temporary Provisions) Act, 1951
7. The Industrial (Development and Regulation) Act, 1951
8. The Industrial Disputes (Amendment) Act, 1952
9. The Industrial Disputes (Amendment) Act, 1953
10. The Industrial Disputes (Amendment) Act, 1954
11. The Industrial Disputes (Amendment and Miscellaneous Provisions) Act, 1956
12. The Industrial Disputes (Amendment) Act, 1956
13. The Industrial Disputes (Amendment) Act, 1957
14. The State Bank of India (Subsidiary Banks) Act, 1959
15. The Deposit Insurance Corporation Act, 1961
16. The Agricultural Refinance Corporation Act, 1963
17. The Unit Trust of India Act, 1963
18. The Industrial Development Bank of India Act, 1964
19. The Industrial Disputes (Amendment) Act, 1964
20. The Industrial Disputes (Amendment) Act, 1965

21. The Food Corporations (Amendment) Act, 1968
22. The Banking Companies (Acquisition and Transfer of Undertakings) Act, 1970
23. The Central Labour Laws (Extension to Jammu and Kashmir) Act, 1970
24. The Industrial Disputes (Amendment) Act, 1971
25. The Industrial Disputes (Amendment) Act, 1972
26. The Banking Service Commission Act, 1975
27. The Regional Rural Banks Act, 1976
28. The Industrial Disputes (Amendment) Act, 1976
29. The Banking Companies (Acquisition and Transfer of Undertakings) Act, 1980
30. The Export-Import Bank of India Act, 1981
31. The National Bank for Agriculture and Rural Development Act, 1981
32. The Industrial Disputes (Amendment) Act, 1982
33. The Industrial Disputes (Amendment) Act, 1984
34. The Industrial Reconstruction Bank of India Act, 1984
35. The National Housing Bank Act, 1987
36. The Small Industries Development Bank of India Act, 1989
37. The Industrial Disputes (Amendment) Act, 1996
38. The Industrial Development Bank (Transfer of Undertaking and Repeal) Act, 2003
39. The Industrial Disputes (Amendment) Act, 2010

CHAPTER I: PRELIMINARY

Short Title, Extent and Commencement (Section 1)

1. This Act may be called the Industrial Disputes Act, 1947.
2. It extends to the whole of India.
3. It shall come into force on the 1st day of April, 1947.

Definitions (Section 2)

In this Act, unless there is anything repugnant in the subject or context,

Appropriate Government [Section 2(a)] Appropriate Government means:

(i) in relation to any industrial dispute concerning any industry carried on by or under the authority of the Central Government, or by a railway company or concerning any such controlled industry as may be specified in this behalf by the Central Government or in relation to an industrial dispute concerning a Dock Labour Board established under Section 5A of the Dock Workers (Regulation of Employment) Act, 1948, or the Industrial Finance Corporation of India Ltd. formed and registered under the Companies Act, 1946, or the Employees' State Insurance Corporation established under Section 3 of the Employees' State Insurance Act, 1948, or the Board of Trustees constituted under Section 3A of the Coal Mines Provident Fund and Miscellaneous Provisions Act, 1948, or the Central Board of Trustees and the State Boards of Trustees constituted under Section 5A and Section 5B, respectively, of the Employees' Provident Fund and Miscellaneous Provisions Act, 1952, or the Life Insurance Corporation of India established under Section 3 of the Life Insurance Corporation Act, 1956, or the Oil and Natural Gas Commission Ltd. registered under the Companies Act, 1946, or the Deposit Insurance and Credit Guarantee Corporation established under Section 3 of the Deposit Insurance and Credit Guarantee Corporation Act, 1961, or the Central Warehousing Corporation established under Section 3 of the Warehousing Corporations Act, 1962, or the Unit Trust of India established under Section 3 of the Unit Trust of India Act, 1963, or the Food Corporation of India established under Section 3, or a Board of Management established for 2 or more contiguous States under Section 16 of the Food Corporations Act, 1964, or the Airports Authority of India constituted under Section 3 of the Airports Authority of India Act, 1994, or a Regional Rural Bank established under Section 3 of the Regional Rural Banks Act, 1976, or the Export Credit and Guarantee Corporation Ltd. or the Industrial Reconstruction Bank of India Ltd., the National Housing Bank established under Section 3 of the National Housing Bank Act, 1987, or an air transport service, or a banking or an insurance company, a mine, an oil-field, a Cantonment Board, or a major port, any company in which not less than 51 per cent of the paid-up share capital is held by the Central Government, or any corporation, not being a corporation referred to in this clause, established by or under any law made by Parliament, or the Central public sector undertaking , subsidiary companies set up by the principal undertaking and autonomous bodies owned or controlled by the Central Government, the Central Government, and

(ii) in relation to any other industrial dispute, including the State public sector undertaking, subsidiary companies set up by the principal undertaking and autonomous bodies owned or controlled by the State Government, the State Government:

Provided that in case of a dispute between a contractor and the contract labour employed through the contractor in any industrial establishment where such dispute first arose, the appropriate Government shall be the Central Government or the State Government, as the case may be, which has control over such industrial establishment.

Arbitrator [Section 2(aa)] Arbitrator includes an umpire;

Average pay [Section 2(aaa)] Average pay means the average of the wages payable to a workman:

(i) in the case of monthly paid workman, in 3 complete calendar months,
(ii) in the case of weekly paid workman, in 4 complete weeks,
(iii) in the case of daily paid workman, in the 12 full working days,

preceding the date on which the average pay becomes payable if the workman had worked for 3 complete calendar months, or 4 complete weeks, or 12 full working days, as the case may be, and where such calculation cannot be made, the average pay shall be calculated as the average of the wages payable to a workman during the period he actually worked;

Award [Section 2(b)] Award means an interim or a final determination of any industrial dispute or of any question relating thereto by any Labour Court, Industrial Tribunal or National Industrial Tribunal and includes an arbitration award made under Section 10A;

Banking company [Section 2(bb)] Banking company means a banking company as defined in Section 5 of the Banking Companies Act, 1949, having branches or other establishments in more than 1 State, and includes the Export-Import Bank of India, the Industrial Reconstruction Bank of India, the Small Industries Development Bank of India established under Section 3 of the Small Industries Development Bank of India Act, 1989, the Reserve Bank of India, the State Bank of India, a corresponding new bank constituted under Section 3 of the Banking Companies (Acquisition and Transfer of Undertakings) Act, 1970, a corresponding new bank constituted under Section 3 of the

Banking Companies (Acquisition and Transfer of Undertakings) Act, 1980, and any subsidiary bank, as defined in the State Bank of India (Subsidiary Banks) Act, 1959.

Board [Section 2(c)] Board means a Board of Conciliation constituted under this Act;

Closure [Section 2(cc)] Closure means the permanent closing down of a place of employment or part thereof;

Conciliation officer [Section 2(d)] Conciliation officer means a conciliation officer appointed under this Act;

Conciliation proceeding [Section 2(e)] Conciliation proceeding means any proceeding held by a conciliation officer or Board under this Act;

Controlled industry [Section 2(ee)] Controlled industry means any industry the control of which by the Union has been declared by any Central Act to be expedient in the public interest;

Court [Section 2(f)] Court means a Court of Inquiry constituted under this Act;

Employer [Section 2(g)] Employer means:

(i) in relation to an industry carried on by or under the authority of any department of the Central Government or a State Government, the authority prescribed in this behalf, or where no authority is prescribed, the head of the department;
(ii) in relation to an industry carried on by or on behalf of a local authority, the chief executive officer of that authority;

Executive [Section 2(gg)] Executive, in relation to a trade union, means the body, by whatever name called, to which the management of the affairs of the trade union is entrusted;

Independent [Section 2(i)] A person shall be deemed to be "independent" for the purpose of his appointment as the Chairman, or other member of a Board, Court or Tribunal, if he is unconnected with the industrial dispute referred to such Board, Court or Tribunal or with any industry directly affected by such dispute:

Provided that no person shall cease to be independent by reason only of the fact that he is a shareholder of an incorporated company which is connected with, or likely to be affected by, such industrial dispute; but in such a case, he shall disclose to the appropriate Government the nature and extent of the shares held by him in such company;

Industry [Section 2(j)] Industry means any systematic activity carried on by co-operation between an employer and his workmen (whether such workmen are employed by such employer directly or by or through any agency, including a contractor) for the production, supply or distribution of goods or services with a view to satisfy human wants or wishes (not being wants or wishes which are merely spiritual or religious in nature), whether or not:

Spotlight
Production in an industry satisfies human wants or wishes that are not spiritual or religious in nature.

(i) any capital has been invested for the purpose of carrying on such activity; or
(ii) such activity is carried on with a motive to make any gain or profit, and includes:
  (a) any activity of the Dock Labour Board established under Section 5A of the Dock Workers (Regulation of Employment) Act, 1948;

(b) any activity relating to the promotion of sales or business or both carried on by an establishment, but does not include:

(1) any agricultural operation except where such agricultural operation is carried on in an integrated manner with any other activity (being any such activity as is referred to in the foregoing provisions of this clause) and such other activity is the predominant one.

Explanation For the purposes of this sub-clause, "agricultural operation" does not include any activity carried on in a plantation as defined in clause (f) of Section 2 of the Plantations Labour Act, 1951; or

(2) hospitals or dispensaries; or

(3) educational, scientific, research or training institutions; or

(4) institutions owned or managed by organisations wholly or substantially engaged in any charitable, social or philanthropic service; or

(5) khadi or village industries; or

(6) any activity of the Government relatable to the sovereign functions of the Government including all the activities carried on by the departments of the Central Government dealing with defence research, atomic energy and space; or

(7) any domestic service; or

(8) any activity, being a profession practised by an individual or body or individuals, if the number of persons employed by the individual or body of individuals in relation to such profession is less than 10; or

(9) any activity, being an activity carried on by a co-operative society or a club or any other like body of individuals, if the number of persons employed by the co-operative society, club or other like body of individuals in relation to such activity is less than 10;

CASE CORNER

The triple test laid down in *Bangalore Water Supply and Sewerage Board, etc. vs. R. Rajappa and Others* (AIR 1978 SC 548) by the Supreme Court is considered to govern the whether a particular activity is an "industry" or not. The test has three ingredients, namely, there should be a systematic activity; there should exist an employer and employee relationship; and the activities should render services to the society at large. Following this test, it was held in *Gujarat Forest Producers, Gatherers and Forest Workers Union vs. State of Gujarat* [(2004) 2 GLR 568] that the Forest and Environment Department of the State Government is not an industry under Section 2(j) of the Industrial Disputes Act, 1947 (hereafter the 'Act') and the question whether any of its unit, establishment or undertaking is an industry or not would depend on the nature of the work done by such entity. Further, only when the activity undertaken amounts to an activity for production or distribution of goods and/or services for satisfying the wants and desires of consumers, it can pass the third ingredient of the triple test, that such unit or establishment or undertaking of the Department can be said to be industry, unless falling in the categories removed by constitutional and competently enacted legislative provisions from the scope of the Act.

(Adapted from: www.indiankanoon.org/doc/1175367/ accessed on 30/12/2013.)

It has been held by the Supreme Court in *State of Bombay and Others vs. The Hospital Mazdoor Sabha and Others* [(1960 SCR (2) 866] that the definition of the word "employer" clearly indicates that the legislature intended the application of the Act to activities of the Government which fall within Section 2(j).

(Adapted from: www.indiankanoon.org/doc/621517/ accessed on 31/12/2013.)

Industrial dispute [Section 2(k)] Industrial dispute means any dispute or difference between employers and employers, or between employers and workmen, or between workmen and workmen, which is connected with the employment or non-employment or the terms of employment or with the conditions of labour, of any person;

CASE CORNER

In *Workmen of Dimakuchi Tea Estate vs. The Management of Dimakuchi Tea Estate* [(1958) AIR 353] the appellants, who were the workmen of Dimakuchi Tea Estate, espoused the cause of one Assistant Medical Officer, who had been dismissed unheard with a month's salary in lieu of notice but had accepted such payment and left the garden. The dispute raised was ultimately referred by the Government for adjudication under Section 10 of the Industrial Disputes Act, 1947 (or the 'Act'). Both the Tribunal and the Appellate Industrial Tribunal took the view that as he was not a workman within the meaning of the Act, the dispute was not an industrial dispute as defined by Section 2(k). The question for decision in this appeal was whether a dispute raised by workmen relating to a person who was not a workman could be an industrial dispute defined by Section 2(k), as it stood before the amendments of 1956.

The Apex Court held that even if an industrial dispute has to be one in which workmen are interested, it is not implied that it can only be a dispute concerning workmen and therefore the words "any person" in Section 2(k) must not mean only workmen. Even if it is necessary to constitute an industrial dispute that workmen must have an interest in, the dispute in this case is one in which the appellants have a direct and substantial interest and it is an industrial dispute. "The words in the Act cannot have a different meaning than their natural meaning because otherwise there would be a possibility of the Act being used for a purpose for which it was not meant. The remedy against this possibility is provided in the Act, in that it has given complete freedom to the Government not to refer such a dispute." The Supreme Court came to the conclusion that a dispute concerning a person who is not a workman may be an industrial dispute within Section 2(k).

(Adapted from: www.indiankanoon.org/doc/1198151/ accessed on 31/12/2013.)

Industrial establishment or undertaking [Section 2(ka)] Industrial establishment or undertaking means an establishment or undertaking in which any industry is carried on:

Provided that where several activities are carried on in an establishment or undertaking and only one or some of such activities is or are an industry or industries, then—

(a) if any unit of such establishment or undertaking carrying on any activity, being an industry, is severable from the other unit or units of such establishment or undertaking, such unit shall be deemed to be a separate industrial establishment or undertaking;

(b) if the predominant activity or each of the predominant activities carried on in such establishment, or undertaking, or any thereof is an industry and the other activity or each of the other activities carried on in such establishment, or undertaking, or unit thereof is not severable from and is, for the purpose of carrying on, or aiding the carrying on of, such predominant activity or activities, the entire establishment or undertaking or, as the case may be, unit thereof shall be deemed to be an industrial establishment or undertaking;

Insurance company [Section 2(kk)] Insurance company means an insurance company as defined in Section 2 of the Insurance Act, 1938, having branches or other establishments in more than 1 State;

Khadi [Section 2(kka)] Khadi has the meaning assigned to it in clause (d) of Section 2 of the Khadi and Village Industries Commission Act, 1956;

Labour Court [Section 2(kkb)] Labour Court means a Labour Court constituted under Section 7;

Lay-off [Section 2(kkk)] Lay-off (with its grammatical variations and cognate expressions) means the failure, refusal or inability of an employer on account of shortage of coal, power or raw materials or the accumulation of stocks or the breakdown of machinery or natural calamity or for any other connected reason to give employment to a workman whose name is borne on the muster rolls of his industrial establishment and who has not been retrenched.

Spotlight

Lay-off does not include a workman who has been retrenched.

Explanation Every workman whose name is borne on the muster rolls of the industrial establishment and who presents himself for work at the establishment at the time appointed for the purpose during normal working hours on any day and is not given employment by the employer within 2 hours of his so presenting himself shall be deemed to have been laid-off for that day within the meaning of this clause:

Provided that if the workman, instead of being given employment at the commencement of any shift for any day is asked to present himself for the purpose during the second half of the shift for the day and is given employment then, he shall be deemed to have been laid-off only for one-half of that day:

Provided further that if he is not given any such employment even after so presenting himself, he shall not be deemed to have been laid-off for the second half of the shift for the day and shall be entitled to full basic wages and dearness allowance for that part of the day;

Lock-out [Section 2(l)] Lock-out means the temporary closing of a place of employment, or the suspension of work, or the refusal by an employer to continue to employ any number of persons employed by him;

Spotlight

Lock-out, as given in Section 2(l), is the temporary closing of a place of employment or the suspension of work, or the refusal by an employer to continue to employ any number of persons employed by him.

Major port [Section 2(la)] Major port means a major port as defined in clause (8) of Section 3 of the Indian Ports Act, 1908;

Mine [Section 2(lb)] Mine means a mine as defined in clause (j) of sub-section (1) of Section 2 of the Mines Act, 1952;

National Tribunal [Section 2(ll)] National Tribunal means a National Industrial Tribunal constituted under Section 7B;

Office bearer [Section 2(lll)] Office bearer, in relation to a trade union, includes any member of the executive thereof, but does not include an auditor;

Prescribed [Section 2(m)] Prescribed means prescribed by rules made under this Act;

Public utility service [Section 2(n)] Public utility service means:

(i) any railway service or any transport service for the carriage of passengers or goods by air;

(ia) any service in, or in connection with the working of, any major port or dock;

(ii) any section of an industrial establishment, on the working of which the safety of the establishment or the workmen employed therein depends;

(iii) any postal, telegraph or telephone service;

(iv) any industry which supplies power, light or water to the public;

(v) any system of public conservancy or sanitation;

(vi) any industry specified in the First Schedule which the appropriate Government may, if satisfied that public emergency or public interest so requires, by notification in the Official Gazette, declare to be a public utility service for the purposes of this Act, for such period as may be specified in the notification:

Provided that the period so specified shall not, in the first instance, exceed 6 months but may, by a like notification, be extended from time to time, by any period not exceeding 6 months, at any 1 time if in the opinion of the appropriate Government public emergency or public interest requires such extension;

Railway company [Section 2(o)] Railway company means a railway company as defined in Section 3 of the Indian Railways Act, 1890;

Retrenchment [Section 2(oo)] Retrenchment means the termination by the employer of the service of a workman for any reason whatsoever, otherwise than as a punishment inflicted by way of disciplinary action, but does not include:

(a) voluntary retirement of the workman; or

(b) retirement of the workman on reaching the age of superannuation if the contract of employment between the employer and the workman concerned contains a stipulation in that behalf; or

(bb) termination of the service of the workman as a result of the non-renewal of the contract of employment between the employer and the workman concerned on its expiry or of such contract being terminated under a stipulation in that behalf contained therein; or

(c) termination of the service of a workman on the ground of continued ill-health;

In *Balbir Singh vs. Kurukshetra Central Co-operative Bank Ltd.* [(1990) ILLJ 443 PH] the Court has observed that the intention of the Parliament in enacting clause (bb) in Section 2(oo) of the Industrial Disputes Act, 1947 was to exclude certain categories of workers from the term 'retrenchment', but there is nothing in this clause which a vent to "unscrupulous employers to shunt out workers in the garb of non-renewal of the contract even when the work subsists". Hence this clause as a whole has to be construed strictly in favour of workmen to ensure that the Act is implemented in the letter and spirit. If termination is meant to exploit a worker or to increase the bargaining power of the employer, then it has to be excluded from the ambit of clause (oo) and the definition of the term 'retrenchment' has to be given full meaning. The contractual clause enshrined in clause (bb) cannot be resorted to frustrate the claim of a workman against uncalled for retrenchment or for denying other benefits. It simply cannot enable an employer to resort to the policy of hire and fire and have unguided power to renew or not to renew an employment contract irrespective of the circumstances in which it was entered into or the nature and extent of work for which the worker was employed.

(Adapted from www.indiankanoon.org/doc/894436/ accessed on 30/12/2013.)

CASE CORNER

In *Punjab Land Development and Reclamation Corporation Ltd., Chandigarh vs. Presiding Officer, Labour Court, Chandigarh etc.* (1990 SCR (3) 111), it has been observed that while the employers' contention is that the term "retrenchment", as defined in Section 2(oo) of the Industrial Disputes Act, 1947, or simply the Act, means termination of service of a workman only by way of surplus labour for any reason whatsoever, workmen contend that "retrenchment" means termination of the service of a workman for any reason whatsoever, other than those expressly excluded by the definition in Section 2(oo). The Court held that the definition of retrenchment in the said section means termination by the employer of the service of a workman for any reason whatsoever otherwise than as a punishment inflicted by way of disciplinary action and those expressly excluded by the definition. This is the wider literal interpretation, as distinguished from the narrow, natural and contextual interpretation of the word to mean termination by the employer of the service of a workman as surplus labour for any reason whatsoever.

(Adapted from: www.indiankanoon.org/doc/67608/ accessed on 30/12/2013.)

Settlement [Section 2(p)] Settlement means a settlement arrived at in the course of conciliation proceeding and includes a written agreement between the employer and workmen arrived at otherwise than in the course of conciliation proceeding where such agreement has been signed by the parties thereto in such manner as may be prescribed and a copy thereof has been sent to an officer authorised in this behalf by the appropriate Government and the conciliation officer;

Strike [Section 2(q)] Strike means a cessation of work by a body of persons employed in any industry acting in combination, or a concerted refusal, or a refusal under a common understanding, of any number of persons who are or have been so employed to continue to work or to accept employment;

Spotlight

Strike is a cessation of work by a body of persons employed in any industry acting in combination, as defined by Section 2(q).

Trade union [Section 2(qq)] Trade union means a trade union registered under the Trade Unions Act, 1926;

Tribunal [Section 2(r)] Tribunal means an Industrial Tribunal constituted under Section 7A and includes an Industrial Tribunal constituted before the 10th day of March, 1957, under this Act;

Unfair labour practice [Section 2(ra)] Unfair labour practice means any of the practices specified in the Fifth Schedule;

Village industries [Section (rb)] Village industries has the meaning assigned to it in clause (h) of Section 2 of the Khadi and Village Industries Commission Act, 1956;

Wages [Section 2(rr)] Wages means all remuneration capable of being expressed in terms of money, which would, if the terms of employment, expressed or implied, were fulfilled, be payable to a workman in respect of his employment or of work done in such employment, and includes:

(i) such allowances (including dearness allowance) as the workman is for the time being entitled to;

(ii) the value of any house accommodation, or of supply of light, water, medical attendance or other amenity or of any service or of any concessional supply of foodgrains or other articles;

(iii) any travelling concession;

(iv) any commission payable on the promotion of sales or business or both;

but does not include:

(a) any bonus;

(b) any contribution paid or payable by the employer to any pension fund or provident fund or for the benefit of the workman under any law for the time being in force;

(c) any gratuity payable on the termination of his service;

Workman [Section 2(s)] Workman means any person (including an apprentice) employed in any industry to do any manual, unskilled, skilled, technical, operational, clerical or supervisory work for hire or reward, whether the terms of employment be express or implied, and for the purposes of any proceeding under this Act in relation to an industrial dispute, includes any such person who has been dismissed, discharged or retrenched in connection with, or as a consequence of, that dispute, or whose dismissal, discharge or retrenchment has led to that dispute, but does not include any such person:

Spotlight
Workman includes an apprentice.

(i) who is subject to the Air Force Act, 1950, or the Army Act, 1950, or the Navy Act, 1957; or

(ii) who is employed in the police service or as an officer or other employee of a prison; or

(iii) who is employed mainly in a managerial or administrative capacity; or

(iv) who, being employed in a supervisory capacity, draws wages exceeding ₹10,000 per mensem or exercises, either by the nature of the duties attached to the office or by reason of the powers vested in him, functions mainly of a managerial nature.

A part-time employee is covered by the definition of 'workman' (*Kan Singh vs. District Ayurved Officer and Another* [(2012) LLR 325] (*Labour Law Reporter*, March, 2012, p. 325).

Dismissal, etc., of an Individual Workman to be Deemed to be an Industrial Dispute (Section 2A)

1. Where any employer discharges, dismisses, retrenches or otherwise terminates the services of an individual workman, any dispute or difference between that workman and his employer connected with, or arising out of, such discharge, dismissal, retrenchment or termination shall be deemed to be an industrial dispute notwithstanding that no other workman nor any union of workmen is a party to the dispute.
2. Notwithstanding anything contained in Section 10, any such workman as is specified in sub-section (1) may make an application direct to the Labour Court or Tribunal for adjudication of the dispute referred to therein after the expiry of 45 days from the date he has made the application to the Conciliation Officer of the appropriate Government for conciliation of the dispute, and in receipt of such application the Labour Court or Tribunal shall have powers and jurisdiction to adjudicate upon the dispute, as if it were a dispute referred to it by the appropriate Government in accordance with the provisions of this Act and all the provisions of this Act shall apply in relation to such adjudication as they apply in relation to an industrial dispute referred to it by the appropriate Government.
3. The application referred to in sub-section (2) shall be made to the Labour Court or Tribunal before the expiry of 3 years from the date of discharge, dismissal, retrenchment or otherwise termination of service as specified in sub-section (1).

CHAPTER II: AUTHORITIES UNDER THIS ACT

Works Committee (Section 3)

1. In the case of any industrial establishment in which 100 or more workmen are employed or have been employed on any day in the preceding 12 months, the appropriate Government may by general or special order require the employer to constitute in the prescribed manner a Works Committee consisting of representatives of employers and workmen engaged in the establishment so however that the number of representatives of workmen on the Committee shall not be less than the number of representatives of the employer. The representatives of the workmen shall be chosen in the prescribed manner from among the workmen engaged in the establishment and in consultation with their trade union, if any, registered under the Indian Trade Unions Act, 1926.
2. It shall be the duty of the Works Committee to promote measures for securing and preserving amity and good relations between the employer and workmen and, to that end, to comment upon matters of their common interest or concern and endeavour to compose any material difference of opinion in respect of such matters.

Spotlight
A Works Committee must have equal number of representatives of workmen and employer, as provided in Section 3.

Conciliation Officers (Section 4)

1. The appropriate Government may, by notification in the Official Gazette, appoint such number of persons as it thinks fit to be conciliation officers, charged with the duty of mediating in and promoting the settlement of industrial disputes.
2. A conciliation officer may be appointed for a specified area or for specified industries in a specified area or for 1 or more specified industries and either permanently or for a limited period.

Boards of Conciliation (Section 5)

1. The appropriate Government may as occasion arises by notification in the Official Gazette constitute a Board of Conciliation for promoting the settlement of an industrial dispute.
2. A Board shall consist of a chairman and 2 or 4 other members, as the appropriate Government thinks fit.
3. The chairman shall be an independent person and the other members shall be persons appointed in equal numbers to represent the parties to the dispute and any person appointed to represent a party shall be appointed on the recommendation of that party:

   Provided that, if any party fails to make a recommendation as aforesaid within the prescribed time, the appropriate Government shall appoint such persons as it thinks fit to represent that party.
4. A Board, having the prescribed quorum, may act notwithstanding the absence of the chairman or any of its members or any vacancy in its number:

   Provided that if the appropriate Government notifies the Board that the services of the chairman or of any other member have ceased to be available, the Board shall not act until a new chairman or member, as the case may be, has been appointed.

Spotlight
A Board of Conciliation shall have a chairman and 2 or 4 other members, as per Section 5.

Courts of Inquiry (Section 6)

Spotlight
Section 6 provides for a Court of Inquiry for inquiring into any matter appearing to be connected with or relevant to an industrial dispute.

1. The appropriate Government may as occasion arises by notification in the Official Gazette constitute a Court of Inquiry for inquiring into any matter appearing to be connected with or relevant to an industrial dispute.
2. A Court may consist of 1 independent person or of such number of independent persons as the appropriate Government may think fit and where a Court consists of 2 or more members, 1 of them shall be appointed as the chairman.
3. A Court, having the prescribed quorum, may act notwithstanding the absence of the chairman or any of its members or any vacancy in its number:

   Provided that, if the appropriate Government notifies the Court that the services of the chairman have ceased to be available, the Court shall not act until a new chairman has been appointed.

Labour Courts (Section 7)

Spotlight
A Labour Court, as per Section 7, shall consist of only 1 person (appointed by the appropriate Government).

1. The appropriate Government may, by notification in the Official Gazette, constitute 1 or more Labour Courts for the adjudication of industrial disputes relating to any matter specified in the Second Schedule and for performing such other functions as may be assigned to them under this Act.
2. A Labour Court shall consist of 1 person only to be appointed by the appropriate Government.
3. A person shall not be qualified for appointment as the presiding officer of a Labour Court, unless-
   (a) he is, or has been, a Judge of a High Court; or
   (b) he has, for a period of not less than 3 years, been a District Judge or an Additional District Judge; or
   (d) he has held any judicial office in India for not less than 7 years; or
   (e) he has been the presiding officer of a Labour Court constituted under any Provincial Act or State Act for not less than 5 years.
   (f) he is or has been a Deputy Chief Labour Commissioner (Central) or Joint Commissioner of the State Labour Department, having a degree in law and at least 7 years' experience in the labour department including 3 years of experience in the labour department including 3 years of experience as Conciliation Officer:

   Provided that no such a Deputy Chief Labour Commissioner or Joint Labour Commissioner shall be appointed unless he resigns from the service of the Central Government or State Government, as the case may be, before being appointed as the presiding officer; or

   (g) he is an officer of Indian Legal Service in Grade III with 3 years' experience in the grade.

Tribunals (Section 7A)

1. The appropriate Government may, by notification in the Official Gazette, constitute 1 or more Industrial Tribunals for the adjudication of industrial disputes relating to any matter, whether specified in the Second Schedule or the Third Schedule and for performing such other functions as may be assigned to them under this Act.
2. A Tribunal shall consist of 1 person only to be appointed by the appropriate Government.

3. A person shall not be qualified for appointment as the presiding officer of a Tribunal unless-
   (a) he is, or has been, a Judge of a High Court; or
   (aa) he has, for a period of not less than 3 years, been a District Judge, or an Additional District Judge;
   (b) he is or has been a Deputy Chief Labour Commissioner (Central) or Joint Commissioner of the State Labour Department, having a degree in law and at least 7 years' experience in the labour department including 3 years of experience in the labour department including 3 years of experience as Conciliation Officer:

       Provided that no such a Deputy Chief Labour Commissioner or Joint Labour Commissioner shall be appointed unless he resigns from the service of the Central Government or State Government, as the case may be, before being appointed as the presiding officer; or
   (c) he is an officer of Indian Legal Service in Grade III with 3 years' experience in the grade.
4. The appropriate Government may, if it so thinks fit, appoint 2 persons as assessors to advise the Tribunal in the proceeding before it.

National Tribunals (Section 7B)

1. The Central Government may, by notification in the Official Gazette, constitute 1 or more National Industrial Tribunals for the adjudication of industrial disputes which, in the opinion of the Central Government, involve questions of national importance or are of such a nature that industrial establishments situated in more than 1 State are likely to be interested in, or affected by, such disputes.

Spotlight

National Industrial Tribunals adjudicate industrial disputes which involve questions of national importance.

2. A National Tribunal shall consist of 1 person only to be appointed by the Central Government.
3. A person shall not be qualified for appointment as the presiding officer of a National Tribunal unless he is, or has been, a judge of a High Court.
4. The Central Government may, if so thinks fit, appoint 2 persons as assessors to advise the National Tribunal in the proceeding before it.

Disqualifications for the Presiding Officers of Labour Courts, Tribunals and National Tribunals (Section 7C)

No person shall be appointed to, or continue in, the office of the presiding officer of a Labour Court, Tribunal or National Tribunal, if:

(a) he is not an independent person; or
(b) he has attained the age of 65 years.

Filling of Vacancies (Section 8)

If, for any reason a vacancy (other than a temporary absence) occurs in the office of the presiding officer of a Labour Court, Tribunal or National Tribunal or in the office of the Chairman or any other member of a Board or Court, then, in the case of a National Tribunal, the Central Government and in any other case, the appropriate Government, shall appoint another person in accordance with the provisions of this Act to fill the vacancy, and the proceeding may be continued before the Labour Court, Tribunal, National Tribunal, Board or Court, as the case may be, from the stage at which the vacancy is filled.

Finality of Orders Constituting Boards, etc. (Section 9)

1. No order of the appropriate Government or of the Central Government appointing any person as the Chairman or any other member of a Board or Court or as the presiding officer of a Labour Court, Tribunal or National Tribunal shall be called in question in any manner; and no act or proceeding before any Board or Court shall be called in question in any manner on the ground merely of the existence of any vacancy in, or defect in the constitution of, such Board or Court.
2. No settlement arrived at in the course of a conciliation proceeding shall be invalid by reason only of the fact that such settlement was arrived at after the expiry of the period referred to in sub-section (6) of Section 12 or sub-section (5) of Section 13, as the case may be.
3. Where the report of any settlement arrived at in the course of conciliation proceeding before a Board is signed by the Chairman and all the other members of the Board, no such settlement shall be invalid by reason only of the casual or unforeseen absence of any of the members (including the Chairman) of the Board during any stage of the proceeding.

CHAPTER IIA: NOTICE OF CHANGE

Notice of Change (Section 9A)

No employer, who proposes to effect any change in the conditions of service applicable to any workman in respect of any matter specified in the Fourth Schedule, shall effect such change:

(a) without giving to the workmen likely to be affected by such change a notice in the prescribed manner of the nature of the change proposed to be effected; or

(b) within 21 days of giving such notice:

Provided that no notice shall be required for effecting any such change:

(a) where the change is effected in pursuance of any settlement or award; or

(b) where the workmen likely to be affected by the change are persons to whom the Fundamental and Supplementary Rules, Civil Services (Classification, Control and Appeal) Rules, Civil Services (Temporary Service) Rules, Revised Leave Rules, Civil Service Regulations, Civilians in Defence Services (Classification, Control and Appeal) Rules or the Indian Railway Establishment Code or any other rules or regulations that may be notified in this behalf by the appropriate Government in the Official Gazette, apply.

Power of Government to Exempt (Section 9B)

Where the appropriate Government is of opinion that the application of the provisions of Section 9A to any class of industrial establishments or to any class of workmen employed in any industrial establishment affect the employers in relation thereto so prejudicially that such application may cause serious repercussion on the industry concerned and that public interest so requires, the appropriate Government may, by notification in the Official Gazette, direct that the provisions of the said section shall not apply or shall apply, subject to such conditions as may be specified in the notification, to that class of industrial establishments or to that class of workmen employed in any industrial establishment.

CHAPTER IIB: GRIEVANCE REDRESSAL MACHINERY

Setting up of Grievance Redressal Machinery (Section 9C)

1. Every industrial establishment employing 20 or more workmen shall have 1 or more Grievance Redressal Committee for the resolution of disputes arising out of individual grievances.
2. The Grievance Redressal Committee shall consist of equal number of members from the employer and the workmen.
3. The chairperson of the Grievance Redressal Committee shall be selected from the employer and from among the workmen alternatively on rotation basis every year.
4. The total number of members of the Grievance Redressal Committee shall not exceed more than 6:

   Provided that there shall be, as far as practicable, 1 woman member if the Grievance Redressal Committee has 2 members and in case the number of members is more than 2, the number of women members may be increased proportionately.
5. Notwithstanding anything contained in this section, the setting up of Grievance Redressal Committee shall not affect the right of the workman to raise industrial dispute on the same matter under the provisions of this Act.
6. The Grievance Redressal Committee may complete its proceedings within 30 days on receipt of a written application by or on behalf of the aggrieved party.
7. The workman who is aggrieved of the decision of the Grievance Redressal Committee may prefer an appeal to the employer against the decision of Grievance Redressal Committee and the employer shall, within 1 month from the date of receipt of such appeal, dispose off the same, and send a copy of his decision to the workman concerned.
8. Nothing contained in this section shall apply to the workmen for whom there is an established Grievance Redressal Mechanism in the establishment concerned.

Spotlight

The Grievance Redressal Committee may complete its proceedings within 30 days on receipt of a written application by or on behalf of the aggrieved party, as given in Section 9C(6).

CHAPTER III: REFERENCE OF DISPUTES TO BOARDS, COURTS OR TRIBUNALS

Reference of Disputes to Boards, Courts or Tribunals (Section 10)

1. Where the appropriate Government is of opinion that any industrial dispute exists or is apprehended, it may at any time, by order in writing:
   (a) refer the dispute to a Board for promoting a settlement thereof; or
   (b) refer any matter appearing to be connected with, or relevant to, the dispute to a Court for inquiry; or
   (c) refer the dispute or any matter appearing to be connected with, or relevant to, the dispute, if it relates to any matter specified in the Second Schedule, to a Labour Court for adjudication; or
   (d) refer the dispute or any matter appearing to be connected with, or relevant to, the dispute, whether it relates to any matter specified, in the Second Schedule or the Third Schedule, to a Tribunal for adjudication:

Spotlight

Chapter III has provisions for reference of disputes to Boards, Courts or Tribunals.

Provided that where the dispute relates to any matter specified in the Third Schedule and is not likely to affect more than 100 hundred workmen, the appropriate Government may, if it so thinks fit, make the reference to a Labour Court under clause (c):

Provided further that where the dispute relates to a public utility service and a notice under Section 22 has been given, the appropriate Government shall, unless it considers that the notice has been frivolously or vexatiously given or that it would be inexpedient so to do, make a reference under this sub-section notwithstanding that any other proceedings under this Act in respect of the dispute may have commenced:

Provided also that where the dispute in relation to which the Central Government is the appropriate Government, it shall be competent for that Government to refer the dispute to a Labour Court or an Industrial Tribunal, as the case may be, constituted by the State Government.

1A. Where the Central Government is of opinion that any industrial dispute exists or is apprehended and the dispute involves any question of national importance or is of such a nature that industrial establishments situated in more than 1 State are likely to be interested in, or affected by, such dispute and that the dispute should be adjudicated by a National Tribunal, then, the Central Government may, whether or not it is the appropriate Government in relation to that dispute, at any time, by order in writing, refer the dispute or any matter appearing to be connected with, or relevant to, the dispute, whether it relates to any matter specified in the Second Schedule or the Third Schedule, to a National Tribunal for adjudication.

2. Where the parties to an industrial dispute apply in the prescribed manner, whether jointly or separately, for a reference of the dispute to a Board, Court, Labour Court, Tribunal or National Tribunal, the appropriate Government, if satisfied that the persons applying represent the majority of each party, shall make the reference accordingly.

2A. An order referring an industrial dispute to a Labour Court, Tribunal or National Tribunal under this section shall specify the period within which such Labour Court, Tribunal or National Tribunal shall submit its award on such dispute to the appropriate Government:

Provided that where such industrial dispute is connected with an individual workman, no such period shall exceed 3 months:

Provided further that where the parties to an industrial dispute apply in the prescribed manner, whether jointly or separately, to the Labour Court, Tribunal or National Tribunal for extension of such period or for any other reason, and the presiding officer of such Labour Court, Tribunal or National Tribunal considers it necessary or expedient to extend such period, he may for reasons to be recorded in writing, extend such period by such further period as he may think fit:

Provided also that in computing any period specified in this sub-section, the period, if any, for which the proceedings before the Labour Court, Tribunal or National Tribunal had been stayed by any injunction or order of a Civil Court shall be excluded:

Provided also that no proceedings before a Labour Court, Tribunal or National Tribunal shall lapse merely on the ground that any period specified under this sub-section had expired without such proceedings being completed.

3. Where an industrial dispute has been referred to a Board, Labour Court, Tribunal or National Tribunal under this section, the appropriate Government may by order prohibit the continuance of any strike or lock-out in connection with such dispute which may be in existence on the date of the reference.

4. Where in an order referring an industrial dispute to a Labour Court, Tribunal or National Tribunal under this section or in a subsequent order, the appropriate Government has specified the points

of dispute for adjudication, the Labour Court or the Tribunal or the National Tribunal, as the case may be, shall confine its adjudication to those points and matters incidental thereto.

5. Where a dispute concerning any establishment or establishments has been, or is to be, referred to a Labour Court, Tribunal or National Tribunal under this section and the appropriate Government is of opinion, whether on an application made to it in this behalf or otherwise, that the dispute is of such a nature that any other establishment, group or class of establishments of a similar nature is likely to be interested in, or affected by, such dispute, the appropriate Government may, at the time of making the reference or at any time thereafter but before the submission of the award, include in that reference such establishment, group, or class of establishments, whether or not at the time of such inclusion any dispute exists, or is apprehended in that establishment, group or class of establishments.
6. Where any reference has been made under sub-section (1A) to a National Tribunal, then notwithstanding anything contained in this Act, no Labour Court or Tribunal shall have jurisdiction to adjudicate upon any matter which is under adjudication before the National Tribunal, and accordingly:
   (a) if the matter under adjudication before the National Tribunal is pending in a proceeding before a Labour Court or Tribunal, the proceeding before the Labour Court or the Tribunal, as the case may be, in so far as it relates to such matter, shall be deemed to have been quashed on such reference to the National Tribunal; and
   (b) it shall not be lawful for the appropriate Government to refer the matter under adjudication before the National Tribunal to any Labour Court or Tribunal for adjudication during the pendency of the proceeding in relation to such matter before the National Tribunal.

   Explanation In this sub-section, "Labour Court" or "Tribunal" includes any Court or Tribunal or other authority constituted under any law relating to investigation and settlement of industrial disputes in force in any State.
7. Where any industrial dispute, in relation to which the Central Government is not the appropriate Government, is referred to a National Tribunal, then notwithstanding anything contained in this Act, any reference in Section 15, Section 17, Section 19, Section 33A, Section 33B and Section 36A to the appropriate Government in relation to such dispute shall be construed as a reference to the Central Government but, save as aforesaid and as otherwise expressly provided in this Act, any reference in any other provision of this Act to the appropriate Government in relation to that dispute shall mean a reference to the State Government.

> **Spotlight**
> No pending proceeding shall lapse due to death of any of the parties to the dispute, as provided in Section 10(8).

8. No proceedings pending before a Labour Court, Tribunal or National Tribunal in relation to an industrial dispute shall lapse merely by reason of the death of any of the parties to the dispute being a workman, and such Labour Court, Tribunal or National Tribunal shall complete such proceedings and submit its award to the appropriate Government.

Voluntary Reference of Disputes to Arbitration (Section 10A)

1. Where any industrial dispute exists or is apprehended and the employer and the workmen agree to refer the dispute to arbitration, they may, at any time before the dispute has been referred under Section 10 to a Labour Court or Tribunal or National Tribunal, by a written agreement, refer the dispute to arbitration and the reference shall be to such person or persons (including the presiding officer of a Labour Court or Tribunal or National Tribunal) as an arbitrator or arbitrators as may be specified in the arbitration agreement.

1A. Where an arbitration agreement provides for a reference of the dispute to an even number of arbitrators, the agreement shall provide for the appointment of another person as umpire who shall enter upon the reference, if the arbitrators are equally divided in their opinion, and the award of the umpire shall prevail and shall be deemed to be the arbitration award for the purposes of this Act.

2. An arbitration agreement referred to in sub-section (1) shall be in such form and shall be signed by the parties thereto in such manner as may be prescribed.

3. A copy of the arbitration agreement shall be forwarded to the appropriate Government and the conciliation officer and the appropriate Government shall, within 1 month from the date of the receipt of such copy, publish the same in the Official Gazette.

> **Spotlight**
> An arbitration agreement must be in prescribed manner and signed by the parties thereto.

3A. Where an industrial dispute has been referred to arbitration and the appropriate Government is satisfied that the persons making the reference represent the majority of each party, the appropriate Government may, within the time referred to in sub-section (3) issue a notification in such manner as may be prescribed; and when any such notification is issued, the employers and workmen who are not parties to the arbitration agreement but are concerned in the dispute, shall be given an opportunity of presenting their case before the arbitrator or arbitrators.

4. The arbitrator or arbitrators shall investigate the dispute and submit to the appropriate Government the arbitration award signed by the arbitrator or all the arbitrators, as the case may be.

4A. Where an industrial dispute has been referred to arbitration and a notification has been issued under sub-section (3A), the appropriate Government may, by order, prohibit the continuance of any strike or lock-out in connection with such dispute which may be in existence on the date of the reference.

5. Nothing in the Arbitration Act, 1940 shall apply to arbitrations under this section.

CHAPTER IV: PROCEDURE, POWERS AND DUTIES OF AUTHORITIES

Procedure and Powers of Conciliation Officers, Boards, Courts and Tribunals (Section 11)

1. Subject to any rules that may be made in this behalf, an arbitrator, a Board, Court, Labour Court, Tribunal or National Tribunal shall follow such procedure as the arbitrator or other authority concerned may think fit.
2. A conciliation officer or a member of a Board, or Court or the presiding officer of a Labour Court, Tribunal or National Tribunal may for the purpose of inquiry into any existing or apprehended industrial dispute, after giving reasonable notice, enter the premises occupied by any establishment to which the dispute relates.
3. Every Board, Court, Labour Court, Tribunal and National Tribunal shall have the same powers as are vested in a Civil Court under the Code of Civil Procedure, 1908, when trying a suit, in respect of the following matters, namely:
   (a) enforcing the attendance of any person and examining him on oath;
   (b) compelling the production of documents and material objects;
   (c) issuing commissions for the examination of witnesses;
   (d) in respect of such other matters as may be prescribed,

and every inquiry or investigation by a Board, Court, Labour Court, Tribunal or National Tribunal, shall be deemed to be a judicial proceeding within the meaning of sections 193 and 228 of the Indian Penal Code.

4. A conciliation officer may enforce the attendance of any person for the purpose of examination of such person, or call for and inspect any document which he has ground for considering to be relevant to the industrial dispute, or to be necessary for the purpose of verifying the implementation of any award, or carrying out any other duty imposed on him under this Act, and for the aforesaid purposes, the conciliation officer shall have the same powers as are vested in a Civil Court under the Code of Civil Procedure, 1908, in respect of enforcing the attendance of any person and examining him or of compelling the production of documents.
5. A Court, Labour Court, Tribunal or National Tribunal may, if it so thinks fit, appoint 1 or more persons having special knowledge of the matter under consideration as assessor or assessors to advise it in the proceeding before it.
6. All conciliation officers, members of a Board or Court and the presiding officers of a Labour Court, Tribunal or National Tribunal shall be deemed to be public servants within the meaning of Section 21 of the Indian Penal Code.
7. Subject to any rules made under this Act, the costs of, and incidental to, any proceeding before a Labour Court, Tribunal, or National Tribunal shall be in the discretion of that Labour Court, Tribunal or National Tribunal and the Labour Court, Tribunal or National Tribunal, as the case may be, shall have full power to determine by and to whom and to what extent and subject to what conditions, if any, such costs are to be paid, and to give all necessary directions for the purposes aforesaid and such costs may, on application made to the appropriate Government by the person entitled, be recovered by that Government in the same manner as an arrear of land revenue.
8. Every Labour Court, Tribunal or National Tribunal shall be deemed to be Civil Court for the purposes of sections 345, 346 and 348 of the Code of Criminal Procedure, 1973.
9. Every award made, order issued or settlement at by or before Labour Court or Tribunal or National Tribunal shall be executed in accordance with the procedure laid down for execution of orders and decree of a Civil Court under Order 21 of the Code of Civil Procedure, 1908.
10. The Labour Court or Tribunal or National Tribunal, as the case may be, shall transmit any award, order or sttlement to a Civil Court having jurisdiction and such Civil Court shall execute the award, order or settlement as if it were a decree passed by it.

In *Punjab General Mazdoor Federation vs. Union of India and Another* (2012 LLR 1102) the reply filed by Union of India against the petition filed has specifically asserted that the newly added subsections (9) and (10) to Section 11 of the Industrial Disputes Act, 1947 (hereafter, the Act), are not in suppression or in derogation to the existing provisions contained in sections 15, 17, 29 and 33C of the Act; rather these subsections are in addition to the existing provisions of the Act. The Court, on inspection of the original record to explore why amendment was necessitated in Section 11 came to the conclusion that deliberation had started way back in 2005, when some labour organisations and the Government perceived that the present provisions to enforce the award takes 30 days and thereafter it cannot be executed within next 30 days; sometimes execution of award would be stayed by notification issued under Section 17A. Therefore an amendment was felt necessary to treat award as decree of the Civil Court for execution thereof in accordance with the provisions of law for execution of Civil Court decree. *(Adapted from: Labour Law Reporter, October, 2012, pp. 1102-1103.)*

Powers of Labour Courts, Tribunals and National Tribunals to Give Appropriate Relief in Case of Discharge or Dismissal of Workmen (Section 11A)

Where an industrial dispute relating to the discharge or dismissal of a workman has been referred to a Labour Court, Tribunal or National Tribunal for adjudication and, in the course of the adjudication proceedings, the Labour Court, Tribunal or National Tribunal, as the case may be, is satisfied that the order of discharge or dismissal was not justified, it may, by its award, set aside the order of discharge or dismissal and direct re-instatement of the workman on such terms and conditions, if any, as it thinks fit, or give such other relief to the workman including the award of any lesser punishment in lieu of discharge or dismissal as the circumstances of the case may require:

Provided that in any proceeding under this section the Labour Court, Tribunal or National Tribunal, as the case may be, shall rely only on the materials on record and shall not take any fresh evidence in relation to the matter.

CASE CORNER

In *A. Chandrappa vs. Management of Bangalore Metropolitan Transport Corporation* (2011 LLR 1277) the petitioner driver/workmen was in drunken state on duty and had used filthy language and misbehaved with the passengers. The police registered a case and arrested him. His misconduct stood proved. Subsequently the respondent corporation initiated enquiry and the appellant participated in the enquiry along with his co-worker. A show-cause notice was issued, for which the appellant did not choose to submit any explanation. The Disciplinary Authority, on exercising the power vested with it, passed an order of dismissal. Thereafter an industrial dispute was referred before the Labour Court, Bangalore by the appellant for adjudication of the points in dispute. The Labour Court, after considering the charges levelled against the appellant and the imposition of sentence on him, rejected the reference and passed award. Aggrieved by such award, the appellant filed the writ petition before the learned Single Judge, which came to be dismissed on the ground that the charge levelled against the appellant is of serious nature as his conduct itself was not only dangerous to the safety of those in the vehicle but also those using the roads.

It was submitted that the appellant had voluntarily confessed about the commission of the offence. He did not contest the case in criminal case; the charge levelled against him is trivial in nature and does not warrant maximum punishment of dismissal from services. Therefore the order passed is liable to be set aside. However, the respondent corporation submitted that the appellant who was employed as driver in the corporation, not only consumed liquor while on duty, but also picked up quarrel and misbehaved with the passengers in the bus.

Section 11A vests the Labour Court with the discretion to substitute the order of discharge or dismissal of a workman into an order of reinstatement of the workman, including the award of lesser punishment in lieu of discharge or dismissal as per circumstances of the case. Hence the Disciplinary Authority and the Labour Court are justified in imposing the punishment of dismissal, which does not warrant any interference by the Court. The appeal filed was hence dismissed.

(Adapted from: www.indiankanoon.org/doc/81752942/ accessed on 1/1/2014.)

Duties of Conciliation Officers (Section 12)

1. Where any industrial dispute exists or is apprehended, the conciliation officer may, or where the dispute relates to a public utility service and a notice under Section 22 has been given, shall hold conciliation proceedings in the prescribed manner.
2. The conciliation officer shall, for the purpose of bringing about a settlement of the dispute, without delay, investigate the dispute and all matters affecting the merits and the right settlement thereof and may do all such things as he thinks fit for the purpose of inducing the parties to come to a fair and amicable settlement of the dispute.
3. If a settlement of the dispute or of any of the matters in dispute is arrived at in the course of the conciliation proceedings the conciliation officer shall send a report thereof to the appropriate Government or an officer authorised in this behalf by the appropriate Government together with a memorandum of the settlement signed by the parties to the dispute.
4. If no such settlement is arrived at, the conciliation officer shall, as soon as practicable after the close of the investigation, send to the appropriate Government a full report setting forth the steps taken by him for ascertaining the facts and circumstances relating to the dispute and for bringing about a settlement thereof, together with a full statement of such facts and circumstances, and the reasons on account of which, in his opinion, a settlement could not be arrived at.

> **Spotlight**
> A conciliation officer, as per Section 12(6), shall submit report within 14 days of commencement of conciliation proceedings.

5. If, on a consideration of the report referred to in sub-section (4), the appropriate Government is satisfied that there is a case for reference to a Board, Labour Court, Tribunal or National Tribunal, it may make such reference. Where the appropriate Government does not make such a reference it shall record and communicate to the parties concerned its reasons therefor.
6. A report under this section shall be submitted within 14 days of the commencement of the conciliation proceedings or within such shorter period as may be fixed by the appropriate Government:

   Provided that, subject to the approval of the conciliation officer, the time for the submission of the report may be extended by such period as may be agreed upon in writing by all the parties to the dispute.

Duties of Board (Section 13)

1. Where a dispute has been referred to a Board under this Act, it shall be the duty of the Board to endeavour to bring about a settlement of the same and for this purpose the Board shall, in such manner as it thinks fit and without delay, investigate the dispute and all matters affecting the merits and the right settlement thereof and may do all such things as it thinks fit for the purpose of inducing the parties to come to a fair and amicable settlement of the dispute.
2. If a settlement of the dispute or of any of the matters in dispute is arrived at in the course of the conciliation proceedings, the Board shall send a report thereof to the appropriate Government together with a memorandum of the settlement signed by the parties to the dispute.
3. If no such settlement is arrived at, the Board shall, as soon as practicable after the close of the investigation, send to the appropriate Government a full report setting for the proceedings and steps taken by the Board for ascertaining the facts and circumstances relating to the dispute and for bringing about a settlement thereof, together with a full statement of such facts and circum-

stances, its findings thereon, the reasons on account of which, in its opinion, a settlement could not be arrived at and its recommendations for the determination of the dispute.

4. If, on the receipt of a report under sub-section (3) in respect of a dispute relating to a public utility service, the appropriate Government does not make a reference to a Labour Court, Tribunal or National Tribunal under Section 10, it shall record and communicate to the parties concerned its reasons therefor.
5. The Board shall submit its report under this section within 2 months of the date on which the dispute was referred to it or within such shorter period as may be fixed by the appropriate Government:

   Provided that the appropriate Government may from time to time extend the time for the submission of the report by such further periods not exceeding 2 months in the aggregate:

   Provided further that the time for the submission of the report may be extended by such period as may be agreed on in writing by all the parties to the dispute.

Duties of Courts (Section 14)

A Court shall inquire into the matters referred to it and report thereon to the appropriate Government ordinarily within a period of 6 months from the commencement of its inquiry.

Spotlight

A Court shall inquire into the matters referred to it and report thereon to the appropriate Government within a period of 6 months from the commencement of its inquiry, as provided in Section 14.

Duties of Labour Courts, Tribunals, and National Tribunals (Section 15)

Where an industrial dispute has been referred to a Labour Court, Tribunal or National Tribunal for adjudication, it shall hold its proceedings expeditiously and shall, within the period specified in the order referring such industrial dispute or the further period extended under the second proviso to sub-section (2A) of Section 10, submit its award to the appropriate Government.

Form of Report or Award (Section 16)

1. The report of a Board or Court shall be in writing and shall be signed by all the members of the Board or Court, as the case may be:

   Provided that nothing in this section shall be deemed to prevent any member of the Board or Court from recording any minute of dissent from a report or from any recommendation made therein.
2. The award of a Labour Court or Tribunal or National Tribunal shall be in writing and shall be signed by its presiding officer.

Publication of Reports and Awards (Section 17)

1. Every report of a Board or Court together with any minute of dissent recorded therewith, every arbitration award and every award of a Labour Court, Tribunal or National Tribunal shall, within a period of 30 days from the date of its receipt by the appropriate Government, be published in such manner as the appropriate Government thinks fit.
2. Subject to the provisions of Section 17A, the award published under sub-section (1) shall be final and shall not be called in question by any Court in any manner whatsoever.

Commencement of the Award (Section 17A)

> **Spotlight**
> An award (including an arbitration award), as per Section 17A, shall become enforceable on the expiry of 30 days from the date it was published.

1. An award (including an arbitration award) shall become enforceable on the expiry of 30 days from the date of its publication under Section 17:
   Provided that:
   (a) if the appropriate Government is of opinion, in any case where the award has been given by a Labour Court or Tribunal in relation to an industrial dispute to which it is a party; or
   (b) if the Central Government is of opinion, in any case where the award has been given by a National Tribunal,

   that it will be inexpedient on public grounds affecting national economy or social justice to give effect to the whole or any part of the award, the appropriate Government, or as the case may be, the Central Government may, by notification in the Official Gazette, declare that the award shall not become enforceable on the expiry of the said period of 30 days.
2. Where any declaration has been made in relation to an award under the proviso to sub-section (1), the appropriate Government or the Central Government may, within 90 days from the date of publication of the award under Section 17, make an order rejecting or modifying the award, and shall, on the first available opportunity, lay the award together with a copy of the order before the Legislature of the State, if the order has been made by a State Government, or before Parliament, if the order has been made by the Central Government.
3. Where any award as rejected or modified by an order made under sub-section (2) is laid before the Legislature of a State or before Parliament, such award shall become enforceable on the expiry of 15 days from the date on which it is so laid; and where no order under sub-section (2) is made in pursuance of a declaration under the proviso to sub-section (1), the award shall become enforceable on the expiry of the period of 90 days referred to in sub-section (2).
4. Subject to the provisions of sub-section (1) and sub-section (3) regarding the enforceability of an award, the award shall come into operation with effect from such date as may be specified therein, but where no date is so specified, it shall come into operation on the date when the award becomes enforceable under sub-section (1) or sub-section (3), as the case may be.

Payment of Full Wages to Workman Pending Proceedings in Higher Courts (Section 17B)

> **Spotlight**
> A workman shall not be paid wages during pendency of proceedings if he is employed in any establishment, as provided in Section 17B.

Where in any case, a Labour Court, Tribunal or National Tribunal by its award directs reinstatement of any workman and the employer prefers any proceedings against such award in a High Court or the Supreme Court, the employer shall be liable to pay such workman, during the period of pendency of such proceedings in the High Court or the Supreme Court, full wages last drawn by him, inclusive of any maintenance allowance admissible to him under any rule if the workman had not been employed in any establishment during such period and an affidavit by such workman had been filed to that effect in such Court:

Provided that where it is proved to the satisfaction of the High Court or the Supreme Court that such workman had been employed and had been receiving adequate remuneration during any such period or part thereof, the Court shall order that no wages shall be payable under this section for such period or part, as the case may be.

Persons on whom Settlements and Awards are Binding (Section 18)

1. A settlement arrived at by agreement between the employer and workman otherwise than in the course of conciliation proceeding shall be binding on the parties to the agreement.
2. Subject to the provisions of sub-section (3), an arbitration award which has become enforceable shall be binding on the parties to the agreement who referred the dispute to arbitration.
3. A settlement arrived at in the course of conciliation proceedings under this Act or an arbitration award in a case where a notification has been issued under sub-section (3A) of Section 10A or an award of a Labour Court, Tribunal or National Tribunal which has become enforceable shall be binding on:
   (a) all parties to the industrial dispute;
   (b) all other parties summoned to appear in the proceedings as parties to the dispute, unless the Board, arbitrator, Labour Court, Tribunal or National Tribunal, as the case may be, records the opinion that they were so summoned without proper cause;
   (c) where a party referred to in clause (a) or clause (b) is an employer, his heirs, successors or assigns in respect of the establishment to which the dispute relates;
   (d) where a party referred to in clause (a) or clause (b) is composed of workmen, all persons who were employed in the establishment or part of the establishment, as the case may be, to which the dispute relates on the date of the dispute and all persons who subsequently become employed in that establishment or part.

Period of Operation of Settlements and Awards (Section 19)

Spotlight

Section 19(3) provides that any award shall remain in operation for 1 year from the date it became enforceable.

1. A settlement shall come into operation on such date as is agreed upon by the parties to the dispute, and if no date is agreed upon, on the date on which the memorandum of the settlement is signed by the parties to the dispute.
2. Such settlement shall be binding for such period as is agreed upon by the parties, and if no such period is agreed upon, for a period of 6 months from the date on which the memorandum of settlement is signed by the parties to the dispute, and shall continue to be binding on the parties after the expiry of the period aforesaid, until the expiry of 2 months from the date on which a notice in writing of an intention to terminate the settlement is given by 1 of the parties to the other party or parties to the settlement.
3. An award shall, subject to the provisions of this section, remain in operation for a period of 1 year from the date on which the award becomes enforceable under Section 17A.

   Provided that the appropriate Government may reduce the said period and fix such period as it thinks fit:

   Provided further that the appropriate Government may, before the expiry of the said period, extend the period of operation by any period not exceeding 1 year at a time as it thinks fit so, however, that the total period of operation of any award does not exceed 3 years from the date on which it came into operation.
4. Where the appropriate Government, whether of its own motion or on the application of any party bound by the award, considers that since the award was made, there has been a material change in the circumstances on which it was based, the appropriate Government may refer the award or a part of it to a Labour Court, if the award was that of a Labour Court or to a Tribunal, if the award was that of a Tribunal or of a National Tribunal, for decision whether the period of opera-

tion should not, by reason of such change, be shortened and the decision of Labour Court or the Tribunal, as the case may be on such reference shall be final.

5. Nothing contained in sub-section (3) shall apply to any award which by its nature, terms or other circumstances does not impose, after it has been given effect to, any continuing obligation on the parties bound by the award.
6. Notwithstanding the expiry of the period of operation under sub-section (3), the award shall continue to be binding on the parties until a period of 2 months has elapsed from the date on which notice is given by any party bound by the award to the other party or parties intimating its intention to terminate the award.
7. No notice given under sub-section (2) or sub-section (6) shall have effect, unless it is given by a party representing the majority of persons bound by the settlement or award, as the case may be.

Commencement and Conclusion of Proceedings (Section 20)

1. A conciliation proceeding shall be deemed to have commenced on the date on which a notice of strike or lock-out under Section 22 is received by the conciliation officer or on the date of the order referring the dispute to a Board, as the case may be.
2. A conciliation proceeding shall be deemed to have concluded:
   (a) where a settlement is arrived at, when a memorandum of the settlement is signed by the parties to the dispute;
   (b) where no settlement is arrived at, when the report of the conciliation officer is received by the appropriate Government or when the report of the Board is published under Section 17, as the case may be; or
   (c) when a reference is made to a Court, Labour Court, Tribunal or National Tribunal under Section 10 during the pendency of conciliation proceedings.
3. Proceedings before an arbitrator under Section 10A or before a Labour Court, Tribunal or National Tribunal shall be deemed to have commenced on the date of the reference of the dispute for arbitration or adjudication, as the case may be, and such proceedings shall be deemed to have concluded on the date on which the award becomes enforceable under Section 17A.

Certain Matters to be Kept Confidential (Section 21)

There shall not be included in any report or award under this Act, any information obtained by a conciliation officer, Board, Court, Labour Court, Tribunal, National Tribunal or an arbitrator in the course of any investigation or inquiry as to a trade union or as to any individual business (whether carried on by a person, firm or company) which is not available otherwise than through the evidence given before such officer, Board, Court, Labour Court, Tribunal, National Tribunal or arbitrator, if the trade union, person, firm or company, in question has made a request in writing to the conciliation officer, Board, Court, Labour Court, Tribunal, National Tribunal or arbitrator, as the case may be, that such information shall be treated as confidential; nor shall such conciliation officer or any individual member of the Board, or Court or the presiding officer of the Labour Court, Tribunal or National Tribunal or the arbitrator or any person present at or concerned in the proceedings disclose any such information without the consent in writing of the secretary of the trade union or the person, firm or company in question, as the case may be:

Provided that nothing contained in this section shall apply to a disclosure of any such information for the purposes of a prosecution under Section 193 of the Indian Penal Code.

CHAPTER V: STRIKES AND LOCK-OUTS

Prohibition of Strikes and Lock-Outs (Section 22)

Spotlight
Notice of 6 weeks is necessary for strike or lock-out in a public utility service.

1. No person employed in a public utility service shall go on strike, in breach of contract–
   (a) without giving to the employer notice of strike, as hereinafter provided, within 6 weeks before striking; or
   (b) within 14 days of giving such notice; or
   (c) before the expiry of the date of strike specified in any such notice as aforesaid; or
   (d) during the pendency of any conciliation proceedings before a conciliation officer and 7 days after the conclusion of such proceedings.
2. No employer carrying on any public utility service shall lock-out any of his workmen–
   (a) without giving them notice of lock-out as hereinafter provided, within 6 weeks before locking out; or
   (b) within 14 days of giving such notice; or
   (c) before the expiry of the date of lock-out specified in any such notice as aforesaid; or
   (d) during the pendency of any conciliation proceedings before a conciliation officer and 7 days after the conclusion of such proceedings.
3. The notice of lock-out or strike under this section shall not be necessary where there is already in existence a strike or, as the case may be, lock-out in the public utility service, but the employer shall send intimation of such lock-out or strike on the day on which it is declared, to such authority as may be specified by the appropriate Government either generally or for a particular area or for a particular class of public utility services.

Spotlight
Notice of lock-out or strike is not necessary when there is already a strike or lock-out in that public utility service.

4. The notice of strike referred to in sub-section (1) shall be given by such number of persons to such person or persons and in such manner as may be prescribed.
5. The notice of lock-out referred to in sub-section (2) shall be given in such manner as may be prescribed.
6. If on any day an employer receives from any persons employed by him any such notices as are referred to in sub-section (1) or gives to any persons employed by him any such notices as are referred to in sub-section (2), he shall within 5 days thereof report to the appropriate Government or to such authority as that Government may prescribe the number of such notices received or given on that day.

General Prohibition of Strikes and Lock-outs (Section 23)

No workman who is employed in any industrial establishment shall go on strike in breach of contract and no employer of any such workman shall declare a lock-out:

(a) during the pendency of conciliation proceedings before a Board and 7 days after the conclusion of such proceedings;
(b) during the pendency of proceedings before a Labour Court, Tribunal or National Tribunal and 2 months after the conclusion of such proceedings;
(bb) during the pendency of arbitration proceedings before an arbitrator and 2 months after the conclusion of such proceedings, where a notification has been issued under sub-section (3A) of Section 10A; or

(c) during any period in which a settlement or award is in operation, in respect of any of the matters covered by the settlement or award.

Illegal Strikes and Lock-outs (Section 24)

1. A strike or a lock-out shall be illegal if:
   (i) it is commenced or declared in contravention of Section 22 or Section 23; or
   (ii) it is continued in contravention of an order made under sub-section (3) of Section 10 or sub-section (4A) of Section 10A.
2. Where a strike or lock-out in pursuance of an industrial dispute has already commenced and is in existence at the time of the reference of the dispute to a Board, an arbitrator, a Labour Court, Tribunal or National Tribunal, the continuance of such strike or lock-out shall not be deemed to be illegal, provided that such strike or lock-out was not at its commencement in contravention of the provisions of this Act or the continuance thereof was not prohibited under sub-section (3) of Section 10 or sub-section (4A) of Section 10A.

> **Spotlight**
> As per Section 24(3), a lock-out declared in consequence of an illegal strike or a strike declared in consequence of an illegal lock-out shall not be deemed to be illegal.

3. A lock-out declared in consequence of an illegal strike or a strike declared in consequence of an illegal lock-out shall not be deemed to be illegal.

   In *Punjab Tractors Workers' Union (Regd.) vs. The Presiding Officer, Industrial Tribunal, Punjab, Chandigarh and Another* [(2011) LLR 1277] a petition was filed against the award passed by the Presiding Officer, wherein the lock-out declared by the second respondent, M/s Swaraj Tractor Division of Punjab Tractors Ltd. was challenged to be unlawful. The counsel for the Industrial Tribunal stated that the lock-out could not be declared unlawful on the basis of the settlement subsequently arrived at between the workmen and the employer, in which the representatives of the union contend that the union gave the assurance that the workmen would not involve themselves in such activities in future. Following sections 23, 24 and 10, once the workmen have accepted that they had indulged in violence, a declaration of lock-out cannot be held to be illegal. *(Adapted from: Labour Law Reporter, December, 2011, p. 1277.)*

Prohibition of Financial Aid to Illegal Strikes and Lock-outs (Section 25)

No person shall knowingly expend or apply any money in direct furtherance or support of any illegal strike or lock-out.

CHAPTER VA: LAY-OFF AND RETRENCHMENT

Application of Sections 25C to 25E (Section 25A)

1. Sections 25C to 25E inclusive shall not apply to industrial establishments to which Chapter VB applies, or–
   (a) to industrial establishments in which less than 50 workmen on an average per working day have been employed in the preceding calendar month; or
   (b) to industrial establishments which are of a seasonal character or in which work is performed only intermittently.

> **Spotlight**
> Chapter VA has provisions related to lay-off and retrenchment.

2. If a question arises whether an industrial establishment is of a seasonal character or whether work is performed therein only intermittently, the decision of the appropriate Government thereon shall be final.

Explanation In this section and in sections 25C, 25D and 25E, "industrial establishment" means-
(i) a factory as defined in clause (m) of Section 2 of the Factories Act, 1948; or
(ii) a mine as defined in clause (j) of Section 2 of the Mines Act, 1952; or
(iii) a plantation as defined in clause (f) of Section 2 of the Plantations Labour Act, 1951.

Definition of Continuous Service (Section 25B)

For the purposes of this Chapter:

1. a workman shall be said to be in continuous service for a period if he is, for that period, in uninterrupted service, including service which may be interrupted on account of sickness or authorised leave or an accident or a strike which is not illegal or a lock-out or a cessation of work which is not due to any fault on the part of the workman;
2. where a workman is not in continuous service within the meaning of clause (1) for a period of 1 year or 6 months, he shall be deemed to be in continuous service under an employer–
   (a) for a period of 1 year, if the workman, during a period of 12 calendar months preceding the date with reference to which calculation is to be made, has actually worked under the employer for not less than:
      (i) 190 days, in the case of a workman employed below ground in a mine; and
      (ii) 240 days, in any other case;
   (b) for a period of 6 months, if the workman, during a period of 6 calendar months preceding the date with reference to which calculation is to be made, has actually worked under the employer for not less than:
      (i) 95 days, in the case of a workman employed below ground in a mine; and
      (ii) 120 days, in any other case.

   Explanation For the purposes of clause (2), the number of days on which a workman has actually worked under an employer shall include the days on which:
      (i) he has been laid-off under an agreement or as permitted by standing orders made under the Industrial Employment (Standing Orders) Act, 1946, or under the Act or under any other law applicable to the industrial establishment;
      (ii) he has been on leave with full wages, earned in the previous years;
      (iii) he has been absent due to temporary disablement caused by accident arising out of and in the course of his employment; and
      (iv) in the case of a female, she has been on maternity leave; so, however, that the total period of such maternity leave does not exceed 12 weeks.

Right of Workmen Laid-off for Compensation (Section 25C)

Whenever a workman (other than a *badli* workman or a casual workman) whose name is borne on the muster rolls of an industrial establishment and who has completed not less than 1 year of continuous service under an employer is laid-off, whether continuously or intermittently, he shall be paid by the employer for all days during which he is so laid-off, except for such weekly holidays as may intervene, compensation which shall be equal to 50 per cent of the total of the basic wages and dearness allowance that would have been payable to him had he not been so laid-off:

Provided that if during any period of 12 months, a workman is so laid-off for more than 45 days, no such compensation shall be payable in respect of any period of the lay-off after the expiry of the first 45 days, if there is an agreement to that effect between the workman and the employer:

Provided further that it shall be lawful for the employer in any case falling within the foregoing proviso to retrench the workman in accordance with the provisions contained in Section 25F at any time after the expiry of the first 45 days of the lay-off and when he does so, any compensation paid to the workman for having been laid-off during the preceding 12 months may be set off against the compensation payable for retrenchment.

Explanation "*Badli* workman" means a workman who is employed in an industrial establishment in the place of another workman whose name is borne on the muster rolls of the establishment, but shall cease to be regarded as such for the purposes of this section, if he has completed 1 year of continuous service in the establishment.

Spotlight

A *badli* workman shall not be considered as such if he has completed 1 year of continuous service in an industrial establishment.

Duty of an Employer to Maintain Muster Rolls of Workmen (Section 25D)

Notwithstanding that workmen in any industrial establishment have been laid-off, it shall be the duty of every employer to maintain for the purposes of this Chapter a muster roll, and to provide for the making of entries therein by workmen who may present themselves for work at the establishment at the appointed time during normal working hours.

Workmen not Entitled to Compensation in Certain Cases (Section 25E)

No compensation shall be paid to a workman who has been laid-off:

(i) if he refuses to accept any alternative employment in the same establishment from which he has been laid-off, or in any other establishment belonging to the same employer situate in the same town or village or situate within a radius of 5 miles from the establishment to which he belongs, if, in the opinion of the employer, such alternative employment does not call for any special skill or previous experience and can be done by the workman, provided that the wages which would normally have been paid to the workman are offered for the alternative employment also;

(ii) if he does not present himself for work at the establishment at the appointed time during normal working hours at least once a day;

(iii) if such laying-off is due to a strike or slowing-down of production on the part of workmen in another part of the establishment.

Conditions Precedent to Retrenchment of Workmen (Section 25F)

No workman employed in any industry who has been in continuous service for not less than 1 year under an employer shall be retrenched by that employer until:

(a) the workman has been given 1 month's notice in writing indicating the reasons for retrenchment and the period of notice has expired, or the workman has been paid in lieu of such notice, wages for the period of the notice:

(b) the workman has been paid, at the time of retrenchment, compensation which shall be equivalent to 15 days' average pay for every completed year of continuous service or any part thereof in excess of 6 months; and

(c) notice in the prescribed manner is served on the appropriate Government or such authority as may be specified by the appropriate Government by notification in the Official Gazette.

CASE CORNER

In *General Manager, Haryana Roadways vs. Rudhan Singh* [(2005) 5 SCC 591] the Supreme Court has held that while dealing with retrenchment under Section 25F of the Industrial Disputes Act, 1947 (or simply the Act) and passing an order of payment of back wages, "There is no rule of thumb that in every case where the Industrial Tribunal gives a finding that the termination of service was in violation of Section 25F of the Act, entire back wages should be awarded." A host of factors like: the manner and method of selection and appointment (i.e., advertisement of the vacancy or inviting applications from the employment exchange), nature of appointment (i.e., whether ad hoc, short term, daily wage, temporary or permanent), any special qualification required for the job, etc. should be weighed and balanced in taking a decision regarding award of back wages.

One of the most important factors to be considered here is the *length of service* the workman had rendered with the employer. In case the workman has rendered a considerable period of service and his services are wrongfully terminated, he may be awarded full or partial back wages, keeping in view the fact that at his age and the qualification he possesses, he may not be in a position to get another employment. However, where the length of service rendered by a workman is very small, the award of back wages for the complete period, i.e., from the date of termination till the date of the award, which may be quite large, would be wholly inappropriate. Another important factor to be considered is the *nature of employment*. A regular service of permanent character cannot be compared to any short or intermittent daily-wage employment, though it may be for 240 days in a calendar year.

(Adapted from: www.indiankanoon.org/doc/1628125/ accessed on 31/12/2013.)

In *Damyanti vs. Presiding Officer, Industrial Tribunal-cum-Labour-Court, Panipat and Another* (2012 LLR 833) the petitioner was employed since 1986; her services were terminated on 27th March 2001 following which, she raised an industrial dispute. Defence of the management was that her service was less than 240 days in the preceding calendar year from the date of termination and that the employer- Forest Department is not an industry. Further, she was a seasonal daily-wager. The Labour Court observed that the petitioner had completed 240 days service within the meaning of Section 25B of the Industrial Disputes Act, 1947. However, the petitioner being a daily-wager not engaged by following norms and procedure as laid down for such appointment, she has no right to reinstatement despite non-compliance of Section 25F. In response, the workman challenged the award of the Labour Court. The Court held that the issue is with regard to the legality and validity of the termination and not for regularisation. A daily-wager or seasonal worker too is a workman with industrial rights. It was also held that the Forest Department is an industry. Further, since management did not quote the rule which was violated by the workman, it was held that the petitioner would go back on the same position as held by her on the date of termination with full back-wages. Award of the Labour Court was quashed. *(Adapted from: Labour Law Reporter, August, 2012, pp. 833-834.)*

Compensation to Workmen in Case of Transfer of Undertakings (Section 25FF)

Where the ownership or management of an undertaking is transferred, whether by agreement or by operation of law, from the employer in relation to that undertaking to a new employer, every workman who has been in continuous service for not less than 1 year in that undertaking immediately before such transfer shall be entitled to notice and compensation in accordance with the provisions of Section 25F, as if the workman had been retrenched:

Provided that nothing in this section shall apply to a workman in any case where there has been a change of employers by reason of the transfer, if:

(a) the service of the workman has not been interrupted by such transfer;
(b) the terms and conditions of service applicable to the workman after such transfer are not in any way less favourable to the workman than those applicable to him immediately before the transfer; and
(c) the new employer is, under the terms of such transfer or otherwise, legally liable to pay to the workman, in the event of his retrenchment, compensation on the basis that his service has been continuous and has not been interrupted by the transfer.

Sixty Days' Notice to be Given of Intention to Close Down Any Undertaking (Section 25FFA)

1. An employer who intends to close down an undertaking shall serve, at least 60 days before the date on which the intended closure is to become effective, a notice in the prescribed manner, on the appropriate Government stating clearly the reasons for the intended closure of the undertaking:

   Provided that nothing in this section shall apply to—

   (a) an undertaking in which—
      (i) less than 50 workmen are employed, or
      (ii) less than 50 workmen were employed on an average per working day in the preceding 12 months,
   (b) an undertaking set up for the construction of buildings, bridges, roads, canals, dams or for other construction work or project.

> **Spotlight**
> Sixty days' notice must be given of intention to close down any undertaking.

2. Notwithstanding anything contained in sub-section (1), the appropriate Government may, if it is satisfied that owing to such exceptional circumstances as accident in the undertaking or death of the employer or the like it is necessary so to do, by order, direct that provisions of sub-section (1) shall not apply in relation to such undertaking for such period as may be specified in the order.

Compensation to Workmen in Case of Closing Down of Undertakings (Section 25FFF)

1. Where an undertaking is closed down for any reason whatsoever, every workman who has been in continuous service for not less than 1 year in that undertaking immediately before such closure shall, subject to the provisions of sub-section (2), be entitled to notice and compensation in accordance with the provisions of Section 25F, as if the workman had been retrenched:

   Provided that where the undertaking is closed down on account of unavoidable circumstances beyond the control of the employer, the compensation to be paid to the workman under clause (b) of Section 25F shall not exceed his average pay for 3 months.

   Explanation An undertaking which is closed down by reason merely of:

   (i) financial difficulties (including financial losses); or
   (ii) accumulation of undisposed of stocks; or
   (iii) the expiry of the period of the lease or licence granted to it; or
   (iv) in a case where the undertaking is engaged in mining operations, exhaustion of the minerals in the area in which such operations are carried on;

   shall not be deemed to be closed down on account of unavoidable circumstances beyond the control of the employer within the meaning of the proviso to this sub-section.

1A. Notwithstanding anything contained in sub-section (1), where an undertaking engaged in mining operations is closed down by reason merely of exhaustion of the minerals in the area in which such operations are carried on, no workman referred to in that sub-section shall be entitled to any notice or compensation in accordance with the provisions of Section 25F, if:
   (a) the employer provides the workman with alternative employment with effect from the date of closure at the same remuneration as he was entitled to receive, and on the same terms and conditions of service as were applicable to him, immediately before the closure;
   (b) the service of the workman has not been interrupted by such alternative employment; and
   (c) the employer is, under the terms of such alternative employment or otherwise, legally liable to pay to the workman, in the event of his retrenchment, compensation on the basis that his service has been continuous and has not been interrupted by such alternative employment.

1B. For the purposes of sub-sections (1) and (1A), the expressions "minerals" and "mining operations" shall have the meanings respectively assigned to them in clauses (a) and (d) of Section 3 of the Mines and Minerals (Regulation and Development) Act, 1957.

2. Where any undertaking set-up for the construction of buildings, bridges, roads, canals, dams or other construction work is closed down on account of the completion of the work within 2 years from the date on which the undertaking had been set-up, no workman employed therein shall be entitled to any compensation under clause (b) of Section 25F, but if the construction work is not so completed within 2 years, he shall be entitled to notice and compensation under that section for every completed year of continuous service or any part thereof in excess of 6 months.

Procedure for Retrenchment (Section 25G)

Where any workman in an industrial establishment, who is a citizen of India, is to be retrenched and he belongs to a particular category of workmen in that establishment, in the absence of any agreement between the employer and the workman in this behalf, the employer shall ordinarily retrench the workman who was the last person to be employed in that category, unless for reasons to be recorded the employer retrenches any other workman.

Re-employment of Retrenched Workmen (Section 25H)

Where any workmen are retrenched, and the employer proposes to take into his employ any persons, he shall, in such manner as may be prescribed, give an opportunity to the retrenched workmen who are citizens of India to offer themselves for re-employment, and such retrenched workmen who offer themselves for re-employment shall have preference over other persons.

Spotlight

As per Section 25H, retrenched workmen who offer themselves for re-employment shall have preference over other persons.

Recovery of Moneys Due from Employers under this Chapter (Section 25I)

Repealed by the Industrial Disputes (Amendment and Miscellaneous Provisions) Act, 1956.

Effect of Laws Inconsistent with this Chapter (Section 25J)

1. The provisions of this Chapter shall have effect notwithstanding anything inconsistent therewith contained in any other law including standing orders made under the Industrial Employment (Standing Orders) Act, 1946:

Provided that where under the provisions of any other Act or rules, orders or notifications issued thereunder or under any standing orders or under any award, contract of service or otherwise, a workman is entitled to benefits in respect of any matter which are more favourable to him than those to which he would be entitled under this Act, the workman shall continue to be entitled to the more favourable benefits in respect of that matter, notwithstanding that he receives benefits in respect of other matters under this Act.

2. For the removal of doubts, it is hereby declared that nothing contained in this Chapter shall be deemed to affect the provisions of any other law for the time being in force in any State in so far as that law provides for the settlement of industrial disputes, but the rights and liabilities of employers and workmen in so far as they relate to lay-off and retrenchment shall be determined in accordance with the provisions of this Chapter.

CHAPTER VB: SPECIAL PROVISIONS RELATING TO LAY-OFF, RETRENCHMENT AND CLOSURE IN CERTAIN ESTABLISHMENTS

Application of Chapter VB (Section 25K)

1. The provisions of this Chapter shall apply to an industrial establishment (not being an establishment of a seasonal character or in which work is performed only intermittently) in which not less than 100 workmen were employed on an average per working day for the preceding 12 months.
2. If a question arises whether an industrial establishment is of a seasonal character or whether work is performed therein only intermittently, the decision of the appropriate Government thereon shall be final.

Spotlight
Chapter VB has special provisions relating to lay-off, retrenchment and closure in certain establishments.

Definitions (Section 25L)

For the purposes of this Chapter:

(a) "industrial establishment" means:
   (i) a factory as defined in clause (m) of Section 2 of the Factories Act, 1948;
   (ii) a mine as defined in clause (i) of sub-section (1) of Section 2 of the Mines Act, 1952; or
   (iii) a plantation as defined in clause (f) of Section 2 of the Plantations Labour Act, 1951;

(b) notwithstanding anything contained in sub-clause (ii) of clause (a) of Section 2,-
   (i) in relation to any company in which not less than 51 per cent of the paid-up share capital is held by the Central Government, or
   (ii) in relation to any corporation not being a corporation referred to in sub-clause (i) of clause (a) of Section 2 established by or under any law made by Parliament,

the Central Government shall be appropriate Government.

Prohibition of Lay-off (Section 25M)

1. No workman (other than a *badli* workman or a casual workman) whose name is borne on the muster rolls of an industrial establishment to which this Chapter applies shall be laid-off by his employer except with the prior permission of the appropriate Government or such authority as may be specified by that Government by notification in the Official Gazette (hereinafter in this

section referred to as the specified authority), obtained on an application made in this behalf, unless such lay-off is due to shortage of power or to natural calamity, and in the case of a mine, such lay-off is due also to fire, flood, excess of inflammable gas or explosion.

2. An application for permission under sub-section (1) shall be made by the employer in the prescribed manner stating clearly the reasons for the intended lay-off and a copy of such application shall also be served simultaneously on the workmen concerned in the prescribed manner.
3. Where the workmen (other than *badli* workmen or casual workmen) of an industrial establishment, being a mine, have been laid-off under sub-section (1) for reasons of fire, flood or excess of inflammable gas or explosion, the employer, in relation to such establishment, shall, within a period of 30 days from the date of commencement of such lay-off, apply, in the prescribed manner, to the appropriate Government or the specified authority for permission to continue the lay-off.
4. Where an application for permission under sub-section (1) or sub-section (3) has been made, the appropriate Government or the specified authority, after making such enquiry as it thinks fit and after giving a reasonable opportunity of being heard to the employer, the workmen concerned and the persons interested in such lay-off, may, having regard to the genuineness and adequacy of the reasons for such lay-off, the interests of the workmen and all other relevant factors, by order and for reasons to be recorded in writing, grant or refuse to grant such permission and a copy of such order shall be communicated to the employer and the workmen.
5. Where an application for permission under sub-section (1) or sub-section (3) has been made and the appropriate Government or the specified authority does not communicate the order granting or refusing to grant permission to the employer within a period of 60 days from the date on which such application is made, the permission applied for shall be deemed to have been granted on the expiration of the said period of 60 days.
6. An order of the appropriate Government or the specified authority granting or refusing to grant permission shall, subject to the provisions of sub-section (7), be final and binding on all the parties concerned and shall remain in force for 1 year from the date of such order.
7. The appropriate Government or the specified authority may, either on its own motion or on the application made by the employer or any workman, review its order granting or refusing to grant permission under sub-section (4) or refer the matter or, as the case may be, cause it to be referred, to a Tribunal for adjudication:

   Provided that where a reference has been made to a Tribunal under this sub-section, it shall pass an award within a period of 30 days from the date of such reference.
8. Where no application for permission under sub-section (1) is made, or where no application for permission under sub-section (3) is made within the period specified therein, or where the permission for any lay-off has been refused, such lay-off shall be deemed to be illegal from the date on which the workmen had been laid-off and the workmen shall be entitled to all the benefits under any law for the time being in force as if they had not been laid-off.
9. Notwithstanding anything contained in the foregoing provisions of this section, the appropriate Government may, if it is satisfied that owing to such exceptional circumstances as accident in the establishment or death of the employer or the like, it is necessary so to do, by order, direct that the provisions of sub-section (1), or, as the case may be, sub-section (3) shall not apply in relation to such establishment for such period as may be specified in the order.
10. The provisions of Section 25C (other than the second proviso thereto) shall apply to cases of lay-off referred to in this section.

Explanation For the purposes of this section, a workman shall not be deemed to be laid-off by an employer if such employer offers any alternative employment (which in the opinion of the employer does not call for any special skill or previous experience and can be done by the workman) in the same establishment from which he has been laid-off or in any other establishment belonging to the same employer, situate in the same town or village, or situate within such distance from the establishment to which he belongs that the transfer will not involve undue hardship to the workman having regard to the facts and circumstances of his case, provided that the wages which would normally have been paid to the workman are offered for the alternative appointment also.

Conditions Precedent to Retrenchment of Workmen (Section 25N)

1. No workman employed in any industrial establishment to which this Chapter applies, who has been in continuous service for not less than 1 year under an employer shall be retrenched by that employer until:
   (a) the workman has been given 3 months' notice in writing indicating the reasons for retrenchment and the period of notice has expired, or the workman has been paid in lieu of such notice, wages for the period of the notice; and
   (b) the prior permission of the appropriate Government or such authority as may be specified by that Government by notification in the Official Gazette (hereafter in this section referred to as the specified authority) has been obtained on an application made in this behalf.
2. An application for permission under sub-section (1) shall be made by the employer in the prescribed manner stating clearly the reasons for the intended retrenchment and a copy of such application shall also be served simultaneously on the workmen concerned in the prescribed manner.
3. Where an application for permission under sub-section (1) has been made, the appropriate Government or the specified authority, after making such enquiry as it thinks fit and after giving a reasonable opportunity of being heard to the employer, the workmen concerned and the person interested in such retrenchment, may, having regard to the genuineness and adequacy of the reasons stated by the employer, the interests of the workmen and all other relevant factors, by order and for reasons to be recorded in writing, grant or refuse to grant such permission and a copy of such order shall be communicated to the employer and the workmen.
4. Where an application for permission has been made under sub-section (1) and the appropriate Government or the specified authority does not communicate the order granting or refusing to grant permission to the employer within a period of 60 days from the date on which such application is made, the permission applied for shall be deemed to have been granted on the expiration of the said period of 60 days.
5. An order of the appropriate Government or the specified authority granting or refusing to grant permission shall, subject to the provisions of sub-section (6), be final and binding on all the parties concerned and shall remain in force for 1 year from the date of such order.
6. The appropriate Government or the specified authority may, either on its own motion or on the application made by the employer or any workman, review its order granting or refusing to grant permission under sub-section (3) or refer the matter or, as the case may be, cause it to be referred, to a Tribunal for adjudication:

   Provided that where a reference has been made to a Tribunal under this sub-section, it shall pass an award within a period of 30 days from the date of such reference.

7. Where no application for permission under sub-section (1) is made, or where the permission for any retrenchment has been refused, such retrenchment shall be deemed to be illegal from the date on which the notice of retrenchment was given to the workman and the workman shall be entitled to all the benefits under any law for the time being in force as if no notice had been given to him.
8. Notwithstanding anything contained in the foregoing provisions of this section, the appropriate Government may, if it is satisfied that owing to such exceptional circumstances as accident in the establishment or death of the employer or the like, it is necessary so to do, by order, direct that the provisions of sub-section (1) shall not apply in relation to such establishment for such period as may be specified in the order.
9. Where permission for retrenchment has been granted under sub-section (3) or where permission for retrenchment is deemed to be granted under sub-section (4), every workman who is employed in that establishment immediately before the date of application for permission under this section shall be entitled to receive, at the time of retrenchment, compensation which shall be equivalent to 15 days' average pay for every completed year of continuous service or any part thereof in excess of 6 months.

> **Spotlight**
> Compensation at the time of retrenchment is equivalent to 15 days' average pay for every year of continuous service or part in excess of 6 months.

Procedure for Closing Down an Undertaking (Section 25-O)

1. An employer who intends to close down an undertaking of an industrial establishment to which this Chapter applies shall, in the prescribed manner, apply, for prior permission at least 90 days before the date on which the intended closure is to become effective, to the appropriate Government, stating clearly the reasons for the intended closure of the undertaking and a copy of such application shall also be served simultaneously on the representatives of the workmen in the prescribed manner:

   Provided that nothing in this sub-section shall apply to an undertaking set up for the construction of buildings, bridges, roads, canals, dams or for other construction work.
2. Where an application for permission has been made under sub-section (1), the appropriate Government, after making such enquiry as it thinks fit and after giving a reasonable opportunity of being heard to the employer, the workmen, and the persons interested in such closure may, having regard to the genuineness and adequacy of the reasons stated by the employer, the interests of the general public and all other relevant factors, by order and for reasons to be recorded in writing, grant or refuse to grant such permission and a copy of such order shall be communicated to the employer and the workmen.
3. Where an application has been made under sub-section (1) and the appropriate Government does not communicate the order granting or refusing to grant permission to the employer within a period of 60 days from the date on which such application is made, the permission applied for shall be deemed to have been granted on the expiration of the said period of 60 days.
4. An order of the appropriate Government granting or refusing to grant permission shall, subject to the provisions of sub-section (5), be final and binding on all the parties and shall remain in force for 1 year from the date of such order.
5. The appropriate Government may, either on its own motion or on the application made by the employer or any workman, review its order granting or refusing to grant permission under sub-section (2) or refer the matter to a Tribunal for adjudication:

> **Spotlight**
> Prior permission must be obtained for closing down an undertaking at least 90 days before, as per Section 25-O(i).

Provided that where a reference has been made to a Tribunal under this sub-section, it shall pass an award within a period of 30 days from the date of such reference.

6. Where no application for permission under sub-section (1) is made within the period specified therein, or where the permission for closure has been refused, the closure of the undertaking shall be deemed to be illegal from the date of closure and the workmen shall be entitled to all the benefits under any law for the time being in force as if the undertaking had not been closed down.
7. Notwithstanding anything contained in the foregoing provisions of this section, the appropriate Government may, if it is satisfied that owing to such exceptional circumstances as accident in the undertaking or death of the employer or the like, it is necessary so to do, by order, direct that the provisions of sub-section (1) shall not apply in relation to such undertaking for such period as may be specified in the order.
8. Where an undertaking is permitted to be closed down under sub-section (2) or where permission for closure is deemed to be granted under sub-section (3), every workman who is employed in that undertaking immediately before the date of application for permission under this section, shall be entitled to receive compensation which shall be equivalent to 15 days' average pay for every completed year of continuous service or any part thereof in excess of 6 months.

Special Provision as to Restarting of Undertakings Closed Down before Commencement of the Industrial Disputes (Amendment) Act, 1976 (Section 25P)

If the appropriate Government is of opinion in respect of any undertaking or an industrial establishment to which this Chapter applies and which closed down before the commencement of the Industrial Disputes (Amendment) Act, 1976:

(a) that such undertaking was closed down otherwise than on account of unavoidable circumstances beyond the control of the employer;
(b) that there are possibilities of restarting the undertaking;
(c) that it is necessary for the rehabilitation of the workmen employed in such undertaking before its closure or for the maintenance of supplies and services essential to the life of the community to restart the undertaking or both; and
(d) that the restarting of the undertaking will not result in hardship to the employer in relation to the undertaking,

it may, after giving an opportunity to such employer and workmen, direct, by order published in the Official Gazette, that the undertaking shall be restarted within such time (not being less than 1 month from the date of the order) as may be specified in the order.

Penalty for Lay-off and Retrenchment without Previous Permission (Section 25Q)

Any employer, who contravenes the provisions of Section 25M or of Section 25N shall be punishable with imprisonment for a term which may extend to 1 month, or with fine which may extend to ₹1,000, or with both.

Spotlight

As per Section 25Q, penalty for lay-off and retrenchment without prior permission is imprisonment up to 1 month or fine up to ₹1,000 or with both.

Penalty for Closure (Section 25R)

1. Any employer, who closes down an undertaking without complying with the provisions of sub-section (1) of Section 25-O shall be punishable with imprisonment for a term which may extend to 6 months, or with fine which may extend to ₹5,000, or with both.
2. Any employer, who contravenes an order refusing to grant permission to close down an undertaking under sub-section (2) of Section 25-O or a direction given under Section 25P, shall be punishable with imprisonment for a term which may extend to 1 year, or with fine which may extend to ₹5,000, or with both, and where the contravention is a continuing one, with a further fine which may extend to ₹2,000 for every day during which the contravention continues after the conviction.

Certain Provisions of Chapter VA to Apply to an Industrial Establishment to which this Chapter Applies (Section 25S)

The provisions of sections 25B, 25D, 25FF, 25G, 25H and 25J in Chapter VA shall, so far as may be, apply also in relation to an industrial establishment to which the provisions of this Chapter apply.

CHAPTER VC: UNFAIR LABOUR PRACTICES

Prohibition of Unfair Labour Practice (Section 25T)

No employer or workman or a trade union, whether registered under the Trade Unions Act, 1926, or not, shall commit any unfair labour practice.

Penalty for Committing Unfair Labour Practices (Section 25U)

Any person who commits any unfair labour practice shall be punishable with imprisonment for a term which may extend to 6 months or with fine which may extend to ₹1,000 or with both.

> **Spotlight**
> Penalty for committing unfair labour practices as per Section 25U is imprisonment upto 6 months and/or fine upto ₹1,000.

CHAPTER VI: PENALTIES

Penalty for Illegal Strikes and Lock-outs (Section 26)

> **Spotlight**
> Chapter VI contains provisions relating to penalties.

1. Any workman who commences, continues or otherwise acts in furtherance of, a strike which is illegal under this Act, shall be punishable with imprisonment for a term which may extend to 1 month, or with fine which may extend to ₹50, or with both.
2. Any employer who commences, continues or otherwise acts in furtherance of a lock-out which is illegal under this Act, shall be punishable with imprisonment for a term which may extend to 1 month, or with fine which may extend to ₹1,000, or with both.

Penalty for Instigation, etc. (Section 27)

Any person who instigates or incites others to take part in, or otherwise acts in furtherance of, a strike or lock-out which is illegal under this Act, shall be punishable with imprisonment for a term which may extend to 6 months, or with fine which may extend to ₹1,000, or with both.

Penalty for Giving Financial Aid to Illegal Strikes and Lock-outs (Section 28)

Any person who knowingly expends or applies any money in direct furtherance or support of any illegal strike or lock-out shall be punishable with imprisonment for a term which may extend to 6 months, or with fine which may extend to ₹1,000, or with both.

Penalty for Breach of Settlement or Award (Section 29)

Any person who commits a breach of any term of any settlement or award, which is binding on him under this Act, shall be punishable with imprisonment for a term which may extend to 6 months, or with fine, or with both, and where the breach is a continuing one, with a further fine which may extend to ₹200 for every day during which the breach continues after the conviction for the first and the Court trying the offence, if it fines the offender, may direct that the whole or any part of the fine realised from him shall be paid, by way of compensation, to any person who, in its opinion, has been injured by such breach.

Penalty for Disclosing Confidential Information (Section 30)

Any person who wilfully discloses any such information as is referred to in Section 21 in contravention of the provisions of that section shall, on complaint made by or on behalf of the trade union or individual business affected, be punishable with imprisonment for a term which may extend to 6 months, or with fine which may extend to ₹1,000, or with both.

Penalty for Closure without Notice (Section 30A)

Any employer who closes down any undertaking without complying with the provisions of Section 25FFA shall be punishable with imprisonment for a term which may extend to 6 months, or with fine which may extend to ₹5,000, or with both.

Spotlight

Penalty for closure without notice, as per Section 30A, is imprisonment up to 6 months or fine up to ₹5,000 or both.

Penalty for Other Offences (Section 31)

1. Any employer who contravenes the provisions of Section 33 shall be punishable with imprisonment for a term which may extend to 6 months, or with fine which may extend to ₹1,000, or with both.
2. Whoever contravenes any of the provisions of this Act or any rule made thereunder shall, if no other penalty is elsewhere provided by or under this Act for such contravention, be punishable with fine which may extend to ₹100.

CHAPTER VII: MISCELLANEOUS

Offence by Companies, etc. (Section 32)

Where a person committing an offence under this Act is a company, or other body corporate, or an association of persons (whether incorporated or not), every director, manager, secretary, agent or other officer or person concerned with the management thereof shall, unless he proves that the offence was committed without his knowledge or consent, be deemed to be guilty of such offence.

Conditions of Service, etc., to Remain Unchanged under Certain Circumstances during Pendency of Proceedings (Section 33)

1. During the pendency of any conciliation proceeding before a conciliation officer or a Board or of any proceeding before an arbitrator, or a Labour Court, or Tribunal, or National Tribunal in respect of an industrial dispute, no employer shall:
   (a) in regard to any matter connected with the dispute, alter, to the prejudice of the workmen concerned in such dispute, the conditions of service applicable to them immediately before the commencement of such proceeding; or
   (b) for any misconduct connected with the dispute, discharge or punish, whether by dismissal or otherwise, any workman concerned in such dispute,

   save with the express permission in writing of the authority before which the proceeding is pending.
2. During the pendency of any such proceeding in respect of an industrial dispute, the employer may, in accordance with standing orders applicable to a workman concerned in such dispute or, where there are no such standing orders, in accordance with the terms of the contract, whether express or implied, between him and the workman:
   (a) alter, in regard to any matter not connected with the dispute, the conditions of service applicable to that workman immediately before the commencement of such proceeding; or
   (b) for any misconduct not connected with the dispute, or discharge or punish, whether by dismissal or otherwise, that workman:

Provided that no such workman shall be discharged or dismissed, unless he has been paid wages for 1 month and an application has been made by the employer to the authority before which the proceeding is pending for approval of the action taken by the employer.

3. Notwithstanding anything contained in sub-section (2), no employer shall, during the pendency of any such proceeding in respect of an industrial dispute, take any action against any protected workman concerned in such dispute:
   (a) by altering, to the prejudice of such protected workman, the conditions of service applicable to him immediately before the commencement of such proceeding; or
   (b) by discharging or punishing, whether by dismissal or otherwise, such protected workman,

   save with the express permission in writing of the authority before which the proceeding is pending.

   Explanation For the purposes of this sub-section, a "protected workman", in relation to an establishment, means a workman who, being a member of the executive or other office bearer of a registered trade union connected with the establishment, is recognised as such in accordance with rules made in this behalf.

> **Spotlight**
> Minimum and maximum number of protected workmen in an establishment are 5 and 10 respectively.

4. In every establishment, the number of workmen to be recognised as protected workmen for the purposes of sub-section (3) shall be 1 per cent of the total number of workmen employed therein subject to a minimum number of five protected workmen and a maximum number of 100 protected workmen and for the aforesaid purpose, the appropriate Government may make rules providing for the distribution of such protected workmen among various trade unions, if any, connected with the establishment and the manner in which the workmen may be chosen and recognised as protected workmen.
5. Where an employer makes an application to a conciliation officer, Board, an arbitrator, a Labour Court, Tribunal or National Tribunal under the proviso to sub-section (2) for approval of the action taken by him, the authority concerned shall, without delay, hear such application and pass,

within a period of 3 months from the date of receipt of such application, such order in relation thereto as it deems fit:

Provided that where any such authority considers it necessary or expedient so to do, it may, for reasons to be recorded in writing, extend such period by such further period as it may think fit:

Provided further that no proceedings before any such authority shall lapse merely on the ground that any period specified in this sub-section had expired without such proceedings being completed.

Special Provision for Adjudication as to Whether Conditions of Service, etc., Changed during Pendency of Proceeding (Section 33A)

Where an employer contravenes the provisions of Section 33 during the pendency of proceedings before a conciliation officer, Board, an arbitrator, a Labour Court, Tribunal or National Tribunal any employee aggrieved by such contravention, may make a complaint in writing, in the prescribed manner:

(a) to such conciliation officer or Board, and the conciliation officer or Board shall take such complaint into account in mediating in, and promoting the settlement of, such industrial dispute; and

(b) to such arbitrator, Labour Court, Tribunal or National Tribunal and on receipt of such complaint, the arbitrator, Labour Court, Tribunal or National Tribunal, as the case may be, shall adjudicate upon the complaint as if it were a dispute referred to or pending before it, in accordance with the provisions of this Act and shall submit his or its award to the appropriate Government and the provisions of this Act shall apply accordingly.

Power to Transfer Certain Proceedings (Section 33B)

1. The appropriate Government may, by order in writing and for reasons to be stated therein, withdraw any proceeding under this Act pending before a Labour Court, Tribunal or National Tribunal and transfer the same to another Labour Court, Tribunal or National Tribunal, as the case may be, for the disposal of the proceeding and the Labour Court, Tribunal or National Tribunal to which the proceeding is so transferred may, subject to special directions in the order of transfer, proceed either *de novo* or from the stage at which it was so transferred:

   Provided that where a proceeding under Section 33 or Section 33A is pending before a Tribunal or National Tribunal, the proceeding may also be transferred to a Labour Court.
2. Without prejudice to the provisions of sub-section (1), any Tribunal or National Tribunal, if so authorised by the appropriate Government, may transfer any proceeding under Section 33 or Section 33A pending before it to any one of the Labour Courts specified for the disposal of such proceedings by the appropriate Government by notification in the Official Gazette and the Labour Court to which the proceeding is so transferred shall dispose off the same.

Recovery of Money Due from an Employer (Section 33C)

1. Where any money is due to a workman from an employer under a settlement or an award or under the provisions of Chapter VA or Chapter VB, the workman himself or any other person authorised by him in writing in this behalf, or, in the case of the death of the workman, his assignee or heirs may, without prejudice to any other mode of recovery, make an application to the appropriate Government for the recovery of the money due to him, and if the appropriate Government is satisfied that any money is so due, it shall issue certificate for that amount to the Collector who shall proceed to recover the same in the same manner as an arrear of land revenue:

Provided that every such application shall be made within 1 year from the date on which the money became due to the workman from the employer:

Provided further that any such application may be entertained after the expiry of the said period of 1 year, if the appropriate Government is satisfied that the applicant had sufficient cause for not making the application within the said period.

2. Where any workman is entitled to receive from the employer any money or any benefit which is capable of being computed in terms of money and if any question arises as to the amount of money due or as to the amount at which such benefit should be computed, then the question may, subject to any rules that may be made under this Act, be decided by such Labour Court as may be specified in this behalf by the appropriate Government within a period not exceeding 3 months:

   Provided that where the presiding officer of a Labour Court considers it necessary or expedient so to do, he may, for reasons to be recorded in writing, extend such period by such further period as he may think fit.
3. For the purposes of computing the money value of a benefit, the Labour Court may, if it so thinks fit, appoint a Commissioner who shall, after taking such evidence as may be necessary, submit a report to the Labour Court and the Labour Court shall determine the amount after considering the report of the Commissioner and other circumstances of the case.
4. The decision of the Labour Court shall be forwarded by it to the appropriate Government and any amount found due by the Labour Court may be recovered in the manner provided for in sub-section (1).
5. Where workmen employed under the same employer are entitled to receive from him any money or any benefit capable of being computed in terms of money, then, subject to such rules as may be made in this behalf, a single application for the recovery of the amount due may be made on behalf of or in respect of any number of such workmen.

Explanation In this section "Labour Court" includes any court constituted under any law relating to investigation and settlement of industrial disputes in force in any State.

CASE CORNER

In *Sarjerao Janardhan Hande and Others vs. Maharashtra State Co-operative Marketing Federation Ltd.* [(2012) LLR 724] both the petitioners were working as drivers with the respondent and had retired under Voluntary Retirement Scheme (VRS). No dispute was raised at that time with regard to the overtime wages; however, they subsequently filed a common application claiming overtime after getting all the benefits of retirement/VRS, referring to the dates and vehicle numbers which they claimed to have worked and the relevant overtime bills. Management resisted the same, denying the validity of the supporting documents, to which the workmen raised industrial dispute under Section 33C(2) of the Industrial Disputes Act, 1947. The Labour Court dismissed their application holding that the petitioners had failed to prove their overtime working. The petitioners then filed writ petition. The High Court held that admittedly the claim of the workmen is not based upon undisputed and/or admitted documents, which were not even original. The forms placed on record were admittedly not countersigned by the officers of the respondent and copies of those documents not considered to be sufficient. The Court thus held that no adverse inference could be drawn against the management on denial of such documents. The Labour Court, therefore, considering the scope and purpose of Section 33(C), had rightly rejected the application.

(*Adapted from: Labour Law Reporter, September, 2012, p. 924.*)

Cognizance of Offences (Section 34)

1. No Court shall take cognizance of any offence punishable under this Act or of the abetment of any such offence, save on complaint made by or under the authority of the appropriate Government.
2. No Court inferior to that of a Metropolitan Magistrate or a Judicial Magistrate of the first class shall try any offence punishable under this Act.

Protection of Persons (Section 35)

1. No person refusing to take part or to continue to take part in any strike or lock-out which is illegal under this Act shall, by reason of such refusal or by reason of any action taken by him under this section, be subject to expulsion from any trade union or society, or to any fine or penalty, or to deprivation of any right or benefit to which he or his legal representatives would otherwise be entitled, or be liable to be placed in any respect, either directly or indirectly, under any disability or at any disadvantage as compared with other members of the union or society, anything to the contrary in the rules of a trade union or society notwithstanding.
2. Nothing in the rules of a trade union or society requiring the settlement of disputes in any manner shall apply to any proceeding for enforcing any right or exemption secured by this section, and in any such proceeding the Civil Court may, in lieu of ordering a person who has been expelled from membership of a trade union or society to be restored to membership, order that he be paid out of the funds of the trade union or society such sum by way of compensation or damages as that Court thinks just.

Representation of Parties (Section 36)

1. A workman who is a party to a dispute shall be entitled to be represented in any proceeding under this Act by:
   (a) any member of the executive or other office bearer of a registered trade union of which he is a member;
   (b) any member of the executive or other office bearer of a federation of trade unions to which the trade union referred to in clause (a) is affiliated;
   (c) where the worker is not a member of any trade union, by any member of the executive or other office bearer of any trade union connected with, or by any other workman employed in, the industry in which the worker is employed and authorised in such manner as may be prescribed.
2. An employer who is a party to a dispute shall be entitled to be represented in any proceeding under this Act by:
   (a) an officer of an association of employers of which he is a member;
   (b) an officer of a federation of association of employers to which the association referred to in clause (a) is affiliated;
   (c) where the employer is not a member of any association of employers, by an officer of any association of employers connected with, or by any other employer engaged in, the industry in which the employer is engaged and authorised in such manner as may be prescribed.
3. No party to a dispute shall be entitled to be represented by a legal practitioner in any conciliation proceedings under this Act or in any proceedings before a Court.

4. In any proceeding before a Labour Court, Tribunal or National Tribunal, a party to a dispute may be represented by a legal practitioner with the consent of the other parties to the proceeding and with the leave of the Labour Court, Tribunal or National Tribunal, as the case may be.

Power to Remove Difficulties (Section 36A)

1. If, in the opinion of the appropriate Government, any difficulty or doubt arises as to the interpretation of any provision of an award or settlement, it may refer the question to such Labour Court, Tribunal or National Tribunal as it may think fit.
2. The Labour Court, Tribunal or National Tribunal to which such question is referred shall, after giving the parties an opportunity of being heard, decide such question and its decision shall be final and binding on all such parties.

Power to Exempt (Section 36B)

Where the appropriate Government is satisfied in relation to any industrial establishment or undertaking or any class of industrial establishments or undertakings carried on by a department of that Government that adequate provisions exist for the investigation and settlement of industrial disputes in respect of workmen employed in such establishment or undertaking or class of establishments or undertakings, it may, by notification in the Official Gazette, exempt, conditionally or unconditionally such establishment or undertaking or class of establishments or undertakings from all or any of the provisions of this Act.

Protection of Action Taken under the Act (Section 37)

No suit, prosecution or other legal proceeding shall lie against any person for anything which is in good faith done or intended to be done in pursuance of this Act, or any rules made thereunder.

Power to Make Rules (Section 38)

1. The appropriate Government may, subject to the condition of previous publication, make rules for the purpose of giving effect to the provisions of this Act.
2. In particular and without prejudice to the generality of the foregoing power, such rules may provide for all or any of the following matters, namely:
   - (a) the powers and procedure of conciliation officers, Boards, Courts, Labour Courts, Tribunals and National Tribunals including rules as to the summoning of witnesses, the production of documents relevant to the subject-matter of an inquiry or investigation, the number of members necessary to form a quorum and the manner of submission of reports and awards;
   - (aa) the form of arbitration agreement, the manner in which it may be signed by the parties, the manner in which a notification may be issued under sub-section (3A) of Section 10A, the powers of the arbitrator named in the arbitration agreement and the procedure to be followed by him;
   - (aaa) the appointment of assessors in proceedings under this Act;
   - (b) the constitution and functions of and the filling of vacancies in Works Committees, and the procedure to be followed by such Committees in the discharge of their duties;
   - (c) the salaries and allowances and the terms and conditions for appointment of the presiding officers of the Labour Court, Tribunal and the National Tribunal including the allowances admissible to members of Courts, Boards and to assessors and witnesses;

(d) the ministerial establishment which may be allotted to a Court, Board, Labour Court, Tribunal, or National Tribunal and the salaries and allowances payable to members of such establishment;
(e) the manner in which and the persons by and to whom notice of strike or lock-out may be given and the manner in which such notices shall be communicated;
(f) the conditions subject to which parties may be represented by legal practitioners in proceedings under this Act before a Court, Labour Court, Tribunal or National Tribunal;
(g) any other matter which is to be or may be prescribed.

3. Rules made under this section may provide that a contravention thereof shall be punishable with fine not exceeding ₹50.
4. All rules made under this section shall, as soon as possible after they are made, be laid before the State Legislature or, where the appropriate Government is the Central Government, before both Houses of Parliament.
5. Every rule made by the Central Government under this section shall be laid, as soon as may be after it is made, before each House of Parliament while it is in session for a total period of 30 days which may be comprised in 1 session or in 2 or more successive sessions, and if, before the expiry of the session immediately following the session or the successive sessions aforesaid both Houses agree in making any modification in the rule, or both Houses agree that the rule should not be made, the rule shall thereafter have effect only in such modified form or be of no effect, as the case may be; so, however, that any such modification or annulment shall be without prejudice to the validity of anything previously done under that rule.

Delegation of Powers (Section 39)

The appropriate Government may, by notification in the Official Gazette, direct that any power exercisable by it under this Act or rules made thereunder shall, in relation to such matters and subject to such conditions, if any, as may be specified in the direction, be exercisable also:

(a) where the appropriate Government is the Central Government, by such officer or authority subordinate to the Central Government or by the State Government or by such officer or authority subordinate to the State Government, as may be specified in the notification; and
(b) where the appropriate Government is a State Government, by such officer or authority subordinate to the State Government as may be specified in the notification.

Power to Amend Schedules (Section 40)

1. The appropriate Government may, if it is of opinion that it is expedient or necessary in the public interest so to do, by notification in the Official Gazette, add to the First Schedule any industry, and on any such notification being issued, the First Schedule shall be deemed to be amended accordingly.
2. The Central Government may, by notification in the Official Gazette, add to or alter or amend the Second Schedule or the Third Schedule and on any such notification being issued, the Second Schedule or the Third Schedule, as the case may be, shall be deemed to be amended accordingly.
3. Every such notification shall, as soon as possible after it is issued, be laid before the Legislature of the State, if the notification has been issued by a State Government, or before Parliament, if the notification has been issued by the Central Government.

ADMINISTRATION OF THE ACT

The Industrial Disputes Act, 1947 is administered by the Ministry of Labour & Employment through its Industrial Relations Division. The Ministry is responsible for protection and safeguarding of the interests of workers in general and the poor, deprived and disadvantaged sections of the society in particular. The Industrial Relations Division is concerned with improving the institutional framework in the country for dispute settlement and for amending labour laws relating to industrial relations. It works in close co-ordination with the Central Industrial Relations Machinery (CIRM), which is an attached office of the Ministry of Labour & Employment. The CIRM is also known as the Chief Labour Commissioner (Central) [CLC(C)] Organisation, headed by the Chief Labour Commissioner (Central).

SUMMARY

- The Industrial Disputes Act, 1947, an Act mainly to make provision for the investigation and settlement of industrial disputes, came into force on and from 1st April 1947.
- Industrial dispute, as per Section 2(k), means any dispute or difference between employers and employers, or between employers and workmen, or between workmen and workmen, which is connected with the employment or non-employment or the terms of employment or with the conditions of labour, of any person.
- Section 2(kkk) defines lay-off as the failure, refusal or inability of an employer on account of shortage of coal, power or raw materials or the accumulation of stocks or the breakdown of machinery or natural calamity or for any other connected reason to give employment to a workman whose name is borne on the muster rolls of his industrial establishment and who has not been retrenched.
- Lock-out, as per Section 2(l), refers to the temporary closing of a place of employment or suspension of work, or refusal by an employer to continue to employ any number of persons employed by him; closure is defined in Section 2(cc) as the permanent closing down of a place of employment or part thereof.
- According to Section 2(oo), retrenchment means the termination by the employer of the service of a workman for any reason whatsoever, otherwise than as a punishment inflicted by way of disciplinary action, but does not include voluntary retirement of the workman; or retirement of the workman on reaching the age of superannuation; or termination of the service of the workman as a result of the non-renewal of the contract of employment; or termination of the service of a workman on the ground of continued ill-health.
- Section 2(q) defines strike as a cessation of work by a body of persons employed in any industry acting in combination, or a concerted refusal, or a refusal under a common understanding, of any number of persons who are or have been so employed to continue to work or to accept employment.
- Section 4 empowers the appropriate Government to appoint conciliation officers charged with the duty of mediating in and promoting the settlement of industrial disputes. Boards of Conciliation, as per Section 5, are constituted for promoting the settlement of an industrial dispute. Other authorities include Courts of Inquiry, Labour Courts, Industrial Tribunals and National Tribunals.
- Works Committees, as per Section 6, must promote measures for securing and preserving amity and good relations between the employer and workmen, comment upon matters of their common interest or concern and endeavour to compose any material difference of opinion in respect of such matters.

- Section 9C mandates every industrial establishment employing 20 or more workmen to have 1 or more Grievance Redressal Committee consisting of equal number of members from the employer and workmen for the resolution of disputes arising out of individual grievances.
- Section 10A provides for voluntary reference of disputes to arbitration on mutual agreement between employer and workmen.
- Chapter IV elaborates on the procedures, powers and duties of conciliation officer, a Board, Court, Labour Court, Tribunal and National Tribunal. Sections 15 to 21 in this chapter have various provisions related to reports and awards given by the various authorities under the Act.
- Section 22 prohibits a person employed in a public utility service from going on strike in breach of contract: without giving to the employer notice of strike within 6 weeks before striking; or within 14 days of giving such notice; or before the expiry of the date of strike specified in any such notice as aforesaid; or during the pendency of any conciliation proceedings before a conciliation officer and 7 days after the conclusion of such proceedings. Similar prohibition is provided in context of an employer carrying on a public utility service for lock-out of any of his workmen.
- Section 24(1) considers a strike or a lock-out to be illegal if it is commenced or declared in contravention of Section 22 or 23; or if it is continued in contravention of an order made under sub-section (3) or (4A) of Section 10. A lock-out declared in consequence of an illegal strike or a strike declared in consequence of an illegal lock-out shall not be deemed to be illegal as per Section 24(3).
- Chapter VA has provisions for lay-off and retrenchment, while Chapter VB has special provisions relating to lay-off, retrenchment and closure in certain establishments. Chapter VC deals with unfair labour practices.
- Chapter VI provides for penalties under different circumstances, namely illegal strikes and lock-outs (Section 26), instigation (Section 27), giving financial aid to illegal strikes and lock-outs (Section 28), breach of settlement or award (Section 29), etc.
- Chapter VII has miscellaneous provisions related to offence by companies (Section 32), power to transfer certain proceedings (Section 33B), etc.
- The Industrial Disputes Act, 1947 is administered by the Ministry of Labour & Employment through its Industrial Relations Division, which works in close co-ordination with the CIRM. The CIRM is also known as the Chief Labour Commissioner (Central) Organisation, headed by the Chief Labour Commissioner (Central).

Key Concepts

Strike	Unfair labour practice	Grievance Redressal Committee
Lock-out	Closure	Award
Public utility service	Conciliation proceeding	Tribunal
Lay-off	Labour Court	Dismissal

Bibliography

Misra, S. N. and Misra, S. K. *An Introduction to Labour and Industrial Laws*, Allahabad: Central Law Publications; 1995.

www.indiankanoon.org

Review Questions

Objective Type Questions

I. State True or False

i. A workman must be paid compensation equivalent to 15 days' average pay for every completed year of continuous service at the time of retrenchment.
ii. A person must have served as a District Judge for a period of not less than 3 years to be the presiding officer of a Labour Court.
iii. Term of imprisonment as penalty for committing unfair labour practices may extend to 6 months.
iv. No person employed in a public utility service shall go on strike without giving notice of strike to the employer within 6 weeks before striking.
v. An auditor of a trade union is considered to be an office bearer.

Answers: i. True, ii. True, iii. True, iv. True, v. False

ii. Fill in the Blanks

i. Total number of members of the Grievance Redressal Committee must not exceed ____.
ii. Notice of ______ days must be given of an intention to close down any undertaking.
iii. No employer should declare a lock-out till _____days after the conclusion of conciliation proceedings before a Board.
iv. No employer shall take any action against any _____workman concerned in a dispute during the pendency of a proceeding in respect of that dispute.
v. Unfair labour practice refers to any of the practices specified in the _____Schedule.

Answers: i. 6, ii. 60, iii. 7, iv. protected, v. Fifth

Discussion Questions

1. State the differences between lay-off, retrenchment and closure.
2. What are the authorities for settlement and investigation of industrial disputes, as per the Industrial Disputes Act, 1947? Discuss the structure and function of each such authority.
3. Discuss the provisions for prohibition of strikes and lock-outs in public utility services. When is a strike or lock-out considered to be illegal?
4. What are unfair labour practices as per the Industrial Disputes Act, 1947?
5. Explain the various penalties for offences under the Industrial Disputes Act, 1947.
6. Discuss the provisions related to compensation of workmen on the event of closing down of an undertaking.
7. Elaborate on the following concepts as per the Industrial Disputes Act, 1947:
   a. Appropriate Government
   b. Industry
   c. Workman
8. Explain the concept of a Grievance Redressal Committee and its role in settlement of disputes.
9. What are the special provisions for adjudication of disputes relating to change of conditions of service?
10. Discuss the provision on reference of disputes to Boards, Courts or Tribunals.

CASE STUDY

CASE STUDY-I

The workmen-respondent in this case was appointed as an accountant in the appellant-company. It was submitted on behalf of the appellant that the respondent was not a workman as per the Industrial Disputes Act, 1947, which excluded any person who is working in managerial or administrative capacity. In fact, the respondent himself in his reply before the Labour Court had admitted that he was handling and dealing with other companies also and was given one scooter with fuel; therefore he was discharging the duty of managerial nature. It was submitted by the appellant that the respondent was not entitled to back-wages because he had failed to prove that he was not engaged in gainful work during the entire period. However, findings based on evidence implied that no managerial function has been assigned to him, and this prompted Labour Court to pass an award in favour of the workman. However, modification was made in the award of back-wages by reducing it by 25 per cent. The applicant-company was aggrieved against such order passed by the Labour Court.

The Court considered the submissions of the parties and perused the reasons given in the award as well as in the impugned order. It was also considered that it was an undisputed fact that the respondent, who was admittedly appointed on the post of accountant, was assigned the duty of realisation of amounts from other companies and for that purpose he was provided with a scooter and fuel.

(Adapted from: Management, M/s. Gajraj Estates (P) Ltd. vs. Workman, A. K. Agarwal and Another [(2012) LLR 1092], Labour Law Reporter, October, 2012, pp. 1092-1093.)

Review Questions

1. As per which section of the Industrial Disputes Act, 1947 can the respondent be classified as a workman or otherwise?
2. Do you think that any managerial function has been assigned to the respondent?
3. Should the Court interfere with the impugned order of reducing the back-wages by 25 per cent by the Labour Court?

CASE STUDY-II

This case is on the basis of a petition filed by a workman under Articles 226 and 227 of the Constitution against the impugned award passed by the Labour Court, Amritsar answering the reference in favour of the respondent-management. The case of the management lies in the testimony of its own witness (MW-1). The petitioner was selected and joined duty at the Government College for Women, Amritsar on 25th September 1991. On 9th May1992, the Head Girl to the Principal reported misconduct of the petitioner, which led to the termination of the services of the latter on 14th May 1992. The foundation of the order lay in misconduct; no charge-sheet was issued to her, nor was any basic fact-finding enquiry held to establish the misconduct before such termination. No opportunity was given to workman to counter the report of Head Girl and the Mess President, or to confront the complainant with a defence at cross-examination. No prior warning letter was placed on record by the management leading to the action taken on 9th May 1992. Consequently, the petitioner served the College from 25th September 1991 to 14th May 1992, i.e., for 233 days.

The MW-1 admitted that the job was perennial in nature and the workman's services were terminated for misconduct. The defence of the management before the Labour Court was that the workman had put in only 233 days of service and thus she had acquired no industrial rights; she was removed from service in terms of her appointment letter under which her service could be terminated at any time, without any notice.

The appointment was a regular one and not contractual. It may have been temporary employment not curtailed by time, but the management could not have so easily resorted to the clause in the appointment letter empowering it to relieve the workman from service at any time, without any prior notice. The Labour Court simply closed the door for the petitioner on the ground that 240 days service had not been put in. It further failed to see or address itself to the core question that putting in of 240 days of continuous service does not arise in case of misconduct.

Subsequently, the Court allowed the writ petition and quashed the impugned award. The petitioner was directed to be reinstated with continuity of service and full back-wages. However the management was given the liberty to hold fresh enquiry on the same allegations in accordance with law but only after implementation of the Court's order.

(Adapted from: Madhu vs. Presiding Officer, Labour Court, Amritsar and Another [(2012) LLR 830], Labour Law Reporter, August, 2012, pp. 830-833.)

Review Questions

1. Do you think that the respondent-management was right in abruptly terminating the services of the petitioner 7 days short of completing 240 days on the ground of misconduct? What were the lacunae on the part of the management in the case?
2. Would termination of services of the petitioner in an admitted case of misconduct, 7 days short of completing 240 days amount to unfair labour practice? Argue with logic.
3. Was the decision of the Labour Court fair? Justify.
4. Which sections of the Industrial Disputes Act, 1947 are relevant in this case?

16

The Industrial Employment (Standing Orders) Act, 1946

An Act to require employers in industrial establishments formally to define conditions of employment under them

Desired Knowledge Competencies

- To understand the emergence of the Industrial Employment (Standing Orders) Act, 1946.
- To gain knowledge of the extent, commencement and application of the Act.
- To discuss concepts like standing orders, model standing orders, certifying officer, subsistence allowance, etc.

CONCEPT OF INDUSTRIAL EMPLOYMENT

Clarity of obligations and privileges play a major role in cordial relations, work satisfaction and performance. The same is true in context of employment conditions in industrial settings. The Labour Investigation Committee (1946) had observed that 'an industrial worker has the right to know the terms and conditions under which he is employed and the rules of discipline which he is expected to follow' *(Source: Labour Investigation Committee Report, 1946, p. 109)*. The Industrial Employment (Standing Orders) Act, 1946 was passed so that employers in industrial establishments define with sufficient precision the conditions of employment under them and to also make the said conditions known to workmen employed in such establishments.

BACKDROP OF INDUSTRIAL EMPLOYMENT (STANDING ORDERS) ACT, 1946

Prior to the Industrial Employment (Standing Orders) Act, 1946, conditions of obtaining employment in several industrial establishments were governed by contracts between employers and employees.

Terms and conditions of employment were not reduced to writing and were even governed by oral agreements. In establishments which had their own standing orders, such terms and conditions would either be ambiguous or inequitable, and would be the root causes of many a case of dissent and industrial disputes. Victimisation and unfair labour practices were frequent to occur, and the industrial worker had no right to know the rules governing his employment.

When workmen realised that at individual level they lacked adequate bargaining strength to secure fair terms and conditions of employment, they organised themselves in the form of trade unions and initiated the process of collective bargaining with employers. The intervention of unions and the process of collective bargaining created new problems in the way to maintaining industrial peace. Soon emerged a situation in which workers would put forth their demands and employers would face the wrath of workmen if they did not define their conditions of service; possibilities of industrial strife became inevitable. The Tripartite Labour Conference held in 1947 pleaded for defining the conditions of employment so as to promote harmonious relations between employers and workmen. There was a consensus of opinion in favour of legislation in the Conference. It was then that the legislature made an attempt to intervene by introducing the Industrial Employment (Standing Orders) Bill, 1946 to provide for the framing of 'standing orders' in all industrial establishments employing 100 or more workers. The Bill was passed by the legislature and it received assent of the President of India on 23rd April 1946. It came on the statute book as the Industrial Employment (Standing Orders) Act, 1946.

With the Trade Unions Act, 1926 intended to provide a foundation for orderly labour-management relations, the Industrial Employment (Standing Orders) Act, 1946 also forms part of the same base. Its principal objective is to define the conditions of recruitment, discharge, disciplinary action, holidays, leave, etc. and to settle and clarify such terms and conditions of employment over which disputes normally arose. It also protects workers from arbitrary actions by employers.

Spotlight

The Industrial Employment (Standing Orders) Act, 1946 is designed to avoid friction and tension between employers and workmen.

As observed in *Shahdara (Delhi)-Saharanpur Light Railway Company Ltd. vs. Shahdara-Saharanpur Railway Workers' Union* [(1969) SCR (2) 131] the Industrial Employment (Standing Orders) Act, 1946 is a beneficent piece of legislation, its object being to require, as its preamble and its long title lay down, employers' industrial establishments to define with sufficient precision the conditions of employment of workmen employed under them and to make them known to such workmen.

(Adapted from: www.indiankanoon.org/doc/80637/ accessed on 6/3/2014.)

It has further been observed in *Agra Electric Supply Co. Ltd vs. Sri Alladin and Others* [(1970) SCR (1) 808] that the object of the Act is to have uniform standing orders providing for the matters enumerated in the Schedule to the Act, that it was not intended that there should be different conditions of service for those who are employed before and those employed after the standing orders came into force, and finally, that once the standing orders come into force, they bind all those presently in the employment of the concerned establishment as well as those who are appointed thereafter.

(Adapted from: www.indiankanoon.org/doc/416759/ accessed on 6/3/2014.)

Following is the list of amending acts and adaptation orders of the Act:

1. The Indian Independence (Adaptation of Central Acts and Ordinances) Order, 1948
2. The Adaptation of Laws Order, 1950

3. The Part B States (Laws) Act, 1951
4. The Industrial Disputes (Amendment and Miscellaneous Provisions) Act, 1956
5. The Industrial Employment (Standing Orders) Amendment Act, 1961
6. The Industrial Employment (Standing Orders) Amendment Act, 1963
7. The Central Labour Laws (Extension to Jammu and Kashmir) Act, 1970
8. The Industrial Employment (Standing Orders) Amendment Act, 1982

ABOUT THE ACT

Short Title, Extent and Application (Section 1)

1. This Act may be called the Industrial Employment (Standing Orders) Act, 1946.
2. It extends to the whole of India.
3. It applies to every industrial establishment wherein 100 or more workmen are employed, or were employed on any day of the preceding 12 months:

   Provided that the appropriate Government may, after giving not less than 2 months' notice of its intention so to do, by notification in the Official Gazette, apply the provisions of this Act to any industrial establishment employing such number of persons less than 100 as may be specified in the notification.
4. Nothing in this Act shall apply to:
   (i) any industry to which the provisions of Chapter VII of the Bombay Industrial Relations Act, 1946 apply; or
   (ii) any industrial establishment to which the provisions of the Madhya Pradesh Industrial Employment (Standing Orders) Act, 1961 apply:

Provided that notwithstanding anything contained in the Madhya Pradesh Industrial Employment (Standing Orders) Act, 1961, the provisions of this Act shall apply to all industrial establishments under the control of the Central Government.

Interpretation (Section 2)

In this Act, unless there is anything repugnant in the subject or context, —

Appellate authority [Section 2(a)] Appellate authority means an authority appointed by the appropriate Government by notification in the Official Gazette to exercise in such area as may be specified in the notification the functions of an appellate authority under this Act:

Provided that in relation to an appeal pending before an Industrial Court or other authority immediately before the commencement of the Industrial Employment (Standing Orders) Amendment Act, 1963, that Court or authority shall be deemed to be the appellate authority;

Appropriate Government [Section 2(b)] Appropriate Government means in respect of industrial establishments under the control of the Central Government or a Railway administration or in a major port, mine or oil-field, the Central Government, and in all other cases the State Government:

Provided that where any question arises as to whether any industrial establishment is under the control of the Central Government, that Government may, either on a reference made to it by the employer or the workman or a trade union or other representative body of the workmen, or on its own motion and after giving the parties an opportunity of being heard, decide the question and such decision shall be final and binding on the parties.

Spotlight

As per Section 2(c), a Certifying Officer is a Labour Commissioner or a Regional Labour Commissioner and includes any other officer appointed by the appropriate Government.

Certifying Officer [Section 2(c)] Certifying Officer means a Labour Commissioner or a Regional Labour Commissioner, and includes any other officer appointed by the appropriate Government, by notification in the Official Gazette, to perform all or any of the functions of a Certifying Officer under this Act;

Employer [Section 2(d)] Employer means the owner of an industrial establishment to which this Act for the time being applies, and includes—

(i) in a factory, any person named under clause (f) of sub-section (1) of Section 7 of the Factories Act, 1948, as manager of the factory;
(ii) in any industrial establishment under the control of any department of any Government in India, the authority appointed by such Government in this behalf, or where no authority is so appointed, the head of the department;
(iii) in any other industrial establishment, any person responsible to the owner for the supervision and control of the industrial establishment;

Industrial Establishment [Section 2(e)] Industrial establishment means—

(i) an industrial establishment as defined in clause (ii) of Section 2 of the Payment of Wages Act, 1936, or
(ii) a factory as defined in clause (m) of Section 2 of the Factories Act, 1948, or
(iii) a railway as defined in clause (4) of Section 2 of the Indian Railway Act, 1890, or
(iv) the establishment of a person who, for the purpose of fulfilling a contract with the owner of any industrial establishment, employs workmen;

CASE CORNER

In *Bharti Bhawan (P and D) vs. State of Bihar and Others* [(2004) IILLJ 920 Pat], the petitioner is an establishment registered under the Bihar Shops and Establishments Act, 1953. According to the petitioner, it is engaged as a publisher and distributor of books. For this purpose, the manuscript given by the author after editing, filming, etc. on computer is sent to the press, where the books are printed and sent to it after binding by independent binders. The petitioner further submitted that it only deals with the intellectual contents of a book but the material for producing the book, i.e., paper, glue, cover printed material, etc. are not handled by it. The Certifying Officer found that the petitioner is engaged in production of books and as such it comes within the definition of an industrial establishment in view of the inclusive definition of an industrial establishment under Section 2(e) of Industrial Employment (Standing Orders) Act, 1946. From a plain reading of Section 2(ii)(f) of the Payment of Wages Act, 1936, it is evident that an establishment in which articles are produced comes within the definition of industrial establishment. In the present case, according to the petitioner itself, the manuscript given by the author is edited by it and filmed on computer, and thereafter sent to the press not belonging to it. After it is so printed, a book is sent to the petitioner subsequent to binding by the independent buyers. The Court held that the act of editing and filming and thereafter getting a book printed and bound even by other printers and binders shall bring the petitioner within the expression "industrial establishment" in which books are produced.

(Adapted from: www.indiankanoon.org/doc/541524/ accessed on 3/3/2014.)

Prescribed [Section 2(f)] Prescribed means prescribed by rules made by the appropriate Government under this Act;

Spotlight
As per Section 2(g), standing orders means rules relating to matters set out in the Schedule.

Standing orders [Section 2(g)] Standing orders means rules relating to matters set out in the Schedule;

Trade union [Section 2(h)] Trade union means a trade union for the time being registered under the Trade Unions Act, 1926;

Wages and workman [Section 2(i)] "Wages" and "workman" have the meanings respectively assigned to them in clauses (rr) and (s) of Section 2 of the Industrial Disputes Act, 1947.

Submission of Draft Standing Orders (Section 3)

1. Within 6 months from the date on which this Act becomes applicable to an industrial establishment, the employer shall submit to the Certifying Officer 5 copies of the draft standing orders proposed by him for adoption in his industrial establishment.
2. Provision shall be made in such draft for every matter set out in the Schedule which may be applicable to the industrial establishment, and where model standing orders have been prescribed, shall be, so far as is practicable, in conformity with such model.
3. The draft standing orders submitted under this section shall be accompanied by a statement giving prescribed particulars of the workmen employed in the industrial establishment including the name of the trade union, if any, to which they belong.
4. Subject to such conditions as may be prescribed, a group of employers in similar industrial establishments may submit a joint draft of standing orders under this section.

Conditions for Certification of Standing Orders (Section 4)

Standing orders shall be certifiable under this Act if—

(a) provision is made therein for every matter set out in the Schedule which is applicable to the industrial establishment, and
(b) the standing orders are otherwise in conformity with the provisions of this Act,

and it shall be the function of the Certifying Officer or appellate authority to adjudicate upon the fairness or reasonableness of the provisions of any standing orders.

Certification of Standing Orders (Section 5)

1. On receipt of the draft under Section 3, the Certifying Officer shall forward a copy thereof to the trade union, if any, of the workmen, or where there is no such trade union, to the workmen in such manner as may be prescribed, together with a notice in the prescribed form requiring objections, if any, which the workmen may desire to make to the draft standing orders to be submitted to him within 15 days from the receipt of the notice.
2. After giving the employer and the trade union or such other representatives of the workmen as may be prescribed an opportunity of being heard, the Certifying Officer shall decide whether or not any modification of or addition to the draft submitted by the employer is necessary to render the draft standing orders certifiable under this Act, and shall make an order in writing accordingly.

3. The Certifying Officer shall thereupon certify the draft standing orders, after making any modifications therein which his order under sub-section (2) may require, and shall within 7 days thereafter send copies of the certified standing orders authenticated in the prescribed manner and of his order under sub-section (2) to the employer and to the trade union or other prescribed representatives of the workmen.

In *S. Alamelu vs. The Superintending Engineer, South Arcot Electricity System* [(1990) IILLJ 96 Mad], it has been stated that certified standing orders have their overriding effect on other service rules and regulations.

Appeals (Section 6)

1. Any employer, workman, trade union or other prescribed representatives of the workmen aggrieved by the order of the Certifying Officer under sub-section (2) of Section 5 may, within 30 days from the date on which copies are sent under sub-section (3) of that section, appeal to the appellate authority, and the appellate authority, whose decision shall be final, shall by order in writing confirm the standing orders either in the form certified by the Certifying Officer or after amending the said standing orders by making such modifications thereof or additions thereto as it thinks necessary to render the standing orders certifiable under this Act.
2. The appellate authority shall, within 7 days of its order under sub-section (1), send copies thereof of the Certifying Officer, to the employer and to the trade union or other prescribed representatives of the workmen, accompanied, unless it has confirmed without amendment the standing orders as certified by the Certifying Officer, by copies of the standing orders as certified by it and authenticated in the prescribed manner.

Date of Operation of Standing Orders (Section 7)

Standing orders shall, unless an appeal is preferred under Section 6, come into operation on the expiry of 30 days from the date on which authenticated copies thereof are sent under sub-section (3) of Section 5, or where an appeal as aforesaid is preferred, on the expiry of 7 days from the date on which copies of the order of the appellate authority are sent under sub-section (2) of Section 6.

Register of Standing Orders (Section 8)

A copy of all standing orders as finally certified under this Act shall be filed by the Certifying Officer in a register in the prescribed form maintained for the purpose, and the Certifying Officer shall furnish a copy thereof to any person applying therefor on payment of the prescribed fee.

Posting of Standing Orders (Section 9)

The text of the standing orders as finally certified under this Act shall be prominently posted by the employer in English and in the language understood by the majority of his workmen on special boards to be maintained for the purpose at or near the entrance through which the majority of the workmen enter the industrial establishment and in all departments thereof where the workmen are employed.

CASE CORNER

In *Indian Express Employees Union vs. Indian Express (Madurai) Ltd. and Others* [(1999) ILLJ 490 Ker], the petitioner is a registered union of workmen under the respondent company. It is contended by the respondent that the petitioner trade union is not a recognised one and that it does not have representative character as it represented only a very thin minority of workmen. Under Section 10(2) of the Industrial Employment (Standing Orders) Act, 1946 (referred to as 'Act' now onwards), an employer or workmen or trade union or other representative body of workmen can apply for modification of standing orders. This shows that the applicant need not be a trade union; it can be workmen who need not be a sizeable number of workmen of the establishment. A trade union can also be an applicant; it needs only to be a trade union registered under the Trade Unions Act, 1926. The Act does not say that such a trade union shall have recognition or a representative character with substantial majority. It is obviously so because notice on such application for modification shall necessarily be given after applied for by the workmen or any one of the trade unions, to other trade unions or such other representatives of the workmen in terms of Section 5(2) read with Section 10(3). If the applicant is not a sizeable majority and the majority of the workmen represented by other trade unions or other body can object to it, necessarily the Certifying Officer can ascertain the will of the workers. Even if application for modification is by a minority union, the majority union can object to such modification. Further if the modification application is filed by a majority union and it is not in conformity with the provisions of the Act, it will not be allowed.

(Adapted from: www.indiankanoon.org/doc/1850116/ accessed on 6/3/2014.)

Duration and Modification of Standing Orders (Section 10)

1. Standing orders finally certified under this Act shall not, except on agreement between the employer and the workmen, or a trade union or other representative body of the workmen, be liable to modification until the expiry of 6 months from the date on which the standing orders or the last modifications thereof came into operation.
2. Subject to the provisions of sub-section (1), an employer or workman or a trade union or other representative body of the workmen may apply to the Certifying Officer to have the standing orders modified, and such application shall be accompanied by 5 copies of the modifications proposed to be made, and where such modifications are proposed to be made by agreement between the employer and the workmen or a trade union or other representative body of the workmen, a certified copy of that agreement shall be filed along with the application.
3. The foregoing provisions of this Act shall apply in respect of an application under sub-section (2) as they apply to the certification of the first standing orders.
4. Nothing contained in sub-section (2) shall apply to an industrial establishment in respect of which the appropriate Government is the Government of the State of Gujarat or the Government of the State of Maharashtra.

Spotlight

As per Section 10(2), an employer or workman or a trade union or other representative body of the workmen may apply to the Certifying Officer to have the standing orders modified.

Payment of Subsistence Allowance (Section 10A)

1. Where any workman is suspended by the employer pending investigation or inquiry into complaints or charges of misconduct against him, the employer shall pay to such workman subsistence allowance—
   (a) at the rate of 50 per cent of the wages which the workman was entitled to immediately preceding the date of such suspension, for the first 90 days of suspension; and
   (b) at the rate of 75 per cent of such wages for the remaining period of suspension if the delay in the completion of disciplinary proceedings against such workman is not directly attributable to the conduct of such workman.
2. If any dispute arises regarding the subsistence allowance payable to a workman under sub-section (1), the workman or the employer concerned may refer the dispute to the Labour Court, constituted under the Industrial Disputes Act, 1947, within the local limits of whose jurisdiction the industrial establishment wherein such workman is employed is situate and the Labour Court to which the dispute is so referred shall, after giving the parties an opportunity of being heard, decide the dispute and such decision shall be final and binding on the parties.
3. Notwithstanding anything contained in the foregoing provisions of this section, where provisions relating to payment of subsistence allowance under any other law for the time being in force in any State are more beneficial than the provisions of this section, the provisions of such other law shall be applicable to the payment of subsistence allowance in that State.

In *Vijaya Bank vs. Shyamal Kumar Lodh* [(2010) 7 SCC 635] it was held that the provisions of the Industrial Employment (Standing Orders) Act, 1946 indicate that a Labour Court constituted under the Industrial Disputes Act, 1947, whether by the State Government or Central Government, would have jurisdiction to entertain a claim of subsistence allowance payable to a workman on an application made to such Labour Court by the concerned workman. The provisions of Section 10A(2) of the Act is a special provision incorporated only for adjudicating on claims relating to payment of subsistence allowance.

(Adapted from: www.indiankanoon.org/doc/1016822/ accessed on 6/3/2014.)

Certifying Officers and Appellate Authorities to have Powers of Civil Court (Section 11)

1. Every Certifying Officer and appellate authority shall have all the powers of a Civil Court for the purposes of receiving evidence, administering oaths, enforcing the attendance of witnesses, and compelling the discovery and production of documents, and shall be deemed to be a Civil Court within the meaning of sections 345 and 346 of the Code of Criminal Procedure, 1973.
2. Clerical or arithmetical mistakes in any order passed by a Certifying Officer or appellate authority, or errors arising therein from any accidental slip or omission may, at any time, be corrected by that Officer or authority or the successor in office of such officer or authority, as the case may be.

Oral Evidence in Contradiction of Standing Orders not Admissible (Section 12)

No oral evidence having the effect of adding to or otherwise varying or contradicting standing orders as finally certified under this Act shall be admitted in any Court.

Temporary Application of Model Standing Orders (Section 12A)

1. Notwithstanding anything contained in sections 3 to 12, for the period commencing on the date on which this Act becomes applicable to an industrial establishment and ending with the date on which the standing orders as finally certified under this Act come into operation under Section 7 in that establishment, the prescribed model standing orders shall be deemed to be adopted in that establishment, and the provisions of Section 9, sub-section (2) of Section 13 and Section 13A shall apply to such model standing orders as they apply to the standing orders so certified.
2. Nothing contained in sub-section (1) shall apply to an industrial establishment in respect of which the appropriate government is the Government of the State of Gujarat or the Government of the State of Maharashtra.

Penalties and Procedure (Section 13)

1. An employer who fails to submit draft standing orders as required by Section 3, or who modifies his standing orders otherwise than in accordance with Section 10, shall be punishable with fine which may extend to ₹5,000, and in the case of a continuing offence with a further fine which may extend to ₹200 for every day after the first during which the offence continues.
2. An employer who does any act in contravention of the standing orders finally certified under this Act for his industrial establishment shall be punishable with fine which may extend to ₹100, and in the case of a continuing offence with a further fine which may extend to ₹25 for every day after the first during which the offence continues.
3. No prosecution for an offence punishable under this section shall be instituted except with the previous sanction of the appropriate Government.
4. No Court inferior to that of a Metropolitan Magistrate or Judicial Magistrate of the second class shall try any offence under this section.

Spotlight

As per Section 13(1), an employer who fails to submit draft standing orders or who modifies his standing orders violating Section 10 shall be punishable with fine up to ₹5,000

Interpretation, etc., of Standing Orders (Section 13A)

If any question arises as to the application or interpretation of a standing order certified under this Act, any employer or workman or a trade union or other representative body of the workmen may refer the question to any one of the Labour Courts constituted under the Industrial Disputes Act, 1947, and specified for the disposal of such proceeding by the appropriate Government by notification in the Official Gazette, and the Labour Court to which the question is so referred shall, after giving the parties an opportunity of being heard, decide the question and such decision shall be final and binding on the parties.

In *Moti Lal vs. Bharat Electronics Limited* [(2003) 2 UPLBEC 1620] it was held that the determination of the Labour Court is made final and binding on the parties. Further, it was held that the language of Section 13A is not very clear; it cannot certainly be understood as creating a forum for adjudication of industrial disputes involving the application and/or interpretation of the Standing Orders.

That is the function of the courts and tribunal constituted under the Industrial Disputes Act, 1947. The limited purpose of Section 13A is to provide a forum for determination of any question arising 'as to the application or interpretation' of the certified Standing Orders as such, in case either the employer or the employee(s) entertain a doubt as to their meaning or their applicability.

(Adapted from: www.indiankanoon.org/doc/601186/ accessed on 6/3/2014.)

Act not to Apply to Certain Industrial Establishments (Section 13B)

Nothing in this Act shall apply to an industrial establishment in so far as the workmen employed therein are persons to whom the Fundamental and Supplementary Rules, Civil Services (Classification, Control and Appeal) Rules, Civil Services (Temporary Services) Rules, Revised Leave Rules, Civil Service Regulations, Civilians in Defence Service (Classification, Control and Appeal) Rules or the Indian Railway Establishment Code or any other rules or regulations that may be notified in this behalf by the appropriate Government in the Official Gazette, apply.

Power to Exempt (Section 14)

The appropriate Government may by notification in the Official Gazette exempt, conditionally or unconditionally, any industrial establishment or class of industrial establishments from all or any of the provisions of this Act.

Delegation of Powers (Section 14A)

The appropriate Government may, by notification in the Official Gazette, direct that any power exercisable by it under this Act or any rules made thereunder shall, in relation to such matters and subject to such conditions, if any, as may be specified in the direction, be exercisable also—

(a) where the appropriate Government is the Central Government, by such officer or authority subordinate to the Central Government or by the State Government, or by such officer or authority subordinate to the State Government, as may be specified in the notification;

(b) where the appropriate government is a State Government, by such officer or authority subordinate to the State Government, as may be specified in the notification.

Power to Make Rules (Section 15)

1. The appropriate Government may, after previous publication, by notification in the Official Gazette, make rules to carry out the purposes of this Act.
2. In particular and without prejudice to the generality of the foregoing power, such rules may:
   (a) prescribe additional matters to be included in the Schedule, and the procedure to be followed in modifying standing orders certified under this Act in accordance with any such addition;
   (b) set out model standing orders for the purposes of this Act;
   (c) prescribe the procedure of Certifying Officers and appellate authorities;
   (d) prescribe the fee which may be charged for copies of standing orders entered in the register of standing orders;
   (e) provide for any other matter which is to be or may be prescribed;

Provided that before any rules are made under clause (a) representatives of both employers and workmen shall be consulted by the appropriate Government.

3. Every rule made by the Central Government under this section shall be laid as soon as may be after it is made, before each House of Parliament while it is in session for a total period of 30 days which may be comprised in 1 session or in 2 or more successive sessions, and if, before the expiry of the session immediately following the session or the successive sessions aforesaid both Houses agree in making any modification in the rule or both Houses agree that the rule should not be made, the rule shall thereafter have effect only in such modified form or be of no effect, as the case may be; so however that any such modification or annulment shall be without prejudice to the validity of anything previously done under that rule.

THE SCHEDULE

[See Sections 2(g) and 3(2)]

Matters to be Provided in Standing Orders under this Act

1. Classification of workmen, e.g., whether permanent, temporary, apprentices, probationers or *badlis*.
2. Manner of intimating to workmen periods and hours of work, holidays, pay-days and wage rates.
3. Shift working.
4. Attendance and late coming.
5. Conditions of, procedure in applying for, and the authority which may grant leave and holidays.
6. Requirement to enter premises by certain gates, and liability to search.
7. Closing and re-opening of sections of the industrial establishment, temporary stoppages of work and the rights and liabilities of the employer and workmen arising therefrom.
8. Termination of employment, and the notice thereof to be given by employer and workmen.
9. Suspension or dismissal for misconduct, and acts or omissions which constitute misconduct.
10. Means of redress for workmen against unfair treatment or wrongful exactions by the employer or his agents or servants.
11. Any other matter which may be prescribed.

ADMINISTRATION OF THE ACT

The Industrial Relations Division of the Ministry of Labour & Employment is entrusted with the responsibility of policy formulation and amendment of various Central Labour Acts which primarily aid in harmonious industrial relations. The Industrial Employment (Standing Orders) Act, 1946 is one of these Central Labour Acts administered by the IR Division. The machinery for the implementation of the Act comprises the Certifying Officer and the appellate authority. The Chief Labour Commissioner (Central) is the appellate authority, while the Deputy Labour Commissioner and Regional Labour Commissioner exercise the power of Certifying Officers in the Central Sphere situated within their respective jurisdiction.

Spotlight

The machinery for the implementation of the Industrial Employment (Standing Orders) Act, 1946 comprises the Certifying Officer and the appellate authority.

RECENT INITIATIVES

The Ministry of Labour & Employment has amended Paragraph 14 of Schedule I and Paragraph 17 of Schedule I(A) of the Industrial Employment (Standing Orders) Central Rules, 1946 in compliance with the directions of the Hon'ble Supreme Court to include 'sexual harassment' as misconduct, that includes such unwelcome sexual determined behaviour (whether directly or by implication), such as physical contact and advances; or demand or request for sexual favours; or sexually coloured remarks; or showing pornography; or any other unwelcome physical, verbal or non-verbal conduct of sexual nature [vide GSR 25(E), dated 19th January 2006 (w.e.f. 19.1.2006)]. Further, the same amendments provide that the Complaints Committee established in each establishment for inquiring into a complaint of sexual harassment shall be deemed to be the inquiring authority appointed by the employer for the purpose of these rules. The Act has also been amended to make the guidelines applicable to the employees in the private sector.

SUMMARY

- The Industrial Employment (Standing Orders) Act, 1946 is designed primarily to avoid friction and tension between employers and workmen employed in an industry. Its principal function is to settle and clarify many terms and conditions of employment over which disputes normally arise. It also protects workers from arbitrary actions by employers.
- As per Section 2(c), a Certifying Officer is a Labour Commissioner or a Regional Labour Commissioner; Section 2(g) defines standing orders as rules relating to matters set out in the Schedule.
- Section 3(1) prescribes that the employer shall submit to the Certifying Officer 5 copies of the draft standing orders proposed by him for adoption in his industrial establishment within 6 months from the date on which this Act becomes applicable to the establishment.
- On receiving the draft standing orders, as per Section 5(1), the Certifying Officer shall forward a copy thereof to the trade union, if any, or where there is no such trade union, to the workmen in such manner as may be prescribed, together with a notice in the prescribed form requiring objections, if any, which the workmen may desire to make to the draft standing orders to be submitted to him within 15 days from the receipt of the notice.
- According to Section 6(1), any employer, workmen, trade union or other prescribed representatives of the workmen aggrieved by the order of the Certifying Officer may, within 30 days from the date on which copies are sent under Section 5(3), appeal to the appellate authority.
- Standing orders finally certified under this Act shall not, except on agreement between the employer and the workmen or a trade union or other representative body of the workmen, be liable to modification until the expiry of 6 months from the date on which the standing orders or the last modifications thereof came into operation, as provided in Section 10(1).
- Section 13(1) provides that an employer who fails to submit draft standing orders as required by Section 3, or who modifies his standing orders otherwise than in accordance with Section 10, shall be punishable with fine which may extend to ₹5,000.
- The Schedule contains matters to be provided in standing orders under this Act, including classification of workmen (e.g., whether permanent, temporary, apprentices, probationers, or *badlis*), manner of intimating to workmen periods and hours of work, holidays, pay-days and wage rates, shift working, etc.

Key Concepts

Standing orders
Certifying Officer
Draft standing orders
Certification
Subsistence allowance
Model standing orders
Termination of employment
Schedule
Appellate authority

Bibliography

Labour Investigation Committee Report, 1946. Retrieved from www.indianlabourarchives.org/usr/locl/gsdl accessed on 6/3/2014.

Mamoria, C. B., Mamoria, S. and Gankar, S. V. *Dynamics of Industrial Relations*, Mumbai: Himalaya Publishing House, 2008.

Misra, S. N. and Misra, S. K. *An Introduction to Labour and Industrial Laws*, Allahabad: Central Law Publications, 1995.

http://hrylabour.gov.in/docs/labourActpdfdocs/Industrial_Employment_Rules.pdf accessed on 5/3/2014.

Review Questions

Objective Type Questions

I. State True or False

(i) Failure to submit draft standing orders by an employer shall make him punishable with fine up to ₹5,000.
(ii) Subsistence allowance is at the rate of 75 per cent of wages for the first 90 days of suspension.
(iii) Certifying Officer means a Labour Commissioner or a Deputy Labour Commissioner.
(iv) A group of employers in similar industrial establishments may submit a joint draft of standing orders.
(v) The text of the standing orders must be prominently posted by the employer only in Hindi.

Answers: i. True, ii. False, iii. False, iv. True, v. False

II. Fill in the Blanks

(i) The employer must submit to the Certifying Officer _____ copies of the draft standing orders for adoption in his industrial establishment.
(ii) Clerical or ____ mistakes in any order passed by a Certifying Officer may be corrected by that Officer.
(iii) Standing orders finally certified shall not be liable to modification until the expiry of ___ months from the date on which the last modifications came into operation.
(iv) No ____ evidence adding to or contradicting standing orders finally certified under this Act shall be admitted in any Court.
(v) Standing orders means ____ relating to matters set out in the Schedule.

Answers: i. five, ii. arithmetical, iii. six, iv. oral, v. rules

Discussion Questions

1. Discuss the matters to be provided in standing orders under the Industrial Employment (Standing Orders) Act, 1946.
2. Clearly mention the provisions of payment of subsistence allowance.
3. Explain the concept of standing orders. Briefly enumerate the historical evolution of the Industrial Employment (Standing Orders) Act, 1946.
4. How can model standing orders be applied temporarily to an industrial establishment?
5. Discuss the machinery for the administration of the Industrial Employment (Standing Orders) Act, 1946.
6. What provisions in the Industrial Employment (Standing Orders) Act, 1946 apply to modification of standing orders of any industrial establishment?
7. What are the prerequisites for certification of standing orders?
8. What is the procedure for appeal against certification?
9. Discuss the provisions with respect to penalties in the Industrial Employment (Standing Orders) Act, 1946.
10. Explain briefly:
    i. Appellate authority
    ii. Certification of standing orders
    iii. Powers of Certifying Officers

CASE I

The respondent company in this case had applied to the Industrial Tribunal under Section 33 of the Industrial Disputes Act, 1947 for permission to dismiss 27 of its employees. Its contention was that there was an illegal strike on 11th November 1953 of the workers of the company, that these 27 employees had participated in the illegal strike, and that they had also refused to obey lawful orders. It was further the contention of the respondent company that a proper inquiry as required by the standing orders had been held, that, the charge of misconduct with regard to these two acts had been established and therefore under the standing orders the company was entitled to inflict the penalty of dismissal upon these 27 workers.

The Industrial Court granted permission with regard to 3 out of the 27 employees and refused permission involving the rest 24. The reason that induced the Industrial Tribunal to come to this conclusion was that no translation in Marathi of the standing orders had been posted on special boards and therefore the 27 employees, who did not know English, had no notice of the standing orders, which were thus not binding upon those 24 employees and no proper inquiry could be deemed to have been held as required by the standing orders. With respect to the other 3 employees, as they knew English, and a copy of the standing orders having been posted on the notice board, the Tribunal took the view that the same were binding on those 3 employees and gave the necessary permission to the respondent company.

There was an appeal from the decision of the Certifying Officer certifying the standing orders and the copies of the Appellate Court's decision were forwarded to the trade unions concerned and also to the employer on 30th September 1953. Therefore the standing orders came into operation on 8th October 1953.

Questions

1. Which of the sections of the Industrial Employment (Standing Orders) Act, 1946 are relevant in this case?
2. Marathi being the language understood by the majority of the second respondent company's workmen, do you think that the workmen affected are not bound by the provisions of the Standing Orders?
3. The illegal strike having taken place on 11th November 1953, do you think that the penalty inflicted upon the employees was a penalty permitted under the Standing Orders to the employer?

(Adapted from: Ismail Papamia and Others vs. Labour Appellate Tribunal (A) (AIR 1956 Bom 584) www.indiankanoon.org/doc/1468795/ accessed on 6/3/2014.)

CASE II

The three petitioners in this case are employees of the Government Training Centre, a State Government establishment, and have questioned the legality of the order by which the subsistence allowance paid during the period of suspension is sought to be recovered from the salary of the petitioner.

Departmental enquiries on certain charges were instituted against the petitioners, who were found guilty of the charges. Punishment by way of reduction of their pay was imposed by the orders dated 19th August 1987.

As far as the validity of the order imposing the penalty is concerned, the petitioners have presented separate writ petitions seeking the quashing of that portion of the order denying subsistence allowance. As the condition imposed in all the three orders is similar, it is sufficient to extract the relevant portion in one of the orders, as follows:

"Since all the charges framed in the charge sheet dated 5th September 1985 have been proved against you and you are found guilty of the said charges, you are deemed to be absent from duty for the period of suspension and shall not be entitled to any remuneration for the said period. Hence the subsistence allowance paid for the period 5th September 1985 till date of reinstatement will be recovered from your salary with effect from September 1987 in suitable instalments. You are hereby reinstated into service with effect from 1st September 1987."

The question therefore is whether the direction to recover subsistence allowance paid during the period of suspension is valid or not?

In support of the legality of the action, the respondent relied upon the certified standing order of the respondent, which reads as follows:

If, on the conclusion of the enquiry, the employee has been found to be guilty of any or all the charges framed against him, the employee shall be deemed to be absent from duty for the period of suspension and shall not be entitled to any remuneration for such period, and the order of punishment shall take effect from the date of suspension. If, however, the employee is found not guilty of any of the charges framed against him he shall be deemed to have been on duty during the period of suspension and shall be entitled to the same remuneration as he would have received if he had not been placed under suspension, after deducting the subsistence allowance paid to him for such period.

The learned counsel for the petitioners, however, contended that the real meaning of the standing order was that in a case in which the disciplinary proceedings instituted against the suspended employee, ends in his exoneration, he would become entitled to full remuneration and in the case where it ends in punishment, he would not be entitled to the same, and standing order does not mean that even the subsistence allowance paid should be recovered.

(Adapted from: R. Govendaraj and Others vs. Government Tool Room and Training Centre (ILR 1989 KAR 1864) www.indiankanoon.org/doc/343511/ accessed on 6/3/2014.)

Questions

1. Can any employer deny the subsistence allowance required to be paid under the Act either during the period of suspension or subsequently after passing of the final order?
2. Do you think that subsistence allowance paid during the period of suspension can be recovered from salary?

17

The Maternity Benefit Act, 1961

An Act to regulate the employment of women in certain establishments for certain period before and after child-birth and to provide for maternity benefit and certain other benefits.

Desired Knowledge Competencies

- To comprehend the concept of maternity benefit and evolution of the Maternity Benefit Act, 1961.
- To discuss the scope and coverage of the Maternity Benefit Act, 1961 and of the various definitions given under the Act.
- To develop clarity of concepts like miscarriage, medical termination of pregnancy, medical bonus and nursing break, as laid down in the Act.

INTRODUCTION

Motherhood and childhood are entitled to special care and assistance. All children whether born in, or out of, wedlock, shall enjoy the same social protection.

Article 25(2), Universal Declaration of Human Rights, 1948

Motherhood is a very special and unique experience to a woman, which brings with itself abundant joy and marks the beginning of a new journey in a woman's life; however, this journey also entails several compromises. In the early days of wage labour system, women who would bear a child were not provided with any relief at work. They were required to work for long hours and thus bear heavy physical strains (Sinha, Sinha and Shekhar, 2006). In many instances employers would even terminate the services of women workers if the productivity of these workers was found to be affected due to maternity. This was a dubious condition for women workers: either they had to strain themselves to safeguard their job and thus jeopardise their own health and the health of their newborns, or forego their employment on account of maternity.

It was thus perceived largely that an employer must be considerate and sympathetic towards women workers, and a legislation that must keep in perspective the physical difficulties a working woman would face in performing her duties during pre- and post-natal periods was also needed. The Maternity Benefit Act, 1961 is an example of the attempts by the Government of India to move legislations to ensure social security of women by allowing them to perform their "social function of child bearing" (Sinha, Sinha and Shekhar, 2006, p. 444), undeterred by the fear of punitive measures for absence during pre- and/or post-natal period(s). It is a Central legislation that addresses the protection of employment of a working woman and her need for leave during pregnancy and after childbirth.

Spotlight
The Maternity Benefit Act, 1961 is a Central legislation that addresses the protection of employment of a working woman and her need for leave during pregnancy and after childbirth.

BACKDROP OF THE MATERNITY BENEFIT ACT, 1961

The history of working women in India reveals that after the first Factories Act in 1881, only a few 'modern' sectors like tea plantations had particular need for women workers (Sen, n.d.). It was a common practice to consider women workers as 'special', mainly because they also had to perform their social role of a wife and a mother. Legislations were sought to regulate the condition of women actually engaged in factory work, covering aspects like hours of work, periods of rest, prohibition of night work and handling of machinery.

The issue of maternity benefit acquired worldwide attention in the First Maternity Protection Conference convened in 1919 by the International Labour Organisation (ILO). The resolution of compulsory maternity leave, non-termination of service and other benefits for women industrial workers during pregnancy and immediately after childbirth passed at the Conference was however turned down by the Government of India on the ground that such a law would not be workable in the country.

It would be worthwhile to mention here the name of N. M. Joshi, who had introduced the Maternity Benefit Bill in the Legislative Assembly in 1924. The Bill aimed at prohibiting the employment of women in factories, mines and tea plantations in the period immediately before and after childbirth. However, the Assembly rejected the Bill.

In spite of long opposition from mill owners and other employers, the first maternity benefit legislation, known as the Bombay Maternity Benefit Act of 1929, was passed in Maharashtra and this was followed by the Madhya Pradesh Maternity Benefit Act of 1930. As a result of the Royal Commission's recommendation on the subject, several State-level legislations for maternity benefit were passed in Madras, Uttar Pradesh, Bengal, Punjab and Assam. However, these legislations varied from each other as regards their scope, qualifying conditions, etc. and a need was perceived for a central legislation for maternity benefit. Thus the Mines Maternity Benefit Act, 1941, enforced in December 1942, came up as the first Central enactment extending maternity benefits to women employed in mines. The Bengal Maternity Benefits (Tea Estates) Bill, 1941 was introduced by the Bengal Government with a view to regularising maternity benefits for women workers in tea factories and plantations. This was followed by the Employees' State Insurance Act, 1948 and the Plantations Labour Act, 1951. The report given by the Labour Investigation Committee (1946) appointed by the Government of India expressed dissatisfaction regarding the enforcement of the State-level Acts. Meanwhile, the Constitution of India was adopted on 27th January 1950. Part IV of the Constitution mentions the Directive Principles of State Policy. Article 39 provides, *inter alia*, that the State shall, in particular, direct its policy towards securing that the citizens, men and women equally, have the right to an adequate means of livelihood; and that the health and strength of workers, men and women, and the tender age of children are not abused and that citizens are not forced by economic necessity to enter avocations unsuited to their age or strength;

Spotlight
Maternity benefit legislations prior to the Maternity Benefit Act, 1961:

- Bombay Maternity Benefit Act, 1929
- Machya Pradesh Maternity Benefit Act, 1930
- Other State-level legislations
- Mines Maternity Benefit Act, 1941
- Employees' State Insurance Act, 1948
- Plantations Labour Act, 1951

Keeping in perspective the philosophy of ILO and understanding that woman workers need legislation towards maternity benefit, care for woman and maternity relief was recognised by the Constitution of India under Article 42, which provides that the State shall make provisions for securing just and humane conditions of work and for maternity relief. Subsequently, the Central Maternity Benefit Act was passed in 1961, replacing the earlier Central and State legislations.

Meanwhile the General Conference of the International Labour Organisation convened at Geneva by the Governing Body of the International Labour Office, and having met in its thirty-fifth Session on 4th June 1952, adopted Convention No. 103 that guaranteed maternity protection with effect from 7th September 1955 (*www.ilo.org*).

Let us highlight some of the relevant excerpts from the Convention here.

Article 2

For the purpose of this Convention, the term woman means any female person, irrespective of age, nationality, race or creed, whether married or unmarried, and the term child means any child whether born of marriage or not.

Article 3

A woman to whom this Convention applies shall, on the production of a medical certificate stating the presumed date of her confinement, be entitled to a period of maternity leave.

The period of maternity leave shall be at least twelve weeks, and shall include a period of compulsory leave after confinement.

Article 4

While absent from work on maternity leave in accordance with the provisions of Article 3, the woman shall be entitled to receive cash and medical benefits.

The rates of cash benefit shall be fixed by national laws or regulations so as to ensure benefits sufficient for the full and healthy maintenance of herself and her child in accordance with a suitable standard of living.

Medical benefits shall include pre-natal, confinement and post-natal care by qualified midwives or medical practitioners as well as hospitalisation care where necessary; freedom of choice of doctor and freedom of choice between a public and private hospital shall be respected.

The Convention No. 103 had worldwide implications and the guarantee of maternity protection with effect from 7th September 1955 became a possible reality in India when the Government of India passed the Maternity Benefit Act, 1961, eleven years after the adoption of the Constitution of India. The Act was eventually extended to all States by the end of the year 1972.

"Women do two third of the world's work, receive ten percent of the world's income, and own one percent of the means of production" (Robbins, 1999, p. 354). Not only at global level, but in India also women are making strides by their increasing participation in workforce. Times have changed since the first Central legislation on maternity benefit was passed, and so has the scenario of working women in India. Gone are the days when women used to be restricted at work due to their physical limitations and would also be unable to uphold their own interests. They are now much more educated and well aware of their rights. As such this Act, though passed in 1961, is finding increasing relevance in modern times, and this is why the Government keeps on amending the Act to make provisions for social security of the new age woman. The Act has been amended several times since 1961, the latest being the Maternity Benefit (Amendment) Act, 2008. Following is the list of Amending Acts:

1. The Central Labour Laws (Extension to Jammu and Kashmir) Act, 1970
2. The Maternity Benefit (Amendment) Act, 1972
3. The Maternity Benefit (Amendment) Act, 1973

4. The Maternity Benefit (Amendment) Act, 1976
5. The Maternity Benefit (Amendment) Act, 1988
6. The Maternity Benefit (Amendment) Act, 1995
7. The Maternity Benefit (Amendment) Act, 2008

ABOUT THE ACT

Short Title, Extent and Commencement (Section 1)

1. This Act may be called the Maternity Benefit Act, 1961.
2. It extends to the whole of India.

   The Act has been extended to Pondicherry by Regulation 7 of 1963, Section 3 and Schedule I and Goa, Daman and Diu by Regulation 11 of 1963, Section 3 and Schedule.

   The words "except the State of Jammu and Kashmir" have been omitted by the Act 51 of 1970, Section 2 and Schedule.
3. It shall come into force on such date as may be notified in this behalf in the Official Gazette—
   (a) in relation to mines and to any other establishment wherein persons are employed for the exhibition of equestrian, acrobatic and other performances, by the Central Government; and.
   (b) in relation to other establishments in a State, by the State Government.

Application of Act (Section 2)

1. It applies, in the first instance, —
   (a) to every establishment being a factory, mine or plantation including any such establishment belonging to Government and to every establishment wherein persons are employed for the exhibition of equestrian, acrobatic and other performances;
   (b) to every shop or establishment within the meaning of any law for the time being in force in relation to shops and establishments in a State, in which 10 or more persons are employed, or were employed, on any day of the preceding 12 months.

   Provided that the State Government may, with the approval of the Central Government, after giving not less than 2 months' notice of its intention of so doing, by notification in the Official Gazette, declare that all or any of the provisions of this Act shall apply also to any other establishment or class of establishments, industrial, commercial, agricultural or otherwise.
2. Save as otherwise provided in sections 5A and 5B, nothing contained in this Act shall apply to any factory or other establishment to which the provisions of the Employees' State Insurance Act, 1948 apply for the time being.

Definitions (Section 3)

In this Act, unless the context otherwise requires—

Appropriate Government [Section 3(a)] Appropriate Government means, in relation to an establishment being a mine, or an establishment where persons are employed for the exhibition of equestrian, acrobatic and other performances, the Central Government and in relation to any other establishment, the State Government;

Child [Section 3(b)] Child includes a still-born child;

Delivery [Section 3(c)] Delivery means the birth of a child;

Employer [Section 3(d)] Employer means–

(i) in relation to an establishment which is under the control of the Government, a person or authority appointed by the Government for the supervision and control of employees or where no person or authority is so appointed, the head of the department;

(ii) in relation to an establishment under any local authority, the person appointed by such authority for the supervision and control of employees or where no person is so appointed, the chief executive officer of the local authority;

(ii) in any other case, the person who, or the authority which, has the ultimate control over the affairs of the establishment and where the said affairs are entrusted to any other person whether called a manager, managing director, managing agent, or by any other name, such person;

Establishment [Section 3(e)] Establishment means–

(i) a factory;

(ii) a mine;

(iii) a plantation;

(iv) an establishment wherein persons are employed for the exhibition of equestrian, acrobatics and other performances;

(iv) a shop or establishment; or

(v) an establishment to which the provisions of this Act have been declared under sub-section (4) of Section 2 to be applicable.

CASE CORNER

In *Parjinder Kaur, wife of Shri Bhupinder Singh, R/o Quarter No.31, Maharaj Aggarsain Medical College, Agroha District Hisar, Haryana vs. State of Haryana, through its Financial Commissioner and Principal Secretary to Government of Haryana, Health Department, Haryana, and Others [Civil Writ Petition No. 13301 of 2011 (0&M)]*, the petitioner, who was an employee as a Staff Nurse in respondent's Medical College, had a grievance that the benefit of maternity leave had not been given to her. She had applied for maternity leave on 30th May 2011 before she had actually delivered the child on 10th May 2011, but the same was denied to her and she was compelled to take casual leave instead of maternity leave which she was entitled to.

On behalf of the College, the contention raised is that the representation said to have been made itself is not available with the records and an application for maternity leave which the petitioner had given, had been taken back by her for whatever reasons. It is also to be considered here whether a medical college should be excluded from an establishment or not.

The first part of Section 2 of the Maternity Benefit Act, 1961 (referred to hereafter as Act) relates to factory, mine or plantation and includes any establishment belonging to government employees for exhibition of equestrian, acrobatic and other performances. Medical College does not fall within the scheme of things under the first part. The second part relates to any shop or establishment and the issue here is whether the College could be stated to fall within any such establishment. The proviso to Section 2(1) of the Act enables the State Government with the approval of the Central Government to declare that all or any of the provisions of the Act shall apply also to any other establishment or class of establishments. No such notification extending the application to the houseman of medical colleges or to doctors employed in hospitals and medical colleges being shown, it was held that the Act does not apply to the petitioner and that she is not entitled to maternity benefit in the manner sought for.

(Adapted from: www.indiankanoon.org/doc/117384487/ accessed on 3/9/2014.)

Factory [Section 3(f)] Factory means a factory as defined in clause (m) of Section 2 of the Factories Act, 1948;

Inspector [Section 3(g)] Inspector means an Inspector appointed under Section 14;

Maternity benefit [Section 3(h)] Maternity benefit means the payment referred to in sub-section (1) of Section 5;

Medical termination of pregnancy [Section 3(ha)] Medical termination of pregnancy means the termination of pregnancy permissible under the provisions of Medical Termination of Pregnancy Act, 1971;

Mine [Section 3(i)] Mine means a mine as defined in clause (j) of Section 2 of the Mines Act, 1952;

Miscarriage [Section 3(j)] Miscarriage means expulsion of the contents of a pregnant uterus at any period prior to or during the 26th week of pregnancy but does not include any miscarriage, the causing of which is punishable under the Indian Penal Code;

> **Spotlight**
> As per Section 3(j), miscarriage means expulsion of the contents of a pregnant uterus at any period prior to or during the 26th week of pregnancy, but does not include any miscarriage the causing of which is punishable under the Indian Penal Code.

Plantation [Section 3(k)] Plantation means a plantation as defined in clause (f) of Section 2 of the Plantations Labour Act, 1951;

Prescribed [Section 3(l)] Prescribed means prescribed by rules made under this Act;

State Government [Section 3(m)] State Government, in relation to a Union Territory, means the Administrator thereof;

Wages [Section 3(n)] Wages means all remuneration paid or payable in cash to a woman, if the terms of the contract of employment, express or implied, were fulfilled and includes–

1. such cash allowances (including dearness allowance and house rent allowance) as a woman is for the time being entitled to;
2. incentive bonus; and
3. the money value of the concessional supply of foodgrains and other articles,

but does not include–

(i) any bonus other than incentive bonus;
(ii) overtime earnings and any deduction or payment made on account of fines;
(iii) any contribution paid or payable by the employer to any pension fund or provident fund or for the benefit of the woman under any law for the time being in force; and
(iv) any gratuity payable on the termination of service;

Woman [Section 3(o)] Woman means a woman employed, whether directly or through any agency, for wages in any establishment.

Let us highlight a specific category of women employees here, i.e., married women Government servants. The Government Order in *G.O.(Ms) No.173,* P& AR Department, dated 27th June 1997 stipulates that on and from 29th June 1993, maternity leave shall be granted to a woman Government servant with less than 2 surviving children. Further, as per the recommendations of the Ninth Pay Revision Commission, married women Government servants, temporary or permanent, are now eligible

CASE CORNER

In *Municipal Corporation of Delhi vs. Female Workers (Muster Roll) and Another* (2000 (2) SCR 171), the female workers (muster roll) engaged by the Municipal Corporation of Delhi (hereafter referred to as 'the Corporation') had raised a demand for grant of maternity leave which was made available only to regular female workers. The same was denied to them on the ground that their services were not regularised and therefore they were not entitled to any maternity leave. Their case was espoused by the Delhi Municipal Workers Union (hereafter referred to as 'the Union') and consequently the following question was referred by the Secretary (Labour), Delhi Administration to the Industrial Tribunal for adjudication: Whether female workers working on muster roll should be given any maternity benefit? If so, what directions are necessary in this regard?

The Union filed a statement of claim in which it was stated that the Corporation employs a large number of persons including female workers on muster roll and they are made to work in that capacity for years together, although they are recruited against the work of perennial nature. It was further stated that the nature of duties and responsibilities performed and undertaken by the employees on muster roll are the same as those of regular employees. It was also argued that the women employed on muster roll have been working with the Municipal Corporation of Delhi for years together; they have to work very hard in construction projects and maintenance of roads, including the work of digging trenches, etc., even during the period of mature pregnancy or soon after the delivery of child. It was pleaded that the female workers required the same maternity benefits as were enjoyed by regular female workers under the Maternity Benefit Act, 1961 (referred to as "Act" hereafter).

The Corporation pleaded that the provisions under the Act or Central Civil Services (Leave) Rules were not applicable to the female workers engaged on muster roll as they were all engaged on daily wages. It was also put up that they were not entitled to any benefit under the Employees' State Insurance Act, 1948. Hence the Corporation contended that the demand of the female workers (muster roll) for grant of maternity leave as liable to be rejected.

The Tribunal, however, allowed the claim of the female workers and directed the Corporation to extend the benefits under the Maternity Benefit Act, 1961 to muster roll female workers who were in continuous service of the Corporation for three years or more.

(Adapted from: www.indiankanoon.org/doc/808569/ accessed on 4/9/2014.)

for maternity leave on full pay for a period of 180 days, subject to the condition that the same would be granted to those with less than 2 surviving children.

Employment of, or Work by, Women Prohibited during Certain Periods (Section 4)

1. No employer shall knowingly employ a woman in any establishment during the 6 weeks immediately following the day of her delivery, miscarriage or medical termination of pregnancy.
2. No woman shall work in any establishment during the 6 weeks immediately following the day of her delivery, miscarriage or medical termination of pregnancy.
3. Without prejudice to the provisions of Section 6, no pregnant woman shall, on a request being made by her in this behalf, be required by her employer to do during the period specified in subsection (4) any work which is of an arduous nature or which involves long hours of standing, or which in any way is likely to interfere with her pregnancy or the normal development of the foetus, or is likely to cause her miscarriage or otherwise to adversely affect her health.

CASE CORNER

In C. Vidya Murthy (Smt.) vs. Bangalore Metro Rail Corporation Ltd. (2012 LLR 602), the petitioner was offered the post of Manager (Finance) purely on contract basis for a period of 3 years. The petitioner joined duty in the respondent-Corporation on 31st August 2007. On becoming pregnant around June 2008, she absented from duty for 106 days between 27th June 2008 and 10th November 2008 on different dates, and worked for 53 days only. On 6th December 2008 the petitioner applied for maternity leave of 180 days, providing proof of her expected date of delivery as 21st March 2009, and the same was refused by the respondent. Her services were terminated by giving one month's notice pay on 23rd March 2009 as per the terms and conditions of her appointment. It was appealed by the petitioner that the action of the respondent in not granting maternity leave as well as regularising the period of absence on different dates (mentioned above) as leave without allowance is patently illegal and in violation of the mandatory provisions of the Maternity Benefit Act, 1961.

Keeping in perspective Article 42 of the Constitution, the beneficent rule of construction which would enable a woman employee not only to subsist, but also to make up her dissipated energy, nurse her child, preserve her efficiency as an employee and maintain her previous efficiency, the Court directed the respondent to pay the petitioner, within a period of one month from the date of verdict, the monetary benefits on account of maternity, from the terms of appointment, for the period from 14th December 2008 to 12th March 2009, and thereafter for a period of one month, being the notice period, commencing from 13th March 2009, i.e., up to 12th April 2009.

(Adapted from: Labour Law Reporter, June 2012, pp. 602-607.)

4. The period referred to in sub-section (3) shall be–
   (a) the period of 1 month immediately preceding the period of 6 weeks, before the date of her expected delivery;
   (b) any period during the said period of 6 weeks for which the pregnant woman does not avail of leave of absence under Section 6.

Right to Payment of Maternity Benefits (Section 5)

Spotlight
Average daily wage means the average of the woman's wages payable to her for the days on which she has worked during the period of 3 calendar months immediately preceding the date from which she absents herself on account of maternity, the minimum rate of wage fixed or revised under the Minimum Wages Act, 1948 or ₹10, whichever is the highest.

1. Subject to the provisions of this Act, every woman shall be entitled to, and her employer shall be liable for, the payment of maternity benefit at the rate of the average daily wage for the period of her actual absence, that is to say, the period immediately preceding the day of her delivery, the actual day of her delivery and any period immediately following that day.
   Explanation. For the purpose of this sub-section, the average daily wage means the average of the woman's wages payable to her for the days on which she has worked during the period of 3 calendar months immediately preceding the date from which she absents herself on account of maternity, the minimum rate of wage fixed or revised under the Minimum Wages Act, 1948 or ₹10, whichever is the highest.
2. No woman shall be entitled to maternity benefit unless she has actually worked in an establishment of the employer from whom she claims maternity benefit, for a period of not less than 80 days in the 12 months immediately preceding the date of her expected delivery:
   Provided that the qualifying period of 80 days aforesaid shall not apply to a woman who has immigrated into the State of Assam and was pregnant at the time of the immigration.

Explanation: For the purpose of calculating under this sub-section the days on which a woman has actually worked in the establishment, the days for which she has been laid-off or was on holidays declared under any law for the time being in force to be holidays with wages during the period of 12 months immediately preceding the date of her expected delivery shall be taken into account.

3. The maximum period for which any woman shall be entitled to maternity benefit shall be 12 weeks of which not more than 6 weeks shall precede the date of her expected delivery:

   Provided that where a woman dies during this period, the maternity benefit shall be payable only for the days up to and including the day of her death:

   Provided further that where a woman, having been delivered a child, dies during her delivery or during the period immediately following the date of her delivery for which she is entitled for the maternity benefit, leaving behind, in either case the child, the employer shall be liable for the maternity benefit for that entire period but if the child also dies during the said period, then, for the days up to, and including the day of the death of the child.

CASE CORNER

In *B. Shah vs. Presiding Officer, Labour Court Coimbatore & Others* (1978 AIR 12), the respondent working in "Mount Stuart Estate" belonging to the appellant was allowed leave of absence on maternity leave. After her delivery, the appellant made a payment to her, on account of maternity benefit, an amount equivalent to what she would have earned on the basis of her average daily wages in 72 working days, falling within 12 weeks of the maternity period and excluding 12 Sundays being wageless holidays which fell during the period of the respondent's actual absence immediately preceding and including the day of her delivery and the 6 weeks immediately following that day. The respondent moved the Labour Court, Coimbatore, on being refused the claim for the benefit of the entire period of 12 weeks (i.e., for 84 days) on the plea that a week consisted of 7 days. The Court allowed the said claim by its order dated 26th February 1969; thereafter the appellant moved the High Court challenging the decision of the Labour Court. The single Judge of the High Court allowed the petition, holding that 12 weeks for which maternity benefit is provided for in sub-section (3) of Section 5 of the Maternity Benefit Act, 1961 must be taken to mean 12 weeks of work and the computation of the benefit had to be made with reference to the actual days on which the woman would have worked but for her inability.

Aggrieved by this decision, the respondent filed an appeal, dismissing which, the Court held that though the Act does not contain any definition of the word "week", it has to be understood in its ordinary dictionary meaning. In the context of sub-sections (1) and (3) of Section 5 of the Act, the term has to be taken to signify a cycle of 7 days including Sundays. By using the words, namely, "for the period of her actual absence immediately preceding and including the day of her delivery and for the 6 weeks immediately following that day", the Legislature intended that computation of maternity benefit is to be made for the entire period of the woman worker's actual absence, that is, for all the days including Sundays which may be wageless holidays falling within that period and not only for the intermittent period of 6 days, thereby excluding Sundays falling within that period. The word "period" occurring in Section 5(1) of the Act emphasises the continuous running of time and recurrence of 7 days. It is also in conformity with paragraphs 1 and 2 of Article 4 of Convention No. 103 of the Maternity Protection Convention (Revised) 1952 adopted by the General Conference of the ILO.

(Adapted from: www.indiankanoon.org/doc/450185/ accessed on 1/9/2014.)

Continuance of Payment of Maternity Benefit in Certain Cases (Section 5A)

Every woman entitled to the payment of maternity benefit under this Act shall, notwithstanding the application of the Employees' State Insurance Act, 1948, to the factory or other establishment in which she is employed, continue to be so entitled until she becomes qualified to claim maternity benefit under Section 50 of that Act.

Payment of Maternity Benefit in Certain Cases (Section 5B)

Every woman–

(a) who is employed in a factory or other establishment to which the provisions of the Employees' State Insurance Act, 1948 apply;

(b) whose wages (excluding remuneration for overtime work) for a month exceed the amount specified in sub-clause (b) of clause (9) of Section 2 of that Act; and

(c) who fulfils the conditions specified in sub-section (2) of Section 5,

shall be entitled to the payment of maternity benefit under this Act.

Notice of Claim for Maternity Benefit and Payment thereof (Section 6)

1. Any woman employed in an establishment and entitled to maternity benefit under the provisions of this Act may give notice in writing in such form as may be prescribed, to her employer, stating that her maternity benefit and any other amount to which she may be entitled under this Act may be paid to her or to such person as she may nominate in the notice and that she will not work in any establishment during the period for which she receives maternity benefit.
2. In the case of a woman who is pregnant, such notice shall state the date from which she will be absent from work, not being a date earlier than 6 weeks from the date of her expected delivery.
3. Any woman who has not given the notice when she was pregnant may give such notice as soon as possible after the delivery.
4. On receipt of the notice, the employer shall permit such woman to absent herself from the establishment during the period for which she receives the maternity benefit.
5. The amount of maternity benefit for the period preceding the date of her expected delivery shall be paid in advance by the employer to the woman on production of such proof as may be prescribed that the woman is pregnant, and the amount due for the subsequent period shall be paid by the employer to the woman within 48 hours of production of such proof as may be prescribed that the woman has been delivered of child.
6. The failure to give notice under this section shall not disentitle a woman to maternity benefit or any other amount under this Act if she is otherwise entitled to such benefit or amount and in any such case an Inspector may either of his own motion or on an application made to him by the woman, order the payment of such benefit or amount within such period as may be specified in the order.

Payment of Maternity Benefit in Case of Death of a Woman (Section 7)

If a woman is entitled to maternity benefit or any other amount under this Act, dies before receiving such maternity benefit or amount, or where the employer is liable for maternity benefit under the second proviso to sub-section (3) of Section 5, the employer shall pay such benefit or amount to the person nominated by the woman in the notice given under Section 6 and in case there is no such nominee, to her legal representative.

Payment of Medical Bonus (Section 8)

Every woman entitled to maternity benefit under this Act shall also be entitled to receive from her employer a medical bonus of ₹1,000, if no pre-natal confinement and post-natal care is provided for by the employer free of charge.

The Central Government may before every 3 years, by notification in the Official Gazette, increase the amount of medical bonus subject to the maximum of ₹20,000.

The Central Government vide notification no. S.O. 2015(E) dated 11th August 2008 has increased the amount of medical bonus from ₹1,000 to ₹2,500. Further, vide notification no. S.O. 2016(E) dated 19th December 2011, the amount of medical bonus has been increased from ₹2,500 to ₹3,500.

Spotlight

As per Section 8, every woman entitled to maternity benefit under this Act shall also be entitled to receive from her employer a medical bonus of ₹3,500 (revised), if no pre-natal confinement and post-natal care is provided for by the employer free of charge.

Leave for Miscarriage, etc (Section 9)

In case of miscarriage or medical termination of pregnancy, a woman shall, on production of such proof as may be prescribed, be entitled to leave with wages at the rate of maternity benefit for a period of 6 weeks immediately following the day of her miscarriage or, as the case may be, her medical termination of pregnancy.

Leave with Wages for Tubectomy Operation (Section 9A)

In case of tubectomy operation, a woman shall, on production of such proof as may be prescribed, be entitled to leave with wages at the rate of maternity benefit for a period of 2 weeks immediately following the day of her tubectomy operation.

Leave for Illness Arising out of Pregnancy, Delivery, Premature Birth of Child, Miscarriage, Medical Termination of Pregnancy or Tubectomy Operation (Section 10)

A woman suffering from illness arising out of pregnancy, delivery, premature birth of child, miscarriage, medical termination of pregnancy or tubectomy operation shall, on production of such proof as may be prescribed, be entitled in addition to the period of absence allowed to her under Section 6, or, as the case may be, under Section 9, to leave with wages at the rate of maternity benefit for a maximum period of 1 month.

Nursing Breaks (Section 11)

Every woman delivered of a child who returns to duty after such delivery shall, in addition to the interval for rest allowed to her, be allowed in the course of her daily work 2 breaks of prescribed duration for nursing the child until the child attains the age of 15 months.

Spotlight

As per Section 11, every woman delivered of a child who returns to duty after such delivery shall, in addition to the interval for rest allowed to her, be allowed in the course of her daily work 2 breaks of prescribed duration for nursing the child until the child attains the age of 15 months.

Dismissal during Absence of Pregnancy (Section 12)

1. Where a woman absents herself from work in accordance with the provisions of this Act, it shall be unlawful for her employer to discharge or dismiss her during or on account of such absence or to give notice of discharge or dismissal on such a day that the notice will expire during such absence, or to vary to her disadvantage any of the conditions of her service.
2. (a) The discharge or dismissal of a woman at any time during her pregnancy, if the woman for such discharge of dismissal would have been entitled to maternity benefit or medical bonus referred to in Section 8, shall not have the effect of depriving her of the maternity benefit or medical bonus:

   Provided that where the dismissal is for any prescribed gross misconduct, the employer may, by order in writing communicated to the woman, deprive her of the maternity benefit or medical bonus or both.

   (b) Any woman deprived of maternity benefit or medical bonus, or both, or discharged or dismissed during or on account of her absence from work in accordance with the provisions of this Act, may, within 60 days from the date on which the order of such deprivation is communicated to her, appeal to such authority as may be prescribed, and the decision of that authority on such appeal, whether the woman should or should not be deprived of maternity benefit or medical bonus or both, or discharged or dismissed shall be final.

   (c) Nothing contained in this sub-section shall affect the provisions contained in sub-section (1).

No Deduction of Wages in Certain Cases (Section 13)

No deduction from the normal and usual daily wages of a woman entitled to maternity benefit under the provisions of this Act shall be made by reason only of–

(a) the nature of work assigned to her by virtue of the provisions contained in sub-section (3) of Section 4; or

(b) breaks for nursing the child allowed to her under the provisions of Section 11.

Appointment of Inspectors (Section 14)

The appropriate Government may, by notification in the Official Gazette, appoint such officers as it thinks fit to be Inspectors for the purposes of this Act and may define the local limits of the jurisdiction within which they shall exercise their functions under this Act.

Powers and Duties of Inspectors (Section 15)

An Inspector may, subject to such restrictions or conditions as may be prescribed, exercise all or any of the following powers, namely:

(a) enter at all reasonable times with such assistants, if any, being persons in the service of the Government or any local or other public authority, as he thinks fit, any premises or place where women are employed or work is given to them in an establishment, for the purposes of examining any registers, records and notices required to be kept or exhibited by or under this Act and require their production for inspection;

(b) examine any person whom he finds in any premises or place and who, he has reasonable cause to believe, is employed in the establishment:

Provided that no person shall be compelled under this section to answer any question or give any evidence tending to incriminate himself;

(c) require the employer to give information regarding the names and addresses of women employed, payments made to them, and applications or notices received from them under this Act; and
(d) take copies of any registers and records or notices or any portions thereof.

Inspectors to be Public Servants (Section 16)

Every Inspector appointed under this Act shall be deemed to be a public servant within the meaning of Section 21 of the Indian Penal Code.

Power of Inspector to Direct Payments to be Made (Section 17)

1. Any woman claiming that:
   (a) maternity benefit or any other amount to which she is entitled under this Act and any person claiming that payment due under Section 7 has been improperly withheld;
   (b) her employer has discharged or dismissed her during or on account of her absence from work in accordance with the provisions of this Act,

   may make a complaint to the Inspector.
2. The Inspector may, of his own motion or on receipt of a complaint referred to in sub-section (1), make an inquiry or cause an inquiry to be made and if satisfied that:
   (a) payment has been wrongfully withheld, may direct the payment to be made in accordance with his orders;
   (b) she has been discharged or dismissed during or on account of her absence from work in accordance with the provisions of this Act, may pass such orders as are just and proper according to the circumstances of the case.
3. Any person aggrieved by the decision of the Inspector under sub-section (2) may, within 30 days from the date on which such decision is communicated to such person, appeal to the prescribed authority.
4. The decision of the prescribed authority where an appeal has been preferred to it under sub-section (3) or of the Inspector where no such appeal has been preferred, shall be final.
5. Any amount payable under this section shall be recoverable by the Collector on a certificate issued for that amount by the Inspector as an arrear of land revenue.

Forfeiture of Maternity Benefit (Section 18)

If a woman works in any establishment after she has been permitted by her employer to absent herself under the provisions of Section 6 for any period during such authorised absence, she shall forfeit her claim to the maternity benefit for such period.

Abstract of Act and Rules thereunder to be Exhibited (Section 19)

An abstract of the provisions of this Act and the rules made thereunder in the language or languages of the locality shall be exhibited in a conspicuous place by the employer in every part of the establishment in which women are employed.

Registers, etc. (Section 20)

Every employer shall prepare and maintain such registers, records and muster-rolls and in such manner as may be prescribed.

Penalty for Contravention of Act by Employer (Section 21)

1. If any employer fails to pay any amount of maternity benefit to a woman entitled under this Act or discharges or dismisses such woman during or on account of her absence from work in accordance with the provisions of this Act, he shall be punishable with imprisonment which shall not be less than 3 months but which may extend to 1 year and with fine which shall not be less than ₹2,000 but which may extend to ₹5,000:

   Provided that the court may, for sufficient reasons to be recorded in writing, impose a sentence of imprisonment for a lesser term or fine only in lieu of imprisonment.
2. If any employer contravenes the provisions of this Act or the rules made thereunder, he shall, if no other penalty is elsewhere provided by or under this Act for such contravention, be punishable with imprisonment which may extend to 1 year, or with fine which may extend to ₹5,000, or with both:

   Provided that where the contravention is of any provision regarding maternity benefit or regarding payment of any other amount and such maternity benefit or amount has not already been recovered, the court shall, in addition, recover such maternity benefit or amount as if it were a fine, and pay the same to the person entitled thereto.

Penalty for Obstructing Inspector (Section 22)

Whoever fails to produce on demand by the Inspector any register or document in his custody kept in pursuance of this Act or the rules made thereunder or conceals or prevents any person from appearing before or being examined by an Inspector, shall be punishable with imprisonment which may extend to 1 year, or with fine which may extend to ₹5,000, or with both.

Cognizance of Offences (Section 23)

1. Any aggrieved woman, an office-bearer of a trade union registered under the Trade Unions Act, 1926 of which such woman is a member or a voluntary organisation registered under the Societies Registration Act, 1860 or an Inspector, may file a complaint regarding the commission of an offence under this Act in any court of competent jurisdiction and no such complaint shall be filed after the expiry of 1 year from the date on which the offence is alleged to have been committed.
2. No court inferior to that of a Metropolitan Magistrate or a Magistrate of the first class shall try any offence under this Act.

Protection of Action Taken in Good Faith (Section 24)

No suit, prosecution or other legal proceeding shall lie against any person for anything which is in good faith done or intended to be done in pursuance of this Act or of any rule or order made thereunder.

Power of Central Government to Give Directions (Section 25)

The Central Government may give such directions as it may deem necessary to a State Government regarding the carrying into execution the provisions of this Act and the State Government shall comply with such directions.

Power to Exempt Establishments (Section 26)

If the appropriate Government is satisfied that having regard to an establishment or a class of establishments providing for the grant of benefit which are not less favourable than those provided in this Act, it is necessary so to do, it may, by notification in the Official Gazette, exempt, subject to such conditions and restrictions, if any, as may be specified in the notification, the establishment or class of establishments from the operation of all or any of the provisions of this Act or of any rule made thereunder.

Effect of Laws and Agreements Inconsistent with this Act (Section 27)

1. The provisions of this Act shall have effect notwithstanding anything inconsistent therewith contained in any other law or in the terms of any award, agreement or contract of service, whether made before or after the coming into force of this Act:

   Provided that where under any such award, agreement, contract of service or otherwise, a woman is entitled to benefits in respect of any matter which are more favourable to her than those to which she would be entitled under this Act, the woman shall continue to be entitled to the more favourable benefits in respect of that matter, notwithstanding that she is entitled to receive benefits in respect of other matters under this Act.
2. Nothing contained in this Act shall be construed to preclude a woman from entering into an agreement with her employer for granting her rights or privileges in respect of any matter which are more favourable to her than those to which she would be entitled under this Act.

Power to Make Rules (Section 28)

1. The appropriate Government may, subject to the condition of previous publication and by notification in the Official Gazette, make rules for carrying out the purposes of this Act.
2. In particular, and without prejudice to the generality of the foregoing power, such rules may provide for–
   (a) the preparation and maintenance of registers, records and muster-rolls;
   (b) the exercise of powers (including the inspection of establishments) and the performance of duties by Inspectors for the purposes of this Act;
   (c) the method of payment of maternity benefit and other benefits under this Act in so far as provision has not been made therefor in this Act;
   (d) the form of notices under Section 6:
   (e) the nature of proof required under the provisions of this Act;
   (f) the duration of nursing breaks referred to in Section 11;
   (g) acts which may constitute gross misconduct for purposes of Section 12;
   (h) the authority to which an appeal under clause (b) of sub-section (2) of Section 12 shall lie, the form and manner in which such appeal may be made and the procedure to be followed in disposal thereof;
   (i) the authority to which an appeal shall lie against the decision of the Inspector under Section 17; the form and manner in which such appeal may be made and the procedure to be followed in disposal thereof;
   (j) the form and manner in which complaints may be made to Inspectors under sub-section (1) of Section 17 and the procedure to be followed by them when making inquiries or causing inquiries to be made under sub-section (2) of that section;
   (k) any other matter which is to be, or may be, prescribed.

3. Every rule made by the Central Government under this section shall be laid as soon as may be after it is made, before each House of Parliament while it is in session for a total period of 30 days which may be comprised in 1 session or in 2 or more successive sessions, and if, before the expiry of the session immediately following the session or the successive sessions, aforesaid, both Houses agree in making any modification in the rule or both Houses agree that the rule should not be made, the rule shall thereafter have effect only in such modified form or be of no effect, as the case may be; so however that any such modification or annulment shall be without prejudice to the validity of anything previously done under that rule.

Amendment of Act 69 of 1951 (Section 29)

In Section 32 of the Plantations Labour Act, 1951—

(a) in sub-section (1), the letter and brackets "(a)" before the words "in the case of sickness," the word "and" after the words "sickness allowance", and clause (b) shall be omitted;
(b) In sub-section (2), the words "or maternity" shall be omitted.

Repeal (Section 30)

On the application of this Act–

(i) to mines, the Mines Maternity Benefit Act, 1941; and
(ii) to factories situate in the Union Territory of Delhi, the Bombay Maternity Benefit Act, 1929, as in force in that territory, shall stand repealed.

ADMINISTRATION OF THE ACT

For organisations where the Central Government is the appropriate Government, the Maternity Benefit Act, 1961 is enforced through the Central Industrial Relation Machinery (CIRM), an attached office of the Ministry of Labour & Employment. This office is also known as the Chief Labour Commissioner (Central) Organisation, and is headed by the Chief Labour Commissioner (Central).

SUMMARY

- The Maternity Benefit Act, 1961 ensures social security of working women by allowing them to perform their social obligation of child bearing, undeterred by the fear of punitive measures for absence during pre- and/or post-natal period(s).
- Maternity benefit legislations prior to the Maternity Benefit Act, 1961 include the Bombay Maternity Benefit Act, 1929, the Madhya Pradesh Maternity Benefit Act, 1930, other State-level legislations, the Mines Maternity Benefit Act, 1941, the Employees' State Insurance Act, 1948 and the Plantations Labour Act, 1951.
- Section 3(ha) defines medical termination of pregnancy as the termination of pregnancy permissible under the provisions of Medical Termination of Pregnancy Act, 1971.
- Miscarriage as per Section 3(j) means expulsion of the contents of a pregnant uterus at any period prior to or during the 26th week of pregnancy, but does not include any miscarriage, the causing of which is punishable under the Indian Penal Code.

- According to Section 4(1), no employer shall knowingly employ a woman in any establishment during the 6 weeks immediately following the day of her delivery, miscarriage or medical termination of pregnancy.
- Section 5(1) states that subject to the provisions of this Act, every woman shall be entitled to, and her employer shall be liable for, the payment of maternity benefit at the rate of the average daily wage for the period of her actual absence immediately preceding and including the day of her delivery and for the 6 weeks immediately following that day.
- According to Section 8(1), every woman entitled to maternity benefit under this Act shall also be entitled to receive from her employer a medical bonus of ₹3,500, if no pre-natal confinement and post-natal care is provided for by the employer free of charge.
- In case of miscarriage or medical termination of pregnancy, a woman shall, on production of such proof as may be prescribed, be entitled to leave with wages at the rate of maternity benefit for a period of 6 weeks immediately following the day of her miscarriage, or her medical termination of pregnancy, as per Section 9; in case of tubectomy operation, a woman shall, on production of such proof as may be prescribed, be entitled to leave with wages at the rate of maternity benefit for a period of 2 weeks immediately following the day of her tubectomy operation, as mentioned in Section 9A.
- Section 11 provides that every woman after delivery of a child and returning to duty after such delivery shall, in addition to the interval for rest allowed to her, be allowed in the course of her daily work, 2 breaks of prescribed duration for nursing the child, until the child attains the age of 15 months.
- If a woman works in any establishment after she has been permitted by her employer to absent herself under the provisions of Section 6 for any period during such authorised absence, she shall forfeit her claim to maternity benefit for such period, as per Section 18.
- For organisations where the Central Government is the appropriate Government, the Act is enforced through the CIRM, an attached office of the Ministry of Labour & Employment.

Key Concepts

Maternity	Tubectomy operation	Medical termination of pregnancy
Maternity benefit	Post-natal	Delivery
Nursing break	Pre-natal	Medical bonus
Miscarriage	Pregnancy	Pre-natal confinement

Bibliography

The Maternity Benefit Act, 1961, Delhi: Universal Law Publishing Co. Pvt. Ltd.

Robbins, R. H. *Global Problems and Culture Capitalism*, Allyn and Bacon, 1999, p. 354.

Sinha, P. R. N., Sinha, I. B. and Shekhar, S. P. *Industrial Relations, Trade Unions and Labour Legislation*, New Delhi: Pearson, 2006.

www.indiankanoon.org

www.indialabourarchives.org/publications/Samita%20Sen.htm accessed on 4/9/2014.

Sen, S. (n.d.) Gender and Class: Women in Indian Industry, 1920–1990. Retrieved from Labour Investigation Committee Report, 1946 www.indianlabourarchives.org/usr/local/gsdl accessed on 4/9/2014.

www.ilo.org/dyn/norm/ex/en/ accessed on 4/9/2014.

REVIEW QUESTIONS

Objective Type Questions

I. State True or False

(i) The notified date from which a woman employee will be absent from work can not be earlier than 12 weeks from the date of her expected delivery.
(ii) An employer need not pay maternity benefit if the woman employee dies before receiving such benefit.
(iii) No woman shall work in any establishment during the 6 weeks immediately following the day of her delivery.
(iv) Wages include any deduction or payment made on account of fines.
(v) Upper limit for revision in medical bonus is ₹25,000.

Answers: (i) False, (ii) False, (iii) True, (iv) False, (v) False

II. Fill in the Blanks

(i) No court inferior to that of a ______Magistrate shall try any offence under the Maternity Benefit Act, 1961.
(ii) Two nursing breaks are permissible until the child attains the age of ____ months.
(iii) If any employer fails to pay any amount of maternity benefit, he shall be punishable with fine which may extend to ₹______.
(iv) Every employer is required to prepare and maintain _____, records and muster-rolls in prescribed manner.
(v) An establishment under the Maternity Benefit Act, 1961 includes one wherein persons are employed for the exhibition of ______, acrobatics and other performances.

Answers: (i) Metropolitan, (ii) fifteen, (iii) 5000, (iv) registers, (v) equestrian

Discussion Questions

1. Discuss the provisions for notice of claim for maternity benefit and payment thereof.
2. Critically explain the historical backdrop of the Maternity Benefit Act, 1961.
3. Describe the various conditions of dismissal during absence of pregnancy in details.
4. What is the purpose of appointment of Inspectors under the Maternity Benefit Act, 1961? What are the powers and duties of Inspectors as per the provisions of the Act?
5. Explain the provision regarding penalty to be imposed in case of contravention of the Act by an employer.
6. Discuss right to payment of maternity benefits in details.
7. What is a nursing break? Discuss the provision for nursing break in the Act.
8. Clearly distinguish between the following cases of leave as permissible in the Act:
   (a) Leave for miscarriage, etc.
   (b) Leave with wages for tubectomy operation
   (c) Leave for illness arising out of pregnancy, delivery, premature birth of child, miscarriage, medical termination of pregnancy or tubectomy operation
9. Explain in brief:
   (a) Payment of maternity in case of death of a woman employee
   (b) Wages as defined in the Maternity Benefit Act, 1961
   (c) Medical bonus

10. Differentiate between:
    (a) Miscarriage and Medical termination of pregnancy
    (b) Continuance of payment of maternity benefit in certain cases and Payment of maternity benefits in certain cases

CASE STUDY-I

The petitioner in this case is a Block Resources Teacher Educator in Mathematics in Thoothukudi District, who had her second delivery during the period between 16th October 2006 and 11th January 2007. She was not given maternity benefit for the aforesaid period, stating that during the first labour, she had given birth to twins and therefore, by the present delivery, she had given birth to a third child. As such, by the order of the Government in G. O. Ms. No. 237, School Education Department, dated 29th June 1993, she will not be paid wages for her leave.

(Adapted from: J. Sharmila vs. The Secretary to Government on 19 October, 2010, www.indiankanoon.org/doc/1925964/ accessed on 4/9/2014.)

Questions

1. Analyse whether the order refusing to grant maternity leave to the petitioner for the birth of her third child in the second delivery was legally justified or not.
2. What logic can the petitioner put up in defence?
3. Is maternity leave confined only to the second delivery and not based on the third child norm?

CASE STUDY-II

In this case the petitioner, a qualified architect, was initially offered contractual appointment for a period of 6 months on 8th October 1997 by the respondents (hereafter referred to as "RITES'). She had continued in the employment of RITES subsequent to her contract being renewed after the expiry of the 6 months period. The petitioner has questioned the impugned order dated 13th December 2000 which states that the contractual engagement ceased from 16th October 2000 and that she was no longer in the rolls of the organisation after that date. The claim in the petition was confined to the release of maternity leave benefits, which was also declined.

The petitioner claimed that her services were continued and she was working uninterruptedly till she applied for maternity leave on 15th October 2000. It is averred by that application RITES was intimated that the petitioner was proceeding on maternity leave from 11th November 2000 onwards till further notice, after which she delivered a baby on 5th December 2000. The petitioner has further mentioned that RITES did not reply to this notice and by the impugned order, referred to the last letter dated 23th May 2000, and stated that the period of her engagement was to come to an end upon expiry of 6 months. The petitioner made representations on 10th November 2001 and 24th December 2001, *inter alia*, for release of maternity benefits. RITES however did not accept the request. Hence she approached this Court for appropriate directions.

The respondents in their counter affidavit have denied the claim. They claimed that the petitioner was engaged on purely contractual basis and that her period of engagement came to an end on 16th October 2000. They have further denied the receipt of letter dated 15th October 2000 and have even alleged that the letter was given to RITES on 17th November 2000. The respondents have also placed on record copies of letters written on 21th June 2000, 17th July 2000, 4th August 2000 and 19th October 2000, by which the petitioner sought medical leave. It is further alleged that the petitioner accepted her termination as evidenced by a duly filled Form No. 19, which was an application for release of provident fund and other dues, furnished to the respondent RITES under cover of a letter dated 11th September 2001, and that the petitioner had collected all her dues on 7th December 2001 from RITES. The record shows that the petitioner continued in employment till 11th November 2000, as per RITES itself.

The pleadings in this case show that apparently the contract was for spells of 6 months. As is evident from an examination of the last contract/order dated 23th May 2000, the RITES was issuing contracts/appointment letters for fresh periods after the expiry of the previous period(s). For instance, the order dated 23th May 2000 states that the term of employment is 6 months from 17th April 2000 to 16th October 2000. The last order, extending the contract of appointment by 6 months, was issued on May, 2000; the previous period had expired on 17th April 2000. Hence, the period commenced on 17th April 2000, and continued till 16th October 2000. Further, the petitioner continued to report for duties after 16th October 2000, though the period of contractual appointment came to an end on 16th October 2000. The letter seeking leave does indicate that the petitioner would be on leave after 11th November 2000. RITES does not dispute the existence of this letter; it only alleges that the letter in fact was given on 17th November 2000.

(Adapted from: Mrs. Bharti Gupta vs. Rail India Technical and Economic Services (2005 (84) DRJ 53) www.indiankanoon.org/doc/1796719/ accessed on 3/9/2014.)

Questions

1. Which section(s) of the Maternity Benefit Act, 1961 is/are relevant to this case?
2. Do you think that RITES is an establishment covered under the Act?
3. Given that the Supreme Court has held that even daily wage employees on muster rolls are entitled to the benefits under the Act, do you think that the petitioner is entitled to leave as well as maternity benefit?

Appendix

Form H

(See Rule 9)

To

The Inspector,
(Under the Maternity Benefit Act, 1961)

Sir,

I, ________________ (Name of woman) employed in _________ (Name and full address of establishment) having fulfilled the conditions laid down in the Maternity Benefit Act, 1961 and the Rules there under am entitled to ₹ _____ being maternity benefit and/or ₹_____ being the medical bonus/or ₹ _____ being wage for leave due under sections 9 and 10 but the same has been improperly withheld by the employer.

He may, therefore, be directed to pay the amount to me.

Date..................

Signature or thumb impression
of the woman

Signature of an attester in case
the woman is unable to sign and
affixes thumb impression.

Full address of the woman

....

Strike out unnecessary portion

Form 'I'

(See Rule 10)

To

The Inspector,
(Under the Maternity Benefit Act, 1961)

I, ________ (name), a person nominated under Section 6 by or a legal representative of ______ (name of woman) employed in _______(name and full address of establishment) have to complain that the said woman having fulfilled the conditions laid down in the Maternity Benefit Act, 1961 and the rules thereunder is entitled to ₹ ______ being maternity benefit and/or ₹______ being the medical bonus and/or ₹_____ being wages for leave due under sections 9 or 10 but the same has been improperly withheld by the employer. He may, therefore, be directed to pay the amount to me.

Signature or thumb impression of the
nominee/legal representative.

Signature of an attester in case the
nominee/legal representative is
unable to sign and affixes
thumb impression.

Full address of the nominee/legal representative

Form 'J'

(See Rule II)

To

____

____

Sir,

Shri __________ Inspector, having directed under sub-section (2) of Section 17 to pay the Maternity Benefit or other amount being _______ (nature of amount) to which ____ (name of woman) is said to be entitled, I prefer this appeal under sub-section (3) of Section 17. In view of the facts mentioned in the memorandum attached hereto and other documents filed herewith it is submitted that the woman is not entitled to the maternity benefit to the said amount and hence the decision of the Inspector in this behalf, copy of which is enclosed may be set aside.

Signature of aggrieved person

Dated.................

Full address......................

18

The Minimum Wages Act, 1948

An Act to provide for fixing minimum rates of wages in certain employments.

Desired Knowledge Competencies

- To discuss the notions of fair wage, minimum wage and living wage and the evolution of the legislation on minimum wages in India.
- To become familiar with the scope and coverage of the Minimum Wages Act, 1948 and of the various definitions given under the Act.
- To comprehend issues like fixing of minimum wage, minimum wage for overtime work, etc.

CONCEPT OF FIXATION OF WAGE

Wage to a worker is a means of livelihood; for an employer, it is an expense. If we consider an economy to comprise only two agents, i.e., firms and households, we can easily visualise an exchange process between them. Physical (or intellectual) labour is supplied by the household to the firm, in return of which, firm pays wage/salary to the household. This process of exchange in reality becomes a process of bargaining between these agents, where workers try to get high wages but employers want to pay less to reduce their cost. Workers often seek the intervention of unions in such bargaining. On the other hand, employers bargain with workers to ensure greater contribution to production. The level of wages employers offer to workers is one of the basic determinants in this process.

The next issue is how much wage should paid to workers in lieu of the work done? In other words, we are referring to the adequacy of wages (which is actually the issue of fair wages). Let us discuss the relevance of fair wages here. The very purpose of seeking employment is to sell labour for earning wages; in return that would enable a worker to achieve a decent standard of living. The primary expectation out of earning wage is both to fulfill one's basic needs and to feel reassured that he/she receives a fair return for the work done. The onus lies on both the society and the State to ensure such a wage is paid to every worker to help prevent starvation and poverty, and also ensure that at least the basic needs of every worker with a standard family size are met.

Fundamental rules of economics propose that the level of wage is determined by the demand for and supply of labour. Interestingly, the labour market is characterised by the dual-existence of a highly skilled segment commanding high wage rate and a low-skilled segment having low wage rate. The reason, again, can be explained by economics—the former has a demand for labour that exceeds its supply, while the latter segment has supply of labour in excess of demand. This is one of the primary reasons behind diversity in wage-levels across skill-sets and industries, especially in India. As the demand for skilled labour would increase, the already existing wage differential between skilled and unskilled labour would rise. Most of the studies of wage differentials in India, comment Sarkar and Mehta (2010), indicate that the labour market generates differences in wage rate and earnings that are based on geographical locations, level of education, industry, social group and gender. Considering the sectors of the Indian economy, we can find wide disparities in wages across organised and unorganised sectors as well. Such disparities are found across rural and urban areas, with urban workers earning more wages than their rural counterparts.

Occupation-wise, non-agricultural wage rate has been historically higher than agricultural wage rate in India. In spite of more and more women joining the labour force, wages paid to women workers are usually lesser than men. Significant gaps in the earnings of men and women still exist; in fact, 2008-2009 figures reveal that wages/salaries per man day worked for directly employed women workers (at ₹131.23) was nearly half of that of their male counterparts (at ₹258.04) (Statistical Profile on Women Labour, 2009-2011). Ownership pattern of industrial enterprises also dictates differences in wages, with the public sector usually offering better fringe benefits than the private sector.

Let us now explore the role of government in fixing the level of wage, which is usually a two-pronged situation. While increased wages would lead to improved standard of living for the masses, it would put pressure on employers due to a higher wage bill. Not to forget that such increase in wage bill would be passed on ultimately to consumers by way of higher price to be paid for goods/services. The situation becomes more difficult if the government also has to ensure uniformity in wage-levels across different sectors of the economy.

BACKDROP OF THE MINIMUM WAGES ACT, 1948

The issue of discrepancies in wage levels across the nation has always been of paramount concern to the Government of India. Article 39 of the Constitution of India holds that the State shall, in particular, direct its policy towards securing that the citizens, men and women equally, have the right to an adequate means of livelihood, and that there is equal pay for equal work for both men and women. Article 43 states that the State shall endeavour to secure, by suitable legislation or economic organisation or in any other way, to all workers, agricultural, industrial or otherwise, work, a living wage, conditions of work ensuring a decent standard of life, and full enjoyment of leisure and social and cultural opportunities.

The beginning of the 19th century had marked the onset of a perceived need for fixing a minimum rate of wages. In its report submitted in 1931, the Royal Commission on Labour had recommended investigations pertaining to fixation of minimum wage rates in certain small industries and establishment of machinery towards this end. A large number of committees were set up thereafter from time to time to address this issue. The most notable of these were the Cawnpore Labour Enquiry Committee and the Bombay Textile Labour Enquiry Committee (both in 1937), the Bihar Labour Enquiry Committee (in 1938), the C.P. and Berar Textile Labour Enquiry Committee and the U.P. Labour Enquiry Committee (both in 1946) set up by the respective provincial governments (Sinha, Sinha and Shekhar, 2006). Investigations made by such committees on the wage levels of workers across industries revealed disparities and fixation of minimum wages was recommended.

Post-Independence, the first notable development in fixation of a minimum wage rate was the formation of a tripartite committee named as the Committee on Fair Wages in the year 1946, to provide guidelines for wage structures in the country. The report of the Committee published in 1948 was a major landmark in the formulation of wage policies. The Committee prescribed clarification of the various concepts of wages (like fair wage, living wage and subsistence wage), standardisation of wages in the organised sector and enactment of a minimum wage legislation. The concepts of wages laid down in the report are as follows:

- **Minimum wage:** Minimum wage was proposed to be paid for the bare subsistence of a worker and should ideally include enough for the efficiency, health and working capability of the worker. For this purpose, the minimum wage must also provide for some measure of education, medical requirements and amenities. The Committee on Fair Wages emphasised that an industry had no right to exist unless this minimum level of wages was paid.

> **Spotlight**
> Minimum **wage** is paid for the bare subsistence of a worker. **Fair wage** aims at the living wage level. **Living wage** is the concept of an ideal wage.

- **Fair wage:** Such wage was proposed to be above the minimum wage level, aiming at living wage level. The actual wage in an industry or organisation should be determined by factors like the capacity of an employer to pay, the position of an industry in the economy, per capita income, etc. The Committee recommended that fair wage should be related with the productivity of labour. Since the prevailing level of wages in India was unable to maintain the workers on subsistence plus standard, it was essential that workers must be first assured a living wage, and only after this, wages should be related to productivity. The Committee further suggested that fair wage should be related with the prevailing rates of wages.
- **Living wage:** Living wage was the concept of an ideal wage; it represented the highest level of wage which could enable a male earner of a family to provide for himself and his family not only the bare necessities of food, clothing and shelter, but also a measure of comfort, education for his children, protection against ill-health, essential social needs and insurance against more important misfortunes, including old age.

Let us quickly analyse the implications of these concepts here. As per the Committee, industrial wages paid out must have a floor-level, namely subsistence wage, below which no industry must pay any worker. It is thus implied that this subsistence wage represents the absolute minimum wage to be paid to workers. This apart, the concept of living wage was introduced in lines with an ideal wage rate. The Committee was of the opinion that when such a wage is to be determined, the considerations of national income and capacity to pay of the industry concerned must also be taken into account. Living wage had to be the ultimate goal or target and a benchmark that all workers and their representative unions should attain. Next arises the question: what should the minimum wage be? Should it be subsistence wage, which may enable a worker to stay alive and maintain his working capacity; or should it be a living wage, which may also provide for the maintenance of health and efficiency, measures of economic comfort and insurance against unforeseen exigencies; or should it be a fair wage, lying somewhere between the levels of subsistence and living wages? It must be noted here that "minimum" is essentially a relative term and minimum wages may have different meanings in different countries, according to their level of social and economic development. Further, it needs to be considered whether there should be a national system of minimum wages providing for a uniform level of wage for all workers, but for regional variations, or a system of fixing different minimum wage rates for different sectors or industries.

Incidentally, the Committee on Fair Wages did not actually prescribe any actual wage rate to be followed uniformly across industries principally due to the large scale disparities in them. This provided industries with enough flexibility to work on determining wage levels on the basis of various parameters, including capacity to pay. On the whole, the Committee provided the much needed momentum to initiate fixation of a minimum level of wage through the legislative machinery.

The issue of a minimum level of wages and the establishment of a machinery for the fixation of such a level has been of concern to the International Labour Organisation (ILO) as well, which has come up with several Conventions and Recommendations to this effect. The Minimum Wage Fixing Machinery Convention, 1928 (Convention No. 26) provided for the creation of wage-fixing machinery in certain trades. The Convention required consultation with representatives of employers and workers before such machinery is applied in a trade and hence imposed an obligation on the ratifying countries to associate both employers and workers in the working of the machinery. Such a machinery was also recommended to conduct investigation into the conditions relevant to the specific trades under the purview of the Recommendation. Further, the Convention laid down the mandate of minimum wages fixed by the machinery to be binding on both employers and workers. India ratified the Convention in 1955, after the enactment of the Minimum Wages Act, 1948. Both the Convention and Recommendation of 1928 were restricted to the non-agriculture sectors of employment. Hence the ILO Conference, in its 34th Session in the year 1957, adopted the Minimum Wage Fixing Machinery (Agriculture) Convention and the Minimum Wage Fixing Machinery Recommendation for agricultural employments. This was followed by the adoption of the Minimum Wage Fixing Machinery Convention in 1970.

The question of the fixation of minimum rates of wages in India was considered by the Standing Labour Committee and the 5th Session of the Indian Labour Conference in 1943, on recommendation of which, a Labour Investigation Committee was appointed in the same year to investigate into the question of wages and other matters like housing, social conditions and employment. The issue drew the attention of the Standing Labour Committee and the 6th and 7th sessions of the Indian Labour Conference again in 1944 and 1945 respectively. A draft bill was considered by the Indian Labour Conference in 1945. The 8th meeting of the Standing Labour Committee in the year 1946 recommended enactment of a separate legislation for the unorganised sector, including working hours, minimum wages and paid holidays. In light of these recommendations, the Government of India introduced the Minimum Wages Bill in the Central Legislative Assembly in 1946, which was passed on 9th February 1948. The Act came into force from 15th March the same year.

The sole purpose of the Minimum Wages Act, 1948 is to prevent exploitation of labour and it provides for fixation and/or periodic revision of minimum wages in employments where labour is vulnerable to exploitation. The Act has been amended several times since its enactment in 1948. Following is the list of amending acts and adaptation orders:

Spotlight

The sole point of the Minimum Wages Act, 1948 is to prevent exploitation of labour. It provides for fixation and/or periodic revision of minimum wages in employments where labour is susceptible to exploitation.

1. The Adaptation of Laws Order, 1950
2. The Minimum Wages (Amendment) Act, 1950
3. The Part B States (Laws) Act, 1951
4. The Minimum Wages (Amendment) Act, 1951
5. The Minimum Wages (Amendment) Act, 1954
6. The Minimum Wages (Amendment) Act, 1957
7. The Minimum Wages (Amendment) Act, 1961
8. The Central Labour Laws (Extension to Jammu and Kashmir) Act, 1970
9. The Child Labour (Prohibition and Regulation) Act, 1986
10. The Delegated Legislation Provisions (Amendment) Act, 2004

ABOUT THE ACT

Short Title and Extent (Section 1)

1. This Act may be called the Minimum Wages Act, 1948.
2. It extends to the whole of India

This Act has been extended to Dadra and Nagar Haveli, Pondicherry, Laccadive, Minicoy and Amindivi Islands and Union Territory of Goa, Daman and Diu.

Interpretation (Section 2)

In this Act, unless there is anything repugnant in the subject or context:

Adolescent [Section 2(a)] Adolescent means a person who has completed his fourteenth year of age but has not completed his eighteenth year;

Adult [Section 2(aa)] Adult means a person who has completed his eighteenth year of age;

Appropriate Government [Section 2(b)] Appropriate Government means,—

(i) in relation to any scheduled employment carried on by or under the authority of the Central Government, or a railway administration, or in relation to a mine, oilfield or major port, or any corporation established by a Central Act, the Central Government, and

(ii) in relation to any other scheduled employment, the State Government;

Child [Section 2(bb)] Child means a person who has not completed his fourteenth year of age;

Competent authority [Section 2(c)] Competent authority means the authority appointed by the appropriate Government by notification in its Official Gazette to ascertain from time to time the cost of living index number applicable to the employees employed in the scheduled employments specified in such notification;

Cost of living index number [Section 2(d)] Cost of living index number, in relation to employees in any scheduled employment in respect of which minimum rates of wages have been fixed, means the index number ascertained and declared by the competent authority by notification in the Official Gazette to be the cost of living index number applicable to employees in such employment;

In *Mangalore Ganesh Beedi and Allied Industries vs. State of Karnataka and Others* [(2003) IIILLJ 861 Kant] it has been mentioned that consumer price index numbers are also known as cost of living index numbers, which are generally intended to represent the average change over time in the prices paid by the ultimate consumer of a specified basket of goods and services. The need for constructing these numbers arises mainly because of the fact general index numbers fail to give an exact idea of the effect of change in the general price level on the cost of living of different classes of people, since a given change in prices affect different classes in different manners.

(Adapted from: www.indiankanoon.org/doc/1971257/ accessed on 12/4/2014.)

Employer [Section 2(e)] Employer means any person who employs, whether directly or through another person, or whether on behalf of himself or any other person, 1 or more employees in any scheduled employment in respect of which minimum rates of wages have been fixed under this Act, and includes, except in sub-section (3) of Section 26–

(i) in a factory where there is carried on any scheduled employment in respect of which minimum rates of wages have been fixed under this Act, any person named as manager of the factory;

(ii) in any scheduled employment under the control of any Government in India in respect of which minimum rates of wages have been fixed under this Act, the person or authority appointed by such Government for the supervision and control of employees or where no person or authority is so appointed, the head of the department;

(iii) in any scheduled employment under any local authority in respect of which minimum rates of wages have been fixed under this Act, the person appointed by such authority for the supervision and control of employees or where no person is so appointed, the chief executive officer of the local authority;

(iv) in any other case where there is carried on any scheduled employment in respect of which minimum rates of wages have been fixed under this Act, any person responsible to the owner for the supervision and control of the employees or for the payment of wages;

Prescribed [Section 2(f)] Prescribed means prescribed by rules made under this Act;

Scheduled employment [Section 2(g)] Scheduled employment means an employment specified in the Schedule, or any process or branch of work forming part of such employment;

CASE CORNER

In *Champak Lal H. Thakkar and Others vs. State of Gujarat and Another* (1980 AIR 1889), the defence of the appellants was on the plea that different types of industries are covered by the Minimum Wages Act, 1948 (or Act) but the company does not run any such industry, and is therefore not liable for any contravention of the Act or the rules framed thereunder. According to the prosecution, the factory run by the company is an oil mill, an industry which is certainly covered by the Act. However, the company is running a mill which manufactures vanaspati and vanaspati is not oil, but is vegetable ghee. Oil extraction is undoubtedly a major operation carried on by the company, but that operation is incidental to the preparation of vanaspati. Vanaspati is manufactured by subjecting oil to the processes of neutralisation, bleaching, deodorisation, hardening, hydrogenation, etc., and is a product quite different from oil. In spite of the sale of oil, therefore, the company remains a vanaspati manufacturer and cannot be considered to be running an oil mill.

The Court was of the view that oil will remain oil if it retains its essential properties, and merely because it has been subjected to certain processes would not convert it into a different substance. In other words, although certain additions have been made to and operations carried out on oil, it will still be classified as oil unless its essential characteristics have undergone change. No doubt, the word 'oil' is not defined in the Act. Taking the dictionary meaning for interpreting the term 'oil mill', in this case it is clear that hydrogenated vegetable oil falls within the said term. The various processes to which oil is subjected for being converted into vanaspati leave its basic characteristics untouched, that is, it remains a cooling medium with vegetable fat as its main ingredient. Thus vanaspati must be regarded as an oil for the purpose of Item 5 in Part-I of the Schedule to the Act, and employment in a vanaspati manufacturing concern is a scheduled employment within the scope of Section 2(g) of the Act.

(Adapted from: www.indiankanoon.org/doc/1480973/ accessed on 9/4/2014.)

Wages [Section 2(h)] Wages means all remuneration, capable of being expressed in terms of money, which would, if the terms of the contract of employment, express or implied, were fulfilled, be payable to a person employed in respect of his employment or of work done in such employment and includes house rent allowance, but does not include–

(i) the value of:
   (a) any house-accommodation, supply of light, water, medical attendance, or
   (b) any other amenity or any service excluded by general or special order of the appropriate Government;

(ii) any contribution paid by the employer to any Pension Fund or Provident Fund or under any scheme of social insurance;

(iii) any travelling allowance or the value of any travelling concession;

(iv) any sum paid to the person employed to defray special expenses entailed on him by the nature of his employment; or

(v) any gratuity payable on discharge;

Employee [Section 2(i)] Employee means any person who is employed for hire or reward to do any work, skilled or unskilled, manual or clerical, in a scheduled employment in respect of which minimum rates of wages have been fixed; and includes an out-worker to whom any articles or materials are given out by another person to be made up, cleaned, washed, altered, ornamented, finished, repaired, adapted or otherwise processed for sale for the purposes of the trade or business of that other person where the process is to be carried out either in the home of the out-worker or in some other premises not being premises under the control and management of that other person; and also includes an employee declared to be an employee by the appropriate Government; but does not include any member of the Armed Forces of the Union.

In *Pali Devi and Others vs. Chairman Managing Committee and Another* [(1996) SCC (3) 296], the High Court took the view that the word 'employee', defined in Section 2(i) of the Act did not include an ex-employee. It was held that a person who is not in the actual employment of the employer at the time of making an application under Section 20(2) of the Act, was not entitled to seek relief.

(Adapted from: www.indiankanoon.org/doc/1604516/ accessed on 13/4/2014.)

Fixing of Minimum Rates of Wages (Section 3)

1. The appropriate Government shall, in the manner hereinafter provided–
   (a) fix the minimum rates of wages payable to employees employed in an employment specified in Part I or Part II of the Schedule and in an employment added to either Part by notification under Section 27:

   Provided that the appropriate Government may, in respect of employees employed in an employment specified in Part II of the Schedule, instead of fixing minimum rates of wages under this clause for the whole State, fix such rates for a part of the State or for any specified class or classes of such employment in the whole State or part thereof;

   (b) review at such intervals as it may think fit, such intervals not exceeding 5 years, the minimum rates of wages so fixed and revise the minimum rates, if necessary:

   Provided that where for any reason the appropriate Government has not reviewed the minimum rates of wages fixed by it in respect of any scheduled employment within any interval of 5 years, nothing contained in this clause shall be deemed to prevent it from reviewing the minimum rates after the expiry of the said period of 5 years and revising them, if necessary, and until they are so revised the minimum rates in force immediately before the expiry of the said period of 5 years shall continue in force.

1A. Notwithstanding anything contained in sub-section (1), the appropriate Government may refrain from fixing minimum rates of wages in respect of any scheduled employment in which there are in the whole State less than 1,000 employees engaged in such employment, but if at any time the appropriate Government comes to a finding after such inquiry as it may make or cause to be made in this behalf that the number of employees in any scheduled employment in respect of which it has refrained from fixing minimum rates of wages has risen to 1,000 or more, it shall fix minimum rates of wages payable to employees in such employment as soon as may be after such finding.

2. The appropriate Government may fix–
   (a) a minimum rate of wages for time work (hereinafter referred to as "a minimum time rate");
   (b) a minimum rate of wages for piece work (hereinafter referred to as "a minimum piece rate");
   (c) a minimum rate of remuneration to apply in the case of employees employed on piece work for the purpose of securing to such employees a minimum rate of wages on a time work basis (hereinafter referred to as "a guaranteed time rate");
   (d) a minimum rate (whether a time rate or a piece rate) to apply in substitution for the minimum rate which would otherwise be applicable, in respect of overtime work done by employees (hereinafter referred to as "overtime rate").

2A. Where in respect of an industrial dispute relating to the rates of wages payable to any of the employees employed in a scheduled employment, any proceeding is pending before a Tribunal or National Tribunal under the Industrial Disputes Act, 1947, or before any like authority under any other law for the time being in force, or an award made by any Tribunal, National Tribunal or such authority is in operation, and a notification fixing or revising the minimum rates of wages in respect of the scheduled employment is issued during the pendency of such proceeding or the operation of the award, then, notwithstanding anything contained in this Act, the minimum rates of wages so fixed or so revised shall not apply to those employees during the period in which the proceeding is pending and the award made therein is in operation or, as the case may be, where the notification is issued during the period of operation of an award, during that period; and where such proceeding or award relates to the rates of wages payable to all the employees in the scheduled employment, no minimum rates of wages shall be fixed or revised in respect of that employment during the said period.

> **Spotlight**
> As per Section 3(3)(a), different minimum rates of wages may be fixed for different scheduled employments; different classes of work in the same scheduled employment; adults, adolescents, children and apprentices; and different localities.

(3) In fixing or revising minimum rates of wages under this section–
   (a) different minimum rates of wages may be fixed for:
      (i) different scheduled employments;
      (ii) different classes of work in the same scheduled employment;
      (iii) adults, adolescents, children and apprentices;
      (iv) different localities;
   (b) minimum rates of wages may be fixed by any one or more of the following wage periods, namely-
      (i) by the hour,
      (ii) by the day,
      (iii) by the month, or
      (iv) by such other larger wage-period as may be prescribed;

and where such rates are fixed by the day or by the month, the manner of calculating wages for a month or for a day, as the case may be, may be indicated:

Provided that where any wage-periods have been fixed under Section 4 of the Payment of Wages Act, 1936, minimum wages shall be fixed in accordance therewith.

CASE CORNER

In *Tamil Nadu Spinning Mills Association vs. The State of Tamil Nadu* (W.P.Nos. 28741, 28749, 28782, 28783 and 28805 of 2008), the State Textile Workers Federation made a representation in February 2006 through the Centre of Indian Trade Unions (CITU), to the Government of Tamil Nadu, alleging that the textile mills in Tamil Nadu were indulging in an exploitative practice of engaging adolescent girls under a scheme known as "Thirumagal Thirumana Thittam", and that the same amounted to forced labour. The Chief Inspector of Factories sent a report in February 2007 to the Government, stating that a camp coolie scheme was prevalent in these mills and young girls above the age of 15 years were being engaged under this scheme for 3 years as apprentices. The Government took into consideration various factors like the existing low wages paid to apprentices, the rapid changes in the consumer price index adversely affecting the living conditions of workers, representations made by various trade unions regarding the plight of apprentices, notice issued by the National Human Rights Commission in this issue, and the direction by the Division Bench of the Honourable Madras High Court to the authorities to take steps to ensure that these apprentices receive wages as per the Minimum Wages Act, 1948. Accordingly, the Government issued a draft notification dated 16th May 2008, proposing to fix the minimum rate of wages payable to these apprentices at ₹110/- per day, apart from Dearness Allowance.

However, the Southern India Mills Association, the South India Small Spinners Association, the Tamil Nadu Spinning Mills Association, the Employers' Federation of South India, around 302 mills, and some other trade unions sent objections and suggestions to this draft notification. One of the contentions of the petitioners was that the power to fix minimum rate of wages under Section 3(1)(a) of the Act does not extend to apprentices, but is limited only to employees. They argued that apprentices are not "employees employed in an employment" and hence the State Government has no power to fix the minimum rate of wages for apprentices in an employment specified in the Schedule.

It was held by the Court that to secure living wages to labour is one of the Directive Principles of State Policy embodied in Article 43 of the Constitution. The challenge to the vires of Section 3(3)(a)(iii) was not validated on any well accepted principles on which such challenges are possible.

(Adapted from: www.indiankanoon.org/doc/1102952/ accessed on 8/4/2014.)

Minimum Rate of Wages (Section 4)

1. Any minimum rate of wages fixed or revised by the appropriate Government in respect of scheduled employments under Section 3 may consist of—
   (i) a basic rate of wages and a special allowance at a rate to be adjusted, at such intervals and in such manner as the appropriate Government may direct, to accord as nearly as practicable with the variation in the cost of living index number applicable to such workers (hereinafter referred to as the "cost of living allowance"); or
   (ii) a basic rate of wages with or without the cost of living allowance, and the cash value of the concessions in respect of supplies of essential commodities at concession rates, where so authorised; or

(iii) an all-inclusive rate allowing for the basic rate, the cost of living allowance and the cash value of the concessions, if any.

2. The cost of living allowance and the cash value of the concessions in respect of supplies of essential commodities at concession rates shall be computed by the competent authority at such intervals and in accordance with such directions as may be specified or given by the appropriate Government.

It has been mentioned in *Mangalore Ganesh Beedi and Allied Industries vs. State of Karnataka and Others* [(2003) IIILLJ 861 Kant] that the concept of "cost of living allowance" is popularly known as Dearness Allowance (DA). The Act makes no specific mention of the term "dearness allowance", but it refers to an allowance paid on the rise of cost of living. Further, Variable Dearness Allowance (VDA) is very much a part and parcel of wages. Once the rates of minimum wages are prescribed under the Act, whether as all-inclusive under Section 4(1)(iii) or by combining basic plus DA under Section 4(1)(i), they are not amenable to split up.

(Adapted from: www.indiankanoon.org/doc/1971257/ accessed on 12/4/2014.)

CASE CORNER

In *Karnataka Film Chamber of Commerce vs. State of Karnataka* [(1987) ILLJ 182 Kant], it has been mentioned that Section 4 of the Minimum Wages Act, 1948 (referred to hereafter as the Act) indicates that basic wage is an integral part of minimum wage, which may consist of a basic rate of wages and a special allowance at a rate to be adjusted at such intervals and in such manner as the appropriate Government may direct. When the question of neutralisation of the cost of living arises by payment of Dearness Allowance, it necessarily follows that the Court should keep in view whether there had been an increase or decrease in the basic wage in a particular industry over a given period of time for the purpose of determining whether the neutralisation factor adopted by the State Government exceeds 100 per cent or 200 per cent or 300 per cent in a given situation.

In its attempt to define "dearness allowance", the DA Commission has referred to it as "a device to protect, to a greater or lesser extent, the real income of wage earners and salaried employees from the effects of rise in prices". Hence DA is a wider concept and is intended to neutralise the erosion of the real income of wage earners. Further, the Commission was of the opinion that DA should protect wage-earners at, or a little above, the subsistence level. It is hence clear that the payment of DA would arise only if the basic wage fixed for a particular category of workmen fell short of the minimum wage which the State Government has to fix, taking into consideration the needs of a worker's family consisting of 3 consumption units.

(Adapted from: www.indiankanoon.org/doc/1000631/ accessed on 10/4/2014.)

Procedure for Fixing and Revising Minimum Wages (Section 5)

1. In fixing minimum rates of wages in respect of any scheduled employment for the first time under this Act or in revising minimum rates of wages so fixed, the appropriate Government shall either:
   (a) appoint as many committees and sub-committees as it considers necessary to hold enquiries and advise it in respect of such fixation or revision, as the case maybe, or
   (b) by notification in the Official Gazette, publish its proposals for the information of persons likely to be affected thereby and specify a date, not less than 2 months from the date of the notification, on which the proposals will be taken into consideration.

2. After considering the advice of the committee or committees appointed under clause (a) of sub-section (1), or as the case may be, all representations received by it before the date specified in the notification under clause (b) of that sub-section, the appropriate Government shall, by notification in the Official Gazette, fix, or, as the case may be, revise the minimum rates of wages in respect of each scheduled employment, and unless such notification otherwise provides, it shall come into force on the expiry of 3 months from the date of its issue:

Provided that where the appropriate Government proposes to revise the minimum rates of wages by the mode specified in clause (b) of subsection (1), the appropriate Government shall consult the Advisory Board also.

In, *Bidi Leaves and Tobacco Merchants Association vs. State of Bombay* [(1959) 61 BOMLR 890], it was held that an Advisory Board is a very large body and it is certainly not convenient that the whole Board should hold an enquiry; instead the Board is allowed to appoint some of its members to conduct such enquiry and submit their report. After all, the function of the Advisory Board is only to advise and not to take a decision. It is open to the Advisory Board to devise its own procedure for obtaining information necessary for the purpose of discharging its advisory duty.

(Adapted from: www.indiankanoon.org/doc/1442165/ accessed on 10/4/2014.)

The Supreme Court in *Edward Mills Co. Ltd., Beawar and Others vs. State of Ajmer and Another* (1955 SCR (1) 735) held that the committee appointed under Section 5 of the Act was only an advisory body and the Government was not bound to accept any of its recommendations.

(Adapted from: www.indiankanoon.org/doc/121478/ accessed on 12/4/2014.)

ADVISORY COMMITTEES AND SUB-COMMITTEES (SECTION 6)

Repealed

Advisory Board (Section 7)

For the purpose of co-ordinating the work of committees and sub-committees appointed under Section 5 and advising the appropriate Government generally in the matter of fixing and revising minimum rates of wages, the appropriate Government shall appoint an Advisory Board.

Central Advisory Board (Section 8)

1. For the purpose of advising the Central and State Governments in the matters of the fixation and revision of minimum rates of wages and other matters under this Act and for co-ordinating the work of the Advisory Boards, the Central Government shall appoint a Central Advisory Board.
2. The Central Advisory Board shall consist of persons to be nominated by the Central Government representing employers and employees in the scheduled employments, who shall be equal in number, and independent persons not exceeding one-third of its total number of members; 1 of such independent persons shall be appointed the Chairman of the Board by the Central Government.

Spotlight

As per Section 8(1), the Central Government shall appoint a Central Advisory Board for advising the Central and State Governments in the matters of fixation and revision of minimum rates of wages and other matters under this Act and for co-ordinating the work of the Advisory Boards.

Composition of Committees, etc. (Section 9)

Each of the committees, sub-committees and the Advisory Board shall consist of persons to be nominated by the appropriate Government representing employers and employees in the scheduled employments, who shall be equal in number, and independent persons not exceeding one-third of its total number of members; 1 of such independent persons shall be appointed the Chairman by the appropriate Government.

Spotlight

As per Section 9, independent persons should not exceed one-third of total number of members of each committee, sub-committee and the Advisory Board.

CASE CORNER

In *State of Andhra Pradesh vs. Narayana Velur Beedi Manufacturing Factory and Others* (1973 SCR (3) 755), the appellant-Government had passed an order revising minimum wages in the *beedi* industry based on the recommendation of a committee of 6 members consisting of persons representing employers and employees and the Chief inspector and Deputy Chief Inspector of Factories. Section 9 of the Minimum Wages Act, 1948 requires that the Committee shall consist of an equal number of representatives of employer and employees, and of independent persons not exceeding one-third of its total number.

On the question whether the 2 Government officials could be regarded as independent persons, it was held that the mere fact that these 2 officials happened to be Government officials or Government servants will not divest them of the character of independent persons. It was further held by the Court that the language of Section 9 does not contain any indication that persons in the employment of the Government would be excluded from the category of 'independent persons'. These words have essentially been employed in contra-distinction to representatives of employers and employees. In other words, apart from the representatives of employers and employees in the committee, there should be persons who should be independent of them.

(Adapted from: www.indiankanoon.org/doc/125924/ accessed on 10/4/2014.)

Correction of Errors (Section 10)

1. The appropriate Government may, at any time, by notification in the Official Gazette, correct clerical or arithmetical mistakes in any order fixing or revising minimum rates of wages under this Act, or errors arising therein from any accidental slip or omission.
2. Every such notification shall, as soon as may be after it is issued, be placed before the Advisory Board for information.

Wages in Kind (Section 11)

1. Minimum wages payable under this Act shall be paid in cash.
2. Where it has been the custom to pay wages wholly or partly in kind, the appropriate Government being of the opinion that it is necessary in the circumstances of the case may, by notification in the Official Gazette, authorise the payment of minimum wages either wholly or partly in kind.
3. If the appropriate Government is of the opinion that provision should be made for the supply of essential commodities at concession rates, the appropriate Government may, by notification in the Official Gazette, authorise the provision of such supplies at concession rates.
4. The cash value of wages in kind and of concessions in respect of supplies of essential commodities at concession rates authorised under sub-sections (2) and (3) shall be estimated in the prescribed manner.

Payment of Minimum Rates of Wages (Section 12)

1. Where in respect of any scheduled employment a notification under Section 5 is in force, the employer shall pay to every employee engaged in a scheduled employment under him wages at a rate not less than the minimum rate of wages fixed by such notification for that class of employees in that employment without any deductions except as may be authorised within such time and subject to such conditions as may be prescribed.
2. Nothing contained in this section shall affect the provisions of the Payment of Wages Act, 1936.

Fixing Hours for a Normal Working Day, etc. (Section 13)

Spotlight

All employees must be allowed a day of rest in every period of 7 days, as provided in Section 13(1)(b).

1. In regard to any scheduled employment minimum rates of wages in respect of which have been fixed under this Act, the appropriate Government may:
   (a) fix the number of hours of work which shall constitute a normal working day, inclusive of 1 or more specified intervals;
   (b) provide for a day of rest in every period of 7 days which shall be allowed to all employees or to any specified class of employees and for the payment of remuneration in respect of such days of rest;
   (c) provide for payment for work on a day of rest at a rate not less than the overtime rate.
2. The provisions of sub-section (1) shall, in relation to the following classes of employees, apply only to such extent and subject to such conditions as may be prescribed–
   (a) employees engaged on urgent work, or in any emergency which could not have been foreseen or prevented;
   (b) employees engaged in work in the nature of preparatory or complementary work which must necessarily be carried on outside the limits laid down for the general working in the employment concerned;
   (c) employees whose employment is essentially intermittent;
   (d) employees engaged in any work which for technical reasons has to be completed before the duty is over;
   (e) employees engaged in a work which could not be carried on except at times dependent on the irregular action of natural forces.
3. For the purposes of clause (c) of sub-section (2), employment of an employee is essentially intermittent when it is declared to be so by the appropriate Government on the ground that the daily hours of duty of the employee, or if there be no daily hours of duty as such for the employee, the hours of duty, normally include periods of inaction during which the employee may be on duty but is not called upon to display either physical activity or sustained attention.

Overtime (Section 14)

1. Where an employee, whose minimum rate of wages is fixed under this Act by the hour, by the day or by such a longer wage-period as may be prescribed, works on any day in excess of the number of hours constituting a normal working day, the employer shall pay him for every hour or for part of an hour so worked in excess at the overtime rate fixed under this Act or under any law of the appropriate Government for the time being in force, whichever is higher.
2. Nothing in this Act shall prejudice the operation of the provisions of Section 59 of the Factories Act, 1948 in any case where those provisions are applicable.

Wages of Worker who Works for Less than Normal Working Day (Section 15)

If an employee whose minimum rate of wages has been fixed under this Act by the day works on any day on which he was employed for a period less than the requisite number of hours constituting a normal working day, he shall, save as otherwise hereinafter provided, be entitled to receive wages in respect of work done by him on that day as if he had worked for a full normal working day:

Provided, however, that he shall not be entitled to receive wages for a full normal working day:

(i) in any case where his failure to work is caused by his unwillingness to work and not by the omission of the employer to provide him with work, and

(ii) in such other cases and circumstances as may be prescribed.

Wages for Two or more Classes of Work (Section 16)

Where an employee does 2 or more classes of work to each of which a different minimum rate of wages is applicable, the employer shall pay to such employee in respect of the time respectively occupied in each such class of work, wages at not less than the minimum rate in force in respect of each such class.

Minimum Time Rate Wages for Piece Work (Section 17)

Where an employee is employed on piece work for which minimum time rate and not a minimum piece rate has been fixed under this Act, the employer shall pay to such employee wages at not less than the minimum time rate.

Maintenance of Registers and Records (Section 18)

1. Every employer shall maintain such registers and records giving such particulars of employees employed by him, the work performed by them, the wages paid to them, the receipts given by them and such other particulars and in such form as may be prescribed.
2. Every employer shall keep exhibited, in such manner as may be prescribed, in the factory, workshop or place where the employees in the scheduled employment may be employed, or in the case of out-workers, in such factory, workshop or place as may be used for giving out-work to them, notices in the prescribed form containing prescribed particulars.
3. The appropriate Government may, by rules made under this Act, provide for the issue of wage books or wage slips to employees employed in any scheduled employment in respect of which minimum rates of wages have been fixed and prescribe the manner in which entries shall be made and authenticated in such wage books or wage slips by the employer or his agent.

Inspectors (Section 19)

1. The appropriate Government may, by notification in the Official Gazette, appoint such persons as it thinks fit to be Inspectors for the purposes of this Act, and define the local limits within which they shall exercise their functions.
2. Subject to any rules made in this behalf, an Inspector may, within the local limits for which he is appointed:

   (a) enter, at all reasonable hours, with such assistants (if any), being persons in the service of the Government or any local or

Spotlight

The appropriate Government may appoint such persons as it thinks fit to be Inspectors, and define the local limits within which they shall exercise their functions, as per Section 19(1).

other public authority, as he thinks fit, any premises or place where employees are employed or work is given out to out-workers in any scheduled employment in respect of which minimum rates of wages have been fixed under this Act, for the purpose of examining any register, record of wages or notices required to be kept or exhibited by or under this Act or rules made thereunder, and require the production thereof for inspection;
(b) examine any person whom he finds in any such premises or place and who, he has reasonable cause to believe, is an employee employed therein or an employee to whom work is given out therein;
(c) require any person giving out-work and any out-workers, to give any information, which is in his power to give, with respect to the names and addresses of the persons to, for and from whom the work is given out or received, and with respect to the payments to be made for the work;
(d) seize or take copies of such register, record of wages or notices or portions thereof as he may consider relevant in respect of an offence under this Act which he has reason to believe has been committed by an employer; and
(e) exercise such other powers as may be prescribed.
3. Every Inspector shall be deemed to be a public servant within the meaning of the Indian Penal Code.
4. Any person required to produce any document or thing or to give any information by an Inspector under sub-section (2) shall be deemed to be legally bound to do so within the meaning of Section 175 and Section 176 of the Indian Penal Code.

Claims (Section 20)

1. The appropriate Government may, by notification in the Official Gazette, appoint any Commissioner for Workmen's (now Employees') Compensation or any officer of the Central Government exercising functions as a Labour Commissioner for any region, or any officer of the State Government not below the rank of Labour Commissioner or any other officer with experience as a Judge of a Civil Court or as a stipendiary Magistrate to be the Authority to hear and decide for any specified area all claims arising out of payment of less than the minimum rates of wages or in respect of the payment of remuneration for days of rest or for work done on such days under clause (b) or clause (c) of sub-section (1) of Section 13 or of wages at the overtime rate under Section 14 to employees employed or paid in that area.
2. Where an employee has any claim of the nature referred to in sub-section (1), the employee himself, or any legal practitioner or any official of a registered trade union authorised in writing to act on his behalf, or any Inspector, or any person acting with the permission of the Authority appointed under sub-section (1), may apply to such Authority for a direction under sub-section (3):

   Provided that every such application shall be presented within 6 months from the date on which the minimum wages or other amount became payable:

   Provided further that any application may be admitted after the said period of 6 months when the applicant satisfies the Authority that he had sufficient cause for not making the application within such period.
3. When any application under sub-section (2) is entertained, the Authority shall hear the applicant and the employer, or give them an opportunity of being heard, and after such further inquiry, if any, as it may consider necessary, may, without prejudice to any other penalty to which the employer may be liable under this Act, direct:

(i) in the case of a claim arising out of payment of less than the minimum rates of wages, the payment to the employee of the amount by which the minimum wages payable to him exceed the amount actually paid, together with the payment of such compensation as the Authority may think fit, not exceeding 10 times the amount of such excess;

(ii) in any other case, the payment of the amount due to the employee, together with the payment of such compensation as the Authority may think fit, not exceeding ₹10,

and the Authority may direct payment of such compensation in cases where the excess or the amount due is paid by the employer to the employee before the disposal of the application.

4. If the Authority hearing any application under this section is satisfied that it was either malicious or vexatious, it may direct that a penalty not exceeding ₹50 be paid to the employer by the person presenting the application.
5. Any amount directed to be paid under this section may be recovered:
   (a) if the Authority is a Magistrate, by the Authority as if it were a fine imposed by the Authority as a Magistrate, or
   (b) if the Authority is not a Magistrate, by any Magistrate to whom the Authority makes application in this behalf, as if it were a fine imposed by such Magistrate.
6. Every direction of the Authority under this section shall be final.
7. Every Authority appointed under sub-section (1) shall have all the powers of a Civil Court under the Code of Civil Procedure, 1908, for the purpose of taking evidence and of enforcing the attendance of witnesses and compelling the production of documents, and every such Authority shall be deemed to be a Civil Court for all the purposes of Section 195 and Chapter XXXV of the Code of Criminal Procedure, 1898.

Single Application in Respect of a Number of Employees (Section 21)

1. Subject to such rules as may be prescribed, a single application may be presented under Section 20 on behalf or in respect of any number of employees employed in the scheduled employment in respect of which minimum rates of wages have been fixed and in such cases the maximum compensation which may be awarded under sub-section (3) of Section 20 shall not exceed 10 times the aggregate amount of such excess or ₹10 per head, as the case may be.
2. The Authority may deal with any number of separate pending applications presented under Section 20 in respect of employees in the scheduled employments in respect of which minimum rates of wages have been fixed, as a single application presented under sub-section (1) of this section and the provisions of that sub-section shall apply accordingly.

Penalties for Certain Offences (Section 22)

Spotlight

Penalties for certain offences for an employer, as per Section 22, may be imprisonment for a term up to 6 months, or fine extending to ₹500, or both.

Any employer who:

(a) pays to any employee less than the minimum rates of wages fixed for that employee's class of work, or less than the amount due to him under the provisions of this Act, or

(b) contravenes any rule or order made under Section 13,

shall be punishable with imprisonment for a term which may extend to 6 months, or with fine which may extend to ₹500, or with both:

Provided that in imposing any fine for an offence under this section, the Court shall take into consideration the amount of any compensation already awarded against the accused in any proceedings taken under Section 20.

General Provision for Punishment of Other Offences (Section 22A)

Any employer who contravenes any provision of this Act or of any rule or order made thereunder shall, if no other penalty is provided for such contravention by this Act, be punishable with fine which may extend to ₹500.

Cognizance of Offences (Section 22B)

1. No Court shall take cognizance of a complaint against any person for an offence:
   (a) under clause (a) of Section 22 unless an application in respect of the facts constituting such offence has been presented under Section 20 and has been granted wholly or in part, and the appropriate Government or an officer authorised by it in this behalf has sanctioned the making of the complaint;
   (b) under clause (b) of Section 22 or under Section 22A except on a complaint made by, or with the sanction of, an Inspector.
2. No Court shall take cognizance of an offence:
   (a) under clause (a) or clause (b) of Section 22, unless complaint thereof is made within 1 month of the grant of sanction under this section;
   (b) under Section 22A, unless complaint thereof is made within 6 months of the date on which the offence is alleged to have been committed.

Offences by Companies (Section 22C)

1. If the person committing any offence under this Act is a company, every person who at the time the offence was committed, was in charge of, and was responsible to, the company for the conduct of the business of the company as well as the company shall be deemed to be guilty of the offence and shall be liable to be proceeded against and punished accordingly:

   Provided that nothing contained in this sub-section shall render any such person liable to any punishment provided in this Act if he proves that the offence was committed without his knowledge or that he exercised all due diligence to prevent the commission of such offence.
2. Notwithstanding anything contained in sub-section (1), where an offence under this Act has been committed by a company and it is proved that the offence has been committed with the consent or connivance of, or is attributable to any neglect on the part of, any director, manager, secretary or other officer of the company, such director, manager, secretary or other officer of the company shall also be deemed to be guilty of that offence and shall be liable to be proceeded against and punished accordingly:

Explanation For the purposes of this section:

(a) "company" means any body corporate and includes a firm or other association of individuals, and
(b) "director" in relation to a firm means a partner in the firm.

Payment of Undisbursed Amounts Due to Employees (Section 22D)

All amounts payable by an employer to an employee as the amount of minimum wages of the employee under this Act or otherwise due to the employee under this Act or any rule or order made thereunder shall, if such amounts could not or cannot be paid to the employee on account of his death before payment or on account of his whereabouts not being known, be deposited with the prescribed authority who shall deal with the money so deposited in such manner as may be prescribed.

Protection against Attachment of Assets of Employer with Government (Section 22E)

Any amount deposited with the appropriate Government by an employer to secure the due performance of a contract with that Government and any other amount due to such employer from that Government in respect of such contract shall not be liable to attachment under any decree or order of any Court in respect of any debt or liability incurred by the employer other than any debt or liability incurred by the employer towards any employee employed in connection with the contract aforesaid.

Application of Payment of Wages Act, 1936, to Scheduled Employments (Section 22F)

1. Notwithstanding anything contained in the Payment of Wages Act, 1936, the appropriate Government may, by notification in the Official Gazette, direct that, subject to the provisions of sub-section (2), all or any of the provisions of the said Act shall with such modifications, if any, as may be specified in the notification, apply to wages payable to employees in such scheduled employments as may be specified in the notification.
2. Where all or any of the provisions of the said Act are applied to wages payable to employees in any scheduled employment under sub-section (1), the Inspector appointed under this Act shall be deemed to be the Inspector for the purpose of enforcement of the provisions so applied within the local limits of his jurisdiction.

Exemption of Employer from Liability in Certain Cases (Section 23)

Where an employer is charged with an offence against this Act, he shall be entitled, upon complaint duly made by him, to have any other person whom he charges as the actual offender, brought before the Court at the time appointed for hearing the charge; and if, after the commission of the offence has been proved, the employer proves to the satisfaction of the Court–

(a) that he has used due diligence to enforce the execution of this Act, and
(b) that the said other person committed the offence in question without his knowledge, consent or connivance,

that other person shall be convicted of the offence and shall be liable to the like punishment as if he were the employer and the employer shall be discharged:

Provided that in seeking to prove, as aforesaid, the employer may be examined on oath, and the evidence of the employer or his witness, if any, shall be subject to cross-examination by or on behalf of the person whom the employer charges as the actual offender and by the prosecution.

Bar of Suits (Section 24)

No Court shall entertain any suit for the recovery of wages in so far as the sum so claimed:

(a) forms the subject of an application under Section 20 which has been presented by or on behalf of the plaintiff, or
(b) has formed the subject of a direction under that section in favour of the plaintiff, or
(c) has been adjudged in any proceeding under that section not to be due to the plaintiff, or
(d) could have been recovered by an application under that section.

Contracting Out (Section 25)

Any contract or agreement, whether made before or after the commencement of this Act, whereby an employee either relinquishes or reduces his right to a minimum rate of wages or any privilege or concession accruing to him under this Act shall be null and void in so far as it purports to reduce the minimum rate of wages fixed under this Act.

Spotlight

As per Section 25, any contract or agreement, whereby an employee either relinquishes or reduces his right to a minimum rate of wages or any privilege or concession accruing to him under this Act, shall be null and void if it purports to reduce the minimum rate of wages fixed under this Act.

In *Gulamahamed Tarasaheb and Others vs. State of Bombay and others* [(1961) 63 BOMLR 32], the Court has emphasised that the object of the Minimum Wages Act, 1948 is to provide for fixation of minimum rates of wages in certain employments to prevent exploitation of workers and to protect them against accepting wages less than the minimum rate. Employers are in a better position to resist any demand put up by employees for higher rates of wages. While the Act makes contracting out void by virtue of Section 25 in the interests of employees themselves, the legislature has provision for penalties in case of breach of Section 12 by employers only because the onus is on employers only to pay the minimum rate of wages fixed by the Government.

(Adapted from: www.indiankanoon.org/doc/1715084 accessed on 13/4/2014.)

Exemptions and Exceptions (Section 26)

1. The appropriate Government may, subject to such conditions, if any as it may think fit to impose, direct that the provisions of this Act shall not apply in relation to the wages payable to disabled employees.
2. The appropriate Government may, if for special reasons it thinks so fit, by notification in the Official Gazette, direct that subject to such conditions and for such period as it may specify the provisions of this Act or any of them shall not apply to all or any class of employees employed in any scheduled employment or to any locality where there is carried on a scheduled employment.

2A. The appropriate Government may, if it is of opinion that, having regard to the terms and conditions of service applicable to any class of employees in a scheduled employment generally or in a scheduled employment in a local area or to any establishment or a part of any establishment in a scheduled employment, it is not necessary to fix minimum wages in respect of such employees of that class or in respect of employees in such establishment or such part of any establishment as are in receipt of wages exceeding such limit as may be prescribed in this behalf, direct, by notification in the Official Gazette and subject to such conditions, if any, as it may think fit to impose, that the provisions of this Act or any of them shall not apply in relation to such employees.

3. Nothing in this Act shall apply to the wages payable by an employer to a member of his family who is living with him and is dependent on him.

Explanation In this sub-section a member of the employer's family shall be deemed to include his/her spouse or child or parent or brother or sister.

Spotlight

A member of an employer's family includes his/her spouse or child or parent or brother or sister.

Power of State Government to add to Schedule (Section 27)

The appropriate Government, after giving by notification in the Official Gazette not less than 3 months' notice of its intention so to do, may, by like notification, add to either part of the Schedule any employment in respect of which it is of opinion that minimum rates of wages should be fixed under this Act, and thereupon the Schedule shall in its application to the State be deemed to be amended accordingly.

It has been clearly stated in *Edward Mills Co. Ltd., Beawar and Others vs. State of Ajmer and Another* (1955 SCR (1) 735) that there is an element of delegation implied in the provisions of Section 27 of the Act, for the legislature, in a sense, authorises another body specified by it, to do something which it might do itself. But such delegation, is not unwarranted and unconstitutional. Further, it does not exceed the limits of permissible delegation.

(Adapted from: www.indiankanoon.org/doc/121478 accessed on 12/4/2014.)

Power of Central Government to Give Directions (Section 28)

The Central Government may give directions to a State Government as to the carrying into execution of this Act in the State.

Power of the Central Government to Make Rules (Section 29)

The Central Government may, subject to the condition of previous publication, by notification in the Official Gazette, make rules prescribing the term of office of the members, the procedure to be followed in the conduct of business, the method of voting, the manner of filling up casual vacancies in membership and the quorum necessary for the transaction of business of the Central Advisory Board.

Power of Appropriate Government to Make Rules (Section 30)

1. The appropriate Government may, subject to the condition of previous publication, by notification in the Official Gazette, make rules for carrying out the purposes of this Act.
2. Without prejudice to the generality of the foregoing power, such rules may:
   (a) prescribe the term of office of the members, the procedure to be followed in the conduct of business, the method of voting, the manner of filling up casual vacancies in membership and the quorum necessary for the transaction of business of the committees, sub-committees, and the Advisory Board;
   (b) prescribe the method of summoning witnesses, production of documents relevant to the subject-matter of the enquiry before the committees, sub-committees, and the Advisory Board;
   (c) prescribe the mode of computation of the cash value of wages in kind and of concessions in respect of supplies of essential commodities at concession rates;
   (d) prescribe the time and conditions of payment of, and the deductions permissible from, wages;
   (e) provide for giving adequate publicity to the minimum rates of wages fixed under this Act;
   (f) provide for a day of rest in every period of 7 days and for the payment of remuneration in respect of such day;
   (g) prescribe the number of hours of work which shall constitute a normal working day;
   (h) prescribe the cases and circumstances in which an employee employed for a period of less than the requisite number of hours constituting a normal working day shall not be entitled to receive wages for a full normal working day;
   (i) prescribe the form of registers and records to be maintained and the particulars to be entered in such registers and records;

(j) provide for the issue of wage books and wage slips and prescribe the manner of making and authenticating entries in wage books and wage slips;
(k) prescribe the powers of Inspectors for purposes of this Act;
(l) regulate the scale of costs that may be allowed in proceedings under Section 20;
(m) prescribe the amount of court-fees payable in respect of proceedings under Section 20; and
(n) provide for any other matter which is to be or may be prescribed.

Rules Made by Central Government to be Laid before Parliament (Section 30A)

Every rule made by the Central Government under this Act shall be laid as soon as may be after it is made before each House of Parliament while it is in session for a total period of 30 days which may be comprised in 1 session or in 2 successive sessions, and if, before the expiry of the session in which it is so laid or the session immediately following, both Houses agree in making any modification in the rule or both Houses agree that the rule should not be made, the rule shall thereafter have effect only in such modified form or be of no effect, as the case may be, so, however, that any such modification or annulment shall be without prejudice to the validity of anything previously done under that rule.

Validation of Fixation of Certain Minimum Rates of Wages (Section 31)

Where during the period:
(a) commencing on the 1st day of April, 1952, and ending with the date of the commencement of the Minimum Wages (Amendment) Act, 1954; or
(b) commencing on the 31st day of December, 1954, and ending with the date of the commencement of the Minimum Wages (Amendment) Act, 1957; or
(c) commencing on the 31st day of December, 1959, and ending with the date of the commencement of the Minimum Wages (Amendment) Act, 1961,

minimum rates of wages have been fixed by an appropriate Government as being payable to employees employed in any employment specified in the Schedule in the belief or purported belief that such rates were being fixed under clause (a) of sub-section (1) of Section 3, as in force immediately before the commencement of the Minimum Wages (Amendment) Act, 1954, or the Minimum Wages (Amendment) Act, 1957, or the Minimum Wages (Amendment) Act, 1961, as the case may be, such rates shall be deemed to have been fixed in accordance with law and shall not be called in question in any court on the ground merely that the relevant date specified for the purpose in that clause had expired at the time the rates were fixed:

Provided that nothing contained in this section shall extend, or be construed to extend, to affect any person with any punishment or penalty whatsoever by reason of the payment by him by way of wages to any of his employees during any period specified in this section of an amount which is less than the minimum rates of wages referred to in this section or by reason of non-compliance during the period aforesaid with any order or rule issued under Section 13.

ADMINISTRATION OF THE ACT

Under the provisions of the Minimum Wages Act, 1948, both Central and State Governments are appropriate Governments to fix, review and revise the minimum wages of workers employed in scheduled employments under their respective jurisdictions. The appropriate Government is also been empowered to notify any employment in the schedule where the number of employees is 1,000 or more, and fix the rates of minimum wages in respect of the employees employed therein.

WORKING OF THE ACT

Country-wide disparity in the level of minimum wage has always been a matter of concern to the Government. In order to reduce this disparity and also to have a uniform wage structure, a concept by the name of National Floor Level Minimum Wage (NFLMW) was designed on the basis of the recommendations of the National Commission on Rural Labour (NCRL) in 1991. However, the National Floor Level Minimum Wage is a non-statutory measure to ensure upward revision of minimum wages in different in States/Union Territories. The State Governments are persuaded to fix minimum wages in such a way that the minimum wage is less than NFLMW in none of the scheduled employments. This method has helped in reducing disparity among different rates of minimum wages to some extent.

Keeping in consideration the recommendation of the NCRL and consecutive rises in price indices over the years, the National Floor Level Minimum Wage was fixed at ₹35 per day in 1996. Subsequent revisions in the NFLMW were ₹40 per day in the year 1998, ₹45 w.e.f. 1st December 1999, ₹50 per day w.e.f. 1st September 2002, ₹66 per day w.e.f. 1st February 2004, and ₹80 per day w.e.f. 1st September 2007. One of the principal reasons behind such revisions is the increase in the Consumer Price Index.

RECENT INITIATIVES

For the Twelfth Five Year Plan (2012-2017), the Planning Commission has constituted the Working Group on Labour Laws and Other Labour Regulations, which has identified an urgent need to protect the interest of around 94 per cent of the workforce in the unorganised sector by providing them with minimum living wage, improved regulatory activities, basic social security and labour welfare schemes and improved health and safety facilities. The living standards of this segment need urgent attention, since the workers in this segment practically have no security of job and are often deprived of the basic rights under various labour laws. As per the Working Group, there should be one single statutory National Floor Level Minimum Wage for the entire nation, below which wages in any employment cannot be paid. Such a floor level would have its own advantages. Firstly, a single wage rate will be easy to understand and implement. Further, standardisation of minimum wages under NFLMW should also reduce procedural complications in implementation of the law and would enhance compliance.

The Minimum Wages Act, 1948 defines wages to include basic, Dearness Allowance and House Rent Allowance (HRA). It has been found that some employers split the consolidated wages announced by the Government into these heads, so that they do not have to pay provident fund, etc. on the full minimum wage announced by the Government. This way, such employers also do not pay gratuity on the component of HRA. The Working Group has come up with the following solutions to this problem:

- Wage in the Minimum Wages Act, 1948 to be defined to consist of basic and DA only.
- Section 20 to be amended to provide for the recovery of the amount determined by the Authority as arrears of land revenue in the same lines as the Payment of Gratuity Act, 1972, so that the Authority does not have to file an application before the Court.
- Filing of claim application and its being upheld, as given in Section 22B(a), should not be a condition precedent to the initiation of prosecution proceedings.

- As per Section 11(1), minimum wage is usually paid in cash. However, the Working Group opines that the Act should also provide for payment of wages by remittance in the bank account of the employee.
- There should be a law for migrant labour, who should be protected, as they are not provided with even minimum wages.
- While supporting that minimum wages should be paid to contract workers, the Working Group has held that it may not be just to equate the wages of a contract worker with wages of a regular worker who would have many more years of experience. Further, the selection process for a contract worker and a regular worker normally differ, and also the quality and skill of both may be different.

(Adapted from: Report on the Working of the Minimum Wages Act, 1948 for the Year 2010, Ministry of Labour & Employment.)

Summary

- Discrepancies in wage rates across the nation have always been a cause of concern to the Government. The report of the Committee on Fair Wages, published in 1948, prescribed clarification of concepts like fair wage, living wage and subsistence wage and enactment of a minimum wage legislation.
- The primary objective of the Minimum Wages Act, 1948 is to prevent exploitation of labour by providing for fixation and/or periodic revision of minimum wages in employments in which labour is susceptible to exploitation.
- Cost of living index number, as per Section 2(d), in relation to employees in any scheduled employment means the index number ascertained and declared by the competent authority by notification in the Official Gazette to be the cost of living index number applicable to employees in such employment.
- According to Section 3(1)(a), the appropriate Government shall fix the minimum rates of wages payable to employees employed in an employment specified in Part I or Part II of the Schedule and in an employment added to either Part by notification under Section 27.
- Section 4(1)(a) lays down that any minimum rate of wages fixed or revised by the appropriate Government may consist of either a basic rate of wages and a special allowance at a rate to be adjusted, at such intervals and in such manner as the appropriate Government may direct, to accord as nearly as practicable with the variation in the cost of living index number applicable to such workers.
- As per Section 8(1), for the purpose of advising the Central and State Governments in the matters of the fixation and revision of minimum rates of wages and other matters and for co-ordinating the work of the Advisory Boards, the Central Government shall appoint a Central Advisory Board.
- Section 14(1) provides that where an employee, whose minimum rate of wages is fixed under this Act by the hour, by the day or by such a longer wage-period as may be prescribed, works on any day in excess of the number of hours constituting a normal working day, the employer shall pay him for every hour or for part of an hour so worked in excess at the overtime rate fixed under this Act or under any law of the appropriate Government for the time being in force, whichever is higher.
- Section 19(1) lays down that the appropriate Government may, by notification in the Official Gazette, appoint Inspectors for the purposes of this Act, and define the local limits within which they shall exercise their functions.

- According to Section 22, any employer who pays to any employee less than the minimum rates of wages fixed for that employee's class of work, or less than the amount due to him under the provisions of this Act, or contravenes any rule or order made under Section 13, shall be punishable with imprisonment up to 6 months, or with fine up to ₹500, or with both.
- Both Central and State Governments are appropriate Governments to fix, review and revise the minimum wages of the workers employed in the scheduled employments under their respective jurisdictions.
- The National Floor Level Minimum Wage has been fixed at ₹80 per day with effect from 1st September 2007.

Key Concepts

Minimum wage
Fair wage
Overtime
Central Advisory Board
Living wage
Time rate
Out-worker
Piece work
Cost of living index number

Bibliography

Report on the Working of the Minimum Wages Act, 1948 for the Year 2010, Ministry of Labour & Employment Labour Bureau, Chandigarh/Shimla, Government of India.

Sarkar, S. and Mehta, B.S. "Income Inequality in India: Pre- and Post-Reform Periods", 2010, *Economic and Political Weekly*, 2010, Vol. XLV, No. 37, pp. 45-55.

Statistical Profile on Women Labour, 2009-2011, Ministry of Labour & Employment, Labour Bureau, Chandigarh/Shimla, Government of India.

Sinha, P.R.N., Sinha, I.B. and Shekhar, S.P., *Industrial Relations, Trade Unions, and Labour Legislation 2006*. New Delhi: Pearson Education.

Review Questions

Objective Type Questions

I. State True or False

i. Members of the Armed Forces come under the purview of the Minimum Wages Act.
ii. The term of imprisonment as a penalty for an employer may extend to 5 months.
iii. Minimum wage rate is fixed only by the hour or day or month.
iv. Wages exclude any contribution paid by the employer to any pension fund.
v. For any scheduled employment the appropriate Government may provide for payment for work on a day of rest at a rate not less than the overtime rate.

Answers: i. False, ii. False, iii. False, iv. True, v. True

II. Fill in the Blanks

i. Number of independent members in each committee should not exceed _______ of the total number of members.

ii. Notice to add to schedule by State Government must not be of less than _______ months.
iii. For any scheduled employment, minimum rates of wages would include employees whose employment is essentially _______.
iv. ______ wage is considered an ideal wage.
v. Child means a person who has not completed his _______ year of age.

Answers: i. one-third, ii. three, iii. intermittent, iv. living, v. fourteenth

Discussion Questions

1. Discuss the concepts of minimum wage, living wage and fair wage as laid down by the Committee on Fair Wages. Which of these is the most realistic, according to you?
2. Explain the term wages as given in the Minimum Wages Act, 1948. Clearly mention what all items do not come under wages.
3. What are the rules for fixing hours for a normal working day?
4. Explain the role of the various committees and boards in fixing or revising minimum rate of wages. Comment on the composition of such committees and boards.
5. Elaborate on the process of fixing of minimum rates of wages.
6. What are the provisions in the Minimum Wages Act, 1948 for offences by companies?
7. Which all items are considered by the appropriate Government in fixing or revising minimum rate of wages in respect of scheduled employments?
8. Are wages always paid in cash? Explain the provisions regarding modes of payment of wages.
9. Critically analyse the recent initiatives by the Planning Commission to protect the interests of the workers of unorganised sector in terms of fixing of minimum wage.
10. Explicate in details:
    a. Cost of living index number
    b. Wages for two or more classes of work
    c. Payment of minimum wage w.r.t. overtime work
    d. Minimum time rate wages for piece work

CASE STUDY-I

The Kozhikode Taluk Central Council of Local Trade Unions representing the workmen employed in the timber industry submitted a memorandum to the Labour Commissioner, Kerala State, requesting the latter to fix the minimum rates of wages for the workmen employed in the timber industry. The State Government, after considering these representations and making inquiries, came to the conclusion that a minimum rate of wage has to be fixed in the said industry. Accordingly, the State Government, by virtue of the powers conferred under Section 27 of the Minimum Wages Act, 1948 (hereafter "the Act") published a notification dated 22nd May 1957, declaring their intention to add employment in the timber industry to Part I of the Schedule to the Act. The notification also stated that the proposals will be taken into consideration after the expiry of 3 months from the date of publication and the objections and suggestions received before the said period will be considered by the State Government.

Finally the Government after a consideration of objections received, published another notification dated 9th October 1957, amending Part I of the Schedule to the Act by adding employment in timber industry as item No. 22.

The State Government appointed a committee by notifications dated 28th January 1958 and 12th March 1958 for holding inquiries and to advise in fixing minimum rates of wages in respect of employment in the timber industry and also nominated the members of the committee. The Chairman of the Committee, by his letter dated 7th February 1958, sought for clarification from the Government regarding the exact scope of the terms of reference. The State Government clarified the position by their communication, dated 24th March 1958, that the terms of reference to the Committee included all types of employment in the timber industry, namely, saw mills, furniture workshops, plywood factories, factories making slate frames, wooden toys, packing cases, etc.

The Committee circulated elaborate questionnaires among the employers and workmen, and collected necessary data regarding the nature of the industry, prevailing rates of wages, its place in the economy of the State and other relevant materials. It examined a large number of employers and employees and after a consideration of all these facts and circumstances, submitted its report, dated 29th January 1959, to the Government. After considering the advice of the Committee, the Government by a notification dated 22nd August 1959, and published in the Kerala State Gazette, dated 1st September 1959, fixed minimum rates of wages in respect of employment in the timber industry.

Writ petitions were filed against this notification, that plywood industry is something different from timber industry and inasmuch as the notifications issued relate only to timber industry and not plywood industry. Further it was mentioned that the State Government has no jurisdiction to fix minimum rates of wages in respect of plywood industry also, as purported to do under the impugned notification.

(Adapted from: D.M.S. Rao and Others vs. The State of Kerala and Another [(1963) ILLJ 176 Ker] www.indiankanoon.org/doc/194079/ accessed on 10/4/2014.)

Review Questions

1. Which sections of the Minimum Wages Act, 1948, in your opinion, are relevant in the following situations as mentioned in this case?
   i. The State Government amended Part I of the Schedule to the Act by adding the employment in timber industry as item No. 22.
   ii. The State Government appointed a committee by proper notifications.
2. Fixation of the minimum rates of wages has been made by Government vide notification dated 22nd August 1959 and vide notification dated 9th October 1957, amending Part I of the Schedule to the Act by adding the employment in timber industry as item No. 22. Do you think that the fixation of minimum rate of wages under the impugned notification is legal? On what basis and w.r.t. which provision of the Act?
3. Do you think that the objection raised in the writ petitions that the State Government has no jurisdiction to fix minimum rates of wages in respect of plywood industry is justified?

CASE STUDY-II

The Government of Kerala issued a draft preliminary notification containing proposals regarding the revision of minimum wages payable to the classes of employees employed in tea, rubber, coffee and cardamom plantations employing approximately 4 lakh persons in the State with effect from 1st April 1995. The last wage revision was made in the year 1985. As per Section 3 of the Minimum Wages Act,

1948 (referred to now on as the Act), the appropriate Government is required to review the minimum rates of wages at intervals not exceeding 5 years. Hence a proposal in the form of draft preliminary notification dated 18th November 1995 was issued for the information of all persons who were likely to be affected, calling upon them to submit their objection and suggestion on or before 20th January 1996. In pursuance to this, the petitioners filed their objection on 16th January 1996, contending that the said notification suffers from jurisdictional error apparent on the face of the records. It has been submitted by the petitioners that the issuance of notification in exercise of jurisdiction conferred on the State as a delegate is ultra vires of the provisions of the Act and rules, arbitrary, unreasonable and against public interest and violative of Articles 14 and 19 (1)(g) of the Constitution of India, on the basis of the following:

(i) giving retrospective effect from 1st April 1995 to the minimum rates of wages;
(ii) fixation of the minimum rate for over-kilos over and above the standard output and incorporate the same as part of minimum wages;
(iii) fixation of service weightage and job differentials for workers.

The Government is yet to issue the final notification.

As per Section 5 of the Act, before revising the minimum rates of wages the State Government has to, by notification, publish the proposal (draft preliminary notification) for the information of persons likely to be affected thereby, and after considering the objections, the State Government shall revise the minimum rates of wages (by final notification). The said final notification unless otherwise provides, shall come into force on the expiry of 3 months from the date of its issue.

The argument on behalf of the petitioners is that if the proposals, viz. the draft preliminary notification, proposing to give effect to the revision from 1st April 1995, is approved and a final notification is issued, it would be ultra vires of Section 5 of the Act. Therefore the petitioners are questioning the proposal (draft notification itself) inasmuch as the Government cannot propose to revise the minimum rates of wages from an anterior date.

(Adapted from: Association of Planters of Kerala vs. State ([1996) IILLJ 267 Ker] www.indiankanoon.org/doc/1579730/ accessed on 13/4/2014.)

Review Questions

1. Given that the Government is yet to issue a final notification after considering the objections, do you think the objection raised in the petition is valid?
2. Do you think that the Government cannot propose to revise the minimum rates of wages from an anterior date?

19

The Payment of Bonus Act, 1965

An Act to provide for the payment of bonus to persons employed in certain establishments on the basis of profits or on the basis of production or productivity and for matters connected therewith.

Desired Knowledge Competencies

- To understand the concept of bonus and its difference from an ex gratia payment.
- To discuss the scope and coverage of the Payment of Bonus Act, 1965 and of the various definitions given under the Act.
- To grasp the notions of set on and set off of allocable surplus, and minimum and maximum bonus payable.

CONCEPT OF BONUS

An industrial enterprise makes profits by the joint contribution of labour and capital. Hence labour should have a share in profits and in the prosperity of the enterprise; bonus represents such share of profits by an employee. In an organisational context, bonus is any payment made beyond the salary of an employee, and is usually linked to productivity, whether individual or collective. It is intended to provide a stimulus to employees.

Let us now touch upon a very common doubt: is bonus an ex gratia payment? Ex gratia is a voluntary payment often given out by an employer as a gesture of compassion; it connotes "gratis" on the part of the employer, implying a payment out of his own free will, kindness or grace, under no obligation of any law. Since the payment is voluntary, it is not bound by any legality; in other words, there is no obligation on the part of an employer to make an ex gratia payment. Because organisations in service industries like hospitals and organisations involved in social work are not covered under the Payment of Bonus Act, 1965, employees of such organisations are provided with ex gratia. What is interesting to note is that there is no ceiling on the payment of ex gratia unlike bonus, and also the percentage of such payment may vary from year to year solely at the discretion of the management.

Spotlight

Ex gratia is a voluntary payment given out by the employer as a gesture of compassion, under no obligation of any law; however, bonus is statutory.

Bonus literally means 'extra'. Unlike ex gratia, bonus is statutory, since the Government of India has fixed the minimum rate of bonus.

BACKDROP OF THE PAYMENT OF BONUS ACT, 1965

The Payment of Bonus Act, 1965 gives an employee the statutory right to a share in the profits of his/her employer. Prior to the enactment of the Act, bonus was given to an employee as a payment out of generosity, at the sole discretion of the employer. The practice of paying bonus in India appears to have originated during the First World War, with instances of payment of bonus at the rate of 10 per cent of wages in textile mills, and also with the inclusion of demand for payment of bonus in some cases of industrial disputes. In 1950, a Full Bench of the Labour Appellate Tribunal, on observing that bonus could no longer be considered as an ex gratia payment, laid down a formula, known as the Full Bench formula for determination of bonus. A plea was made to raise that formula in 1959. Eventually, due to a perceived need to address the issue of bonus in a comprehensive manner a Tripartite Commission was set up in 1961 by the Government of India with the objective of considering the question of payment of bonus based on profits of an establishment to employees of such an establishment. The Commission rejected the argument that the payment of bonus is meant to fill up the existing gap between actual and living wages, though in the process of sharing the prosperity this gap is narrowed down or closed. It did not approve of linking of available surplus set apart for the payment of bonus with wages. The Payment of Bonus Act, 1965 is an outcome of the recommendations of the Commission, which were accepted with a few modifications. The Payment of Bonus Ordinance, 1965 was promulgated on 29th May 1965, which was replaced by the Payment of Bonus Bill. The Bill received assent of the President of India on 25th September 1965 and the Payment of Bonus Act, 1965 came into force. Since then, the Act has witnessed several changes through multiple amendments. Following is the list of amending Acts:

1. The Insurance (Amendment) Act, 1968
2. The Payment of Bonus (Amendment) Act, 1969
3. The Central Labour Laws (Extension of Jammu and Kashmir) Act, 1970
4. The Payment of Bonus (Amendment) Act, 1972
5. The Payment of Bonus (Amendment) Act, 1973
6. The Payment of Bonus (Second Amendment) Act, 1973
7. The Payment of Bonus (Amendment) Act, 1974
8. The Payment of Bonus (Amendment) Act, 1976
9. The Payment of Bonus (Amendment) Act, 1978
10. The Payment of Bonus (Second Amendment) Act, 1980
11. The National Bank for Agriculture and Rural Development Act, 1981
12. The Payment of Bonus (Amendment) Act, 1985
13. The Payment of Bonus (Second Amendment) Act, 1985
14. The National Housing Bank Act, 1987
15. The Small Industries Development Bank of India Act, 1989
16. The Payment of Bonus (Amendment) Act, 1995
17. The Payment of Bonus (Amendment) Act, 2007

Spotlight

The objective of the Act is to reward employees for their performance and share the fruits of joint contribution of labour and capital with employees.

The Payment of Bonus Act, 1965 is the principal act for the payment of bonus to employees, with the objective of rewarding employees for their performance and sharing the fruits of joint contribution of labour and capital with employees. The object of the Act, as observed in *Jalan Trading Co.*

(Pvt. Ltd.) vs. Mill Mazdoor Union [(1967) SCR(1) 15], is to make an equitable distribution of the surplus profits of the establishment with a view to maintain peace and harmony between the three agencies (capital, management and labour) which contribute to the earning of profits. The scheme of the Act has the following four dimensions:

- To impose a statutory obligation upon the employer of every establishment defined in the Act to pay bonus to all eligible employees working in such establishment.
- To outline the principles of payment of bonus according to the formula prescribed.
- To provide for payment of minimum and maximum bonus, and linking such payment with the scheme of "set on" and "set off".
- To provide machinery for enforcement of the liability for payment of bonus.

(Adapted from: www.indiankanoon.org/doc/493792 accessed on 10/7/2014.)

ABOUT THE ACT

Short Title, Extent and Application (Section 1)

1. This Act may be called the Payment of Bonus Act, 1965.
2. It extends to the whole of India.

   The words "except the State of Jammu and Kashmir" were omitted by the Central Labour Laws (Extension to Jammu and Kashmir) Act, 1970, and the Act has been extended to Goa, Daman and Diu.
3. Save as otherwise provided in this Act, it shall apply to:
   (a) every factory; and
   (b) every other establishment in which 20 or more persons are employed on any day during an accounting year.

   Provided that the appropriate Government may, after giving not less than 2 months' notice of its intention so to do, by notification in the Official Gazette, apply the provisions of this Act with effect from such accounting year as may be specified in the notification, to any establishment or class of establishments including an establishment being a factory within the meaning of sub-clause (ii) of clause (m) of Section 2 of the Factories Act, 1948 employing such number of persons less than 20 as may be specified in the notification, so however, that the number of persons so specified shall in no case be less than 10.
4. Save as otherwise provided in this Act, the provisions of this Act shall, in relation to a factory or other establishment to which this Act applies, have effect in respect of the accounting year commencing on any day in the year 1964, and in respect of every subsequent accounting year:

   Provided that in relation to the State of Jammu and Kashmir, the reference to the accounting year commencing on any day in the year 1964, and every subsequent accounting year shall be construed as reference to the accounting year commencing on any day in the year 1968, and every subsequent accounting year.

   Provided further that when the provisions of this Act have been made applicable to any establishment or class of establishments, by the issue of a notification under the proviso to sub-section (3), the reference to the accounting year commencing on any day in the year 1964 and every subsequent accounting year or, as the case may be, the reference to the accounting year commencing on any day in the year 1968 and every subsequent accounting year, shall, in relation to such establishment or class of establishments, be construed as a reference to the accounting year specified in such notification and every subsequent accounting year.

5. An establishment to which this Act applies shall continue to be governed by this Act notwithstanding that the number of persons employed therein falls below 20 or, as the case may be, the number specified in the notification issued under the proviso to sub-section (3).

In *Jalan Trading Co. (Pvt. Ltd.) vs. Mill Mazdoor Union* [(1967) SCR(1) 15], the retrospective operation of the Act was made by Section 33, the provisions of which were held to be violative of Article 14, to depend on the pendency on that date of any dispute regarding payment of bonus relating to any accounting year from 1962 onwards. The year 1962 had apparently no connection with the date on which the Act came into operation, which was 29th May 1965.

Definitions (Section 2)

In this Act, unless the context otherwise requires,

Accounting year [Section 2(1)] Accounting year means:

(i) in relation to a corporation, the year ending on the day on which the books and accounts of the corporation are to be closed and balanced;

(ii) in relation to a company, the period in respect of which any profit and loss account of the company laid before it in annual general meeting is made up, whether that period is a year or not;

(iii) in any other case:

   (a) the year commencing on the 1st day of April; or

   (b) if the accounts of an establishment maintained by the employer thereof are closed and balanced on any day other than the 31st day of March, then, at the option of the employer, the year ending on the day on which its accounts are so closed and balanced.

Provided that an option once exercised by the employer under paragraph (b) of this sub-clause shall not again be exercised except with the previous permission in writing of the prescribed authority and upon such conditions as that authority may think fit;

Agricultural income [Section 2(2)] Agricultural income shall have the same meaning as in the Income-tax Act;

Agricultural income-tax law [Section 2(3)] Agricultural income-tax law means any law for the time being in force relating to the levy of tax on agricultural income.

Allocable surplus [Section 2(4)] Allocable surplus means:

(a) in relation to an employer, being a company other than a banking company which has not made the arrangements prescribed under the Income-tax Act for the declaration and payment within India of the dividends payable out of its profits in accordance with the provisions of Section 194 of that Act, 67 per cent of the available surplus in an accounting year;

(b) in any other case, 60 per cent of such available surplus;

Appropriate Government [Section 2(5)] Appropriate Government means:

(i) in relation to an establishment in respect of which the appropriate Government under the Industrial Disputes Act, 1947, the Central Government;

(ii) in relation to any other establishment, the Government of the State in which that other establishment is situate;

Available surplus [Section 2(6)] Available surplus means the available surplus computed under Section 5;

Award [Section 2(7)] Award means an interim or a final determination of any industrial dispute or of any question relating thereto by any Labour Court, Industrial Tribunal or National Tribunal constituted under the Industrial Disputes Act, 1947, or by any other authority constituted under any corresponding law relating to investigation and settlement of industrial disputes in force in a State and includes an arbitration award made under Section 10A of that Act or under that law;

Banking company [Section 2(8)] Banking company means a banking company as defined in Section 5 of the Banking Companies Act, 1949, and includes the State Bank of India, any subsidiary bank as defined in the State Bank of India (Subsidiary Banks) Act, 1959, any corresponding new bank specified in the First Schedule to the Banking Companies (Acquisition and Transfer of Undertakings) Act, 1970, any corresponding new bank constituted under Section 3 of the Banking Companies (Acquisition and Transfer of Undertakings) Act, 1980, any co-operative bank as defined in clause (bii) of Section 2 of the Reserve Bank of India Act, 1934, and any other banking institution which may be notified in this behalf by the Central Government;

Company [Section 2(9)] Company means any company as defined in Section 3 of the Companies Act, 1956, and includes a foreign company within the meaning of Section 591 of that Act;

Co-operative society [Section 2(10)] Co-operative society means a society registered or deemed to be registered under the Co-operative Societies Act, 1912, or any other law for the time being in force in any State relating to co-operative societies;

CASE CORNER

In *Air Corporation Employees' Co-operative Bank Ltd. vs. Co-operative Bank Employees' Union* [(1984) ILLJ 207 Bom], the petitioners are a co-operative bank. The first respondents are a trade union of co-operative bank employees, which made a demand for payment of 20 per cent bonus to the petitioners' employees for the year 1976-1977. Of the 3 deductions claimed by the bank, as disputed by the union, one was on account of return at the rate of 8 per cent on the capital invested. A reference was made and was heard by the Industrial Tribunal. The union alleged that the bank had made substantial profit and should be required to pay bonus at the rate of 20 per cent. The bank contended that on the basis of its profits for the relevant year the bonus payable worked out at not more than 6.5 per cent, but it was willing to pay at the rate of 8.33 per cent. Both parties filed statements of bonus calculations based on the balance-sheet and profit and loss account of the bank for the relevant year. The bank claimed that it was entitled to deduct 8.5 per cent of the capital invested by it in its establishment, based on Item 4 of Schedule III to the Payment of Bonus Act, 1965, or simply, the Act. The union, on the other hand, contended that the bank was entitled to such deduction at the rate of only 7.5 per cent and based its claim upon Item 2 of the Schedule III. Section 2(8) of the Act defines a banking company as including any co-operative bank. Item 2 of Schedule III is applied to an employer which is a banking company and Item 4 applies to an employer which is a co-operative society. In this case, co-operative bank being a banking company, Item 2 of Schedule III is specifically applicable and not the more general category of co-operative society specified in Item 4. As such, the bank is entitled to a deduction only of 7.5 per cent of the capital invested and the Tribunal was right in its decision.

(Adapted from: www.indiankanoon.org/doc/924929/ accessed on 14/7/2014.)

Corporation [Section 2(11)] Corporation means any body corporate established by or under any Central, Provincial or State Act but does not include a company or a co-operative society.

Direct tax [Section 2(12)] Direct tax means:

(a) Any tax chargeable under:
 (i) the Income-tax Act;
 (ii) the Super Profits Tax Act, 1963;
 (iii) the Companies (Profits) Surtax Act, 1964 ;
 (iv) the Agricultural Income-tax Law; and

(b) any other tax which, having regard to its nature or incidence, may by declared by the Central Government, by notification in the Official Gazette, to be a direct tax for the purposes of this Act;

Employee [Section 2(13)] Employee means any person (other than an apprentice) employed on a salary or wage not exceeding ₹10,000 per mensem in any industry to do any skilled or unskilled, manual, supervisory, managerial, administrative, technical or clerical work for hire or reward, whether the terms of employment be express or implied;

Spotlight
The definition of employee in Section 2(13) excludes an apprentice.

Employer [Section 2(14)] Employer includes:

(i) in relation to an establishment which is a factory, the owner or occupier of the factory, including the agent of such owner or occupier, the legal representative of a deceased owner or occupier and where a person has been named as a manager of the factory under clause (f) of sub-section (1) of Section 7 of the Factories Act, 1948, the person so named; and

(ii) in relation to any other establishment, the person who, or the authority which, has the ultimate control over the affairs of the establishment and where the said affairs are entrusted to a manager, managing director or managing agent, such manager, managing director or managing agent.

Establishment in private sector [Section 2(15)] Establishment in private sector means any establishment other than an establishment in public sector;

Establishment in public sector [Section 2(16)] Establishment in public sector means an establishment owned, controlled or managed by:

(a) a Government company as defined in Section 617 of the Companies Act, 1956;

(b) a corporation in which not less than 40 per cent of its capital is held (whether singly or taken together) by:
 (i) the Government; or
 (ii) the Reserve Bank of India; or
 (iii) a corporation owned by the Government or the Reserve Bank of India;

Factory [Section 2(17)] A factory shall have the same meaning as in clause (m) of Section 2 of the Factories Act, 1948;

Gross profits [Section 2(18)] Gross profits means the gross profits calculated under Section 4;

Income-tax Act [Section 2(19)] Income-tax Act means the Income-tax Act, 1961;

Prescribed [Section 2(20)] Prescribed means prescribed by rules made under this Act;

Salary or wage [Section 2(21)] Salary or wage means all remuneration (other than remuneration in respect of overtime work) capable of being expressed in terms of money, which would, if the terms of employment, express or implied, were fulfilled, be payable to an employee in respect of his employment or of work done in such employment and includes dearness allowance (that is to say, all cash payments, by whatever name called, paid to an employee on account of a rise in the cost of living), but does not include:

(i) any other allowance which the employee is for the time being entitled to;

(ii) the value of any house accommodation or supply of light, water, medical attendance or other amenity, or of any service or of any concessional supply of food grains or other articles;

(iii) any travelling concession;

(iv) any bonus (including incentive, production and attendance bonus);

(v) any contribution paid or payable by the employer to any pension fund or provident fund or for the benefit of the employee under any law for the time being in force;

(vi) any retrenchment compensation or any gratuity or other retirement benefit payable to the employee or any ex gratia payment made to him;

(vii) any commission payable to the employee.

Spotlight

Any bonus (including incentive, production and attendance bonus) is excluded from salary or wage by Section 2(21).

Explanation Where an employee is given in lieu of the whole or part of the salary or wage payable to him, free food allowance or free food by his employer, such food allowance or the value of such food shall, for the purpose of this clause, be deemed to form part of the salary or wage of such employee.

CASE CORNER

As laid down in *Gopalan vs. Angamali Chit Fund (P) Ltd.* [(1975) IILLJ 296 Ker], the Court deduced the following principles:

1. The Civil Procedure Code has not defined "wages". The word "wages" is used in a general sense without any qualification, including all payments made to an employee arising out of the relationship, but wages has also a narrower or special meaning, connoting periodical payment. The phrase "wages of labour" has to be understood in the context of the particular case before the court.
2. "Bonus" paid to a labour is an "ex gratia" payment and is not a wage deferred or otherwise, and as such cannot be a part of wages which has a permanence and a periodicity.
3. The definition of "wages" in enactments of a special nature made with a special purpose for giving the employee certain amount of protection cannot be imported by reference into Section 60(1)(h) of the Civil Procedure Code.
4. Payment of bonus may also assume permanence and periodicity if it is the result of an agreement between the employer and an employee or is the result of a statute.
5. Bonus declared under the Payment of Bonus Act, 1965 being the result of a statute, acquires permanence and periodicity, and is a part of wages within the meaning of the Civil Procedure Code.

It is true that the definition of "wages" in the Payment of Bonus Act, 1965 does not include bonus. But that is because for the purpose of that Act bonus has to be distinguished from wages and has to be determined in relation to the wages paid to the employee. The fact that bonus is specifically excluded from the definition of wages in Section 2(21) of the Act itself signifies that but for such exclusion bonus would fall under "wages".

(Adapted from: www.indiankanoon.org/doc/499296/ accessed on 14/7/2014.)

Words not defined [Section 2(22)] Words and expressions used but not defined in this Act and defined in the Industrial Disputes Act, 1947, shall have the meanings respectively assigned to them in that Act.

Establishments to Include Departments, Undertakings and Branches (Section 3)

Where an establishment consists of different departments or undertakings or has branches, whether situated in the same place or in different places, all such departments or undertakings or branches shall be treated as parts of the same establishment for the purpose of computation of bonus under this Act:

Provided that where for any accounting year a separate balance-sheet and profit and loss account are prepared and maintained in respect of any such department or undertaking or branch, then such department or undertaking or branch shall be treated as a separate establishment for the purpose of computation of bonus under this Act for that year, unless such department or undertaking or branch was, immediately before the commencement of that accounting year treated as part of the establishment for the purpose of computation of bonus.

In *K.C.P.E. Association, Madras vs. K.C.P.E. Ltd.* (AIR 1978 SC 474), the Supreme Court had held that the workmen of the industrial unit located at Madras (now Chennai) could not claim bonus on the basis of single establishment and proviso to Section 3 was attracted on the ground that separate balance sheet and profit and loss accounts of the unit have been prepared and maintained in the past and during the relevant years of accounting also.

Computation of Gross Profits (Section 4)

Gross profits derived by an employer from an establishment in respect of any accounting year shall:

(a) in the case of a banking company, be calculated in the manner specified in the First Schedule;

(b) in any other case, be calculated in the manner specified in the Second Schedule.

Spotlight

As per Section 4, gross profits shall be calculated as:

- in case of a banking company: First Schedule
- in any other case: Second Schedule

Computation of Available Surplus (Section 5)

The available surplus in respect of any accounting year shall be the gross profits for that year after deducting therefrom the sums referred to in Section 6:

Provided that the available surplus in respect of the accounting year commencing on any day in the year 1968 and in respect of every subsequent accounting year shall be the aggregate of:

(a) the gross profits for that accounting year after deducting therefrom the sums referred to in Section 6; and

(b) an amount equal to the difference between:

(i) the direct tax, calculated in accordance with the provisions of Section 7, in respect of an amount equal to the gross profits of the employer for the immediately preceding accounting year; and

(ii) the direct tax, calculated in accordance with the provisions of Section 7, in respect of an amount equal to the gross profits of the employer for such preceding accounting year after deducting therefrom the amount of bonus which the employer has paid or is liable to pay to his employees in accordance with the provisions of this Act for that year.

Sums Deductible from Gross Profits (Section 6)

The following sums shall be deducted from gross profits as prior charges, namely:

(a) any amount by way of depreciation admissible in accordance with the provisions of sub-section (1) of Section 32 of the Income-tax Act, or in accordance with the provisions of the agricultural income-tax law, as the case may be:

Provided that where an employer has been paying bonus to his employees under a settlement or an award or agreement made before the 29th May 1965, and subsisting on that date after deducting from the gross profits notional normal depreciation, then, the amount of depreciation to be deducted under this clause shall, at the option of such employer (such option to be exercised once and within 1 year from that date) continue to be such notional normal depreciation;

(b) any amount by way of development rebate or investment allowance or development allowance which the employer is entitled to deduct from his income under the Income-tax Act;

(c) subject to the provisions of Section 7, any direct tax which the employer is liable to pay for the accounting year in respect of his income, profits and gains during that year;

(d) such further sums as are specified in respect of the employer in the Third Schedule.

CASE CORNER

In the case of companies other than a banking company, gross profits are to be calculated in the manner specified in the Second Schedule. While computing gross profits, the Second Schedule requires adding back the following to the net profits shown in the prcfit and loss account: bonus to employees, depreciation, direct taxes including the provision (if any) for previous accounting years, development rebate/investment allowance/development allowance reserve, and any other reserves. In *Metal Box Co. of India Ltd. vs. Their Workmen* [(1969) SCR(1) 750], it was held by the Court that the notional tax liability is to be worked out by first working out the gross profits and deducting therefrom the prior charges under Section 6 of the Payment of Bonus Act, 1965, or simply, the Act, but not the bonus payable to the employees. It is clear from the above decision that an employer is entitled to deduct his tax liability without deducting first the amount of bonus he would be liable to pay from and out of the amount computed under Sections 4 and 6 of the Act.

(Adapted from: www.indiankanoon.org/doc/756197/ accessed on 10/7/2014.)

Calculation of Direct Tax Payable by the Employer (Section 7)

Any direct tax payable by the employer for any accounting year shall, subject to the following provisions, be calculated at the rates applicable to the income of the employer for that year, namely:

(a) in calculating such tax no account shall be taken of:

  (i) any loss incurred by the employer in respect of any previous accounting year and carried forward under any law for the time being in force relating to direct taxes;

  (ii) any arrears of depreciation which the employer is entitled to add to the amount of the allowance for depreciation for any following accounting year or years under sub-section (2) of Section 32 of the Income-tax Act;

(iii) any exemption conferred on the employer under Section 84 of the Income-tax Act or of any deduction to which he is entitled under sub-section (1) of Section 101 of that Act, as in force immediately before the commencement of the Finance Act, 1965;

(b) where the employer is a religious or a charitable institution to which the provisions of Section 32 do not apply and the whole or any part of its income is exempt from tax under the Income-tax Act, then, with respect to the income so exempted, such institution shall be treated as if it were a company in which the public are substantially interested within the meaning of that Act;

(c) where the employer is an individual or a Hindu Undivided Family, the tax payable by such employer under the Income-tax Act shall be calculated on the basis that the income derived by him from the establishment is his only income;

(d) where the income of any employer includes any profits and gains derived from the export of any goods or merchandise out of India and any rebate on such income is allowed under any law for the time being in force relating to direct taxes, then, no account shall be taken of such rebate;

(e) no account shall be taken of any rebate other than development rebate or investment allowance or development allowance or credit or relief or deduction (not herein before mentioned in this section) in the payment of any direct tax allowed under any law for the time being in force relating to direct taxes or under the relevant annual Finance Act, for the development of any industry.

Eligibility for Bonus (Section 8)

Every employee shall be entitled to be paid by his employer in an accounting year, bonus, in accordance with the provisions of this Act, provided he has worked in the establishment for not less than 30 working days in that year.

Spotlight

As per Section 8, every employee shall be entitled for bonus in an accounting year, provided he has worked in the establishment for not less than 30 working days in that year.

Disqualification for Bonus (Section 9)

Notwithstanding anything contained in this Act, an employee shall be disqualified from receiving bonus under this Act, if he is dismissed from service for:

(a) fraud; or

(b) riotous or violent behaviour while on the premises of the establishment; or

(c) theft, misappropriation or sabotage of any property of the establishment.

Payment of Minimum Bonus (Section 10)

Subject to the other provisions of this Act, every employer shall be bound to pay to every employee in respect of the accounting year commencing on any day in the year 1979 and in respect of every subsequent accounting year, a minimum bonus which shall be 8.33 per cent of the salary or wage earned by the employee during the accounting year or ₹100, whichever is higher, whether or not the employer has any allocable surplus in the accounting year:

Spotlight

Section 10 mandates a minimum bonus of 8.33 percent of salary/wage of an employee or ₹100, whichever is higher.

Provided that where an employee has not completed 15 years of age at the beginning of the accounting year, the provisions of this section shall have effect in relation to such employee as if for the words "₹100", the words "₹60" were substituted.

As laid down in *D. P Kelkar vs. Ambadas Keshav Bajaj and Others* [1971 (22) FLR 268], bonus is payable "whether there are profits in the accounting year or not"; thus the payment of minimum bonus under the Act is not dependent upon the establishment of the employer making a profit at all.

On the contrary, even though the establishment may incur a loss, the payment of minimum bonus is compulsory under the Act, as long as its requirements are fulfilled. A right is thus created in the favour of the employee on the one hand, and a duty enjoined upon the employer on the other, to pay bonus. By this legislation a term of employment has been introduced as binding on the employer, and in favour of the employee.

(Adapted from: www.indiankanoon.org/doc/1353003 accessed on 15/7/2014.)

Payment of Maximum Bonus (Section 11)

1. Where in respect of any accounting year referred to in Section 10, the allocable surplus exceeds the amount of minimum bonus payable to the employees under that section, the employer shall, in lieu of such minimum bonus, be bound to pay to every employee in respect of that accounting year bonus which shall be an amount in proportion to the salary or wage earned by the employee during the accounting year subject to a maximum of 20 per cent of such salary or wage.
2. In computing the allocable surplus under this section, the amount set on or the amount set off under the provisions of Section 15 shall be taken into account in accordance with the provisions of that section.

Calculation of Bonus with Respect to Certain Employees (Section 12)

Where the salary or wage of an employee exceeds ₹3,500 per mensem, the bonus payable to such employee under Section 10 or, as the case may be, under Section 11, shall be calculated as if his salary or wage were ₹3,500 per mensem.

Proportionate Reduction in Bonus in Certain Cases (Section 13)

Where an employee has not worked for all the working days in an accounting year, the minimum bonus of ₹100 or, as the case may be, of ₹60, if such bonus is higher than 8.33 per cent, of his salary or wage for the days he has worked in that accounting year, shall be proportionately reduced.

Computation of Number of Working Days (Section 14)

For the purposes of Section 13, an employee shall be deemed to have worked in an establishment in any accounting year also on the days on which:

(a) he has been laid off under an agreement or as permitted by standing orders under the Industrial Employment (Standing Orders) Act, 1946, or under the Industrial Disputes Act, 1947, or under any other law applicable to the establishment;
(b) he has been on leave with salary or wage;
(c) he has been absent due to temporary disablement caused by accident arising out of and in the course of his employment; and
(d) the employee has been on maternity leave with salary or wage,

during the accounting year.

Set on and Set off of Allocable Surplus (Section 15)

1. Where for any accounting year, the allocable surplus exceeds the amount of maximum bonus payable to the employees in the establishment under Section 11, then, the excess shall, subject to

a limit of 20 per cent of the total salary or wage of the employees employed in the establishment in that accounting year, be carried forward for being set on in the succeeding accounting year and so on up to and inclusive of the fourth accounting year, to be utilised for the purpose of payment of bonus in the manner illustrated in the Fourth Schedule.

2. Where for any accounting year, there is no available surplus or the allocable surplus in respect of that year falls short of the amount of minimum bonus payable to the employees in the establishment under Section 10, and there is no amount or sufficient amount carried forward and set on under sub-section (1) which could be utilised for the purpose of payment of minimum bonus, then, such minimum amount or the deficiency, as the case may be, shall be carried forward for being set off in the succeeding accounting year and so on up to and inclusive of the fourth accounting year in the manner illustrated in the Fourth Schedule.
3. The principle of set on and set off as illustrated in the Fourth Schedule shall apply to all other cases not covered by sub-section (1) or sub-section (2) for the purpose of payment of bonus under this Act.
4. Where in any accounting year any amount has been carried forward and set on or set off under this section, then, in calculating bonus for the succeeding accounting year, the amount of set on or set off carried forward from the earliest accounting year shall first be taken into account.

Special Provisions with Respect to Certain Establishments (Section 16)

1. Where an establishment is newly set up, whether before or after the commencement of this Act, the employees of such establishment shall be entitled to be paid bonus under this Act in accordance with the provisions of sub-section (1A), (1B) and (1C).

1A. In the first 5 accounting years following the accounting year in which the employer sells the goods produced or manufactured by him or renders services, as the case may be, from such establishment, bonus shall be payable only in respect of the accounting year in which the employer derives profit from such establishment and such bonus shall be calculated in accordance with the provisions of this Act in relation to that year, but without applying the provisions of Section 15.

In *Deputy Commissioner of Income-tax vs. Kicha Sugar Co. Ltd.* [(1996) 57 ITD 11 Delhi], the assessee is a co-operative society, running and maintaining a sugar mill at Kicha in Nainital District, Uttar Pradesh (UP) (now in Uttarakhand). It is an undertaking of the UP State Government and is being run as a subsidiary of the UP State Sugar Corporation Ltd. Production in the assessee's co-operative sugar mill started in the accounting year/previous year 1973-1974, relevant to the assessment year 1975-1976. For the first time it closed its accounts on 30th September 1992. In none of the accounting years relevant to the assessment years 1975-1976, 1976-1977, and 1977-1978 the assessee paid any bonus or customary bonus to its employees or workers. Even the liability of minimum bonus was not there for the assessee as it had started production only in the assessment year 1975-1976 and in accordance with the provisions of Section 16(1A) of the Act, the employers were exempted from payment of bonus for 5 years subsequent to the start of its production.

(Adapted from: www.indiankanoon.org/doc/559618/ accessed on 12/7/2014.)

1B. For the sixth and seventh accounting years following the accounting year in which the employer sells the goods produced or manufactured by him or renders services, as the case may be, from such establishment, the provisions of Section 15 shall apply subject other following modifications, namely:

(i) for the sixth accounting year:
set on or set off, as the case may be, shall be made in the manner illustrated in the Fourth Schedule taking into account the excess or deficiency, if any, as the case may be, of the allocable surplus set on or set off in respect of the fifth and sixth accounting years;

Spotlight
Reason of change in its location, management, name or ownership shall not make an establishment deemed to be newly set up.

(ii) for the seventh accounting year:
set on or set off, as the case may be, shall be made in the manner illustrated in the Fourth Schedule taking into account the excess or deficiency, if any, as the case may be, of the allocable surplus set on or set off in respect of the fifth, sixth and seventh accounting years.

1C. From the eighth accounting year following the accounting year in which the employer sells the goods produced or manufactured by him or renders services, as the case may be, from such establishment, the provisions of Section 15 shall apply in relation to such establishment as they apply in relation to any other establishment.

Explanation I For the purpose of sub-section (1), an establishment shall not be deemed to be newly set up merely by reason of a change in its location, management, name or ownership.

Explanation II For the purpose of sub-section (1A), an employer shall not be deemed to have derived profit in any accounting year unless–

(a) he has made provision for that year's depreciation to which he is entitled under the Income-tax Act or, as the case may be, under the Agricultural Income-tax law; and
(b) the arrears of such depreciation and losses incurred by him in respect of the establishment for the previous accounting years have been fully set off against his profits.

Explanation III For the purpose of sub-sections (1A), (1B) and (1C), sale of the goods produced or manufactured during the course of the trial running of any factory or of the prospecting stage of any mine or any oil field shall not be taken into consideration and where any question arises with regard to such production or manufacture, the decision of the appropriate Government, made after giving the parties a reasonable opportunity of representing the case, shall be final and shall not be called in question by any court or other authority.

2. The provisions of sub-sections (1), (1A), (1B) and (1C) shall, so far as may be, apply to new departments or undertakings or branches set up by existing establishments:

Provided that if an employer in relation to an existing establishment consisting of different departments or undertakings or branches (whether or not in the same industry) set up at different periods has, before the 29th May 1965, been paying bonus to the employees of all such departments or undertakings or branches, irrespective of the date on which such departments or undertakings or branches were set up, on the basis of the consolidated profits computed in respect of all such departments or undertakings or branches, then, such employer shall be liable to pay bonus in accordance with the provisions of this Act to the employees of all such departments or undertakings or branches (whether set up before or after that date) on the basis of the consolidated profits computed as aforesaid.

Adjustment of Customary or Interim Bonus against Bonus Payable under the Act (Section 17)

Where in any accounting year:

(a) an employer has paid any puja bonus or other customary bonus to an employee; or
(b) an employer has paid a part of the bonus payable under this Act to an employee before the date on which such bonus becomes payable,

then, the employer shall be entitled to deduct the amount of bonus so paid from the amount of bonus payable by him to the employee under this Act in respect of that accounting year and the employee shall be entitled to receive only the balance.

Deduction of Certain Amounts from Bonus Payable under the Act (Section 18)

Where in any accounting year, an employee is found guilty of misconduct causing financial loss to the employer, then, it shall be lawful for the employer to deduct the amount of loss from the amount of bonus payable by him to the employee under this Act in respect of that accounting year only and the employee shall be entitled to receive the balance, if any.

Time-limit for Payment of Bonus (Section 19)

All amounts payable to an employee by way of bonus under this Act shall be paid in cash by his employer:

(a) where there is a dispute regarding payment of bonus pending before any authority under Section 22, within a month from the date on which the award becomes enforceable or the settlement comes into operation, in respect of such dispute;

(b) in any other case, within a period of 8 months from the close of the accounting year:

Provided that the appropriate Government or such authority as the appropriate Government may specify in this behalf may, upon an application made to it by the employer and for sufficient reasons, by order, extended the said period of 8 months to such further period or periods as it thinks fit; so, however, that the total period so extended shall not in any case exceed 2 years.

Spotlight

As per Section 19, bonus shall be paid in cash to an employee within a period of 8 months from the close of the accounting year..

As observed in *Binny Ltd vs. Their Workmen* [(1972) SCR (3) 462], the claim for bonus can be made only after the close of the accounting year and in accordance with the provisions of the Act. The gross profits can be calculated only at the end of the accounting year and the available and allocable surplus can also be worked out only at the end of the accounting year. There is no question of an employer computing the gross profits, available surplus and allocable surplus in the middle of an accounting year or at any time before the close of the relevant accounting year.

(Adapted from: www.indiankanoon.org/doc/10682/ accessed on 12/7/2014.)

Application of Act to Establishments in Public Sector in Certain Cases (Section 20)

1. If in any accounting year an establishment in public sector sells any goods produced or manufactured by it or renders any services, in competition with an establishment in private sector, and the income from such sale or services or both is not less than 20 per cent of the gross income of the establishment in public sector for that year, then, the provisions of this Act shall apply in relation to such establishment in public sector as they apply in relation to a like establishment in private sector.
2. Save as otherwise provided in sub-section (1), nothing in this Act shall apply to the employees employed by any establishment in public sector.

Recovery of Bonus Due from an Employer (Section 21)

Where any money is due to an employee by way of bonus from his employer under a settlement or an award or agreement, the employee himself or any other person authorised by him in writing in this behalf, or in the case of the death of the employee, his assignee or heirs may, without prejudice to any other mode of recovery, make an application to the appropriate Government for the recovery of the money due to him, and if the appropriate Government or such authority as the appropriate Government may specify in this behalf, is satisfied that any money is so due, it shall issue a certificate for that amount to the Collector who shall proceed to recover the same in the same manner as an arrear of land revenue:

Provided that every such application shall be made within 1 year from the date on which the money became due to the employee from the employer:

Provided further that any such application may be entertained after the expiry of the said period of 1 year, if the appropriate Government is satisfied that the applicant had sufficient cause for not making the application within the said period.

Explanation In this section and in sections 22, 23, 24 and 25, "employee" includes a person who is entitled to the payment of bonus under this Act but who is no longer in employment.

Reference of Disputes under the Act (Section 22)

Where any dispute arises between an employer and his employees with respect to the bonus payable under this Act or with respect to the application of this Act to an establishment in public sector, then, such dispute shall be deemed to be an industrial dispute within the meaning of the Industrial Disputes Act, 1947, or of any corresponding law relating to investigation and settlement of industrial disputes in force in a State and the provisions of that Act or, as the case may be, such law, shall, save as otherwise expressly provided, apply accordingly.

Spotlight

Section 22 categorises any dispute under this Act as deemed to be an industrial dispute under the Industrial Disputes Act, 1947.

Presumption about Accuracy of Balance-sheet and Profit and Loss Account of Corporations and Companies (Section 23)

1. Where, during the course of proceedings before any arbitrator or Tribunal under the Industrial Disputes Act, 1947, or under any corresponding law relating to investigation and settlement of industrial disputes in force in a State (hereinafter in this section and in sections 24 and 25 referred to as the "said authority") to which any dispute of the nature specified in Section 22 has been referred, the balance-sheet and the profit and loss account of an employer, being a corporation or a company (other than a banking company), duly audited by the Comptroller and Auditor-General of India or by auditors duly qualified to act as auditors of companies under sub-section (1) of Section 226 of the Companies Act, 1956, are produced before it, then, the said authority may presume the statements and particulars contained in such balance-sheet and profit and loss account to be accurate and it shall not be necessary for the corporation or the company to prove the accuracy of such statements and particulars by the filing of an affidavit or by any other mode:

   Provided that where the said authority is satisfied that the statements and particulars contained in the balance-sheet or the profit and loss account of the corporation or the company are not accurate, it may take such steps as it thinks necessary to find out the accuracy of such statement and particulars.

2. When an application is made to the said authority by any trade union being a party to the dispute or where there is no trade union, by the employees being a party to the dispute, requiring any clarification relating to any item in the balance-sheet or the profit and loss account, it may, after satisfying itself that such clarification is necessary, by order, direct the corporation or, as the case may be, the company, to furnish to the trade union or the employees such clarification within such time as may be specified in the direction and the corporation or, as the case may be, the company, shall comply with such direction.

Audited Accounts of Banking Companies not to be Questioned (Section 24)

1. Where any dispute of the nature specified in Section 22 between an employer, being a banking company, and its employees has been referred to the said authority under that section and during the course of proceedings the accounts of the banking company duly audited are produced before it, the said authority shall not permit any trade union or employees to question the correctness of such accounts, but the trade union or the employees may be permitted to obtain from the banking company such information as is necessary for verifying the amount of bonus due under this Act.
2. Nothing contained in sub-section (1) shall enable the trade union or the employees to obtain any information which the banking company is not compelled to furnish under the provisions of Section 34A of the Banking Regulation Act, 1949.

Audit of Accounts of Employers, not Being Corporations or Companies (Section 25)

1. Where any dispute of the nature specified in Section 22 between an employer, not being a corporation or a company, and his employees has been referred to the said authority under that section and the accounts of such employer audited by any auditor duly qualified to act as auditor of companies under sub-section (1) of Section 226 of the Companies Act, 1956, are produced before the said authority, the provisions of Section 23, shall, so far as may be, apply to the accounts so audited.
2. When the said authority finds that the accounts of such employer have not been audited by any such auditor and it is of opinion that an audit of the accounts of such employer is necessary for deciding the question referred to it, then, it may, by order, direct the employer to get his accounts audited within such time as may be specified in the direction or within such further time as it may allow by such auditor or auditors as it thinks fit and thereupon the employer shall comply with such direction.
3. Where an employer fails to get the accounts audited under sub-section (2) the said authority may, without prejudice to the provisions of Section 28, get the accounts audited by such auditor or auditors as it thinks fit.
4. When the accounts are audited under sub-section (2) or sub-section (3) the provisions of Section 23 shall, so far as may be, apply to the accounts so audited.
5. The expenses of, and incidental to, any audit under sub-section (3) (including the remuneration of the auditor or auditors) shall be determined by the said authority (which determination shall be final) and paid by the employer and in default of such payment shall be recoverable from the employer in the manner provided in Section 21.

Maintenance of Registers, Records, etc. (Section 26)

Every employer shall prepare and maintain such registers, records and other documents in such form and in such manner as may be prescribed.

Inspectors (Section 27)

1. The appropriate Government may, by notification in the Official Gazette, appoint such persons as it thinks fit to be Inspectors for the purposes of this Act and may define the limits within which they shall exercise jurisdiction.
2. An Inspector appointed under sub-section (1) may, for the purpose of ascertaining whether any of the provisions of this Act has been complied with:
   (a) require an employer to furnish such information as he may consider necessary;
   (b) at any reasonable time and with such assistance, if any, as he thinks fit, enter any establishment or any premises connected therewith and require any one found in charge thereof to produce before him for examination any accounts, books, registers and other documents relating to the employment of persons or the payment of salary or wage or bonus in the establishment;
   (c) examine with respect to any matter relevant to any of the purposes aforesaid, the employer, his agent or servant or any other person found in charge of the establishment or any premises connected therewith or any person whom the Inspector has reasonable cause to believe to be or to have been an employee in the establishment;
   (d) make copies of, or take extracts from, any book, register or other document maintained in relation to the establishment; and
   (e) exercise such other powers as may be prescribed.
3. Every Inspector shall be deemed to be a public servant within the meaning of the Indian Penal Code.
4. Any person required to produce any accounts, books, register or other document or to give information by an Inspector under sub-section (1) shall be legally bound to do so.
5. Nothing contained in this section shall enable an Inspector to require a banking company to furnish or disclose any statement or information or to produce or give inspection of any of its books of account or other documents which a banking company cannot be compelled to furnish, disclose, produce or give inspection of, under the provisions of Section 34A of the Banking Regulation Act, 1949.

Penalty (Section 28)

If any person:
(a) contravenes any of the provisions of this Act or any rule made thereunder; or
(b) to whom a direction is given or a requisition is made under this Act fails to comply with the direction or requisition,

he shall be punishable with imprisonment for a term which may extend to 6 months, or with fine which may extend to ₹1,000, or with both.

Offences by Companies (Section 29)

1. If the person committing an offence under this Act is a company, every person who, at the time the offence was committed, was in charge of, and was responsible to, the company for the con-

duct of business of the company, as well as the company, shall be deemed to be guilty of the offence and shall be liable to be proceeded against and punished accordingly:

Provided that nothing contained in this sub-section shall render any such person liable to any punishment if he proves that the offence was committed without his knowledge or that he exercised all due diligence to prevent the commission of such offence.

2. Notwithstanding anything contained in sub-section (1), where an offence under this Act has been committed by a company and it is proved that the offence has been committed with the consent or connivance of, or is attributable to any neglect on the part of any director, manager, secretary or other officer of the company, such director, manager, secretary or other officer shall also be deemed to be guilty of that offence and shall be liable to be proceeded against and punished accordingly.

Explanation For the purposes of this section,

(a) "company" means any body corporate and includes a firm or other association of individuals; and
(b) "director", in relation to a firm, means a partner in the firm.

Cognizance of Offences (Section 30)

1. No court shall take cognizance of any offence punishable under this Act, save on complaint made by or under the authority of the appropriate Government or an officer of that Government (not below the rank of a Regional Labour Commissioner in the case of an officer of the Central Government, and not below the rank of a Labour Commissioner in the case of an officer of the State Government) specially authorised in this behalf by that Government
2. No court inferior to that of a presidency magistrate or a magistrate of the first class shall try any offence punishable under this Act.

Protection of Action Taken under the Act (Section 31)

No suit, prosecution or other legal proceeding shall lie against the Government or any officer of the Government for anything which is in good faith done or intended to be done in pursuance of this Act or any rule made thereunder.

Special Provision with Respect to Payment of Bonus Linked with Production or Productivity (Section 31A)

Notwithstanding anything contained in this Act,

(i) where an agreement or a settlement has been entered into by the employees with their employer before the commencement of the Payment of Bonus (Amendment) Act, 1976, or
(ii) where the employees enter into any agreement or settlement with their employer after such commencement,

for payment of an annual bonus linked with production or productivity in lieu of bonus based on profits payable under this Act, then, such employees shall be entitled to receive bonus due to them under such agreement or settlement, as the case may be:

Provided that any such agreement or settlement whereby the employees relinquish their right to receive the minimum bonus under Section 10 shall be null and void in so far as it purports to deprive them of such right:

Provided further that such employees shall not be entitled to be paid such bonus in excess of 20 per cent of the salary or wage earned by them during the relevant accounting year.

Act not to Apply to Certain Classes of Employees (Section 32)

Nothing in this Act shall apply to:

(i) employees employed by the Life Insurance Corporation of India;

(ii) seamen as defined in clause (42) of Section 3 of the Merchant Shipping Act, 1958;

(iii) employees registered or listed under any scheme made under the Dock Workers (Regulation of Employment) Act, 1948, and employed by registered or listed employers;

(iv) employees employed by an establishment engaged in any industry carried on by or under the authority of any department of the Central Government or a State Government or a local authority;

(v) employees employed by:

- (a) the Indian Red Cross Society or any other institution of a like nature (including its branches);
- (b) universities and other educational institutions;
- (c) institutions (including hospitals, chambers of commerce and social welfare institutions) established not for purposes of profit;

(viii) employees employed by the Reserve Bank of India;

(ix) employees employed by:

- (a) the Industrial Finance Corporation of India;
- (b) any Financial Corporation established under Section 3, or any joint Financial Corporation established under Section 3A of the State Financial Corporations Act, 1951;
- (c) the Deposit Insurance Corporation;
- (d) the National Bank for Agriculture and Rural Development;
- (e) the Unit Trust of India;
- (f) the Industrial Development Bank of India;
- (fa) the Small Industries Development Bank of India established under Section 3 of the Small Industries Development Bank of India Act, 1989;
- (ff) the National Housing Bank;
- (g) any other financial institution other than a banking company, being an establishment in public sector, which the Central Government may, by notification in the Official Gazette, specify, having regard to–
  - (i) its capital structure;
  - (ii) its objectives and the nature of its activities;
  - (iii) the nature and extent of financial assistance or any concession given to it by the Government; and
  - (iv) any other relevant factor;

(xi) employees employed by inland water transport establishments operating on routes passing through any other country.

In *Union of India and Others vs. R. C. Jain and Others* (1981 SCR (2) 854), the Delhi Development Authority, a statutory body created under the Delhi Development Act, 1957 for the development of Delhi, paid bonus to its employees for a period of 10 years up to the year 1973-1974, but later discontinued such payment on the advice of the Ministry of Law. The employees' petition impugning the action of the Authority in stopping the payment of bonus was allowed by the High Court. On the question whether the Delhi Development Authority is a 'local authority' and whether the provisions of the Payment of Bonus Act, 1965 are attracted, it was held that the expression 'local authority' is not defined in the Act. The Delhi Development Authority is endowed with all the usual attributes and characteristics of a 'local authority' and therefore the provisions of the Act are not attracted.

(Adapted from: www.indiankanoon.org/doc/769281 accessed on 14/07/2014.)

In *Maharashtra State Electricity Board vs. M.C. Chitale and Others* [(1981) ILLJ 462 Bom] serious dispute was raised whether Maharashtra State Electricity Board is an "establishment in public sector" and hence exempted from the provisions of the Payment of Bonus Act, 1965 under sections 32(iv) and 32(v)(c) of the Act. Under Section 32(iv), however large the powers of the State Government may be, the determining factor will be whether the Board has independent legal existence or not and whether the State Government is running the industry as its own department. Section 32(v)(c) provides two facets: whether the petitioner is an "institution" as contemplated under this provision; and whether it is "established not for the purpose of profit". It is not possible to conclude that the Board is established not for profit, and is exempt in terms of Section 32(v)(c) of the Act.

(Adapted from: www.indiankanoon.org/doc/1935562 accessed on 15/7/2014.)

Act to Apply to Certain Pending Disputes Regarding Payment of Bonus (Section 33)

Repealed by the Payment of Bonus (Amendment) Act, 1976.

Effect of Laws and Agreements Inconsistent with the Act (Section 34)

Subject to the provisions of Section 31A, the provisions of this Act shall have effect notwithstanding anything inconsistent therewith contained in any other law for the time being in force or in the terms of any award, agreement, settlement or contract of service.

Saving (Section 35)

Nothing contained in this Act shall be deemed to affect the provisions of the Coal Mines Provident Fund and Bonus Schemes Act, 1948, or of any scheme made thereunder.

Power of Exemption (Section 36)

If the appropriate Government, having regard to the financial position and other relevant circumstances of any establishment or class of establishments, is of opinion that it will not be in public interest to apply all or any of the provisions of this Act thereto, it may, by notification in the Official Gazette, exempt for such period as may be specified therein and subject to such conditions as it may think fit to impose, such establishment or class of establishments from all or any of the provisions of this Act.

Power to Remove Difficulties (Section 37)

Repealed by the Payment of Bonus (Amendment) Act, 1976.

Power to Make Rules (Section 38)

1. The Central Government may make rules for the purpose of carrying into effect the provisions of this Act.
2. In particular, and without prejudice to the generality of the foregoing power, such rules may provide for–
   (a) the authority for granting permission under the proviso to sub-clause (iii) of clause (1) of Section 2;

(b) the preparation of registers, records and other documents and the form and manner in which such registers, records and documents may be maintained under Section 26;
(c) the powers which may be exercised by an Inspector under clause (e) of sub-section (2) of Section 27;
(d) any other matter which is to be, or may be prescribed.

(3) Every rule made under this section shall be laid as soon as may be after it is made, before each House of Parliament while it is in session for a total period of 30 days, which may be comprised in 1 session or in 2 or more successive sessions, and if before the expiry of the session immediately following the session or the successive sessions aforesaid both Houses agree in making any modification in the rule or both Houses agree that the rule should not be made, the rule shall thereafter have effect only in such modified form or be of no effect, as the case may be; so, however, that any such modification or annulment shall be without prejudice to the validity of anything previously done under that rule.

Application of Certain Laws not Barred (Section 39)

Save as otherwise expressly provided, the provisions of this Act shall be in addition to and not in derogation of the Industrial Disputes Act, 1947, or any corresponding law relating to investigation and settlement of industrial disputes in force in a State.

Repeal and Saving (Section 40)

1. The Payment of Bonus Ordinance, 1965 is hereby repealed.
2. Notwithstanding such repeal, anything done or any action taken under the said Ordinance shall be deemed to have been done or taken under this Act as if this Act had commenced on the 29th May 1965.

ADMINISTRATION OF THE ACT

The Payment of Bonus Act, 1965 is enforced through the Central Industrial Relation Machinery (CIRM), Ministry of Labour & Employment.

SUMMARY

- Bonus is any payment made in an organisation beyond the salary of an employee, and is usually linked to productivity, whether individual or collective.
- The Payment of Bonus Act, 1965 is the principal act for the payment of bonus to employees, with the objective of rewarding them for their performance and sharing the fruits of joint contribution of labour and capital with employees. It gives an employee the statutory right to a share in the profits of an employer.
- The Act applies to every factory and every other establishment in which 20 or more persons are employed on any day during an accounting year.
- As per Section 3, where an establishment consists of different departments or undertakings or has branches, whether situated in the same place or in different places, all such departments or undertakings or branches shall be treated as parts of the same establishment for the purpose of computation of bonus under this Act.

- As laid down in Section 5, the available surplus in respect of any accounting year shall be the gross profits for that year after deducting therefrom the sums referred to in Section 6.
- Subject to the other provisions of this Act, every employer shall be bound to pay to every employee in respect of the accounting year commencing on any day in the year 1979 and in respect of every subsequent accounting year, a minimum bonus which shall be 8.33 per cent of the salary or wage earned by the employee during the accounting year or ₹100, whichever is higher, whether or not the employer has any allocable surplus in the accounting year.
- Where in respect of any accounting year referred to in Section 10, the allocable surplus exceeds the amount of minimum bonus payable to the employees under that section, the employer shall, in lieu of such minimum bonus, be bound to pay to every employee in respect of that accounting year bonus which shall be an amount in proportion to the salary or wage earned by the employee during the accounting year subject to a maximum of 20 per cent of such salary or wage.
- Where for any accounting year, the allocable surplus exceeds the amount of maximum bonus payable to the employees in the establishment under Section 11, then, the excess shall, subject to a limit of 20 per cent of the total salary or wage of the employees employed in the establishment in that accounting year, be carried forward for being set on in the succeeding accounting year and so on up to and inclusive of the fourth accounting year, to be utilised for the purpose of payment of bonus in the manner illustrated in the Fourth Schedule.

Key Concepts

Bonus	Set on	Direct tax
Available surplus	Set off	Accounting year
Allocable surplus	Gross profits	Interim bonus

Bibliography

Misra, S. N. and Misra, S. K. *An Introduction to Labour and Industrial Laws*, Allahabad: Central Law Publications; 1995.

www.indiankanoon.org

Review Questions

Objective Type Questions

I. Write True or False

(i) Any court inferior to that of a magistrate of the first class may try any offence punishable under the Payment of Bonus Act.
(ii) The excess of allocable surplus is carried forward for being set on up to and inclusive of the fourth accounting year for the payment of bonus.
(iii) Salary or wage is inclusive of remuneration in respect of overtime work.
(iv) An apprentice is eligible for bonus as per the Payment of Bonus Act.
(v) The Payment of Bonus Act does not have retrospective operations.

Answers: (i) False, (ii) True, (iii) False, (iv) False, (v) False

II. Fill in the Blanks

(i) An employee shall be disqualified from receiving bonus if he is dismissed from service for _____ or violent behaviour while on the premises of the establishment.

(ii) Director, in relation to a firm, means a ____ in the firm.

(iii) Gross profits by a banking company in respect of any accounting year shall be calculated in the manner specified in the _____ Schedule.

(iv) An employee is entitled to be paid bonus in an accounting year, provided he has worked in that establishment for not less than ____ working days in that year.

(v) Any amount by way of _____ rebate is deducted from gross profits.

Answers: (i) riotous, (ii) partner, (iii) First, (iv) thirty, (v) development

Discussion Questions

1. Discuss the cases of adjustment of customary or interim bonus against bonus payable.
2. Clearly explain the principle of set on and set off of allocable surplus.
3. Explain all the sums deductible from gross profits in details.
4. What are the various items that are not included in salary or wages in context of bonus?
5. Discuss the special provisions with respect to certain establishments as per Section 16 of the Payment of Bonus Act, 1965.
6. How would you compute the number of working days for an employee for the purpose of payment of bonus?
7. Elaborate on all provisions regarding audit of accounts of employers, not being corporations or companies and audited accounts of banking companies.
8. Discuss the different categories of employees who are not eligible for bonus.
9. Explain in brief:
   (a) Recovery of bonus due from an employer
   (b) Time-limit for payment of bonus
   (c) Special provision with respect to payment of bonus linked with production or productivity
   (d) Payment of maximum bonus
10. Differentiate between:
    (a) Available surplus and Allocable surplus
    (b) Bonus and Ex gratia payment
    (c) Power of exemption and Power to make rules
    (d) Offences by companies and Cognizance of offences

CASE STUDY-I

The petitioner in this case is Hutti Gold Mines Kamgar Sangh, a registered trade union of employees working in Hutti Gold Mines Company Ltd., Raichur, Mysore State, the respondent, which is a company governed by the provisions contained in the Companies Act, 1956, engaged in mining of gold. This company became a Government company with the Government of Mysore purchasing more than 51 per cent of shares. The Payment of Bonus Act, 1965 (hereinafter referred to as "the Act") came into force w.e.f. from the accounting year 1964. The petitioner raised a dispute regarding payment of bonus for the year 1968-1969 at the rate of 20 per cent of the total annual wages of every worker under the Act. The management resisted the said claim mainly on the ground that the Act is not applicable to them as they are a public sector establishment, and also on the additional ground that there is no allocable surplus.

The petitioner submitted that the respondent became a Government company as per Section 617 of the Companies Act, 1956. The business of the respondent is gold mining; there is another gold mining establishment in India known as Kolar Gold Fields Company, which was nationalised by the Government. Barring these two establishments, there is no other establishment doing gold mining in the country. Hence there is no scope for the respondent-establishment in the private sector so as to come within the scope of Section 20 of the Act. The employees of the respondent-company are thus denied the benefit of maximum and minimum bonus under the Act, though it is an establishment employing more than 20 persons. According to the petitioner, no distinction can be drawn between employees of a company in private sector and those in Government companies in public sector as regards payment of bonus.

(Adapted from: The Hutti Gold Mines Kamgar Sangh vs. Government of India and Others [(1973) ILLJ 46 AP] www.indiankanoon.org/doc/251302/ accessed on 12/7/2014.)

Review Questions

1. Which of the Sections 1(2) and 20, in your opinion, gives a stronger argument in favour of payment of bonus in the case?
2. What reasons has the petitioner put up for paying bonus?

CASE STUDY-II

The assessee in this case is a registered partnership firm engaged in the business of manufacturing and selling carborandum (a part used in petrochemicals) on wholesale basis and its turnover of sales during the year amounted to over ₹4 lakhs. The assessee had claimed deduction under Sections 80HH and 80J of the Income-tax Act, 1961 as it is an industrial undertaking which carries on manufacturing activity. However, on scrutiny of manufacturing account it is seen that the assessee has not employed 10 or more persons in manufacturing process. It has got certain processes done from outsiders on piecemeal basis. The assessee has not provided regular employment to any person in its manufacturing process. Mere providing of job work to some persons cannot be said to be regular employment and, therefore, the Income-Tax Officer (ITO) rejected the claim.

On appeal, the assessee submitted the following factual data for consideration:

The industrial undertaking has employed workers and paid ₹91,502.45, which has duly been debited in the trading and manufacturing account in the account "Majuri-Pagar Kharch". The workers are doing work in the factory and whatever work that is done by them is measured and on the basis of the quantity of work done and rate, voucher is made and payment against that voucher is made to the worker. The full details of Majuri-Pagar Kharch of the payments made to the workers are prepared and filed and a summary of the workers month-wise is also prepared. From the details of the workers and payments made to them and the month-wise summary, it is quite evident that more than 10 workers were working. When an industrial undertaking has provided work and workers are paid on the basis of the work done, the relief claimed should have been allowed. It is, therefore, claimed that more than 10 workers were working in the factory.

(Adapted from: V.B. Narania and Co. vs. Income-Tax Officer (1986 16 ITD 334 Ahd) www.indiankanoon.org/doc/1475692/ accessed on 10/7/2014.)

Review Questions

1. Which section of the Payment of Bonus Act, 1965 is relevant to this case?
2. Do you think the ITO was justified in rejecting the claim made by the assessee?
3. Is the assessee depriving the workers of various benefits by not engaging them on permanent basis?

The First Schedule

[*See Section 4(a)*]

Computation OF Gross Profits

Accounting year ending.............

Item No.	Particulars	Amount of sub-items ₹	Amount of main items ₹	Remarks
*1.	Net Profit as shown in the Profit and Loss Account after making usual and necessary provisions.			
2.	Add back provision for:			
	(a) Bonus to employees.			
	(b) Depreciation.			
	(c) Development Rebate Reserve.			See foot-note (1)
	(d) Any other reserves.			See foot-note (1)
	Total of Item No. 2	₹		
		₹	₹	
3.	Add back also:			
	(a) Bonus paid to employees in respect of previous accounting years.			
	(b) The amount debited in respect of gratuity paid or payable to employees in excess of the aggregate of –			
	(i) the amount, if any, paid to, or provided for payment to, an approved gratuity fund; and			
	(ii) the amount actually paid to employees on their retirement or on termination of their employment for any reason.			
	(c) Donations in excess of the amount admissible for income-tax.			
	(d) Capital expenditure (other than capital expenditure on scientific research which is allowed as a deduction under any law for the time being in force relating to direct taxes) and capital losses (other than losses on sale of capital assets on which depreciation has been allowed for income-tax).			See foot-note (1)
	(e) Any amount certified by the Reserve Bank of India in terms of sub-section (2) of Section 34A of the Banking Regulation Act, 1949 (10 of 1949)			
	(f) Losses of, or expenditure relating to, any business situated outside India.			
	Total of Item No. 3	₹		

*Where the profit subject to taxation is shown in the Profit and Loss Account and the provisions made for taxes on income is shown, the actual provisions for taxes as income shall be deducted from the profit.

4.	Add also income, profits or gains (if any) credited directly to published or disclosed reserves, other than— (i) capital receipts and capital profits (including profits on the sale of capital assets on which depreciation has not been allowed for income-tax); (ii) profits of, and receipts relating to, any business situated outside India; (iii) income of foreign banking companies from investment outside India. Net Total of Item No. 4	₹		
5.	Total of Item Nos. 1,2.3 and 4			
6.	Deduct:	₹		
	(a) Capital receipts and capital profits (other than profits on the sale of assets on which depreciation has been allowed for income-tax			See foot-note (2)
	(b) Profits of, and receipts relating to, any business situated outside India.			See foot-note (2)
	(c) Income of foreign banking companies from investments outside India			See foot-note (2)
	(d) Expenditure or losses (if any debited directly to published or disclosed reserves, other than– (i) capital expenditure and capital losses (other than losses on sale of capital assets on which depreciation has not been allowed for income-tax) (ii) Losses of any business situated outside India.	₹		
	(e) In the case of foreign banking companies proportionate administrative (overhead) expenses of head Office allocable to Indian business.			See foot-note (3)
	(f) Refund of any excess direct tax paid for previous accounting years and excess provision, if any, of previous accounting years, relating to bonus, depreciation, or development rebate, if written back.			See foot-note (2)
	(g) Cash subsidy, if any, given by the Government or by anybody corporate established by any law for the time being in force or by any other agency through budgetary grants, whether given directly or through any agency for specified purposes and the proceeds of which are reserved for such purposes. Total of Item No. 6......			See foot-note (2)
7.	Gross Profits for purposes of bonus (Item No. 5 minus Item No. 6)	₹	₹	

Explanation– In sub-item (b) of item 3, 'approved gratuity fund' has the same meaning assigned to it in clause (5) of Section 2 of the Income-Tax Act.

Footnotes: (1) If, and to the extent charged to Profit and Loss Account.

(2) If, and to the extent, credited to Profit and Loss Account.

(3) In the proportion of Indian Gross Profit (Item No. 7) to Total World Gross Profit (as per Consolidated Profit and Loss Account, adjusted as in Item No. 2 above only).

The Second Schedule

[See Section 4(a)]

Computation of Gross Profits

Accounting year ending................

Item No.	*Particulars*	*Amount of sub-items* ₹	*Amount of main items* ₹	*Remarks*
1.	Net Profit as per Profit and Loss Account.			
2.	Add back provision for:			
	(a) Bonus to employees.			
	(b) Depreciation			
	(c) Direct taxes, including the provision (if any) for previous accounting years.			
	(d) Development Rebate/Investment allowance/ Development Allowance reserve.			See foot-note (1)
	(e) Any other reserves.			
	Total of Item No. 2			See foot-note (1)
3.	Add back also:			
	(a) Bonus paid to employees in respect of previous accounting years.	₹		
	(aa)The amount debited in respect of gratuity paid or payable to employees in excess of the aggregate of – (i) the amount , if any, paid to, or provided for payment to, an approved gratuity fund; and (ii) the amount actually paid to employees on their retirement or on termination of their employment for any reason			See foot-note (1)
	(b) Donations in excess of the amount admissible for income- tax.			
	(c) Any annuity due, or commuted value of any annuity paid, under the provisions of section 280D of the Income-tax Act during the accounting year.			
	(d) Capital expenditure (other than capital expenditure on scientific research which is allowed as a deduction under any law for the time being in force relating to direct taxes) and capital losses (other than losses on sale of capital assets on which depreciation has been allowed for income-tax).			See foot-note (1)
	(e) Losses of, or expenditure relating to, any business situated outside India.			
	Total of Item No. 3	₹		

4.	Add also income, profits or gains (if any) credited directly to published or disclosed reserves, other than— (i) capital receipts and capital profits (including profits on the sale of capital assets on which depreciation has not been allowed for income-tax or agricultural Income-Tax); (ii) profits of, and receipts relating to, any business situated outside India; (iii) income of foreign concerns from investment outside India.			
	Net Total of Item No. 4......	₹		
		₹		
5.	Total of Item Nos. 1, 2, 3 and 4			
6.	Deduct:			See foot-note (2)
	(a) Capital receipts and capital profits (other than profits on the sale of assets on which depreciation has been allowed for income-tax or agricultural income-tax)			See foot-note (2)
	(b) Profits of, and receipts relating to, any business situated outside India.			See foot-note (2)
	(c) Income of foreign concerns from investments outside India			
	(d) Expenditure or losses (if any debited directly to published or disclosed reserves, other than- (i) capital expenditure and capital losses (other than losses on sale of capital assets on which depreciation has not been allowed for income-tax.) (ii) losses of any business situated outside India.			
	(e) In the case of foreign banking companies proportionate administrative (overhead) expenses of head office allocable to Indian business.			See foot-note (3)
				See foot-note (3)
	(f) Refund of any direct tax paid for previous accounting years and excess provision, if any, of previous accounting years, relating to bonus, depreciation, taxation or development rebate or development allowance, if written back.			
	(g) Cash subsidy, if any, given by the Government or by anybody corporate established by any law for the time being in force or by any other agency through budgetary grants, whether given directly or through any agency for specified purposes and the proceeds of which are reserved for such purposes			
7.	(j) Total of Item No. 6......	₹		
	Gross Profits for purposes of bonus (Item No. 5 minus Item No. 6)	₹		

Explanation– In sub-item (aa) of item 3, 'approved gratuity fund' has the same meaning assigned to it in clause (5) of Section 2 of the Income-Tax Act.

Foot-Notes: (1) If, and to the extent charged to Profit and Loss Account.

(2) If, and to the extent, credited to Profit and Loss Account.

(3) In the proportion of India Gross Profit (Item No. 7) to Total World Gross Profit (as per Consolidated Profit and Loss Account adjusted as in Item No. 2 above only).

THE THIRD SCHEDULE

[*See Section 6(d)*]

Item No.	*Category of employer*	*Further sums to be deducted*
(1)	*(2)*	*(3)*
1.	Company, other than a banking company	(i) The dividends payable on its preference share capital for the accounting year calculated at the actual rate at which such dividends are payable; (ii) 8.5 per cent of its paid up equity share capital as at the commencement of the accounting year; (iii) 6 per cent of its reserves shown in its balance-sheet as at the commencement of the accounting year, including any profits carried forward from the previous accounting year. Provided that where the employer is a foreign company within the meaning of Section 591 of the Companies Act, 1956 (1 of 1956), the total amount to be deducted under this Item shall be 8.5 per cent on the aggregate of the value of the net fixed assets and the current assets of their company in India after deducting the amount of its current liabilities (other than any amount shown as payable by the company to its Head Office whether towards any advance made by the Head Office or otherwise or any interest paid by the company to its Head Office) in India.
2.	Banking company	(i) The dividends payable on its preference share capital for the accounting year calculated at the rate at which such dividends are payable; (ii) 7.5 per cent of its paid up equity share capital as at the commencement of the accounting year; (iii) 5 per cent of its reserves shown in its balance-sheet as at the commencement of the accounting year, including any profits carried forward from the previous accounting year. (iv) any sum which in respect of the accounting year, is transferred by it- (a) to a reserve fund under sub-section (1) of section 17 of the Banking Regulation Act, 1949 (10 of 1949); or (b) to any reserves in India in pursuance of any direction or advise given by the Reserve bank of India, whichever is higher: Provided that where the banking company is a foreign company within the meaning of Section 591 of the Companies Act, 1956 (1 of 1956), the amount to be deducted under this item shall be aggregate of– (i) the dividends payable on its preference shareholders for the accounting year at the rate at which such dividends are payable on such amount as bears the same proportion to its total preference share capital as its total working funds in India bear to its total world working funds;

		(ii) 7.5 per cent of such amount as bears the same proportion to its total paid up equity share capital as its total working funds in India bear to its total working funds in India bear to its total world working funds; (iii) 5 per cent of such amount as bears the same proportion to its total disclosed reserves as its total working funds in India bear to its total world working funds; (iv) any sum which, in respect of the accounting year, is deposited by it with the Reserve Bank of India under sub-clause (ii) of clause (b) of sub-section (2) of Section 11 of the Banking Regulation Act, 1949 (10 of 1949), not exceeding the amount required under the aforesaid provision to be so deposited.]
3.	Corporation	(i) 8.5 per cent of its paid up capital as at the commencement of the accounting year. (ii) 6 per cent of its reserves, if any, shown in its balance sheet as at the commencement of the accounting, year including any profits carried forward from the previous accounting year.
4.	Co-operative society	(i) 8.5 per cent of the capital invested by such society in its establishment as evidenced from its books of accounts at the commencement of the accounting year; (ii) such sum as has been carried forward in respect of the accounting year to a reserve fund under any law relating to co-operative societies for the time being in force.
5.	Any other employer not falling under any of the aforesaid categories.	8.5 per cent of the capital invested by him in his establishment as evidence from his books of accounts at the commencement of the accounting year. Provided that where such employer is a person to whom Chapter XXIIA of the Income-tax Act applies, the annuity deposit payable by him under the provisions of that Chapter during the accounting year shall also be deducted. Provided further that where such employer is a firm, an amount equal to 25 per cent, of the gross profits derived by it from the establishment in respect of the accounting year after deducting depreciation in accordance with the provision of clause (a) of Section 6 by way of remuneration to all the partners taking part in the conduct of business of the establishment shall also be deducted, but where the partnership agreement, whether oral or written, provides for the payment of remuneration to any such partner, and – (i) the total remuneration payable to all such partners is less than the said 25 per cent the amount payable, subject to a maximum of ₹48,000 to each such partner; or (ii) the total remuneration payable to all such partners is higher than the said 25 per cent such percentage, or a sum calculated at the rate of ₹48,000 to each such partner, whichever is less, shall be deducted under this proviso; Provided also that where such employer is an individual or a Hindu undivided family- (i) an amount equal to 25 per cent of the gross profits derived by such employer from the establishment in respect of the accounting year after deducting depreciation in accordance with the provisions of clause (a) of Section 6; or (ii) ₹48,000; whichever is less, by way of remuneration to such employer, shall also be deducted.

6.	Any employer failing under Item No. 1 or Item No. 3 or Item No. 4 or Item No. 5 and being a license within the meaning of the Electricity (Supply) Act, 1948 (54 of 1948)	In addition to the sums deductible under any of the aforesaid items, such sums as are required to be appropriate by the license in respect of the accounting year to a reserve under the Sixth Schedule to that Act shall also be deducted.

Explanation: The expression 'reserves" occurring in column (3) against item Nos. 1(iii), 2(iii) and 3(ii)] shall not include any amount set apart for the purpose of–

(i) Payment of any direct tax which, according to the balance–sheet, would be payable;

(ii) meeting any depreciation admissible in accordance with the provisions of clause(a) of Section 6;

(iii) payment of dividends which have been declared; but shall include–

(a) any amount, over and above the amount referred to in clause (i) of this Explanation.

(b) any amount set apart for meeting any depreciation in excess of the amount admissible in accordance with the provisions of clause (a) of Section 6.

THE FOURTH SCHEDULE

[*See sections 15 and 16*]

In this Schedule, the total amount of bonus equal to 8.33 per cent of the annual salary or wage payable to all the employees is assumed to be ₹1,04,167. Accordingly, the maximum bonus to which all the employees are entitled to the paid (20 per cent of the annual salary or wage of all the employees) would be ₹2,50,000.

Year	*Amount equal to 60 per cent, or 67 per cent, as the case may be, or available surplus allocable as bonus*	*Amount payable as bonus*	*Set on or set off of the year carried forward*	*Total set on or set off carried forward*
(1)	*(2)*	*(3)*	*(4)*	*(5)*
	₹	₹	₹	₹ of (year)
1.	1,04,167	1.04,167**	Nil	NIl
2.	6,35,000	2,50,000*	Set on 2,50,000*	Set on 2,50,000* (2)
3.	2,20,000	2,50,000* (inclusive of 30,000 from year–2)	Nil	Set on (2) 2,20,000
4.	3,75,000	2,50,000*	Set on 1,25,000*	Set on 2,20,000 (2) 1,25,000 (4)
5.	1,40,000	2,50,000* (inclusive of 1,10,000 from year-2)	Nil	Set on 1,10,000 (2) 1,25,000 (4)
6.	3,10,000	2,50,000*	Set on 60,000	Set on Nil+ (2) 1,25,00 (4) 60,000 (6)

7.	1,00,000	2,50,000* (inclusive of 1,25,000 from year–4 and 25,000 from year-6)	Nil	Set on 35,000 (6)
8.	Nil (due to loss)	1,04,167** (inclusive of 35,000 from year-6)	Set off 69,167	Set off 69,167 (8)
9.	10,000	1,04,167**	Set off 94,167	Set off 69,167 (8) 94,167 (9)
10.	2,15,000	1,04,167** (after setting of 69,167 from year-8 and 41,666 from year-9)	Nil	Set off 52,501 (9)

Notes-
* Maximum amount admissible
** Minimum amount admissible
+ The balance of ₹1,10,000 set on from year-2 lapses.

20

The Payment of Gratuity Act, 1972

An Act to provide for a scheme for the payment of gratuity to employees engaged in factories, mines, oilfields, plantations, ports, railway companies, shops or other establishments and for matters connected therewith or incidental thereto.

Desired Knowledge Competencies

- To discuss the concept of gratuity.
- To comprehend the scope and coverage of the Payment of Gratuity Act, 1972 and various definitions under the Act.
- To grasp the cases of forfeiture, nomination and penalties as per the Act.

INTRODUCTION

The dictionary meaning of gratuity is "something voluntarily given in return for a favour or service, recompense, and an acknowledgement". Going back in time we may see that payment of gratuity in India was earlier on the will of the employer; there would be a few employers who would give gratuity for the "good" and "meritorious" services rendered by employees for a prolonged period of time with such employers. It was thus largely a gratuitous payment made by an employer at his pleasure. However, as an outcome of a long series of discussions in Industrial Tribunals, gratuity came to be regarded as a legitimate claim of workmen, which, in certain cases, can give rise to industrial disputes.

Gratuity is thus a kind of retirement benefit; in common practice it is a lump sum payment made to an employee on attaining the age of superannuation or termination of service or on account of death or disability, provided the employee has rendered continuous service for a period of 5 years to the employer concerned. It is thus evident that the concept and practice of payment of gratuity has undergone an evolution from being a favour or gift to a matter of right for a worker. The concept of gratuity is, however, different from that of pension. A pension is a steady income given to a person, usually after retirement; it is a form of deferred compensation, usually to the advantage of both the employee and employer.

Spotlight

Gratuity is a lump sum payment, while pension is a steady income given to a person.

BACKDROP OF THE PAYMENT OF GRATUITY ACT, 1972

The earliest instance of payment of gratuity by legislation was through the Working Journalists (Conditions of Service and Miscellaneous Provisions) Act, 1955 which had provisions for gratuity payment to journalists. However, there was no such legislation for industrial workers. Before the Payment of Gratuity Act, 1972 was enacted gratuity was in practice in only 2 States, namely West Bengal and Kerala, through the West Bengal Employees' Payment of Compulsory Gratuity Act, 1971 and the Kerala Industrial Employees Payment of Gratuity Act, 1970 respectively, apart from the Working Journalists (Conditions of Service and Miscellaneous Provisions) Act, 1955. Eventually there was a perceived need for a central legislation on the subject and other States expressed their concern in this issue, so that gratuity could be paid to workmen across the nation in a uniform pattern. Accordingly, the Payment of Gratuity Act, 1972 came into force on 16th September 1972, largely based on the West Bengal legislation. The Act has undergone several amendments since its enactment; following is the list of such amendments:

> **Spotlight**
> The Payment of Gratuity Act, 1972 came into force on 16th September 1972.

1. The Payment of Gratuity (Amendment) Act, 1984
2. The Payment of Gratuity (Second Amendment) Act, 1984
3. The Payment of Gratuity (Amendment) Act, 1987
4. The Payment of Gratuity (Amendment) Act, 1994
5. The Payment of Gratuity (Amendment) Act, 1998
6. The Payment of Gratuity (Amendment) Act, 2009
7. The Payment of Gratuity (Amendment) Act, 2010

ABOUT THE ACT

Short Title, Extent, Application and Commencement (Section 1)

1. This Act may be called the Payment of Gratuity Act, 1972.
2. It extends to the whole of India:
   Provided that in so far as it relates to plantations or ports, it shall not extend to the State of Jammu and Kashmir.
3. It shall apply to-
   (a) every factory, mine, oilfield, plantation, port and railway company;
   (b) every shop or establishment within the meaning of any law for the time being in force in relation to shops and establishments in a State, in which 10 or more persons are employed, or were employed, on any day of the preceding 12 months;
   (c) such other establishments or class of establishments, in which 10 or more employees are employed, or were employed, on any day of the preceding 12 months, as the Central Government may, by notification, specify in this behalf.

3A. A shop or establishment to which this Act has once become applicable, shall continue to be governed by this Act, even though the number of persons employed therein at any time after it has become so applicable falls below 10.

4. It shall come into force on such date as the Central Government may, by notification, appoint.

The Act initially provided for payment of gratuity to employees drawing wages up to ₹1,000 per month. However such wage-ceiling has been abolished as per amendment in 1994.

Definitions (Section 2)

In this Act, unless the context otherwise requires,-

Appropriate Government [Section 2(a)] Appropriate Government means,-

(i) in relation to an establishment-
  (a) belonging to, or under the control of, the Central Government,
  (b) having branches in more than 1 State,
  (c) of a factory belonging to, or under the control of, the Central Government,
  (d) of a major port, mine, oilfield or railway company, the Central Government,

(ii) in any other case, the State Government;

Completed year of service [Section 2(b)] Completed year of service means continuous service for 1 year.

Continuous service [Section 2(c)] Continuous service means continuous service as defined in Section 2A;

Duncan Agro Industries Ltd. vs. Subbanna, B. [(1984) ILLJ 96 (AP)] discusses computation of service rendered anterior to the enforcement of the Act. In view of the provisions of Section 2(c), it was held that gratuity shall be payable to an employee who has rendered continuous service of not less than 5 years, irrespective of whether such period of service is prior to or after the commencement of the Act.

(Adapted from: www.indiankanoon.org/doc/241087/ accessed on 10/7/2014.)

Controlling authority [Section 2(d)] Controlling authority means an authority appointed by the appropriate Government under Section 3;

Employee [Section 2(e)] Employee means any person (other than an apprentice) employed on wages, in any establishment, factory, mine, oilfield, plantation, port, railway company or shop to do any skilled, semi-skilled, or unskilled, manual, supervisory, technical or clerical work, whether the terms of such employment are express or implied, and whether or not such person is employed in a managerial or administrative capacity, but does not include any such person who holds a post under the Central Government or a State Government and is governed by any other Act or by any rules providing for payment of gratuity.

As laid down in *General Manager, Yellamma Cotton, Woollen & Silk Mills vs. Regional Labour Commissioner (Central)* (2006 LLR 1029), a trainee is not an "employee" to be paid wages as an employee. In the absence of any statutory provision under the Act, a trainee cannot be held entitled to gratuity. As per *K. Velukutty Acharya vs. Harrisons Malayalam Ltd.* [1993 66 FLR 423 (Ker) (DB)], any workman engaged for work on temporary basis, according to the availability of work is not an "employee" within the meaning of Section 2(e). Any person subject to the Air Force Act, 1950, the Army Act, 1950 or the Navy Act, 1957 also does not come under the definition of employee under the Act.

A workman employed in managerial or administrative capacity was earlier not eligible for gratuity. However, subsequent to an amendment in 1984, such persons have been made eligible for gratuity. In *Anand Bazar Patrika (P) Ltd. vs. The Workmen* [(1969) (18) FLR 186 (SC)], it has been held that if the main work done by an employee is of a clerical nature, the mere fact that some supervisory duties are also performed incidentally or as a small fraction of the work done by him will not convert his employment from clerical to supervisory capacity.

CASE CORNER

In *Patel Hiralal Ramlal & Co. vs. Chandbibi Pirubhai and Others* [(1981) Lab IC 790 (Guj. HC)], the petitioner is engaged in manufacturing *beedis* and in selling *beedis* and loose tea, while the workmen were rolling out (or manufacturing) *beedis* for the petitioner. After leaving his service, they applied for payment of gratuity. The controlling authority under the Payment of Gratuity Act, 1972 (referred to now onwards as 'the Act'), ordered the payment of gratuity to these workmen in terms of the orders which he made. The petitioner appealed against such orders to the Appellate Authority. It was contended on behalf of the petitioner that the workmen were not "employees" within the meaning of the definition given in the Act; this contention was negated by the Appellate Authority. It appears these workmen worked in the premises of the petitioner for a few years, and that thereafter they started taking raw material home for rolling out *beedis* for the petitioner. The question which was raised is whether a workman who does not work at the business premises of his employer but works for him at his home, indeed for the benefit of his employer, can be said to be an employee "in any establishment" as per the Act. The Court held that there is no reason to make a distinction between a workman who rolls out *beedis* for the manufacturer at the premises of the manufacturer and the one who rolls out *beedis* for him at his own home. This is because both are engaged directly by the manufacturer, and both work for his benefit and satisfaction. It was thus observed that the residential premises of a workman where he rolls out *beedis* for the manufacturer is, for the purpose of the Act, an extension of the *beedi* manufacturer's establishment. The Court was thus of the opinion that these workmen were employees of the petitioner and are entitled to the payment of gratuity.

(Adapted from: www.indiankanoon.org/doc/704216/ accessed on 9/6/2014.)

The definition of employees has been widened to extend the benefit of gratuity to teachers as per the Payment of Gratuity (Amendment) Act, 2009 and the amendment is applicable retrospectively with effect from 3rd April 1997.

Employer [Section 2(f)] Employer means, in relation to any establishment, factory, mine, oilfield, plantation, port, railway company or shop:

(i) belonging to, or under the control of, the Central Government or a State Government, a person or authority appointed by the appropriate Government for the supervision and control of employees, or where no person or authority has been so appointed, the head of the Ministry or Department concerned,

(ii) belonging to, or under the control of, any local authority, the person appointed by such authority for the supervision and control of employees, or where no person has been so appointed, the chief executive officer of the local authority,

(iii) in any other case, such person, who, or the authority which has the ultimate control over the affairs of the establishment, factory, mine, oilfield, plantation, port, railway company or shop, and where the said affairs are entrusted to any other person, whether called a manager, managing director or by any other name such person;

Factory [Section 2(g)] Factory has the meaning assigned to it in clause (m) of Section 2 of the Factories Act, 1948;

Family [Section 2(h)] Family in relation to an employee, shall be deemed to consist of-

(i) in the case of a male employee, himself, his wife, his children, whether married or unmarried, his dependent parents and the dependent parents of his wife and the widow and children of his predeceased son, if any,

(ii) in the case of a female employee, herself, her husband, her children, whether married or unmarried, her dependent parents and the dependent parents of her husband and the widow and children of her predeceased son, if any;

Explanation Where the personal law of an employee permits the adoption by him of a child, any child lawfully adopted by him shall be deemed to be included in his family, and where a child of an employee has been adopted by another person and such adoption is, under the personal law of the person making such adoption, lawful, such child shall be deemed to be excluded from the family of the employee;

Major port [Section 2(i)] Major port has the meaning assigned to it in clause (8) of Section 3 of the Indian Ports Act, 1908;

Mine [Section 2(j)] Mine has the meaning assigned to it in clause (j) of sub-section (1) of Section 2 of the Mines Act, 1952;

Notification [Section 2(k)] Notification means a notification published in the Official Gazette;

Oilfield [Section 2(l)] Oilfield has the meaning assigned to it in clause (e) of Section 3 of the Oilfields (Regulation and Development) Act, 1948;

Plantation [Section 2(m)] Plantation has the meaning assigned to it in clause (f) of Section 2 of the Plantations Labour Act, 1951;

Port [Section 2(n)] Port has the meaning assigned to it in clause (4) of Section 3 of the Indian Ports Act, 1908;

Prescribed [Section 2(o)] Prescribed means prescribed by rules made under this Act;

Railway company [Section 2(p)] Railway company has the meaning assigned to it in clause (5) of Section 3 of the Indian Railways Act, 1890;

Retirement [Section 2(q)] Retirement means termination of the service of an employee, otherwise than on superannuation;

Spotlight

Section 2(q) defines retirement as termination of the service of an employee, otherwise than on superannuation.

Superannuation [Section 2(r)] Superannuation, in relation to an employee, means the attainment by the employee of such age as is fixed in the contract or conditions of service at the age on the attainment of which the employee shall vacate the employment;

Wages [Section 2(s)] Wages means all emoluments which are earned by an employee while on duty or on leave in accordance with the terms and conditions of his employments and which are paid or are payable to him in cash and includes dearness allowance but does not include any bonus, commission, house rent allowance, overtime wages and any other allowance.

Continuous service (Section 2A)

For the purposes of this Act,-

1. an employee shall be said to be in continuous service for a period if he has, for that period, been in uninterrupted service, including service which may be interrupted on account of sickness, accident, leave, absence from duty without leave (not being absence in respect of which an order treating the absence as break in service has been passed in accordance with the standing orders, rules or regulations governing the employees of the establishment), lay-off, strike or a lock-out or cessation of work not due to any fault of the employee, whether such uninterrupted or interrupted service was rendered before or after the commencement of this Act;
2. where an employee (not being an employee employed in a seasonal establishment) is not in continuous service within the meaning of clause (1), for any period of 1 year or 6 months, he shall be deemed to be in continuous service under the employer-
   (a) for the said period of 1 year, if the employee during the period of 12 calendar months preceding the date with reference to which calculation is to be made, has actually worked under the employer for not less than-
      (i) 190 days, in the case of any employee employed below the ground in a mine or in an establishment which works for less than 6 days in a week; and
      (ii) 240 days, in any other case;
   (b) for the said period of 6 months, if the employee during the period of 6 calendar months preceding the date with reference to which the calculation is to be made, has actually worked under the employer for not less than-
      (i) 95 days, in the case of an employee employed below the ground in a mine or in an establishment which works for less than 6 days in a week; and
      (ii) 120 days, in any other case.

   Explanation For the purposes of clause (2) the number of days on which an employee has actually worked under an employer shall include the days on which-
   (i) he has been laid-off under an agreement or as permitted by standing orders made under the Industrial Employment (Standing Orders) Act, 1946, or under the Industrial Disputes Act, 1947, or under any other law applicable to the establishment;
   (ii) he has been on leave with full wages, earned in the previous year;
   (iii) he has been absent due to temporary disablement caused by accident arising out of and in the course of his employment; and
   (iv) in the case of a female, she has been on maternity leave; so, however, that the total period of such maternity leave does not exceed 12 weeks.
3. where an employee, employed in a seasonal establishment, is not in continuous service within the meaning of clause (1), for any period of 1 year or 6 months, he shall be deemed to be in continuous service under the employer for such period if he has actually worked for not less than 75 per cent of the number of days on which the establishment was in operation during such period.

As per *Texmaco Ltd. vs. Shri Ram Dhan* [(1992) LLR 369 (Del)], an employee resigning from service is entitled to gratuity. Following *State of Punjab vs. Labour Court* [(1980) I SDR 953], a retrenched employee is entitled to gratuity. As laid down in *Mettur Spinning Mills vs. Deputy Commissioner of Labour* [(1983) II LU 188], non-acceptance of resignation is no hurdle in the way of an employee to claim his gratuity. It has been laid down in *Pattathurila K. Damodaran vs. M. Kassim Kanju* [(1993) ILLJ 1211 (Ker)] that by change of ownership, the relationship between employer and

CASE CORNER

In *Jeevanlal (1929) Ltd. and Others vs. Controlling Authority* [(1982) ILLJ 86 (Mad)], the employees concerned had reached the age of superannuation, which was 58 years well before the Payment of Gratuity Act, 1972 (or, the Act) came into force. They were, however, re-employed on a yearly basis, and eventually their employment came to an end on 31st December 1972 or 31st December 1973, as the case may be. Having regard to this factor, the employees claimed that they were entitled to payment of gratuity according to the terms of the Act. However the management contended that their employment had come to a termination on their reaching the age of superannuation long before the Act came into force; as such, they will be entitled to get gratuity only in accordance with the terms of the scheme or award which was in force earlier.

It was finally decided that an employee who is re-employed without any break in service will be eligible for gratuity, and he cannot be denied gratuity simply on the ground of change in employment.

(Adapted from: www.indiankanoon.org/doc/1399016/ accessed on 11/6/2014.)

employee subsists, and the new employer cannot escape from the liability of payment of gratuity to the employee. As per *Travancore Plywood Industries Pvt. Ltd. vs. Regional Joint Labour Commissioner* [(1996) II LLJ 85 (Ker)], refusal of employee to surrender land belonging to the employer is not a ground to withhold gratuity.

Controlling Authority (Section 3)

The Appropriate Government may, by notification, appoint any officer to be a controlling authority, who shall be responsible for the administration of this Act and different authorities may be appointed for different areas.

Payment of Gratuity (Section 4)

1. Gratuity shall be payable to an employee on the termination of his employment after he has rendered continuous service for not less than 5 years,-
   (a) on his superannuation, or
   (b) on his retirement or resignation, or
   (c) on his death or disablement due to accident or disease:

   Provided that the completion of continuous service of 5 years shall not be necessary where the termination of the employment of any employee is due to death or disablement:

   Provided further that in the case of death of the employee, gratuity payable to him shall be paid to his nominee or, if no nomination has been made, to his heirs, and where any such nominees or heirs is a minor, the share of such minor, shall be deposited with the controlling authority who shall invest the same for the benefit of such minor in such bank or other financial institution, as may be prescribed, until such minor attains majority.

   Explanation For the purposes of this section, disablement means such disablement as incapacitates an employee for the work which he was capable of performing before the accident or disease resulting in such disablement.

2. For every completed year of service or part thereof in excess of 6 months, the employer shall pay gratuity to an employee at the rate of 15 days' wages based on the rate of wages last drawn by the employee concerned:

   Provided that in the case of a piece-rated employee, daily wages shall be computed on the average of the total wages received by him for a period of 3 months immediately preceding the termination of his employment, and, for this purpose, the wages paid for any overtime work shall not be taken into account:

   Provided further that in the case of an employee who is employed in a seasonal establishment and who is not so employed throughout the year, the employer shall pay the gratuity at the rate of 7 days' wages for each season.

   Explanation In the case of a monthly rated employee, the 15 days' wages shall be calculated by dividing the monthly rate of wages last drawn by him by 26 and multiplying the quotient by 15.
3. The amount of gratuity payable to an employee shall not exceed ₹10 lakh.
4. For the purpose of computing the gratuity payable to an employee who is employed, after his disablement, on reduced wages, his wages for the period preceding his disablement shall be taken to be the wages received by him during that period, and his wages for the period subsequent to his disablement shall be taken to be the wages as so reduced.

Spotlight

The amount of gratuity payable to an employee is not to exceed ₹10 lakhs as per an amendment by the Government, with effect from 24th May 2010. The earlier ceiling was ₹3.5 lakhs.

5. Nothing in this section shall affect the right of an employee to receive better terms of gratuity under any award or agreement or contract with the employer.
6. Notwithstanding anything contained in sub-section (1),-
   (a) the gratuity of an employee, whose services have been terminated for any act, willful omission or negligence causing any damage or loss to, or destruction of, property belonging to the employer shall be forfeited to the extent of the damage or loss so caused;
   (b) the gratuity payable to an employee may be wholly or partially forfeited-
      (i) if the services of such employee have been terminated for his riotous or disorderly conduct or any other act of violence on his part, or
      (ii) if the services of such employee have been terminated for any act which constitutes an offence involving moral turpitude, provided that such offence is committed by him in the course of his employment.

Let us now have a quick formula on the amount of gratuity that would serve as a ready reckoner:

Gratuity payable (for all non-seasonal establishments) = 15 days wages × Number of completed years of service (not exceeding ₹10 lakhs)

Gratuity payable (for seasonal establishments) = 7 days wages × Number of seasons for which employed, (not exceeding ₹10 lakhs)

$$\text{In case of an employee drawing monthly wages, 15 days wages} = \frac{\text{Monthly wages last drawn}}{26} \times 15$$

In the case of *Narayan Rao Bhosekar vs. Municipal Corporation Mumbai* [(2002) 94 FLR 55], the Bombay High Court held that if there was dismissal from services on grounds of dishonesty and taking bribe, etc., it involved moral turpitude, and therefore forfeiture of gratuity under Section 4(6)(b) of the Act was correct and tenable.

Compulsory Insurance (Section 4A)

1. With effect from such date as may be notified by the appropriate Government in this behalf, every employer, other than an employer or an establishment belonging to, or under the control of, the Central Government or a State Government, shall, subject to the provisions of sub-section (2), obtain an insurance in the manner prescribed, for his liability for payment towards the gratuity under this Act, from the Life Insurance Corporation of India established under the Life Insurance Corporation of India Act, 1956 or any other prescribed insurer.

   Provided that different dates may be appointed for different establishments or class of establishments or for different areas.
2. The appropriate Government may, subject to such conditions as may be prescribed, exempt every employer who had already established an approved gratuity fund in respect of his employees and who desires to continue such arrangement, and every employer employing five hundred or more persons who establishes an approved gratuity fund in the manner prescribed from the provisions of sub-section (1).
3. For the purpose of effectively implementing the provisions of this section, every employer shall within such time as may be prescribed get his establishment registered with the controlling authority in the prescribed manner and no employer shall be registered under the provisions of this section unless he has taken an insurance referred to in sub-section (1) or has established an approved gratuity fund referred to in sub-section (2).
4. The appropriate Government may, by notification, make rules to give effect to the provisions of this section and such rules may provide for the composition of the Board of Trustees of the approved gratuity fund and for the recovery by the controlling authority of the amount of the gratuity payable to an employee from the Life Insurance Corporation of India or any other insurer with whom an insurance has been taken under sub-section (1), or as the case may be, the Board of Trustees of the approved gratuity fund.
5. Where an employer fails to make any payment by way of premium to the insurance referred to in sub-section (1) or by way of contribution to an approved gratuity fund referred to in sub-section (2), he shall be liable to pay the amount of gratuity due under this Act (including interest, if any, for delayed payments) forthwith to the controlling authority.
6. Whoever contravenes the provisions of sub-section (5) shall be punishable with fine which may extend to ₹10,000 and in the case of a continuing offence with a further fine which may extend to ₹1,000 for each day during which the offence continues.

Explanation In this section, "approved gratuity fund" shall have the same meaning as in clause (5) of Section 2 of the Income-tax Act, 1961.

Power to Exempt (Section 5)

1. The appropriate Government may, by notification, and subject to such conditions as may be specified in the notification, exempt any establishment, factory, mine, oilfield, plantation, port, railway company or shop to which this Act applies from the operation of the provisions of this Act if, in the opinion of the appropriate Government, the employees in such establishment factory, mine, oilfield, plantation, port, railway company or shop are in receipt of gratuity or pensionary benefits not less favourable than the benefits conferred under this Act.
2. The appropriate Government may, by notification and subject to such conditions as may be specified in the notification, exempt any employee or class of employees employed in any establish-

ment, factory, mine, oilfield, plantation, port, railway company or shop to which this Act applies from the operation of the provisions of this Act, if, in the opinion of the appropriate Government, such employee or class of employees are in receipt of gratuity or pensionary benefits not less favourable than the benefits conferred under this Act.

3. A notification issued under sub-section (1) or sub-section (2) may be issued retrospectively a date not earlier than the date of commencement of this Act, but no such notification shall be issued so as to prejudicially, affect the interests of any person.

Nomination (Section 6)

1. Each employee, who has completed 1 year of service, shall make, within such time, in such form and in such manner, as may be prescribed, nomination for the purpose of the second proviso to sub-section (1) of Section 4.
2. An employee may, in his nomination, distribute the amount of gratuity payable to him under this Act amongst more than 1 nominee.
3. If an employee has a family at the time of making a nomination, the nomination shall be made in favour of 1 or more members of his family, and any nomination made by such employee in favour of a person who is not a member of his family shall be void.
4. If at the time of making a nomination the employee has no family, the nomination may be made in favour of any person or person but if the employee subsequently acquires a family, such nomination shall forthwith become invalid and the employee shall make within such time as may be prescribed, a fresh nomination in favour of 1 or more members of his family.
5. A nomination may, subject to the provisions of sub-sections (3) and (4), be modified by an employee at any time, after giving to his employer a written notice in such form and in such manner as may be prescribed, of his intention to do so.
6. If a nominee predeceases the employee, the interest of the nominee shall revert to the employee who shall make a fresh nomination, in the prescribed form, in respect of such interest.
7. Every nomination, fresh nomination or alteration of nomination, as the case may be, shall be sent by the employee to his employer, who shall keep the same in his safe custody.

Spotlight
Gratuity is payable to an employee when his services are terminated during his lifetime; however, the said amount is paid to his successors on the unfortunate event of his death, for which the Act has provision for nomination.

Nomination shall be in Form F, and submitted in duplicate by personal service by the employee, after taking proper receipt, or by sending through registered post, acknowledgment due to the employer. Fresh nomination is made in Form G, in favour of 1 or more members of family and must be submitted within 90 days of acquiring family. Notice for modification of nomination must be submitted in duplicate in Form H to the employer.

Determination of the Amount of Gratuity (Section 7)

1. A person who is eligible for payment of gratuity under this Act or any person authorised, in writing to act on his behalf shall send a written application to the employer, within such time and in such form, as may be prescribed, for payment of such gratuity.
2. As soon as gratuity becomes payable, the employer shall, whether an application referred to in sub-section (1) has been made or not, determine the amount of gratuity and give notice in writing to the

Spotlight
An employee eligible for gratuity shall apply in Form J to the employer; a nominee of an employee needs to apply in Form J; a legal heir must apply in Form K.

person to whom the gratuity is payable and also to the controlling authority specifying the amount of gratuity so determined.

3. The employer shall arrange to pay the amount of gratuity within 30 days from the date it becomes payable to the person to whom the gratuity is payable.

Spotlight

The employer shall give notice in Form L to the person to whom gratuity is payable.

3A. If the amount of gratuity payable under sub-section (3) is not paid by the employer within the period specified in sub-section (3), the employer shall pay, from the date on which the gratuity becomes payable to the date on which it is paid, simple interest at such rate, not exceeding the rate notified by the Central Government from time to time for repayment of long-term deposits, as that Government may, by notification specify:

Provided that no such interest shall be payable if the delay in the payment is due to the fault of the employee and the employer has obtained permission in writing from the controlling authority for the delayed payment on this ground.

6. (a) If there is any dispute to the amount of gratuity payable to an employee under this Act or as to the admissibility of any claim of, or in relation to, an employee for payment of gratuity, or as to the person entitled to receive the gratuity, the employer shall deposit with the controlling authority such amount as he admits to be payable by him as gratuity.
   (b) Where there is a dispute with regard to any matter or matters specified in clause (a), the employer or employee or any other person raising the dispute may make an application to the controlling authority for deciding the dispute.
   (c) The controlling authority shall, after due inquiry and after giving the parties to the dispute a reasonable opportunity of being heard, determine the matter or matters in dispute and if, as a result of such inquiry any amount is found to be payable to the employee, the controlling authority shall direct the employer to pay such amount or, as the case may be, such amount as reduced by the amount already deposited by the employer.
   (d) The controlling authority shall pay the amount deposited, including the excess amount, if any, deposited by the employer, to the person entitled thereto.
   (e) As soon as may be after a deposit is made under clause (a), the controlling authority shall pay the amount of the deposit-
      (i) to the applicant where he is the employee; or
      (ii) where the applicant is not the employee, to the nominee or, as the case may be, the guardian of such nominee or heir of the employee if the controlling authority is satisfied that there is no dispute as to the right of the applicant to receive the amount of gratuity.

5. For the purpose of conducting an inquiry under sub-section (4), the controlling authority shall have the same powers as are vested in a court, while trying a suit, under the Code of Civil Procedure, 1908, in respect of the following matters, namely:-
   (a) enforcing the attendance of any person or examining him on oath;
   (b) requiring the discovery and production of documents;
   (c) receiving evidence on affidavits;
   (d) issuing commissions for the examination of witnesses.

6. Any inquiry under this section shall be a judicial proceeding within the meaning of sections 193 and 228, and for the purpose of Section 196 of the Indian Penal Code.

7. Any person aggrieved by an order under sub-section (4) may, within 60 days from the date of the receipt of the order, prefer an appeal to the appropriate Government or such other authority as may be specified by the appropriate Government in this behalf:

Provided that the appropriate Government or the appellate authority, as the case may be, may, if it is satisfied that the appellant was prevented by sufficient cause from preferring the appeal within the said period of 60 days, extend the said period by a further period of 60 days:

Provided further that no appeal by an employer shall be admitted unless at the time of preferring the appeal, the appellant either produces a certificate of the controlling authority to the effect that the appellant has deposited with him an amount equal to the amount of gratuity required to be deposited under sub-section (4), or deposits with the appellate authority such amount.

8. The appropriate Government or the appellate authority, as the case may be, may, after giving the parties to the appeal a reasonable opportunity of being heard, confirm, modify, or reverse the decision of the controlling authority.

Inspectors (Section 7A)

1. The appropriate Government may, by notification, appoint as many Inspectors, as it deems fit, for the purposes of this Act.
2. The appropriate Government may, by general or special order, define the area to which the authority of an Inspector so appointed shall extend and where 2 or more Inspectors are appointed for the same area, also provide, by such order, for the distribution or allocation of work to be performed by them under this Act.
3. Every Inspector shall be deemed to be a public servant within the meaning of Section 21 of the Indian Penal Code.

Powers of Inspectors (Section 7B)

1. Subject to any rules made by the appropriate Government in this behalf, an Inspector may, for the purpose of ascertaining whether any of the provisions of this Act or the conditions, if any, of any exemption granted thereunder, have been complied with, exercise all or any of the following powers, namely:-
   (a) require an employer to furnish such information as he may consider necessary;
   (b) enter and inspect, at all reasonable hours, with such assistants (if any), being persons in the service of the Government or local or any public authority, as he thinks fit, any premises of or place in any factory, mine, oilfield, plantation, port, railway company, shop or other establishment to which this Act, applies, for the purpose of examining any register, record or notice or other document required to be kept or exhibited under this Act or the rules made thereunder, or otherwise kept or exhibited in relation to the employment of any person or the payment of gratuity to the employees, and require the production thereof for inspection;
   (c) examine with respect to any matter relevant to any of the purposes aforesaid, the employer or any person whom he finds in such premises or place and who, he has reasonable cause to believe, is an employee employed therein;
   (d) make copies of, or take extracts from, any register, record, notice or other document, as he may consider relevant, and where he has reason to believe that any offence under this Act has been committed by an employer search and seize with such assistance as he may think fit, such register, record, notice or other document as he may consider relevant in respect of that offence;
   (e) exercise such other powers as may be prescribed.

2. Any person required to produce any register, record, notice or other document or to give any information by an Inspector under sub-section (1) shall be deemed to be legally bound to do so within the meaning of sections 175 and 176 of the Indian Penal Code.
3. The provisions of the Code of Criminal Procedure, 1973, shall so far as may be, apply to any search or seizure under this section as they apply to any search or seizure made under the authority of a warrant issued under Section 94 of the Code.

Recovery of Gratuity (Section 8)

If the amount of gratuity payable under this Act is not paid by the employer, within the prescribed time, to the person entitled thereto, the controlling authority shall, on an application made to it in this behalf by the aggrieved person, issue a certificate for that amount to the Collector who shall recover the same, together with compound interest thereon at such rate as the Central Government may, by notification, specify, from the date of expiry of the prescribed time as arrears of land revenue and pay the same to the person entitled thereto:

Provided that the controlling authority shall, before issuing a certificate under this section, give the employer a reasonable opportunity of showing cause against the issue of such certificate:

Provided further that the amount of interest payable under this section shall, in no case exceed the amount of gratuity payable under this Act.

An aggrieved person make an application made to the controlling authority in duplicate in Form T. The Collector shall recover the same, together with compound interest thereon at the rate of 9 per cent (with effect from 1st October 1987) from the date of expiry of the prescribed time and pay the same to the person entitled to it.

Mode of Payment of Gratuity

The amount of gratuity payable under the Act is to be paid in cash, or if so desired by the payee, in the form of demand draft or bank cheque to the employee or nominee, or legal heir, as the case may be. If the amount of gratuity is less than ₹1,000, then such payment may be made by postal money order, if the employee or nominee or legal heir so desires. The commission on the postal money order may be deducted from the amount of gratuity payable.

> **Spotlight**
> The amount of gratuity is to be paid in cash, or in the form of demand draft or bank cheque.

The employer must also intimate the controlling authority of that area about the details of such payment. If the nominee or legal heir is a minor, the controlling authority shall invest the amount of gratuity deposited with him for the benefit of such minor in a term deposit with the State Bank of India, or any of its subsidiaries, or any nationalised bank.

Penalties (Section 9)

1. Whoever, for the purpose of avoiding any payment to be made by himself under this Act or of enabling any other person to avoid such payment, knowingly makes or causes to be made any false statement or false representation shall be punishable with imprisonment for a term which may extend to 6 months or with fine which may extend to ₹10,000 or with both.
2. An employer who contravenes, or make default in complying with, any of the provisions of this Act or any rule or order made thereunder shall be punishable with imprisonment for a term which

shall not be less than 3 months but which may extend to 1 year, or with fine which shall not be less than ₹10,000 but which may extend to ₹20,000, or with both:

Provided that where the offence relates to non-payment of any gratuity payable under this Act, the employer shall be punishable with imprisonment for a term which shall not be less than 6 months but which may extend to 2 years unless the court trying the offence, for reasons to be recorded by it in writing, is of opinion that a lesser term of imprisonment or the imposition of a fine would meet the ends of justice.

Exemption of Employer from Liability in Certain Cases (Section 10)

Where an employer is charged with an offence punishable under this Act, he shall be entitled, upon complaint duly made by him and on giving to the complainant not less than 3 clear days' notice in writing of his intention to do so, to have any other person whom he charges as the actual offender brought before the court at the time appointed for hearing the charge; and if, after the commission of the offence has been proved, the employer proves to the satisfaction of the court-

(a) that he has used due diligence to enforce the execution of this Act, and

(b) that the said other person committed the offence in question without his knowledge, consent or connivance, that other person shall be convicted of the offence and shall be liable to the like punishment as if he were the employer and the employer shall be discharged from any liability under this Act in respect of such offence:

Provided that in seeking to prove as aforesaid, the employer may be examined on oath and his evidence and that of any witness whom he calls in his support shall be subject to cross-examination on behalf of the person he charges as the actual offender and by the prosecutor:

Provided further that, if the person charged as the actual offender by the employer cannot be brought before the court at the time appointed for hearing the charge, the court shall adjourn the hearing from time to time for a period not exceeding 3 months and if by the end of the said period the person charged as the actual offender cannot still be brought before the court, the court shall proceed to hear the charge against the employer and shall, if the offence be proved, convict the employer.

Cognizance of Offences (Section 11)

1. No court shall take cognizance of any offence punishable under this Act save on a complaint made by or under the authority of the appropriate Government:

   Provided that where the amount of gratuity has not been paid, or recovered, within 6 months from the expiry of the prescribed time, the appropriate Government shall authorise the controlling authority to make a complaint against the employer, where-upon the controlling authority shall within 15 days from the date of such authorisation, make such complaint to a magistrate having jurisdiction to try the offence.
2. No court inferior to that of a Metropolitan Magistrate or a Judicial Magistrate of the first class shall try any offence punishable under this Act.

Protection of Action Taken in Good Faith (Section 12)

No suit or other legal proceeding shall lie against the controlling authority or any other person in respect of anything which is in good faith done or intended to be done under this Act or any rule or order made thereunder.

Protection of Gratuity (Section 13)

No gratuity payable under this Act and no gratuity payable to an employee employed in any establishment, factory, mine, oilfield, plantation, port, railway company or shop exempted under Section 5 shall be liable to attachment in execution of any decree or order of any civil, revenue or criminal court.

Act to Override other Enactments, etc. (Section 14)

The provisions of this Act or any rule made thereunder shall have effect notwithstanding anything inconsistent therewith contained in any enactment other than this Act or in any instrument or contract having effect by virtue of any enactment other than this Act.

Power to Make Rules (Section 15)

1. The appropriate Government may, by notification, make rules for the purpose of carrying out the provisions of this Act.
2. Every rule made by the Central Government under this Act shall be laid, as soon as may be after it is made, before each House of Parliament while it is in session, for a total period of 30 days which may be comprised in 1 session or in 2 or more successive sessions, and if, before the expiry of the session immediately following the session or the successive sessions aforesaid, both Houses agree in making any modification in the rule or both Houses agree that the rule should not be made, the rule shall, thereafter, have effect only in such modified form or be of no effect, as the case may be; so, however, that any such modification or annulment shall be without prejudice to the validity of anything previously done under that rule.

TAX EXEMPTION OF GRATUITY RECEIVED

As per Section 10(10) of the Income-tax Act, employees have been divided into 3 categories in context of tax exemption of gratuity received:

i. **Employees of Central or State Government and local bodies:** Gratuity received by such employees is fully exempted without any limit.

ii. **Employees covered under the Payment of Gratuity Act, 1972:** Amount as per the Payment of Gratuity Act, 1972 is fully exempted.

iii. **Other employees:** For other employees, the earlier limit was 3.5 lakhs as per the Income-tax Act. Many Public Sector Undertakings (PSUs) not covered under the Central or State Government have started paying gratuity as per the Sixth Pay Commission, up to a maximum of 10 lakhs. In case of such employees, the amount in excess of 3.5 lakhs is taxable.

The Government has enhanced the exemption limit for PSU employees retired after 24th May 2010. The increased limit is also available for claiming income tax exemption for employees of private sector establishments, who receive gratuity as per Payment of Gratuity Act, 1972.

(Adapted from: www.sriramconsultancyservices.com accessed on 10/6/2014.)

ADMINISTRATION OF THE ACT

The Central Industrial Relations Machinery (CIRM) of the Ministry of Labour & Employment is responsible for enforcing this Act. The Central Government has appointed the Chief Labour

Commissioner (Central), Regional Labour Commissioner (Central) and Assistant Labour Commissioner (Central) as the Controlling or Appellate Authorities under the Act for their respective areas.

Any claim or complaint under the Act shall be filed before the Assistant Labour Commissioner of the concerned area. The Deputy Labour Commissioner of such area is the Appellate Authority.

Summary

- The Payment of Gratuity Act, 1972 is an enactment towards social security that applies to every factory, mine, oilfield, plantation, port, railway company, and shop or other establishment in which 10 or more persons are employed.
- The benefits of the Act are available not only to employees regardless of their wages, but also to people working in managerial or administrative capacity.
- Section 2(A) of the Act defines the term "continuous service" to mean uninterrupted service that includes service which is interrupted, among others, by leave or cessation of work, not due to any fault of the employee concerned. Completed year of service means continuous service for 1 year.
- Gratuity is payable to an employee covered under the Act on termination of his employment after having rendered continuous service for not less than 5 years at the time of superannuation; or on his retirement or resignation; or on his death or disablement due to accident or disease.
- For every completed year of service or part thereof, in excess of 6 months, the employer has to pay gratuity to an employee at the rate of 15 days' wages, based on the rate of wages he has last drawn; for an employee in a seasonal establishment gratuity is paid at the rate of 7 days' wages for each season.
- As per Section 4(6)(a), the amount of gratuity payable to an employee whose services have been terminated for any act, willful omission or negligence, causing any damage or loss to, or destruction of, property belonging to the employer shall be forfeited to the extent of the damage or loss so caused.
- Under normal circumstances gratuity is payable to an employee when his services are terminated during his lifetime; however, the said amount is paid to his successors on the unfortunate event of his death, for which the Act has a provision for nomination.
- An employer must arrange to pay the amount of gratuity within 30 days from the date it becomes due.

Key Concepts

Gratuity	Superannuation	Retirement
Controlling authority	Continuous service	Compulsory insurance
Forfeiture	Nomination	Recovery

BIBLIOGRAPHY

Misra, S. N. and Misra, S. K. *An Introduction to Labour and Industrial Laws,* Allahabad: Central Law Publications, 1995.

The Payment of Gratuity Act, 1972, New Delhi: Universal Law Publishing Co. Pvt. Ltd.

www.indiankanoon.org

www.sriramconsultancyservices.com/files/Gratuity%20exemption%20Limit%20enhanced%2010%20Lakh%20Income%20tax%20wef%2024.pdf accessed on 10/6/2014.

Review Questions

Objective Type Questions

I. State True or False

(i) Any person employed in managerial or administrative capacity is not eligible for gratuity.

(ii) If the amount of gratuity is less than ₹5,000, then such payment may be made by postal money order.

(iii) The notice to modify a nomination must be submitted in duplicate in Form G to the employer.

(iv) Wages paid to a worker for any overtime work are not taken into account in computation of gratuity.

(v) Completed year of service means continuous service for 1 year.

Answers: (i) False, (ii) False, (iii) False, (iv) True, (v) True

II. Fill in the Blanks

(i) If an employer fails to pay the amount of gratuity, the same can be recovered as arrears of land _______.

(ii) An employer shall be punishable for non-payment of gratuity with imprisonment for a minimum term of _______ months.

(iii) Retirement implies termination of the service of an employee, otherwise than on _______.

(iv) Nomination for gratuity is made in Form _______.

(v) _______ is a steady income given to a person, usually after his retirement.

Answers: (i) revenue, (ii) 6, (iii) superannuation, (iv) F, (v) Pension

Discussion Questions

1. What, in your opinion, prompted the transformation of gratuity into a legitimate claim of a worker from a gratuitous act of an employer?
2. Distinguish between retirement and superannuation. Discuss their relevance in the qualifying conditions of the Payment of Gratuity Act, 1972.
3. Explain the types of workers who are not considered as employees under the Payment of Gratuity Act, 1972.
4. What are the various forms that are used in Payment of Gratuity Act, 1972? Discuss the context of each.
5. What is completed year of service? Relate it to continuous service as regards qualifying condition for payment of gratuity.
6. What are the powers conferred upon inspectors by the Payment of Gratuity Act, 1972?
7. How would you account for an employee who has worked for more than 6 months in a year, beyond 5 years of continuous service while calculating gratuity?
8. Under which conditions is an employer exempted from the liability of payment of gratuity?
9. Discuss the formulae for calculating gratuity for different categories of employees.
10. Explain in brief:
    (a) Computation of wage for an employee who has been re-employed after disablement
    (b) Forfeiture of gratuity under different circumstances
    (c) Family, as per the Payment of Gratuity Act, 1972
    (d) Nomination, as per Payment of Gratuity Act, 1972

CASE STUDY

CASE STUDY-I

The respondent in this case was a workman in the service of the appellant, Bharath Gold Mines. Disciplinary proceedings were instituted against him on the charge that he had committed theft of gold worth ₹15,561.00 in the course of his employment with the appellant. In the inquiry he was found guilty of the charge. The Disciplinary Authority accepted the findings and imposed the penalty of dismissal from service against the respondent w.e.f. 18th August 1981, forfeiting all rights and privileges accrued to him, including gratuity, from the 26 years of service which he had put in before the date of termination of his service. The order of dismissal has not been challenged by the respondent in any proceeding and consequently it has become final.

(Adapted from: Bharath Gold Mines Ltd. vs. Regional Labour Commissioner [(1994) III LLJ 54 Kant] www.indiankanoon.org/doc/732409 accessed on 10/7/2014.)

Review Questions

1. On what ground do you think gratuity of this workman has been forfeited?
2. Given the circumstance that no show cause notice was issued to the respondent, would forfeiting of the gratuity amount be wrong?
3. On what basis can the workman appeal for payment of the gratuity amount?

CASE STUDY-II

While calculating gratuity, the petitioner-employee claimed that an equivalent money for free supply of food should form a part and be added to the cash salary paid to him to form total wages for computing the amount of gratuity payable to him. The respondent-company argued that the definition of wages in the Payment of Gratuity Act, 1972 refers only to the amount paid in cash and shall not include the food allowance or amount equivalent to the food or tiffin given along with wages as conditions of employment. The petitioner's claim was rejected on the plea that merely an amenity could not form a part of and be added to the cash salary paid to him to form his total wages for computing the amount of gratuity payable to him.

(Adapted from: N. Sivadasan vs. Appellate Authority under Payment of Gratuity Act, Madras & Others [(1992) IILLJ 794 Mad.] www.indiankanoon.org/doc/449861 accessed on 12/7/2014)

Review Questions

1. Do you think the employee in this case is correct in claiming for free supply of food by the employer in computation of gratuity?
2. Following Section 2(s) of the Act, wages does not include any bonus, commission, house rent allowance, overtime wages and any other allowance. Do you think value of food provided to the employee should be a part of wage?
3. Can you link this with any of the other labour legislations you have come across?

21

The Payment of Wages Act, 1936

An Act to regulate the payment of wages to certain classes of employed persons.

Desired Knowledge Competencies

- To gauge the importance of payment of wages and the evolution of the legislation on payment of wages in India.
- To discuss the scope and coverage of the Payment of Wages Act, 1936 and of the various definitions given under the Act.
- To comprehend issues like fixation of wage-periods, time of payment of wages and authorised deductions from wages.

CONCEPT OF WAGE AND PAYMENT OF WAGES

Wages refer to the total pay package an employee receives from his/her employer on a periodic basis in return of the physical labour supplied to the firm. A robust and fair wage structure is instrumental for attracting and retaining employees. The following factors must be taken into consideration by any organisation while determining wage rates: its own bargaining capacity and that of its employees; its financial capacity to pay higher wages; the on-going wage rate for similar type of work in the market (i.e., level of competition) as well as the prevailing condition of the economy; requirement of specialised skills and training in a job; nature and type of work done by the workers (e.g., hazardous jobs demanding higher wage rates); and productivity of workers (e.g., workers who are more efficient and experienced should get higher wages).

(Adapted from: www.business.gov.in accessed on 4/6/2014.)

Given the above considerations, there can be 3 important methods of wage payment, namely:

- **Time-rate system:** This is one of the simplest and oldest methods of wage payment. As is suggestive from the name itself, remuneration following this system is based upon the amount of time

Spotlight

Three important methods of wage payment are:

- Time-rate system
- Piece-rate system
- Incentive wage plan

spent on work. Wages are calculated on hourly, daily, weekly, monthly or yearly basis, and wage rate increases with an increase in hours of work done.

- **Piece-rate system:** This method takes into consideration the efficiency of workers and wages are based on the amount of work done. Wage rate is prescribed per piece and rises or falls with increase or decrease in the output of the worker.

Spotlight

Incentive wage plan is the co-ordinated from of time-rate and piece-rate systems

- **Incentive wage plan:** This wage plan is actually the co-ordinated form of time-rate and piece-rate systems for wage payment. Under this method, workers get additional wages on the basis of their efficiency, in addition to the minimum guaranteed wages. Incentive wage rate rises or falls with increase or decrease in the quantity of production.

We have already discussed in Chapter 18 about the Committee on Fair Wages as a major landmark in the history of formulation of wage policy in India. The recommendations of the Committee have been instrumental in formulation of the concepts of living wage, minimum wage and fair wage, besides laying down the guidelines for wage fixation. In this chapter we would be focusing on the Payment of Wages Act, 1936 as the key legislation enacted to regulate payment of wages to workers employed in industries and to ensure speedy and effective remedies against illegal deductions and/or unjustified delays in such payments.

BACKDROP OF THE PAYMENT OF WAGES ACT, 1936

It may be little known to large number of people in modern times that the concept of fair wages paid at regular intervals with commonly known and acceptable deductions was unthinkable at the beginning of the 20th century. Industrialisation in India had created enormous employment opportunities but industrialists used it as a tool for undue exploitation of workers by not paying their due in return of work done; hence the issue of payment of wages brought forth new challenges to authorities. As a general practice wages were not paid at regular intervals, and delay in payment was routine. Further, wages paid were not uniform across industries. Deductions were made from wages at the discretion of employers without any justification; various kinds of fines were also imposed on workers. In fact, employers had the sole authority to decide and execute the mode and manner of all such payments. Workers were thus subjected to severe exploitation. An urgent need for legislation to protect the rights of workers in matters of wages and compensation was hence perceived.

The anomalies in payment of wages were first addressed in 1925 by way of a private member's bill called the "Weekly Payment Bill", which suggested the need for legislation for payment of wages. The Bill was however withdrawn on assurance by the government that remedial measures would be initiated towards regularisation of payment of wages. In fact, in the year 1926, the government wrote to local governments to ascertain the delays in the payment of wages to the persons employed in industry and the practice of imposing fines on them. Investigations revealed the existence of abuses in both directions and the findings were placed before the Royal Commission on Labour which was appointed in 1929. The report of the Commission recommended the necessity of legislation to address all these problems related to payment of wages. Following such recommendations, the government re-examined the matter and in February 1933 the Payment of Wages Bill was introduced in the Legislative Assembly, though it lapsed eventually. This was followed by the Payment of Wages Bill, 1935, based upon the same principles as the Bill of 1933 but thoroughly revised, and was introduced in the Legislative Assembly on 15th February 1935. Having been passed by the Legislative

Assembly, the Payment of Wages Bill, 1935 received its assent on 23rd April 1936, and it came on the Statute Book as The Payment of Wages Act, 1936.

The Payment of Wages Act, 1936 was introduced for the broad purpose of safeguarding wages of workers under certain conditions laid down in the Act. The specific objectives of the Act are:

- regulation of payment of wages and imposition of fines and deductions from wages, and
- elimination of all malpractices by laying down wage-periods and time and mode of payment of wages.

Spotlight

The Payment of Wages Act, 1936 was introduced for the broad purpose of safeguarding wages of workers under certain conditions laid down in the Act.

The Act therefore ensures payment of wages in a particular form at regular intervals, without unauthorised deductions. It has been amended several times according to the needs of the situation. Following is the list of amending acts, ordinances and adaptation orders:

1. The Government of India (Adaptation of Indian Laws) Order, 1937
2. The Repealing and Amending Act, 1937
3. The Payment of Wages (Amendment) Act, 1937
4. The Payment of Wages (Amendment) Ordinance, 1940
5. The Indian Independence (Adaptation of Central Acts and Ordinances) Order, 1948
6. The Adaptation of Laws Order, 1950
7. The Part B States (Laws) Act, 1951
8. The Payment of Wages (Amendment) Act, 1957
9. The Payment of Wages (Amendment) Act, 1964
10. The Central Labour Laws (Extension to Jammu and Kashmir) Act, 1970
11. The Repealing and Amending Act, 1974
12. The Payment of Wages (Amendment) Act, 1976
13. The Payment of Wages (Amendment) Act, 1977
14. The Payment of Wages (Amendment) Act, 1982
15. The Payment of Wages (Amendment) Act, 2005

ABOUT THE ACT

Short Title, Extent, Commencement and Application (Section 1)

1. This Act may be called the Payment of Wages Act, 1936.
2. It extends to the whole of India.
3. It shall come into force on such date as the Central Government may, by notification in the Official Gazette, appoint.
4. It applies in the first instance to the payment of wages to persons employed in any factory, to persons employed (otherwise than in a factory) upon any railway by a railway administration or, either directly or through a sub-contractor, by a person fulfilling a contract with a railway administration, and to persons employed in an industrial or other establishment specified in sub-clauses (a) to (g) of clause (ii) of Section 2.
5. The appropriate Government may, after giving 3 months' notice of its intention of so doing, by notification in the Official Gazette, extend the provisions of this Act or any of them to the payment of wages to any class of persons employed in any establishment or class of establishments specified by the appropriate Government under sub-clause (h) of clause (ii) of Section 2.

Provided that in relation to any such establishment owned by the Central Government, no such notification shall be issued except with the concurrence of that Government.

6. This Act applies to wages payable to an employed person in respect of a wage-period, if such wages for that wage-period do not exceed ₹6,500 per month or such other higher sum which, on the basis of the figures of Consumer Expenditure Survey published by the National Sample Survey Office, the Central Government may, after every 5 years, by notification in the Official Gazette, specify.

Definitions (Section 2)

In this Act, unless there is anything repugnant in the subject or context,

Appropriate Government [Section 2(i)] Appropriate Government means, in relation to railways, air transport services, mines and oilfields, the Central Government and, in relation to all other cases, the State Government;

Employed person [Section 2(ia)] Employed person includes the legal representative of a deceased employed person;

Employer [Section 2(ib)] Employer includes the legal representative of a deceased employer;

Factory [Section 2(ic)] Factory means a factory as defined in clause (m) of Section 2 of the Factories Act, 1948, and includes any place to which the provisions of that Act have been applied under sub-section (1) of Section 85 thereof;

Industrial or other establishment [Section 2(ii)] Industrial or other establishment means any:

(a) tramway service, or motor transport service engaged in carrying passengers or goods or both by road for hire or reward;

(aa) air transport service other than such service belonging to, or exclusively employed in the military, naval or air forces of the Union or the Civil Aviation Department of the Government of India;

(b) dock, wharf or jetty;

(c) inland vessel, mechanically propelled;

(d) mine, quarry or oilfield;

(e) plantation;

(f) workshop or other establishment in which articles are produced, adapted or manufactured, with a view to their use, transport or sale;

(g) establishment in which any work relating to the construction, development or maintenance of buildings, roads, bridges or canals, or relating to operations connected with navigation, irrigation or the supply of water, or relating to the generation, transmission and distribution of electricity or any other form of power is being carried on;

(h) any other establishment or class of establishments which the appropriate Government may, having regard to the nature thereof, the need for protection of persons employed therein and other relevant circumstances, specify, by notification in the Official Gazette.

CASE CORNER

In *K.L. Garg vs. New India Assurance Co. Ltd. and Others* [(1991) (62) FLR 869] the petitioner had submitted that the respondent, New India Assurance Co. Ltd. was an "industry", with reference to the definition of "industrial or other establishment" in the Payment of Wages Act, 1936 (referred to as the Act now onwards); therefore, it was submitted further that the provisions of the Act were applicable to the petitioner. On the other hand, the respondent pleaded that the definition of "industrial or other establishment" in the Act does not include insurance companies and, therefore, the Act, as such, was not applicable to them. It was further submitted that in the said definition in clause (h), it has been provided that an industrial or other establishment shall mean any other establishment or class of establishments which the Central Government or the State Government may specify by notification in the Official Gazette. However, no such notification has been issued by either the Central Government or the State Government in this behalf. Hence the learned authority had wrongly relied on the said notification to come to the conclusion that the insurance business was an industry under the Act.

(Adapted from: www.indiankanoon.org/doc/1069135/ accessed on 14/6/2014.)

Mine [Section 2(iia)] Mine has the meaning assigned to it in clause (j) of sub-section (1) of Section 2 of the Mines Act, 1952.

Plantation [Section 2(iii)] Plantation has the meaning assigned to it in clause (f) of Section 2 of the Plantations Labour Act, 1951;

Prescribed [Section 2(iv)] Prescribed means prescribed by rules made under this Act;

Railway administration [Section 2(v)] Railway administration has the meaning assigned to it in clause (32) of Section 2 of the Railways Act, 1989.

Wages [Section 2(vi)] Wages means all remuneration (whether by way of salary, allowances or otherwise) expressed in terms of money or capable of being so expressed which would, if the terms of employment, express or implied, were fulfilled, be payable to a person employed in respect of his employment or of work done in such employment, and includes–

(a) any remuneration payable under any award or settlement between the parties or order of a Court;
(b) any remuneration to which the person employed is entitled in respect of overtime work or holidays or any leave period;
(c) any additional remuneration payable under the terms of employment (whether called a bonus or by any other name);
(d) any sum which by reason of the termination of employment of the person employed is payable under any law, contract or instrument which provides for the payment of such sum, whether with or without deductions, but does not provide for the time within which the payment is to be made;
(e) any sum to which the person employed is entitled under any scheme framed under any law for the time being in force;

Spotlight

As per Section 2(vi), wages means all remuneration (whether by way of salary, allowances or otherwise) expressed in terms of money or capable of being so expressed which would be payable to a person employed in respect of his employment or of work done in such employment.

but does not include–

1. any bonus (whether under a scheme of profit sharing or otherwise) which does not form part of the remuneration payable under the terms of employment or which is not payable under any award or settlement between the parties or order of a Court;
2. the value of any house-accommodation, or of the supply of light, water, medical attendance or other amenity or of any service excluded from the computation of wages by a general or special order of the appropriate Government;
3. any contribution paid by the employer to any pension or provident fund, and the interest which may have accrued thereon;
4. any travelling allowance or the value of any travelling concession;
5. any sum paid to the employed person to defray special expenses entailed on him by the nature of his employment; or
6. any gratuity payable on the termination of employment in cases other than those specified in sub-clause (d).

In *Md. Qasim Larry, Factory Manager, Sasamusa Sugar Works vs. Muhammad Samsuddin and Another* [(1964) AIR 1699], it was pointed out that the amendment in the payment of Wages Act, 1936 in 1958 expressly provides by Section 2(vi)(a) that any remuneration payable under any award or settlement between the parties or order of a Court, would be included in the main definition of wages under Section 2(vi). When an award is made and it prescribes a new wage structure, in law the old contractual wage structure becomes inoperative and is replaced by the one prescribed by the award. In other words, the latter wage structure must be deemed to be a contract between the parties, because that, in substance, is the effect of industrial adjudication. When industrial disputes are decided by industrial adjudication and awards are made, such awards replace contractual terms in respect of matters covered by them and are substituted for them.

(Adapted from: www.indiankanoon.org/doc/435033/ accessed on 10/6/2014.)

In *Balaram Abaji Patil vs. M.C. Ragojiwalla* [(1960) IILLJ 491 Bom], it was held by the Court that all remuneration would be "wages" if such remuneration satisfies two conditions; first: it should be payable to "a person employed in respect of his employment or of work done in such employment", and second: it should be payable "if the terms of the contract of employment, express or implied, were fulfilled". The definition of "wages" given in Section 2(h) of the Minimum Wages Act, 1948 is identical with that in Section 2(vi) of the Payment of Wages Act, 1936. Under the Minimum Wages Act, 1948, minimum wages are undoubtedly "wages" and in view of the identity of the definition of the term "wages" in both the Acts, it must follow that minimum wages are also wages under the Payment of Wages Act, 1936.

(Adapted from: www.indiankanoon.org/doc/1736060/ accessed on 12/6/2014.)

Responsibility for Payment of Wages (Section 3)

1. Every employer shall be responsible for the payment of all wages required to be paid under this Act to persons employed by him and in case of persons employed,–
   (a) in factories, if a person has been named as the manager of the factory under clause (f) of sub-section (1) of Section 7 of the Factories Act, 1948;

(b) in industrial or other establishments, if there is a person responsible to the employer for the supervision and control of the industrial or other establishment;

(c) upon railways (otherwise than in factories), if the employer is the railway administration and the railway administration has nominated a person in this behalf for the local area concerned;

(d) in the case of a contractor, a person designated by such contractor who is directly under his charge; and

(e) in any other case, a person designated by the employer as a person responsible for complying with the provisions of the Act;

the person so named, the person so responsible to the employer, or the person so nominated, or the person so designated, as the case may be, shall be responsible for such payment.

2. Notwithstanding anything contained in sub-section (1), it shall be the responsibility of the employer to make payment of all wages required to be made under this Act in case the contractor or the person designated by the employer fails to make such payment.

CASE CORNER

In *Cominco Binani Zinc Ltd. vs. Pappachan* [(1989) ILLJ 452 Ker], the petitioner-company is having more than 250 workers on its rolls, and as per Section 46 of the Factories Act, 1948, the company had to provide and maintain a canteen for its employees. The right to conduct the canteen was being given on contract to others from time to time, and at no point of time had the company run the canteen by itself. The contractors who took up the responsibility of running the canteen were engaging their own workmen, who were paid by the contractors.

As per the Industrial Tribunal, the mere fact that the petitioner had the responsibility to provide and maintain a canteen under Section 46 of the Factories Act, 1948 cannot make it the ultimate employer of the workers engaged in the canteen for all purposes. When the management has entrusted the responsibility of running the canteen with a contractor, then the workmen employed and paid by such contractor cannot be treated as workmen of the management. There is no employer-employee relationship between the management and such workmen. All claims of these workmen are to be met by the contractor, who would be the employer in this case.

However, it was held that even in a case where the canteen is run by the contractor, the management of the factory cannot absolve itself from the liability to pay wages to the workers engaged in the canteen. The principal-employer's liability to pay wages is recognised in Section 21(4) of the Contract Labour (Regulation and Abolition) Act, 1970, by which, if the contractor fails to pay the wages the petitioner shall be bound to pay the same.

(Adapted from: www.indiankanoon.org/doc/1387153/ accessed on 15/6/2014.)

Fixation of Wage-periods (Section 4)

1. Every person responsible for the payment of wages under Section 3 shall fix periods (in this Act referred to as wage-periods) in respect of which such wages shall be payable.
2. No wage-period shall exceed 1 month.

Time of Payment of Wages (Section 5)

Spotlight
Wages in any railway, factory or industrial or other establishment upon or in which less than 1,000 persons are employed shall be paid before the expiry of the 7th day after the last day of the respective wage-period, as provided in Section 5(1)(a).

1. The wages of every person employed upon or in-
   (a) any railway, factory or industrial or other establishment. upon or in which less than 1,000 persons are employed, shall be paid before the expiry of the seventh day,
   (b) any other railway, factory or industrial or other establishment, shall be paid before the expiry of the tenth day,

   after the last day of the wage-period in respect of which the wages are payable:

   Provided that in the case of persons employed on a dock, wharf or jetty or in a mine, the balance of wages found due on completion of the final tonnage account of the ship or wagons loaded or unloaded, as the case may be, shall be paid before the expiry of the seventh day from the day of such completion.
2. Where the employment of any person is terminated by or on behalf of the employer, the wages earned by him shall be paid before the expiry of the second working day from the day on which his employment is terminated:

   Provided that where the employment of any person in an establishment is terminated due to the closure of the establishment for any reason other than a weekly or other recognised holiday, the wages earned by him shall be paid before the expiry of the second day from the day on which his employment is so terminated.
3. The appropriate Government may, by general or special order, exempt, to such extent and subject to such conditions as may be specified in the order, the person responsible for the payment of wages to persons employed upon any railway (otherwise than in a factory) or to persons employed as daily-rated workers in the Public Works Department of the Central Government or the State Government from the operation of this section in respect of the wages of any such persons or class of such persons:

   Provided that in the case of persons employed as daily-rated workers as aforesaid, no such order shall be made except in consultation with the Central Government.
4. Save as otherwise provided in sub-section (2), all payments of wages shall be made on a working day.

Wages to be Paid in Current Coin or Currency Notes (Section 6)

All wages shall be paid in current coin or currency notes or in both:

Provided that the employer may, after obtaining the written authorisation of the employed person, pay him the wages either by cheque or by crediting the wages in his bank account.

Deductions which May be Made from Wages (Section 7)

Spotlight
Section 7 lays down the deductions which may be made from wages.

1. Notwithstanding the provisions of the Railways Act, 1989 the wages of an employed person shall be paid to him without deductions of any kind except those authorised by or under this Act.

Explanation 1 Every payment made by the employed person to the employer or his agent shall, for the purposes of this Act, be deemed to be a deduction from wages.

CASE CORNER

In *General Manager, Northern Railway*, New Delhi *vs. Sajjan Raj and Another* (AIR (1957) Raj 78), it has been pointed out that there is a seeming contradiction between Section 2(vi) and Section 6 of the Payment of Wages Act, 1936 (or, "the Act"). It was further held that perhaps the definition of wages was left wide by the framers of the Act to cover remuneration which was paid in kind by employers to employees before the enforcement of the Act, so that it may be possible to convert the same into cash and include it in wages afterwards. Sections 6, 20 and 23 read together clearly exclude payments in kind from "wages" which can be paid only in current coin or currency notes after the enforcement of the Act.

If Section 6 of the Act envisages that payment in kind, according to earlier practice or agreement made before the Act, could be converted into cash according to its value before payment, the Court held that this could be done by a subsequent agreement between an employer and his employees. In such a case, there would be no contravention of Section 6 of the Act and Section 23 would not apply unless the contract or agreement expressly forbids such conversion into cash. Anything agreed to be paid in kind in circumstances contemplated by the definition of "wages" is covered by the expression "capable of being so expressed", which implies, capable of being expressed in terms of money but, as required by Section 6, it has to be converted into money according to its value and then paid in coins or currency notes.

(Adapted from: www.indiankanoon.org/doc/1708747/ accessed on 14/6/2014.)

Explanation II Any loss of wages resulting from the imposition, for good and sufficient cause, upon a person employed of any of the following penalties, namely:

(i) the withholding of increment or promotion (including the stoppage of increment at an efficiency bar);

(ii) the reduction to a lower post or time scale or to a lower stage in a time scale; or

(iii) suspension;

shall not be deemed to be a deduction from wages in any case where the rules framed by the employer for the imposition of any such penalty are in conformity with the requirements, if any, which may be specified in this behalf by the State Government by notification in the Official Gazette.

2. Deductions from the wages of an employed person shall be made only in accordance with the provisions of this Act, and may be of the following kinds only, namely:

   (a) fines;

   (b) deductions for absence from duty;

   (c) deductions for damage to or loss of goods expressly entrusted to the employed person for custody, or for loss of money for which he is required to account, where such damage or loss is directly attributable to his neglect or default;

   (d) deductions for house-accommodation supplied by the employer or by Government or any housing board set up under any law for the time being in force (whether the Government or the board is the employer or not) or any other authority engaged in the business of subsidising house-accommodation which may be specified in this behalf by the State Government by notification in the Official Gazette;

   (e) deductions for such amenities and services supplied by the employer as the State Government or any officer specified by it in this behalf may, by general or special order, authorise;

Explanation The word "services" in this clause does not include the supply of tools and raw materials required for the purposes of employment;

(f) deductions for recovery of advances of whatever nature (including advances for travelling allowance or conveyance allowance), and the interest due in respect thereof, or for adjustment of over-payments of wages;

(ff) deductions for recovery of loans made from any fund constituted for the welfare of labour in accordance with the rules approved by the State Government, and the interest due in respect thereof;

(fff) deductions for recovery of loans granted for house-building or other purposes approved by the State Government, and the interest due in respect thereof;

(g) deductions of income-tax payable by the employed person;

(h) deductions required to be made by order of a Court or other authority competent to make such order;

(i) deductions for subscriptions to, and for repayment of advances from any provident fund to which the Provident Funds Act, 1925, applies or any recognised provident fund as defined in clause (38) of Section 2 of the Income-tax Act, 1961, or any provident fund approved in this behalf by the appropriate Government, during the continuance of such approval;

(j) deductions for payments to co-operative societies approved by the appropriate Government or any officer specified by it in this behalf or to a scheme of insurance maintained by the Indian Post Office; and

(k) deductions, made with the written authorisation of the person employed for payment of any premium on his life insurance policy to the Life Insurance Corporation of India established under the Life Insurance Corporation Act, 1956, or for the purchase of securities of the Government of India or of any State Government or for being deposited in any Post Office Savings Bank in furtherance of any savings scheme of any such Government;

(kk) deductions made, with the written authorisation of the employed person, for the payment of his contribution to any fund constituted by the employer or a trade union registered under the Trade Unions Act, 1926, for the welfare of the employed persons or the members of their families, or both, and approved by the appropriate Government or any officer specified by it in this behalf, during the continuance of such approval;

(kkk) deductions made, with the written authorisation of the employed person, for payment of the fees payable by him for the membership of any trade union registered under the Trade Unions Act, 1926;

(l) deductions for payment of insurance premia on Fidelity Guarantee Bonds;

(m) deductions for recovery of losses sustained by a railway administration on account of acceptance by the employed person of counterfeit or base coins or mutilated or forged currency notes;

(n) deductions for recovery of losses sustained by a railway administration on account of the failure of the employed person to invoice, to bill, to collect or to account for the appropriate charges due to that administration, whether in respect of fares, freight, demurrage, wharfage and cranage or in respect of sale of food in catering establishments or in respect of sale of commodities in grain shops or otherwise;

(o) deductions for recovery of losses sustained by a railway administration on account of any rebates or refunds incorrectly granted by the employed person where such loss is directly attributable to his neglect or default;

(p) deductions, made with the written authorisation of the employed person, for contribution to the Prime Minister's National Relief Fund or to such other Fund as the Central Government may, by notification in the Official Gazette, specify;

(q) deductions for contributions to any insurance scheme framed by the Central Government for the benefit of its employees.

3. Notwithstanding anything contained in this Act, the total amount of deductions which may be made under sub-section (2) in any wage-period from the wages of any employed person shall not exceed:
   (i) in cases where such deductions are wholly or partly made for payments to co-operative societies under clause (j) of sub-section (2), 75 per cent of such wages, and
   (ii) in any other case, 50 per cent of such wages:

   Provided that where the total deductions authorised under sub-section (2) exceed 75 per cent, or, as the case may be, 50 per cent of the wages, the excess may be recovered in such manner as may be prescribed.
4. Nothing contained in this section shall be construed as precluding the employer from recovering from the wages of the employed person or otherwise any amount payable by such person under any law for the time being in force other than the Railways Act, 1989.

Fines (Section 8)

1. No fine shall be imposed on any employed person save in respect of such acts and omissions on his part as the employer, with the previous approval of the appropriate Government or of the prescribed authority, may have specified by notice under sub-section (2).
2. A notice specifying such acts and omissions shall be exhibited in the prescribed manner on the premises in which the employment is carried on or in the case of person employed upon a railway (otherwise than in a factory), at the prescribed place or places.
3. No fine shall be imposed on any employed person until he has been given an opportunity of showing cause against the fine, or otherwise than in accordance with such procedure as may be prescribed for the imposition of fines.
4. The total amount of fine which may be imposed in any 1 wage-period on any employed person shall not exceed an amount equal to 3 per cent of the wages payable to him in respect of that wage-period.
5. No fine shall be imposed on any employed person who is under the age of 15 years.
6. No fine imposed on any employed person shall be recovered from him by instalments or after the expiry of 90 days from the day on which it was imposed.
7. Every fine shall be deemed to have been imposed on the day of the act or omission in respect of which it was imposed.
8. All fines and all realisations thereof shall be recorded in a register to be kept by the person responsible for the payment of wages under Section 3 in such form as may be prescribed; and all such realisations shall be applied only to such purposes beneficial to the persons employed in the factory or establishment as are approved by the prescribed authority.

Spotlight

No fine, as per section 8(5), shall be imposed on an employed person under 15 years of age.

Explanation When the persons employed upon or in any railway, factory or industrial or other establishment are part only of a staff employed under the same management, all such realisations may be credited to a common fund maintained for the staff as a whole, provided that the fund shall be applied only to such purposes as are approved by the prescribed authority.

Deductions for Absence from Duty (Section 9)

1. Deductions may be made under clause (b) of sub-section (2) of Section 7 only on account of the absence of an employed person from the place or places where, by the terms of his employment, he is required to work, such absence being for the whole or any part of the period during which he is so required to work.
2. The amount of such deduction shall in no case bear to the wages payable to the employed person in respect of the wage-period for which the deduction is made a larger proportion than the period for which he was absent bears to the total period, within such wage-period, during which by the terms of his employment, he was required to work:

   Provided that, subject to any rules made in this behalf by the appropriate Government, if 10 or more employed persons acting in concert absent themselves without due notice (that is to say without giving the notice which is required under the terms of their contracts of employment) and without reasonable cause, such deduction from any such person may include such amount not exceeding his wages for 8 days as may be any such terms be due to the employer in lieu of due notice.

Explanation For the purposes of this section, an employed person shall be deemed to be absent from the place where he is required to work if, although present in such place, he refuses, in pursuance of a stay-in strike or for any other cause which is not reasonable in the circumstances, to carry out his work.

Deductions for Damage or Loss (Section 10)

1. A deduction under clause (c) or clause (o) of sub-section (2) of Section 7 shall not exceed the amount of the damage or loss caused to the employer by the neglect or default of the employed person.

1A. A deduction shall not be made under clause (c) or clause (m) or clause (n) or clause (o) of sub-section (2) of Section 7 until the employed person has been given an opportunity of showing cause against the deduction, or otherwise than in accordance with such procedure as may be prescribed for the making of such deductions.

2. All such deductions and all realisations thereof shall be recorded in a register to be kept by the person responsible for the payment of wages under Section 3 in such form as may be prescribed.

Deductions for Services Rendered (Section 11)

A deduction under clause (d) or clause (e) of sub-section (2) of Section 7 shall not be made from the wages of an employed person, unless the house-accommodation amenity or service has been accepted by him, as a term of employment or otherwise, and such deduction shall not exceed an amount equivalent to the value of the house-accommodation amenity or service supplied and, in the case of a deduction under the said clause (e), shall be subject to such conditions as the appropriate Government may impose.

Deductions for Recovery of Advances (Section 12)

Deductions under clause (f) of sub-section (2) of Section 7 shall be subject to the following conditions, namely:

(a) recovery of an advance of money given before employment began shall be made from the first payment of wages in respect of a complete wage-period, but no recovery shall be made of such advances given for travelling expenses;

(aa) recovery of an advance of money given after employment began shall be subject to such conditions as the appropriate Government may impose;

(b) recovery of advances of wages not already earned shall be subject to any rules made by the appropriate Government regulating the extent to which such advances may be given and the instalments by which they may be recovered.

Deductions for Recovery of Loans (Section 12A)

Deductions for recovery of loans granted under clause (fff) of sub-section (2) of Section 7 shall be subject to any rules made by the appropriate Government regulating the extent to which such loans may be granted and the rate of interest payable thereon.

Deductions for Payments to Co-operative Societies and Insurance Schemes (Section 13)

Deductions under clause (j) and clause (k) of sub-section (2) of Section 7 shall be subject to such conditions as the appropriate Government may impose.

Maintenance of Registers and Records (Section 13A)

1. Every employer shall maintain such registers and records giving such particulars of persons employed by him, the work performed by them, the wages paid to them, the deductions made from their wages, the receipts given by them and such other particulars and in such form as may be prescribed.
2. Every register and record required to be maintained under this section shall, for the purposes of this Act, be preserved for a period of 3 years after the date of the last entry made therein.

Inspectors (Section 14)

1. An Inspector of Factories appointed under sub-section (1) of Section 8 of the Factories Act, 1948, shall be an Inspector for the purposes of this Act in respect of all factories within the local limits assigned to him.
2. The appropriate Government may appoint Inspectors for the purposes of this Act in respect of all persons employed upon a railway (otherwise than in a factory) to whom this Act applies.
3. The appropriate Government may, by notification in the Official Gazette, appoint such other persons as it thinks fit to be Inspectors for the purposes of this Act, and may define the local limits within which and the class of factories and industrial or other establishments in respect of which they shall exercise their functions.
4. An Inspector may:
   (a) make such examination and inquiry as he thinks fit in order to ascertain whether the provisions of this Act or rules made thereunder are being observed;
   (b) with such assistance, if any, as he thinks fit, enter, inspect and search any premises of any railway, factory or industrial or other establishment at any reasonable time for the purpose of carrying out the objects of this Act;

(c) supervise the payment of wages to persons employed upon any railway or in any factory or industrial or other establishment;
(d) require by a written order the production at such place, as may be prescribed, of any register or record maintained in pursuance of this Act and take on the spot or otherwise statements of any persons which he may consider necessary for carrying out the purposes of this Act;
(e) seize or take copies of such registers or documents or portions thereof as he may consider relevant in respect of an offence under this Act which he has reason to believe has been committed by an employer;
(f) exercise such other powers as may be prescribed:

Provided that no person shall be compelled under this sub-section to answer any question or make any statement tending to incriminate himself.

4A. The provisions of the Code of Criminal Procedure, 1973 shall, so far as may be, apply to any search or seizure under this sub-section as the apply to any search or seizure made under the authority of a warrant issued under Section 94 of the said Code.

(5) Every Inspector shall be deemed to be a public servant within the meaning of the Indian Penal Code.

Facilities to be Afforded to Inspectors (Section 14A)

Every employer shall afford an Inspector all reasonable facilities for making any entry, inspection, supervision, examination or inquiry under this Act.

Claims Arising out of Deductions from Wages or Delay in Payment of Wages and Penalty for Malicious or Vexatious Claims (Section 15)

1. The appropriate Government may, by notification in the Official Gazette, appoint:
   (a) any Commissioner for Workmen's (or Employees') Compensation; or
   (b) any officer of the Central Government exercising functions as,-
      (i) Regional Labour Commissioner; or
      (ii) Assistant Labour Commissioner with at least 2 years' experience; or
   (c) any officer of the State Government not below the rank of Assistant Labour Commissioner with at least 2 years' experience; or
   (d) a presiding officer of any Labour Court or Industrial Tribunal, constituted under the Industrial Disputes Act, 1947, or under any corresponding law relating to the investigation and settlement of industrial disputes in force in the State; or
   (e) any other officer with experience as a Judge of a Civil Court or a Judicial Magistrate,

   as the authority to hear and decide for any specified area all claims arising out of deductions from the wages, or delay in payment of the wages, of persons employed or paid in that area, including all matters incidental to such claims:

   Provided that where the appropriate Government considers it necessary so to do, it may appoint more than 1 authority for any specified area and may, by general or special order, provide for the distribution or allocation of work to be performed by them under this Act.
2. Where contrary to the provisions of this Act any deduction has been made from the wages of an employed person, or any payment of wages has been delayed, such person himself, or any legal practitioner or any official of a registered trade union authorised in writing to act on his behalf, or any Inspector under this Act, or any other person acting with the permission of the authority

CASE CORNER

In *A. V. D' Costa, Divisional Engineer, G.I.P. Railway vs. B.C. Patel and Another* [(1955) AIR SC 412], the respondent was employed as a carpenter on daily wages basis with the Railway Administration. The Railway Administration had introduced a scheme which created a cadre of skilled labourers on the scale of monthly-rated pay and admitted only those persons to it who would pass a test. The respondent could not pass the test and continued to serve as an employee on daily wages. He subsequently filed an application under Section 15(2) of the Payment of Wages Act, 1936 (now onwards referred to as "the Act") before the Authority under the Act to recover the additional amount of wages that would have become payable to him had he been taken on the cadre of monthly-rated employee.

The Supreme Court held that "If the parties entered into the contract of service, say by correspondence and the contract is to be determined with reference to the letters that passed between them, it may be open to the Authority to decide the controversy and find-out what the terms of contract with reference to these letters were. But if an employee were to say that his wages were ₹100 per month, which he actually received as and when they fall due, but that he would be entitled to higher wages, if his claims to be placed on the higher wages scheme had been recognised and given effect to, that would not, in our opinion, be a matter within the ambit of jurisdiction."

In other words, the Authority has the jurisdiction to decide what actually the terms of the contract between the parties were, that is, to determine the actual wages; but the Authority has no jurisdiction to determine the question of potential wages.

(Adapted from: www.indiankanoon.org/doc/924929/ accessed on 14/6/2014.)

appointed under sub-section (1), may apply to such authority for a direction under sub-section (3):

Provided that every such application shall be presented within 12 months from the date on which the deduction from the wages was made or from the date on which the payment of the wages was due to be made, as the case may be:

Provided further that any application may be admitted after the said period of 12 months when the applicant satisfies the authority that he had sufficient cause for not making the application within such period.

3. When any application under sub-section (2) is entertained, the authority shall hear the applicant and the employer or other person responsible for the payment of wages under Section 3, or give them an opportunity of being heard, and, after such further inquiry, if any, as may be necessary, may, without prejudice to any other penalty to which such employer or other person is liable under this Act, direct the refund to the employed person of the amount deducted, or the payment of the delayed wages, together with the payment of such compensation as the authority may think fit, not exceeding 10 times the amount deducted in the former case and not exceeding ₹3,000 in the latter, and even if the amount deducted or the delayed wages are paid before the disposal of the application, direct the payment of such compensation, as the authority may think fit, not exceeding ₹2,000:

Provided that a claim under this Act shall be disposed of as far as practicable within a period of 3 months from the date of registration of the claim by the authority:

Provided further that the period of 3 months may be extended if both the parties to the dispute agree for a *bona fide* reason to be recorded by the authority that the said period of 3 months may be extended to such period as may be necessary to dispose off the application in a just manner:

Provided also that no direction for the payment of compensation shall be made in the case of delayed wages if the authority is satisfied that the delay was due to–

(a) a *bona fide* error or *bona fide* dispute as to the amount payable to the employed person; or
(b) the occurrence of an emergency, or the existence of exceptional circumstances, such that the person responsible for the payment of the wages was unable, in spite of exercising reasonable diligence; or
(c) the failure of the employed person to apply for or accept payment.

4. If the authority hearing an application under this section is satisfied:
   (a) that the application was either malicious or vexatious, the authority may direct that a penalty not exceeding ₹375 be paid to the employer or other person responsible for the payment of wages by the person presenting the application; or
   (b) that in any case in which compensation is directed to be paid under sub-section (3), the applicant ought not to have been compelled to seek redress under this section, the authority may direct that a penalty not exceeding ₹375 be paid to the appropriate Government by the employer or other person responsible for the payment of wages.

4A. Where there is any dispute as to the person or persons being the legal representative or representatives of the employer or of the employed person, the decision of the authority on such dispute shall be final.

4B. Any inquiry under this section shall be deemed to be a judicial proceeding within the meaning of sections 193, 219 and 228 of the Indian Penal Code.

5. Any amount directed to be paid under this section may be recovered–
   (a) if the authority is a Magistrate, by the authority as if it were a fine imposed by him as Magistrate, and
   (b) if the authority is not a Magistrate, by any Magistrate to whom the authority makes application in this behalf, as if it were a fine imposed by such Magistrate.

Single Application in Respect of Claims from Unpaid Group (Section 16)

1. Employed persons are said to belong to the same unpaid group if they are borne on the same establishment and if deductions have been made from their wages in contravention of this Act for the same cause and during the same wage-period or periods or if their wages for the same wage-period or periods have remained unpaid after the day fixed by Section 5.
2. A single application may be presented under Section 15 on behalf or in respect of any number of employed persons belonging to the same unpaid group, and in such case every person on whose behalf such application is presented may be awarded maximum compensation to the extent specified in sub-section (3) of Section 15.
3. The authority may deal with any number of separate pending applications, presented under Section 15 in respect of persons belonging to the same unpaid group, as a single application presented under sub-section (2) of this section, and the provisions of that sub-section shall apply accordingly.

Spotlight

As per Section 16(1), employed persons are said to belong to the same unpaid group if they are borne on the same establishment and if deductions have been made from their wages in contravention of this Act for the same cause and during the same wage-period(s) or if their wages for the same wage-period(s) have remained unpaid after the day fixed by Section 5.

Appeal (Section 17)

1. An appeal against an order dismissing either wholly or in part an application made under sub-section (2) of Section 15, or against a direction made under sub-section (3) or sub-section (4) of that section may be preferred, within 30 days of the date on which the order or direction was made, in a Presidency-town before the Court of Small Causes and elsewhere before the District Court–
   (a) by the employer or other person responsible for the payment of wages under Section 3, if the total sum directed to be paid by way of wages and compensation exceeds ₹300 or such direction has the effect of imposing on the employer or the other person a financial liability exceeding ₹1,000, or
   (b) by an employed person or any legal practitioner or any official of a registered trade union authorised in writing to act on his behalf or any Inspector under this Act, or any other person permitted by the authority to make an application under sub-section (2) of Section 15, if the total amount of wages claimed to have been withheld from the employed person exceeds ₹20 or from the unpaid group to which the employed person belongs or belonged exceeds ₹50, or
   (c) by any person directed to pay a penalty under sub-section (4) of Section 15.

1A. No appeal under clause (a) of sub-section (1) shall lie unless the memorandum of appeal is accompanied by a certificate by the authority to the effect that the appellant has deposited the amount payable under the direction appealed against.

2. Save as provided in sub-section (1), any order dismissing either wholly or in part an application made under sub-section (2) of Section 15, or a direction made under sub-section (3) or sub-section (4) of that section shall be final.
3. Where an employer prefers an appeal under this section, the authority against whose decision the appeal has been preferred may, and if so directed by the court referred to in sub-section (1) shall, pending the decision of the appeal, withhold payment of any sum in deposit with it.
4. The court referred to in sub-section (1) may, if it thinks fit, submit any question of law for the decision of the High Court and, if it so does, shall decide the question in conformity with such decision.

Conditional Attachment of Property of Employer or Other Persons Responsible for Payment of Wages (Section 17A)

1. Where at any time after an application has been made under sub-section (2) of Section 15 the authority, or where at any time after an appeal has been filed under Section 17 by an employed person or any legal practitioner or any official of a registered trade union authorised in writing to act on his behalf or any Inspector under this Act or any other person permitted by the authority to make an application under sub-section (2) of Section 15 the Court referred to in that section, is satisfied that the employer or other person responsible for the payment of wages under section 3 is likely to evade payment of any amount that may be directed to be paid under Section 15 or Section 17, the authority or the Court, as the case may be, except in cases where the authority or Court is of opinion that the ends of justice would be defeated by the delay, after giving the employer or other person an opportunity of being heard, may direct the attachment of so much of the property of the employer or other person responsible for the payment of wages as is, in the opinion of the authority or Court, sufficient to satisfy the amount which may be payable under the direction.

2. The provisions of the Code of Civil Procedure, 1908, relating to attachment before judgment under that Code shall, so far as may be, apply to any order for attachment under sub-section (1).

Powers of Authorities Appointed under Section 15 (Section 18)

Every authority appointed under sub-section (1) of Section 15 shall have all the powers of a Civil Court under the Code of Civil Procedure, 1908, for the purpose of taking evidence and of enforcing the attendance of witnesses and compelling the production of documents, and every such authority shall be deemed to be a Civil Court for all the purposes of Section 195 and of Chapter XXVI of the Code of Criminal Procedure, 1973.

Power to Recover from Employer in Certain Cases (Section 19)

Repealed by the Payment of Wages (Amendment) Act, 1964.

Penalty for Offences under the Act (Section 20)

1. Whoever being responsible for the payment of wages to an employed person contravenes any of the provisions of any of the following sections, namely, Section 5 except sub-section (4) thereof, Section 7, Section 8 except sub-section (8) thereof, Section 9, Section 10 except sub-section (2) thereof, and Sections 11 to 13, both inclusive, shall be punishable with fine which shall not be less than ₹1,500 but which may extend to ₹7,500.
2. Whoever contravenes the provisions of Section 4, sub-section (4) of Section 5, Section 6, sub-section (8) of Section 8, sub-section (2) of Section 10 or Section 25 shall be punishable with fine which may extend to ₹3,750.

2A. Whoever being required to nominate or designate a person under Section 3 fails to do so, such person shall be punishable with fine which may extend to ₹3,000.

3. Whoever being required under this Act to maintain any records or registers or to furnish any information or return:
   (a) fails to maintain such register or record; or
   (b) wilfully refuses or without lawful excuse neglects to furnish such information or return; or
   (c) wilfully furnishes or causes to be furnished any information or return which he knows to be false; or
   (d) refuses to answer or wilfully gives a false answer to any question necessary for obtaining any information required to be furnished under this Act,

   shall, for each such offence, be punishable with fine which shall not be less than ₹1,500 but which may extend to ₹7,500.
4. Whoever:
   (a) wilfully obstructs an Inspector in the discharge of his duties under this Act; or
   (b) refuses or wilfully neglects to afford an Inspector any reasonable facility for making any entry, inspection, examination, supervision, or inquiry authorised by or under this Act in relation to any railway, factory or industrial or other establishment; or
   (c) wilfully refuses to produce on the demand of an Inspector any register or other document kept in pursuance of this Act; or

(d) prevents or attempts to prevent or does anything which he has any reason to believe is likely to prevent any person from appearing before or being examined by an Inspector acting in pursuance of his duties under this Act,

shall be punishable with fine which shall not be less than ₹1,500 but which may extend to ₹7,500.

5. If any person who has been convicted of any offence punishable under this Act is again guilty of an offence involving contravention of the same provision, he shall be punishable on a subsequent conviction with imprisonment for a term which shall not be less than 1 month but which may extend to 6 months and with fine which shall not be less than ₹3,750 but which may extend to ₹22,500 or with both:

   Provided that for the purpose of this sub-section, no cognizance shall be taken of any conviction made more than 2 years before the date on which the commission of the offence which is being punished came to the knowledge of the Inspector.

6. If any person fails or wilfully neglects to pay the wages of any employed person by the date fixed by the authority in this behalf, he shall, without prejudice to any other action that may be taken against him, be punishable with an additional fine which may extend to ₹750 for each day for which such failure or neglect continues.

Procedure in Trial of Offences (Section 21)

1. No Court shall take cognizance of a complaint against any person for an offence under sub-section (1) of Section 20 unless an application in respect of the facts constituting the offence has been presented under Section 15 and has been granted wholly or in part and the authority empowered under the latter section or the Appellate Court granting such application has sanctioned the making of the complaint.
2. Before sanctioning the making of a complaint against any person for an offence under sub-section (1) of Section 20, the authority empowered under Section 15 or the Appellate Court, as the case may be, shall give such person an opportunity of showing cause against the granting of such sanction, and the sanction shall not be granted if such person satisfies the authority or Court that his default was due to:
   (a) a *bona fide* error or *bona fide* dispute as to the amount payable to the employed person, or
   (b) the occurrence of an emergency, or the existence of exceptional circumstances, such that the person responsible for the payment of the wages was unable, though exercising reasonable diligence, to make prompt payment, or
   (c) the failure of the employed person to apply for or accept payment.
3. No Court shall take cognizance of a contravention of Section 4 or of Section 6 or of a contravention of any rule made under Section 26 except on a complaint made by or with the sanction of an Inspector under this Act.

3A. No Court shall take cognizance of any offence punishable under sub-section (3) or sub-section (4) of Section 20 except on a complaint made by or with the sanction of an Inspector under this Act.

4. In imposing any fine for an offence under sub-section (1) of Section 20 the Court shall take into consideration the amount of any compensation already awarded against the accused in any proceedings taken under Section 15.

CASE CORNER

In *Mining Engineer (Vig.) vs. Akhlesh Kumar Sharma and Another* [(2006) IIILLJ 992 Raj], it has been stated that while Section 20 of the Payment of Wages Act, 1936 (or the Act) is only in regard to penalty for various offences under different sections of the Act, Section 21 further provides for procedure in trial of offences. Under the procedure as provided under Section 21, it is only a Court which can make cognizance of the offence and impose penalty as provided under Section 20. The Authority under the Act has been defined under Section 15 of the Act itself. However, the Payment of Wages Authority, Bharatpur (the Authority in the present case), cannot be treated as the Court as referred to under Section 21. The Authority could only grant sanction to the concerned workman for prosecution of the defaulting employer; it could not have imposed penalty on its own.

(Adapted from: www.indiankanoon.org/doc/31322/ accessed on 14/6/2014.)

Bar of Suits (Section 22)

No Court shall entertain any suit for the recovery of wages or of any deduction from wages in so far as the sum so claimed:

(a) forms the subject of an application under Section 15 which has been presented by the plaintiff and which is pending before the authority appointed under that section or of an appeal under Section 17; or
(b) has formed the subject of a direction under Section 15 in favour of the plaintiff; or
(c) has been adjudged, in any proceeding under Section 15, not to be owed to the plaintiff; or
(d) could have been recovered by an application under Section 15.

Protection of Action Taken in Good Faith (Section 22A)

No suit, prosecution or other legal proceeding shall lie against the Government or any officer of the Government for anything which is in good faith done or intended to be done under this Act.

Contracting out (Section 23)

Any contract or agreement, whether made before or after the commencement of this Act, whereby an employed person relinquishes any right conferred by this Act shall be null and void in so far as it purports to deprive him of such right.

Delegation of Powers (Section 24)

The appropriate Government may, by notification in the Official Gazette, direct that any power exercisable by it under this Act shall, in relation to such matters and subject to such conditions, if any, as may be specified in the direction, be exercisable:

(a) where the appropriate Government is the Central Government, by such officer or authority subordinate to the Central Government or by the State Government or by such officer or authority subordinate to the State Government, as may be specified in the notification;
(b) where the appropriate Government is a State Government, by such officer or authority subordinate to the State Government as may be specified in the notification.

Display by Notice of Abstracts of the Act (Section 25)

The person responsible for the payment of wages to persons employed in a factory or an industrial or other establishment shall cause to be displayed in such factory or industrial or other establishment a notice containing such abstracts of this Act and of the rules made thereunder in English and in the language of the majority of the persons employed in the factory, or industrial or other establishment, as may be prescribed.

Spotlight

A notice containing the abstracts of this Act and of the rules made thereunder in English and in the language of the majority of the persons employed in the factory, or industrial or other establishment must be displayed in such establishment, as provided in Section 25.

Payment of Undisbursed Wages in Cases of Death of Employed Person (Section 25A)

1. Subject to the other provisions of the Act, all amounts payable to an employed person as wages shall, if such amounts could not or cannot be paid on account of his death before payment or on account of his whereabouts not being known,
   (a) be paid to the person nominated by him in this behalf in accordance with the rules made under this Act; or
   (b) where no such nomination has been made or where for any reasons such amounts cannot be paid to the person so nominated, be deposited with the prescribed authority who shall deal with the amounts so deposited in such manner as may be prescribed.
2. Where, in accordance with the provisions of sub-section (1), all amounts payable to an employed person as wages:
   (a) are paid by the employer to the person nominated by the employed person; or
   (b) are deposited by the employer with the prescribed authority, or the employer shall be discharged of his liability to pay those wages.

Rule-making Power (Section 26)

1. The appropriate Government may make rules to regulate the procedure to be followed by the authorities and Courts referred to in sections 15 and 17.
2. The appropriate Government may, by notification in the Official Gazette, make rules for the purpose of carrying into effect the provisions of this Act.
3. In particular and without prejudice to the generality of the foregoing power, rules made under sub-section (2) may:
   (a) require the maintenance of such records, registers, returns and notices as are necessary for the enforcement of the Act prescribe the form thereof and the particulars be entered in such registers or records;
   (b) require the display in a conspicuous place on premises where employment is carried on of notices specifying rates of wages payable to persons employed on such premises;
   (c) provide for the regular inspection of the weights, measures and weighing machines used by employers in checking or ascertaining the wages of persons employed by them;
   (d) prescribe the manner of giving notice of the days on which wages will be paid;
   (e) prescribe the authority competent to approve under sub-section (1) of Section 8 acts and omissions in respect of which fines may be imposed;
   (f) prescribe the procedure for the imposition of fines under Section 8 and for the making of the deductions referred to in Section 10;

(g) prescribe the conditions subject to which deductions may be made under the proviso to sub-section (2) of Section 9;

(h) prescribe the authority competent to approve the purposes on which the proceeds of fines shall be expended;

(i) prescribe the extent to which advances may be made and the instalments by which they may be recovered with reference to clause (b) of Section 12;

(ia) prescribe the extent to which loans may be granted and the rate of interest payable thereon with reference to Section 12A;

(ib) prescribe the powers of Inspectors for the purposes of this Act;

(j) regulate the scales of costs which may be allowed in proceedings under this Act;

(k) prescribe the amount of court-fees payable in respect of any proceedings under this Act;

(l) prescribe the abstracts to be contained in the notices required by Section 25;

(la) prescribe the form and manner in which nominations may be made for the purposes of sub-section (1) of Section 25A, the cancellation or variation of any such nomination, or the making of any fresh nomination in the event of the nominee predeceasing the person making nomination, and other matters connected with such nominations;

(lb) specify the authority with whom amounts required to be deposited under clause (b) of sub-section (1) of Section 25A shall be deposited, and the manner in which such authority shall deal with the amounts deposited with it under that clause;

(m) provide for any other matter which is to be or may be prescribed.

4. In making any rule under this section the State Government may provide that a contravention of the rule shall be punishable with fine which shall not be less than ₹750 but which may extend to ₹1,500.
5. All rules made under this section shall be subject to the condition of previous publication, and the date to be specified under clause (3) of Section 23 of the General Clauses Act, 1897, shall not be less than 3 months from the date on which the draft of the proposed rules was published.
6. Every rule made by the Central Government under this section shall be laid, as soon as may be after it is made, before each House of Parliament while it is in session for a total period of 30 days which may be comprised in 1 session or in 2 or more successive sessions, and if, before the expiry of the session immediately following the session or the successive sessions aforesaid, both Houses agree in making any modification in the rule, or both Houses agree that the rule should not be made, the rule shall thereafter have effect only in such modified form or be of no effect, as the case may be; so, however, that any such modification or annulment shall be without prejudice to the validity of anything previously done under that rule.
7. All rules made under this section by the State Government shall, as soon as possible after they are made, be laid before the State Legislature.

ADMINISTRATION OF THE ACT

We have already mentioned about the Chief Labour Commissioner's (Central) Organisation in previous chapters. Also known as the Central Industrial Relation Machinery (CIRM), the CLC(C) Organisation enforces among others, the Payment of Wages Act, 1936 and Rules made thereunder for mines, railways, air transport services and docks, wharves and jetties.

RECENT INITIATIVES

The wage ceiling under the Payment of Wages Act, 1936 was fixed at ₹1,600 per month in the year 1982. With a view to enhance the wage ceiling to ₹6,500 per month for applicability of the Act, to empower the Central Government to further increase the ceiling in future by way of notification, and to enhance the penal provisions, etc., the Payment of Wages (Amendment) Act, 2005 was notified on 6th September 2005 as Act 41 of 2005 by the Ministry of Law and Justice. It was made effective from 9th November 2005.

Further, exercising the powers conferred by sub-section (6) of Section 1 of the Act, the Central Government, on the basis of the figures of the Consumer Expenditure Survey published by the National Sample Survey Office, has enhanced the wage ceiling further to ₹10,000 per month (Ministry of Labour & Employment, 2011).

SUMMARY

- Wages refer to the total pay package an employee receives from his/her employer on a periodic basis in return of the physical labour supplied to the firm. The important methods of wage payment are: time-rate system, piece-rate system, and incentive wage plan.
- With the onset of industrialisation in India, industrialists were found to be unduly exploiting workers by not paying their due in return of their labour. The Payment of Wages Act, 1936 was introduced for the broad purpose of safeguarding the wages of workers under certain conditions laid down in the Act. The Act ensures payment of wages in a particular form at regular intervals, without unauthorised deductions.
- On the basis of the figures of the Consumer Expenditure Survey published by NSSO, the Central Government has enhanced the wage ceiling to ₹10,000 per month.
- Section 2(vi) defines wages as all remuneration (whether by way of salary, allowances or otherwise) expressed in terms of money or capable of being so expressed which would, if the terms of employment, express or implied, were fulfilled, be payable to a person employed in respect of his employment or of work done in such employment.
- Section 3 mandates every employer to pay wages required to be paid under this Act to persons employed by him and even in case the contractor or the person designated by him fails to make such payment.
- As per Section 5(1), the wages of every person employed upon or in any railway, factory or industrial, or other establishment upon or in which less than 1,000 persons are employed, shall be paid before the expiry of the seventh day, and in any other railway, factory or industrial or other establishment, wages shall be paid before the expiry of the tenth day, after the last day of the wage-period.
- Section 7 lays down the deductions which may be made from wages.
- According to Section 8(1), no fine shall be imposed on any employed person save in respect of such acts and omissions on his part as the employer, with the previous approval of the appropriate Government or of the prescribed authority, may have specified by notice under sub-section (2). The total amount of fine which may be imposed in any wage-period on any employed person shall not exceed an amount equal to 3 per cent of the wages payable to him in respect of that wage-period, as provided in Section 8(4).
- Section 15 provides for claims arising out of deductions from wages or delay in payment of wages and penalty for malicious and vexation claims.

- As per Section 16(1), employed persons are said to belong to the same unpaid group if they are borne on the same establishment and if deductions have been made from their wages in contravention of this Act for the same cause and during the same wage-period(s) or if their wages for the same wage-period(s) have remained unpaid after the day fixed by Section 5.
- Whoever responsible for the payment of wages to an employed person, as laid down in Section 20(1), contravenes any of the given provisions shall be punishable with fine which shall not be less than ₹1,500, but which may extend to ₹7,500.
- According to Section 25, notice containing the abstracts of the Act and of the rules made thereunder in English and in the language of the majority of the persons employed in the factory, or industrial or other establishment must be displayed in such establishment.

Key Concepts

Wage
Unpaid group
Deductions
Wage-period
Undisbursed wages
Recovery of advances
Absence from duty
Wage ceiling
Time of payment of wages

Bibliography

Indian Labour Statistics (2009 and 2010), Ministry of Labour & Employment, Labour Bureau, Shimla Chandigarh, Government of India, 2011.

Misra, S. N. and Misra, S. K. *An Introduction to Labour and Industrial Laws*, Allahabad: Central Law Publications, 1995.

The Payment of Wages Act, 1936, Bare Acts, New Delhi: Universal Law Publishing Co. Pvt. Ltd.

www.indiankanoon.org

www.business.gov.in/manage_business/wages.php accessed on 14/6/2014.

Review Questions

Objective Type Questions

I. State True or False

i. A person who is required to nominate or designate a person fails to do so, shall be punishable with fine up to ₹3,000.

ii. Every register and record required to be maintained shall be preserved for a period of 3 years after the date of the last entry made therein.

iii. No fine shall be imposed on any employed person below 18 years of age.

iv. Maximum limit for a wage-period is 60 days.

v. Abstracts of the Act must be displayed in a notice only in the language of the majority of the persons employed in the establishment.

Answers: i. True, ii. True, iii. False, iv. False, v. False

II. Fill in the Blanks

i. A claim under the Act shall be disposed of within a period of ____ months from the date of registration of the claim by the authority.
ii. No fine imposed on any employed person shall be recovered from him by instalments or after the expiry of ____ days from the day on which it was imposed.
iii. The present wage ceiling is ₹ ______ per month.
iv. Every employer shall afford an Inspector all reasonable facilities for making any entry, inspection, _______, examination or inquiry under this Act.
v. Wages in an establishment in which less than 1,000 persons are employed, shall be paid before the expiry of the ______ day after the last day of the wage-period.

Answers: i. 3, ii. 90, iii. 10,000, iv. supervision, v. seventh

Discussion Questions

1. Critically explain the circumstances that had led to the enactment of the Payment of Wages Act, 1936.
2. What is deduction from wages? Discuss all permissible deductions from wages as per the Payment of Wages Act, 1936.
3. Explain the term wages as given in the Payment of Wages Act, 1936. Clearly mention items that are included in and those which do not come under wages.
4. What are the rules for time of payment of wages?
5. Discuss in details all provisions on penalty for offences.
6. What is an unpaid group? How can compensation be awarded to the members of such a group?
7. What are the provisions in the Payment of Wages Act, 1936 for fines to be imposed on any employed person?
8. Differentiate between deductions for absence from duty and for damage or loss.
9. Are wages always paid in cash? Explain the provisions regarding payment of wages.
10. Explain the provision for claims arising out of deductions from wages or delay in payment of wages and penalty for malicious or vexatious claims.

CASE STUDY-I

The appellant is a nationalised bank and two of the respondents are its employees. The other two are the trade unions representing the Bank's employees. In furtherance of certain demands for wage revision made by the employees in June 1977 the All the India Bank Employees' Association gave a call for an all-India strike on certain days. The Bank issued a circular dated 23rd September 1977 to its managers and agents directing them to deduct the wages of such of the employees who participated in the strike on the principle of 'no work no pay'. There was a 4-hour strike on 25th December 1977. The Bank issued an administrative circular dated 27th December 1977 to its managers and agents that such employees who participated in the 4-hour strike would be committing a breach of their contract of service and would not draw salary for the entire day.

The employees struck work for 4 hours on 29th December 1977. On 16th January 1978 the Bank issued a circular to its managers and agents directing them to deduct the full day's wages of such employees who had participated in the 4-hour strike. The respondents filed a writ petition for rescinding that circular. The petition was allowed. Hence the present appeal was made by the Bank.

(Adapted from: The Bank of India, Bombay and Another vs. T.S. Kelawala, Bombay and Others [(1990) SCR(3)214) www.indiankanoon.org/doc/398653/ accessed on 13/6/2014.)

Review Questions

1. Was it permissible for the Bank, by means of the impugned administrative circular, to deduct a full day's wages (or even a part thereof) of the employees who participated in the 4-hour strike on 29th December 1977?
2. Given that strikes are recognised as a legitimate form of protest for workers, do you think that the bank is justified in suppressing such a legitimate mode of protest by an administrative circular?
3. Which all sections of the Payment of Wages Act, 1936 are relevant in this case?

CASE STUDY-II

The State Electricity Board had revoked the license of a company and taken over the undertaking. The first respondent, who was the director of the company, served notices on the employees that their services would not be required. Thereupon, the appellant filed an application under Section 15(2) of the Payment of Wages Act, 1936 (hereby "the Act"), on behalf of the employees, for recovering wages for the notice month and retrenchment compensation under Section 25FF of the Industrial Disputes Act, 1947. The first respondent contested the claim as well as the jurisdiction of the authority under the Payment of Wages Act to deal with the application on the ground that he was not the person responsible for payment of compensation and that the right of the workmen was defeated by reason of the proviso to Section 25FF of the Industrial Disputes Act, because there was no interruption in their employment and the new employer (the Electricity Board) was responsible for payment of the compensation. In response the Authority held against the first respondent, who then filed a writ petition in the High Court and the High Court held that Section 15 of the Act did not apply and that the proper forum for such an application was the Labour Court under Section 33C(2) of the Industrial Disputes Act, 1947.

Note: The 3 sections, namely Section 25F introduced into the Industrial Disputes Act, 1947 by Act 43 of 1951 and sections 25FF and 25FFF incorporated by Act 18 of 1957, involve termination of service in consequence of retrenchment, transfer and closure respectively. In sections 25FF and 25FFF, notice and compensation have been provided for "in accordance with the provisions of Section 25F". These words are used only as a measure of compensation and not for laying down any time within which the employer must pay compensation.

(Adapted from: Payment of Wages Inspector vs. Surajmal Mehta and Another (1969 SCR (3) 1051) www.indiankanoon.org/doc/1757386/ accessed on 14/6/2014.)

Review Questions

1. Referring to compensation payable under Section 25FF of the Industrial Disputes Act, 1947, justify if it can fall under the amended definition of wages in the Payment of Wages Act, 1936.
2. Do you think that the authority under Section 15 of the Payment of Wages Act, 1936 had jurisdiction to entertain the application?
3. Which all sections of the Payment of Wages Act, 1936 are relevant in this case?

22

The Trade Unions Act, 1926

An Act to provide .for the registration of Trade Unions and in certain respects to define the law relating to registered Trade Unions.

Desired Knowledge Competencies

- To comprehend the scope and coverage of the Trade Unions Act, 1926 and of the various definitions given under the Act.
- To develop an understanding of registration of trade unions, minimum requirement about membership and types of funds of a registered trade union.
- To grasp the notions of amalgamation and dissolution of a union, penalties and procedures imposed on a registered trade union and other related concepts.

CONCEPT AND RELEVANCE OF TRADE UNIONS

Management and workers are the two indispensible components of organised industrial world, and prosperity of industry is contingent upon their joint contribution. Whenever the conditions at work create divergence of interest between these two components, the natural outcome is conflict. It is here that trade unions play a significant role by bridging the notional and functional gap between the interests of management and workers and by maintaining cordial relations between them.

Reflection

Trade unionism provides a platform to workers to express their views and voice their grievances regarding problems at work.

Unions are a legitimate system to organise workers and to voice their rights and grievances. Union representation and collective bargaining are the keys to the growth of a stable workforce through which workers are able to gain a more equitable share of the wealth that they create; they are also able to improve their working conditions and gain job security. Protection of basic worker and human rights in industrial settings thus necessitates unionisation, so that the working population can reap the benefits from economic growth (Ghosh and Geetika, 2007).

BACKDROP OF THE TRADE UNIONS ACT, 1926

The concept of trade unions and the emergence of trade unionism in India has already been discussed in Chapter 3. Let us now touch briefly upon the historical backdrop of the Trade Unions Act, 1926.

The main protagonist in the movement for trade union legislation was N. M. Joshi, who was the founder of the All India Trade Union Congress (AITUC) and the then General Secretary of the AITUC. In March 1921, Joshi moved a resolution in the Central Legislative Assembly with the recommendation that the government should introduce a legislation towards protection of trade unions. However, the very idea of such a legislative measure faced severe opposition from employers and it took the government 5 long years to pass the Indian Trade Unions Act. The Indian Trade Unions Bill, 1925, passed by the Legislature, received assent on 25th March 1926, though it came into force only on and from 1st June 1927, as the Indian Trade Unions Act, 1926.

The Trade Unions Act, 1926 is a legislation that has provisions for registration of trade unions, their rights, liabilities and responsibilities. It gives corporate status to a registered trade union, with a common seal and having perpetual succession. The Act gives guidelines on the utilisation of funds of registered unions as well. Further, as per the Act, the Societies Registration Act, 1860, the Co-operative Societies Act, 1912 and the Companies Act, 1956 shall not apply to any registered trade union, and the registration of any union under any such Act shall be void.

> **Spotlight**
> The Trade Unions Act, 1926 provides for registration of trade unions, their rights, liabilities and responsibilities.

The Trade Unions Act, 1926 has undergone several amendments ever since it has been passed. In 1929 it was amended to make provisions for the procedure of appeal against the decision of the Registrar to refuse to register a trade union or to withdraw registration of a union. The Royal Commission on Labour (1929) examined the working of the Act and made the following recommendations:

(i) The Act was to be re-examined within 3 years. Further, the limitations imposed upon the activities of trade unions and their office-bearers were to be reconsidered, so as to ensure that under no circumstances shall a *bona fide* trade union be prevented from registration.
(ii) The accounts of trade unions would be audited by government officials free of charge.
(iii) Minimum two-thirds of the members of the executive of a trade union should be persons who are actually engaged or employed in the industry to which the union belongs.
(iv) No union shall be deprived of initiating and carrying out cooperative societies.

Among the above recommendations made by the Commission, the government reserved the first one, while it did not consider the legislation necessary as regards the second recommendation.

As we have mentioned earlier, the Trade Unions Act, 1926 provides for registration of a trade union subject to fulfilment of specific requirements. However, the original Act did not provide for any obligation on the part of an employer to recognise or deal with a union, even if it was registered either in spirit or in letter. The Act was again amended in the year 1947. The Amendment provided for recognition of trade unions by employers; it was laid down that recognition would be granted if the union applying for recognition was representative of all the workers in the establishment or industry concerned, though it did not have any provision for inspection of books of trade unions by the Registrar. However, the Indian Trade Unions (Amendment) Act, 1947 was neither notified, nor brought into force.

Issues related to amending the Indian Trade Unions Act, 1926 were discussed in the 11th Session of the Standing Labour Committee in January 1949, on the basis of which, the Trade Unions Bill was introduced in the Parliament in February 1950. However the Bill lapsed with the dissolution of the Parliament. Minor amendments were made to the original Act in 1960 and the word "Indian" was deleted from the Act by the Amendment Act of 1964. This was followed by the Trade Unions (Amendment)

Bill, 1982, that contained provisions relating to machineries for the resolution of inter-union and intra-union disputes; this Bill also could not be passed.

The next effective amendment to the Act happened after a long gap of almost 20 years, with the Trade Unions (Amendment) Act, 2001. Some of the notable modifications included in the Amending Act are: minimum requirement of 10 per cent or 100 of the workmen, whichever is less, subject to a minimum of 7, for registration of a trade union; binding of a minimum 7 workmen as the members of a trade union making an application for registration, etc. Following is the list of amending Acts and Adaptation Orders:

1. The Indian Trade Unions (Amendment) Act, 1928
2. The Government of India (Adaptation of Indian Laws) Order, 1937
3. The Repealing and Amending Act, 1942
4. The Indian Independence (Adaptation of Central Acts and Ordinances) Order, 1948
5. The Adaptation of Laws Order, 1950
6. The Part B States (Laws) Act, 1951
7. The Indian Trade Unions (Amendment) Act, 1960
8. The Indian Trade Unions (Amendment) Act, 1964
9. The Central Labour Laws (Extension to Jammu and Kashmir) Act, 1970
10. The Trade Unions (Amendment) Act, 2001

ABOUT THE ACT

CHAPTER I: PRELIMINARY

Short Title, Extent and Commencement (Section 1)

1. This Act may be called the Trade Unions Act, 1926.
2. It extends to the whole of India.

   This Act has been extended to Goa, Daman and Diu, to Pondicherry, and to Laccadive, Minicoy and Amindivi Islands. It has been amended in Madhya Pradesh and in Maharashtra.
3. It shall come into force on such date as the Central Government may, by notification in the Official Gazette, appoint.

Definitions (Section 2)

In this Act "the appropriate Government" means, in relation to Trade Unions whose objects are not confined to one State, the Central Government, and in relation to other Trade Unions, the State Government, and unless there is anything repugnant in the subject or context,-

Executive [Section 2(a)] Executive means the body, by whatever name called, to which the management of the affairs of a Trade Union is entrusted;

Office-bearer [Section 2(b)] Office-bearer, in the case of a Trade Union, includes any member of the executive thereof, but does not include an auditor;

Prescribed [Section 2(c)] Prescribed means prescribed by regulations made under this Act;

Registered office [Section 2(d)] Registered office means that office of a Trade Union which is registered under this Act as the head office thereof;

Registered trade union [Section 2(e)] Registered Trade Union means a Trade Union registered under this Act;

Registrar [Section 2(f)] Registrar means:

(i) a Registrar of Trade Unions appointed by the appropriate Government under Section 3, and includes any Additional or Deputy Registrar of Trade Unions; and

(ii) in relation to any Trade Union, the Registrar appointed for the State in which the head or registered office, as the case may be, of the Trade Union is situated.

Trade dispute [Section 2(g)] Trade dispute means any dispute between employers and workmen or between workmen and workmen, or between employers and employers which is connected with the employment or non-employment, or the terms of employment or the conditions of labour, of any person, and "workmen" means all persons employed in trade or industry whether or not in the employment of the employer with whom the trade dispute arises; and

Trade union [Section 2(h)] Trade Union means any combination, whether temporary or permanent, formed primarily for the purpose of regulating the relations between workmen and employers or between workmen and workmen, or between employers and employers, or for imposing restrictive conditions on the conduct of any trade or business, and includes any federation of 2 or more Trade Unions:

Spotlight

A trade union, as per Section 2(h), includes a federation of 2 or more unions.

Provided that this Act shall not affect:

(i) any agreement between partners as to their own business;

(ii) any agreement between an employer and those employed by him as to such employment; or

(iii) any agreement in consideration of the sale of the goodwill of a business or of instruction in any profession, trade or handicraft.

CASE CORNER

In *I. Srinivasa Rao and Others vs. The Commissioner of Labour* (Writ Petition No. 28054 of 2009, dated 12.3.2010), a writ petition was filed seeking a Mandamus. This Mandamus declared the action of the second respondent in not including the names of 147 *badli* workers to participate in the ensuing elections as arbitrary, illegal, amounting to unfair labour practice and also violative of Articles 14 and 16 of the Constitution of India. The question that arises for consideration here is: *whether badli workers/employees are workmen for the purpose of the Trade Unions Act, 1926, and whether they are entitled to participate in voting when verification of membership of the unions is being conducted?*

According to the petitioners, there are 147 *badli* workers working under the control of the third respondent from 2005 onwards. Given that the petitioners and others have paid subscription and joined as members in the fourth and fifth respondent unions, and have been paying subscription every month, the second respondent issued a notice to conduct secret ballot election to determine the status of majority union operating under the control of the third respondent. The fourth and fifth respondent unions have also made representations stating that these workers were not included in the voters list and that they may be included for the purpose of their participation in the verification process. However, on the basis of the representation of the third respondent that *badli* workers are working in the place of permanent workers, their names were not included in the voters list. The second respondent hence denied these workers to participate in the verification process.

A *badli* worker is also a worker within the meaning of Section 2(s) of the Industrial Disputes Act, 1947 (though the term '*badli* workers' is not defined in the Act), and he can be a member of a trade union. In relation to a trade union, any action on the part of the employer/workmen to discourage a workman from participating in a trade union activity is unfair labour practice. *Badli* workmen are workmen and, therefore if any management disapproves a trade union of such workers, or discourages them to join a trade union, or does not permit them to participate in any trade union activity, or denies them voting rights, the same would amount to unfair labour practice, apart from being arbitrary and illegal.

(Adapted from: www.indiankanoon.org/doc/1749312/ accessed on 15/8/2014.)

CHAPTER II: REGISTRATION OF TRADE UNIONS

Appointment of Registrars (Section 3)

1. The appropriate Government shall appoint a person to be the Registrar of Trade Unions for each State.
2. The appropriate Government may appoint as many Additional and Deputy Registrars of Trade Unions as it thinks fit for the purpose of exercising and discharging, under the superintendence and direction of the Registrar, such powers and functions of the Registrar under this Act as it may, by order, specify and define the local limits within which any such Additional or Deputy Registrar shall exercise and discharge the powers and functions so specified.
3. Subject to the provisions of any order under sub-section (2), where an Additional or Deputy Registrar exercises and discharges the powers and functions of a Registrar in an area within which the registered office of a Trade Union is situated, the Additional or Deputy Registrar shall be deemed to be the Registrar in relation to the Trade Union for the purposes of this Act.

Spotlight

As per Section 3(1), the appropriate Government shall appoint a person to be the Registrar of Trade Unions for each State.

Mode of Registration (Section 4)

1. Any 7 or more members of a Trade Union may, by subscribing their names to the rules of the Trade Union and by otherwise complying with the provisions of this Act with respect to registration, apply for registration of the Trade Union under this Act:

   Provided that no Trade Union of workmen shall be registered unless at least 10 per cent or 100 of the workmen, whichever is less, engaged or employed in the establishment or industry with which it is connected are the members of such Trade Union on the date of making of application of registration:

   Provided further that no Trade Union of workmen shall be registered unless it has on the date of making application not less than 7 persons as its members, who are workmen engaged or employed in the establishment or industry with which it is connected.

Spotlight

As per Section 4(1), no trade union shall be registered unless at least 10 per cent or 100 of the workmen, whichever is less, engaged or employed in the establishment or industry with which it is connected, are the members of such union on the date of making such application.

2. Where an application has been made under sub-section (1) for the registration of a Trade Union, such application shall not be deemed to have become invalid merely by reason of the fact that, at any time after the date of the application, but before the registration of the Trade Union, some of the applicants, but not exceeding half of the total number of persons who made the application, have ceased to be members of the Trade Union or have given notice in writing to the Registrar dissociating themselves from the application.

Application for Registration (Section 5)

1. Every application for registration of a Trade Union shall be made to the Registrar, and shall be accompanied by a copy of the rules of the Trade Union and a statement of the following particulars, namely:
   (a) the names, occupations and addresses of the members making the application;
   (aa) in the case of a Trade Union of workmen, the names, occupations and addresses of the place of work of the members of the Trade Union making the application;
   (b) the name of the Trade Union and the address of its head office; and
   (c) the titles, names, ages, addresses and occupations of the office-bearers of the Trade Union.
2. Where a Trade Union has been in existence for more than 1 year before the making of an application for its registration, there shall be delivered to the Registrar, together with the application, a general statement of the assets and liabilities of the Trade Union prepared in such form and containing such particulars as may be prescribed.

Provisions to be Contained in the Rules of a Trade Union (Section 6)

A Trade Union shall not be entitled to registration under this Act, unless the executive thereof is constituted in accordance with the provisions of this Act, and the rules thereof provide for the following matters, namely:

(a) the name of the Trade Union;
(b) the whole of the objects for which the Trade Union has been established;
(c) the whole of the purposes for which the general funds of the Trade Union shall be applicable, all of which purposes shall be purposes to which such funds are lawfully applicable under this Act;
(d) the maintenance of a list of the members of the Trade Union and adequate facilities for the inspection thereof by the office-bearers and members of the Trade Union;
(e) the admission of ordinary members who shall be persons actually engaged or employed in an industry with which the Trade Union is connected, and also the admission of the number of honourary or temporary members as office-bearers required under Section 22 to form the executive of the Trade Union;

Spotlight
The minimum subscription fee shall not be less than ₹1 per annum for rural workers.

(ee) the payment of a minimum subscription by members of the Trade Union which shall be not less than–
   (i) ₹1 per annum for rural workers;
   (ii) ₹3 per annum for workers in other unorganised sectors; and
   (iii) ₹12 per annum for workers in any other case
(f) the conditions under which any member shall be entitled to any benefit assured by the rules and under which any fine or forfeiture may be imposed on the members;

(g) the manner in which the rules shall be amended, varied or rescinded;

(h) the manner in which the members of the executive and the other office-bearers of the Trade union shall be elected and removed;

(hh) the duration of period being not more than 3 years, for which the members of the executive and other office-bearers of the Trade Union shall be elected;

(i) the safe custody of the funds of the Trade Union, an annual audit, in such manner as may be prescribed, of the accounts thereof, and adequate facilities for the inspection of the account books by the office-bearers and members of the Trade Union; and

(j) the manner in which the Trade Union may be dissolved.

It was held in *Standard Chartered Bank vs. Chartered Bank Employees Union* [(1996) IILLJ 52 (Del)] that every registered bank employees' union shall furnish, from time-to-time, the bank with the names of the president, vice-president and the secretaries of the union. Further, with the exception of very special cases, whenever the transfer of any of the above-mentioned officer bearers is contemplated, at least 5 clear working days' notice of such contemplated action should be put up on the notice boards of the bank.

(Adapted from: www.indiankanoon.org/doc/69981/ accessed on 15/8/2014.)

Power to Call for Further Particulars and to Require Alterations of Names (Section 7)

1. The Registrar may call for further information for the purpose of satisfying himself that any application complies with the provisions of Section 5, or that the Trade Union is entitled to registration under Section 6, and may refuse to register the Trade Union until such information is supplied.
2. If the name under which a Trade Union is proposed to be registered is identical with that by which any other existing Trade Union has been registered or, in the opinion of the Registrar, so nearly resembles such name as to be likely to deceive the public or the members of either Trade Union, the Registrar shall require the persons applying for registration to alter the name of the Trade Union stated in the application, and shall refuse to register the Union until such alteration has been made.

Registration (Section 8)

The Registrar, on being satisfied that the Trade Union has complied with all the requirements of this Act in regard to registration, shall register the Trade Union by entering in a register, to be maintained in such form as may be prescribed, the particulars relating to the Trade Union contained in the statement accompanying the application for registration.

Certificate of Registration (Section 9)

The Registrar, on registering a Trade Union under Section 8, shall issue a certificate of registration in the prescribed form which shall be conclusive evidence that the Trade Union has been duly registered under this Act.

Minimum Requirement about Membership of a Trade Union (Section 9A)

A registered Trade Union of workmen shall at all times continue to have not less than 10 per cent or 100 of the workmen, whichever is less, subject to a minimum of 7, engaged or employed in an establishment or industry with which it is connected, as its members.

Spotlight

A registered union must have a minimum of 7 workmen as its members, as mandated by Section 9A.

Cancellation of Registration (Section 10)

A certificate of registration of a Trade Union may be withdrawn or cancelled by the Registrar–

(a) on the application of the Trade Union to be verified in such manner as may be prescribed, or

(b) if the Registrar is satisfied that the certificate has been obtained by fraud or mistake, or that the Trade Union has ceased to exist or has wilfully and after notice from the Registrar contravened any provision of this Act or allowed any rule to continue in force which is inconsistent with any such provision, or has rescinded any rule providing for any matter provision for which is required by Section 6;

(c) If the Registrar is satisfied that a registered Trade Union of workmen ceases to have the requisite number of members.

Provided that not less than 2 months' previous notice in writing specifying the ground on which it is proposed to withdraw or cancel the certificate shall be given by the Registrar to the Trade Union before the certificate is withdrawn or cancelled otherwise than on the application of the Trade Union.

Appeal (Section 11)

1. Any person aggrieved by any refusal of the Registrar to register a Trade Union or by the withdrawal or cancellation of a certificate of registration may, within such period as may be prescribed, appeal–
   (a) where the head office of the Trade Union is situated within the limits of a Presidency town, to the High Court, or
   (aa) where the head office is situated in an area, falling within the jurisdiction of a Labour Court or an Industrial Tribunal, to that Court or Tribunal, as the case may be;
   (b) where the head office is situated in any other area, to such Court, not inferior to the Court of an additional or assistant Judge of a principal Civil Court of original jurisdiction, as the appropriate Government may appoint in this behalf for that area.
2. The appellate Court may dismiss the appeal, or pass an order directing the Registrar to register the Union and to issue a certificate of registration under the provisions of Section 9 or setting aside the order for withdrawal or cancellation of the certificate, as the case may be, and the Registrar shall comply with such order.
3. For the purpose of an appeal under sub-section (1) an appellate Court shall, so far as may be, follow the same procedure and have the same power as it follows and has when trying a suit under the Code of Civil Procedure, 1908, and may direct by whom the whole or any part of the costs of the appeal shall be paid, and such costs shall be recovered as if they had been awarded in a suit under the said Code.
4. In the event of the dismissal of an appeal by any Court appointed under clause (b) of sub-section (1), the person aggrieved shall have a right of appeal to the High Court, and the High Court shall, for the purpose of such appeal, have all the powers of an appellate Court under sub-sections (2) and (3), and the provisions of those sub-sections shall apply accordingly.

CASE CORNER

In *Rangaswami and Another vs. Registrar of Trade Unions and Another* [(1961) ILLJ 599 (Mad)], a petition was made under Section 11 of the Trade Unions Act, 1926 (referred hereafter as "the Act"), seeking to set aside the order of the Registrar of Trade Unions, Madras (now Chennai) refusing to register the union of employees of the Madras Raj Bhavan as a trade union under the Act.

In the Raj Bhavan at Guindy, a number of persons are employed in various capacities such as household, staff, peons, chauffeurs, tailors, carpenters, maistries, gardeners, sweepers, etc. Maistries and gardeners are employed at the Raj Bhavan at Ootacamund; they are employed for doing domestic and other services, maintenance of the Governor's household, and to attend to the needs of the Governor, the members of his family, staff and State guests. Their service is not pensionable but they are entitled to gratuity at certain rates. With the object of securing better service conditions and to facilitate collective bargaining with the employer, the employees formed themselves into a union called the Madras Raj Bhavan Workers' Union, and 7 of the employees applied to the Registrar of Trade Unions, Madras for registration of their union under the Trade Unions Act, 1926. The applicants did not however claim before the Registrar that the employees were engaged in either trade or an industry; the claim was that their services could not be held to be purely domestic services and that their union would hence be entitled to the benefits of registration under the Act.

The Registrar was of the view that before a union can be registered, the members thereof must be connected with a trade or industry or business of an employer, and that condition not being fulfilled in this case, the employees could not be held to be workmen within the meaning of the Act to entitle them to the registration; the application for registration was hence rejected.

The Court held that the services rendered by these employees to the State guests are personal in nature, indirectly to the employer, and would not be indicative of any co-operation between the employer and the employees for the purpose of a trade or business. Further, the occasional sale of unserviceable articles and garden products are incidents of the ordinary administration of Government property, and would not amount to a trade or business. The union of such workers would hence not come within the scope of the Act, so as to entitle it to registration. The order of the Register of Trade Unions rejecting the application of the petitioner was hence considered to be correct.

(Adapted from: www.indiankanoon.org/doc/1314449/ accessed on 16/8/2014.)

Registered Office (Section 12)

All communications and notices to a registered Trade Union may be addressed to its registered office. Notice of any change in the address of the head office shall be given within 14 days of such change to the Registrar in writing, and the changed address shall be recorded in the register referred to in Section 8.

Incorporation of Registered Trade Unions (Section 13)

Every registered Trade Union shall be a body corporate by the name under which it is registered, and shall have perpetual succession and a common seal with power to acquire and hold both movable and immovable property and to contract, and shall by the said name sue and be sued.

CASE CORNER

In *State Bank of Travancore Employees Union vs. Wealth-Tax Officer* [(1984) 8 ITD 529 (Mad)], the point for determination is whether the assessee, State Bank of Travancore Employees Union, a trade union registered under the (Indian) Trade Unions Act, 1926 (hereafter "the Act"), is liable to wealth-tax (in context of the Wealth-tax Act, 1957) in the status of an individual.

The representative of the assessee pointed out that Section 13 of the Act states that every registered trade union shall be a body corporate. According to him, a body corporate is not an assessable entity under the Act; in fact, the expression "body corporate" is wider in context than the expression "company" and a body corporate is distinct and apart from the members constituting it. In his submission, all body corporates are not individuals and holding of assets by a body corporate cannot be equated to holding of assets by an individual. Artificial persons are not contemplated to be included in the term "individual", and only normal human beings are to be included in the expression "individual" for the purpose of charge to wealth-tax. It was also pointed out that the assessee-trade union has not been declared by the Board as a company for the purpose of the Act.

The Court however pointed out the authorities of both the High Courts and the Supreme Court affirming and reaffirming the proposition that the term 'individual' is not confined in its meaning or connotation to a natural human being, but includes every entity, such as a body corporate, not only for purposes of income-tax, but also for assessment under the Wealth-tax Act, 1957. The status of the assessee can only be "individual" and it clearly follows, therefore, that the assessee-trade union, which is a body corporate having independent legal existence and personality, is chargeable to wealth-tax in the status of "individual". The Court therefore rejected the objection of the assessee.

(Adapted from: www.indiankanoon.org/doc/369494/ accessed on 15/8/2014.)

Certain Acts Not to Apply to Registered Trade Unions (Section 14)

The following Acts, namely:

(a) The Societies Registration Act, 1860;
(b) The Co-operative Societies Act, 1912;
(c) The Companies Act, 1956,

shall not apply to any registered Trade Union, and the registration of any such Trade Union under any such Act shall be void.

CHAPTER III: RIGHTS AND LIABILITIES OF REGISTERED TRADE UNIONS

Objects on which General Funds May be Spent (Section 15)

The general funds of a registered Trade Union shall not be spent on any other objects than the following, namely:

(a) the payment of salaries, allowances and expenses to office-bearers of the Trade Union;
(b) the payment of expenses for the administration of the Trade Union, including audit of the accounts of the general funds of the Trade Union;

(c) the prosecution or defence of any legal proceeding to which the Trade Union or any member thereof is a party, when such prosecution or defence is undertaken for the purpose of securing or protecting any rights of the Trade Union as such or any rights arising out of the relations of any member with his employer or with a person whom the member employs;
(d) the conduct of trade disputes on behalf of the Trade Union or any member thereof;
(e) the compensation of members for loss arising out of trade disputes;
(f) allowances to members or their dependants on account of death, old age, sickness, accidents or unemployment of such members;
(g) the issue of, or the undertaking of liability under, policies of assurance on the lives of members, or under policies insuring members against sickness, accident or unemployment;
(h) the provision of educational, social or religious benefits for members (including the payment of the expenses of funeral or religious ceremonies for deceased members) or for the dependants of members;
(i) the upkeep of a periodical published mainly for the purpose of discussing questions affecting employers or workmen as such;
(j) the payment, in furtherance of any of the objects on which the general funds of the Trade Union may be spent, of contributions to any cause intended to benefit workmen in general, provided that the expenditure in respect of such contributions in any financial year shall not at any time during that year be in excess of one-fourth of the combined total of the gross income which has up to that time accrued to the general funds of the Trade Union during that year and of the balance at the credit of those funds at the commencement of that year; and
(k) subject to any conditions contained in the notification, any other object notified by the appropriate Government in the Official Gazette.

Constitution of a Separate Fund for Political Purposes (Section 16)

Spotlight
Section 16 provides for constitution of a separate fund for promotion of civic and political interests of union members.

1. A registered Trade Union may constitute a separate fund, from contributions separately levied for or made to that fund, from which payments may be made, for the promotion of the civic and political interests of its members, in furtherance of any of the objects specified in sub-section (2).
2. The objects referred to in sub-section (1) are:
   (a) the payment of any expenses incurred, either directly or indirectly, by a candidate or prospective candidate for election as a member of any legislative body constituted under the Constitution or of any local authority, before, during, or after the election in connection with his candidature or election; or
   (b) the holding of any meeting or the distribution of any literature or documents in support of any such candidate or prospective candidate; or
   (c) the maintenance of any person who is a member of any legislative body constituted under the Constitution or for any local authority; or
   (d) the registration of electors or the election of a candidate for any legislative body constituted under the Constitution or for any local authority; or
   (e) the holding of political meetings of any kind, or the distribution of political literature or political documents of any kind.

2A. In its application to the State of Jammu and Kashmir, references in sub-section (2) to any legislative body constituted under the Constitution shall be construed as including references to the Legislature of that State.

3. No member shall be compelled to contribute to the fund constituted under sub-section (1); and a member who does not contribute to the said fund shall not be excluded from any benefits of the Trade Union, or placed in any respect either directly or indirectly under any disability or at any disadvantage as compared with other members of the Trade Union (except in relation to the control or management of the said fund) by reason of his not contributing to the said fund; and contribution to the said fund shall not be made a condition for admission to the Trade Union.

Criminal Conspiracy in Trade Disputes (Section 17)

No office-bearer or member of a registered Trade Union shall be liable to punishment under sub-section (2) of Section 120B of the Indian Penal Code, 1860, in respect of any agreement made between the members for the purpose of furthering any such object of the Trade Union as is specified in Section 15, unless the agreement is an agreement to commit an offence.

Immunity from Civil Suit in Certain Cases (Section 18)

1. No suit or other legal proceeding shall be maintainable in any Civil Court against any registered Trade Union or any office-bearer or member thereof in respect of any act done in contemplation or furtherance of a trade dispute to which a member of the Trade Union is a party on the ground only that such act induces some other person to break a contract of employment, or that it is in interference with the trade, business or employment of some other person or with the right of some other person to dispose of his capital or of his labour as he wills.
2. A registered Trade Union shall not be liable in any suit or other legal proceeding in any Civil Court in respect of any tortious act done in contemplation or furtherance of a trade dispute by an agent of the Trade Union if it is proved that such person acted without the knowledge of, or contrary to express instructions given by, the executive of the Trade Union.

Enforceability of Agreements (Section 19)

Notwithstanding anything contained in any other law for the time being in force, an agreement between the members of a registered Trade Union shall not be void or voidable merely by reason of the fact that any of the objects of the agreement are in restraint of trade:

Provided that nothing in this section shall enable any Civil Court to entertain any legal proceeding instituted for the express purpose of enforcing or recovering damages for the breach of any agreement concerning the conditions on which any members of a Trade Union shall or shall not sell their goods, transact business, work, employ or be employed.

Right to Inspect Books of Trade Union (Section 20)

The account books of a registered Trade Union and the list of members thereof shall be open to inspection by an office-bearer or member of the Trade Union at such times as may be provided for in the rules of the Trade Union.

Rights of Minors to Membership of Trade Unions (Section 21)

Any person who has attained the age of 15 years may be a member of a registered Trade Union subject to any rules of the Trade Union to the

Spotlight

Minimum age for membership of union is 15 years.

contrary, and may, subject as aforesaid, enjoy all the rights of a member and execute all instruments and give all acquittances necessary to be executed or given under the rules.

Disqualifications of Office-Bearers of Trade Unions (Section 21)

1. A person shall be disqualified for being chosen as, and for being a member of the executive or any other office-bearer of a registered Trade Union if:
   (i) he has not attained the age of 18 years;
   (ii) he has been convicted by a Court in India of any offence involving moral turpitude and sentenced to imprisonment, unless a period of 5 years has elapsed since his release.
2. Any member of the executive or other office-bearer of a registered Trade Union who, before the commencement of the Indian Trade Unions (Amendment) Act, 1964, has been convicted of any offence involving moral turpitude and sentenced to imprisonment, shall on the date of such commencement cease to be such member or office-bearer unless a period of 5 years has elapsed since his release before that date.
3. In its application to the State of Jammu and Kashmir, reference in sub-section (2) to the commencement of the Indian Trade Unions (Amendment) Act, 1964, shall be construed as reference to the commencement of this Act in the said State.

Proportion of Officer-Bearers to be Connected with the Industry (Section 22)

1. Not less than one-half of the total number of the office-bearers of every registered Trade Union in an unorganised sector shall be persons actually engaged or employed in an industry with which the Trade Union is connected:

   Provided that the appropriate Government may, by special or general order, declare that the provisions of this section shall not apply to any Trade Union or class of Trade Unions specified in the order.

   Explanation For the purposes of this section, "unorganised sector" means any sector which the appropriate Government may, by notification in the Official Gazette, specify.
2. Save as otherwise provided in sub-section (1), all office-bearers of a registered Trade Union, except not more than one-third of the total number of the office-bearers or 5, whichever is less, shall be persons actually engaged or employed in the establishment or industry with which the Trade Union is connected.

   Explanation For the purposes of this sub-section, an employee who has retired or has been retrenched shall not be construed as outsider for the purpose of holding an office in a Trade Union.
3. No member of the Council of Ministers or a person holding an office of profit (not being an engagement or employment in an establishment or industry with which the Trade Union is connected), in the Union or a State, shall be a member of the executive or other office-bearer of a registered Trade Union.

> **Spotlight**
> As per Section 22(1), not less than one-half of the total number of the office-bearers of every registered union in unorganised sector shall be persons actually engaged or employed in an industry with which the union is connected.

Change of Name (Section 23)

Any registered Trade Union may, with the consent of not less than two-thirds of the total number of its members and subject to the provisions of Section 25, change its name.

> **Spotlight**
> A minimum of two-thirds of members' consent is required to change the name of a union, as provided in Section 23.

Amalgamation of Trade Unions (Section 24)

Any 2 or more registered Trade Unions may become amalgamated together as 1 Trade Union with or without dissolution or division of the funds of such Trade Unions or either or any of them, provided that the votes of at least one-half of the members of each or every such Trade Union entitled to vote are recorded, and that at least 60 per cent of the votes recorded are in favour of the proposal.

As laid down in *Rattan Kumar Dey vs. Union of India* [(1991) 63 FLR 463 (Gau)], a trade union and its office-bearers do not lose their identity on merger.

Notice of Change of Name or Amalgamation (Section 25)

1. Notice in writing of every change of name and of every amalgamation signed, in the case of a change of name, by the Secretary and by 7 members of the Trade Union changing its name, and, in the case of an amalgamation, by the Secretary and by 7 members of each and every Trade Union which is a party thereto, shall be sent to the Registrar, and where the head office of the amalgamated Trade Union is situated in a different State, to the Registrar of such State.
2. If the proposed name is identical with that by which any other existing Trade Union has been registered or, in the opinion of the Registrar, so nearly resembles such name as to be likely to deceive the public or the members of either Trade Union, the Registrar shall refuse to register the change of name.
3. Save as provided in sub-section (2), the Registrar shall, if he is satisfied that the provisions of this Act in respect of change of name have been complied with, register the change of name in the register referred to in Section 8, and the change of name shall have effect from the date of such registration.
4. The Registrar of the State in which the head office of the amalgamated Trade Union is situated shall, if he is satisfied that the provisions of this Act in respect of amalgamation have been complied with and that the Trade Union formed thereby is entitled to registration under Section 6, register the Trade Union in the manner provided in Section 8, and the amalgamation shall have effect from the date of such registration.

Effects of Change of Name and of Amalgamation (Section 26)

1. The change in the name of a registered Trade Union shall not affect any rights or obligations of the Trade Union or render defective any legal proceeding by or against the Trade Union, and any legal proceeding which might have been continued or commenced by or against it by its former name may be continued or commenced by or against it by its new name.
2. An amalgamation of 2 or more registered Trade Unions shall not prejudice any right of any of such Trade Unions or any right of a creditor of any of them.

Dissolution (Section 27)

1. When a registered Trade Union is dissolved, notice of the dissolution signed by 7 members and by the Secretary of the Trade Union shall, within 14 days of the dissolution be sent to the Registrar, and shall be registered by him if he is satisfied that the dissolution has been effected in accordance with the rules of the Trade Union, and the dissolution shall have effect from the date of such registration.

Spotlight

As per Section 27(1), when a registered union is dissolved, notice of the dissolution signed by 7 members and by the Secretary of the union shall, within 14 days of the dissolution be sent to the Registrar.

2. Where the dissolution of a registered Trade Union has been registered and the rules of the Trade Union do not provide for the distribution of funds of the Trade Union on dissolution, the Registrar shall divide the funds amongst the members in such manner as may be prescribed.

Returns (Section 28)

1. There shall be sent annually to the Registrar, on or before such date as may be prescribed, a general statement, audited in the prescribed manner, of all receipts and expenditure of every registered Trade Union during the year ending on the 31st day of December next preceding such prescribed date, and of the assets and liabilities of the Trade Union existing on such 31st day of December. The statement shall be prepared in such form and shall comprise such particulars as may be prescribed.
2. Together with the general statement there shall be sent to the Registrar a statement showing all changes of office-bearers made by the Trade Union during the year to which the general statement refers, together also with a copy of the rules of the Trade Union corrected up to the date of the despatch thereof to the Registrar.
3. A copy of every alteration made in the rules of a registered Trade Union shall be sent to the Registrar within 15 days of the making of the alteration.
4. For the purpose of examining the documents referred to in sub-sections (1), (2) and (3), the Registrar, or any officer authorised by him, by general or special order, may at all reasonable times inspect the certificate of registration, account books, registers, and other documents, relating to a Trade Union, at its registered office or may require their production at such place as he may specify in this behalf, but no such place shall be at a distance of more than 10 miles from the registered office of a Trade Union.

In *Rashtriya Mukund Employees' Union vs. Mukund Iron and Steel Works Ltd.* [(1995) IIILLJ 200 (Bom)], registration of the union was cancelled on account of failing to send an annual return in accordance with the provisions contained in Section 28 of the Trade Unions Act, 1926. It was held that the order of cancellation of the registration of a trade union cannot be withdrawn or revoked by the Registrar; the only remedy is to go in for appeal or apply for re-registration.

(Adapted from: www.indiankanoon.org/doc/447380/ accessed on 16/8/2014.)

CHAPTER IV: REGULATIONS

Power to Make Regulations (Section 29)

1. The appropriate Government may make regulations for the purpose of carrying into effect the provisions of this Act.
2. In particular and without prejudice to the generality of the foregoing power, such regulations may provide for all or any of the following matters, namely:
   (a) the manner in which Trade Unions and the rules of Trade Unions shall be registered and the fees payable on registration;
   (b) the transfer of registration in the case of any registered Trade Union which has changed its head office from one State to another;
   (c) the manner in which, and the qualifications of persons by whom, the accounts of registered Trade Unions or of any class of such Unions shall be audited;

(d) the conditions subject to which inspection of documents kept by Registrars shall be allowed and the fees which shall be chargeable in respect of such inspections; and
(e) any matter which is to be or may be prescribed.

3. Every notification made by the Central Government under sub-section (1) of Section 22, and every regulation made by it under sub-section (1), shall be laid, as soon as may be after it is made, before each House of Parliament, while it is in session, for a total period of 30 days which may be comprised in 1 session or in 2 or more successive sessions, and if, before the expiry of the session immediately following the session or the successive sessions aforesaid, both Houses agree in making any modification in the notification or regulation, or both Houses agree that the notification or regulation should not be made, the notification or regulation shall thereafter have effect only in such modified form or be of no effect, as the case may be; so, however, that any such modification or annulment shall be without prejudice to the validity of anything previously done under that notification or regulation.
4. Every notification made by the State Government under sub-section (1) of Section 22 and every regulation made by it under sub-section (1) shall be laid, as soon as may be after it is made, before the State Legislature.

Publication of Regulations (Section 30)

1. The power to make regulations conferred by Section 29 is subject to the condition of the regulations being made after previous publication.
2. The date to be specified in accordance with clause (3) of Section 23 of the General Clauses Act, 1897, as that after which a draft of regulations proposed to be made will be taken into consideration shall not be less than 3 months from the date on which the draft of the proposed regulations was published for general information.
3. Regulations so made shall be published in the Official Gazette, and on such publication shall have effect as if enacted in this Act.

CHAPTER V: PENALTIES AND PROCEDURE

Failure to Submit Returns (Section 31)

1. If default is made on the part of any registered Trade Union in giving any notice or sending any statement or other document as required by or under any provision of this Act, every office-bearer or other person bound by the rules of the Trade Union to give or send the same, or, if there is no such office-bearer or person every member of the executive of the Trade Union, shall be punishable with fine which may extend to ₹5 and, in the case of a continuing default, with an additional fine which may extend to ₹5 for each week after the first during which the default continues:

   Provided that the aggregate fine shall not exceed ₹50.
2. Any person who wilfully makes, or causes to be made, any false entry in, or any omission from, the general statement required by Section 28, or in or from any copy of rules or of alterations of rules sent to the Registrar under that section, shall be punishable with fine which may extend to ₹500.

Supplying False Information Regarding Trade Unions (Section 32)

Any person who, with intent to deceive, gives to any member of a registered Trade Union or to any person intending or applying to become a member of such Trade Union any document purporting to be a copy of the rules of the Trade Union or of any alterations to the same which he knows, or has reason to believe, is not a correct copy of such rules or alterations as are for the time being in force, or any person who, with the like intent, gives a copy of any rules of an unregistered Trade Union to any person on the pretence that such rules are the rules of a registered Trade Union, shall be punishable with fine which may extend to ₹200.

Cognizance of Offences (Section 33)

1. No Court inferior to that of a Presidency Magistrate or a Magistrate of the First Class shall try any offence under this Act.
2. No Court shall take cognizance of any offence under this Act, unless complaint thereof has been made by, or with the previous sanction of, the Registrar or, in the case of an offence under Section 32, by the person to whom the copy was given, within 6 months of the date on which the offence is alleged to have been committed.

ADMINISTRATION OF THE ACT

The Trade Unions Act, 1926 is administered by the Ministry of Labour & Employment, through its Industrial Relations Division, which is concerned with the amendment of labour laws and improvement of the procedure of settlement of grievances in industrial relations. Towards this end, the Division works in close tandem with the Central Industrial Relation Machinery (CIRM), an attached office of the Ministry. We have already talked about the CIRM and its functions in the previous chapters.

Summary

- The Trade Unions Act, 1926 is a legislation to provide for the registration of trade unions, their rights, liabilities and responsibilities.
- Section 2(h) defines a trade union as any combination, whether temporary or permanent, formed primarily for the purpose of regulating the relations between workmen and employers, or between workmen and workmen, or between employers and employers, or for imposing restrictive conditions on the conduct of any trade or business, and includes any federation of 2 or more unions. Registrar of Trade Unions for each State is appointed by the appropriate Government as per Section 3(1).
- Section 4(1) lays down that any 7 or more members of a trade union may, by subscribing their names to the rules of the union and by otherwise complying with the provisions of this Act with respect to registration, apply for registration of the union under this Act. No Trade Union shall be registered unless at least 10 per cent or 100 of the workmen, whichever is less, engaged or employed in the establishment or industry with which it is connected are the members of such union on the date of making of application of registration, as per Section 4(2).
- Section 9A provides that a registered trade union shall at all times continue to have not less than 10 per cent or 100 of the workmen, whichever is less, subject to a minimum of 7, engaged or employed in an establishment or industry with which it is connected, as its members.

- As per Section 13, every registered trade union shall be a body corporate by the name under which it is registered, have perpetual succession and a common seal with power to acquire and hold both movable and immovable property and to contract, and shall by the said name sue and be sued. The Societies Registration Act, 1860, the Co-operative Societies Act, 1912 and the Companies Act, 1956 shall not apply to any registered trade union, and the registration of any such union under any such Act shall be void, according to Section 14.
- Section 21 lays down that any person who has attained the age of 15 years may be a member of a registered trade union subject to any rules of the union to the contrary.
- Any 2 or more registered trade unions may become amalgamated together as one union with or without dissolution or division of the funds of such trade unions or either or any of them, provided that the votes of at least one-half of the members of each or every such trade union entitled to vote are recorded, and that at least 60 per cent of the votes recorded are in favour of the proposal, according to Section 24.
- Section 27(1) provides that when a registered Trade Union is dissolved, notice of the dissolution, signed by 7 members and by the Secretary of the Trade Union shall, within 14 days of the dissolution be sent to the Registrar.
- The Trade Unions Act, 1926 is administered by the Ministry of Labour & Employment through its Industrial Relations Division.

Key Concepts

Trade union	Registrar	General funds
Registration	Amalgamation	Membership
Office bearers	Dissolution	Perpetual succession
Registered office	Certificate of registration	Application for registration

Bibliography

Ghosh, P. and Geetika. Unionisation: A Feasibility Study for the Indian Software Industry, *Russian Management Journal*, 2007, Issue 2, pp. 45-56.

Misra, S. N. and Misra, S. K. *An Introduction to Labour and Industrial Laws*, Allahabad: Central Law Publications; 1995.

Review Questions

Objective Type Questions

I. State True or False

(i) Union subscription fee for rural workers must be a minimum of ₹3 per annum.

(ii) A retrenched employee shall be an outsider for the purpose of holding an office in a trade union.

(iii) A member who does not contribute to the fund for political purposes shall be summarily excluded from any benefits of the union.

(iv) Application for registration of a trade union must be accompanied by the names, occupations and age of the members making the application.

(v) A person shall be disqualified for being chosen as an office-bearer of a registered trade union if he has not attained the age of 18 years.

Answers: (i) False, (ii) False, (iii) False, (iv) False, (v) True

II. Fill in the Blanks

(i) Consent of not less than _____ of the total number of members is required for change of name of a registered trade union.
(ii) Notice of change in the address of the head office of a union must be given within ____ days of such change to the Registrar in writing.
(iii) Every registered trade union shall have perpetual _____.
(iv) Minimum age to be a member of a registered trade union is ____ years.
(v) Notice of dissolution of a union must be sent to the Registrar within _____ days of the dissolution.

Answers: (i) two-thirds, (ii) 14, (iii) succession, (iv) 15, (v) 14

Discussion Questions

1. What are the different funds maintained by a union? Discuss the provisions for each, as per the Trade Unions Act, 1926.
2. On what grounds may the Registrar cancel the certificate of registration of a union?
3. Discuss the provision given in the Trade Unions Act, 1926 with respect to notice of change of name or amalgamation of a trade union.
4. What is the procedure for application by a trade union for its registration?
5. Explain the provision given in the Trade Unions Act, 1926 for appeal by any person aggrieved by any refusal of the Registrar to register a union.
6. Discuss the proportion of officer-bearers to be connected with the industry, as per the Trade Unions Act, 1926.
7. Elaborate on the provision regarding disqualification of office-bearers of a registered trade union.
8. Discuss penalties and procedure on a registered trade union as laid down in the Trade Unions Act, 1926.
9. What are the provisions to be contained in the rules of a trade union?
10. Explain in brief:
    (a) Amalgamation of trade unions
    (b) Dissolution of trade unions
    (c) Supplying false information regarding trade unions
    (d) Appointment of Registrars

CASE STUDY-I

The case of the appellant here, the Neyveli National Workers Union (hereafter referred to as "the Union") registered under the Trade Unions Act, 1926 (in short "the Act") and affiliated to the INTUC, is that, an impugned order cancelling the registration of the appellant has been passed by the first respondent, i.e., Additional Registrar-II Registered in 1976, the Union was started with the object of securing rights, privilege and immunities and other protection to its members, and also to maintain industrial peace in the Neyveli Lignite Corporation Ltd., a Government of India undertaking. After complying with the requirements and the provisions of the Act, a certificate was issued. The Union submitted its annual report of 1996 in Form 'E'. However, neither had it received any communication from the first respondent, nor was it issued any notice for the non-compliance of the provisions of the Act. It is further stated that when the petitioner approached the first respondent on 9th June 1998, the latter issued an order dated 21st January 1997, stating that the petitioner had failed to submit the annual report for the years 1992 to 1995. Hence the first respondent had cancelled the registration of the petitioner's union.

(Adapted from: Neyveli National Workers Union vs. The Additional Registrar-II of Trade Unions and Deputy Commissioner of Labour-II [(1999 (81) FLR 1008] www.indiankanoon.org/doc/280417/ accessed on 17/8/2014.)

Review Questions

1. Under which section(s) of the Trade Unions Act, 1926, in your opinion, has the registration of the union discussed here been cancelled?
2. What arguments can the petitioner put up for stating that cancellation of registration is illegal?

CASE STUDY-II

In this case the petitioner is a union called the ACC Rajanka Limestone Quarries Mazdoor Union (hereafter referred to as "the Union"). It is alleged that the Union consisted of workers employed in the ACC Rajanka Limestone Quarries' of the Associated Cement Company Ltd. at Jhinkpani in the district of Singhbhum. The Union was formed at the meeting of the workers on 5th July 1957, and on 31st July 1957, the petitioner sent an application for registration of the Union to the Registrar of Trade Unions, Government of Bihar, Patna, under a registered postal cover with acknowledgment due. The application was duly received by the Registrar on 3rd August 1957. As the matter was kept pending for a long time, reminders were sent to the Registrar to expedite registration, but no action was taken. Even a telegraphic reminder was sent on 23rd September 1957, but there was no reply to that telegram also. In these circumstances the petitioner applied to the High Court for grant of a writ in the nature of Mandamus calling upon the respondent to perform his statutory duty of registering or refusing to register the union under the provisions of the Trade Unions Act, 1926. There is a counter-affidavit filed on behalf of the respondent and in paragraph 5 of the counter-affidavit it is said that the Inspector of Trade Unions had passed the following order on 26th October 1957: "Perused the list. Original copy of the constitution of the already registered Union at the Establishment has not been made available. However, a spot enquiry may be necessary and at that time the discrepancy noticed in the draft constitution can be removed. Put up when I draw up my programme to visit that side sometime in November/December, 1957."

It is the admitted position in the present case that though the application for registration was made on 31st July 1957, no action has as yet been taken by the Registrar to call for further particulars.

(Adapted from: ACC Rajanka Limestone Quarries' Mazdoor Union vs. Registrar of Trade Unions Government of Bihar, Patna [(1958) IILLJ 458 (Pat)] www.indiankanoon.org/doc/1875176/ accessed on 15/8/2014.)

Review Questions

1. Which sections of the Trade Unions Act, 1926 are relevant in this case?
2. Do you think that the writ of Mandamus by the petitioner is valid, keeping in perspective the statutory duties imposed on the Registrar?
3. Give your opinion on the order passed by the Inspector of Trade Unions.
4. What statutory duties of the Registrar are relevant in this case?

23

The Employees' Provident Fund and Miscellaneous Provisions Act, 1952

An Act to provide for the institution of provident funds, pension fund and deposit-linked insurance fund for employees in factories and other establishments.

Desired Knowledge Competencies

- To understand the concept of provident fund, pension fund and deposit-linked insurance fund.
- To discuss the application of the Employees' Provident Fund and Miscellaneous Provisions Act, 1952 and the various definitions and schemes given in the Act.
- To comprehend the notions of contribution, EPF, EPS, EDLIS, etc.

CONCEPT OF PROVIDENT FUND

Social protection denotes major branches of social security like pensions, healthcare, work injury and social assistance. We have talked about social security in Chapter 9. The main objectives of any social security (or social protection) system are: smoothing of consumption over an individual's lifetime; insurance (particularly against longevity and inflation risks); income redistribution for the society as a whole; and poverty relief (Asher, 2009). All social security benefits comprise transfers, either in cash or in kind, i.e., they represent a transfer of income or services. The recipients of such transfers may be in a position to receive them from a specific social security scheme on fulfilling conditions like contribution to such a scheme (contributory scheme), or meeting specific age criteria (categorical schemes), or experiencing specific resource conditions (social assistance schemes), etc. (ILO, 2010-2011). Of the various schemes available, contributory schemes may also have some non-contributory elements in entitlement to benefits, being financed either by other contributors (redistribution within the scheme) or by the State. These schemes are also described as "social insurance schemes". Provident funds are an example of such contributory schemes. Conversely, non-contributory schemes or "social assistance schemes" normally do not require direct contribution from beneficiaries or their employers as a condition of entitlement to receive relevant benefits.

According to the International Labour Organisation (ILO), provident funds which exist primarily in developing countries are essentially compulsory savings programmes in which regular contributions withheld from employees' wages are enhanced by, and often matched, with employers' contributions. Contributions are set aside and invested for each employee in a single, publicly managed fund for future repayment to employees when defined contingencies occur. "Typically, benefits are paid in a lump sum with accrued interest, although in certain circumstances drawdown provisions enable partial access to savings prior to retirement or other defined contingencies. On retirement, some provident funds also permit beneficiaries to purchase an annuity or opt for a pension. Some provide pensions for survivors." (ILO, 2010-2011, p. 232).

A provident fund scheme may be mandatory or voluntary. In the case of defined contribution schemes in which contributions are defined but benefits are left undefined, individual members have to bear investment and other risks. Participants usually receive a lump sum at a specified retirement age, though annuity features can be easily incorporated in such schemes. Contributions are typically by employers and employees, though in some cases the government may also contribute to the fund. While they are primarily used for retirement financing, many provident and pension fund schemes permit a member to borrow for housing, education or other purposes, but such loans need to be repaid. This reduces the power of compound interest (Asher, 2009).

Spotlight
Provident funds are compulsory savings programmes.

BACKDROP OF THE EMPLOYEES' PROVIDENT FUND AND MISCELLANEOUS PROVISIONS ACT, 1952

Towards meeting the objective of social security, the question of providing for the future of industrial workers after their retirement or for their dependents in the event of their premature death had been preoccupying the attention of the government since long. The first Provident Fund Act passed in 1925 for regulating the provident funds of Railways and government industrial establishments was limited in scope. In 1929, the Royal Commission on Labour emphasised the need for provisions against old age of industrial workers by formulation of schemes for instituting provident funds. The issue was raised at the Third Conference of Labour Ministers in 1942, in which the proposal for instituting provident funds was generally accepted. It was however considered that such funds should be on voluntary rather than on compulsory basis. A recommendation was made that the Central Government should frame model rules and accordingly model rules were circulated to employers in the year 1945 for adoption in industrial establishments. This was followed by establishment of voluntary provident funds by some progressive employers, though the general response was rather disappointing.

In 1947, the issue of provident fund was reviewed at the Asian Regional Conference of ILO. It was reiterated that in view of the financial and administrative conditions in India, a contributory provident fund scheme was the most preferable out of the options available, instead of a scheme of old age pension as adopted in the industrially advanced nations. The main difficulty in a gratuity scheme is that a worker, with his meagre means, would not be making any contribution to the fund; the amount paid to him or his dependents would hence be small. The most appropriate course of action was hence the institution of a compulsory contributory provident fund, in which both workers and employers would contribute. Such a scheme would have, *inter-alia*, benefits like inculcation of a spirit of thrift among workers and stabilisation of the labour force.

(Adapted from: Annual Report, EPF India, 2012-2013.)

In accordance with the recommendations of the Asian Regional Conference, the matter was discussed at the 10th Session of the Indian Labour Conference in 1948, in which it was generally agreed that the introduction of a statutory provident fund scheme for industrial workers must be undertaken. The Coal Mines Provident Fund (CMPF) was launched in the same year, mainly to test the feasibility of such a scheme in a restricted field. The success of CMPF led to the demand for its expansion to other industries as well. With a growing consensus on the formation of legislation for instituting provident funds in industrial undertakings, the Employees' Provident Fund (EPF) came into existence with the promulgation of the Employees' Provident Funds Ordinance on 15th November 1951. It was replaced by the Employees' Provident Funds Act, 1952. The Employees' Provident Funds Scheme, 1952, framed under Section 5 of the Act was brought into force in stages and was enforced in its entirety by 1st November 1952. The working of the Scheme highlighted certain defects in the Act, such as lack of provision for inspection of exempted factories, recovery of dues from such factories and payment of damages. In order to rectify such defects, an amending Bill was introduced in the Council of States on 14th September 1952. As some of the amendments necessitated urgent implementation and because the Employees' Provident Funds (Amendment) Bill could not be passed during that session of the Parliament, an amending Ordinance was promulgated, which was subsequently replaced by the Employees' Provident Funds (Amendment) Act, 1953. It received the assent of the President on 12th December 1953 and is now referred to the Employees' Provident Funds and Miscellaneous Provisions (EPF & MP) Act, 1952, extending to the whole of India except Jammu and Kashmir.

"The Employees' Provident Funds and Miscellaneous Provisions Act, 1952 is a welfare legislation enacted mainly for the purpose of instituting provident funds, pension fund and deposit-linked insurance fund for employees working in factories and other establishments. The Act aims at providing social security and timely monetary assistance to industrial employees and their families when they are in distress and/or are unable to meet family and social obligations. It also aims to protect them in old age, disablement, early death of the bread winner and in some other contingencies." (Ministry of Labour & Employment, 2009-10, p. 75)

"The Act covers all types of employees employed directly and indirectly, permanent or casual. It is a piece of social legislation conferring certain retiral benefits on the working class of people. It is a beneficial enactment pursuant to constitutional mandate keeping in view the basic human rights of individuals in a democratic country."

(Adapted from: www.indiankanoon.org/doc/867786/ accessed on 1/5/2014.)

Spotlight

The EPF & MP Act, 1952 is a welfare legislation enacted for the purpose of instituting provident fund, pension fund and deposit-linked insurance fund for employees working in factories and other establishments.

The Act has undergone a number of changes over the years in view of changes in the industrial milieu. Following is the list of amending Acts that have been enacted over the years:

1. The Employees' Provident Funds (Amendment) Act, 1953
2. The Employees' Provident Funds (Amendment) Act, 1956
3. The Repealing and Amending Act, 1957
4. The Employees' Provident Funds (Amendment) Act, 1958
5. The Employees' Provident Funds (Amendment) Act, 1960
6. The Employees' Provident Funds (Amendment) Act, 1963
7. The Employees' Provident Funds (Amendment) Act, 1965
8. The Labour Provident Fund Laws (Amendment) Act, 1971
9. The Employees' Provident Fund and Family Pension Fund (Amendment) Act, 1973
10. The Labour Provident Fund Laws (Amendment) Act, 1976
11. The Delegated Legislation Provisions (Amendment) Act, 1985

12. The Employees' Provident Funds and Miscellaneous Provisions (Amendment) Act, 1988
13. The Employees' Provident Funds and Miscellaneous Provisions (Amendment) Act, 1996
14. The Employees' Provident Funds and Miscellaneous Provisions (Amendment) Act, 1998
15. The Repealing and Amendment Act, 2001

ABOUT THE ACT

Short Title, Extent and Application (Section 1)

1. This Act may be called the Employees' Provident Funds and Miscellaneous Provisions Act, 1952.
2. It extends to the whole of India except the State of Jammu and Kashmir.
3. Subject to the provisions contained in Section 16, it applies–
   (a) to every establishment which is a factory engaged in any industry specified in Schedule I and in which 20 or more persons are employed, and
   (b) to any other establishment employing 20 or more persons or class of such establishments which the Central Government may, by notification in the Official Gazette, specify, in this behalf:

   It is held in *Shri Jain Swetamber Nakoda Paraswnath Teerth, Mewanagar, Barmer vs. Regional Provident Fund Commissioner and Others* [(2009) LLR 295] that a religious trust managing a temple does not fall under the definition given in Section 1(3)(b) of the Act. In *M/s P. M. Patel & Sons and Others vs. Union of India and Others, etc.* [(1985) SCR Supl. (3) 55], the Court has held that the provisions of the Act and the Scheme are applicable to home workers.

   (Adapted from www.indiankanoon.org/doc/1050814 accessed on 1/5/2014.)

   Provided that the Central Government may, after giving not less than 2 months' notice of its intention so to do, by notification in the Official Gazette, apply the provisions of this Act to any establishment employing such number of persons less than 20 as may be specified in the notification.
4. Notwithstanding anything contained in sub-section (3) of this section or sub-section (1) of Section 16, where it appears to the Central Provident Fund Commissioner, whether on an application made to him in this behalf or otherwise, that the employer and the majority of employees in relation to any establishment have agreed that the provisions of this Act should be made applicable to the establishment, he may, by notification in the Official Gazette, apply the provisions of this Act to that establishment on and from the date of such agreement or from any subsequent date specified in such agreement.
5. An establishment to which this Act applies shall continue to be governed by this Act notwithstanding that the number of persons employed therein at any time falls below 20.

In *Joseph vs. Regional Provident Fund Commissioner, Trivandrum* [(1962) ILLJ 745 Ker], the Court has held that the Act contemplates the employment of 50 or more persons for the Act to apply. This is more or less an essential condition which should be satisfied, for not only the Act applying in the first instance, but also for the Act continuing to apply at all times. When there is a reduction due to some reason or the other, there may be a hardship. But in the face of the clear provisions of the statute, considerations of hardship have no place in the construction of the particular section. The sub-section (5) of Section 1 categorically provides for the continued application of the Act, notwithstanding that there has been a reduction in the number of employees. This gives an indication that the Parliament was aware of the difficulty in applying the provisions of the main Act, as it stood originally to establishments when there has been a reduction in the number of employees due to any reason whatsoever.

(Adapted from: www.indiankanoon.org/doc/1687219/ accessed on 2/5/2014.)

DEFINITIONS (Section 2)

In this Act, unless the context otherwise requires,

Appropriate Government [Section 2(a)] Appropriate Government means:

(i) in relation to an establishment belonging to, or under the control of, the Central Government or in relation to an establishment connected with a railway company, a major port, a mine or an oil-field or a controlled industry or in relation to an establishment having departments or branches in more than 1 State, the Central Government; and

(ii) in relation to any other establishment, the State Government;

Authorised officer [Section 2(aa)] Authorised officer means the Central Provident Fund Commissioner, Additional Central Provident Fund Commissioner, Deputy Provident Fund Commissioner, Regional Provident Fund Commissioner, or such other officer as may be authorised by the Central Government, by notification in the Official Gazette;

Basic wages [Section 2(b)] Basic wages means all emoluments which are earned by an employee while on duty or on leave or on holidays with wages in either case in accordance with the terms of the contract of employment and which are paid or payable in cash to him, but does not include:

> **Spotlight**
> Basic wages, defined in Section 2(b), does not include cash value of any food concession.

(i) the cash value of any food concession;

(ii) any dearness allowance (that is to say, all cash payments by whatever named called paid to an employee on account of a rise in the cost of living), house-rent allowance, overtime allowance, bonus, commission or any other similar allowance payable to the employee in respect of his employment or of work done in such employment;

(iii) any presents made by the employer;

CASE CORNER

In *Bridge and Roof Co. (India) Ltd vs. Union of India* (1963 SCR (3) 978), the issue before the Supreme Court was as to whether "production bonus" could be included in basic wages for the purposes of the Act. The Apex Court observed that clause (ii) of Section 2(b) excludes, from the definition of "basic wages" amongst other allowances, bonus payable to an employee in respect of his employment or of work done in such employment. This exception suggests that even though the main part of the definition includes all emoluments which are earned as per the terms of the contract of employment, there are certain payments which are the price of labour and earned as per the terms of the contract of employment, and are excluded from the main part of the definition. Since the word "bonus" has been used in this clause without any qualification, it could be inferred that the legislature had referred to every kind of bonus that may be payable to an employee. It was, therefore, held that production bonus is outside the definition of "basic wages" in Section 2(b).

(Adapted from: www.indiankanoon.org/doc/698659/ accessed on 1/5/2014.)

Contribution [Section 2(c)] Contribution means a contribution payable in respect of a member under a Scheme or the contribution payable in respect of an employee to whom the Insurance Scheme applies;

Controlled industry [Section 2(d)] Controlled industry means any industry the control of which by the Union has been declared by a Central Act to be expedient in the public interest;

Employer [Section 2(e)] Employer means:

(i) in relation to an establishment which is a factory, the owner or the occupier of the factory, including the agent of such owner or occupier, the legal representative of a deceased owner or occupier and, where a person has been named as a manager of the factory under clause (f) of sub-section (1) of Section 7 of the Factories Act, 1948, the person so named; and

(ii) in relation to any other establishment, the person who, or the authority which, has the ultimate control over the affairs of the establishment, and where the said affairs are entrusted to a manager, managing director or managing agent, such manager, managing director or managing agent;

Employee [Section 2(f)] Employee means any person who is employed for wages in any kind of work, manual or otherwise, in or in connection with the work of an establishment, and who gets his wages directly or indirectly from the employer, and includes any person:

(i) employed by or through a contractor in or in connection with the work of the establishment;

(ii) engaged as an apprentice, not being an apprentice engaged under the Apprentices Act, 1961 or under the standing orders of the establishment;

CASE CORNER

In *Madathupatti Weavers Co-operative Production and Sales Society Ltd. vs. Regional Provident Fund Commissioner, Madurai and Others* [(1998) ILLJ 824 Mad], the petitioner is a handloom weaving cooperative society with weavers as the members of the society. Yarn is directly supplied to the members who weave the yarn in their home and supply the finished cloth to the society. It is contended that all persons who supply yarn are only the members of the petitioner-society and as such, there being no master and servant relationship, the Employees' Provident Funds and Miscellaneous Provisions Act, 1952 will not apply to the petitioner-society.

The Court held that the weavers are paid wages on the basis of their work. Yarn is supplied to the weavers by the petitioner-society, which sells the cloth woven by the weavers. Thus, it can be concluded that the weavers are engaged in work connected with that of the petitioner-society. Therefore, there is an employer-employee relationship between the petitioner establishment and their weaver workers. Hence, these workers are entitled for provident fund benefits and the petitioner-establishment has to enroll them and remit the provident fund contributions in respect of them.

(Adapted from: www.indiankanoon.org/doc/867786/ accessed on 1/5/2014.)

Exempted employee [Section 2(ff)] Exempted employee means an employee to whom a Scheme or the Insurance Scheme, as the case may be would, but for the exemption granted under Section 17, have applied;

Exempted establishment [Section 2(fff)] Exempted establishment means an establishment in respect of which an exemption has been granted under Section 17 from the operation of all or any of the provisions of any Scheme or the Insurance Scheme, as the case may be, whether such exemption has been granted to the establishment as such or to any person or class of persons employed therein;

Factory [Section 2(g)] Factory means any premises, including the precincts thereof, in any part of which a manufacturing process is being carried on or is ordinarily so carried on, whether with the aid of power or without the aid of power;

Fund [Section 2(h)] Fund means the provident fund established under a Scheme;

Industry [Section 2(i)] Industry means any industry specified in Schedule I, and includes any other industry added to the Schedule by notification under Section 4;

Insurance fund [Section (ia)] Insurance Fund means the Deposit-Linked Insurance Fund established under sub-section (2) of Section 6C;

Insurance Scheme [Section (ib)] Insurance Scheme means the Employees' Deposit-linked Insurance Scheme framed under sub-section (1) of Section 6C;

Manufacture or Manufacturing process [Section 2[(ic)] Manufacture or manufacturing process means any process for making, altering, repairing, ornamenting, finishing, packing, oiling, washing, cleaning, breaking up, demolishing or otherwise treating or adapting any article or substance with a view to its use, sale, transport, delivery or disposal;

CASE CORNER

In *Bharat Board Mills Ltd. vs. The Regional Provident Fund Commissioner, West, Bengal* (AIR 1957 Cal 702), the petitioner had commenced business of manufacturing and dealing of all kinds of board paper and pulp from 31st July 1950. By a deed of agreement, it purchased machineries from India Paper and Board Mills Co. and by a deed of sale it had purchased a one-storied brick built house. By certain awards made by the Industrial Tribunal, the petitioner-company was treated as a new concern. It was pointed out by the Regional Provident Fund Commissioner, West Bengal that the petitioner's factory came within the purview of the Employees' Provident Funds and Miscellaneous Provision Act, 1952 and the Scheme framed thereunder. The petitioner-company made a representation to the first respondent, requesting to keep the question of contribution in abeyance as it had remained closed for about 4 months from 1st April 1952.

A criminal case was started as the petitioner-company did not submit returns prescribed under the Employees' Provident Fund Scheme, and did not remit the contributions and other charges payable in respect of the period from 1st November 1952 to 31st March 1954. It was ascertained upon proper investigation made into the affairs of the petitioner-company, that the factory which was originally established by India Paper and Board Mills Co. was continued by the petitioner-company after it had purchased the said factory and no new factory had been established by the petitioner after it commenced business in 1950. As the date of establishment of the factory was sometime in the year 1936 the Court held that the petitioner-company had started production after the establishment of the factory sometime in the year 1936 and that there is nothing to show that production had stopped at any time prior to 12th May 1950. This factory ran into production in 1938 and is still manufacturing goods, though its ownership had changed hands meanwhile. The petitioner is a new concern since 29th June 1950, but the factory continues to be the same. The date of establishment of a factory is held to be the date when the factory starts its manufacturing process. The fact that a new company or concern has subsequently taken over or acquired the factory does not shift its date of establishment to the date of such take over or acquisition; nor does the fact that the factory had ceased to produce goods for certain time and resumed production after certain brief intervals would result in extinction of the old factory and establishment of a new one.

(Adapted from: www.indiankanoon.org/doc/1972649/ accessed on 2/5/2014.)

Member [Section 2(j)] Member means a member of the Fund;

Occupier of a factory [Section 2(k)] Occupier of a factory means the person who has ultimate control over the affairs of the factory, and, where the said affairs are entrusted to a managing agent, such agent shall be deemed to be the occupier of the factory;

Pension Fund [Section 2(kA)] Pension Fund means the Employees' Pension Fund established under sub-section (2) of Section 6A;

Pension Scheme [Section 2(kB)] Pension Scheme means the Employees' Pension Scheme framed under sub-section (1) of Section 6A;

Prescribed [Section 2(ka)] Prescribed means prescribed by rules made under this Act;

Recovery Officer [Section 2(kb)] Recovery Officer means any officer of the Central Government, State Government or the Board of Trustees constituted under Section 5A, who may be authorised by the Central Government, by notification in the Official Gazette, to exercise the powers of a Recovery Officer under this Act;

Scheme [Section 2(l)] Scheme means the Employees' Provident Fund Scheme framed under Section 5;

Superannuation [Section 2(ll)] Superannuation, in relation to an employee who is the member of the Pension Scheme, means the attainment, by the said employee, of the age of 58 years;

Tribunal [Section 2(m)] Tribunal means the Employees' Provident Funds Appellate Tribunal constituted under Section 7D;

Spotlight

As per Section 2(m), Tribunal means the Employees' Provident Funds Appellate Tribunal.

Establishment to Include All Departments and Branches (Section 2A)

For the removal of doubts, it is hereby declared that where an establishment consists of different departments or has branches, whether situate in the same place or in different places, all such departments or branches shall be treated as parts of the same establishment.

Power to Apply Act to an Establishment which has a Common Provident Fund with another Establishment (Section 3)

Where immediately before this Act becomes applicable to an establishment there is in existence a provident fund which is common to the employees employed in that establishment, and employees in any other establishment, the Central Government may, by notification in the Official Gazette, direct that the provisions of this Act shall also apply to such other establishment.

Power to Add to Schedule I (Section 4)

1. The Central Government may, by notification in the Official Gazette, add to Schedule I any other industry in respect of the employees whereof it is of opinion that a Provident Fund Scheme should be framed under this Act, and thereupon the industry so added shall be deemed to be an industry specified in Schedule I for the purposes of this Act.
2. All notifications under sub-section (1) shall be laid before Parliament, as soon as may be, after they are issued.

Employees' Provident Fund Scheme (Section 5)

1. The Central Government may, by notification in the Official Gazette, frame a Scheme to be called the Employees' Provident Fund Scheme for the establishment of provident funds under this Act for employees or for any class of employees and specify the establishments or class of establishments to which the said scheme shall apply and there shall be established, as soon as may be after the framing of the scheme, a fund in accordance with the provisions of this Act and the Scheme.

1A. The fund shall vest in, and be administered by, the Central Board constituted under Section 5A.

1B. Subject to the provisions of this Act, a Scheme framed under sub-section (1) may provide for all or any of the matters specified in Schedule II.

2. A scheme framed under sub-section (1) may provide that any of its provisions shall take effect either prospectively or retrospectively on such date as may be specified in this behalf in the Scheme.

Central Board (Section 5A)

1. The Central Government may, by notification in the Official Gazette, constitute with effect from such date as may be specified therein, a Board of Trustees for the territories to which this Act extends (hereinafter in this Act referred to as the Central Board) consisting of the following persons as members, namely:
   - (a) a Chairman and a Vice-Chairman to be appointed by the Central Government;
   - (aa) the Central Provident Fund Commissioner, *ex officio*;
   - (b) not more than 5 persons appointed by the Central Government from amongst its officials;
   - (c) not more than 15 persons representing Governments of such States as the Central Government may specify in this behalf, appointed by the Central Government;
   - (d) 10 persons representing employers of the establishments to which the Scheme applies, appointed by the Central Government after consultation with such organisations of employers as may be recognised by the Central Government in this behalf; and

Spotlight

The Chairman and Vice-Chairman of the Central Board are appointed by the Central Government.

(e) 10 persons representing employees in the establishments to which the Scheme applies, appointed by the Central Government after consultation with such organisations of employees as may be recognised by the Central Government in this behalf.

2. The terms and conditions subject to which a member of the Central Board may be appointed and the time, place and procedure of the meetings of the Central Board shall be such as may be provided for in the Scheme.
3. The Central Board shall, subject to the provisions of Section 6A and Section 6C administer the fund vested in it in such manner as may be specified in the Scheme.
4. The Central Board shall perform such other functions as it may be required to perform by or under any provisions of the Scheme, the Pension Scheme and the Insurance Scheme.
5. The Central Board shall maintain proper accounts of its income and expenditure in such form and in such manner as the Central Government may, after consultation with the Comptroller and Auditor-General of India, specify in the Scheme.
6. The accounts of the Central Board shall be audited annually by the Comptroller and Auditor-General of India and any expenditure incurred by him in connection with such audit shall be payable by the Central Board to the Comptroller and Auditor-General of India.
7. The Comptroller and Auditor-General of India and any person appointed by him in connection with the audit of the accounts of the Central Board shall have the same rights and privileges and authority in connection with such audit as the Comptroller and Auditor-General has, in connection with the audit of Government accounts and, in particular, shall have the right to demand the production of books, accounts, connected vouchers, documents and papers and inspect any of the offices of the Central Board.
8. The accounts of the Central Board as certified by the Comptroller and Auditor-General of India or any other person appointed by him in this behalf together with the audit report thereon shall be forwarded to the Central Board which shall forward the same to the Central Government along with its comments on the report of the Comptroller and Auditor-General.
9. It shall be the duty of the Central Board to submit also to the Central Government an annual report of its work and activities and the Central Government shall cause a copy of the annual report, the audited accounts together with the report of the Comptroller and Auditor-General of India and the comments of the Central Board thereon to be laid before each House of Parliament.

Executive Committee (Section 5AA)

1. The Central Government may, by notification in the Official Gazette, constitute, with effect from such date as may be specified therein, an Executive Committee to assist the Central Board in the performance of its functions.

Spotlight
The Executive Committee assists the Central Board in the performance of its functions.

2. The Executive Committee shall consist of the following persons as members, namely:
   (a) a Chairman appointed by the Central Government from amongst the members of the Central Board;
   (b) 2 persons appointed by the Central Government from amongst the persons referred to in clause (b) of sub-section (1) of Section 5A;
   (c) 3 persons appointed by the Central Government from amongst the persons referred to in clause (c) of sub-section (1) of Section 5A;
   (d) 3 persons representing the employers elected by the Central Board from amongst the persons referred to in clause (d) of sub-section (1) of Section 5A;

(e) 3 persons representing the employees elected by the Central Board from amongst the persons referred to in clause (e) of sub-section (1) of Section 5A;
(f) the Central Provident Fund Commissioner, *ex officio*.

3. The terms and conditions subject to which a member of the Central Board may be appointed or elected to the Executive Committee and the time, place and procedure of the meetings of the Executive Committee shall be such as may be provided for in the Scheme.

State Board (Section 5B)

1. The Central Government may, after consultation with the Government of any State, by notification in the Official Gazette, constitute for that State a Board of Trustees (hereinafter in this Act referred to as the State Board), in such manner as may be provided for in the Scheme.
2. A State Board shall exercise such powers and perform such duties as the Central Government may assign to it from time to time.
3. The terms and conditions subject to which a member of a State Board may be appointed and the time, place and procedure of the meetings of a State Board shall be such as may be provided for in the Scheme.

Board of Trustees to be Body Corporate (Section 5C)

Every Board of Trustees constituted under Section 5A or Section 5B shall be a body corporate under the name specified in the notification constituting it, having perpetual succession and a common seal and shall by the said name sue and be sued.

Spotlight

Every Board of Trustees shall be a body corporate, as per Section 5C.

Appointment of Officers (Section 5D)

1. The Central Government shall appoint a Central Provident Fund Commissioner who shall be the Chief Executive Officer of the Central Board and shall be subject to the general control and superintendence of that Board.
2. The Central Government may also appoint a Financial Adviser and Chief Accounts Officer to assist the Central Provident Fund Commissioner in the discharge of his duties.
3. The Central Board may appoint subject to the maximum scale of pay, as may be specified in the Scheme, as many Additional Central Provident Fund Commissioners, Deputy Provident Fund Commissioners, Regional Provident Fund Commissioners, Assistant Provident Fund Commissioners, and such other officers and employees as it may consider necessary for the efficient administration of the Scheme, the Pension Scheme and the Insurance Scheme.
4. No appointment to the post of the Central Provident Fund Commissioner or an Additional Central Provident Fund Commissioner or a Financial Adviser and Chief Accounts Officer or any other post under the Central Board carrying a scale of pay equivalent to the scale of pay of any Group 'A' or Group 'B' post under the Central Government shall be made except after consultation with the Union Public Service Commission:

   Provided that no such consultation shall be necessary in regard to any such appointment:

   (a) for a period not exceeding 1 year; or
   (b) if the person to be appointed is at the time of his appointment:
      (i) a member of the Indian Administrative Service, or

(ii) in the service of the Central Government or a State Government or the Central Board in a Group 'A' or Group 'B' post.

5. A State Board may, with the approval of the State Government concerned, appoint such staff as it may consider necessary.

Spotlight

Section 5D(1) provides that a State Board may appoint staff with the approval of the State Government.

6. The method of recruitment, salary and allowances, discipline and other conditions of service of the Central Provident Fund Commissioner, and the Financial Adviser and Chief Accounts Officer shall be such as may be specified by the Central Government and such salary and allowances shall be paid out of the Fund.
7. (a) The method of recruitment, salary and allowances, discipline and other conditions of service of the Additional Central Provident Fund Commissioner, Deputy Provident Fund Commissioner, Regional Provident Fund Commissioner, Assistant Provident Fund Commissioner and other officers and employees of the Central Board shall be such as may be specified by the Central Board in accordance with the rules and orders applicable to the officers and employees of the Central Government drawing corresponding scales of pay:

   Provided that where the Central Board is of the opinion that it is necessary to make a departure from the said rules or orders in respect of any of the matters aforesaid, it shall obtain the prior approval of the Central Government.

   (b) In determining the corresponding scales of pay of officers and employees under clause (a), the Central Board shall have regard to the educational qualifications, method of recruitment, duties and responsibilities of such officers and employees under the Central Government and in case of any doubt, the Central Board shall refer the matter to the Central Government whose decision thereon shall be final.
8. The method of recruitment, salary and allowances, discipline and other conditions of service of officers and employees of a State Board shall be such as may be specified by that Board, with the approval of the State Government concerned.

Acts and Proceedings of the Central Board or its Executive Committee or the State Board Not to be Invalidated on Certain Grounds (Section 5DD)

No act done or proceeding taken by the Central Board or the Executive Committee constituted under Section 5AA or the State Board shall be questioned on the ground merely of the existence of any vacancy in, or any defect in the constitution of, the Central Board or the Executive Committee or the State Board, as the case may be.

Delegation (Section 5E)

The Central Board may delegate to the Executive Committee or to the Chairman of the Board or to any of its officers and a State Board may delegate to its Chairman or to any of its officers, subject to such conditions and limitations, if any, as it may specify, such of its powers and functions under this Act as it may deem necessary for the efficient administration of the Scheme, the Pension Scheme and the Insurance Scheme.

Contribution and Matters which May be Provided for in Schemes (Section 6)

The contribution which shall be paid by the employer to the Fund shall be 10 per cent of the basic wages, dearness allowance and retaining allowance (if any), for the time being payable to each of the employees (whether employed by him directly or by or through a contractor), and the employee's contribution shall be equal to the contribution payable by the employer in respect of him and may, if any employee so desires, be an amount exceeding 10 per cent of his basic wages, dearness allowance and retaining allowance (if any), subject to the condition that the employer shall not be under an obligation to pay any contribution over and above his contribution payable under this section:

Provided that in its application to any establishment or class of establishments which the Central Government, after making such enquiry as it deems fit, may, by notification in the Official Gazette specify, this section shall be subject to the modification that for the words "10 per cent", at both the places where they occur, the words "12 per cent" shall be substituted:

Provided further that where the amount of any contribution payable under this Act involves a fraction of a rupee, the Scheme may provide for the rounding off of such fraction to the nearest rupee, half of a rupee or quarter of a rupee.

Explanation I For the purposes of this section, dearness allowance shall be deemed to include also the cash value of any food concession allowed to the employee.

Explanation II For the purposes of this section, "retaining allowance" means an allowance payable for the time being to an employee of any factory or other establishment during any period in which the establishment is not working, for retaining his services.

Spotlight

Employer's contribution to the Fund is 10 per cent of the basic wages, dearness allowance and retaining allowance payable to each employee, as laid down in Section 6.

Employees' Pension Scheme (Section 6A)

1. The Central Government may, by notification in the Official Gazette, frame a scheme to be called the Employees' Pension Scheme for the purpose of providing for:
   (a) superannuation pension, retiring pension or permanent total disablement pension to the employees of any establishment or class of establishments to which this Act applies; and
   (b) widow or widower's pension, children pension or orphan pension payable to the beneficiaries of such employees.
2. Notwithstanding anything contained in Section 6, there shall be established, as soon as may be after framing of the Pension Scheme, a Pension Fund into which there shall be paid, from time to time, in respect of every employee who is a member of the Pension Scheme,
   (a) such sums from the employer's contribution under Section 6, not exceeding 8 and 1/3 per cent of the basic wages, dearness allowance and retaining allowance, if any, of the concerned employees, as may be specified in the Pension Scheme;
   (b) such sums as are payable by the employers of exempted establishments under sub-section (6) of Section 17;
   (c) the net assets of the Employees' Family Pension Fund as on the date of the establishment of the Pension Fund;
   (d) such sums as the Central Government may, after due appropriation by Parliament by law in this behalf, specify.

Spotlight

The Employees' Pension Scheme provides superannuation pension, retiring pension, permanent total disablement pension, widow or widower's pension, and children pension or orphan pension.

CASE CORNER

In *Hindustan Lever Employees' Union vs. Regional Provident Fund Commissioner* (1995 (71) FLR 46), the petitioners are trade unions representing the employees of the respondent, Hindustan Lever Ltd. For several years, the latter had been including the amount of leave encashment for the purpose of calculating employer's as well as employees' contribution towards payment of provident fund. The Regional Provident Fund Commissioner, Maharashtra and Goa informed that according to the provisions of Section 6 of the Employees' Provident Funds and Miscellaneous Provisions Act, 1952 (hereinafter referred to as "the Act"), provident fund contribution is payable on basic wages, dearness allowance and retaining allowance, if any. Further, as per the Commissioner, leave encashment is not earned wages and therefore deduction of provident fund contribution on it is not envisaged.

However, the Court held that the amount of leave encashment forms a part of basic wages, as defined in Section 2(b) of the Act. The decision of the Commissioner that provident fund is not liable to be deducted on such wages, i.e., encashment of leave, is quashed and set aside.

(Adapted from: www.indiankanoon.org/doc/1970061/ accessed on 4/5/2014.)

3. On the establishment of the Pension Fund, the Family Pension Scheme (hereinafter referred to as the ceased scheme) shall cease to operate and all assets of the ceased scheme shall vest in and shall stand transferred to, and all liabilities under the ceased scheme shall be enforceable against, the Pension Fund and the beneficiaries under the ceased scheme shall be entitled to draw the benefits, not less than the benefits they were entitled to under the ceased scheme, from the Pension Fund.
4. The Pension Fund shall vest in and be administered by the Central Board in such manner as may be specified in the Pension Scheme.
5. Subject to the provisions of this Act, the Pension Scheme may provide for all or any of the matters specified in Schedule III.
6. The Pension Scheme may provide that all or any of its provisions shall take effect either prospectively or retrospectively on such date as may be specified in that behalf in that Scheme.
7. A Pension Fund Scheme, framed under sub-section (l) shall be laid, as soon as may be after it is made, before each House of Parliament, while it is in session, for a total period of 30 days which may be comprised in 1 session or in 2 or more successive sessions, and if, before the expiry of the session immediately following the session or the successive sessions aforesaid, both Houses agree in making any modification in the scheme or both Houses agree that the scheme should not be made, the scheme shall thereafter have effect only in such modified form or be of no effect, as the case may be; so, however, that any such modification or annulment shall be without prejudice to the validity of anything previously done under that scheme.

Employees' Deposit-Linked Insurance Scheme (Section 6C)

1. The Central Government may, by notification in the Official Gazette, frame a scheme to be called the Employees' Deposit-Linked Insurance Scheme for the purpose of providing life insurance benefits to the employees of any establishment or class of establishments to which this Act applies.
2. There shall be established, as soon as may be after the framing of the Insurance Scheme, a Deposit-Linked Insurance Fund into which shall be paid by the employ-

Spotlight
The Employees' Deposit-Linked Insurance Scheme provides life insurance benefits to employees.

er from time to time in respect of every such employee in relation to whom he is the employer, such amount, not being more than 1 per cent of the aggregate of the basic wages, dearness allowance and retaining allowance (if any) for the time being payable in relation to such employee, as the Central Government may, by notification in the Official Gazette, specify.

Explanation For the purposes of this sub-section, the expressions 'dearness allowance' and 'retaining allowance' have the same meaning as in Section 6.

4. (a) The employer shall pay into the Insurance Fund such further sums of money, not exceeding one-fourth of the contribution which he is required to make under sub-section (2), as the Central Government may, from time to time, determine to meet all the expenses in connection with the administration of the Insurance Scheme other than the expenses towards the cost of any benefits provided by or under that scheme.
5. The Insurance Fund shall vest in the Central Board and be administered by it in such manner as may be specified in the Insurance Scheme.
6. The Insurance Scheme may provide for all or any of the matters specified in Schedule IV.
7. The Insurance Scheme may provide that any of its provisions shall take effect either prospectively or retrospectively on such date as may be specified in this behalf in that Scheme

In *Ram Singh vs. State of Uttar Pradesh* [(2005) LLR 349 (All)] it has been laid that an employee, having withdrawn the entire amount from the Employees' Provident Fund Scheme, cannot be permitted to switch over to the Employees' Pension Scheme.

Laying of Schemes before Parliament (Section 6D)

Every scheme framed under Section 5, Section 6A and Section 6C shall be laid, as soon as may be after it is framed, before each House of Parliament, while it is in session, for a total period of 30 days which may be comprised in 1 session or in 2 or more successive sessions, and if, before the expiry of the session immediately following the session or the successive sessions aforesaid, both Houses agree in making any modification in the scheme, or both Houses agree that the scheme should not be framed, the scheme shall thereafter have effect only in such modified form or be of no effect, as the case may be; so, however, that any such modification or annulment shall be without prejudice to the validity of anything previously done under that scheme.

Modification of Scheme (Section 7)

1. The Central Government may, by notification in the Official Gazette, add to, amend or vary, either prospectively or retrospectively, the Scheme, the Pension Scheme or the Insurance Scheme, as the case may be.
2. Every notification issued under sub-section (1) shall be laid, as soon as may be after it is issued, before each House of Parliament while it is in session, for a total period of 30 days, which may be comprised in 1 session or in 2 or more successive sessions, and if, before the expiry of the session immediately following the sessions or the successive sessions aforesaid, both Houses agree in making any modification in the notification, or both Houses agree that the notification should not be issued, the notification shall thereafter have effect only in such modified form or be of no effect, as the case may be; so, however, that any such modification or annulment shall be without prejudice to the validity of anything previously done under that notification.

Determination of Moneys Due from Employers (Section 7A)

1. The Central Provident Fund Commissioner, any Additional Central Provident Fund Commissioner, any Deputy Provident Fund Commissioner, any Regional Provident Fund Commissioner or any Assistant Provident Fund Commissioner may, by order,
   (a) in a case where a dispute arises regarding the applicability of this Act to an establishment, decide such dispute; and
   (b) determine the amount due from any employer under any provision of this Act, the Scheme or the Pension Scheme or the Insurance Scheme, as the case may be,

   and for any of the aforesaid purposes may conduct such inquiry as he may deem necessary.
2. The officer conducting the inquiry under sub-section (1) shall, for the purposes of such inquiry, have the same powers as are vested in a Court under the Code of Civil Procedure, 1908, for trying a suit in respect of the following matters, namely:
   (a) enforcing the attendance of any person or examining him on oath;
   (b) requiring the discovery and production of documents;
   (c) receiving evidence on affidavit;
   (d) issuing commissions for the examination of witnesses;

   and any such inquiry shall be deemed to be a judicial proceeding within the meaning of sections 193 and 228, and for the purpose of Section 196, of the Indian Penal Code, 1860.
3. No order shall be made under sub-section (1), unless the employer concerned is given a reasonable opportunity of representing his case.

3A. Where the employer, employee or any other person required to attend the inquiry under sub-section (1) fails to attend such inquiry without assigning any valid reason or fails to produce any document or to file any report or return when called upon to do so, the officer conducting the inquiry may decide the applicability of the Act or determine the amount due from any employer, as the case may be, on the basis of the evidence adduced during such inquiry and other documents available on record.

4. Where an order under sub-section (1) is passed against an employer *ex parte*, he may, within 3 months from the date of communication of such order, apply to the officer for setting aside such order and if he satisfies the officer that the show cause notice was not duly served or that he was prevented by any sufficient cause from appearing when the inquiry was held, the officer shall make an order setting aside his earlier order and shall appoint a date for proceeding with the inquiry:

   Provided that no such order shall be set aside merely on the ground that there has been an irregularity in the service of the show cause notice if the officer is satisfied that the employer had notice of the date of hearing and had sufficient time to appear before the officer.

   Explanation Where an appeal has been preferred under this Act against an order passed *ex parte* and such appeal has been disposed of otherwise than on the ground that the appellant has withdrawn the appeal, no application shall lie under this sub-section for setting aside the *ex parte* order.
5. No order passed under this section shall be set aside on any application under sub-section (4) unless notice thereof has been served on the opposite party.

In *Food Corporation of India vs. Provident Fund Commissioner and Others* [(1990) 1 SCC 68] it is held that "...the Commissioner is authorised to enforce attendance in person and also to examine any person on oath. He has the power requiring the discovery and production of documents. This power was given to the Commissioner to decide not abstract question of law, but only to determine actual concrete differences in payment of contribution and other dues by identifying the workmen. The Commissioner should exercise all his power to collect all evidence and collate all material before coming to proper conclusion. That is the legal duty of the Commissioner."

(Adapted from: Labour Law Reporter, October, 2012, p. 1097.)

In *K. S. Engineers & Contractors vs. Assistant Provident Fund Commissioner and Another* [(2012) LLR 809] the petitioner has alleged to have employed 4 to 5 persons since 1997 to 2003. When the number of persons in 2003 reached 20, it applied for EPF code number and has been making contributions regularly thereafter. The EPF Authority initiated proceedings under Section 7A and ordered to pay the outstanding amount from 1997 to March, 2003. The Court has held that when an employer fails to submit relevant records like attendance register, salary register and balance sheet before the designated authority in enquiry under Section 7A of the Act so as to satisfy the authority with regard to non-applicability of the Act by proving that at the relevant point of time, the employees engaged were less than 20 and the provisions of the Act were not applicable during the relevant period, the liability has to be determined on the basis of the available material.

(Adapted from: Labour Law Reporter, August, 2012, p. 809.)

CASE CORNER

In *Sushil Choudhury vs. Union of India* [(2007) IIILLJ 925 Gau], the writ petitioner is the proprietor of two establishments, viz. a newspaper, *Dainik Ganadoot*, and a printing press under the name "Pioneer Press". The writ petition is in response to the order of the Regional Provident Fund Commissioner under Section 7A of the Employees' Provident Funds and Miscellaneous Provisions Act, 1952, (in short, Act) for recovery of dues as provided under Section 8 of the Act. The present writ petition claimed that the provision of the Act and the Scheme are not applicable to *Dainik Ganadoot*, being a newspaper establishment. It also contended that Pioneer Press and *Dainik Ganadoot* are separate and independent establishments. It is the case of the petitioner that Pioneer Press is registered and licensed under the Factories Act, 1948, having 9 workers, while *Dainik Ganadoot* is a newspaper establishment with 14 workers, out of whom 4 are casual and temporary workers recruited on daily basis. The petitioner has argued that even if the said two establishments are taken to be one and the same total number of persons employed taken together is less than 20 persons, as 4 casual employees cannot be counted for determining the number of employees under Section 1(3).

The representation submitted by the petitioner before the Regional Provident Fund Commissioner in the proceedings under Section 7A of the Act does not clearly mention that 4 workers employed in the *Dainik Ganadoot* are casual and as such they could not be counted in calculating the total number of persons employed in *Dainik Ganadoot* under Section 1(3). The Regional Provident Fund Commissioner passed the final order under Section 7A with a finding that Pioneer Press and *Dainik Ganadoot* came under the list of industry or class of establishments coverable under the Act. They are to be treated as 1 establishment for application of the provisions of the Act and schemes framed thereunder due to factual situations like: they are situated in the same premises with common address; they have common office management; they are owned by the same proprietor/occupier; there is functional integrity as the newspaper is printed in the press; attendance of the employees for both are recorded in one and the same register; there is inter-transferability of employees; there was only 1 balance sheet up to 1990-1991 for both the units; there is financial, management, functional and locational integrity between them; and both together employed 23 persons on 1st July 1993.

The Court held that in absence of materials and/or reasons for classifying the said employees as casual employees of *Dainik Ganadoot*, the said submissions for the petitioner cannot be accepted.

(Adapted from: www.indiankanoon.org/doc/1053526/ accessed on 1/5/2014.)

Review of Orders Passed under Section 7A (Section 7B)

1. Any person aggrieved by an order made under sub-section (1) of Section 7A, but from which no appeal has been preferred under this Act, and who, from the discovery of new and important matter or evidence which, after the exercise of due diligence was not within his knowledge or could not be produced by him at the time when the order was made, or on account of some mistake or error apparent on the face of the record or for any other sufficient reason, desires to obtain a review of such order may apply for a review of that order to the officer who passed the order:

   Provided that such officer may also on his own motion review his order if he is satisfied that it is necessary so to do on any such ground.
2. Every application for review under sub-section (1) shall be filed in such form and manner and within such time as may be specified in the Scheme.
3. Where it appears to the officer receiving an application for review that there is no sufficient ground for a review, he shall reject the application.
4. Where the officer is of the opinion that the application for review should be granted, he shall grant the same:

   Provided that,

   (a) no such application shall be granted without previous notice to all the parties before him to enable them to appear and be heard in support of the order in respect of which a review is applied for, and

   (b) no such application shall be granted on the ground of discovery of new matter or evidence which the applicant alleges was not within his knowledge or could not be produced by him when the order was made, without proof of such allegation.
5. No appeal shall lie against the order of the officer rejecting an application for review, but an appeal under this Act shall lie against an order passed under review as if the order passed under review were the original order passed by him under Section 7A.

Determination of Escaped Amount (Section 7C)

Where an order determining the amount due from an employer under Section 7A or Section 7B has been passed and if the officer who passed the order–

(a) has reason to believe that by reason of the omission or failure on the part of the employer to make any document or report available, or to disclose, fully and truly, all material facts necessary for determining the correct amount due from the employer, any amount so due from such employer for any period has escaped his notice;

(b) has, in consequence of information in his possession, reason to believe that any amount to be determined under Section 7A or Section 7B has escaped from his determination for any period notwithstanding that there has been no omission or failure as mentioned in clause (a) on the part of the employer, he may, within a period of 5 years from the date of communication of the order passed under Section 7A or Section 7B, re-open the case and pass appropriate orders re-determining the amount due from the employer in accordance with the provisions of this Act:

Provided that no order re-determining the amount due from the employer shall be passed under this section unless the employer is given a reasonable opportunity of representing his case.

Employees' Provident Funds Appellate Tribunal (Section 7D)

1. The Central Government may, by notification in the Official Gazette, constitute 1 or more Appellate Tribunals to be known as the Employees' Provident Funds Appellate Tribunal to exercise the powers and discharge the functions conferred on such Tribunal by this Act and every such Tribunal shall have jurisdiction in respect of establishments situated in such area as may be specified in the notification constituting the Tribunal.
2. A Tribunal shall consist of 1 person only to be appointed by the Central Government.
3. A person shall not be qualified for appointment as a Presiding Officer of a Tribunal (hereinafter referred to as the Presiding Officer) unless he is, or has been, or is qualified to be,
   (i) a Judge of a High Court; or
   (ii) a District Judge.

Spotlight
The Central Government may constitute 1 or more EPF Appellate Tribunals to exercise the powers and discharge the functions conferred on it by the Act, as given in Section 7D(1).

Term of Office (Section 7E)

The Presiding Officer of a Tribunal shall hold office for a term of 5 years from the date on which he enters upon his office or until he attains the age of 62 years, whichever is earlier.

Resignation (Section 7F)

1. The Presiding Officer may, by notice in writing under his hand addressed to the Central Government, resign his office:

   Provided that the Presiding Officer shall, unless he is permitted by the Central Government to relinquish his office sooner, continue to hold office until the expiry of 3 months from the date of receipt of such notice or until a person duly appointed as his successor enters upon his office or until the expiry of his term of office, whichever is the earliest.
2. The Presiding Officer shall not be removed from his office except by an order made by the President on the ground of proved misbehaviour or incapacity after an inquiry made by a Judge of the High Court in which such Presiding Officer had been informed of the charges against him and given a reasonable opportunity of being heard in respect of those charges.
3. The Central Government may, by rules, regulate the procedure for the investigation of misbehaviour or incapacity of the Presiding Officer.

Salary and Allowances and Other Terms and Conditions of Service of Presiding Officer (Section 7G)

The salary and allowances payable to, and the other terms and conditions of service (including pension, gratuity and other retirement benefits) of the Presiding Officer shall be such as may be prescribed:

Provided that neither the salary and allowances nor the other terms and conditions of service of the Presiding Officer shall be varied to his disadvantage after his appointment.

Staff of the Tribunal (Section 7H)

1. The Central Government shall determine the nature and categories of the officers and other employees required to assist a Tribunal in the discharge of its functions and provide the Tribunal with such officers and other employees as it may think fit.
2. The officers and other employees of a Tribunal shall discharge their functions under the general superintendence of the Presiding Officer.
3. The salaries and allowances and other conditions of service of the officers and other employees of a Tribunal shall be such as may be prescribed.

Appeals to Tribunal (Section 7I)

1. Any person aggrieved by a notification issued by the Central Government, or an order passed by the Central Government or any authority, under the proviso to sub-section (3), or sub-section (4), of Section 1, or Section 3, or sub-section (1) of Section 7A, or Section 7B except an order rejecting an application for review referred to in sub-section (5) thereof, or Section 7C, or Section 14B, may prefer an appeal to a Tribunal against such notification or order.
2. Every appeal under sub-section (1) shall be filed in such form and manner, within such time and be accompanied by such fees, as may be prescribed.

Spotlight

As per Section 7I(1), any person aggrieved by a notification issued or an order passed by the Central Government or any authority may prefer an appeal to a Tribunal against such notification or order.

Procedure of Tribunals (Section 7J)

1. A Tribunal shall have power to regulate its own procedure in all matters arising out of the exercise of its powers or of the discharge of its functions including the places at which the Tribunal shall have its sittings.
2. A Tribunal shall, for the purposes of discharging its functions, have all the powers which are vested in the officers referred to in Section 7A and any proceeding before the Tribunal shall be deemed to be a judicial proceeding within the meaning of sections 193 and 228, and for the purpose of Section 196 of the Indian Penal Code, 1860, the Tribunal shall be deemed to be a civil court for all the purposes of Section 195 and Chapter XXVI of the Code of Criminal Procedure, 1973.

Right of Appellant to Take Assistance of Legal Practitioner and of Government etc., to Appoint Presenting Officers (Section 7K)

1. A person preferring an appeal to a Tribunal under this Act may either appear in person or take the assistance of a legal practitioner of his choice to present his case before the Tribunal.
2. The Central Government or a State Government or any other authority under this Act may authorise one or more legal practitioners or any of its officers to act as presenting officers and every person so authorised may present the case with respect to any appeal before a Tribunal.

Orders of Tribunal (Section 7L)

1. A Tribunal may, after giving the parties to the appeal, an opportunity of being heard, pass such orders thereon as it thinks fit, confirming, modifying or annulling the order appealed against or may refer the case back to the authority which passed such order with such directions as the Tribunal may think fit, for a fresh adjudication or order, as the case may be, after taking additional evidence, if necessary.
2. A Tribunal may, at any time within 5 years from the date of its order, with a view to rectifying any mistake apparent from the record, amend any order passed by it under sub-section (1) and shall make such amendment in the order if the mistake is brought to its notice by the parties to the appeal:

   Provided that an amendment which has the effect of enhancing the amount due from, or otherwise increasing the liability of, the employer shall not be made under this sub-section, unless the Tribunal has given notice to him of its intention to do so and has allowed him a reasonable opportunity of being heard.
3. A Tribunal shall send a copy of every order passed under this section to the parties to the appeal.
4. Any order made by a Tribunal finally disposing of an appeal shall not be questioned in any court of law.

Filling up of Vacancies (Section 7M)

If, for any reason, a vacancy occurs in the office of the Presiding Officer, the Central Government shall appoint another person in accordance with the provisions of this Act, to fill the vacancy and the proceedings may be continued before a Tribunal from the stage at which the vacancy is filled.

Finality of Orders Constituting a Tribunal (Section 7N)

No order of the Central Government appointing any person as the Presiding Officer shall be called in question in any manner, and no act or proceeding before a Tribunal shall be called in question in any manner on the ground merely of any defect in the constitution of such Tribunal.

Deposit of Amount Due, on Filing Appeal (Section 7O)

No appeal by the employer shall be entertained by a Tribunal unless he has deposited with it 75 per cent of the amount due from him as determined by an officer referred to in Section 7A:

Provided that the Tribunal may, for reasons to be recorded in writing, waive or reduce the amount to be deposited under this section.

Transfer of Certain Applications to Tribunals (Section 7P)

All applications which are pending before the Central Government under Section 19A, before its repeal, shall stand transferred to a Tribunal exercising jurisdiction in respect of establishment in relation to which such applications had been made as if such applications were appeals preferred to the Tribunal.

Interest Payable by the Employer (Section 7Q)

The employer shall be liable to pay simple interest at the rate of 12 per cent per annum or at such higher rate as may be specified in the Scheme on any amount due from him under this Act from the date on which the amount has become so due till the date of its actual payment:

Provided that higher rate of interest specified in the Scheme shall not exceed the lending rate of interest charged by any scheduled bank.

Mode of Recovery of Moneys Due from Employers (Section 8)

Any amount due:

(a) from the employer in relation to an establishment to which any Scheme or the Insurance Scheme applies in respect of any contribution payable to the Fund or, as the case may be, the Insurance Fund, damages recoverable under Section 14B, accumulations required to be transferred under sub-section (2) of Section 15 or under sub-section (5) of Section 17 or any charges payable by him under any other provision of this Act or of any provision of the Scheme or the Insurance Scheme; or

(b) from the employer in relation to any exempted establishment in respect of any damages recoverable under Section 14B or any charges payable by him to the appropriate Government under any provision of this Act or under any of the conditions specified under Section 17 or in respect of the contribution payable by him towards the Pension Scheme under the said Section 17

may, if the amount is in arrear, be recovered in the manner specified in sections 8B to 8G.

Recovery of Moneys by Employers and Contractors (Section 8A)

1. The amount of contribution (that is to say the employer's contribution as well as the employee's contribution in pursuance of any Scheme and the employer's contribution in pursuance of the Insurance Scheme), and any charges for meeting the cost of administering the Fund paid or payable by an employer in respect of an employee employed by or through a contractor may be recovered by such employer from the contractor, either by deduction from any amount payable to the contractor under any contract or as a debt payable by the contractor.
2. A contractor from whom the amounts mentioned in sub-section (1) may be recovered in respect of any employee employed by or through him, may recover from such employee the employee's contribution under any Scheme by deduction from the basic wages, dearness allowance and retaining allowance (if any) payable to such employee.
3. Notwithstanding any contract to the contrary, no contractor shall be entitled to deduct the employer's contribution or the charges referred to in sub-section (1) from the basic wages, dearness allowance and retaining allowance (if any) payable to an employee employed by or through him or otherwise to recover such contribution or charges from such employee.

Spotlight

No contractor, provides Section 8A(3), is entitled to deduct the employer's contribution from the basic wages, dearness allowance and retaining allowance (if any) payable to an employee employed by or through him.

Explanation In this section, the expressions, 'dearness allowance' and 'retaining allowance' shall have the same meanings as in Section 6.

Issue of Certificate to the Recovery Officer (Section 8B)

1. Where any amount is in arrear under Section 8, the authorised officer may issue, to the Recovery Officer, a certificate under his signature specifying the amount of arrears and the Recovery Officer, on receipt of such certificate, shall proceed to recover the amount specified therein from the

establishment or, as the case may be, the employer by 1 or more of the modes mentioned below:
(a) attachment and sale of the movable or immovable property of the establishment or as the case may be, the employer;
(b) arrest of the employer and his detention in prison;
(c) appointing a receiver for the management of the movable or immovable properties of the establishment or, as the case may be, the employer:

Provided that the attachment and sale of any property under this section shall first be effected against the properties of the establishment and where such attachment and sale is insufficient for recovering the whole of the amount of arrears specified in the certificate, the Recovery Officer may take such proceedings against the property of the employer for recovery of the whole or any part of such arrears.

2. The authorised officer may issue a certificate under sub-section (1), notwithstanding that proceedings for recovery of the arrears by any other mode have been taken.

Recovery Officer to Whom Certificate is to be Forwarded (Section 8C)

1. The authorised officer may forward the certificate referred to in Section 8B to the Recovery Officer within whose jurisdiction the employer:
   (a) carries on his business or profession or within whose jurisdiction the principal place of his establishment is situate; or
   (b) resides or any movable or immovable property of the establishment or the employer is situate.
2. Where an establishment or the employer has property within the jurisdiction of more than 1 Recovery Officers and the Recovery Officer to whom a certificate is sent by the authorised officer:
   (a) is not able to recover the entire amount by the sale of the property, movable or immovable, within his jurisdiction; or
   (b) is of the opinion that, for the purpose of expediting or securing the recovery of the whole or any part of the amount, it is necessary so to do,

   he may send the certificate or, where only a part of the amount is to be recovered, a copy of the certificate certified in the prescribed manner and specifying the amount to be recovered to the Recovery Officer within whose jurisdiction the establishment or the employer has property or the employer resides, and thereupon that Recovery Officer shall also proceed to recover the amount due under this section as if the certificate or the copy thereof had been the certificate sent to him by the authorised officer.

Validity of Certificate and Amendment thereof (Section 8D)

1. When the authorised officer issues a certificate to a Recovery Officer under Section 8B, it shall not be open to the employer to dispute before the Recovery Officer the correctness of the amount, and no objection to the certificate on any other ground shall also be entertained by the Recovery Officer.
2. Notwithstanding the issue of a certificate to a Recovery Officer, the authorised officer shall have power to withdraw the certificate or correct any clerical or arithmetical mistake in the certificate by sending intimation to the Recovery Officer.
3. The authorised officer shall intimate to the Recovery Officer any orders withdrawing or cancelling a certificate or any correction made by him under sub-section (2) or any amendment made under sub-section (4) of Section 8E.

Stay of Proceedings under Certificate and Amendment or Withdrawal thereof (Section 8E)

1. Notwithstanding that a certificate has been issued to the Recovery Officer for the recovery of any amount, the authorised officer may grant time for the payment of the amount, and thereupon the Recovery Officer shall stay the proceedings until the expiry of the time so granted.
2. Where a certificate for the recovery of amount has been issued, the authorised officer shall keep the Recovery Officer informed of any amount paid or time granted for payment, subsequent to the issue of such certificate.
3. Where the order giving rise to a demand of amount for which a certificate for recovery has been issued has been modified in appeal or other proceeding under this Act, and, as a consequence thereof, the demand is reduced but the order is the subject-matter of a further proceeding under this Act, the authorised officer shall stay the recovery of such part of the amount of the certificate as pertains to the said reduction for the period for which the appeal or other proceeding remains pending.
4. Where a certificate for the recovery of amount has been issued and subsequently the amount of the outstanding demand is reduced as a result of an appeal or other proceeding under this Act, the authorised officer shall, when the order which was the subject-matter of such appeal or other proceeding has become final and conclusive, amend the certificate or withdraw it, as the case may be.

Other Modes of Recovery (Section 8F)

1. Notwithstanding the issue of a certificate to the Recovery Officer under Section 8B, the Central Provident Fund Commissioner or any other officer authorised by the Central Board may recover the amount by any one or more of the modes provided in this section.
2. If any amount is due from any person to any employer who is in arrears, the Central Provident Fund Commissioner or any other officer authorised by the Central Board in this behalf may require such person to deduct from the said amount the arrears due from such employer under this Act, and such person shall comply with any such requisition and shall pay the sum so deducted to the credit of the Central Provident Fund Commissioner or the officer so authorised, as the case may be:

   Provided that nothing in this sub-section shall apply to any part of the amount exempt from attachment in execution of a decree of a civil court under Section 60 of the Code of Civil Procedure, 1908.
3. (i) The Central Provident Fund Commissioner or any other officer authorised by the Central Board in this behalf may, at any time or from time to time, by notice in writing, require any person from whom money is due or may become due to the employer or, as the case may be, the establishment or any person who holds or may subsequently hold money for or on account of the employer or, as the case may be, the establishment to pay to the Central Provident Fund Commissioner either forthwith upon the money becoming due or being held or at or within the time specified in the notice (not being before the money becomes due or is held) so much of the money as is sufficient to pay the amount due from the employer in respect of arrears or the whole of the money when it is equal to or less than that amount.

   (ii) A notice under this sub-section may be issued to any person who holds or may subsequently hold any money for or on account of the employer jointly with any other person and for the purposes of this sub-section, the shares of the joint holders in such account shall be presumed, until the contrary is proved, to be equal.

(iii) A copy of the notice shall be forwarded to the employer at his last address known to the Central Provident Fund Commissioner, or as the case may be, the officer so authorised and in the case of a joint account to all the joint holders at their last addresses known to the Central Provident Fund Commissioner or the officer so authorised.

(iv) Save as otherwise provided in this sub-section, every person to whom a notice is issued under this sub-section shall be bound to comply with such notice, and, in particular, where any such notice is issued to a post office, bank or an insurer, it shall not be necessary for any pass book, deposit receipt, policy or any other document to be produced for the purpose of any entry, endorsement or the like being made before payment is made notwithstanding any rule, practice or requirement to the contrary.

(v) Any claim respecting any property in relation to which a notice under this sub-section has been issued arising after the date of the notice shall be void as against any demand contained in the notice.

(vi) Where a person to whom a notice under this sub-section is sent objects to it by a statement on oath that the sum demanded or any part thereof is not due to the employer or that he does not hold any money for or on account of the employer, then, nothing contained in this sub-section shall be deemed to require such person to pay any such sum or part thereof, as the case may be, but if it is discovered that such a statement was false in any material particular, such person shall be personally liable to the Central Provident Fund Commissioner or the officer so authorised to the extent of his own liability to the employer on the date of the notice, or to the extent of the employer's liability for any sum due under this Act, whichever is less.

(vii) The Central Provident Fund Commissioner or the officer so authorised may, at any time or from time to time, amend or revoke any notice issued under this sub-section or extend the time for making any payment in pursuance of such notice.

(viii) The Central Provident Fund Commissioner or the officer so authorised shall grant a receipt for any amount paid in compliance with a notice issued under this sub-section, and the person so paying shall be fully discharged from his liability to the employer to the extent of the amount so paid.

(ix) Any person discharging any liability to the employer after the receipt of a notice under this sub-section shall be personally liable to the Central Provident Fund Commissioner or the officer so authorised to the extent of his own liability to the employer so discharged or to the extent of the employer's liability for any sum due under this Act, whichever is less.

(x) If the person to whom a notice under this sub-section is sent fails to make payment in pursuance thereof to the Central Provident Fund Commissioner or the officer so authorised, he shall be deemed to be an employer in default in respect of the amount specified in the notice and further proceedings may be taken against him for the realisation of the amount as if it were an arrear due from him, in the manner provided in sections 8B to 8E and the notice shall have the same effect as an attachment of a debt by the Recovery Officer in exercise of his powers under Section 8B.

4. The Central Provident Fund Commissioner or the officer authorised by the Central Board in this behalf may apply to the court in whose custody there is money belonging to the employer for payment to him of the entire amount of such money, or if it is more than the amount due, an amount sufficient to discharge the amount due.

5. The Central Provident Fund Commissioner or any officer not below the rank of Assistant Provident Fund Commissioner may, if so authorised by the Central Government by general or special order, recover any arrears of amount due from an employer or, as the case may be, from the establishment by distraint and sale of his or its movable property in the manner laid down in the Third Schedule to the Income-tax Act, 1961.

Application of Certain Provisions of Income-tax Act (Section 8G)

The provisions of the Second and Third Schedules to the Income-tax Act, 1961 and the Income Tax (Certificate Proceeding) Rules, 1962, as in force from time to time, shall apply with necessary modifications as if the said provisions and the rules referred to the arrears of the amount mentioned in Section 8 of this Act instead of to the income-tax:

Provided that any reference in the said provisions and the rules to the "assessee" shall be construed as a reference to an employer as defined in this Act.

Fund to be Recognised under Act 11 of 1922 (Section 9)

For the purposes of the Indian Income-tax Act, 1922, the Fund shall be deemed to be a recognised provident fund within the meaning of Chapter IXA of the Act:

Provided that nothing contained in the said Chapter shall operate to render ineffective any provision of the Scheme (under which the Fund is established) which is repugnant to any of the provisions of that Chapter or of the rules made thereunder.

Protection against Attachment (Section 10)

1. The amount standing to the credit of any member in the Fund or of any exempted employee in a provident fund shall not in any way be capable of being assigned or charged and shall not be liable to attachment under any decree or order of any Court in respect of any debt or liability incurred by the member or the exempted employee, and neither the official assignee appointed under the Presidency Towns Insolvency Act, 1909, or any receiver appointed under the Provincial Insolvency Act, 1920, shall be entitled to, or have any claim on, any such amount.
2. Any amount standing to the credit of a member in the fund or of an exempted employee in a provident fund at the time of his death and payable to his nominee under the Scheme or the rules of the provident fund shall, subject to any deduction authorised by the said Scheme or rules, vest in the nominee and shall be free from any debt or other liability incurred by the deceased or the nominee before the death of the member or of the exempted employee, and shall also not be liable to attachment under any decree or order of any Court.
3. The provisions of sub-section (1) and sub-section (2) shall, so far as may be, apply in relation to the pension or any other amount payable under the Pension Scheme and also in relation to any amount payable under the Insurance Scheme as they apply in relation to any amount payable out of the Fund.

Priority of Payment of Contributions over Other Debts (Section 11)

1. Where any employer is adjudicated insolvent or, being a company, an order for winding up is made, the amount due:
   (a) from the employer in relation to an establishment to which any Scheme or the Insurance Scheme applies in respect of any contribution payable to the Fund or, as the case may be,

the Insurance Fund, damages recoverable under Section 14B, accumulations required to be transferred under sub-section (2) of Section 15 or any charges payable by him under any other provision of this Act or of any provision of the Scheme or the Insurance Scheme; or

(b) from the employer in relation to an exempted establishment in respect of any contribution to the provident fund or any insurance fund (in so far as it relates to exempted employees), under the rules of the provident fund or any insurance fund, any contribution payable by him towards the Pension Fund under sub-section (6) of Section 17, damages recoverable under Section 14B or any charges payable by him to the appropriate Government under any provision of this Act or under any of the conditions specified under Section 17,

shall, where the liability therefor has accrued before the order of adjudication or winding up is made, be deemed to be included among the debts which under Section 49 of the Presidency-Towns Insolvency Act, 1909 or under Section 61 of the Provincial Insolvency Act, 1920 or under Section 530 of the Companies Act, 1956, are to be paid in priority to all other debts in the distribution of the property of the insolvent or the assets of the company being wound up, as the case may be.

Explanation In this sub-section and in Section 17, "insurance fund" means any fund established by an employer under any scheme for providing benefits in the nature of life insurance to employees, whether linked to their deposits in provident fund or not, without payment by the employees of any separate contribution or premium in that behalf.

2. Without prejudice to the provisions of sub-section (1), if any amount is due from an employer whether in respect of the employee's contribution (deducted from the wages of the employee) or the employer's contribution, the amount so due shall be deemed to be the first charge on the assets of the establishment, and shall, notwithstanding anything contained in any other law for the time being in force, be paid in priority to all other debts.

Employer not to Reduce Wages, etc. (Section 12)

No employer in relation to an establishment to which any Scheme or the Insurance Scheme applies shall, by reason only of his liability for the payment of any contribution to the Fund or the Insurance Fund or any charges under this Act or the Scheme or the Insurance Scheme reduce whether directly or indirectly, the wages of any employee to whom the Scheme or the Insurance Scheme applies or the total quantum of benefits in the nature of old age pension, gratuity, provident fund or life insurance to which the employee is entitled under the terms of his employment, express or implied.

Spotlight

Section 12 provides that no employer shall, because of his liability for the payment of any contribution to the Fund or the Insurance Fund, reduce, directly or indirectly, the wages of any employee to whom the Scheme or the Insurance Scheme applies.

Inspectors (Section 13)

1. The appropriate Government may, by notification in the Official Gazette, appoint such persons as it thinks fit to be Inspectors for the purposes of this Act, the Scheme, the Pension Scheme or the Insurance Scheme, and may define their jurisdiction.
2. Any Inspector appointed under sub-section (1) may, for the purpose of inquiring into the correctness of any information furnished in connection with this Act or with any Scheme or the Insurance Scheme or for the purpose of ascertaining whether any of the provisions of this Act or of any Scheme or the Insurance Scheme have been complied with in respect of an establishment to which any Scheme or the Insurance Scheme applies or for the purpose of ascertaining whether

the provisions of this Act or any Scheme or the Insurance Scheme are applicable to any establishment to which the Scheme or the Insurance Scheme has not been applied or for the purpose of determining whether the conditions subject to which exemption was granted under Section 17 are being complied with by the employer in relation to an exempted establishment–

(a) require an employer or any contractor from whom any amount is recoverable under Section 8A to furnish such information as he may consider necessary;

(b) at any reasonable time and with such assistance, if any, as he may think fit, enter and search any establishment or any premises connected therewith and require any one found in charge thereof to produce before him for examination any accounts, books, registers and other documents relating to the employment of persons or the payment of wages in the establishment;

(c) examine, with respect to any matter relevant to any of the purposes aforesaid, the employer or any contractor from whom any amount is recoverable under Section 8A, his agent or servant or any other person found in charge of the establishment or any premises connected therewith or whom the Inspector has reasonable cause to believe to be or to have been an employee in the establishment;

(d) make copies of, or take extracts from, any book, register or other document maintained in relation to the establishment and, where he has reason to believe that any offence under this Act has been committed by an employer, seize with such assistance as he may think fit, such book, register or other document or portions thereof as he may consider relevant in respect of that offence;

(e) exercise such other powers as the Scheme or the Insurance Scheme may provide.

2A. Any Inspector appointed under sub-section (1) may, for the purpose of inquiring into the correctness of any information furnished in connection with the Pension Scheme or for the purpose of ascertaining whether any of the provisions of this Act or of the Pension Scheme have been complied with in respect of an establishment to which the Pension Scheme applies, exercise all or any of the powers conferred on him under clause (a), clause (b), clause (c) or clause (d) of sub-section (2).

2B. The provisions of the Code of Criminal Procedure, 1974, shall, so far as may be, apply to any search or seizure under sub-section (2) or under sub-section (2A), as the case may be, as they apply to any search or seizure made under the authority of a warrant issued under Section 98 of the said Code.

Penalties (Section 14)

1. Whoever, for the purpose of avoiding any payment to be made by himself under this Act , the Scheme the Pension Scheme or the Insurance Scheme or of enabling any other person to avoid such payment, knowingly makes or causes to be made any false statement or false representation shall be punishable with imprisonment for a term which may extend to 1 year, or with fine of ₹5,000, or with both.

Spotlight

Penalty for false statement or false representation is imprisonment for a term up to 1 year, or with fine of ₹5,000, or with both, as provided in Section 14(1).

1A. An employer who contravenes, or makes default in complying with, the provisions of Section 6 or clause (a) of sub-section (3) of Section 17 in so far as it relates to the payment of inspection charges, or paragraph 38 of the Scheme in so far as it relates to the payment of administrative charges, shall be punishable with imprisonment for a term which may extend to 3 years, but–

(a) which shall not be less than 1 year and a fine of ₹10,000 in case of default in payment of the employees' contributions which has been deducted by the employer from the employees' wages;

(b) which shall not be less than 6 months and a fine of ₹5,000 in any other case:

Provided that the Court may, for any adequate and special reasons to be recorded in the judgment, impose a sentence of imprisonment for a lesser term.

1B. An employer who contravenes, or makes default in complying with, the provisions of Section 6C, or clause (a) of sub-section (3A) of Section 17 in so far as it relates to the payment of inspection charges, shall be punishable with imprisonment for a term which may extend to 1 year but which shall not be less than 6 months and shall also be liable to fine which may extend to ₹5,000:

Provided that the Court may, for any adequate and special reasons to be recorded in the judgment, impose a sentence of imprisonment for a lesser term.

2. Subject to the provisions of this Act, the Scheme, the Pension Scheme or the Insurance Scheme may provide that any person who contravenes, or makes default in complying with, any of the provisions thereof shall be punishable with imprisonment for a term which may extend to 1 year, or with fine which may extend to ₹4,000, or with both.

2A. Whoever contravenes or makes default in complying with any provision of this Act or of any condition subject to which exemption was granted under Section 17 shall, if no other penalty is elsewhere provided by or under this Act for such contravention or non-compliance, be punishable with imprisonment which may extend to 6 months, but which shall not be less than 1 month and shall also be liable to fine which may extend to ₹5,000.

Offences by Companies (Section 14A)

1. If the person committing an offence under this Act, the Scheme or the Pension Scheme or the Insurance Scheme is a company, every person, who at the time the offence was committed was in charge of, and was responsible to, the company for the conduct of the business of the company, as well as the company, shall be deemed to be guilty of the offence and shall be liable to be proceeded against and punished accordingly:

   Provided that nothing contained in this sub-section shall render any such person liable to any punishment, if he proves that the offence was committed without his knowledge or that he exercised all due diligence to prevent the commission of such offence.

2. Notwithstanding anything contained in sub-section (1), where an offence under this Act, the Scheme or the Pension Scheme or the Insurance Scheme has been committed by a company and it is proved that the offence has been committed with the consent or connivance of, or is attributable to, any neglect on the part of, any director or manager, secretary or other officer of the company, such director, manager, secretary or other officer shall be deemed to be guilty of that offence and shall be liable to be proceeded against and punished accordingly.

Explanation For the purposes of this section,

(a) "company" means any body corporate and includes a firm and other association of individuals; and

(b) "director" in relation to a firm, means a partner in the firm.

Enhanced Punishment in Certain Cases after Previous Conviction (Section 14AA)

Whoever, having been convicted by a court of an offence punishable under this Act, the Scheme or the Pension Scheme or the Insurance Scheme, commits the same offence shall be subject for every such subsequent offence to imprisonment for a term which may extend to 5 years, but which shall not be less than 2 years, and shall also be liable to a fine of ₹25,000.

Certain Offences to be Cognizable (Section 14AB)

Notwithstanding anything contained in the Code of Criminal Procedure, 1898, an offence relating to default in payment of contribution by the employer punishable under this Act shall be cognizable.

Cognizance and Trial of Offences (Section 14AC)

1. No court shall take cognizance of any offence punishable under this Act, the Scheme or the Pension Scheme or the Insurance Scheme, except on a report in writing of the facts constituting such offence made with the previous sanction of the Central Provident Fund Commissioner or such other officer as may be authorised by the Central Government, by notification in the Official Gazette, in this behalf, by an Inspector appointed under Section 13.
2. No court inferior to that of a Presidency Magistrate or a Magistrate of the first class shall try any offence under this Act or the Scheme or the Pension Scheme or the Insurance Scheme.

Power to Recover Damages (Section 14B)

> **Spotlight**
> Recovery of damages from the employer by way of penalty should not exceed the amount of arrears.

Where an employer makes default in the payment of any contribution to the Fund, the Pension Fund or the Insurance Fund or in the transfer of accumulations required to be transferred by him under sub-section (2) of Section 15 or sub-section (5) of Section 17 or in the payment of any charges payable under any other provision of this Act or of any Scheme or Insurance Scheme or under any of the conditions specified under Section 17, the Central Provident Fund Commissioner or such other officer as may be authorised by the Central Government, by notification in the Official Gazette, in this behalf may recover from the employer by way of penalty such damages, not exceeding the amount of arrears, as may be specified in the Scheme:

Provided that before levying and recovering such damages, the employer shall be given a reasonable opportunity of being heard:

Provided further that the Central Board may reduce or waive the damages levied under this section in relation to an establishment which is a sick industrial company and in respect of which a scheme for rehabilitation has been sanctioned by the Board for Industrial and Financial Reconstruction established under Section 4 of the Sick Industrial Companies (Special Provisions) Act, 1985, subject to such terms and conditions as may be specified in the Scheme.

In *Organo Chemical Industries and Another vs. Union of India and Others* [(1980) SCR (1) 61], the Court puts forth the fact that the authorities had noticed in the working of the Act and the Scheme that an employer could delay payment of provident fund dues without any additional financial liability. Accordingly the Act was amended and Section 14B was inserted for recovery of damages on the amount of arrears. The object and purpose of such insertion was to authorise the Regional Provident Fund Commissioners to impose exemplary punitive damages and thereby to prevent employers from making defaults. In its original form Section 14B provided for imposition of such damages 'not exceeding 25 per cent on the amount of arrears'. This however did not prove to be sufficiently deterrent and employers were still making defaults in making contributions to the provident fund. In fact, they were utilising both their own contribution as well as the employees' contributions in their business. The National Commission on Labour recommended that in order to check the growth of arrears, penalties for default in payment of provident fund dues should be made more stringent and that the default should be made cognizable. Accordingly, the Act was further amended by the Act 40 of 1973, and the words '25 per cent' were omitted from Section 14B and were substituted by the words "not exceeding the amount of arrears".

(Adapted from: www.indiankanoon.org/doc/1672252/ accessed on 1/5/2014.)

CASE CORNER

In *Organo Chemical Industries and Another vs. Union of India* [(1980) SCR (1) 61], the employer, a chemical industry, had failed to deposit the amount of Provident Fund and Family Pension Scheme dues. The Regional Provident Fund Commissioner imposed a penalty of nearly ₹1 lakh on the employer, which was equivalent to the amount payable by the petitioner-company. The Commissioner opined that in absence of any convincing case to justify the delay in making the deposits, and being 'habitual defaulters', their case should be severely dealt with. In the writ petition to the Court, the petitioner contended that Section 14B of the Act is violative of Article 14 of the Constitution, as it confers unguided, uncontrolled and arbitrary powers on the Regional Provident Fund Commissioner to impose damages which may be to the extent of 100 per cent, i.e., equal to the amount of arrears. It also contended that this section deals with the power to recover damages and the damages imposed must have correlation with the loss suffered as a result of delayed payment.

The Court held that the expression 'damages' occurring in Section 14B is, in substance, a penalty imposed on the employer for the breach of the statutory obligation. The object of imposition of penalty is not merely 'to provide compensation for the employees'. It was also held that the imposition of damages under this section serves the twin purposes of penalising defaulting employers and providing reparation for the amount of loss suffered by employees. It is thus not only a warning to employers in general not to commit a breach of the statutory requirements, but it is also meant to provide compensation to the employees for the loss sustained by them. There is nothing in the Section to show that damages must bear relationship to the loss which is caused to the beneficiaries under the Scheme, who would get damages commensurate with their loss, i.e., the amount of interest on delayed payments. The remaining amount should go to augment the fund constituted under Section 5, for implementing the Scheme under the Act.

(Adapted from: www.indiankanoon.org/doc/1672252/ accessed on 1/5/2014.)

Power of Court to Make Orders (Section 14C)

1. Where an employer is convicted of an offence of making default in the payment of any contribution to the Fund, the Pension Fund or the Insurance Fund or in the transfer of accumulations required to be transferred by him under sub-section (2) of Section 15 or sub-section (5) of Section 17, the court may, in addition to awarding any punishment, by order in writing require him within a period specified in the order (which the court may, if it thinks fit and on application in that behalf, from time to time, extend), to pay the amount of contribution or transfer the accumulations, as the case may be, in respect of which the offence was committed.

2. Where an order is made under sub-section (1), the employer shall not be liable under this Act in respect of the continuation of the offence during the period or extended period, if any, allowed by the court, but if, on the expiry of such period or extended period, as the case may be, the order of the court has not been fully complied with, the employer shall be deemed to have committed a further offence and shall be punished with imprisonment in respect thereof under Section 14 and shall also be liable to pay fine which may extend to ₹100 for every day after such expiry on which the order has not been complied with.

Special Provisions Relating to Existing Provident Funds (Section 15)

1. Subject to the provisions of Section 17, every employee who is a subscriber to any provident fund of an establishment to which this Act applies shall, pending the application of a Scheme to the establishment in which he is employed, continue to be entitled to the benefits accruing to him under the provident fund, and the provident fund shall continue to be maintained in the same manner and subject to the same conditions as it would have been if this Act had not been passed.
2. On the application of any Scheme to an establishment, the accumulations in any provident fund of the establishment, standing to the credit of the employees who become members of the Fund established under the Scheme shall, notwithstanding anything to the contrary contained in any law for the time being in force or in any deed or other instrument establishing the provident fund but subject to the provisions, if any, contained in the Scheme, be transferred to the fund established under the Scheme, and shall be credited to the accounts of the employees entitled thereto in the Fund.

Act not to Apply to Certain Establishments (Section 16)

1. This Act shall not apply:
   (a) to any establishment registered under the Co-operative Societies Act, 1912, or under any other law for the time being in force in any State relating to co-operative societies, employing less than 50 persons and working without the aid of power; or
   (b) to any other establishment belonging to or under the control of the Central Government or a State Government and whose employees are entitled to the benefit of contributory provident fund or old age pension in accordance with any Scheme or rule framed by the Central Government or the State Government governing such benefits; or
   (c) to any other establishment set up under any Central, Provincial or State Act and whose employees are entitled to the benefits of contributory provident fund or old age pension in accordance with any scheme or rule framed under that Act governing such benefits;
2. If the Central Government is of opinion that having regard to the financial position of any class of establishments or other circumstances of the case, it is necessary or expedient so to do, it may, by notification in the Official Gazette, and subject to such conditions, as may be specified in the notification, exempt whether prospectively or retrospectively, that class of establishments from the operation of this Act for such period as may be specified in the notification.

In *Bharat Board Mills Ltd. vs. The Regional Provident Fund Commissioner, West, Bengal* (AIR 1957 Cal 702), the petitioner-company had made representation for keeping the question of contribution in abeyance on the ground that it had suffered financial loss and was therefore not in a position to pay the contributions and other charges as asked for. In response, the Deputy Secretary, Government of West Bengal informed the petitioner that no company could be granted exemption on the ground of financial stringency and under Section 16(2) of the Act it is only a class of factory which could be exempted on the grounds specified in the said section.

(Adapted from: www.indiankanoon.org/doc/1972649/ accessed on 3/5/2014.)

In *Vegetable Products Ltd. vs. Regional Provident Fund Commissioner, West Bengal and Others* (AIR 1959 Cal 783) the Court had held that for the purpose of determining exemption under Section 16 of the Act Courts are not concerned with the owners of the factory but with the factory itself. It was pointed out that each time the factory changes hands it cannot be said that it was newly established. For the consideration as to when such a factory was established, the facts and circumstances of each case must be dealt with individually.

(Adapted from: www.indiankanoon.org/doc/548299/ accessed on 3/5/2014.)

Authorising Certain Employers to Maintain Provident Fund Accounts (Section 16A)

1. The Central Government may, on an application made to it in this behalf by the employer and the majority of employees in relation to an establishment employing 100 or more persons, authorise the employer by an order in writing, to maintain a provident fund account in relation to the establishment, subject to such terms and conditions as may be specified in the Scheme:

   Provided that no authorisation shall be made under this sub-section if the employer of such establishment had committed any default in the payment of provident fund contribution or had committed any other offence under this Act during the 3 years immediately preceding the date of such authorisation.
2. Where an establishment is authorised to maintain a provident fund account under sub-section (1), the employer in relation to such establishment shall maintain such account, submit such return, deposit the contribution in such manner, provide for such facilities for inspection, pay such administrative charges, and abide by such other terms and conditions as may be specified in the Scheme.
3. Any authorisation made under this section may be cancelled by the Central Government by order in writing if the employer fails to comply with any of the terms and conditions of the authorisation or where he commits any offence under any provision of this Act.

   Provided that before canceling the authorisation the Central Government shall give the employer a reasonable opportunity of being heard.

> **Spotlight**
> As per Section 16A(1), the employer of an establishment with 100 or more persons may be authorised to maintain a PF account in relation to the establishment.

Power to Exempt (Section 17)

1. The appropriate Government may, by notification in the Official Gazette, and subject to such conditions as may be specified in the notification, exempt, whether prospectively or retrospectively, from the operation of all or any of the provisions of any Scheme:
   (a) any establishment to which this Act applies if, in the opinion of the appropriate Government, the rules of its provident fund with respect to the rates of contribution are not less favourable than those specified in Section 6 and the employees are also in enjoyment of other provident fund benefits which on the whole are not less favourable to the employees than the benefits, provided under this Act or any Scheme in relation to the employees in any other establishment of a similar character; or

(b) any establishment if the employees of such establishment are in enjoyment of benefits in the nature of provident fund, pension or gratuity and the appropriate Government is of opinion that such benefits, separately or jointly, are on the whole not less favourable to such employees than the benefits provided under this Act or any Scheme in relation to employees in any other establishment of a similar character.

Provided that no such exemption shall be made except after consultation with the Central Board which on such consultation shall forward its views on exemption to the appropriate Government within such time limit as may be specified in the Scheme.

1A. Where an exemption has been granted to an establishment under clause (a) of sub-section (1),

(a) the provisions of sections 6, 7, 8 and 14B shall, so far as may be, apply to the employer of the exempted establishment in addition to such other conditions as may be specified in the notification granting such exemption, and where such employer contravenes, or makes default in complying with any of the said provisions or conditions or any other provisions of this Act, he shall be punishable under Section 14 as if the said establishment had not been exempted under the said clause (a);

(b) the employer shall establish a Board of Trustees for the administration of the provident fund consisting of such number of members as may be specified in the Scheme;

(c) the terms and conditions of service of members of the Board of Trustees shall be such as may be specified in the Scheme:

(d) the Board of Trustees constituted under clause (b) shall:

(i) maintain detailed accounts to show the contributions credited, withdrawals made and interest accrued in respect of each employee;

(ii) submit such returns to the Regional Provident Fund Commissioner or any other officer as the Central Government may direct from time to time;

(iii) invest the provident fund monies in accordance with the directions issued by the Central Government from time to time;

(iv) transfer, where necessary, the provident fund account of any employee; and

(v) perform such other duties as may be specified in the Scheme.

1B. Where the Board of Trustees established under clause (b) of sub-section (1A) contravenes, or makes default in complying with, any provisions of clause (d) of that sub-section, the Trustees of the said Board shall be deemed to have committed an offence under sub-section (2A) of Section 14 and shall be punishable with the penalties provided in that sub-section.

1C. The appropriate Government may, by notification in the Official Gazette, and subject to the condition on the pattern of investment of pension fund and such other conditions as may be specified therein, exempt any establishment or class of establishments from the operation of the Pension Scheme, if the employees of such establishment or class of establishments are either members of any other pension scheme or propose to be members of such pension scheme, where the pensionary benefits are at par or more favourable than the Pension Scheme under this Act.

2. Any Scheme may make provision for exemption of any person or class of persons employed in any establishment to which the Scheme applies from the operation of all or any of the provisions of the Scheme, if such person or class of persons is entitled to benefits in the nature of provident fund, gratuity or old age pension and such benefits, separately or jointly, are on the whole not less favourable than the benefits provided under this Act or the Scheme:

Provided that no such exemption shall be granted in respect of a class of persons unless the appropriate Government is of opinion that the majority of persons constituting such class desire to continue to be entitled to such benefits.

2A. The Central Provident Fund Commissioner may, if requested so to do by the employer, by notification in the Official Gazette, and subject to such conditions as may be specified in the notification, exempt, whether prospectively or retrospectively, any establishment from the operation of all or any of the provisions of the Insurance Scheme, if he is satisfied that the employees of such establishment are, without making any separate contribution or payment of premium, in enjoyment of benefits in the nature of life insurance, whether linked to their deposits in provident fund or not, and such benefits are more favourable to such employees than the benefits admissible under the Insurance Scheme.

2B. Without prejudice to the provisions of sub-section (2A), the Insurance Scheme may provide for the exemption of any person or class of persons employed in any establishment and covered by that scheme from the operation of all or any of the provisions thereof, if the benefits in the nature of life insurance admissible to such person or class of persons are more favourable than the benefits provided under the Insurance Scheme.

3. Where in respect of any person or class of persons employed in an establishment an exemption is granted under this section from the operation of all or any of the provisions of any Scheme (whether such exemption has been granted to the establishment wherein such person or class of persons is employed, or to the person or class of persons as such), the employer in relation to such establishment:

(a) shall, in relation to the provident fund, pension and gratuity to which any such person or class of persons is entitled, maintain such accounts, submit such returns, make such investment, provide for such facilities for inspection and pay such inspection charges, as the Central Government may direct;

(b) shall not, at any time after the exemption, without the leave of the Central Government, reduce the total quantum of benefits in the nature of pension, gratuity or provident fund to which any such person or class of persons was entitled at the time of the exemption; and

(c) shall, where any such person leaves his employment and obtains reemployment in another establishment to which this Act applies, transfer within such time as may be specified in this behalf by the Central Government, the amount of accumulations to the credit of that person in the provident fund of the establishment left by him to the credit of that person's account in the provident fund of the establishment in which he is re-employed or, as the case may be, in the Fund established under the Scheme applicable to the establishment.

3A. Where, in respect of any person or class of persons employed in any establishment, an exemption is granted under sub-section (2A) or sub-section (2B) from the operation of all or any of the provisions of the Insurance Scheme (whether such exemption is granted to the establishment wherein such person or class of persons is employed or to the person or class of persons as such), the employer in relation to such establishment:

(a) shall, in relation to the benefits in the nature of life insurance, to which any such person or class of persons are entitled, or any insurance fund, maintain such accounts, submit such returns, make such investments, provide for such facilities for inspection and pay such inspection charges, as the Central Government may direct;

(b) shall not, at any time after the exemption without the leave of the Central Government, reduce the total quantum of benefits in the nature of life insurance to which any such person or class of persons was entitled immediately before the date of the exemption,

4. Any exemption granted under this section may be cancelled by the authority which granted it, by order in writing, if an employer fails to comply,

(a) in the case of an exemption granted under sub-section (1), with any of the conditions imposed under that sub-section or sub-section (1A) or with any of the provisions of sub-section (3);

(aa) in the case of an exemption granted under sub-section (1C) with any of the conditions imposed under that sub-section; and
(b) in the case of an exemption granted under sub-section (2), with any of the provisions of sub-section (3);
(c) in the case of an exemption granted under sub-section (2A), with any of the conditions imposed under that sub-section or with any of the provisions of sub-section (3A);
(d) in the case of an exemption granted under sub-section (2B), with any of the provisions of sub-section (3A).

5. Where any exemption granted under sub-section (1), sub-section (1C), sub-section (2), sub-section (2A) or sub-section (2B) is cancelled, the amount of accumulations to the credit of every employee to whom such exemption applied, in the provident fund, the Pension Fund or the Insurance Fund of the establishment in which he is employed together with any amount forfeited from the employer's share of contribution to the credit of the employee who leaves the employment before the completion of the full period of service shall be transferred within such time and in such manner as may be specified in the Scheme or the Pension Scheme or the Insurance Scheme to the credit of his account in the Fund or the Pension Fund or the Insurance Fund, as the case may be.
6. Subject to the provisions of sub-section (1C), the employer of an exempted establishment or of an exempted employee of an establishment to which the provisions of the Pension Scheme apply, shall, notwithstanding any exemption granted under sub-section (1) or sub-section (2), pay to the Pension Fund such portion of the employer's contribution to its provident fund within such time and in such manner as may be specified in the Pension Scheme.

In *The Bharatkhand Textile Manufacturing Co. Ltd. and Others vs. The Textile Labour Association, Ahmedabad* [(1960) SCR (3) 329], it was held that the statutory provident fund created by the Act could be no bar to the respondent's claim for a gratuity scheme. However, in awarding such a scheme, Industrial Courts must make due allowance for it. Provisions of Section 17 of the Act clearly indicate that the statutory benefits under the Act are the minimum to which employees are entitled, and that these are no bar to any additional benefits claimed by the employees. A scheme for gratuity is, by its very nature, an integrated scheme, and covers all classes of termination of service where gratuity benefit can be legitimately claimed.

(Adapted from: www.indiankanoon.org/doc/1936107 accessed on 1/5/2014.)

Transfer of Accounts (Section 17A)

1. Where an employee employed in an establishment to which this Act applies leaves his employment and obtains re-employment in another establishment to which this Act does not apply, the amount of accumulations to the credit of such employee in the Fund, or as the case may be, in the provident fund of the establishment left by him shall be transferred, within such time as may be specified by the Central Government in this behalf, to the credit of his account in the provident fund of the establishment in which he is re-employed, if the employee so desires and the rules in relation to that provident fund permit such transfer.

Spotlight

The accumulation is transferred to the credit of an employee from the PF of the establishment left by him in the PF of the establishment in which he is re-employed, as per Section 17A.

2. Where an employee employed in an establishment to which this Act does not apply leaves his employment and obtains re-employment in another establishment to which this Act applies, the amount of accumulations to the credit of such employee in the provident fund of the establish-

ment left by him may, if the employee so desires and the rules in relation to such provident fund permit, be transferred to the credit of his account in the Fund or, as the case may be, in the provident fund of the establishment in which he is re-employed.

Act to Have Effect Notwithstanding Anything Contained in Act 31 of 1956 (Section 17AA)

The provisions of this Act shall have effect notwithstanding anything inconsistent therewith contained in the Life Insurance Corporation Act, 1956.

Liability in Case of Transfer of Establishment (Section 17B)

Where an employer, in relation to an establishment, transfers that establishment in whole or in part, by sale, gift, lease or licence or in any other manner whatsoever, the employer and the person to whom the establishment is so transferred shall jointly and severally be liable to pay the contribution and other sums due from the employer under any provision of this Act or the Scheme or the Pension Scheme or the Insurance Scheme, as the case may be, in respect of the period up to the date of such transfer:

> **Spotlight**
> Section 17B limits the liability of the transferee to the value of the assets he obtains by such transfer.

Provided that the liability of the transferee shall be limited to the value of the assets obtained by him by such transfer.

Protection of Action Taken in Good Faith (Section 18)

No suit, prosecution or other legal proceeding shall lie against the Central Government, a State Government, the Presiding Officer of a Tribunal, any authority referred to in Section 7A, an Inspector or any other person for anything which is in good faith done or intended to be done in pursuance of this Act, the Scheme, the Pension Scheme or the Insurance Scheme.

Presiding Officer and Other Officers to be Public Servants (Section 18A)

The Presiding Officer of a Tribunal, its officers and other employees, the authorities referred to in Section 7A and every Inspector shall be deemed to be public servants within the meaning of Section 21 of the Indian Penal Code.

Delegation of Powers (Section 19)

The appropriate Government may direct that any power or authority or jurisdiction exercisable by it under this Act, the Scheme, the Pension Scheme or the Insurance Scheme shall, in relation to such matters and subject to such conditions, if any, as may be specified in the direction, be exercisable also:

(a) where the appropriate Government is the Central Government, by such officer or authority subordinate to the Central Government or by the State Government, or by such officer or authority subordinate to the State Government, as may be specified in the notification; and

(b) where the appropriate Government is a State Government, by such officer or authority subordinate to the State Government as may be specified in the notification.

Power of Central Government to Give Directions (Section 20)

The Central Government may, from time to time, give such directions to the Central Board as it may think fit for the efficient administration of this Act and when any such direction is given, the Central Board shall comply with such direction.

Power to Make Rules (Section 21)

1. The Central Government may, by notification in the Official Gazette, make rules to carry out the provisions of this Act.
2. Without prejudice to the generality of the foregoing power, such rules may provide for all or any of the following matters, namely:
   (a) the salary and allowances and other terms and conditions of service of the Presiding Officer and the employees of a Tribunal;
   (b) the form and the manner in which, and the time within which, an appeal shall be filed before a Tribunal and the fees payable for filing such appeal;
   (c) the manner of certifying the copy of the certificate, to be forwarded to the Recovery Officer under sub-section (2) of Section 8C; and
   (d) any other matter which has to be, or may be, prescribed by rules under this Act.
3. Every rule made under this Act shall be laid, as soon as may be after it is made, before each House of Parliament, while it is in session, for a total period of 30 days which may be comprised in 1 session or in 2 or more successive sessions, and if, before the expiry of the session immediately following the session or the successive sessions aforesaid, both Houses agree in making any modification in the rule or both Houses agree that the rule should not be made, the rule shall thereafter have effect only in such modified form or be of no effect, as the case may be; so, however, that any such modification or annulment shall be without prejudice to the validity of anything previously done under that rule.

Power to Remove Difficulties (Section 22)

1. If any difficulty arises in giving effect to the provisions of this Act, as amended by the Employees' Provident Funds and Miscellaneous Provisions (Amendment) Act, 1988, the Central Government may, by order published in the Official Gazette, make such provisions, not inconsistent with the provisions of this Act, as appear to it to be necessary or expedient for the removal of the difficulty:

   Provided that no such order shall be made after the expiry of a period of 3 years from the date on which the said amendment Act receives the assent of the President.
2. Every order made under this section shall, as soon as may be after it is made, be laid before each House of Parliament.

Repeal of Ordinance VIII of 1951 (Section 23)

Repealed by the Repealing and Amending Act, 1957.

ADMINISTRATION OF THE ACT

Spotlight
The Act is administered through the Employees' Provident Fund Organisation (EPFO).

The Employees' Provident Funds and Miscellaneous Provisions Act, 1952 is administered through the Employees' Provident Fund Organisation (EPFO), consisting of offices at 123 locations across the country. The EPFO is under the administrative control of the Ministry of Labour & Employment. As on 31st March 2012, the organisation had a structure consisting of 10 zonal offices, 40 regional offices and 83 sub-regional offices. The EPFO also has 122 district offices and 14 service centers across India. It has a well-equipped training set up with the National Academy for Training and Research in Social Security (NATRSS), New Delhi, at the apex level, and Zonal Training Institutes (ZTIs) at Faridabad (North Zone), Chennai (South Zone), Kolkata (East Zone), Ujjain (West Zone) and Shillong (Sub-Zonal).

The EPF & MP Act, 1952 and Schemes framed thereunder are administered by the Central Board of Trustees, Employees' Provident Fund, which is a tripartite board consisting of representatives of the Government (5 members of Central Government and 15 members from State Governments), and 10 representatives each of employers and employees. The Board administers a contributory provident fund, a pension scheme and an insurance scheme for the workforce engaged in the organised sector in India. The Board is assisted by the EPFO.

Spotlight
The Central Board of Trustees, EPF, operates 3 schemes, viz., the EPF Scheme, 1952, the EPS, 1995 and the EDLI Scheme, 1976.

Establishments covered by the Act are required to statutorily comply in respect of all employees drawing wages up to ₹6,500 per month. Towards addressing the 3 core areas of provisioning of provident funds, pension and insurance, the Board operates 3 schemes, viz. the Employees' Provident Funds (EPF) Scheme, 1952, the Employees' Pension Scheme (EPS), 1995 replacing the Family Pension Scheme, 1971 and the Employees' Deposit-Linked Insurance Scheme (EDLI), 1976. Of these, Provident Fund is a defined contribution scheme in which both employees and employers contribute their mandated share. The Pension Scheme has a mix of "defined contribution" and "defined benefit" forms; employees do not have to contribute to this scheme. Lastly, the Insurance Scheme is a deposit-linked scheme that provides for benefits up to ₹1,30,000 without any contribution from employees. The benefits admissible under each of the three schemes, nominations and declarations are indicated in Table 23.1.

TABLE 23.1 Benefits, Nominations and Declarations of Schemes Offered by the Employees' Provident Fund

	Employees' Provident Fund Scheme, 1952	*Employees' Pension Scheme, 1995*	*Employees' Deposit-Linked Insurance Scheme, 1976*
Benefits	• Accumulation plus interest upon retirement, resignation and death • Partial withdrawals allowed for specific expenses like house construction, higher education, marriage, illness, etc.	• Monthly benefits for superannuation or retirement and disability for survivor, widow(er) and children • Amount of pension based on average salary during the preceding 12 months from the date of exit and total years of employment. • Minimum pension on disablement • Past service benefit to participants of erstwhile Family Pension Scheme, 1971	• Benefit provided in case of death of an employee who was member of the Scheme at the time of death • Family will get 20 times the average wages of the last 12 months of the member • According to the revised scheme, maximum benefits under the scheme will now be ₹1,30,000, as the wage ceiling up to which contribution can be paid under the scheme is ₹6,500.

(contd.)

(contd.)

Nomination	• There is a common form for all the 3 Schemes, i.e., Form 2(R). • The nominations in case of EPF Scheme are also applicable for the EDLI Scheme. • Member having family can nominate any one or more of the family members as defined under Para 2(f) of the EPF Scheme, 1952. • Member not having any family member as defined in the said para can nominate any other person, but the nomination will become invalid in case of the member acquiring family.	• Member has to give the names of spouse and all children in the prescribed form. • In case the member has no family, any other person can be nominated. • However, such nomination will become invalid once the member acquires a family.	• Nomination under the EPF Scheme will be applicable for EDLI Scheme also.
Declaration	Any person joining an establishment, to which the Act applies, shall compulsorily submit a declaration (Form 11) to his/her employer, whether he/she is already a member of Provident Fund. This will ensure continuity of service and consequential benefits. In case he/she was a member, he/she shall also apply in Form 13 for getting the old account details and the fund balance to the new account.		

(Adapted from: www.epfindia.com accessed on 2/5/2014.)

The contribution rates for financing and administering the benefits under the Act are given in Table 23.2.

Table 23.2 Contribution Rates

	Contribution Accounts			*Administration Accounts*		*Total*
	EPF	*EPS*	*EDLI*	*EPF*	*EDLI*	
Employee	12	0	0	0	0	12
Employer	3.67	8.33	0.5	1.10	0.01	13.61
Central Government	0	1.16	0	0	0	1.16
Total	15.67	9.49	0.5	1.10	0.01	26.77

(Adapted from: www.epfindia.com accessed on 2/5/2014.)

Thus employers and employees both contribute at the rate of 12 per cent of wages in contribution accounts. Further, employers also contribute towards administration of the benefits under the Act. The rate of contribution for certain category of establishments is 10 per cent. These are:

- Any establishment in which less than 20 employees are employed.
- Any sick industrial company and which has been declared as such by the Board for Industrial and Financial Reconstruction.
- Any establishment which has, at the end of any financial year, accumulated losses equal to or exceeding its entire net worth, and
- Any establishment in jute, *beedi*, brick, coir industries and guar gum factories.

(Adapted from: www.epfindia.com accessed on 2/5/2014.)

A member of the Employees' Provident Fund Scheme is entitled to withdraw the amount lying in his account along with interest on quitting service. The Scheme also provides for partial withdrawals from the Provident Fund Account to meet contingencies like illness and invalidation and also to provide financial assistance to members in discharging their social responsibilities like marriage of self or children, or higher education of children and construction of dwelling house. During the year 2009-2010, 36.60 lakh EPF claims were settled (Ministry of Labour & Employment, 2010-11).

RECENT INITIATIVES

At present 187 industries or classes of establishments are covered under the Act, including factories or establishments engaged in trading and commercial activities and the service sector. Out of these, the maximum percentage of members is concentrated in 8 categories, accounting for 73.06 per cent of the total establishments and 72.78 per cent of the total membership, as on 31st March 2013. With 63.48 per cent of the members concentrated in 5 States, Tamil Nadu has the largest number of members, followed by Maharashtra, Karnataka, Gujarat and Haryana. There were 15 categories having 10 lakhs or more members as on 31st March 2013.

As on 31st March 2013, the number of voluntarily covered establishments was 25,683, i.e., 3.46 per cent of the total number of establishments. During the year 2012-2013, additional 39 establishments were notified for voluntary coverage under the Act, as against 259 establishments notified during the year 2010-2011 and 162 establishments during 2011-12.

EMPLOYEES' PENSION SCHEME, 1995

The Employees' Pension Scheme aims at providing for economic sustenance during old age and survivorship coverage to a member and his family. The Employees' Pension Scheme, 1995 came into effect from 16th November 1995, on the introduction of which the erstwhile Employees' Family Pension Scheme, 1971 ceased to operate and all the assets and liabilities of the old scheme were transferred and merged with the Employees' Pension Fund.

Spotlight

With the introduction of EPS, 1995, the erstwhile Employees' Family Pension Scheme, 1971 has ceased to operate.

Benefits under Employees' Pension Scheme, 1995

Under the Employees' Family Pension Scheme, 1971 only widow/widower pension was payable in case of death of a member-employee while in reckonable service and prior to the completion of 60 years of age. In the absence of a widow or on cessation of widow pension, pension was payable to the eldest child up to the age of 25 years and then it was passed on to the younger children, one at a time, subject to the age limit of 25 years. There was no provision for pension to member on retirement or disablement pension. On leaving service, an employee was entitled to withdrawal benefit only. However, the Employees' Pension Scheme, 1995 provides the following benefits to the members and their families: member pension, disablement pension, widow/widower pension, children pension, orphan pension, disabled children/orphan pension, nominee pension, pension to dependent father or mother and withdrawal benefit.

Eligibility for Benefits under Employees' Pension Scheme, 1995

Superannuation or early pension under the Employees' Pension Scheme, 1995 is payable on fulfilling the following conditions:

(i) minimum 10 years of eligible service and

(ii) attainment of 58/50 years age

Spotlight

Superannuation or early pension under EPS, 1995 is payable on fulfilling minimum 10 years of eligible service and attainment of 58/50 years age.

On cessation of employment and before completing 58 years of age, a member can opt for early pension, but only after completing 50 years of age, subject to a discounting factor at the rate of 4 per cent (w.e.f. 26th September 2008) for every year falling short of 58 years. No member pension is payable before attaining the age of 50 years. However, no such age or minimum eligibility service criteria shall apply for pension entitlement in case of disablement or death of the member; membership with 1 month's contribution will suffice in such cases. The quantum of pension payable to a member on superannuation and/or exit from service on attaining the age of 58/50 years shall correspond to the period of pensionable service rendered by the member and his pensionable salary, i.e., the average pay of last 12 months drawn at the time of exit.

The Employees' Pension Scheme, 1995 derives its financial resources by partial diversion at the rate of 8.33 per cent of the employer's share of Provident Fund contribution. The Central Government contributes at the rate of 1.16 per cent of wages, similar to Employees' Family Pension Scheme, 1971 (refer to Table 23.2). On its introduction, the Scheme applies compulsorily to all the existing members of the Provident Fund who were contributing to the Employees' Family Pension Scheme, 1971. The benefits and entitlements to the members under the old scheme are protected and continued under the new scheme. Any new entrant to the membership of Provident Fund from 16th November 1995 onwards shall also acquire membership of the Scheme on compulsory basis. The existing members of Provident Fund, as on 15th November 1995 who did not opt for joining the erstwhile Employees' Family Pension Scheme, 1971, have the option to join the EPS, 1995, as per the provisions laid down. Further, the Pension Scheme has a provision for retrospective application from 1st April 1993, in selective cases for outgoing members of the ceased Employees' Family Pension Scheme, 1971, although it is effective from 16th November 1995, and its beneficiaries during the period between 1st April 1993 and 15th November 1995. Members of the old scheme, who have died between 1st April 1993 and 16th November 1995 are deemed to have joined the new scheme; their beneficiaries are entitled for pensionary benefits under EPS, 1995.

For disbursement of monthly pension and other benefits, the Regional Offices have entered into arrangement with nationalised and commercial banks. Centralised arrangements have also been made with HDFC Bank, ICICI Bank, Axis Bank and post offices to disburse pension and other benefits all over India.

(Adapted from: Annual Report, EPF India, 2012-13.)

During the year 2009-2010, ₹10,924.52 crore were received as Pension Fund contributions, out of which, ₹9,930.52 crore were collected from employers' share and ₹994 crore were in the form of contribution by the Central Government. At the end of 2009-2010, the Employees' Provident Fund had cumulative investments of ₹1,23,790.43 crore under the EPS Scheme (Ministry of Labour & Employment, 2010-11).

Pension Beneficiaries

The classification of beneficiaries under Employees' Pension Scheme, 1995 as on 31st March 2013 is given in Table 23.3.

TABLE 23.3 Classification of Pension Beneficiaries

Pension Beneficiaries		
i. Members Pension		
S. No.	Early Pension (50-57 years)	16,70,625
a.	Superannuation Pension	12,98,120
b.	Disablement Pension	2,115
Sub-Total		29,70,860
ii. Widow/Widower Pension		
a.	Death in Service	7,06,179
b.	Death away from Service	1,17,678
Sub-Total		8,23,857
iii.	Nominee Pension	8,894
iv.	Parent Pension	15,663
v.	Orphan Pension	15,670
vi.	Children Pension	5,65,287
Sub-Total		6,05,514
Grand Total		44,00,231

Note: Figures include widow/widower pensioners and children pensioners drawing pension under the ceased Employees' Family Pension Scheme, 1971

(Adapted from: Annual Report, EPF India, 2012-13.)

Provisions for International Workers

As a consequence of concerns regarding provisions of adequate social security cover to Indian employees working abroad, the Government of India has signed Social Security Agreements (SSAs) with some countries with the objective of providing exemption to such employees from the mandatory social security contributions in those countries. A Social Security Agreement is a bilateral instrument to protect the social security interests of international workers. It covers 3 important provisions: *detachment* (by which Indian employees working in countries with which India has SSAs are exempted from contributing to their social security systems, provided they are complying with the Indian Social Security System); *totalisation of benefits* (by which the period of service rendered by an employee in another country is counted for determining his/her eligibility for pension); and *portability of pension* (by which pension benefits are payable direct to the beneficiaries choosing to reside in the home country or in any other country, without any reduction). The Ministry of Overseas Indian Affairs, Government of India is the nodal ministry for initiating negotiations for SSA. The EPFO has been duly identified as the competent agency and liaison agency in India. As a competent agency, it is required to implement the provisions of the agreement in respect of all the employees covered or coverable under the purview of the EPF & MP Act, 1952. As a liaison agency, the EPFO has the responsibility of coordination with other social security providers like banks, institutions, Coal Mines Provident Fund, Sea Men's Provident Fund, etc.

Spotlight

Any SSA covers 3 provisions: detachment, totalisation of benefits and portability of pension.

Withdrawal of provident fund accumulations by international workers is permitted only after they attain 58 years of age. Withdrawal benefit under the Employees' Pension Scheme, 1995 is available only to those covered under any SSA. Further, employer's contribution of 8.33 per cent to the Pension Fund is now payable to international workers on full salary.

EMPLOYEES' DEPOSIT-LINKED INSURANCE SCHEME

The Employees' Deposit-Linked Insurance Scheme, 1976 came into force from 1st August 1976. The Scheme is supported by a nominal contribution by employers at the rate of 0.5 per cent of pay, i.e., basic wages, dearness allowance including cash value of food concession and retaining allowance, if any. Employees, however, need not pay any contribution for availing the insurance cover. This scheme is applicable to all factories or establishments to which the EPF & MP Act, 1952 applies. All employees who are members of the Provident Fund are members of this Scheme by default.

Benefits under the Scheme

As per the revisions during the year 2010-2011, in case of death of an employee who was member of the Scheme at the time of his death, his/her family will get 20 times of the average wages of the last 12 months of the member as benefits under the EDLI Scheme. According to the revised scheme, maximum benefits under the Scheme will now be ₹1,30,000 and the wage ceiling up to which contribution can be paid under the scheme is ₹6,500.

Spotlight

Maximum benefit under EDLI Scheme is ₹1,30,000, as the wage ceiling up to which contribution can be paid is ₹6,500.

(Adapted from: Annual Report, EPF India, 2012-13.)

During the year 2009-2010, a sum of ₹423.22 crore comprising employers' contribution was deposited and at the end of 2009-2010, the EPFO had cumulative investments worth ₹7,880.91 crore under this Scheme (Ministry of Labour & Employment, 2010-11).

SUMMARY

- The Employees' Provident Funds and Miscellaneous Provisions Act, 1952 is a welfare legislation enacted mainly for the purpose of instituting provident funds, pension fund and deposit-linked insurance fund for employees working in factories and other establishments.
- Contribution, as defined by Section 2(c), means a contribution payable in respect of a member under a scheme or the contribution payable in respect of an employee to whom the Insurance Scheme applies.
- Section 2(f) defines an employee as any person who is employed for wages in any kind of work, manual or otherwise, in or in connection with the work of an establishment, including any person employed by or through a contractor and one engaged as an apprentice.
- As per Section 5(1), the Central Government may frame a Scheme to be called the Employees' Provident Fund Scheme for the establishment of provident funds. The fund shall vest in, and be administered by, the Central Board. The contribution paid by the employer to the Fund shall be 10 per cent of the basic wages, dearness allowance and retaining allowance (if any).

- A member of the EPF Scheme is entitled to withdraw the amount lying in his account along with interest on quitting service. The Scheme also provides for partial withdrawals from the PF Account to meet contingencies like illness and invalidation and also to provide financial assistance to members in discharging their social responsibilities like marriage of self, or children, or higher education of children and construction of dwelling house.
- The Central Government may constitute a Board of Trustees, called the Central Board, which shall administer the fund vested in it and perform other functions, as laid down in Section 5A(1). The Board is assisted by an Executive Committee in the performance of its functions. As per Section 5B(1), the Central Government may, after consultation with the Government of any State, constitute a Board of Trustees for that State, referred to as the State Board.
- As per provisions of Section 5D, the Central Government shall appoint a Central Provident Fund Commissioner, who shall be the Chief Executive Officer of the Board, a Financial Adviser and Chief Accounts Officer to assist the Commissioner in the discharge of his duties.
- The Employees' Pension Scheme provides superannuation pension, retiring pension or permanent total disablement pension to employees and widow or widower's pension, children pension or orphan pension to the beneficiaries of such employees, as per Section 6A. Employer's contribution is 8.33 per cent of the basic wages, dearness allowance and retaining allowance, if any, of the concerned employees. On the establishment of the Pension Fund, the Family Pension Scheme has ceased to operate and all assets of the ceased scheme have been transferred to the Pension Fund.
- Superannuation or early pension under EPS, 1995 is payable on fulfilling minimum 10 years of eligible service and attainment of 58/50 years age. On cessation of employment and before completing 58 years of age, a member can opt for early pension, but only after completing 50 years of age, subject to a discounting factor at the rate of 4 per cent (w.e.f. 26th September 2008) for every year falling short of 58 years.
- According to Section 6C(1), the Employees' Deposit-Linked Insurance (EDLI) Scheme provides life insurance benefits to employees. Employer's contribution to the Deposit-Linked Insurance Fund is 1 per cent of the aggregate of basic wages, dearness allowance and retaining allowance (if any). Employees need not pay any contribution for availing the insurance cover. Maximum benefits under EDLI Scheme is ₹1,30,000, as the current wage ceiling up to which contribution can be paid is ₹6,500.
- Section 7D(1) empowers the Central Government to constitute 1 or more EPF Appellate Tribunals to exercise the powers and discharge the functions conferred on it by the Act. As per Section 7I(1), any person aggrieved by a notification issued or an order passed by the Central Government or any authority may prefer an appeal to a Tribunal against such notification or order.
- Section 12 provides that no employer shall, because of his liability for the payment of any contribution to the Fund or the Insurance Fund, reduce, directly or indirectly, the wages of any employee to whom the Scheme or the Insurance Scheme applies.
- Recovery of damages from the employer by way of penalty should not exceed the amount of arrears, as per Section 14B. However, before levying and recovering such damages, the employer shall be given a reasonable opportunity of being heard.
- Section 16A(1) provides that the employer of an establishment with 100 or more persons may be authorised to maintain a PF account in relation to the establishment.
- As per Section 17A(1), when an employee employed in an establishment to which this Act applies leaves his employment and obtains re-employment in another establishment to which this Act does not apply, the amount of accumulations to the credit of such employee in the Fund shall be transferred to the credit of his account in the provident fund of the establishment in which he is re-employed.

- The Government of India has signed Social Security Agreements (SSAs), which are bilateral instruments to protect the social security interests of international workers. An SSA covers three important provisions: *detachment*, *totalisation of benefits,* and *portability of pension*.
- As a competent agency, the EPFO is required to implement the provisions of the agreement in respect of all the employees covered or coverable under the purview of the EPF & MP Act, 1952. As a liaison agency, the EPFO has the responsibility of coordination with other social security providers like banks, institutions, Coal Mines Provident Fund, Sea Men's Provident Fund, etc.

Key Concepts

Contribution
Provident Fund
EPF Scheme
Employees' Pension Scheme
Insurance Fund
EDLI Scheme
EPF Appellate Tribunal
EPFO
Social Security Agreement

Bibliography

Annual Report, 2009-10, Ministry of Labour & Employment, Government of India.

Annual Report, EPF India, 2012-13, Retrieved from http://www.epfindia.com/Annual_Reports/AR_2012-13.pdf accessed on 1/5/2014.

Annual Report, EPF India, 2011-12, Retrieved from http://www.epfindia.com/Annual_Reports/AR_2011-12.pdf accessed on 1/5/2014.

Annual Report, 2010-11, Ministry of Labour & Employment, Government of India.

Asher, Mukul G. Pension Plans, Provident Fund Schemes and Retirement Policies: India's Social Security Reform Imperative, *ASCI Journal of Management*, September 2009, Vol. 39, No. 1, pp. 1-18.

http://www.epfindia.gov.in/epfbrief.html

ILO World Social Security Report 2010/11: Providing Coverage in Times of Crisis and beyond, International Labour Office, Geneva.

Review Questions

Objective Type Questions

I. State True or False

(i) Any presents made by the employer are excluded from basic wages for the purpose of this Act.

(ii) Employees' contribution to Employees' Deposit-Linked Insurance Scheme is at the rate of 0.5 per cent of pay.

(iii) Nomination under the EPF Scheme will be applicable for EDLI Scheme as well.

(iv) Penalty for knowingly making any false representation may be up to ₹10,000.

(v) Any person employed by a contractor in connection with the work of the establishment is covered under the Act.

Answers: (i) True, (ii) False, (iii) True, (iv) False, (v) True

II. Fill in the Blanks

(i) Wage ceiling up to which contribution can be paid under the EDLI Scheme is ₹ _____.
(ii) Co-operative societies employing less than _____persons and working without the aid of power are not covered under the Act.
(iii) The Central Board must have a maximum of ____ persons appointed by the Central Government from amongst its officials.
(iv) The Executive Committee shall consist of ___ persons representing the employers as members.
(v) The 3 important provisions of an SSA are____, totalisation of benefits, and portability of pension.

Answers: (i) 6,500, (ii) 50, (iii) 5, (iv) 3, (v) detachment

Discussion Questions

1. Describe the membership structure of the Central Board and Executive Committee.
2. What is the provision for recovery of damages?
3. In what way are international workers benefitted by the EPF & MP Act, 1952?
4. What are the provisions in the Act for transfer of accounts of an employee who obtains re-employment?
5. On what grounds can an establishment be exempted from the operation of scheme(s) under the Act? What are the duties of the employer of such an establishment on such exemption been granted?
6. Discuss the provision for recovery of money by employers and contractors? What is the provision for other modes of recovery in the Act?
7. What are the various penalties that may be imposed on an employer?
8. Discuss the various benefits under the EPS and EDLI Scheme. Mention the eligibility criteria for both the schemes.
9. Define a Recovery Officer. What are the duties and responsibilities of a Recovery Officer, as given in various provisions of the Act?
10. Explain the following concepts:
    (a) Escaped amount
    (b) Protection against attachment
    (c) EPF Appellate Tribunal
    (d) Enhanced punishment

CASE STUDY-I

In this case, the respondent-establishment, M/s Miraj Minerals, was proceeded against in pursuance to an enquiry report, for assessment of dues for the period from April 2003 to July 2004 and was found liable for an amount of ₹1,95,475 for damages. The liability was arrived at on a finding that on a physical verification by the Squad, 32 employees were found to be working on the day of inspection. The inspecting team, taking note of 18 employees working and the statement of the Mines Manager that he and a *chowkidar* are also employed, recorded that in addition to 18 employees, 12 employees were also found working in the premises of the establishment for loading of material of the establishment for crushing from Pooja Minerals.

Relying on this report and observing that 32 employees were found to be working on the day of the inspection, the Assistant Provident Fund Commissioner, Jabalpur held the respondent-establishment liable for the dues from April 2003 to July 2004. In an appeal under the Act, the said order has been revised by the Tribunal for the reason that the 2 respondents, i.e., M/s Miraj Minerals and M/s Pooja Minerals were wrongly clubbed for ascertaining the strength of employees. The main contention is that, as per the inspection report, 20 persons including the Mine Manager and the *chowkidar* were engaged, which is being ignored by the Tribunal. However, there is no explanation as to why when 20 persons are employed, the inspection team has recorded on physical verification 18 persons and further in a proceeding, 32 persons are recorded to be employed. No material is brought on record to show that an enquiry has been taken recourse to as would substantiate the findings recorded by the Assistant Provident Fund Commissioner.

(Adapted from: Regional Provident Fund Commissioner vs. M/s Miraj Minerals, Labour Law Reporter, October, 2012, pp. 137-138.)

Review Questions

1. Even if the said two establishments are taken to be one and the same, total number of persons employed taken together is less than 20. Do you think that the respondent-establishment may be held liable for the dues on this ground?
2. What is the provision for clubbing of establishments for coverage under the Employees' Provident Funds and Miscellaneous Provisions Act, 1952?
3. Which all sections of the Act are relevant in this case?

CASE STUDY-II

The petitioner in this case was earlier carrying on his business from rented premises bearing House No. 1337, Sector 28, Faridabad. Later on he constructed his own building and shifted to the new place of business, bearing Plot No. 454, Sector 21-D, Faridabad in March 2002. The impugned order was passed by the Assistant Provident Fund Commissioner on 27th December 2007 without serving any notice to the petitioner, as the notices were sent to him on his old address. When the petitioner came to know about passing of the order, he immediately filed an appeal before the Tribunal. However the same has been dismissed at time barred. Delay in depositing provident fund was on account of the fact that the petitioner firm was in financial crisis due to recession.

The counsel for the respondents submitted that notices were sent to the petitioner at the address available on record in the office of the Provident Fund Commissioner. In case there was any change of address, the petitioner-establishment was duty bound to bring it to the notice of the Office immediately. It further submitted that after passing of the impugned order, the petitioner had represented to the Regional Provident Fund Commissioner, Faridabad. He stated that because of poor financial conditions, he will not be able to pay the damages in lump sum; rather the same will be paid in installments of ₹1 lakh per month from April 2009 onwards. In terms thereof, some cheques issued by the petitioner were cleared, whereas one of the cheques was dishonoured, on account of which a complaint under Section 138 of the Negotiable Instruments Act has been filed against the petitioner. In his letter the petitioner has clearly established that he was in knowledge of the order passed by the Assistant Provident Fund Commissioner; he admitted therein that he had received information about passing the order on 16th February 2009 through M/s Havell's India Limited, Faridabad. As is evident from the impugned order passed by the Tribunal, the appeal was filed on 16th November 2009, i.e., 9 months after the date of knowledge of the order passed against the petitioner.

(Adapted from: C. B. Sharma vs. The Employees' Provident Fund Appellate Tribunal and Others, Indian Labour Law Reporter, October, 2012, pp. 138-140.)

Review Questions

1. The Tribunal has been empowered to condone any delay in filing an appeal. What is the time limit given in the Act for such delay? Do you think that in this case the delay by the respondent-establishment could be condoned?
2. Do you think that the Provident Fund Commissioner is at fault in not sending the notice at the changed address of the petitioner?
3. Which all sections of the Employees' Provident Funds and Miscellaneous Provisions Act, 1952 are relevant in this case?

SCHEDULE I

[See Sections 2(I) and 4]

Any industry engaged in the manufacture of any of the following, namely:

Cement
Cigarettes
Electrical, mechanical or general engineering products
Iron and steel
Paper
Textiles (made wholly or in part of cotton or wool or jute or silk, whether natural or artificial)

1. Matches
2. Edible oils and fats
3. Sugar
4. Rubber and rubber products
5. Electricity including the generation, transmission and distribution thereof
6. Tea
7. Printing other than printing industry relating to newspaper establishment as defined in the Working Journalists (Conditions of Service) and Miscellaneous Provisions Act, 1955, including the process of composing types for printing, printing by letterpress, lithography, photogravure or other similar process or book-binding.
8. Glass
9. Stone-ware pipes
10. Sanitary wares
11. Electrical porcelain insulators of high and low tension
12. Refractories
13. Tiles

1. Heavy and fine chemicals, including:
    (i) Fertilisers
    (ii) Turpentine
    (iii) Resin

(iv) Medical and pharmaceutical preparations
(v) Toilet preparations
(vi) Soaps
(vii) Inks
(viii) Intermediates, dyes, colour lacs and toners
(ix) Fatty acids, and
(x) Oxygen, acetylene, and carbon-dioxide gases industry

2. Indigo
3. Lac including shellac
4. Non-edible vegetable and animal oils and fats

Mineral oil refining industry

(i) Industrial and Power Alcohol industry; and
(ii) Asbestos Cement Sheets industry

Biscuit making industry including composite units making biscuit and products such as bread, confectionery, milk and milk powder

Mica industry

Plywood industry

Automobile repairing and servicing industry

1. Rice Milling
2. Flour Milling
3. Dal Milling

Starch industry

1. Petroleum or natural gas exploration, prospecting, drilling or production
2. Petroleum or natural gas refining

Leather and leather products industry

1. Stone-ware jars

Crockery

The fruit and vegetable preservation industry, that is to say, any industry which is engaged in the preparation or production of any of the following articles, namely:

(i) canned and bottled fruits, juices and pulps
(ii) canned and bottled vegetables
(iii) frozen fruits and vegetables
(iv) jams, jellies and marmalades
(v) tomato products, ketchups and sauces
(vi) squashes, crushes, cordials and ready-to-serve beverages or any other beverages containing fruit juice or fruit pulp
(vii) preserved, candied and crystallised fruits and peels
(viii) chutneys
(ix) any other unspecified item relating to the preservation or canning of fruits and vegetables

Cashewnut industry

Confectionery industry

1. Buttons
2. Brushes
3. Plastic and plastic products
4. Stationery products

The aerated water industry (i.e., any industry engaged in the manufacture of aerated water, soft drinks or carbonated water)

Distilling and rectifying of spirits (not falling under industrial and power alcohol) and blending of spirits industry

Paint and varnish industry

Bone crushing industry

Pickers industry

Milk and milk products industry

Non-ferrous metals and alloys in the form of ingots industry

Bread industry

Stemming or redrying of tobacco leaf industry (i.e., any industry engaged in the stemming, re-drying, handling, sorting, grading or packing of tobacco leaf

Agarbatee (including dhoop and dhoopbatee) industry

Coir (excluding the spinning sector) industry

Tobacco industry, that is to say, any industry engaged in the manufacture of cigars, zarda, snuff, quivam and guraku from tobacco

Paper products industry

Licensed salt industry (i.e., any industry engaged in the manufacture of salt for which a licence is necessary and which has land not less than 4.05 hectares

Linoleum industry and Indoleum industry

Explosives industry

Jute bailing or pressing industry

Fire-works and percussion cap works industry

Tent-making industry

Ferro-manganese industry

Ice or ice-cream industry

Winding of thread and yarn reeling industry

Cotton ginning, baling and pressing industry

Katha making industry

Beer manufacturing industry, that is to say, any industry engaged in the manufacture of the product of alcoholic fermentation of a mash in potable water of malted barley and hops, or of hops concentrated with or without the addition of other malted or unmalted cereals or other carbohydrate preparations

Beedi industry, that is to say, any industry engaged in the manufacture of beedis

Ferro-chrome industry, i.e., any industry engaged in manufacture of ferrochrome

Diamond cutting industry

Industries engaged in the manufacture of myrobalan extract powder, myrobalan extract solid and vegetable tanin blended extract

Bricks industry, i.e., any industry engaged in manufacture of bricks

All industries based on asbestos as principal raw material

Industries manufacturing iron ore pellets

Explanation In this Schedule, without prejudice to the ordinary meaning of expressions used therein,

(a) the expression "electrical, mechanical or general engineering products" includes:

(1) machinery and equipment for the generation, transmission, distribution or measurement of electrical energy and motors including cables and wires

(2) telephones, telegraph and wireless communication apparatus
(3) electric lamps (not including glass bulbs)
(4) electric fans and electrical domestic appliances
(5) storage and dry batteries
(6) radio receivers and sound reproducing instruments
(7) machinery used in industry (including textile machinery) other than electrical machinery and machine tools
(8) boilers and prime movers, including internal combustion engines, marine engines, and locomotives
(9) machine tools, that is to say, metal and wood working machinery
(10) grinding wheels
(11) ships
(12) automobiles and tractors
(13) bolts, nuts and rivets
(14) power-driven pumps
(15) bicycles
(16) hurricane lanterns
(17) sewing and knitting machines
(18) mathematical and scientific instruments
(19) products of metal rolling and re-rollings
(20) wires, pipes, tubes and fittings
(21) ferrous and non-ferrous castings
(22) safes, vaults and furniture made of iron or steel or steel alloys
(23) cutlery and surgical instruments
(24) drums and containers
(25) parts and accessories of products specified in items 1 to 24

(b) the expression "Iron and Steel" includes pig iron, ingots, blooms, billets and rolled or re-rolled products into basic forms and tool and alloy steel
(c) the expression "Paper" includes pulp, paperboards and strawboard
(d) the expression "textiles" includes the products of carding, spinning, weaving, finishing and dyeing yarn and fabrics, printing, knitting and embroidering

SCHEDULE II

[See Section 5(1B)]

MATTERS FOR WHICH PROVISION MAY BE MADE IN A SCHEME

1. The employees or class of employees who shall join the Fund, and the conditions under which employees may be exempted from joining the Fund or from making any contribution.
2. The time and manner in which contribution shall be made to the Fund by employers and by, or on behalf of, employees, (whether employed by him directly or by or through a contractor,) the contributions which an employee may, if he so desires, make under Section 6, and the manner in which such contributions may be recovered.

2A. The manner in which employee's contributions may be recovered by contractors from employees employed by or through such contractors.

3. The payment by the employer of such sums of money as may be necessary to meet the cost of administering the Fund and the rate at which and the manner in which the payment shall be made.
4. The constitution of any committee for assisting any Board of Trustees.
5. The opening of regional and other offices of any Board of Trustees.
6. The manner in which accounts shall be kept, the investment of moneys belonging to the Fund in accordance with any directions issued or conditions specified by the Central Government, the preparation of the budget, the audit of accounts and the submission of reports to the Central Government or to any specified State Government.
7. The conditions under which withdrawal from the Fund may be permitted and any deduction or forfeiture may be made and the maximum amount of such deduction or forfeiture.
8. The fixation by the Central Government in consultation with the boards of trustees concerned of the rate of interest payable to members.
9. The form in which an employee shall furnish particulars about himself and his family whenever required.
10. The nomination of a person to receive the amount standing to the credit of a member after his death and the cancellation or variation of such nomination.
11. The registers and records to be maintained with respect to employees and the returns to be furnished by employers or contractors.
12. The form or design of any identity card, token or disc for the purpose of identifying any employee, and for the issue, custody and replacement thereof.
13. The fees to be levied for any of the purposes specified in this Schedule.
14. The contraventions or default which shall be punishable under sub-section (2) of Section 14.
15. The further powers if any, which may be exercised by Inspectors.
16. The manner in which accumulations in any existing provident fund shall be transferred to the Fund under Section 15, and the mode of valuation of any assets which may be transferred by the employers in this behalf.
17. The conditions under which a member may be permitted to pay premia on life insurance, from the Fund.
18. Any other matter which is to be provided for in the Scheme or which may be necessary or proper for the purpose of implementing the Scheme.

SCHEDULE III

[See Section 6A(5)]

MATTERS FOR WHICH PROVISION MAY BE MADE IN THE PENSION SCHEME

1. The employees or class of employees to whom the Pension Scheme shall apply.
2. The time within which the employees who are not members of the Pension Scheme under Section 6A as it stood before the commencement of the Employees' Provident Funds and Miscellaneous Provisions (Amendment) Act, 1996, (hereinafter, in this Schedule, referred to as the amending Act) shall opt for the Pension Scheme.
3. The portion of employers' contribution to the Provident Fund which shall be credited to the Pension Fund and the manner in which it is credited.

4. The minimum qualifying service for being eligible for pension and the manner in which the employees may be granted the benefits of their past service under Section 6A, as it stood before the commencement of the amending Act.
5. The regulation of the manner in which, the period of service for which no contribution is received.
6. The manner in which employees' interest will be protected against default in payment of contribution by the employer.
7. The manner in which the accounts of the pension fund shall be kept and investment of moneys belonging to pension fund to be made subject to such pattern of investment as may be determined by the Central Government.
8. The form in which an employee shall furnish particulars about himself and the members of his family whenever required.
9. The forms, registers and records to be maintained in respect of employees, required for the administration of the Pension Scheme.
10. The scale of pension and pensionary benefits and the conditions relating to grant of such benefits to the employees.
11. The manner in which the exempted establishments have to pay contribution towards the Pension Scheme and the submission of returns relating thereto.
12. The mode of disbursement of pension and arrangements to be entered into with such disbursing agencies as may be specified for the purpose.
13. The manner in which the expenses for administering the Pension Scheme will be met from the income of the Pension Fund.
14. Any other matter which is to be provided for in the Pension Scheme or which may be necessary or proper for the purpose of implementation of the Pension Scheme.

SCHEDULE IV

[See Section 6C(6)]

MATTERS TO BE PROVIDED FOR IN THE EMPLOYEES' DEPOSIT-LINKED INSURANCE SCHEME

1. The employees or class of employees who shall be covered by the Insurance Scheme.
2. The manner in which the accounts of the Insurance Fund shall be kept and the investment of moneys belonging to the Insurance Fund subject to such pattern of investment as may be determined, by order, of the Central Government.
3. The form in which an employee shall furnish particulars about himself and the members of his family whenever required.
4. The nomination of a person to receive the insurance amount due to the employee after his death and the cancellation or variation of such nomination.
5. The registers and records to be maintained in respect of employees; the form or design of any identity card, token or disc or the purpose of identifying any employee or his nominee or member of his family entitled to receive the insurance amount.
6. The scales of insurance benefits and conditions relating to the grant of such benefits to the employees.

7. The manner in which the amount due to the nominee or the member of the family of the employee under the scheme is to be paid including a provision that the amount shall not be paid otherwise than in the form of a deposit in a savings bank account, in the name of such nominee or member of family in any corresponding new bank specified in the First Schedule to the Banking Companies (Acquisition and Transfer of Undertakings) Act, 1970.
8. Any other matter which is to be provided for in the Employees' Deposit-Linked Insurance Scheme or which may be necessary or proper for the purpose of implementing that Scheme.

24

The Employees' State Insurance Act, 1948

An Act to provide for certain benefits to employees in case of sickness, maternity and employment injury and to make provision for certain other matters in relation thereto.

Desired Knowledge Competencies

- To sketch the evolution of the Employees' State Insurance Act, 1948.
- To comprehend the extent and application of the Act and interpretation of the various definitions given in the Act.
- To discuss concepts of sickness, contribution, various organisations related to the Act, ESI Scheme, etc.

CONCEPT OF SOCIAL SECURITY

Referring to Maslow's hierarchy of needs we can quickly recall that food, shelter and clothing are the primary needs of any individual, while the next higher level of needs, i.e., safety needs include the need for freedom from threats caused by the environment, animals and people. Safety needs also cover the need for shelter, security and peace. These apart, an individual needs protection from distresses that may arise out of unforeseen exigencies like death or disablement due to accident at work.

We have talked about social security in previous chapters. The underlying theme of a social security system is that an individual on his/her own may not be capable enough to meet the exigencies of life. This becomes more pronounced for a wage-earner with little means to support himself and his family. Benefits provided by such a system are important not only for an individual worker and his/her family, but also for the

Reflection

According to the ILO, a social security system provides for basic income in cases of unemployment, illness and injury, old age and retirement, invalidity, family responsibilities such as pregnancy and childcare, and loss of the breadwinner of the family.

community. By providing healthcare, income security and social services, social security enhances productivity and contributes to the dignity and full realisation of the individual. For employers and enterprises, social security helps maintain a stable workforce that is adaptable to change. Further, by way of providing a safety net in case of economic crisis, social security serves as a fundamental element of social cohesion, thereby ensuring social peace and a positive engagement with globalisation and economic development (*www.ilo.org*).

Spotlight
Social security provides a safety net in case of economic crisis and serves as a fundamental element of social cohesion.

BACKDROP OF THE EMPLOYEES' STATE INSURANCE ACT, 1948

The first document on social insurance, "Report on Health Insurance" submitted to the Tripartite Labour Conference headed by B.P. Adarkar in 1943, was acclaimed as a worthy document and a precursor to the social security scheme in India. The Factories Act, 1948 was meant for ensuring the health, safety, welfare and leaves of workers employed in the factory premises only; there was no legislation that would cover aspects like sickness of workmen and medical benefits they may earn. There was thus a need for a legislation that would provide a multi-dimensional social security system.

Efforts all round were being made to provide organised social protection to the working class of the country through statutory provisions. The Employees' State Insurance Bill, having been passed by the Legislature, received its assent on 19th April 1948 and came on the Statute Book as The Employees' State Insurance (ESI) Act, 1948. In fact, the promulgation of the ESI Act by the Parliament was the first major legislation on social security for workers in independent India. The Act encompasses certain health-related eventualities that workers are generally exposed to, namely, sickness, maternity, temporary or permanent disablement, occupational disease or death due to employment injury, resulting in loss of wages or earning capacity (total or partial). Social security provisions made in the Act to counterbalance or negate the resulting physical or financial distress in such contingencies are thus aimed at upholding human dignity in times of crises through protection from deprivation, destitution, and social degradation, while enabling the society the retention and continuity of a socially useful and productive manpower (*www.esic.nic.in*). Further, this Act goes beyond the coverage of workers under the Factories Act, 1948 as the benefits of this Act extend to all workers, whether working inside the factory or establishment or elsewhere, or whether they are directly employed by the principal employer or through an intermediate agency, whether the employment is incidental or in connection with the factory or establishment.

"The Employees' State Insurance Act, 1948 entails a scheme of health insurance for industrial workers providing compulsory state insurance that renders certain benefits in the event of sickness, maternity and employment injury to workmen employed in or in connection with the work in factories other than seasonal factories. The broad object of the Act was to plan a scheme of this nature on an all-India basis, to be administered uniformly throughout the country. Hence the administration of the scheme was proposed to be entrusted to a corporation (known as the Employees' State Insurance Corporation) constituted by central legislation. The functions of the Corporation will be performed by a Central Board with representatives of Central and Provincial Governments, and of employers, workers and members from the medical profession. The Board will also include certain members elected by the Central Legislative Assembly. A Standing Committee of the Board will act as the

Spotlight
The broad object of the ESI Act, 1948 is to plan a scheme of health insurance on an all-India basis and administered uniformly throughout the country.

Executive of the Board, and a Medical Benefit Council will also be set up to advise on matters relating to the administration of medical benefit. As per the object of the Act, there would be an insurance fund mainly derived from contributions from employers and workmen. The contributions payable in respect of each workman will be based on his average wages and will be payable in the first instance by the employer. The employer will be entitled to recover the workman's share from the wages of the workman concerned. Workmen whose earnings do not exceed 10 annas a day will be totally exempt from payment of any share of the contribution; the entire contribution on account of such workmen being met by employer. Provision has been made for the preparation of proper budgets and the audit of accounts."

(Adapted from: Statement of Objects and Reasons, Gazette of India, 1946, Pt. V, pp. 319-357.)

The ESI Scheme was inaugurated in Kanpur on 24th February 1952 by the then Prime Minister, Pandit Jawahar Lal Nehru. It was simultaneously launched at Delhi as well and the initial coverage for both the centres was of 1,20,000 employees. Thereafter the Scheme was implemented in a phased manner across the country with the active involvement of State Governments.

The Employees' State Insurance Act, 1948 has been amended several times. Following is the list of amending acts and adaptation orders:

1. The Adaptation of Laws Order, 1950
2. The Employees' State Insurance (Amendment) Act, 1951
3. The Adaptation of Laws (No. 3) Order, 1956
4. The Adaptation of Laws (No. 4) Order, 1957
5. The Employees' State Insurance (Amendment) Act, 1966
6. The Central Labour Laws (Extension to Jammu and Kashmir) Act, 1970
7. The Employees' State Insurance (Amendment) Act, 1975
8. The Employees' State Insurance (Amendment) Act, 1984
9. The Employees' State Insurance (Amendment) Act, 1989
10. The Employees' State Insurance (Amendment) Act, 2010

Spotlight

The latest amendment in the Act is the ESI (Amendment) Act, 2010.

Considering the changes that have happened in the economic scenario in the country since the Act was amended last in 1989, the ESI Corporation in 2007 had decided to bring comprehensive amendments in the Act. The ESI (Amendment) Bill, 2010 received assent of the President of India on 24th May 2010 and has been enacted as the Employees' State Insurance (Amendment) Act, 2010. All the provisions of the Amendment Act (except Section 18) have come into effect from 1st June 2010 vide Notification SO No. 1296 (E) dated 1st June 2010.

ABOUT THE ACT
CHAPTER I: PRELIMINARY

Short Title, Extent, Commencement and Application (Section 1)

1. This Act may be called the Employees' State Insurance Act, 1948.
2. It extends to the whole of India.
3. It shall come into force on such date or dates as the Central Government may, by notification in the Official Gazette, appoint, and different dates may be appointed for different provisions of this Act and for different States or for different parts thereof.
4. It shall apply, in the first instance, to all factories (including factories belonging to the Government) other than seasonal factories.

Provided that nothing contained in this sub-section shall apply to a factory or establishment belonging to or under the control of the Government whose employees are otherwise in receipt of benefits substantially similar or superior to the benefits provided under this Act.

5. The appropriate Government may, in consultation with the Corporation and where the appropriate Government is a State Government, with the approval of the Central Government, after giving 1 months' notice of its intention of so doing by notification in the Official Gazette, extend the provisions of this Act or any of them, to any other establishment, or class of establishments, industrial, commercial, agricultural or otherwise.

   Provided that where the provisions of this Act have been brought into force in any part of a State, the said provisions shall stand extended to any such establishment or class of establishments within that part if the provisions have already been extended to similar establishment or class of establishments in another part of that State.
6. A factory or an establishment to which this Act applies shall continue to be governed by this Act notwithstanding that the number of persons employed therein at any time falls below the limit specified by or under this Act or the manufacturing process therein ceases to be carried on with the aid of power.

Definitions (Section 2)

In this Act, unless there is anything repugnant in the subject or context:

Appropriate Government [Section 2(1)] Appropriate Government means, in respect of establishments under the control of the Central Government or a railway administration or a major port or a mine or oilfield, the Central Government, and in all other cases, the State Government;

Confinement [Section 2(3)] Confinement means labour resulting in the issue of a living child or labour after 26 weeks of pregnancy resulting in the issue of a child whether alive or dead;

Contribution [Section 2(4)] Contribution means the sum of money payable to the Corporation by the principal employer in respect of an employee and includes any amount payable by or on behalf of the employee in accordance with the provisions of this Act;

> **Spotlight**
> As per Section 2(4), contribution is the sum of money payable to the Corporation by the principal employer in respect of an employee.

Corporation [Section 2(6)] Corporation means the Employees' State Insurance Corporation set up under this Act;

Dependant [Section 2(6A)] Dependant means any of the following relatives of a deceased insured person, namely:

(i) a widow, a legitimate or adopted son who has not attained the age of 25 years, an unmarried legitimate or adopted daughter;

(ia) a widowed mother;

(ii) if wholly dependent on the earnings of the insured person at the time of his death, a legitimate or adopted son or daughter who has attained the age of 25 years and who is infirm;

(iii) if wholly or in part dependent on the earnings of the insured person at the time of his death:

  (a) a parent other than a widowed mother,

  (b) a minor illegitimate son, an unmarried illegitimate daughter or a daughter legitimate or adopted or illegitimate if married and a minor or if widowed and a minor,

  (c) a minor brother or an unmarried sister or a widowed sister if a minor,

(d) a widowed daughter-in-law,
(e) a minor child of a pre-deceased son,
(f) a minor child of a pre-deceased daughter where no parent of the child is alive, or
(g) a paternal grand-parent if no parent of the insured person is alive;

Duly appointed [Section 2(7)] Duly appointed means appointed in accordance with the provisions of this Act or with the rules or regulations made thereunder;

Employment injury [Section 2(8)] Employment injury means a personal injury to an employee caused by accident or an occupational disease arising out of and in the course of his employment, being an insurable employment, whether the accident occurs or the occupational disease is contracted within or outside the territorial limits of India;

Spotlight
Employment injury as per Section 2(8) may be caused by accident occurring even outside the territorial limits of India.

In *Bhagubai vs. General Manager, Central Railway, Bombay* [(1954) 56 BOMLR 509] the deceased was employed in the Central Railway at Kurla station and he lived in the railway quarters adjoining the railway station. He had left his quarters a few minutes before midnight in order to join duty. He went through the compound of the railway quarters and was stabbed by some unknown person. The dispute is that whether the accident arise out of the employment of the deceased. It was held that there must be a causal connection between the accident and the employment in order that the Court can say that the accident arose out of the employment of the deceased. In this case it is established that the employee was in the place where he was murdered by reason of his employment. The connection between the employment and the accident was hence established.

(Adapted from: www.indiankanoon.org/doc/130571/ accessed on 15/4/2014.)

CASE CORNER

In *The Regional Director, ESI Corporation and Another vs. Francis De Costa and Another*, the first respondent was hit by a lorry belonging to his employer while on the way to his place of employment on his bicycle, at a place about 1 kilometre away from the factory. His collar-bone was fractured and he had to remain in hospital for 12 days. The only dispute in this case is whether the injury will amount to "employment injury" within the meaning of Section 2(8) of the ESI Act, so as to enable the respondent to claim benefit under the Act.

The employee, in the order to succeed in this case, had to prove that the injury that he had suffered arose out of and was in the course of his employment. It did not appear that the injury suffered by the employee arose in any way out of his employment. Unless it can be said that his employment began as soon as he set out for the factory from his home, it cannot be held conclusively that the injury was caused by an accident "arising out of and in the course of his employment". A road accident may happen anywhere at any time. But such accident cannot be said to have arisen out of employment. Further, the bicycle belonged to the respondent and not the employer. If he meets with an accident while riding his own bicycle on the way to his place of work, it cannot be said that the accident was reasonably incidental to the employment and was in the course of his employment.

The employee was unable to prove that the accident had any causal connection with the work he was doing at the factory and in any event, it was not suffered in the course of employment.

(Adapted from: www.indiankanoon.org/doc/1095646/ accessed on 12/4/2014.)

There can also be cases where an employee has to go out of his workplace in the usual course of his employment. In *South Maitland Railways Proprietary Limited vs. James* (67 CLR 496) it was observed that when the workmen had to go for a short time to drink cool water on a hot day in course of their employment, in order to enable them to continue to work, and without which they could not have otherwise continued, they were in such cases doing something in the course of their employment.

(Adapted from: www.indiankanoon.org/doc/1095646/ accessed on 12/4/2014.)

CASE CORNER

In *Saurashtra Salt Manufacturing Co. vs. Bai Valu Raja* [AIR (1958) SC 881], the Court held that as a rule, the employment of a workman does not commence until he has reached the place of employment and does not continue when he has left that place, the journey to and from the place of employment being excluded. There might however be some reasonable extension in both time and place to this principle. A workman might be considered as in the course of his employment even though he had not reached or had left his employer's premises in some special cases. The facts and circumstances of each case would have to be examined very carefully in order to ascertain whether the accident arose out of and in the course of the employment of a workman, keeping in view at all times this theory of notional extension. The Court observed that when a workman is on a public road or a public place or on a public transport, he is there as any other member of the public, and is not there in the course of his employment unless the very nature of his employment makes it necessary for him to be there. Further, a workman is not in the course of his employment from the moment he leaves his home and is on his way to his place of work. He certainly is in the course of his employment if he reaches the place of work or a point or an area which comes within the theory of notional extension, outside of which the employer is not liable to pay compensation for any accident happening to him.

(Adapted from: www.indiankanoon.org/doc/1095646/ accessed on 12/4/2014.)

Employee [Section 2(9)] Employee means any person employed for wages in or in connection with the work of a factory or establishment to which this Act applies and:

(i) who is directly employed by the principal employer on any work of, or incidental or preliminary to or connected with the work of, the factory or establishment, whether such work is done by the employee in the factory or establishment or elsewhere; or

(ii) who is employed by or through an immediate employer on the premises of the factory or establishment or under the supervision of the principal employer or his agent on work which is ordinarily part of the work of the factory or establishment or which is preliminary to the work carried on in or incidental to the purpose of the factory or establishment; or

(iii) whose services are temporarily lent or let on hire to the principal employer by the person with whom the person whose services are so lent or let on hire has entered into a contract of service;

and includes any person employed for wages on any work connected with the administration of the factory or establishment or any part, department or branch thereof or with the purchase of raw materials for, or the distribution or sale of the products of, the factory or establishment or any person engaged as an apprentice, not being an apprentice engaged under the Apprentices Act, 1961, and includes such person engaged as apprentice whose training period is extended to any length of time but does not include:–

(a) any member of the Indian naval, military or air forces; or
(b) any person so employed whose wages (excluding remuneration for overtime work) exceed such wages as may be prescribed by the Central Government:

Provided that an employee whose wages (excluding remuneration for overtime work) exceed such wages as may be prescribed by the Central Government at any time after (and not before) the beginning of the contribution period, shall continue to be an employee until the end of that period;

CASE CORNER

In *Royal Talkies, Hyderabad and Others vs. Employees' State Insurance Corporation* [(1979 SCR (1) 80], the contractors of the canteen and cycle stand attached to the theatre (Royal Talkies), which were leased out to them, had employed certain persons. The question that arose was whether the Cinema Theatre Manager can be held liable to pay contribution as the principal employer of the workers engaged in the canteen or cycle stand. The Supreme Court held that keeping a cycle stand and running a canteen are incidental or adjunct to the primary purpose of the theatre within the meaning of clause (ii) of Section 2(9). While referring to the definition of 'employee' in Section 2(9) it was pointed out that: "The reach and range of the definition is apparently wide and deliberately transcends pure contractual relationships."

The Supreme Court also held that Section 2(9) contains 2 substantive parts; unless the person employed qualifies under both, he is not an 'employee'. Firstly, he must be "employed" in or in connection with the work of an establishment. The expression "in connection with the work of an establishment" includes in a wide variety of workmen who may not be employed in the establishment as such, but may be engaged only in connection with the work of the establishment. Merely being employed in connection with the work of an establishment in itself does not entitle a person to be an employee of such establishment. He must not only be employed in connection with the work of the establishment, but also be shown to be employed in one or the other of the 3 categories mentioned in Section 2(9).

(Adapted from: www.indiankanoon.org/doc/983834/ accessed on 13/4/2014.)

Exempted employee [Section 2(10)] Exempted employee means an employee who is not liable under this Act to pay the employee's contribution;

Family [Section 2(11)] Family means all or any of the following relatives of an insured person, namely:

(i) a spouse;
(ii) a minor legitimate or adopted child dependent upon the insured person;
(iii) a child who is wholly dependent on the earnings of the insured person and who is:
    (a) receiving education, till he or she attains the age of 21 years,
    (b) an unmarried daughter;
(iv) a child who is infirm by reason of any physical or mental abnormality or injury and is wholly dependent on the earnings of the insured person, so long as the infirmity continues;
(v) dependant parents, whose income from all sources does not exceed such income as may be prescribed by the Central Government;

Spotlight

An exempted employee as per Section 2(10) is not liable to pay the employees contribution.

(vi) in case the insured person is unmarried and his or her parents are not alive, a minor brother or sister wholly dependant upon the earnings of the insured person;

Factory [Section 2(12)] Factory means any premises including the precincts thereof whereon 10 or more persons are employed or were employed on any day of the preceding 12 months, and in any part of which a manufacturing process is being carried on or is ordinarily so carried on, but does not include a mine subject to the operation of the Mines Act, 1952, or a railway running shed;

Immediate employer [Section 2(13)] Immediate employer in relation to employees employed by or through him, means a person who has undertaken the execution on the premises of a factory or an establishment to which this Act applies or under the supervision of the principal employer or his agent, of the whole or any part of any work which is ordinarily part of the work of the factory, or establishment of the principal employer or is preliminary to the work carried on in, or incidental to the purpose of, any such factory or establishment and includes a person by whom the services of an employee who has entered into a contract of service with him are temporarily lent or let on hire to the principal employer and includes a contractor.

Insurable employment [Section 2(13A)] Insurable employment means an employment in a factory or establishment to which this Act applies;

Spotlight

Insurable employment defined in Section 2(13A) means an employment in a factory or establishment to which this Act applies.

Insured person [Section 2(14)] Insured person means a person who is or was an employee in respect of whom contributions are or were payable under this Act and who is, by reason thereof, entitled to any of the benefits provided by this Act;

Managing agent [Section 2(14A)] Managing agent means any person appointed or acting as the representative of another person for the purpose of carrying on such other person's trade or business, but does not include an individual manager subordinate to an employer;

Manufacturing process [Section 2(14AA)] Manufacturing process shall have the meaning assigned to it in the Factories Act, 1948;

Miscarriage [Section 2(14B)] Miscarriage means expulsion of the contents of a pregnant uterus at any period prior to or during the twenty-sixth week of pregnancy but does not include any miscarriage, the causing of which is punishable under the Indian Penal Code;

Occupier [Section 2(15)] Occupier of the factory shall have the meaning assigned to it in the Factories Act, 1948;

Permanent partial disablement [Section 2(15A)] Permanent partial disablement means such disablement of a permanent nature, as reduces the earning capacity of an employee in every employment which he was capable of undertaking at the time of the accident resulting in the disablement:

Spotlight

Every injury specified in Part II of the Second Schedule shall be deemed to result in permanent partial disablement.

Provided that every injury specified in Part II of the Second Schedule shall be deemed to result in permanent partial disablement;

Permanent total disablement [Section 2(15B)] Permanent total disablement means such disablement of a permanent nature as incapacitates an employee for all work which he was capable of performing at the time of the accident resulting in such disablement:

Provided that permanent total disablement shall be deemed to result from every injury specified in Part I of the Second Schedule or from any combination of injuries specified in Part II thereof where the aggregate percentage of the loss of earning capacity, as specified in the said Part II against those injuries, amounts to 100 per cent or more;

Power [Section 2(15C)] Power shall have the meaning assigned to it in the Factories Act, 1948;

Prescribed [Section 2(16)] Prescribed means prescribed by rules made under this Act;

Principal employer [Section 2(17)] Principal employer means:

(i) in a factory, the owner or occupier of the factory and includes the managing agent of such owner or occupier, the legal representative of a deceased owner or occupier, and where a person has been named as the manager of the factory under the Factories Act, 1948, the person so named;

(ii) in any establishment under the control of any department of any Government in India, the authority appointed by such Government in this behalf or where no authority is so appointed, the head of the department ;

(iii) in any other establishment, any person responsible for the supervision and control of the establishment;

CASE CORNER

In *The Regional Director, ESI Corporation, Jaipur vs. P. C. Kasliwal and Others* [(1981) WLN 460], P. C. Kasliwal is an active partner of M/s Vijay Metal Industries, Jaipur, a partnership firm. He draws a monthly allowance of ₹400. The ESI Corporation, Jaipur, taking Kasliwal as an employee within the meaning of Section 2(9) of the ESI Act (or. the Act), required the firm to pay employees' contribution amounting to ₹211.25 and employer's special contribution amounting to ₹472 for the period from 28th January 1968 to 30th January 1971. When the firm did not make the said payment, the Regional Director, ESI Corporation obtained a certificate from the Collector, Jaipur, under the Public Demands Recovery Act. An application was filed by Kasliwal before the Court, and the main contention raised therein was that he was only a partner of the firm and not an employee within the meaning of the Act. The ESI Corporation contested the application and a preliminary issue was whether an employer/partner can be an employee of his own firm.

The Court held that a partner who draws emoluments and actively works in the factory is an 'employee' within the meaning of Section 2(9) of the Act and he can have different capacities as 'principal employer' and 'employee' and both capacities are not contradictory to each other. Employees' contribution as well as 'employer's special contribution' is payable in respect of such partner. In Kasliwal's case it is not disputed that he was actively working in the factory and was drawing a monthly allowance. As such, for the purpose of 'employees' contribution as well as 'employer's special contribution', he is an employee within the meaning of Section 2(9) of the Act.

(Adapted from: www.indiankanoon.org/doc/756309/ accessed on 13/4/2014.)

Regulation [Section 2(18)] Regulation means a regulation by the Corporation;

Schedule [Section 2(19)] Schedule means a Schedule to this Act;

Seasonal factory [Section 2(19A)] Seasonal factory means a factory which is exclusively engaged in 1 or more of the following manufacturing processes, namely, cotton ginning, cotton or jute pressing, decortication of ground-nuts, the manufacture of coffee, indigo, lac, rubber, sugar (including gur) or tea or any manufacturing process which is incidental to or connected with any of the aforesaid processes and includes a factory which is engaged for a period not exceeding 7 months in a year–

(a) in any process of blending, packing or repacking of tea or coffee; or
(b) in such other manufacturing process as the Central Government may, by notification in the Official Gazette, specify;

Sickness [Section 2(20)] Sickness means a condition which requires medical treatment and attendance and necessitates abstention from work on medical grounds;

Temporary disablement [Section 2(21)] Temporary disablement means a condition resulting from an employment injury which requires medical treatment and renders an employee, as a result of such injury, temporarily incapable of doing the work which he was doing prior to or at the time of the injury;

Wages [Section 2(22)] Wages means all remuneration paid or payable in cash to an employee, if the terms of the contract of employment, express or implied, were fulfilled and includes any payment to an employee in respect of any period of authorised leave, lock-out, strike which is not illegal or layoff and other additional remuneration, if any, paid at intervals not exceeding 2 months, but does not include:

(a) any contribution paid by the employer to any pension fund or provident fund, or under this Act;
(b) any travelling allowance or the value of any travelling concession;
(c) any sum paid to the person employed to defray special expenses entailed on him by the nature of his employment; or
(d) any gratuity payable on discharge;

Spotlight
Wages, as per Section 2(22), excludes any gratuity payable on discharge.

Wage period [Section 2(23)] Wage period in relation to an employee means the period in respect of which wages are ordinarily payable to him whether in terms of the contract of employment, express or implied or otherwise;

Section 2(24) All other words and expressions used but not defined in this Act and defined in the Industrial Disputes Act, 1947 shall have the meanings respectively assigned to them in that Act.

Registration of Factories and Establishments (Section 2A)

Every factory or establishment to which this Act applies shall be registered within such time and in such manner as may be specified in the regulations made in this behalf.

CHAPTER II: CORPORATION, STANDING COMMITTEE AND MEDICAL BENEFIT COUNCIL

Establishment of Employees' State Insurance Corporation (Section 3)

1. With effect from such date as the Central Government may, by notification in the Official Gazette, appoint in this behalf, there shall be established for the administration of the scheme of

Employees' State Insurance in accordance with the provisions of this Act a Corporation to be known as the Employees' State Insurance Corporation.

2. The Corporation shall be a body corporate by the name of Employees' State Insurance Corporation having perpetual succession and a common seal and shall by the said name sue and be sued.

Spotlight

As per Section 3(2), the ESIC shall be a body corporate having perpetual succession and a common seal, and shall sue and be sued by the said name.

Constitution of Corporation (Section 4)

The Corporation shall consist of the following members, namely:

(a) a Chairman to be appointed by the Central Government;
(b) a Vice-Chairman to be appointed by the Central Government;
(c) not more than 5 persons to be appointed by the Central Government,
(d) 1 person each representing each of the States in which this Act is in force to be appointed by the State Government concerned;
(e) 1 person to be appointed by the Central Government to represent the Union territories;
(f) 10 persons representing employers to be appointed by the Central Government in consultation with such organisations of employers as may be recognised for the purpose by the Central Government;
(g) 10 persons representing employees to be appointed by the Central Government in consultation with such organisations of employees as may be recognised for the purpose by the Central Government;
(h) 2 persons representing the medical profession to be appointed by the Central Government in consultation with such organisations of medical practitioners as may be recognised for the purpose by the Central Government;
(i) 3 members of Parliament of whom 2 shall be members of the House of the People (Lok Sabha) and 1 shall be a member of the Council of States (Rajya Sabha) elected respectively by the members of the House of the People and the members of the Council of States; and
(j) the Director-General of the Corporation, *ex-officio*.

Term of Office of the Members of the Corporation (Section 5)

1. Save as otherwise expressly provided in this Act, the term of office of members of the Corporation, other than the members referred to in clauses (a), (b), (c), (d) and (e) of Section 4 and the *ex-officio* member, shall be 4 years commencing from the date on which their appointment or election is notified.

   Provided that a member of the Corporation shall, notwithstanding the expiry of the said period of 4 years, continue to hold office until the appointment or election of his successor is notified.
2. The members of the Corporation referred to in clauses (a), (b), (c), (d) and (e) of Section 4 shall hold office during the pleasure of the Government appointing them.

Eligibility for Re-appointment or Re-election (Section 6)

An outgoing member of the Corporation, the Standing Committee, or the Medical Benefit Council shall be eligible for re-appointment or re-election as the case may be.

Authentication of Orders, Decisions, etc. (Section 7)

All orders and decisions of the Corporation shall be authenticated by the signature of the Director General of the Corporation and all other instruments issued by the Corporation shall be authenticated by the signature of the Director-General or such other officer of the Corporation as may be authorised by him.

Constitution of Standing Committee (Section 8)

Spotlight
The Chairman of the Standing Committee is appointed by the Central Government.

A Standing Committee of the Corporation shall be constituted from among its members, consisting of-

(a) a Chairman appointed by the Central Government;
(b) 3 members of the Corporation, appointed by the Central Government;
(bb) 3 members of the Corporation representing such 3 State Governments thereon as the Central Government may, by notification in the Official Gazette, specify from time to time;
(c) 8 members elected by the Corporation as follows:
   (ii) 3 members from among the members of the Corporation representing employers;
   (iii) 3 members from among the members of the Corporation representing employees;
   (iv) 1 member from among the members of the Corporation representing the medical profession; and
   (v) 1 member from among the members of the Corporation elected by Parliament;
(d) the Director-General of the Corporation, *ex-officio*.

Term of Office of Members of Standing Committee (Section 9)

1. Save as otherwise expressly provided in this Act, the term of office of a member of the Standing Committee, other than a member referred to in clause (a) or clause (b) or clause (bb) of Section 8, shall be 2 years from the date on which his election is notified:

   Provided that a member of the Standing Committee shall, notwithstanding the expiry of the said period of 2 years, continue to hold office until the election of his successor is notified:

   Provided further that a member of the Standing Committee shall cease to hold office when he ceases to be a member of the Corporation.
2. A member of the Standing Committee referred to in clause (a) or clause (b) or clause (bb) of Section 8 shall hold office during the pleasure of the Central Government.

Medical Benefit Council (Section 10)

1. The Central Government shall constitute a Medical Benefit Council consisting of:
   (a) the Director-General, the Employees' State Insurance Corporation, *ex-officio* as Chairman;
   (b) the Director-General, Health Services, *ex-officio* as Co-Chairman;
   (c) the Medical Commissioner of the Corporation, *ex-officio*;
   (d) 1 member each representing each of the States (other than Union territories) in which this Act is in force to be appointed by the State Government concerned;
   (e) 3 members representing employers to be appointed by the Central Government in consultation with such organisations of employers as may be recognised for the purpose by the Central Government;
   (f) 3 members representing employees to be appointed by the Central Government in consultation with such organisations of employees as may be recognised for the purpose by the Central Government; and

(g) 3 members, of whom not less than 1 shall be a woman, representing the medical profession, to be appointed by the Central Government in consultation with such organisations of medical practitioners as may be recognised for the purpose by the Central Government.

2. Save as otherwise expressly provided in this Act, the term of office of a member of the Medical Benefit Council, other than a member referred to in any of the clauses (a) to (d) of sub-section (1), shall be 4 years from the date on which his appointment is notified:

   Provided that a member of the Medical Benefit Council shall, notwithstanding the expiry of the said period of 4 years continue to hold office until the appointment of his successor is notified.

3. A member of the Medical Benefit Council referred to in clauses (b) and (d) of sub-section (1) shall hold office during the pleasure of the Government appointing him.

Resignation of Membership (Section 11)

A member of the Corporation, the Standing Committee or the Medical Benefit Council may resign his office by notice in writing to the Central Government and his seat shall fall vacant on the acceptance of the resignation by that Government.

Cessation of Membership (Section 12)

1. A member of the Corporation, the Standing Committee or the Medical Benefit Council shall cease to be a member of that body if he fails to attend 3 consecutive meetings thereof:

   Provided that the Corporation, the Standing Committee or the Medical Benefit Council, as the case may be, may, subject to rules made by the Central Government in this behalf, restore him to membership.

2. Where in the opinion of the Central Government any person appointed or elected to represent employers, employees or the medical profession on (*sic.*) the Corporation, the Standing Committee or the Medical Benefit Council, as the case may be, has ceased to represent such employers, employees or the medical profession, the Central Government may, by notification in the Official Gazette, declare that with effect from such date as may be specified therein such person shall cease to be a member of the Corporation, the Standing Committee or the Medical Benefit Council, as the case may be.

3. A person referred to in clause (i) of Section 4 shall cease to be a member on becoming a Minister or Speaker or Deputy Speaker of the House of the People or Deputy Chairman of the Council of States or when he ceases to be a member of Parliament.

Disqualification (Section 13)

A person shall be disqualified for being chosen as or for being a member of the Corporation, the Standing Committee or the Medical Benefit Council:

(a) if he is declared to be of unsound mind by a competent Court; or

(b) if he is an undischarged insolvent; or

(c) if he has directly or indirectly by himself or by his partner any interest in subsisting contract with, or any work being done for, the Corporation except as a medical practitioner or as a share-holder (not being a Director) of a company; or

(d) if before or after the commencement of this Act, he has been convicted of an offence involving moral turpitude.

Filling of Vacancies (Section 14)

1. Vacancies in the office of appointed or elected members of the Corporation, the Standing Committee or the Medical Benefit Council shall be filled by appointment or election, as the case may be.
2. A member of the Corporation, the Standing Committee or the Medical Benefit Council appointed or elected to fill a casual vacancy shall hold office only so long as the member in whose place he is appointed or elected would have been entitled to hold office if the vacancy had not occurred.

Fees and Allowances (Section 15)

Members of the Corporation, the Standing Committee and the Medical Benefit Council shall receive such fees and allowances as may from time to time be prescribed by the Central Government.

Principal Officers (Section 16)

1. The Central Government may, in consultation with the Corporation, appoint a Director-General and a Financial Commissioner.
2. The Director-General shall be the Chief Executive Officer of the Corporation.
3. The Director-General and the Financial Commissioner shall be whole-time officers of the Corporation and shall not undertake any work unconnected with their office without the sanction of the Central Government and of the Corporation.
4. The Director-General or the Financial Commissioner shall hold office for such period, not exceeding 5 years, as may be specified in the order appointing him. An outgoing Director General or Financial Commissioner shall be eligible for re-appointment if he is otherwise qualified.
5. The Director-General or the Financial Commissioner shall receive such salary and allowances as may be prescribed by the Central Government.
6. A person shall be disqualified from being appointed as or for being the Director General or the Financial Commissioner if he is subject to any of the disqualifications specified in Section 13.
7. The Central Government may at any time remove the Director General or the Financial Commissioner from office and shall do so if such removal is recommended by a resolution of the Corporation passed at a special meeting called for the purpose and supported by the votes of not less than two-third is of the total strength of the Corporation.

Spotlight

The Director-General shall be the Chief Executive Officer of the Corporation.

Staff (Section 17)

1. The Corporation may employ such other staff of officers and servants as may be necessary for the efficient transaction of its business provided that the sanction of the Central Government shall be obtained for the creation of any post the maximum monthly salary of which exceeds such salary as may be prescribed by the Central Government.
2. (a) The method of recruitment, salary and allowances, discipline and other conditions of service of the members of the staff of the Corporation shall be such as may be specified in the regulations made by the Corporation in accordance with the rules and orders applicable to the officers and employees of the Central Government drawing corresponding scales of pay:

   Provided that where the Corporation is of the opinion that it is necessary to make a departure from the said rules or orders in respect of any of the matters aforesaid, it shall obtain the prior approval of the Central Government.

Provided further that this sub-section shall not apply to appointment of consultants and specialists in various fields appointed on contract basis.

(b) In determining the corresponding scales of pay of the members of the staff under clause (a), the Corporation shall have regard to the educational qualifications, method of recruitment, duties and responsibilities of such officers and employees under the Central Government and in case of any doubt, the Corporation shall refer the matter to the Central Government whose decision thereon shall be final.

3. Every appointment to posts (other than medical posts) corresponding to Group A and Group B posts under the Central Government shall be made in consultation with the Union Public Service Commission:

   Provided that this sub-section shall not apply to an officiating or temporary appointment for a period not exceeding 1 year.

   Provided further that any such officiating or temporary appointment shall not confer any claim for regular appointment and the services rendered in that capacity shall not count towards seniority or minimum qualifying service specified in the regulations for promotion to next higher grade.

4. If any question arises whether a post corresponds to a Group A and Group B posts under the Central Government, the question shall be referred to that Government whose decision thereon shall be final.

Powers of the Standing Committee (Section 18)

1. Subject to the general superintendence and control of the Corporation, the Standing Committee shall administer the affairs of the Corporation and may exercise any of the powers and perform any of the functions of the Corporation.

Spotlight

Section 18(1) provides that the Standing Committee shall administer the affairs of the corporation.

2. The Standing Committee shall submit for the consideration and decision of the Corporation all such cases and matters as may be specified in the regulations made in this behalf.
3. The Standing Committee may, in its discretion, submit any other case or matter for the decision of the Corporation.

Corporation's Power to Promote Measures for Health, etc., of Insured Persons (Section 19)

The Corporation may, in addition to the scheme of benefits specified in this Act, promote measures for the improvement of the health and welfare of insured persons and for the rehabilitation and re-employment of insured persons who have been disabled or injured and may incur in respect of such measures expenditure from the funds of the Corporation within such limits as may be prescribed by the Central Government.

Meetings of Corporation, Standing Committee and Medical Benefit Council (Section 20)

Subject to any rules made under this Act, the Corporation, the Standing Committee and the Medical Benefit Council shall meet at such times and places and shall observe such rules or procedure in regard to transaction of business at their meetings as may be specified in the regulations made in this behalf.

Supersession of the Corporation and Standing Committee (Section 21)

1. If in the opinion of the Central Government, the Corporation, or the Standing Committee persistently makes default in performing the duties imposed on it by or under this Act or abuses its powers, that Government may, by notification in the official Gazette, supersede the Corporation, or in the case of the Standing Committee, supersede in consultation with the Corporation, the Standing Committee:

   Provided that before issuing a notification under this sub-section the Central Government shall give a reasonable opportunity to the Corporation or the Standing Committee, as the case may be, to show cause why it should not be superseded and shall consider the explanations and objections, if any, of the Corporation or the Standing Committee, as the case may be.
2. Upon the publication of a notification under sub-section (1) superseding the Corporation or the Standing Committee, all the members of the Corporation or the Standing Committee, as the case may be, shall, as from the date of such publication, be deemed to have vacated their offices.
3. When the Standing Committee has been superseded, a new Standing Committee shall be immediately constituted in accordance with Section 8.

> **Spotlight**
> When the Standing Committee has been superseded, a new Standing Committee shall be immediately constituted, as provided in Section 21(3).

4. When the Corporation has been superseded, the Central Government may:
   (a) immediately appoint or cause to be appointed or elected new members to the Corporation in accordance with Section 4 and may constitute a new Standing Committee under Section 8;
   (b) in its discretion, appoint such agency, for such period as it may think fit, to exercise the powers and perform the functions of the Corporation and such agency shall be competent to exercise all the powers and perform all the functions of the Corporation.
5. The Central Government shall cause a full report of any action taken under this section and the circumstances leading to such action to be laid before Parliament at the earliest opportunity and in any case not later than 3 months from the date of the notification superseding the Corporation or the Standing Committee, as the case may be.

Duties of Medical Benefit Council (Section 22)

The Medical Benefit Council shall:

(a) advise the Corporation and the Standing Committee on matters relating to the administration of medical benefit, the certification for purposes of the grant of benefits and other connected matters;
(b) have such powers and duties of investigation as may be prescribed in relation to complaints against medical practitioners in connection with medical treatment and attendance; and
(c) perform such other duties in connection with medical treatment and attendance as may be specified in the regulations.

Duties of Director-General and the Financial Commissioner (Section 23)

The Director-General and the Financial Commissioner shall exercise such powers and discharge such duties as may be prescribed. They shall also perform such other functions as may be specified in the regulations.

Acts of Corporation, etc., not Invalid by Reason of Defect in Constitution, etc. (Section 24)

No act of the Corporation, the Standing Committee or the Medical Benefit Council shall be deemed to be invalid by reason of any defect in the constitution of the Corporation, the Standing Committee or the Medical Benefit Council, or on the ground that any member thereof was not entitled to hold or continue in office by reason of any disqualification or of any irregularity in his appointment or election, or by reason of such act having been done during the period of any vacancy in the office of any member of the Corporation, the Standing Committee, or the Medical Benefit Council.

Regional Board, Local Committees, Regional and Local Medical Benefit Councils (Section 25)

The Corporation may appoint Regional Boards, Local Committees, and Regional and Local Medical Benefit Councils in such areas and in such manner, and delegate to them such powers and functions, as may be provided by the regulations.

CHAPTER III: FINANCE AND AUDIT

Employees' State Insurance Fund (Section 26)

1. All contributions paid under this Act and all other moneys received on behalf of the Corporation shall be paid into a fund called the Employees' State Insurance Fund which shall be held and administered by the Corporation for the purposes of this Act.
2. The Corporation may accept grants, donations and gifts from the Central or any State Government, local authority, or any individual or body whether incorporated or not, for all or any of the purposes of this Act.
3. Subject to the other provisions contained in this Act and to any rules or regulations made in this behalf, all moneys accruing or payable to the said Fund shall be paid into the Reserve Bank of India or such other bank as may be approved by the Central Government to the credit of an account styled the account of the Employees' State Insurance Fund.
4. Such account shall be operated on by such officers as may be authorised by the Standing Committee with the approval of the Corporation.

Spotlight

As per Section 26(1), all contributions and all other moneys received on behalf of the Corporation shall be paid into a fund called the Employees' State Insurance Fund.

Grant by the Central Government (Section 27)

Repealed by the Employees' State Insurance (Amendment) Act, 1966.

Purposes for which the Fund May be Expended (Section 28)

Subject to the provisions of this Act and of any rules made by the Central Government in that behalf, the Employees' State Insurance Fund shall be expended only for the following purposes, namely:

(i) payment of benefits and provision of medical treatment and attendance to insured persons and, where the medical benefit is extended to their families, the provision of such medical benefit to their families, in accordance with the provisions of this Act and defraying the charges and costs in connection therewith;

(ii) payment of fees and allowances to members of the Corporation, the Standing Committee and the Medical Benefit Council, the Regional Boards Local Committees and Regional and Local Medical Benefit Councils;

(iii) payment of salaries, leave and joining time allowances, travelling and compensatory allowances, gratuities and compassionate allowances, pensions, contributions to provident or other benefit fund of officers and servants of the Corporation and meeting the expenditure in respect of officers and other services set up for the purpose of giving effect to the provisions of this Act;

(iv) establishment and maintenance of hospitals, dispensaries and other institutions and the provision of medical and other ancillary services for the benefit of insured persons and, where the medical benefit is extended to their families, their families;

(v) payment of contributions to any State Government, local authority or any private body or individual, towards the cost of medical treatment and attendance provided to insured persons and, where the medical benefit is extended to their families, including the cost of any building and equipment, in accordance with any agreement entered into by the Corporation;

(vi) defraying the cost (including all expenses) of auditing the accounts of the Corporation and of the valuation of its assets and liabilities;

(vii) defraying the cost (including all expenses) of the Employees' State Insurance Courts set up under this Act;

(viii) payment of any sums under any contract entered into for the purposes of this Act by the Corporation or the Standing Committee or by any officer duly authorised by the Corporation or the Standing Committee in that behalf;

(ix) payment of sums under any decree, order or award of any Court or Tribunal against the Corporation or any of its officers or servants for any act done in the execution of his duty or under a compromise or settlement of any suit or other legal proceeding or claim instituted or made against the Corporation;

(x) defraying the cost and other charges of instituting or defending any civil or criminal proceedings arising out of any action taken under this Act;

(xi) defraying expenditure, within the limits prescribed, on measures for the improvement of the health and welfare of insured persons and for the rehabilitation and re-employment of insured persons who have been disabled or injured; and

(xii) such other purposes as may be authorised by the Corporation with the previous approval of the Central Government.

Administrative Expenses (Section 28A)

The types of expenses which may be termed as administrative expenses and the percentage of the income of the Corporation which may be spent for such expenses shall be such as may be prescribed by the Central Government and the Corporation shall keep its administrative expenses within the limit so prescribed by the Central Government.

Spotlight

Section 28A mandates the Corporation to limit its administrative expenses as prescribed by the Central Government.

Holding of Property, etc. (Section 29)

1. The Corporation may, subject to such conditions as may be prescribed by the Central Government, acquire and hold property both movable and immovable, sell or otherwise transfer any movable or immovable property which may have become vested in or have been acquired by it and do all things necessary for the purposes for which the Corporation is established.

2. Subject to such conditions as may be prescribed by the Central Government, the Corporation may from time to time invest any moneys which are not immediately required for expenses properly defrayable under this Act and may, subject as aforesaid, from time to time re-invest or realise such investments.
3. The Corporation may, with the previous sanction of the Central Government and on such terms as may be prescribed by it, raise loans and take measures for discharging such loans.
4. The Corporation may constitute for the benefit of its staff or any class of them, such provident or other benefit fund as it may think fit.

Vesting of the Property in the Corporation (Section 30)

All property acquired before the establishment of the Corporation shall vest in the Corporation and all income derived and expenditure incurred in this behalf shall be brought into the books of the Corporation.

Expenditure by Central Government to be Treated as a Loan (Section 31)

Repealed by the Employees' State Insurance (Amendment) Act, 1966.

Budget Estimates (Section 32)

The Corporation shall in each year frame a budget showing the probable receipts and the expenditure which it proposes to incur during the following year and shall submit the copy of the budget for the approval of the Central Government before such date as may be fixed by it in that behalf. The budget shall contain provisions adequate in the opinion of the Central Government for the discharge of the liabilities incurred by the Corporation and for the maintenance of the working balance.

Accounts (Section 33)

The Corporation shall maintain correct accounts of its income and expenditure in such form and in such manner as may be prescribed by the Central Government.

Audit (Section 34)

1. The accounts of the Corporation shall be audited annually by the Comptroller and Auditor-General of India and any expenditure incurred by him in connection with such audit shall be payable by the Corporation to the Comptroller and Auditor-General of India.
2. The Comptroller and Auditor-General of India and any person appointed by him in connection with the audit of the accounts of the Corporation shall have the same rights and privileges and authority in connection with such audit as the Comptroller and Auditor-General has, in connection with the audit of Government accounts and in particular shall have the right to demand the production of books, accounts, connected vouchers and other documents and papers and to inspect any of the Offices of the Corporation.
3. The accounts of the Corporation as certified by the Comptroller and Auditor-General of India or any other person appointed by him in this behalf together with the audit report thereon shall

Spotlight

As per Section 34(1), the accounts of the Corporation shall be audited annually by the Comptroller and Auditor-General of India.

be forwarded to the Corporation which shall forward the same to the Central Government along with its comments on the report of the Comptroller and Auditor-General.

Annual Report (Section 35)

The Corporation shall submit to the Central Government an annual report of its work and activities.

Budget, Audited Accounts and the Annual Report to be Placed before Parliament (Section 36)

The annual report, the audited accounts of the Corporation together with the report of the Comptroller and Auditor-General of India thereon and the comments of the Corporation on such report and the budget as finally adopted by the Corporation shall be placed before Parliament.

Valuation of Assets and Liabilities (Section 37)

The Corporation shall, at intervals of 3 years, have a valuation of its assets and liabilities made by the valuer appointed with the approval of the Central Government:

Provided that it shall be open to the Central Government to direct a valuation to be made at such other times as it may consider necessary.

CHAPTER IV: CONTRIBUTIONS

All Employees to be Insured (Section 38)

Subject to the provisions of this Act, all employees in factories or establishments to which this Act applies shall be insured in the manner provided by this Act.

Contributions (Section 39)

1. The contributions payable under this Act in respect of an employee shall comprise contribution payable by the employer (hereinafter referred to as the employer's contribution) and contribution payable by the employee (hereinafter referred to as the employee's contribution) and shall be paid to the Corporation.
2. The contribution shall be paid at such rates as may be prescribed by the Central Government:

   Provided that the rates so prescribed shall not be more than the rates which were in force immediately before the commencement of the Employees' State Insurance (Amendment) Act, 1989.
3. The wage period in relation to an employee shall be the unit in respect of which all contributions shall be payable under this Act.
4. The contributions payable in respect of each wage period shall ordinarily fall due on the last day of the wage period and where an employee is employed for part of the wage period or is employed under 2 or more employers during the same wage period the contributions shall fall due on such days as may be specified in the regulations.
5. (a) If any contribution payable under this Act is not paid by the principal employer on the date on which such contribution has become due, he shall be liable to pay simple interest at the

Spotlight

As per Section 39(1), the contributions payable in respect of an employee shall comprise employer's contribution and employee's contribution.

rate of 12 per cent per annum or at such higher rate as may be specified in the regulations till the date of its actual payment:

Provided that higher interest specified in the regulations shall not exceed the lending rate of interest charged by any scheduled bank.

(b) Any interest recoverable under clause (a) may be recovered as an arrear of land revenue or under Section 45C to Section 45I.

Explanation In this sub-section, "scheduled bank" means a bank for the time being included in the Second Schedule to the Reserve Bank of India Act, 1934;

Principal Employer to Pay Contributions in the First Instance (Section 40)

1. The principal employer shall pay in respect of every employee, whether directly employed by him or by or through an immediate employer, both the employer's contribution and the employee's contribution.
2. Notwithstanding anything contained in any other enactment but subject to the provisions of this Act and the regulations, if any, made thereunder the principal employer shall, in the case of an employee directly employed by him (not being an exempted employee), be entitled to recover from the employee the employee's contribution by deduction from his wages and not otherwise:

   Provided that no such deduction shall be made from any wages other than such as relate to the period or part of the period in respect of which the contribution is payable, or in excess of the sum representing the employee's contribution for the period.
3. Notwithstanding any contract to the contrary, neither the principal employer nor the immediate employer shall be entitled to deduct the employer's contribution from any wage payable to an employee or otherwise to recover it from him.
4. Any sum deducted by the principal employer from wages under this Act shall be deemed to have been entrusted to him by the employee for the purpose of paying the contribution in respect of which it was deducted.
5. The principal employer shall bear the expenses of remitting the contributions to the Corporation.

Spotlight

In the case of a directly employed employee, the principal employer shall be entitled to recover the employee's contribution by deduction from his wages, as per Section 40(2).

CASE CORNER

The Court has held in *Employees' State Insurance Corporation vs. Hotel Kalpaka International* [(1993) SCR (1) 219] that under Section 40 the primary liability is on the employer to pay not only his contribution but also the employees' contribution. As such the employer cannot plead that since he had not deducted the employees' contribution from their wages, he could not be made liable for the same. After all, when he makes employees' contribution, he is entitled to deduct such amount from their wages.

(Adapted from: www.indiankanoon.org/doc/1590128/ accessed on 17/4/2014.)

Recovery of Contribution from Immediate Employer (Section 41)

1. A principal employer, who has paid contribution in respect of an employee employed by or through an immediate employer, shall be entitled to recover the amount of the contribution so

paid (that is to say the employer's contribution as well as the employee's contribution, if any) from the immediate employer, either by deduction from any amount payable to him by the principal employer under any contract or as a debt payable by the immediate employer.

1A. The immediate employer shall maintain a register of employees employed by or through him as provided in the regulations and submit the same to the principal employer before the settlement of any amount payable under sub-section (1).

2. In the case referred to in sub-section (1), the immediate employer shall be entitled to recover the employee's contribution from the employee employed by or through him by deduction from wages and not otherwise, subject to the conditions specified in the proviso to sub-section (2) of Section 40.

General Provisions as to Payment of Contributions (Section 42)

1. No employee's contribution shall be payable by or on behalf of an employee whose average daily wages during a wage period are below such wages as may be prescribed by the Central Government.

Explanation The average daily wages of an employee shall be calculated in such manner as may be prescribed by the Central Government;

2. Contribution (both the employer's contribution and the employee's contribution) shall be payable by the principal employer for each wage period in respect of the whole or part of which wages are payable to the employee and not otherwise.

Method of Payment of Contribution (Section 43)

Subject to the provisions of this Act, the Corporation may make regulations for any matter relating or incidental to the payment and collection of contribution payable under this Act and without prejudice to the generality of the foregoing power such regulations may provide for–

(a) the manner and time of payment of contributions;

(b) the payment of contributions by means of adhesive or other stamps affixed to or impressed upon books, cards or otherwise and regulating the manner, times and conditions in, at and under which, such stamps are to be affixed or impressed;

(bb) the date by which evidence of contributions having been paid is to be received by the Corporation;

(c) the entry in or upon books or cards of particulars of contributions paid and benefits distributed in the case of the insured person to whom such books or cards relate; and

(d) the issue, sale, custody, production, inspection and delivery of books or cards and the replacement of books or cards which have been lost, destroyed or defaced.

Employers to Furnish Returns and Maintain Registers in Certain Cases (Section 44)

Spotlight

Section 44 provides for employers to furnish returns and maintain registers in certain cases.

1. Every principal and immediate employer shall submit to the Corporation or to such officer of the Corporation as it may direct such returns in such form and containing such particulars relating to persons employed by him or to any factory or establishment in respect of which he is the principal or immediate employer as may be specified in regulations made in this behalf.

2. Where in respect of any factory or establishment the Corporation has reason to believe that a return should have been submitted under sub-section (1) but has not been so submitted, the Corporation may require any person in charge of the factory or establishment to furnish such particulars as it may consider necessary for the purpose of enabling the Corporation to decide whether the factory or establishment is a factory or establishment to which this Act applies.
3. Every principal and immediate employer shall maintain such registers or records in respect of his factory or establishment as may be required by regulations made in this behalf.

Social Security Officers, their Functions and Duties (Section 45)

1. The Corporation may appoint such persons as Social Security Officers, as it thinks fit, for the purposes of this Act, within such local limits as it may assign to them.
2. Any Social Security Officer appointed by the Corporation under sub-section (1) (hereinafter referred to as Social Security Officer), or other official of the Corporation authorised in this behalf by it, may for the purposes of enquiring into the correctness of any of the particulars stated in any return referred to in Section 44 or for the purpose of ascertaining whether the any provisions of this Act has been complied with–
   (a) require any principal or immediate employer to furnish to him such information as he may consider necessary for the purposes of this Act; or
   (b) at any reasonable time enter any office, establishment, factory or other premises occupied by such principal or immediate employer and require any person found in charge thereof to produce to such Social Security Officer or other official and allow him to examine such accounts, books and other documents relating to the employment of persons and payment of wages or to furnish to him such information as he may consider necessary; or
   (c) examine, with respect to any matter relevant to the purposes aforesaid, the principal or immediate employer, his agent or servant, or any person found in such factory, establishment, office or other premises, or any person whom the said Social Security Officer or other official has reasonable cause to believe to be or to have been an employee;
   (d) make copies of, or take extracts from, any register, account book or other document maintained in such factory, establishment, office or other premises;
   (e) exercise such other powers as may be prescribed.
3. A Social Security Officer shall exercise such functions and perform such duties as may be authorised by the Corporation or as may be specified in the regulations.
4. Any officer of the Corporation authorised in this behalf by it may, carry out re-inspection or test inspection of the records and returns submitted under Section 44 for the purpose of verifying the correctness and quality of the inspection carried out by a Social Security Officer.

Determination of Contributions in Certain Cases (Section 45A)

1. Where in respect of a factory or establishment no returns, particulars, registers or records are submitted, furnished or maintained in accordance with the provisions of Section 44 or any Social Security Officer or other official of the Corporation referred to in sub-section (2) of Section 45 is prevented in any manner by the principal or immediate employer or any other person in exercising his functions or discharging his duties under Section 45, the Corporation may, on the basis of information available to it, by order, determine the amount of contributions payable in respect of the employees of that factory or establishment:

Provided that no such order shall be passed by the Corporation unless the principal or immediate employer or the person in charge of the factory or establishment has been given a reasonable opportunity of being heard:

Provided further that no such order shall be passed by the Corporation in respect of the period beyond 5 years from the date on which the contribution shall become payable.

2. An order made by the Corporation under sub-section (1) shall be sufficient proof of the claim of the Corporation under Section 75 or for recovery of the amount determined by such order as an arrear of land revenue under Section 45B or the recovery under Section 45C to Section 45I.

Appellate Authority (Section 45AA)

If an employer is not satisfied with the order referred to in Section 45A, he may prefer an appeal to an appellate authority as may be provided by regulation, within 60 days of the date of such order after depositing 25 per cent of the contribution so ordered or the contribution as per his own calculation, whichever is higher, with the Corporation:

Provided that if the employer finally succeeds in the appeal, the Corporation shall refund such deposit to the employer together with such interest as may be specified in the regulation.

CASE CORNER

It has been held in *E.I.D. Parry (India) Ltd. vs. The Regional Director, Tamil Nadu [(1995) 1 MLJ 261]*, that failure to submit returns, particulars, etc. or obstruction of the Corporation inspectors or officials provide the occasion for invoking the power under Section 45A of the ESI Act, 1948. The very basis for invoking the power is thus non-cooperation on the part of the employer in voluntarily providing information and data required to be furnished, on the basis of which the employer should have but failed to make the contributions. If the liability is disputed, it is for the employer to seek adjudication under Section 75.

Sections 45A and 45B were introduced into the Act by Section 17 of the amending Act of 1976 (w.e.f. 17th June 1976). The object of introducing these provisions was to enable the Corporation to take speedy action against the defaulting employers without having to resort to adjudication by the ESI Court. Before an order under Section 45A is made, a show cause notice is to be served on the employer, so that the latter has an opportunity to meet the case set out in the show cause notice. Provision is also made for personal hearing if the same is sought by the employer.

Liability to pay contribution is not a liability under the general law, but is one created for the first time by this special statute. The amenities and benefits to be provided to workmen have to be paid from the contributions required to be paid under the Act. Section 45A does not provide an alternate mode of recovery of any liability created under the general law, nor does it prescribe any period of limitation. The Legislature has chosen not to prescribe any period of limitation for exercising the power under this section apparently because employers who fail to submit returns or obstruct the respondent from obtaining the necessary information by carrying out inspection through its officials should not be allowed to avoid contributions required to be paid by them and thus benefit themselves from their own wrongful actions. The authorities have therefore been vested with the jurisdiction and power to determine the liability and enforce recovery so that the object of the enactment could be better effectuated with the aid of the funds thus recovered.

(Adapted from: www.indiankanoon.org/doc/1603070/ accessed on 12/4/2014.)

Recovery of Contribution (Section 45B)

Any contribution payable under this Act may be recovered as an arrear of land revenue.

Issue of Certificate to the Recovery Officer (Section 45C)

1. Where any amount is in arrear under this Act, the authorised officer may issue to the Recovery Officer, a certificate under his signature specifying the amount of arrears and the Recovery Officer, on receipt of such certificate, shall proceed to recover the amount specified therein from the factory or establishment or, as the case may be, the principal or immediate employer by 1 or more of the modes mentioned below–
   (a) attachment and sale of the movable or immovable property of the factory or establishment or, as the case may be, the principal or immediate employer;
   (b) arrest of the employer and his detention in prison;
   (c) appointing a receiver for the management of the movable or immovable properties of the factory or establishment or, as the case may be, the employer:

   Provided that the attachment and sale of any property under this section shall first be effected against the properties of the factory or establishment and where such attachment and sale is insufficient for recovering the whole of the amount of arrears specified in the certificate, the Recovery Officer may take such proceedings against the property of the employer for recovery of the whole or any part of such arrears.
2. The authorised officer may issue a certificate under sub-section (1) notwithstanding that proceedings for recovery of the arrears by any other mode have been taken.

Recovery Officer to whom Certificate is to be Forwarded (Section 45D)

1. The authorised officer may forward the certificate referred to in Section 45C to the Recovery Officer within whose jurisdiction the employer:
   (a) carries on his business or profession or within whose jurisdiction the principal place of his factory or establishment is situate; or
   (b) resides or any movable or immovable property of the factory or establishment or the principal or immediate employer is situate.
2. Where a factory or an establishment or the principal or immediate employer has property within the jurisdiction of more than 1 Recovery Officer and the Recovery Officer to whom a certificate is sent by the authorised officer:
   (a) is not able to recover the entire amount by the sale of the property, movable or immovable, within his jurisdiction; or
   (b) is of the opinion that for the purpose of expediting or securing the recovery of the whole or any part of the amount, it is necessary so to do,

   he may send the certificate or, where only a part of the amount is to be recovered, a copy of the certificate certified in the manner prescribed by the Central Government and specifying the amount to be recovered to the Recovery Officer within whose jurisdiction the factory or establishment or the principal or immediate employer has property or the employer resides, and thereupon that Recovery Officer shall also proceed to recover the amount due under this section as if the certificate or the copy thereof had been the certificate sent to him by the authorised officer.

Validity of Certificate and Amendment thereof (Section 45E)

1. When the authorised officer issues a certificate to a Recovery Officer under Section 45C, it shall not be open to the factory or establishment or the principal or immediate employer to dispute before the Recovery Officer the correctness of the amount, and no objection to the certificate on any other ground shall also be entertained by the Recovery Officer.
2. Notwithstanding the issue of a certificate to a Recovery Officer, the authorised officer shall have power to withdraw the certificate or correct any clerical or arithmetical mistake in the certificate by sending an intimation to the Recovery Officer.
3. The authorised officer shall intimate to the Recovery Officer any orders, withdrawing or cancelling a certificate or any correction made by him under sub-section (2) or any amendment made under sub-section (4) of Section 45F.

Stay of Proceedings under Certificate and Amendment or Withdrawal thereof (Section 45F)

1. Notwithstanding that a certificate has been issued to the Recovery Officer for the recovery of any amount, the authorised officer may grant time for the payment of the amount, and thereupon the Recovery Officer shall stay the proceedings until the expiry of the time so granted.
2. Where a certificate for the recovery of amount has been issued, the authorised officer shall keep the Recovery Officer informed of any amount paid or time granted for payment, subsequent to the issue of such certificate.
3. Where the order giving rise to demand of amount for which a certificate for recovery has been issued has been modified in appeal or other proceedings under this Act, and, as a consequence thereof, the demand is reduced but the order is the subject-matter of a further proceeding under this Act, the authorised officer shall stay the recovery of such part of the amount of the certificate as pertains to the said reduction for the period for which the appeal or other proceeding remains pending.
4. Where a certificate for the recovery of amount has been issued and subsequently the amount of the outstanding demand is reduced as a result of an appeal or other proceeding under this Act, the authorised officer shall, when the order which was the subject-matter of such appeal or other proceeding has become final and conclusive, amend the certificate or withdraw it, as the case may be.

Other Modes of Recovery (Section 45G)

1. Notwithstanding the issue of a certificate to the Recovery Officer under Section 45C, the Director- General or any other officer authorised by the Corporation may recover the amount by any 1 or more of the modes provided in this section.
2. If any amount is due from any person to any factory or establishment or, as the case may be the principal or immediate employer who is in arrears, the Director-General or any other officer authorised by the Corporation in this behalf may require such person to deduct from the said amount the arrears due from such factory or establishment or, as the case may be, the principal or immediate employer under this Act and such person shall comply with any such requisition and shall pay the sum so deducted to the credit of the Corporation:

Spotlight

Section 45G provides for other modes of recovery of arrears.

Provided that nothing in this sub-section shall apply to any part of the amount exempt from attachment in execution of a decree of a civil court under Section 60 of the Code of Civil Procedure, 1908.

3. (i) The Director-General or any other officer authorised by the Corporation in this behalf may, at any time or from time to time, by notice in writing, require any person from whom money is due or may become due to the factory or establishment or, as the case may be, the principal or immediate employer, or any person who holds or may subsequently hold money for or on account of the factory or establishment or, as the case may be, the principal or immediate employer, to pay to the Director-General either forthwith upon the money becoming due or being held or at or within the time specified in the notice (not being before the money becomes due or is held) so much of the money as is sufficient to pay the amount due from the factory or establishment or, as the case may be, the principal or immediate employer in respect of arrears or the whole of the money when it is equal to or less than that amount.

(ii) A notice under this sub-section may be issued to any person who holds or may subsequently hold any money for or on account of the principal or immediate employer jointly with any other person and for the purposes of this sub-section, the shares of the joint holders in such account shall be presumed, until the contrary is proved to be equal.

(iii) A copy of the notice shall be forwarded to the principal or immediate employer at his last address known to the Director-General or, as the case may be, the officer so authorised and in the case of a joint account to all the joint-holders at their last addresses known to the Director General or the officer so authorised.

(iv) Save as otherwise provided in this sub-section, every person to whom a notice is issued under this sub-section shall be bound to comply with such notice, and, in particular, where any such notice is issued to a post office, bank or an insurer, it shall not be necessary for any pass book, deposit receipt, policy or any other document to be produced for the purpose of any entry, endorsement or the like being made before payment is made notwithstanding any rule, practice or requirement to the contrary.

(v) Any claim respecting any property in relation to which a notice under this sub-section has been issued arising after the date of the notice shall be void as against any demand contained in the notice.

(vi) Where a person to whom a notice under this sub-section is sent objects to it by a statement on oath that the sum demanded or any part thereof is not due to the principal or immediate employer or that he does not hold any money for or on account of the principal or immediate employer, then, nothing contained in this sub-section shall be deemed to require such person to pay any such sum or part thereof, as the case may be, but if it is discovered that such statement was false in any material particular, such person shall be personally liable to the Director General or the officer so authorised to the extent of his own liability to the principal or immediate employer on the date of the notice, or to the extent of the principal or immediate employer's liability for any sum due under this Act, whichever is less.

(vii) The Director-General or the officer so authorised may, at any time or from time to time amend or revoke any notice issued under this sub-section or extend the time for making any payment in pursuance of such notice.

(viii) The Director-General or the officer so authorised shall grant a receipt for any amount paid in compliance with a notice issued under this sub-section and the person so paying shall be fully discharged from his liability to the principal or immediate employer to the extent of the amount so paid.

(ix) Any person discharging any liability to the principal or immediate employer after the receipt of a notice under this sub-section shall be personally liable to the Director-General or the officer so authorised to the extent of his own liability to the principal or immediate employer so discharged or to the extent of the principal or immediate employer's liability for any sum due under this Act, whichever is less.

(x) If the person to whom a notice under this sub-section is sent fails to make payment in pursuance thereof to the Director-General or the officer so authorised, he shall be deemed to be a principal or immediate employer in default in respect of the amount specified in the notice and further proceeding may be taken against him for the realisation of the amount as if it were an arrear due from him, in the manner provided in sections 45C to 45F and the notice shall have the same effect as an attachment of a debt by the Recovery Officer in exercise of his powers under Section 45C.

4. The Director-General or the officer authorised by the Corporation in this behalf may apply to the court in whose custody there is money belonging to the principal or immediate employer for payment to him of the entire amount of such money, or if it is more than the amount due, an amount sufficient to discharge the amount due.
5. The Director-General or any officer of the Corporation may, if so authorised by the Central Government by general or special order, recover any arrears of amount due from a factory or an establishment or, as the case may be, from the principal or immediate employer by distraint and sale of its or his movable property in the manner laid down in the Third Schedule to the Income-tax Act, 1961.

Application of Certain Provisions of the Income-tax Act (Section 45H)

The provisions of the Second and the Third Schedules to the Income-tax Act, 1961 and the Income-tax (Certificate Proceedings) Rules, 1962, as in force from time to time, shall apply with necessary modifications, as if the said provisions and the rules referred to the arrears of the amount of contributions, interests or damages under this Act instead of to the income-tax:

Provided that any reference in the said provisions and the rules to the "assessee" shall be construed as a reference to a factory or an establishment or the principal or immediate employer under this Act.

Definitions (Section 45I)

For the purposes of Sections 45C to 45H:

(a) "authorised Officer" means the Director-General, Insurance Commissioner, Joint Insurance Commissioner, Regional Director or such other officer as may be authorised by the Central Government, by notification in the Official Gazette;

(b) "Recovery Officer" means any officer of the Central Government, State Government or the Corporation, who may be authorised by the Central Government, by notification in the Official Gazette, to exercise the powers of a Recovery Officer under this Act.

CHAPTER V: BENEFITS

Benefits (Section 46)

1. Subject to the provisions of this Act, the insured persons, their dependents or the persons hereinafter mentioned, as the case may be, shall be entitled to the following benefits, namely:-

(a) periodical payments to any insured person in case of his sickness certified by a duly appointed medical practitioner or by any other person possessing such qualifications and experience as the Corporation may, by regulations, specify in this behalf (hereinafter referred to as sickness benefit);
(b) periodical payments to an insured woman in case of confinement or miscarriage or sickness arising out of pregnancy, confinement, premature birth of child or miscarriage, such woman being certified to be eligible for such payments by an authority specified in this behalf by the regulations (hereinafter referred to as maternity benefit);
(c) periodical payments to an insured person suffering from disablement as a result of an employment injury sustained as an employee under this Act and certified to be eligible for such payments by an authority specified in this behalf by the regulations (hereinafter referred to as disablement benefit);
(d) periodical payments to such dependants of an insured person who dies as a result of an employment injury sustained as an employee under this Act, as are entitled to compensation under this Act (hereinafter referred to as dependants' benefit);
(e) medical treatment for an attendance on insured persons (hereinafter referred to as medical benefit); and
(f) payment to the eldest surviving member of the family of an insured person who has died, towards the expenditure on the funeral of the deceased insured person or, where the insured person did not have a family or was not living with his family at the time of his death, to the person who actually incurs the expenditure on the funeral of the deceased insured person (to be known as funeral expenses):

Provided that the amount of such payment shall not exceed such amount as may be prescribed by the Central Government and the claim for such payment shall be made within 3 months of the death of the insured person or within such extended period as the Corporation or any officer of authority authorised by it in this behalf may allow.

Spotlight

Claim for payment of funeral expense must be made within 3 months of the death of the insured person as provided in Section 46(1)(f).

2. The Corporation may, at the request of the Appropriate Government, and subject to such conditions as may be laid down in the regulations, extend the medical benefits to the family of an insured person.

When Person Eligible for Sickness Benefit (Section 47)

Repealed by the Employees' State Insurance (Amendment) Act, 1966.

When Person Deemed Available for Employment (Section 48)

Repealed by the Employees' State Insurance (Amendment) Act, 1966.

Sickness Benefit (Section 49)

The qualification of a person to claim sickness benefit, the conditions subject to which such benefit may be given, the rates and period thereof shall be such as may be prescribed by the Central Government.

Maternity Benefit (Section 50)

The qualification of an insured woman to claim maternity benefit, the conditions subject to which such benefit may be given, the rates and period thereof shall be such as may be prescribed by the Central Government.

Disablement Benefit (Section 51)

Subject to the provisions of this Act:

(a) a person who sustains temporary disablement for not less than 3 days (excluding the day of accident), shall be entitled to periodical payment at such rates and for such periods and subject to such conditions as may be prescribed by the Central Government;

(b) a person who sustains permanent disablement, whether total or partial, shall be entitled to periodical payment at such rates and for such period and subject to such conditions as may be prescribed by the Central Government.

Spotlight

As per Section 51A, an accident arising in the course of employment is presumed to have also arisen out of that employment.

Presumption as to Accident Arising in Course of Employment (Section 51A)

For the purposes of this Act, an accident arising in the course of an employee's employment shall be presumed, in the absence of evidence to the contrary, also to have arisen out of that employment.

Accidents Happening while Acting in Breach of Regulations, etc. (Section 51B)

An accident shall be deemed to arise out of and in the course of an employee's employment notwithstanding that he is at the time of the accident acting in contravention of the provisions of any law applicable to him, or of any orders given by or on behalf of his employer or that he is acting without instructions from his employer, if:

(a) the accident would have been deemed so to have arisen had the act not been done in contravention as aforesaid on or without instructions from his employer, as the case may be; and

(b) the act is done for the purpose of and in connection with the employer's trade or business.

Accidents Happening while Travelling in Employer's Transport (Section 51C)

1. An accident happening while an employee is, with the express or implied permission of his employer, travelling as a passenger by any vehicle to or from his place of work shall, notwithstanding that he is under no obligation to his employer to travel by that vehicle, be deemed to arise out of and in the course of his employment, if:
   (a) the accident would have been deemed so to have arisen had he been under such obligation; and
   (b) at the time of the accident, the vehicle:
      (i) is being operated by or on behalf of his employer or some other person by whom it is provided in pursuance of arrangements made with his employer, and
      (ii) is not being operated in the ordinary course of public transport service.
2. In this section "vehicle" includes a vessel and an aircraft.

Accidents Happening while Meeting Emergency (Section 51D)

An accident happening to an employee in or about any premises at which he is for the time being employed for the purpose of his employer's trade or business shall be deemed to arise out of and in the course of his employment, if it happens while he is taking steps, on an actual or supposed emergency at those premises, to rescue, succour or protect persons who are, or are thought to be, or possibly to be, injured or imperiled, or to avert or minimise serious damage to property.

Accidents Happening while Commuting to the Place of Work and Vice Versa (Section 51E)

An accident occurring to an employee while commuting from his residence to the place of employment for duty or from the place of employment to his residence after performing duty, shall be deemed to have arisen out of and in the course of employment if nexus between the circumstances, time and place in which the accident occurred and the employment is established.

Dependants' Benefit (Section 52)

1. If an insured person dies as a result of an employment injury sustained as an employee under this Act (whether or not he was in receipt of any periodical payment for temporary disablement in respect of the injury) dependants' benefit shall be payable at such rates and for such period and subject to such conditions as may be prescribed by the Central Government to his dependants specified in sub-clause (i), sub-clause (ia) and sub-clause (ii) of clause (6A) of Section 2.
2. In case the insured person dies without leaving behind him the dependants as aforesaid, the dependants' benefit shall be paid to the other dependants of the deceased at such rates and for such period and subject to such conditions as may be prescribed by the Central Government.

In *Employees' State Insurance Corporation vs. Amina Bee* [(1993) (2) ALT 278], when an employee in the boiler house of Sirsilk Ltd. had died while in service, his widowed mother filed a case before the Insurance Court, claiming benefit under the Act. The Court found that the petitioner was entitled to dependants' benefit and allowed the petition, directing the Corporation to pay the benefit to the petitioner. Complaining that instead of paying her a sum of ₹3.15 towards dependants' benefit, the employer was paying only ₹0.37 per day, the petitioner filed an application. The defence of the Corporation is that the widowed mother is entitled to receive dependent's benefit as per the rates prescribed in the First Schedule, which is 3/10ths of the full rate, i.e., 75/2 paise, equivalent to ₹0.35 per day. The Court held that a parent which includes a widowed mother is only entitled to an amount equivalent to 3/10ths of the full rate.

(Adapted from: www.indiankanoon.org/doc/40784/ accessed on 15/4/2014.)

Occupational Disease (Section 52A)

1. If an employee employed in any employment specified in Part A of the Third Schedule contracts any disease specified therein as an occupational disease peculiar to that employment, or if an employee employed in the employment specified in Part B of that Schedule for a continuous period of not less than 6 months contracts any disease specified therein as an occupational disease peculiar to that employment or if an employee employed in any employment specified in Part C of that Schedule for such continuous period as the Corporation may specify in respect of each such employment, contracts any disease specified therein as an occupational disease peculiar to

that employment, the contracting of the disease shall, unless the contrary is proved, be deemed to be an 'employment injury' arising out of and in the course of employment.

2. (i) Where the Central Government or a State Government, as the case may be, adds any description of employment to the employments specified in Schedule III to the Workmen's (now Employees') Compensation Act, 1923 by virtue of the powers vested in it under sub-section (3) of Section 3 of the said Act, the said description of employment and the occupational diseases specified under that sub-section as peculiar to that description of employment shall be deemed to form part of the Third Schedule.

   (ii) Without prejudice to the provisions of clause (i), the Corporation after giving, by notification in the Official Gazette, not less than 3 months' notice of its intention so to do, may, by a like notification, add any description of employment to the employments specified in the Third Schedule and shall specify in the case of employments so added the diseases which shall be deemed for the purposes of this section to be occupational diseases peculiar to those employments respectively and thereupon the provisions of this Act shall apply, as if such diseases had been declared by this Act to be occupational diseases peculiar to those employments.

3. Save as provided by sub-sections (1) and (2), no benefit shall be payable to an employee in respect of any disease unless the disease is directly attributable to a specific injury by accident arising out of and in the course of his employment.

4. The provisions of Section 51A shall not apply to the cases to which this section applies.

Bar against Receiving or Recovery of Compensation or Damages under any other Law (Section 53)

An insured person or his dependants shall not be entitled to receive or recover, whether from the employer of the insured person or from any other person, any compensation or damages under the Workmen's (now Employees') Compensation Act, 1923, or any other law for the time being in force or otherwise, in respect of an employment injury sustained by the insured person as an employee under this Act.

CASE CORNER

In *United India Insurance Co. Ltd. vs. Som Wati and Others* [(2012) LLR 383], the appeal by the insurance company is on the ground that the claimants had already availed a benefit under the ESI Act, 1948, the deceased being a person covered by the ESI scheme. It has been held that the object of Section 53 is that the employer is not foisted with more than one claim for the same accident, and once the claim has had the benefit under the ESI Act, a separate claim under the Motor Vehicles (MV) Act shall not be permitted The Tribunal, while considering the objection of the insurer regarding non-maintainability of the petition in terms of Section 53 of the ESI Act, held that the bar will operate for securing award only under the Employees' Compensation Act, and not when the provision of the MV Act are invoked. The claimants could not have been duplicated the claim before the Tribunal also, without forsaking the benefit under the ESI Act.

(Adapted from: Labour Law Reporter, April 2012, p. 383.)

Determination of Question of Disablement (Section 54)

Any question:

(a) whether the relevant accident has resulted in permanent disablement; or
(b) whether the extent of loss of earning capacity can be assessed provisionally or finally; or
(c) whether the assessment of the proportion of the loss of earning capacity is provisional or final; or
(d) in the case of provisional assessment, as to the period for which such assessment shall hold good,

shall be determined by a medical board constituted in accordance with the provisions of the regulations and any such question shall hereinafter be referred to as the "disablement question."

References to Medical Boards and Appeals to Medical Appeal Tribunals and Employees' Insurance Courts (Section 54A)

1. The case of any insured person for permanent disablement benefit shall be referred by the Corporation to a medical board for determination of the disablement question and if, on that or any subsequent reference, the extent of loss of earning capacity of the insured person is provisionally assessed, it shall again be so referred to the medical board not later than the end of the period taken into account by the provisional assessment.
2. If the insured person or the Corporation is not satisfied with the decision of the medical board, the insured person or the Corporation may appeal in the prescribed manner and within the prescribed time to–
   (i) the medical appeal tribunal constituted in accordance with the provisions of the regulations with a further right of appeal in the prescribed manner and within the prescribed time to the Employees' Insurance Court, or
   (ii) the Employees' Insurance Court directly:

Provided that no appeal by an insured person shall lie under this sub-section if such person has applied for commutation of disablement benefit on the basis of the decision of the medical board and received the commuted value of such benefit:

Provided further that no appeal by the Corporation shall lie under this sub-section if the Corporation paid the commuted value of the disablement benefit on the basis of the decision of the medical board.

Review of Decisions by Medical Board or Medical Appeal Tribunal (Section 55)

1. Any decision under this Act of a medical board or a medical appeal tribunal may be reviewed at any time by the medical board or the medical appeal tribunal, as the case may be, if it is satisfied by fresh evidence that the decision was given in consequence of the non-disclosure or misrepresentation by the employee or any other person of a material fact (whether the non-disclosure or misrepresentation was or was not fraudulent).
2. Any assessment of the extent of the disablement resulting from the relevant employment injury may also be reviewed by a medical board if it is satisfied that since the making of the assessment there has been a substantial and unforeseen aggravation of the results of the relevant injury:

   Provided that an assessment shall not be reviewed under this sub-section unless the medical board is of opinion that with regard to the period taken into account by the assessment and the probable duration of the aggravation aforesaid, substantial injustice will be done by not reviewing it.

3. Except with the leave of a medical appeal tribunal, an assessment shall not be reviewed under sub-section (2) on any application made less than 5 years, or in the case of a provisional assessment, 6 months, from the date thereof and on such a review the period to be taken into account by any revised assessment shall not include any period before the date of the application.
4. Subject to the foregoing provisions of this section, a medical board may deal with a case of review in any manner in which it could deal with it on an original reference to it, and in particular may make a provisional assessment notwithstanding that the assessment under review was final; and the provisions of Section 54A shall apply to an application for review under this section and to a decision of a medical board in connection with such application as they apply to a case for disablement benefit under this section and to a decision of the medical board in connection with such case.

Review of Dependants' Benefit (Section 55A)

1. Any decision awarding dependants' benefit under this Act may be reviewed at any time by the Corporation if it is satisfied by fresh evidence that the decision was given in consequence of non-disclosure or misrepresentation by the claimant or any other person of a material fact (whether the non-disclosure or misrepresentation was or was not fraudulent) or that the decision is no longer in accordance with this Act due to any birth or death or due to the marriage, re-marriage or cessor of infirmity of, or attainment of the age of 18 years by, a claimant.
2. Subject to the provisions of this Act, the Corporation may, on such review as aforesaid, direct that the dependants' benefit be continued, increased, reduced or discontinued.

Spotlight

As per Section 55A, the Corporation, may direct after review that dependents' benefit be increased, reduced or discontinued.

Medical Benefit (Section 56)

1. An insured person or (where such medical benefit is extended to his family) a member of his family whose condition requires medical treatment and attendance shall be entitled to receive medical benefit.
2. Such medical benefit may be given either in the form of out-patient treatment and attendance in a hospital or dispensary, clinic or other institution or by visits to the home of the insured person or treatment as in-patient in a hospital or other institution.
3. A person shall be entitled to medical benefit during any period for which contributions are payable in respect of him or in which he is qualified to claim benefit or maternity benefit or is in receipt of such disablement benefit as does not disentitle him to medical benefit under the regulations:

   Provided that a person in respect of whom contribution ceases to be payable under this Act may be allowed medical benefit for such period and of such nature as may be provided under the regulations:

   Provided further that an insured person who ceases to be in insurable employment on account of permanent disablement shall continue, subject to payment of contribution and such other conditions as may be prescribed by the Central Government, to receive medical benefit till the date on which he would have vacated the employment on attaining the age of superannuation had he not sustained such permanent disablement:

   Provided also that an insured person who has attained the age of superannuation, a person who retires under a Voluntary Retirement Scheme or takes premature retirement, and his spouse shall be eligible to receive medical benefits subject to payment of contribution and such other conditions as may be prescribed by the Central Government.

Explanation In this section, "superannuation", in relation to an insured person, means the attainment by that person of such age as is fixed in the contract or conditions of service as the age on the attainment of which he shall vacate the insurable employment or the age of 60 years where no such age is fixed and the person is no more in the insurable employment.

Scale of Medical Benefit (Section 57)

1. An insured person and (where such medical benefit is extended to his family) his family shall be entitled to receive medical benefit only of such kind and on such scale as may be provided by the State Government or by the Corporation, and an insured person or, where such medical benefit is extended to his family, his family shall not have a right to claim any medical treatment except such as is provided by the dispensary, hospital, clinic or other institution to which he or his family is allotted, or as may be provided by the regulations.
2. Nothing in this Act shall entitle an insured person and (where such medical benefit is extended to his family) his family to claim reimbursement from the Corporation of any expenses incurred in respect of any medical treatment, except as may be provided by the regulations.

Provision of Medical Treatment by State Government (Section 58)

1. The State Government shall provide for insured persons and (where such benefit is extended to their families) their families in the State, reasonable medical, surgical, and obstetric treatment:

   Provided that the State Government may, with the approval of the Corporation, arrange for medical treatment at clinics of medical practitioners on such scale and subject to such terms and conditions as may be agreed upon.

Spotlight

Section 58(2) provides that the Corporation may waive the recovery of the whole or a part of the share borne by the State Government.

2. Where the incidence of sickness benefit payment to insured persons in any State is found to exceed the all-India average, the amount of such excess shall be shared between the Corporation and the State Government in such proportion as may be fixed by agreement between them:

   Provided that the Corporation may in any case waive the recovery of the whole or any part of the share which is to be borne by the State Government.
3. The Corporation may enter into an agreement with a State Government in regard to the nature and scale of the medical treatment that should be provided to insured persons and (where such medical benefit is extended to the families) their families (including provision of buildings, equipment, medicines and staff) and for the sharing of the cost thereof and of any excess in the incidence of sickness benefit to insured persons between the Corporation and the State Government.
4. In default of agreement between the Corporation and any State Government as aforesaid the nature and extent of the medical treatment to be provided by the State Government and the proportion in which the cost thereof and of the excess in the incidence of sickness benefit, shall be shared between the Corporation and that Government, shall be determined by an arbitrator (who shall be or shall have been a Judge of the High Court of a State) appointed by the Chief Justice of India and the award of the arbitrator shall be binding on the Corporation and the State Government.
5. The State Government may, in addition to the Corporation under this Act, with the previous approval of the Central Government, establish such organisation (by whatever name called) to provide for certain benefits to employees in case of sickness, maternity and employment injury:

Provided that any reference to the State Government in the Act shall also include reference to the organisation as and when such organisation is established by the State Government.

6. The organisation referred to in sub-section (5) shall have such structure and discharge functions, exercise powers and undertake such activities as may be prescribed.

CASE CORNER

In *Regional Director, ESI Corporation, Bangalore vs. Lakshmi Biradar and Others [(2011) LLR 1271]* the respondent's son, while working in the establishment of National Aluminium Company Ltd., had developed breathlessness and swelling in feet. He was admitted to a private hospital, where he was diagnosed with congenital heart disease, requiring replacement of heart valve; he eventually died in the hospital. The respondent approached the Insurance Court for reimbursement of the sum insured by her for her son's treatment. The Court held that the State Government is duty-bound to reimburse the expenses incurred by employees working in such establishments whenever they have spent money for such specialised treatment in private hospitals, when such treatment is unavailable in ESI hospitals.

(Adapted from: Labour Law Reporter, December, 2011, p. 1271.)

Establishment and Maintenance of Hospitals, etc. by Corporation (Section 59)

1. The Corporation may, with the approval of the State Government, establish and maintain in a State such hospitals, dispensaries and other medical and surgical services as it may think fit for the benefit of insured persons and (where such medical benefit is extended to their families) their families.
2. The Corporation may enter into agreement with any local authority, private body or individual in regard to the provision of medical treatment and attendance for insured persons and (where such medical benefit extended to their families) their families, in any area and sharing the cost thereof.
3. The Corporation may also enter into agreement with any local authority, local body or private body for commissioning and running Employees' State Insurance hospitals through third party participation for providing medical treatment and attendance to insured persons and where such medical benefit has been extended to their families, to their families.

Provision of Medical Benefit by the Corporation in Lieu of State Government (Section 59A)

1. Notwithstanding anything contained in any other provision of this Act, the Corporation may, in consultation with the State Government, undertake the responsibility for providing medical benefit to insured persons and where such medical benefit is extended to their families, to the families of such insured persons in the State subject to the condition that the State Government shall share the cost of such medical benefit in such proportion as may be agreed upon between the State Government and the Corporation.
2. In the event of the Corporation exercising its power under sub-section (1), the provisions relating to medical benefit under this Act shall apply, so far as may be, as if a reference therein to the State Government were a reference to the Corporation.

Medical and Para-Medical Education (Section 59B)

The Corporation may establish medical colleges, nursing colleges and training institutes for its para-medical staff and other employees with a view to improve the quality of services provided under the Employees' State Insurance Scheme.

Spotlight

Section 59B empowers the Corporation to establish medical colleges, nursing colleges and training institutes for its paramedical staff.

GENERAL

Benefit not Assignable or Attachable (Section 60)

1. The right to receive any payment of any benefit under this Act shall not be transferable or assignable.
2. No cash benefit payable under this Act shall be liable to attachment or sale in execution of any decree or order of any Court.

Bar of Benefits under other Enactments (Section 61)

When a person is entitled to any of the benefits provided by this Act, he shall not be entitled to receive any similar benefit admissible under the provisions of any other enactment.

Persons not to Commute Cash Benefits (Section 62)

Save as may be provided in the regulations, no person shall be entitled to commute for a lump sum any disablement benefit admissible under this Act.

Persons not Entitled to Receive Benefit in Certain Cases (Section 63)

Save as may be provided in the regulations, no person shall be entitled to sickness benefit or disablement benefit for temporary disablement on any day on which he works or remains on leave or on a holiday in respect of which he receives wages or on any day on which he remains on strike.

Recipients of Sickness or Disablement Benefit to Observe Conditions (Section 64)

A person who is in receipt of sickness benefit or disablement benefit (other than benefit granted on permanent disablement):

(a) shall remain under medical treatment at a dispensary, hospital, clinic or other institution provided under this Act and shall carry out the instructions given by the medical officer or medical attendant in charge thereof;

(b) shall not while under treatment do anything which might retard or prejudice his chances of recovery;

(c) shall not leave the area in which medical treatment provided by this Act is being given, without the permission of the medical officer, medical attendant or such other authority as may be specified in this behalf by the regulations; and

(d) shall allow himself to be examined by any duly appointed medical officer or other person authorised by the Corporation in this behalf.

Benefits not to be Combined (Section 65)

> **Spotlight**
> As per Section 65(2) where a person is entitled to more than 1 benefits, he shall be entitled to choose the one he shall receive.

1. An insured person shall not be entitled to receive for the same period:
   (a) both sickness benefit and maternity benefit; or
   (b) both sickness benefit and disablement benefit for temporary disablement; or
   (c) both maternity benefit and disablement benefit for temporary disablement.
2. Where a person is entitled to more than 1 of the benefits mentioned in sub-section (1), he shall be entitled to choose which benefit he shall receive.

Corporation's Right to Recover Damages from Employer in Certain Cases (Section 66)

Repealed by the Employees' State Insurance (Amendment) Act, 1966.

Corporation's Right to be Indemnified in Certain Cases (Section 67)

Repealed by the Employees' State Insurance (Amendment) Act, 1966.

Corporation's Right where a Principal Employer Fails or Neglects to Pay any Contribution (Section 68)

1. If any principal employer fails or neglects to pay any contribution which under this Act he is liable to pay in respect of any employee and by reason thereof such person becomes disentitled to any benefit or entitled to a benefit on a lower scale, the Corporation may, on being satisfied that the contribution should have been paid by the principal employer, pay to the person the benefit at the rate to which he would have been entitled if the failure or neglect had not occurred and the Corporation shall be entitled to recover from the principal employer either:
   (i) the difference between the amount of benefit which is paid by the Corporation to the said person and the amount of the benefit which would have been payable on the basis of the contributions which were in fact paid by the employer; or
   (ii) twice the amount of the contribution which the employer failed or neglected to pay, whichever is greater.
2. The amount recoverable under this section may be recovered as if it were an arrear of land-revenue or under sections 45C to 45I.

Liability of Owner or Occupier of Factories, etc. for Excessive Sickness Benefit (Section 69)

1. Where the Corporation considers that the incidence of sickness among insured persons is excessive by reason of:
   (i) insanitary working conditions in a factory or establishment or the neglect of the owner or occupier of the factory or establishment to observe any health regulations enjoined on him by or under any enactment, or

(ii) insanitary conditions of any tenements or lodgings occupied by insured persons and such insanitary conditions are attributable to the neglect of the owner of the tenements or lodgings to observe any health regulations enjoined on him by or under any enactment,

the Corporation may send to the owner or occupier of the factory or establishment or to the owner of the tenements or lodgings, as the case may be, a claim for the payment of the amount of the extra expenditure incurred by the Corporation as sickness benefit; and if the claim is not settled by agreement, the Corporation may refer the matter, with a statement in support of its claim, to the appropriate Government.

2. If the appropriate Government is of opinion that a *prima facie* case for inquiry is disclosed, it may appoint a competent person or persons to hold an inquiry into the matter.
3. If upon such inquiry it is proved to the satisfaction of the person or persons holding the inquiry that the excess in incidence of sickness among the insured persons is due to the default or neglect of the owner or occupier of the factory or establishment or the owner of the tenements or lodgings, as the case may be, the said person or persons shall determine the amount of the extra expenditure incurred as sickness benefit, and the person or persons by whom the whole or any part of such amount shall be paid to the Corporation.
4. A determination under sub-section (3) may be enforced as if it were a decree for payment of money passed in a suit by a Civil Court.
5. For the purposes of this section, "owner" of tenements or lodgings shall include any agent of the owner and any person who is entitled to collect the rent of the tenements or lodgings as a lessee of the owner.

Repayment of Benefit Improperly Received (Section 70)

1. Where any person has received any benefit or payment under this Act when he is not lawfully entitled thereto, he shall be liable to repay to the Corporation the value of the benefit or the amount of such payment, or in the case of his death his representative shall be liable to repay the same from the assets of the deceased, if any, in his hands.
2. The value of any benefits received other than cash payments shall be determined by such authority as may be specified in the regulations made in this behalf and the decision of such authority shall be final.
3. The amount recoverable under this section may be recovered as if it were an arrear of land revenue or under sections 45C to 45I.

Benefit Payable upto and Including Day of Death (Section 71)

If a person dies during any period for which he is entitled to a cash benefit under this Act, the amount of such benefit up to and including the day of his death shall be paid to any person nominated by the deceased person in writing in such form as may be specified in the regulations or, if there is no such nomination, to the heir or legal representative of the deceased person.

Employer not to Reduce Wages, etc. (Section 72)

No employer by reason only of his liability for any contributions payable under this Act shall, directly or indirectly, reduce the wages of any employee, or except as provided by the regulations, discontinue or reduce benefits payable to him under the conditions of his service which are similar to the benefits conferred by this Act.

Employer not to Dismiss or Punish Employee During the Period of Sickness, etc. (Section 73)

> **Spotlight**
> Section 73 prohibits an employer from dismissing or punishing an employee during the period of sickness, etc.

1. No employer shall dismiss discharge or reduce or otherwise punish an employee during the period the employee is in receipt of sickness benefit or maternity benefit, nor shall he, except as provided under the regulations, dismiss, discharge or reduce or otherwise punish an employee during the period he is in receipt of disablement benefit for temporary disablement or is under medical treatment for sickness or is absent from work as a result of illness duly certified in accordance with the regulations to arise out of the pregnancy or confinement rendering the employee unfit for work.
2. No notice of dismissal or discharge or reduction given to an employee during the period specified in sub-section (1) shall be valid or operative.

CHAPTER VA: SCHEME FOR OTHER BENEFICIARIES

Definitions (Section 73A)

In this Chapter:

(a) "other beneficiaries" means persons other than the person insured under this Act;
(b) "Scheme" means any Scheme framed by the Central Government from time to time under Section 73B for the medical facility for other beneficiaries;
(c) "underutilised hospital" means any hospital not fully utilised by the persons insured under this Act;
(d) "user charges" means the amount which is to be charged from the other beneficiaries for medical facilities as may be notified by the Corporation in consultation with the Central Government from time to time.

Power to Frame Schemes (Section 73B)

Notwithstanding anything contained in this Act, the Central Government may, by notification in the Official Gazette, frame Scheme for other beneficiaries and the members of their families for providing medical facility in any hospital established by the Corporation in any area which is under-utilised on payment of user charges.

Collection of User Charges (Section 73C)

The user charges collected from the other beneficiaries shall be deemed to be the contribution and shall form part of the Employees' State Insurance Fund.

Scheme for other Beneficiaries (Section 73D)

The Scheme may provide for all or any of the following matters, namely:

(i) the other beneficiaries who may be covered under this Scheme;
(ii) the time and manner in which the medical facilities may be availed by the other beneficiaries;
(iii) the form in which the other beneficiary shall furnish particulars about himself and his family whenever required as may be specified by the Corporation;
(iv) any other matter which is to be provided for in the Scheme or which may be necessary or proper for the purpose of implementing the Scheme.

Power to Amend Scheme (Section 73E)

The Central Government may, by notification in the Official Gazette, add to, amend, vary or rescind the Scheme.

Spotlight
As per Section 73E, the Central Government is empowered to add to, amend, vary or rescind the scheme.

Laying of Scheme Framed under this Chapter (Section 73F)

Every Scheme framed under this chapter shall be laid, as soon as may be after it is made, before each House of Parliament while it is in session, for a total period of 30 days which may be comprised in 1 session or in 2 or more successive sessions, and if, before the expiry of the session immediately following the session or the successive sessions aforesaid, both Houses agree in making any modification in the Scheme or both Houses agree that the Scheme should not be made, the Scheme shall thereafter have effect only in such modified form or to be of no effect, as the case may be; so, however, that any such modification or annulment shall be without prejudice to the validity of anything previously done under that Scheme.

CHAPTER VI: ADJUDICATION OF DISPUTE AND CLAIMS

Constitution of Employees' Insurance Court (Section 74)

1. The State Government shall, by notification in the Official Gazette, constitute an Employees' Insurance Court for such local area as may be specified in the notification.
2. The Court shall consist of such number of judges as the State Government may think fit.
3. Any person who is or has been a judicial officer or is a legal practitioner of 5 years' standing shall be qualified to be a Judge of the Employees' Insurance Court.
4. The State Government may appoint the same Court for 2 or more local areas or 2 or more Courts for the same local area.
5. Where more than one Court has been appointed for the same local area, the State Government may, by general or special order, regulate the distribution of business between them.

Matters to be Decided by Employees' Insurance Court (Section 75)

1. If any question or dispute arises as to:
   (a) whether any person is an employee within the meaning of this Act or whether he is liable to pay the employee's contribution, or
   (b) the rate of wages or average daily wages of an employee for the purposes of this Act, or
   (c) the rate of contribution payable by a principal employer in respect of any employee, or
   (d) the person who is or was the principal employer in respect of any employee, or
   (e) the right of any person to any benefit and as to the amount and duration thereof, or
   (ee) any direction issued by the Corporation under Section 55A on a review of any payment of dependants benefits, or
   (g) any other matter which is in dispute between a principal employer and the Corporation, or between a principal employer and an immediate employer, or between a person and the

Spotlight
Section 75 provides for matters to be decided by Employees' Insurance Courts.

Corporation or between an employee and a principal or immediate employer, in respect of any contribution or benefit or other dues payable or recoverable under this Act, or any other matter required to be or which may be decided by the Employees' Insurance Court under this Act,

such a question or dispute subject to the provisions of sub-section (2A), shall be decided by the Employees' Insurance Court in accordance with the provisions of this Act.

2. Subject to the provisions of sub-section (2A), the following claims shall be decided by the Employees' Insurance Court, namely:
   (a) claim for the recovery of contribution from the principal employer;
   (b) claim by a principal employer to recover contributions from any immediate employer;
   (d) claim against a principal employer under Section 68;
   (e) claim under Section 70 for the recovery of the value or amount of the benefits received by a person when he is not lawfully entitled thereto; and
   (f) any claim for the recovery of any benefit admissible under this Act.

2A. If in any proceedings before the Employees' Insurance Court a disablement question arises and the question of a medical board or a medical appeal tribunal has not been obtained on the same and the decision of such question is necessary for the determination of the claim or question before the Employees' Insurance Court, that Court shall direct the Corporation to have the question decided by this Act and shall thereafter proceed with the determination of the claim or question before it in accordance with the decision of the medical board or the medical appeal tribunal, as the case may be, except where an appeal has been filed before the Employees' Insurance Court under sub-section (2) of Section 54A in which case the Employees' Insurance Court may itself determine all the issues arising before it.

2B. No matter which is in dispute between a principal employer and the Corporation in respect of any contribution or any other dues shall be raised by the principal employer in the Employees' Insurance Court unless he has deposited with the Court 50 per cent of the amount due from him as claimed by the Corporation:

   Provided that the Court may, for reasons to be recorded in writing waive or reduce the amount to be deposited under this sub-section.

3. No Civil Court shall have jurisdiction to decide or deal with any question or dispute as aforesaid or to adjudicate on any liability which by or under this Act is to be decided by a medical board, or by a medical appeal tribunal or by the Employees' Insurance Court.

Institution of Proceedings, etc. (Section 76)

1. Subject to the provisions of this Act and any rules made by the State Government, all proceedings before the Employees' Insurance Court shall be instituted in the Court appointed for the local area in which the insured person was working at the time the question or dispute arose.
2. If the Court is satisfied that any matter arising out of any proceeding pending before it can be more conveniently dealt with by any other Employees' Insurance Court in the same State, it may, subject to any rules made by the State Government in this behalf, order such matter to be transferred to such other Court for disposal and shall forthwith transmit to such other Court the records connected with that matter.
3. The State Government may transfer any matter pending before any Employees' Insurance Court in the State to any such Court in another State with the consent of the State Government of that State.

4. The Court to which any matter is transferred under sub-section (2) or sub-section (3) shall continue the proceedings as if they had been originally instituted in it.

Commencement of Proceedings (Section 77)

1. The proceedings before an Employees' Insurance Court shall be commenced by application.

1A. Every such application shall be made within a period of 3 years from the date on which the cause of action arose.

Spotlight

Section 77(1) provides that proceedings before an EI court shall be commenced by application.

Explanation For the purpose of this sub-section:

(a) the cause of action in respect of a claim for benefit shall not be deemed to arise unless the insured person or in the case of dependants' benefit, the dependants of the insured person claims or claim that benefit in accordance with the regulations made in that behalf within a period of 12 months after the claim became due or within such further period as the Employees' Insurance Court may allow on grounds which appear to it to be reasonable;

(b) the cause of action in respect of a claim by the Corporation for recovering contributions (including interest and damages) from the principal employer shall be deemed to have arisen on the date on which such claim is made by the Corporation for the first time:

Provided that no claim shall be made by the Corporation after 5 years of the period to which the claim relates;

(c) the cause of action in respect of a claim by the principal employer for recovering contributions from an immediate employer shall not be deemed to arise till the date by which the evidence of contributions having been paid is due to be received by the Corporation under the regulations.

2. Every such application shall be in such form and shall contain such particulars and shall be accompanied by such fee, if any, as may be prescribed by rules made by the State Government in consultation with the Corporation.

CASE CORNER

In *Rajrani Omprakash Shukla and Another vs. Director, Employees' State Insurance Corporation and Others [(2012) LLR 807]* the deceased workman was working with his employer at Indore; he died at Ahmedabad. The appellants (i.e., mother and sister of the deceased) filed an application for compensation under the Act in Employees' Insurance (EI) Court at Ahmedabad. The application was rejected on the ground of jurisdiction. In response to the appeal the Court held that Section 76 of the Act refers to the institution of proceedings in the EI Court of local areas where the insured was working at that time. The application ought to have been returned to the applicant instead of rejecting for presenting the same to the Court at Indore, in which it could have been instituted. Hence the Court ordered that the application must be returned to the applicant for presenting the same to the EI Court at Indore in accordance with law and be disposed of as early as possible, preferably within 3 months.

(Adapted from: Labour Law Reporter, August, 2012, p. 807.)

Powers of Employees' Insurance Court (Section 78)

1. The Employees' Insurance Court shall have all the powers of a Civil Court for the purposes of summoning and enforcing the attendance of witnesses, compelling the discovery and production of documents and material objects, administering oath and recording evidence and such Court shall be deemed to be a Civil Court within the meaning of Section 195 and Chapter XXVI of the Code of Criminal Procedure, 1973.
2. The Employees' Insurance Court shall follow such procedure as may be prescribed by rules made by the State Government.
3. All costs incidental to any proceeding before an Employees' Insurance Court shall, subject to such rules as may be made in this behalf by the State Government, be in the discretion of the Court.
4. An order of the Employees' Insurance Court shall be enforceable as if it were a decree passed in a suit by a Civil Court.

Appearance by Legal Practitioners, etc. (Section 79)

Any application, appearance or act required to be made or done by any person to or before an Employees' Insurance Court (other than appearance of a person required for the purpose of his examination as witness) may be made or done by a legal practitioner or by an officer of a registered trade union authorised in writing by such person or with the permission of the Court, by any other person so authorised.

Benefit not Admissible unless Claimed in Time (Section 80)

Repealed by the Employees' State Insurance (Amendment) Act, 1966.

Reference to High Court (Section 81)

An Employees' Insurance Court may submit any question of law for the decision of the High Court and if it does so, shall decide the question pending before it in accordance with such decision.

Appeal (Section 82)

1. Save as expressly provided in this section, no appeal shall lie from an order of an Employees' Insurance Court.
2. An appeal shall lie to the High Court from an order of an Employees' Insurance Court if it involves a substantial question of law.
3. The period of limitation for an appeal under this section shall be 60 days.
4. The provisions of sections 5 and 12 of the Limitation Act, 1963 shall apply to appeals under this section.

> **Spotlight**
> As per Section 82(3), the period of limitation for an appeal is 60 days.

In *Employees' State Insurance Corporation vs. Cheeran's Auto Agencies* [(1992) (1) LLJ 704] it was held that "Section 82 makes it clear that an appeal lies to the High Court from an order of the Insurance Court only if it involves a substantial question of law. The question whether 2 persons are employees or not is a question which has to be decided on an assessment of facts and it is a question of fact. It cannot be treated as a substantial question of law."

(Adapted from: www.indiankanoon.org/doc/1684660/ accessed on 17/4/2014.)

CASE CORNER

In *Employees' State Insurance Corporation, Patna and Others vs. R. K. Tekriwal s/o Late Matadin Tekriwal Director, M/s Azad Transport Company Pvt. Ltd. and Another* [(2012) LLR 84]), an appeal is directed against the order passed by the ESI Court, holding that the demand for contribution made by the ESI Corporation is not tenable. The respondent, M/s Azad Transport Company Pvt. Ltd., on receiving such demand, filed an application under Section 75(1)(g) of the ESI Act, 1948. Demand of ESI contribution by the petitioner-corporation in respect of employees engaged for loading and unloading of goods as and when required was challenged by the respondent-company before the EI Court. It is contended by the appellants that relevant documents were not considered by the Labour Court while giving a finding against the Corporation. The respondent-company has contended that on perusal of the order under appeal it would appear that the matter in issue was whether the employees for whom demands were made by the Corporation were covered under the provisions or not. The latter could not bring any positive evidence on record to show that they were the employees of the respondent by engaging them through any appointment letter, nor could it produce any document to show that they were engaged by the company.

The Court considered this aspect of the matter and discussed the order under appeal. The contention advanced on behalf of the appellants is that those documents were not considered by the Court. However, on perusal of the order under appeal, it was concluded that the all materials on record were considered by the Court in its correct perspective.

(Adapted from: Labour Law Reporter, August, 2012, pp. 842-844.)

Stay of Payment Pending Appeal (Section 83)

Where the Corporation has presented an appeal against an order of the Employees' Insurance Court, that Court may, and if so directed by the High Court, shall, pending the decision of the appeal, withhold the payment of any sum directed to be paid by the order appealed against.

CHAPTER VII: PENALTIES

Punishment for False Statement (Section 84)

Whoever, for the purpose of causing any increase in payment or benefit under this Act, or for the purpose of causing any payment or benefit to be made where no payment or benefit is authorised by or under this Act, or for the purpose of avoiding any payment to be made by himself under this Act or enabling any other person to avoid any such payment, knowingly makes or causes to be made any false statement or false representation, shall be punishable with imprisonment for a term which may extend to 6 months, or with fine not exceeding ₹2000, or with both:

Spotlight

Imprisonment as punishment for false statement can be up to 6 months, as per Section 84.

Provided that where an insured person is convicted under this section, he shall not be entitled for any cash benefit under this Act for such period as may be prescribed by the Central Government.

Punishment for Failure to Pay Contributions, etc. (Section 85)

If any person–

(a) fails to pay any contribution which under this Act he is liable to pay, or
(b) deducts or attempts to deduct from the wages of an employee the whole or any part of the employer's contribution, or
(c) in contravention of Section 72 reduces the wages or any privileges or benefits admissible to an employee, or
(d) in contravention of Section 73 or any regulation dismisses, discharges, reduces or otherwise punishes an employee, or
(e) fails or refuses to submit any return required by the regulations, or makes a false return, or
(f) obstructs any Inspector or other official of the Corporation in the discharge of his duties, or
(g) is guilty of any contravention of or non-compliance with any of the requirements of this Act or the rules or the regulations in respect of which no special penalty is provided,

he shall be punishable:

(i) where he commits an offence under clause (a), with imprisonment for a term which may extend to 3 years but–
   (a) which shall not be less than 1 year, in case of failure to pay the employee's contribution which has been deducted by him from the employee's wages and shall also be liable to fine of ₹10,000;
   (b) which shall not be less than 6 months, in any other case and shall also be liable to fine of ₹5,000:

Provided that the Court may, for any adequate and special reasons to be recorded in the judgment, impose a sentence of imprisonment for a lesser term;

(ii) where he commits an offence under any of the clauses (b) to (g) (both inclusive), with imprisonment for a term which may extend to 1 year or with fine which may extend to ₹4,000, or with both.

CASE CORNER

In *Employees' State Insurance Corporation vs. Hotel President* [(2012) LLR 105], the respondent was called upon to pay contribution for the year 1992-1993 and 1994-1995 along with computed interest and damages within 15 days of receipt of notice. Only partial payment was made without disputing the liability. Therefore another statutory notice was issued and served upon the respondent giving details of the period of default and damages due upon such default. The Court held that the provision of Section 76(2B) of the ESI Act, 1948 is a measure provided for fulfilling the aims and objects of the Act. The language is explicit and it is imperative for the employer to deposit 50 per cent of the amount due from him as claimed by the Corporation before the Court undertakes to decide any dispute that the amount would include not only the contribution but also the penalty and/or damages as given in Section 85B.

(Adapted from: Labour Law Reporter, October, 2012, pp. 1050-1052.)

Enhanced Punishment in Certain Cases after Previous Conviction (Section 85A)

Whoever, having been convicted by a Court of an offence punishable under this Act, commits the same offence shall, for every such subsequent offence, be punishable with imprisonment for a term which may extend to 2 years and with fine of ₹5,000.

Provided that where such subsequent offence is for failure by the employer to pay any contribution which under this Act he is liable to pay, he shall, for every such subsequent offence, be punishable with imprisonment for a term which may extend to 5 years but which shall not be less than 2 years and shall also be liable to fine of ₹25,000.

Power to Recover Damages (Section 85B)

> **Spotlight**
> Section 85B(1) provides that an employer shall be given a reasonable opportunity of being heard before recovery of damages.

1. Where an employer fails to pay the amount due in respect of any contribution or any other amount payable under this Act, the Corporation may recover from the employer by way of penalty such damages not exceeding the amount of arrears as may be specified in the regulations:

   Provided that before recovering such damages, the employer shall be given a reasonable opportunity of being heard:

   Provided further that the Corporation may reduce or waive the damages recoverable under this section in relation to an establishment which is a sick industrial company in respect of which a scheme for rehabilitation has been sanctioned by the Board for Industrial and Financial Reconstruction established under Section 4 of the Sick Industrial Companies (Special Provisions) Act, 1985 subject to such terms and conditions as may be specified in regulations.
2. Any damages recoverable under sub-section (1) may be recovered as an arrear of land revenue or under Section 45C to Section 45I.

Power of Court to Make Orders (Section 85C)

1. Where an employer is convicted of an offence for failure to pay any contribution payable under this Act, the Court may, in addition to awarding any punishment, by order, in writing, require him within a period specified in the order (which the Court may if it thinks fit and an application in that behalf, from time to time, extend), to pay the amount of contribution in respect of which the offence was committed and to furnish the return relating to such contributions.
2. Where an order is made under sub-section (1), the employer shall not be liable under this Act in respect of the continuation of the offence during the period or extended period, if any, allowed by the Court, but if, on the expiry of such period or extended period, as the case may be, the order of the Court has not been fully complied with, the employer shall be deemed to have committed a further offence and shall be punishable with imprisonment in respect thereof under Section 85 and shall also be liable to pay fine which may extend to ₹1,000 for every day after such expiry on which the order has not been complied with.

Prosecutions (Section 86)

1. No prosecution under this Act shall be instituted except by or with the previous sanction of the Insurance Commissioner or of such other officer of the Corporation as may be authorised in this behalf by the Director General of the Corporation.
2. No Court inferior to that of a Metropolitan Magistrate or Judicial Magistrate of the first class shall try any offence under this Act.
3. No Court shall take cognizance of any offence under this Act except on a complaint made in writing in respect thereof.

Offences by Companies (Section 86A)

1. If the person committing an offence under this Act is a company, every person, who at the time the offence was committed was in charge of, and was responsible to, the company for the conduct of the business of the company, as well as the company, shall be deemed to be guilty of the offence and shall be liable to be proceeded against and punished accordingly:

   Provided that nothing contained in this sub-section shall render any person liable to any punishment, if he proves that the offence was committed without his knowledge or that he exercised all due diligence to prevent the commission of such offence.
2. Notwithstanding anything contained in sub-section (1), where an offence under this Act has been committed with the consent or connivance of, or is attributable to, any neglect on the part of, any director or manager, secretary or other officer of the company, such director, manager, secretary or other officer shall be deemed to be guilty of that offence and shall be liable to be proceeded against and punished accordingly.

Explanation For the purposes of this section:

(i) "company" means any body corporate and includes a firm and other associations of individuals; and

(ii) "director" in relation to:

  (a) a company, other than a firm, means the managing director or a whole-time director;

  (b) a firm means a partner in the firm.

CHAPTER VIII: MISCELLANEOUS

Exemption of a Factory or Establishment or Class of Factories or Establishments (Section 87)

The appropriate Government may, by notification in the Official Gazette and subject to such conditions as may be specified in the notification, exempt any factory or establishment or class of factories or establishments in any specified area from the operation of this Act for a period not exceeding 1 year and may from time to time by like notification renew any such exemption for periods not exceeding 1 year at a time:

Provided that such exemptions may be granted only if the employees in such factories or establishments are otherwise in receipt of benefits substantially similar or superior to the benefits provided under this Act:

Provided further that an application for renewal shall be made 3 months before the date of expiry of the exemption period and a decision on the same shall be taken by the appropriate Government within 2 months of receipt of such application.

In *Kancor Ingredients Ltd. vs. ESI Corporation* [(2012) LLR 351] it was held that "granting or denying exemption under Section 87 from the coverage of the Act is open to judicial review under Article 226 of Constitution of India. A detailed order is warranted to be passed under Section 37 of the Act while granting or disallowing exemption by analysing the benefit under the Act and provided by the employer, showing item-wise comparison since the interest of a large section of workers, the actual beneficiaries, is involved."

(Adapted from: Labour Law Reporter, April 2012, p. 351.)

Exemption of Persons or Class of Persons (Section 88)

The appropriate Government may, by notification in the Official Gazette and subject to such conditions as it may deem fit to impose, exempt any persons or class of persons employed in any factory, or establishment or class of factories or establishments to which this Act applies from the operation of the Act.

Corporation to Make Representation (Section 89)

No exemption shall be granted or renewed under Section 87 or Section 88, unless a reasonable opportunity has been given to the Corporation to make any representation it may wish to make in regard to the proposal and such representation has been considered by the appropriate Government.

Exemption of Factories or Establishments Belonging to Government or any Local Authority (Section 90)

The appropriate government may, after consultation with the Corporation, by notification in the Official Gazette and subject to such conditions as may be specified in the notification, exempt any factory or establishment belonging to any local authority, from the operation of this Act if the employees in any such factory or establishment are otherwise in receipt of benefits substantially similar or superior to the benefits provided under this Act.

Exemption from One or More Provisions of the Act (Section 91)

The appropriate Government may, with the consent of the Corporation, by notification in the Official Gazette, exempt any employees or class of employees in any factory or establishment or class of factories or establishments from 1 or more of the provisions relating to the benefits provided under this Act.

Exemptions to be either Prospective or Retrospective (Section 91A)

Any notification granting exemption under Section 87, Section 88, Section 90 or Section 91 may be issued so as to take effect prospectively on such date as may be specified therein.

Central Government to be Appropriate Government (Section 91AA)

Notwithstanding anything contained in this Act, in respect of establishments located in the States where medical benefit is provided by the Corporation, the Central Government shall be the appropriate Government.

Misuse of Benefits (Section 91B)

If the Central Government is satisfied that the benefits under this Act are being misused by insured persons in a factory or establishment, that Government may, by order, published in the Official Gazette, disentitle such persons from such of the benefits at it thinks fit:

Provided that no such order shall be passed unless a reasonable opportunity of being heard is given to the concerned factory or establishment, insured persons and the trade unions registered under the Trade Unions Act, 1926 having members in the factory or establishment.

Writing off of Losses (Section 91C)

Subject to the conditions as may be prescribed by the Central Government, where the Corporation is of opinion that the amount of contribution, interest and damages due to the Corporation is irrecoverable, the Corporation may sanction the writing off finally of the said amount.

Power of Central Government to Give Directions (Section 92)

1. The Central Government may give directions to a State Government as to the carrying into execution of this Act in the State.
2. The Central Government may, from time to time, give such directions to the Corporation as it may think fit for the efficient administration of the Act, and if any such direction is given, the Corporation shall comply with such direction.

Corporation Officers and Servants to be Public Servants (Section 93)

All officers and servants of the Corporation shall be deemed to be public servants within the meaning of Section 21 of the Indian Penal Code.

Liability in Case of Transfer of Establishment (Section 93A)

Where an employer, in relation to a factory or establishment, transfers that factory or establishment in whole or in part, by sale, gift, lease or license or in any other manner whatsoever, the employer and the person to whom the factory or establishment is so transferred shall jointly and severally be liable to pay the amount due in respect of any contribution or any other amount payable under this Act in respect of the periods up to the date of such transfer:

> **Spotlight**
> Section 93A limits the liability of the transferee to the value of assets he has obtained by such transfer.

Provided that the liability of the transferee shall be limited to the value of the assets obtained by him by such transfer.

Contributions, etc., due to Corporation to Have Priority over other Debts (Section 94)

There shall be deemed to be included among the debts which, under Section 49 of the Presidency towns Insolvency Act, 1909, or under Section 61 of the Provincial Insolvency Act, 1920, or under any law relating to insolvency in force in the territories which, immediately before the 1st November, 1956, were comprised in a Part B State, or under Section 530 of the Companies Act, 1956, in the distribution of the property of the insolvent or in the distribution of the assets of a company being wound up, to be paid in priority to all other debts, the amount due in respect of any contribution or any other amount payable under this Act the liability where for accrued before the date of the order of adjudication of the insolvent or the date of the winding up, as the case may be.

Delegation of Powers (Section 94A)

The Corporation, and, subject to any regulations made by the Corporation in this behalf, the Standing Committee may direct that all or any of the powers and functions which may be exercised or performed by the Corporation or the Standing Committee, as the case may be, may, in relation to such matters and subject to such conditions, if any, as may be specified, be also exercisable by any officer or authority subordinate to the Corporation.

Power of Central Government to Make Rules (Section 95)

1. The Central Government may, after consultation with the Corporation and subject to the condition of previous publication, make rules not inconsistent with this Act for the purpose of giving effect to the provisions thereof.
2. In particular and without prejudice to the generality of the foregoing power, such rules may provide for all or any of the following matters, namely:
   (a) the limit of wages beyond which a person shall not be deemed to be an employee;
   (ab) the limit of maximum monthly salary for the purpose of sub-section (1) of Section 17;
   (ac) the manner in which appointments and elections of members of the Corporation, the Standing Committee and the Medical Benefit Council shall be made;
   (b) the quorum at meetings of the Corporation, the Standing Committee and the Medical Benefit Council and the minimum number of meetings of those bodies to be held in a year;
   (c) the records to be kept of the transaction of business by the Corporation, the Standing Committee and the Medical Benefit Council;
   (d) the powers and duties of the Director-General and the Financial Commissioner and the conditions of their service;
   (e) the powers and duties of the Medical Benefit Council;
   (ea) the types of expenses which may be termed as administrative expenses, the percentage of income of the Corporation which may be spent for such expenses;
   (eb) the rates of contributions and limits of wages below which employees are not liable to pay contribution;
   (ec) the manner of calculation of the average daily wage;
   (ed) the manner of certifying the certificate to recover amount by the Recovery Officer;
   (ee) the amount of funeral expenses;
   (ef) the qualifications, conditions, rates and period of sickness benefit, maternity benefit, disablement benefit and dependants' benefit;
   (eff) the income of dependant parents from all sources;
   (eg) the conditions for grant of medical benefits for insured persons who cease to be in insurable employment on account of permanent disablement;
   (eh) the conditions for grant of medical benefits for persons who have attained the age of superannuation;
   (ehh) the conditions under which the medical benefits shall be payable to the insured person and spouse of an insured person who has attained the age of superannuation, the person who retires under Voluntary Retirement Scheme and the person who takes pre-mature retirement;
   (ei) the manner in which and the time within which appeals may be filed to medical appeal tribunals or Employees' Insurance Courts;
   (f) the procedure to be adopted in the execution of contracts;
   (g) the acquisition, holding and disposal of property by the Corporation;
   (h) the raising and repayment of loans;
   (i) the investment of the funds of the Corporation and of any provident or other benefit fund and their transfer or realisation;
   (j) the basis on which the periodical valuation of the assets and liabilities of the Corporation shall be made;

(k) the bank or banks in which the funds of the Corporation may be deposited, the procedure to be followed in regard to the crediting of moneys accruing or payable to the Corporation and the manner in which any sums may be paid out of the Corporation funds and the officers by whom such payment may be authorised;

(l) the accounts to be maintained by the Corporation and the forms in which such accounts shall be kept and the times at which such accounts shall be audited;

(m) the publication of the accounts of the Corporation and the report of auditors, the action to be taken on the audit report, the powers of auditors to disallow and surcharge items of expenditure and the recovery of sums so disallowed or surcharged;

(n) the preparation of budget estimates and supplementary estimates and the manner in which such estimates shall be sanctioned and published;

(o) the establishment and maintenance of provident or other benefit fund for officers and servants of the Corporation;

(oa) the period of non-entitlement for cash benefit in case of conviction of an insured person;

(p) any matter which is required or allowed by this Act to be prescribed by the Central Government.

2A. The power to make rules conferred by this section shall include the power to give retrospective effect, from a date not earlier than the date of commencement of this Act, to the rules or any of them but no retrospective effect shall be given to any rules so as to prejudicially affect the interest of any person other than the Corporation to whom such rule may be applicable.

3. Rules made under this section shall be published in the Official Gazette and thereupon shall have effect as if enacted in this Act.

4. Every rule made under this section shall be laid, as soon as may be after it is made, before each House of Parliament while it is in session for a total period of 30 days which may be comprised in 1 session or in 2 or more successive sessions, and if, before the expiry of the session immediately following the session or the successive sessions aforesaid, both Houses agree in making any modification in the rule or both Houses agree that the rule should not be made, the rule shall thereafter have effect only in such modified form or be of no effect, as the case may be; so however, that any such modification or annulment shall be without prejudice to the validity of anything previously done under that rule.

Power of State Government to Make Rules (Section 96)

1. The State Government may, after consultation with the Corporation and subject to the condition of previous publication, make rules not inconsistent with this Act in regard to all or any of the following matters, namely:

   (a) the constitution of Employees' Insurance Courts, the qualifications of persons who may be appointed Judges thereof, and the conditions of service of such Judges;

   (b) the procedure to be followed in proceedings before such Courts and the execution of orders made by such Courts;

   (c) the fee payable in respect of applications made to the Employees' Insurance Court, the costs incidental to the proceedings in such Court, the form in which applications should be made to it and the particulars to be specified in such applications;

   (d) the establishment of hospitals, dispensaries and other institutions, the allotment of insured persons or their families to any such hospital, dispensary or other institution;

   (e) the scale of medical benefit which shall be provided at any hospital, clinic, dispensary or institution, the keeping of medical records and the furnishing of statistical returns;

(ee) the organisational structure, functions, powers, activities and other matters for the establishment of the organisation;
(f) the nature and extent of the staff, equipment and medicines that shall be provided at such hospitals, dispensaries and institutions;
(g) the conditions of service of the staff employed at such hospitals, dispensaries and institutions; and
(h) any other matter which is required or allowed by this Act to be prescribed by the State Government.

2. Rules made under this section shall be published in the Official Gazette and thereupon shall have effect as if enacted in this Act.
3. Every rule made under this section shall be laid as soon as may be after it is made, before each House of the State Legislature where it consists of 2 Houses, or, where such Legislature consists of 1 House, before that House.

Power of Corporation to Make Regulations (Section 97)

1. The Corporation may, subject to the condition to previous publication, make regulations, not inconsistent with this Act and the rules made thereunder, for the administration of the affairs of the Corporation and for carrying into effect the provisions of this Act.
2. In particular and without prejudice to the generality of the foregoing power, such regulations may provide for all or any of the following matters, namely:
   (i) the time and place of meetings of the Corporation, the Standing Committee and the Medical Benefit Council and the procedure to be followed at such meetings;
   (ia) the time within which and the manner in which a factory or establishment shall be registered;
   (ii) the matters which shall be referred by the Standing Committee to the Corporation for decision;
   (iii) the manner in which any contribution payable under this Act shall be assessed and collected;
   (iiia) the rate of interest higher than 12 per cent on delayed payment of contributions;
   (iv) reckoning of wages for the purpose of fixing the contribution payable under this Act;
   (iva) the register of employees to be maintained by the immediate employer;
   (ivb) the entitlement of sickness benefit or disablement benefit for temporary disablement on any day on which person works or remains on leave or on holiday and in respect of which he receives wages or for any day on which he remains on strike;
   (v) the certification of sickness and eligibility for any cash benefit;
   (vi) the method of determining whether an insured person is suffering from 1 or more of the diseases specified in the Third Schedule;
   (vii) the assessing of the money value of any benefit which is not a cash benefit;
   (viii) the time within which and the form and manner in which any claim for a benefit may be made and the particulars to be specified in such claim;
   (ix) the circumstances in which an employee in receipt of disablement benefit may be dismissed, discharged, reduced or otherwise punished;
   (x) the manner in which and the place and time at which any benefit shall be paid;
   (xi) the method of calculating the amount of cash benefit payable and the circumstances in which and the extent to which commutation of disablement and dependants' benefits, may be allowed and the method of calculating the commutation value;

(xii) the notice of pregnancy or of confinement and notice and proof of sickness;

(xiia) specifying the authority competent to give certificate of eligibility for maternity benefit;

(xiib) the manner of nomination by an insured woman for payment of maternity benefit in case of her or her child's death;

(xiic) the production of proof in support of claim for maternity benefit or additional maternity benefit;

(xiii) the conditions under which any benefit may be suspended;

(xiv) the conditions to be observed by a person when in receipt of any benefit and the periodical medical examination of such persons;

(xvi) the appointment of medical practitioners for the purposes of this Act, the duties of such practitioners and the form of medical certificates;

(xvia) the qualifications and experience which a person should possess for giving certificate of sickness;

(xvib) the constitution of medical boards and medical appeal tribunals;

(xvii) the penalties for breach of regulations by fine (not exceeding 2 days' wages for a first breach and not exceeding 3 days' wages for any subsequent breach) which may be imposed on employees;

(xviia) the amount of damages to be recovered as penalty;

(xviib) the terms and conditions for reduction or waiver of damages in relation to a sick industrial company;

(xviii) the circumstances in which and the conditions subject to which any regulation may be relaxed, the extent of such relaxation, and the authority by whom such relaxation may be granted;

(xix) the returns to be submitted and the registers or records to be maintained by the principal and immediate employers, the forms of such returns, registers or records, and the times at which such returns should be submitted and the particulars which such returns, registers and records should contain;

(xx) the duties and powers of Social Security Officers and other officers and servants of the Corporation;

(xxa) the constitution of the appellate authority and the interest on amount deposited by the employer with the Corporation;

(xxi) the method of recruitment, pay and allowances, discipline, superannuation benefits and other conditions of service of the officers and servants of the Corporation other than the Director General and Financial Commissioner;

(xxii) the procedure to be followed in remitting contributions to the Corporation; and

(xxiii) any matter in respect of which regulations are required or permitted to be made by this Act.

2A. The condition of previous publication shall not apply to any regulations of the nature specified in clause (xxi) of sub-section (2).

3. Regulations made by the Corporation shall be published in the Gazette of India and thereupon shall have effects as if enacted in this Act.

4. Every regulation shall, as soon as may be, after it is made by the Corporation, be forwarded to the Central Government and that Government shall cause a copy of the same to be laid before each House of Parliament, while it is in session for a total period of 30 days, which may be comprised in 1 session or in 2 or more successive sessions, and if, before the expiry of the session immediately following the session or the successive sessions aforesaid, both Houses agree in making any modification in the regulation or both Houses agree that the regulation should not be made, the

regulation shall thereafter have effect only in such modified form or be of no effect, as the case may be, so, however, that any such modification or annulment shall be without prejudice to the validity of anything previously done under that regulation.

Corporation May Undertake Duties in Part B States (Section 98)

Repealed by the Employees' State Insurance (Amendment) Act, 1951.

Medical Care for the Families of Insured Persons (Section 99)

At any time when its funds so permit, the Corporation may provide or contribute towards the cost of medical care for the families of insured persons.

Power to Remove Difficulties (Section 99A)

1. If any difficulty arises in giving effect to the provisions of this Act, the Central Government may, by order published in the Official Gazette, make such provisions or give such directions, not inconsistent with the provisions of this Act, as appears to it to be necessary or expedient for removing the difficulty.
2. Any order made under this section shall have effect notwithstanding anything inconsistent therewith in any rules or regulations made under this Act.

Repeals and Savings (Section 100)

If, immediately before the day on which this Act comes into force in any part of the territories which, immediately before the 1st November 1956, were comprised in a Part B State, there is in force in that part any law corresponding to this Act, that law shall, on such day, stand repealed:

Provided that the repeal shall not affect:

(a) the previous operations of any such law, or

(b) any penalty, forfeiture or punishment incurred in respect of any offence committed against any such law, or

(c) any investigation or remedy in respect of any such penalty, forfeiture or punishment;

and any such investigation, legal proceeding or remedy may be instituted, continued or enforced and any such penalty, forfeiture or punishment may be imposed, as if this Act had not been passed:

Provided further that subject to the preceding proviso anything done or any action taken under any such law shall be deemed to have been done or taken under the corresponding provision of this Act and shall continue in force accordingly unless and until superseded by anything done or any action taken under this Act.

SOCIAL SECURITY BENEFITS

In exercise of the powers conferred by Section 95 of the Employees' State Insurance Act, 1948, the Central Government has framed the Employees' State Insurance (Central) Rules, 1950. Employees covered under the scheme are entitled to medical facilities for self and dependants and cash benefits in specified contingencies resulting in loss of wages or earning capacity. Insured women are entitled to maternity benefit for confinement. In the event of death of an insured employee due to employment injury or any occupational disease, his/her dependants are entitled to family pension. Following are the various benefits that insured employees and their dependants are entitled to:

- **Sickness benefit:** Subject to the provisions of the Act, sickness benefit is payable to an insured person in cash in the event of sickness resulting in absence from work and duly certified by an authorised insurance medical officer or practitioner. The benefit is admissible only after contribution in respect of the insured has been paid for at least 78 days in a contribution period of 6 months. Sickness benefit is payable for a maximum of 91 days in 2 consecutive contribution periods. The daily rate of sickness benefits in respect of an insured person during any benefit period shall be 20 per cent more than "the standard benefit rate" corresponding to the average daily wages of that person during the corresponding contribution period.
- **Maternity benefit:** Maternity benefit is payable to an insured woman in case of confinement occurring or expected to occur in a benefit period or miscarriage, or sickness related thereto. For claiming this benefit, contribution in respect of her should have been paid for at least 70 days in the immediately preceding 2 consecutive contribution periods. Maternity benefit is normally payable for a period of 12 weeks, of which not more than 6 weeks shall precede the expected date of confinement. In case of sickness arising out of pregnancy, confinement, premature birth of child or miscarriage or medical termination of pregnancy, an insured woman qualified to claim such maternity benefit shall be entitled to an additional period not exceeding 1 month on medical grounds. The daily rate of payment of the benefit is equal to twice the "standard benefit rate". In case the insured woman dies during her delivery or during the period immediately following the date of her delivery for which she is entitled to maternity benefits, leaving behind in either case, the child, maternity benefit shall be paid for the whole of that period, but if the child also dies during the said period, then for the days up to and including the day of the death of the child, to the person nominated by the insured woman, and if there is no such nominee, to her legal representative.
- **Disablement benefits:** Disablement benefit is payable to insured employees suffering from physical disablement due to employment injury or occupational disease. Temporary disablement benefit at 70 per cent of the wages is payable for not less than 3 days (excluding the day of accident) till the temporary disablement lasts and is duly certified by an authorised insurance medical officer. In case of permanent disablement, whether total or partial, cash benefit is payable for life. The daily rate of disablement benefit shall be 50 per cent more than the "standard benefit rate" in the contribution period corresponding to the benefit period in which the employment injury has occurred, rounded to the next higher rupee. The amount payable is worked out on the basis of earning capacity determined by a medical board.
- **Dependants' benefits:** Dependants' benefit is payable to the dependants (widow, children and widowed mother) of a insured person who has died due to an employment injury or an occupational disease. A widow can receive this benefit on a monthly basis for life or till remarriage. A legitimate or adopted son can receive this benefit till 18 years of age; a legitimate or adopted unmarried daughter may receive this benefit till 18 years of age or until her marriage, whichever is earlier. Other dependants like parents including a widowed mother can also receive the benefit under certain conditions. The daily rate of dependant's benefit shall be 50 per cent more than the "standard benefit rate" in the contribution period corresponding to the benefit period in which the employment injury occurs.
- **Funeral expenses:** The amount of funeral expenses (earlier known as funeral "benefits") on the death of an insured person shall be ₹5,000.

- **Medical benefits to retired insured persons:** An insured person who leaves the insurable employment on attaining the age of superannuation or retires under a Voluntary Retirement Scheme or takes premature retirement after being insured for not less than 5 years in all such cases, shall be eligible to receive medical benefits for himself and his spouse at the scale prescribed under the Act and the regulations made thereunder.

In exercise of the powers conferred by Section 97 of the Employees' State Insurance Act, 1948, the Employees' State Insurance Corporation has framed the Employees' State Insurance (General) Regulations, 1950. Following are the various benefits under the Regulations that insured employees and their dependants are entitled to:

- **Extended sickness benefit:** Extended sickness benefit is payable to insured persons for the period of certified sickness in case of any of the specified 34 malignant and long-term diseases that need prolonged treatment and absence from work on medical advice. In order to be entitled for this benefit, an insured person should have been in insurable employment for at least 2 years, and should have paid contribution for a minimum of 156 days in the preceding 4 contribution periods. Such benefit is payable at an enhanced rate of 80 per cent of wages for a maximum period of 2 years on the basis of proper medical certification and authentication by the designated authority.
- **Enhanced sickness benefit:** This cash benefit is payable to insured persons in the productive age group for undergoing sterilisation operation, for 14 days in case of tubectomy and for 7 days in case of vasectomy. The amount payable is double the standard sickness benefit rate, i.e., full wages.
- **Medical benefit to families of insured persons**: The family of an insured person shall become entitled to medical benefit from the day the insured person himself becomes entitled to medical benefit and shall continue to be so entitled so long as the insured person is entitled to receive medical benefit for himself, or in the case of death of the insured person till such date up to which the insured person would have remained entitled to medical care, had he survived.

ADMINISTRATION OF THE ACT

The social security programme of ESI Scheme under the Employees' State Insurance Act, 1948 is administered by an apex corporate body called the Employee' State Insurance Corporation (ESIC). With its central headquarters at New Delhi, the Corporation comprises members representing vital stakeholders that include employees, employers and the Central and State Governments, along with representatives of the Parliament and medical profession. The Corporation is headed by the Union Minister of Labour as its Chairman, and the Director-General, appointed by the Central Government, functions as its Chief Executive Officer. A Standing Committee constituted from amongst the members of the Corporation acts as the Executive Body. The Medical Benefit Council, constituted by the Central Government, is another statuary body that advises the Corporation on matters related to the effective delivery of services to the beneficiaries. The Corporation operates through a network of 52 regional, sub-regional and divisional offices located in various States. The respective State Governments take care of the administration of medical benefits under the Scheme, except in case of Delhi and Noida/ Greater Noida areas of Uttar Pradesh, where the Corporation administers medical facilities directly. The Corporation has taken over the administration of 23 ESI Hospitals in various States for developing them as ESIC Model Hospitals *(www.esic.nic.in)*.

SUMMARY

- The Employees' State Insurance (ESI) Act, 1948 entails a scheme of health insurance for industrial workers. It provides compulsory state insurance that renders certain benefits in the event of sickness, maternity and employment injury to workmen employed in or in connection with work in factories other than seasonal factories.
- Employees covered under the scheme are entitled to medical facilities for self and dependants and cash benefits in the event of specified contingencies resulting in loss of wages or earning capacity. Insured women are entitled to maternity benefit for confinement.
- In the event of death of an insured employee due to employment injury or any occupational disease, his/her dependants are entitled to family pension. Other benefits include medical benefits to retired insured persons, medical benefit to families of insured persons, extended sickness benefit, enhanced sickness benefit and funeral expenses.
- Section 2(4) of the Act defines contribution as the sum of money payable to the ESI Corporation by the principal employer in respect of an employee and includes any amount payable by or on behalf of the employee in accordance with the provisions of this Act. Contributions in respect of an employee shall comprise contribution payable by the employer and contribution payable by the employee, as provided in Section 39(1).
- Permanent partial disablement is defined in Section 2(15A) as such disablement of a permanent nature, as reduces the earning capacity of an employee in every employment which he was capable of undertaking at the time of the accident resulting in the disablement.
- Section 2(15B) defines permanent total disablement as such disablement of a permanent nature as incapacitates an employee for all work which he was capable of performing at the time of the accident resulting in such disablement.
- Chapter II of the Act has provisions related to the ESI Corporation, Standing Committee and Medical Benefit Council.
- The Standing Committee, as per Section 18, shall administer the affairs of the Corporation and may exercise any of the powers and perform any of the functions of the Corporation.
- Section 26(1) mandates that all contributions paid under this Act and all other moneys received on behalf of the Corporation shall be paid into a fund called the Employees' State Insurance Fund, held and administered by the Corporation.
- All employees in factories or establishments to which this Act applies shall be insured in the manner provided by this Act, as laid down in Section 38.
- As per Section 40(1), the principal employer shall pay in respect of every employee, whether directly employed by him or by or through an immediate employer, both the employer's contribution and the employee's contribution.
- The State Government shall, by notification in the Official Gazette, constitute an Employees' Insurance Court for such local area as may be specified in the notification, as laid down in Section 74(1). Section 76(1) provides that all proceedings before the Employees' Insurance Court shall be instituted in the Court appointed for the local area in which the insured person was working at the time the question or dispute arose.
- According to Section 84, whoever knowingly makes or causes to be made any false statement or false representation, shall be punishable with imprisonment for a term which may extend to 6 months or with fine not exceeding ₹2000, or with both.
- In exercise of the powers conferred by Section 95 of the ESI Act, 1948, the Central Government has framed the Employees' State Insurance (Central) Rules, 1950. Employees covered under the

scheme are entitled to medical facilities for self and dependants and cash benefits in the event of specified contingencies resulting in loss of wages or earning capacity. Insured women are entitled to maternity benefit for confinement. In the event of death of an insured employee due to employment injury or any occupational disease, the dependants are entitled to family pension.

- In exercise of the powers conferred by Section 97 of the ESI Act, 1948, the ESIC has framed the Employees' State Insurance (General) Regulations, 1950, under which insured employees and their dependants are entitled to benefits like extended sickness benefit, enhanced sickness benefit and medical benefit to families of insured persons.
- The ESI Scheme is administered by ESIC. With its central headquarters at New Delhi, the Corporation comprises members that include employees, employers, and the Central and State Governments, along with representatives of the Parliament and medical profession. ESIC operates through a network of 52 regional, sub-regional and divisional offices located in various States.

Key Concepts

Contribution
ESI Corporation
Employment injury
Insured person
Sickness
Standing Committee
Medical Benefit Council
Principal officer
ESI Fund
Benefits
Occupational disease
Funeral expense

Bibliography

Misra, S. N. and Misra, S. K.. *An Introduction to Labour and Industrial Laws*, Allahabad: Central Law Publications; 1995.

Statement of Objects and Reasons, Gazette of India, 1946, Pt. V, pp. 319-357

http://www.esic.nic.in/about_us.php accessed on 11/4/2014.

http://www.esic.nic.in/administration.php accessed on 11/4/2014.

http://www.ilo.org/wcmsp5/groups/public/---dgreports/---dcomm/documents/publication/wcms_067588.pdf accessed on 12/4/2014.

Review Questions

Objective Type Questions

I. State True or False

(i) An individual manager subordinate to an employer is considered to be a managing agent.
(ii) Enhanced sickness benefit is payable for 14 days in case of tubectomy.
(iii) There can be 2 or more Employees' Insurance Courts for the same local area.
(iv) Exemption of any factory from the operation of this Act is granted for a period not exceeding 1 year.
(v) Medical Benefit Council must have 3 members representing the medical profession.

Answers: (i) False, (ii) False, (iii) True, (iv) True, (v) True

I. Fill in the Blanks

(i) The period of limitation for an appeal is _____ days.
(ii) An insured person who takes premature retirement must be insured for not less than ___ years to be eligible to receive medical benefits.
(iii) Claim for payment of funeral expenses must be made within ___ months of the death of the insured person.
(iv) The Act specifies ___ malignant and long-term diseases that need prolonged treatment.
(v) For proceedings before an Employees' Insurance Court to commence, an application must be made within ___ years from the date on which the cause of action arose.

Answers: (i) 60, (ii) 5, (iii) 3, (iv) 34, (v) 3

Discussion Questions

1. Discuss the provisions related to maternity benefit and sickness benefit as given in the Act.
2. Clearly explain the power of the Central Government to make rules under this Act.
3. Discuss the concept of Social Security Officers, their functions and duties.
4. What are the types of disablement discussed in the Act? Discuss the benefits under such types.
5. What are the duties and obligations of an employer as regards contributions payable under this Act?
6. Elaborate on the machinery for the administration of the Employees' State Insurance Act, 1948.
7. What conditions need to be observed by a recipient of sickness or disablement benefit?
8. What are the provisions for punishment in case of:
   (a) Furnishing false statements
   (b) Failure to pay contributions
9. Discuss the constitution of the following:
   (a) Employees' State Insurance Corporation
   (b) Standing Committee
   (c) Medical Benefit Council
10. Explain the following terms in brief:
    (a) Occupational disease
    (b) Principal officers
    (c) Powers of Certifying Officers

CASE STUDY-I

The respondent-company in this case is engaged in milling wheat into wheat products in its flour mill. It had commenced the construction of another building in the compound of the existing factory for the expansion of the factory and it also engaged workmen for such construction on daily wage basis. The appellant-Corporation called upon the respondent-company to make contribution in respect of the workmen employed for the construction work of the factory building as required by the Employees' State Insurance Act, 1948 (or simply 'the Act'). The respondent-company disputed its liability and filed a petition. The Court, allowing the petition, took the view that the persons employed in the construction of a new unit of the factory were not employees within the meaning of the definition of the term 'employee' under the Act.

Incidentally, it is because of this additional building that the existing factory will be expanded and consequently, there will be increase in the production of the factory concerned. So the work of construction of an additional building has a link with the work of the factory. Further, the expression 'work of the factory' should be understood in the sense of any work necessary for the expansion of the factory or establishment for augmenting or increasing the work of that factory or establishment. Such work is incidental or preliminary to or connected with the work of the factory or establishment.

(Adapted from: Regional Director, Employees' State Insurance Corporation, Madras vs. South India Flour Mills (P) Ltd. [(1986) SCR (2) 863]www.indiankanoon.org/doc/1399397/ accessed on 15/4/2014.)

Review Questions

1. Given that the definition of 'employee' under the Act is very wide, what are the various types of employees brought within its purview? Specifically, do construction workers, who are admittedly casual workers, come within the purview of the Act?
2. Which of the sections envisage the case of casual employees?
3. Do you think that the construction of factory buildings for the expansion of the existing factories is incidental or preliminary to or connected with the work of the factory?

CASE STUDY-II

The appellants in this case were appointed as drivers and had put in long service to the satisfaction of the respondent-corporation. Subsequently on their medical examination it was found that they had developed defective eye-sight, i.e., they did not have the required vision for driving buses. The respondent-corporation issued notices to them and after considering their explanation, terminated their services on the ground that they were unfit for driving buses. The appellants filed writ petitions in the High Court challenging their termination order, though the High Court dismissed the writ petitions. Hence these appeals have been made by the workmen-drivers. In a connected appeal, the concerned driver had developed weak eye-sight on account of an accident in the course of his employment. He was given employment as a helper but subsequently his services as a helper were terminated. He filed a writ petition in the High Court challenging his termination, which was dismissed. Hence the appeal was filed by the workmen-driver.

In the appeals it was contended on behalf of the appellants that since the expression "continued ill-health" as used in clause (c) of Section 2(oo) of the Industrial Disputes Act, 1947 does not cover the cases of a loss of limb or an organ or its permanent use and covers cases only of a general physical or mental debility or incapacity to execute the work, their termination not being covered by the said clause amounted to retrenchment which was illegal for non-compliance with Section 25F. The appellants have pleaded that they should have been given alternative jobs irrespective of the fact whether there was an agreement or not between the Corporation and the union to provide alternative jobs to unfit drivers.

There is no dispute that the drivers developed a weak or subnormal eye-sight or lost their required vision on account of their occupation as drivers in the respondent-corporation. Due to the very nature of their job, they are required to strain their eye-sight, which takes its inevitable toil on vision. However, these workmen are and will be able to do any work other than that of a driver with the eye-sight they possess.

(Adapted from: Anand Bihari and Others vs. Rajasthan State Road Transport Corporation [(1991) AIR 100] www.indiankanoon.org/doc/1727786/ accessed on 12/4/2014.)

Review Questions

1. Which sections of the Employees' State Insurance Act, 1948 are relevant in this case?
2. Do you think that the cases of sub-normal eye-sight or loss of the required vision to work as a driver may be considered as an employment injury or as an occupational disease?
3. Can these workmen be said to have suffered either a permanent, total or partial disablement to carry on any job?

SCHEDULE II

[Section 2 (15A) and (15B)]

PART I List of Injuries Deemed to Result in Permanent Total Disablement

S. No.	*Description of injury*	*%age of loss of earning capacity*
1.	Loss of both hands or amputation at higher sites	100
2.	Loss of a hand and a foot	100
3.	Double amputation through leg or thigh, or amputation through leg or thigh on one side and loss of other foot	100
4.	Loss of sight to such an extent as to render the claimant unable to perform any work for which eyesight is essential	100
5.	Very severe facial disfigurement	100
6.	Absolute deafness	100

PART II List of Injuries Deemed to Result in Permanent Partial Disablement

S. No.	*Description of injury*	*%age of loss of earning capacity*
Amputation-Upper limbs (either arm)		
7.	Amputation through shoulder joint	90
8.	Amputation below shoulder with stump less than 20.32 cm from tip of acromion	80
9.	Amputation from 20.32 cm from tip of acromion to less than 11.43 cm below tip of olecranon	70
10.	Loss of a hand or of the thump and four fingers of one hand or amputation from 11.43 cm. below tip of olecranon	60
11.	Loss of thumb	30
12.	Loss of thumb and its metacarpal bone	40
13.	Loss of four fingers of one hand	50
14.	Loss of three fingers of one hand	30
15.	Loss of two fingers of one hand	20
16.	Loss of terminal phalanx of thumb	20
16A.	Guillotine amputation of the tip of the thumb without loss of bone	10

(Contd.)

Amputation-Lower limbs		
17	Amputation of both feet resulting in end-bearing stumps	90
18.	Amputation through both feet proximal to the metatarso-phalangeal joint	80
19.	Loss of all toes of both feet through the metatarso-phalangeal joint	40
20.	Loss of all toes of both feet proximal to the proximal inter phalangeal joint	30
21.	Loss of all toes of both feet distal to the proximal inter phalangeal joint	20
22.	Amputation at hip	90
23.	Amputation below hip with stump not exceeding 12.70 cm. in length measured from tip of great trochanter	80
24.	Amputation below hip with stump exceeding 12.70 cm. in length measured from tip of great trochanter but not beyond middle thigh	70
25.	Amputation below middle thigh to 8.89 cm. below knee	60
26.	Amputation below knee with stump exceeding 8.89 cm. but not exceeding 12.70 cm.	50
27.	Amputation below knee with stump exceeding 12.70 cm.	50
28.	Amputation of one foot resulting in end-bearing	50
29.	Amputation through one foot proximal to the metatarso-phalangeal joint	50
30	Loss of all toes of one foot through metatarso-phalangeal joint	20
Other injuries		
31.	Loss of one eye, without complications, the other being normal	40
32.	Loss of vision of one eye without complications or disfigurement of eye-ball, the other being normal	30
32A.	Partial loss of vision of one eye	10
Loss of	**A- Fingers of right or left hand** **Index finger**	
33	Whole	14
34.	Two phalanges	11
35.	One phalanx	9
36.	Guillotine amputation of tip without loss of bone	5
	Middle finger	
37	Whole	12
38.	Two phalanges	9
39.	One phalanx	7
40.	Guillotine amputation of tip without loss of bone	4

(*Contd.*)

	Ring or little finger	
41.	Whole	7
42.	Two phalanges	6
43.	One phalanx	5
44.	Guillotine amputation of tip without loss of bone	2
	B- Toes of right or left foot **Great toe**	
45.	Through metatarso-phalangeal joint	14
46.	Part, with some loss of bone	3
	Any other toe	
47.	Through metatarso-phalangeal joint	3
48.	Part, with some loss of bone	1
	Two toes of one foot, excluding great toe	
49.	Through metatarso-phalangeal joint	5
50.	Part, with some loss of bone	2
	Three toes of one foot, excluding great toe	
51.	Through metatarso-phalangeal joint	6
52.	Part, with some loss of bone	3
	Four toes of one foot, excluding great toe	
53.	Through metatarso-phalangeal joint	9
54.	Part, with some loss of bone	3

Note: Complete and permanent loss of the use of any limb or member referred to in this Schedule shall be deemed to be the equivalent of the loss of that limb or member.

SCHEDULE III

[Section 52A]

List of Occupational Diseases

Sl. No.	*Occupational disease*	*Employment*
	PART A	
1.	Infectious and parasitic diseases contracted in an occupation where there is a particular risk of contamination	(a) All work involving exposure to health or laboratory work; (b) All work involving exposure to veterinary work; (c) Work relating to handling animals; animal carcasses, part of such. Carcasses, or merchandise which may have been contaminated by animals or animal carcasses; (d) Other work carrying a particular risk of contamination.

(*Contd.*)

2.	Diseases caused by work in compressed air.	All work involving exposure to the risk concerned.
3.	Diseases caused by lead or its toxic compounds.	All work involving exposure to the risk concerned.
4.	Poisoning by nitrous fumes.	All work involving exposure to the risk concerned.
5.	Poisoning by organo phosphorus compounds.	All work involving exposure to the risk concerned.
	PART B	
1.	Diseases caused by phosphorus or its toxic compounds.	All work involving exposure to the risk concerned.
2.	Diseases caused by mercury or its toxic compounds.	All work involving exposure to the risk concerned.
3.	Diseases caused by benzene or its toxic homologues.	All work involving exposure to the risk concerned.
4.	Diseases caused by nitro and amido toxic derivatives of benzene or its homologues.	All work involving exposure to the risk concerned.
5.	Diseases caused by chromium or its toxic compounds.	All work involving exposure to the risk concerned.
6.	Diseases caused by arsenic or its toxic compounds.	All work involving exposure to the risk concerned.
7.	Diseases caused by radioactive substances and ionising radiations.	All work involving exposure to the action of radioactive substances or ionising radiations.
8.	Primary epithelomatous cancer of the skin caused by tar, pitch, bitumen, mineral oil, anthracene, or the compounds, products or residues of these substances.	All work involving exposure to the risk concerned.
9.	Diseases caused by the toxic halogen derivatives of hydrocarbons (of the aliphatic and aromatic series)	All work involving exposure to the risk concerned.
10.	Diseases caused by carbon disulphide.	All work involving exposure to the risk concerned.
11.	Occupational cataract due to infra-red radiations.	All work involving exposure to the risk concerned.
12.	Diseases caused by manganese or its toxic compounds.	All work involving exposure to the risk concerned.
13.	Skin diseases caused by physical, chemical, or biological agents not included in other items.	All work involving exposure to the risk concerned.
14.	Hearing impairment caused by noise.	All work involving exposure to the risk concerned.
15.	Poisoning by dinitrophenol or a homologue or by substituted dinitrophenol or by the salts of such substances.	All work involving exposure to the risk concerned.
16.	Diseases caused by beryllium or its toxic compounds.	All work involving exposure to the risk concerned.
17.	Diseases caused by cadmium or its toxic compounds.	All work involving exposure to the risk concerned.
18.	Occupational asthma caused by recognised sensitising agents inherent to the work process.	All work involving exposure to the risk concerned.
19.	Diseases caused by fluorine or its toxic compound	All work involving exposure to the risk concerned.

(Contd.)

20.	Diseases caused by nitroglycerine or other nitro acid esters.	All work involving exposure to the risk concerned.
21.	Diseases caused by alcohols and ketones.	All work involving exposure to the risk concerned.
22.	Diseases caused by asphyxiants; carbon monoxide and its toxic derivatives, hydrogen sulphide.	All work involving exposure to the risk concerned.
23.	Lung cancer and mesotheliomas caused by asbestos.	All work involving exposure to the risk concerned.
24.	Primary neoplasm of the epithelial lining of the urinary bladder or the kidney or the ureter.	All work involving exposure to the risk concerned.
	PART C	
1.	Pneumoconiosis caused by sclerogenic mineral dust (silicosis, anthracosilicosis asbestosis) and silico- tuberculosis provided that silicosis is an essential factor in causing the resultant incapacity or death..	All work involving exposure to the risk concerned.
2.	Bagassosis	All work involving exposure to the risk concerned.
3.	Bronchopulmonary diseases caused by cotton, flax, hemp and sisal dust (Byssinosis)	All work involving exposure to the risk concerned.
4.	Extrinsic allergic alveolitis caused by the inhalation of organic dusts.	All work involving exposure to the risk concerned.
5.	Bronchopulmonary diseases caused by hard metals.	All work involving exposure to the risk concerned.

25

The Employees' Compensation Act, 1923

An Act to provide for the payment by certain classes of employers to their employees of compensation for injury by accident.

Desired Knowledge Competencies

- To comprehend the notion of compensation paid in case of accident, different types of disablement and the amount of compensation paid under different conditions.
- To discuss the scope and coverage of the Employees' Compensation Act, 1923, and of the various definitions given under the Act.
- To develop clarity on issues like special provisions relat ng to certain categories of employees, penalty and rules related to compensation.

CONCEPT OF COMPENSATION

To compensate is to counterbalance. In general parlance, compensation is the remuneration employees receive in return for their contribution to an organisation. However, in this chapter, by compensation we would be referring to damages paid by an employer to an employee (or his/her heir), who has met with an injury out of an accident at work (or has deceased out of such accident). The scheme of the Employees' Compensation Act, 1923 is not to compensate an employee in lieu of wages. Rather, the guiding principle of this Act is that a worker, who suffers an injury in the course of his/her employment, resulting in any disablement, should be entitled to compensation. Further, in the case of a fatal injury, his/her dependants should be compensated. Let us mention at the outset that the meaning of compensation in the Act is limited to compensation granted under the Act for employment injuries sustained during the course of work. It is also limited specifically to monetary compensation other than salary, travel allowance and any other form of remuneration that could be paid under normal circumstances of employment (*The Workmen's Compensation Act, A Guide for Activists, 2005).*

Many a times a workman may have to face unprecedented events like accidents, leading to disability and even death while on duty. Hence the necessity of social insurance to provide adequate protection to workmen from losses incurred through accidents, etc. The Workmen's Compensation Act, 1923, now termed as Employees' Compensation Act, 1923, is one of the earliest legislations aimed at social security, adopted to benefit workers who would undergo losses out of accidents at work.

Before we move on to the historical backdrop of the Act, let us touch upon the concepts of social security and social insurance, discussed broadly in Chapter 9. Generally speaking, social security refers to action programmes of the government of any nation aimed at providing security and protecting the population from the insecurities of poverty, illness, etc. Social security was established as a basic human right in the Declaration of Philadelphia (1944) of the International Labour Organisation (ILO) and its Income Security Recommendation (1944). Chapters III and IV of the Constitution of India mention the relevance of dignity of human labour and the need for protecting and safeguarding the interest of labour as human beings.

Spotlight

Social security refers to action programmes of a government to prove security and protection to the population from the insecurities of poverty, illness, etc.

Social insurance, on the other hand, is broadly a method of social security in which people receive benefits or securities by financing through the contributions made by employers, workers and other beneficiaries. Such financing may even be supplemented by State grants. It is thus evident that people who are in receipt of such benefits need to participate in insurance programmes which are mostly established compulsorily by law.

BACKDROP OF THE EMPLOYEES' COMPENSATION ACT, 1923

The historical evolution of the Employees' Compensation Act, 1923 can be traced back to the time when Indian industries had already tasted the flavour of industrialisation and mechanisation of production processes. These brought along with an obvious evil, that of accidents, injuries at workplace, and even death. According to Dr. Panandikar, compensation schemes were not unknown in India (Bhattacharya, 1970). "As far back as 1884, workers in Bombay made a demand for compensation in a petition to the Government of India, but nothing came out of it" (Hasan, 1972, p. 65). The issue of payment of compensation to workmen who would meet with fatal accidents was raised when the Factory and Mining Inspectors drew the attention of the government to this serious problem, pointing immediate attention to it. So, long cases of injuries and accidents were to be treated in the same manner as the Common Law in the United Kingdom, which was naturally adopted with the establishment of British rule in India.

Let us briefly talk about the Common Law here. Broadly speaking, the Common Law was a system of law in place in England and its colonies. Under the Common Law, any workman who had suffered an injury at workplace in the course of his employment, or his dependent heir in case of his death due to such accident, had to file a suit in a civil court, claiming damages for the losses incurred. What is worth noting here is that, the court would award damages in favour of the workman or his dependent heirs if the claimant could prove that such accident was due to negligence on the part of the employer. Workers being an illiterate lot could not put up a stiff opposition against the employers. Employers, even though actually negligent, could avail of three Common Law defences, namely assumption of risk, fellow servant rule and contributory negligence (Law Commission of India, 1974).

Specifically the fellow servant rule was based on a fictitious implied term in the contract of service to the effect that the servant had agreed to run the risk naturally incident to his employment, and that one of these risks was that of harm due to the negligence of a fellow-servant (Salmond, 1965 as cited in Law Commission of India, 1974). It is thus obvious that the Common Law was pro-employer and it brought only miseries to the workman. These shortcomings, coupled with the callous attitude of employers towards the increasing number of accidents at workplace, fuelled a movement for reforms in the Common Law. As pointed out by Dr. Panandikar, the Indian worker was always at the mercy of the employer as regards compensation; it was paid only as an act of gesture by the employer, not as a matter of the worker's right (Bhattacharya, 1970). With time, compensation gained significance, and this resulted in agitations; workers went on a number of strikes across the nation.

In June 1922, a committee was constituted consisting of members of the Legislative Assembly, employers, workers or their representatives and medical and insurance experts. After considering the numerous replies and opinions received by the government, the Committee was unanimously in favour of a legislation, and it drew up detailed recommendations regarding the lines which the legislation should follow (Law Commission of India, 1974). The Workmen's Compensation Act was enacted on the basis of the recommendations of this committee (Misra and Misra, 1995).

One serious lacunae of the Common Law was that it was difficult for the workman to prove that the injury inflicted on him was due to the negligence of any one at all, or to understand the root cause behind it. The Workmen's Compensation Act, 1923 reversed the situation in favour of the workman by ensuring payment of compensation more or less automatically. An employer could evade such compensation only if he could prove that the accident was due to the negligence of the workman himself. Let us explain this further here. In case of Common Law, a workman or his heir had to prove the negligence of the employer in order to get compensation. On the contrary, as per the Act, the employer is responsible to pay compensation by default, only if he is unable to prove that the accident was due to the negligence of the workman. We can thus infer that while the Common Law was pro-employer, the Workmen's Compensation Act, 1923 is pro-workmen.

> **Spotlight**
> The Common Law was pro-employer and the Workmen's Compensation Act, 1923 is pro-workmen.

The Workmen's Compensation Bill having been passed by the Legislature received its assent on 5th March 1923. It came into force on 1st July 1924 as The Workmen's Compensation Act, 1923, with a view to provide compensation to workmen who would undergo any injury due to an accident arising out of and in the course of employment. Let us refer to the "Statement of Objects and Reasons" published with the Act in 1923, for better understanding of the Act.

"...the growing complexity of industry in this country with the increasing use of the machinery and consequent danger to workmen, along with the comparative poverty to workmen themselves renders it advisable that they should be protected, as far as possible from hardship arising out of accidents. An additional advantage of a legislation of this type is that by increasing the importance for employers of adequate safety devises, it reduces the number of accidents to workmen in a manner that cannot be achieved by official inspection. Further, the encouragement given to employers to provide adequate medical treatment for their workmen should mitigate the effects of such accidents as does occur. The benefits so conferred added to the increased sense of security, which he will enjoy, should render industrial life more attractive and thus increase the available supply of labour. At the same time a corresponding increase in the efficiency of the average workmen may be expected."

Ever since its enactment, the Act has undergone several amendments mainly in response to changes in work complexities and living standards. Efforts have always been made to bring more and more categories of workmen under the ambit of the Act, and to ensure enhanced amount of compensation, commensurate with the changing times. The latest of the amending acts is the Workmen's Compensation (Amendment) Act, 2009, whereby for the words "workman" and "workmen", wherever they occur, the words "employee" and "employees" have respectively been substituted, along with other consequential amendments as per rules of grammar. Following is the list of amending acts and adaptation orders:

1. The Repealing and Amending Act, 1924
2. The Repealing and Amending Act, 1925
3. The Workmen's Compensation (Amendment) Act, 1926
4. The Workmen's Compensation (Amendment) Act, 1929
5. The Workmen's Compensation (Amendment) Act, 1933
6. The Government of India (Adaptation of Indian Laws) Order, 1937
7. The Workmen's Compensation (Amendment) Act, 1937
8. The Workmen's Compensation (Amendment) Act, 1938
9. The Workmen's Compensation (Amendment) Act, 1939
10. The Workmen's Compensation (Second Amendment) Act, 1939
11. The Workmen's Compensation (Amendment) Act, 1942
12. The Workmen's Compensation (Amendment) Act, 1946
13. The Indian Independence (Adaptation of Central Acts and Ordinances) Order, 1948
14. The Adaptation of Laws Order, 1950
15. The Part B States (Laws) Act, 1951
16. The Adaptation of Laws (No. 3) Order, 1956
17. The Repealing and Amending Act, 1957
18. The Workmen's Compensation (Amendment) Act, 1959
19. The Repealing and Amending Act, 1960
20. The Workmen's Compensation (Amendment) Act, 1962
21. The Central Labour Laws (Extension to Jammu and Kashmir) Act, 1970
22. The Workmen's Compensation (Amendment) Act, 1976
23. The Workmen's Compensation (Amendment) Act, 1984
24. The Delegated Legislation Provisions (Amendment) Act, 1985
25. The Workmen's Compensation (Amendment) Act, 1995
26. The Workmen's Compensation (Amendment) Act, 2000
27. The Workmen's Compensation (Amendment) Act, 2009

ABOUT THE ACT
CHAPTER I: PRELIMINARY

Short Title, Extent and Commencement (Section 1)

1. This Act may be called the Employees' Compensation Act, 1923.
2. It extends to the whole of India.
3. It shall come into force on the first day of July 1924.

DEFINITIONS (Section 2)

1. In this Act, unless there is anything repugnant in the subject or context:—

Commissioner [Section 2(1)(b)] Commissioner means a Commissioner for Employees' Compensation appointed under Section 20;

Compensation [Section 2(1)(c)] Compensation means compensation as provided for by this Act;

Dependant [Section 2(1)(d)] Dependant means any of the following relatives of a deceased employee, namely:

(i) a widow, a minor legitimate or adopted son, and unmarried legitimate or adopted daughter, or a widowed mother; and

(ii) if wholly dependent on the earnings of the employee at the time of his death, a son or a daughter who has attained the age of 18 years and who is infirm;

(iii) if wholly or in part dependent on the earnings of the employee at the time of his death,

- (a) a widower,
- (b) a parent other than a widowed mother,
- (c) a minor illegitimate son, an unmarried illegitimate daughter or a daughter legitimate or illegitimate or adopted if married and a minor or if widowed and a minor,
- (d) a minor brother or an unmarried sister or a widowed sister if a minor,
- (e) a widowed daughter-in-law,
- (f) a minor child of a pre-deceased son,
- (g) a minor child of a pre-deceased daughter where no parent of the child is alive, or
- (h) a paternal grandparent if no parent of the employee is alive.

Explanation For the purposes of sub-clause (ii) and items (f) and (g) of sub-clause (iii), references to a son, daughter or child include an adopted son, daughter or child respectively.

Employee [Section 2(1)(dd)] Employee means a person, who is:

(i) a railway servant as defined in clause (34) of Section 2 of the Railways Act, 1989, not permanently employed in any administrative district or sub-divisional office of a railway and not employed in any such capacity as is specified in Schedule II; or

(ii) (a) a master, seaman or other members of the crew of a ship,

- (b) a captain or other member of the crew of an aircraft,
- (c) a person recruited as driver, helper, mechanic, cleaner or in any other capacity in connection with a motor vehicle,
- (d) a person recruited for work abroad by a company,

and who is employed outside India in any such capacity as is specified in Schedule II and the ship, aircraft or motor vehicle, or company, as the case may be, is registered in India; or

(iii) employed in any such capacity as is specified in Schedule II, whether the contract of employment was made before or after the passing of this Act and whether such contract is expressed or implied, oral or in writing; but does not include any person working in the capacity of a member of the Armed Forces of the Union; and

> **Spotlight**
> The definition of employee excludes any member of the Armed Forces of the Union.

any reference to any employee who has been injured shall, where the employee is dead, include a reference to his dependants or any of them.

Employer [Section 2(1)(e)] Employer includes any body of persons whether incorporated or not and any managing agent of an employer and the legal representative of a deceased employer, and, when the services of an employee are temporarily lent or let on hire to another person by the person with whom the employee has entered into a contract of service or apprenticeship, means such other person while the employee is working for him;

Managing agent [Section 2(1)(f)] Managing agent means any person appointed or acting as the representative of another person for the purpose of carrying on such other person's trade or business, but does not include an individual manager subordinate to an employer;

Minor [Section 2(1)(ff)] Minor means a person who has not attained the age of 18 years.

Partial disablement [Section 2(1)(g)] Partial disablement means, where the disablement is of a temporary nature, such disablement as reduces the earning capacity of an employee in any employment in which he was engaged at the time of the accident resulting in the disablement, and, where the disablement is of a permanent nature, such disablement as reduces his earning capacity in every employment which he was capable of undertaking at that time:

Provided that every injury specified in Part II of Schedule I shall be deemed to result in permanent partial disablement;

Spotlight

As per Section 2(1)(g), partial temporary disablement reduces the earning capacity of an employee in any employment in which he was engaged at the time of the accident resulting in the disablement.

Prescribed [Section 2(1)(h)] Prescribed means prescribed by rules made under this Act;

Qualified medical practitioner [Section 2(1)(i)] Qualified medical practitioner means any person registered under any Central Act, Provincial Act, or an Act of the Legislature of a State providing for the maintenance of a register of medical practitioners, or, in any area where no such last-mentioned Act is in force, any person declared by the State Government, by notification in the Official Gazette, to be a qualified medical practitioner for the purposes of this Act;

Seaman [Section 2(1)(k)] Seaman means any person forming part of the crew of any ship, but does not include the master of the ship;

Total disablement [Section 2(1)(l)] Total disablement means such disablement, whether of a temporary or permanent nature, as incapacitates an employee for all work which he was capable of performing at the time of the accident resulting in such disablement:

Provided that permanent total disablement shall be deemed to result from every injury specified in Part I of Schedule I or from any combination of injuries specified in Part II thereof where the aggregate percentage of the loss of earning capacity, as specified in the said Part II against those injuries, amounts to 100 per cent or more.

Spotlight

As per Section 2(1)(l), total disablement, whether temporary or permanent, incapacitates an employee for all work which he was capable of performing at the time of the accident resulting in such disablement.

In *Pratap Narain Singh Deo vs. Srinivas Sabata and Another* (1976 AIR 222), there was personal injury to a carpenter in the course of employment, leading to amputation of his left hand above elbow. Since a carpenter cannot work with 1 hand, it was held that this disablement is total and not partial. According to the Apex Court, it has been argued that the injury did not result in permanent total disablement of the respondent. Further, the Commissioner committed a gross error of law in taking that view as there was only partial disablement within the meaning of Section 2(1)(g) of the Act, which should have been deemed to have resulted in permanent partial disablement of the nature referred to in Item 3 of Part II of Schedule I of the Act. This argument has been advanced on the ground that the amputation was from 8 inches from tip of acromion and less than 4½ inches below tip of olecranon.

(Adapted from: www.indiankanoon.org/doc/1640530/ accessed on 24/7/2014.)

Wages [Section 2(1)(m)] Wages includes any privilege or benefit which is capable of being estimated in money, other than a travelling allowance or the value of any travelling concession or a contribution paid by the employer of an employee towards any pension or provident fund or a sum paid to an employee to cover any special expenses entailed on him by the nature of his employment;

CHAPTER II: EMPLOYEES' COMPENSATION

Employer's Liability for Compensation (Section 3)

Spotlight
If personal injury is caused to an employee by any accident arising out of and in the course of his employment, his employer shall be liable to pay compensation.

1. If personal injury is caused to an employee by accident arising out of and in the course of his employment, his employer shall be liable to pay compensation in accordance with the provisions of this chapter:

   Provided that the employer shall not be so liable:

   (a) in respect of any injury which does not result in the total or partial disablement of the employee for a period exceeding 3 days;

   (b) in respect of any injury, not resulting in death or permanent total disablement caused by an accident which is directly attributable to:

   (i) the employee having been at the time thereof under the influence of drink or drugs, or

   (ii) the wilful disobedience of the employee to an order expressly given, or to a rule expressly framed, for the purpose of securing the safety of employees, or

   (iii) the wilful removal or disregard by the employee of any safety guard or other device which he knew to have been provided for the purpose of securing the safety of employees.

In *P. Kalyani vs. The Divisional Manager, Southern Railway (Personal Branch), Divisional Office, Madras* (*II* (2004) ACC 388), it was stated that in order to attract the provision in sub-section (1) of Section 3, three conditions mentioned therein are to be fulfilled, i.e., (i) personal injury; (ii) accident; and (iii) arising out of and in the course of employment. Let us take up each of these points with relevant examples.

First let us explain the concept of "accident". In *Shakuntala Chandrakant Shreshti vs. Prabhakar Maruti Carvali and another* [2007 LLR 185 (SC)], the Apex Court had held that: "Accident, ordinarily, would have to be understood as unforeseen or uncomprehended or as that which could not be foreseen or comprehended. A finding of fact, thus, has to be arrived at, *inter alia*, having regard to the nature of work and the situation in which the deceased was placed. An accident may lead to death but that an accident had taken place must be proved. Only because a death has taken place in course of employment will not amount to accident. Death must arise out of accident. There is no presumption that an accident had occurred."

(Adapted from: Labour Law Reporter, October 2012, p. 1063.)

Next in turn is the concept of "personal injury". In *Leela Devi vs. Ramlal Rahu* [1990 LLR 213 (HP)], it was held that injury sustained by a workman must be a physical injury on account of an accident. Further, in *Jyothi Ademma vs. Plant Engineer, Nellore and Another* (2006 LLR 890 SC), the Apex Court held that the expression "accident" means an untoward mishap, which is not expected or designed, while "injury" means physiological injury. The causal connection between the death of the workman and the nature of his employment has to be established.

(Adapted from: Labour Law Reporter, October 2012, p. 1065.)

Let us now look at the terms: "arising out of employment" and "in the course of employment". The expression "arising out of employment" applies as such to employment, its nature, its conditions, its obligations and its incidents, and the words "in the course of employment" mean in the course of work which the workman is employed to do and which is incidental to it. An accident is said to have arisen out of employment if it has occurred by reason of the nature of employment, or by reason of anything incidental to the employment; however, it is not confined to the mere nature of the employment. If by reason of any of the factors stated above, any workman is brought within the ambit of special danger, the injury would be one which arises "out of employment". In other words, if the accident had occurred on account of a risk which is an incident of the employment, the claim for compensation must succeed, unless of course the workman has exposed himself to an added peril by his own imprudent act *[Executive Engineer 19th Div. R.C.P., Bikaner vs. Heeraram (*1982 (44) FLR 179 Raj)]. Further, there must be causal relationship between the accident and employment. As stated in *Oriental Insurance Co. Ltd. vs. Nanguli Singh* [1995 LLJ HC ORS (298)], if the accident has occurred on account of the risk which is an incident to employment, it has to be held that the same has arisen "out of employment".

In *Nisbet vs. Rayne and Burn* [(1910) 2 KB 689 C], Nisbet was a cashier employed by the appellants and in the course of his duty he was carrying a large sum of money to pay the wages of colliers. While travelling in train in the discharge of his duty, the bag of money was stolen and he was killed. Though it was a criminal act, the claim for compensation claimed by the widow of Nisbet was allowed considering that it was an accident arising out of and in the course of employment.

(Adapted from: Labour Law Reporter, October 2012, p. 1065.)

In the same lines, as held in *TNCS Corporation Ltd. vs. S. Poomalai* [1995 LLR 63 (Mad)], if the deceased employee met with death while travelling to his place of work, and the death has arisen during the course of employment, then the employer is liable for compensation. Let us give an interesting contrast to this judgement. In *State Bank vs. Vijay Laxmi* (1998 LLR 319), the deceased employee had met with a fatal accident while travelling by public transport to his place of work. However, since neither there was anything brought on record that the deceased was obliged to travel in any particular manner under the terms of employment, nor was her travelling by official transport, the claimant was held not to be entitled to any compensation.

CASE CORNER

In *National Insurance Co. Ltd. vs. Padmavathy* [(2012) LLR 815 Kerala HC], the driver who took the vehicle for cleaning to the riverside drowned in the river while taking a dip after cleaning the vehicle. The insurer's plea was that the death of the victim was not on account of any activity that arose in the course of employment. However, the Commissioner held that cleaning and maintaining the vehicle is very much a part of the course of the duties of the driver. As such, taking a dip was considered to have reasonable nexus to the continuity of the duties of the deceased driver. The appeal was hence dismissed with costs.

(Adapted from: Labour Law Reporter, August 2012, pp. 815-817.)

2. If an employee employed in any employment specified in Part A of Schedule III contracts any disease specified therein as an occupational disease peculiar to that employment, or if an employee whilst in the service of an employer in whose service he has been employed for a continuous period of not less than 6 months (which period shall not include a period of service under any other employer in the same kind of employment) in any employment specified in Part B of Schedule III, contracts any disease specified therein as an occupational disease peculiar to that employment, or if an employee whilst in the service of one or more employers in any employment specified in Part C of Schedule III for such continuous period as the Central Government may specify in respect of each such employment, contracts any disease specified therein as an occupational disease peculiar to that employment, the contracting of the disease shall be deemed to be an injury by accident within the meaning of this section and, unless the contrary is proved, the accident shall be deemed to have arisen out of, and in the course of, the employment:

   Provided that if it is proved:

   (a) that an employee whilst in the service of 1 or more employers in any employment specified in Part C of Schedule III has contracted a disease specified therein as an occupational disease peculiar to that employment during a continuous period which is less than the period specified under this sub-section for that employment; and
   (b) that the disease has arisen out of and in the course of the employment, the contracting of such disease shall be deemed to be an injury by accident within the meaning of this Section:

   Provided further that if it is proved that an employee who having served under any employer in any employment specified in Part B of Schedule III or who having served under one or more employers in any employment specified in Part C of that Schedule, for a continuous period specified under this sub-section for that employment and he has after the cessation of such service contracted any disease specified in the said Part B or the said Part C, as the case may be, as an occupational disease peculiar to the employment and that such disease arose out of the employment, the contracting of the disease shall be deemed to be an injury by accident within the meaning of this section.

2A. If an employee employed in any employment specified in Part C of Schedule III contracts any occupational disease peculiar to that employment, the contracting whereof is deemed to be an injury by accident within the meaning of this section, and such employment was under more than 1 employer, all such employers shall be liable for the payment of the compensation in such proportion as the Commissioner may, in the circumstances, deem just.

3. The Central Government or the State Government, after giving, by notification in the Official Gazette, not less than 3 months' notice of its intention so to do, may, by a like notification, add any description of employment to the employments specified in Schedule III, and shall specify in the case of employments so added the diseases which shall be deemed for the purposes of this section to be occupational diseases peculiar to those employments respectively, and thereupon the provisions of sub-section (2) shall apply, in the case of a notification by the Central Government, within the territories to which this Act extends or, in case of a notification by the State Government, within the State as if such diseases had been declared by this Act to be occupational diseases peculiar to those employments.
4. Save as provided by sub-sections (2), (2A) and (3), no compensation shall be payable to an employee in respect of any disease unless the disease is directly attributable to a specific injury by accident arising out of and in the course of his employment.
5. Nothing herein contained shall be deemed to confer any right to compensation on an employee in respect of any injury if he has instituted in a Civil Court a suit for damages in respect of the injury against the employer or any other person; and no suit for damages shall be maintainable by an employee in any Court of law in respect of any injury:
   (a) if he has instituted a claim to compensation in respect of the injury before a Commissioner; or
   (b) if an agreement has been come to between the employee and his employer providing for the payment of compensation in respect of the injury in accordance with the provisions of this Act.

In *Jyothi Ademma vs. Plant Engineer, Nellore and Another* [2006 LLR 890 (SC)], the Apex Court held that if a workman dies as a natural result of any disease he was suffering from, or while suffering from a disease he dies of that disease out of wear and tear of the employment, no liability will be fixed upon the employer. But if the employment is a contributory cause, or has accelerated the death of the employee, or if the death was due not only to the disease, but also the disease coupled with the employment, then it can be said that the death arose out of the employment and the employer would be liable.

(Adapted from: Labour Law Reporter, October 2012, p. 1065)

CASE CORNER

In *Divisional Manager, National Insurance Co. Ltd. vs. P. Krishna Reddy Bin Channa Reddy and another* [(2012) LLR 1054 Karnataka HC], the claimant, working as a conductor in a bus, sustained injuries when the bus met with an accident on 19th November 2003. The Commissioner held that the claimant as conductor fell within the definition of "workman" and the policy of insurance being valid on the date of accident, the appellant is liable to pay compensation to the injured, who had suffered permanent disability. However, the conductor's license of the injured was not renewed subsequent to 4th March 2003, which implies that it had expired about 8 months prior to the accident. It was hence held that the insurance company cannot be fastened with the liability to pay compensation to such a person.

(Adapted from: Labour Law Reporter, October 2012, pp. 1054-1059.)

Amount of Compensation (Section 4)

1. Subject to the provisions of this Act, the amount of compensation shall be as follows, namely:

(a) where death results from the injury: an amount equal to 50 per cent of the monthly wages of the deceased employee multiplied by the relevant factor; or an amount of ₹1,20,000, whichever is more;

(b) where permanent total disablement results from the injury: an amount equal to 60 per cent of the monthly wages of the injured employee multiplied by the relevant factor; or an amount of ₹1,40,000, whichever is more.

Provided that the Central Government may, by notification in the Official Gazette, from time to time, enhance the amount of compensation mentioned in clauses (a) and (b);

Explanation I For the purposes of clause (a) and clause (b), "relevant factor", in relation to an employee means the factor specified in the second column of Schedule IV against the entry in the first column of that Schedule specifying the number of years which are the same as the completed years of the age of the employee on his last birthday immediately preceding the date on which the compensation fell due.

Spotlight

Relevant factor for an employee is the factor specified in the 2nd column of Schedule IV against the entry in the 1st column of that Schedule specifying the number of years which are the same as the completed years of the age of the employee on his last birthday immediately preceding the date on which the compensation fell due.

(c) where permanent partial disablement results from the injury:

(i) in the case of an injury specified in Part II of Schedule I, such percentage of the compensation which would have been payable in the case of permanent total disablement as is specified therein as being the percentage of the loss of earning capacity caused by that injury; and

(ii) in the case of an injury not specified in Schedule I, such percentage of the compensation payable in the case of permanent total disablement as is proportionate to the loss of earning capacity (as assessed by the qualified medical practitioner) permanently caused by the injury;

Explanation I Where more injuries than 1 are caused by the same accident, the amount of compensation payable under this head shall be aggregated but not so in any case as to exceed the amount which would have been payable if permanent total disablement had resulted from the injuries.

Explanation II In assessing the loss of earning capacity for the purposes of sub-clause (ii), the qualified medical practitioner shall have due regard to the percentages of loss of earning capacity in relation to different injuries specified in Schedule I;

(d) where temporary disablement, whether total or partial, results from the injury: a half-monthly payment of the sum equivalent to 25 per cent of monthly wages of the employee to be paid in accordance with the provisions of sub-section (2).

1A. Notwithstanding anything contained in sub-section (1), while fixing the amount of compensation payable to an employee in respect of an accident occurred outside India, the Commissioner shall take into account the amount of compensation, if any, awarded to such employee in accordance with the law of the country in which the accident occurred and shall reduce the amount fixed by him by the amount of compensation awarded to the employee in accordance with the law of that country.

1B. The Central Government may, by notification in the Official Gazette, specify, for the purposes of sub-section (1), such monthly wages in relation to an employee as it may consider necessary.

2. The half-monthly payment referred to in clause (d) of sub-section (1) shall be payable on the sixteenth day:
   (i) from the date of disablement where such disablement lasts for a period of 28 days or more, or
   (ii) after the expiry of a waiting period of 3 days from the date of disablement where such disablement lasts for a period of less than 28 days; and thereafter half-monthly during the disablement or during a period of 5 years, whichever period is shorter:

   Provided that:
   (a) there shall be deducted from any lump sum or half-monthly payments to which the employee is entitled the amount of any payment or allowance which the employee has received from the employer by way of compensation during the period of disablement prior to the receipt of such lump sum or of the first half-monthly payment, as the case may be; and
   (b) no half-monthly payment shall in any case exceed the amount, if any, by which half the amount of the monthly wages of the employee before the accident exceeds half the amount of such wages which he is earning after the accident.

Explanation Any payment or allowance which the employee has received from the employer towards his medical treatment shall not be deemed to be a payment or allowance received by him by way of compensation within the meaning of clause (a) of the proviso.

2A. The employee shall be reimbursed the actual medical expenditure incurred by him for treatment of injuries caused during the course of employment.

3. On the ceasing of the disablement before the date on which any half-monthly payment falls due, there shall be payable in respect of that half-month a sum proportionate to the duration of the disablement in that half-month.

4. If the injury of the employee results in his death, the employer shall, in addition to the compensation under sub-section (1), deposit with the Commissioner a sum of not less than ₹5,000 for payment of the same to the eldest surviving dependant of the employee towards the expenditure of the funeral of such employee or where the employee did not have a dependant or was not living with his dependant at the time of his death to the person who actually incurred such expenditure.

   Provided that the Central Government may, by notification in the Official Gazette, from time to time, enhance the amount specified in this sub-section.

Compensation to be Paid when Due and Penalty for Default (Section 4A)

1. Compensation under Section 4 shall be paid as soon as it falls due.
2. In cases where the employer does not accept the liability for compensation to the extent claimed, he shall be bound to make provisional payment based on the extent of liability which he accepts, and, such payment shall be deposited with the Commissioner or made to the employee as the case may be, without prejudice to the right of the employee to make any further claim.

3. Where any employer is in default in paying the compensation due under this Act within 1 month from the date it fell due, the Commissioner shall:
   (a) direct that the employer shall, in addition to the amount of the arrears, pay simple interest thereon at the rate of 12 per cent per annum or at such higher rate not exceeding the maximum of the lending rates of any scheduled bank as may be specified by the Central Government, by notification in the Official Gazette, on the amount due; and
   (b) if, in his opinion, there is no justification for the delay, direct that the employer shall, in addition to the amount of the arrears and interest thereon, pay a further sum not exceeding 50 per cent of such amount by way of penalty:

   Provided that an order for the payment of penalty shall not be passed under clause (b) without giving a reasonable opportunity to the employer to show cause why it should not be passed.

Spotlight

In case of default in paying compensation within 1 month from the due date, the Commissioner shall direct that the employer shall, in addition to the amount of the arrears, pay simple interest at the rate of 12 per cent per annum, as given in Section 4A(3)(a).

Explanation For the purposes of this sub-section, "scheduled bank" means a bank for the time being included in the Second Schedule to the Reserve Bank of India Act, 1934.

3A. The interest and the penalty payable under sub-section (3) shall be paid to the employee or his dependant, as the case may be.

CASE CORNER

In *Pratap Narain Singh Deo vs. Srinivas Sabata and Another* [(1976) AIR 222], the respondent, a carpenter by profession, had suffered an injury by an accident arising out of and in the course of his employment with the appellant. This resulted in the amputation of his left arm from above the elbow. It was held that in consequence he had become unfit for the work of carpenter, as carpentry cannot be carried on with one hand only, and that, he had lost 100 per cent of his earning capacity and suffered total disablement. Hence the Commissioner awarded compensation and also ordered the payment of penalty under Section 4A(3) of the Employees' Compensation Act, 1923, together with interest at 6 per cent per annum.

As per Section 4A(1), it was the duty of the appellant to pay the compensation at the rate provided in Section 4, as soon as the personal injury was caused to the respondent. Not only did the appellant not do so or even make a provisional payment under Section 4A(2), but also he took the false pleas that the respondent was a casual contractor and that the accident was caused solely by the respondent's own negligence. Further, the appellant raised frivolous objections before the Commissioner that he had no jurisdiction and even prevailed on the respondent to file a memorandum of agreement settling the claim at a grossly inadequate sum. He was therefore liable to pay the penalty and the interest.

(Adapted from: www.indiankanoon.org/doc/1640530/ accessed on 24/7/2014.)

Method of Calculating Wages (Section 5)

In this Act and for the purposes thereof the expression "monthly wages" means the amount of wages deemed to be payable for a month's service (whether the wages are payable by the month or by whatever other period or at piece rates), and calculated as follows, namely:

(a) where the employee has, during a continuous period of not less than 12 months immediately preceding the accident, been in the service of the employer who is liable to pay compensation, the monthly wages of the employee hall be one-twelfth of the total wages which have fallen due for payment to him by the employer in the last 12 months of that period;

(b) where the whole of the continuous period of service immediately preceding the accident during which the employee was in the service of the employer who is liable to pay the compensation was less than 1 month, the monthly wages of the employee shall be the average monthly amount which, during the 12 months immediately preceding the accident, was being earned by an employee employed on the same work by the same employer, or, if there was no employee so employed, by an employee employed on similar work in the same locality;

(c) in other cases including cases in which it is not possible for want of necessary information to calculate the monthly wages under clause (b), the monthly wages shall be 30 times the total wages earned in respect of the last continuous period of service immediately preceding the accident from the employer who is liable to pay compensation, divided by the number of days comprising such period.

Explanation A period of service shall, for the purposes of this section be deemed to be continuous which has not been interrupted by a period of absence from work exceeding 14 days.

Review (Section 6)

1. Any half-monthly payment payable under this Act, either under an agreement between the parties or under the order of a Commissioner, may be reviewed by the Commissioner, on the application either of the employer or of the employee accompanied by the certificate of a qualified medical practitioner that there has been a change in the condition of the employee or, subject to rules made under this Act, on application made without such certificate.
2. Any half-monthly payment may, on review under this section, subject to the provisions of this Act, be continued, increased, decreased or ended, or if the accident is found to have resulted in permanent disablement, be converted to the lump sum to which the employee is entitled less any amount which he has already received by way of half-monthly payments.

Commutation of Half-monthly Payments (Section 7)

Any right to receive half-monthly payments may, by agreement between the parties or, if the parties cannot agree and the payments have been continued for not less than 6 months, on the application of either party to the Commissioner, be redeemed by the payment of a lump sum of such amount as may be agreed to by the parties or determined by the Commissioner, as the case may be.

Distribution of Compensation (Section 8)

1. No payment of compensation in respect of an employee whose injury has resulted in death, and no payment of a lump sum as compensation to an employee or a person under a legal disability, shall be made otherwise than by deposit with the Commissioner, and no such payment made directly by an employer shall be deemed to be a payment of compensation:

   Provided that, in the case of a deceased employee an employer may make to any dependant advances on account of compensation of an amount equal to 3 months' wages of such employee and so much of such amount as does not exceed the compensation payable to that dependant shall be deducted by the Commissioner from such compensation and repaid to the employer.
2. Any other sum amounting to not less than ₹10 which is payable as compensation may be deposited with the Commissioner on behalf of the person entitled thereto.

3. The receipt of the Commissioner shall be a sufficient discharge in respect of any compensation deposited with him.
4. On the deposit of any money under sub-section (1), as compensation in respect of a deceased employee the Commissioner shall, if he thinks necessary, cause notice to be published or to be served on each dependant in such manner as he thinks fit, calling upon the dependants to appear before him on such date as he may fix for determining the distribution of the compensation. If the Commissioner is satisfied after any inquiry which he may deem necessary, that no dependant exists, he shall repay the balance of the money to the employer by whom it was paid. The Commissioner shall, on application by the employer, furnish a statement showing in detail all disbursements made.

Spotlight

As per section 8(4), the Commissioner shall repay the balance to the employer in case the deceased employee is found to have no dependant.

5. Compensation deposited in respect of a deceased employee shall, subject to any deduction made under sub-section (4), be apportioned among the dependants of the deceased employee or any of them in such proportion as the Commissioner thinks fit, or may, in the discretion of the Commissioner, be allotted to any 1 dependant.
6. Where any compensation deposited with the Commissioner is payable to any person, the Commissioner shall, if the person to whom the compensation is payable is not a woman or a person under a legal disability, and may, in other cases, pay the money to the person entitled thereto.
7. Where any lump sum deposited with the Commissioner is payable to a woman or a person under a legal disability, such sum may be invested, applied or otherwise dealt with for the benefit of the woman, or of such person during his disability, in such manner as the Commissioner may direct; and where a half-monthly payment is payable to any person under a legal disability, the Commissioner may, of his own motion or on an application made to him in this behalf, order that the payment be made during the disability to any dependant of the employee or to any other person, whom the Commissioner thinks best fitted to provide for the welfare of the employee.
8. Where, on application made to him in this behalf or otherwise, the Commissioner is satisfied that, on account of neglect of children on the part of a parent or on account of the variation of the circumstances of any dependant or for any other sufficient cause, an order of the Commissioner as to the distribution of any sum paid as compensation or as to the manner in which any sum payable to any such dependant is to be invested, applied or otherwise dealt with, ought to be varied, the Commissioner may make such orders for the variation of the former order as he thinks just in the circumstances of the case:

   Provided that no such order prejudicial to any person shall be made unless such person has been given an opportunity of showing cause why the order should not be made, or shall be made in any case in which it would involve the repayment by a dependant of any sum already paid to him.
9. Where the Commissioner varies any order under sub-section (8) by reason of the fact that payment of compensation to any person has been obtained by fraud, impersonation or other improper means, any amount so paid to or on behalf of such person may be recovered in the manner hereinafter provided in Section 31.

Compensation not to be Assigned, Attached or Charged (Section 9)

Save as provided by this Act, no lump sum or half-monthly payment payable under this Act shall in any way be capable of being assigned or charged or be liable to attachment or pass to any person other than the employee by operation of law, nor shall any claim be set off against the same.

Notice and Claim (Section 10)

Spotlight

As per Section 10(1), no claim for compensation shall be entertained by a Commissioner unless preferred before him within 2 years of the occurrence of the accident or from the date of death.

1. No claim for compensation shall be entertained by a Commissioner unless notice of the accident has been given in the manner hereinafter provided as soon as practicable after the happening thereof and unless the claim is preferred before him within 2 years of the occurrence of the accident or, in case of death, within 2 years from the date of death:

   Provided that, where the accident is the contracting of a disease in respect of which the provisions of sub-section (2) of Section 3 are applicable, the accident shall be deemed to have occurred on the first of the days during which the employee was continuously absent from work in consequence of the disablement caused by the disease:

   Provided further that in case of partial disablement due to the contracting of any such disease and which does not force the employee to absent himself from work, the period of 2 years shall be counted from the day the employee gives notice of the disablement to his employer:

   Provided further that if an employee who, having been employed in an employment for a continuous period, specified under sub-section (2) of Section 3 in respect of that employment, ceases to be so employed and develops symptoms of an occupational disease peculiar to that employment within 2 years of the cessation of employment, the accident shall be deemed to have occurred on the day on which the symptoms were first detected.

   Provided further that the want of or any defect or irregularity in a notice shall not be a bar to the entertainment of a claim:

   (a) if the claim is preferred in respect of the death of an employee resulting from an accident which occurred on the premises of the employer, or at any place where the employee at the time of the accident was working under the control of the employer or of any person employed by him, and the employee died on such premises or at such place, or on any premises belonging to the employer, or died without having left the vicinity of the premises or place where the accident occurred, or

   (b) if the employer or any one of several employers or any person responsible to the employer for the management of any branch of the trade or business in which the injured employee was employed had knowledge of the accident from any other source at or about the time when it occurred:

   Provided further that the Commissioner may entertain and decide any claim to compensation in any case notwithstanding that the notice has not been given, or the claim has not been preferred in due time as provided in this sub-section, if he is satisfied that the failure so to give the notice or prefer the claim, as the case may be, was due to sufficient cause.

2. Every such notice shall give the name and address of the person injured and shall state in ordinary language the cause of the injury and the date on which the accident happened, and shall be served on the employer or upon any one of several employers, or upon any person responsible to the employer for the management of any branch of the trade or business in which the injured employee was employed.

3. The State Government may require that any prescribed class of employers shall maintain at their premises at which employees are employed a notice-book, in the prescribed form, which shall be readily accessible at all reasonable times to any injured employee employed on the premises and to any person acting *bona fide* on his behalf.

4. A notice under this section may be served by delivering it at, or sending it by registered post addressed to, the residence or any office or place of business of the person on whom it is to be served, or, where a notice-book is maintained, by entry in the notice-book.

Power to Require from Employers Statements Regarding Fatal Accidents (Section 10A)

1. Where a Commissioner receives information from any source that an employee has died as a result of an accident arising out of and in the course of his employment, he may send by registered post a notice to the employee's employer requiring him to submit, within 30 days of the service of the notice, a statement, in the prescribed form, giving the circumstances attending the death of the employee and indicating whether, in the opinion of the employer, he is or is not liable to deposit compensation on account of the death.
2. If the employer is of opinion that he is liable to deposit compensation, he shall make the deposit within 30 days of the service of the notice.
3. If the employer is of opinion that he is not liable to deposit compensation, he shall in his statement indicate the grounds on which he disclaims liability.
4. Where the employer has so disclaimed liability, the Commissioner, after such inquiry as he may think fit, may inform any of the dependants of the deceased employee that it is open to the dependants to prefer a claim for compensation, and may give them such other further information as he may think fit.

Spotlight

If the employer is of the opinion that he is liable to deposit compensation, then as per Section 10A(2), he shall deposit the same within 30 days of service of notice.

Reports of Fatal Accidents and Serious Bodily Injuries (Section 10B)

1. Where, by any law for the time being in force, notice is required to be given to any authority, by or on behalf of an employer, of any accident occurring on his premises which results in death or serious bodily injury, the person required to give the notice shall, within 7 days of the death or serious bodily injury, send a report to the Commissioner giving the circumstances attending the death or serious bodily injury:

   Provided that where the State Government has so prescribed the person required to give the notice may instead of sending such report to the Commissioner send it to the authority to whom he is required to give the notice.

Explanation "Serious bodily injury" means an injury which involves, or in all probability will involve the permanent loss of the use of, or permanent injury to, any limb, or the permanent loss of or injury to the sight or hearing, or the fracture of any limb, or the enforced absence of the injured person from work for a period exceeding 20 days.

2. The State Government may, by notification in the Official Gazette, extend the provisions of sub-section (1) to any class of premises other than those coming within the scope of that sub-section, and may, by such notification, specify the persons who shall send the report to the Commissioner.
3. Nothing in this section shall apply to factories to which the Employees' State Insurance Act, 1948 applies.

Spotlight

Serious bodily injury means an injury which involves, or in all probability, will involve the permanent loss of the use of, or permanent injury to, any limb, or the permanent loss of or injury to the sight or hearing, or the fracture of any limb, or the enforced absence of the injured person from work for a period exceeding 20 days.

CASE CORNER

In *A. Trehan vs. Associated Electrical Agencies and Another* [1996 SCC (4) 255], the claimant was the worker himself and the claim petition was in respect of an injury sustained in the course of his employment, on account of which he was said to have lost the vision of his left eye. This employee was also an insured person under the Employees' State Insurance (ESI) Act, 1948, and he became entitled to the benefit of Section 46(c) of the said Act. He approached the Employees' State Insurance Corporation and obtained the benefit available to him under the said Act. Thereafter he served a notice on the management, demanding ₹7 lakhs as compensation, and followed the same by filing an application under the provisions of the Workmen's (Employees') Compensation Act, 1923, claiming ₹1 lakh and odd with penalty, penal interest and costs.

As per Section 53 of the ESI Act, 1948, an insured person or his dependents shall not be entitled to receive or recover, whether from the employer of the insured person or from any other person, any compensation or damages under the Employees' Compensation Act (or, EC Act), 1923 or any other law for the time being in force or otherwise, in respect of an employment injury sustained by the insured person as an employee under the ESI Act. Further, Section 61 of the same Act states that when a person is entitled to any of the benefits provided by this Act, he shall not be entitled to receive any similar benefit admissible under the provisions of any other enactment. In view of the clear language of the section, the Supreme Court found no justification in construing it as not taking away the right of the workman who is an insured person and an employee under the ESI Act to claim compensation under the EC Act. The Court was hence of the opinion that the High Court was right in holding that in view the bar created by Section 53 the application for compensation filed by the appellant under the EC Act was not maintainable.

(Adapted from: www.indiankanoon.org/doc/1787127/ accessed on 1/7/2014.)

Medical Examination [Section 11]

1. Where an employee has given notice of an accident, he shall, if the employer, before the expiry of 3 days from the time at which service of the notice has been effected, offers to have him examined free of charge by a qualified medical practitioner, submit himself for such examination, and any employee who is in receipt of a half-monthly payment under this Act shall, if so required, submit himself for such examination from time to time:

   Provided that an employee shall not be required to submit himself for examination by a medical practitioner otherwise than in accordance with rules made under this Act, or at more frequent intervals than may be prescribed.
2. If an employee, on being required to do so by the employer under sub-section (1) or by the Commissioner at any time, refuses to submit himself for examination by a qualified medical practitioner or in any way obstructs the same, his right to compensation shall be suspended during the continuance of such refusal or obstruction unless, in the case of refusal, he was prevented by any sufficient cause from so submitting himself.
3. If an employee, before the expiry of the period within which he is liable under sub-section (1) to be required to submit himself for medical examination, voluntarily leaves without having been so examined the vicinity of the place in which he was employed, his right to compensation shall be suspended until he returns and offers himself for such examination.

4. Where an employee, whose right to compensation has been suspended under sub-section (2) or sub-section (3), dies without having submitted himself for medical examination as required by either of those sub-sections, the Commissioner may, if he thinks fit, direct the payment of compensation to the dependants of the deceased employee.
5. Where under sub-section (2) or sub-section (3) a right to compensation is suspended, no compensation shall be payable in respect of the period of suspension, and, if the period of suspension commences before the expiry of the waiting period referred to in clause (d) of sub-section (1) of Section 4, the waiting period shall be increased by the period during which the suspension continues.
6. Where an injured employee has refused to be attended by a qualified medical practitioner whose services have been offered to him by the employer free of charge or having accepted such offer has deliberately disregarded the instructions of such medical practitioner, then, if it is proved that the employee has not thereafter been regularly attended by a qualified medical practitioner or having been so attended has deliberately failed to follow his instructions and that such refusal, disregard or failure was unreasonable in the circumstances of the case and that the injury has been aggravated thereby, the injury and resulting disablement shall be deemed to be of the same nature and duration as they might reasonably have been expected to be if the employee had been regularly attended by a qualified medical practitioner, whose instructions he had followed, and compensation, if any, shall be payable accordingly.

Contracting (Section 12)

1. Where any person (hereinafter in this section referred to as the principal) in the course of or for the purposes of his trade or business contracts with any other person (hereinafter in this section referred to as the contractor) for the execution by or under the contractor of the whole or any part of any work which is ordinarily part of the trade or business of the principal, the principal shall be liable to pay to any employee employed in the execution of the work any compensation which he would have been liable to pay if that employee had been immediately employed by him; and where compensation is claimed from the principal, this Act shall apply as if references to the principal were substituted for references to the employer except that the amount of compensation shall be calculated with reference to the wages of the employee under the employer by whom he is immediately employed.
2. Where the principal is liable to pay compensation under this section, he shall be entitled to be indemnified by the contractor, or any other person from whom the employee could have recovered compensation and where a contractor who is himself a principal is liable to pay compensation or to indemnify a principal under this section he shall be entitled to be indemnified by any person standing to him in the relation of a contractor from whom the employee could have recovered compensation, and all questions as to the right to and the amount of any such indemnity shall, in default of agreement, be settled by the Commissioner.
3. Nothing in this section shall be construed as preventing an employee from recovering compensation from the contractor instead of the principal.
4. This section shall not apply in any case where the accident occurred elsewhere than on, in or about the premises on which the principal has undertaken or usually undertakes, as the case may be, to execute the work or which are otherwise under his control or management.

Remedies of Employer against Stranger (Section 13)

Where an employee has recovered compensation in respect of any injury caused under circumstances creating a legal liability of some person other than the person by whom the compensation was paid to pay damages in respect thereof, the person by whom the compensation was paid and any person who has been called on to pay an indemnity under Section 12 shall be entitled to be indemnified by the person so liable to pay damages as aforesaid.

Insolvency of Employer (Section 14)

1. Where any employer has entered into a contract with any insurers in respect of any liability under this Act to any employee, then in the event of the employer becoming insolvent or making a composition or scheme of arrangement with his creditors or, if the employer is a company, in the event of the company having commenced to be wound up, the rights of the employer against the insurers as respects that liability shall, notwithstanding anything in any law for the time being in force relating to insolvency or the winding up of companies, be transferred to and vest in the employee, and upon any such transfer the insurers shall have the same rights and remedies and be subject to the same liabilities as if they were the employer, so, however, that the insurers shall not be under any greater liability to the employee than they would have been under the employer.
2. If the liability of the insurers to the employee is less than the liability of the employer to the employee, the employee may prove for the balance in the insolvency proceedings or liquidation.
3. Where in any case such as is referred to in sub-section (1) the contract of the employer with the insurers is void or voidable by reason of non-compliance on the part of the employer with any terms or conditions of the contract (other than a stipulation for the payment of premia), the provisions of that sub-section shall apply as if the contract were not void or voidable, and the insurers shall be entitled to prove in the insolvency proceedings or liquidation for the amount paid to the employee:

   Provided that the provisions of this sub-section shall not apply in any case in which the employee fails to give notice to the insurers of the happening of the accident and of any resulting disablement as soon as practicable after he becomes aware of the institution of the insolvency or liquidation proceedings.
4. There shall be deemed to be included among the debts which under Section 49 of the Presidency-towns Insolvency Act, 1909, or under Section 61 of the Provincial Insolvency Act, 1920, or under Section 530 of the Companies Act, 1956, are in the distribution of the property of an insolvent or in the distribution of the assets of a company being wound up to be paid in priority to all other debts, the amount due in respect of any compensation the liability where for accrued before the date of the order of adjudication of the insolvent or the date of the commencement of the winding up, as the case may be, and those Acts shall have effect accordingly.
5. Where the compensation is a half-monthly payment, the amount due in respect thereof shall, for the purposes of this section, be taken to be the amount of the lump sum for which the half-monthly payment could, if redeemable, be redeemed if applications were made for that purpose under Section 7, and a certificate of the Commissioner as to the amount of such sum shall be conclusive proof thereof.
6. The provisions of sub-section (4) shall apply in the case of any amount for which an insurer is entitled to prove under sub-section (3), but otherwise those provisions shall not apply where the insol-

Spotlight

Section 14 shall not apply where a company is wound up voluntarily for reconstruction or of amalgamation with another company.

vent or the company being wound up has entered into such a contract with insurers as is referred to in sub-section (1).

7. This section shall not apply where a company is wound up voluntarily merely for purposes of reconstruction or of amalgamation with another company.

Compensation to be First Charge on Assets Transferred by Employer (Section 14A)

Where an employer transfers his assets before any amount due in respect of any compensation, the liability wherefor accrued before the date of the transfer, has been paid, such amount shall, notwithstanding anything contained in any other law for the time being in force, be a first charge on that part of the assets so transferred as consists of immovable property.

Special Provisions Relating to Masters and Seamen [Section 15]

This Act shall apply in the case of employees of ships or seamen subject to the following modifications, namely:

1. The notice of the accident and the claim for compensation may, except where the person injured is the master of the ship, be served on the master of the ship as if he were the employer, but where the accident happened and the disablement commenced on board the ship, it shall not be necessary for any seaman to give any notice of the accident.
2. In the case of the death of a master or seaman, the claim for compensation shall be made within 1 year after the news of the death has been received by the claimant or, where the ship has been or is deemed to have been lost with all hands, within 18 months of the date on which the ship was, or is deemed to have been, so lost:

   Provided that the Commissioner may entertain any claim to compensation in any case notwithstanding that the claim has not been preferred in due time as provided in this sub-section, if he is satisfied that the failure so to prefer the claim was due to sufficient cause.
3. Where an injured master or seaman is discharged or left behind in any part of India or in any foreign country any depositions taken by any Judge or Magistrate in that part or by any Consular Officer in the foreign country and transmitted by the person by whom they are taken to the Central Government or any State Government shall, in any proceedings for enforcing the claim, be admissible in evidence:
   (a) if the deposition is authenticated by the signature of the Judge, Magistrate or Consular Officer before whom it is made;
   (b) if the defendant or the person accused, as the case may be, had an opportunity by himself or his agent to cross-examine the witness; and
   (c) if the deposition was made in the course of a criminal proceeding, on proof that the deposition was made in the presence of the person accused,

   and it shall not be necessary in any case to prove the signature or official character of the person appearing to have signed any such deposition and a certificate by such person that the defendant or the person accused had an opportunity of cross-examining the witness and that the deposition if made in a criminal proceeding was made in the presence of the person accused shall, unless the contrary is proved, be sufficient evidence that he had that opportunity and that it was so made.
4. No half-monthly payment shall be payable in respect of the period during which the owner of the ship is, under any law in force for the time being relating to merchant shipping, liable to defray the expenses of maintenance of the injured master or seaman.

5. No compensation shall be payable under this Act in respect of any injury in respect of which provision is made for payment of a gratuity, allowance or pension under the War Pensions and Detention Allowances (Mercantile Marine, etc.) Scheme, 1939, or the War Pensions and Detention Allowances (Indian Seamen, etc.) Scheme, 1941, made under the Pensions (Navy, Army, Air Force and Mercantile Marine) Act, 1939, or under War Pensions and Detention Allowances (Indian Seamen) Scheme, 1942, made by the Central Government.
6. Failure to give a notice or make a claim or commence proceedings within the time required by this Act shall not be a bar to the maintenance of proceedings under this Act in respect of any personal injury, if:
   (a) an application has been made for payment in respect of the injury under any of the schemes referred to in the preceding clause, and
   (b) the State Government certifies that the said application was made in the reasonable belief that the injury was one in respect of which the scheme under which the application was made makes provision for payments, and that the application was rejected or that payments made in pursuance of the application were discontinued on the ground that the injury was not such an injury, and
   (c) the proceedings under this Act are commenced within 1 month from the date on which the said certificate of the State Government was furnished to the person commencing the proceedings.

Special Provisions Relating to Captains and other Members of Crew of Aircrafts (Section 15A)

Spotlight
Notice of accident is not necessary if such accident happened and disablement commenced on board the aircraft, as provided in Section 15A(1).

This Act shall apply in the case of employees who are captains or other members of the crew of aircrafts subject to the following modifications, namely:

1. The notice of the accident and the claim for compensation may, except where the person injured is the captain of the aircraft, be served on the captain of the aircraft and if he were the employer, but where the accident happened and the disablement commenced on board the aircraft it shall not be necessary for any member of the crew to give notice of the accident.
2. In the case of the death of the captain or other member of the crew, the claim for compensation shall be made within 1 year after the news of the death has been received by the claimant or, where the aircraft has been or is deemed to have been lost with all hands, within 18 months of the date on which the aircraft was, or is deemed to have been, so lost:

   Provided that the Commissioner may entertain any claim for compensation in any case notwithstanding that the claim had not been preferred in due time as provided in this sub-section, if he is satisfied that the failure so to prefer the claim was due to sufficient cause.
3. Where an injured captain or other member of the crew of the aircraft is discharged or left behind in any part of India or in any other country, any depositions taken by any Judge or Magistrate in that part or by any Consular Officer in the foreign country and transmitted by the person by whom they are taken to the Central Government or any State Government shall, in any proceedings for enforcing the claim, be admissible in evidence:
   (a) if the deposition is authenticated by the signature of the Judge, Magistrate or Consular Officer before whom it is made;
   (b) if the defendant or the person accused, as the case may be, had an opportunity by himself or his agent to cross-examine the witness;

(c) if the deposition was made in the course of a criminal proceeding, on proof that the deposition was made in the presence of the person accused,

and it shall not be necessary in any case to prove the signature or official character of the person appearing to have signed any such deposition and a certificate by such person that the defendant or the person accused had an opportunity of cross-examining the witness and that the deposition if made in a criminal proceeding was made in the presence of the person accused shall, unless the contrary is proved, be sufficient evidence that he had that opportunity and that it was so made.

Special Provisions Relating to Employees Abroad of Companies and Motor Vehicles (Section 15B)

This Act shall apply:

(i) in the case of employees who are persons recruited by companies registered in India and working as such abroad, and

(ii) persons sent for work abroad along with motor vehicles registered under the Motor Vehicles Act, 1988 as drivers, helpers, mechanics, cleaners or other employees subject to the following modifications, namely:

1. The notice of the accident and the claim for compensation may be served on the local agent of the company, or the local agent of the owner of the motor vehicle, in the country of accident, as the case may be.
2. In the case of death of the employee in respect of whom the provisions of this section shall apply, the claim for compensation shall be made within 1 year after the news of the death has been received by the claimant:

   Provided that the Commissioner may entertain any claim for compensation in any case notwithstanding that the claim had not been preferred in due time as provided in this sub-section, if he is satisfied that the failure so to prefer the claim was due to sufficient cause.
3. Where an injured employee is discharged or left behind in any part of India or in any other country any depositions taken by any Judge or Magistrate in that part or by any Consular Officer in the foreign country and transmitted by the person by whom they are taken to the Central Government or any State Government shall, in any proceedings for enforcing the claims, be admissible in evidence:

   (a) if the deposition is authenticated by the signature of the Judge, Magistrate or Consular Officer before whom it is made;

   (b) if the defendant or the person accused, as the case may be, had an opportunity by himself or his agent to cross-examine the witness;

   (c) if the deposition was made in the course of a criminal proceeding, on proof that the deposition was made in the presence of the person accused,

   and it shall not be necessary in any case to prove the signature or official character of the person appearing to have signed any such deposition and a certificate by such person that the defendant or the person accused had an opportunity of cross-examining the witness and that the deposition if made in a criminal proceeding was made in the presence of the person accused shall, unless the contrary is proved, be sufficient evidence that he had that opportunity and that it was so made.

Returns as to Compensation (Section 16)

The State Government may, by notification in the Official Gazette, direct that every person employing employees, or that any specified class of such persons, shall send at such time and in such form and to such authority, as may be specified in the notification, a correct return specifying the number of injuries in respect of which compensation has been paid by the employer during the previous year and the amount of such compensation together with such other particulars as to the compensation as the State Government may direct.

Contracting out (Section 17)

Any contract or agreement whether made before or after the commencement of this Act, whereby an employee relinquishes any right of compensation from the employer for personal injury arising out of or in the course of the employment, shall be null and void in so far as it purports to remove or reduce the liability of any person to pay compensation under this Act.

Proof of Age (Section 18)

Repealed by the Workmen's compensation (Amendment) Act, 1959.

Penalties (Section 18A)

1. Whoever:
   (a) fails to maintain a notice-book which he is required to maintain under sub-section (3) of Section 10, or
   (b) fails to send to the Commissioner a statement which he is required to send under sub-section (1) of Section 10A, or
   (c) fails to send a report which he is required to send under Section 10B, or
   (d) fails to make a return which he is required to make under Section 16,
   shall be punishable with fine which may extend to ₹5,000.
2. No prosecution under this section shall be instituted except by or with the previous sanction of a Commissioner, and no Court shall take cognizance of any offence under this section, unless complaint thereof is made within 6 months of the date on which the alleged commission of the offence came to the knowledge of the Commissioner.

CHAPTER III: COMMISSIONERS

Reference to Commissioners (Section 19)

1. If any question arises in any proceedings under this Act as to the liability of any person to pay compensation (including any question as to whether a person injured is or is not an employee or as to the amount or duration of compensation (including any question as to the nature or extent of disablement), the question shall, in default of agreement, be settled by a Commissioner:
2. No Civil Court shall have jurisdiction to settle, decide or deal with any question which is by or under this Act required to be settled, decided or dealt with by a Commissioner or to enforce any liability incurred under this Act.

CASE CORNER

In *State of Punjab and Others vs. Vidya Devi and Others* [(1991) ILLJ 305 PH], deceased Mansha Ram was employed as a workman at Anandpur Sahib Hydel Project as a Dumper Operator. He met with an accident which proved fatal, subsequent to which, his widow and minor children have claimed compensation to the tune of ₹73,516.62 together with penalty equivalent to 50 per cent of the amount of compensation. Prayer was also made for grant of interest at the rate of 1 per cent per annum from the date of accident till payment. This petition was contested on behalf of the employer and the State of Punjab on the ground that the monthly wages of Mansha Ram exceeded ₹1,000, hence he was not covered by the definition of a workman. Also, that the said accident took place due to his negligence as he touched the electric wire and the employer was not liable to pay compensation to the heirs of the deceased.

There was ample evidence on the record that at time of his death, the deceased was getting wages which did not exceed ₹1000 per month. However, as a result of subsequent revision, his wages exceeded ₹1,000 per month. Mansha Ram was an *ad hoc* employee; hence it is obvious that the revision of pay was made with an ulterior motive to escape the liability for payment of compensation. The provisions of the Employees' Compensation Act, 1923 (or, the Act) cannot be permitted to be set at naught by revision of pay scale with retrospective effect by employers. Further it was held that the employer, instead of giving adequate compensation to the dependents of the deceased, has gone out of the way to escape the liability of payment in respect of the claim of the worker, who died while he was on duty in the course of his employment. His dependents cannot be deprived of compensation under the Act. They were granted compensation to the tune of ₹24,000 with interest at the rate of 6 per cent per annum from the date of accident till actual payment.

(Adapted from: www.indiankanoon.org/doc/161282/ accessed on 31/7/2014.)

Appointment of Commissioners (Section 20)

1. The State Government may, by notification in the Official Gazette, appoint any person who is or has been a member of a State Judicial Service for a period of not less than 5 years or is or has been for not less than 5 years an advocate or a pleader or is or has been a Gazetted Officer for not less than 5 years having educational qualifications and experience in personnel management, human resource development and industrial relations to be a Commissioner for Employees' Compensation for such area as may be specified in the notification.
2. Where more than 1 Commissioner has been appointed for any area, the State Government may, by general or special order, regulate the distribution of business between them.
3. Any Commissioner may, for the purpose of deciding any matter referred to him for decision under this Act, choose 1 or more persons possessing special knowledge of any matter relevant to the matter under inquiry to assist him in holding the inquiry.
4. Every Commissioner shall be deemed to be a public servant within the meaning of the Indian Penal Code.

Spotlight

Section 20(2) empowers the State Government to regulate distribution of business if more than 1 Commissioner is appointed for an area.

Venue of Proceedings and Transfer (Section 21)

1. Where any matter under this Act is to be done by or before a Commissioner, the same shall, subject to the provisions of this Act and to any rules made hereunder, be done by or before the Commissioner for the area in which:
   (a) the accident took place which resulted in the injury; or
   (b) the employee or in case of his death, the dependant claiming the compensation ordinarily resides; or
   (c) the employer has his registered office:

   Provided that no matter shall be processed before or by a Commissioner, other than the Commissioner having jurisdiction over the area in which the accident took place, without his giving notice in the manner prescribed by the Central Government to the Commissioner having jurisdiction over the area and the State Government concerned:

   Provided further that, where the employee, being the master of a ship or a seaman or the captain or a member of the crew of an aircraft or an employee in a motor vehicle or a company, meets with the accident outside India any such matter may be done by or before a Commissioner for the area in which the owner or agent of the ship, aircraft or motor vehicle resides or carries on business or the registered office of the company is situate, as the case may be.

1A. If a Commissioner, other than the Commissioner with whom any money has been deposited under Section 8, proceeds with a matter under this Act, the former may for the proper disposal of the matter call for transfer of any records or money remaining with the latter and on receipt of such a request, he shall comply with the same.

2. If a Commissioner is satisfied that any matter arising out of any proceedings pending before him can be more conveniently dealt with by any other Commissioner, whether in the same State or not, he may, subject to rules made under this Act, order such matter to be transferred to such other Commissioner either for report or for disposal, and, if he does so, shall forthwith transmit to such other Commissioner all documents relevant for the decision of such matter and, where the matter is transferred for disposal, shall also transmit in the prescribed manner any money remaining in his hands or invested by him for the benefit of any party to the proceedings:

   Provided that the Commissioner shall not, where any party to the proceedings has appeared before him, make any order of transfer relating to the distribution among dependants of a lump sum without giving such party an opportunity of being heard.

3. The Commissioner to whom any matter is so transferred shall, subject to rules made under this Act, inquire there into and, if the matter was transferred for report, return his report thereon or, if the matter was transferred for disposal, continue the proceedings as if they had originally commenced before him.
4. On receipt of a report from a Commissioner to whom any matter has been transferred for report under sub-section (2), the Commissioner by whom it was referred shall decide the matter referred in conformity with such report.
5. The State Government may transfer any matter from any Commissioner appointed by it to any other Commissioner appointed by it.

Form of Application (Section 22)

1. Where an accident occurs in respect of which liability to pay compensation under this Act arises, a claim for such compensation may, subject to the provisions of this Act, be made before the Commissioner.

1A. Subject to the provisions of sub-section (1), no application for the settlement of any matter by a Commissioner, other than an application by a dependant or dependants for compensation shall be made unless and until some question has arisen between the parties in connection therewith which they have been unable to settle by agreement.

2. An application to a Commissioner may be made in such form and shall be accompanied by such fee, if any, as may be prescribed, and shall contain, in addition to any particulars which may be prescribed, the following particulars, namely:
   (a) a concise statement of the circumstances in which the application is made and the relief or order which the applicant claims;
   (b) in the case of a claim for compensation against an employer, the date of service of notice of the accident on the employer and, if such notice has not been served or has not been served in due time, the reason for such omission;
   (c) the names and addresses of the parties; and
   (d) except in the case of an application by dependants for compensation a concise statement of the matters on which agreement has and of those on which agreement has not been come to.

Spotlight

As per Section 22(1), where an accident occurs in respect of which liability to pay compensation under this Act arises, a claim for such compensation may be made before the Commissioner.

3. If the applicant is illiterate or for any other reason is unable to furnish the required information in writing, the application shall, if the applicant so desires, be prepared under the direction of the Commissioner.

Power of Commissioner to Require Further Deposit in Cases of Fatal Accident (Section 22A)

1. Where any sum has been deposited by an employer as compensation payable in respect of an employee whose injury has resulted in death, and in the opinion of the Commissioner such sum is insufficient, the Commissioner may, by notice in writing stating his reasons, call upon the employer to show cause why he should not make a further deposit within such time as may be stated in the notice.
2. If the employer fails to show cause to the satisfaction of the Commissioner, the Commissioner may make an award determining the total amount payable, and requiring the employer to deposit the deficiency.

Powers and Procedure of Commissioners (Section 23)

The Commissioner shall have all the powers of a Civil Court under the Code of Civil Procedure, 1908, for the purpose of taking evidence on oath (which such Commissioner is hereby empowered to impose) and of enforcing the attendance of witnesses and compelling the production of documents and material objects and the Commissioner shall be deemed to be a Civil Court for all the purposes of Section 195 and of Chapter XXVI of the Code of Criminal Procedure, 1973.

Appearance of Parties (Section 24)

Any appearance, application or act required to be made or done by any person before or to a Commissioner (other than an appearance of a party which is required for the purpose of his examination as a witness) may be made or done on behalf of such person by a legal practitioner or by an official of an

Insurance Company or a registered Trade Union or by an Inspector appointed under sub-section (1) of Section 8 of the Factories Act, 1948, or under sub-section (1) of Section 5 of the Mines Act, 1952, or by any other officer specified by the State Government in this behalf, authorised in writing by such person, or, with the permission of the Commissioner, by any other person so authorised.

Method of Recording Evidence (Section 25)

The Commissioner shall make a brief memorandum of the substance of the evidence of every witness as the examination of the witness proceeds, and such memorandum shall be written and signed by the Commissioner with his own hand and shall form part of the record:

Provided that, if the Commissioner is prevented from making such memorandum, he shall record the reason of his inability to do so and shall cause such memorandum to be made in writing from his dictation and shall sign the same, and such memorandum shall form a part of the record:

Provided further that the evidence of any medical witness shall be taken down as nearly as may be word for word.

Time Limit for Disposal of Cases Relating to Compensation (Section 25A)

The Commissioner shall dispose of the matter relating to compensation under this Act within a period of 3 months from the date of reference and intimate the decision in respect thereof within the said period to the employee.

Spotlight

Time limit for disposal of cases relative to compensation is 3 months.

Costs (Section 26)

All costs, incidental to any proceedings before a Commissioner, shall, subject to rules made under this Act, be in the discretion of the Commissioner.

Power to Submit Cases (Section 27)

A Commissioner may, if he thinks fit, submit any question of law for the decision of the High Court and, if he does so, shall decide the question in conformity with such decision.

Registration of Agreements (Section 28)

1. Where the amount of any lump sum payable as compensation has been settled by agreement, whether by way of redemption of a half-monthly payment or otherwise, or where any compensation has been so settled as being payable to a woman or a person under a legal disability, a memorandum thereof shall be sent by the employer to the Commissioner, who shall, on being satisfied as to its genuineness, record the memorandum in a register in the prescribed manner:

   Provided that:

   (a) no such memorandum shall be recorded before 7 days after communication by the Commissioner of notice to the parties concerned;

   (c) the Commissioner may at any time rectify the register;

   (d) where it appears to the Commissioner that an agreement as to the payment of a lump sum whether by way of redemption of a half-monthly payment or otherwise, or an agreement as to the amount of compensation payable, to a woman, or a person under a legal disability-ought not to be registered by reason of the inadequacy of the sum or amount, or by reason of the agreement having been obtained by fraud or undue influence or other improper means, he may refuse to record the memorandum of the agreement and may make such order, including an order as to any sum already paid under the agreement, as he thinks just in the circumstances.

2. An agreement for the payment of compensation which has been registered under sub-section (1) shall be enforceable under this Act notwithstanding anything contained in the Indian Contract Act, 1872, or in any other law for the time being in force.

Effect of Failure to Register Agreement (Section 29)

Where a memorandum of any agreement, the registration of which is required by Section 28, is not sent to the Commissioner as required by that section, the employer shall be liable to pay the full amount of compensation which he is liable to pay under the provisions of this Act, and notwithstanding anything contained in the proviso to sub-section (1) of Section 4, shall not, unless the Commissioner otherwise directs, be entitled to deduct more than half of any amount paid to the employee by way of compensation whether under the agreement or otherwise.

Appeals (Section 30)

1. An appeal shall lie to the High Court from the following orders of a Commissioner, namely:
   (a) an order awarding as compensation a lump sum whether by way of redemption of a half-monthly payment or otherwise or disallowing a claim in full or in part for a lump sum;
   (aa) an order awarding interest or penalty under Section 4A;
   (b) an order refusing to allow redemption of a half-monthly payment;
   (c) an order providing for the distribution of compensation among the dependants of a deceased employee, or disallowing any claim of a person alleging himself to be such dependant;
   (d) an order allowing or disallowing any claim for the amount of an indemnity under the provisions of sub-section (2) of Section 12; or
   (e) an order refusing to register a memorandum of agreement or registering the same or providing for the registration of the same subject to conditions:

   Provided that no appeal shall lie against any order unless a substantial question of law is involved in the appeal and, in the case of an order other than an order such as is referred to in clause (b), unless the amount in dispute in the appeal is not less than ₹300:

   Provided further that no appeal shall lie in any case in which the parties have agreed to abide by the decision of the Commissioner, or in which the order of the Commissioner gives effect to an agreement come to by the parties:

CASE CORNER

In *Oriental Insurance Company through its Senior Divisional Manager vs. Bhagat Singh s/o Late Shiv Ram and Others* [(2012) LLR 952 Himachal Pradesh HC], the claimants claimed compensation pleading that the deceased, their son, who was a driver, had met with an accident and died on the spot, was drawing a salary of ₹5,500 per month. The owner, however, admitted paying a salary of ₹3,800 per month and ₹50 daily for food, etc. On conclusion that the accident had taken place during the course of employment, the Commissioner had awarded a sum of ₹4,31,160 taking wages of ₹4,000 per month.

The insurer/appellant filed an appeal against the Award on the ground that wages/salary and driving license have not been proved. The Commissioner held that no evidence was led by the appellant on ground of an invalid licence. Records of Licensing Authority showed that the driver was having a valid licence. No driver can be employed for less than ₹4,000 per month. Further, daily allowance was held to be counted for the purpose of calculating the wages/salary of the driver.

The appeal was as such dismissed.

(Adapted from: Labour Law Reporter, September 2012, pp. 952-953.)

Provided further that no appeal by an employer under clause (a) shall lie unless the memorandum of appeal is accompanied by a certificate by the Commissioner to the effect that the appellant has deposited with him the amount payable under the order appealed against.

2. The period of limitation for an appeal under this section shall be 60 days.
3. The provision of Section 5 of the Limitation Act, 1963 shall be applicable to appeals under this section.

Withholding of Certain Payments Pending Decision of Appeal (Section 30A)

Where an employer makes an appeal under clause (a) of sub-section (1) of Section 30, the Commissioner may, and if so directed by the High Court shall, pending the decision of the appeal, withhold payment of any sum in deposit with him.

Recovery (Section 31)

The Commissioner may recover as an arrear of land revenue any amount payable by any person under this Act, whether under an agreement for the payment of compensation or otherwise, and the Commissioner shall be deemed to be a public officer within the meaning of Section 5 of the Revenue Recovery Act, 1890.

Spotlight

As per Section 31, the Commissioner may recover any amount payable by any person under this Act as an arrear of land revenue, whether under an agreement for the payment of compensation or otherwise.

CHAPTER IV: RULES

Power of the State Government to Make Rules (Section 32)

1. The State Government may make rules to carry out the purposes of this Act.
2. In particular and without prejudice to the generality of the foregoing power, such rules may provide for all or any of the following matters, namely:
   (a) for prescribing the intervals at which and the conditions subject to which an application for review may be made under Section 6 when not accompanied by a medical certificate;
   (b) for prescribing the intervals at which and the conditions subject to which an employee may be required to submit himself for medical examination under sub-section (1) of Section 11;
   (c) for prescribing the procedure to be followed by Commissioners in the disposal of cases under this Act and by the parties in such cases;
   (d) for regulating the transfer of matters and cases from one Commissioner to another and the transfer of money in such cases;

(e) for prescribing the manner in which money in the hands of a Commissioner may be invested for the benefit of dependants of a deceased employee and for the transfer of money so invested from one Commissioner to another;
(f) for the representation in proceedings before Commissioners of parties who are minors or are unable to make an appearance;
(g) for prescribing the form and manner in which memoranda of agreements shall be presented and registered;
(h) for the withholding by Commissioners, whether in whole or in part of half-monthly payments pending decision on applications for review of the same;
(i) for regulating the scales of costs which may be allowed in proceedings under this Act;
(j) for prescribing and determining the amount of the fees payable in respect of any proceedings before a Commissioner under this Act;
(k) for the maintenance by Commissioners of registers and records of proceedings before them;
(l) for prescribing the classes of employers who shall maintain notice-books under sub-section (3) of Section 10, and the form of such notice-books;
(m) for prescribing the form of statement to be submitted by employers under Section 10A;
(n) for prescribing the cases in which the report referred to in Section 10B may be sent to an authority other than the Commissioner;
(o) for prescribing abstracts of this Act and requiring the employers to display notices containing such abstracts;
(p) for prescribing the manner in which diseases specified as occupational diseases may be diagnosed;
(q) for prescribing the manner in which diseases may be certified for any of the purposes of this Act;
(r) for prescribing the manner in which, and the standards by which, incapacity may be assessed.

3. Every rule made under this section shall be laid, as soon as may be after it is made, before the State Legislature.

Power of Local Government to Make Rules (Section 33)

Repealed by A.O. 1937

Publication of Rules (Section 34)

1 The power to make rules conferred by Section 32 shall be subject to the condition of the rules being made after previous publication.
2. The date to be specified in accordance with clause (3) of Section 23 of the General Clauses Act, 1897, as that after which a draft of rules proposed to be made under Section 32 will be taken into consideration, shall not be less than 3 months from the date on which the draft of the proposed rules was published for general information.
3. Rules so made shall be published in the Official Gazette and, on such publication, shall have effect as if enacted in this Act.

Rules to Give Effect to Arrangements with other Countries for the Transfer of Money Paid as Compensation (Section 35)

1. The Central Government may, by notification in the Official Gazette, make rules for the transfer to any foreign country of money deposited with a Commissioner under this Act which has been awarded to or may be due to any person residing or about to reside in such foreign country and for the receipt, distribution and administration in any State of any money deposited under the law relating to employees' compensation in any foreign country which has been awarded to, or may be due to any person residing or about to reside in any State:

   Provided that no sum deposited under this Act in respect of fatal accidents shall be so transferred without the consent of the employer concerned until the Commissioner receiving the sum has passed orders determining its distribution and apportionment under the provisions of sub-sections (4) and (5) of Section 8.
2. Where money deposited with a Commissioner has been so transferred in accordance with the rules made under this section, the provisions elsewhere contained in this Act regarding distribution by the Commissioner of compensation deposited with him shall cease to apply in respect of any such money.

Rules Made by Central Government to be Laid before Parliament (Section 36)

Every rule made under this Act by the Central Government shall be laid as soon as may be after it is made before each House of Parliament while it is in session for a total period of 30 days which may be comprised in 1 session or in 2 or more successive sessions, and if, before the expiry of the session immediately following the session or the successive sessions aforesaid, both Houses agree in making any modification in the rule or both Houses agree that the rule should not be made, the rule shall thereafter have effect only in such modified form or be of no effect, as the case may be; so however that any such modification or annulment shall be without prejudice to the validity of anything previously done under that rule.

ADMINISTRATION OF THE ACT

The State Governments administer the provisions of the Employees' Compensation Act, 1923 through the Commissioners appointed for specified areas. The State Governments also make rules for ensuring that the provisions of the Act are complied with.

SUMMARY

- The Workmen's (now Employees') Compensation Act, 1923 is one of the earliest legislations aimed at social security, aimed to benefit workers who would undergo losses out of accidents arising out of and in the course of employment.
- As per Section 2(1)(g), temporary partial disablement reduces the earning capacity of an employee in any employment in which he was engaged at the time of the accident resulting in the disablement. Permanent partial disablement reduces the earning capacity of an employee in every employment which he was capable of undertaking at that time.

- Total disablement, according to Section 2(1)(l), means such disablement, whether of a temporary or permanent nature, as incapacitates an employee for all work which he was capable of performing at the time of the accident resulting in such disablement.
- As per Section 3(1), if personal injury is caused to an employee by accident arising out of and in the course of his employment, his employer shall be liable to pay compensation. Exceptions are in respect of any injury which does not result in total or partial disablement for a period exceeding 3 days, or not resulting in death or permanent total disablement caused by an accident which is directly attributable to (i) if the employee was under the influence of drink or drugs, or (ii) the wilful disobedience of the employee to an order expressly given, or to a rule expressly framed, for the purpose of securing the safety of employees, or (iii) the wilful removal or disregard by the employee of any safety guard or other device which he knew to have been provided for the purpose of securing the safety of employees.
- According to Section 4(1), where death results from the injury, compensation shall be an amount equal to 50 per cent of the monthly wages of the deceased employee multiplied by the relevant factor or an amount of ₹1,20,000, whichever is more. Where permanent total disablement results from the injury, compensation is an amount equal to 60 per cent of the monthly wages of the injured employee multiplied by the relevant factor or an amount of ₹1,40,000, whichever is more.
- Where temporary disablement, whether total or partial, results from the injury, a half-monthly payment of the sum equivalent to 25 per cent of monthly wages of the employee is to be paid in accordance with the provisions of Section 4(2).
- Compensation shall be paid as soon as it falls due, as per Section 4A(1).
- Section 10(1) lays down that no claim for compensation shall be entertained by a Commissioner unless notice of the accident has been given in prescribed manner as soon as practicable after the happening thereof and unless the claim is preferred before him within 2 years of the occurrence of the accident or from the date of death.
- Sections 15, 15A and 15B give out special provisions of the application of the Act relating to masters and seamen, captains and other members of crew of aircrafts, and employees abroad of companies and motor vehicles respectively.
- Whoever fails to maintain a notice-book required under Section 10(3), or fails to send to the Commissioner a statement required to send under Section10A(1), or fails to send a report required to send under Section 10B, or fails to make a return required to make under Section 16, shall be punishable with fine which may extend to ₹5,000, as laid down in Section 18(1).
- Section 20(1) empowers the State Government to appoint any person who is or has been a member of a State Judicial Service for a period of not less than 5 years or is or has been for not less than 5 years an advocate or a pleader or is or has been a Gazetted Officer for not less than 5 years having educational qualifications and experience in personnel management, human resource development and industrial relations to be a Commissioner for such area as may be specified in the notification in the Official Gazette.
- Where an accident occurs in respect of which liability to pay compensation under this Act arises, a claim for such compensation may, subject to the provisions of this Act, be made before the Commissioner, according to Section 22(1).
- The State Governments administer the provisions of the Act through the Commissioners appointed for specified areas. The State Governments also make rules for ensuring that the provisions of the Act are complied with.

Key Concepts

Compensation
Dependant
Accident
Partial disablement
Total disablement
Commissioner
Out of employment
In the course of employment
Occupational disease
Liability
Injury
Death

Bibliography

Bhattacharya, V. R. *Some Aspects of Social Security Measures in India: Towards Democracy and Social Justice*, Delhi: Metropolitan Book Co.; 1970.

Hasan, N. *Social Security Measures in India*, New Delhi: S.Chand & Co. Pvt. Ltd.; 1972, p. 65.

Misra, S. N. and Misra, S. K. *An Introduction to Labour and Industrial Laws*, Allahabad: Central Law Publications; 1995.

Panandikar's Industrial Labour in India, cited by Bhattacharya, V. R. *Social Security Measures in India*, 1970.

Sixty-Second Report on the Workmen's Compensation Act 1923, Law Commission of India, 1974

The Workmen's Compensation Act: A Guide for Activists, Bangalore: Alternative Law Forum; 2005.

Review Questions

Objective Type Questions

I. State True or False

(i) Any member of the crew of an aircraft may not give notice of an accident in case the accident happened and the disablement commenced on board.

(ii) The Commissioner shall dispose of the matter relating to compensation within 3 months from the date of reference.

(iii) An employer who fails to send a report required under Section 16 shall be punishable with fine up to ₹5,000.

(iv) Permanent partial disablement of an employee reduces his earning capacity in every employment which he was capable of undertaking at that time.

(v) A railway servant permanently employed in any sub-divisional office of a railway is an employee under the Act.

Answers: (i) True, (ii) True, (iii) False, (iv) True, (v) False

II. Fill in the Blanks

(i) Where permanent total disablement results from the injury, compensation is equal to ___ per cent of the monthly wages of the injured employee multiplied by the relevant factor.

(ii) In case of the death of a master or ______, the claim for compensation shall be made within 1 year after the news of the death has been received by the claimant.

(iii) An employer in default in paying due compensation must pay simple interest at the rate of ____ per cent per annum.

(iv) Dependant of a deceased employee includes, if wholly dependent on the earnings of the employee, a son or a daughter who has attained the age of 18 years and is ____.

(v) Half-monthly payment is payable on the _____ day from the date of disablement where such disablement lasts for a period of 28 days or more.

Answers: (i) 60, (ii) seaman, (iii) 12, (iv) infirm, (v) sixteenth

Discussion Questions

1. You have already got a fair idea about the Employees' State Insurance (ESI) Act, 1948. Discuss how the Employees' Compensation Act, 1923 is different from ESI Act, 1948.
2. Explain the conditions in which an employer shall not liable to pay compensation.
3. Discuss in details the method of calculation of wages for payment of compensation.
4. State the different matters in which the State Government has the power to make rules.
5. Explain in details the amount of compensation where:
   (a) death results from the injury
   (b) permanent total disablement results from the injury
   (c) permanent partial disablement results from the injury
   (d) temporary disablement, whether total or partial, results from the injury
6. Discuss the special provisions for forms of application in case of claim for compensation.
7. What are the provisions for provisional payment and penalties in case of an employer in default of payment of compensation?
8. Describe your understanding of the terms "arising out of employment" and "in the course of employment". Further, discuss the situations which may not be considered under either of these two terms.
9. Explain in brief:
   (a) Dependant
   (b) Appeals
   (c) Liability of compensation in case of contracting
   (d) Notice of accident
10. Differentiate between:
    (a) Partial disablement and Total disablement
    (b) Statements regarding fatal accidents and Reports of fatal accidents and serious bodily injuries
    (c) Special provisions relating to masters and seamen and Special provisions relating to captains and other members of crew of aircrafts

CASE STUDY-I

The deceased in this case, working as assistant-cum-cleaner of a vehicle, had voluntarily consumed ethyl alcohol in heavy quantity and died of myocardial heart failure inside the vehicle when it was parked. The appellant, brother of the deceased, presented a petition for granting him adequate compensation for the death of his brother, arising out and in the course of employment. It was stated that the deceased earned ₹2,500 (besides TA, DA) per month as wages. He performed strenuous job in cleaning and loading the vehicle, and he had died of cardiac failure due to heavy exhaustion. The first respondent, i.e., the owner of the vehicle, admitted the employment of the deceased and further stated that he had died due to consumption ethyl alcohol; further, there was no accident at all in the course of employment. Therefore, as per the owner, the claim for compensation was not entertainable. There is however no dispute that the death took place in the course of employment.

(Adapted from: Shri Shankar Kal vs. Sri Sunil Kumar Saha [(2012) IVLLJ629 Gau], Labour Law Reporter, October 2012, pp. 1060-1066.)

Review Questions

1. Which sections of the Employees' Compensation Act, 1923, in your opinion, are relevant in this case?
2. Discuss the applicability of the terms "accident" and "arising out of employment" to the case.
3. Do you think that the claim for compensation is justifiable?

CASE STUDY-II

The husband of the respondent Ashiya Begam, namely, Vazir Ahmad, was employed as a Senior Cook with the appellants and was performing duty in the Running Room. He used to cook on cooking gas. On 19th April 1984, while working in the Running Room, there was an accident on account of the excessive gas inhaled by him and he was admitted to hospital for treatment. However, he died on 27th April 1984. It is alleged that the deceased received personal injury by accident arising out of and in the course of his employment, which resulted in his death. In reply, the appellants submitted that the deceased had died on account of his old disease and not due to any accident arising out of or in the course of his employment. According to the appellants, there was no accident in connection with the services of the deceased, but the death was on account of hypertension, hemiparesis, left side renal failure and pulmonary arrest, according to the certificate issued by the Director.

The Commissioner under the Employees' Compensation Act, 1923 looked into the pleadings as well as the evidence produced in the case and held that working on the cooking stove could not be the immediate cause of the death but a situation could arise where hard work on cooking stove can lead to strain and accelerate the death. He did not accept that the deceased was regularly ill or suffering from any disease. He was of the opinion that the deceased died during the course of his employment and the real cause of his death was excessive working on cooking gas. Thus, a sum of ₹35,600 was awarded by way of compensation. However the same has not been paid.

The learned counsel for the appellants has contended that unless it is shown that death had occurred due to the injury by accident arising out of and in the course of employment, the employer cannot be made liable for compensation. On the other hand, the learned counsel for the respondent has contended that the death occurred during the course of employment on account of the fact that the working conditions were such which accelerated the death of a person who was suffering from hypertension but the disease was not as such as to claim his life; however, the strenuous duty and condition of working had accelerated his death.

(Adapted from: Divisional Personnel Officer, Western Railway vs. Ashiya Begam [(1994) IILLJ 795 Raj] www.indiankanoon.org/doc/1058687/ accessed on 3/7/2014.)

Review Questions

1. Did the deceased workman die on account of personal injury caused to him by accident arising out of and in the course of his employment?
2. Do you think that strenuous duties and working condition in which the deceased was working had accelerated his death?
3. Can you draw a causal relationship between the accident and employment?
4. Are the dependents, in your opinion, entitled to get the compensation?

SCHEDULE I

[See Sections 2(1) and (4)]

PART I List of Injuries Deemed to Result in Permanent Total Disablement

Serial No.	*Description of injury*	*Percentage of loss of earning capacity*
1	*2*	*3*
1.	Loss of both hands or amputation at higher sites	100
2.	Loss of a hand and foot	100
3.	Double amputation through leg or thigh, or amputation through leg or thigh on one side and loss of other foot	100
4.	Loss of sight to such an extent as to render the claimant unable to perform any work for which eye sight is essential.	100
5.	Very severe facial disfigurement	100
6.	Absolute deafness	100

PART II List of Injuries Deemed to Result In Permanent Partial Disablement

Serial No.	*Description of injury*	*Percentage of loss of earning capacity*
1.	Amputation through shoulder joint	90
2.	Amputation below shoulder with stump less than 20.32 cm. from tip of acromion	80
3.	Amputation from 20.32 cm. from tip of acromion to less than 11.43 cm. below tip of olecranon	70
4.	Loss of a hand or of the thumb and four fingers of one hand or amputation from 11.43 cm. below tip of olecranon	60
5.	Loss of thumb	30
6.	Loss of thumb and its metacarpal bone	40
7.	Loss of four fingers of one hand	50

(contd.)

(contd.)

8.	Loss of three fingers of one hand	30
9.	Loss of two fingers of one hand	20
10.	Loss of terminal phalanx of thumb	20
10A.	Guillotine amputation of tip of thumb without loss of bone.	10
	Amputation cases - lower limbs	
11.	Amputation of both feet resulting in end-bearing stumps	90
12.	Amputation through both feet proximal to the metatarso-phalangeal joint	80
13.	Loss of all toes of both feet through the metatarso-phalangeal joint	40
14.	Loss of all toes of both feet proximal to the proximal inter-phalangeal joint	30
15.	Loss of all toes of both feet distal to the proximal inter-phalangeal joint	20
16.	Amputation at hip	90
17.	Amputation below hip with stump not exceeding 12.70 cm. in length measured from tip of great trenchanter	80
18.	Amputation below hip with stump exceeding 12.70 cm. in length measured from tip of great trenchanter but not beyond middle thigh	70
19.	Amputation below middle thigh to 8.89 cm. below knee	60
20.	Amputation below knee with stump exceeding 8.89 cms. but not exceeding 12.70 cm.	50
21.	Amputation below knee with stump exceeding 12.70 cm.	50
22.	Amputation of one foot resulting in end-bearing	50
23.	Amputation through one foot proximal to the metatarso-phalangeal joint	50
24.	Loss of all toes of one foot through the metatarso-phalangeal joint	20
	Other injuries	
25.	Loss of one eye, without complications, the other being normal	40
26.	Loss of vision of one eye. without complications or disfigurement of eye-ball, the other being normal	30
26A.	Loss of partial vision of one eye	10
	Loss of - A. Fingers of right or left hand index finger	
27.	Whole	14
28.	Two phalanges	11
29.	One phalanx	9
30.	Guillotine amputation of tip without loss of bone	5
	Middle finger	
31.	Whole	12
32.	Two phalanges	9
33.	One phalanx	7

(contd.)

(contd.)

34.	Guillotine amputation of tip without loss of bone	4
	Ring or little finger	
35.	Whole	7
36.	Two phalanges	6
37.	One phalanx	5
38.	Guillotine amputation of tip without loss of bone	2
	B. Toes of right or left foot great toe	
39.	Through metatarso-phalangeal joint	14
40.	Part, with some loss of bone	3
	Any other toe	
41.	Through metatarso-phalangeal joint	3
42.	Part, with some loss of bone	1
	Two toes of one foot, excluding great toe	
43.	Through metatarso-phalangeal joint	5
44.	Part, with some loss of bone	2
	Three toes of one foot, excluding great toe	
45.	Through metatarso-phalangeal joint	6
46.	Part, with some loss of bone	3
	Four toes of one foot, excluding great toe	
47.	Through metatarso-phalangeal joint	9
48.	Part, with some loss of bone	3

Note - Complete and permanent loss of the use of any limb or member referred to in this Schedule shall be deemed to be equivalent to the loss of that limb or member

SCHEDULE II

See [Section 2(1)(dd)]

LIST OF PERSONS WHO SUBJECT TO THE PROVISIONS OF SECTION 2(1)(dd) ARE INCLUDED IN THE DEFINITION OF EMPLOYEES

The following persons are employees within the meaning of Section 2(1)(dd) and subject to the provisions of that section, that is to say, any person who is:

(i) employed in railways in connection with the operation, repair or maintenance of a lift or a vehicle propelled by steam or other mechanical power or by electricity or in connection with the loading or unloading of any such vehicle; or

(ii) employed, in any premises wherein or within the precincts whereof a manufacturing process as defined in clause (k) of Section 2 of the Factories Act, 1948, is being carried on, or in any kind of work whatsoever incidental to or connected with any such manufacturing process or with the article made whether or not employment in any such work is within such premises or precincts, and steam, water or other mechanical power or electrical power is used; or

(iii) employed for the purpose of making, altering, repairing, ornamenting, finishing or otherwise adapting for use, transport or sale of any article or part of an article in any premises

Explanation For the purposes of this clause, persons employed outside such premises or precincts but in any work incidental to, or connected with, the work relating to making, altering, repairing, ornamenting, finishing or otherwise adapting for use, transport or sale of any articles or part of an article shall be deemed to be employed within such premises or precincts; or

(iv) employed in the manufacture or handling of explosives in connection with the employer's trade or business; or

(v) employed, in any mine as defined in clause (j) of Section 2 of the Mines Act, 1952, in any mining operation or in any kind of work, incidental to or connected with any mining operation or with the mineral obtained, or in any kind of work whatsoever below ground; or

(vi) employed as the master or as a seaman of:

- (a) any ship which is propelled wholly or in part by steam or other mechanical power or by electricity or which is towed or intended to be towed by a ship so propelled; or
- (c) any sea-going ship not included in sub-clause (a) provided with sufficient area for navigation under sails alone; or

(vii) employed for the purpose of:

- (a) loading, unloading, fuelling, constructing, repairing, demolishing, cleaning or painting any ship of which he is not the master or a member of the crew, or handling or transport within the limits of any port subject to the Ports Act, 1908, or the Major Port Trusts Act, 1963, of goods which have been discharged from or are to be loaded into any vessel; or
- (b) warping a ship through the lock; or
- (c) mooring and unmooringships at harbour wall berths or in pier; or
- (d) removing or replacing dry dock caissons when vessels are entering or leaving dry docks; or
- (e) the docking or undocking of any vessel during an emergency; or
- (f) preparing splicing coir springs and check wires, painting depth marks on lock-sides, removing or replacing fenders whenever necessary, landing of gangways, maintaining life-buoys up to standard or any other maintenance work of a like nature; or
- (g) any work on jolly-boats for bringing a ship's line to the wharf; or

(viii) employed in the construction, maintenance, repair or demolition of—

- (a) any building which is designed to be or is or has been more than 1 storey in height above the ground or 12 feet or more from the ground level to the apex of the roof; or
- (b) any dam or embankment which is 12 feet or more in height from its lowest to its highest point; or
- (c) any road, bridge, tunnel or canal; or
- (d) any wharf, quay, sea-wall or other marine work including any moorings of ships; or

(ix) employed in setting up, maintaining, repairing or taking down any telegraph or telephone line or post or any overhead electric line or cable or post or standard or fittings and fixtures for the same; or

(x) employed, in the construction, working, repair or demolition of any aerial ropeway, canal, pipeline or sewer; or

(xi) employed in the service of any fire brigade; or

(xii) employed upon a railway as defined in clause (31) of Section 2 and sub-section (1) of Section 197 of the Railways Act, 1989, either directly or through a sub-contractor, by a person fulfilling a contract with the railway administration; or

(xiii) employed as an inspector, mail guard, sorter or van peon in the Railway Mail Service, or as a telegraphist or as a postal or railway signaller, or employed in any occupation ordinarily involving outdoor work in the Indian Posts and Telegraphs Department; or

(xiv) employed, in connection with operations for winning natural petroleum or natural gas; or

(xv) employed in any occupation involving blasting operations; or

(xvi) employed in the making of any excavation or explosives have been used, or whose depth from its highest to its lowest point exceeds 12 feet; or

(xvii) employed in the operation of any ferry boat capable of carrying more than 10 persons; or

(xviii) employed on any estate which is maintained for the purpose of growing cardamom, cinchona, coffee, rubber or tea; or

(xix) employed, in the generating, transforming, transmitting or distribution of electrical energy or in generation or supply of gas; or

(xx) employed in a lighthouse as defined in clause (d) of Section 2 of the Indian Lighthouse Act, 1927; or

(xxi) employed in producing cinematograph pictures intended for public exhibition or in exhibiting such pictures; or

(xxii) employed in the training, keeping or working of elephants or wild animals; or

(xxiii) employed in the tapping of palm-trees or the felling or logging of trees, or the transport of timber by inland waters, or the control or extinguishing of forest fires; or

(xxiv) employed in operations for the catching or hunting of elephants or other wild animals; or

(xxv) employed as a diver; or

(xxvi) employed in the handling or transport of goods in, or within the precincts of,

(a) any warehouse or other place in which goods are stored, or,

(b) any market, or

(xxvii) employed in any occupation involving the handling and manipulation of radium or X-rays apparatus, or contact with radio-active substances or

(xxviii) employed in or in connection with the construction, erection, dismantling, operation or maintenance of an aircraft as defined in Section 2 of the Indian Aircraft Act, 1934; or

(xxix) employed in horticultural operations, forestry, bee-keeping or farming by tractors or other contrivances driven by steam or other mechanical power or by electricity; or

(xxx) employed, in the construction, working, repair or maintenance of a tube well; or

(xxxi) employed in the maintenance, repair or renewal of electric fittings in any building; or

(xxxii) employed in a circus; or

(xxxiii) employed as watchman in any factory or establishment; or

(xxxiv) employed in any operation in the sea for catching fish; or

(xxxv) employed in any employment which requires handling of snakes for the purpose of extraction of venom or for the purpose of looking after snakes or handling any other poisonous animal or insect; or

(xxxvi) employed in handling animals like horses, mules and bulls; or

(xxxvii) employed for the purpose of loading or unloading any mechanically propelled vehicle or in the handling or transport of goods which have been loaded in such vehicles; or

(xxxviii) employed in cleaning of sewer lines or septic tanks within the limits of a local authority; or

(xxxix) employed on surveys and investigation, exploration or gauge or discharge observation of rivers including drilling operations, hydro-logical observations and flood forecasting activities ground, water surveys and exploration; or

(xl) employed in cleaning of jungles or reclaiming land or ponds; or (xli) employed in cultivation of land or rearing and maintenance of livestock or forest operations or fishing;

(xlii) employed in installation, maintenance or repair of pumping equipment used for lifting of water from wells, tube-wells, ponds, lakes, streams and the like; or

(xliii) employed in the construction, boring or deepening of an open well or dug well, bore well, bore-cum-dug well, filter-point and the like; or

(xliv) employed in spraying and dusting of insecticides or pesticides in agricultural operations or plantations; or

(xlv) employed in mechanised harvesting and threshing operations; or

(xlvi) employed in working or repair or maintenance of bulldozers, tractors, power tillers and the like; or

(xlvii) employed as artist for drawing pictures on advertisement boards at a height of 3.66 metres or more from the ground level; or

(xlviii) employed in any newspaper establishment as defined in the Working Journalists and Other Newspaper Employees (Conditions of Service) and Miscellaneous Provisions Act, 1955 and engaged in outdoor work;

(xlix) employed as divers for work under water.

SCHEDULE III

[See Section 3]

LIST OF OCCUPATIONAL DISEASES

S. No.	*Occupational disease*	*Employment*
(1)	*(2)*	*(3)*
	PART A	
1.	Infectious and parasitic diseases contracted in an occupation where there is a particular risk of contamination.	(*a*) All work involving exposure to health or laboratory work;
		(*b*) All work involving exposure to veterinary work;
		(*c*) Work relating to handling animals, animal carcasses, part of such carcasses, or merchandise which may have been contaminated by animals or animal carcasses;
		(*d*) Other work carrying a particular risk of contamination.
2.	Diseases caused by work in compressed air.	All work involving exposure to the risk concerned.

(contd.)

(contd.)

3.	Diseases caused by lead or its toxic compounds.	All work involving exposure to the risk concerned.
4.	Poisoning by nitrous fumes.	All work involving exposure to the risk concerned.
5.	Poisoning by organo phosphorus compounds.	All work involving exposure to the risk concerned.
	PART B	
1.	Diseases caused by phosphorus or its toxic compounds.	All work involving exposure to the risk concerned.
2.	Diseases caused by mercury or its toxic compounds.	All work involving exposure to the risk concerned.
3.	Diseases caused by benzene or its toxic homologues.	All work involving exposure to the risk concerned.
4.	Diseases caused by nitro and amido toxic derivatives of benzene or its homologues.	All work involving exposure to the risk concerned.
5.	Diseases caused by chromium or its toxic compounds.	All work involving exposure to the risk concerned.
6.	Diseases caused by arsenic or its toxic compounds.	All work involving exposure to the risk concerned.
7.	Diseases caused by radioactive substances and ionising radiations.	All work involving exposure to the action of radioactive substances or ionising radiations.
8.	Primary epitheliomatous cancer of the skin caused by tar, pitch, bitumen, mineral oil, anthracene, or the compounds, products or residues of these substances.	All work involving exposure to the risk concerned.
9.	Disease caused by the toxic halogen derivatives of hydrocarbons (of the aliphatic and aromatic series).	All work involving exposure to the risk concerned.
10.	Diseases caused by carbon disulphide.	All work involving exposure to the risk concerned.
11.	Occupational cataract due to infra-red radiations.	All work involving exposure to the risk concerned.
12.	Diseases caused by manganese or its toxic compounds.	All work involving exposure to the risk concerned.
13.	Skin diseases caused by physical, chemical or biological agents not included in other items.	All work involving exposure to the risk concerned.
14.	Hearing impairment caused by noise.	All work involving exposure to the risk concerned.

(contd.)

(contd.)

15.	Poisoning by dinitrophenol or a homologue or by substituted dinitrophenol or by the salts of such substances.	All work involving exposure to the risk concerned.
16.	Diseases caused by beryllium or its toxic compounds.	All work involving exposure to the risk concerned.
17.	Diseases caused by cadmium or its toxic compounds	All work involving exposure to the risk concerned.
18.	Occupational asthma caused by recognised sensitising agents inherent to the work process.	All work involving exposure to the risk concerned.
19.	Diseases caused by fluorine or its toxic compounds.	All work involving exposure to the risk concerned.
20.	Diseases caused by nitroglycerine or other nitroacid esters.	All work involving exposure to the risk concerned.
21.	Diseases caused by alcohols and ketones.	All work involving exposure to the risk concerned.
22.	Diseases caused by asphyxiants, carbon monoxide, and its toxic derivatives, hydrogen sulphide.	All work involving exposure to the risk concerned.
23.	Lung cancer and mesotheliomas caused by asbestos.	All work involving exposure to the risk concerned.
24.	Primary neoplasm of the epithelial lining of the urinary bladder or the kidney or the ureter.	All work involving exposure to the risk concerned.
25.	Snow blindness in snow bound areas.	All work involving exposure to the risk concerned.
26.	Disease due to effect of heat in extreme hot climate.	All work involving exposure to the risk concerned.
27.	Disease due to effect of cold in extreme cold climate.	All work involving exposure to the risk concerned.
	PART C	
1.	Pneumoconioses caused by sclerogenic mineral dust (silicosis, anthracosilicosis, asbestosis) and silico-tuberculosis provided that silicosis is an essential factor in causing the resultant incapacity or death.	All work involving exposure to the risk concerned.
2.	Bagassosis	All work involving exposure to the risk concerned.
3.	Bronchopulmonary diseases caused by cotton, flax hemp and sisal dust (Byssinosis).	All work involving exposure to the risk concerned.
4.	Extrinsic allergic alveolitis caused by the inhalation of organic dusts.	All work involving exposure to the risk concerned.
5.	Bronchopulmonary diseases caused by hard metals.	All work involving exposure to the risk concerned.
6.	Acute Pulmonary Oedema of high altitude.	All work involving exposure to the risk concerned.

SCHEDULE IV

[See Section 4]

FACTORS FOR WORKING OUT LUMP SUM EQUIVALENT OF COMPENSATION AMOUNT IN CASE OF PERMANENT DISABLEMENT AND DEATH

Completed years of age on the last birthday of the employee immediately preceding the date on which the compensation fell due	*Factors*
(1)	*(2)*
Not more than 16	228.54
17	227.49
18	226.38
19	225.22
20	224.00
21	222.71
22	221.37
23	219.95
24	218.47
25	216.91
26	215.28
27	213.57
28	211.79
29	209.92
30	207.98
31	205.95
32	203.85
33	201.66
34	199.40
35	197.06
36	194.64
37	192.14
38	189.56
39	186.90
40	184.17
41	181.37

(contd.)

42	178.49
43	175.54
44	172.52
45	169.44
46	166.29
47	163.07
48	159.80
49	156.47
50	153.09
51	149.67
52	146.20
53	142.68
54	139.13
55	135.56
56	131.95
57	128.33
58	124.70
59	121.05
60	117.41
61	113.77
62	110.14
63	106.52
64	102.93
65 or more	99.37

26

The Contract Labour (Regulation and Abolition) Act, 1970

An Act to regulate the employment of contract labour in certain establishments and to provide for its abolition in certain circumstances and for matters connected therewith.

Desired Knowledge Competencies

- To clarify the concept of contract labour and understand the background behind the emergence of the Contract Labour (Regulation and Abolition) Act, 1970.
- To discuss the extent, commencement and application of the Act and of the various definitions given under the Act.
- To comprehend the notions of principal employer, Advisory Boards, licenses, welfare and health issues of contract labour.

CONCEPT OF CONTRACT LABOUR

As per the World Development Report 2013, part time and temporary wage employment are now major features of industrialised and developing countries, and that in India, the number of temporary workers that employment agencies recruit has grown more than 10 per cent in 2009 and 18 per cent in 2010. The report released by the Press Information Bureau dated 4th March 2013 shows that part time work is showing a rising trend in the country, with the share of informal workers in total employment in organised firms having grown from 32 per cent in 2000 to 52 per cent in 2005 and to 68 per cent in 2010. *(Adapted from: Indian Labour Journal, May, 2013)*

To compete in a customer-driven market economy, domestic companies have adopted strategies of cost-cutting and are consequently getting dependant on contract labour. The primary motive behind hiring labour on contract basis is to have greater flexibility in adjusting the size of the workforce in order to address occasional surges or slowdown in demand. With contract workers gradually occupying significant portion of the workforce, organisations are encouraged to keep many of their workers off the books, albeit the risk of lesser worker loyalties. However, such changes in the workforce composition are being obstructed by the dated and rigid Indian labour legislations, enacted several decades back. These legislations restrict right-sizing of manpower and are creating hurdles in the smooth functioning of industries.

Let us now understand the concept of contract labour. A workman is deemed to be a contract labour when he/she is hired in connection with the work or "contract for service" of an establishment by or through a contractor or a contracting agency. Contract labour are indirect employees; persons who are hired, supervised and remunerated by a contractor who, in turn, is compensated by the establishment. Such labour is neither borne on pay roll nor on muster roll nor on wages paid directly to the labour *(Adapted from: Report of the National Commission on Labour, 1969).*

Spotlight

A workman is deemed to be a contract labour when he/she is hired in connection with the work or "contract for service" of an establishment by or through a contractor or a contracting agency.

This segment of the industrial workforce suffers from anxiety of job security, lack of social security, exploitation in the hands of contractors, low wages, unequal treatment by trade unions and often abusive behaviour of the permanent workers and supervisors, and consequently develops rebellious feelings *(Adapted from: All India Organisation of Employers', 2012).* A recent and perhaps the worst form of industrial unrest was witnessed in the Manesar plant of Maruti Suzuki India Ltd., where workers resorted to riotous behaviour, creating one of the most violent instances of strikes in the history of India's industrial relations. The immediate implication of such industrial unrests is in production and financial losses and damage of investors' confidence in the country. If left unchecked, such unrests are bound to send wrong signals to foreign and domestic investors, which will directly affect the country's economy and employment generation targets.

BACKDROP OF THE CONTRACT LABOUR (REGULATION AND ABOLITION) ACT, 1970

The Constitution of India mandates the State to improve the lot of its workforce. The Directive Principle of State Policy in Chapter IV has laid down principles that are fundamental in the governance of the country and it shall be the duty of the State to apply these principles in making laws. More specifically, Article 38 mandates the State to secure a social order for the promotion of welfare of the people and to establish an egalitarian society. According to Article 43, State should endeavour to secure, by suitable legislation or economic organisation or in any other way, to all workers, agricultural, industrial or otherwise, work, a living wage, conditions of work ensuring a decent standard of life and full enjoyment of leisure and social and cultural opportunities. Article 43A mandates the State to take steps by suitable legislation or in any other way to secure participation of workers in the management of undertakings, establishments or other organisations engaged in any industry.

In the previous chapters we have mentioned that the Government of India has adopted a two-pronged strategy, i.e., legislative measures and welfare schemes and programmes, for the promotion of welfare of the working class. A major landmark in the direction of attaining fair treatment to labour and industrial peace was the enactment of the Industrial Disputes Act, 1947. The growing size of contract labour in the industrial workforce and the probabilities of abuse and exploitation of contractual workers had necessitated the enactment of another piece of legislation. Hence the Contract Labour (Regulation and Abolition) Act, 1970 was introduced to deal with the abuses of contract labour system. The Parliament had adopted twin measures to curb the abuses of employment of contract labour: the first is to regulate employment of contract labour suitably, and the second is to abolish it in certain circumstances Adapted from: (*Steel Authority of India Ltd. and Others vs. National Union Water Front Workers and Others*).

Looking at the historical aspect of contract labour in India we can infer that as a practice, employing contract labour has its roots from time immemorial. However the size of contract labour in India has significantly expanded in the post-Independence period, with the expansion of construction activities following substantial investment in the Plans. During the early period of industrialisation, industrial establishments were plagued with problems of labour recruitment. Some of the most prominent inhibitors were low status of factory workers, lack of labour mobility, caste and religious taboo and language. Therefore they had to depend on "middlemen" who helped them in recruitment and control of labour. These middlemen or contractors were known by different names in various parts of the country, and they contributed significantly in the growth of contract labour.

Right from the emergence and growth of this segment of the workforce, the lot of contract labour was considered to be victims of exploitation in the hands of employers, mainly due to lack of organisation on their part. Besides such exploitation, the Workman's Breach of Contract Act, 1859 operated in holding such workers criminally responsible in the event of a breach of contract service *(Adapted from: All India Organisation of Employers', 2012)*. Miseries of contract labour had been growing with time, and soon caught the attention of the government. In 1860 the Whitley Commission recommended abolition of contract labour by implication. Subsequently the government constituted various committees to study the socio-economic conditions of contract labour. These included the Bombay Textile Labour Enquiry Committee (1938), the Bihar Labour Enquiry Committee (1941) and the Rege Committee (1946). All these committees reported the rampant practice of contract labour in various industries and unanimously condemned the practice. The Government of India responded to such recommendations and as a result of these findings, the scope of the definition of "workers" in the Factories Act (1948), the Mines Act (1952) and the Plantations Labour Act (1951) was enlarged to include contract labour. In the Second Five Year Plan the Planning Commission laid down the necessity of examining where contract labour could be progressively eliminated, securing gradual abolition of the contract system wherever feasible and ensuring that the displaced labour is provided with alternative employment.

The issue of contract labour came up at various meetings of tripartite committees in which State Governments were also represented. There was a general consensus of opinion on abolishing the system wherever possible and practicable, and that in cases where it could not be abolished altogether, the working conditions of contract labour should be regulated so as to ensure payment of wages and provision of essential amenities. Based on these views, the Contract Labour (Regulation and Abolition) Bill was passed by both the Houses of Parliament. The Contract Labour (Regulation and Abolition) Act received the assent of the President on 5th September 1970, and it came into force from 10th February 1971. Since enactment, it has been amended twice, as follows:

Spotlight

The Contract Labour (Regulation and Abolition) Act received the assent of the President on 5th September 1970 and came into force from 10th February 1971.

1. The Contract Labour (Regulation and Abolition) (Amendment) Act, 1986.
2. The Delegated Legislation Provisions (Amendment) Act, 2004.

As mentioned in *Dena Nath and Others vs. National Fertilizers Ltd. and Others* [(1992) AIR 457], the Statement of Objects and Reasons of the Act mentions that the system of employment of contract labour has tended itself to various abuses and the question of its abolition had been under consideration of the Government for a long time. A close review of the Statement shows that in respect of such categories as may be notified by the appropriate Government, in light of the prescribed criteria, contract labour will be abolished, and in respect of the other categories the service conditions of contract labour will be regulated. The Act serves a twofold purpose: it aims for regulation of the conditions of service of workers employed by the contractor who is engaged by a principal employer; and it also provides for the appropriate Government to abolish contract labour altogether in certain notified processes, operations or other works in any establishment.

ABOUT THE ACT

CHAPTER I: PRELIMINARY

Short Title, Extent, Commencement and Application (Section 1)

1. This Act may be called the Contract Labour (Regulation and Abolition) Act, 1970.
2. It extends to the whole of India.
3. It shall come into force on such date as the Central Government may, by notification in the Official Gazette, appoint and different dates may be appointed for different provisions of this Act.
4. It applies:
   (a) to every establishment in which 20 or more workmen are employed or were employed on any day of the preceding 12 months as contract labour;
   (b) to every contractor who employees or who employed, on any day of the preceding 12 months, 20 or more workmen:

   Provided that the appropriate Government may, after giving not less than 2 months' notice of its intention so to do, by notification in the Official Gazette, apply the provisions of this Act to any establishment or contractor employing such number of workmen less than 20 as may be specified in the notification.
5. (a) It shall not apply to establishments in which work only of an intermittent or casual nature is performed.
   (b) If a question arises whether work performed in an establishment is of an intermittent or casual nature, the appropriate Government shall decide that question after consultation with the Central Board or, as the case may be, a State Board, and its decision shall be final.

   Explanation For the purpose of this sub-section, work performed in an establishment shall not be deemed to be of an intermittent nature:
   (i) if it was performed for more than 120 in the preceding 12 months, or
   (ii) if it is of a seasonal character and is performed for more than 60 days in a year.

Spotlight

The Act applies to every establishment in which 20 or more workmen are (or were) employed on any day of the preceding 12 months as contract labour;

Definitions (Section 2)

1. In this Act, unless the context otherwise requires:

Appropriate Government [Section 2(1)(a)] Appropriate Government means:
(i) in relation to an establishment in respect of which the appropriate Government under the Industrial Disputes Act, 1947, is the Central Government, the Central Government;
(ii) in relation to any other establishment, the Government of the State in which that other establishment is situated.

Contract labour [Section 2(1)(b)] A workman shall be deemed to be employed as "contract labour" in or in connection with the work of an establishment when he is hired in or in connection with such work by or through a contractor, with or without the knowledge of the principal employer;

Spotlight

A workman shall be deemed to be employed as "contract labour" as per Section 2(1)(b) when he is hired by or through a contractor, with or without the knowledge of the principal employer.

CASE CORNER

As per the Supreme Court in *Steel Authority of India Ltd. and Others vs. National Union Water Front Workers and Others*, in order to hold that the Central Government is the appropriate Government in relation to an establishment, the court must be satisfied that the particular industry in question is carried on by or under the authority of the Central Government. Keeping this aspect in mind, it would be clear that the Central Government will be the appropriate Government under the Contract Labour (Regulation and Abolition) Act, 1970 and the Industrial Disputes Act, 1947, provided the industry in question is carried on by a Central Government company or an undertaking under the authority of the Central Government. Such an authority may be conferred, either by a Statute, or by virtue of relationship of principal and agent or delegation of power.

Incidentally, in this case, the Supreme Court has overruled the judgment on *Air India Statutory Corporation vs. United Labour Union and Others*, and has held that neither Section 10 of the Act nor any other provision in the Act expressly or by necessary implication provides for automatic absorption of contract labour on issuing a notification by the appropriate Government under sub-section (1) of Section 10 prohibiting employment of contract labour in any process or operation or other work in any establishment. Thus the principal employer cannot be required to order absorption of contract labour working in the concerned establishment.

(Adapted from: www.indiankanoon.org/doc/277653/ accessed on 27/6/2014.)

As stated in *Shri J.R. Prabhu, Principal, College of Agricultural Banking, Pune vs. The State Represented by Shri Satpute* [(2001) 2 BOMLR 803], workers employed by catering contractors are workmen as defined by Section 2(1)(i) of the Act, and since employed through contractor, they are contract labour within the purview of Section 2(1)(b) of the Act. *(Adapted from: www.indiankanoon.org/doc/874874/ accessed on 26/6/2014.)*

Spotlight

The definition of contractor, as per Section 2(1)(c), includes a sub-contractor;

Contractor [Section 2(1)(c)] Contractor, in relation to an establishment, means a person who undertakes to produce a given result for the establishment, other than a mere supply of goods of articles of manufacture to such establishment, through contract labour or who supplies contract labour for any work of the establishment and includes a sub-contractor;

Controlled industry [Section 2(1)(d)] Controlled industry means any industry the control of which by the Union has been declared by any Central Act to be expedient in the public interest;

Establishment [Section 2(1)(e)] Establishment means:

(i) any office or department of the Government or a local authority, or

(ii) any place where any industry, trade, business, manufacture or occupation is carried on;

Prescribed [Section 2(1)(f)] Prescribed means prescribed by rules made under this Act;

Principal employer [Section 2(1)(g)] Principal employer means:

(i) in relation to any office or department of the Government or a local authority, the head of that office or department or such other officer as the Government or the local authority, as the case may be, may specify in this behalf,

(ii) in a factory, the owner or occupier of the factory and where a person has been named as the manager of the factory under the Factories Act, 1948 the person so named,

(iii) in a mine, the owner or agent of the mine and where a person has been named as the manager of the mine, the person so named,

(iv) in any other establishment, any person responsible for the supervision and control of the establishment.

Explanation For the purpose of sub-clause (iii) of this clause, the expressions "mine", "owner" and "agent" shall have the meanings respectively assigned to them in clause (j), clause (l) and clause (c) of sub-section (1) of Section 2 of the Mines Act, 1952;

In *Shri J.R. Prabhu, Principal, College of Agricultural Banking, Pune vs. The State Represented by Shri Satpute* [(2001) 2 BOMLR 803], the Court has pointed out that sub-clause (g) of Section 2(1) of the Act classifies the group of "principal employers" into four categories. Although the fourth clause is a residuary clause, on reference to sub-clauses (i) and (ii), it can be seen that Government departments or local authorities on one hand and factories, etc. on the other, which are grouped separately by the definition of "establishment", are also kept on different pedestal while defining "principal employer". In relation to any office or department of the Government or a local authority, the head of that office or department or such other officer as the Government or the local authority, as the case may be, may specify in this behalf, as the principal employer.

(Adapted from: www.indiankanoon.org/doc/874874/ accessed on 26/6/2014.)

Wages [Section 2(1)(h)] Wages shall have the meaning assigned to it in clause (vi) of Section 2 of the Payment of Wages Act, 1936;

Workman [Section 2(1)(i)] Workman means any person employed in or in connection with the work of any establishment to do any skilled, semiskilled or un-skilled manual, supervisory, or clerical work for hire or reward, whether the terms of employment be express or implied, but does not include any such person–

> **Spotlight**
> A person employed in managerial or administrative capacity is not a workman as per the Act.

(A) who is employed mainly in a managerial or administrative capacity; or

(B) who, being employed in a supervisory capacity draws wages exceeding ₹500 per mensem or exercises, either by the nature of the duties attached to the office or by reason of the powers vested in him, functions mainly of a managerial nature; or

(C) who is an out-worker, that is to say, a person to whom any articles or materials are given out by or on behalf of the principal employer to be made up, cleaned, washed, altered, ornamented, finished, repaired, adapted or otherwise processed for sale for the purposes of the trade or business of the principal employer and the process is to be carried out either in the home of the out-worker or in some other premises, not being premises under the control and management of the principal employer.

2. Any reference in this Act to a law, which is not in force in the State of Jammu and Kashmir, shall, in relation to that State, be construed as a reference to the corresponding law, if any, in force in that State.

CHAPTER II: THE ADVISORY BOARDS

Central Advisory Board (Section 3)

1. The Central Government shall, as soon as may be, constitute a board to be called the Central Advisory Contract Labour Board (hereinafter referred to as the Central Board) to advise the Central Government on such matters arising out of the administration of this Act as may be referred to it and to carry out other functions assigned to it under this Act.
2. The Central Board shall consist of:
   (a) a Chairman to be appointed by the Central Government;
   (b) the Chief Labour Commissioner (Central), *ex-officio*;
   (c) such number of members, not exceeding 17 but not less than 11, as the Central Government may nominate to represent that Government, the railways, the coal industry, the mining industry, the contractors, the workmen and any other interests which, the opinion of the Central Government, ought to be represented on the Central Board.
3. The number of persons to be appointed as members from each of the categories specified in sub-section (2), the term of office and other conditions of service of, the procedure to be followed in the discharge of their functions by, and the manner of filling vacancies among, the members of the Central Board shall be such as may be prescribed:

   Provided that the number of members nominated to represent the workmen shall not be less than the number of members nominated to represent the principal employers and the contractors.

Spotlight

As per Section 3(1), the Central Advisory Contract Labour Board shall advise the Central Government on matters arising out of the administration of this Act as referred to it.

State Advisory Board (Section 4)

1. The State Government may constitute a board to be called the State Advisory Contract Labour Board (hereinafter referred to as the State Board) to advise the State Government on such matters arising out of the administration of this Act as may be referred to it and to carry out other functions assigned to it under this Act.
2. The State Board shall consist of:
   (a) a Chairman to be appointed by the State Government;
   (b) the Labour Commissioner, *ex-officio*, or in his absence any other officer nominated by the State Government in that behalf;
   (c) such number of members, not exceeding 11 but not less than 9, as the State Government may nominate to represent that Government, the industry, the contractors, the workmen and any other interests which, in the opinion of the State Government, ought to be represented on the State Board.
3. The number of persons to be appointed as members from each of the categories specified in sub-section (2), the term of office and other conditions of service of, the procedure to be followed in the discharge of their functions by, and the manner of filling vacancies among, the members of the State Board shall be such as may be prescribed:

   Provided that the number of members nominated to represent the workmen shall not be less than the number of members nominated to represent the principal employers and the contractors.

Power to Constitute Committees (Section 5)

1. The Central Board or the State Board, as the case may be, may constitute such committees and for such purpose or purposes as it may think fit.
2. The committee constituted under sub-section (1) shall meet at such times and places and shall observe such rules of procedure in regard to the transaction of business at its meetings as may be prescribed.
3. The members of a committee shall be paid such fees and allowances for attending its meetings as may be prescribed:

   Provided that no fees shall, be payable to a member who is an officer of Government or of any corporation established by any law for the time being in force.

CHAPTER III: REGISTRATION OF ESTABLISHMENTS EMPLOYING CONTRACT LABOUR

Appointment of Registering Officers (Section 6)

The appropriate Government may, by an order notified in the Official Gazette:

(a) appoint such persons, being Gazetted Officers of Government, as it thinks fit to be registering officers for the purposes of this chapter; and

(b) define the limits, within which a registering officer shall exercise the powers conferred on him by or under this Act.

Registration of Certain Establishments (Section 7)

1. Every principal employer of an establishment to which this Act applies shall, within such period as the appropriate Government may, by notification in the Official Gazette, fix in this behalf with respect to establishments generally or with respect to any class of them, make an application to the registering officer in the prescribed manner for registration of the establishment:

   Provided that the registering officer may entertain any such application for registration after expiry of the period fixed in this behalf, if the registering officer is satisfied that the applicant was prevented by sufficient cause from making the application in time.
2. If the application for registration is complete in all respects, the registering officer shall register the establishment and issue to the principal employer of the establishment a certificate of registration containing such particulars as may be prescribed.

Revocation of Registration in Certain Cases (Section 8)

If the registering officer is satisfied, either on a reference made to him in this behalf or otherwise, that the registration of any establishment has been obtained by misrepresentation or suppression of any material fact, or that for any other reason the registration has become useless or ineffective and, therefore, requires to be revoked, the registering officer may, after giving an opportunity to the principal employer of the establishment to be heard and with the previous approval of the appropriate Government, revoke the registration.

Effect of Non-registration (Section 9)

No principal employer of an establishment, to which this Act applies, shall:

(a) in the case of an establishment required to be registered under Section 7, but which has not been registered within the time fixed for the purpose under that section,

(b) in the case of an establishment the registration in respect of which has been revoked under Section 8,

employ contract labour in the establishment after the expiry of the period referred to in clause (a) or after the revocation of registration referred to in clause (b), as the case may be.

Prohibition of Employment of Contract Labour (Section 10)

1. Notwithstanding anything contained in this Act, the appropriate Government may, after consultation with the Central Board or, as the case may be, a State Board, prohibit, by notification in the Official Gazette, employment of contract labour in any process, operation or other work in any establishment.
   In *Jamshedpur Contractors' Workers' Union vs. State of Bihar and Others* [(1991) SCC Supl. (1)158], the contract workers engaged by the management of Tata Iron and Steel Company Ltd., Jamshedpur in various permanent and regular nature of work sought permanent employment under the principal employer. The dispute was referred by the State Government under Section 10 of the Industrial Disputes Act, 1947 to the Industrial Tribunal. The Tribunal held that the workmen constituted contract labour and, therefore, the reference was not maintainable. It further held that action, if any, had to be taken under Section 10 of the Contract Labour (Regulation and Abolition) Act, 1970, power to take steps for which is vested in the State Government and not in the Tribunal.

Spotlight

Section 10(1) empowers the appropriate Government to prohibit, by notification in the Official Gazette, employment of contract labour in any process, operation or other work in any establishment.

(Adapted from: www.indiankanoon.org/doc/523430/ accessed on 25/6/2014.)

CASE CORNER

In *Air India Statutory Corporation vs. United Labour Union and Others*, the appellants were engaged as contract labour for sweeping, cleaning, dusting and watching of the building owned and occupied by the appellant. The appellant had obtained on 20th September 1971 a certificate of registration from the Regional Labour Commissioner (Central) under Contract Labour (Regulation and Abolition) Act, 1970 (hereafter, the Act). The Central Government, exercising the power under Section 10 of the Act, on the basis of recommendation and in consultation with the Central Advisory Board constituted under Section 10(1) of the Act, issued a notification on 9th December 1976, prohibiting employment of contract labour on and from 9th December 1976 for sweeping, cleaning, dusting and watching of buildings owned or occupied by the establishment in respect of which the appropriate Government is the Central Government. However, the said prohibition was not to apply to outside cleaning and other maintenance operations of multi-storeyed building where such cleaning or maintenance cannot be carried out expect with specialised experience.

The Court turned down the request that the management may be left with the discretion to absorb contract labour on the ground that this would keep the workmen at the whim of the establishment. In this behalf, the Court has recapitulated that on abolition of the contract labour system, by necessary implication, the principal employer is under statutory obligation to absorb contract labour. The linkage between contractor and employees was snapped and the direct relationship between principal employer and contract labour as its employees stood restored. Considered from this perspective, all the workmen in the respective services working on contract labour were required to be absorbed in the establishment of the appellant.

(Adapted from: www.indiankanoon.org/doc/784921/ accessed on 24/6/2014.)

2. Before issuing any notification under sub-section (1) in relation to an establishment, the appropriate Government shall have regard to the conditions of work and benefits provided for the contract labour in that establishment and other relevant factors, such as:
   (a) whether the process, operation or other work is incidental to, or necessary for the industry, trade, business, manufacture, or occupation that is carried on in the establishment:
   (b) whether it is of perennial nature, that is to say, it is of sufficient duration having regard to the nature of industry, trade, business, manufacture or occupation carried on in that establishment;
   (c) whether it is done ordinarily through regular workmen in that establishment or an establishment similar thereto;
   (d) whether it is sufficient to employ considerable number of whole-time workmen.

Explanation If a question arises whether any process or operation or other work is of perennial nature, the decision of the appropriate Government thereon shall be final.

It appears to the Court in *Shri J.R. Prabhu, Principal, College of Agricultural Banking, Pune vs. The State Represented by Shri Satpute* [(2001) 2 BOMLR 803] that the legislation did not feel it expedient to do away with contract labour altogether. There are several fields of employment in which it is otherwise not possible to have continuous employment, hence considering the necessities of the situation, the Contract Labour (Regulation and Abolition) Act, 1970 provides for continuation of contract labour. The legislation in the enactment itself has provided various provisions pertaining to the working conditions of contract labour and has also provided employment of contract labour being necessary in the interest of the concerned industry. In the event of contract labour being employed in an establishment for seasonal work, the question of its abolition would obviously not arise. But in case the same is of perennial nature, the Legislature steps in to abolish the same.

(Adapted from: www.indiankanoon.org/doc/874874/ accessed on 26/6/2014.)

CASE C

In *BHEL Workers' Association Hardwar and Others vs. Union of India and Others* [(1985) SCR(2) 611] a writ petition was filed by the workmen under Article 32 of the Constitution. It was contended by the workmen's association that out of the 16,000-odd workmen working within the premises of the respondent-company, about a thousand workers were treated as contract labour. They were placed under the control and at the mercy of contractors. Though they did the same work as the workers directly employed by the company, they were not paid the same wages, nor were their conditions of service same as that of the latter. It was further alleged that the management paid to the contractors, and in turn, the contractors paid salary to them, after deducting substantial commission, and the wages paid did not bear comparison to the wages paid to those directly employed by the company. Hence it was alleged that the rights of the contract workers were infringed under Articles 14 and 19(1)(f) of the Constitution. Further, a declaration was sought from the Court that the system of contract labour prevalent in the respondent-company was illegal, and that the contract employees were direct employees of the respondent-company and were entitled to equal pay as the workmen directly employed.

The respondent-company opposed the petition by contending that on behalf of the company certain jobs, though required to be done within the plant area, could more conveniently and efficiently be done on a contract basis, and this was actually due to the introduction of a new technology for expansion of production with foreign collaboration. The jobs themselves were entrusted to contractors and it was not appropriate to say that contractors merely supplied labour. They were required to do the total job and payment was made on the basis of the quantum of work involved and not on the basis of the workers employed by the contractor.

The Court dismissed the writ petition by holding that the Contract Labour (Regulation and Abolition) Act, 1970 (hereafter, the Act) does not provide for the total abolition of contract labour, but for its abolition only in certain circumstances, and for the regulation of the employment of contract labour in certain establishments. The Act is not confined to private employers only. The Parliament has not abolished contract labour but has provided for its abolition by the Central Government in appropriate cases under Section 10 of the Act. It is not for the court to enquire into the question and to decide whether the employment of contract labour in any process, operation or other work in any establishment should be abolished or not. This is a matter for the decision of the Government after considering the matters required to be considered under Section 10 of the Act.

(Adapted from: www.indiankanoon.org/doc/1114147/ accessed on 23/6/2014.)

CHAPTER IV: LICENSING OF CONTRACTORS

Appointment of Licensing Officers (Section 11)

The appropriate Government may, by an order notified in the Official Gazette:

(a) appoint such persons, being Gazetted Officers of Government, as it thinks fit to be licensing officers for the purposes of this Chapter; and

(b) define the limits, within which a licensing officer shall exercise the powers conferred on licensing officers by or under this Act.

Licensing of Contractors (Section 12)

1. With effect from such date as the appropriate Government may, by notification in the Official Gazette, appoint, no contractor to whom this Act applies, shall undertake or execute any work through contract labour except under and in accordance with a licence issued in that behalf by the licensing officer.

Spotlight

According to Section 12(1), no contractor to whom this Act applies, shall undertake or execute any work through contract labour except under and in accordance with a licence issued in that behalf by the licensing officer.

In *Labourers Working on Salal Hydro-Project vs. State of Jammu and Kashmir and Others* [(1983) SCR (2) 473] the Court held that not only a contractor but also a sub-contractor who comes within the definition of the term "contractor" in Section 2(c) of the Contract Labour Regulation and Abolition) Act, 1970, is bound to obtain a licence under sub-section (1) of Section 12 thereof, before he can undertake or execute any work through contract labour. If sub-contractors undertake or execute any work through contract labour without obtaining a licence under sub-section (1) of Section 12, they would be guilty of criminal offence punishable under Section 23 or 24.

(Adapted from: www.indiankanoon.org/doc/320547/ accessed on 24/6/2014.)

2. Subject to the provisions of this Act, a licence under sub-section (1) may contain such conditions including, in particular, conditions as to hours of work, fixation of wages and other essential amenities in respect of contract labour as the appropriate Government may deem fit to impose in accordance with the rules, if any, made under Section 35 and shall be issued on payment of such fees and on the deposit of such sum, if any, as security for the due performance of the conditions as may be prescribed.

Grant of Licences (Section 13)

1. Every application for the grant of a licence under sub-section of Section 12 shall be made in the prescribed form and shall contain the particulars regarding the location of the establishment, the nature of process, operation or work for which contract labour is to be employed and such other particulars as may be prescribed.
2. The licensing officer may make such investigation in respect of the application received under sub-section (1) and in making any such investigation the licensing officer shall follow such procedure as may be prescribed.
3. A licence granted under this Chapter shall be valid for the period specified therein and may be renewed from time to time for such period and on payment of such fees and on such conditions as may be prescribed.

Revocation, Suspension and Amendment of Licences (Section 14)

1. If the licensing officer is satisfied, either on a reference made to him in this behalf or otherwise, that:
   (a) a licence granted under Section 12 has been obtained by misrepresentation or suppression of any material fact, or
   (b) the holder of a licence has, without reasonable cause, failed to comply with the conditions subject to which the licence has been granted or has contravened any of the provisions of this Act or the rules made thereunder,

   then, without prejudice to any other penalty to which the holder of the licence may be liable under this Act, the licensing officer may, after giving the holder of the licence an opportunity of showing cause, revoke or suspend the licence or forfeit the sum, if any, or any portion thereof deposited as security for the due performance of the conditions subject to which the licence has been granted.
2. Subject to any rules that may be made in this behalf, the licensing officer may vary or amend a licence granted under Section 12.

Appeal (Section 15)

1. Any person aggrieved by an order made under Section 7, Section 8, Section 12 or Section 14 may, within 30 days from the date on which the order is communicated to him, prefer an appeal to an appellate officer who shall be a person nominated in this behalf by the appropriate Government:

   Provided that the appellate officer may entertain the appeal after the expiry of the said period of 30 days, if he is satisfied that the appellant was prevented by sufficient cause from filing the appeal in time.
2. On receipt of an appeal under sub-section (1), the appellate officer shall, after giving the appellant an opportunity of being heard dispose of the appeal as expeditiously as possible.

CHAPTER V: WELFARE AND HEALTH OF CONTRACT LABOUR

Canteens (Section 16)

1. The appropriate Government may make rules requiring that in every establishment:
   (a) to which this Act applies,
   (b) wherein work requiring employment of contract labour is likely to continue for such period as may be prescribed, and
   (c) wherein contract labour numbering 100 or more is ordinarily employed by a contractor,

   1 or more canteens shall be provided and maintained by the contractor for the use of such contract labour.
2. Without prejudice to the generality of the foregoing power, such rules may provide for:
   (a) the date by which the canteens shall be provided;
   (b) the number of canteens that shall be provided, and the standards in respect of construction, accommodation, furniture and other equipment of the canteens; and
   (c) the foodstuffs which may be served therein and the charges which may be made thereof.

Rest-rooms (Section 17)

Spotlight

Sections 16 to 19 mandate provision of canteens, restrooms, first-aid and other facilities in an establishment employing contract labour.

1. In every place wherein contract labour is required to halt at night in connection with the work of an establishment:
   (a) to which this Act applies, and
   (b) in which work requiring employment of contract labour is likely to continue for such period as may be prescribed,

   there shall be provided and maintained by the contractor for the use of the contract labour such number of rest-rooms or such other suitable alternative accommodation within such time as may be prescribed.
2. The rest-rooms or the alternative accommodation to be provided under sub-section (1) shall be sufficiently lighted and ventilated and shall be maintained in a clean and comfortable condition.

Other Facilities (Section 18)

It shall be the duty of every contractor employing contract labour in connection with the work of an establishment to which this Act applies, to provide and maintain:

(a) a sufficient supply of wholesome drinking water for the contract labour at convenient places;
(b) a sufficient number of latrines and urinals of the prescribed types so situated as to be convenient and accessible to the contract labour in the establishment; and
(c) washing facilities.

Spotlight

If any amenity mandatory under sections 16 to 19 is not provided by the contractor within the time prescribed, such amenity shall be provided by the principal employer within prescribed time, as per Section 20(1).

First-aid Facilities (Section 19)

There shall be provided and maintained by the contractor so as to be readily accessible during all working hours a first-aid box equipped with the prescribed contents at every place where contract labour is employed by him.

Liability of Principal Employer in Certain Cases (Section 20)

1. If any amenity required to be provided under Section 16, Section 17, Section 18 or Section 19 for the benefit of the contract labour employed in an establishment is not provided by the contractor within the time prescribed thereof, such amenity shall be provided by the principal employer within such time as may be prescribed.
2. All expenses incurred by the principal employer in providing the amenity may be recovered by the principal employer from the contractor either by deduction from any amount payable to the contractor under any contract or as a debt payable by the contractor.

CASE CORNER

In *People's Union for Democratic Rights and Others vs. Union of India and Others* [(1983) SCR (1) 456], the various authorities to whom the execution of the different projects of the Asian Games was entrusted, had engaged contractors for the purpose of carrying out construction work of the projects. They were registered as principal employers under Section 7 of the Contract Labour (Regulation and Abolition) Act, 1970 (or, "the Act").These contractors engaged workers through *jamadars* who brought them from different parts of India. It was alleged in a Public Interest Litigation that there was violation of the provisions of the Act, which resulted in deprivation and exploitation of the workers and denial of their right to proper living condition and medical and other facilities under the Act.

The Court held that the rights and benefits conferred on workmen employed by a contractor under the provisions of the Contract Labour (Regulation and Abolition) Act, 1970 and the Inter-State Migrant Workmen (Regulation of Employment and Conditions of Service) Act, 1979 are clearly intended to ensure basic human dignity to workmen. Further, such deprivation of any of these rights and benefits under the provisions of these two pieces of social welfare legislation would clearly be a violation of Article 21 by the Union of India. Hence, the Delhi Administration and the Delhi Development Authority as principal employers are made statutorily responsible for securing such rights and benefits to workmen.

(Adapted from www.indiankanoon.org/doc/496663/ accessed on 23/6/2014.)

Responsibility for Payment of Wages (Section 21)

1. A contractor shall be responsible for payment of wages to each worker employed by him as contract labour and such wages shall be paid before the expiry of such period as may be prescribed.

2. Every principal employer shall nominate a representative duly authorised by him to be present at the time of disbursement of wages by the contractor and it shall be the duty of such representative to certify the amounts paid as wages in such manner as may be prescribed.
3. It shall be the duty of the contractor to ensure the disbursement of wages in the presence of the authorised representative of the principal employer.

Spotlight

As per Section 21(3), the contractor must ensure the disbursement of wages in the presence of the authorised representative of the principal employer.

In *People's Union for Democratic Rights and Others vs. Union of India and Others* [(1983) SCR (1) 456], the Court has held that under sub-section (3) of Section 21 of the Act, wages due to workmen employed by the 'piece-wagers' or sub-contractors must be paid directly to the workmen without the intervention of *khatedars*, and no deductions can be made from the wages on account of any advances alleged to have been made by the *khatedars* to the workmen.

(Adapted from: www.indiankanoon.org/doc/496663/ accessed on 23/6/2014.)

4. In case the contractor fails to make payment of wages within the prescribed period or makes short payment, then the principal employer shall be liable to make payment of wages in full or the unpaid balance due, as the case may be, to the contract labour employed by the contractor and recover the amount so paid from the contractor either by deduction from any amount payable to the contractor under any contract or as a debt payable by the contractor.

In *Hindustan Steelworks Construction Ltd. vs. Commissioner of Labour and Others* [(1996) LabIC 2520] it has been laid down that the definition of wages under Section 2 of the Contract Labour (Regulation and Abolition) Act, 1970 (or, the Act) read with that under the Payment of Wages Act, 1936 does not cover any additional amount found payable under Rule 25(v)(a) of the Andhra Pradesh Contract Labour (Regulation and Abolition) Rules, 1971 if the principal employer has its own workers doing similar work. More specifically, one of the conditions that Rule 25 imposes on the contractor, subject to which a licence is granted to him, is that he shall not pay to the contract labour in his employment wages which are lower than the wages paid by the principal employer to his own workers which do the same or similar kind of work. Such contingencies are not covered by Section 21 of the Act. The contractor cannot recover any such additional amount from the principal employer under Section 21(4).

(Adapted from www.indiankanoon.org/doc/795632/ accessed on 25/6/2014.)

CHAPTER VI: PENALTIES AND PROCEDURE

Obstructions (Section 22)

1. Whoever obstructs an inspector in the discharge of his duties under this Act or refuses or wilfully neglects to afford the inspector any reasonable facility for making any inspection, examination, inquiry or investigation authorised by or under this Act in relation to an establishment to which, or a contractor to whom, this Act applies, shall be punishable with imprisonment for a term which may extend to 3 months, or with fine which may extend to ₹500, or with both.

2. Whoever wilfully refuses to produce on the demand of an inspector any register or other document kept in pursuance of this Act, or prevents or attempts to prevent or does anything which he has reason to believe is likely to prevent any person from appearing before or being examined by an inspector acting in pursuance of his duties under this Act, shall be punishable with imprisonment for a term which may extend to 3 months, or with fine which may extend to ₹500, or with both.

Contravention of Provisions Regarding Employment of Contract Labour (Section 23)

Whoever contravenes any provision of this Act or of any rules made thereunder prohibiting, restricting or regulating the employment of contract labour, or contravenes any condition of a licence granted under this Act, shall be punishable with imprisonment for a term which may extend to 3 months, or with fine which may extend to ₹1,000, or with both, and in the case of a continuing contravention with an additional fine which may extend to ₹100 for every day during which such contravention continues after conviction for the first such contravention.

Spotlight

As per Section 23, contravention of any provision or of any rules prohibiting, restricting or regulating the employment of contract labour, or of any condition of a licence granted, would be punishable with imprisonment up to 3 months, or with fine up to ₹1,000, or with both.

Other Offences (Section 24)

If any person contravenes any of the provisions of this Act or of any rules made thereunder for which no other penalty is elsewhere provided, he shall be punishable with imprisonment for a term which may extend to 3 months, or with fine which may extend to ₹1,000, or with both.

Offences by Companies (Section 25)

1. If the person committing an offence under this Act is a company, the company as well as every person in charge of, and responsible to, the company for the conduct of its business at the time of the commission of the offence shall be deemed to be guilty of the offence and shall be liable to be proceeded against and punished accordingly:

   Provided that nothing contained in this sub-section shall render any such person liable to any punishment if he proves that the offence was committed without his knowledge or that he exercised all due diligence to prevent the commission of such offence.
2. Notwithstanding anything contained in sub-section (1), where an offence under this Act has been committed by a company and it is proved that the offence has been committed with the consent or connivance of, or that the commission of the offence is attributable to any neglect on the part of any director, manager, managing agent, or any other officer of the company, such director, manager, managing agent or such other officer shall also be deemed to be guilty of that offence and shall be liable to be proceeded against and punished accordingly.

Explanation For the purpose of this section:

(a) "company" means any body corporate and includes a firm or other association of individuals; and

(b) "director", in relation to a firm, means a partner in the firm.

Cognizance of Offences (Section 26)

No court shall take cognizance of any offence under this Act except on a complaint made by, or with the previous sanction in writing of, the inspector and no court inferior to that of a Presidency Magistrate or a Magistrate of the first class shall try any offence punishable under this Act.

Limitation of Prosecutions (Section 27)

No court shall take cognizance of an offence punishable under this Act unless the complaint thereof is made within 3 months from the date on which the alleged commission of the offence came to the knowledge of an inspector:

Provided that where the offence consists of disobeying a written order made by an inspector, complaint thereof may be made within 6 months of the date on which the offence is alleged to have been committed.

CHAPTER VII: MISCELLANEOUS

Inspecting Staff (Section 28)

1. The appropriate Government may, by notification in the Official Gazette, appoint such persons as it thinks fit to be inspectors for the purposes of this Act, and define the local limits within which they shall exercise their powers under this Act.
2. Subject to any rules made in this behalf, an inspector may, within the local limits for which he is appointed:
   (a) enter, at all reasonable hours, with such assistance (if any), being persons in the service of the government or any local or other public authority as he thinks fit, any premises or place where contract labour is employed, for the purpose of examining any register or record or notices required to be kept or exhibited by or under this Act or rules made thereunder, and require the production thereof for inspection;
   (b) examine any person whom he finds in any such premises or place and who, he has reasonable cause to believe, is a workman employed therein;
   (c) require any person giving out work and any workman, to give any information, which is in his power to give with respect to the names and addresses of the persons to, for and from whom the work is given out or received, and with respect to the payments to be made for the work;
   (d) seize or take copies of such register, record of wages or notices or portions thereof as he may consider relevant in respect of an offence under this Act which he has reason to believe has been committed by the principal employer or contractor; and
   (e) exercise such other powers as may be prescribed.
3. Any person required to produce any document or thing or to give any information required by an inspector under sub-section (2) shall be deemed to be legally bound to do so within the meaning of Section 175 and Section 176 of the Indian Penal Code.
4. The provisions of the Code of Criminal Procedure, 1898, shall, so far as may be, apply to any search or seizure under sub-section (2) as they apply to any search or seizure made under the authority of a warrant issued under Section 98 of the said Code.

Registers and other Records to be Maintained (Section 29)

1. Every principal employer and every contractor shall maintain such registers and records giving such particulars of contract labour employed, the nature of work performed by the contract labour, the rates of wages paid to the contract labour and such other particulars in such form as may be prescribed.
2. Every principal employer and every contractor shall keep exhibited in such manner as may be prescribed within the premises of the establishment where the contract labour is employed, notices in the prescribed form containing particulars about the hours of work, nature of duty and such other information as may be prescribed.

Effect of Laws and Agreements Inconsistent with this Act (Section 30)

1. The provisions of this Act shall have effect notwithstanding anything inconsistent therewith contained in any other law or in the terms of any agreement or contract of service, or in any standing orders applicable to the establishment whether made before or after the commencement of this Act:

   Provided that where under any such agreement, contract of service or standing orders the contract labour employed in the establishment are entitled to benefits in respect of any matter which are more favourable to them than those to which they would be entitled under this Act, the contract labour shall continue to be entitled to the more favourable benefits in respect of that matter, notwithstanding that they receive benefits in respect of other matters under this Act.
2. Nothing contained in this Act shall be construed as precluding any such contract labour from entering into an agreement with the principal employer or the contractor, as the case may be, for granting them rights or privileges in respect of any matter, which are more favourable to them than those to which they would be entitled under this Act.

Power to Exempt in Special Cases (Section 31)

The appropriate Government may, in the case of an emergency, direct, by notification in the Official Gazette, that subject to such conditions and restrictions, if any, and for such period or periods, as may be specified in the notification, all or any of the provisions of this Act or the rules made thereunder shall not apply to any establishment or class of establishments or any class of contractors.

Spotlight

The appropriate Government may, in the case of an emergency, direct that all or any of the provisions of this Act or the rules made thereunder shall not apply to any establishment or class of establishments or any class of contractors, as per Section 31.

Protection of Action Taken under this Act (Section 32)

1. No suit, prosecution or other legal proceedings shall lie against any registering officer, licensing officer or any other Government servant or against any member of the Central Board or the State Board, as the case may be, for anything which is in good faith done or intended to be done in pursuance of this Act or any rule or order made thereunder.
2. No suit or other legal proceeding shall lie against the Government for any damage caused or likely to be caused by anything which is in good faith done or intended to be done in pursuance of this Act or any rule or order made thereunder.

Power to Give Directions (Section 33)

The Central Government may give directions to the Government of any State as to the carrying into execution in the State of the provisions contained in this Act.

Power to Remove Difficulties (Section 34)

If any difficulty arises in giving effect to the provisions of this Act, the Central Government may, by order published in the Official Gazette, make such provisions not inconsistent with the provisions of this Act, as appears to it to be necessary or expedient for removing the difficulty.

Power to Make Rules (Section 35)

Spotlight

As per Section 35(1), the appropriate Government may make rules for carrying out the purposes of this Act.

1. The appropriate Government may, subject to the condition of previous publication, make rules for carrying out the purposes of this Act.
2. In particular, and without prejudice to the generality of the foregoing power, such rules may provide for all or any of the following matters, namely:
   - (a) the number of persons to be appointed as members representing various interests on the Central Board and the State Board, the term of their office and other conditions of service, the procedure to be followed in the discharge of their functions and the manner of filling vacancies;
   - (b) the times and places of the meetings of any committee constituted under this Act, the procedure to be followed at such meetings including the quorum necessary for the transaction of business, and the fees and allowances that may be paid to the members of a committee;
   - (c) the manner in which establishments may be registered under Section 7, the levy of a fee thereof and the form of certificate of registration;
   - (d) the form of application for the grant or renewal of a licence under Section 13 and the particulars it may contain;
   - (e) the manner in which an investigation is to be made in respect of an application for the grant of a licence and the matters to be taken into account in granting or refusing a licence;
   - (f) the form of a licence which may be granted or renewed under Section 12 and the conditions subject to which the licence may be granted or renewed, the fees to be levied for the grant or renewal of a licence and the deposit of any sum as security for the performance of such conditions;
   - (g) the circumstances under which licences may be varied or amended under Section 14;
   - (h) the form and manner in which appeals may be filed under Section 15 and the procedure to be followed by appellate officers in disposing of the appeals;
   - (i) the time within which facilities required by this Act to be provided and maintained may be so provided by the contractor and in case of default on the part of the contractor, by the principal employer;
   - (j) the number and types of canteens, rest rooms, latrines and urinals that should be provided and maintained;
   - (k) the type of equipment that should be provided in the first-aid boxes;
   - (l) the period within which wages payable to contract labour should be paid by the contractor under sub-section (1) Section 21;
   - (m) the form of registers and records to be maintained by principal employers and contractors;

(n) the submission of returns, forms in which, and the authorities to which, such returns, may be submitted;

(o) the collection of any information or statistics in relation to contract labour; and

(p) any other matter which has to be, or may be, prescribed under this Act.

3. Every rule made by the Central Government under this Act shall be laid as soon as may be after it is made, before each House of Parliament while it is in session for a total period of 30 days which may be comprised in 1 session or in 2 successive sessions, and if before the expiry of the session in which it is so laid or the session immediately following, both Houses agree in making any modification in the rule or both Houses agree that the rule should not be made, the rule shall thereafter have effect only in such modified form or be of no effect, as the case may be; so, however, that any such modification or annulment shall be without prejudice to the validity of anything previously done under that rule.

ADMINISTRATION OF THE ACT

The Contract Labour (Regulation and Abolition) Act, 1970 is enforced through the Central Industrial Relations Machinery (CIRM).

RECENT INITIATIVES

The Labour Bureau, Ministry of Labour & Employment, has been conducting all-India, industry-specific Contract Labour Surveys since 1956-1957. These surveys aim at studying the extent and nature of problems and working conditions of contract labour employed in different segments of industries vis-à-vis the provisions given in the Act. Under these surveys, information is collected on parameters like employment, wages and earnings, working conditions, labour welfare, social security, industrial relations, etc. So far 45 surveys have been conducted in 39 industries (including repeat surveys conducted in 6 industries, *viz.* iron ore mines, rice milling, petroleum refineries and oil fields, building and construction, iron and steel and mica mines). Reports on all these surveys have been released.

Spotlight

Contract Labour Surveys on all-India, industry-specific basis are conducted by the Labour Bureau, Ministry of Labour & Employment since 1956-1957.

The Government of India has tried to bring about effective compliance mechanisms in the Contract Labour (Regulation and Abolition) Act, 1970, and in the Rules, 1971 from time to time for safeguarding the interest of contract workers. But the bitter reality is that the Government itself employs more contract labour than the private sector; almost 32 per cent of the labour force in the public sector is on contract, as against 30 per cent in the private sector, while average wage of contract labour in public sector at ₹185.28 is higher than that paid by the private sector at ₹143.45. *(Contract Labour: Govt. Gains More, The Economic Times, 10th March 2011.)*

A large number of casual or temporary workers are also employed by the Government ministries or departments and their attached and subordinate offices and there is no legislation exclusively for regulating engagement of such workers. *(Adapted from: All India Organisation of Employers', 2012).*

It has been speculated that the Government might soon ask companies to disclose information on the number and percentage of workers they have hired on contract, the minimum monthly wages paid to the contractual workers, and the non-discriminatory employment policies followed by them. Firms would also be expected to include this information in their annual financial statements. *(The Economic Times, 17th January 2011.)*

In the 42nd Session of the Indian Labour Conference, a Tripartite Task Force was constituted to examine the provisions in the Contract Labour (Regulation and Abolition) Act, 1970, and to suggest amendments to the Act. However, the Task Force could not arrive to a consensus due to wide divergence of views. *(Adapted from: All India Organisation of Employers,' 2012.)*

In the State Labour Ministers' Conference held on 22nd January 2010, it was proposed to amend the Act and introduce the following provisions as part of the Act *(www.labour.nic.in)*:

(i) In case where the contract labour perform the same or similar kind of work as the workmen directly appointed by the principal employer, the wage rates, holidays, hours of work, social security and other conditions of service of contract labour shall be the same as is available to the workmen on the rolls of the principal employer. In case same or similar kind of work is not being performed by the workmen directly employed by the principal employer, the appropriate Government will notify the wage rates, holidays, hours of work, social security and other conditions of service.

(ii) Whenever a contract is given to a contractor, the contract agreement between the principal employer and the contractor should clearly indicate the wages contribution towards social security schemes and other benefits that are to be paid by the contractor to the contracted workman.

The Ministry of Labour & Employment in 2011 had proposed to provide contract workers the same salary and other benefits as regular workers, but the proposal was kept on hold by the Cabinet Secretariat, looking at its implications. The proposed amendment would have entitled contract labour to the same wage rate, holidays, hours of work and social security provisions as that given to regular employees doing similar jobs. The only difference between contract and regular workers would have been security of tenure. *('Tussle Sends Contract Labour Pay Parity Plan to Cabinet Secy', The Economic Times. 14th December 2011.)*

In the 43rd Session of State Labour Ministers' Conference held on 27th September 2012, it has been pointed out that quarterly progress reports of major labour laws, including the Contract Labour (Regulation and Abolition) Act, 1970 are not being sent regularly to the Ministry of Labour & Employment by the State Governments, though it was so decided in the meeting of the Labour Ministers and Senior Officers of State Governments on 20th February 2009.

Overall it is increasingly becoming apparent that in spite of attracting debates and generating conflict of interest among the social partners, employment of contract labour in India has come to stay in the changing global economic scenario. It thus becomes the responsibility of the State to see that the interests of the contract workers are protected and their exploitation is prevented. Addressing the issues of contract labour through a sustainable method and avoiding future industrial unrest is the need of the time; the only remedy is by bringing this segment of workers under the ambit of social security.

Summary

- A workman is deemed to be a contract labour when he/she is hired in connection with the work or "contract for service" of an establishment by or through a contractor. Contract labour are indirect employees; persons who are hired, supervised and remunerated by a contractor who, in turn, is compensated by the establishment.
- Employment of contract labour has become a debatable issue of late, and a key reason for increasing labour unrest in the economy. Such unrests are presumed to stem from rebellious feelings harboured in contract workers due to anxiety of job security, lack of social security, exploitation in the hands of contractors, low wages, unequal treatment by trade unions and even abusive behaviour of permanent workers and supervisors.
- The Contract Labour (Regulation and Abolition) Act received the assent of the President on 5th September 1970, and it came into force from 10th February 1971. The Statement of Objects

and Reasons of the Act shows that in respect of such categories as may be notified by the appropriate Government, in the light of the prescribed criteria, contract labour will be abolished, and in respect of the other categories the service conditions of contract labour will be regulated.

- Section 1(4) makes the Act applicable to every establishment in which 20 or more workmen are employed or were employed on any day of the preceding 12 months as contract labour, and to every contractor who employees or who employed on any day of the preceding 12 months 20 or more workmen.
- As defined in Section 2(1)(b), a workman shall be deemed to be employed as "contract labour" in or in connection with the work of an establishment when he is hired in or in connection with such work by or through a contractor, with or without the knowledge of the principal employer.
- Section 3(1) lays down that the Central Government shall, as soon as may be, constitute a board to be called the Central Advisory Contract Labour Board to advise it on such matters arising out of the administration of this Act as may be referred to it and to carry out other functions assigned to it under this Act. Similarly, a State Advisory Contract Labour Board may be constituted by the State Government, as per Section 4(1).
- According to Section 10(1), the appropriate Government may, after consultation with the Central Board or, as the case may be, a State Board, prohibit, by notification in the Official Gazette, employment of contract labour in any process, operation or other work in any establishment.
- Sections 16 to 19 mandate provision of canteens, restrooms, first-aid and other facilities in an establishment employing contract labour. If any of such amenities is not provided by the contractor within the time prescribed, the same shall be provided by the principal employer within prescribed time, as given in Section 20(1).
- According to Section 21(1), a contractor shall be responsible for payment of wages to each worker employed by him as contract labour, before the expiry of prescribed period. It shall be the duty of the contractor to ensure the disbursement of wages in the presence of the authorised representative of the principal employer, as given in Section 21(3).
- Section 23 lays down that contravention of any provision or of any rules prohibiting, restricting or regulating the employment of contract labour, or of any condition of a licence granted, would be punishable with imprisonment for a term extending to 3 months, or with fine extending to ₹1,000, or with both.
- Inspectors may be appointed by the appropriate Government, as provided in Section 28(1), by notification in the Official Gazette, which shall define the local limits within which they shall exercise their powers under this Act.

Key Concepts

Contract labour	Licensing	Inspecting staff
Contractor	Central Advisory Board	State Advisory Board
Principal employer	Obstructions	Registering officers

Bibliography

All India Organisation of Employers', 2012, Retrieved from http://www.ficci.com/spdocument/20189/Industrial-Relations-and-Contract-Labour-in-India.pdf on 23/6/2014.

Indian Labour Journal, May 2013, Vol. 54, No. 3.
Report of the National Commission on Labour (2002, 1991–1967). Academic Foundation, New Delhi.
http://planningcommission.nic.in/plans/planrel/fiveyr/2nd/2planch27.html accessed on 24/6/2014.
www.labour.nic.in
www.indiankanoon.org/doc/277653/ accessed on 26/6/2014.

Review Questions

Objective Type Questions

I. State True or False

(i) An out-worker is included in the definition of a workman.
(ii) The minimum number of members of a State Advisory Board is 11.
(iii) The member of a committee who is an officer of Government shall be paid prescribed fees and allowances for attending its meetings.
(iv) If an offence consists of disobeying a written order made by an inspector, a complaint may be made within 6 months of such date.
(v) Every rule made by the Central Government under this Act shall be laid before each House of Parliament while it is in session for a total period of 60 days.

Answers: (i) False, (ii) False, (iii) False, (iv) True, (v) False

II. Fill in the Blanks

(i) Contravention of any condition of a licence granted under the Act shall be punishable with imprisonment for a term up to _____ months.
(ii) The minimum number of members of Central Advisory Board should be _____.
(iii) ______ must be provided at every place wherein contract labour is required to halt at night in connection with the work of an establishment.
(iv) Any obstruction is punishable with imprisonment up to 3 months, or with fine up to ₹ ______, or with both.
(v) One or more canteens shall be provided and maintained by the contractor wherein ______ or more contract labour is ordinarily employed by a contractor.

Answers: (i) 3, (ii) 11, (iii) rest-room, (iv) 500, (v) 100

Discussion Questions

1. Discuss the miscellaneous provisions for the health and welfare of contract workers.
2. Critically discuss the recent measures taken by the Government to regulate contract labour with the intervention of the Contract Labour (Regulation and Abolition) Act, 1970.
3. Which all matters are covered under the rules the appropriate Government may make for carrying out the purposes of the Act?
4. Define workman in context of the Act. Who all are not included in such definition?
5. Which powers are vested on inspecting staff under this Act?
6. What are the penalties laid down for obstruction and contravention of the provisions regarding employment of contract labour?
7. Elaborate on all provisions regarding licenses given in the Contract Labour (Regulation and Abolition) Act, 1970.

8. Discuss responsibility of both contractor and employer for the payment of wages.
9. In light of the various judgements discussed in the chapter, critically appraise the provision of prohibition of employment of contract labour as given in Section 10.
10. Explain the role of various Advisory Boards laid down in the Act.

CASE STUDY-I

In this case the Labour Court had held that the concerned workmen were employees of the appellant and not of the contractor. The reasons given by the Labour Court to come to this finding were also found to be convincing. In fact, it has held that these workmen were working under the orders of the officers of the appellant, and were being paid ₹70 per day, whereas the workmen/employees of the contractor were paid ₹56 per day. The High Court has rightly refused to interfere with this finding of fact recorded by the Labour Court. The counsel for the appellant submitted that the High Court has wrongly held that the appellant had resorted to a subterfuge, when there was no such finding by the Labour Court.

(Adapted from: Bhilwara Dugdh Utpadak Sahakari S. Ltd. vs. Vinod Kumar Sharma Dead by Lrs & Ors. www.indiankanoon.org/doc/294074/ accessed on 28/6/2014.)

Review Questions

1. Do you think there is any infirmity in the impugned judgment of the High Court?
2. Refer to the judgment in *Steel Authority of India vs. National Union Waterfront Workers*. Do you think that this judgment has any application in the present case? Defend on the basis of facts and comparison of the cases.
3. Which all sections of the Contract Labour (Regulation and Abolition) Act, 1970 are relevant in this case?

CASE STUDY-II

The petitioner, which is a union of employees of the Food Corporation of India (Respondent 1, hereafter referred to as "Corporation"), has approached the Court by way of a writ petition under Article 226 of the Constitution of India, praying *inter alia* to hold that the employees of the petitioner-union working in 11 depots of the Corporation, situated in Gujarat State, are employees of the Food Corporation of India. It also prayed to issue a suitable writ, direction and/or order to give these employees necessary benefits of back wages and all other consequential benefits.

According to the petitioner, for the past 14 years, about 1,600 employees are doing the loading and unloading, re-stacking, breaking, weighment and other incidental work (including railway siding), in connection with the food-grains received and sent by the aforesaid depots. This is argued to be a perennial type of work because this is one of the main objects of the Corporation to see that the food-grains are properly kept and dispatched in a proper manner. The said work is being done by the Corporation through various labour contractors, but these contractors are changed from time to time after a period of about two years or so. From 1st March 1985 as such there is no contractor, though on paper the Corporation might have shown the names of some contractors. In fact, the entire control and supervision was done directly by the Corporation qua its employees in the aforesaid depots. It is also stated by the petitioner-union that the contractors shown by the Corporation on record were not having any valid licence required under the Contract Labour (Regulation and Abolition) Act, 1970 (hereinafter referred to as "the Act") and, hence all these employees working in the 11 depots served through contractors who were not holding valid licence in the eye of law at least since 28th January 1986, when the definition of the term "appropriate Government" under the Act was changed. Therefore, the employees of the petitioner-union must be treated as the employees of the Corporation itself.

Incidentally it has been pointed out that since the petitioner-union made a demand for giving the employees the permanency benefits, the Corporation closed these depots by way of illegal lock-out since March 1987. This resulted in wastage of food-grains worth crores of rupees without proper handling. According to the petitioner-union, thereafter conciliation proceedings were started, wherein it took the stand that after the change in the definition of term "appropriate Government" under the Act, there is no contractor with the Corporation and, in fact, the payments have also been made directly by the Corporation to the employees, as there was no contractor having a valid licence at the relevant time as required under the Act and the Rules made thereunder. It was therefore submitted on behalf of the petitioner that there was no contractor in the eye of law at the relevant time for the last 3 years and if during that period to workers worked for the Corporation, they were required to be treated as employees of the Corporation.

On the other hand, the Corporation contended that the contractors had obtained a valid licence and hence the contract is valid and legal and contract labour is not entitled to be treated as direct employees of the respondent-Corporation. Thus it is contended that the employees can approach the contractors for redressal of their grievances. It was further submitted that the Corporation was holding the Certificate from the State Government (of Gujarat) and the appropriate Government was changed from State Government to Central Government. The said certificate was obtained on 21st May 1987 from the competent authority appointed by the Central Government. According to the respondents, the contractors have also obtained licences after the change of the "appropriate Government" from State Government to Central Government.

(Adapted from: Food Corporation of India vs. Food Corporation of India and Others [(1990) 1 GLR 384] www.indiankanoon.org/doc/530621/ accessed on 25/6/2014.)

Review Questions

1. Which sections of the Contract Labour (Regulation and Abolition) Act, 1970 are relevant to this case?
2. What relief, according to you, may be granted to the petitioner?
3. From 28th January 1986 till 21st May 1987 (in case of Baroda Division) and up to 4th June 1987 (in case of Sabarmati, Ahmedabad Division) there was no valid Certificate of Registration for the Corporation. Similarly, the contractors through whom the workmen were engaged also did not possess licence. Hence, in relation to this period, do you think that the workmen can claim that they were employed directly by the principal employer?
4. Can the Food Corporation of India, without incurring the liability of employing workmen where work is of an intermittent nature, employ a contractor for supply of labour or for handling certain works of the Corporation? Defend your answer.

The Sexual Harassment of Women at Workplace (Prevention, Prohibition and Redressal) Act, 2013

An Act to provide protection against sexual harassment of women at workplace and for the prevention and redressal of complaints of sexual harassment and for matters connected therewith or incidental thereto.

The Sexual Harassment of Women at Workplace (Prevention, Prohibition and Redressal) Act, 2013 has received assent of the President of India on 22nd April 2013.

ABOUT THE ACT
CHAPTER I: PRELIMINARY

Short Title, Extent and Commencement (Section 1)

1. This Act may be called the Sexual Harassment of Women at Workplace (Prevention, Prohibition and Redressal) Act, 2013.
2. It extends to the whole of India.
3. It shall come into force on such date as the Central Government may, by notification in the Official Gazette, appoint.

Definitions (Section 2)

In this Act, unless the context otherwise requires,

Aggrieved woman [Section 2(a)] Aggrieved woman means:

(i) in relation to a workplace, a woman, of any age whether employed or not, who alleges to have been subjected to any act of sexual harassment by the respondent;

(ii) in relation to a dwelling place or house, a woman of any age who is employed in such a dwelling place or house;

Appropriate Government [Section 2(b)] Appropriate Government means:

(i) in relation to a workplace which is established, owned, controlled or wholly or substantially financed by funds provided directly or indirectly:
   (A) by the Central Government or the Union Territory administration, the Central Government;
   (B) by the State Government, the State Government;

(ii) in relation to any workplace not covered under sub-clause (i) and falling within its territory, the State Government;

Chairperson [Section 2(c)] Chairperson means the Chairperson of the Local Complaints Committee nominated under sub-section (1) of Section 7;

District Officer [Section 2(d)] District Officer means an officer notified under Section 5;

Domestic worker [Section 2(e)] Domestic worker means a woman who is employed to do the household work in any household for remuneration whether in cash or kind, either directly or through any agency on a temporary, permanent, part time or full time basis, but does not include any member of the family of the employer;

Employee [Section 2(f)] Employee means a person employed at a workplace for any work on regular, temporary, *ad hoc* or daily wage basis, either directly or through an agent, including a contractor, with or without the knowledge of the principal employer, whether the terms of employment are express or implied and includes a co-worker, a contract worker, probationer, trainee, apprentice or called by any other such name;

Employer [Section 2(g)] Employer means:

(i) in relation to any department, organisation, undertaking, establishment, enterprise, institution, office, branch or unit of the appropriate Government or a local authority, the head of that department, organisation, undertaking, establishment, enterprise, institution, office, branch or unit or such other officer as the appropriate Government or the local authority, as the case may be, may by an order specify in this behalf;

(ii) in any workplace not covered under sub-clause (i), any person responsible for the management, supervision and control of the workplace.

Explanation For the purposes of this sub-clause "management" includes the person or board or committee responsible for formulation and administration of policies for such organisation;

(iii) in relation to workplace covered under sub-clauses (i) and (ii), the person discharging contractual obligations with respect to his or her employees;

(iv) in relation to a dwelling place or house, a person or a household who employs or benefits from the employment of domestic worker, irrespective of the number, time period or type of such worker employed, or the nature of the employment or activities performed by the domestic worker;

Internal Committee [Section 2(h)] Internal Committee means an Internal Complaints Committee constituted under Section 4;

Local Committee [Section 2(i)] Local Committee means the Local Complaints Committee constituted under Section 6;

Member [Section 2(j)] Member means a Member of the Internal Committee or the Local Committee, as the case may be;

Prescribed [Section 2(k)] Prescribed means prescribed by rules made under this Act;

Presiding Officer [Section 2(l)] Presiding Officer means the Presiding Officer of the Internal Complaints Committee nominated under sub-section (2) of Section 4;

Respondent [Section 2(m)] Respondent means a person against whom the aggrieved woman has made a complaint under Section 9;

Sexual harassment [Section 2(n)] Sexual harassment includes any 1 or more of the following unwelcome acts or behaviour (whether directly or by implication) namely:

(i) physical contact and advances; or
(ii) a demand or request for sexual favours; or
(iii) making sexually coloured remarks; or
(iv) showing pornography; or
(v) any other unwelcome physical, verbal, or non-verbal conduct of sexual nature;

Workplace [Section 2(o)] Workplace includes:

(i) any department, organisation, undertaking, establishment, enterprise, institution, office, branch or unit which is established, owned, controlled or wholly or substantially financed by funds provided directly or indirectly by the appropriate Government or the local authority or a Government company or a corporation or a cooperative society;
(ii) any private sector organisation or a private venture, undertaking, enterprise, institution, establishment, society, trust, non-governmental organisation, unit or service provider carrying on commercial, professional, vocational, educational, entertainment, industrial, health services or financial activities including production, supply, sale, distribution or service;
(iii) hospitals or nursing homes;
(iv) any sports institute, stadium, sports complex or competition or games venue, whether residential or not used for training, sports or other activities relating thereto;
(v) any place visited by the employee arising out of or during the course of employment including transportation provided by the employer for undertaking such journey;
(vi) a dwelling place or a house;

Unorganised sector [Section 2(p)] Unorganised sector in relation to a workplace means an enterprise owned by individuals or self-employed workers and engaged in the production or sale of goods or providing service of any kind whatsoever, and where the enterprise employs workers, the number of such workers is less than 10.

Prevention of Sexual Harassment (Section 3)

1. No woman shall be subjected to sexual harassment at any workplace.
2. The following circumstances, among other circumstances, if it occurs or is present in relation to or connected with any act or behaviour of sexual harassment may amount to sexual harassment:-
   (i) implied or explicit promise of preferential treatment in her employment; or
   (ii) implied or explicit threat of detrimental treatment in her employment; or
   (iii) implied or explicit threat about her present or future employment status; or

(iv) interference with her work or creating an intimidating or offensive or hostile work environment for her; or
(v) humiliating treatment likely to affect her health or safety.

CHAPTER II: CONSTITUTION OF INTERNAL COMPLAINTS COMMITTEE

Constitution of Internal Complaints Committee (Section 4)

1. Every employer of a workplace shall, by an order in writing, constitute a Committee to be known as the "Internal Complaints Committee":

   Provided that where the offices or administrative units of the workplace are located at different places or divisional or sub-divisional level, the Internal Committee shall be constituted at all administrative units or offices.
2. The Internal Committee shall consist of the following members to be nominated by the employer, namely:
   (a) a Presiding Officer who shall be a woman employed at a senior level at workplace from amongst the employees:

   Provided that in case a senior level woman employee is not available, the Presiding Officer shall be nominated from other offices or administrative units of the workplace referred to in sub-section (1);

   Provided further that in case the other offices or administrative units of the workplace do not have a senior level woman employee, the Presiding Officer shall be nominated from any other workplace of the same employer or other department or organisation;
   (b) not less than 2 members from amongst employees preferably committed to the cause of women or who have had experience in social work or have legal knowledge;
   (c) 1 member from amongst non-governmental organisations or associations committed to the cause of women or a person familiar with the issues relating to sexual harassment:

   Provided that at least one-half of the total members so nominated shall be women.
3. The Presiding Officer and every Member of the Internal Committee shall hold office for such period, not exceeding 3 years, from the date of their nomination as may be specified by the employer.
4. The Member appointed from amongst the non-governmental organisations or associations shall be paid such fees or allowances for holding the proceedings of the Internal Committee, by the employer, as may be prescribed.
5. Where the Presiding Officer or any Member of the Internal Committee:-
   (a) contravenes the provisions of Section 16; or
   (b) has been convicted for an offence or an inquiry into an offence under any law for the time being in force is pending against him; or
   (c) he has been found guilty in any disciplinary proceedings or a disciplinary proceeding is pending against him; or
   (d) has so abused his position as to render his continuance in office prejudicial to the public interest,

   such Presiding Officer or Member, as the case may be, shall be removed from the Committee and the vacancy so created or any casual vacancy shall be filled by fresh nomination in accordance with the provisions of this section.

CHAPTER III: CONSTITUTION OF LOCAL COMPLAINTS COMMITTEE

Notification of District Officer (Section 5)

The appropriate Government may notify a District Magistrate or Additional District Magistrate, or the Collector or Deputy Collector as a District Officer for every District to exercise powers or discharge functions under this Act.

Constitution and Jurisdiction of Local Complaints Committee (Section 6)

1. Every District Officer shall constitute in the district concerned, a committee to be known as the "Local Complaints Committee" to receive complaints of sexual harassment from establishments where the Internal Complaints Committee has not been constituted due to having less than 10 workers or if the complaint is against the employer himself.
2. The District Officer shall designate 1 nodal officer in every block, taluka and tehsil in rural or tribal area and ward or municipality in the urban area, to receive complaints and forward the same to the concerned Local Complaints Committee within a period of 7 days.
3. The jurisdiction of the Local Complaints Committee shall extend to the areas of the district where it is constituted.

Composition, Tenure and other Terms and Conditions of Local Complaints Committee (Section 7)

1. The Local Complaints Committee shall consist of the following members to be nominated by the District Officer, namely:
   (a) a Chairperson to be nominated from amongst the eminent women in the field of social work and committed to the cause of women;
   (b) 1 Member to be nominated from amongst the women working in block, taluka or tehsil or ward or municipality in the district;
   (c) 2 Members, of whom at least 1 shall be a woman, to be nominated from amongst such non-governmental organisations or associations committed to the cause of women or a person familiar with the issues relating to sexual harassment, which may be prescribed:
   Provided that at least 1 of the nominees should, preferably, have a background in law or legal knowledge;
   Provided further that at least 1 of the nominees shall be a woman belonging to the Scheduled Castes or the Scheduled Tribes or the Other Backward Classes or minority community notified by the Central Government, from time to time;
   (d) the concerned officer dealing with the social welfare or women and child development in the district, shall be a member *ex officio*.
2. The Chairperson and every Member of the Local Committee shall hold office for such period, not exceeding 3 years, from the date of their appointment as may be specified by the District Officer.
3. Where the Chairperson or any Member of the Local Complaints Committee-
   (a) contravenes the provisions of Section 16; or
   (b) has been convicted for an offence or an inquiry into an offence under any law for the time being in force is pending against him; or
   (c) has been found guilty in any disciplinary proceedings or a disciplinary proceeding is pending against him; or

(d) has so abused his position as to render his continuance in office prejudicial to the public interest,

such Chairperson or Member, as the case may be, shall be removed from the Committee and the vacancy so created or any casual vacancy shall be filled by fresh nomination in accordance with the provisions of this section.

4. The Chairperson and Members of the Local Committee other than the Members nominated under clauses (b) and (d) of sub-section (1) shall be entitled to such fees or allowances for holding the proceedings of the Local Committee as may be prescribed.

Grants and Audit (Section 8)

1. The Central Government may, after due appropriation made by Parliament by law in this behalf, make to the State Government grants of such sums of money as the Central Government may think fit, for being utilised for the payment of fees or allowances referred to in sub-section (4) of Section 7.
2. The State Government may set up an agency and transfer the grants made under sub-section (1) to that agency.
3. The agency shall pay to the District Officer, such sums as may be required for the payment of fees or allowances referred to in sub-section (4) of Section 7.
4. The accounts of the agency referred to in sub-section (2) shall be maintained and audited in such manner as may, in consultation with the Accountant General of the State, be prescribed and the person holding the custody of the accounts of the agency shall furnish, to the State Government, before such date, as may be prescribed, its audited copy of accounts together with auditors' report thereon.

CHAPTER IV: COMPLAINT

Complaint of Sexual Harassment (Section 9)

1. Any aggrieved woman may make, in writing, a complaint of sexual harassment at workplace to the Internal Committee if so constituted, or the Local Committee, in case it is not so constituted, within a period of 3 months from the date of incident and in case of a series of incidents, within a period of 3 months from the date of last incident:

   Provided that where such complaint cannot be made in writing, the Presiding Officer, or any Member of the Internal Committee or the Chairperson, or any Member of the Local Committee, as the case may be, shall render all reasonable assistance to the woman for making complaint in writing:

   Provided further that the Internal Committee or, as the case may be, the Local Committee may, for the reason to be recorded in writing, extend the time limit not exceeding 3 months, if it is satisfied that the circumstances were such which prevented the woman from filing a complaint within the said period.
2. Where the aggrieved woman is unable to make a complaint on account of her physical or mental incapacity or death or otherwise, her legal heir or such other person as may be prescribed may make a complaint under this section.

Conciliation [Section 10]

1. The Internal Committee or, as the case may be, the Local Committee, may, before initiating an enquiry under Section 11 and at the request of the aggrieved woman take steps to settle the matter between her and the respondents through conciliation:

   Provided that no monetary settlement shall be made as a basis of conciliation.
2. Where a settlement is arrived at under sub-section (1), the Internal Committee or the Local Committee, as the case may be, shall record the settlement so arrived and forward the same to the employer or the District Officer to take action as specified in the recommendation.
3. The Internal Committee or the Local Committee, as the case may be, shall provide the copies of the settlement as recorded under sub-section (2) to the aggrieved woman and the respondent.
4. Where a settlement is arrived at under sub-section (1), no further inquiry shall be conducted by the Internal Committee or the Local Committee, as the case may be.

Inquiry into Complaint (Section 11)

1. Subject to the provisions of Section 10, the Internal Committee or the Local Committee, as the case may be, shall, where the respondent is an employee, proceed to make inquiry into the complaint in accordance with provisions of the service rules applicable to the respondent and where no such rules exist, in such manner as may be prescribed or in case of a domestic worker, the Local Committee shall, if *prima facie* case exist, forward the complaint to the police, within a period of 7 days for registering the case under Section 509 of the Indian Penal Code, and any other relevant provisions of the said code where applicable:

   Provided that where the aggrieved woman informs the Internal Committee or the Local Committee, as the case may be, that any term or condition of the settlement arrived at under sub-section (2) of Section 10 has not been complied with by the respondent, the Internal Committee or the Local Committee shall proceed to make an enquiry into the complaint or, as the case may be, forward the complaint to the police:

   Provided further that where both parties are employees, the parties shall, during the course of inquiry, be given an opportunity of being heard and a copy of the findings shall be made available to both the parties enabling them to make representation against the findings before the Committee.
2. Notwithstanding anything contained in Section 509 of the Indian Penal Code, the court may, when the respondent is convicted of the offence, order payment of such sums as it may consider appropriate, to the aggrieved woman by the respondent, having regard to the provisions of Section 15.
3. For the purpose of making an inquiry under sub-section (1), the Internal Committee or the Local Committee, as the case may be, shall have the same powers as are vested in a civil court under the Code of Civil Procedure, 1908, when trying a suit in respect of the following matters, namely:
   (a) summoning and enforcing the attendance of any person and examining him on oath;
   (b) requiring the discovery and production of documents; and
   (c) any other matter which may be prescribed.
4. The inquiry under sub-section (1) shall be completed within a period of 90 days.

CHAPTER V: INQUIRY INTO COMPLAINT

Action during Pendency of Inquiry (Section 12)

1. During the pendency of an inquiry, on a written request made by the aggrieved woman, the Internal Committee or the Local Committee, as the case may be, may recommend to the employer to:
   (a) transfer the aggrieved woman or the respondent to any other workplace; or
   (b) grant leave to the aggrieved woman up to a period of 3 months; or
   (c) grant such other relief to the aggrieved woman as may be prescribed.
2. The leave granted to the aggrieved woman under this section shall be in addition to the leave she would be otherwise entitled.
3. On the recommendation of the Internal Committee or the Local Committee, as the case may be, under sub-section (1), the employer shall implement the recommendations made under sub-section (1) and send the report of such implementation to the Internal Committee or the Local Committee, as the case may be.

Inquiry Report (Section 13)

1. On completion of an inquiry under in this Act, the Internal Committee or the Local Committee, as the case may be, shall provide a report of its findings to the employer, or, as the case may be, the District Officer within a period of 10 days from the date of completion of the inquiry and such report be made available to the concerned parties.
2. Where the Internal Committee or the Local Committee, as the case may be, arrives at the conclusion that the allegation against the respondent has not been proved, it shall recommend to the employer and the District Officer that no action is required to be taken in the matter.
3. Where the Internal Committee or the Local Committee, as the case may be, arrives at the conclusion that the allegation against the respondent has not been proved, it shall recommend to the employer and the District Officer, as the case may be:
   (i) to take action for sexual harassment as a misconduct in accordance with the provisions of the service rules applicable to the respondent or where no such service rules have been made, in such manner as may be prescribed;
   (ii) to deduct, notwithstanding anything in the service rules applicable to the respondent, from the salary or wages of the respondent such sum as it may consider appropriate to be paid to the aggrieved woman or to her legal heirs, as it may determine, in accordance with the provisions of Section 15;

   Provided that in case the employer is unable to make such deduction from the salary of the respondent due to his being absent from the duty or cessation of employment it may direct to the respondent to pay such sum to the aggrieved woman:

   Provided further that in case the respondent fails to pay the sum referred to in clause (ii), the Internal Committee or, as the case may be, the Local Committee may forward the order for recovery of the sum as an arrear of land revenue to the concerned District Officer.
4. The employer or the District Officer shall act upon the recommendation within 60 days of its receipt by him.

Punishment for False or Malicious Complaint and False Evidence (Section 14)

1. Where the Internal Committee or the Local Committee, as the case may be, arrives at the conclusion that the allegation against the respondent is malicious or the aggrieved woman or any other person making the complaint has made the complaint knowing it to be false or the aggrieved woman or any other person making the complaint has produced any forged or misleading document, it may recommend to the employer or the District Officer, as the case may be, to take action against the woman or the other person who had made the complaint under sub-section (1) or sub-section (2) of Section 9, as the case may be, in accordance with the provisions of the service rules applicable to her or him or where no such service rules exist, in such manner as may be prescribed:

   Provided that a mere inability to substantiate a complaint or provide adequate proof need not attract action against the complainant under this section.

   Provided further that the malicious intent on part of the complainant shall be established after an enquiry in accordance with the procedure prescribed, before any action is recommended.
2. Where the Internal Committee or the Local Committee, as the case may be, arrives at a conclusion that during the inquiry any witness has given false evidence or produced any forged or misleading document, it may recommend to the employer of the witness or the District Officer, as the case may be, to take action in accordance with the provision of the service rules applicable to the said witness or where no such service rules exist, in such manner as may be prescribed.

Determination of Compensation (Section 15)

For the purpose of determining the sums to be paid to the aggrieved woman under clause (ii) of sub-section (3) of Section 13, the Internal Committee or the Local Committee, as the case may be, shall have regard to:

(a) the mental trauma, pain, suffering and emotional stress caused to the aggrieved woman;
(b) the loss in the career opportunity due to the incident of sexual harassment;
(c) medical expenses incurred by the victim for physical and psychiatric treatment;
(d) the income and financial status of the respondent;
(e) feasibility of such payment in lump sum or in instalments.

Prohibition of Publication or Making Known Contents of Complaint and Inquiry Proceedings (Section 16)

Notwithstanding anything contained in the Right to Information Act, 2005, the contents of the complaint made under Section 9, the identity and addresses of the aggrieved woman, respondent and witnesses, any information relating to conciliation and inquiry proceedings, recommendation of the Internal Committee or the Local Committee, as the case may be, and action taken by the employer or the District Officer under the provisions of this Act shall not be published, communicated or made known to the public, press and media in any manner:

Provided that information may be disseminated regarding the justice secured to any victim of sexual harassment under this Act without disclosing the name, address, identity or any other particulars calculated to lead to the identification of the aggrieved woman and witnesses.

Penalty for Publication or Making Known Contents of Complaint and Inquiry Proceedings (Section 17)

Where any person entrusted with the duty to handle or deal with the complaint, inquiry or any recommendations or action to be taken under the provisions of this Act, contravenes the provisions of Section 16, he shall be liable for penalty in accordance with the provisions of the service rules applicable to the said person or where no such service rules exist, in such manner as may be prescribed.

Appeal (Section 18)

1. Any person aggrieved from the recommendations made under sub-section (2) of Section 13 or under clause (i) or clause (ii) of sub-section (3) of Section 13 or sub-section (1) or sub-section (2) of Section 14 or Section 17 or non-implementation of such recommendations may prefer an appeal to the court or tribunal in accordance with the provisions of the service rules applicable to the said person or where no such service rules exist then, without prejudice to provisions contained in any other law for the time being in force, the person aggrieved may prefer an appeal in such manner as may be prescribed.
2. The appeal under sub-section (1) shall be preferred within a period of 90 days of the recommendations.

CHAPTER VI: DUTIES OF EMPLOYER

Duties of Employer (Section 19)

Every employer shall:

(a) provide a safe working environment at the workplace which shall include safety from the persons coming into contact at the workplace;

(b) display at any conspicuous place in the workplace, the penal consequences of sexual harassments; and the order constituting, the Internal Committee under sub-section (1) of Section 4;

(c) organise workshops and awareness programmes at regular intervals for sensitising the employees with provisions of the Act and orientation programmes for the members of the Internal Committee in the manner as may be prescribed;

(d) provide necessary facilities to the Internal Committee or the Local Committee, as the case may be, for dealing with complaints and conducting an inquiry;

(e) assist in securing the attendance of respondent and witnesses before the Internal Committee or the Local Committee, as the case may be;

(f) make available such information to the Internal Committee or the Local Committee, as the case may be, as it may require having regard to the complaint made under sub-section (1) of Section 9;

(g) provide assistance to the woman if she so chooses to file a complaint in relation to the offence under Indian Penal Code or any other law for the time being in force;

(h) cause to initiate action, under the Indian Penal Code or any other law for the time being in force, against the perpetrator, or if the aggrieved woman so desires, where the perpetrator is not an employee, in the workplace at which the incident of sexual harassment took place;

(i) treat sexual harassment as a misconduct under the service rules and initiate action for such misconduct;

(j) monitor the timely submission of reports by the Internal Committee.

CHAPTER VII: DUTIES AND POWERS OF DISTRICT OFFICER

Duties and Powers of District Officer (Section 20)

The District Officer shall:

(a) monitor the timely submission of reports furnished by the Local Committee;
(b) take such measures as may be necessary for engaging non-governmental organisations for creation of awareness on sexual harassment and the rights of the women.

CHAPTER VIII: MISCELLANEOUS

Committee to Submit Annual Report (Section 21)

1. The Internal Committee or the Local Committee, as the case may be, shall in each calendar year prepare, in such form and at such time as may be prescribed, an annual report and submit the same to the employer and the District Officer.
2. The District Officer shall forward a brief report on the annual reports received under sub-section (1) to the State Government.

Employer to Include Information in Annual Report (Section 22)

The employer shall include in its report the number of cases filed, if any, and their disposal under this Act in the annual report of his organisation or where no such report is required to be prepared, intimate such number of cases, if any, to the District Officer.

Appropriate Government to Monitor Implementation and Maintain Data (Section 23)

The appropriate Government shall monitor the implementation of this Act and maintain data on the number of cases filed and disposed of in respect of all cases of sexual harassment at workplace.

Appropriate Government to Take Measures to Publicise the Act (Section 24)

The appropriate Government may, subject to the availability of financial and other resources,—

(a) develop relevant information, education, communication and training materials, and organise awareness programmes, to advance the understanding of the public of the provisions of this Act providing for protection against sexual harassment of women at workplace,
(b) formulate orientation and training programmes for the members of the Local Complaints Committee.

Power to Call for Information and Inspection of Records (Section 25)

1. The appropriate Government, on being satisfied that it is necessary in the public interest or in the interest of women employees at a workplace to do so, by order in writing:
   (a) call upon any employer or District Officer to furnish in writing such information relating to sexual harassment as it may require,
   (b) authorise any officer to make inspection of the records and workplace in relation to sexual harassment, who shall submit a report of such inspection to it within such period as may be specified in the order.

2. Every employer and District Officer shall produce on demand before the officer making the inspection all information, records and other documents in his custody having a bearing on the subject matter of such inspection.

Penalty for Non-compliance with Provisions of Act (Section 26)

1. Where the employer fails to:
   (a) constitute an Internal Committee under sub-section (1) of Section 4;
   (b) take action under sections 13, 14 and 22; and
   (c) contravenes or attempts to contravene or abets contravention of other provisions of this Act or any rules made thereunder,

   he shall be punishable with fine which may extend to ₹50,000.
2. If any employer, after having been previously convicted of an offence punishable under this Act subsequently commits and is convicted of the same offence, he shall be liable to:
   (i) twice the punishment, which might have been imposed on a first conviction, subject to the punishment being maximum provided for the same offence;

   Provided that in case a higher punishment is prescribed under any other law for the time being in force, for the offence for which the accused is being prosecuted, the court shall take due cognizance of the same while awarding the punishment;

   (ii) cancellation, of his license or withdrawal, or non-renewal, or approval, or cancellation of the registration, as the case may be, by the Government or local authority required for carrying on his business or activity.

Cognizance of Offence by Courts (Section 27)

1. No court shall take cognizance of any offence punishable under this Act or any rules made thereunder, save on a complaint made by the aggrieved woman or any person authorised by the Internal Committee or Local Committee in this behalf.
2. No court inferior to that of a Metropolitan Magistrate or a Judicial Magistrate of the first class try any offence punishable under this Act.
3. Every offence under this Act shall be non-cognizable.

Act not in Derogation of any other Law (Section 28)

The provisions of this Act shall be in addition to and not in derogation of the provisions of any other law for the time being in force.

Power of Appropriate Government to Make Rules (Section 29)

1. The Central Government may, by notification in the Official Gazette, make rules for carrying out the provisions of this Act.
2. In particular and without prejudice to the generality of the foregoing power, such rules may provide for all or any of the following matters, namely:
   (a) the fees or allowances to be paid to the members under sub-section (4) of Section 4;
   (b) nomination of members under clause (c) of sub- section (1) of Section 7;
   (c) the fees and allowances to be paid to the Chairperson, and Members under sub-section (4) of Section 7;

(d) the person who may make complaints under sub-section (2) of Section 9;
(e) the manner of inquiry under sub-section (1) of Section 11;
(f) the powers for making an inquiry under clause (c) of sub-section (2) of Section 11;
(g) the relief to be recommended under clause (c) of sub-section (1) of Section 12;
(h) the manner of action to be taken under clause (i) of sub-section (3) of Section 13;
(i) the manner of action to be taken under sub-sections (1) and (2) of Section 14;
(j) the manner of action to be taken under Section 17;
(k) the manner of appeal under sub-section (1) of Section 18;
(l) the manner of organising workshops, awareness programmes for sensitising the employees, and orientation programmes for the members of the Internal Committee under clause (c) of Section 19; and
(m) the form and time for preparation of annual report by Internal Committee and the Local Committee under sub-section (1) of Section 21.

3. Every rule made by the Central Government under this Act shall be laid as soon as may be after it is made, before each House of Parliament, while it is in session, for a total period of 30 days which may be comprised in 1 session or in 2 or more successive sessions, and if, before the expiry of the session immediately following the session or the successive sessions aforesaid, both Houses agree in making any modification in the rule or both Houses agree that the rule should not be made, the rule shall thereafter have effect only in such modified form or be of no effect, as the case may be, so, however, that any such modification or annulment shall be without prejudice to the validity of anything previously done under that rule.
4. Any rule made under sub-section (4) of Section 8 by the State Government shall be laid, as soon as may be after it is made, before each House of the State Legislature where it consists of 2 Houses, or where such legislature consists of 1 House, before that House.

Power to Remove Difficulties (Section 30)

1. If any difficulty arises in giving effect to the provisions of this Act, the Central Government may, by order published in the Official Gazette, make such provisions of this Act, not inconsistent with the provisions of this Act, as may appear to it to be necessary for removing the difficulty.

   Provided that no such order shall be made under this section after the expiry of a period of 2 years from the commencement of this Act.
2. Every order made under this section shall be laid, as soon as may be after it is made, before each House of Parliament.

Index

C

D

E

I

J

K

L

M

N

O

P

Q

R

S